ONE WEEK LOAN

The material covered in *An Introduction to Database Systems* is organized into six major parts:

- **Part I** (four chapters) provides a broad introduction to the concepts of database systems in general and relational systems in particular. It also introduces the standard database language, SQL.

- **Part II** (six chapters) consists of a detailed and very careful description of the relational model, which is not only the theoretical foundation underlying relational systems but is, in fact, the theoretical foundation for the entire database field.

- **Part III** (four chapters) discusses the general question of database design. Three chapters are devoted to design theory, and the fourth considers semantic modeling and the entity/relationship model.

- **Part IV** (two chapters) is concerned with transaction management (i.e., recovery and concurrency controls).

- **Part V** (eight chapters) shows how relational concepts are relevant to a variety of further aspects of database technology—security, distributed databases, temporal data, decision support, and so on.

- **Part VI** (three chapters) describes the impact of object technology on database systems. Chapter 25 describes object systems specifically; Chapter 26 considers the possibility of a *rapprochement* between object and relational technologies and discusses object/relational systems; and Chapter 27 addresses the relevance to databases of XML.

About the Author

C. J. DATE is an author, lecturer, researcher, and independent consultant specializing in relational database systems. An active member of the database community for nearly 35 years, C. J. Date devotes the major part of his career to exploring, expanding, and expounding the theory and practice of relational technology. He enjoys a reputation second to none for his ability to explain complex technical material in a clear and understandable fashion.

Database Place ▲▼▼

Free Access! } As a reader of this database concepts book, you are entitled to six months of free access to Database Place! Database Place will be a key resource in helping you succeed in your database course.

This access allows you to use all the student support areas of Database Place, including:

- Interactive tutorial environments for practicing database modelling, normalization problems, and writing SQL queries

- Automatically graded practice questions in the areas of Normalization, SQL, database modeling, and relational algebra to help you assess your basic understanding of the material

- And more!

To access Database Place for the first time:

You will need to register online using a computer with an Internet connection and a Web browser. The process takes just a couple of minutes and only needs to be completed once.

1) Go to **http://www.aw.com/databaseplace**

2) Click **Enter Database Place**

3) Click the **Register** button

4) Use a coin to scratch off the gray coating below and reveal your student access code*. Do not use a knife or other sharp object, which can damage the code.

Scratch Here! }

5) On the registration page, enter your student access code. Do not type the dashes. You can use lowercase or uppercase.

6) Follow the on-screen instructions. If you need help at any time during the online registration process, simply click the **Need Help?** icon.

7) Once your personal Login Name and Password are confirmed, you can begin using Database Place!

To Log into Database Place After You Register:

You can access Database Place anytime by going to http://www.aw.com/databaseplace, clicking "Enter Database Place," and providing your Login Name and Password when prompted.

*Important: The Access Code on this page can only be used once to establish a subscription to Database Place. This subscription is valid for six months upon activation, and is not transferable. If this access code has already been scratched off, it may no longer be valid. If this is the case, you can purchase a subscription by going to http://www.aw.com/databaseplace and clicking "Enter Database Place."

EIGHTH EDITION

An Introduction to

Database Systems

EIGHTH EDITION

An Introduction to
Database Systems

C.J. Date

PEARSON

Addison
Wesley

Boston San Francisco New York
London Toronto Sydney Tokyo Singapore Madrid
Mexico City Munich Paris Cape Town Hong Kong Montreal

Senior Acquisitions Editor: Maite Suarez-Rivas
Project Editor: Katherine Harutunian
Marketing Manager: Nathan Schultz
Production Supervisor: Marilyn Lloyd
Project Management: Elisabeth Beller
Composition: Nancy Logan
Technical Art: Dartmouth Publishing, Inc.
Copyeditor: Daril Bentley
Proofreader: Jennifer McClain
Design Manager: Joyce Cosentino Wells
Cover Design: Night & Day Design
Cover Image: Lindy Date
Prepress and Manufacturing: Caroline Fell

Access the latest information about Addison-Wesley titles from our World Wide Web site:
http://www.aw.com/cs

ISBN 0-321-18956-6

4 5 6 7 8 9 10-HAM-0605

*This book is dedicated to my wife Lindy
and to the memory of my mother Rene—*

*also to the memory of Ted Codd, who, sadly,
passed away as this book was going to press*

Those who cannot remember the past
are condemned to repeat it

Usually quoted in the form:

Those who don't know history are
doomed to repeat it

—George Santayana

I would like to see computer science
teaching set deliberately
in a historical framework. . .
Students need to understand
how the present situation has come
about, what was tried,
what worked and what did not, and
how improvements in hardware
made progress possible. The absence
of this element in
their training causes people to
approach every problem from
first principles. They are apt to
propose solutions that
have been found wanting in the past.
Instead of standing
on the shoulders of their precursors,
they try to go it alone.

—Maurice V. Wilkes

About the Author

C. J. Date is an independent author, lecturer, researcher, and consultant, specializing in relational database technology. He is based in Healdsburg, California.

In 1967, following several years as a mathematical programmer and programming instructor for Leo Computers Ltd. (London, England), Mr. Date moved to the IBM (UK) Development Laboratories, where he worked on the integration of database functionality into PL/I. In 1974 he transferred to the IBM Systems Development Center in California, where he was responsible for the design of a database language known as the Unified Database Language, UDL, and worked on technical planning and externals design for the IBM products SQL/DS and DB2. He left IBM in May, 1983.

Mr. Date has been active in the database field for well over 30 years. He was one of the first people anywhere to recognize the significance of Codd's pioneering work on the relational model. He has lectured widely on technical subjects—principally on database topics, and especially on relational database—throughout North America and also in Europe, Australia, Latin America, and the Far East. In addition to the present book, he is author or coauthor of a number of other database texts, including, from Morgan Kaufmann, *Temporal Data and the Relational Model* (2003) and, from Addison-Wesley, *Foundation for Future Database Systems: The Third Manifesto* (2nd edition, 2000), a detailed proposal for the future direction of the field; *Database: A Primer* (1983), which treats database systems from the nonspecialist's point of view; a series of *Relational Database Writings* books (1986, 1990, 1992, 1995, 1998), which deal with various aspects of relational technology in depth; and another series of books on specific systems and languages—*A Guide to DB2* (4th edition, 1993), *A Guide to SYBASE and SQL Server* (1992), *A Guide to SQL/DS* (1988), *A Guide to INGRES* (1987), and *A Guide to the SQL Standard* (4th edition, 1997). His books have been translated into several languages, including Braille, Chinese, Dutch, French, German, Greek, Italian, Japanese, Korean, Polish, Portuguese, Russian, and Spanish.

Mr. Date has also produced over 300 technical articles and research papers and has made a variety of original contributions to database theory. For several years, he was a regular columnist for the magazine *Database Programming & Design*. He also contributes regularly to the website *http://www.dbdebunk.com*. His professional seminars on database technology, offered both in North America and overseas, are widely considered to be second to none for the quality of the subject matter and the clarity of the exposition.

Mr. Date holds an Honours Degree in Mathematics from Cambridge University, England (BA 1962, MA 1966) and the honorary degree of Doctor of Technology from De Montfort University, England (1994).

Contents

PART III   DATABASE DESIGN   329

PART IV   TRANSACTION MANAGEMENT   443

PART V   FURTHER TOPICS   501

APPENDIXES   939

Preface to the Eighth Edition

This book is a comprehensive introduction to the now very large field of database systems. It provides a solid grounding in the foundations of database technology and gives some idea as to how the field is likely to develop in the future. The book is meant primarily as a textbook, not a work of reference (though I hope and believe it can be useful as a reference also, to some extent). The emphasis throughout is on **insight** and **understanding**, not just on formalisms.

PREREQUISITES

The book as a whole is meant for anyone professionally interested in computing in some way who wants to gain an understanding of what database systems are all about. I assume you have at least a basic knowledge of both:

- The storage and file management capabilities (indexing, etc.) of a modern computer system
- The features of at least one high-level programming language (Java, Pascal, PL/I, etc.)

Regarding the first of these prerequisites, however, please note that a detailed tutorial on such matters can be found in the online Appendix D, "Storage Structures and Access Methods."

STRUCTURE

I have to say that I am a little embarrassed at the size of this book. The fact is, however, that database technology has become a very large field, and it is not possible to do it justice in fewer than 1,000 pages or so (indeed, most of the book's competitors are also about 1,000 pages). Be that as it may, the book overall is divided into six major parts:

   I. Basic Concepts
  II. The Relational Model
 III. Database Design
 IV. Transaction Management

V. Further Topics

VI. Objects, Relations, and XML

Each part in turn is divided into several chapters:

- Part I (four chapters) provides a broad introduction to the concepts of database systems in general and relational systems in particular. It also introduces the standard database language **SQL**.

- Part II (six chapters) consists of a detailed and very careful description of **the relational model**, which is not only the theoretical foundation underlying relational systems, but is in fact the theoretical foundation for the entire database field.

- Part III (four chapters) discusses the general question of **database design**; three chapters are devoted to design theory, the fourth considers semantic modeling and the entity/relationship model.

- Part IV (two chapters) is concerned with **transaction management** (i.e., recovery and concurrency controls).

- Part V (eight chapters) is a little bit of a *potpourri*. In general, however, it shows how relational concepts are relevant to a variety of further aspects of database technology—**security**, **distributed databases**, **temporal data**, **decision support**, and so on.

- Finally, Part VI (three chapters) describes the impact of **object technology** on database systems. Chapter 25 describes **object systems** specifically; Chapter 26 considers the possibility of a *rapprochement* between object and relational technologies and discusses **object/relational** systems; and Chapter 27 addresses the relevance to databases of **XML**.

There are also four appendixes. The first is an overview of a dramatic new and radically different implementation technology called **The TransRelational™ Model**; the next gives a **BNF grammar** for SQL expressions; the third contains a **glossary** of the more important abbreviations, acronyms, and symbols introduced in the body of the text; and the last is, as already explained, an online tutorial on **storage structures and access methods**.

ONLINE MATERIALS

The following instructor supplements are available only to qualified instructors. For information on accessing them, please contact your local Addison-Wesley Sales Representative, or send e-mail to *aw.cse@aw.com*.

- An Instructor's Manual provides guidance on how to use the book as a basis for teaching a database course. It consists of a series of notes, hints, and suggestions on each part, chapter, and appendix, as well as other supporting material.

- Answers to exercises (included in Instructor's Manual)

- Lecture slides in PowerPoint format

The following supplements are available to all readers of this book at *http://www.aw .com/cssupport*.

- Appendix D on storage structures and access methods (as already mentioned)
- Answers to a selected subset of the exercises

HOW TO READ THIS BOOK

The book overall is meant to be read in sequence more or less as written, but you can skip later chapters, and later sections within chapters, if you choose. A suggested plan for a first reading would be:

- Read Chapters 1 and 2 "once over lightly."
- Read Chapters 3 and 4 very carefully (except perhaps for Sections 4.6 and 4.7).
- Read Chapter 5 "once over lightly."
- Read Chapters 6, 7, 9, and 10 carefully, but skip Chapter 8 (except perhaps for Section 8.6 on SQL).
- Read Chapter 11 "once over lightly."
- Read Chapters 12 and 14 carefully,[1] but skip Chapter 13.
- Read Chapters 15 and 16 carefully (except perhaps for Section 15.6 on two-phase commit).
- Read subsequent chapters selectively (but in sequence), according to taste and interest.

Each chapter opens with an introduction and closes with a summary; in addition, most chapters include exercises, and the online answers often give additional information about the topic of the exercise. Most chapters also include a set of references, many of which are annotated. This structure allows the subject matter to be treated in a layered fashion, with the most important concepts and results being presented "in line" in the main body of the text and various subsidiary issues and more complex aspects being deferred to the exercises or answers or references (as appropriate). *Note:* References are identified by two-part numbers in square brackets. For example, the reference "[3.1]" refers to the first item in the list of references at the end of Chapter 3: namely, a paper by E. F. Codd published in *CACM 25,* No. 2, in February, 1982. (For an explanation of abbreviations used in references—e.g., "CACM"—see Appendix C.)

COMPARISON WITH EARLIER EDITIONS

We can summarize the major differences between this edition and its immediate predecessor as follows:

- *Part I:* Chapters 1–4 cover roughly the same ground as Chapters 1-4 in the seventh edition, but they have been significantly revised at the detail level. In particular,

---

[1] You could also read Chapter 14 earlier if you like, possibly right after Chapter 4.

Chapter 4, the introduction to SQL, has been upgraded to the level of the current standard SQL:1999, as indeed has SQL coverage throughout the entire book. (This fact all by itself caused major revisions to more than half the chapters from the seventh edition.) *Note:* Facilities likely to be included in the next version of the standard—which will probably be ratified in late 2003—are also mentioned where appropriate.

- *Part II:* Chapters 5–10, on the relational model, are a totally rewritten, considerably expanded, and very much improved version of Chapters 5–9 from the seventh edition. In particular, the material on types—also known as domains—has been expanded into a chapter of its own (Chapter 5), and the material on integrity (Chapter 9) has been completely restructured and rethought. I hasten to add that the changes in these chapters do not represent changes in the underlying concepts but, rather, changes in how I have chosen to present them, based on my practical experience in teaching this material in live presentations.

  Note: Some further words of explanation are in order here. Earlier editions of the book used SQL as a basis for teaching relational concepts, in the belief that it was easier on the student to show the concrete before the abstract. Unfortunately, however, the gulf between SQL and the relational model grew and continued to grow, ultimately reaching a point where I felt it would be actively misleading to use SQL for such a purpose any longer. The sad truth is that SQL is now so far from being a true embodiment of relational principles—it suffers from so many sins of both omission and commission—that I would frankly prefer not to discuss it at all! However, SQL is obviously important from a commercial point of view; thus, every database professional needs to have some familiarity with it, and it would just not be appropriate to ignore it in a book of this nature. I therefore settled on the strategy of including (a) a chapter on SQL basics in Part I of the book and (b) individual sections in other chapters, as applicable, describing those aspects of SQL that are specific to the subject of the chapter in question. In this way the book still provides comprehensive—indeed, extensive—coverage of SQL material, but puts that coverage into what I feel is the proper context.

- *Part III:* Chapters 10–13 are a mostly cosmetic revision of Chapters 9–12 from the seventh edition. There are detail-level improvements throughout, however.

  Note: Again some further explanation is in order. Some reviewers of earlier editions complained that database design issues were treated too late. But it is my feeling that students are not ready to design databases properly or to appreciate design issues fully until they have some understanding of what databases are and how they are used; in other words, I believe it is important to spend some time on the relational model and related matters before exposing the student to design questions. Thus, I still believe Part III is in the right place. (That said, I do recognize that many instructors prefer to treat the entity/relationship material much earlier. To that end, I have tried to make Chapter 14 more or less self-contained, so that they can bring it in immediately after, say, Chapter 4.)

- *Part IV:* The two chapters of this part, Chapters 15 and 16, are completely rewritten, extended, and improved versions of Chapters 14 and 15 from the seventh edition. In particular, Chapter 16 now includes a careful analysis of—and some unorthodox conclusions regarding—the so-called ACID properties of transactions.

- *Part V:* Chapter 20 on type inheritance and Chapter 23 on temporal databases have been totally rewritten to reflect recent research and developments in those areas. Revisions to other chapters are mostly cosmetic, though there are improvements in explanations and examples throughout and new material here and there.

- *Part VI:* Chapters 25 and 26 are improved and expanded versions of Chapters 24 and 25 from the seventh edition. Chapter 27 is new.

Finally, Appendix A is also new, while Appendixes B and C are revised versions of Appendixes A and C, respectively, from the seventh edition (the material from Appendix B in that edition has been incorporated into the body of the book). Appendix D is a significantly revised version of Appendix A from the *sixth* edition.

WHAT MAKES THIS BOOK DIFFERENT?

Every database book on the market has its own individual strengths and weaknesses, and every writer has his or her own particular ax to grind. One concentrates on transaction management issues; another stresses entity/relationship modeling; another looks at everything through an SQL lens; yet another takes a pure "object" point of view; still another views the field exclusively in terms of some commercial product; and so on. And, of course, I am no exception to this rule—I too have an ax to grind: what might be called the **foundation** ax. I believe very firmly that we must get the foundation right, and understand it properly, before we try to build on that foundation. This belief on my part explains the heavy emphasis in this book on the relational model; in particular, it explains the length of Part II—the most important part of the book—where I present my own understanding of the relational model as carefully as I can. I am interested in foundations, not fads and fashions. Products change all the time, but principles endure.

In this regard, I would like to draw your attention to the fact that there are several important ("foundation") topics for which this book, virtually alone among the competition, includes an entire in-depth chapter (or an appendix, in one case). The topics in question include:

- Types
- Integrity
- Views
- Missing information
- Inheritance
- Temporal databases
- The TransRelational™ Model

In connection with that same point (the importance of foundations), I have to admit that the overall tone of the book has changed over the years. The first few editions were mostly descriptive in nature; they described the field as it actually was in practice, "warts and all." Later editions, by contrast, were much more *pre*scriptive; they talked about the way the field *ought* to be and the way it ought to develop in the future, if we did things right. And the present edition is certainly prescriptive in this sense (so it is a text with an attitude!). Since the first part of that "doing things right" is surely educating oneself as to what those right things are, I hope this new edition can help in that endeavor.

Yet another related point: As you might know, I recently published, along with my colleague Hugh Darwen, another "prescriptive" book, *Foundation for Future Database Systems: The Third Manifesto* (reference [3.3] in the present book).[2] That book, which we call *The Third Manifesto* or just the *Manifesto* for short, builds on the relational model to offer a detailed technical proposal for future database systems; it is the result of many years of teaching and thinking about such matters on the part of both Hugh and myself. And, not surprisingly, the ideas of the *Manifesto* permeate the present book. Which is not to say the *Manifesto* is a prerequisite to the present book—it is not; but it *is* directly relevant to much that is in the present book, and further related information is often to be found therein.

Note: Reference [3.3] uses a language called **Tutorial D** for illustrative purposes, and the present book does the same. **Tutorial D** syntax and semantics are intended to be more or less self-explanatory (the language might be characterized, loosely, as "Pascal-like"), but individual features are explained when they are first used if such explanation seems necessary.

A CLOSING REMARK

I would like to close these prefatory notes with the following lightly edited extract from another preface—Bertrand Russell's own preface to *The Bertrand Russell Dictionary of Mind, Matter and Morals* (ed., Lester E. Denonn), Citadel Press, 1993, reprinted here by permission:

> *I have been accused of a habit of changing my opinions . . . I am not myself in any degree ashamed of [that habit]. What physicist who was already active in 1900 would dream of boasting that his opinions had not changed during the last half century? . . . [The] kind of philosophy that I value and have endeavoured to pursue is scientific, in the sense that there is some definite knowledge to be obtained and that new discoveries can make the admission of former error inevitable to any candid mind. For what I have said, whether early or late, I do not claim the kind of truth which theologians claim for their creeds. I claim only, at best, that the opinion expressed was a sensible one to hold at the time . . . I should be much surprised if subsequent research did not show that it needed to be modified. [Such opinions were not] intended as pontifical pronouncements, but only as the best I could do at the time towards the promotion of clear and accurate thinking. Clarity, above all, has been my aim.*

---

[2] There is a website, too: *http://www.thethirdmanifesto.com*. See also *http://www.dbdebunk.com* for much related material.

If you compare earlier editions of this book with this eighth edition, you will find that I too have changed my opinions on many matters (and no doubt will continue to do so). I hope you will accept the remarks just quoted as adequate justification for this state of affairs. I share Bertrand Russell's perception of what the field of scientific inquiry is all about, but he expresses that perception far more eloquently than I could.

ACKNOWLEDGMENTS

Once again it is a pleasure to acknowledge my debt to the many people involved, directly or indirectly, in the production of this book:

- First of all, I must thank my friends David McGoveran and Nick Tindall for their major involvement in this edition; David contributed the first draft of Chapter 22 on decision support, and Nick contributed the first draft of Chapter 27 on XML. I must also thank my friend and colleague Hugh Darwen for major help (in a variety of forms) with all SQL portions of the manuscript. Nagraj Alur and Fabian Pascal also provided me with a variety of technical background material. A special vote of thanks goes to Steve Tarin for inventing the technology described in Appendix A and for his help in getting me to understand it fully.

- Second, the text has benefited from the comments of students on the seminars I have been teaching over the past several years. It has also benefited enormously from the comments of, and discussions with, numerous friends and reviewers, including Hugh Darwen, IBM; Guy de Tré, Ghent University; Carl Eckberg, San Diego State University; Cheng Hsu, Rensselaer Polytechnic Institute; Abdul-Rahman Itani, The University of Michigan-Dearborn; Vijay Kanabar, Boston University; Bruce O. Larsen, Stevens Institute of Technology; David Livingstone, University of Northumbria at Newcastle; David McGoveran, Alternative Technologies; Steve Miller, IBM; Fabian Pascal, independent consultant; Martin K. Solomon, Florida Atlantic University; Steve Tarin, Required Technologies; and Nick Tindall, IBM. Each of these people reviewed at least some part of the manuscript or made technical material available or otherwise helped me find answers to my many technical questions, and I am very grateful to all of them.

- I would also like to thank my wife Lindy for contributing the cover art once again and for her support throughout this and all my other database-related projects over the years.

- Finally, I am grateful (as always) to everyone at Addison-Wesley—especially Maite Suarez-Rivas and Katherine Harutunian—for all of their encouragement and support throughout this project, and to my packager Elisabeth Beller for another sterling job.

Healdsburg, California   C. J. Date
2003

PRELIMINARIES

Part I consists of four introductory chapters:

- Chapter 1 sets the scene by explaining what a database is and why database systems are desirable. It also briefly discusses the difference between relational systems and others.

- Next, Chapter 2 presents a general architecture for database systems, the so-called ANSI/SPARC architecture. That architecture serves as a framework on which the rest of the book will build.

- Chapter 3 then presents an overview of relational systems (the aim is to serve as a gentle introduction to the much more comprehensive discussions of the same subject in Part II and later parts of the book). It also introduces and explains the running example, the suppliers-and-parts database.

- Finally, Chapter 4 introduces the standard relational language SQL (more precisely, SQL:1999).

CHAPTER **1**

An Overview of Database Management

1.1 INTRODUCTION

A **database system** is basically just a *computerized record-keeping system.* The **database** itself can be regarded as a kind of electronic filing cabinet; that is, it is a repository or container for a collection of computerized data files. Users of the system can perform (or request the system to perform, rather) a variety of operations involving such files—for example:

- Adding new files to the database
- Inserting data into existing files
- Retrieving data from existing files
- Deleting data from existing files
- Changing data in existing files
- Removing existing files from the database

Fig. 1.1 shows a very small database containing just one file, called CELLAR, which in turn contains data concerning the contents of a wine cellar. Fig. 1.2 shows an example of a **retrieval** request against that database, together with the data returned by that request. (Throughout this book we show database requests, file names, and other such material in uppercase for clarity. In practice it is often more convenient to enter such material in lowercase. Most systems will accept both.) Fig. 1.3 gives examples, all more or less self-explanatory, of **insert**, **delete**, and **change** requests on the wine cellar database. Examples of adding and removing entire files are given in later chapters.

Several points arise immediately from Figs. 1.1–1.3:

1. First of all, the SELECT, INSERT, DELETE, and UPDATE requests (also called *statements, commands,* or *operators*) in Figs. 1.2 and 1.3 are all expressed in a language called **SQL**. Originally a proprietary language from IBM, SQL is now an international standard that is supported by just about every database product commercially available; in fact, the market is totally dominated by SQL products at the time of writing. Because of its commercial importance, therefore, Chapter 4 presents a general overview of the SQL standard, and most subsequent chapters include a section called "SQL Facilities" that describes those aspects of that standard that are pertinent to the topic of the chapter in question.

   By the way, the name SQL originally stood for *Structured Query Language* and was pronounced *sequel.* Now that it is a standard, however, the name is officially just a name—it is not supposed to be an abbreviation for anything at all—and it is officially pronounced *ess-cue-ell.* We will assume this latter pronunciation throughout this book.

2. Note from Fig. 1.3 that SQL uses the keyword UPDATE to mean "change" specifically. This fact can cause confusion, because the term *update* is also used to refer to the three operators INSERT, DELETE, and UPDATE considered as a group. We will distinguish between the two meanings in this book by using lowercase when the generic meaning is intended and uppercase to refer to the UPDATE operator specifically.

   Incidentally, you might have noticed that we have now used both the term *operator* and the term *operation.* Strictly speaking, there is a difference between the two (the *operation* is what is performed when the *operator* is invoked); in informal discussions, however, the terms tend to be used interchangeably.

3. In SQL, computerized files such as CELLAR in Fig. 1.1 are called **tables** (for obvious reasons); the **rows** of such a table can be thought of as the *records* of the file, and the **columns** can be thought of as the *fields*. In this book, we will use the terminology of files, records, and fields when we are talking about database systems in general (mostly just in the first two chapters); we will use the terminology of tables, rows, and columns when we are talking about SQL systems in particular. (And when we get to our more formal discussions in Chapter 3 and later parts of the book, we will meet yet another set of terms: *relations, tuples,* and *attributes* instead of tables, rows, and columns.)

BIN#	WINE	PRODUCER	YEAR	BOTTLES	READY
2	Chardonnay	Buena Vista	2001	1	2003
3	Chardonnay	Geyser Peak	2001	5	2003
6	Chardonnay	Simi	2000	4	2002
12	Joh. Riesling	Jekel	2002	1	2003
21	Fumé Blanc	Ch. St. Jean	2001	4	2003
22	Fumé Blanc	Robt. Mondavi	2000	2	2002
30	Gewürztraminer	Ch. St. Jean	2002	3	2003
43	Cab. Sauvignon	Windsor	1995	12	2004
45	Cab. Sauvignon	Geyser Peak	1998	12	2006
48	Cab. Sauvignon	Robt. Mondavi	1997	12	2008
50	Pinot Noir	Gary Farrell	2000	3	2003
51	Pinot Noir	Fetzer	1997	3	2004
52	Pinot Noir	Dehlinger	1999	2	2002
58	Merlot	Clos du Bois	1998	9	2004
64	Zinfandel	Cline	1998	9	2007
72	Zinfandel	Rafanelli	1999	2	2007

Fig. 1.1   The wine cellar database (file CELLAR)

```
Retrieval:
SELECT  WINE, BIN#, PRODUCER
FROM    CELLAR
WHERE   READY = 2004 ;
```

Result (as shown on, e.g., a display screen):

WINE	BIN#	PRODUCER
Cab. Sauvignon	43	Windsor
Pinot Noir	51	Fetzer
Merlot	58	Clos du Bois

Fig. 1.2   Retrieval example

```
Inserting new data:
INSERT
INTO    CELLAR ( BIN#, WINE, PRODUCER, YEAR, BOTTLES, READY )
VALUES ( 53, 'Pinot Noir', 'Saintsbury', 2001, 6, 2005 ) ;

Deleting existing data:
DELETE
FROM    CELLAR
WHERE   BIN# = 2 ;

Changing existing data:
UPDATE CELLAR
SET     BOTTLES = 4
WHERE   BIN# = 3 ;
```

Fig. 1.3   Insert, delete, and change examples

4. With respect to the CELLAR table, we have made a tacit assumption for simplicity that columns WINE and PRODUCER contain character-string data and all other columns contain integer data. In general, however, columns can contain data of arbitrary

complexity. For example, we might extend the CELLAR table to include additional columns as follows:

- LABEL (photograph of the wine bottle label)
- REVIEW (text of a review from some wine magazine)
- MAP (map showing where the wine comes from)
- NOTES (audio recording containing our own tasting notes)

and many other things. For obvious reasons, the majority of examples in this book involve only very simple kinds of data, but do not lose sight of the fact that more exotic possibilities are always available. We will consider this question of column **data types** in more detail in later chapters (especially Chapters 5–6 and 26–27).

5. Column BIN# constitutes the **primary key** for table CELLAR (meaning, loosely, that no two CELLAR rows ever contain the same BIN# value). In figures like Fig. 1.1 we use *double underlining* to indicate primary key columns.

One last point to close this preliminary section: While a full understanding of this chapter and the next is necessary to a proper appreciation of the features and capabilities of a modern database system, it cannot be denied that the material is somewhat abstract and rather dry in places (also, it does tend to involve a large number of concepts and terms that might be new to you). In Chapters 3 and 4 you will find material that is much less abstract and hence more immediately understandable, perhaps. You might therefore prefer just to give these first two chapters a "once over lightly" reading for now, and to reread them more carefully later as they become more directly relevant to the topics at hand.

1.2   WHAT IS A DATABASE SYSTEM?

To repeat from the previous section, a database system is basically a computerized record-keeping system; in other words, it is a computerized system whose overall purpose is to store information and to allow users to retrieve and update that information on demand. The information in question can be anything that is of significance to the individual or organization concerned—anything, in other words, that is needed to assist in the general process of running the business of that individual or organization.

Incidentally, please note that we treat the terms *data* and *information* as synonyms in this book. Some writers prefer to distinguish between the two, using *data* to refer to what is actually stored in the database and *information* to refer to the *meaning* of that data as understood by some user. The distinction is clearly important—so important that it seems preferable to make it explicit, where appropriate, instead of relying on a somewhat arbitrary differentiation between two essentially synonymous terms.

Fig. 1.4 is a simplified picture of a database system. As the figure shows, such a system involves four major components: **data**, **hardware**, **software**, and **users**. We consider these four components briefly here. Later we will discuss each in much more detail (except for the hardware component, details of which are mostly beyond the scope of this book).

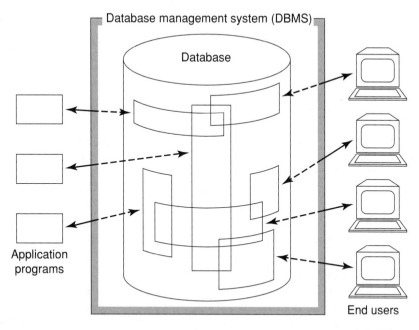

Fig. 1.4   Simplified picture of a database system

Data

Database systems are available on machines that range all the way from the smallest hand-held or personal computers to the largest mainframes or clusters of mainframes. Needless to say, the facilities provided by any given system are determined to some extent by the size and power of the underlying machine. In particular, systems on large machines ("large systems") tend to be *multi-user,* whereas those on smaller machines ("small systems") tend to be *single-user.* A **single-user system** is a system in which at most one user can access the database at any given time; a **multi-user system** is a system in which many users can access the database at the same time. As Fig. 1.4 suggests, we will normally assume the latter case in this book, for generality; in fact, however, the distinction is largely irrelevant so far as most users are concerned, because it is precisely an objective of multi-user systems in general to allow each user to behave as if he or she were working with a *single*-user system instead. The special problems of multi-user systems are prima-rily problems that are internal to the system, not ones that are visible to the user (see Part IV of this book, especially Chapter 16).

Now, it is convenient to assume for the sake of simplicity that the totality of data in the system is all stored in a single database, and we will usually make that assumption in this book, since it does not materially affect any of our other discussions. In practice, however, there might be good reasons, even in a small system, why the data should be split across several distinct databases. We will touch on some of those reasons later, in Chapter 2 and elsewhere.

In general, then, the data in the database—at least in a large system—will be both *integrated* and *shared*. As we will see in Section 1.4, these two aspects, data integration and data sharing, represent a major advantage of database systems in the "large" environment, and data integration, at least, can be significant in the "small" environment as well. Of course, there are many additional advantages also, to be discussed later, even in the small environment. But first let us explain what we mean by the terms *integrated* and *shared:*

- By **integrated**, we mean the database can be thought of as a unification of several otherwise distinct files, with any redundancy among those files partly or wholly eliminated. For example, a given database might contain both an EMPLOYEE file, giving employee names, addresses, departments, salaries, and so on, and an ENROLL-MENT file, representing the enrollment of employees in training courses (refer to Fig. 1.5). Now suppose that, in order to carry out the process of training course administration, it is necessary to know the department for each enrolled student. Then there is clearly no need to include that information redundantly in the ENROLL-MENT file, because it can always be discovered by referring to the EMPLOYEE file instead.

- By **shared**, we mean the database can be shared among different users, in the sense that different users can have access to the same data, possibly even at the same time ("concurrent access"). Such sharing, concurrent or otherwise, is partly a consequence of the fact that the database is integrated. In the example of Fig. 1.5, for instance, the department information in the EMPLOYEE file would typically be shared by users in the Personnel Department and users in the Education Department. (A database that is not shared in the foregoing sense is sometimes said to be "personal" or "application-specific.")

Another consequence of the foregoing facts—that the database is integrated and shared—is that any given user will typically be concerned only with some small portion of the total database; moreover, different users' portions will overlap in various ways. In other words, a given database will be perceived by different users in many different ways. In fact, even when two users share the same portion of the database, their views of that portion might differ considerably at a detailed level. This latter point is discussed more fully in Section 1.5 and in later chapters (especially Chapter 10).

We will have more to say regarding the nature of the data component of the system in Section 1.3.

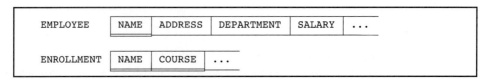

Fig. 1.5   The EMPLOYEE and ENROLLMENT files

Hardware

The hardware components of the system consist of:

- The secondary storage volumes—typically magnetic disks—that are used to hold the stored data, together with the associated I/O devices (disk drives, etc.), device controllers, I/O channels, and so forth

- The hardware processor(s) and associated main memory that are used to support the execution of the database system software (see the next subsection)

This book does not concern itself very much with the hardware aspects of the system, for the following reasons among others: First, those aspects form a major topic in their own right; second, the problems encountered in this area are not peculiar to database systems; and third, those problems have been very thoroughly investigated and documented elsewhere.

Software

Between the physical database itself—that is, the data as physically stored—and the users of the system is a layer of software, known variously as the **database manager** or **database server** or, most commonly, the **database management system** (DBMS). All requests for access to the database are handled by the DBMS; the facilities sketched in Section 1.1 for adding and removing files (or tables), retrieving data from and updating data in such files or tables, and so on, are all facilities provided by the DBMS. One general function provided by the DBMS is thus *the shielding of database users from hardware-level details* (much as programming language systems shield application programmers from hardware-level details). In other words, the DBMS provides users with a perception of the database that is elevated somewhat above the hardware level, and it supports user operations (such as the SQL operations discussed briefly in Section 1.1) that are expressed in terms of that higher-level perception. We will discuss this function, and other functions of the DBMS, in considerably more detail throughout the body of the book.

A couple of further points:

- The DBMS is easily the most important software component in the overall system, but it is not the only one. Others include utilities, application development tools, design aids, report writers, and (most significant) the *transaction manager* or *TP monitor*. See Chapters 2, 3, and especially 15 and 16 for further discussion of these components.

- The term *DBMS* is also used to refer generically to some particular product from some particular vendor—for example, IBM's DB2 Universal Database product. The term *DBMS instance* is then sometimes used to refer to the particular copy of such a product that happens to be running at some particular computer installation. As you will surely appreciate, sometimes it is necessary to distinguish carefully between these two concepts.

That said, you should be aware that people often use the term *database* when they really mean *DBMS* (in either of the foregoing senses). Here is a typical example: "Vendor *X*'s database outperformed vendor *Y*'s database by a factor of two to one." This usage is sloppy, and deprecated, but very, very common. (The problem is: If we call the DBMS the database, what do we call the database? *Caveat lector!*)

Users

We consider three broad (and somewhat overlapping) classes of users:

- First, there are **application programmers**, responsible for writing database application programs in some programming language, such as COBOL, PL/I, C++, Java, or some higher-level "fourth-generation" language (see Chapter 2). Such programs access the database by issuing the appropriate request (typically an SQL statement) to the DBMS. The programs themselves can be traditional batch applications, or they can be **online** applications, whose purpose is to allow an end user—see the next paragraph—to access the database interactively (e.g., from an online workstation or terminal or a personal computer). Most modern applications are of the online variety.

- Next, there are **end users**, who access the database interactively as just described. A given end user can access the database via one of the online applications mentioned in the previous paragraph, or he or she can use an interface provided as an integral part of the system. Such vendor-provided interfaces are also supported by means of online applications, of course, but those applications are **built in**, not user-written. Most systems include at least one such built-in application, called a **query language processor**, by which the user can issue database requests such as SELECT and INSERT to the DBMS interactively. SQL is a typical example of a database query language. (As an aside, we remark that the term *query language,* common though it is, is really a misnomer, inasmuch as the verb "to query" suggests *retrieval* only, whereas query languages usually—not always—provide update and other operators as well.)

   Most systems also provide additional built-in interfaces in which end users do not issue explicit database requests such as SELECT and INSERT at all, but instead operate by (e.g.) choosing items from a menu or filling in boxes on a form. Such **menu-** or **forms-driven** interfaces tend to be easier to use for people who do not have a formal training in IT (IT = information technology; the abbreviation IS, short for information systems, is also used with much the same meaning). By contrast, **command-driven interfaces**—that is, query languages—do tend to require a certain amount of professional IT expertise, though perhaps not much (obviously not as much as is needed to write an application program in a language like COBOL). Then again, a command-driven interface is likely to be more flexible than a menu- or forms-driven one, in that query languages typically include certain features that are not supported by those other interfaces.

- The third class of user, not illustrated in Fig. 1.4, is the **database administrator** or DBA. Discussion of the database administration function—and the associated (very important) **data** administration function—is deferred to Section 1.4 and Chapter 2 (Section 2.7).

This completes our preliminary description of the major aspects of a database system. We now go on to discuss the ideas in more detail.

1.3   WHAT IS A DATABASE?

Persistent Data

It is customary to refer to the data in a database as "persistent" (though it might not actually persist for very long!). By *persistent,* we mean, intuitively, that database data differs in kind from other more ephemeral data, such as input data, output data, work queues, software control blocks, SQL statements, intermediate results, and more generally any data that is transient in nature. More precisely, we say that data in the database "persists" because, once it has been accepted by the DBMS for entry into the database in the first place, *it can subsequently be removed from the database only by some explicit request to the DBMS,* not as a mere side effect of (e.g.) some program completing execution. This notion of persistence thus allows us to give a slightly more precise definition for the term *database:*

- A **database** is a collection of persistent data that is used by the application systems of some given enterprise.

The term *enterprise* here is simply a convenient generic term for any reasonably self-contained commercial, scientific, technical, or other organization. An enterprise might be a single individual (with a small personal database), or a complete corporation or similar large body (with a large shared database), or anything in between. Here are some examples:

1. A manufacturing company
2. A bank
3. A hospital
4. A university
5. A government department

Any enterprise must necessarily maintain a lot of data about its operation. That data is the "persistent data" referred to in the definition. The enterprises just mentioned would typically include the following (respectively) among their persistent data:

1. Product data
2. Account data
3. Patient data
4. Student data
5. Planning data

Note: The first six editions of this book used the term *operational data* in place of *persistent data.* That earlier term reflected the original emphasis in database systems on **operational** or **production** applications—that is, routine, highly repetitive applications that were executed over and over again to support the day-to-day operation of the enterprise (for example, an application to support the deposit or withdrawal of cash in a banking system). The term **online transaction processing** (OLTP) has come to be used to refer to this kind of environment. However, databases are now increasingly used for other kinds of applications as well—that is, **decision support** applications—and the term *operational data* is thus no longer entirely appropriate. Indeed, enterprises nowadays frequently maintain two separate databases, one containing operational data and one, often called the **data warehouse**, containing decision support data. The data warehouse often includes *summary information* (e.g., totals, averages), where the summary information in question is extracted from the operational database on a periodic basis—say once a day or once a week. See Chapter 22 for an in-depth treatment of decision support databases and applications.

Entities and Relationships

We now consider the example of a manufacturing company ("KnowWare Inc.") in a little more detail. Such an enterprise will typically wish to record information about the *projects* it has on hand; the *parts* that are used in those projects; the *suppliers* who are under contract to supply those parts; the *warehouses* in which those parts are stored; the *employees* who work on those projects; and so on. Projects, parts, suppliers, and so on, thus constitute the basic **entities** about which KnowWare Inc. needs to record information (the term *entity* is commonly used in database circles to mean any distinguishable object that is to be represented in the database). Refer to Fig. 1.6.

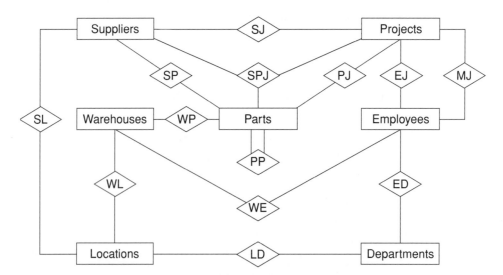

Fig. 1.6 Entity/relationship (E/R) diagram for KnowWare Inc.

In addition to the basic entities themselves (suppliers, parts, and so on, in the example), there will also be **relationships** linking those basic entities together. Such relationships are represented by diamonds and connecting lines in Fig. 1.6. For example, there is a relationship ("SP" or *shipments*) between suppliers and parts: Each supplier supplies certain parts, and conversely each part is supplied by certain suppliers (more accurately, each supplier supplies certain *kinds* of parts, each *kind* of part is supplied by certain suppliers). Similarly, parts are used in projects, and conversely projects use parts (relationship PJ); parts are stored in warehouses, and warehouses store parts (relationship WP); and so on. Note that these relationships are all *bidirectional*—that is, they can be traversed in either direction. For example, relationship SP between suppliers and parts can be used to answer both of the following queries:

- Given a supplier, get the parts supplied by that supplier.
- Given a part, get the suppliers who supply that part.

The significant point about this relationship (and all of the others illustrated in the figure) is that *they are just as much a part of the data as are the basic entities*. They must therefore be represented in the database, just like the basic entities.[1]

We note in passing that Fig. 1.6 is an example of what is called (for obvious reasons) an **entity/relationship diagram** (E/R diagram for short). We will consider such diagrams in detail in Chapter 14.

Fig. 1.6 also illustrates a number of other important points:

1. Although most of the relationships in that figure involve two entity types—that is, they are *binary* relationships—it is by no means the case that all relationships are binary in this sense. In the example there is one relationship ("SPJ") involving three entity types (suppliers, parts, and projects): a *ternary* relationship. The intended interpretation is that certain suppliers supply certain parts to certain projects. Note carefully that this ternary relationship ("suppliers supply parts to projects") is *not* equivalent, in general, to the combination of the three binary relationships "suppliers supply parts," "parts are used in projects," and "projects are supplied by suppliers." For example, the statement[2] that

    a. Smith supplies monkey wrenches to the Manhattan project

    tells us *more* than the following three statements do:

    b. Smith supplies monkey wrenches

    c. Monkey wrenches are used in the Manhattan project

    d. The Manhattan project is supplied by Smith

---

[1] In a relational database specifically (see Section 1.6), the basic entities and the relationships connecting them are both represented by means of *relations,* or in other words by tables like the one shown in Fig. 1.1, loosely speaking. Note carefully, therefore, that the term *relationship* as used in the present section and the term *relation* as used in the context of relational databases do not mean the same thing.

[2] The term *statement* is unfortunately used in the database world to mean two rather different things: It can be used, as here, to mean an *assertion of fact,* or what logicians call a *proposition* (see the subsection "Data and Data Models" later in this section); it can also be used, as we already know from earlier discussions, as a synonym for *command,* as in the expression "SQL statement."

—we cannot (validly!) infer *a* knowing only *b, c,* and *d.* More precisely, if we know *b, c,* and *d,* then we might be able to infer that Smith supplies monkey wrenches to *some* project (say project *Jz*), that *some* supplier (say supplier *Sx*) supplies monkey wrenches to the Manhattan project, and that Smith supplies *some* part (say part *Py*) to the Manhattan project—but we cannot validly infer that *Sx* is Smith or *Py* is monkey wrenches or *Jz* is the Manhattan project. False inferences such as these are examples of what is sometimes called **the connection trap**.

2. The figure also shows one relationship (PP) involving just *one* entity type (parts). The relationship here is that certain parts include other parts as immediate components (the so-called **bill-of-materials** relationship); for example, a screw is a component of a hinge assembly, which is also a part and might in turn be a component of some higher-level part such as a lid. Note that this relationship is still binary; it is just that the two entity types involved, parts and parts, happen to be one and the same.

3. In general, a given set of entity types might be involved in any number of distinct relationships. In the example in Fig. 1.6, there are two distinct relationships involving projects and employees: One (EJ) represents the fact that employees are assigned to projects; the other (MJ) represents the fact that employees manage projects.

We now observe that *a relationship can be regarded as an entity in its own right.* If we take as our definition of entity "any object about which we wish to record information," then a relationship certainly fits the definition. For instance, "part P4 is stored in warehouse W8" is an entity about which we might well wish to record information—for example, the corresponding quantity. Moreover, there are definite advantages (beyond the scope of the present chapter) to be obtained by not making any unnecessary distinctions between entities and relationships. In this book, therefore, we will tend to treat relationships as just a special kind of entity.

Properties

As just indicated, an entity is any object about which we wish to record information. It follows that entities (relationships included) can be regarded as having **properties,** corresponding to the information we wish to record about them. For example, suppliers have *locations;* parts have *weights;* projects have *priorities;* assignments (of employees to projects) have *start dates;* and so on. Such properties must therefore be represented in the database. For example, an SQL database might include a table called S representing suppliers, and that table might include a column called CITY representing supplier locations.

Properties in general can be as simple or as complex as we please. For example, the "supplier location" property is presumably quite simple, consisting as it does of just a city name, and can be represented in the database by a simple character string. By contrast, a warehouse might have a "floor plan" property, and that property might be quite complex, consisting perhaps of an entire architectural drawing and associated descriptive text. As noted in Section 1.1, in other words, the kinds of data we might want to keep in (for example) columns of SQL tables can be arbitrarily complex. As also noted in that same section, we will return to this topic later (principally in Chapters 5–6 and 26–27); until then, we will mostly assume, where it makes any difference, that properties are "simple" and can be represented by "simple" data types. Examples of such "simple" types include numbers, character strings, dates, times, and so forth.

Data and Data Models

There is another (and important) way of thinking about what data and databases really are. The word *data* derives from the Latin for "to give"; thus, data is really *given facts,* from which additional facts can be inferred. (Inferring additional facts from given facts is exactly what the DBMS does when it responds to a user query.) A "given fact" in turn corresponds to what logicians call a *true proposition;* for example, the statement "Supplier S1 is located in London" might be such a true proposition. (A proposition in logic is something that is either true or false, unequivocally. For instance, "William Shakespeare wrote *Pride and Prejudice*" is a proposition—a false one, as it happens.) It follows that a database is really **a collection of true propositions**.

Now, we have already said that SQL products have come to dominate the marketplace. One reason for this state of affairs is that SQL products are based on a formal theory called **the relational model of data**, and that theory in turn supports the foregoing interpretation of data and databases very directly—almost trivially, in fact. To be specific, in the relational model:

1. Data is represented by means of rows in tables,[3] and such rows can be directly interpreted as true propositions. For example, the row for BIN# 72 in Fig. 1.1 can be interpreted in an obvious way as the following true proposition:

   Bin number 72 contains two bottles of 1999 Rafanelli Zinfandel, which will be ready to drink in 2007

2. Operators are provided for operating on rows in tables, and those operators directly support the process of inferring additional true propositions from the given ones. As a simple example, the relational *project* operator (see Section 1.6) allows us to infer, from the true proposition just quoted, the following additional true proposition among others:

   Some bottles of Zinfandel will be ready to drink in 2007

   (More precisely: "Some bottles of Zinfandel in some bin, produced by some producer in some year, will be ready to drink in 2007.")

The relational model is not the only data model, however; others do exist (see Section 1.6)—though most of them differ from the relational model in being *ad hoc* to a degree, instead of being firmly based as the relational model is on formal logic. Be that as it may, the question arises: What in general *is* a data model? Following reference [1.1] (but paraphrasing considerably), we can define the concept thus:

- A **data model** is an abstract, self-contained, logical definition of the objects, operators, and so forth, that together constitute the *abstract machine* with which users

---

[3] More precisely, by *tuples* in *relations* (see Chapter 3).

interact. The objects allow us to model the *structure* of data. The operators allow us to model its *behavior.*

We can then draw a useful (and very important!) distinction between the model and its *implementation:*

- An **implementation** of a given data model is a physical realization on a real machine of the components of the abstract machine that together constitute that model.

In a nutshell: The model is what users have to know about; the implementation is what users do not have to know about.

As you can see from the foregoing, the distinction between model and implementation is really just a special case—a very important special case—of the familiar distinction between *logical* and *physical.* Sadly, however, many of today's database systems, even ones that profess to be relational, do not make these distinctions as clearly as they should. Indeed, there seems to be a fairly widespread lack of understanding of these distinctions and the importance of making them. As a consequence, there is all too often a gap between database *principles* (the way database systems ought to be) and database *practice* (the way they actually are). In this book we are concerned primarily with principles, but it is only fair to warn you that you might therefore be in for a few surprises, mostly of an unpleasant nature, if and when you start using a commercial product.

In closing this section, we should mention the fact that *data model* is another term that is used in the literature with two quite different meanings. The first meaning is as already explained. The second is as follows: A data model (second sense) is *a model of the persistent data of some particular enterprise* (e.g., the manufacturing company KnowWare Inc. discussed earlier in this section). The difference between the two meanings can be characterized thus:

- A data model in the first sense is like a *programming language*—albeit one that is somewhat abstract—whose constructs can be used to solve a wide variety of specific problems, but in and of themselves have no direct connection with any such specific problem.

- A data model in the second sense is like a *specific program* written in that language. In other words, a data model in the second sense takes the facilities provided by some model in the first sense and applies them to some specific problem. It can be regarded as *a specific application* of some model in the first sense.

In this book, the term *data model* will be used only in the first sense from this point forward, barring explicit statements to the contrary.

1.4   WHY DATABASE?

Why use a database system? What are the advantages? To some extent the answer to these questions depends on whether the system in question is single- or multi-user (or rather, to be more accurate, there are numerous *additional* advantages in the multi-user case). We consider the single-user case first.

Refer back to the wine cellar example once again (Fig. 1.1), which we can regard as illustrative of the single-user case. Now, that particular database is so small and so simple that the advantages might not be all that obvious. But imagine a similar database for a large restaurant, with a stock of perhaps thousands of bottles and very frequent changes to that stock; or think of a liquor store, with again a very large stock and high turnover on that stock. The advantages of a database system over traditional, paper-based methods of record-keeping are perhaps easier to see in these cases. Here are some of them:

- *Compactness:* There is no need for possibly voluminous paper files.

- *Speed:* The machine can retrieve and update data far faster than a human can. In particular, *ad hoc,* spur-of-the-moment queries (e.g., "Do we have more Zinfandel than Pinot Noir?") can be answered quickly without any need for time-consuming manual or visual searches.

- *Less drudgery:* Much of the sheer tedium of maintaining files by hand is eliminated. Mechanical tasks are always better done by machines.

- *Currency:* Accurate, up-to-date information is available on demand at any time.

- *Protection:* The data can be better protected against unintentional loss and unlawful access.

The foregoing benefits apply with even more force in a multi-user environment, where the database is likely to be much larger and more complex than in the single-user case. However, there is one overriding additional advantage in such an environment: *The database system provides the enterprise with centralized control of its data* (which, as you should realize by now, is one of its most valuable assets). Such a situation contrasts sharply with that found in an enterprise without a database system, where typically each application has its own private files—quite often its own private tapes and disks, too—so that the data is widely dispersed and difficult to control in any systematic way.

Data Administration and Database Administration

We elaborate briefly on this concept of centralized control. The concept implies that there will be some identifiable person in the enterprise who has this central responsibility for the data, and that person is the **data administrator** (DA for short) mentioned briefly at the end of Section 1.2. Given that, to repeat, the data is one of the enterprise's most valuable assets, it is imperative that there should be some person who understands that data, and the needs of the enterprise with respect to that data, *at a senior management level.* The data administrator is that person. Thus, it is the data administrator's job to decide what data should be stored in the database in the first place, and to establish policies for maintaining and dealing with that data once it has been stored. An example of such a policy might be one that dictates who can perform what operations on what data in what circumstances—in other words, a *data security* policy (see the next subsection).

Note carefully that the data administrator is a manager, not a technician (although he or she certainly does need to have some broad appreciation of the capabilities of database systems at a technical level). The *technical* person responsible for implementing the data administrator's decisions is the **database administrator** (DBA for short). The DBA, unlike the data administrator, is thus an information technology (IT) professional. The job of the DBA is to create the actual database and to put in place the technical controls needed to enforce the various policy decisions made by the data administrator. The DBA is also responsible for ensuring that the system operates with adequate performance and for providing a variety of other technical services. The DBA will typically have a staff of system programmers and other technical assistants (i.e., the DBA function will typically be performed in practice by a team of people, not just by one person); for simplicity, however, it is convenient to assume that the DBA is indeed a single individual. We will discuss the DBA function in more detail in Chapter 2.

Benefits of the Database Approach

In this subsection we identify some more specific advantages that accrue from the foregoing notion of centralized control.

- *The data can be shared.*

  We discussed this point in Section 1.2, but for completeness we mention it again here. Sharing means not only that existing applications can share the data in the database, but also that new applications can be developed to operate against that same data. In other words, it might be possible to satisfy the data requirements of new applications without having to add any new data to the database.

- *Redundancy can be reduced.*

  In nondatabase systems each application has its own private files. This fact can often lead to considerable redundancy in stored data, with resultant waste in storage space. For example, a personnel application and an education records application might both own a file that includes department information for employees. As suggested in Section 1.2, however, those two files can be integrated, and the redundancy eliminated, as long as the data administrator is aware of the data requirements for both applications—that is, as long as the enterprise has the necessary overall control.

  Note: We do not mean to say that *all* redundancy can or necessarily should be eliminated. Sometimes there are sound business or technical reasons for maintaining several distinct copies of the same data. However, we do mean that any such redundancy should be carefully **controlled**; that is, the DBMS should be aware of it, if it exists, and should assume responsibility for "propagating updates" (see the point immediately following).

- *Inconsistency can be avoided (to some extent).*

  This is really a corollary of the previous point. Suppose a given fact about the real world—say the fact that employee E3 works in department D8—is represented by two distinct entries in the database. Suppose also that the DBMS is not aware of this duplication (i.e., the redundancy is not controlled). Then there will necessarily be occasions on which the two entries will not agree: namely, when one of the two has been updated and the other not. At such times the database is said to be *inconsistent*. Clearly, a database that is in an inconsistent state is capable of supplying incorrect or contradictory information to its users.

Of course, if the given fact is represented by a single entry (i.e., if the redundancy is removed), then such an inconsistency cannot occur. Alternatively, if the redundancy is not removed but is *controlled* (by making it known to the DBMS), then the DBMS can guarantee that the database is never inconsistent *as seen by the user,* by ensuring that any change made to either of the two entries is automatically applied to the other one as well. This process is known as **propagating updates**.

■ *Transaction support can be provided.*

A **transaction** is a logical unit of work (more precisely, a logical unit of *database* work), typically involving several database operations—in particular, several update operations. The standard example involves the transfer of a cash amount from one account *A* to another account *B*. Clearly two updates are required here, one to withdraw the cash from account *A* and the other to deposit it to account *B*. If the user has made the two updates part of the same transaction, then the system can effectively guarantee that either both of them are done or neither is—even if, for example, the system fails (say because of a power outage) halfway through the process.

Note: The transaction *atomicity* feature just illustrated is not the only benefit of transaction support, but unlike some of the others it is one that applies, at least in principle, even in the single-user case. (On the other hand, single-user systems often do not provide any transaction support at all but simply leave the problem to the user.) A full description of all of the various advantages of transaction support and how they can be achieved appears in Chapters 15 and 16.

■ *Integrity can be maintained.*

The problem of integrity is the problem of ensuring (as far as possible) that the data in the database is correct. Inconsistency between two entries that purport to represent the same fact is an example of lack of integrity (see the discussion of this point earlier in this subsection); of course, this particular problem can arise only if redundancy exists in the stored data. Even if there is no redundancy, however, the database might still contain incorrect information. For example, an employee might be shown as having worked 400 hours in the week instead of 40, or as belonging to a department that does not exist. Centralized control of the database can help in avoiding such problems— insofar as they can be avoided—by permitting the data administrator to define, and the DBA to implement, **integrity constraints** to be checked when update operations are performed.

It is worth pointing out that data integrity is even more important in a database system than it is in a "private files" environment, precisely because the data is shared. For without appropriate controls it would be possible for one user to update the database incorrectly, thereby generating bad data and so "infecting" other innocent users of that data. It should also be mentioned that most database products are still quite weak in their support for integrity constraints (though there have been some recent improvements in this area). This fact is unfortunate, given that (as we will see in Chapter 9) integrity constraints are both fundamental and crucially important—much more so than is usually realized, in fact.

- *Security can be enforced.*

  Having complete jurisdiction over the database, the DBA (under appropriate direction from the data administrator) can ensure that the only means of access to the database is through the proper channels, and hence can define **security constraints** to be checked whenever access is attempted to sensitive data. Different constraints can be established for each type of access (retrieve, insert, delete, etc.) to each piece of information in the database. Note, however, that without such constraints the security of the data might actually be more at risk than in a traditional (dispersed) filing system; that is, the centralized nature of a database system in a sense *requires* that a good security system be in place also.

- *Conflicting requirements can be balanced.*

  Knowing the overall requirements of the enterprise, as opposed to the requirements of individual users, the DBA (again under the data administrator's direction) can so structure the system as to provide an overall service that is "best for the enterprise." For example, a physical representation can be chosen for the data in storage that gives fast access for the most important applications (possibly at the cost of slower access for certain other applications).

- *Standards can be enforced.*

  With central control of the database, the DBA (under the direction of the data administrator once again) can ensure that all applicable standards are observed in the representation of the data, including any or all of the following: departmental, installation, corporate, industry, national, and international standards. Standardizing data representation is particularly desirable as an aid to *data interchange,* or movement of data between systems (this consideration is becoming particularly important with the advent of distributed systems—see Chapters 2, 21, and 27). Likewise, data naming and documentation standards are also very desirable as an aid to data sharing and understandability.

  Now, most of the advantages listed so far are probably fairly obvious. However, one further point—which might not be as obvious, although it is in fact implied by several of the others—needs to be added to the list: *the provision of data independence.* (Strictly speaking, this is an *objective* for database systems, rather than an advantage as such.) The concept of data independence is so important that we devote a separate section to it.

1.5   DATA INDEPENDENCE

We begin by observing that there are two kinds of data independence, physical and logical [1.3, 1.4]; for the time being, however, we will concern ourselves with the physical kind only. Until further notice, therefore, the unqualified term *data independence* should be understood to mean physical data independence specifically. (We should perhaps add that the term *data independence* is not very apt—it does not capture very well the essence of what is really going on—but it is the term traditionally used, and we will stay with it in this book.)

Data independence can most easily be understood by first considering its opposite. Applications implemented on older systems—prerelational or even predatabase systems—tend to be *data-dependent*. What this means is that the way the data is physically represented in secondary storage, and the techniques used to access it, are both dictated by the requirements of the application under consideration, and moreover that *knowledge of that physical representation and those access techniques is built into the application code.* For example, suppose we have an application that uses the EMPLOYEE file of Fig. 1.5, and suppose it is decided, for performance reasons, that the file is to be indexed on its "employee name" field (see Appendix D, online). In an older system, the application in question will typically be aware of the fact that the index exists, and aware also of the sequence of records as defined by that index, and the internal structure of the application will be built around that knowledge. In particular, the precise form of the various data access and exception-checking routines within the application will depend very heavily on details of the interface presented to the application by the data management software.

We say that an application such as the one in this example is **data-dependent**, because it is impossible to change the physical representation (how the data is physically represented in storage) and access techniques (how it is physically accessed) without affecting the application, probably drastically. For instance, it would not be possible to replace the index in the example by a hashing scheme without making major modifications to the application code. What is more, the portions of that code requiring alteration in such a situation are precisely those portions that communicate with the data management software; the difficulties involved are quite irrelevant to the problem the application was originally written to solve—that is, they are difficulties *introduced* by the nature of the data management interface.

In a database system, however, it would be extremely undesirable to allow applications to be data-dependent in the foregoing sense, for at least the following two reasons:

1. Different applications will require different views of the same data. For example, suppose that before the enterprise introduces its integrated database there are two applications, *A* and *B,* each owning a private file that includes the field "customer balance." Suppose, however, that application *A* stores that field in decimal, whereas application *B* stores it in binary. It will still be possible to integrate the two files, and to eliminate the redundancy, provided the DBMS is ready and able to perform all necessary conversions between the stored representation chosen (which might be decimal or binary or something else again) and the form in which each application wishes to see it. For example, if it is decided to store the field in decimal, then every access by *B* will require a conversion to or from binary.

   This is a fairly trivial example of the kind of difference that might exist in a database system between the data as seen by a given application and the data as physically stored. We will consider many other possible differences later in this section.

2. The DBA—or possibly the DBMS—must have the freedom to change the physical representation and access technique in response to changing requirements, without existing applications having to be modified. For example, new kinds of data might be added to the database; new standards might be adopted; application priorities (and therefore relative performance requirements) might change; new storage devices

might become available; and so on. If applications are data-dependent, such changes will typically require corresponding changes to program code, thus tying up programmer effort that would otherwise be available for the creation of new applications. It is still not uncommon, even today, to find a significant fraction of the available programming effort devoted to this kind of maintenance (think of all the work that went into addressing the "Year 2000" problem)—hardly the best use of a scarce and valuable resource.

It follows that the provision of data independence is a major objective for database systems. Data independence can be defined as **the immunity of applications to change in physical representation and access technique**—which implies that the applications in question do not depend on any particular physical representation or access technique. In Chapter 2, we describe an architecture for database systems that provides a basis for achieving this objective. Before then, however, let us consider in more detail some examples of the types of changes that the DBA might wish to make, and that we might therefore wish applications to be immune to.

We start by defining three terms: *stored field, stored record,* and *stored file* (refer to Fig. 1.7).

- A **stored field** is, loosely, the smallest unit of stored data. The database will contain many **occurrences** (or **instances**) of each of several **types** of stored field. For example, a database containing information about different kinds of parts might include a stored field type called "part number," and then there would be one occurrence of that stored field for each kind of part (screw, hinge, lid, etc.).

  Note: The foregoing paragraph notwithstanding, you should be aware that it is common in practice to drop the qualifiers *type* and *occurrence* and to rely on context to indicate which is meant. Despite a small risk of confusion, the practice is convenient, and we will adopt it ourselves from time to time in what follows. (These remarks apply to stored records as well—see the paragraph immediately following.)

- A **stored record** is a collection of related stored fields. Again we distinguish between type and occurrence. A stored record **occurrence** (or **instance**) consists of a group of related stored field occurrences. For example, a stored record occurrence in the "parts" database might consist of an occurrence of each of the following stored fields: part number, part name, part color, and part weight. We say that the database contains many occurrences of the "part" stored record **type**—again, one occurrence for each kind of part.

- Finally, a **stored file** is the collection of all currently existing occurrences of one type of stored record. (We assume for simplicity that any given stored file contains just one type of stored record. This simplification does not materially affect any of our subsequent discussions.)

Now, in nondatabase systems it is normally the case that any given *logical* record as seen by some application is identical to some corresponding *stored* record. As we have already seen, however, this is not necessarily the case in a database system, because the DBA might need to be able to make changes to the stored representation of data—that is,

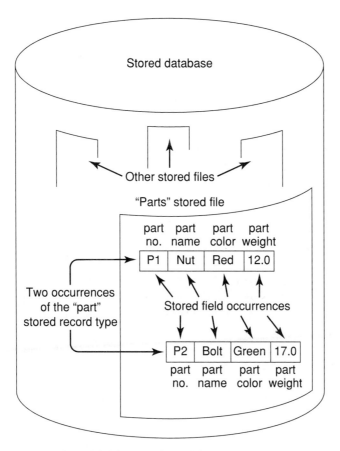

Fig. 1.7   Stored fields, records, and files

to the stored fields, records, and files—while the data as seen by applications does *not* change. For example, the SALARY field in the EMPLOYEE file might be stored in binary to economize on storage space, whereas a given COBOL application might see it as a character string. And later the DBA might decide for some reason to change the stored representation of that field from binary to decimal, say, and yet still allow the COBOL application to see it in character form.

As stated earlier, a difference such as this one—involving data type conversion on some field on each access—is comparatively minor. In general, however, the difference between what the application sees and what is physically stored might be quite considerable. To amplify this remark, we briefly consider some aspects of the stored representation that might be subject to change. You should consider in each case what the DBMS would have to do to make applications immune to such change (and indeed whether such immunity can always be achieved).

- *Representation of numeric data*

  A numeric field might be stored in internal arithmetic form (e.g., packed decimal) or as a character string. Either way, the DBA must choose whether to use *fixed* or *floating point;* what *base* or *radix* (e.g., binary or decimal) to use; what the *precision* (number of digits) should be; and, if fixed point, what the *scale factor* (number of digits after the radix point) should be. Any of these aspects might need to be changed to improve performance or to conform to a new standard or for many other reasons.

- *Representation of character data*

  A character string field might be stored using any of several distinct coded character sets—for example, ASCII, EBCDIC, or Unicode.

- *Units for numeric data*

  The units in a numeric field might change—from inches to centimeters, for example, during a process of metrication.

- *Data coding*

  In some situations it might be desirable to represent data in storage by coded values. For example, the "part color" field, which an application sees as a character string ("Red" or "Blue" or "Green" . . .), might be stored as a single decimal digit, interpreted according to the coding scheme 1 = "Red," 2 = "Blue," and so on.

- *Data materialization*

  In practice the logical field seen by an application usually does correspond directly to some specific stored field (although there might be differences in data type, coding, and so on, as we have seen). If it does, then the process of *materialization*—that is, constructing an occurrence of the logical field from the corresponding stored field occurrence and presenting it to the application—is said to be *direct.* Sometimes, however, a logical field will have no single stored counterpart; instead, its values will be materialized by means of some computation, perhaps on several stored field occurrences. For example, values of the logical field "total quantity" might be materialized by summing a number of individual stored quantities. In such a case, the materialization process is said to be *indirect.*

- *Structure of stored records*

  Two existing stored records might be combined into one. For example, the stored records

part no.	part color

  and

part no.	part weight

  might be combined to form

part no.	part color	part weight

  Such a change might occur as new applications are integrated into the database system. The implication is that a given application's logical record might consist of a proper subset of the corresponding stored record—that is, certain fields in that stored record would be invisible to the application in question.

Alternatively, a single stored record type might be split into two. Reversing the previous example, the stored record

part no.	part color	part weight

might be split into

part no.	part color

and

part no.	part weight

Such a split would allow less frequently used portions of the original record to be stored on a slower device, for example. The implication is that a given application's logical record might contain fields from several distinct stored records—that is, it might be a proper superset of any given one of those stored records.

- *Structure of stored files*

  A given stored file can be physically implemented in storage in a wide variety of ways (see Appendix D, online). For example, it might be entirely contained within a single storage volume (e.g., a single disk), or it might be spread across several volumes (possibly on several different device types); it might or might not be physically sequenced according to the values of some stored field; it might or might not be sequenced in one or more additional ways by some other means (e.g., by one or more indexes or one or more embedded pointer chains or both); it might or might not be accessible via some hashing scheme; the stored records might or might not be physically grouped into blocks; and so on. But none of these considerations should affect applications in any way (other than performance, of course).

This concludes our partial list of aspects of the stored data representation that are subject to possible change. Note that the list implies in particular that the database should be able to **grow** without impairing existing applications; indeed, enabling the database to grow without logically impairing existing applications is one of the most important reasons for requiring data independence in the first place. For example, it should be possible to extend an existing stored record by the addition of new stored fields, representing, typically, further information concerning some existing type of entity (e.g., a "unit cost" field might be added to the "part" stored record). Such new fields should simply be invisible to existing applications. Likewise, it should be possible to add entirely new stored record types and new stored files, again without requiring any change to existing applications; such new records and files would typically represent new entity types (e.g., a "supplier" record type might be added to the "parts" database). Again, such additions should be invisible to existing applications.

As you might have realized by now, data independence is one of the reasons why separating the data model from its implementation, as discussed near the end of Section 1.3, is so important: To the extent we do *not* make that separation, we will not achieve data independence. The widespread failure to make the separation properly, in today's SQL systems in particular, is thus particularly distressing. *Note:* We do not mean to suggest by these remarks that today's SQL systems provide no data independence at all—only that they provide much less than relational systems are theoretically capable of.[4] In other words, data independence is not an absolute; different systems provide it to different degrees, and few if any provide none at all. Today's SQL systems typically provide more data independence than older systems did, but they are still far from perfect, as we will see in the chapters to come.

1.6   RELATIONAL SYSTEMS AND OTHERS

We have said that SQL systems have come to dominate the DBMS marketplace, and that one important reason for this state of affairs is that such systems are based on *the relational model of data.* Informally, indeed, SQL systems are often referred to as *relational systems* specifically.[5] In addition, the vast majority of database research over the last 30 years or so has also been based (albeit a little indirectly, in some cases) on the relational model. Indeed, it is fair to say that the introduction of the relational model in 1969–70 was *the single most important event in the entire history of the database field.* For these reasons, plus the fact that the relational model is solidly based on logic and mathematics and therefore provides an ideal vehicle for teaching database foundations and principles, the emphasis in this book is heavily on relational systems.

What then exactly is a relational system? It is obviously not possible to answer this question properly at this early point in the book—but it is possible, and desirable, to give a rough and ready answer, which we can make more precise later. Briefly, then (albeit very loosely), a relational system is a system in which:

1. The data is perceived by the user as tables (and nothing but tables).

2. The operators available to the user for (e.g.) retrieval are operators that derive "new" tables from "old" ones. For example, there is one operator, *restrict,* which extracts a subset of the rows of a given table, and another, *project,* which extracts a subset of the columns—and a row subset and a column subset of a table can both be regarded in turn as tables in their own right, as we will see in just a moment.

So why are such systems called "relational"? The reason is that *relation* is basically just a mathematical term for a table. (Indeed, the terms *relation* and *table*—sometimes *relational* table for emphasis—can be taken as synonymous, at least for informal purposes. See Chapters 3 and 6 for further discussion.) Please note that the reason is definitely *not* that *relation* is "basically just a mathematical term for" a *relationship* in the sense of entity/relationship diagrams as described in Section 1.3; in fact, as noted in that section, there is very little direct connection between relational systems and such diagrams.

As promised, we will make the foregoing definitions much more precise later, but they will serve for the time being. Fig. 1.8 provides an illustration. The data—see part *a* of the figure—consists of a single table, named CELLAR (in fact, it is a scaled-down version

---

[4] A striking example of what relational systems *are* capable of in this respect is described in Appendix A.

[5] Despite the fact that in many respects SQL is quite notorious for its *departures* from the relational model, as we will see.

```
a. Given table:              CELLAR   ┌──────────────┬───────┬──────────┐
                                      │ WINE         │ YEAR  │ BOTTLES  │
                                      ├──────────────┼───────┼──────────┤
                                      │ Zinfandel    │ 1999  │        2 │
                                      │ Fumé Blanc   │ 2000  │        2 │
                                      │ Pinot Noir   │ 1997  │        3 │
                                      │ Zinfandel    │ 1998  │        9 │
                                      └──────────────┴───────┴──────────┘

b. Operators (examples):

1. Restrict:            Result:       ┌──────────────┬───────┬──────────┐
                                      │ WINE         │ YEAR  │ BOTTLES  │
   SELECT WINE, YEAR, BOTTLES         ├──────────────┼───────┼──────────┤
   FROM CELLAR                        │ Zinfandel    │ 1999  │        2 │
   WHERE YEAR > 1998 ;                │ Fumé Blanc   │ 2000  │        2 │
                                      └──────────────┴───────┴──────────┘

2. Project:             Result:       ┌──────────────┬──────────┐
                                      │ WINE         │ BOTTLES  │
   SELECT WINE, BOTTLES               ├──────────────┼──────────┤
   FROM CELLAR ;                      │ Zinfandel    │        2 │
                                      │ Fumé Blanc   │        2 │
                                      │ Pinot Noir   │        3 │
                                      │ Zinfandel    │        9 │
                                      └──────────────┴──────────┘
```

Fig. 1.8   Data structure and operators in a relational system (examples)

of the CELLAR table from Fig. 1.1, reduced in size to make it more manageable). Two sample retrievals, one involving a *restriction* or row-subsetting operation and the other a *projection* or column-subsetting operation, are shown in part *b* of the figure. The examples are expressed in SQL once again.

We can now distinguish between relational and nonrelational systems. In a relational system, the user sees the data as tables, and nothing but tables (as already explained). In a nonrelational system, by contrast, the user sees *other data structures* (either instead of or as well as the tables of a relational system). Those other structures, in turn, require other operators to access them. For example, in a hierarchic system like IBM's IMS, the data is represented to the user in the form of trees (hierarchies), and the operators provided for accessing such trees include operators for *following pointers* (namely, the pointers that implement the hierarchic paths up and down the trees). By contrast, as the examples in this chapter have shown, it is precisely an important distinguishing characteristic of relational systems that **they involve no pointers** (at least, no pointers visible to the user—i.e., no pointers at the model level—though there might well be pointers at the level of the physical implementation).

As the foregoing discussion suggests, database systems can be conveniently categorized according to the data structures and operators they present to the user. According to this scheme, the oldest (prerelational) systems fall into three broad categories: **inverted list**, **hierarchic**, and **network** systems.[6] (*Note:* The term *network* here has nothing to do

---

[6] By analogy with the relational model, earlier editions of this book referred to inverted list, hierarchic, and network *models* (and much of the literature still does). To talk in such terms is a little misleading, however, because—unlike the relational model—the inverted list, hierarchic, and network "models" were all invented *after the fact;* that is, commercial inverted list, hierarchic, and network products were implemented *first,* and the corresponding "models" were defined *subsequently* by a process of induction (in this context, a polite term for guesswork) from those existing implementations. See the annotation to reference [1.1] for further discussion.

with networks in the data communications sense, as described in the next chapter.) We do not discuss these categories in detail in this book because—from a technological point of view, at least—they must be regarded as obsolete. You can find tutorial descriptions of all three in reference [1.5] if you are interested.

As an aside, we remark that network systems are sometimes called either **CODASYL** systems or **DBTG** systems, after the committee that proposed them: namely, the Data Base Task Group (DBTG) of the Conference on Data Systems Languages (CODASYL). Probably the best-known example of such a system is IDMS, from Computer Associates International Inc. Like hierarchic systems (but unlike relational ones), such systems all expose pointers to the user.

The first **relational** products began to appear in the late 1970s and early 1980s. At the time of writing, the vast majority of database systems are relational (at least, they support SQL), and they run on just about every kind of hardware and software platform available. Leading examples include, in alphabetical order, DB2 (various versions) from IBM Corp., Ingres II from Computer Associates International Inc., Informix Dynamic Server from Informix Software Inc.,[7] Microsoft SQL Server from Microsoft Corp., Oracle 9i from Oracle Corp., and Sybase Adaptive Server from Sybase Inc. *Note:* When we have cause to refer to any of these products later in this book, we will refer to them (as most of the industry does, informally) by the abbreviated names DB2, Ingres (pronounced "ingress"), Informix, SQL Server, Oracle, and Sybase, respectively.

Subsequently, **object** and **object/relational** products began to become available—object systems in the late 1980s and early 1990s, object/relational systems in the late 1990s. The object/relational systems are extended versions of certain of the original SQL products (e.g., DB2, Informix); the object—sometimes *object-oriented*—systems represent attempts to do something entirely different, as in the case of GemStone from GemStone Systems Inc. and Versant ODBMS from Versant Object Technology. Such systems are discussed in Part VI of this book. (We should note that the term *object* as used in this paragraph has a rather specific meaning, which we will explain when we get to Part VI. Prior to that point, we will use the term in its normal generic sense, barring explicit statements to the contrary.)

In addition to the approaches already mentioned, research has proceeded over the years on a variety of alternative schemes, including the **multi-dimensional** approach and the **logic-based** (also called *deductive* or *expert*) approach. We discuss multi-dimensional systems in Chapter 22 and logic-based systems in Chapter 24. Also, the recent explosive growth of the World Wide Web and the use of XML has generated much interest in what has become known (not very aptly) as the **semistructured** approach. We discuss "semistructured" systems in Chapter 27.

1.7 SUMMARY

We close this introductory chapter by summarizing the main points discussed. First, a **database system** can be thought of as a computerized record-keeping system. Such a sys-

---

[7] The DBMS division of Informix Software Inc. was acquired by IBM Corp. in 2001.

tem involves the **data** itself (stored in the **database**), **hardware**, **software** (in particular the **database management system** or DBMS), and—most important!—**users**. Users in turn can be divided into **application programmers**, **end users**, and the **database administrator** or DBA. The DBA is responsible for administering the database and database system in accordance with policies established by the **data administrator** or DA.

Databases are **integrated** and (usually) **shared**; they are used to store **persistent data**. Such data can usefully, albeit informally, be considered as representing **entities**, together with **relationships** among those entities—although in fact a relationship is really just a special kind of entity. We very briefly examined the idea of **entity/relationship diagrams**.

Database systems provide a number of benefits, of which one of the most important is (physical) **data independence**. Data independence can be defined as the immunity of application programs to changes in the way the data is physically stored and accessed. Among other things, data independence requires that a sharp distinction be made between the **data model** and its **implementation**. (We remind you in passing that the term *data model,* perhaps unfortunately, has two rather different meanings.)

Database systems also usually support **transactions** or logical units of work. One advantage of transactions is that they are guaranteed to be **atomic** (all or nothing), even if the system fails in the middle of the transaction in question.

Finally, database systems can be based on a number of different approaches. Relational systems in particular are based on a formal theory called **the relational model**, according to which data is represented as rows in tables (interpreted as **true propositions**), and operators are provided that directly support the process of **inferring** additional true propositions from the given ones. From both an economic and a theoretical perspective, relational systems are easily the most important (and this state of affairs is not likely to change in the foreseeable future). We have seen a few simple examples of **SQL**, the standard language for relational systems (in particular, examples of the SQL **SELECT**, **INSERT**, **DELETE**, and **UPDATE** statements). This book is heavily based on relational systems, although—for reasons explained in the preface—not so much on SQL *per se.*

EXERCISES

1.1 Explain the following in your own words:

binary relationship	menu-driven interface
command-driven interface	multi-user system
concurrent access	online application
data administration	persistent data
database	property
database system	query language
data independence	redundancy
DBA	relationship
DBMS	security

entity   sharing
entity/relationship diagram   stored field
forms-driven interface   stored file
integration   stored record
integrity   transaction

1.2   What are the advantages of using a database system? What are the disadvantages?

1.3   What do you understand by the term *relational system?* Distinguish between relational and nonrelational systems.

1.4   What do you understand by the term *data model?* Explain the difference between a data model and its implementation. Why is the difference important?

1.5   Show the effects of the following SQL retrieval operations on the wine cellar database of Fig. 1.1:

```
a. SELECT WINE, PRODUCER
   FROM    CELLAR
   WHERE   BIN# = 72 ;

b. SELECT WINE, PRODUCER
   FROM    CELLAR
   WHERE   YEAR > 2000 ;

c. SELECT BIN#, WINE, YEAR
   FROM    CELLAR
   WHERE   READY < 2003 ;

d. SELECT WINE, BIN#, YEAR
   FROM    CELLAR
   WHERE   PRODUCER = 'Robt. Mondavi'
   AND     BOTTLES > 6 ;
```

1.6   Give in your own words an interpretation as a true proposition of a typical row from each of your answers to Exercise 1.5.

1.7   Show the effects of the following SQL update operations on the wine cellar database of Fig. 1.1:

```
a. INSERT
   INTO    CELLAR ( BIN#, WINE, PRODUCER, YEAR, BOTTLES, READY )
   VALUES ( 80, 'Syrah', 'Meridian', 1998, 12, 2003 ) ;

b. DELETE
   FROM    CELLAR
   WHERE   READY > 2004 ;

c. UPDATE  CELLAR
   SET     BOTTLES = 5
   WHERE   BIN# = 50 ;

d. UPDATE  CELLAR
   SET     BOTTLES = BOTTLES + 2
   WHERE   BIN# = 50 ;
```

1.8   Write SQL statements to perform the following operations on the wine cellar database:

a. Get bin number, name of wine, and number of bottles for all Geyser Peak wines.

b. Get bin number and name of wine for all wines for which there are more than five bottles in stock.

c. Get bin number for all red wines.

   d. Add three bottles to bin number 30.

   e. Remove all Chardonnay from stock.

   f. Add an entry for a new case (12 bottles) of Gary Farrell Merlot: bin number 55, year 2000, ready in 2005.

1.9 Suppose you have a music collection consisting of CDs and/or minidiscs and/or LPs and/or audiotapes, and you want to build a database that will let you find which recordings you have for a specific composer (e.g., Sibelius) or conductor (e.g., Simon Rattle) or soloist (e.g., Arthur Grumiaux) or work (e.g., Beethoven's Fifth) or orchestra (e.g., the New York Philharmonic) or kind of work (e.g., violin concerto) or chamber group (e.g., the Kronos Quartet). Draw an entity/relationship diagram like that of Fig. 1.6 for this database.

REFERENCES AND BIBLIOGRAPHY

1.1 E. F. Codd: "Data Models in Database Management," Proc. Workshop on Data Abstraction, Databases, and Conceptual Modelling, Pingree Park, Colo. (June 1980), *ACM SIGMOD Record 11*, No. 2 (February 1981) and elsewhere.

> Codd was the inventor of the relational model, which he first described in reference [6.1]. Reference [6.1], however, did not in fact define the term *data model* as such—but the present much later paper does. It also addresses the question: What purposes are data models in general, and the relational model in particular, intended to serve? And it goes on to offer evidence to support the claim that, contrary to popular belief, the relational model was in fact the first data model to be defined. In other words, Codd has some claim to being the inventor of the data model concept in general, as well as of the relational data model in particular.

1.2 Hugh Darwen: "What a Database *Really* Is: Predicates and Propositions," in C. J. Date, Hugh Darwen, and David McGoveran, *Relational Database Writings 1994–1997*. Reading, Mass.: Addison-Wesley (1998).

> This paper gives a very approachable (informal but accurate) explanation of the idea, discussed briefly near the end of Section 1.3, that a database is best thought of as a collection of true propositions.

1.3 C. J. Date and P. Hopewell: "Storage Structures and Physical Data Independence," Proc. 1971 ACM SIGFIDET Workshop on Data Definition, Access, and Control, San Diego, Calif. (November 1971).

1.4 C. J. Date and P. Hopewell: "File Definition and Logical Data Independence," Proc. 1971 ACM SIGFIDET Workshop on Data Definition, Access, and Control, San Diego, Calif. (November 1971).

> References [1.3] and [1.4] were the first papers to define and distinguish between physical and logical data independence.

1.5 C. J. Date: *Relational Database Writings 1991–1994*. Reading, Mass.: Addison-Wesley (1995).

CHAPTER 2

Database System Architecture

2.1 INTRODUCTION

We are now in a position to present an architecture for a database system. Our aim in presenting this architecture is to provide a framework on which subsequent chapters can build. Such a framework is useful for describing general database concepts and for explaining the structure of specific database systems—but we do not claim that every system can neatly be matched to this particular framework, nor do we mean to suggest that this particular architecture provides the only possible framework. In particular, "small" systems (see Chapter 1) will probably not support all aspects of the architecture. However, the architecture does seem to fit most systems reasonably well; moreover, it is basically identical to the architecture proposed by the ANSI/SPARC Study Group on Data Base Management Systems (the so-called ANSI/SPARC architecture—see references [2.1] and [2.2]). We choose not to follow the ANSI/SPARC terminology in every detail, however.

Caveat: This chapter resembles Chapter 1 inasmuch as, while an understanding of the material it contains is essential to a full appreciation of the structure and capabilities of a modern database system, it is again somewhat abstract and dry. As with Chapter 1, therefore, you might prefer just to give the material a "once over lightly" reading for now and come back to it later as it becomes more directly relevant to the topics at hand.

2.2   THE THREE LEVELS OF THE ARCHITECTURE

The ANSI/SPARC architecture is divided into three levels, usually referred to as the internal level, the external level, and the conceptual level (see Fig. 2.1), though other names are also used. Broadly speaking:

- The **internal level** (also known as the *storage* level) is the one closest to physical storage—that is, it is the one concerned with the way the data is stored inside the system.
- The **external level** (also known as the *user logical* level) is the one closest to the users—that is, it is the one concerned with the way the data is seen by individual users.
- The **conceptual level** (also known as the *community logical* level, or sometimes just the *logical* level, unqualified) is a level of indirection between the other two.

Observe that the external level is concerned with *individual* user perceptions, while the conceptual level is concerned with a *community* user perception. As we saw in Chapter 1, most users will not be interested in the total database, but only in some restricted

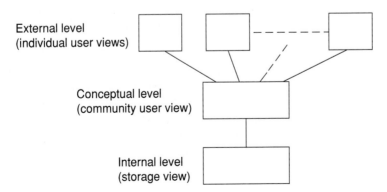

Fig. 2.1   The three levels of the architecture

portion of it; thus, there will be many distinct "external views," each consisting of a more or less abstract representation of some portion of the total database, and there will be precisely one "conceptual view," consisting of a similarly abstract representation of the database in its entirety. And then there will be precisely one "internal view," representing the database as stored internally. Note that (to use the terminology of Chapter 1) the external and conceptual levels are both *model* levels, while the internal level is an *implementation* level; in other words, the external and conceptual levels are defined in terms of user-oriented constructs such as records and fields, while the internal level is defined in terms of machine-oriented constructs such as bits and bytes.

An example will help to make these ideas clearer. Fig. 2.2 shows the conceptual view, the corresponding internal view, and two corresponding external views (one for a PL/I user and one for a COBOL user[1]), all for a simple personnel database. Of course, the example is completely hypothetical—it is not intended to resemble any real system—and many irrelevant details have deliberately been omitted. *Explanation:*

1. At the conceptual level, the database contains information concerning an entity type called EMPLOYEE. Each individual employee has an EMPLOYEE_NUMBER (six characters), a DEPARTMENT_NUMBER (four characters), and a SALARY (five decimal digits).

2. At the internal level, employees are represented by a stored record type called STORED_EMP, 20 bytes long. STORED_EMP contains four stored fields: a 6-byte prefix (presumably containing control information such as codes, flags, or pointers), and three data fields corresponding to the three properties of employees. In addition, STORED_EMP records are indexed on the EMP# field by an index called EMPX, whose definition is not shown.

```
┌─────────────────────────────┬─────────────────────────────────┐
│ External (PL/I)             │ External (COBOL)                │
│ DCL 1 EMPP,                 │     01 EMPC.                     │
│     2 EMP# CHAR(6),         │        02 EMPNO PIC X(6).        │
│     2 SAL FIXED BIN(31);    │        02 DEPTNO PIC X(4).       │
├─────────────────────────────┴─────────────────────────────────┤
│ Conceptual                                                     │
│         EMPLOYEE                                               │
│             EMPLOYEE_NUMBER      CHARACTER(6)                  │
│             DEPARTMENT_NUMBER    CHARACTER(4)                  │
│             SALARY               DECIMAL(5)                    │
├────────────────────────────────────────────────────────────────┤
│ Internal                                                       │
│         STORED_EMP       BYTES=20                              │
│             PREFIX       BYTES=6,OFFSET=0                      │
│             EMP#         BYTES=6,OFFSET=6,INDEX=EMPX           │
│             DEPT#        BYTES=4,OFFSET=12                     │
│             PAY          BYTES=4,ALIGN=FULLWORD,OFFSET=16      │
└────────────────────────────────────────────────────────────────┘
```

Fig. 2.2   An example of the three levels

---

[1] We apologize for using such ancient languages as the basis for this example, but the fact is that PL/I and COBOL are both still widely used in commercial installations.

3. The PL/I user has an external view of the database in which each employee is represented by a PL/I record containing two fields (department numbers are of no interest to this user and have therefore been omitted). The record type is defined by an ordinary PL/I structure declaration in accordance with normal PL/I rules.

4. Similarly, the COBOL user has an external view in which each employee is represented by a COBOL record containing, again, two fields (this time, salaries have been omitted). The record type is defined by an ordinary COBOL record description in accordance with normal COBOL rules.

Notice that corresponding data items can have different names at different points in the foregoing scheme. For example, the employee number is called EMP# in the PL/I external view, EMPNO in the COBOL external view, EMPLOYEE_NUMBER in the conceptual view, and EMP# again in the internal view. Of course, the system must be aware of the correspondences; for example, it must be told that the COBOL field EMPNO is derived from the conceptual field EMPLOYEE_NUMBER, which in turn is derived from the stored field EMP# at the internal level. Such correspondences, or **mappings**, are not explicitly shown in Fig. 2.2; see Section 2.6 for further discussion.

Now, it makes little difference for the purposes of the present chapter whether the system under consideration is relational or otherwise. However, it might be helpful to indicate briefly how the three levels of the architecture are typically realized in a relational system specifically:

- First, the conceptual level in such a system will definitely be relational, in the sense that the objects visible at that level will be relational tables and the operators will be relational operators (including in particular the *restrict* and *project* operators discussed briefly in Chapter 1).

- Second, a given external view will typically be relational too, or something very close to it; for example, the PL/I and COBOL record declarations of Fig. 2.2 might loosely be regarded as PL/I and COBOL analogs of the declaration of a relational table in a relational system. *Note:* We should mention in passing that the term *external view* (usually abbreviated to just *view*) unfortunately has a rather specific meaning in relational contexts that is *not* identical to the meaning assigned to it in this chapter. See Chapters 3 and (especially) 10 for an explanation and discussion of the relational meaning.

- Third, the internal level will *not* be relational, because the objects at that level will not be just (stored) relational tables—instead, they will be the same kinds of objects found at the internal level of any other kind of system (stored records, pointers, indexes, hashes, etc.). In fact, the relational model as such has **nothing whatsoever to say** about the internal level; it is, to repeat from Chapter 1, concerned with how the database looks to the *user.*

We now proceed to discuss the three levels of the architecture in considerably more detail, starting with the external level. Throughout our discussions we will be making repeated references to Fig. 2.3, which shows the major components of the architecture and their interrelationships.

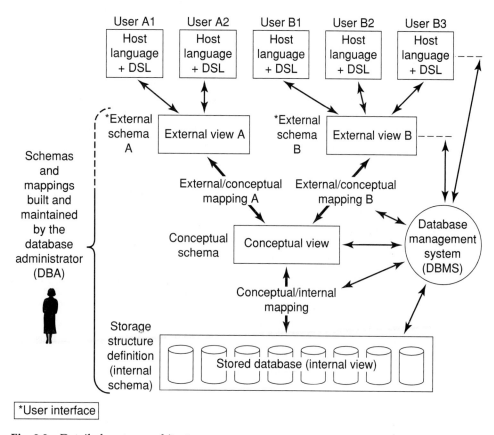

Fig. 2.3   Detailed system architecture

2.3   THE EXTERNAL LEVEL

The external level is the individual user level. As explained in Chapter 1, a given user can be an application programmer or an end user of any degree of sophistication. (The DBA is an important special case; unlike other users, however, the DBA will need to be interested in the conceptual and internal levels also. See the next two sections.)

Each user has a **language** at his or her disposal:

- For the application programmer, that language will be either a conventional programming language (e.g., Java, C++, or PL/I) or perhaps a proprietary language that is specific to the system in question. Such proprietary languages are sometimes called *fourth-generation* languages or 4GLs, on the (fuzzy!) grounds that (a) machine code, assembler language, and languages such as Java or C++ or PL/I can be regarded as three earlier language "generations," and (b) the proprietary languages represent the same kind of improvement over third-generation languages (3GLs) as those languages did over assembler language and assembler language did over machine code.

- For the end user, the language will be either a query language (probably SQL) or some special-purpose language, perhaps forms- or menu-driven, tailored to that user's requirements and supported by some online application as explained in Chapter 1.

For our purposes, the important thing about all such languages is that they will include a **data sublanguage**—that is, a subset of the total language that is concerned specifically with database objects and operations. The data sublanguage (abbreviated DSL in Fig. 2.3) is said to be **embedded** within the corresponding **host language**. The host language is responsible for providing various nondatabase facilities, such as local variables, computational operations, branching logic, and so on. A given system might support any number of host languages and any number of data sublanguages; however, one particular data sublanguage that is supported by almost all current systems is the language SQL, discussed briefly in Chapter 1. Most such systems allow SQL to be used both *interactively* as a stand-alone query language and also *embedded* in other languages such as Java or C++ or PL/I (see Chapter 4 for further discussion).

Now, although it is convenient for architectural purposes to distinguish between the data sublanguage and its containing host language, the two might in fact *not* be distinct as far as the user is concerned; indeed, it is probably preferable from the user's perspective if they are not. If they are not distinct, or if they can be distinguished only with difficulty, we say they are **tightly coupled** (and the combination is called a *database programming language*[2]). If they are clearly and easily separable, we say they are **loosely** coupled. Some commercial systems—including in particular certain SQL products, such as Oracle—support tight coupling, but not all do (tight coupling provides a more uniform set of facilities for the user but obviously involves more effort on the part of the system implementers, a fact that presumably accounts for the *status quo*).

In principle, any given data sublanguage is really a combination of at least two subordinate languages—a **data definition language** (DDL), which supports the *definition* or "declaration" of database objects, and a **data manipulation language** (DML), which supports the *processing* or "manipulation" of such objects.[3] For example, consider the PL/I user of Fig. 2.2 in Section 2.2. The data sublanguage for that user consists of those PL/I features that are used to communicate with the DBMS:

- The DDL portion consists of those declarative constructs of PL/I that are needed to declare database objects—the DECLARE (DCL) statement itself, certain PL/I data types, and possibly special extensions to PL/I to deal with new kinds of objects not supported by existing PL/I.

- The DML portion consists of those executable statements of PL/I that transfer information into and out of the database—again, possibly including special new statements.

---

[2] The language **Tutorial D** that we will be using in later chapters as a basis for examples—see the remarks on this topic in the preface to this book—is a database programming language in this sense.

[3] This rather inappropriate use of the term *manipulation* has become sanctioned by usage.

(In the interest of accuracy, we should make it clear that PL/I does not in fact include any specific database features at the time of writing. The "DML" statements in particular are typically just PL/I CALL statements that invoke the DBMS—though those calls might be syntactically disguised in some way to make them a little more user-friendly; see the discussion of *embedded SQL* in Chapter 4.)

To return to the architecture: We have already indicated that an individual user will generally be interested only in some portion of the total database; moreover, that user's view of that portion will generally be somewhat abstract when compared with the way the data is physically stored. The ANSI/SPARC term for an individual user's view is an **external view**. An external view is thus the content of the database as seen by some particular user; to that user, in other words, the external view *is* the database. For example, a user from the Personnel Department might regard the database as a collection of department and employee record occurrences, and might be quite unaware of the supplier and part record occurrences seen by users in the Purchasing Department.

In general, then, an external view consists of many occurrences of many types of **external record** (*not* necessarily the same thing as a stored record).[4] The user's data sublanguage is thus defined in terms of external records; for example, a DML *retrieve* operation will retrieve external record occurrences, not stored record occurrences. (Incidentally, we can now see that the term *logical record* used a couple of times in Chapter 1 actually referred to an external record. From this point forward, in fact, we will generally avoid the term *logical record.*)

Each external view is defined by means of an **external schema**, which consists basically of definitions of each of the various external record types in that external view (again, refer back to Fig. 2.2 for a couple of simple examples). The external schema is written using the DDL portion of the user's data sublanguage. (That DDL is therefore sometimes referred to as an **external DDL**.) For example, the employee external record type might be defined as a six-character employee number field plus a five-digit (decimal) salary field, and so on. In addition, there must be a definition of the *mapping* between the external schema and the underlying *conceptual* schema (see the next section). We will consider that mapping later, in Section 2.6.

2.4　THE CONCEPTUAL LEVEL

The **conceptual view** is a representation of the entire information content of the database, again (as with an external view) in a form that is somewhat abstract in comparison with the way in which the data is physically stored. It will also be quite different, in general, from the way in which the data is viewed by any particular user. Broadly speaking, the

---

[4] We are assuming here that all information is represented at the external level in the form of records specifically. However, some systems allow information to be represented in other ways instead of or as well as records. For a system using such alternative methods, the definitions and explanations given in this section will require suitable modification. Analogous remarks apply to the conceptual and internal levels also. Detailed consideration of such matters is beyond the scope of this early part of the book; see Chapters 14 (especially the "References and Bibliography" section) and 25 for further discussion. See also—in connection with the internal level in particular—Appendix A.

conceptual view is intended to be a view of the data "as it really is," rather than as users are forced to see it by the limitations of (for example) the particular language or hardware they might be using.

The conceptual view consists of many occurrences of many types of **conceptual record**. For example, it might consist of a collection of department record occurrences, plus a collection of employee record occurrences, plus a collection of supplier record occurrences, plus a collection of part record occurrences, and so on. A conceptual record is not necessarily the same as either an external record, on the one hand, or a stored record, on the other.

The conceptual view is defined by means of the **conceptual schema**, which includes definitions of each of the various conceptual record types (again, refer to Fig. 2.2 for a simple example). The conceptual schema is written using another data definition language, the **conceptual DDL**. If physical data independence is to be achieved, then those conceptual DDL definitions must not involve any considerations of physical representation or access technique at all—they must be definitions of information content *only*. Thus, there must be no reference in the conceptual schema to stored field representation, stored record sequence, indexes, hashing schemes, pointers, or any other storage and access details. If the conceptual schema is made truly data-independent in this way, then the external schemas, which are defined in terms of the conceptual schema (see Section 2.6), will *a fortiori* be data-independent too.

The conceptual view, then, is a view of the total database content, and the conceptual schema is a definition of that view. However, it would be misleading to suggest that the conceptual schema is nothing more than a set of definitions much like the simple record definitions found in (e.g.) a COBOL program today. The definitions in the conceptual schema are intended to include a great many additional features, such as the security and integrity constraints mentioned in Chapter 1. Some authorities would go as far as to suggest that the ultimate objective of the conceptual schema is to describe the complete enterprise—not just its data *per se,* but also how that data is used: how it flows from point to point within the enterprise, what it is used for at each point, what audit or other controls are to be applied at each point, and so on [2.3]. It must be emphasized, however, that no system today actually supports a conceptual schema of anything approaching this degree of comprehensiveness;[5] in most existing systems, the "conceptual schema" is little more than a simple union of all of the individual external schemas, plus certain security and integrity constraints. But it is certainly possible that systems of the future will be much more sophisticated in their support of the conceptual level.

2.5   THE INTERNAL LEVEL

The third level of the architecture is the internal level. The **internal view** is a low-level representation of the entire database; it consists of many occurrences of many types of **internal record**. *Internal record* is the ANSI/SPARC term for the construct that we have

---

[5] Some might argue that the so-called *business rule* systems come close (see Chapters 9 and 14).

been calling a *stored* record (and we will continue to use this latter term). The internal view is thus still at one remove from the physical level, since it does not deal in terms of *physical* records—also called **blocks** or **pages**—nor with any device-specific consider- ations such as cylinder or track sizes. In other words, the internal view effectively assumes an unbounded linear address space; details of how that address space is mapped to physi- cal storage are highly system-specific and are deliberately omitted from the general archi- tecture. *Note:* In case you are not familiar with the term, we should explain that the block, or page, is the **unit of I/O**—that is, it is the amount of data transferred between secondary storage and main memory in a single I/O operation. Typical page sizes can be anywhere from 1KB or less to 64KB or so, where (as we will see later) 1KB = one kilobyte = 1024 bytes.

The internal view is described by means of the **internal schema**, which not only defines the various stored record types but also specifies what indexes exist, how stored fields are represented, what physical sequence the stored records are in, and so on (once again, see Fig. 2.2 for a simple example; see also Appendix D, online). The internal schema is written using yet another data definition language—the **internal DDL**.

Note: In what follows, we will tend to use the more intuitive terms *stored database* and *stored database definition* in place of *internal view* and *internal schema,* respectively. Also, we observe that, in certain exceptional situations, application programs—in particu- lar, those of a utility nature (see Section 2.11)—might be permitted to operate directly at the internal level rather than at the external level. Needless to say, the practice is not rec- ommended; it represents a security risk (since the security constraints are bypassed) and an integrity risk (since the integrity constraints are bypassed likewise), and the program will be data-dependent to boot; but sometimes it might be the only way to obtain the required functionality or performance—just as an application programmer might occa- sionally have to descend to assembler language in order to satisfy certain functionality or performance objectives in a programming language system.

2.6   MAPPINGS

In addition to the three levels *per se,* the architecture of Fig. 2.3 involves certain **map- pings**—one conceptual/internal mapping and several external/conceptual mappings, in general:

- The *conceptual/internal* mapping defines the correspondence between the conceptual view and the stored database; it specifies how conceptual records and fields are repre- sented at the internal level. If the structure of the stored database is changed—that is, if a change is made to the stored database definition—then the conceptual/internal mapping must be changed accordingly, so that the conceptual schema can remain invariant. (It is the responsibility of the DBA, or possibly the DBMS, to manage such changes.) In other words, the effects of such changes must be isolated below the con- ceptual level, in order to preserve physical data independence.

- An *external/conceptual* mapping defines the correspondence between a particular external view and the conceptual view. In general, the differences that can exist between these two levels are analogous to those that can exist between the conceptual view and the stored database. For example, fields can have different data types; field and record names can be changed; several conceptual fields can be combined into a single external field; and so on. Any number of external views can exist at the same time; any number of users can share a given external view; different external views can overlap.

Without going into too much detail, it should be clear that, just as the conceptual/ internal mapping is the key to providing physical data independence, so the external/ conceptual mappings are the key to providing *logical* data independence. As we saw in Chapter 1, a system provides physical data independence [1.3] if users and user programs are immune to changes in the physical structure of the stored database. Analogously, a system provides **logical** data independence [1.4] if users and user programs are also immune to changes in the *logical* structure of the database (meaning changes at the conceptual or "community logical" level). We will have more to say on this important issue in Chapters 3 and 10.

■ In addition to the foregoing, most systems permit some external views to be defined in terms of others (in effect, via *external/external* mappings), rather than always requiring an explicit definition of the mapping to the conceptual level—a useful feature if several external views are rather similar to one another. Relational systems in particular provide such a capability.

2.7 THE DATABASE ADMINISTRATOR

As explained in Chapter 1, the *data* administrator (DA) is the person who makes the strategic and policy decisions, and the data*base* administrator (DBA) is the person who provides the necessary technical support for implementing those decisions. Thus, the DBA is responsible for the overall control of the system at a technical level. We can now describe some of the tasks of the DBA in a little more detail. In general, those tasks will include at least all of the following:

■ *Defining the conceptual schema*

It is the *data* administrator's job to decide exactly what information is to be held in the database—in other words, to identify the entities of interest to the enterprise and to identify the information to be recorded about those entities. This process is usually referred to as **logical**—sometimes *conceptual*—**database design**. Once the data administrator has thus decided the content of the database at an abstract level, the DBA will then create the corresponding conceptual schema, using the conceptual DDL. The object (compiled) form of that schema will be used by the DBMS in responding to user requests. The source (uncompiled) form will act as a reference document for the users of the system.

We should add that, in practice, matters might not be as clearcut as the foregoing remarks suggest. In some cases, the data administrator might create the conceptual schema directly. In others, the DBA might do the logical design.

■ *Defining the internal schema*

The DBA must also decide how the data is to be represented in the stored database. This process is usually referred to as **physical** database design. Having done the physical design, the DBA must then create the corresponding stored database definition (i.e., the internal schema), using the internal DDL. In addition, he or she must also define the associated conceptual/internal mapping. In practice, either the conceptual DDL or the internal DDL—most likely the former—will probably include the means for defining that mapping, but the two functions (creating the schema and defining the mapping) should be clearly separable. Like the conceptual schema, the internal schema and corresponding mapping will exist in both source and object form.

By the way, observe the sequence: Decide what data you want first, then decide how to represent it in storage. Physical design should always be done *after* logical design.

■ *Liaising with users*

It is the business of the DBA to liaise with users to ensure that the data they need is available and to write (or help the users write) the necessary external schemas, using the applicable external DDL. (As already indicated, a given system might support several distinct external DDLs.) In addition, the corresponding external/conceptual mappings must also be defined. In practice, the external DDL will probably include the means for specifying those mappings, but once again the schemas and the mappings should be clearly separable. Each external schema and corresponding mapping will exist in both source and object form.

Other aspects of the user liaison function include consulting on application design; providing technical education; assisting with problem determination and resolution; and similar professional services.

■ *Defining security and integrity constraints*

As already explained, security and integrity constraints can be regarded as part of the conceptual schema. The conceptual DDL must include facilities for specifying such constraints.

■ *Defining dump/restore schemes*

Once an enterprise is committed to a database system, it becomes critically dependent on the successful operation of that system. In the event of damage to any portion of the database—caused by human error, say, or a failure in the hardware or operating system—it is essential to be able to repair the data concerned with the minimum of delay and with as little effect as possible on the rest of the system. For example, the availability of data that has not been damaged should ideally not be affected. The DBA must define and implement an appropriate damage control scheme, typically involving (a) periodic unloading or "dumping" of the database to backup storage and (b) reloading or "restoring" the database when necessary from the most recent dump.

As an aside, we note that the need for quick data repair is one reason why it might be a good idea to spread the total data collection across several databases, instead of keeping it all in one place; the individual database might very well form the unit for dump/restore purposes. In this connection, note that *multi-terabyte systems*[6]—that is, commercial database installations that store several trillions of bytes of data, loosely speaking—already exist, and systems of the future are predicted to be much larger. It goes without saying that such *VLDB* ("very large database") systems require very careful and sophisticated administration, especially if there is a requirement for continuous availability (which there usually is). Nevertheless, we will continue to talk (for the sake of simplicity) as if there were in fact just a single database.

- *Monitoring performance and responding to changing requirements*

  As indicated in Chapter 1, the DBA is responsible for organizing the system in such a way as to get the performance that is "best for the enterprise," and for making the appropriate adjustments—that is, **tuning**—as requirements change. For example, it might be necessary to **reorganize** the stored database from time to time to ensure that performance levels remain acceptable. As already mentioned, any change to the internal level of the system must be accompanied by a corresponding change to the definition of the conceptual/internal mapping, so that the conceptual schema can remain constant.

Of course, the foregoing is not an exhaustive list—it is merely intended to give some idea of the extent and nature of the DBA's responsibilities.

2.8 THE DATABASE MANAGEMENT SYSTEM

The **database management system** (DBMS) is the software that handles all access to the database. Conceptually, what happens is the following (refer to Fig. 2.3 once again):

1. A user issues an access request, using some particular data sublanguage (typically SQL).

2. The DBMS accepts that request and analyzes it.

3. The DBMS inspects, in turn, (the object versions of) the external schema for that user, the corresponding external/conceptual mapping, the conceptual schema, the conceptual/internal mapping, and the stored database definition.

4. The DBMS executes the necessary operations on the stored database.

By way of an example, consider what is involved in the retrieval of a particular external record occurrence. In general, fields will be required from several conceptual record occurrences, and each conceptual record occurrence in turn will require fields from several stored record occurrences. Conceptually, then, the DBMS must first retrieve all required stored record occurrences, then construct the required conceptual record occur-

---

[6] 1024 bytes = 1 kilobyte (KB); 1024KB = 1 megabyte (MB); 1024MB = 1 gigabyte (GB); 1024GB = 1 terabyte (TB); 1024TB = 1 petabyte (PB); 1024PB = 1 exabyte (EB or XB); 1024XB = 1 zettabyte (ZB); 1024ZB = 1 yottabyte (YB). Note in particular that a gigabyte is a billion bytes, loosely speaking (the abbreviation BB is sometimes used instead of GB). Incidentally (and contrary to popular belief), *gigabyte* is pronounced with a soft initial *g* and the *i* is long (as in *gigantic*).

rences, and then construct the required external record occurrence. At each stage, data type or other conversions might be necessary.

Of course, the foregoing description is very much simplified; in particular, it suggests that the entire process is interpretive, inasmuch as it describes the processes of analyzing the request, inspecting the various schemas, and so on, as if they were all done at run time. Interpretation, in turn, often implies poor performance, because of the run-time overhead. In practice, however, it might be possible for access requests to be *compiled* prior to run time (in particular, several of today's SQL products do this—see, for example, the annotation to references [4.13] and [4.27] in Chapter 4).

Let us now examine the functions of the DBMS in a little more detail. Those functions will include support for at least all of the following (refer to Fig. 2.4, overleaf):

■ *Data definition*

The DBMS must be able to accept data definitions (external schemas, the conceptual schema, the internal schema, and all associated mappings) in source form and convert them to the appropriate object form. In other words, the DBMS must include **DDL processor** or **DDL compiler** components for each of the various data definition languages (DDLs). The DBMS must also "understand" the DDL definitions, in the sense that, for example, it "understands" that EMPLOYEE external records include a SALARY field, and it must be able to use this knowledge in analyzing and responding to data manipulation requests (e.g., "Get employees with salary < $50,000").

■ *Data manipulation*

The DBMS must be able to handle requests to retrieve, update, or delete existing data in the database or to add new data to the database. In other words, the DBMS must include a **DML processor** or **DML compiler** component to deal with the data manipulation language (DML).

In general, DML requests can be planned or unplanned:

a. A **planned** request is one for which the need was foreseen in advance of the time at which the request is made. The DBA will probably have tuned the physical database design in such a way as to guarantee good performance for planned requests.

b. An **unplanned** request, by contrast, is an *ad hoc* query or (less likely) update— that is, a request for which the need was not seen in advance, but instead arose in a spur-of-the-moment fashion. The physical database design might or might not be well suited for the specific request under consideration.

To use the terminology introduced in Chapter 1 (Section 1.3), planned requests are characteristic of *operational* or *production* applications, while unplanned requests are characteristic of *decision support* applications. Furthermore, planned requests will typically be issued from prewritten application programs, whereas unplanned requests, by definition, will be issued interactively, typically via some *query language processor.* (In fact, as we saw in Chapter 1, the query language processor is really a built-in online application, not part of the DBMS *per se;* we include it in Fig. 2.4 only for completeness.)

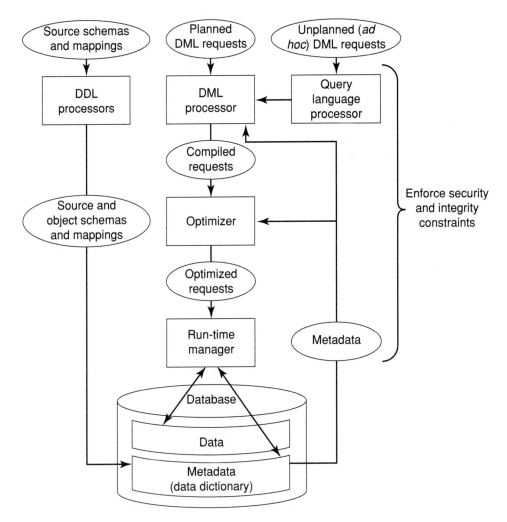

Fig. 2.4 Major DBMS functions and components

- *Optimization and execution*

  DML requests, planned or unplanned, must be processed by the **optimizer** component, whose purpose is to determine an efficient way of implementing the request.[7]
  Optimization is discussed in detail in Chapter 18. The optimized requests are then executed under the control of the **run-time manager**. (In practice, the run-time manager
  will probably invoke some kind of *file* or *storage manager* to access the stored data.
  File managers are discussed briefly at the end of the present section.)

---

[7] Throughout this book we take the term *optimization* to refer to the optimization of DML requests specifically, barring explicit statements to the contrary.

- *Data security and integrity*

  The DBMS, or some subsystem invoked by the DBMS, must monitor user requests and reject any attempt to violate the security and integrity constraints defined by the DBA (see the previous section). These tasks can be carried out at compile time or run time or some mixture of the two.

- *Data recovery and concurrency*

  The DBMS—or, more likely, another related software component called the **transaction manager** or **TP monitor**—must enforce certain recovery and concurrency controls. Details of these aspects of the system are beyond the scope of this chapter; see Part IV of this book for an in-depth discussion. The transaction manager is not shown in Fig. 2.4 because it is usually not part of the DBMS *per se.*

- *Data dictionary*

  The DBMS must provide a **data dictionary** function. The data dictionary can be regarded as a database in its own right (but a system database rather than a user database); it contains "data about the data" (sometimes called **metadata** or **descriptors**)—that is, *definitions* of other objects in the system, instead of just "raw data." In particular, all of the various schemas and mappings (external, conceptual, etc.) and all of the various security and integrity constraints will be kept, in both source and object form, in the dictionary. A comprehensive dictionary will also include much additional information, showing, for instance, which programs use which parts of the database, which users require which reports, and so on. The dictionary might even—in fact, probably should—be integrated into the database it defines and thus include its own definition. Certainly it should be possible to query the dictionary just like any other database, so that, for example, it is possible to tell which programs and/or users are likely to be affected by some proposed change to the system. See Chapter 3 for further discussion.

  Note: We are touching here on an area in which there is much terminological confusion. Some people would refer to what we are calling the dictionary as a *directory* or a *catalog*—with the tacit implication that directories and catalogs are somehow inferior to a genuine dictionary—and would reserve the term *dictionary* to refer to a specific (important) kind of application development tool. Other terms that are also sometimes used to refer to this latter kind of object are *data repository* (see Chapter 14) and *data encyclopedia.*

- *Performance*

  It goes without saying that the DBMS should perform all of its tasks as efficiently as possible.

We can summarize all of the foregoing by saying that the overall purpose of the DBMS is to provide the **user interface** to the database system. The user interface can be defined as a boundary in the system below which everything is invisible to the user. By definition, therefore, the user interface is at the *external* level. In today's SQL products, however, there are some situations—mostly having to do with update operations—in which the external level is unlikely to differ very significantly from the relevant portion of the underlying conceptual level. We will elaborate on this issue in Chapter 10.

We conclude this section by briefly contrasting database management systems (DBMSs) with *file* management systems (*file managers* or *file servers* for short). Basically, the **file manager** is that component of the underlying operating system that manages stored files; loosely speaking, therefore, it is "closer to the disk" than the DBMS is. (In fact, Appendix D, online, explains how the DBMS is often built *on top of* some kind of file manager.) Thus, the user of a file management system will be able to create and destroy stored files and perform simple retrieval and update operations on stored records in such files. In contrast to the DBMS, however:

- File managers are not aware of the internal structure of stored records and hence cannot handle requests that rely on a knowledge of that structure.

- File managers typically provide little or no support for security and integrity constraints.

- File managers typically provide little or no support for recovery and concurrency controls.

- There is no genuine data dictionary concept at the file manager level.

- File managers provide much less data independence than the DBMS does.

- Files are typically not "integrated" or "shared" in the same sense that the database is, but instead are usually private to some particular user or application.

2.9   DATA COMMUNICATIONS

In this section, we briefly consider the topic of **data communications**. Database requests from an end user are actually transmitted from the user's computer or workstation—which might be physically remote from the database system itself—to some online application, built-in or otherwise, and thence to the DBMS, in the form of *communication messages.* Likewise, responses back from the DBMS and online application to the user's workstation are also transmitted in the form of such messages. All such message transmissions take place under the control of another software component, the **data communications manager** (DC manager).

The DC manager is not part of the DBMS but is an autonomous system in its own right. However, since it is clearly required to work in harmony with the DBMS, the two are sometimes regarded as equal partners in a higher-level cooperative venture called a **database/data-communications system** (DB/DC system), in which the DBMS looks after the database and the DC manager handles all messages to and from the DBMS, or more accurately to and from applications that use the DBMS. In this book, however, we will have comparatively little to say about message handling as such (it is a large subject in its own right). Section 2.12 does briefly discuss the question of communication *between distinct systems* (e.g., between distinct machines in a communications network such as the Internet), but that is really a separate topic.

2.10   CLIENT/SERVER ARCHITECTURE

So far in this chapter we have been discussing database systems from the point of view of the so-called ANSI/SPARC architecture. In particular, we gave a simplified picture of that architecture in Fig. 2.3. In this section we offer a slightly different perspective on the subject.

The overall purpose of a database system is to support the development and execution of database applications. From a high-level point of view, therefore, such a system can be regarded as having a very simple two-part structure, consisting of a *server,* also called the *back end,* and a set of *clients,* also called the *front ends* (refer to Fig. 2.5). *Explanation:*

1. The **server** is just the DBMS itself. It supports all of the basic DBMS functions discussed in Section 2.8—data definition, data manipulation, data security and integrity, and so on. In other words, "server" in this context is just another name for the DBMS.

2. The **clients** are the various applications that run on top of the DBMS—both user-written applications and built-in applications (i.e., applications provided by the DBMS vendor or some third party). As far as the server is concerned, of course, there is no difference between user-written and built-in applications; they all use the same interface to the server—namely, the external-level interface discussed in Section 2.3. (We note as an aside that, as mentioned in Section 2.5, certain special "utility" applications might constitute an exception to the foregoing, inasmuch as they might sometimes need to operate directly at the *internal* level of the system. Such utilities are

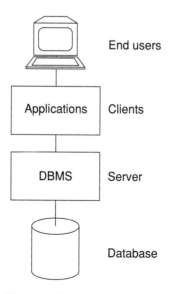

Fig. 2.5   Client/server architecture

best regarded as integral components of the DBMS, rather than as applications in the usual sense. They are discussed in more detail in the next section.)

We elaborate briefly on the question of user-written *vs.* vendor-provided applications:

- **User-written applications** are basically regular application programs, written (typically) either in a conventional 3GL such as C++ or COBOL or in some proprietary 4GL—though in both cases the language needs to be coupled somehow with an appropriate data sublanguage, as explained in Section 2.3.

- **Vendor-provided applications** (often called **tools**) are applications whose basic purpose is to assist in the creation and execution of other applications! The applications that are created are applications that are tailored to some specific task (they might not look much like applications in the conventional sense; indeed, the whole point of the tools is to allow users, especially end users, to create applications *without* having to write programs in a conventional programming language). For example, one of the vendor-provided tools will be a *report writer,* whose purpose is to allow end users to obtain formatted reports from the system on request. Any given report request can be regarded as a small application program, written in a very high-level (and special-purpose) *report writer language.*

  Vendor-provided tools can be divided into several more or less distinct classes:

  a. Query language processors

  b. Report writers

  c. Business graphics subsystems

  d. Spreadsheets

  e. Natural language processors

  f. Statistical packages

  g. Copy management or "data extract" tools

  h. Application generators (including 4GL processors)

  i. Other application development tools, including computer-aided software engineering (CASE) products

  j. Data mining and visualization tools

  and many others. Details of most such tools are beyond the scope of this book; however, we remark that since (as stated near the opening of this section) the whole point of a database system is to support the creation and execution of applications, the quality of the available tools is, or should be, a major factor in "the database decision" (i.e., the process of choosing the right database product). In other words, the DBMS *per se* is not the only factor that needs to be taken into account, nor even necessarily the most significant factor.

We close this section with a forward reference. Since the overall system can be so neatly divided into two parts, server and clients, the possibility arises of running the two on different machines. In other words, the potential exists for **distributed processing**.

Distributed processing means that distinct machines can be connected into some kind of communications network in such a way that a single data processing task can be spread across several machines in the network. In fact, so attractive is this possibility—for a variety of reasons, mainly economic—that the term *client/server* has come to apply almost exclusively to the case where client and server are indeed on different machines. We will discuss distributed processing in more detail in Section 2.12.

2.11 UTILITIES

Utilities are programs designed to help the DBA with various administration tasks. As mentioned in the previous section, some utility programs operate at the external level of the system, and thus are effectively nothing more than special-purpose applications; some might not even be provided by the DBMS vendor, but rather by some third party. Other utilities, however, operate directly at the internal level (in other words, they are really part of the server), and hence must be provided by the DBMS vendor.

Here are some examples of the kind of utilities that are typically needed in practice:

- **Load** routines, to create the initial version of the database from regular data files
- **Unload/reload** (or **dump/restore**) routines, to unload the database or portions thereof to backup storage and to reload data from such backup copies (of course, the "reload utility" is basically identical to the load utility just mentioned)
- **Reorganization** routines, to rearrange the data in the stored database for various reasons (usually having to do with performance)—for example, to cluster data in some particular way on the disk, or to reclaim space occupied by logically deleted data
- **Statistical** routines, to compute various performance statistics such as file sizes, value distributions, I/O counts, and so on
- **Analysis** routines, to analyze the statistics just mentioned

Of course, this list represents just a small sample of the range of functions that utilities typically provide; numerous other possibilities exist.

2.12 DISTRIBUTED PROCESSING

To repeat from Section 2.10, the term *distributed processing* means that distinct machines can be connected into a communications network—the Internet provides the obvious example—such that a single data processing task can span several machines in the network. (The term *parallel processing* is also used with essentially the same meaning, except that the distinct machines tend to be physically close together in a "parallel" system and need not be so in a "distributed" system; that is, they might be geographically dispersed in the latter case.) Communication among the various machines is handled by some kind of network management software, possibly an extension of the DC manager (discussed in Section 2.9), more likely a separate software component.

Many levels or varieties of distributed processing are possible. To repeat from Section 2.10, one simple case involves running the DBMS back end (the server) on one machine and the application front ends (the clients) on another. Refer to Fig. 2.6.

As mentioned at the end of Section 2.10, *client/server,* though strictly speaking a purely architectural term, has come to be almost synonymous with the arrangement illustrated in Fig. 2.6, in which client and server run on different machines. Indeed, there are many arguments in favor of such a scheme:

- The first is basically just the usual parallel processing argument: namely, two or more machines are now being applied to the overall task, and server (database) and client (application) processing are being done in parallel. Response time and throughput should thus be improved.

- Furthermore, the server machine might be a custom-built machine that is tailored to the DBMS function (a "database machine") and might thus provide better DBMS performance.

- Likewise, the client machine might be a personal workstation, tailored to the needs of the end user and thus able to provide better interfaces, high availability, faster responses, and overall improved ease of use to the user.

- Several different client machines might be able—in fact, typically will be able—to access the same server machine. Thus, a single database might be shared across several distinct clients (see Fig. 2.7).

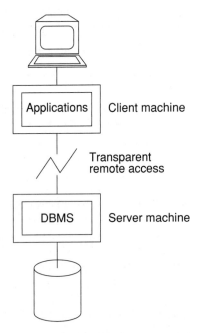

Fig. 2.6 Client(s) and server running on different machines

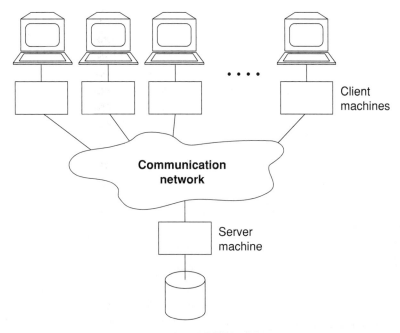

Fig. 2.7 One server machine, many client machines

In addition to the foregoing arguments, there is also the point that running the client(s) and the server on separate machines matches the way enterprises actually operate. It is quite common for a single enterprise—a bank, for example—to operate many computers, such that the data for one portion of the enterprise is stored on one computer and the data for another portion is stored on another. It is also quite common for users on one computer to need at least occasional access to data stored on another. To pursue the banking example for a moment, it is very likely that users at one branch office will occasionally need access to data stored at another. Note, therefore, that the client machines might have stored data of their own, and the server machine might have applications of its own. In general, therefore, each machine will act as a server for some users and a client for others (see Fig. 2.8); in other words, each machine will support *an entire database system,* in the sense of earlier sections of this chapter.

The final point is that a single client machine might be able to access several different server machines (the converse of the case illustrated in Fig. 2.7). This capability is desirable because, as already mentioned, enterprises do typically operate in such a manner that the totality of their data is not stored on one single machine but rather is spread across many distinct machines, and applications will sometimes need the ability to access data from more than one machine. Such access can basically be provided in two different ways:

- A given client might be able to access any number of servers, but only one at a time (i.e., each individual database request must be directed to just one server). In such a system it is not possible, within a single request, to combine data from two or more

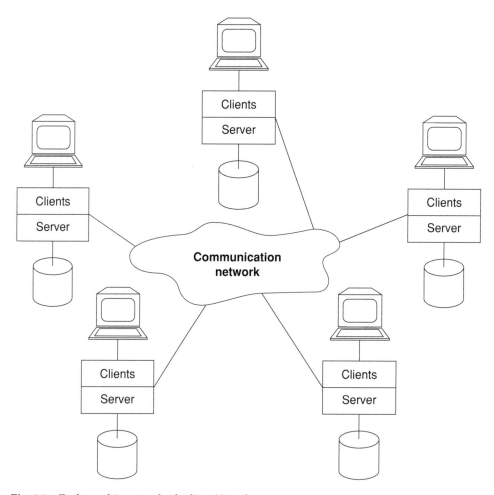

Fig. 2.8   Each machine runs both client(s) and server

different servers. Furthermore, the user in such a system has to know which particular machine holds which pieces of data.

- The client might be able to access many servers simultaneously (i.e., a single database request might be able to combine data from several servers). In this case, the servers look to the client from a logical point of view as if they were really a single server, and the user does not have to know which machines hold which pieces of data.

This latter case constitutes what is usually called a **distributed database system**. Distributed database is a big topic in its own right; carried to its logical conclusion, full distributed database support implies that a single application should be able to operate "transparently" on data that is spread across a variety of different databases, managed by a variety of different DBMSs, running on a variety of different machines, supported by a variety of different operating systems, and connected by a variety of different communication networks—where "transparently" means the application operates from a logical point of view as if the data were all managed by a single DBMS running on a single machine. Such a capability might sound like a pretty tall order, but it is highly desirable from a practical perspective, and much effort has been devoted to making such systems a reality. We will discuss such systems in detail in Chapter 21.

2.13 SUMMARY

In this chapter we have looked at database systems from an architectural point of view. First, we described the **ANSI/SPARC architecture**, which divides a database system into three levels, as follows: The **internal** level is the one closest to physical storage (i.e., it is the one concerned with the way the data is stored); the **external** level is the one closest to the users (i.e., it is the one concerned with the way the data is viewed by individual users); and the **conceptual** level is a level of indirection between the other two (it provides a *community view* of the data). The data as perceived at each level is described by a **schema** (or several schemas, in the case of the external level). **Mappings** define the correspondence between (a) a given external schema and the conceptual schema, and (b) the conceptual schema and the internal schema. Those mappings are the key to the provision of **logical** and **physical data independence**, respectively.

Users—that is, end users and application programmers, both of whom operate at the external level—interact with the data by means of a **data sublanguage**, which consists of at least two components, a **data definition language** (DDL) and a **data manipulation language** (DML). The data sublanguage is embedded in a **host language**. Please note, however, that the boundaries (a) between the host language and the data sublanguage and (b) between the DDL and the DML are primarily conceptual in nature; ideally they should be "transparent to the user."

We also took a closer look at the functions of the **DBA** and the **DBMS**. Among other things, the DBA is responsible for creating the internal schema (**physical database design**); by contrast, creating the conceptual schema (**logical** or **conceptual** database design) is the responsibility of the *data* administrator. And the DBMS is responsible, among other things, for implementing DDL and DML requests from the user. The DBMS is also responsible for providing some kind of **data dictionary** function.

Database systems can also be conveniently thought of as consisting of a **server** (the DBMS itself) and a set of **clients** (the applications). Client and server can and often will run on distinct machines, thus providing one simple kind of **distributed processing**. In general, each server can serve many clients, and each client can access many servers. If the system provides total "transparency"—meaning that each client can behave as if it were dealing with a single server on a single machine, regardless of the overall physical state of affairs—then we have a genuine **distributed database system**.

EXERCISES

2.1 Draw a diagram of the database system architecture presented in this chapter (the ANSI/ SPARC architecture).

2.2 Explain the following in your own words:

back end	front end
client	host language
conceptual DDL, schema, view	load
conceptual/internal mapping	logical database design
data definition language	internal DDL, schema, view
data dictionary	physical database design
data manipulation language	planned request
data sublanguage	reorganization
DB/DC system	server
DC manager	stored database definition
distributed database	unload/reload
distributed processing	unplanned request
external DDL, schema, view	user interface
external/conceptual mapping	utility

2.3 Describe the sequence of steps involved in retrieving a particular external record occurrence.

2.4 List the major functions performed by the DBMS.

2.5 Distinguish between logical and physical data independence.

2.6 What do you understand by the term *metadata*?

2.7 List the major functions performed by the DBA.

2.8 Distinguish between the DBMS and a file management system.

2.9 Give some examples of vendor-provided tools.

2.10 Give some examples of database utilities.

2.11 Examine any database system that might be available to you. Try to map that system to the ANSI/SPARC architecture as described in this chapter. Does it cleanly support the three levels of the architecture? How are the mappings between levels defined? What do the various DDLs (external, conceptual, internal) look like? What data sublanguage(s) does the system support? What host languages? Who performs the DBA function? Are there any security or integrity facilities? Is there a dictionary? Is it self-describing? What vendor-provided applications does the system support? What utilities? Is there a separate DC manager? Are there any distributed processing capabilities?

REFERENCES AND BIBLIOGRAPHY

Most of the following references are fairly old by now, but they are still relevant to the concepts introduced in the present chapter. See also the references in Chapter 14.

2.1 ANSI/X3/SPARC Study Group on Data Base Management Systems: Interim Report, *FDT* (bulletin of ACM SIGMOD) *7,* No. 2 (1975).

2.2 Dionysios C. Tsichritzis and Anthony Klug (eds.): "The ANSI/X3/SPARC DBMS Framework: Report of the Study Group on Data Base Management Systems," *Information Systems 3* (1978).

References [2.1] and [2.2] are the Interim and Final Report, respectively, of the so-called ANSI/SPARC Study Group. The ANSI/X3/SPARC Study Group on Data Base Management Systems (to give it its full title) was established in late 1972 by the Standards Planning and Requirements Committee (SPARC) of the American National Standards Institute (ANSI) Committee on Computers and Information Processing (X3). (*Note:* Some 25 years later, the name X3 was changed to NCITS—National Committee on Information Technology Standards. A few years later again, it was changed to INCITS—IN for International instead of National.) The objectives of the Study Group were to determine which areas, if any, of database technology were appropriate for standardization, and to produce a set of recommendations for action in each such area. In working to meet these objectives, the Study Group took the reasonable position that *interfaces* were the only aspect of a database system that could possibly be suitable for standardization, and accordingly defined a generalized database system architecture, or framework, that emphasized the role of such interfaces. The Final Report provides a detailed description of that architecture and of some of the 42 (!) identified interfaces. The Interim Report is an earlier working document that is still of some interest; in some areas it provides additional detail.

2.3 J. J. van Griethuysen (ed.): "Concepts and Terminology for the Conceptual Schema and the Information Base," International Organization for Standardization (ISO) Technical Report ISO/TR 9007:1987(E) (March 1982; revised July 1987).

This document is the report of an ISO Working Group whose objectives included "the definition of concepts for conceptual schema languages." It includes an introduction to three competing candidates (more accurately, three *sets* of candidates) for an appropriate set of formalisms, and applies each of the three to a common example involving the activities of a hypothetical car registration authority. The three sets of contenders are (1) "entity-attribute-relationship" schemes, (2) "binary relationship" schemes, and (3) "interpreted predicate logic" schemes. The report also includes a discussion of the fundamental concepts underlying the notion of the conceptual schema, and suggests some principles as a basis for implementation of a system that properly supports that notion. Heavy going in places, but an important document for anyone seriously interested in the conceptual level of the system.

2.4 William Kent: *Data and Reality.* Amsterdam, Netherlands: North-Holland/New York, N.Y.: Elsevier Science (1978).

A stimulating and thought-provoking discussion of the nature of information, and in particular of the conceptual schema. "This book projects a philosophy that life and reality are at bottom amorphous, disordered, contradictory, inconsistent, nonrational, and nonobjective" (excerpt from the final chapter). The book can be regarded in large part as a compendium of real-world problems that (it is suggested) existing database formalisms—in particular, formalisms that are based on conventional record-like structures, which includes the relational model—have difficulty dealing with. Recommended.

2.5 Odysseas G. Tsatalos, Marvin H. Solomon, and Yannis E. Ioannidis: "The GMAP: A Versatile Tool for Physical Data Independence," Proc. 20th Int. Conf. on Very Large Data Bases, Santiago, Chile (September 1994).

GMAP stands for *Generalized Multi-level Access Path.* The authors of the paper note correctly that today's database products "force users to frame their queries in terms of a logical schema that is directly tied to physical structures," and hence are rather weak on physical data independence. In their paper, therefore, they propose a conceptual/internal mapping language (to use the terminology of the present chapter) that can be used to specify far more kinds of mappings than are typically supported in products today. Given a particular "logical schema," the language (which is based on relational algebra—see Chapter 7—and is therefore declarative, not procedural, in nature) allows the specification of numerous different "physical" or internal schemas, all of them formally derived from that logical schema. Among other things, those physical schemas can include vertical and horizontal partitioning (or "fragmentation"—see Chapter 21), any number of physical access paths, clustering, and controlled redundancy.

The paper also gives an algorithm for transforming user operations against the logical schema into equivalent operations against the physical schema. A prototype implementation shows that the DBA can tune the physical schema to "achieve significantly better performance than is possible with conventional techniques."

CHAPTER 3

An Introduction
to Relational Databases

3.1   INTRODUCTION

As explained in Chapter 1, the emphasis in this book is heavily on relational systems. In particular, Part II covers the theoretical foundations of such systems—that is, the relational model—in considerable depth. The purpose of the present chapter is to give a preliminary, intuitive, and very informal introduction to the material to be addressed in Part II (and to some extent in subsequent parts too), in order to pave the way for a better understanding of those later parts of the book. Most of the topics mentioned will be discussed much more formally, and in much more detail, in those later chapters.

3.2   AN INFORMAL LOOK AT THE RELATIONAL MODEL

We claimed in Chapter 1 that relational systems are based on a formal foundation, or theory, called *the relational model of data*. The relational model is often described as having the following three aspects:

- *Structural aspect:* The data in the database is perceived by the user as tables, and nothing but tables.

- *Integrity aspect:* Those tables satisfy certain integrity constraints, to be discussed toward the end of this section.

- *Manipulative aspect:* The operators available to the user for manipulating those tables—for example, for purposes of data retrieval—are operators that derive tables from tables. Of those operators, three particularly important ones are *restrict, project,* and *join.*

A simple relational database, the departments-and-employees database, is shown in Fig. 3.1. As you can see, that database is indeed "perceived as tables" (and the meanings of those tables are intended to be self-evident). Fig. 3.2 shows some sample restrict, project, and join operations against the database of Fig. 3.1. Here are (very loose!) definitions of those operations:

- The *restrict* operation extracts specified rows from a table. *Note:* Restrict is sometimes called *select;* we prefer *restrict* because the operator is not the same as the SELECT of SQL.

- The *project* operation extracts specified columns from a table.

- The *join* operation combines two tables into one on the basis of common values in a common column.

Of the examples in Fig. 3.2, the only one that seems to need any further explanation is the join example. Join requires the two tables to have a common column, which tables DEPT and EMP do (they both have a column called DEPT#), and so they can be joined on

DEPT

DEPT#	DNAME	BUDGET
D1	Marketing	10M
D2	Development	12M
D3	Research	5M

EMP

EMP#	ENAME	DEPT#	SALARY
E1	Lopez	D1	40K
E2	Cheng	D1	42K
E3	Finzi	D2	30K
E4	Saito	D2	35K

Fig. 3.1   The departments-and-employees database (sample values)

```
Restrict:                    Result:  | DEPT# | DNAME        | BUDGET |
                                      |-------|--------------|--------|
DEPTs where BUDGET > 8M               | D1    | Marketing    |   10M  |
                                      | D2    | Development  |   12M  |
```

```
Project:                     Result:  | DEPT# | BUDGET |
                                      |-------|--------|
DEPTs over DEPT#, BUDGET              | D1    |   10M  |
                                      | D2    |   12M  |
                                      | D3    |    5M  |
```

```
Join:

DEPTs and EMPs over DEPT#
```

Result:

DEPT#	DNAME	BUDGET	EMP#	ENAME	SALARY
D1	Marketing	10M	E1	Lopez	40K
D1	Marketing	10M	E2	Cheng	42K
D2	Development	12M	E3	Finzi	30K
D2	Development	12M	E4	Saito	35K

Fig. 3.2 Restrict, project, and join (examples)

the basis of common values in that column. To be specific, a given row from table DEPT will join to a given row in table EMP (to yield a row of the result table) if and only if the two rows in question have a common DEPT# value. For example, the DEPT and EMP rows

DEPT#	DNAME	BUDGET
D1	Marketing	10M

EMP#	ENAME	DEPT#	SALARY
E1	Lopez	D1	40K

(column names shown for explicitness) join together to produce the result row

DEPT#	DNAME	BUDGET	EMP#	ENAME	SALARY
D1	Marketing	10M	E1	Lopez	40K

because they have the same value, D1, in the common column. Note that the common value appears once, not twice, in the result row. The overall result of the join contains all possible rows that can be obtained in this manner, and no other rows. Observe in particular that since no EMP row has a DEPT# value of D3 (i.e., no employee is currently assigned to that department), no row for D3 appears in the result, even though there *is* a row for D3 in table DEPT.

Now, one point that Fig. 3.2 clearly shows is that *the result of each of the three operations is another table* (in other words, the operators are indeed "operators that derive tables from tables," as required). This is the **closure** property of relational systems, and it is very important. Basically, because the output of any operation is the same kind of object as the input—they are all tables—*the output from one operation can become input* *to another.* Thus it is possible, for example, to take a projection of a join, a join of two restrictions, a restriction of a projection, and so on. In other words, it is possible to write *nested relational expressions*—that is, relational expressions in which the operands themselves are represented by relational expressions, not necessarily just by simple table names. This fact in turn has numerous important consequences, as we will see later, both in this chapter and in many subsequent ones.

By the way, when we say that the output from each operation is another table, it is important to understand that we are talking *from a conceptual point of view.* We do not mean to imply that the system actually has to materialize the result of every individual operation in its entirety.[1] For example, suppose we are trying to compute a restriction of a join. Then, as soon as a given row of the join is formed, the system can immediately test that row against the specified restriction condition to see whether it belongs in the final result, and immediately discard it if not. In other words, the intermediate result that is the output from the join might never exist as a fully materialized table in its own right at all. As a general rule, in fact, the system tries very hard *not* to materialize intermediate results in their entirety, for obvious performance reasons. *Note:* If intermediate results are fully materialized, the overall expression evaluation strategy is called (unsurprisingly) **materialized evaluation**; if intermediate results are passed piecemeal to subsequent operations, it is called **pipelined evaluation**.

Another point that Fig. 3.2 also clearly illustrates is that the operations are all **set-at-a-time**, not row-at-a-time; that is, the operands and results are whole tables, not just single rows, and tables contain *sets* of rows. (A table containing a set of just one row is legal, of course, as is an *empty* table, i.e., one containing no rows at all.) For example, the join in Fig. 3.2 operates on two tables of three and four rows respectively, and returns a result table of four rows. By contrast, the operations in nonrelational systems are typically at the row- or record-at-a-time level; thus, this *set processing capability* is a major distinguishing characteristic of relational systems (see further discussion in Section 3.5).

Let us return to Fig. 3.1 for a moment. There are a couple of additional points to be made in connection with the sample database of that figure:

- First, note that relational systems require only that the database be *perceived by the user* as tables. Tables are the logical structure in a relational system, not the physical structure. At the physical level, in fact, the system is free to store the data any way it likes—using sequential files, indexing, hashing, pointer chains, compression, and so on—provided only that it can map that stored representation to tables at the logical level. Another way of saying the same thing is that tables represent an *abstraction* of the way the data is physically stored—an abstraction in which numerous storage-level details (such as stored record placement, stored record sequence, stored data value representations, stored record prefixes, stored access structures such as indexes, and so forth) are all *hidden from the user.*

  Incidentally, the term *logical structure* in the foregoing paragraph is intended to encompass both the conceptual and external levels, in ANSI/SPARC terms. The point is that—as explained in Chapter 2—the conceptual and external levels in a relational

---

[1] In other words, to repeat from Chapter 1, the relational model is indeed a *model*—it has nothing to say about implementation.

system will both be relational, but the internal level will not be. In fact, relational theory as such has nothing to say about the internal level at all; it is, to repeat, concerned with how the database looks to the *user.*[2] The only requirement is that, to repeat, whatever physical structure is chosen at the internal level must fully support the required logical structure.

- Second, relational databases abide by a very nice principle, called ***The Information Principle:*** *The entire information content of the database is represented in one and only one way—namely, as explicit values in column positions in rows in tables.* This method of representation is the *only* method available (at the logical level, that is) in a relational system. In particular, **there are no *pointers*** connecting one table to another. In Fig. 3.1, for example, there is a connection between the D1 row of table DEPT and the E1 row of table EMP, because employee E1 works in department D1; but that connection is represented, not by a pointer, but by the appearance of the *value* D1 in the DEPT# position of the EMP row for E1. In nonrelational systems such as IMS or IDMS, by contrast, such information is typically represented—as mentioned in Chapter 1—by some kind of *pointer* that is explicitly visible to the user.

    Note: We will explain in Chapter 26 just why allowing such user-visible pointers would constitute a violation of *The Information Principle.* Also, when we say there are no pointers in a relational database, we do not mean there cannot be pointers at the *physical level*—on the contrary, there certainly can, and indeed there almost certainly will. But, to repeat, all such physical storage details are concealed from the user in a relational system.

So much for the structural and manipulative aspects of the relational model; now we turn to the integrity aspect. Consider the departments-and-employees database of Fig. 3.1 once again. In practice, that database might be required to satisfy any number of integrity constraints—for example, employee salaries might have to be in the range 25K to 95K (say), department budgets might have to be in the range 1M to 15M (say), and so on. Certain of those constraints are of such major pragmatic importance, however, that they enjoy some special nomenclature. To be specific:

1. Each row in table DEPT must include a unique DEPT# value; likewise, each row in table EMP must include a unique EMP# value. We say, loosely, that columns DEPT# in table DEPT and EMP# in table EMP are the **primary keys** for their respective tables. (Recall from Chapter 1 that we indicate primary keys in our figures by double underlining.)

2. Each DEPT# value in table EMP must exist as a DEPT# value in table DEPT, to reflect the fact that every employee must be assigned to an existing department. We say, loosely, that column DEPT# in table EMP is a **foreign** key, referencing the primary key of table DEPT.

---

[2] It is an unfortunate fact that most of today's SQL products do not support this aspect of the theory properly. To be more specific, they typically support only rather restrictive conceptual/internal mappings; typically, in fact, they map one logical table directly to one stored file. This is one reason why (as noted in Chapter 1) those products do not provide as much data independence as relational technology is theoretically capable of. See Appendix A for further discussion.

A More Formal Definition

We close this section with a somewhat more formal definition of the relational model, for purposes of subsequent reference (despite the fact that the definition is quite abstract and will not make much sense at this stage). Briefly, **the relational model** consists of the following five components:

1. An open-ended collection of **scalar types** (including in particular the type *boolean* or *truth value*)

2. A **relation type generator** and an intended interpretation for relations of types generated thereby

3. Facilities for defining **relation variables** of such generated relation types

4. A **relational assignment** operation for assigning relation values to such relation variables

5. An open-ended collection of generic **relational operators** ("the relational algebra") for deriving relation values from other relation values

As you can see, the relational model is very much more than just "tables plus restrict, project, and join," though it is often characterized in such a manner informally.

By the way, you might be surprised to see no explicit mention of integrity constraints in the foregoing definition. The fact is, however, such constraints represent just one application of the relational operators (albeit a very important one); that is, such constraints are formulated in terms of those operators, as we will see in Chapter 9.

3.3 RELATIONS AND RELVARS

If it is true that a relational database is basically just a database in which the data is perceived as tables—and of course it *is* true—then a good question to ask is: Why exactly do we call such a database relational? The answer is simple (in fact, we mentioned it in Chapter 1): *Relation* is just a mathematical term for a table—to be precise, a table of a specific kind (details to be pinned down in Chapter 6). Thus, for example, we can say that the departments-and-employees database of Fig. 3.1 contains two *relations*.

Now, in informal contexts it is usual to treat the terms *relation* and *table* as if they were synonymous; in fact, the term *table* is used much more often than the term *relation* in practice. But it is worth taking a moment to understand why the term *relation* was introduced in the first place. Briefly:

■ As we have seen, relational systems are based on the relational model. The relational model in turn is an abstract theory of data that is based on certain aspects of mathematics (mainly set theory and predicate logic).

■ The principles of the relational model were originally laid down in 1969–70 by E. F. Codd, at that time a researcher at IBM. It was late in 1968 that Codd, a mathematician by training, first realized that the discipline of mathematics could be used to inject some solid principles and rigor into a field (database management) that prior to that time was all too deficient in any such qualities. Codd's ideas were first widely disseminated in a now classic paper, "A Relational Model of Data for Large Shared Data Banks" (reference [6.1] in Chapter 6).

■ Since that time, those ideas—by now almost universally accepted—have had a wide-ranging influence on just about every aspect of database technology, and indeed on other fields as well, such as the fields of artificial intelligence, natural language processing, and hardware design.

Now, the relational model as originally formulated by Codd very deliberately made use of certain terms, such as the term *relation* itself, that were not familiar in IT circles at that time (even though the concepts in some cases were). The trouble was, many of the more familiar terms were very fuzzy—they lacked the precision necessary to a formal theory of the kind that Codd was proposing. For example, consider the term *record*. At different times and in different contexts, that single term can mean either a record *occurrence* or a record *type;* a *logical* record or a *physical* record; a *stored* record or a *virtual* record; and perhaps other things besides. The relational model therefore does not use the term *record* at all—instead, it uses the term *tuple* (rhymes with *couple*), to which it gives a very precise definition. We will discuss that definition in detail in Chapter 6; for present purposes, it is sufficient to say that the term *tuple* corresponds approximately to the notion of a row (just as the term *relation* corresponds approximately to the notion of a table).

In the same kind of way, the relational model does not use the term *field;* instead, it uses the term *attribute,* which for present purposes we can say corresponds approximately to the notion of a column in a table.

When we move on to study the more formal aspects of relational systems in Part II, we will make use of the formal terminology, but in this chapter we are not trying to be so formal (for the most part, at any rate), and we will mostly stick to terms such as *row* and *column* that are reasonably familiar. However, one formal term we will start using a lot from this point forward is the term *relation* itself.

We return to the departments-and-employees database of Fig. 3.1 to make another important point. The fact is, DEPT and EMP in that database are really relation **variables**: variables, that is, whose values are relation **values** (different relation values at different times). For example, suppose EMP currently has the value—the *relation* value, that is— shown in Fig. 3.1, and suppose we delete the row for Saito (employee number E4):

```
DELETE EMP WHERE EMP# = EMP# ('E4') ;
```

The result is shown in Fig. 3.3.

EMP	EMP#	ENAME	DEPT#	SALARY
	E1	Lopez	D1	40K
	E2	Cheng	D1	42K
	E3	Finzi	D2	30K

Fig. 3.3 Relation variable EMP after deleting E4 row

Conceptually, what has happened here is that *the old relation value of EMP has been replaced* en bloc *by an entirely new relation value.* Of course, the old value (with four rows) and the new one (with three) are very similar, but conceptually they *are* different values. Indeed, the delete operation in question is basically just shorthand for a certain **relational assignment** operation that might look like this:

```
EMP   :=   EMP WHERE NOT ( EMP# = EMP# ('E4') ) ;
```

As in all assignments, what is happening here, conceptually, is that (a) the *expression* on the right side is evaluated, and then (b) the result of that evaluation is assigned to the *variable* on the left side (naturally that left side must identify a variable specifically). As already stated, the net effect is thus to replace the "old" EMP value by a "new" one. (As an aside, we remark that we have now seen our first examples of the use of the **Tutorial D** language—both the original DELETE and the equivalent assignment are expressed in that language.)

In analogous fashion, relational INSERT and UPDATE operations are also basically shorthand for certain relational assignments. See Chapter 6 for further details.

Now, it is an unfortunate fact that much of the literature uses the term *relation* when what it really means is a relation *variable* (as well as when it means a relation *per se*— that is, a relation *value*). Historically, however, this practice has certainly led to some confusion. Throughout this book, therefore, we will distinguish very carefully between relation variables and relations *per se;* following reference [3.3], in fact, we will use the term **relvar** as a convenient shorthand for *relation variable,* and we will take care to phrase our remarks in terms of relvars, not relations, when it really is relvars that we mean.[3] Please note, therefore, that from this point forward we take the unqualified term *relation* to mean a relation value specifically (just as we take, e.g., the unqualified term *integer* to mean an integer value specifically), though we will also use the qualified term *relation value* on occasion, for emphasis.

Before going any further, we should warn you that the term *relvar* is not in common usage—but it should be! We really do feel it is important to be clear about the distinction between relations *per se* and relation variables. (We freely admit that earlier editions of this book failed in this respect, but then so did the rest of the literature. What is more, most of it still does.) Note in particular that, by definition, update operations and integrity constraints—see Chapters 6 and 9, respectively—both apply specifically to relvars, not relations.

3.4 WHAT RELATIONS MEAN

In Chapter 1, we mentioned the fact that columns in relations have associated **data types** (*types* for short, also known as *domains*). And at the end of Section 3.2, we said that the relational model includes "an open-ended set of . . . types." Note carefully that the fact that the set is open-ended implies among other things that **users will be able to define their**

---

[3] The distinction between relation values and relation variables is actually a special case of the distinction between values and variables in general. We will examine this latter distinction in depth in Chapter 5.

own types (as well as being able to make use of system-defined or *built-in* types, of course). For example, we might have user-defined types as follows (**Tutorial D** syntax again; the ellipses ". . ." denote portions of the definitions that are not germane to the present discussion):

```
TYPE EMP# ... ;
TYPE NAME ... ;
TYPE DEPT# ... ;
TYPE MONEY ... ;
```

Type EMP#, for example, can be regarded (among other things) as *the set of all possible employee numbers;* type NAME as *the set of all possible names;* and so on.

Now consider Fig. 3.4, which is basically the EMP portion of Fig. 3.1 expanded to show the column data types. As the figure indicates, every relation—to be more precise, every relation *value*—has two parts, a set of column-name:type-name pairs (the **heading**), together with a set of rows that conform to that heading (the **body**). *Note:* In practice we often ignore the type-name components of the heading, as indeed we have done in all of our examples prior to this point, but you should understand that, conceptually, they are always there.

Now, there is a very important (though perhaps unusual) way of thinking about relations, and that is as follows:

1. Given a relation *r,* the heading of *r* denotes a certain **predicate** (where a predicate is just a *truth-valued function* that, like all functions, takes a set of *parameters*).

2. As mentioned briefly in Chapter 1, each row in the body of *r* denotes a certain **true proposition**, obtained from the predicate by substituting certain *argument* values of the appropriate type for the parameters of the predicate ("instantiating the predicate").

In the case of Fig. 3.4, for example, the predicate looks something like this:

Employee EMP# is named ENAME, works in department DEPT#, and earns salary SALARY

(the parameters are EMP#, ENAME, DEPT#, and SALARY, corresponding of course to the four EMP columns). And the corresponding true propositions are:

Employee E1 is named Lopez, works in department D1, and earns salary 40K

(obtained by substituting the EMP# value E1, the NAME value Lopez, the DEPT# value D1, and the MONEY value 40K for the appropriate parameters);

EMP# : EMP#	ENAME : NAME	DEPT# : DEPT#	SALARY : MONEY
E1	Lopez	D1	40K
E2	Cheng	D1	42K
E3	Finzi	D2	30K
E4	Saito	D2	35K

Fig. 3.4 Sample EMP relation value, showing column types

Employee E2 is named Cheng, works in department D1, and earns salary 42K

(obtained by substituting the EMP# value E2, the NAME value Cheng, the DEPT# value D1, and the MONEY value 42K for the appropriate parameters); and so on. In a nutshell, therefore:

- *Types* **are (sets of) things we can talk about.**
- *Relations* **are (sets of) things we say about the things we can talk about.**

(There is a nice analogy here that might help you appreciate and remember these important points: *Types are to relations as nouns are to sentences.*) Thus, in the example, the things we can talk about are employee numbers, names, department numbers, and money values, and the things we say are true utterances of the form "The employee with the specified employee number has the specified name, works in the specified department, and earns the specified salary."

It follows from all of the foregoing that:

1. Types and relations are both *necessary* (without types, we have nothing to talk about; without relations, we cannot say anything).

2. Types and relations are *sufficient,* as well as necessary—that is, we do not need anything else, logically speaking.

3. *Types and relations are not the same thing.* It is an unfortunate fact that certain commercial products—not relational ones, by definition!—are confused over this very point. We will discuss this confusion in Chapter 26 (Section 26.2).

By the way, it is important to understand that *every* relation has an associated predicate, including relations that are derived from others by means of operators such as join. For example, the DEPT relation of Fig. 3.1 and the three result relations of Fig. 3.2 have predicates as follows:

- DEPT: *Department DEPT# is named DNAME and has budget BUDGET*
- Restriction of DEPT where BUDGET > 8M: *Department DEPT# is named DNAME and has budget BUDGET, which is greater than eight million dollars*
- Projection of DEPT over DEPT# and BUDGET: *Department DEPT# has some name and has budget BUDGET*
- Join of DEPT and EMP over DEPT#: *Department DEPT# is named DNAME and has budget BUDGET and employee EMP# is named ENAME, works in department DEPT#, and earns salary SALARY* (note that this predicate has six parameters, not seven—the two references to DEPT# denote the same parameter)

Finally, we observe that relvars have predicates too: namely, the predicate that is common to all of the relations that are possible values of the relvar in question. For example, the predicate for relvar EMP is:

Employee EMP# is named ENAME, works in department DEPT#, and earns salary SALARY

3.5   OPTIMIZATION

As explained in Section 3.2, the relational operators (restrict, project, join, and so on) are all *set-level.* As a consequence, relational languages are often said to be **nonprocedural**, on the grounds that users specify *what,* not *how*—that is, they say what they want, without specifying a procedure for getting it. The process of "navigating" around the stored data in order to satisfy user requests is performed automatically by the system, not manually by the user. For this reason, relational systems are sometimes said to perform **automatic navigation**. In nonrelational systems, by contrast, navigation is generally the responsibility of the user. A striking illustration of the benefits of automatic navigation is shown in Fig. 3.5, which contrasts a certain SQL INSERT statement with the "manual navigation" code the user might have to write to achieve an equivalent effect in a nonrelational system (actually a CODASYL network system; the example is taken from the chapter on network databases in reference [1.5]). *Note:* The database is the well-known suppliers-and-parts database. See Section 3.9 for further explanation.

```
INSERT INTO SP ( S#, P#, QTY )
       VALUES ( 'S4', 'P3', 1000 ) ;

MOVE 'S4' TO S# IN S
FIND CALC S
ACCEPT S-SP-ADDR FROM S-SP CURRENCY
FIND LAST SP WITHIN S-SP
while SP found PERFORM
    ACCEPT S-SP-ADDR FROM S-SP CURRENCY
    FIND OWNER WITHIN P-SP
    GET P
    IF P# IN P < 'P3'
       leave loop
    END-IF
    FIND PRIOR SP WITHIN S-SP
END-PERFORM
MOVE 'P3' TO P# IN P
FIND CALC P
ACCEPT P-SP-ADDR FROM P-SP CURRENCY
FIND LAST SP WITHIN P-SP
while SP found PERFORM
    ACCEPT P-SP-ADDR FROM P-SP CURRENCY
    FIND OWNER WITHIN S-SP
    GET S
    IF S# IN S < 'S4'
       leave loop
    END-IF
    FIND PRIOR SP WITHIN P-SP
END-PERFORM
MOVE 1000 TO QTY IN SP
FIND DB-KEY IS S-SP-ADDR
FIND DB-KEY IS P-SP-ADDR
STORE SP
CONNECT SP TO S-SP
CONNECT SP TO P-SP
```

Fig. 3.5   Automatic *vs.* manual navigation

Despite the remarks of the previous paragraph, it has to be said that *nonprocedural* is not a very satisfactory term, common though it is, because procedurality and nonprocedurality are not absolutes. The best that can be said is that some language *A* is either more or less procedural than some other language *B*. Perhaps a better way of putting matters would be to say that relational languages are at *a higher level of abstraction* than nonrelational languages (as Fig. 3.5 suggests). Fundamentally, it is this raising of the level of abstraction that is responsible for the increased productivity that relational systems can provide.

Deciding just how to perform the automatic navigation referred to above is the responsibility of a very important DBMS component called the **optimizer** (we mentioned this component briefly in Chapter 2). In other words, for each access request from the user, it is the job of the optimizer to choose an efficient way to implement that request. By way of an example, let us suppose the user issues the following query (**Tutorial D** once again):

```
( EMP WHERE EMP# = EMP# ('E4') ) { SALARY }
```

Explanation: The expression inside the outer parentheses ("EMP WHERE . . .") denotes a restriction of the current value of relvar EMP to just the row for employee E4. The column name in braces ("SALARY") then causes the result of that restriction to be projected over the SALARY column. The result of that projection is a single-column, single-row relation that contains employee E4's salary. (Incidentally, note that we are implicitly making use of the relational *closure* property in this example—we have written a nested relational expression, in which the input to the projection is the output from the restriction.)

Now, even in this very simple example, there are probably at least two ways of performing the necessary data access:

1. By doing a physical sequential scan of (the stored version of) relvar EMP until the required data is found

2. If there is an index on (the stored version of) the EMP# column—which in practice there probably will be, because EMP# values are supposed to be unique, and many systems in fact *require* an index in order to enforce uniqueness—then by using that index to go directly to the required data

The optimizer will choose which of these two strategies to adopt. More generally, given any particular request, the optimizer will make its choice of strategy for implementing that request on the basis of considerations such as the following:

- Which relvars are referenced in the request
- How big those relvars currently are
- What indexes exist
- How selective those indexes are
- How the data is physically clustered on the disk
- What relational operations are involved

and so on. To repeat, therefore: Users specify only what data they want, not how to get to that data; the access strategy for getting to that data is chosen by the optimizer ("automatic navigation"). Users and user programs are thus independent of such access strategies, which is of course essential if data independence is to be achieved.

We will have a lot more to say about the optimizer in Chapter 18.

3.6   THE CATALOG

As explained in Chapter 2, the DBMS must provide a **catalog** or **dictionary** function. The catalog is the place where—among other things—all of the various schemas (external, conceptual, internal) and all of the corresponding mappings (external/conceptual, conceptual/internal, external/external) are kept. In other words, the catalog contains detailed information, sometimes called *descriptor information* or *metadata,* regarding the various objects that are of interest to the system itself. Examples of such objects are relvars, indexes, users, integrity constraints, security constraints, and so on. Descriptor information is essential if the system is to do its job properly. For example, the optimizer uses catalog information about indexes and other auxiliary structures, as well as much other information, to help it decide how to implement user requests (see Chapter 18). Likewise, the authorization subsystem uses catalog information about users and security constraints to grant or deny such requests in the first place (see Chapter 17).

Now, one of the nice features of relational systems is that, in such a system, *the catalog itself consists of relvars* (more precisely, *system* relvars, so called to distinguish them from ordinary user ones). As a result, users can interrogate the catalog in exactly the same way they interrogate their own data. For example, the catalog in an SQL system might include two system relvars called TABLE and COLUMN, the purpose of which is to describe the tables (or relvars) in the database and the columns in those tables. For the departments-and-employees database of Fig. 3.1, the TABLE and COLUMN relvars might look in outline as shown in Fig. 3.6.[4]

Note: As mentioned in Chapter 2, the catalog should normally be self-describing—that is, it should include entries describing the catalog relvars themselves (see Exercise 3.3).

Now suppose some user of the departments-and-employees database wants to know exactly what columns relvar DEPT contains (obviously we are assuming that for some reason the user does not already have this information). Then the expression

```
( COLUMN WHERE TABNAME = 'DEPT' ) { COLNAME }
```

does the job.

Here is another example: "Which relvars include a column called EMP#?"

```
( COLUMN WHERE COLNAME = 'EMP#' ) { TABNAME }
```

---

[4] Note that the presence of column ROWCOUNT in Fig. 3.6 suggests that INSERT and DELETE operations on the database will cause an update to the catalog as a side effect. In practice, ROWCOUNT might be updated only on request (e.g., when some utility is run), meaning that values of that column might not always be current.

TABLE	TABNAME	COLCOUNT	ROWCOUNT	. . . . .
	DEPT	3	3	. . . . .
	EMP	4	4	. . . . .
	. . . .	. . . .	. . . .	. . . . .

COLUMN	TABNAME	COLNAME	. . . . .
	DEPT	DEPT#	. . . . .
	DEPT	DNAME	. . . . .
	DEPT	BUDGET	. . . . .
	EMP	EMP#	. . . . .
	EMP	ENAME	. . . . .
	EMP	DEPT#	. . . . .
	EMP	SALARY	. . . . .
	. . . .	. . . .	. . . . .

Fig. 3.6   Catalog for the departments-and-employees database (in outline)

Exercise: What does the following do?

```
( ( TABLE JOIN COLUMN )
        WHERE COLCOUNT < 5 ) { TABNAME, COLNAME }
```

3.7   BASE RELVARS AND VIEWS

We have seen that, starting with a set of relvars such as DEPT and EMP, together with a set of relation values for those relvars, relational expressions allow us to obtain further relation values from those given ones. It is time to introduce a little more terminology. The original (given) relvars are called **base relvars**, and their values are called **base relations**; a relation that is not a base relation but can be obtained from the base relations by means of some relational expression is called a **derived**, or **derivable**, relation. *Note:* Base relvars are called real relvars in reference [3.3].

Now, relational systems obviously have to provide a means for creating the base relvars in the first place. In SQL, for example, this task is performed by the CREATE TABLE statement (TABLE here meaning, very specifically, a base relvar, or what SQL calls a base table). And base relvars obviously have to be *named*—for example:

```
CREATE TABLE EMP ... ;
```

However, relational systems usually support another kind of named relvar also, called a **view**, whose value at any given time is a *derived* relation (and so a view can be thought of, loosely, as a **derived relvar**). The value of a given view at a given time is whatever results from evaluating a certain relational expression at that time; the relational expression in question is specified when the view in question is created. For example, the statement

```
CREATE VIEW TOPEMP AS
    ( EMP WHERE SALARY > 33K ) { EMP#, ENAME, SALARY } ;
```

TOPEMP	EMP#	ENAME	DEPT#	SALARY
	E1	Lopez	D1	40K
	E2	Cheng	D1	42K
	E3	Finzi	D2	30K
	E4	Saito	D2	35K

Fig. 3.7   TOPEMP as a view of EMP (unshaded portions)

might be used to define a view called TOPEMP. (For reasons that are unimportant at this juncture, this example is expressed in a mixture of SQL and **Tutorial D**.)

When this statement is executed, the relational expression following the AS—the **view-defining expression**—is not evaluated but is merely remembered by the system in some way (actually by saving it in the catalog, under the specified name TOPEMP). To the user, however, it is now as if there really were a relvar in the database called TOPEMP, with current value as indicated in the unshaded portions (only) of Fig. 3.7. And the user should be able to operate on that view exactly as if it were a base relvar. *Note:* If (as suggested previously) DEPT and EMP are thought of as real relvars, then TOPEMP might be thought of as a *virtual* relvar—that is, a relvar that appears to exist in its own right, but in fact does not (its value at any given time depends on the value(s) of certain other relvar(s)). In fact, views are called virtual relvars in reference [3.3].

Note carefully, however, that although we say that the value of TOPEMP is the relation that would result if the view-defining expression were evaluated, we do *not* mean we now have *a separate copy* of the data; that is, we do not mean the view-defining expression actually *is* evaluated and the result materialized. On the contrary, the view is effectively just a kind of "window" into the underlying base relvar EMP. As a consequence, any changes to that underlying relvar will be automatically and instantaneously visible through that window (assuming they lie within the unshaded portion). Likewise, changes to TOPEMP will automatically and instantaneously be applied to relvar EMP, and hence be visible through the window (see later for an example).

Here is a sample retrieval operation against view TOPEMP:

```
( TOPEMP WHERE SALARY < 42K ) { EMP#, SALARY }
```

Given the sample data of Fig. 3.7, the result will look like this:

EMP#	SALARY
E1	40K
E4	35K

Conceptually, operations against a view like the retrieval operation just shown are handled by replacing references to the view name by the view-defining expression (i.e., the expression that was saved in the catalog). In the example, therefore, the original expression

```
( TOPEMP WHERE SALARY < 42K ) { EMP#, SALARY }
```

is modified by the system to become

```
( ( ( EMP WHERE SALARY > 33K ) { EMP#, ENAME, SALARY } )
         WHERE SALARY < 42K ) { EMP#, SALARY }
```

(we have italicized the view name in the original expression and the replacement text in the modified version). The modified expression can then be simplified to just

```
( EMP WHERE SALARY > 33K AND SALARY < 42K ) { EMP#, SALARY }
```

(see Chapter 18), and this latter expression when evaluated yields the result shown earlier. In other words, the original operation against the view is effectively converted into an equivalent operation against the underlying base relvar, and that equivalent operation is then executed in the normal way (more accurately, *optimized* and executed in the normal way).

By way of another example, consider the following DELETE operation:

```
DELETE TOPEMP WHERE SALARY < 42K ;
```

The DELETE that is actually executed looks something like this:

```
DELETE EMP WHERE SALARY > 33K AND SALARY < 42K ;
```

Now, the view TOPEMP is very simple, consisting as it does just of a row-and-column subset of a single underlying base relvar (loosely speaking). In principle, however, a view definition, since it is essentially just a named relational expression, can be *of arbitrary complexity* (it can even refer to other views). For example, here is a view whose definition involves a join of two underlying base relvars:

```
CREATE VIEW JOINEX AS
     ( ( EMP JOIN DEPT ) WHERE BUDGET > 7M ) { EMP#, DEPT# } ;
```

We will return to the whole question of view definition and view processing in Chapter 10.

Incidentally, we can now explain the remark in Chapter 2, near the end of Section 2.2, to the effect that the term *view* has a rather specific meaning in relational contexts that is not identical to the meaning assigned to it in the ANSI/SPARC architecture. At the external level of that architecture, the database is perceived as an "external view," defined by an external schema (and different users can have different external views). In relational systems, by contrast, a view is, specifically, a *named, derived, virtual relvar,* as previously explained. Thus, the relational analog of an ANSI/SPARC "external view" is (typically) a collection of several relvars, each of which is a view in the relational sense, and the "external schema" consists of definitions of those views. (It follows that views in the relational sense are the relational model's way of providing **logical data independence**, though once again it has to be said that today's SQL products are sadly deficient in this regard. See Chapter 10.)

Now, the ANSI/SPARC architecture is quite general and allows for arbitrary variability between the external and conceptual levels. In principle, even the *types* of data structures supported at the two levels could be different; for example, the conceptual level could be relational, while a given user could have an external view that was hierarchic.[5] In practice, however, most systems use the same type of structure as the basis for both levels, and relational products are no exception to this general rule—views are still relvars, just like the base relvars are. And since the same type of object is supported at both levels, the same data sublanguage (usually SQL) applies at both levels. Indeed, the fact that a view is a relvar is precisely one of the strengths of relational systems; it is important in just the same way as the fact that a subset is a set is important in mathematics. *Note:* SQL products and the SQL standard (see Chapter 4) often seem to miss this point, however, inasmuch as they refer repeatedly to "tables and views," with the tacit implication that a view is not a table. You are strongly advised *not* to fall into this common trap of taking "tables" (or "relvars") to mean, specifically, *base* tables (or relvars) only.

There is one final point that needs to be made on the subject of base relvars *vs.* views, as follows. The base relvar *vs.* view distinction is frequently characterized thus:

- Base relvars "really exist," in the sense that they represent data that is physically stored in the database.

- Views, by contrast, do not "really exist" but merely provide different ways of looking at "the real data."

However, this characterization, though perhaps useful in informal contexts, does not accurately reflect the true state of affairs. It is true that users can *think* of base relvars as if they were physically stored; in a way, in fact, the whole point of relational systems is to allow users to think of base relvars as physically existing, while not having to concern themselves with how those relvars are actually represented in storage. But—and it is a big but—this way of thinking should *not* be construed as meaning that a base relvar is physically stored in any kind of direct way (e.g., as a single stored file). As explained in Section 3.2, base relvars are best thought of as an *abstraction* of some collection of stored data—an abstraction in which all storage-level details are concealed. In principle, there can be an arbitrary degree of differentiation between a base relvar and its stored counterpart.[6]

A simple example might help to clarify this point. Consider the departments-and-employees database once again. Most of today's relational systems would probably implement that database with two stored files, one for each of the two base relvars. But there is absolutely no logical reason why there should not be just one stored file of *hierarchic* stored records, each consisting of (a) the department number, name, and budget for some given department, together with (b) the employee number, name, and salary for each employee who happens to be in that department. In other words, the data can be physically stored in whatever way seems appropriate (see Appendix A for a discussion of further possibilities), but it always looks the same at the logical level.

---

[5] We will see an example of this possibility in Chapter 27.

[6] The following quote from a recent book displays several of the confusions discussed in this paragraph, as well as others discussed in Section 3.3 earlier: "[It] is important to make a distinction between stored relations, which are *tables,* and virtual relations, which are *views* . . . [We] shall use *relation* only where a table or a view could be used. When we want to emphasize that a relation is stored, rather than a view, we shall sometimes use the term *base relation* or *base table*." The quote is, regrettably, not at all atypical.

3.8   TRANSACTIONS

Note: The topic of this section is not peculiar to relational systems. We cover it here never-theless, because an understanding of the basic idea is needed in order to appreciate certain aspects of the material to come in Part II. However, our coverage at this point is deliberately not very deep.

In Chapter 1 we said that a transaction is a "logical unit of work," typically involving several database operations. Clearly, the user needs to be able to inform the system when distinct operations are part of the same transaction, and the BEGIN TRANSACTION, COMMIT, and ROLLBACK operations are provided for this purpose. Basically, a transaction begins when a BEGIN TRANSACTION operation is executed, and terminates when a corresponding COMMIT or ROLLBACK operation is executed. For example (pseudocode):

```
BEGIN TRANSACTION ; /* move $$$ from account A to account B */
UPDATE account A ;                         /* withdrawal   */
UPDATE account B ;                         /* deposit      */
IF everything worked fine
    THEN COMMIT ;                          /* normal end */
    ELSE ROLLBACK ;                        /* abnormal end */
END IF ;
```

Points arising:

1. Transactions are guaranteed to be **atomic**—that is, they are guaranteed (from a logical point of view) either to execute in their entirety or not to execute at all,[7] even if (say) the system fails halfway through the process.

2. Transactions are also guaranteed to be **durable**, in the sense that once a transaction successfully executes COMMIT, its updates are guaranteed to appear in the database, even if the system subsequently fails at any point. (It is this durability property of transactions that makes the data in the database *persistent,* in the sense of Chapter 1.)

3. Transactions are also guaranteed to be **isolated** from one another, in the sense that database updates made by a given transaction *T1* are not made visible to any distinct transaction *T2* until and unless *T1* successfully executes COMMIT. COMMIT causes database updates made by the transaction to become visible to other transactions; such updates are said to be *committed,* and are guaranteed never to be canceled. If the transaction executes ROLLBACK instead, all database updates made by the transaction are canceled (*rolled back*). In this latter case, the effect is as if the transaction never ran in the first place.

4. The interleaved execution of a set of concurrent transactions is usually guaranteed to be **serializable**, in the sense that it produces the same result as executing those same transactions one at a time in some unspecified serial order.

Chapters 15 and 16 contain an extended discussion of all of the foregoing points, and much else besides.

---

[7] Since a transaction is the execution of some piece of code, a phrase such as "the execution of a transaction" is really a solecism (if it means anything at all, it has to mean the execution of an execution). However, such phraseology is common and useful, and for want of anything better we will use it ourselves in this book.

3.9 THE SUPPLIERS-AND-PARTS DATABASE

Most of our examples in this book are based on the well-known **suppliers-and-parts** database. The purpose of this section is to explain that database, in order to serve as a point of reference for later chapters. Fig. 3.8 shows a set of sample data values; subsequent examples will actually assume these specific values, where it makes any difference.[8] Fig. 3.9 shows the database definition, expressed in **Tutorial D** once again (the **Tutorial D** keyword VAR means "variable"). Note the primary and foreign key specifications in particular. Note too that (a) several columns have data types of the same name as the column in question; (b) the STATUS column and the two CITY columns are defined in terms of system-defined types—INTEGER (integers) and CHAR (character strings of arbitrary length)—instead of user-defined ones. Note finally that there is an important point that needs to be made regarding the column values as shown in Fig. 3.8, but we are not yet in a position to make it; we will come back to it in Chapter 5, Section 5.3, near the end of the subsection "Possible Representations."

The database is meant to be understood as follows:

- Relvar S represents *suppliers* (more accurately, suppliers *under contract*). Each supplier has a supplier number (S#), unique to that supplier; a supplier name (SNAME), not necessarily unique (though the SNAME values do happen to be unique in Fig. 3.8); a rating or status value (STATUS); and a location (CITY). We assume that each supplier is located in exactly one city.

- Relvar P represents *parts* (more accurately, *kinds* of parts). Each kind of part has a part number (P#), which is unique; a part name (PNAME); a color (COLOR); a

S	S#	SNAME	STATUS	CITY		SP	S#	P#	QTY
	S1	Smith	20	London			S1	P1	300
	S2	Jones	10	Paris			S1	P2	200
	S3	Blake	30	Paris			S1	P3	400
	S4	Clark	20	London			S1	P4	200
	S5	Adams	30	Athens			S1	P5	100
							S1	P6	100
							S2	P1	300
							S2	P2	400
							S3	P2	200
							S4	P2	200
							S4	P4	300
							S4	P5	400

P	P#	PNAME	COLOR	WEIGHT	CITY
	P1	Nut	Red	12.0	London
	P2	Bolt	Green	17.0	Paris
	P3	Screw	Blue	17.0	Oslo
	P4	Screw	Red	14.0	London
	P5	Cam	Blue	12.0	Paris
	P6	Cog	Red	19.0	London

Fig. 3.8 The suppliers-and-parts database (sample values)

---

[8] For ease of reference, Fig. 3.8 is repeated on the inside back cover. For the benefit of readers who might be familiar with the sample data values from earlier editions, we note that part P3 has moved from Rome to Oslo. The same change has also been made in Fig. 4.5 in the next chapter.

```
TYPE S# ... ;
TYPE NAME ... ;
TYPE P# ... ;
TYPE COLOR ... ;
TYPE WEIGHT ... ;
TYPE QTY ... ;

VAR S BASE RELATION
    { S#      S#,
      SNAME   NAME,
      STATUS  INTEGER,
      CITY    CHAR }
    PRIMARY KEY { S# } ;

VAR P BASE RELATION
    { P#      P#,
      PNAME   NAME,
      COLOR   COLOR,
      WEIGHT  WEIGHT,
      CITY    CHAR }
    PRIMARY KEY { P# } ;

VAR SP BASE RELATION
    { S#      S#,
      P#      P#,
      QTY     QTY }
    PRIMARY KEY { S#, P# }
    FOREIGN KEY { S# } REFERENCES S
    FOREIGN KEY { P# } REFERENCES P ;
```

Fig. 3.9   The suppliers-and-parts database (data definition)

weight (WEIGHT); and a location where parts of that kind are stored (CITY). We assume where it makes any difference that part weights are given in pounds (but see the discussion of *units of measure* in Chapter 5, Section 5.4). We also assume that each kind of part comes in exactly one color and is stored in a warehouse in exactly one city.

■ Relvar SP represents *shipments*. It serves in a sense to link the other two relvars together, logically speaking. For example, the first row in SP as shown in Fig. 3.8 links a specific supplier from relvar S (namely, supplier S1) to a specific part from relvar P (namely, part P1)—in other words, it represents a shipment of parts of kind P1 by the supplier called S1 (and the shipment quantity is 300). Thus, each shipment has a supplier number (S#), a part number (P#), and a quantity (QTY). We assume there is at most one shipment at any given time for a given supplier and a given part; for a given shipment, therefore, the combination of S# value and P# value is unique with respect to the set of shipments currently appearing in SP. Note that the database of Fig. 3.8 includes one supplier, supplier S5, with no shipments at all.

We remark that (as already pointed out in Chapter 1, Section 1.3) suppliers and parts can be regarded as **entities**, and a shipment can be regarded as a **relationship** between a particular supplier and a particular part. As also pointed out in that chapter, however, a relationship is best regarded as just a special case of an entity. One advantage of relational databases over all other known kinds is precisely that all entities, regardless of whether they are in fact relationships, are represented in the same uniform way: namely, by means of rows in relations, as the example indicates.

A couple of final remarks:

- First, the suppliers-and-parts database is clearly very simple, much simpler than any real database is likely to be; most real databases will involve many more entities and relationships (and, more important, many more *kinds* of entities and relationships) than this one does. Nevertheless, it is at least adequate to illustrate most of the points that we need to make in the rest of the book, and (as already stated) we will use it as the basis for most—not all—of our examples as we proceed.

- Second, there is nothing wrong with using more descriptive names such as SUPPLIERS, PARTS, and SHIPMENTS in place of the rather terse names S, P, and SP in Figs. 3.8 and 3.9; indeed, descriptive names are generally to be recommended in practice. But in the case of the suppliers-and-parts database specifically, the relvars are referenced so frequently in what follows that very short names seemed desirable. Long names tend to become irksome with much repetition.

3.10 SUMMARY

This brings us to the end of our brief overview of relational technology. Obviously we have barely scratched the surface of what by now has become a very extensive subject, but the whole point of the chapter has been to serve as a gentle introduction to the much more comprehensive discussions to come. Even so, we have managed to cover quite a lot of ground. Here is a summary of the major topics we have discussed.

A **relational database** is a database that is perceived by its users as a collection of **relation variables**—that is, *relvars*—or, more informally, **tables**. A **relational system** is a system that supports relational databases and operations on such databases, including in particular the operations **restrict, project,** and **join.** These operations, and others like them, are collectively known as **the relational algebra,**[9] and they are all **set-level.** The **closure** property of relational systems means the output from every operation is the same kind of object as the input (they are all relations), which means we can write **nested relational expressions**. Relvars can be updated by means of the **relational assignment** operation; the familiar update operations **INSERT, DELETE,** and **UPDATE** can be regarded as shorthands for certain common relational assignments.

The formal theory underlying relational systems is called **the relational model of data**. The relational model is concerned with logical matters only, not physical matters. It addresses three principal aspects of data: data **structure**, data **integrity**, and data **manipulation**. The *structural* aspect has to do with relations *per se;* the *integrity* aspect has to do with (among other things) **primary and foreign keys**; and the *manipulative* aspect has to do with the operators (restrict, project, join, etc.). ***The Information Principle***—which we

---

[9] We mentioned this term in the formal definition of the relational model in Section 3.2. However, we will not start using it in earnest until we reach Chapter 6.

now observe might better be called *The Principle of Uniform Representation*—states that the entire information content of a relational database is represented in one and only one way, as explicit values in column positions in rows in relations. Equivalently: *The only variables allowed in a relational database are, specifically, relvars.*

Every relation has a **heading** and a **body**; the heading is a set of column-name:type-name pairs, the body is a set of rows that conform to the heading. The heading of a given relation can be regarded as a **predicate**, and each row in the body denotes a certain **true proposition**, obtained by substituting certain **arguments** of the appropriate type for the **parameters** of the predicate. Note that these remarks are true of derived relations as well as base ones; they are also true of relvars, *mutatis mutandis*. In other words, *types* are (sets of) things we can talk about, and *relations* are (sets of) things we say about the things we can talk about. Together, types and relations are **necessary** and **sufficient** to represent any data we like (at the logical level, that is).

The **optimizer** is the system component that determines how to implement user requests (which are concerned with *what,* not *how*). Since relational systems therefore assume responsibility for navigating around the stored database to locate the desired data, they are sometimes described as **automatic navigation** systems. Optimization and automatic navigation are prerequisites for **physical data independence**.

The **catalog** is a set of system relvars that contain **descriptors** for the various items that are of interest to the system (base relvars, views, indexes, users, etc.). Users can interrogate the catalog in exactly the same way they interrogate their own data.

The original (given) relvars in a given database are called **base relvars**, and their values are called **base relations**; a relation that is not a base relation but is obtained from the base relations by means of some relational expression is called a **derived** relation (collectively, base and derived relations are sometimes referred to as **expressible** relations). A **view** is a relvar whose value at any given time is such a derived relation (loosely, it can be thought of as a **derived relvar**); the value of such a relvar at any given time is whatever results from evaluating the associated **view-defining expression** at that time. Note, therefore, that base relvars have *independent existence,* but views do not—they depend on the applicable base relvars. (Another way of saying the same thing is that base relvars are *autonomous,* but views are not.) Users can operate on views in exactly the same way as they operate on base relvars, at least in theory. The system implements operations on views by replacing references to the name of the view by the view-defining expression, thereby converting the operation into an equivalent operation on the underlying base relvar(s).

A **transaction** is a *logical unit of work,* typically involving several database operations. A transaction begins when **BEGIN TRANSACTION** is executed and terminates when **COMMIT** (normal termination) or **ROLLBACK** (abnormal termination) is executed. Transactions are **atomic, durable,** and **isolated** from one another. The interleaved execution of a set of concurrent transactions is usually guaranteed to be **serializable**.

Finally, the base example for most of the book is **the suppliers-and-parts database**. It is worth taking the time to familiarize yourself with that example now, if you have not done so already; that is, you should at least know which relvars have which columns and what the primary and foreign keys are (it is not as important to know exactly what the sample data values are!).

EXERCISES

3.1   Explain the following in your own words:

automatic navigation	primary key
base relvar	projection
catalog	proposition
closure	relational database
commit	relational DBMS
derived relvar	relational model
foreign key	restriction
join	rollback
optimization	set-level operation
predicate	view

3.2   Sketch the contents of the catalog relvars TABLE and COLUMN for the suppliers-and-parts database.

3.3   As explained in Section 3.6, the catalog is self-describing—that is, it includes entries for the catalog relvars themselves. Extend Fig. 3.6 to include the necessary entries for the TABLE and COLUMN relvars themselves.

3.4   Here is a query on the suppliers-and-parts database. What does it do? What is the predicate for the result?

```
( ( S JOIN SP ) WHERE P# = P# ('P2') ) { S#, CITY }
```

3.5   Suppose the expression in Exercise 3.4 is used in a view definition:

```
CREATE VIEW V AS
    ( ( S JOIN SP ) WHERE P# = P# ('P2') ) { S#, CITY } ;
```

Now consider this query:

```
( V WHERE CITY = 'London' ) { S# }
```

What does this query do? What is the predicate for the result? Show what is involved on the part of the DBMS in processing this query.

3.6   What do you understand by the terms *atomicity, durability, isolation,* and *serializability* as applied to transactions?

3.7   State *The Information Principle*.

3.8   If you are familiar with the hierarchic data model, identify as many differences as you can between it and the relational model as briefly described in this chapter.

REFERENCES AND BIBLIOGRAPHY

3.1   E. F. Codd: "Relational Database: A Practical Foundation For Productivity," *CACM 25,* No. 2 (February 1982). Republished in Robert L. Ashenhurst (ed.), *ACM Turing Award Lectures: The First Twenty Years 1966–1985*. Reading, Mass.: Addison-Wesley (*ACM Press Anthology Series,* 1987).

This is the paper Codd presented on the occasion of his receiving the 1981 ACM Turing Award for his work on the relational model. It discusses the well-known *application backlog* problem. To quote: "The demand for computer applications is growing fast—so fast that information systems departments (whose responsibility it is to provide those applications) are lagging further and further behind in their ability to meet that demand." There are two complementary ways of attacking this problem:

1. Provide IT professionals with new tools to increase their productivity.
2. Allow end users to interact directly with the database, thus bypassing the IT professional entirely.

Both approaches are needed, and in this paper Codd gives evidence to suggest that the necessary foundation for both is provided by relational technology.

3.2 C. J. Date: "Why Relational?" in *Relational Database Writings 1985–1989.* Reading, Mass.: Addison-Wesley (1990).

An attempt to provide a succinct yet reasonably comprehensive summary of the major advantages of relational systems. The following observation from the paper is worth repeating here: Among all the numerous advantages of "going relational," there is one in particular that cannot be overemphasized, and that is *the existence of a sound theoretical base.* To quote: "Relational really is different. It is different because it is not *ad hoc.* Older systems, by contrast, were *ad hoc;* they may have provided solutions to certain important problems of their day, but they did not rest on any solid theoretical base. Relational systems, by contrast, do rest on such a base . . . which means [they] are *rock solid* . . . Thanks to this solid foundation, relational systems behave in well-defined ways; and (possibly without realizing the fact) users have a simple model of that behavior in their mind, one that enables them to predict with confidence what the system will do in any given situation. There are (or should be) no surprises. This predictability means that user interfaces are easy to understand, document, teach, learn, use, and remember."

3.3 C. J. Date and Hugh Darwen: *Foundation for Future Database Systems: The Third Manifesto* (2d edition). Reading, Mass.: Addison-Wesley (2000). See also *http://www.thethirdmanifesto.com,* which contains certain formal extracts from the book, an errata list, and much other relevant material. Reference [20.1] is also relevant.

The Third Manifesto is a detailed, formal, and rigorous proposal for the future direction of databases and DBMSs. It can be seen as an abstract blueprint for the design of a DBMS and the language interface to such a DBMS. It is based on the classical core concepts **type, value, variable**, and **operator.** For example, we might have a *type* INTEGER; the integer "3" might be a *value* of that type; N might be a *variable* of that type, whose value at any given time is some integer value (i.e., some value of that type); and "+" might be an *operator* that applies to integer values (i.e., to values of that type). *Note:* The emphasis on types in particular is brought out by the book's subtitle: *A Detailed Study of the Impact of Type Theory on the Relational Model of Data, Including a Comprehensive Model of Type Inheritance.* Part of the point here is that type theory and the relational model are more or less independent of each other. To be more specific, the relational model does not prescribe support for any particular types (other than type *boolean*); it merely says that attributes of relations must be of some type, thus implying that *some* (unspecified) types must be supported.

The term *relvar* is taken from this book. In this connection, the book also says this: "The first version of this *Manifesto* drew a distinction between database values and database variables, analogous to the distinction between relation values and relation variables. It also introduced the term *dbvar* as shorthand for *database variable.* While we still believe this distinction to be a valid one, we found it had little direct relevance to other aspects of these proposals. We therefore decided, in the interest of familiarity, to revert to more traditional terminology." This decision subsequently turned out to be a bad one . . . To quote reference [23.4]: "With hindsight, it would have been much better to bite the bullet and adopt the more logically correct terms *database value* and *database variable* (or dbvar), despite their lack of familiarity." In the present book we do stay with the familiar term *database,* but we decided to do so only against our own better judgment (somewhat).

One more point. As the book itself says: "We [confess] that we do feel a little uncomfortable with the idea of calling what is, after all, primarily a technical document a *manifesto.* According to *Chambers Twentieth Century Dictionary,* a manifesto is *a written declaration of the intentions, opinions, or motives* of some person or group (e.g., a political party). By contrast, *The Third Manifesto* is . . . a matter of science and logic, not mere intentions, opinions, or motives." However, *The Third Manifesto* was specifically written to be compared and contrasted with two previous ones, *The Object-Oriented Database System Manifesto* [20.2, 25.1] and *The Third-Generation Database System Manifesto* [26.44], and our title was thus effectively chosen for us.

3.4 C. J. Date: "Great News, The Relational Model Is Very Much Alive!," *http://www.dbdebunk.com* (August 2000).

Ever since it first appeared in 1969, the relational model has been subjected to an extraordinary variety of attacks by a number of different writers. One recent example was entitled, not at all atypically, "Great News, The Relational Model Is Dead!" This article was written as a rebuttal to this position.

3.5 C. J. Date: "There's Only One Relational Model!" *http://www.dbdebunk.com* (February 2001).

Ever since it first appeared in 1969, the relational model has been subjected to an extraordinary variety of misrepresentation and obfuscation by a number of different writers. One recent example was a book chapter titled "Different Relational Models," the first sentence of which read: "There is no such thing as *the* relational model for databases anymore [*sic*] than there is just one geometry." This article was written as a rebuttal to this position.

CHAPTER 4

An Introduction to SQL

4.1   INTRODUCTION

As noted in Chapter 1, SQL is the standard language for relational systems, and it is supported by just about every database product on the market today. SQL was originally developed by IBM Research in the early 1970s [4.9, 4.10]; it was first implemented on a large scale in an IBM prototype called System R [4.1–4.3, 4.12–4.14], and subsequently reimplemented in numerous commercial products from both IBM [4.8, 4.14, 4.21] and many other vendors. In this chapter we present an overview of the major features of the SQL language (more detailed aspects, having to do with such matters as integrity, security, etc., are deferred to the chapters devoted to those topics). Throughout our discussions, we take the unqualified name SQL to refer to the current version of the standard (*viz.*, **SQL:1999**), barring explicit statements to the contrary.[1] Reference [4.23] is the formal SQL:1999 specification; reference [4.24] is an extensive set of corrections to that specification.

---

[1] A new version of the standard ("SQL:2003") is anticipated in late 2003, and we will occasionally make explicit reference to that version as well.

Note: The previous version of the standard was SQL:1992, and SQL:1999 is meant to be a compatible extension to that previous version. However, it is only fair to point out that no product today supports even SQL:1992 in its entirety; instead, products typically support what might be called "a superset of a subset" of the standard (either SQL:1999 or, more likely, SQL:1992). To be more specific, most products fail to support the standard in some respects and yet go beyond it in others.[2] For example, IBM's DB2 product does not support all of the standard integrity features, but it does support an operator to rename a base table, which the standard does not.

A few additional preliminary remarks:

- SQL was originally intended to be a "data sublanguage" specifically (see Chapter 2). However, with the addition in 1996 of the **SQL Persistent Stored Modules** feature (SQL/PSM, *PSM* for short), the standard became computationally complete—it now includes statements such as CALL, RETURN, SET, CASE, IF, LOOP, LEAVE, WHILE, and REPEAT, as well as several related features such as the ability to declare variables and exception handlers. Further details of PSM are beyond the scope of this book, but a tutorial description can be found in reference [4.20].

- SQL uses the term *table* in place of both of the terms *relation* and *relvar,* and the terms *row* and *column* in place of *tuple* and *attribute,* respectively. For consistency with the SQL standard and SQL products, therefore, we will do likewise in this chapter (and throughout this book whenever we are concerned with SQL specifically).

- SQL is an enormous language. The specification [4.23] is well over 2,000 pages long—not counting the more than 300 hundred pages of corrigenda in reference [4.24]. As a consequence, it is not possible, or even desirable, to treat the subject exhaustively in a book of this nature, and we have not attempted to do so; rather, we have omitted many features and simplified many others.

- Finally, it has to be said that (as already indicated at various points in Chapters 1–3) SQL is very far from being the perfect relational language—it suffers from sins of both omission and commission. Nevertheless, it is the standard, it is supported by just about every product on the market, and every database professional needs to know something about it. Hence the coverage in this book.

4.2 OVERVIEW

SQL includes both data definition and data manipulation operations. We consider **definitional** operations first. Fig. 4.1 gives an SQL definition for the suppliers-and-parts database (compare and contrast Fig. 3.9 in Chapter 3). As you can see, the definition includes one **CREATE TYPE** statement for each of the six user-defined types (UDTs) and one **CREATE TABLE** statement for each of the three base tables (as noted in Chapter 3, the keyword TABLE in CREATE TABLE means a base table specifically). Each such

---

[2] In fact, no product possibly could support the standard in its entirety, because there are simply too many gaps, mistakes, and inconsistencies in references [4.23] and [4.24]. Reference [4.20] includes a detailed discussion of this problem at the SQL:1992 level.

```
CREATE TYPE S# ... ;
CREATE TYPE NAME ... ;
CREATE TYPE P# ... ;
CREATE TYPE COLOR ... ;
CREATE TYPE WEIGHT ... ;
CREATE TYPE QTY ... ;

CREATE TABLE S
     ( S#      S#,
       SNAME   NAME,
       STATUS  INTEGER,
       CITY    CHAR(15),
     PRIMARY KEY ( S# ) ) ;

CREATE TABLE P
     ( P#      P#,
       PNAME   NAME,
       COLOR   COLOR,
       WEIGHT  WEIGHT,
       CITY    CHAR(15),
     PRIMARY KEY ( P# ) ) ;

CREATE TABLE SP
     ( S#      S#,
       P#      P#
       QTY     QTY,
     PRIMARY KEY ( S#, P# ),
     FOREIGN KEY ( S# ) REFERENCES S,
     FOREIGN KEY ( P# ) REFERENCES P ,
```

Fig. 4.1   The suppliers-and-parts database (SQL definition)

CREATE TABLE statement specifies the name of the base table to be created, the names and types of the columns of that table, and the primary key and any foreign keys in that table (possibly some additional information also, not illustrated in Fig. 4.1). Also, please note the following:

■ We often make use of the "#" character in (e.g.) type names and column names, but in fact that character is not legal in the standard.

■ We use the semicolon ";" as a statement terminator. Whether SQL actually uses such terminators depends on the context. The specifics are beyond the scope of this book.

■ The built-in type CHAR in SQL requires an associated *length*—15 in the figure—to be specified.

Having defined the database, we can now start operating on it by means of the SQL **manipulative** operations SELECT, INSERT, DELETE, and UPDATE. In particular, we can perform relational restrict, project, and join operations on the data, in each case by using the SQL data manipulation statement **SELECT**. Some examples are given in Fig. 4.2. *Note:* The join example in that figure illustrates the point that **dot-qualified names** (e.g., S.S#, SP.S#) are sometimes necessary in SQL to "disambiguate" column references. The general rule—though there are exceptions—is that qualified names are always acceptable, but unqualified names are acceptable too as long as they cause no ambiguity.

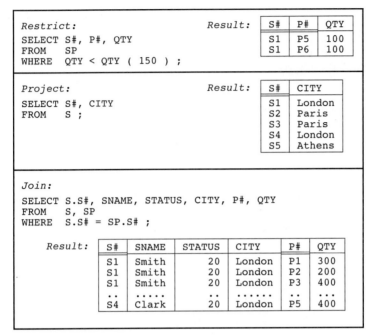

Fig. 4.2   Restrict, project, and join examples in SQL

We remark that SQL also supports a shorthand form of the SELECT clause as illustrated by the following example:

```
SELECT *                      /* or "SELECT S.*" (i.e., the */
FROM   S ;                    /* "*" can be dot-qualified)  */
```

The result is a copy of the entire S table; the star or asterisk is shorthand for a "comma-list"—see Section 4.6 for a formal explanation of this term—of (a) names of all columns in the first table referenced in the FROM clause, in the left-to-right order in which those columns are defined within that table, followed by (b) names of all columns in the second table referenced in the FROM clause, in the left-to-right order in which those columns are defined within that table (and so on for all of the other tables referenced in the FROM clause). *Note:* The expression SELECT * FROM *T,* where *T* is a table name, can be further abbreviated to just TABLE *T.*

The SELECT statement is discussed at much greater length in Chapter 8, Section 8.6.

Turning now to **update** operations: Examples of the SQL INSERT, DELETE, and UPDATE statements have already been given in Chapter 1, but those examples deliberately involved single-row operations only. Like SELECT, however, **INSERT, DELETE,** and **UPDATE** are all *set-level* operations, in general (and some of the exercises in Chapter 1 did in fact illustrate this point). Here are some set-level update examples for the suppliers-and-parts database:

```
INSERT
INTO    TEMP ( P#, WEIGHT )
        SELECT P#, WEIGHT
        FROM    P
        WHERE   COLOR = COLOR ('Red') ;
```

This example assumes that we have already created another table TEMP with two columns, P# and WEIGHT. The INSERT statement inserts into that table part numbers and corresponding weights for all red parts.

```
DELETE
FROM    SP
WHERE   P# = P# ('P2') ;
```

This DELETE statement deletes all shipments for part P2.

```
UPDATE S
SET     STATUS = 2 * STATUS ,
        CITY = 'Rome'
WHERE   CITY = 'Paris' ;
```

This UPDATE statement doubles the status for all suppliers in Paris and moves those suppliers to Rome.

Note: SQL does not include a direct analog of the **relational assignment** operation. However, we can simulate that operation by first deleting all rows from the target table and then performing an INSERT . . . SELECT . . . (as in the first example above) into that table.

4.3 THE CATALOG

The SQL standard does include specifications for a standard catalog called the **Information Schema**. In fact, the conventional terms *catalog* and *schema* are both used in SQL, but with highly SQL-specific meanings; loosely speaking, an SQL **catalog** consists of the descriptors for an individual database,[3] and an SQL **schema** consists of the descriptors for that portion of that database that belongs to some individual user. In other words, there can be any number of catalogs (one per database), each consisting of any number of schemas. However, each catalog is required to include exactly one schema called INFORMATION_SCHEMA, and from the user's perspective it is that schema that, as already indicated, performs the normal catalog function.

The Information Schema thus consists of a set of SQL tables whose contents effectively echo, in a precisely defined way, all of the definitions from all of the other schemas in the catalog in question. More precisely, the Information Schema is defined to contain a set of *views* of a hypothetical "Definition Schema." The implementation is not required to support the Definition Schema as such, but it is required (a) to support *some* kind of "Definition Schema" and (b) to support views of that "Definition Schema" that do look like those of the Information Schema. Points arising:

---

[3] In the interest of accuracy, we should also say that there is no such thing as a "database" in the SQL standard! Exactly what the collection of data is called that is described by a catalog is implementation-defined. However, it is not unreasonable to think of it as a database.

1. The rationale for stating the requirement in terms of two separate constructs as just described is as follows. First, existing products certainly do support something akin to the "Definition Schema." However, those "Definition Schemas" vary widely from one product to another (even when the products in question come from the same vendor). Hence the idea of requiring only that the implementation support certain predefined views of its "Definition Schema" does make sense.

2. We should really say "an" (not "the") Information Schema, since as we have seen there is one such in every catalog. In general, therefore, the totality of data available to a given user will *not* be described by a single Information Schema. For simplicity, however, we will continue to talk as if there were just one.

It is not worth going into great detail on the content of the Information Schema here; instead, we simply list some of the more important Information Schema views, in the hope that their names alone will be sufficient to give some idea of what those views contain. One point that is worth calling out explicitly, however, is that the TABLES view contains information for *all* named tables, views as well as base tables, while the VIEWS view contains information for views only.

```
ASSERTIONS                    TABLES
CHECK_CONSTRAINTS             TABLE_CONSTRAINTS
COLUMNS                       TABLE_PRIVILEGES
COLUMN_PRIVILEGES             USAGE_PRIVILEGES
COLUMN_UDT_USAGE              USER_DEFINED_TYPES
CONSTRAINT_COLUMN_USAGE       UDT_PRIVILEGES
CONSTRAINT_TABLE_USAGE        VIEWS
KEY_COLUMN_USAGE              VIEW_COLUMN_USAGE
REFERENTIAL_CONSTRAINTS       VIEW_TABLE_USAGE
SCHEMATA
```

Reference [4.20] gives more details; in particular, it shows how to formulate queries against the Information Schema (which is not quite as simple as you might expect).

4.4   VIEWS

Here is an example of an SQL view definition:

```
CREATE VIEW GOOD_SUPPLIER
    AS SELECT S#, STATUS, CITY
       FROM   S
       WHERE  STATUS > 15 ;
```

And here is an example of an SQL query against this view:

```
SELECT S#, STATUS
FROM   GOOD_SUPPLIER
WHERE  CITY = 'London' ;
```

Substituting the view definition for the reference to the view name, we obtain an expression that looks something like this (note the **subquery** in the FROM clause):

```
SELECT GOOD_SUPPLIER.S#, GOOD_SUPPLIER.STATUS
FROM ( SELECT S#, STATUS, CITY
       FROM   S
       WHERE  STATUS > 15 ) AS GOOD_SUPPLIER
WHERE  GOOD_SUPPLIER.CITY = 'London' ;
```

And this expression can then be simplified to something like this:

```
SELECT  S#, STATUS
FROM    S
WHERE   STATUS > 15
AND     CITY = 'London' ;
```

This latter query is what is actually executed.

By way of another example, consider the following DELETE operation:

```
DELETE
FROM    GOOD_SUPPLIER
WHERE   CITY = 'London' ;
```

The DELETE actually executed looks something like this:

```
DELETE
FROM    S
WHERE   STATUS > 15
AND     CITY = 'London' ;
```

4.5 TRANSACTIONS

SQL includes direct analogs of the BEGIN TRANSACTION, COMMIT, and ROLL-BACK statements from Chapter 3, called **START TRANSACTION**, **COMMIT WORK**, and **ROLLBACK WORK**, respectively (the keyword WORK is optional).

4.6 EMBEDDED SQL

Most SQL products allow SQL statements to be executed both **directly** (i.e., interactively from an online terminal) and as part of an application program (i.e., the SQL statements can be **embedded**, meaning they can be intermixed with the programming language statements of such a program). In the embedded case, moreover, the application program can typically be written in a variety of host languages; the SQL standard includes support for Ada, C, COBOL, Fortran, Java, M (formerly known as MUMPS), Pascal, and PL/I. In this section we consider the embedded case specifically.

A fundamental principle underlying embedded SQL, which we call **the dual-mode principle**, is that *any SQL statement that can be used interactively can also be embedded in an application program.* Of course, there are various differences of detail between a given interactive SQL statement and its embedded counterpart, and retrieval operations in particular require significantly extended treatment in the embedded case—see later in this section—but the principle is nevertheless broadly true. (Its converse is not, by the way; several embedded SQL statements cannot be used interactively, as we will see.)

Before we can discuss the actual statements of embedded SQL, it is necessary to cover a number of preliminary details. Most of those details are illustrated by the program

```
EXEC SQL BEGIN DECLARE SECTION ;

   DCL SQLSTATE CHAR(5) ;
   DCL P#       CHAR(6) ;
   DCL WEIGHT   FIXED DECIMAL(5,1) ;

EXEC SQL END DECLARE SECTION ;

P# = 'P2' ;                        /* for example                */
EXEC SQL SELECT P.WEIGHT
         INTO   :WEIGHT
         FROM   P
         WHERE  P.P# = P# ( :P# ) ;
IF SQLSTATE = '00000'
THEN ... ;                         /* WEIGHT = retrieved value */
ELSE ... ;                         /* some exception occurred  */
```

Fig. 4.3   Fragment of a PL/I program with embedded SQL

fragment shown in Fig. 4.3. (To fix our ideas we assume the host language is PL/I. Most of the ideas translate into other host languages with only minor changes.) Points arising:

1. Embedded SQL statements are prefixed by **EXEC SQL**, to distinguish them from statements of the host language, and are terminated by a special **terminator** symbol (a semicolon for PL/I).

2. An *executable* SQL statement (for the rest of this section we will mostly drop the "embedded" qualifier) can appear wherever an executable host statement can appear. Note that "executable," by the way: Unlike interactive SQL, embedded SQL includes some statements that are purely declarative, not executable. For example, DECLARE CURSOR is not an executable statement (see the subsection "Operations Involving Cursors" later), nor are BEGIN and END DECLARE SECTION (see point 5), and nor is WHENEVER (see point 9).

3. SQL statements can include references to **host variables**; such references must include a **colon prefix** to distinguish them from SQL column names. Host variables can appear in embedded SQL wherever a literal can appear in interactive SQL. They can also appear in an INTO clause on SELECT (see point 4) or FETCH (again, see the subsection "Operations Involving Cursors" later) to designate targets for retrieval operations.

4. Notice the **INTO** clause on the SELECT statement in Fig. 4.3. The purpose of that clause is (as just indicated) to specify the target variables into which values are to be retrieved; the *i*th target variable mentioned in the INTO clause corresponds to the *i*th value to be retrieved, as specified by the SELECT clause.

5. All host variables referenced in SQL statements must be declared (DCL in PL/I) within an **embedded SQL declare section**, which is delimited by the **BEGIN** and **END DECLARE SECTION** statements.

6. Every program containing embedded SQL statements must include a host variable called **SQLSTATE**. After any SQL statement has been executed, a status code is returned to the program in that variable; a value of 00000 means the statement exe-

cuted successfully, and a value of 02000 means the statement did execute but no data was found to satisfy the request (see reference [4.23] for details of other values). In principle, therefore, every SQL statement in the program should be followed by a test on SQLSTATE, and appropriate action taken if the value is not what was expected. In practice, however, such testing can often be implicit (see point 9).

7. Every host variable must have a **data type** appropriate to the uses to which it is put. For example, a host variable that is to be used as a target (e.g., on SELECT) must have a data type that is compatible with that of the expression that provides the value to be assigned to that target; likewise, a host variable that is to be used as a source (e.g., on INSERT) must have a data type that is compatible with that of the SQL column to which values of that source are to be assigned. The details are a little complicated, however, and we therefore ignore the issue for the remainder of this chapter (for the most part, at any rate), deferring further discussion to Chapter 5, Section 5.7.

8. Host variables and SQL columns can have the same name.

9. As already mentioned, every SQL statement should in principle be followed by a test of the returned SQLSTATE value. The **WHENEVER** statement is provided to simplify this process. The WHENEVER statement takes the form:

```
EXEC SQL WHENEVER <condition> <action> ;
```

Possible *<condition>*s include NOT FOUND, SQLWARNING, and SQLEXCEPTION (others include specific SQLSTATE values and violation of specified integrity constraints); *<action>* is either CONTINUE or a GO TO statement. WHENEVER is not an executable statement—rather, it is a directive to the SQL compiler: "WHENEVER *<condition>* GO TO *<label>*" causes the compiler to insert a statement of the form "IF *<condition>* THEN GO TO *<label>* . . ." after each executable SQL statement it encounters; "WHENEVER *<condition>* CONTINUE" causes it not to insert any such statements, the implication being that the programmer will insert appropriate statements by hand. The *<condition>*s NOT FOUND, SQLWARNING, and SQLEXCEPTION are defined as follows:

NOT FOUND	*means*	no data was found —SQLSTATE = 02xxx
SQLWARNING	*means*	a minor error occurred —SQLSTATE = 01xxx
SQLEXCEPTION	*means*	a major error occurred —see reference [4.23] for SQLSTATE

Each WHENEVER statement the compiler encounters on its sequential scan through the program text for a particular condition overrides the previous one it found for that condition.

10. Note finally that, to use the terminology of Chapter 2, embedded SQL constitutes a *loose coupling* between SQL and the host language.

So much for the preliminaries. In the rest of this section we concentrate on data manipulation operations specifically. As already indicated, most of those operations can be handled in a fairly straightforward fashion (i.e., with only minor changes to their syntax). Retrieval operations require special treatment, however. The problem is that such operations retrieve many rows (in general), not just one, and host languages are generally not equipped to handle the retrieval of more than one row at a time. It is therefore necessary to provide some kind of bridge between the set-level retrieval capabilities of SQL and the row-level retrieval capabilities of the host. Such is the purpose of **cursors**. A cursor consists essentially of a kind of (logical) *pointer*—a pointer in the application, that is, not one in the database—that can be used to run through a collection of rows, pointing to each of the rows in turn and thereby providing addressability to those rows one at a time. However, we defer detailed discussion of cursors to the subsection "Operations Involving Cursors," and consider first those statements that have no need of them.

Operations Not Involving Cursors

The data manipulation statements that do not need cursors are as follows:

- Singleton SELECT
- INSERT
- DELETE (except the CURRENT form—see the next subsection)
- UPDATE (except the CURRENT form—see the next subsection)

We give examples of each in turn.

Singleton SELECT: Get status and city for the supplier whose supplier number is given by the host variable GIVENS#.

```
EXEC SQL SELECT  STATUS, CITY
         INTO    :RANK, :TOWN
         FROM    S
         WHERE   S# = S# ( :GIVENS# ) ;
```

We use the term *singleton SELECT* to mean a SELECT expression that evaluates to a table containing at most one row. In the example, if there is exactly one row in table S satisfying the condition in the WHERE clause, then the STATUS and CITY values from that row will be assigned to the host variables RANK and TOWN as requested, and SQLSTATE will be set to 00000; if no S row satisfies the WHERE condition, SQLSTATE will be set to 02000; and if more than one does, the program is in error, and SQLSTATE will be set to an error code.

INSERT: Insert a new part (part number, name, and weight given by host variables P#, PNAME, PWT, respectively; color and city unknown) into table P.

```
EXEC SQL INSERT
         INTO    P ( P#, PNAME, WEIGHT )
         VALUES ( :P#, :PNAME, :PWT ) ;
```

The COLOR and CITY values for the new part will be set to the applicable *default* values (see Chapter 6, Section 6.6). *Note:* For reasons beyond the scope of this book, the default for a column that is of some user-defined type will necessarily be *null*. (We defer detailed discussion of nulls to Chapter 19. Occasional references prior to that point are unavoidable, however.)

DELETE: Delete all shipments for suppliers whose city is given by the host variable CITY.

```
EXEC SQL DELETE
         FROM    SP
         WHERE   :CITY =
                 ( SELECT CITY
                   FROM   S
                   WHERE  S.S# = SP.S# ) ;
```

If no supplier rows satisfy the WHERE condition, SQLSTATE will be set to 02000. Again, note the subquery (in the WHERE clause this time).

UPDATE: Increase the status of all London suppliers by the amount given by the host variable RAISE.

```
EXEC SQL UPDATE S
         SET     STATUS = STATUS + :RAISE
         WHERE   CITY = 'London' ;
```

Again SQLSTATE will be set to 02000 if no SP rows satisfy the WHERE condition.

Operations Involving Cursors

Now we turn to the question of set-level retrieval—that is, retrieval of a set containing an arbitrary number of rows, instead of at most one row as in the singleton SELECT case discussed in the previous subsection. As explained earlier, what is needed here is a mechanism for accessing the rows in the set one by one, and **cursors** provide such a mechanism. The process is illustrated in outline by the example of Fig. 4.4, which is intended to retrieve S#, SNAME, and STATUS information for all suppliers in the city given by the host variable Y.

Explanation: The statement "DECLARE X CURSOR . . ." defines a cursor called X, with an associated *table expression* (i.e., an expression that evaluates to a table), specified by the SELECT that forms part of that DECLARE. That table expression is not evaluated at this point; DECLARE CURSOR is a purely declarative statement. The expression *is*

```
EXEC SQL DECLARE X CURSOR FOR        /* define the cursor   */
         SELECT S.S#, S.SNAME, S.STATUS
         FROM    S
         WHERE   S.CITY = :Y
         ORDER   BY S# ASC ;

EXEC SQL OPEN X ;                      /* execute the query   */
         DO for all S rows accessible via X ;
            EXEC SQL FETCH X INTO :S#, :SNAME, :STATUS ;
                                     /* fetch next supplier */
            .........
         END ;
EXEC SQL CLOSE X ;                     /* deactivate cursor X */
```

Fig. 4.4 Multi-row retrieval example

evaluated when the cursor is opened ("OPEN X"). The statement "FETCH X INTO . . ." is then used to retrieve rows one at a time from the resulting set, assigning retrieved values to host variables in accordance with the specifications of the INTO clause in that state- ment. (For simplicity we have given the host variables the same names as the correspond- ing database columns. Notice that the SELECT in the cursor declaration does not have an INTO clause of its own.) Since there will be many rows in the result set, the FETCH will normally appear inside a loop; the loop will be repeated as long as there are more rows still to come in that result set. On exit from the loop, cursor X is closed ("CLOSE X").

Now we consider cursors and cursor operations in more detail. First of all, a cursor is declared by means of a **DECLARE CURSOR** statement, which takes the general form

```
EXEC SQL DECLARE <cursor name> CURSOR
        FOR <table exp> [ <ordering> ] ;
```

(we are ignoring a few optional specifications in the interest of brevity). The optional *<ordering>* takes the form

```
ORDER BY <order item commalist>
```

where (a) the commalist contains at least one *<order item>* and (b) each *<order item>* con- sists of a column name—unqualified, please note[4]—optionally followed by ASC (ascend- ing) or DESC (descending), where ASC is the default. If no ORDER BY clause is speci- fied, the ordering is system-determined. (As a matter of fact the same is true if an ORDER BY clause *is* specified, at least as far as rows with the same value for the specified *<order item commalist>* are concerned.)

Note: The useful term *commalist* is defined as follows. Let *<xyz>* denote an arbitrary syntactic category (i.e., anything that appears on the left side of some BNF production rule). Then the expression *<xyz commalist>* denotes a sequence of zero or more *<xyz>*s in which each pair of adjacent *<xyz>*s is separated by a comma (and optionally one or more blanks). We will be making extensive use of the commalist shorthand in future syn- tax rules (all syntax rules, that is, not just SQL ones).

As previously stated, the DECLARE CURSOR statement is declarative, not execut- able; it declares a cursor with the specified name and having the specified table expression and ordering permanently associated with it. The table expression can include host vari- able references. A program can include any number of DECLARE CURSOR statements, each of which must (of course) be for a different cursor.

Three executable statements are provided to operate on cursors: **OPEN, FETCH,** and **CLOSE**.

- The statement

```
EXEC SQL OPEN <cursor name> ;
```

---

[4] Actually, the column name *can* be qualified if the specified *<table exp>* abides by a rather complex set of rules. The rules in question were introduced with SQL:1999, which also introduced rules according to which an *<order item>* can sometimes specify either (a) a computational expression, as in (e.g.) ORDER BY A+B, or (b) the name of a column that is not part of the result table, as in (e.g.) SELECT CITY FROM S ORDER BY STATUS. Details of these rules are beyond the scope of this book.

opens the specified cursor (which must not currently be open). In effect, the table expression associated with the cursor is evaluated (using the current values for any host variables referenced within that expression); a set of rows is thus identified and becomes the current **active set** for the cursor. The cursor also identifies a **position** within that active set: namely, the position just before the first row. *Note:* Active sets are always considered to have an ordering—see the earlier discussion of ORDER BY—and so the concept of position has meaning.[5]

- The statement

```
EXEC SQL FETCH <cursor name>
        INTO <host variable reference commalist> ;
```

advances the specified cursor (which must be open) to the next row in the active set and then assigns the *i*th value from that row to the *i*th host variable referenced in the INTO clause. If there is no next row when FETCH is executed, SQLSTATE is set to 02000 and no data is retrieved.

- The statement

```
EXEC SQL CLOSE <cursor name> ;
```

closes the specified cursor (which must currently be open). The cursor now has no current active set. However, it can subsequently be opened again, in which case it will acquire another active set—probably not exactly the same one as before, especially if the values of any host variables referenced in the cursor declaration have changed in the meantime. Note that changing the values of those host variables while the cursor is open has no effect on the current active set.

Two further statements can include references to cursors, the **CURRENT** forms of **DELETE** and **UPDATE**. If a cursor, X say, is currently positioned on a particular row, then it is possible to DELETE or UPDATE "the current of X"—that is, the row on which X is positioned. For example:

```
EXEC SQL UPDATE S
        SET    STATUS = STATUS + :RAISE
        WHERE  CURRENT OF X ;
```

The CURRENT forms of DELETE and UPDATE are not permitted if the *<table exp>* in the cursor declaration would define a nonupdatable view if it were part of a CREATE VIEW statement (see Chapter 10, Section 10.6).

4.7   DYNAMIC SQL AND SQL/CLI

The previous section tacitly assumed we could compile any given program in its entirety—SQL statements and all—"ahead of time," as it were (i.e., prior to run time). For certain applications, however, that assumption is unwarranted. By way of example, consider an online application (recall from Chapter 1 that an online application is one that

---

[5] Sets *per se* do not have an ordering (see Chapter 6), so an "active set" is not really a set, as such, at all. It would be better to think of it as an *ordered list* or *array* (of rows).

supports access to the database from an online terminal or something analogous). Typically, the steps such an application must go through are as follows (in outline):

1. Accept a command from the terminal.
2. Analyze that command.
3. Execute appropriate SQL statements on the database.
4. Return a message and/or results to the terminal.

Now, if the set of commands the program can accept in Step 1 is fairly small, as in the case of (perhaps) a program handling airline reservations, then the set of possible SQL statements to be executed will probably also be small and can be "hardwired" into the program. In this case, Steps 2 and 3 will consist simply of logic to examine the input command and then branch to the part of the program that issues the predefined SQL statement(s). On the other hand, if there can be great variability in the input, then it might not be practicable to predefine and "hardwire" SQL statements for every possible command. Instead, what we need to do is *construct* the necessary SQL statements dynamically, and then compile and execute those constructed statements dynamically. The SQL facilities described in this section are provided to assist in this process.

Dynamic SQL

Dynamic SQL is part of embedded SQL. It consists of a set of "dynamic statements"—which themselves *are* compiled ahead of time—whose purpose is precisely to support the compilation and execution of regular SQL statements that are constructed at run time. Thus, the two principal dynamic statements are PREPARE (in effect, *compile*) and EXECUTE. Their use is illustrated in the following unrealistically simple, but accurate, PL/I example.

```
DCL SQLSOURCE CHAR VARYING (65000) ;

SQLSOURCE = 'DELETE FROM SP WHERE QTY < QTY ( 300 )' ;
EXEC SQL PREPARE SQLPREPPED FROM :SQLSOURCE ;
EXEC SQL EXECUTE SQLPREPPED ;
```

Explanation:

1. The name SQLSOURCE identifies a PL/I variable (of type "varying length character string") in which, at run time, the program will somehow construct the source form of some SQL statement—a DELETE statement, in our particular example—as a character string.
2. The name SQLPREPPED, by contrast, identifies an *SQL* variable, not a PL/I variable, that will be used to hold the compiled form of the SQL statement whose source form is given in SQLSOURCE. (The names SQLSOURCE and SQLPREPPED are arbitrary, of course.)
3. The PL/I assignment statement "SQLSOURCE = . . . ;" assigns to SQLSOURCE the source form of an SQL DELETE statement. In practice, the process of constructing such a source statement is likely to be much more complex—perhaps involving the

input and analysis of some request from the end user, expressed in natural language or some other form more user-friendly than SQL.

4. The PREPARE statement then takes that source statement and "prepares" (compiles) it to produce an executable version, which it stores in SQLPREPPED.

5. Finally, the EXECUTE statement executes that SQLPREPPED version and thus causes the actual DELETE to occur. SQLSTATE information from the DELETE is returned exactly as if the DELETE had been executed directly in the normal way.

Note that because it denotes an SQL variable, not a PL/I variable, the name SQLPREPPED does not have a colon prefix when it is referenced in the PREPARE and EXECUTE statements. Note too that such SQL variables do not have to be explicitly declared.

By the way, the process just described is essentially what happens when SQL statements themselves are entered interactively. Most systems provide some kind of interactive SQL query processor. That query processor is in effect just a particular online application; it is ready to accept an extremely wide variety of input—*viz.*, any valid (or invalid!) SQL statement. It then uses the facilities of dynamic SQL to construct suitable SQL statements corresponding to its input, to compile and execute those constructed statements, and to return messages and results back to the terminal.

Of course, there is much more to dynamic SQL than the PREPARE and EXECUTE statements as just described; for example, there are mechanisms for parameterizing the statements to be prepared and providing arguments to be substituted for those parameters when those statements are executed, and there are counterparts to the cursor facilities as described in the previous section. In particular, there is an EXECUTE IMMEDIATE statement, which effectively combines the functions of PREPARE and EXECUTE into a single operation.

Call-Level Interfaces

The **SQL Call-Level Interface** feature (SQL/CLI, *CLI* for short) was added to the standard in 1995. SQL/CLI is heavily based on Microsoft's *Open Database Connectivity* interface, ODBC. Both permit an application written in one of the usual host languages to issue database requests, not via embedded SQL, but rather by invoking certain vendor-provided routines. Those routines, which must have been linked to the application in question, then use dynamic SQL to perform the requested database operations on the application's behalf. (From the DBMS's point of view, in other words, those routines can be thought of as just another application.)

As you can see, SQL/CLI and ODBC both address the same general problem as dynamic SQL does: They both allow applications to be written for which the exact SQL statements to be executed are not known until run time. However, they actually represent a better approach to the problem than dynamic SQL does. There are two principal reasons for this state of affairs:

■ Dynamic SQL is a *source code* standard. Any application using dynamic SQL thus requires the services of some kind of SQL compiler in order to process the operations—PREPARE, EXECUTE, and so on—prescribed by that standard. SQL/CLI, by contrast, merely standardizes the details of certain *routine invocations* (i.e., subroutine calls, basically); no special compiler services are needed, only the regular services of the standard host language compiler. As a result, applications can be distributed (perhaps by third-party software vendors) in "shrink-wrapped" *object code* form.

- What is more, those applications can be *DBMS-independent;* that is, SQL/CLI includes features that permit the creation (again, perhaps by third-party software vendors) of generic applications that can be used with several different DBMSs, instead of having to be specific to some particular DBMS.

Here by way of illustration is an SQL/CLI analog of the dynamic SQL example from the previous subsection:

```
char sqlsource [65000] ;

strcpy ( sqlsource,
         "DELETE FROM SP WHERE QTY < QTY ( 300 )" ) ;
rc = SQLExecDirect ( hstmt, (SQLCHAR *)sqlsource, SQL_NTS ) ;
```

Explanation:

1. Since real-world SQL/CLI applications tend to use C as host language, we use C instead of PL/I as the basis for this example. We also follow the SQL/CLI specification in using lowercase (or mixed uppercase and lowercase) for variable names, routine names, and the like, instead of all uppercase as elsewhere in this book (and we show such names in **boldface** in these explanatory notes in order to set them off from surrounding material). Note too that, precisely because it is a standard for invoking routines from a host language, SQL/CLI syntax—though not of course the corresponding semantics—will vary from one host language to another, in general.

2. The C function **strcpy** is invoked to copy the source form of a certain SQL DELETE statement into the C variable **sqlsource**.

3. The C assignment statement ("=") invokes the SQL/CLI routine **SQLExecDirect**— the analog of dynamic SQL's EXECUTE IMMEDIATE—to execute the SQL statement contained in **sqlsource**, and assigns the return code resulting from that invocation to the C variable **rc**.

As you would probably expect, SQL/CLI includes analogs of more or less everything in dynamic SQL, plus a few extra things as well. Further details are beyond the scope of this book. However, you should be aware that interfaces such as SQL/CLI, ODBC, and JDBC (which is a Java variant of ODBC, in effect) are becoming increasingly important in practice, for reasons to be discussed in Chapter 21, Section 21.6.

4.8   SQL IS NOT PERFECT

As stated in Section 4.1, SQL is very far from being the "perfect" relational language—it suffers from numerous sins of both omission and commission. Specific criticisms will be offered at appropriate points in subsequent chapters, but the overriding issue is simply that SQL fails in all too many ways to support the relational model properly. As a consequence, it is not at all clear that today's SQL products really deserve to be called "relational" at all! Indeed, as far as this writer is aware, *there is no product on the market today that supports the relational model in its entirety.*[6] This is not to say that some parts of the model are unimportant; on the contrary, every detail of the model is important, and important, moreover, for genuinely practical reasons. Indeed, the point cannot be stressed too strongly that the purpose of relational theory is not just "theory for its own sake"; rather, the purpose is to provide a base on which to build systems that are *100 percent practical.* But the sad fact is that the vendors have not yet really stepped up to the challenge of implementing the theory in its entirety. As a consequence, the "relational" products of today regrettably all fail, in one way or another, to deliver on the full promise of relational technology.

4.9 SUMMARY

This concludes our introduction to some of the major features of the SQL standard. We have stressed the fact that SQL is important from a commercial perspective, though it is sadly deficient from a relational one.

SQL includes both a **data definition** language (DDL) component and a **data manipulation** language (DML) component. The SQL DML can operate at both the external level (on views) and the conceptual level (on base tables). Likewise, the SQL DDL can be used to define objects at the external level (views), the conceptual level (base tables), and even—in most commercial systems, though not in the standard *per se*—the internal level as well (indexes or other auxiliary structures). Moreover, SQL also provides certain *data control* facilities—that is, facilities that cannot really be classified as belonging to either the DDL or the DML. An example of such a facility is the GRANT statement, which allows users to grant *access privileges* to each other (see Chapter 17).

We showed how SQL can be used to create base tables, using the **CREATE TABLE** statement (we also touched on the **CREATE TYPE** statement in passing). We then gave some examples of the **SELECT, INSERT, DELETE,** and **UPDATE** statements, showing in particular how SELECT can be used to express the relational restrict, project, and join operations. We also briefly described the **Information Schema**, which consists of a set of prescribed views of a hypothetical "Definition Schema," and we took a quick look at the SQL facilities for dealing with **views** and **transactions**.

A large part of the chapter was concerned with **embedded SQL**. The basic idea behind embedded SQL is **the dual-mode principle**—that is, the principle that (insofar as possible) *any SQL statement that can be used interactively can also be used in an application program.* The major exception to this principle arises in connection with **multi-row retrieval operations**, which require the use of a **cursor** to bridge the gap between the set-level retrieval capabilities of SQL and the row-level retrieval capabilities of a host language such as PL/I.

Following a number of necessary, though mostly syntactic, preliminaries (including in particular a brief explanation of **SQLSTATE**), we considered those operations— **singleton SELECT, INSERT, DELETE,** and **UPDATE**—that have no need for cursors.

---

[6] But see reference [20.1].

Then we turned to the operations that *do* need cursors, and discussed **DECLARE CURSOR**, **OPEN**, **FETCH**, **CLOSE**, and the **CURRENT** forms of **DELETE** and **UPDATE**. (The standard refers to the CURRENT forms of these operators as *positioned* DELETE and UPDATE, and uses the term *searched* DELETE and UPDATE for the non-CURRENT or "out of the blue" forms.) Finally, we introduced the concept of **dynamic SQL**, describing the **PREPARE** and **EXECUTE** statements in particular, and we also briefly explained the **SQL Call-Level Interface**, SQL/CLI (we also mentioned ODBC and JDBC).

EXERCISES

4.1   Fig. 4.5 shows some sample data values for an extended form of the suppliers-and-parts database called the suppliers-parts-projects database.[7] Suppliers (S), parts (P), and projects (J) are uniquely identified by supplier number (S#), part number (P#), and project number (J#), respectively. The predicate for SPJ (shipments) is: *Supplier S# supplies part P# to project J# in quantity QTY* (the combination {S#,P#,J#} is the primary key, as the figure indicates). Write an appropriate set of SQL definitions for this database. *Note:* This database will be used as the basis for numerous exercises in subsequent chapters.

S

S#	SNAME	STATUS	CITY
S1	Smith	20	London
S2	Jones	10	Paris
S3	Blake	30	Paris
S4	Clark	20	London
S5	Adams	30	Athens

P

P#	PNAME	COLOR	WEIGHT	CITY
P1	Nut	Red	12.0	London
P2	Bolt	Green	17.0	Paris
P3	Screw	Blue	17.0	Oslo
P4	Screw	Red	14.0	London
P5	Cam	Blue	12.0	Paris
P6	Cog	Red	19.0	London

J

J#	JNAME	CITY
J1	Sorter	Paris
J2	Display	Rome
J3	OCR	Athens
J4	Console	Athens
J5	RAID	London
J6	EDS	Oslo
J7	Tape	London

SPJ

S#	P#	J#	QTY
S1	P1	J1	200
S1	P1	J4	700
S2	P3	J1	400
S2	P3	J2	200
S2	P3	J3	200
S2	P3	J4	500
S2	P3	J5	600
S2	P3	J6	400
S2	P3	J7	800
S2	P5	J2	100
S3	P3	J1	200
S3	P4	J2	500
S4	P6	J3	300
S4	P6	J7	300
S5	P2	J2	200
S5	P2	J4	100
S5	P5	J5	500
S5	P5	J7	100
S5	P6	J2	200
S5	P1	J4	100
S5	P3	J4	200
S5	P4	J4	800
S5	P5	J4	400
S5	P6	J4	500

Fig. 4.5   The suppliers-parts-projects database (sample values)

[7] For ease of reference, Fig. 4.5 is repeated (along with Fig. 3.8) on the inside back cover of the book.

4.2   In Section 4.2 we described the CREATE TABLE statement as defined by the SQL standard *per se*. Many commercial SQL products support additional options on that statement, however, typically having to do with indexes, disk space allocation, and other implementation matters (thereby undermining the objectives of physical data independence and intersystem compatibility). Investigate any SQL product that might be available to you. Do the foregoing criticisms apply to that product? Specifically, what additional CREATE TABLE options does that product support?

4.3   Once again, investigate any SQL product that might be available to you. Does that product support the Information Schema? If not, what *does* its catalog support look like?

4.4   Give SQL formulations for the following updates to the suppliers-parts-projects database:

  a. Insert a new supplier S10 into table S (the name and city are Smith and New York, respectively; the status is not yet known).

  b. Delete all projects for which there are no shipments.

  c. Change the color of all red parts to orange.

4.5   Again using the suppliers-parts-projects database, write a program with embedded SQL statements to list all suppliers in supplier number order. Each supplier should be immediately followed in the listing by all projects supplied by that supplier, in project number order.

4.6   Let tables PART and PART_STRUCTURE be defined as follows:

```
CREATE TABLE PART
    ( P# P#, DESCRIPTION CHAR(100),
      PRIMARY KEY ( P# ) ) ;

CREATE TABLE PART_STRUCTURE
    ( MAJOR_P# P#, MINOR_P# P#, QTY QTY,
      PRIMARY KEY ( MAJOR_P#, MINOR_P# ),
      FOREIGN KEY ( MAJOR_P# ) REFERENCES PART,
      FOREIGN KEY ( MINOR_P# ) REFERENCES PART ) ;
```

Table PART_STRUCTURE shows which parts (MAJOR_P#) contain which other parts (MINOR_P#) as first-level components. Write an SQL program to list all component parts of a given part, to all levels (the so-called **part explosion** problem). *Note:* The sample data shown in Fig. 4.6 might help you visualize this problem. We remark that table PART_STRUCTURE shows how *bill-of-materials* data—see Section 1.3, subsection "Entities and Relationships"—is typically represented in a relational system.

PART_STRUCTURE	MAJOR_P#	MINOR_P#	QTY
	P1	P2	2
	P1	P3	4
	P2	P3	1
	P2	P4	3
	P3	P5	9
	P4	P5	8
	P5	P6	3

Fig. 4.6   Table PART_STRUCTURE (sample value)

REFERENCES AND BIBLIOGRAPHY

Appendix H of reference [3.3] gives a detailed comparison between SQL:1999 and the proposals of *The Third Manifesto*. See also Appendix B of the present book.

4.1 M. M. Astrahan and R. A. Lorie: "SEQUEL-XRM: A Relational System," Proc. ACM Pacific Regional Conf., San Francisco, Calif. (April 1975).

> Describes the first prototype implementation of SEQUEL [4.9], the earliest version of SQL. See also references [4.2] and [4.3], which perform an analogous function for System R.

4.2 M. M. Astrahan *et al.*: "System R: Relational Approach to Database Management," *ACM TODS 1,* No. 2 (June 1976).

> System R was the major prototype implementation of the SEQUEL/2 (later SQL) language [4.10]. This paper describes the architecture of System R as originally planned. See also reference [4.3].

4.3 M. W. Blasgen *et al.*: "System R: An Architectural Overview," *IBM Sys. J. 20,* No. 1 (February 1981).

> This paper describes the architecture of System R as it became by the time the system was fully implemented (compare and contrast reference [4.2]).

4.4 Joe Celko: *SQL for Smarties: Advanced SQL Programming.* San Francisco, Calif.: Morgan Kaufmann (1995).

> "This is the first advanced SQL book available that provides a comprehensive presentation of the techniques necessary to support your progress from casual user of SQL to expert programmer" (from the book's own cover).

4.5 Surajit Chaudhuri and Gerhard Weikum: "Rethinking Database System Architecture: Towards a Self-Tuning RISC-Style Database System," Proc. 26th Int. Conf. on Very Large Data Bases, Cairo, Egypt (September 2000).

> This paper includes some severe criticisms of SQL. To quote: *"SQL is painful.* A big headache that comes with a database system is the SQL language. It is the union of all conceivable features (many of which are rarely used or should be discouraged [from] use anyway) and is way too complex for the typical application developer. Its core, say selection-projection-join queries and aggregation, is extremely useful, but we doubt that there is wide and wise use of all the bells and whistles. Understanding semantics of [SQL:1992, let alone SQL:1999], covering all combinations of nested (and correlated) subqueries, [nulls], triggers, ADT functions, etc. is a nightmare. Teaching SQL typically focuses on the core, and leaves the featurism as a 'learning-on-the-job' life experience. Some trade magazines occasionally pose SQL quizzes where the challenge is to express a complicated information request in a single SQL request. Those statements run over several pages, and are hardly comprehensible."

4.6 Andrew Eisenberg and Jim Melton: "SQL:1999, Formerly Known as SQL3," *ACM SIGMOD Record 28, No. 1* (March 1999).

> A brief introduction to the new features that were added to the SQL standard with the publication of SQL:1999.

4.7 Andrew Eisenberg and Jim Melton: "SQLJ Part 0, Now Known as SQL/OLB (Object Language Bindings)," *ACM SIGMOD Record 27,* No. 4 (December 1998); "SQLJ—Part 1: SQL Routines Using the Java™ Programming Language," *ACM SIGMOD Record 28,* No. 4 (December 1999). See also Gray Clossman *et al.*: "Java and Relational Databases: SQLJ," Proc. 1998 ACM SIGMOD Int. Conf. on Management of Data, Seattle, Wash. (June 1998).

The name *SQLJ* originally referred to a project to consider possible degrees of integration between SQL and Java (a joint effort involving some of the best-known SQL vendors). Part 0 of that project dealt with embedded SQL in Java programs; Part 1 was concerned with the idea of invoking Java from SQL (e.g., calling a stored procedure—see Chapter 21—that is written in Java); and Part 2 addressed the possibility of using Java classes as SQL data types (e.g., as a basis for defining columns in SQL tables). Part 0 was included in SQL:1999, and Parts 1 and 2 will almost certainly be included in SQL:2003 (see the annotation to reference [4.23]).

4.8 Donald D. Chamberlin: *Using the New DB2*. San Francisco, Calif.: Morgan Kaufmann (1996).

A readable and comprehensive description of a state-of-the-art commercial SQL product, by one of the principal designers of the original SQL language [4.9–4.11]. *Note:* The book also discusses "some controversial decisions" that were made in the design of SQL—primarily the decisions to support (a) nulls and (b) duplicate rows. "My [i.e., Chamberlin's] purpose . . . is historical rather than persuasive—I recognize that nulls and duplicates are religious issues . . . For the most part, the designers of [SQL] were practical people rather than theoreticians, and this orientation was reflected in many [design] decisions." This position is very different from ours! Nulls and duplicates are *scientific* issues, not religious ones; they are discussed, scientifically, in this book in Chapters 19 and 6, respectively. As for "practical . . . rather than [theoretical]," we categorically reject the suggestion that theory is not practical; we have already stated in Section 4.8 our position that relational theory, at least, is very practical indeed.

4.9 Donald D. Chamberlin and Raymond F. Boyce: "SEQUEL: A Structured English Query Language," Proc. 1974 ACM SIGMOD Workshop on Data Description, Access, and Control, Ann Arbor, Mich. (May 1974).

The paper that first introduced the SQL language (or SEQUEL, as it was originally called; the name was subsequently changed for legal reasons).

4.10 Donald D. Chamberlin *et al.*: "SEQUEL/2: A Unified Approach to Data Definition, Manipulation, and Control," *IBM J. R&D. 20,* No. 6 (November 1976). See also the errata in *IBM J. R&D. 21,* No. 1 (January 1977).

Experience from the early prototype implementation of SEQUEL discussed in reference [4.1] and results from certain usability tests led to the design of a revised version of the language called SEQUEL/2. The language supported by System R [4.2, 4.3] was basically SEQUEL/2 (with the conspicuous absence of the so-called "assertion" and "trigger" facilities—see Chapter 9), plus certain extensions suggested by early user experience [4.11].

4.11 Donald D. Chamberlin: "A Summary of User Experience with the SQL Data Sublanguage," Proc. Int. Conf. on Databases, Aberdeen, Scotland (July 1980). Also available as IBM Research Report RJ2767 (April 1980).

Discusses early user experience with System R and proposes some extensions to the SQL language in light of that experience. Certain of those extensions—EXISTS, LIKE, PREPARE, and EXECUTE—were in fact implemented in the final version of System R. They are described in Section 8.6 (EXISTS), Appendix B (LIKE), and Section 4.7 (PREPARE and EXECUTE).

4.12 Donald D. Chamberlin *et al.*: "Support for Repetitive Transactions and *Ad Hoc* Queries in System R," *ACM TODS 6,* No. 1 (March 1981).

Gives some measurements of System R performance in both the *ad hoc* query and "canned transaction" environments. (A "canned transaction" is a simple application that accesses only a small part of the database and is compiled prior to execution time. It corresponds to what we called a *planned request* in Chapter 2, Section 2.8.) The paper shows, among other things, that in a system like System R (a) compilation is almost always superior to interpretation, even for *ad hoc* queries, and (b) as long as appropriate indexes exist in the database, many transactions can be executed per second. The paper is notable because it was one of the first to give the lie to the claim, frequently heard at the time, that "relational systems will never perform." Commercial SQL products subsequently achieved transaction rates in the hundreds and even thousands of transactions per second.

4.13 Donald D. Chamberlin *et al.*: "A History and Evaluation of System R," *CACM 24,* No. 10 (October 1981).

Describes the three principal phases of the System R project (preliminary prototype, multi-user prototype, evaluation), with emphasis on the technologies of compilation and optimization that were pioneered in System R. There is some overlap between this paper and reference [4.14].

4.14 Donald D. Chamberlin, Arthur M. Gilbert, and Robert A. Yost: "A History of System R and SQL/Data System," Proc. 7th Int. Conf. on Very Large Data Bases, Cannes, France (September 1981).

Discusses the lessons learned from the System R prototype and describes the evolution of that prototype into the first of IBM's DB2 product family, SQL/DS (subsequently renamed "DB2 for VM and VSE").

4.15 C. J. Date: "A Critique of the SQL Database Language," *ACM SIGMOD Record 14,* No. 3 (November 1984). Republished in *Relational Database: Selected Writings.* Reading, Mass.: Addison-Wesley (1986).

As noted in the body of the chapter, SQL is not perfect. This paper presents a critical analysis of a number of the language's principal shortcomings, mainly from the standpoint of formal computer languages in general rather than database languages specifically. *Note:* Certain of this paper's criticisms do not apply to SQL:1999.

4.16 C. J. Date: "What's Wrong with SQL?" in *Relational Database Writings 1985–1989.* Reading, Mass.: Addison-Wesley (1990).

Discusses some additional shortcomings of SQL, over and above those identified in reference [4.15], under the headings "What's Wrong with SQL *per se,*" "What's Wrong with the SQL Standard," and "Application Portability." *Note:* Again, certain of this paper's criticisms do not apply to SQL:1999.

4.17 C. J. Date: "SQL Dos and Don'ts," in *Relational Database Writings 1985–1989.* Reading, Mass.: Addison-Wesley (1990).

This paper offers some practical advice on how to use SQL in such a way as (a) to avoid some of the potential pitfalls arising from the problems discussed in references [4.15], [4.16], and [4.19] and (b) to realize the maximum possible benefits in terms of productivity, portability, connectivity, and so forth.

4.18 C. J. Date: "How We Missed the Relational Boat," in *Relational Database Writings 1991–1994.* Reading, Mass.: Addison-Wesley (1995).

A succinct summary of SQL's shortcomings with respect to its support (or lack thereof) for the structural, integrity, and manipulative aspects of the relational model.

4.19 C. J. Date: "Grievous Bodily Harm" (in two parts), *DBP&D 11,* No. 5 (May 1998) and No. 6 (June 1998); "Fifty Ways to Quote Your Query," *http://www.dbpd.com* (July 1998).

SQL is an extremely redundant language, in the sense that all but the most trivial of queries can be expressed in many different ways. These papers illustrate this point and discuss some of its implications. In particular, they show that the GROUP BY clause, the HAVING clause, and range variables could all be dropped from the language with effectively no loss of functionality (and the same is true of the "IN <*subquery*>" construct). *Note:* All of these SQL constructs are explained in Chapter 8, Section 8.6.

4.20 C. J. Date and Hugh Darwen: *A Guide to the SQL Standard* (4th edition). Reading, Mass.: Addison-Wesley (1997).

A comprehensive tutorial on the SQL standard (1992 version), including SQL/CLI (1995), SQL/PSM (1996), and a preliminary look at SQL:1999. In particular, the book contains an appendix, Appendix D, that documents "many aspects of the standard that appear to be inadequately defined, or even incorrectly defined, at this time." Most of the problems identified in that appendix still exist in SQL:1999.

4.21 C. J. Date and Colin J. White: *A Guide to DB2* (4th edition). Reading, Mass.: Addison-Wesley (1993).

Provides an extensive and thorough overview of IBM's original DB2 product (as of 1993) and some of its companion products. DB2 was based on System R, though not as closely as SQL/DS was [4.14].

4.22 Neal Fishman: "SQL *du Jour,*" *DBP&D 10,* No. 10 (October 1997).

A depressing survey of some of the incompatibilities to be found among SQL products that all claim to "support the SQL standard."

4.23 International Organization for Standardization (ISO): *Information Technology—Database Languages—SQL,* Document ISO/IEC 9075:1999. *Note:* See also reference [22.21].

The original ISO SQL:1999 definition (known to the cognoscenti as *ISO/IEC 9075,* or sometimes just *ISO 9075*). Note, however, that the original monolithic document has since been replaced by an open-ended series of separate "parts" (ISO/IEC 9075-1, -2, etc.). At the time of writing, the following parts have been defined:

Part 1: Framework (SQL/Framework)
Part 2: Foundation (SQL/Foundation)
Part 3: Call-Level Interface (SQL/CLI)
Part 4: Persistent Stored Modules (SQL/PSM)
Part 5: Host Language Bindings (SQL/Bindings)
Part 6: *There is no Part 6*
Part 7: *There is no Part 7*
Part 8: *There is no Part 8*
Part 9: Management of External Data (SQL/MED)
Part 10: Object Language Bindings (SQL/OLB)

As noted earlier in the chapter, the next edition of the standard is expected in 2003, at which time the following changes to the foregoing list are likely:

- The material from Part 5 will be folded into Part 2 and Part 5 will be dropped.
- The material from Part 2 defining the standard database catalog (the "Information Schema") will be moved to a new Part 11, "SQL Schemata."
- A new Part 13, "Java Routines and Types (SQL/JRT)," will standardize further integration of Java with SQL (see the annotation to reference [4.7]).
- A new Part 14, "XML-Related Specifications (SQL/XML)," will standardize features having to do with the relationship between SQL and XML (see Chapter 27).

By the way, it is worth mentioning that, although SQL is widely recognized as the international "relational" database standard, the standard document does not describe itself as such; in fact, it never actually uses the term *relation* at all! (As mentioned in a footnote earlier in this chapter, it does not use the term *database* either, come to that.)

4.24 International Organization for Standardization (ISO): *(ISO Working Draft)—Database Language SQL—Technical Corrigendum 5,* Document ISO/IEC JTC1/SC32/WG3 (December 2, 2001).

Contains a large number of revisions and corrections to the specifications of reference [4.23].

4.25 Raymond A. Lorie and Jean-Jacques Daudenarde: *SQL and Its Applications.* Englewood Cliffs, N.J.: Prentice-Hall (1991).

An SQL "how to" book (almost half the book consists of a detailed series of case studies involving realistic applications).

4.26 Raymond A. Lorie and J. F. Nilsson: "An Access Specification Language for a Relational Data Base System," *IBM J. R&D. 23,* No. 3 (May 1979).

Gives more details on one particular aspect of the System R compilation mechanism [4.12, 4.27]. For any given SQL statement, the System R optimizer generates a program in an internal language called ASL (Access Specification Language). ASL serves as the interface between the optimizer and the *code generator.* (The code generator, as its name implies, converts an ASL program into machine code.) ASL consists of operators such as "scan" and "insert" on objects such as indexes and stored files. The purpose of ASL is to make the overall translation process more manageable, by breaking it down into a set of well-defined subprocesses.

4.27 Raymond A. Lorie and Bradford W. Wade: "The Compilation of a High-Level Data Language," IBM Research Report RJ2598 (August 1979).

System R pioneered a scheme for compiling queries ahead of run time and then automatically recompiling them if the physical database structure had changed significantly in the interim. This paper describes the System R compilation and recompilation mechanism in some detail, without however getting into questions of optimization. See reference [18.33] for information on this latter topic.

4.28 Jim Melton and Alan R. Simon: *SQL:1999—Understanding Relational Components.* San Francisco, Calif.: Morgan Kaufmann (2002).

A tutorial on SQL:1999 (basics only—advanced topics are deferred to reference [26.32]). Melton is the editor of the SQL standard at the time of writing.

4.29 David Rozenshtein, Anatoly Abramovich, and Eugene Birger: *Optimizing Transact-SQL: Advanced Programming Techniques.* Fremont, Calif.: SQL Forum Press (1995).

Transact-SQL is the dialect of SQL supported by the Sybase and SQL Server products. This book presents a series of programming techniques for Transact-SQL based on the use of *characteristic functions* (defined by the authors as "devices that allow programmers to encode conditional logic as . . . expressions within SELECT, WHERE, GROUP BY, and SET clauses"). Although expressed in terms of Transact-SQL specifically, the ideas are actually of wider applicability. *Note:* We should perhaps add that the "optimizing" mentioned in the book's title refers not to the DBMS optimizer component but rather to "optimizations" that can be done by users themselves by hand.

THE RELATIONAL MODEL

The foundation of modern database technology is without question the relational model; it is that foundation that makes the field a science. Thus, any book on the fundamentals of database technology that does not include thorough coverage of the relational model is by definition shallow. Likewise, any claim to expertise in the database field can hardly be justified if the claimant does not understand the relational model in depth. Not that the material is at all "difficult," we hasten to add—it is not—but, to repeat, it *is* the foundation, and will remain so for as far out as anyone can see.

As explained in Chapter 3, the relational model is concerned with three principal aspects of data: data *structure,* data *manipulation,* and data *integrity.* In this part of the book, we consider each of these aspects in turn:

- Chapters 5 and 6 discuss structure (Chapter 5 deals with *types* and Chapter 6 with *relations*).

- Chapters 7 and 8 discuss manipulation (Chapter 7 deals with the *relational algebra* and Chapter 8 with the *relational calculus*).

- Chapter 9 discusses integrity.

Finally, Chapter 10 discusses the important topic of *views. Note:* Perhaps we should add that the division of the relational model into three parts, useful though it can be at a high conceptual level, tends to break down once we start looking more closely. As you will soon see, in fact, individual components of the model are highly interconnected and rely on one another in a variety of ways; thus, it is not possible in general (even in principle) to remove any given component without wrecking the entire model. One consequence of this fact is that Chapters 5–10 include numerous cross-references to one another.

It is also important to understand that the model is not a static thing—it has evolved and expanded over the years, and it continues to do so.[1] The text that follows reflects the current thinking of the author and other workers in this field (in particular, as mentioned in the preface, it is informed throughout by the ideas of *The Third Manifesto* [3.3]). The treatment is meant to be fairly complete, even definitive (as of the time of writing),

---

[1] It resembles mathematics in this respect (mathematics is not static, either, but grows over time); in fact, the relational model can be regarded itself as a small branch of mathematics.

though of course it is pedagogic in style, but you should not take what follows as the last word on the subject.

To say it again, the relational model is not hard to understand—but it is a theory, and most theories come equipped with their own special terminology, and (for reasons already explained in Section 3.3) the relational model is no exception in this regard. And we will be using that special terminology in this part of the book, naturally. However, it cannot be denied that the terminology can be a little bewildering at first, and indeed can serve as a barrier to understanding. (This latter fact is particularly unfortunate, given that the underlying ideas are not really difficult at all.) So, if you are having trouble in understanding some of the material that follows, please be patient; you will probably find that the concepts do become very straightforward, once you have become familiar with the terminology.

Now, it has to be said that the chapters that follow are very long (they almost form a book in their own right). But the length reflects the importance of the subject matter! It would be quite possible to provide an overview of the topic in just one or two pages; indeed, it is a major strength of the relational model that its basic ideas can be explained and understood very easily. However, a one- or two-page treatment cannot do justice to the subject, nor illustrate its wide range of applicability. The considerable length of this part of the book should thus be seen, not as a comment on the model's complexity, but as a tribute to its importance and its success as a foundation for numerous far-reaching developments. Effort invested in fully understanding the material will repay the reader many times over in his or her subsequent database activities.

Finally, a word regarding SQL. We have already said in Part I of this book that SQL is the standard "relational" database language, and just about every database product on the market supports it (or, more accurately, some dialect of it—see reference [4.22]). As a consequence, no modern database book would be complete without extensive coverage of SQL. The chapters that follow on various aspects of the relational model therefore do also discuss the relevant SQL facilities, where applicable (they build on Chapter 4, which covers basic SQL concepts).

Types

5.1 INTRODUCTION

Note: You might want to give this chapter a "once over lightly" reading on a first pass. The chapter does logically belong here, but large parts of the material are not really needed very much prior to Chapter 20 in Part V and Chapters 25–27 in Part VI.

The data type concept (*type* for short) is fundamental; every value, every variable, every parameter, every read-only operator, and in particular every relational attribute is of some type. So what is a type? Among other things, it is **a set of values**. Examples include type INTEGER (the set of all integers), type CHAR (the set of all character strings), type S# (the set of all supplier numbers), and so on. Thus, when we say that, for example, the suppliers relvar S has an attribute STATUS of type INTEGER, what we mean is that values of that attribute are integers, and nothing but integers.

Note: Two points arise immediately:

- First, types are also called *domains,* especially in relational contexts; in fact, we used this latter term ourselves in earlier editions of this book, but we now prefer *types*.

- Second, a caveat: We are trying to be reasonably precise in this part of the book. Therefore, instead of saying that, for example, type INTEGER is the set of *all* integers, we ought really to say that it is the set of *all integers that are capable of representation in the computer system under consideration* (there will obviously be some integers that are beyond the representational capability of any given computer system). An analogous qualification applies to many subsequent statements and examples in this chapter, as you might expect; we will not bother to spell the point out explicitly every time, but will let this one caveat do duty for all.

Any given type is either **system-defined** (i.e., built in) or **user-defined**. We assume for the purposes of this chapter that, of the three types mentioned earlier, INTEGER and CHAR are system-defined and S# is user-defined. Any type whatsoever, regardless of whether it is system- or user-defined, can be used as the basis for declaring relational attributes (and variables, parameters, and read-only operators—see Section 5.2).

Any given type has an associated set of **operators** that can validly be applied to values of the type in question; that is, values of a given type can be operated upon *solely* by means of the operators defined for that type (where by "defined for that type" we mean, precisely, that the operator in question has a parameter that is declared to be of that type). For example, in the case of the system-defined type INTEGER:

- The system provides operators "=", "<", and so on, for comparing integers.
- It also provides operators "+", "∗", and so on, for performing arithmetic on integers.
- It does *not* provide operators "||" (concatenate), SUBSTR (substring), and so on, for performing string operations on integers (in other words, string operations on integers are not supported).

By contrast, in the case of the user-defined type S#, we would probably define operators "=", "<", and so on, for comparing supplier numbers. However, we would probably not define operators "+", "∗", and so on, which would mean that arithmetic on supplier numbers would not be supported (why would we ever want to add or multiply two supplier numbers?).

We now proceed to explore the foregoing ideas in depth, using the type theory of reference [3.3] as a basis.

5.2 VALUES *VS.* VARIABLES

The first thing we need to do is pin down the crucial, and fundamental, *logical difference*[1] between values and variables (there is a surprising amount of confusion on this issue in the literature). Following reference [5.1], we adopt the following definitions:

- A **value** is an "individual constant"—for example, the individual constant that is the integer 3. A value has *no location in time or space.* However, values can be represented in memory by means of some encoding, and such representations, or (our preferred term) *appearances,* do have locations in time and space. Indeed, distinct

---

[1] See reference [3.3] for an explanation of this useful and important concept.

appearances of the same value can exist at any number of distinct locations in time and space, meaning, loosely, that any number of different variables can have the same value, at the same time or different times. Note in particular that, by definition, **a value cannot be updated**; for if it could, then after such an update it would not be that value any longer.

■ A **variable** is a holder for an appearance of a value. A variable does have a location in time and space. Also, of course, variables, unlike values, **can be updated;** that is, the current value of the variable in question can be replaced by another value, probably different from the previous one. (Of course, the variable in question is still the same variable after the update.)

Please note very carefully that it is not just simple things like the integer 3 that are legitimate values. On the contrary, values can be arbitrarily complex; for example, a value might be a geometric point, or a polygon, or an X ray, or an XML document, or a fingerprint, or an array, or a stack, or a list, or a relation (and on and on). Analogous remarks apply to variables too, of course.

Next, observe that it is important to distinguish between a value *per se,* on the one hand, and an appearance of that value in some particular context (in particular, as the current value of some variable), on the other. As already explained, the very same value can appear in many different contexts simultaneously. Each of those appearances consists, internally, of some *encoding* or *physical representation* of the value in question; furthermore, those encodings are not necessarily all the same. For example, the integer value 3 occurs exactly once in the set of integers (there is exactly one integer 3 "in the universe," as it were), but any number of variables might simultaneously contain an appearance of that integer as their current value. Furthermore, some of those appearances might be physically represented by means of (say) a decimal encoding, and others by means of a binary encoding, of that particular integer. Thus, there is also a logical difference between an **appearance** of a value, on the one hand, and the internal **encoding** or **physical representation** of that appearance, on the other.

The foregoing remarks notwithstanding, we usually find it convenient, for fairly obvious reasons, to abbreviate "encoding of an appearance of a value" to just "appearance of a value," or (more often) to just "value," as long as there is no risk of ambiguity in doing so. Note that "appearance of a value" is a *model* concept, whereas "encoding of an appearance" is an *implementation* concept. For example, users certainly might need to know whether two distinct variables contain appearances of the same value (i.e., whether they "compare equal"); however, they do not need to know whether those two appearances make use of the same physical encoding.

Values and Variables Are Typed

Every value has (equivalently, is of) some type. In other words, if *v* is a value, then *v* can be thought of as carrying around with it a kind of flag that announces "I am an integer" or "I am a supplier number" or "I am a geometric point" (etc.). Note that, by definition, any given value always has exactly one type,[2] which never changes. It follows that distinct types are *disjoint,* meaning they have no values in common. Moreover:

- Every variable is explicitly declared to be of some type, meaning that every possible value of the variable in question is a value of the type in question.

- Every attribute of every relvar—see Chapter 6—is explicitly declared to be of some type, meaning that every possible value of the attribute in question is a value of the type in question.

- Every operator—see Section 5.5—that returns a result is explicitly declared to be of some type, meaning that every possible result that can be returned by an invocation of the operator in question is a value of the type in question.

- Every parameter of every operator—again, see Section 5.5—is explicitly declared to be of some type, meaning that every possible argument that can be substituted for the parameter in question is a value of the type in question. (Actually, this statement is not quite precise enough. Operators in general fall into two disjoint classes, read-only *vs.* update operators; read-only operators return a result, while update operators update one or more of their arguments instead. For an update operator, any argument that is subject to update is required to be a *variable,* not a *value,* of the same type as the corresponding parameter.)

- More generally, every expression is at least implicitly declared to be of some type: namely, the type declared for the outermost operator involved, where by "outermost operator" we mean the operator executed last in the evaluation of the expression in question. For example, the declared type of the expression $a * (b + c)$ is the declared type of the operator "$*$" (multiply).

As an aside, we observe that the foregoing remarks concerning operators and operator parameters need some slight refinement if the operators in question are **polymorphic**. An operator is said to be polymorphic if it is defined in terms of some parameter P and the arguments corresponding to P can be of different types on different invocations. The equality operator "=" is an obvious example: We can test *any* two values $v1$ and $v2$ for equality (just as long as $v1$ and $v2$ are of the same type), and so "=" is polymorphic—it applies to integers, and to character strings, and to supplier numbers, and in fact to values of every possible type. Analogous remarks apply to the assignment operator ":=" (which is also defined for every type): We can assign any value v to any variable V, just as long as v and V are of the same type. (Of course, the assignment will fail if it violates some integrity constraint—see Chapter 9—but it cannot fail on a type error as such.[3]) We will meet further examples of polymorphic operators in Chapter 20 and elsewhere.

---

[2] Except possibly if type inheritance is supported, a possibility we ignore until Chapter 20.

[3] More precisely, it cannot fail on a type error *at run time*. We are assuming here, reasonably enough, that the system does do "static" or compile-time type checking; clearly, a run-time error cannot occur if the compile-time check succeeds.

5.3   TYPES *VS.* REPRESENTATIONS

We have already touched on the fact that there is a logical difference between a type *per se,* on the one hand, and the physical representation of values of that type inside the system, on the other. In fact, types are a *model* issue, while physical representations are an *implementation* issue. For example, supplier numbers might be physically represented as character strings, but it does not follow that we can perform character string operations on supplier numbers; rather, we can perform such operations only if appropriate operators have been defined for the type. And the operators we define for a given type will naturally depend on the intended meaning of the type in question, not on the way values of that type happen to be physically represented—indeed, those physical representations should be **hidden from the user**. In other words, the distinction we draw between type and physical representation is one important aspect of *data independence* (see Chapter 1).

We note in passing that data types (especially user-defined ones) are sometimes called **abstract** data types or ADTs in the literature, to stress the foregoing point: the point, that is, that types must be distinguished from their physical representation. We do not use this term ourselves, however, because it suggests there might be some types that are not "abstract" in this sense, and we believe a distinction should *always* be drawn between a type and its physical representation.

Scalar *vs.* Nonscalar Types

Any given type is either *scalar* or *nonscalar:*

- A **nonscalar** type is a type whose values are explicitly defined to have a set of user-visible, directly accessible components. In particular, relation types (see Chapter 6) are nonscalar in this sense, since relations have both tuples and attributes as user-visible components. (Moreover, tuple types are nonscalar in turn, since tuples have attribute values as user-visible components.)

- A **scalar** type is a type that is not nonscalar (!). *Note:* The terms **encapsulated** and **atomic** are also sometimes used instead of *scalar; atomic* in particular tends to be used in relational contexts (including earlier editions of this book). Regarding *encapsulated,* see Chapter 25.

Values of type *T* are *scalar* or *nonscalar* according as *T* is scalar or nonscalar; thus, a nonscalar value has a set of user-visible components, while a scalar value does not. Analogous remarks apply to variables, attributes, operators, parameters, and expressions in general, *mutatis mutandis.*

Possible Representations, Selectors, and THE_ Operators

Let *T* be a scalar type. We have seen that the physical representation of values of type *T* is hidden from the user. In fact, such representations can be arbitrarily complex—in particular, they can certainly have components—but, to repeat, any such components will be hidden from the user. However, we do require that values of type *T* have at least one **possible**

representation[4] (declared as part of the definition of type *T*), and such possible representations are *not* hidden from the user; in particular, they have user-visible components. Understand, however, that the components in question are *not* components of the type, they are components of the possible representation—the type as such is still scalar in the sense already explained. By way of illustration, consider the user-defined type QTY ("quantity"), whose definition in **Tutorial D** might look like this:

```
TYPE QTY POSSREP { INTEGER } ;
```

This type definition says, in effect, that quantities can "possibly be represented" by integers. Thus, the declared possible representation ("possrep") certainly does have user-visible components—in fact, it has exactly one such, of type INTEGER—but quantities *per se* do not.

Here is another example to illustrate the same point:

```
TYPE POINT      /* geometric points in two-dimensional space */
     POSSREP CARTESIAN { X RATIONAL, Y RATIONAL }
     POSSREP POLAR { R RATIONAL, θ RATIONAL } ;
```

The definition of type POINT here includes declarations of two distinct possible representations, CARTESIAN and POLAR, reflecting the fact that points in two-dimensional space can indeed "possibly be represented" by either Cartesian or polar coordinates. Each of those possible representations in turn has two components, both of which are of type RATIONAL.[5] Note carefully, however, that (to spell it out once again) type POINT *per se* is still scalar—it has no user-visible components.

Syntax: We adopt the convention that if a given type *T* has a possible representation with no explicit name, then that possible representation is named *T* by default. We also adopt the convention that if a given possible representation *PR* has a component with no explicit name, then that component is named *PR* by default. In addition, each POSSREP declaration causes automatic definition of the following more or less self-explanatory operators:

- A **selector** operator, which allows the user to specify or *select* a value of the type in question by supplying a value for each component of the possible representation
- A set of **THE_** operators (one such for each component of the possible representation), which allow the user to access the corresponding possible-representation components of values of the type in question

Note: When we say a POSSREP declaration causes "automatic definition" of these operators, we mean that whatever agency—possibly the system, possibly some human user—is responsible for implementing the type in question is also responsible for implementing the operators.

---

[4] Unless type *T* is a "dummy type" (see Chapter 20).

[5] **Tutorial D** uses the more accurate RATIONAL over the more familiar REAL. We remark in passing that RATIONAL might well be an example of a *built-in* type with more than one declared possible representation. For example, the expressions 530.00 and 5.3E2 might well denote the same RATIONAL value—that is, they might constitute distinct, but equivalent, invocations of two distinct RATIONAL selectors (see subsequent discussion).

Here by way of example are some sample selector and THE_ operator invocations for type POINT:

```
CARTESIAN ( 5.0, 2.5 )
/* selects the point with x = 5.0, y = 2.5 */

CARTESIAN ( X1, Y1 )
/* selects the point with x = X1, y = Y1, where */
/* X1 and Y1 are variables of type RATIONAL     */

POLAR ( 2.7, 1.0 )
/* selects the point with r = 2.7, θ = 1.0 */

THE_X ( P )
/* denotes the x coordinate of the point in */
/* P, where P is a variable of type POINT    */

THE_R ( P )
/* denotes the r coordinate of the point in P */

THE_Y ( exp )
/* denotes the y coordinate of the point denoted  */
/* by the expression exp (which is of type POINT) */
```

Note that (a) selectors have the same name as the corresponding possible representation; (b) THE_ operators have names of the form THE_*C*, where *C* is the name of the corresponding component of the corresponding possible representation. Note too that selectors—or, more precisely, selector *invocations*—are a generalization of the more familiar concept of a **literal** (all literals are selector invocations, but not all selector invocations are literals; in fact, a selector invocation is a literal if and only if all of its arguments are literals in turn).

To see how the foregoing might work in practice, suppose the physical representation of points is in fact Cartesian coordinates (though there is no need, in general, for a physical representation to be identical to any of the declared possible ones). Then the system will provide certain highly protected operators, denoted in what follows by *italic pseudocode,* that effectively expose that physical representation, and the *type implementer* will use those operators to implement the necessary CARTESIAN and POLAR selectors. (Obviously the type implementer is—in fact, must be—an exception to the general rule that users are not aware of physical representations.) For example:

```
OPERATOR CARTESIAN ( X RATIONAL, Y RATIONAL ) RETURNS POINT ;
    BEGIN ;
        VAR P POINT ;    /* P is a variable of type POINT */
        X component of physical representation of P  :=  X ;
        Y component of physical representation of P  :=  Y ;
        RETURN ( P ) ;
    END ;
END OPERATOR ;

OPERATOR POLAR ( R RATIONAL, θ RATIONAL ) RETURNS POINT ;
    RETURN ( CARTESIAN ( R * COS ( θ ), R * SIN ( θ ) ) ) ;
END OPERATOR ;
```

Observe that the POLAR definition makes use of the CARTESIAN selector, as well as the (presumably built-in) operators SIN and COS. Alternatively, the POLAR definition could be expressed directly in terms of the protected operators, as follows:

```
OPERATOR POLAR ( R RATIONAL, θ RATIONAL ) RETURNS POINT ;
   BEGIN ;
      VAR P POINT ;
      X component of physical representation of P
                              :=  R * COS ( θ ) ;
      Y component of physical representation of P
                              :=  R * SIN ( θ ) ;
      RETURN ( P ) ;
   END ;
END OPERATOR ;
```

The type implementer will also use those protected operators to implement the necessary THE_ operators, thus:

```
OPERATOR THE_X ( P POINT ) RETURNS RATIONAL ;
   RETURN ( X̄ component of physical representation of P ) ;
END OPERATOR ;

OPERATOR THE_Y ( P POINT ) RETURNS RATIONAL ;
   RETURN ( Ȳ component of physical representation of P ) ;
END OPERATOR ;

OPERATOR THE_R ( P POINT ) RETURNS RATIONAL ;
   RETURN ( S̄QRT ( THE_X ( P ) ** 2 + THE_Y ( P ) ** 2 ) ) ;
END OPERATOR ;

OPERATOR THE_θ ( P POINT ) RETURNS RATIONAL ;
   RETURN ( ĀRCTAN ( THE_Y ( P ) / THE_X ( P ) ) ) ;
END OPERATOR ;
```

Observe that the definitions of THE_R and THE_θ make use of THE_X and THE_Y, as well as the (presumably built-in) operators SQRT and ARCTAN. Alternatively, THE_R and THE_θ could be defined directly in terms of the protected operators (details left as an exercise).

So much for the POINT example. However, it is important to understand that all of the concepts discussed apply to simpler types as well[6]—for example, type QTY. Here are some sample selector invocations for that type:

```
QTY ( 100 )

QTY ( N )

QTY ( N1 - N2 )
```

And here are some sample THE_ operator invocations:

```
THE_QTY ( Q )

THE_QTY ( Q1 - Q2 )
```

Note: We are assuming in these examples that (a) N, N1, and N2 are variables of type INTEGER, (b) Q, Q1, and Q2 are variables of type QTY, and (c) "–" is a polymorphic operator—it applies to both integers and quantities.

Now, since values are always typed, it is strictly incorrect to say that (e.g.) the quantity for a certain shipment is 100. A quantity is a value of type QTY, not a value of type

---

[6] Including built-in types in particular, although (partly for historical reasons) the corresponding selectors and THE_ operators might deviate somewhat from the syntactic and other rules we have prescribed in this section. See reference [3.3] for further discussion.

INTEGER! For the shipment in question, therefore, we should more properly say the quantity is QTY(100), not simply 100 as such. In informal contexts, however, we usually do not bother to be quite as precise, thus using (e.g.) 100 as a convenient shorthand for QTY(100). Note in particular that we have used such shorthands in the suppliers-and-parts and suppliers-parts-projects databases (see Figs. 3.8 and 4.5, both repeated on the inside back cover).

We give one further example of a type definition:

```
TYPE LINESEG POSSREP { BEGIN POINT, END POINT } ;
```

Type LINESEG denotes line segments. The example illustrates the point that a given possible representation can be defined in terms of *user-defined* types, not just system-defined types as in all of our previous examples (in other words, a user-defined type is indeed a type).

Finally, note that all of our examples in this subsection on possible representations and related matters have involved scalar types specifically. However, nonscalar types have possible representations, too. We will return to this issue in Section 5.6.

5.4 TYPE DEFINITION

New types can be introduced in **Tutorial D** either by means of the TYPE statement already illustrated in several examples in previous sections or by means of some *type generator.* We defer discussion of type generators, and the related question of how to define nonscalar types, to Section 5.6; in this section, we discuss the TYPE statement specifically. Here by way of example is a definition for the scalar type WEIGHT:

```
TYPE WEIGHT POSSREP { D DECIMAL (5,1)
                      CONSTRAINT D > 0.0 AND D < 5000.0 } ;
```

Explanation: Weights can possibly be represented by decimal numbers of five digits precision with one digit after the decimal point, where the decimal number in question is greater than zero and less than 5,000. *Note:* The foregoing sentence in its entirety constitutes a **type constraint** for type WEIGHT. In general, a type constraint for type *T* is, precisely, a definition of the set of values that make up type *T*. If a given POSSREP declaration contains no explicit CONSTRAINT specification, then CONSTRAINT TRUE is assumed by default (in the example, omitting the CONSTRAINT specification would thus mean that valid WEIGHT values are precisely those that can be represented by decimal numbers of five digits precision with one digit after the decimal point).

The WEIGHT example raises another point, however. In Chapter 3, Section 3.9, we said part weights were given in pounds. But it might not be a good idea to bundle the type notion *per se* with the somewhat separate *units* notion (where by the term *units* we mean units of measure). Indeed, following reference [3.3], we can allow users to think of weights as being measured *either* in pounds *or* in (say) grams, by providing a distinct possible representation for each, thus:

```
TYPE WEIGHT
     POSSREP LBS { L DECIMAL (5,1)
                        CONSTRAINT L > 0.0 AND L < 5000.0 }
     POSSREP GMS { G DECIMAL (7,1)
                        CONSTRAINT G > 0.0 AND G < 2270000.0
                             AND MOD ( G, 45.4 ) = 0.0 } ;
```

Note that both POSSREP declarations include a CONSTRAINT specification, and those two specifications are logically equivalent (MOD is an operator that takes two numeric operands and returns the remainder that results after dividing the first by the second; we are assuming for simplicity that one pound = 454 grams). Given this definition:

- If W is an expression of type WEIGHT, then THE_L(W) will return a DECIMAL (5,1) value denoting the corresponding weight in pounds, while THE_G(W) will return a DECIMAL(7,1) value denoting the same weight in grams.

- If N is an expression of type DECIMAL(5,1), then the expressions LBS(N) and GMS(454*N) will both return the same WEIGHT value.

Here then is the **Tutorial D** syntax for defining a scalar type:

```
<type def>
    ::=   TYPE <type name> <possrep def list> ;

<possrep def>
    ::=   POSSREP [ <possrep name> ]
              { <possrep component def commalist>
                     [ <possrep constraint def> ] }

<possrep component def>
    ::=   [ <possrep component name> ] <type name>

<possrep constraint def>
    ::=   CONSTRAINT <bool exp>
```

Points arising from this syntax (most of which are illustrated by the two WEIGHT examples shown earlier):

1. The syntax makes use of both lists and commalists. The term *commalist* was defined in Chapter 4 (Section 4.6); the term *list* is defined analogously, as follows. Let *<xyz>* denote an arbitrary syntactic category (i.e., anything that appears on the left side of some BNF production rule). Then the expression *<xyz list>* denotes a sequence of zero or more *<xyz>*s in which each pair of adjacent *<xyz>*s is separated by one or more blanks.

2. The *<possrep def list>* must contain at least one *<possrep def>*. The *<possrep component def commalist>* must contain at least one *<possrep component def>*.

3. Brackets "[" and "]" indicate that the material they enclose is optional (as is normal with BNF notation). By contrast, braces "{" and "}" stand for themselves; that is, they are symbols in the language being defined, not (as they usually are) symbols of the metalanguage. To be specific, we use braces to enclose commalists of items when the commalist in question is intended to denote a *set* of some kind (implying among

other things that the order in which the items appear within the commalist is immaterial, and implying also that no item can appear more than once).

4. In general, a *<bool exp>* ("boolean expression") is an expression that denotes a truth value (TRUE or FALSE). In the context at hand, the *<bool exp>* must not mention any variables, but *<possrep component name>*s from the containing *<possrep def>* can be used to denote the corresponding components of the applicable possible representation of an arbitrary value of the scalar type in question. *Note:* Boolean expressions are also called *conditional, truth-valued,* or *logical* expressions.

5. Observe that *<type def>*s have absolutely nothing to say about physical representations. Rather, such representations must be specified as part of the conceptual/internal mapping (see Chapter 2, Section 2.6).

6. Defining a new type causes the system to make an entry in the catalog to describe that new type (refer to Chapter 3, Section 3.6, if you need to refresh your memory regarding the catalog). Analogous remarks apply to operator definitions also (see Section 5.5).

Here for future reference are definitions for the scalar types used in the suppliers-and-parts database (except for type WEIGHT, which has already been discussed). CONSTRAINT specifications are omitted for simplicity.

```
TYPE S#    POSSREP { CHAR } ;
TYPE NAME  POSSREP { CHAR } ;
TYPE P#    POSSREP { CHAR } ;
TYPE COLOR POSSREP { CHAR } ;
TYPE QTY   POSSREP { INTEGER } ;
```

(Recall from Chapter 3 that the supplier STATUS attribute and the supplier and part CITY attributes are defined in terms of built-in types instead of user-defined ones, so no type definitions are shown corresponding to these attributes.)

Of course, it must also be possible to get rid of a type if we have no further use for it:

```
DROP TYPE <type name> ;
```

The *<type name>* must identify a user-defined type, not a built-in one. The operation causes the catalog entry describing the type to be deleted, meaning the type in question is no longer known to the system. For simplicity, we assume that DROP TYPE will fail if the type in question is still being used somewhere—in particular, if some attribute of some relvar somewhere is defined on it.

We close this section by pointing out that the operation of defining a type does not actually create the corresponding set of values; conceptually, those values already exist, and always will exist (think of type INTEGER, for example). Thus, all the "define type" operation—for example, the TYPE statement, in **Tutorial D**—really does is introduce a *name* by which that set of values can be referenced. Likewise, the DROP TYPE statement does not actually drop the corresponding values, it merely drops the name that was introduced by the corresponding TYPE statement.

5.5 OPERATORS

All of the operator definitions we have seen in this chapter so far have been either for selectors or for THE_ operators; now we take a look at operator definitions in general. Our first example shows a user-defined operator, ABS, for the built-in type RATIONAL:

```
OPERATOR ABS ( Z RATIONAL ) RETURNS RATIONAL ;
   RETURN ( CASE
               WHEN Z ≥ 0.0 THEN +Z
               WHEN Z < 0.0 THEN –Z
            END CASE ) ;
END OPERATOR ;
```

Operator ABS ("absolute value") is defined in terms of just one parameter, Z, of type RATIONAL, and returns a result of that same type. Thus, an invocation of ABS—for example, ABS (AMT1 + AMT2)—is, by definition, an expression of type RATIONAL.

The next example, DIST ("distance between"), takes two parameters of one user-defined type (POINT) and returns a result of another (LENGTH):

```
OPERATOR DIST ( P1 POINT, P2 POINT ) RETURNS LENGTH ;
   RETURN ( WITH THE_X ( P1 ) AS X1 ,
                 THE_X ( P2 ) AS X2 ,
                 THE_Y ( P1 ) AS Y1 ,
                 THE_Y ( P2 ) AS Y2 :
            LENGTH ( SQRT ( ( X1 – X2 ) ** 2
                          + ( Y1 – Y2 ) ** 2 ) ) ) ;
END OPERATOR ;
```

We are assuming that the LENGTH selector takes an argument of type RATIONAL. Also, note the use of a WITH clause to introduce names for the results of certain subexpressions. We will be making heavy use of this construct in the chapters to come.

Our next example is the required "=" (equality[7]) comparison operator for type POINT:

```
OPERATOR EQ ( P1 POINT, P2 POINT ) RETURNS BOOLEAN ;
   RETURN ( THE_X ( P1 ) = THE_X ( P2 ) AND
            THE_Y ( P1 ) = THE_Y ( P2 ) ) ;
END OPERATOR ;
```

Observe that the expression in the RETURN statement here makes use of the *built-in* "=" operator for type RATIONAL. For simplicity, we will assume from this point forward that the usual infix notation "=" can be used for the equality operator (for all types, that is, not just type POINT); we omit consideration of how such an infix notation might be specified in practice, since it is basically just a matter of syntax.

Here is the ">" operator for type QTY:

```
OPERATOR GT ( Q1 QTY, Q2 QTY ) RETURNS BOOLEAN ;
   RETURN ( THE_QTY ( Q1 ) > THE_QTY ( Q2 ) ) ;
END OPERATOR ;
```

The expression in the RETURN statement here makes use of the built-in ">" operator for type INTEGER. Again, we will assume from this point forward that the usual infix notation can be used for this operator—for all "ordinal types," that is, not just type QTY. (An

---

[7] Our "equality" operator might better be called *identity,* since *v1* = *v2* is true if and only if *v1* and *v2* are in fact the very same value.

ordinal type is, by definition, a type to which ">" applies. A simple example of a "nonordinal" type is POINT.)

Here finally is an example of an *update* operator definition (all previous examples have been of *read-only* operators, which are not allowed to update anything except possibly local variables).[8] As you can see, the definition involves an UPDATES specification instead of a RETURNS specification; update operators do not return a value and must be invoked by explicit CALLs [3.3].

```
OPERATOR REFLECT ( P POINT ) UPDATES P ;
   BEGIN ;
      THE_X ( P )   :=  - THE_X ( P ) ;
      THE_Y ( P )   :=  - THE_Y ( P ) ;
      RETURN ;
   END ;
END OPERATOR ;
```

The REFLECT operator effectively moves the point with Cartesian coordinates (x,y) to the inverse position $(-x,-y)$; it does this by updating its point argument appropriately. Note the use of **THE_ pseudovariables** in this example. A THE_ pseudovariable is an invocation of a THE_ operator in a target position (in particular, on the left side of an assignment). Such an invocation actually *designates*—rather than just returning the value of—the specified component of (the applicable possible representation of) its argument. Within the REFLECT definition, for instance, the assignment

```
THE_X ( P )   :=  ... ;
```

actually assigns a value to the X component of (the Cartesian possible representation of) the argument variable corresponding to the parameter P. Of course, any argument to be updated by an update operator—by assignment to a THE_ pseudovariable in particular—must be specified as a variable specifically, not as some more general expression.

Pseudovariables can be nested, as here:

```
VAR LS LINESEG ;

THE_X ( THE_BEGIN ( LS ) )   :=  6.5 ;
```

We now observe that THE_ pseudovariables are in fact logically unnecessary. Consider the following assignment once again:

```
THE_X ( P )   :=  - THE_X ( P ) ;
```

This assignment, which uses a pseudovariable, is logically equivalent to the following one, which does not:

```
P   :=  CARTESIAN ( - THE_X ( P ), THE_Y ( P ) ) ;
```

Similarly, the assignment

```
THE_X ( THE_BEGIN ( LS ) )   :=  6.5 ;
```

is logically equivalent to this one:

---

[8] Read-only and update operators are also known as *observers* and *mutators,* respectively, especially in object systems (see Chapter 25). *Function* is another synonym for *read-only operator* (and is occasionally used as such in this book).

```
LS   :=   LINESEG ( CARTESIAN ( 6.5,
                                 THE_Y ( THE_BEGIN ( LS ) ) ) ,
               THE_END ( LS ) ) ;
```

In other words, pseudovariables *per se* are not strictly necessary in order to support the kind of component-level updating we are discussing here. However, the pseudovariable approach does seem intuitively more attractive than the alternative (for which it can be regarded as a shorthand); moreover, it also provides a higher degree of imperviousness to changes in the syntax of the corresponding selector. (It might also be easier to implement efficiently.)

While we are on the subject of shorthands, we should point out that the only update operator that is logically necessary is in fact assignment (":="); all other update operators can be defined in terms of assignment alone (as in fact we already know from Chapter 3, in the case of relational update operators in particular). However, we do require support for a **multiple** form of assignment, which allows any number of individual assignments to be performed "simultaneously" [3.3]. For example, we could replace the two assignments in the definition of the operator REFLECT by the following multiple assignment:

```
THE_X ( P )   :=   - THE_X ( P ) ,
THE_Y ( P )   :=   - THE_Y ( P ) ;
```

(note the comma separator). The semantics are as follows: First, all of the source expressions on the right sides are evaluated; second, all of the individual assignments are then executed in sequence as written.[9] *Note:* Since multiple assignment is considered to be a single operation, no integrity checking is performed "in the middle of" such an assignment; indeed, this fact is the major reason why we require multiple assignment support in the first place. See Chapters 9 and 16 for further discussion.

Finally, it must be possible to get rid of an operator if we have no further use for it. For example:

```
DROP OPERATOR REFLECT ;
```

The specified operator must be user-defined, not built in.

Type Conversions

Consider the following type definition once again:

```
TYPE S# POSSREP { CHAR } ;
```

By default, the possible representation here has the inherited name S#, and hence the corresponding selector operator does, too. The following is thus a valid selector invocation:

```
S# ('S1')
```

(it returns a certain supplier number). Note, therefore, that the S# selector might be regarded, loosely, as a **type conversion** operator that converts character strings to supplier

---

[9] This definition requires some refinement in the case where two or more of the individual assignments refer to the same target variable. The details are beyond the scope of this book; suffice it to say they are carefully specified to give the desired result when—as in the example, in fact—distinct individual assignments update distinct parts of the same target variable (an important special case).

numbers. Analogously, the P# selector might be regarded as a conversion operator that converts character strings to part numbers; the QTY selector might be regarded as a conversion operator that converts integers to quantities; and so on.

By the same token, THE_ operators might be regarded as operators that perform type conversion in the opposite direction. For example, recall the definition of type WEIGHT from the beginning of Section 5.4:

```
TYPE WEIGHT POSSREP { D DECIMAL (5,1)
                      CONSTRAINT D > 0.0 AND D < 5000.0 } ;
```

If W is of type WEIGHT, then the expression

```
THE_D ( W )
```

effectively converts the weight denoted by W to a DECIMAL(5,1) number.

Now, we said in Section 5.2 that (a) the source and target in an assignment must be of the same type, and (b) the comparands in an equality comparison must be of the same type. In some systems, however, these rules are not directly enforced; thus, it might be possible in such a system to request, for example, a comparison between a part number and a character string—in a WHERE clause, perhaps, as here:

```
... WHERE P# = 'P2'
```

Here the left comparand is of type P# and the right comparand is of type CHAR; on the face of it, therefore, the comparison should fail on a **type error** (a *compile-time* type error, in fact). Conceptually, however, what happens is that the system realizes that it can use the P# "conversion operator" (in other words, the P# selector) to convert the CHAR comparand to type P#, and so it effectively rewrites the comparison as follows:

```
... WHERE P# = P# ('P2')
```

The comparison is now valid.

Invoking a conversion operator implicitly in this way is known as **coercion**. However, it is well known that coercion can lead to program bugs. For that reason, we adopt the conservative position in this book that *coercions are not permitted*—operands must always be of the appropriate types, not merely coercible to those types. Of course, we do allow type conversion operators (or "CAST" operators, as they are usually called) to be defined and invoked explicitly when necessary—for example:

```
CAST_AS_CHAR ( 530.00 )
```

As we have already pointed out, selectors (at least, those that take just one argument) can also be thought of as explicit conversion operators, of a kind.

Now, you might have realized that what we are talking about here is what is known in programming language circles as **strong typing**. Different writers have slightly different definitions for this term; as we use it, however, it means, among other things, that (a) every value *has* a type, and (b) whenever we try to perform an operation, the system checks that the operands are of the right types for the operation in question. For example, consider the following expressions:

```
WEIGHT + QTY    /* e.g., part weight plus shipment quantity  */

WEIGHT * QTY    /* e.g., part weight times shipment quantity */
```

The first of these expressions makes no sense, and the system should reject it. The second, on the other hand, does make sense—it denotes the total weight for all parts involved in the shipment. So the operators we would define for weights and quantities in combination would presumably include "*" but not "+".

Here are a couple more examples, involving comparison operations this time:

```
WEIGHT > QTY

EVEN > ODD
```

(In the second example, we are assuming that EVEN is of type EVEN_INTEGER and ODD is of type ODD_INTEGER, with the obvious semantics.) Again, then, the first expression makes no sense, but the second does make sense. So the operators we would define for weights and quantities in combination presumably would not include ">", but those for even and odd integers presumably would.[10] (With respect to this question of deciding which operators are valid for which types, incidentally, we note that historically most of the database literature—the first few editions of this book included—considered comparison operators only and ignored other operators, such as "+" and "*".)

Concluding Remarks

Complete support for operators along the lines sketched in the present section has a number of significant implications, which we briefly summarize here:

- First, and most important, it means the system will know (a) exactly **which expressions are valid**, and (b) the **type of the result** for each such valid expression.

- It also means that the total collection of types for a given database will be a **closed set**—that is, the type of the result of every valid expression will be a type that is known to the system. Observe in particular that this closed set of types must include the type *boolean* or *truth value,* if comparisons are to be valid expressions!

- In particular, the fact that the system knows the type of the result of every valid expression means it knows which **assignments** are valid, and also which **comparisons**.

We close this section with a forward reference. We have claimed that what the relational community has historically called *domains* are really data types, system- or user-defined, of arbitrary internal complexity, whose values can be operated on solely by means of the operators defined for the type in question (and whose physical representation is therefore hidden from the user). Now, if we turn our attention for a moment to **object** systems, we find that the most fundamental object concept, the *object class,* is really a data type, system- or user-defined, of arbitrary internal complexity, whose values can be operated on solely by means of the operators defined for the type in question (and whose physical representation is therefore hidden from the user) . . . In other words, domains and

---

[10] In practice EVEN_INTEGER and ODD_INTEGER might both be subtypes of type INTEGER, in which case the ">" operator would probably be *inherited* from this latter type (see Chapter 20).

object classes are the *same thing!*—and so we have here the key to marrying the two technologies (relations and objects) together. We will elaborate on this important issue in Chapter 26.

5.6   TYPE GENERATORS

We turn now to types that are not defined by means of the TYPE statement but are obtained by invoking some **type generator**. Abstractly, a type generator is just a special kind of operator; it is special because it returns a type instead of, for example, a simple scalar value. In a conventional programming language, for example, we might write

```
VAR SALES ARRAY INTEGER [12] ;
```

to define a variable called SALES whose valid values are one-dimensional arrays of 12 integers. In this example, the expression ARRAY INTEGER [12] can be regarded as an invocation of the ARRAY type generator, and it returns a specific array type. That specific array type is a **generated type**. Points arising:

1. Type generators are known by many different names in the literature, including *type constructors, parameterized types, polymorphic types, type templates,* and *generic types.* We will stay with the term *type generator.*

2. Generated types are indeed types, and can be used wherever ordinary "nongenerated" types can be used. For example, we might define some relvar to have some attribute of type ARRAY INTEGER [12]. By contrast, type generators as such are *not* types.

3. Most generated types, though not all, will be *nonscalar* types specifically (array types are a case in point). As promised in Section 5.4, therefore, we have now shown how nonscalar types might be defined. *Note:* While it might be possible to define nonscalar types without directly invoking some type generator, we do not consider such a possibility any further in this book.

4. For definiteness, we regard generated types as *system-defined* types specifically, since they are obtained by invoking a system-defined type generator. *Note:* Actually we are oversimplifying slightly here. In particular, we do not rule out the possibility of users being able to define their own type generators. However, we do not consider such a possibility any further in this book.

Now, generated types clearly have possible representations ("possreps" for short) that are derived in the obvious way from (a) a *generic* possrep that applies to the type generator in question and (b) the specific possrep(s) of the user-visible component(s) of the specific generated type in question. In the case of ARRAY INTEGER [12], for example:

- There will be some generic possrep defined for one-dimensional arrays in general, probably as a contiguous sequence of *array elements* that can be identified by subscripts in the range from *lower* to *upper* (where *lower* and *upper* are the applicable bounds—1 and 12, in our example).

■ The user-visible components are precisely the 12 array elements just mentioned, and they have whatever possrep(s) are defined for type INTEGER.

In like manner, there will be operators that provide the required selector and THE_ operator functionality. For example, the expression

```
ARRAY INTEGER ( 2, 5, 9, 9, 15, 27, 33, 32, 25, 19, 5, 1 )
```

—an array literal, in fact—might be used to specify a particular value of type ARRAY INTEGER [12] ("selector functionality"). Likewise, the expression

```
SALES [3]
```

might be used to access the third component (i.e., the third array element) of the array value that happens to be the current value of the array variable SALES ("THE_ operator functionality"). It might also be used as a pseudovariable.

Assignment and equality comparison operators also apply. For example, here is a valid assignment:

```
SALES  :=  ARRAY INTEGER (  2,   5,   9,   9, 15, 27,
                           33, 32, 25, 19,   5,   1 ) ;
```

And here is a valid equality comparison:

```
SALES  =  ARRAY INTEGER (  2,   5,   9,   9, 15, 27,
                          33, 32, 25, 19,   5,   1 )
```

Note: Any given type generator will also have a set of generic constraints and operators associated with it (generic, in the sense that the constraints and operators in question will apply to every specific type obtained via invocation of the type generator in question). For example, in the case of the ARRAY type generator:

■ There might be a generic constraint to the effect that the lower bound *lower* must not be greater than the upper bound *upper.*

■ There might be a generic "reverse" operator that takes an arbitrary one-dimensional array as input and returns as output another such array containing the elements of the given one in reverse order.

(In fact, the "selectors," "THE_ operators," and assignment and equality comparison operators discussed previously are also effectively derived from certain generic operators.)

Note finally that two type generators that are of particular importance in the relational world are TUPLE and RELATION. They are discussed in detail in the next chapter.

5.7 SQL FACILITIES

Built-In Types

SQL provides the following more or less self-explanatory built-in types:

```
BOOLEAN                         NUMERIC (p,q)    DATE
BIT [ VARYING ] (n)             DECIMAL (p,q)    TIME
BINARY LARGE OBJECT (n)         INTEGER          TIMESTAMP
CHARACTER [ VARYING ] (n)       SMALLINT         INTERVAL
CHARACTER LARGE OBJECT (n)      FLOAT (p)
```

A number of defaults, abbreviations, and alternative spellings—for example, CHAR for CHARACTER, CLOB for CHARACTER LARGE OBJECT, BLOB for BINARY LARGE OBJECT—are also supported; we omit the details. Points arising:

1. BIT and BIT VARYING were added in SQL:1992 and will be dropped again in SQL:2003 (!).

2. Their names notwithstanding, (a) CLOB and BLOB are really *string* types (they have nothing to do with objects in the sense of Chapter 25); (b) BLOB in particular is really a *byte* or "octet" string type (it has nothing to do with binary numbers). Also, since values of such types can be very large—they are sometimes referred to, informally, as *long strings*—SQL provides a construct called a *locator* that (among other things) allows them to be accessed piecemeal.

3. Assignment and equality comparison operators are available for all of these types. Equality comparison is essentially straightforward (but see point 5). The assignment statement looks like this:

   ```
   SET <target> = <source> ;
   ```

   Of course, assignments are also performed implicitly when database retrievals and updates are executed. However, relational assignment as such is not supported. Multiple assignment also is not supported, except as follows:[11] If row *r* is updated by means of a statement of the form

   ```
   UPDATE T SET C1 = exp1, ..., Cn = expn WHERE p ;
   ```

   (*r* here being a row in the result of *T* WHERE *p*), all of the expressions *exp1, ..., expn* are evaluated before any of the individual assignments to *C1, ..., Cn* are executed.

4. Strong typing is supported, but only to a limited extent. To be specific, a certain taxonomy can be imposed on the built-in types that divides them into 10 disjoint categories, thus:

   - boolean
   - bit string
   - binary
   - character string
   - numeric
   - date
   - time
   - timestamp
   - year/month interval
   - day/time interval

   Type checking is performed on the basis of these 10 categories (on assignment and equality comparison operations in particular). Thus, for example, an attempt to compare a number and a character string is illegal; however, an attempt to compare two

---

[11] Two further exceptions are explained briefly in Chapter 9, Section 9.12, subsection "Base Table Constraints," and Chapter 10, Section 10.6, subsection "View Updates." These exceptions apart, we know of no product on the market today that supports multiple assignment. We do believe such support is desirable, however, and ultimately required; indeed, it is planned for inclusion in SQL:2003, though not for relations.

numbers is legal, even if those numbers are of different numeric types, say INTEGER and FLOAT (in this example, the INTEGER value will be coerced to type FLOAT before the comparison is done).

5. For character string types in particular—CHAR(n), CHAR VARYING(n), and CLOB(n)—the type checking rules are quite complex. Full details are beyond the scope of this book, but we do need to elaborate briefly on the case of fixed-length character strings (i.e., type CHAR(n)) in particular:

   ▪ *Comparison*: If values of type CHAR($n1$) and CHAR($n2$) are compared, the shorter is conceptually padded at the right with blanks to make it the same length as the longer before the comparison is done.[12] Thus, for example, the strings 'P2' (of length two) and 'P2 ' (of length 3) are considered to "compare equal."

   ▪ *Assignment:* If a value of type CHAR($n1$) is assigned to a variable of type CHAR($n2$), then, before the assignment is done, the CHAR($n1$) value is padded at the right with blanks if $n1 < n2$, or truncated at the right if $n1 > n2$, to make it of length $n2$. It is an error if any nonblank characters are lost in any such truncation.

For further explanation and discussion, see reference [4.20].

DISTINCT Types

SQL supports two kinds of user-defined types, *DISTINCT* types and *structured* types, both of which are defined by means of the **CREATE TYPE** statement.[13] We consider DISTINCT types in this subsection and structured types in the next (we set "DISTINCT" in uppercase to stress the point that the word is not being used in this context in its usual natural language sense). The following is an SQL definition for the DISTINCT type WEIGHT (compare and contrast the various **Tutorial D** definitions for this type in Section 5.4):

```
CREATE TYPE WEIGHT AS DECIMAL (5,1) FINAL ;
```

In its simplest form (i.e., ignoring a variety of optional specifications), the syntax is:

```
CREATE TYPE <type name> AS <representation> FINAL ;
```

Points arising:

1. The required FINAL specification is explained in Chapter 20.

2. The *<representation>* is the name of another type (and the type in question must not be either user-defined or generated). Note in particular that, given these rules regarding the *<representation>*, we cannot define our POINT type from Section 5.3 as an SQL DISTINCT type.

3. Note further that the *<representation>* specifies, not a possible representation as discussed earlier in this chapter, but rather the actual *physical* representation of the

---

[12] We are assuming here that PAD SPACE applies to such comparisons [4.20].

[13] It also supports something it calls a *domain,* but SQL's domains have nothing to do with domains in the relational sense. Reference [4.20] discusses SQL's domains in detail.

DISTINCT type in question. In fact, SQL does not support the "possrep" notion at all. One consequence of this omission is that it is not possible to define a DISTINCT type—or a structured type, come to that—with two or more distinct possreps.

4. There is nothing analogous to the **Tutorial D** CONSTRAINT specification. In the case of type WEIGHT, for example, there is no way to specify that for each WEIGHT value, the corresponding DECIMAL(5,1) value must be greater than zero (!) or less than 5,000.

5. The comparison operators that apply to the DISTINCT type being defined are precisely those that apply to the underlying physical representation. *Note:* Apart from assignment (see point 8), other operators that apply to the physical representation do *not* apply to the DISTINCT type. For example, none of the following expressions is valid, even if WT is of type WEIGHT:

```
WT + 14.7     WT * 2     WT + WT
```

6. "Selector" and "THE_" operators *are* supported. For example, if NW is a host variable of type DECIMAL(5,1), then the expression WEIGHT(:NW) returns the corresponding weight value; and if WT is a column of type WEIGHT, then the expression DECIMAL(WT) returns the corresponding DECIMAL(5,1) value.[14] Hence, the following are valid SQL statements:

```
DELETE
FROM    P
WHERE   WEIGHT = WEIGHT ( 14.7 ) ;

EXEC SQL DELETE
         FROM    P
         WHERE   WEIGHT = WEIGHT ( :NW ) ;

EXEC SQL DECLARE Z CURSOR FOR
         SELECT DECIMAL ( WEIGHT ) AS DWT
         FROM    P
         WHERE   WEIGHT > WEIGHT ( :NW ) ;
```

7. With one important exception (see point 8), strong typing does apply to DISTINCT types. Note in particular that comparisons between values of a DISTINCT type and values of the underlying representation type are not legal. Hence, the following are *not* valid SQL statements, even if (as before) NW is of type DECIMAL(5,1):

```
DELETE
FROM    P
WHERE   WEIGHT = 14.7 ;              /* warning -- invalid !!! */

EXEC SQL DELETE
         FROM    P
         WHERE   WEIGHT = :NW ;      /* warning -- invalid !!! */

EXEC SQL DECLARE Z CURSOR FOR
         SELECT DECIMAL ( WEIGHT ) AS DWT
         FROM    P
         WHERE   WEIGHT > :NW ;      /* warning -- invalid !!! */
```

8. The exception mentioned under point 7 has to do with assignment operations. For example, if we want to retrieve some WEIGHT value into some DECIMAL(5,1)

---

[14] Actually DECIMAL(WT) is not syntactically valid in SQL:1999 but is expected to become so in SQL: 2003. Note, however, that (unlike **Tutorial D**'s THE_ operators) it cannot be used as a pseudovariable.

variable, some type conversion has to occur. Now, we can certainly perform that conversion explicitly, as here:

```
SELECT DECIMAL ( WEIGHT ) AS DWT
INTO   :NW
FROM   P
WHERE  P# = P# ('P1') ;
```

However, the following is also legal (and an appropriate coercion will occur):

```
SELECT WEIGHT
INTO   :NW
FROM   P
WHERE  P# = P# ('P1') ;
```

Analogous remarks apply to INSERT and UPDATE operations.

9. Explicit CAST operators can also be defined for converting to, from, or between DISTINCT types. We omit the details here.

10. Additional operators can be defined (and subsequently dropped) as required. *Note:* The SQL term for operators is *routines,* and there are three kinds: *functions, procedures,* and *methods.* (Functions and procedures correspond very roughly to our read-only and update operators, respectively; methods behave like functions, but are invoked using a different syntactic style.[15]) So we could define a function—a polymorphic function, in fact—called ADDWT ("add weight") that would allow two values to be added regardless of whether they were WEIGHT values or DECIMAL(5,1) values or a mixture of the two. All of the following expressions would then be legal:

```
ADDWT ( WT, 14.7 )
ADDWT ( 14.7, WT )
ADDWT ( WT, WT )
ADDWT ( 14.7, 3.0 )
```

More information regarding SQL routines can be found in references [4.20] and [4.28]. Further details are beyond the scope of this book.

11. The following statement is used to drop a user-defined type:

```
DROP TYPE <type name> <behavior> ;
```

Here *<behavior>* is either RESTRICT or CASCADE; loosely, RESTRICT means the DROP will fail if the type is currently in use anywhere, while CASCADE means the DROP will always succeed and will cause an implicit DROP . . . CASCADE for everything currently using the type (!).

Structured Types

Now we turn to structured types. Here are a couple of examples:

```
CREATE TYPE POINT AS ( X FLOAT, Y FLOAT ) NOT FINAL ;

CREATE TYPE LINESEG AS ( BEGIN POINT, END POINT ) NOT FINAL ;
```

---

[15] They also, unlike functions and procedures, involve some *run-time binding* (see Chapter 20). *Note:* The term *method,* and the slightly strange meaning that must be ascribed to it in contexts like the one at hand, derive from the world of object orientation (see Chapter 25).

(Actually the second example fails because BEGIN and END are reserved words in SQL, but we choose to overlook this point.) In its simplest form, then—that is, ignoring a variety of optional specifications—the syntax for creating a structured type is:

```
CREATE TYPE <type name> AS <representation> NOT FINAL ;
```

Points arising:

1. The required NOT FINAL specification is explained in Chapter 20. *Note:* SQL:2003 is expected to allow the alternative FINAL to be specified instead.

2. The *<representation>* is an *<attribute definition commalist>* enclosed in parentheses, where an *<attribute>* consists of an *<attribute name>* followed by a *<type name>*. Note carefully, however, that those "attributes" are not attributes in the relational sense, in part because structured types are not relation types (see Chapter 6). Moreover, that *<representation>* is the actual physical representation, not just some possible representation, of the structured type in question. *Note:* The type designer can effectively conceal that fact, however—the fact, that is, that the representation is physical—by a judicious choice and design of operators. For example, given the foregoing definition of type POINT, the system will automatically provide operators to expose the Cartesian representation (see points 3 and 6), but the type designer could provide operators "manually" to expose a polar representation as well.

3. Each attribute definition causes automatic definition of two associated operators (actually "methods"), one *observer* and one *mutator,* that provide functionality analogous to that of **Tutorial D**'s THE_ operators.[16] For example, if LS, P, and Z are of types LINESEG, POINT, and FLOAT, respectively, the following assignments are valid:

```
SET Z = P.X ;               /* "observes" X attribute of P */
SET P.X = Z ;               /* "mutates" X attribute of P  */
SET X = LS.BEGIN.X ;        /* "observes" X attribute of   */
                            /* BEGIN attribute of LS        */
SET LS.BEGIN.X = Z ;        /* "mutates" X attribute of     */
                            /* BEGIN attribute of LS        */
```

4. There is nothing analogous to the **Tutorial D** CONSTRAINT specification.

5. The comparison operators that apply to the structured type being defined are specified by means of a separate **CREATE ORDERING** statement. Here are two examples:

```
CREATE ORDERING FOR POINT EQUALS ONLY BY STATE ;
```

```
CREATE ORDERING FOR LINESEG EQUALS ONLY BY STATE ;
```

EQUALS ONLY means that "=" and "≠" (or "<>", rather, this latter being the SQL syntax for "not equals") are the only valid comparison operators for values of the type in question. BY STATE means that two values of the type in question are equal if and only if, for all *i,* their *i*th attributes are equal. Other possible CREATE ORDERING specifications are beyond the scope of this book; suffice it to say that, for example, the

---

[16] In the interest of accuracy, we should say that SQL's mutators are not really mutators in the conventional sense of the term (i.e., they are not update operators), but they can be used in such a way as to achieve conventional mutator functionality. For example, "SET P.X = Z" (which in fact does not explicitly contain a mutator invocation!) is defined to be shorthand for "SET P = P.X(Z)" (which does).

semantics of ">" can also be defined for a structured type if desired. Note, however, that if a given structured type has no associated "ordering," then no comparisons at all, **not even equality comparisons**, can be performed on values of that type—a state of affairs with far-reaching consequences, as you might imagine.

6. No selectors are provided automatically, but their effect can be achieved as follows. First, SQL does automatically provide what it calls *constructor functions,* but such functions return the same value on every invocation—namely, that value of the type in question whose attributes all have the applicable *default* value.[17] For example, the constructor function invocation

```
POINT ()
```

returns the point with default X and Y values. Now, however, we can immediately invoke the X and Y mutators (see point 3) to obtain whatever point we want from the result of that constructor function invocation. Moreover, we can bundle the initial "construction" and the subsequent "mutations" into a single expression, as illustrated by the following example:

```
POINT () . X ( 5.0 ) . Y ( 2.5 )
```

Here is a more complex example:

```
LINESEG () . BEGIN ( POINT () . X ( 5.0 ) . Y ( 2.5 ) )
           . END   ( POINT () . X ( 7.3 ) . Y ( 0.8 ) )
```

Note: Constructor function invocations can optionally be preceded by the noiseword NEW without changing the semantics. For example:

```
NEW LINESEG () . BEGIN ( NEW POINT () . X ( 5.0 ) . Y ( 2.5 ) )
               . END   ( NEW POINT () . X ( 7.3 ) . Y ( 0.8 ) )
```

7. Strong typing does apply to structured types, except possibly as described in Chapter 6, Section 6.6 (subsection "Structured Types").

8. Operators in addition to those already mentioned can be defined (and subsequently dropped) as required.

9. Structured types and orderings can be dropped. Such types can be "altered," too, via an ALTER TYPE statement—for example, new attributes can be added or existing ones dropped (in other words, the representation can be changed).

We will have more to say regarding SQL's structured types in the next chapter (Section 6.6) and in Chapters 20 and 26.

---

[17] The default value for a given attribute can be specified as part of the corresponding attribute definition. If no such value is specified explicitly, the default value—the "default default"—will be null. *Note:* For reasons beyond the scope of this book, the default *must* be null if the type of the attribute is either a row type or a user-defined type (like POINT), and it must be either null or empty—specified as ARRAY[]—if it is an array type. Thus, for example, the constructor function invocation LINESEG() will necessarily return the line segment whose BEGIN and END components are both null.

Type Generators

SQL supports three type generators (the SQL term is *type constructors*): REF, ROW, and ARRAY.[18] In this chapter we discuss ROW and ARRAY only, deferring REF to Chapter 26. Here is an example illustrating the use of ROW:

```
CREATE TABLE CUST
     ( CUST# CHAR(3),
       ADDR   ROW ( STREET CHAR(50),
                    CITY    CHAR(25),
                    STATE   CHAR(2),
                    ZIP     CHAR(5) )
   PRIMARY KEY ( CUST# ) ) ;
```

STREET, CITY, STATE, and ZIP here are the *fields* of the generated row type. In general, such fields can be of any type, including other row types. Field-level references make use of dot qualification, as in the following example (the syntax is *<exp>.<field name>,* where the *<exp>* must be row-valued):

```
SELECT CX.CUST#
FROM   CUST AS CX
WHERE  CX.ADDR.STATE = 'CA' ;
```

Note: CX here is a *correlation name.* Correlation names are discussed in detail in Chapter 8 (Section 8.6); here we simply note that SQL requires explicit correlation names to be used in field references, in order to avoid a certain syntactic ambiguity that might otherwise occur.

Here now is an INSERT example:

```
INSERT INTO CUST ( CUST#, ADDR )
VALUES ( '666', ROW ( '1600 Pennsylvania Ave.',
                      'Washington', 'DC', '20500' ) ) ;
```

Note the row literal in this example (actually, that should be "row literal," in quotes—formally, there is no such thing as a row literal in SQL, and the expression in the example is a *row value constructor*).

One more example:

```
UPDATE CUST AS CX
SET     CX.ADDR.STATE = 'TX'
WHERE   CUST# = '999' ;
```

Note: In fact the standard does not currently permit field-level updating as in this example, but the omission looks like an oversight.

The ARRAY type generator is somewhat similar. Here is an example:

```
CREATE TABLE ITEM_SALES
     ( ITEM# CHAR(5),
       SALES INTEGER ARRAY [12],
       PRIMARY KEY ( ITEM# ) ) ;
```

---

[18] SQL:2003 is likely to add MULTISET.

Types generated by means of ARRAY are always one-dimensional; the specified element type (INTEGER in the example) can be anything except another array type.[19] Let *a* be a value of some array type. Then *a* can contain any number *n* of elements ($n \geq 0$), up to but not greater than the specified upper bound (12 in the example). If *a* contains exactly *n* elements ($n > 0$), then those elements are precisely—and can be referenced as—*a*[1], *a*[2], ..., *a*[*n*]. The expression CARDINALITY(*a*) returns the value *n*.

Here now are some examples that use the ITEM_SALES table. Note the array literal (or "array literal," rather—officially, it is an *array value constructor*) in the second example.

```
SELECT  ITEM#
FROM    ITEM_SALES
WHERE   SALES [3] > 10 ;

INSERT INTO ITEM_SALES ( ITEM#, SALES )
VALUES ( 'X4320',
         ARRAY [ 0, 0, 0, 0, 0, 0, 0, 0, 0, 0, 0, 0 ] ) ;

UPDATE ITEM_SALES
SET     SALES [3] = 10
WHERE   ITEM# = 'Z0564' ;
```

We close this section by noting that assignment and equality comparison operators do apply, for both ROW and ARRAY types—unless the ROW or ARRAY type in question involves an element type for which equality comparision is not defined, in which case it is not defined for the ROW or ARRAY type in question either.

5.8   SUMMARY

In this chapter we have taken a comprehensive look at the crucial notion of **data types** (also known as domains or simply types). A type is **a set of values**: namely, the set of all values that satisfy a certain **type constraint** (specified in **Tutorial D** by a **POSSREP** clause, including an optional **CONSTRAINT** specification). Every type has an associated set of **operators** (both *read-only* and *update* operators) for operating on values and variables of the type in question. Types can be as simple or as complex as we like; thus, we can have types whose values are numbers, or strings, or dates, or times, or audio recordings, or maps, or video recordings, or geometric points (etc.). Types **constrain operations**, in that the operands to any given operation are required to be of the types defined for that operation (**strong typing**). Strong typing is a good idea because it allows certain logical errors to be caught, and caught moreover at compile time instead of run time. Note that strong typing has important implications for the relational operations in particular (join, union, etc.), as we will see in Chapter 7.

---

[19] This restriction is likely to be removed in SQL:2003. In any case, the element type can be a row type, and that row type can include a field of some array type. Thus (e.g.) the following is a legal variable definition:

```
VX ROW (FX INTEGER ARRAY [12]) ARRAY [12]
```

And then (e.g.) VX[3].FX[5] refers to the fifth element of the array that is the sole field value within the row that is the third element of the array that is the value of the variable VX.

We also discussed the important *logical difference* between **values** and **variables**, and pointed out that the essential property of a value is that *it cannot be updated.* Values and variables are always typed; so also are (relational) *attributes,* (read-only) *operators, parameters,* and more generally *expressions* of arbitrary complexity.

Types can be **system-** or **user-defined**; they can also be **scalar** or **nonscalar**. A scalar type has no user-visible components. (The most important *non*scalar types in the relational model are relation types, which are discussed in the next chapter.) We distinguish carefully between a type and its **physical representation** (types are a *model* issue, physical representations are an *implementation* issue). However, we do require that every type have at least one declared **possible** representation (possibly more than one). Each such possible representation causes automatic definition of one **selector** operator and, for each component of that possible representation, one **THE_** operator (including a THE_ **pseudovariable**). We support explicit type **conversions** but no implicit type **coercions**. We also support the definition of any number of additional operators for scalar types, and we require that **equality comparison** and (multiple) **assignment** be defined for every type.

We also discussed **type generators**, which are operators that return types (ARRAY is an example). The constraints and operators that apply to generated types are derived from the *generic* constraints and operators that are associated with the applicable type generator.

Finally, we sketched SQL's type facilities. SQL provides a variety of **built-in** types—BOOLEAN, INTEGER, DATE, TIME, and so on (each with its associated set of operators, of course)—but supports only a limited form of strong typing in connection with those types. It also allows users to define their own types, which it divides into **DISTINCT** types and **structured** types, and it supports certain **type generators** (ARRAY and ROW, also REF). We offered an analysis of all of this SQL functionality in terms of the ideas presented earlier in the chapter.

EXERCISES

5.1 State the type rules for the assignment (":=") and equality comparison ("=") operators.

5.2 Distinguish:

value	*vs.* variable
type	*vs.* representation
physical representation	*vs.* possible representation
scalar	*vs.* nonscalar
read-only operator	*vs.* update operator

5.3 Explain the following in your own words:

coercion	pseudovariable
generated type	selector
literal	strong typing
ordinal type	THE_ operator
polymorphic operator	type generator

5.4   Why are pseudovariables logically unnecessary?

5.5   Define an operator that, given a rational number, returns the cube of that number.

5.6   Define a read-only operator that, given a point with Cartesian coordinates *x* and *y,* returns the point with Cartesian coordinates *f*(*x*) and *g*(*y*), where *f* and *g* are predefined operators.

5.7   Repeat Exercise 5.6 but make the operator an update operator.

5.8   Give a type definition for a scalar type called CIRCLE. What selectors and THE_ operators apply to this type? Also:

a. Define a set of read-only operators to compute the diameter, circumference, and area of a given circle.

b. Define an update operator to double the radius of a given circle (more precisely, to update a given CIRCLE variable in such a way that its circle value is unchanged except that the radius is twice what it was before).

5.9   Give some examples of types for which it might be useful to define two or more distinct possible representations. Can you think of an example where distinct possible representations for the same type have different numbers of components?

5.10   Given the catalog for the departments-and-employees database shown in outline in Fig. 3.6 in Chapter 3, how could that catalog be extended to take account of user-defined types and operators?

5.11   What types are the catalog relvars themselves defined on?

5.12   Give an appropriate set of scalar type definitions for the suppliers-parts-projects database (see Fig. 4.5 on the inside back cover). Do not attempt to write the relvar definitions.

5.13   We pointed out in Section 5.3 that it is strictly incorrect to say that (e.g.) the quantity for a certain shipment is 100 ("a quantity is a value of type QTY, not a value of type INTEGER"). As a consequence, Fig. 4.5 is rather sloppy, inasmuch as it pretends that it *is* correct to think of, for example, quantities as integers. Given your answer to Exercise 5.12, show the correct way of referring to the various scalar values in Fig. 4.5.

5.14   Given your answer to Exercise 5.12, which of the following scalar expressions are legal? For the legal ones, state the type of the result; for the others, show a legal expression that will achieve what appears to be the desired effect.

a. `J.CITY = P.CITY`

b. `JNAME || PNAME`

c. `QTY * 100`

d. `QTY + 100`

e. `STATUS + 5`

f. `J.CITY < S.CITY`

g. `COLOR = P.CITY`

h. `J.CITY = P.CITY || 'burg'`

5.15   It is sometimes suggested that types are really variables too, like relvars. For example, legal employee numbers might grow from three digits to four as a business expands, so we might need to update "the set of all possible employee numbers." Discuss.

5.16 Give SQL analogs of all type definitions from Sections 5.3 and 5.4.

5.17 Give an SQL answer to Exercise 5.12.

5.18 In SQL:

a. What is a DISTINCT type? What are values of a DISTINCT type called generically? Is there such a thing as an indistinct type?

b. What is a structured type? What are values of a structured type called generically? Is there such a thing as an unstructured type?

5.19 Explain the terms *observer, mutator,* and *constructor function* as used in SQL.

5.20 What are the consequences of the "=" operator not being defined for some given type?

5.21 A type is a set of values, so we might define the *empty* type to be the (necessarily unique) type where the set in question is empty. Can you think of any uses for such a type?

5.22 "SQL has no formal row or array literals." Explain and justify this observation.

5.23 Consider the SQL type POINT as defined in the subsection "Structured Types" in Section 5.7. That type has a representation involving Cartesian coordinates X and Y. What happens if we replace that type by a revised type POINT with a representation involving polar coordinates R and θ instead?

5.24 What is the difference between the SQL COUNT and CARDINALITY operators? *Note:* COUNT is discussed in Chapter 8, Section 8.6.

REFERENCES AND BIBLIOGRAPHY

5.1 J. Craig Cleaveland: *An Introduction to Data Types*. Reading, Mass.: Addison-Wesley (1986).

CHAPTER **6**

Relations

6.1 INTRODUCTION

In the previous chapter, we discussed types, values, and variables in general; now we turn our attention to relation types, values, and variables in particular. And since relations are built out of tuples (speaking a trifle loosely), we need to examine tuple types, values, and variables as well. Note immediately, however, that tuples are not all that important in themselves, at least from a relational perspective; their significance lies primarily in the fact that they form a necessary stepping-stone on the way to relations.

6.2 TUPLES

We begin by defining the term *tuple* precisely. Given a collection of types Ti ($i = 1, 2, ...,$ n), not necessarily all distinct, a **tuple value** (tuple for short) on those types—t, say—is a set of ordered triples of the form $<Ai,Ti,vi>$, where Ai is an **attribute name**, Ti is a **type name**, and vi is a **value** of type Ti, and:

- The value n is the **degree** or **arity** of t.
- The ordered triple $<Ai,Ti,vi>$ is a **component** of t.

■ The ordered pair *<Ai,Ti>* is an **attribute** of *t,* and it is uniquely identified by the attribute name *Ai* (attribute names *Ai* and *Aj* are the same only if *i = j*). The value *vi* is the **attribute value** for attribute *Ai* of *t*.[1] The type *Ti* is the corresponding **attribute type**.

■ The complete set of attributes is the **heading** of *t*.

■ The **tuple type** of *t* is determined by the heading of *t,* and the heading and that tuple type both have the same attributes (and hence the same attribute names and types) and the same degree as *t* does. The **tuple type name** is precisely:

```
TUPLE { A1 T1, A2 T2, ..., An Tn }
```

Here is a sample tuple:

MAJOR_P# : P#	MINOR_P# : P#	QTY : QTY
P2	P4	7

The attribute names here are MAJOR_P#, MINOR_P#, and QTY; the corresponding type names are P#, P# again, and QTY; and the corresponding values are P#('P2'), P#('P4'), and QTY(7) (for simplicity, these values have been abbreviated to just P2, P4, and 7, respectively, in the picture). The degree of this tuple is three. Its heading is:

MAJOR_P# : P#	MINOR_P# : P#	QTY : QTY

And its type is:

```
TUPLE { MAJOR_P# P#, MINOR_P# P#, QTY QTY }
```

Note: It is common in informal contexts to omit the type names from a tuple heading, showing just the attribute names. Informally, therefore, we might represent the foregoing tuple thus:

MAJOR_P#	MINOR_P#	QTY
P2	P4	7

In **Tutorial D**, the following expression could be used to denote the tuple we have been discussing:

```
TUPLE { MAJOR_P# P#('P2'), MINOR_P# P#('P4'), QTY QTY(7) }
```

(an example of a tuple selector invocation—see the next subsection but one). Observe in particular in this expression that the types of the tuple attributes are determined unambiguously by the specified attribute values (e.g., attribute MINOR_P# is of type P# because the corresponding attribute value is of type P#).

---

[1] There is, of course, a logical difference between an attribute name and an attribute *per se*. This fact notwithstanding, we often use expressions such as "attribute *Ai*," informally, to mean the attribute whose *name* is *Ai* (indeed, we did exactly this several times in the previous chapter).

Properties of Tuples

Tuples satisfy a variety of important properties, all of them immediate consequences of the definitions given in this section so far. To be specific:

- Every tuple contains exactly one value (of the appropriate type) for each of its attributes.

- There is no left-to-right ordering to the components of a tuple. This property follows because a tuple is defined to involve a *set* of components, and sets in mathematics have no ordering to their elements.

- Every subset of a tuple is a tuple (and every subset of a heading is a heading). What is more, these remarks are true of the empty subset in particular!—see the next paragraph.

More terminology: A tuple of degree one is said to be *unary,* a tuple of degree two *binary,* a tuple of degree three *ternary* (and so on); more generally, a tuple of degree *n* is said to be *n-ary.*[2] A tuple of degree zero (i.e., a tuple with no components) is said to be *nullary.* We elaborate briefly on this last possibility. Here is a nullary tuple in **Tutorial D** notation:

```
TUPLE { }
```

Sometimes we refer to a tuple of degree zero more explicitly as a "0-tuple," in order to emphasize the fact that it has no components. Now, it might seem that a 0-tuple is not likely to be very useful in practice; in fact, however, it turns out that the concept is crucially important. We will have more to say about it in Section 6.4.

The TUPLE Type Generator

Tutorial D provides a TUPLE type generator that can be invoked in the definition of (e.g.) some relvar attribute or some tuple variable.[3] Here is an example of the latter case:

```
VAR ADDR TUPLE { STREET CHAR,
                 CITY    CHAR,
                 STATE   CHAR,
                 ZIP     CHAR } ;
```

A TUPLE type generator invocation takes the general form

```
TUPLE { <attribute commalist> }
```

(where each *<attribute>* consists of an *<attribute name>* followed by a *<type name>*). The tuple type produced by a specific invocation of the TUPLE type generator—for example, the one just shown in the definition of variable ADDR—is, of course, a generated type.

Every tuple type has an associated *tuple selector* operator. Here is an example of a selector invocation for the tuple type shown in the definition of variable ADDR:

---

[2] The term *n-tuple* is sometimes used in place of *tuple* (and so we speak of, e.g., 4-tuples, 2-tuples, and so on). However, it is usual to drop the "*n-*" prefix.

[3] Tuple variables are not part of the relational model, and they are not permitted within a relational database. But a system that supports the relational model fully will probably support tuple variables within individual applications (i.e., tuple variables that are "application-local").

```
TUPLE { STREET '1600 Pennsylvania Ave.',
        CITY 'Washington', STATE 'DC', ZIP '20500' }
```

The tuple denoted by this expression could be assigned to the tuple variable ADDR, or tested for equality with another tuple of the same type. Note in particular that, in order for two tuples to be of the same type, it is necessary and sufficient that they have the same attributes. Note too that the attributes of a given tuple type can be of any type whatsoever (they can even be of some relation type or some other tuple type).

Operators on Tuples

We have already mentioned the tuple selector, assignment, and equality comparison operators briefly. However, it is worth spelling out the semantics of tuple equality in detail, since so much in later chapters depends on it. To be specific, all of the following are defined in terms of it:

- Essentially all of the operators of the relational algebra (see Chapter 7)
- Candidate keys (see Chapter 9)
- Foreign keys (again, see Chapter 9)
- Functional and other dependencies (see Chapters 11–13)

and more besides. Here then is a precise definition:

- **Tuple equality:** Tuples *t1* and *t2* are **equal** (i.e., *t1* = *t2* is true) if and only if they have the same attributes *A1, A2, ..., An* and, for all *i* (*i* = 1, 2, ..., *n*), the value *v1* of *Ai* in *t1* is equal to the value *v2* of *Ai* in *t2*.

- Furthermore—this might seem obvious but it needs to be said—tuples *t1* and *t2* are **duplicates** of each other if and only if they are equal (meaning they are in fact the very same tuple).

Note that it is an immediate consequence of the foregoing definition that all 0-tuples are duplicates of one another! For this reason, we are justified in talking in terms of *the* 0-tuple instead of "a" 0-tuple, and indeed we usually do.

Note too that the comparison operators "<" and ">" do *not* apply to tuples (i.e., tuple types are not "ordinal types").

In addition to the foregoing, reference [3.3] proposes analogs of certain of the well-known relational operators (to be discussed in Chapter 7)—tuple project, tuple join, and so on. These operators are mostly self-explanatory; we content ourselves here with just one example, a tuple project (that operator being probably the most useful in practice). Let variable ADDR be as defined in the previous subsection, and let its current value be as follows:

```
TUPLE { STREET '1600 Pennsylvania Ave.',
        CITY 'Washington', STATE 'DC', ZIP '20500' }
```

Then the **tuple projection**

```
ADDR { CITY, ZIP }
```

denotes the tuple

```
TUPLE { CITY 'Washington', ZIP '20500' }
```

We also need to be able to **extract** a given attribute value from a given tuple. By way of example, if ADDR is as before, then the expression

```
ZIP FROM ADDR
```

denotes the value

```
'20500'
```

Tuple type inference: One important advantage of the tuple type naming scheme, as defined near the start of this section, is that it facilitates the task of determining the type of the result of an arbitrary tuple expression. For example, consider this tuple projection again:

```
ADDR { CITY, ZIP }
```

As we have seen, this expression evaluates to a tuple that is derived from the current value of ADDR by "projecting away" attributes STREET and STATE. And the tuple type of that derived tuple is precisely:

```
TUPLE { CITY CHAR, ZIP CHAR }
```

Analogous remarks apply to all possible tuple expressions.

WRAP and UNWRAP: Consider the following tuple types:

```
TUPLE { NAME NAME, ADDR TUPLE { STREET CHAR, CITY CHAR,
                                STATE  CHAR, ZIP  CHAR } }
TUPLE { NAME NAME, STREET CHAR, CITY CHAR,
                   STATE  CHAR, ZIP  CHAR }
```

Let us refer to these tuple types as *TT1* and *TT2*, respectively. Observe in particular that type *TT1* includes an attribute that is itself of some tuple type (the degree of *TT1* is two, not five). Now let NADDR1 and NADDR2 be tuple variables of types *TT1* and *TT2*, respectively. Then:

- The expression

  ```
  NADDR2 WRAP { STREET, CITY, STATE, ZIP } AS ADDR
  ```

  takes the current value of NADDR2 and *wraps* the STREET, CITY, STATE, and ZIP components of that value to yield a single tuple-valued ADDR component. The result of the expression is thus of type *TT1*, and so (e.g.) the following assignment is valid:

  ```
  NADDR1  :=  NADDR2 WRAP { STREET, CITY, STATE, ZIP } AS ADDR ;
  ```

- The expression

  ```
  NADDR1 UNWRAP ADDR
  ```

  takes the current value of NADDR1 and *unwraps* the (tuple-valued) ADDR component of that value to yield four separate components STREET, CITY, STATE, and ZIP. The result of the expression is thus of type *TT2*, and so (e.g.) the following assignment is valid:

  ```
  NADDR2  :=  NADDR1 UNWRAP ADDR ;
  ```

Tuple Types *vs.* Possible Representations

You might have noticed a certain similarity between our *TUPLE type generator* syntax as described in this section and our *declared possible representation* syntax as described in Chapter 5—both involve a commalist of items, where each item specifies the name of something and a corresponding type name—and you might be wondering whether there are two concepts here or only one. In fact there are two (and the syntactic similarity is unimportant). For example, if *X* is a tuple type, then we might very well want to take a projection of some value of that type, as described in the previous subsection. However, if *X* is a possible representation for some scalar type *T*, then there is no question of wanting to take a projection of a value of that scalar type *T*. For further discussion, see reference [3.3].

6.3   RELATION TYPES

Now we turn to relations. Our treatment parallels that for tuples in the previous section; however, we have rather more to say regarding relations than we had for tuples, and we have therefore split the material over several sections—Section 6.3 discusses relation types, Section 6.4 relation values, and Section 6.5 relation variables (relvars).

Here first is a precise definition of the term *relation*. A **relation value** (relation for short), *r* say, consists of a *heading* and a *body*,[4] where:

- The **heading** of *r* is a tuple heading as defined in Section 6.2. Relation *r* has the same attributes (and hence the same attribute names and types) and the same degree as that heading does.

- The **body** of *r* is a set of tuples, all having that same heading; the cardinality of that set is said to be the **cardinality** of *r*. (In general, the *cardinality* of a set is the number of elements in the set.)

The **relation type** of *r* is determined by the heading of *r*, and it has the same attributes (and hence attribute names and types) and degree as that heading does. The **relation type name** is precisely:

```
RELATION { A1 T1, A2 T2, ..., An Tn }
```

Here is a sample relation (it is similar but not identical to the relation shown in Fig. 4.6 in Chapter 4):

MAJOR_P# : P#	MINOR_P# : P#	QTY : QTY
P1	P2	5
P1	P3	3
P2	P3	2
P2	P4	7
P3	P5	4
P4	P6	8

---

[4] In terms of the usual tabular picture of a relation, the heading corresponds to the row of column names and the body to the set of data rows. The heading is also referred to in the literature as a (relation) **schema,** or sometimes **scheme**. It is also referred to as the **intension** (note the spelling), in which case the body is referred to as the **extension**.

The type of this relation is:

```
RELATION { MAJOR_P# P#, MINOR_P# P#, QTY QTY }
```

It is common in informal contexts to omit the type names from a relation heading, showing just the attribute names. Informally, therefore, we might represent the foregoing relation thus:

MAJOR_P#	MINOR_P#	QTY
P1	P2	5
P1	P3	3
P2	P3	2
P2	P4	7
P3	P5	4
P4	P6	8

In **Tutorial D**, the following expression could be used to denote this relation:

```
RELATION {
   TUPLE { MAJOR_P# P#('P1'), MINOR_P# P#('P2'), QTY QTY(5) } ,
   TUPLE { MAJOR_P# P#('P1'), MINOR_P# P#('P3'), QTY QTY(3) } ,
   TUPLE { MAJOR_P# P#('P2'), MINOR_P# P#('P3'), QTY QTY(2) } ,
   TUPLE { MAJOR_P# P#('P2'), MINOR_P# P#('P4'), QTY QTY(7) } ,
   TUPLE { MAJOR_P# P#('P3'), MINOR_P# P#('P5'), QTY QTY(4) } ,
   TUPLE { MAJOR_P# P#('P4'), MINOR_P# P#('P6'), QTY QTY(8) } }
```

This expression is an example of a relation selector invocation. The general format is:

```
RELATION [ <heading> ] { <tuple exp commalist> }
```

(where the optional *<heading>*, which is a commalist of *<attribute>*s enclosed in braces, is required only if the *<tuple exp commalist>* is empty). Of course, all of the *<tuple exp>*s must be of the same tuple type, and that tuple type must be exactly the one determined by the *<heading>* if a *<heading>* is specified.

Note that, strictly speaking, a relation does not contain tuples—it contains a body, and that body in turn contains tuples. Informally, however, it is convenient to talk as if relations contained tuples directly, and we will follow this simplifying convention throughout this book.

As with tuples, a relation of degree one is said to be *unary,* a relation of degree two *binary,* a relation of degree three *ternary* (and so on); more generally, a relation of degree *n* is said to be *n-ary*. A relation of degree zero—that is, a relation with no attributes—is said to be *nullary* (we will discuss this last possibility in detail in the next section). Also, observe that:

- Every subset of a heading is a heading (as with tuples).
- Every subset of a body is a body.

In both cases, the subset in question might be the empty subset in particular.

The RELATION Type Generator

Tutorial D provides a RELATION type generator that can be invoked in (e.g.) the definition of some relvar. Here is an example:

```
VAR PART_STRUCTURE ...
     RELATION { MAJOR_P# P#, MINOR_P# P#, QTY QTY } ... ;
```

(We have omitted irrelevant portions of this definition for simplicity.) In general, the RELATION type generator takes the same form as the TUPLE type generator, except for the appearance of RELATION in place of TUPLE. The relation type produced by a specific invocation of the RELATION type generator—for example, the one just shown in the definition of relvar PART_STRUCTURE—is, of course, a generated type.

Every relation type has an associated *relation selector* operator. We have already seen an example of a selector invocation for the relation type just illustrated. The relation denoted by that selector invocation could be assigned to the relvar PART_STRUCTURE, or tested for equality with another relation of the same type. Note in particular that, in order for two relations to be of the same type, it is necessary and sufficient that they have the same attributes. Note too that the attributes of a given relation type can be of any type whatsoever (they can even be of some tuple type or some other relation type).

6.4 RELATION VALUES

Now we can begin to take a more detailed look at relations as such (relation *values,* that is). The first point to note is that relations satisfy certain properties, all of them immediate consequences of the definition of *relation* given in the previous section, and all of them very important. We first state the properties in question, then discuss them in detail. They are as follows. Within any given relation:

1. Every tuple contains exactly one value (of the appropriate type) for each attribute.
2. There is no left-to-right ordering to the attributes.
3. There is no top-to-bottom ordering to the tuples.
4. There are no duplicate tuples.

We use the suppliers relation from Fig. 3.8 (see the inside back cover) to illustrate these properties. For convenience we show that relation again in Fig. 6.1, except that now we have expanded the heading to include the type names. *Note:* By rights we should have expanded the body, too, to include the attribute and type names. For example, the S# entry for supplier S1 should really look something like this:

```
S# S# S#('S1')
```

S# : S#	SNAME : NAME	STATUS : INTEGER	CITY : CHAR
S1	Smith	20	London
S2	Jones	10	Paris
S3	Blake	30	Paris
S4	Clark	20	London
S5	Adams	30	Athens

Fig. 6.1 The suppliers relation from Fig. 3.8

For simplicity, however, we have left the body as originally shown in Fig. 3.8.

1. *Relations Are Normalized*

As we know from Section 6.2, every tuple contains exactly one value for each of its attributes; thus, it certainly follows that every tuple in every relation contains exactly one value for each of its attributes. A relation that satisfies this property is said to be **normalized**, or equivalently to be in **first normal form**, 1NF.[5] The relation of Fig. 6.1 is normalized in this sense.

  Note: This first property might seem very obvious, and indeed so it is—especially since, as you must have realized, *all* relations are normalized according to the definition! Nevertheless, the property does have some important consequences. See the subsection "Relation-Valued Attributes" later in this section, also Chapter 19 (on missing information).

2. *Attributes Are Unordered, Left to Right*

We already know that the components of a tuple have no left-to-right ordering, and the same is true for the attributes of a relation (for essentially the same reason—namely, that the heading of a relation involves a *set* of attributes, and sets in mathematics have no ordering to their elements). Now, when we represent a relation as a table on paper, we are naturally forced to show the columns of that table in some left-to-right order, but you should ignore that order if you can. In Fig. 6.1, for example, the columns could just as well have been shown in (say) the left-to-right order SNAME, CITY, STATUS, S#—the figure would still have represented the same relation, at least as far as the relational model is concerned.[6] Thus, there is no such thing as "the first attribute" or "the second attribute" (etc.), and there is no "next attribute" (i.e., there is no concept of "nextness"); attributes are always referenced by name, never by position. As a result, the scope for errors and obscure programming is reduced. For example, there is no way to subvert the system by somehow "flopping over" from one attribute into another. This situation contrasts with that found in many programming systems, where it often is possible to exploit the physical adjacency of logically discrete items, deliberately or otherwise, in a variety of subversive ways.

3. *Tuples Are Unordered, Top to Bottom*

This property follows from the fact that the body of the relation is also a set (of tuples); to say it again, sets in mathematics are not ordered. When we represent a relation as a table on paper, we are forced to show the rows of that table in some top-to-bottom order, but again you should ignore that order if you can. In Fig. 6.1, for example, the rows could just as well have been shown in reverse order—the figure would still have represented the same relation. Thus, there is no such thing as "the first tuple" or "the fifth tuple" or "the 97th tuple" of a relation, and there is no such thing as "the next tuple"; in other words,

---

[5] So called because certain "higher" normal forms—second, third, and so on—can also be defined (see Chapters 12 and 13).

[6] For reasons that need not concern us here, relations in mathematics, unlike their counterparts in the relational model, do have a left-to-right order to their attributes (and likewise for tuples, of course).

there is no concept of positional addressing, and there is no concept of "nextness." Note that if we did have such concepts, we would need certain additional operators as well—for example, "retrieve the *n*th tuple," "insert this new tuple *here*," "move this tuple from *here* to *there*," and so on. It is a very strong feature of the relational model (and a direct consequence of Codd's *Information Principle*) that, because there is one and only one way to represent information in that model, we need one and only one set of operators to deal with it.

To pursue this latter point a moment longer: In fact, it is axiomatic that if we have N different ways to represent information, then we need N different sets of operators. And if $N > 1$, then we have more operators to implement, document, teach, learn, remember, and use. But those extra operators add complexity, not power! There is nothing useful that can be done if $N > 1$ that cannot be done if $N = 1$. We will revisit this issue in Chapter 26 (see references [26.12–26.14] and [26.17]), and it will crop up again in Chapter 27.

Back to relations specifically. Of course, some notion of top-to-bottom tuple ordering—and of left-to-right attribute ordering too, come to that—is required in the interface between the database and a host language such as C or COBOL (see the discussion of SQL cursors and ORDER BY in Chapter 4). But it is the host language, not the relational model, that imposes that requirement; in effect, the host language requires unordered relations to be converted into ordered lists or arrays (of tuples), precisely so that operations such as "retrieve the *n*th tuple" can have a meaning. Likewise, some notion of tuple ordering is also needed when results of queries are presented to the end user. However, such notions are not part of the relational model as such; rather, they are part of the environment in which the relational implementation resides.

4. *There Are No Duplicate Tuples*

This property also follows from the fact that the body of the relation is a set; sets in mathematics do not contain duplicate elements (equivalently, the elements are all distinct). *Note:* This property serves yet again to illustrate the point that a relation and a table are not the same thing, because a table might contain duplicate rows (in the absence of any discipline to prevent such a possibility), whereas a relation, by definition, *never* contains any duplicate tuples.

As a matter of fact, it is (or should be) obvious that the concept of "duplicate tuples" makes no sense. Suppose for simplicity that the relation of Fig. 6.1 had just two attributes, S# and CITY, with the intended interpretation—see Section 6.5—"Supplier S# is located in city CITY," and suppose the relation contained a tuple showing that it is a "true fact" that supplier S1 is located in London. Then if the relation contained a duplicate of that tuple (if that were possible), it would simply be informing us of that same "true fact" a second time. But if something is true, saying it twice does not make it *more* true!

Extended discussions of the problems that duplicate tuples cause can be found in references [6.3] and [6.6].

Relations *vs.* Tables

For purposes of reference, we present in this subsection a list of some of the main differences between (a) the formal object that is a relation as such and (b) the informal object that is a table, which is an informal picture on paper of that formal object:

1. Each attribute in the heading of a relation involves a type name, but those type names are usually omitted from tabular pictures.

2. Each component of each tuple in the body of a relation involves a type name and an attribute name, but those type and attribute names are usually omitted from tabular pictures.

3. Each attribute value in each tuple in the body of a relation is a value of the applicable type, but those values are usually shown in some abbreviated form—for example, S1 instead of S#('S1')—in tabular pictures.

4. The columns of a table have a left-to-right ordering, but the attributes of a relation do not. *Note:* One implication of this point is that columns might have duplicate names, or even no names at all. For example, consider this SQL query:

```
SELECT S.CITY, S.STATUS * 2, P.CITY
FROM   S, P ;
```

What are the column names in the result of this query?

5. The rows of a table have a top-to-bottom ordering, but the tuples of a relation do not.

6. A table might contain duplicate rows, but a relation does not contain duplicate tuples.

The foregoing is not an exhaustive list of the differences. Others include:

■ The fact that tables are usually regarded as having at least one column, while relations are not required to have at least one attribute (see the subsection "Relations with No Attributes" later in this section)

■ The fact that tables—at least in SQL—are allowed to include nulls, while relations are certainly not (see Chapter 19)

■ The fact that tables are "flat" or two-dimensional, while relations are *n*-dimensional (see Chapter 22)

It follows from all of the foregoing that, in order to agree that a tabular picture can properly be regarded as representing a relation, *we have to agree on how to "read" such a picture;* in other words, we have to agree on certain **rules of interpretation** for such pictures. To be specific, we have to agree that there is an underlying type for each column; that each attribute value is a value of the relevant type; that row and column orderings are irrelevant; and that duplicate rows are not allowed. If we can agree on all of these rules of interpretation, then—*and only then*—we can agree that a table is a reasonable picture of a relation.

So we can now see that a table and a relation are indeed not quite the same thing (even though it is often convenient to pretend they are). Rather, a **relation** is what the definition says it is, a rather abstract kind of object, and a **table** is a concrete picture, typically on paper, of such an abstract object. They are not (to repeat) quite the same. Of course, they are very similar . . . and in informal contexts, at least, it is usual, and perfectly acceptable, to say they are the same. But when we are trying to be precise—and right now we *are* trying to be precise—then we do have to recognize that the two concepts are not exactly identical.

That said, it is worth pointing out too that in fact it is a major advantage of the relational model that its basic abstract object, the relation, does have such a simple representation on paper. It is that simple representation that makes relational systems easy to use and easy to understand, and makes it easy to reason about the way relational systems behave. Nevertheless, it is unfortunately also the case that that simple representation does suggest some things that are not true (e.g., that there is a top-to-bottom tuple ordering).

Relation-Valued Attributes

As noted in Section 6.3, any type whatsoever can be used as the basis for defining relational attributes, in general. It follows that relation types in particular, since they are certainly types, can be used as the basis for defining attributes of relations; in other words, attributes can be **relation-valued**, meaning we can have relations with attributes whose values are relations in turn. In other words, we can have relations that have other relations nested inside themselves. An example of such a relation is shown in Fig. 6.2. Observe with respect to that relation that (a) attribute PQ is relation-valued; (b) the cardinality and degree are both five; and in particular (c) the empty set of parts supplied by supplier S5 is represented by a PQ value that is an empty set (more precisely, an empty relation).

The main reason we mention the possibility of relation-valued attributes here is that, historically, such a possibility has usually been regarded as illegal. Indeed, it was so regarded in earlier editions of this book. For example, here is a lightly edited excerpt from the sixth edition:

<table>
<tr><th>S#</th><th>SNAME</th><th>STATUS</th><th>CITY</th><th>PQ</th></tr>
<tr><td>S1</td><td>Smith</td><td>20</td><td>London</td><td><table><tr><th>P#</th><th>QTY</th></tr><tr><td>P1</td><td>300</td></tr><tr><td>P2</td><td>200</td></tr><tr><td>..</td><td>...</td></tr><tr><td>P6</td><td>100</td></tr></table></td></tr>
<tr><td>S2</td><td>Jones</td><td>10</td><td>Paris</td><td><table><tr><th>P#</th><th>QTY</th></tr><tr><td>P1</td><td>300</td></tr><tr><td>P2</td><td>400</td></tr></table></td></tr>
<tr><td>..</td><td>.....</td><td>..</td><td>......</td><td>........</td></tr>
<tr><td>S5</td><td>Adams</td><td>30</td><td>Athens</td><td><table><tr><th>P#</th><th>QTY</th></tr><tr><td></td><td></td></tr></table></td></tr>
</table>

Fig. 6.2 A relation with a relation-valued attribute

Note that *all column values are atomic* . . . That is, at every row-and-column position [*sic*] in every table [*sic*] there is always exactly one data value, never a group of several values. Thus, for example, in table EMP, we have

DEPT#	EMP#
D1	E1
D1	E2
. .	. .

instead of

DEPT#	EMP#
D1	E1,E2
. .	. .

Column EMP# in the second version of this table is an example of what is usually called a **repeating group**. A repeating group is a column . . . that contains several values in each row (different numbers of values in different rows, in general). *Relational databases do not allow repeating groups;* the second version of the table above would not be permitted in a relational system.

And later in the same book, we find: "Domains (i.e., types) contain atomic values only . . . [Therefore,] *relations do not contain repeating groups.* A relation satisfying this condition is said to be normalized, or equivalently to be in first normal form . . . The term *relation* is always taken to mean a normalized relation in the context of the relational model."

These remarks are not correct, however (at least not in their entirety): They arose from a misunderstanding on this writer's part of the true nature of types (domains). For reasons to be discussed in Chapter 12 (Section 12.6), it is unlikely that this mistake will have caused any very serious errors in practice; nevertheless, apologies are still due to anyone who might have been misled. At least the sixth edition was correct when it said that relations in the relational model are always normalized! Again, see Chapter 12 for further discussion.

Relations with No Attributes

Every relation has a set of attributes; and, since the empty set is certainly a set, it follows that it must be possible for a relation to have the empty set of attributes, or in other words no attributes at all. (Do not be confused: We often talk about "empty relations," meaning relations whose body is an empty set of tuples, but here, by contrast, we are talking about relations whose *heading* is an empty set of *attributes*.) Thus, relations with no attributes are at least respectable from a mathematical point of view. What is perhaps more surprising is that they turn out to be extremely important from a practical point of view as well!

In order to examine this notion more closely, we first need to consider the question of whether a relation with no attributes can contain any tuples. The answer (again perhaps surprisingly) is *yes.* To be more specific, such a relation can contain *at most one* tuple:

namely, the 0-tuple (i.e., the tuple with no components; it cannot contain more than one such tuple, because all 0-tuples are duplicates of one another). There are thus precisely two relations of degree zero—one that contains just one tuple, and one that contains no tuples at all. So important are these two relations that, following Darwen [6.5], we have pet names for them: We call the first TABLE_DEE and the other TABLE_DUM, or DEE and DUM for short (DEE is the one with one tuple, DUM is the empty one). *Note:* It is hard to draw pictures of these relations! Thinking of relations as conventional tables breaks down, somewhat, in the case of DEE and DUM.

Why are DEE and DUM so important? There are several more or less interrelated answers to this question. One is that they play a role in the relational algebra—see Chapter 7—that is akin, somewhat, to the role played by the empty set in set theory or zero in ordinary arithmetic. Another has to do with what the relations mean (see reference [6.5]); essentially, DEE means TRUE, or *yes,* and DUM means FALSE, or *no.* In other words, they have *the most fundamental meanings of all.* (A good way to remember which is which is that the "E"s in DEE match the "e" in *yes.*)

In **Tutorial D**, the expressions TABLE_DEE and TABLE_DUM can be used as shorthand for the relation selector invocations

```
RELATION { } { TUPLE { } }
```

and

```
RELATION { } { }
```

respectively.

It is not possible to go into more detail on this topic at this juncture; suffice it to say that you will encounter DEE and DUM many times in the pages ahead. For further discussion, see reference [6.5].

Operators on Relations

We mentioned the relational selector, assignment, and equality comparison operators briefly in Section 6.3. Of course, the comparison operators "<" and ">" do *not* apply to relations; however, relations are certainly subject to other kinds of comparisons in addition to simple equality, as we now explain.

Relational comparisons: We begin by defining a new kind of *<bool exp>*, *<relation comp>*, with syntax as follows:

```
<relation exp> <relation comp op> <relation exp>
```

The relations denoted by the two *<relation exp>*s must be of the same type, and *<relation comp op>* must be one of the following:

$=$ (equals)
$\neq$ (not equals)
$\subseteq$ (subset of)
$\subset$ (proper subset of)
$\supseteq$ (superset of)
$\supset$ (proper superset of)

Then we allow a *<relation comp>* to appear wherever a *<bool exp>* is expected—for example, in a WHERE clause. Here are a couple of examples:

1. `S { CITY } = P { CITY }`
   Meaning: Is the projection of suppliers over CITY equal to the projection of parts over CITY?

2. `S { S# } ⊃ SP { S# }`
   Meaning (considerably paraphrased): Are there any suppliers who supply no parts at all?

One particular relational comparison often needed in practice is a test to see whether a given relation is equal to an empty relation of the same type (i.e., one that contains no tuples). It is useful to have a shorthand for this particular case. We therefore define the expression

   `IS_EMPTY ( <relation exp> )`

to return TRUE if the relation denoted by the *<relation exp>* is empty and FALSE otherwise.

Other operators: Another common requirement is to be able to test whether a given tuple *t* appears in a given relation *r:*

   $t \in r$

This expression returns TRUE if *t* appears in *r* and FALSE otherwise ("∈" is the *set membership* operator; the expression $t \in r$ can be pronounced "*t* belongs to *r*" or "*t* is a member of *r*" or, more simply, just "*t* [is] in *r*").

We also need to be able to extract the single tuple from a relation of cardinality one:

   `TUPLE FROM r`

This expression raises an exception if *r* does not contain exactly one tuple; otherwise, it returns just that one tuple.

In addition to the operators discussed so far, there are also all of the generic operators—join, restrict, project, and so on—that go to make up the relational algebra. We defer detailed treatment of these operators to the next chapter.

Relation type inference: Just as the tuple type naming scheme described in Section 6.2 facilitates the task of determining the type of the result of an arbitrary tuple expression, so the relation type naming scheme described in Section 6.3 facilitates the task of determining the type of the result of an arbitrary relational expression. Chapter 7 goes into detail on this issue; here we content ourselves with one simple example. Given the suppliers relvar S, the expression

   `S { S#, CITY }`

yields a result (a relation) whose type is:

   `RELATION { S# S#, CITY CHAR }`

Analogous remarks apply to all possible relational expressions.

ORDER BY: For presentation purposes it is highly desirable to support an ORDER BY operator, as SQL does (see Chapter 3). We omit a detailed definition here, since the semantics are surely obvious. Note, however, that:

- ORDER BY works (effectively) by sorting tuples into some specified sequence, and yet "<" and ">" are not defined for tuples (!).
- ORDER BY is not a *relational* operator, since what it returns is not a relation.
- ORDER BY is also not a *function,* since there are many possible outputs for a given input, in general.

As an example of this last point, consider the effect of the operation ORDER BY CITY on the suppliers relation of Fig. 6.1. Clearly, this operation can return any of four distinct results. By contrast, the operators of the relational algebra certainly are functions—for any given input, there is always just one possible output.

6.5   RELATION VARIABLES

Now we turn to relation variables (*relvars* for short). Recall from Chapter 3 that relvars come in two varieties, *base relvars* and *views* (also called real and virtual relvars, respectively). In this section, we are primarily concerned with base relvars specifically (views are discussed in detail in Chapter 10); note, however, that anything we say here that talks in terms of *relvars,* unqualified, is true of relvars in general, views included.

Base Relvar Definition

Here is the syntax for defining a base relvar:

```
VAR <relvar name> BASE <relation type>
                  <candidate key def list>
                [ <foreign key def list> ] ;
```

The *<relation type>* takes the form

```
RELATION { <attribute commalist> }
```

(it is in fact an invocation of the RELATION type generator, as discussed in Section 6.3). The *<candidate key def list>* and optional *<foreign key def list>* are explained later. Here by way of example are the base relvar definitions for the suppliers-and-parts database (repeated from Fig. 3.9):

```
VAR S BASE RELATION
    { S#     S#,
      SNAME  NAME,
      STATUS INTEGER,
      CITY   CHAR }
    PRIMARY KEY { S# } ;
```

```
VAR P BASE RELATION
    { P#     P#,
      PNAME  NAME,
      COLOR  COLOR,
      WEIGHT WEIGHT,
      CITY   CHAR }
    PRIMARY KEY { P# } ;

VAR SP BASE RELATION
    { S#     S#,
      P#     P#,
      QTY    QTY }
    PRIMARY KEY { S#, P# }
    FOREIGN KEY { S# } REFERENCES S
    FOREIGN KEY { P# } REFERENCES P ;
```

Explanation:

1. These three base relvars have (relation) types as follows:
   ```
   RELATION { S# S#, SNAME NAME, STATUS INTEGER, CITY CHAR }

   RELATION { P# P#, PNAME NAME, COLOR COLOR,
                            WEIGHT WEIGHT, CITY CHAR }

   RELATION { S# S#, P# P#, QTY QTY }
   ```

2. The terms *heading, body, attribute, tuple, degree* (and so on) previously defined for relation values are all interpreted in the obvious way to apply to relvars as well.

3. All possible values of any given relvar are of the same relation type—namely, the relation type specified (indirectly, if the given relvar is a view) in the relvar definition—and therefore have the same heading.

4. When a base relvar is defined, it is given an initial value that is the empty relation of the applicable type.

5. Candidate key definitions are explained in detail in Chapter 9. Prior to that point, we will simply assume that each base relvar definition includes exactly one *<candidate key def>*, of the following particular form:
   ```
   PRIMARY KEY { <attribute name commalist> }
   ```

6. Foreign key definitions are also explained in Chapter 9.

7. Defining a new relvar causes the system to make entries in the catalog to describe that relvar.

8. As noted in Chapter 3, relvars, like relations, have a corresponding **predicate**: namely, the predicate that is common to all of the relations that are possible values of the relvar in question. In the case of the suppliers relvar S, for example, the predicate looks something like this:

   The supplier with supplier number S# is under contract, is named SNAME, has status STATUS, and is located in city CITY

9. We assume that a means is available for specifying **default values** for attributes of base relvars. The default value for a given attribute is a value that is to be placed in the applicable attribute position if the user does not provide an explicit value when inserting some tuple. Suitable **Tutorial D** syntax for specifying defaults might take

the form of a new clause on the base relvar definition, DEFAULT { *<default spec commalist>* } say, where each *<default spec>* takes the form *<attribute name> <default>*. For example, we might specify DEFAULT { STATUS 0, CITY '' } in the definition of the suppliers relvar S. *Note:* Candidate key attributes will usually, though not invariably, have no default (see Chapter 19).

Here is the syntax for dropping an existing base relvar:

```
DROP VAR <relvar name> ;
```

This operation sets the value of the specified relvar to "empty" (i.e., it deletes all tuples in the relvar, loosely speaking); it then deletes all catalog entries for that relvar. The relvar is now no longer known to the system. *Note:* For simplicity, we assume the DROP will fail if the relvar in question is still being used somewhere—for example, if it is referenced in some view definition somewhere.

Updating Relvars

The relational model includes a **relational assignment** operation for assigning values to—that is, *updating*—relvars (base relvars in particular). Here, slightly simplified, is the **Tutorial D** syntax:

```
<relation assignment>
    ::=    <relation assign commalist> ;

<relation assign>
    ::=    <relvar name> := <relation exp>
```

The semantics are as follows:[7] First, all of the *<relation exp>*s on the right sides of the *<relation assign>*s are evaluated; second, the *<relation assign>*s are executed in sequence as written. Executing an individual *<relation assign>* involves assigning the relation resulting from evaluation of the *<relation exp>* on the right side to the relvar identified by the *<relvar name>* on the left side (replacing the previous value of that relvar). Of course, the relation and relvar must be of the same type.

By way of example, suppose we are given two further base relvars S' and SP' of the same types as the suppliers relvar S and the shipments relvar SP, respectively:

```
VAR S' BASE RELATION
    { S# S#, SNAME NAME, STATUS INTEGER, CITY CHAR } ... ;

VAR SP' BASE RELATION
    { S# S#, P# P#, QTY QTY } ... ;
```

Here then are some valid examples of *<relation assignment>*:

1. S' := S , SP' := SP ;
2. S' := S WHERE CITY = 'London' ;
3. S' := S WHERE NOT (CITY = 'Paris') ;

Note that each individual *<relation assign>* can be regarded as both (a) *retrieving* the relation specified on the right side and (b) *updating* the relvar specified on the left side.

---

[7] Except as noted in footnote 9 in Chapter 5.

Now suppose we change the second and third examples by replacing relvar S' on the left side by relvar S in each case:

```
2. S   :=  S WHERE CITY = 'London' ;
3. S   :=  S WHERE NOT ( CITY = 'Paris' ) ;
```

Observe that these two assignments are both effectively *updates to relvar S*—one effectively deletes all suppliers not in London, the other effectively deletes all suppliers in Paris. For convenience **Tutorial D** does support explicit INSERT, DELETE, and UPDATE operations, but each of these operations is defined to be shorthand for a certain *<relation assign>*. Here are some examples:

```
1. INSERT S RELATION { TUPLE { S#      S# ('S6'),
                               SNAME   NAME ('Smith'),
                               STATUS 50,
                               CITY    'Rome' } } ;
```

Assignment equivalent:

```
S   :=  S UNION RELATION { TUPLE { S#      S# ('S6'),
                                   SNAME   NAME ('Smith'),
                                   STATUS 50,
                                   CITY    'Rome' } } ;
```

Note, incidentally, that this assignment will succeed if the specified tuple for supplier S6 already exists in relvar S. In practice, we might want to refine the semantics of INSERT in such a way as to raise an exception if an attempt is made "to insert a tuple that already exists." For simplicity, however, we ignore this refinement here. Analogous remarks apply to DELETE and UPDATE also.

```
2. DELETE S WHERE CITY = 'Paris' ;
```

Assignment equivalent:

```
S   :=  S WHERE NOT ( CITY = 'Paris' ) ;
```

```
3. UPDATE S WHERE CITY = 'Paris'
              { STATUS := 2 * STATUS,
                CITY   := 'Rome' } ;
```

Assignment equivalent:

```
S   :=  WITH ( S WHERE CITY = 'Paris' ) AS T1 ,
             ( EXTEND T1 ADD ( 2 * STATUS AS NEW_STATUS,
                               'Rome' AS NEW_CITY ) ) AS T2 ,
             T2 { ALL BUT STATUS, CITY } AS T3 ,
             ( T3 RENAME ( NEW_STATUS AS STATUS,
                           NEW_CITY AS CITY ) ) AS T4 :
        ( S MINUS T1 ) UNION T4 ;
```

As you can see, the assignment equivalent is a little complicated in this case—in fact, it relies on several features that will not be explained in detail until the next chapter. For that reason, we omit further discussion here.

For purposes of reference, here is a slightly simplified summary of the syntax of INSERT, DELETE, and UPDATE:

```
INSERT <relvar name> <relation exp> ;

DELETE <relvar name> [ WHERE <bool exp> ] ;
```

```
UPDATE <relvar name> [ WHERE <bool exp> ]
                { <attribute update commalist> } ;
```

An *<attribute update>* in turn takes the form

```
<attribute name> := <exp>
```

Also, the *<bool exp>* in DELETE and UPDATE can include references to attributes of the target relvar, with the obvious semantics.

We close this subsection by stressing the point that relational assignment, and hence INSERT, DELETE, and UPDATE, are all **set-level** operations.[8] UPDATE, for example, updates a *set* of tuples in the target relvar, loosely speaking. Informally, we often talk of (e.g.) updating some individual tuple, but it must be clearly understood that:

1. We are really talking about updating a *set* of tuples, a set that just happens to have cardinality one.

2. Sometimes updating a set of tuples of cardinality one is impossible!

Suppose, for example, that the suppliers relvar is subject to the integrity constraint (see Chapter 9) that suppliers S1 and S4 must have the same status. Then any "single-tuple" UPDATE that tries to change the status of just one of those two suppliers *must fail*. Instead, both must be updated simultaneously, as here:

```
UPDATE S WHERE S# = S# ('S1') OR S# = S# ('S4')
      { STATUS := some value } ;
```

To pursue the point a moment longer, we should now add that to talk (as we have just been doing) of "updating a tuple"—or set of tuples—in a relvar is really rather sloppy. Like relations, tuples are *values* and *cannot* be updated, by definition. Thus, what we really mean when we talk of (for example) "updating tuple t to t'" is that we are **replacing** the tuple t (the tuple *value t,* that is) by another tuple t' (which is, again, a tuple *value*).[9] Analogous remarks apply to phrases such as "updating attribute *A*" within some tuple. In this book, we will continue to talk in terms of "updating tuples" and "updating attributes of tuples"—the practice is convenient—but it must be understood that such usage is only shorthand, and rather sloppy shorthand at that.

Relvars and Their Interpretation

We conclude this section with a reminder to the effect that (as explained in Chapter 3, Section 3.4) (a) the heading of any given relvar can be regarded as a **predicate**, and (b) the tuples appearing in that relvar at any given time can be regarded as **true propositions**, obtained from the predicate by substituting arguments of the appropriate type for the

---

[8] In passing, we note that, by definition, the CURRENT forms of DELETE and UPDATE in SQL—see Section 4.6—are *tuple*-level (or row-level, rather), and are therefore contraindicated.

[9] Of course, none of this is to say that we cannot update tuple *variables*. As explained in Section 6.2, however, the notion of a tuple variable is not part of the relational model, and relational databases do not contain such variables.

parameters of that predicate ("instantiating the predicate"). We can say that the predicate corresponding to a given relvar is **the intended interpretation**, or meaning, for that relvar, and the propositions corresponding to tuples of that relvar are understood by convention to be true ones. In fact, the **Closed World Assumption** (also known as the **Closed World Interpretation**) says that if an otherwise valid tuple—that is, one that conforms to the relvar heading—does *not* appear in the body of the relvar, then we can assume the corresponding proposition is false. In other words, the body of the relvar at any given time contains *all* and *only* the tuples that correspond to true propositions at that time. We will have considerably more to say on such matters in Chapter 9.

6.6 SQL FACILITIES

Rows

SQL does not support tuples, as such, at all; instead, it supports *rows,* which have a left-to-right ordering to their components. Within a given row, the component values—which are called *column values* if the row is immediately contained in a table, or *field values* otherwise—are thus identified primarily by their ordinal position (even when they also have names, which is not always the case). Row types have no explicit row type name. A row value can be "selected" (the SQL term is *constructed*) by means of an expression—actually a *<row value constructor>*—of the form:

```
[ ROW ] ( <exp commalist> )
```

The parentheses can be omitted if the commalist contains just one *<exp>*; the keyword ROW must be omitted in this case, and is optional otherwise. The commalist must not be empty (SQL does not support a "0-row"). Here is an example:

```
ROW ( P#('P2'), P#('P4'), QTY(7) )
```

This expression denotes a row of degree three.

As we saw in Chapter 5, SQL also supports a ROW *type constructor* (its counterpart to the **Tutorial D** TUPLE type generator) that can be invoked in the definition of, for example, some table column or some variable.[10] Here is an example of the latter case:

```
DECLARE ADDR ROW ( STREET CHAR(50),
                   CITY   CHAR(25),
                   STATE  CHAR(2),
                   ZIP    CHAR(5) ) ;
```

Row assignments and comparisons are supported, with the caveat that the only strong typing that applies is the limited form described in Chapter 5, Section 5.7. Note in particular, therefore, that the fact that $r1 = r2$ is true does not imply that rows $r1$ and $r2$ are the same row. Moreover, "<" and ">" are legal row comparison operators! The details of such comparisons are complicated, however, and we omit them here; see reference [4.20] for further discussion.

---

[10] Do not be confused: SQL's "row *value* constructor" is basically a tuple selector, while its "row *type* constructor" is basically the TUPLE type generator (speaking very loosely!).

SQL does not support row versions of any of the regular relational operators ("row project," "row join," etc.), nor does it provide direct counterparts to WRAP and UNWRAP. It also does not support any "row type inferencing"—but this latter point is perhaps unimportant, given that SQL supports almost no row operators anyway.

Table Types

SQL does not support relations, as such, at all; instead, it supports *tables*. The body of a table in SQL is not a set of tuples but a *bag* of *rows* instead (a bag, also known as a *multiset*, is a collection that like a set has no ordering, but unlike a set permits duplicate elements); thus, the columns of such a table have a left-to-right ordering, and there can be duplicate rows. (Throughout this book, however, we will apply certain disciplines to guarantee that duplicate rows never occur, even in SQL contexts.) SQL does not use the terms *heading* or *body*.

Table types have no explicit table type name. A table value can be "selected" (once again, the SQL term is *constructed*) by means of an expression—actually a *<table value constructor>*—of the form:

```
VALUES <row value constructor commalist>
```

(where the commalist must not be empty). Thus, for example, the expression

```
VALUES ( P#('P1'), P#('P2'), QTY(5) ) ,
       ( P#('P1'), P#('P3'), QTY(3) ) ,
       ( P#('P2'), P#('P3'), QTY(2) ) ,
       ( P#('P2'), P#('P4'), QTY(7) ) ,
       ( P#('P3'), P#('P5'), QTY(4) ) ,
       ( P#('P4'), P#('P6'), QTY(8) )
```

evaluates to a table looking something like the relation shown in Section 6.3, except that it has no explicit column names.

SQL does not really support an explicit counterpart to the RELATION type generator at all. It also does not support an explicit table assignment operator (though it does support explicit INSERT, DELETE, and UPDATE statements). Nor does it support any table comparison operators (not even "="). However, it does support an operator for testing whether a given row appears in a given table:

```
<row value constructor> IN <table exp>
```

It also supports a counterpart to the TUPLE FROM operator:

```
( <table exp> )
```

If such an expression appears where an individual row is required, and if the *<table exp>* denotes a table that contains exactly one row, then that row is returned; otherwise, an exception is raised. *Note:* We remark in passing that *<table name>* is not a valid *<table exp>* (!).

Table Values and Variables

SQL unfortunately uses the same term *table* to mean both a table value and a table variable. In the present section, therefore, the term *table* must be understood to mean either a table value or a table variable, as the context demands. Here first, then, is the SQL syntax for defining a base table:

```
CREATE TABLE <base table name>
            ( <base table element commalist> ) ;
```

Each *<base table element>* is either a *<column definition>* or a *<constraint>*:[11]

- The *<constraint>*s specify certain integrity constraints that apply to the base table in question. We defer detailed discussion of such constraints to Chapter 9, except to note that, since they permit duplicate rows, SQL tables do not necessarily have a primary key (or, more fundamentally, any candidate keys).

- The *<column definition>*s—there must be at least one—take the following general form:

```
<column name> <type name> [ <default spec> ]
```

The optional *<default spec>* specifies the *default value,* or simply *default,* that is to be placed in the applicable column if the user does not provide an explicit value on INSERT (see Chapter 4, Section 4.6, subsection "Operations Not Involving Cursors," for an example). It takes the form DEFAULT *<default>*, where *<default>* is a literal, a niladic built-in operator name,[12] or the keyword NULL (see Chapter 19). If a given column does not have an explicit default, it is implicitly assumed to have a default of null—that is, null is the "default default" (as in fact is always the case in SQL). *Note:* For reasons beyond the scope of this book, the default *must* be null if the column is of a user-defined type (as already mentioned in Chapter 4). It must also be null if the column is of some row type, and it must be either null or empty (specified as ARRAY[]) if the column is of an array type.

For some examples of CREATE TABLE, see, for example, Fig. 4.1 in Chapter 4. Note that (as we already know) SQL does not support table-valued columns, nor does it support tables with no columns at all. It does support ORDER BY, together with analogs of most of the operators of the relational algebra (see Chapters 7 and 8). However, its rules for "table type inferencing" (though they do necessarily exist) are at least partly implicit; they are also complicated, and we omit the specifics here.

An existing base table can be dropped. Here is the syntax:

```
DROP TABLE <base table name> <behavior> ;
```

where (as in the case of DROP TYPE in Chapter 5) *<behavior>* is either RESTRICT or CASCADE. Loosely, RESTRICT means the DROP will fail if the table is currently in use

---

[11] A *<base table element>* can also take the form LIKE *T,* which allows some or all of the column definitions for the base table being defined to be copied from some existing named table *T.*

[12] A niladic operator is one that takes no explicit operands. CURRENT_DATE is an example.

anywhere, while CASCADE means the DROP will always succeed and will cause an implicit DROP . . . CASCADE for everything currently using the table.

An existing base table can also be *altered* by means of the statement ALTER TABLE. The following kinds of "alterations" are supported:

- A new column can be added.
- A new default can be defined for an existing column (replacing the previous one, if any).
- An existing column default can be deleted.
- An existing column can be deleted.
- A new integrity constraint can be specified.
- An existing integrity constraint can be deleted.

We give an example of the first case only:

```
ALTER TABLE S ADD COLUMN DISCOUNT INTEGER DEFAULT -1 ;
```

This statement adds a DISCOUNT column (of type INTEGER) to the suppliers base table. All existing rows in that table are extended from four columns to five; the initial value of the new fifth column is –1 in every case.

Finally, the SQL INSERT, DELETE, and UPDATE statements have already been discussed in Chapter 4.

Structured Types

Caveat: The portions of the SQL standard that are relevant to this subsection are hard to understand. What follows is this writer's best attempt to make sense of the material.

Here first, then, repeated from Chapter 5 (Section 5.7), is an example of a structured type definition:

```
CREATE TYPE POINT AS ( X FLOAT, Y FLOAT ) NOT FINAL ;
```

Type POINT can now be used in the definition of variables and columns. For example:

```
CREATE TABLE NADDR
     ( NAME ... ,
       ADDR ... ,
       LOCATION POINT ... ,
       ... ) ;
```

Now, we never said as much explicitly in Chapter 5, but we at least implied that SQL's structured types were scalar types specifically, just as the **Tutorial D** analog of the foregoing POINT type was a scalar type. In some respects, however, they are closer to **Tutorial D**'s *tuple* types.[13] Certainly it is true that we can access the components ("attributes") of a given POINT value, rather as if it were a tuple. Dot qualification syntax is used for this purpose, as in the following examples (note that explicit correlation names are required, as the examples indicate):

---

[13] Except that structured types have a left-to-right ordering to their attributes, whereas tuple types do not.

```
SELECT NT.LOCATION.X, NT.LOCATION.Y
FROM   NADDR AS NT
WHERE  NAME = ... ;

UPDATE NADDR AS NT
SET    NT.LOCATION.X = 5.0
WHERE  NAME = ... ;
```

When used as in the foregoing example, an SQL structured type effectively behaves as if it were a simple row type (again, see Section 5.7 in Chapter 5), except that:

■ The components are called attributes instead of fields.

■ More importantly, structured types, unlike row types, have *names* (we will revisit this point at the very end of this section).

So far, then, SQL's structured types look as if they might not be too hard to understand. But—and it is a big but!—the foregoing is not the end of the story.[14] In addition to the foregoing, SQL also allows a base table to be defined to be "OF" some structured type, in which case a number of further considerations come into play. In order to discuss some of those considerations, let us first extend the definition of type POINT as follows:

```
CREATE TYPE POINT AS ( X FLOAT, Y FLOAT ) NOT FINAL
       REF IS SYSTEM GENERATED ;
```

Now we can define a base table to be "OF" this type—for example:

```
CREATE TABLE POINTS OF POINT
       ( REF IS POINT# SYSTEM GENERATED ... ) ;
```

Explanation:

1. When we define a structured type *T*, the system automatically defines an associated *reference type* ("REF type") called REF(*T*). Values of type REF(*T*) are "references" to rows within some base table[15] that has been defined to be "OF" type *T* (see point 3). In the example, then, the system automatically defines a type called REF(POINT), whose values are references to rows within base tables that are defined to be "OF" type POINT.

2. The specification REF IS SYSTEM GENERATED in a CREATE TYPE statement means the actual values of the associated REF type are provided by the system (other options—for example, REF IS USER GENERATED—are available, but we omit the details here). *Note:* In fact, REF IS SYSTEM GENERATED is the default; in our example, therefore, we could have left our original definition of type POINT unchanged if we had wanted.

3. Base table POINTS has been defined to be "OF" the structured type POINT. The keyword OF is really not very appropriate, however, because the table is *not* actually "of" the type in question, and neither are its rows![16]

---

[14] Nor is what follows! See Chapters 20 and 26 for further discussion.

[15] Or possibly some view. Details of the view case are beyond the scope of this book.

[16] Note in particular, therefore, that if the declared type of some parameter *P* to some operator *Op* is some structured type *ST*, a row from a base table that has been defined to be "OF" type *ST* cannot be passed as a corresponding argument to an invocation of that operator *Op*.

- First of all, if the table had just one column and that column were of the structured type in question, *ST* say, then we *might* say—though not in SQL!—something to the effect that the table is of type TABLE(*ST*) and its rows are of type ROW(*ST*).

- But the table does not have just one column, in general; rather, it has one column for each attribute of *ST*. Thus, in the example, base table POINTS has two columns X and Y; it explicitly does *not* have a column of type POINT.

- Furthermore, that table has one extra column as well: namely, a column of the applicable REF type. However, the syntax for defining that column is not the normal column definition syntax but instead looks like this:

  ```
  REF IS <column name> SYSTEM GENERATED
  ```

  This extra column is called a *self-referencing column;* it is used to contain unique IDs or "references" for the rows of the base table in question. The ID for a given row is assigned when the row is inserted and remains associated with that row until it is deleted. In the example, therefore, base table POINTS actually has *three* columns (POINT#, X, and Y, in that order), not just two. *Note:* It is not at all clear why it should be necessary to define the table to be "OF" some structured type in the first place, instead of just defining an appropriate column in the usual way, in order to obtain this "unique ID" functionality, but our explanations are in accordance with the way SQL is defined.

As an aside, we note that (perhaps surprisingly) a SYSTEM GENERATED column can be a target column in an INSERT or UPDATE operation, though special considerations apply. We omit the details here.

4. Table POINTS is an example of what the standard calls, not very aptly, both a *typed table* and a *referenceable table*. As the standard puts it: "A table ... whose row type is derived from a structured type is called a *typed table*. Only a base table or a view can be a typed table." And elsewhere: "A referenceable table is necessarily also a *typed table* . . . A typed table is called a referenceable table."

Now, it seems that the foregoing features were introduced in SQL:1999 primarily to serve as a basis for incorporating some kind of "object functionality" into SQL,[17] and we will discuss that functionality in detail in Chapter 26. But nothing in the standard says the features in question can be used only in connection with that functionality, which is why we describe them in this chapter.

One final point: Recall from Chapter 5 that there is no explicit "define tuple type" operator in **Tutorial D**; instead, there is a TUPLE type generator, which can be invoked in (e.g.) the definition of a tuple variable. As a consequence, the only names tuple types have in **Tutorial D** are names of the form:

```
TUPLE { A1 T1, A2 T2, ..., An Tn }
```

One important consequence is that it is immediately clear when two tuple types are in fact one and the same, and when two tuples are of the same type.

---

[17] The fact that SQL structured types *always* have an associated REF type, even though that REF type serves no purpose except when the structured type in question is used as the basis for defining a "typed table," strongly suggests this conjecture is correct.

Now, row types in SQL are similar to **Tutorial D**'s tuple types in the foregoing respect. But structured types are different; there *is* an explicit "define structured type" operator, and structured types do have additional explicit names. By way of example, consider the following SQL definitions:

```
CREATE TYPE POINT1 AS ( X FLOAT, Y FLOAT ) NOT FINAL ;

CREATE TYPE POINT2 AS ( X FLOAT, Y FLOAT ) NOT FINAL ;

DECLARE V1 POINT1 ;

DECLARE V2 POINT2 ;
```

Note carefully that variables V1 and V2 are of different types. Thus, they cannot be compared with one another, nor can either one be assigned to the other.

6.7 SUMMARY

In this chapter we have taken a comprehensive look at relations and related matters. We began by defining **tuples** precisely, stressing the points that (a) every tuple contains exactly one value for each of its attributes, (b) there is no left-to-right ordering to the attributes, and (c) every subset of a tuple is a tuple, and every subset of a heading is a heading. And we discussed the **TUPLE type generator**, tuple **selectors**, tuple **assignment** and **equality**, and other generic tuple operators.

Then we turned to **relations** (meaning, more specifically, relation *values*). We gave a precise definition, and pointed out that every subset of a body is a body, and (as with tuples) every subset of a heading is a heading. We discussed the **RELATION type generator** and relation **selectors,** and we observed that the attributes of a given relation type can be of **any type whatsoever**, in general.

Note: It is worth elaborating on this last point briefly, since there is so much confusion surrounding it in the industry. You will often hear claims to the effect that relational attributes can only be of very simple types (numbers, strings, and so forth). The truth is, however, that there is absolutely nothing in the relational model to support such claims. As noted in Chapter 5, in fact, types can be as simple or as complex as we like, and so we can have attributes whose values are numbers, or strings, or dates, or times, or audio recordings, or maps, or video recordings, or geometric points (etc.).

The foregoing message is so important—and so widely misunderstood—that we state it again in different terms:

> **The question of what data types are supported is orthogonal to the question of support for the relational model.**

Back to our summary. Next, we went on to state certain properties that all relations satisfy:

1. They are always normalized.

2. They have no left-to-right ordering to their attributes.

3. They have no top-to-bottom ordering to their tuples.

4. They never contain any duplicate tuples.

We also identified some of the main differences between relations and **tables**; we discussed **relation-valued attributes**; and we briefly considered **TABLE_DEE** and **TABLE_DUM**, which are the only possible relations with no attributes at all. We described **relational comparisons** in some detail, and we took a quick look at certain other operators on relations (including **ORDER BY** in particular).

In connection with operators on relations, by the way, you might have noticed that we discussed the question of user-defined operators for scalar types in some depth in Chapter 5, but did not do the same for relation types. The reason is that most of the relational operators we need—restrict, project, join, relational comparisons, and so forth—are in fact built into the relational model itself and do not require any "user definition." (What is more, those operations are *generic,* in that they apply to relations of all types, loosely speaking.) However, there is no reason why those built-in operators should not be augmented with a set of user-defined ones, if the system provides a means for defining them.

We remind you that the heading of any given relation can be regarded as a predicate and the tuples of that relation can be regarded as true propositions, derived from that predicate by supplying argument values of the appropriate types for the parameters of the predicate.

Next, we went on to consider **base relvars**, pointing out that, like relations, relvars have **predicates**. The **Closed World Assumption** says we can assume that if an otherwise valid tuple does not appear in the body of the relvar, then the corresponding proposition is false.

Next, we discussed relational **assignment** (and the **INSERT**, **DELETE**, and **UPDATE** shorthands) in some detail. We emphasized the point that relational assignment was a **set-level** operation; we also noted that it was not really correct to speak of "updating tuples" or "updating attributes."

Finally, we sketched the SQL counterparts to the foregoing ideas, where applicable. An SQL table is not a set of tuples but a **bag** of **rows** (also, SQL uses the same term *table* for both table values and table variables). Base tables can be "altered" by means of **ALTER TABLE**. They can also be defined in terms of **structured types**, a possibility that we will be considering in much more detail later in this book (in Chapter 26).

EXERCISES

6.1   What do you understand by the term *cardinality?*

6.2   Define as precisely as you can the terms *tuple* and *relation*.

6.3   State as precisely as you can what it means for (a) two tuples to be equal; (b) two tuple types to be equal; (c) two relations to be equal; (d) two relation types to be equal.

6.4   Write (a) a set of predicates and (b) a set of **Tutorial D** relvar definitions for the suppliers-parts-projects database of Fig. 4.5 (see the inside back cover).

6.5   Write tuple selector invocations for a typical tuple from each of the relvars in the suppliers-parts-projects database.

6.6 Define a local tuple variable into which an individual tuple could be retrieved from the shipments relvar in the suppliers-parts-projects database.

6.7 What do the following **Tutorial D** expressions denote?

a. `RELATION { S# S#, P# P#, J# J#, QTY QTY } { }`

b. `RELATION { TUPLE { S# S#('S1'), P# P#('P1'),`
   `                    J# J#('J1'), QTY QTY(200) } }`

c. `RELATION { TUPLE { } }`

d. `RELATION { } { TUPLE { } }`

e. `RELATION { } { }`

6.8 What do you understand by the term *first normal form?*

6.9 List as many differences as you can think of between relations and tables.

6.10 Give an example of your own of a relation with (a) one relation-valued attribute and (b) two such attributes. Also, give two more relations that represent the same information as those relations but do not involve relation-valued attributes.

6.11 Write an expression that returns TRUE if the current value of the parts relvar P is empty and FALSE otherwise. Do not use the IS_EMPTY shorthand.

6.12 In what respects is ORDER BY a rather unusual operator?

6.13 State the **Closed World Assumption**.

6.14 It is sometimes suggested that a relvar is really just a traditional computer file, with "tuples" instead of records and "attributes" instead of fields. Discuss.

6.15 Give **Tutorial D** formulations for the following updates to the suppliers-parts-projects database:

a. Insert a new shipment with supplier number S1, part number P1, project number J2, quantity 500.

b. Insert a new supplier S10 (the name and city are Smith and New York, respectively; the status is not yet known).

c. Delete all blue parts.

d. Delete all projects for which there are no shipments.

e. Change the color of all red parts to orange.

f. Replace all appearances of supplier number S1 by appearances of supplier number S9 instead.

6.16 We have seen that data definition operations cause updates to be made to the catalog. But the catalog is only a collection of relvars, just like the rest of the database; so could we not use the regular update operations INSERT, DELETE, and UPDATE to update the catalog appropriately? Discuss.

6.17 In the body of the chapter, we said that any type whatsoever can be used as the basis for defining relational attributes, in general. That qualifier "in general" was there for a reason, however. Can you think of any exceptions to this general rule?

6.18 What do you understand by the SQL terms *column, field,* and *attribute?*

6.19 *(Modified version of Exercise 5.23)* Consider the SQL type POINT and the SQL table POINTS as defined in the subsection "Structured Types" in Section 6.6. Type POINT has a representation involving Cartesian coordinates X and Y. What happens if we replace that type by a revised type POINT with a representation involving polar coordinates R and θ instead?

REFERENCES AND BIBLIOGRAPHY

Most of the following references are applicable to all aspects of the relational model, not just to relations as such.

6.1 E. F. Codd: "A Relational Model of Data for Large Shared Data Banks," *CACM 13,* No. 6 (June 1970). Republished in *Milestones of Research—Selected Papers 1958–1982* (*CACM 25th Anniversary Issue*), *CACM 26,* No. 1 (January 1983). See also the earlier version, "Derivability, Redundancy, and Consistency of Relations Stored in Large Data Banks," IBM Research Report RJ599 (August 19, 1969), which was Codd's very first publication on the relational model.

> The paper that started it all. Although now over 30 years old, it stands up remarkably well to repeated rereading. Of course, many of the ideas have been refined somewhat since the paper was first published, but by and large the changes have been evolutionary, not revolutionary, in nature. Indeed, there are some ideas in the paper whose implications have still not been fully explored.
>
> We remark on a small matter of terminology. In his paper, Codd uses the term *time-varying relations* in place of our preferred *relation variables* (relvars). But *time-varying relations* is really not a very good term. First, relations as such are *values* and simply do not "vary with time" (there is no notion in mathematics of a relation having different values at different times). Second, if we say in some programming language, for example,
>
> ```
> DECLARE N INTEGER ;
> ```
>
> we do not call N a "time-varying integer," we call it an *integer variable*. In this book, therefore, we use our "relation variable" terminology, not the "time-varying" terminology; however, you should at least be aware of the existence of this latter.

6.2 E. F. Codd: *The Relational Model for Database Management Version 2.* Reading, Mass.: Addison-Wesley (1990).

> Codd spent much of the late 1980s revising and extending his original model (which he renamed "the Relational Model Version 1" or RM/V1), and this book is the result. It describes "the Relational Model Version 2" (RM/V2). The essential difference between RM/V1 and RM/V2 is as follows: Whereas RM/V1 was intended as an abstract blueprint for one particular aspect of the total database problem (essentially the foundational aspect), RM/V2 was intended as an abstract blueprint for *the entire system.* Thus, where RM/V1 had just three parts—structure, integrity, and manipulation—RM/V2 had 18; and those 18 parts include not only the original three (of course), but also parts having to do with the catalog, authorization, naming, distributed database, and various other aspects of database management. For purposes of reference, here is a complete list of the 18 parts:

A	Authorization	M	Manipulation
B	Basic operators	N	Naming
C	Catalog	P	Protection
D	Principles of DBMS design	Q	Qualifiers
E	Commands for the DBA	S	Structure
F	Functions	T	Data types
I	Integrity	V	Views
J	Indicators	X	Distributed database
L	Principles of language design	Z	Advanced operators

The ideas advocated in this book are by no means universally accepted, however [6.7, 6.8]. We comment on one particular issue here. As we saw in Chapter 5, domains (i.e., types) constrain comparisons. In the case of suppliers and parts, for instance, the comparison S.S# = SP.P# is not valid, because the comparands are of different types; hence, an attempt to join suppliers and shipments over matching supplier and part numbers will fail. Codd therefore proposes "**domain check override**" (DCO) versions of certain of the relational algebra operations, which allow the operations in question to be performed even if they involve a comparison between values of different types. A DCO version of the join just mentioned, for example, will cause the join to be done even though attributes S.S# and SP.P# are of different types (presumably it will be done on the basis of matching *representations* instead of matching *types*).

But therein lies the problem. *The whole DCO idea is based on a confusion between types and representations.* Recognizing domains for what they are (i.e., types)—with all that such recognition entails—gives us the domain checking we want *and* gives us something like the DCO capability as well. For example, the following expression constitutes a valid representation-level comparison between a supplier number and a part number:

```
THE_S# ( S# ) = THE_P# ( P# )
```

(both comparands here are of type CHAR). Thus, it is our claim that the kind of mechanism discussed in Chapter 5 gives us all the facilities we want, but does so in a manner that is clean, systematic (i.e., not *ad hoc*), and fully orthogonal. In particular, there is now no need to clutter up the relational model with new constructs such as "DCO join" (etc.).

6.3 Hugh Darwen: "The Duplicity of Duplicate Rows," in C. J. Date and Hugh Darwen, *Relational Database Writings 1989–1991*. Reading, Mass.: Addison-Wesley (1992).

This paper was written as further support for the arguments previously presented in reference [6.6] (first version) in support of the prohibition against duplicate rows. The paper not only offers novel versions of some of those same arguments, it also manages to come up with some additional ones. In particular, it stresses the fundamental point that, in order to discuss in any intelligent manner the question of whether two objects are duplicates, it is essential to have a clear *criterion of equality* (called a criterion of *identity* in the paper) for the class of objects under consideration. In other words, what does it mean for two objects, be they rows in a table or anything else, to be "the same"?

6.4 Hugh Darwen: "Relation-Valued Attributes," in C. J. Date and Hugh Darwen, *Relational Database Writings 1989–1991*. Reading, Mass.: Addison-Wesley (1992).

6.5 Hugh Darwen: "The Nullologist in Relationland," in C. J. Date and Hugh Darwen, *Relational Database Writings 1989–1991*. Reading, Mass.: Addison-Wesley (1992).

Nullology is, as Darwen puts it, "the study of nothing at all"—in other words, the study of the empty set. (It has nothing to do with SQL-style nulls!) Sets are ubiquitous in relational theory, and the question of what happens if such a set happens to be empty is far from a frivolous one. In fact, it turns out that very often the empty-set case turns out to be absolutely fundamental. *Note:* As far as the present chapter is concerned, the most immediately applicable portions of this paper are Sections 2 ("Tables with No Rows") and 3 ("Tables with No Columns").

6.6 C. J. Date: "Double Trouble, Double Trouble" (in two parts), *http://www.dbdebunk.com* (April 2002). An earlier version of this paper, "Why Duplicate Rows Are Prohibited," appeared in *Relational Database Writings 1985–1989*. Reading, Mass.: Addison-Wesley (1990).

Presents an extensive series of arguments, with examples, in support of the prohibition against duplicate rows. In particular, the paper shows that duplicate rows constitute a major *optimization inhibitor* (see Chapter 18). See also reference [6.3].

6.7 C. J. Date: "Notes Toward a Reconstituted Definition of the Relational Model Version 1 (RM/V1)," in C. J. Date and Hugh Darwen, *Relational Database Writings 1989–1991.* Reading, Mass.: Addison-Wesley (1992).

Summarizes and criticizes Codd's "RM/V1" (see the annotation to reference [6.2]) and offers an alternative definition. The assumption is that it is crucially important to get "Version 1" right before we can even think about moving on to some "Version 2." *Note:* The version of the relational model described in the present book is based on the "reconstituted" version as sketched in this paper, and further clarified and described in reference [3.3].

6.8 C. J. Date: "A Critical Review of the Relational Model Version 2 (RM/V2)," in C. J. Date and Hugh Darwen, *Relational Database Writings 1989–1991.* Reading, Mass.: Addison-Wesley (1992).

Summarizes and criticizes Codd's "RM/V2" [6.2].

6.9 C. J. Date: *The Database Relational Model: A Retrospective Review and Analysis.* Reading, Mass.: Addison-Wesley (2001).

This short book (160 pages) is offered as a careful, unbiased, retrospective review and assessment of Codd's relational contribution as documented in his 1970s publications. To be specific, it examines the following papers in detail (as well as touching on several others in passing):

- "Derivability, Redundancy, and Consistency of Relations Stored in Large Data Banks" (the first version of reference [6.1])
- "A Relational Model of Data for Large Shared Data Banks" [6.1]
- "Relational Completeness of Data Base Sublanguages" [7.1]
- "A Data Base Sublanguage Founded on the Relational Calculus" [8.1]
- "Further Normalization of the Data Base Relational Model" [11.6]
- "Extending the Relational Database Model to Capture More Meaning" [14.7]
- "Interactive Support for Nonprogrammers: The Relational and Network Approaches" [26.12]

6.10 Mark A. Roth, Henry F. Korth, and Abraham Silberschatz: "Extended Algebra and Calculus for Nested Relational Databases," *ACM TODS 13,* No. 4 (December 1988).

Many people over the years have proposed the possibility of supporting relation-valued attributes; this paper is a case in point. Such proposals usually go by the name of "NF^2 relations," where NF^2 (pronounced "NF squared") is short for NFNF and stands for "non first normal form." However, there are at least two major differences between such proposals and support for relation-valued attributes as described in this chapter:

- First, NF^2 relation advocates assume that relation-valued attributes are prohibited in the relational model and therefore advertise their proposals as "extensions" to that model (in this connection, note the title of reference [6.10]).
- Second, the NF^2 advocates are correct—they *are* extending the relational model! For example, Roth *et al.* propose an extended form of union that, in our terms, (a) ungroups both operands recursively until they involve no relation-valued attributes at all, either directly or indirectly; (b) performs a regular union on those ungrouped operands; and (c) finally, recursively (re)groups the result again. And it is the recursion that constitutes the extension. That is, while any *specific* extended union is shorthand for some *specific* combination of existing relational operators, it is not possible to say that extended union *in general* is just shorthand for some combination of existing operators.

CHAPTER 7

Relational Algebra

7.1   INTRODUCTION

The relational algebra is a collection of operators that take relations as their operands and return a relation as their result. The first version of the algebra was defined by Codd in references [5.1] and [7.1]; reference [7.1] in particular has come to be regarded as the source of the "original" algebra. That original algebra had eight operators, two groups of four each:

1. The traditional set operators *union, intersection, difference,* and *Cartesian product* (all of them modified somewhat to take account of the fact that their operands are, specifically, relations instead of arbitrary sets)

2. The special relational operators *restrict* (also known as *select*), *project, join,* and *divide*

Fig. 7.1 gives an informal picture of how these operators work.

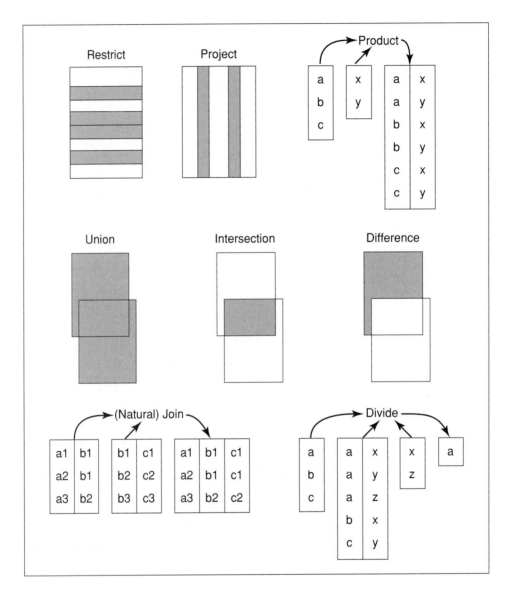

Fig. 7.1   The original eight operators (overview)

Now, Codd had a very specific purpose in mind, which we will examine in the next chapter, for defining just the eight operators he did. But those eight operators are not the end of the story; rather, *any number* of operators can be defined that satisfy the simple requirement of "relations in, relations out," and many additional operators have indeed been defined, by many different writers. In this chapter, we will discuss the original eight operators first—not exactly as they were originally defined but as they have since become—and use them as the basis for discussing a variety of algebraic ideas; then we will go on to consider some of the many useful operators that have subsequently been added to the original set.

Before we can discuss the algebra in detail, however, there are a few more preliminary remarks we need to make:

- First of all, the operators apply to all relations, loosely speaking; in fact, they are really *generic* operators, associated with the RELATION type generator and hence applicable to any specific relation type obtained by invoking that type generator.

- Second, almost all of the operators we will be discussing are really just shorthand anyway! We will have more to say on this important point in Section 7.10.

- Third, the operators are all *read-only* (i.e., they "read" but do not update their operands). Thus, they apply specifically to *values*—relation values, of course—and hence, harmlessly, to those relation values that happen to be the current values of relvars.

- Last, it follows from the previous point that it makes sense to talk about, for example, "the projection over attribute *A* of relvar *R*," meaning the relation that results from taking the projection over that attribute *A* of the current value of that relvar *R*. Occasionally, however, it is convenient to use expressions like "the projection over attribute *A* of relvar *R*" in a slightly different sense. For example, suppose we define a view SC of the suppliers relvar S that consists of just the S# and CITY attributes of that relvar. Then we might say, loosely but very conveniently, that relvar SC is "the projection over S# and CITY of relvar S"—meaning, more precisely, that the value of SC at any given time is the projection over S# and CITY of the value of relvar S at that time. In a sense, therefore, we can talk in terms of projections of relvars *per se,* rather than just in terms of projections of current values of relvars. We hope this kind of dual usage of the terminology on our part does not cause any confusion.

The plan of the chapter is as follows. Following this introductory section, Section 7.2 revisits the question of relational closure and elaborates on it considerably. Sections 7.3 and 7.4 then discuss Codd's original eight operators in detail, and Section 7.5 gives examples of how those operators can be used to formulate queries. Next, Section 7.6 considers the more general question of what the algebra is for. Section 7.7 discusses a number of miscellaneous points. Then Section 7.8 describes some useful additions to Codd's original algebra, including in particular the important EXTEND and SUMMARIZE operators. Section 7.9 discusses operators for mapping between relations with relation-valued attributes and relations without such attributes. Finally, Section 7.10 offers a brief summary. *Note:* We defer discussion of the pertinent SQL facilities to Chapter 8, for reasons to be explained in that chapter.

7.2   CLOSURE REVISITED

As we saw in Chapter 3, the fact that the output from any given relational operation is another relation is referred to as the relational *closure* property. To recap briefly, closure means we can write nested relational expressions—that is, relational expressions in which the operands are themselves represented by relational expressions of arbitrary complexity. (There is an obvious analogy between the ability to nest relational expressions in the relational algebra and the ability to nest arithmetic expressions in ordinary arithmetic; indeed, the fact that relations are closed under the algebra is important for exactly the same kinds of reasons that the fact that numbers are closed under ordinary arithmetic is important.)

Now, when we discussed closure in Chapter 3, there was one very significant point we deliberately glossed over. Recall that every relation has two parts, a heading and a body; loosely speaking, the heading is the attributes and the body is the tuples. The heading for a base relation—where, as you will recall from Chapter 5, a *base relation* is the value of a base relvar—is obviously known to the system, because it is specified as part of the relevant base relvar definition. But what about derived relations? For example, consider the expression

```
S JOIN P
```

(which represents the join of suppliers and parts over matching cities, CITY being the only attribute common to the two relations). We know what the body of the result looks like—but what about the heading? Closure dictates that it must *have* a heading, and the system needs to know what it is (in fact the user does too, as we will see in a moment). In other words, that result must—of course!—be of some well-defined relation type. If we are to take closure seriously, therefore, we need to define the relational operations in such a way as to guarantee that every operation produces a result with a proper relation type: in particular, with proper attribute names. (We remark in passing that this is an aspect of the algebra that has been much overlooked in the literature—and also, regrettably, in the SQL language and hence in SQL products—with the notable exception of the treatment found in references [7.2] and [7.10]. The algebra as presented in this chapter is very much influenced by these two references.)

One reason we require every result relation to have proper attribute names is to allow us to refer to those attributes in subsequent operations—in particular, in operations invoked elsewhere within the overall nested expression. For example, we could not sensibly even write an expression such as

```
( S JOIN P ) WHERE CITY = 'Athens'
```

if we did not know that the result of evaluating the expression S JOIN P had an attribute called CITY.

What we need, therefore, is a set of **relation type inference rules** built into the algebra, such that if we know the type(s) of the input relation(s) for any given relational operation, we can infer the type of the output from that operation. Given such rules, it will follow that an arbitrary relational expression, no matter how complex, will produce a result that also has a well-defined type, and in particular a well-defined set of attribute names.

As a preparatory step to achieving this goal, we introduce a new operator, RENAME, whose purpose is (loosely) to rename attributes within a specified relation. More precisely, the RENAME operator takes a given relation and returns another that is identical to the given one except that one of its attributes has a different name. (The given relation is

specified by means of a relational expression, possibly involving other relational operations.) For example, we might write:

```
S RENAME CITY AS SCITY
```

This expression—please note that it *is* an expression, not a "command" or statement,
and hence that it can be nested inside other expressions—yields a relation with the same
heading and body as the relation that is the current value of relvar S, except that the city
attribute is named SCITY instead of CITY:

S#	SNAME	STATUS	SCITY
S1	Smith	20	London
S2	Jones	10	Paris
S3	Blake	30	Paris
S4	Clark	20	London
S5	Adams	30	Athens

Important: Please note that this RENAME expression has *not* changed the suppliers
relvar in the database! It is just an expression (exactly as, e.g., S JOIN SP is just an
expression), and like any other expression it simply denotes a certain value—a value that,
in this particular case, happens to look very much like the current value of the suppliers
relvar.

Here is another example (a "multiple renaming" this time):

```
P RENAME ( PNAME AS PN, WEIGHT AS WT )
```

This expression is shorthand for the following:

```
( P RENAME PNAME AS PN ) RENAME WEIGHT AS WT
```

The result looks like this:

P#	PN	COLOR	WT	CITY
P1	Nut	Red	12.0	London
P2	Bolt	Green	17.0	Paris
P3	Screw	Blue	17.0	Oslo
P4	Screw	Red	14.0	London
P5	Cam	Blue	12.0	Paris
P6	Cog	Red	19.0	London

It is worth noting that the availability of RENAME means that the relational algebra,
unlike SQL, has no need for (and in fact does not support) dot-qualified attribute names
such as S.S#.

7.3 THE ORIGINAL ALGEBRA: SYNTAX

In this section, we present a concrete syntax, based on **Tutorial D**, for relational algebra
expressions that use the original eight operators, plus RENAME. The syntax is included
here primarily for purposes of subsequent reference. A few notes on semantics are also

included. *Note:* Most database texts use a "mathematical" or "Greek" notation for the relational operators: σ for restriction ("selection"), π for projection, ∩ for intersection, ⋈ ("bow tie") for join, and so on. As you can see, we prefer to use keywords such as JOIN and WHERE. Keywords make for lengthier expressions, but we think they also make for more user-friendly ones.

```
<relation exp>
   ::=    RELATION { <tuple exp commalist> }
     |    <relvar name>
     |    <relation op inv>
     |    <with exp>
     |    <introduced name>
     |    ( <relation exp> )
```

A *<relation exp>* is an expression that denotes a relation (i.e., a relation *value*). The first format is a relation selector invocation (see Chapter 6); we do not spell out the syntax of *<tuple exp>* in detail here, since examples should be sufficient to give the general idea. The *<relvar name>* and *(<relation exp>)* formats are self-explanatory; the others are explained in what follows.

```
<relation op inv>
   ::=    <project> | <nonproject>
```

A relational operator invocation, *<relation op inv>,* is either a *<project>* or a *<nonproject>. Note:* We distinguish these two cases in the syntax merely for operator precedence reasons (it is convenient to assign a high precedence to projection).

```
<project>
   ::=    <relation exp>
              { [ ALL BUT ] <attribute name commalist> }
```

The *<relation exp>* must not be a *<nonproject>*.

```
<nonproject>
   ::=    <rename> | <union> | <intersect> | <minus> | <times>
     |    <where> | <join> | <divide>

<rename>
   ::=    <relation exp> RENAME ( <renaming commalist> )
```

The *<relation exp>* must not be a *<nonproject>*. The individual *<renaming>*s are executed in sequence as written (for the syntax of *<renaming>,* see the examples in the previous section). The parentheses can be omitted if the commalist contains just one *<renaming>*.

```
<union>
   ::=    <relation exp> UNION <relation exp>
```

The *<relation exp>*s must not be *<nonproject>*s, except that either or both can be another *<union>*.

```
<intersect>
   ::=    <relation exp> INTERSECT <relation exp>
```

The *<relation exp>*s must not be *<nonproject>*s, except that either or both can be another *<intersect>*.

```
<minus>
    ::=    <relation exp> MINUS <relation exp>
```

The *<relation exp>*s must not be *<nonproject>*s.

```
<times>
    ::=    <relation exp> TIMES <relation exp>
```

The *<relation exp>*s must not be *<nonproject>*s, except that either or both can be another *<times>*.

```
<where>
    ::=    <relation exp> WHERE <bool exp>
```

The *<relation exp>* must not be a *<nonproject>*. The *<bool exp>* can include references to attributes of the relation denoted by the *<relation exp>*, with the obvious semantics.

```
<join>
    ::=    <relation exp> JOIN <relation exp>
```

The *<relation exp>*s must not be *<nonproject>*s, except that either or both can be another *<join>*.

```
<divide>
    ::=    <relation exp> DIVIDEBY <relation exp> PER <per>
```

The *<relation exp>*s must not be *<nonproject>*s.

```
<per>
    ::=    <relation exp> | ( <relation exp>, <relation exp> )
```

The *<relation exp>*s must not be *<nonproject>*s.

```
<with exp>
    ::=    WITH <name intro commalist> : <exp>
```

The *<with exp>*s we are primarily concerned with in this book are relational expressions specifically, which is why we are discussing them in this chapter. However, scalar and tuple *<with exp>*s are supported too; in fact, a given *<with exp>* is a *<relation exp>*, a *<tuple exp>,* or a *<scalar exp>* according as the *<exp>* after the colon is a *<relation exp>*, a *<tuple exp>*, or a *<scalar exp>* in turn. In all cases, the individual *<name intro>*s are executed in sequence as written, and the semantics of the *<with exp>* are defined to be the same as those of a version of *<exp>* in which each occurrence of each introduced name is replaced by a reference to a variable whose value is the result of evaluating the corresponding expression. *Note:* WITH is not really an operator of the relational algebra as such; it is really just a device to help with the formulation of what otherwise might be rather complicated expressions (especially ones involving common subexpressions). Several examples are given in Section 7.5.

```
<name intro>
    ::=    <exp> AS <introduced name>
```

The *<introduced name>* can be used within the containing *<with exp>* wherever the *<exp>* (enclosed in parentheses if necessary) would be allowed.

7.4   THE ORIGINAL ALGEBRA: SEMANTICS

Union

In mathematics, the union of two sets is the set of all elements belonging to either or both of the given sets. Since a relation is—or, rather, contains—a set (namely, a set of tuples), it is obviously possible to construct the union of two such sets; the result will be a set consisting of all tuples appearing in either or both of the given relations. For example, the union of the set of supplier tuples currently appearing in relvar S and the set of part tuples currently appearing in relvar P is certainly a set.

However, although that result is a set, *it is not a relation;* relations cannot contain a mixture of different kinds of tuples, they must be "tuple-homogeneous." And we do want the result to be a relation, because we want to preserve the closure property. Therefore, the union in the relational algebra is not the completely general mathematical union; rather, it is a special kind of union, in which we require the two input relations to be **of the same type**—meaning, for example, that they both contain supplier tuples, or both part tuples, but not a mixture of the two. If the two relations are of the same type, then we can take their union, and the result will also be a relation of the same type; in other words, the closure property will be preserved. *Note:* Historically, much of the database literature (earlier editions of this book included) used the term *union compatibility* to refer to the notion that two relations must be of the same type. This term is not very apt, however, for a variety of reasons, the most obvious of which is that the notion does not apply just to union.

Here, then, is a definition of the relational union operator: Given two relations *a* and *b* of the same type, the **union** of those two relations, *a* UNION *b,* is a relation of the same type, with body consisting of all tuples *t* such that *t* appears in *a* or *b* or both.

Example: Let relations A and B be as shown in Fig. 7.2 opposite (both are derived from the current value of the suppliers relvar S; A is the suppliers in London, and B is the suppliers who supply part P1, intuitively speaking). Then A UNION B (see part 1 of the figure) is the suppliers who either are located in London or supply part P1, or both. Notice that the result has three tuples, not four; relations never contain duplicate tuples, by definition (we say, loosely, that union "eliminates duplicates"). We remark in passing that the only other operation of the original eight for which this question of duplicate elimination arises is projection (see later in this section).

By the way, observe how the definition of union relies on the concept of tuple equality. Here is a different but equivalent definition that makes the point very clear (the revised text is highlighted): Given two relations *a* and *b* of the same type, the union of those two relations, *a* UNION *b,* is a relation of the same type, with body consisting of all tuples *t* such that *t* **is equal to (i.e., is a duplicate of) some tuple** in *a* or *b* or both. Analogous remarks apply directly to the intersect and difference operations, as you will soon see.

Intersect

Like union, and for essentially the same reason, the relational intersection operator requires its operands to be of the same type. Given two relations *a* and *b* of the same type,

A

S#	SNAME	STATUS	CITY
S1	Smith	20	London
S4	Clark	20	London

B

S#	SNAME	STATUS	CITY
S1	Smith	20	London
S2	Jones	10	Paris

1. *Union*
   (A UNION B)

S#	SNAME	STATUS	CITY
S1	Smith	20	London
S4	Clark	20	London
S2	Jones	10	Paris

2. *Intersection*
   (A INTERSECT B)

S#	SNAME	STATUS	CITY
S1	Smith	20	London

3. *Difference*
   (A MINUS B)

S#	SNAME	STATUS	CITY
S4	Clark	20	London

4. *Difference*
   (B MINUS A)

S#	SNAME	STATUS	CITY
S2	Jones	10	Paris

Fig. 7.2   Union, intersection, and difference examples

then, the **intersection** of those two relations, *a* INTERSECT *b*, is a relation of the same type, with body consisting of all tuples *t* such that *t* appears in both *a* and *b*.

Example: Again, let A and B be as shown in Fig. 7.2. Then A INTERSECT B (see part 2 of the figure) is the suppliers who are located in London and supply part P1.

Difference

Like union and intersection, the relational difference operator also requires its operands to be of the same type. Given two relations *a* and *b* of the same type, then, the **difference** between those two relations, *a* MINUS *b* (in that order), is a relation of the same type, with body consisting of all tuples *t* such that *t* appears in *a* and not *b*.

Example: Let A and B again be as shown in Fig. 7.2. Then A MINUS B (see part 3 of the figure) is the suppliers who are located in London and do not supply part P1, and B MINUS A (see part 4 of the figure) is the suppliers who supply part P1 and are not located in London. Observe that MINUS has a directionality to it, just as subtraction does in ordinary arithmetic (e.g., "5 − 2" and "2 − 5" are not the same thing).

Product

In mathematics, the Cartesian product (product for short) of two sets is the set of all ordered pairs such that, in each pair, the first element comes from the first set and the second element comes from the second set. Thus, the Cartesian product of two relations would be a set of ordered pairs of *tuples,* loosely speaking. But again we want to preserve the closure property; in other words, we want the result to contain tuples *per se,* not *ordered pairs* of tuples. Therefore, the relational version of Cartesian product is an *extended form* of the operation, in which each ordered pair of tuples is replaced by the single tuple that is the *union* of the two tuples in question (using "union" in its normal set theory sense, not its special relational sense). That is, given the tuples[1]

```
{ A1 a1, A2 a2, ..., Am am }
```

and

```
{ B1 b1, B2 b2, ..., Bn bn }
```

the union of the two is the single tuple

```
{ A1 a1, A2 a2, ..., Am am, B1 b1, B2 b2, ..., Bn bn }
```

Note: We are assuming for simplicity here that the two tuples have no attribute names in common. The paragraph immediately following elaborates on this point.

Another problem that occurs in connection with Cartesian product is that, of course, we require the result relation to have a well-formed heading (i.e., to be of a proper relation type). Now, clearly the heading of the result consists of all of the attributes from both of the two input headings. A problem will therefore arise if the two input headings have any attribute names in common; if we were allowed to form the product, the result heading would then have two attributes with the same name and so would not be well-formed. If we need to construct the Cartesian product of two relations that do have any such common attribute names, therefore, we must use the RENAME operator first to rename attributes appropriately.

We therefore define the (relational) **Cartesian product** of two relations *a* and *b, a* TIMES *b,* where *a* and *b* have no common attribute names, to be a relation with a heading that is the (set theory) union of the headings of *a* and *b* and with a body consisting of the set of all tuples *t* such that *t* is the (set theory) union of a tuple appearing in *a* and a tuple appearing in *b*. Note that the cardinality of the result is the product of the cardinalities, and the degree of the result is the sum of the degrees, of the input relations *a* and *b*.

Example: Let relations A and B be as shown in Fig. 7.3 opposite (A is all current supplier numbers and B is all current part numbers, intuitively speaking). Then A TIMES B—see the lower part of the figure—is all current supplier-number/part-number pairs.

Restrict

Let relation *a* have attributes *X* and *Y* (and possibly others), and let θ be an operator—typically "=", "≠", ">", "<", and so on—such that the boolean expression $X \, \theta \, Y$ is well-formed and, given particular values for *X* and *Y,* evaluates to a truth value (TRUE or FALSE). Then the **θ-restriction**, or just *restriction* for short, of relation *a* on attributes *X* and *Y* (in that order)—

```
a WHERE X θ Y
```

---

[1] **Tutorial D** would require the keyword TUPLE to appear in front of each of these expressions.

```
                A   ┌──────┐              B   ┌──────┐
                    │ S#   │                  │ P#   │
                    ├──────┤                  ├──────┤
                    │ S1   │                  │ P1   │
                    │ S2   │                  │ P2   │
                    │ S3   │                  │ P3   │
                    │ S4   │                  │ P4   │
                    │ S5   │                  │ P5   │
                    └──────┘                  │ P6   │
                                              └──────┘

    Cartesian product (A TIMES B)

    ┌──────┬──────┐
    │ S#   │ P#   │
    ├──────┼──────┤
    │ S1   │ P1   │   ┌───────────┐  ┌───────────┐  ┌───────────┐  ┌───────────┐
    │ S1   │ P2   │   │ S2 │ P1   │  │ S3 │ P1   │  │ S4 │ P1   │  │ S5 │ P1   │
    │ S1   │ P3   │   │ S2 │ P2   │  │ S3 │ P2   │  │ S4 │ P2   │  │ S5 │ P2   │
    │ S1   │ P4   │   │ S2 │ P3   │  │ S3 │ P3   │  │ S4 │ P3   │  │ S5 │ P3   │
    │ S1   │ P5   │   │ S2 │ P4   │  │ S3 │ P4   │  │ S4 │ P4   │  │ S5 │ P4   │
    │ S1   │ P6   │   │ S2 │ P5   │  │ S3 │ P5   │  │ S4 │ P5   │  │ S5 │ P5   │
    └──────┴──────┘   │ S2 │ P6   │  │ S3 │ P6   │  │ S4 │ P6   │  │ S5 │ P6   │
                      └───────────┘  └───────────┘  └───────────┘  └───────────┘
```

Fig. 7.3   Cartesian product example

—is a relation with the same heading as *a* and with body consisting of all tuples of *a* such that the expression $X \theta Y$ evaluates to TRUE for the tuple in question.

Note: The foregoing is essentially the definition of restriction given in most of the literature (including earlier editions of this book). However, it is possible to generalize it, and we will, as follows. Let relation *a* have attributes $X, Y, ..., Z$ (and possibly others), and let *p* be a truth-valued function whose parameters are, precisely, some subset of $X, Y, ..., Z$. Then the restriction of *a* according to *p*—

    a WHERE p

—is a relation with the same heading as *a* and with body consisting of all tuples of *a* such that *p* evaluates to TRUE for the tuple in question.

The restriction operator effectively yields a "horizontal" subset of a given relation: that is, that subset of the tuples of the given relation for which some specified condition is satisfied. Some examples (all of them illustrating the generalized version of restriction as just defined) are given in Fig. 7.4, overleaf.

Points arising:

1. The expression *p* following the keyword WHERE is, of course, a boolean expression; in fact, it is a *predicate,* in a sense to be discussed in detail in Chapter 9.

2. We refer to that predicate as a **restriction condition**. If that condition is such that it can be evaluated for a given tuple *t* without examining any tuple other than *t* (and hence *a fortiori* without examining any relation other than *a*), then it is a **simple** restriction condition. All of the restriction conditions in Fig. 7.4 are simple in this sense. Here by contrast is an example that involves a nonsimple restriction condition:

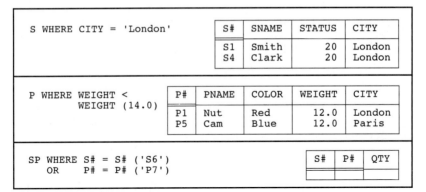

Fig. 7.4 Restriction examples

```
S WHERE ( ( SP RENAME S# AS X ) WHERE X = S# ) { P# } = P { P# }
```

We will examine this example in detail later in this section, following the discussion of divide.

3. The following equivalences are worthy of note:

```
a WHERE p1 OR p2   ≡   ( a WHERE p1 ) UNION ( a WHERE p2 )

a WHERE p1 AND p2  ≡   ( a WHERE p1 ) INTERSECT ( a WHERE p2 )

a WHERE NOT ( p )  ≡   a MINUS ( a WHERE p )
```

Project

Let relation *a* have attributes *X, Y, ..., Z* (and possibly others). Then the **projection** of relation *a* on *X, Y, ..., Z*—

```
a { X, Y, ..., Z }
```

—is a relation with:

- A heading derived from the heading of *a* by removing all attributes not mentioned in the set { *X, Y, ..., Z* }
- A body consisting of all tuples { *X x, Y y, ..., Z z* } such that a tuple appears in *a* with *X* value *x, Y* value *y, ...,* and *Z* value *z*

The projection operator thus effectively yields a "vertical" subset of a given relation: namely, that subset obtained by removing all attributes not mentioned in the specified commalist of attribute names and then eliminating duplicate (sub)tuples from what is left.

Points arising:

1. No attribute can be mentioned more than once in the attribute name commalist (why not?).

2. In practice, it is often convenient to be able to specify, not the attributes over which the projection is to be taken, but rather the ones that are to be "projected away" (i.e.,

removed). Instead of saying "project relation P over the P#, PNAME, COLOR, and CITY attributes," for example, we might say "project the WEIGHT attribute away from relation P," as here:

```
P { ALL BUT WEIGHT }
```

Further examples are given in Fig. 7.5. Notice in the first one (the projection of suppliers over CITY) that, although relvar S currently contains five tuples, there are only three tuples in the result ("duplicates are eliminated"). Analogous remarks apply to the other examples also, of course. Note too the reliance on tuple equality once again.

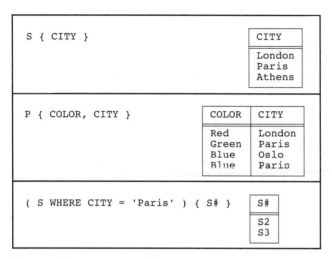

Fig. 7.5 Projection examples

Join

Join comes in several different varieties. Easily the most important, however, is the so-called *natural* join—so much so, in fact, that the unqualified term *join* is almost always taken to mean the natural join specifically, and we adopt that usage in this book. Here then is the definition (it is a little abstract, but you should already be familiar with natural join at an intuitive level from our discussions in Chapter 3). Let relations *a* and *b* have attributes

$$X1, X2, \ldots, Xm, Y1, Y2, \ldots, Yn$$

and

$$Y1, Y2, \ldots, Yn, Z1, Z2, \ldots, Zp$$

respectively; that is, the *Y* attributes *Y1, Y2, ..., Yn* (only) are common to the two relations, the *X* attributes *X1, X2, ..., Xm* are the other attributes of *a*, and the *Z* attributes *Z1, Z2, ..., Zp* are the other attributes of *b*. Observe that:

- We can and do assume without loss of generality, thanks to the availability of the attribute RENAME operator, that no attribute Xi ($i = 1, 2, ..., m$) has the same name as any attribute Zj ($j = 1, 2, ..., p$).

- Every attribute Yk ($k = 1, 2, ..., n$) has the same type in both a and b (for otherwise it would not be a common attribute, by definition).

Now consider { $X1, X2, ..., Xm$ }, { $Y1, Y2, ..., Yn$ }, and { $Z1, Z2, ..., Zp$ } as three *composite* attributes X, Y, and Z, respectively. Then the (natural) **join** of a and b—

    a JOIN b

—is a relation with heading { X, Y, Z } and body consisting of all tuples { $X x, Y y, Z z$ } such that a tuple appears in a with X value x and Y value y and a tuple appears in b with Y value y and Z value z.

An example of a natural join (the natural join S JOIN P, over the common attribute CITY) is given in Fig. 7.6.

Note: We have illustrated the point several times—indeed, it is illustrated by Fig. 7.6—but it is still worth stating explicitly that joins are *not* always between a foreign key and a matching primary (or candidate) key, even though such joins are a very common and important special case.

Incidentally, note how the definition of natural join relies on tuple equality yet again. Note too with respect to that definition that:

- If $n = 0$ (meaning a and b have no common attributes), then a JOIN b degenerates to a TIMES b.[2]

- If $m = p = 0$ (meaning a and b are of the same type), then a JOIN b degenerates to a INTERSECT b.

Now we turn to the *θ-join* operation. This operation is intended for those occasions (comparatively rare, but by no means unknown) where we need to join two relations on the basis of some comparison operator other than equality. Let relations a and b satisfy the

S#	SNAME	STATUS	CITY	P#	PNAME	COLOR	WEIGHT
S1	Smith	20	London	P1	Nut	Red	12.0
S1	Smith	20	London	P4	Screw	Red	14.0
S1	Smith	20	London	P6	Cog	Red	19.0
S2	Jones	10	Paris	P2	Bolt	Green	17.0
S2	Jones	10	Paris	P5	Cam	Blue	12.0
S3	Blake	30	Paris	P2	Bolt	Green	17.0
S3	Blake	30	Paris	P5	Cam	Blue	12.0
S4	Clark	20	London	P1	Nut	Red	12.0
S4	Clark	20	London	P4	Screw	Red	14.0
S4	Clark	20	London	P6	Cog	Red	19.0

Fig. 7.6 The natural join S JOIN P

---

[2] The version of **Tutorial D** defined in reference [3.3] includes no direct support for the TIMES operator for this very reason.

requirements for Cartesian product (i.e., they have no attribute names in common); let *a* have an attribute *X* and let *b* have an attribute *Y;* and let *X, Y,* and θ satisfy the requirements for θ-restriction. Then the **θ-join** of relation *a* on attribute *X* with relation *b* on attribute *Y* is defined to be the result of evaluating the expression:

```
( a TIMES b ) WHERE X θ Y
```

In other words, it is a relation with the same heading as the Cartesian product of *a* and *b,* and with a body consisting of the set of all tuples *t* such that *t* appears in that Cartesian product and the expression $X \theta Y$ evaluates to TRUE for that tuple *t.*

By way of example, suppose we wish to compute the *greater-than join* of relation S on CITY with relation P on CITY (so θ here is ">"; since the CITY attributes are defined to be of type CHAR, ">" simply means "greater in alphabetic ordering"). An appropriate relational expression is as follows:

```
( ( S RENAME CITY AS SCITY ) TIMES
  ( P RENAME CITY AS PCITY ) )
WHERE SCITY > PCITY
```

Note the attribute renaming in this example. (Of course, it would be sufficient to rename just one of the two CITY attributes; the only reason for renaming both is symmetry.) The result of the overall expression is shown in Fig. 7.7.

If θ is "=", the θ-join is called an **equijoin.** It follows from the definition that the result of an equijoin must include two attributes with the property that the values of those two attributes are equal in every tuple in the relation. If one of those two attributes is projected away and the other renamed appropriately (if necessary), the result is the natural join! For example, the expression representing the natural join of suppliers and parts (over cities)—

```
S JOIN P
```

—is equivalent to the following more complex expression:

```
( ( S TIMES ( P RENAME CITY AS PCITY ) )
                  WHERE CITY = PCITY )
                        { ALL BUT PCITY }
```

Note: **Tutorial D** does not include direct support for the θ-join operator because (a) it is not needed very often in practice and in any case (b) it is not a primitive operator (i.e., it can be defined in terms of other operators, as we have seen).

S#	SNAME	STATUS	SCITY	P#	PNAME	COLOR	WEIGHT	PCITY
S2	Jones	10	Paris	P1	Nut	Red	12.0	London
S2	Jones	10	Paris	P3	Screw	Blue	17.0	Oslo
S2	Jones	10	Paris	P4	Screw	Red	14.0	London
S2	Jones	10	Paris	P6	Cog	Red	19.0	London
S3	Blake	30	Paris	P1	Nut	Red	12.0	London
S3	Blake	30	Paris	P3	Screw	Blue	17.0	Oslo
S3	Blake	30	Paris	P4	Screw	Red	14.0	London
S3	Blake	30	Paris	P6	Cog	Red	19.0	London

Fig. 7.7 Greater-than join of suppliers and parts on cities

Divide

Reference [7.4] defines two distinct "divide" operators that it calls the Small Divide and the Great Divide, respectively. In **Tutorial D**, a *<divide>* in which the *<per>* consists of just one *<relation exp>* is a Small Divide, a *<divide>* in which it consists of a parenthesized commalist of two *<relation exp>*s is a Great Divide. The description that follows applies to the Small Divide only, and only to a particular limited form of the Small Divide at that; see reference [7.4] for a discussion of the Great Divide and for further details regarding the Small Divide as well.

We should say too that the version of the Small Divide as discussed here is not the same as Codd's original operator; in fact, it is an improved version that overcomes certain difficulties that arose with that original operator in connection with empty relations. It is also not the same as the version discussed in the first few editions of this book.

Here then is the definition. Let relations *a* and *b* have attributes

```
X1, X2, ..., Xm
```

and

```
Y1, Y2, ..., Yn
```

respectively, where no attribute Xi ($i = 1, 2, ..., m$) has the same name as any attribute Yj ($j = 1, 2, ..., n$), and let relation *c* have attributes

```
X1, X2, ..., Xm, Y1, Y2, ..., Yn
```

(i.e., *c* has a heading that is the union of the headings of *a* and *b*). Let us now regard { *X1, X2, ..., Xm* } and { *Y1, Y2, ..., Yn* } as *composite* attributes *X* and *Y*, respectively. Then the **division** of *a* by *b* per *c* (where *a* is the dividend, *b* is the divisor, and *c* is the "mediator")—

```
a DIVIDEBY b PER c
```

—is a relation with heading { *X* } and body consisting of all tuples { *X x* } appearing in *a* such that a tuple { *X x, Y y* } appears in *c* for *all* tuples { *Y y* } appearing in *b*. In other words, the result consists of those *X* values from *a* whose corresponding *Y* values in *c* include all *Y* values from *b*, loosely speaking. Note the reliance on tuple equality yet again!

Fig. 7.8 shows some examples of division. The dividend (DEND) in each case is the projection of the current value of relvar S over S#; the mediator (MED) in each case is the projection of the current value of relvar SP over S# and P#; and the three divisors (DOR) are as indicated in the figure. Notice the last example in particular, in which the divisor is a relation containing part numbers for all currently known parts; the result (obviously enough) shows supplier numbers for suppliers who supply all of those parts. As this example suggests, the DIVIDEBY operator is intended for queries of this general nature; in fact, whenever the natural language version of the query contains the word "all" in the conditional part ("Get suppliers who supply *all* parts"), there is a strong likelihood that division will be involved. (Indeed, division was specifically intended by Codd to be an algebraic counterpart to the *universal quantifier,* much as projection was intended to be an algebraic counterpart to the *existential* quantifier. See Chapter 8 for further explanation.)

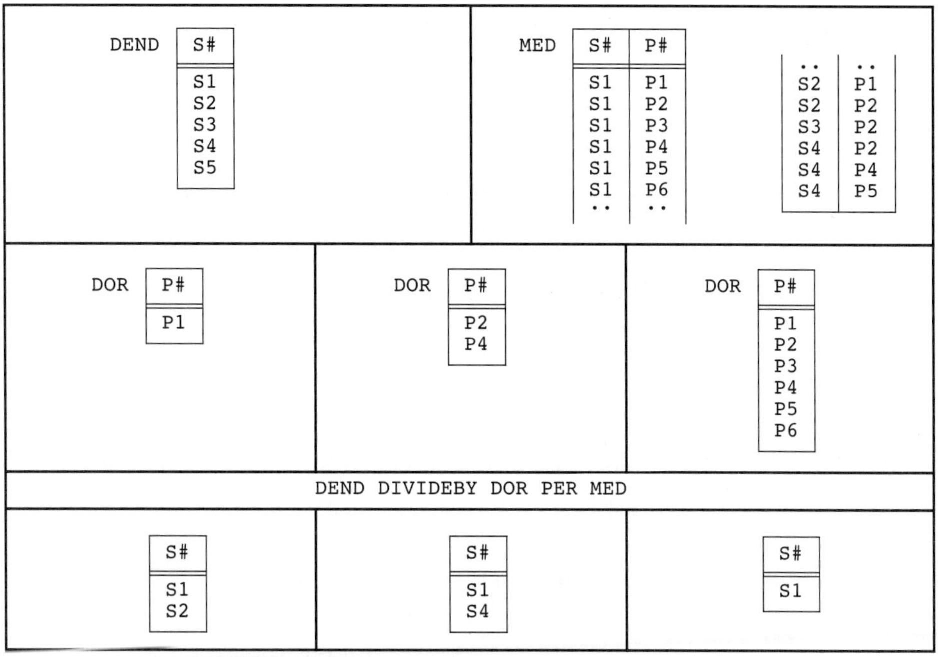

Fig. 7.8 Division examples

In connection with that last example, however, we should point out that queries of that general nature are often more readily expressed in terms of *relational comparisons*. For example:

```
S WHERE ( ( SP RENAME S# AS X ) WHERE X = S# ) { P# } = P { P# }
```

This expression evaluates to a relation containing all and only the supplier tuples for suppliers who supply all currently known parts. *Explanation:*

1. For a given supplier, the expression

   ```
   ( ( SP RENAME S# AS X ) WHERE X = S# ) { P# }
   ```

   yields the set of part numbers for parts supplied by that supplier.

2. That set of part numbers is then compared with the set of all currently known part numbers.

3. If and only if the two sets are equal, the corresponding supplier tuple appears in the result.

   Here by contrast is the DIVIDEBY version, now spelled out in detail:

   ```
   S JOIN ( S { S# } DIVIDEBY P { P# } PER SP { S#, P# } )
   ```

You might well feel that the relational comparison version is conceptually easier to deal with. In fact, there is some doubt as to whether DIVIDEBY would ever have been defined if the relational model had included relational comparisons in the first place—but it did not.

7.5 EXAMPLES

In this section we present a few examples of the use of relational algebra expressions in formulating queries. We recommend that you check these examples against the sample data of Fig. 3.8 (see the inside back cover).

7.5.1 Get supplier names for suppliers who supply part P2:

```
( ( SP JOIN S ) WHERE P# = P# ('P2') ) { SNAME }
```

Explanation: First the join of relations SP and S over supplier numbers is constructed, which has the effect, conceptually, of extending each SP tuple with the corresponding supplier information (i.e., the appropriate SNAME, STATUS, and CITY values). That join is then restricted to just those tuples for part P2. Finally, that restriction is projected over SNAME. The final result has just one attribute, called SNAME.

7.5.2 Get supplier names for suppliers who supply at least one red part:

```
( ( ( P WHERE COLOR = COLOR ('Red') )
                    JOIN SP ) { S# } JOIN S ) { SNAME }
```

The sole attribute of the result is SNAME again.

Here by the way is a different formulation of the same query:

```
( ( ( P WHERE COLOR = COLOR ('Red') ) { P# }
                    JOIN SP ) JOIN S ) { SNAME }
```

This example thus illustrates the important point that there will often be several different ways of formulating any given query. See Chapter 18 for a discussion of some of the implications of this point.

7.5.3 Get supplier names for suppliers who supply all parts:

```
( ( S { S# } DIVIDEBY P { P# } PER SP { S#, P# } )
                                    JOIN S ) { SNAME }
```

Or:

```
( S WHERE
( ( SP RENAME S# AS X ) WHERE X = S# ) { P# } = P { P# } )
{ SNAME }
```

Once again the result has a sole attribute called SNAME.

7.5.4 Get supplier numbers for suppliers who supply at least all those parts supplied by supplier S2:

```
S { S# } DIVIDEBY ( SP WHERE S# = S# ('S2') ) { P# }
                                    PER SP { S#, P# }
```

The result has a sole attribute called S#.

7.5.5 Get all pairs of supplier numbers such that the suppliers concerned are "colocated" (i.e., located in the same city):

```
( ( ( S RENAME S# AS SA ) { SA, CITY } JOIN
    ( S RENAME S# AS SB ) { SB, CITY } )
        WHERE SA < SB ) { SA, SB }
```

The result here has two attributes, called SA and SB (actually it would be sufficient to rename just one of the two S# attributes; we have renamed both for symmetry). We have assumed that the operator "<" has been defined for type S#. The purpose of the restriction condition SA < SB is twofold:

- It eliminates pairs of supplier numbers of the form (x,x).
- It guarantees that the pairs (x,y) and (y,x) will not both appear.

We show another formulation of this query to show how WITH can be used to simplify the business of writing what otherwise might be rather complicated expressions:[3]

```
WITH ( S RENAME S# AS SA ) { SA, CITY } AS T1,
     ( S RENAME S# AS SB ) { SB, CITY } AS T2,
     T1 JOIN T2 AS T3,
     T3 WHERE SA < SB AS T4 :
     T4 { SA, SB }
```

WITH allows us to think about large, complicated expressions in a kind of step-at-a-time fashion, and yet it does not in any way violate the nonprocedurality of the relational algebra. We will expand on this point in the discussion following the next example.

7.5.6 Get supplier names for suppliers who do not supply part P2:

```
( ( S { S# } MINUS ( SP WHERE P# = P# ('P2') ) ) { S# } )
                                            JOIN S ) { SNAME }
```

The result has a sole attribute called SNAME.

As promised, we elaborate on this example in order to illustrate another point. It is not always easy to see immediately how to formulate a given query as a single nested expression. Nor should it be necessary to do so, either. Here is a step-at-a-time formulation of the example:

```
WITH S { S# } AS T1,
     SP WHERE P# = P# ('P2') AS T2,
     T2 { S# } AS T3,
     T1 MINUS T3 AS T4,
     T4 JOIN S AS T5,
     T5 { SNAME } AS T6 :
     T6
```

T6 denotes the desired result. *Explanation:* Names introduced by a WITH clause—that is, names of the form T*i*, in the example—are assumed to be local to the statement containing that clause. Now, if the system supports "lazy evaluation" (as, for example, the PRTV system did [7.9]), then breaking the overall query down into a sequence of steps in this fashion need have *no* undesirable performance implications. Instead, the query can be processed as follows:

---

[3] In fact, we used the *scalar* form of WITH in the definition of operator DIST in Chapter 5, Section 5.5; we also showed the relational form in the expansion of the UPDATE shorthand in Chapter 6, Section 6.5.

- The expressions preceding the colon require no immediate evaluation by the system—all the system has to do is remember them, along with the names introduced by the corresponding AS clauses.

- The expression following the colon denotes the final result of the query (in the example, that expression is just "T6"). When it reaches this point, the system cannot delay evaluation any longer but instead must somehow compute the desired value (i.e., the value of T6).

- In order to evaluate T6, which is the projection of T5 over SNAME, the system must first evaluate T5; in order to evaluate T5, which is the join of T4 and S, the system must first evaluate T4; and so on. In other words, the system effectively has to evaluate the original nested expression, exactly as if the user had written that nested expression in the first place.

See the next section for a brief discussion of the general question of evaluating such nested expressions, and Chapter 18 for an extended treatment of the same topic.

7.6   WHAT IS THE ALGEBRA FOR?

To summarize this chapter so far: We have defined a *relational algebra,* that is, a collection of operations on relations. The operations in question are union, intersect, difference, product, restrict, project, join, and divide, plus an attribute renaming operator, RENAME (this is essentially the set that Codd originally defined in reference [7.1], except for RENAME). We have also presented a syntax for those operations, and used that syntax as a basis for a number of examples and illustrations.

As our discussions have implied, however, Codd's eight operators do not constitute a *minimal* set (nor were they ever meant to), because some of them are not primitive—they can be defined in terms of the others. For example, the operators join, intersect, and divide can be defined in terms of the other five (see Exercise 7.6), and they could therefore be dropped without any loss of functionality. Of the remaining five, however, none can be defined in terms of the other four, so we can regard those five as constituting a **primitive** or minimal set (not necessarily the only one, please note).[4] In practice, however, the other operators (especially join) are so useful that a good case can be made for supporting them directly.

We are now in a position to clarify an important point. Although we never said as much explicitly, the body of the chapter thus far has certainly suggested that the primary purpose of the algebra is merely *data retrieval.* Such is not the case, however. The funda-

---

[4] This sentence requires a certain amount of qualification. First, since we have seen that product is a special case of join, we could replace product by join in the stated set of primitives. Second, we really need to include RENAME, because our algebra (unlike that of reference [7.1]) relies on attribute naming instead of ordinal position. Third, reference [3.3] describes a kind of "reduced instruction set" version of the algebra, called **A**, that allows the entire functionality of Codd's original algebra (as well as RENAME and several other useful operators) to be achieved with just two primitives, called *remove* and *nor.*

mental intent of the algebra is to allow **the writing of relational expressions**. Those expressions in turn are intended to serve a variety of purposes, including retrieval but not limited to retrieval alone. The following list—which is not meant to be exhaustive—indicates some possible applications for such expressions:

- Defining a scope for **retrieval**—that is, defining the data to be fetched in some retrieval operation (as already discussed at length)

- Defining a scope for **update**—that is, defining the data to be inserted, changed, or deleted in some update operation (see Chapter 6)

- Defining **integrity constraints**—that is, defining some constraint that the database must satisfy (see Chapter 9)

- Defining **derived relvars**—that is, defining the data to be included in a view or snapshot (see Chapter 10)

- Defining **stability requirements**—that is, defining the data that is to be the scope of some concurrency control operation (see Chapter 16)

- Defining **security constraints**—that is, defining the data over which authorization of some kind is to be granted (see Chapter 17)

In general, in fact, the expressions serve as *a high-level, symbolic representation of the user's intent* (with regard to some particular query, for example). And precisely because they are high-level and symbolic, they can be subjected to a variety of high-level, symbolic **transformation rules**. For example, the expression

```
( ( SP JOIN S ) WHERE P# = P# ('P2') ) { SNAME }
```

("Get supplier names for suppliers who supply part P2"—Example 7.5.1) can be transformed into the logically equivalent but probably more efficient expression

```
( ( SP WHERE P# = P# ('P2') ) JOIN S ) { SNAME }
```

(*Exercise:* In what sense is the second expression probably more efficient? Why only "probably"?)

The algebra thus serves as a convenient basis for **optimization** (refer back to Chapter 3, Section 3.5, if you need to refresh your memory regarding this notion). Thus, even if the user states the query in the first of the two forms just shown, the optimizer should convert it into the second form before executing it (ideally, the performance of a given query should *not* depend on the particular form in which the user happens to state it). See Chapter 18 for further discussion.

We conclude this section by noting that, precisely because of its fundamental nature, the algebra is often used as a kind of *yardstick* against which the expressive power of some given language can be measured. Basically, a language is said to be **relationally complete** [7.1] if it is at least as powerful as the algebra—that is, if its expressions permit the definition of every relation that can be defined by means of expressions of the algebra (the *original* algebra, that is, as described in previous sections). We will examine this notion of relational completeness in more detail in the next chapter.

7.7   FURTHER POINTS

This section covers a few miscellaneous issues related to the original eight operators.

Associativity and Commutativity

It is easy to verify that UNION is **associative**—that is, if *a, b,* and *c* are arbitrary relations of the same type, then the expressions

        (*a* UNION *b*) UNION *c*

and

        a UNION (*b* UNION *c*)

are logically equivalent. For convenience, therefore, we allow a sequence of UNIONs to be written without any parentheses; as a consequence, each of the foregoing expressions can be unambiguously abbreviated to just

        a UNION *b* UNION *c*

Analogous remarks apply to INTERSECT, TIMES, and JOIN (but not MINUS). *Note:* For such reasons among others, some kind of prefix notation, as in, for example, UNION (*a,b,c*), might be preferable in practice to the infix style used in **Tutorial D**. But we stay with that infix style in this book.

UNION, INTERSECT, TIMES, and JOIN (but not MINUS) are also **commutative**—that is, the expressions

        a UNION *b*

and

        b UNION *a*

are also logically equivalent, and similarly for INTERSECT, TIMES, and JOIN.

We will revisit the whole question of associativity and commutativity in Chapter 18. Regarding TIMES, incidentally, we note that the set theory version of Cartesian product is neither associative nor commutative, but (as we have just seen) the relational version is both.

Some Equivalences

In this subsection we simply list a few important equivalences, with little by way of further comment. In what follows, *r* denotes an arbitrary relation, and *empty* denotes the empty relation of the same type as *r*.

- *r* WHERE TRUE ≡ *r* (an *identity* restriction)
- *r* WHERE FALSE ≡ *empty*
- *r* { X, Y, ..., Z } ≡ *r* if *X, Y, ..., Z* are all of the attributes of *r* (an *identity* projection)

- r { } ≡ TABLE_DUM if r = *empty,* TABLE_DEE otherwise (a *nullary* projection)
- r JOIN r ≡ r UNION r ≡ r INTERSECT r ≡ r
- r JOIN TABLE_DEE ≡ TABLE_DEE JOIN r ≡ r
  (i.e., DEE is the *identity* with respect to join, just as zero is the identity with respect to addition, or one is the identity with respect to multiplication, in ordinary arithmetic)
- r TIMES TABLE_DEE ≡ TABLE_DEE TIMES r ≡ r
  (this equivalence is just a special case of the previous one)
- r UNION *empty* ≡ r MINUS *empty* ≡ r
- *empty* INTERSECT r ≡ *empty* MINUS r ≡ *empty*

Some Generalizations

JOIN, UNION, and INTERSECT were all defined originally as *dyadic* operators (i.e., each took exactly two relations as operands);[5] as we have seen, however, they can be unambiguously generalized to become *n*-adic operators for arbitrary $n > 1$. But what about $n = 1$? Or $n = 0$? It turns out to be desirable, at least from a conceptual point of view, to be able to perform "joins," "unions," and "intersections" of (a) just a single relation and (b) no relations at all (even though **Tutorial D** provides no direct syntactic support for any such operations). Here are the definitions. Let s be a set of relations (all of the same relation type RT in the case of union and intersection). Then:

- If s contains just one relation r, then the join, union, and intersection of all relations in s are all defined to be simply r.
- If s contains no relations at all, then:
  - The join of all relations in s is defined to be TABLE_DEE (the identity with respect to join).
  - The union of all relations in s is defined to be the empty relation of type RT.
  - The intersection of all relations in s is defined to be the "universal" relation of type RT—that is, that unique relation of type RT that contains all possible tuples with heading H, where H is the heading of relation type RT.[6]

7.8 ADDITIONAL OPERATORS

Numerous writers have proposed new algebraic operators since Codd defined his original eight. In this section we examine a few such operators—SEMIJOIN, SEMIMINUS, EXTEND, SUMMARIZE, and TCLOSE—in some detail. In terms of our **Tutorial D** syntax, these operators involve five new forms of *<nonproject>*, with specifics as follows:

---

[5] MINUS is dyadic, too. By contrast, restrict and project are *monadic* operators.

[6] We note in passing that the term *universal relation* is usually used in the literature with a very different meaning. See, for example, reference [13.20].

```
<semijoin>
    ::=    <relation exp> SEMIJOIN <relation exp>

<semiminus>
    ::=    <relation exp> SEMIMINUS <relation exp>

<extend>
    ::=    EXTEND <relation exp> ADD ( <extend add commalist> )
```

The parentheses can be omitted if the commalist contains just one *<extend add>*.

```
<extend add>
    ::=    <exp> AS <attribute name>

<summarize>
    ::=    SUMMARIZE <relation exp> PER <relation exp>
               ADD ( <summarize add commalist> )
```

The parentheses can be omitted if the commalist contains just one *<summarize add>*.

```
<summarize add>
    ::=    <summary type> [ ( <scalar exp> ) ]
                       AS <attribute name>

<summary type>
    ::=    COUNT  | SUM  | AVG  | MAX | MIN | ALL | ANY
         | COUNTD | SUMD | AVGD | ...

<tclose>
    ::=    TCLOSE <relation exp>
```

The various *<relation exp>*s mentioned in the foregoing BNF production rules must not be *<nonproject>*s.

Semijoin

Let *a, b, X,* and *Y* be as defined in the subsection "Join" in Section 7.4. Then the **semijoin** of *a* with *b* (in that order), *a* SEMIJOIN *b,* is defined to be equivalent to:

```
( a JOIN b ) { X, Y }
```

In other words, the semijoin of *a* with *b* is the join of *a* and *b,* projected over the attributes of *a.* The body of the result is thus, loosely, the tuples of *a* that have a counterpart in *b.*
  Example: Get S#, SNAME, STATUS, and CITY for suppliers who supply part P2:

```
S SEMIJOIN ( SP WHERE P# = P# ('P2') )
```

We note in passing that many real-world queries that call for the use of join are really semijoin queries in disguise—implying that direct support for SEMIJOIN might be desirable in practice. An analogous remark applies to SEMIMINUS (see the next subsection).

Semidifference

The **semidifference** between *a* and *b* (in that order), *a* SEMIMINUS *b,* is defined to be equivalent to:

```
a MINUS ( a SEMIJOIN b )
```

The body of the result is thus, loosely, the tuples of *a* that have no counterpart in *b*.

   Example: Get S#, SNAME, STATUS, and CITY for suppliers who do not supply part P2:

```
S SEMIMINUS ( SP WHERE P# = P# ('P2') )
```

Extend

You might have noticed that the algebra as we have described it so far has no computational capabilities, as that term is conventionally understood. In practice, however, such capabilities are obviously desirable. For example, we would like to be able to retrieve the value of an arithmetic expression such as WEIGHT * 454, or to refer to such a value in a WHERE clause (we are assuming here—the discussion of units in Section 5.4 notwithstanding—that part weights are given in pounds and 1 pound = 454 grams[7]). The purpose of the **extend** operation is to support such capabilities. More precisely, EXTEND takes a relation and returns another that is identical to the given one except that it includes an additional attribute, values of which are obtained by evaluating some specified computational expression. For example, we might write:

```
EXTEND P ADD ( WEIGHT * 454 ) AS GMWT
```

This expression—please note that it *is* an expression, not a command or statement, and hence can be nested inside other expressions—yields a relation with the same heading as P, except that it includes an additional attribute called GMWT. Each tuple of that relation is the same as the corresponding tuple of P, except that it additionally includes a GMWT value, computed in accordance with the specified arithmetic expression WEIGHT * 454. See Fig. 7.9.

   Important: Please note that this EXTEND expression has *not* changed the parts relvar in the database; it is just an expression, and like any other expression it simply denotes a certain value—a value that, in this particular case, happens to look rather like the current value of the parts relvar. (In other words, EXTEND is *not* a relational algebra analog of SQL's ALTER TABLE ... ADD COLUMN.)

P#	PNAME	COLOR	WEIGHT	CITY	GMWT
P1	Nut	Red	12.0	London	5448.0
P2	Bolt	Green	17.0	Paris	7718.0
P3	Screw	Blue	17.0	Oslo	7718.0
P4	Screw	Red	14.0	London	6356.0
P5	Cam	Blue	12.0	Paris	5448.0
P6	Cog	Red	19.0	London	8626.0

Fig. 7.9   An example of EXTEND

---

[7] We are also assuming that "*" is a legal operation between weights and integers. What is the type of the result of such an operation?

Now we can use attribute GMWT in projections, restrictions, and so on. For example:

```
( ( EXTEND P ADD ( WEIGHT * 454 ) AS GMWT )
        WHERE GMWT > WEIGHT ( 10000.0 ) ) { ALL BUT GMWT }
```

Note: Of course, a more user-friendly language would allow the computational expression to appear directly in the WHERE clause, as here:

```
P WHERE ( WEIGHT * 454 ) > WEIGHT ( 10000.0 )
```

(see the discussion of restrict in Section 7.4). However, such a feature is really just syntactic sugar.

In general, then, the value of the **extension**

```
EXTEND a ADD exp AS Z
```

is a relation defined as follows:

- The heading of the result consists of the heading of *a* extended with the attribute *Z*.
- The body of the result consists of all tuples *t* such that *t* is a tuple of *a* extended with a value for attribute *Z*, computed by evaluating *exp* on that tuple of *a*.

Relation *a* must not have an attribute called *Z*, and *exp* must not refer to *Z*. Observe that the result has cardinality equal to that of *a* and degree equal to that of *a* plus one. The type of *Z* in that result is the type of *exp*.

Here are some more examples:

1. `EXTEND S ADD 'Supplier' AS TAG`

   This expression effectively tags each tuple of the current value of relvar S with the character string "Supplier" (a literal—or, more generally, a selector invocation—is a legal computational expression, of course).

2. `EXTEND ( P JOIN SP ) ADD ( WEIGHT * QTY ) AS SHIPWT`

   This example illustrates the application of EXTEND to the result of a relational expression that is more complicated than just a simple relvar name.

3. `( EXTEND S ADD CITY AS SCITY ) { ALL BUT CITY }`

   An attribute name such as CITY is also a legal computational expression. Observe that this particular example is equivalent to:

   `S RENAME CITY AS SCITY`

   In other words, RENAME is not primitive!—it can be defined in terms of EXTEND (and project). We would not want to discard our useful RENAME operator, of course, but it is at least interesting to note that it is really just shorthand.

4. `EXTEND P ADD ( WEIGHT * 454 AS GMWT, WEIGHT * 16 AS OZWT )`

   This example illustrates a "multiple EXTEND."

5. ```
   EXTEND S
   ADD COUNT ( ( SP RENAME S# AS X ) WHERE X = S# )
   AS NP
   ```

   The result of this expression is shown in Fig. 7.10. *Explanation:*
   ```

S#	SNAME	STATUS	CITY	NP
S1	Smith	20	London	6
S2	Jones	10	Paris	2
S3	Blake	30	Paris	1
S4	Clark	20	London	3
S5	Adams	30	Athens	0

Fig. 7.10   Another EXTEND example

a. For a given supplier, the expression

```
( ( SP RENAME S# AS X ) WHERE X = S# )
```

yields the set of shipments for that supplier.

b. The *aggregate operator* COUNT is then applied to that set of shipments and returns the corresponding cardinality (a scalar value).

Attribute NP in the result thus represents the number of parts supplied by the supplier identified by the corresponding S# value. Notice the NP value for supplier S5 in particular; the set of shipments for supplier S5 is empty, and so the COUNT invocation returns zero.

We elaborate briefly on this question of **aggregate operators**. The purpose of such an operator, in general, is to derive a single scalar value from the values appearing in some specified attribute of some specified relation (usually a *derived* relation). Typical examples are COUNT, SUM, AVG, MAX, MIN, ALL, and ANY. In **Tutorial D**, an aggregate operator invocation, *<agg op inv>*—which, since it returns a scalar value, is a special kind of *<scalar exp>*—takes the general form:

```
<agg op name> ( <relation exp> [, <attribute name> ] )
```

If the *<agg op name>* is COUNT, the *<attribute name>* is irrelevant and must be omitted; otherwise, it can be omitted if and only if the *<relation exp>* denotes a relation of degree one, in which case the sole attribute of the result of that *<relation exp>* is assumed by default. Here are a couple of examples:

```
SUM ( SP WHERE S# = S# ('S1'), QTY )

SUM ( ( SP WHERE S# = S# ('S1') ) { QTY } )
```

Note the difference between these two expressions—the first gives the total of all shipment quantities for supplier S1, the second gives the total of all *distinct* shipment quantities for supplier S1.

If the argument to an aggregate operator happens to be an empty set, COUNT (as we have seen) returns zero, and so does SUM; MAX and MIN return, respectively, the lowest and the highest value of the applicable type; ALL and ANY return TRUE and FALSE, respectively; and AVG raises an exception.

Summarize

We should begin this subsection by saying that the version of SUMMARIZE discussed here is not the same as that discussed in earlier editions of this book—in fact, it is an improved version that overcomes certain difficulties that arose with the earlier version in connection with empty relations.

As we have seen, the *extend* operator provides a way of incorporating "horizontal" or "tuple-wise" computations into the relational algebra. The **summarize** operator performs the analogous function for "vertical" or "attribute-wise" computations. For example, the expression

```
SUMMARIZE SP PER P { P# } ADD SUM ( QTY ) AS TOTQTY
```

evaluates to a relation with attributes P# and TOTQTY, in which there is one tuple for each P# value in the projection of P over P#, containing that P# value and the corresponding total quantity (see Fig. 7.11). In other words, relation SP is conceptually partitioned into groups or sets of tuples (one such group for each part number in P), and then each such group is used to generate one tuple in the overall result.

In general, the value of the **summarization**

```
SUMMARIZE a PER b ADD summary AS Z
```

is a relation defined as follows:

- First, *b* must be of the same type as some projection of *a* (i.e., every attribute of *b* must be an attribute of *a*). Let the attributes of that projection (equivalently, of *b*) be *A1, A2, ..., An*.

- The heading of the result consists of the heading of *b* extended with the attribute *Z*.

- The body of the result consists of all tuples *t* such that *t* is a tuple of *b* extended with a value for attribute *Z*. That *Z* value is computed by evaluating *summary* over all tuples of *a* that have the same values for attributes { *A1, A2, ..., An* } as tuple *t* does. (Of course, if no tuples of *a* have the same value for { *A1, A2, ..., An* } as tuple *t* does, then *summary* is evaluated over an empty set.)

Relation *b* must not have an attribute called *Z*, and *summary* must not refer to *Z*. Observe that the result has cardinality equal to that of *b* and degree equal to that of *b* plus one. The type of *Z* in that result is the type of *summary*.

P#	TOTQTY
P1	600
P2	1000
P3	400
P4	500
P5	500
P6	100

Fig. 7.11   An example of SUMMARIZE

Here is another example:

```
SUMMARIZE ( P JOIN SP ) PER P { CITY } ADD COUNT AS NSP
```

The result looks like this:

CITY	NSP
London	5
Oslo	1
Paris	6

In other words, the result contains one tuple for each of the three part cities (London, Oslo, and Paris), showing in each case the number of shipments of parts stored in that city.

Points arising:

1. Observe yet again that here we have an operator whose definition relies on the notion of tuple equality.

2. Our syntax allows "multiple SUMMARIZEs"—for example:

```
SUMMARIZE SP PER P { P# } ADD ( SUM ( QTY ) AS TOTQTY,
                                AVG ( QTY ) AS AVGQTY )
```

3. The general form of *<summarize>* (to repeat) is as follows:

```
SUMMARIZE <relation exp> PER <relation exp>
                         ADD ( <summarize add commalist> )
```

Each *<summarize add>* in turn takes the form:

```
<summary type> [ ( <scalar exp> ) ] AS <attribute name>
```

Typical *<summary type>*s are COUNT, SUM, AVG, MAX, MIN, ALL, ANY, COUNTD, SUMD, and AVGD. The "D" ("distinct") in COUNTD, SUMD, and AVGD means "eliminate redundant duplicate values before performing the summary." The *<scalar exp>* can include references to attributes of the relation denoted by the *<relation exp>* immediately following the keyword SUMMARIZE. The *<scalar exp>* and enclosing parentheses can and must be omitted only if the *<summary type>* is COUNT.

Incidentally, please note that a *<summarize add>* is *not* the same thing as an aggregate operator invocation. An *<agg op inv>* is a scalar expression and can appear wherever a literal of the appropriate type can appear. A *<summarize add>,* by contrast, is merely a SUMMARIZE operand; it is *not* a scalar expression, it has no meaning outside the context of SUMMARIZE, and in fact it cannot appear outside that context.

4. As you might have already realized, SUMMARIZE is not a primitive operator—it can be simulated by means of EXTEND. For example, the expression

```
SUMMARIZE SP PER S { S# } ADD COUNT AS NP
```

is defined to be shorthand for the following:

```
( EXTEND S { S# }
         ADD ( ( ( SP RENAME S# AS X ) WHERE X = S# ) AS Y,
               COUNT ( Y ) AS NP ) )
  { S#, NP }
```

Or equivalently:

```
WITH ( S { S# } ) AS T1,
     ( SP RENAME S# AS X ) AS T2,
     ( EXTEND T1 ADD ( T2 WHERE X = S# ) AS Y ) AS T3,
     ( EXTEND T3 ADD COUNT ( Y ) AS NP ) AS T4 :
T4 { S#, NP }
```

By the way, attribute Y here is relation-valued. Refer to Section 6.4 if you need to refresh your memory regarding such a possibility.

5. Here is another example:

```
SUMMARIZE S PER S { CITY } ADD AVG ( STATUS ) AS AVG_STATUS
```

Here the PER relation is not just "of the same type as" some projection of the relation to be summarized, it actually *is* such a projection. In such a case, we allow the following shorthand:

```
SUMMARIZE S BY { CITY } ADD AVG ( STATUS ) AS AVG_STATUS
```

(We have replaced PER *<relation exp>* by BY *<attribute name commalist>*. The attributes named must all be attributes of the relation being summarized.)

6. Consider the following example:

```
SUMMARIZE SP PER SP { } ADD SUM ( QTY ) AS GRANDTOTAL
```

In accordance with the previous point, we can alternatively write this expression thus:

```
SUMMARIZE SP BY { } ADD SUM ( QTY ) AS GRANDTOTAL
```

Either way, the grouping and summarization here are being done on the basis of a relation that has no attributes at all. Let *sp* be the current value of relvar SP, and assume for the moment that relation *sp* does contain at least one tuple. Then all of those *sp* tuples have the same value for no attributes at all (namely, the 0-tuple); hence there is just one group, and so just one tuple in the overall result (in other words, the aggregate computation is performed precisely once for the entire relation *sp*). The expression thus evaluates to a relation with one attribute and one tuple; the attribute is called GRANDTOTAL, and the single scalar value in the single result tuple is the total of all QTY values in the original relation *sp*.

If on the other hand the original relation *sp* has no tuples at all, then there are no groups, and hence no result tuples (i.e., the result relation is empty too). By contrast, the following expression—

```
SUMMARIZE SP PER TABLE_DEE ADD SUM ( QTY ) AS GRANDTOTAL
```

—will "work" (i.e., it will return the correct result, zero) even if *sp* is empty. More precisely, it will return a relation with one attribute, called GRANDTOTAL, and one tuple, containing the value zero. We therefore suggest that it should be possible to omit the PER clause entirely, as here:

```
SUMMARIZE SP ADD SUM ( QTY ) AS GRANDTOTAL
```

Omitting the PER clause is defined to be equivalent to specifying PER TABLE_DEE.

Tclose

"Tclose" stands for *transitive closure*. We mention it here mainly for completeness; detailed discussion is beyond the scope of this chapter. However, we do at least define the operation, as follows. Let *a* be a binary relation with attributes *X* and *Y*, both of the same type *T*. Then the **transitive closure** of *a*, TCLOSE *a*, is a relation a^+ with heading the same as that of *a* and body a superset of that of *a*, defined as follows: The tuple

```
{ X x, Y y }
```

appears in a^+ if and only if it appears in *a* or there exists a sequence of values *z1, z2, ..., zn,* all of type *T*, such that the tuples

```
{ X x, Y z1 }, { X z1, Y z2 }, ..., { X zn, Y y }
```

all appear in *a*. (In other words, if we think of relation *a* as representing a *graph*, then the "(*x,y*)" tuple appears in a^+ only if there is a path in that graph from node *x* to node *y*. Note that the body of a^+ necessarily includes the body of *a* as a subset.)

For further discussion of transitive closure, see Chapter 24.

7.9 GROUPING AND UNGROUPING

The fact that we can have relations with attributes whose values are relations in turn leads to the need for operators, here called *group* and *ungroup*, for mapping between relations that contain such attributes and relations that do not. For example:

```
SP GROUP { P#, QTY } AS PQ
```

Given our usual sample data, this expression yields the result shown in Fig. 7.12. *Note:* You will probably find it helpful to use that figure to check the explanations that follow, since they are (regrettably, but unavoidably) a little abstract.

We begin by observing that the original expression

```
SP GROUP { P#, QTY } AS PQ
```

might be read as "group SP *by* S#," S# being the sole attribute of SP not mentioned in the GROUP specification. The result is a relation defined as follows. First, the heading looks like this:

```
{ S# S#, PQ RELATION { P# P#, QTY QTY } }
```

In other words, it consists of a relation-valued attribute PQ (where PQ values in turn have attributes P# and QTY), together with all of the other attributes of SP (of course, "all of the other attributes of SP" here just means attribute S#). Second, the body contains exactly one tuple for each distinct S# value in SP (and no other tuples). Each tuple in that body consists of the applicable S# value (*s*, say), together with a PQ value (*pq*, say) obtained as follows:

- Each SP tuple is replaced by a tuple (*x*, say) in which the P# and QTY components have been "wrapped" into a tuple-valued component (*y*, say).

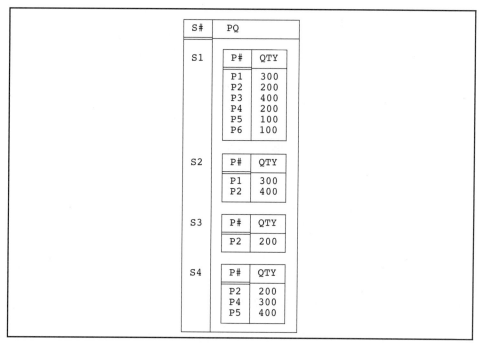

Fig. 7.12   Grouping SP by S#

- The *y* components of all such tuples *x* in which the S# value is equal to *s* are "grouped" into a relation, *pq,* and a result tuple with S# value equal to *s* and PQ value equal to *pq* is thereby obtained.

The overall result is thus indeed as shown in Fig. 7.12. Note in particular that the result includes no tuple for supplier S5 (because relvar SP does not currently do so either).

Observe that the result of *R* GROUP { *A1, A2, ..., An* } AS *B* has degree equal to *nR–n*+1, where *nR* is the degree of *R*.

Now we turn to *ungroup.* Let SPQ be the relation shown in Fig. 7.12. Then the expression

```
SPQ UNGROUP PQ
```

(perhaps unsurprisingly) gives us back our usual sample SP relation. To be more specific, it yields a relation defined as follows. First, the heading looks like this:

```
{ S# S#, P# P#, QTY QTY }
```

In other words, the heading consists of attributes P# and QTY (derived from attribute PQ), together with all of the other attributes of SPQ (i.e., just attribute S#, in the example). Second, the body contains exactly one tuple for each combination of a tuple in SPQ and a tuple in the PQ value within that SPQ tuple (and no other tuples). Each tuple in that body consists of the applicable S# value (*s,* say), together with P# and QTY values (*p* and *q,* say) obtained as follows:

- Each SPQ tuple is replaced by an "ungrouped" set of tuples, one such tuple (*x*, say) for each tuple in the PQ value in that SPQ tuple.

- Each such tuple *x* contains an S# component (*s*, say) equal to the S# component from the SPQ tuple in question and a tuple-valued component (*y*, say) equal to some tuple from the PQ component from the SPQ tuple in question.

- The *y* components of each such tuple *x* in which the S# value is equal to *s* are "unwrapped" into separate P# and QTY components (*p* and *q*, say), and a result tuple with S# value equal to *s*, P# value equal to *p*, and QTY value equal to *q* is thereby obtained.

The overall result is thus, as claimed, our usual sample SP relation.

Observe that the result of *R* UNGROUP *B* (where the relations that are values of the relation-valued attribute *B* have heading { *A1, A2, ..., An* }) has degree equal to *nR+n*−1, where *nR* is the degree of *R*.

As you can see, GROUP and UNGROUP together provide what are more usually referred to as relational "nest" and "unnest" capabilities. We prefer our group/ungroup terminology, however, because the nest/unnest terminology is strongly associated with the concept of NF^2 relations [6.10], a concept we do not endorse.

For completeness, we close this section with some remarks concerning reversibility of the GROUP and UNGROUP operations (though we realize the remarks in question might not be fully comprehensible on a first reading). If we group some relation *r* in some way, there is always an inverse ungrouping that will take us back to *r* again. However, if we *un*group some relation *r* in some way, an inverse grouping to take us back to *r* again might or might not exist. Here is an example (based on one given in reference [6.4]). Suppose we start with relation TWO (see Fig. 7.13) and ungroup it to obtain THREE. If we now group THREE by A (and name the resulting relation-valued attribute RVX once again), we obtain not TWO but ONE.

If we now ungroup ONE, we return to THREE, and we have already seen that THREE can be grouped to give ONE; thus, the group and ungroup operations are indeed inverses of each other for this particular pair of relations. Note that, in ONE, RVX is

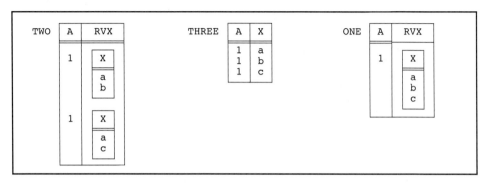

Fig. 7.13 Ungrouping and (re)grouping are not necessarily reversible

functionally dependent on A[8] (necessarily so, since ONE is of cardinality one). In general, in fact, we can say that if relation *r* has a relation-valued attribute *RVX,* then *r* is reversibly ungroupable with respect to *RVX* if and only if the following are both true:

- No tuple of *r* has an empty relation as its *RVX* value.
- *RVX* is functionally dependent on the combination of all other attributes of *r.*

7.10 SUMMARY

We have discussed the **relational algebra**. We began by reemphasizing the importance of **closure** and **nested relational expressions**, and explained that if we are going to take closure seriously, then we need some **relation type inference rules**. Such considerations led us to introduce the **RENAME** operator.

The original algebra consisted of eight operators—the traditional set operators **union**, **intersect**, **difference**, and **product** (all of them modified somewhat to take account of the fact that their operands are very specifically relations, not arbitrary sets), and the special relational operators **restrict**, **project**, **join**, and **divide**. (In the case of divide, however, we remarked that queries involving divide can always be formulated in terms of *relational comparisons* instead, and many people find such formulations intuitively easier to understand.) To that original set we added **RENAME** (as already mentioned), **SEMIJOIN**, **SEMIMINUS**, **EXTEND**, and **SUMMARIZE**, and we also mentioned **TCLOSE** and discussed **GROUP** and **UNGROUP**. EXTEND in particular is extremely important (in some ways it is as important as join).

Next, we pointed out that the algebraic operators are **not all primitive** (i.e., many of them can be defined in terms of others)—a most satisfactory state of affairs, in our opinion. As reference [7.3] puts it: "A language definition should start with a few judiciously chosen primitive operators . . . Subsequent development is, where possible, by defining new operators in terms of . . . previously defined [ones]"—in other words, by defining useful **shorthands**. If the shorthands in question are well chosen, then not only do they save us a great deal of writing, they also effectively **raise the level of abstraction**, by allowing us to talk in terms of certain "bundles" of concepts that fit together naturally. (They also pave the way for more efficient implementation.) In this connection, we remind you that, as noted in Section 7.6, reference [3.3] describes a kind of "reduced instruction set" algebra called **A** that is specifically intended to support the systematic definition of more powerful operators in terms of a very small number of primitives; in fact, it shows that the entire functionality of the original algebra, together with RENAME, EXTEND, SUMMARIZE, GROUP, and UNGROUP, can all be achieved with just two primitives called *remove* and *nor*.

Back to our summary. We went on to show how the algebraic operators can be combined into expressions that serve a variety of purposes: **retrieval**, **update**, and several others. We also very briefly discussed the idea of **transforming** such expressions for **optimization** purposes (but we will examine this idea in much more detail in Chapter 18).

---

[8] See Chapter 11, and note in particular that we are appealing here to that form of functional dependence that applies to relation values (as opposed to the more usual form, which applies to relation variables).

And we explained how the use of **WITH** could simplify the formulation of complex expressions; WITH effectively allows us to introduce names for subexpressions, thereby allowing us to formulate those complex expressions one step at a time, and yet does not compromise the algebra's fundamental nonprocedurality.

We also pointed out that certain of the operators were **associative** and **commutative**, and we showed certain **equivalences** (e.g., we showed that any relation *R* is equivalent to a certain restriction of *R* and a certain projection of *R*). We also considered what it means to perform joins, unions, and intersections on just one relation and on no relations at all.

EXERCISES

7.1 Which of the relational operators defined in this chapter have a definition that does not rely on tuple equality?

7.2 Given the usual suppliers-and-parts database, what is the value of the expression S JOIN SP JOIN P? What is the corresponding predicate? *Warning:* There is a trap here.

7.3 Let *r* be a relation of degree *n*. How many different projections of *r* are there?

7.4 Union, intersection, product, and natural join are all both commutative and associative. Verify these claims.

7.5 Consider the expression *a* JOIN *b*. If *a* and *b* have disjoint headings, this expression is equivalent to *a* TIMES *b;* if they have the same heading, it is equivalent to *a* INTERSECT *b*. Verify these claims. What is the expression equivalent to if the heading of *a* is a proper subset of that of *b?*

7.6 Of Codd's original set of eight operators, union, difference, product, restrict, and project can be considered as primitives. Give definitions of natural join, intersect, and (harder!) divide in terms of those primitives.

7.7 In ordinary arithmetic, multiplication and division are inverse operations. Are TIMES and DIVIDEBY inverse operations in the relational algebra?

7.8 In ordinary arithmetic there are two special numbers, 1 and 0, with the properties that

```
n * 1  =  1 * n  =  n
```

and

```
n * 0  =  0 * n  =  0
```

for all numbers *n*. What relations (if any) play analogous roles in the relational algebra? Investigate the effect of the algebraic operations discussed in this chapter on those relations.

7.9 In Section 7.2, we said the relational closure property was important for the same kind of reason that the arithmetic closure property was important. In arithmetic, however, there is one unpleasant situation where the closure property breaks down—namely, division by zero. Is there any analogous situation in the relational algebra?

7.10 Given that intersect is a special case of join, why do not both operators give the same result when applied to no relations at all?

7.11 Which (if any) of the following expressions are equivalent?

a. SUMMARIZE *r* PER *r* { } ADD COUNT AS CT

b. SUMMARIZE *r* ADD COUNT AS CT

c. SUMMARIZE *r* BY { } ADD COUNT AS CT

    d. `EXTEND TABLE_DEE ADD COUNT ( r ) AS CT`

7.12 Let *r* be the relation denoted by the following expression:

    `SP GROUP { } AS X`

Show what *r* looks like, given our usual sample value for SP. Also, show the result of:

    `r UNGROUP X`

Query Exercises

The remaining exercises are all based on the suppliers-parts-projects database. In each case you are asked to write a relational algebra expression for the indicated query. (By way of an interesting variation, you might like to try looking at some of the online answers first and stating what the given expression means in natural language.) For convenience, we repeat the structure of the database in outline here:

```
S     { S#, SNAME, STATUS, CITY }
      PRIMARY KEY { S# }
P     { P#, PNAME, COLOR, WEIGHT, CITY }
      PRIMARY KEY { P# }
J     { J#, JNAME, CITY }
      PRIMARY KEY { J# }
SPJ   { S#, P#, J#, QTY }
      PRIMARY KEY { S#, P#, J# }
      FOREIGN KEY { S# } REFERENCES S
      FOREIGN KEY { P# } REFERENCES P
      FOREIGN KEY { J# } REFERENCES J
```

7.13 Get full details of all projects.

7.14 Get full details of all projects in London.

7.15 Get supplier numbers for suppliers who supply project J1.

7.16 Get all shipments where the quantity is in the range 300 to 750 inclusive.

7.17 Get all part-color/part-city pairs. *Note:* Here and subsequently, the term "all" means "all currently represented in the database," not "all possible."

7.18 Get all supplier-number/part-number/project-number triples such that the indicated supplier, part, and project are all colocated (i.e., all in the same city).

7.19 Get all supplier-number/part-number/project-number triples such that the indicated supplier, part, and project are not all colocated.

7.20 Get all supplier-number/part-number/project-number triples such that no two of the indicated supplier, part, and project are colocated.

7.21 Get full details for parts supplied by a supplier in London.

7.22 Get part numbers for parts supplied by a supplier in London to a project in London.

7.23 Get all pairs of city names such that a supplier in the first city supplies a project in the second city.

7.24 Get part numbers for parts supplied to any project by a supplier in the same city as that project.

7.25 Get project numbers for projects supplied by at least one supplier not in the same city.

7.26 Get all pairs of part numbers such that some supplier supplies both the indicated parts.

7.27 Get the total number of projects supplied by supplier S1.

7.28 Get the total quantity of part P1 supplied by supplier S1.

7.29 For each part being supplied to a project, get the part number, the project number, and the corresponding total quantity.

7.30 Get part numbers of parts supplied to some project in an average quantity of more than 350.

7.31 Get project names for projects supplied by supplier S1.

7.32 Get colors of parts supplied by supplier S1.

7.33 Get part numbers for parts supplied to any project in London.

7.34 Get project numbers for projects using at least one part available from supplier S1.

7.35 Get supplier numbers for suppliers supplying at least one part supplied by at least one supplier who supplies at least one red part.

7.36 Get supplier numbers for suppliers with a status lower than that of supplier S1.

7.37 Get project numbers for projects whose city is first in the alphabetic list of such cities.

7.38 Get project numbers for projects supplied with part P1 in an average quantity greater than the greatest quantity in which any part is supplied to project J1.

7.39 Get supplier numbers for suppliers supplying some project with part P1 in a quantity greater than the average shipment quantity of part P1 for that project.

7.40 Get project numbers for projects not supplied with any red part by any London supplier.

7.41 Get project numbers for projects supplied entirely by supplier S1.

7.42 Get part numbers for parts supplied to all projects in London.

7.43 Get supplier numbers for suppliers who supply the same part to all projects.

7.44 Get project numbers for projects supplied with at least all parts available from supplier S1.

7.45 Get all cities in which at least one supplier, part, or project is located.

7.46 Get part numbers for parts that are supplied either by a London supplier or to a London project.

7.47 Get supplier-number/part-number pairs such that the indicated supplier does not supply the indicated part.

7.48 Get all pairs of supplier numbers, S*x* and S*y* say, such that S*x* and S*y* supply exactly the same set of parts each. *Note:* For simplicity, you might want to use the original suppliers-and-parts database for this exercise, instead of the expanded suppliers-parts-projects database.

7.49 Get a "grouped" version of all shipments showing, for each supplier-number/part-number pair, the corresponding project numbers and quantities in the form of a binary relation.

7.50 Get an "ungrouped" version of the relation produced in Exercise 7.49.

REFERENCES AND BIBLIOGRAPHY

7.1 E. F. Codd: "Relational Completeness of Data Base Sublanguages," in Randall J. Rustin (ed.), *Data Base Systems, Courant Computer Science Symposia Series 6.* Englewood Cliffs, N.J.: Prentice-Hall (1972).

This is the paper in which Codd first *formally* defined the original algebraic operators (definitions did appear in reference [6.1] also, but they were somewhat less formal, or at least less complete). *Note:* One slightly unfortunate aspect of the paper is that it assumes "for notational and expository convenience" that the attributes of a relation have a left-to-right ordering and hence can be identified by their ordinal position (though Codd does say that "names rather than position numbers [should] be used . . . when actually storing or retrieving information"—and he had previously said much the same thing in reference [6.1]). The paper therefore does not mention an attribute RENAME operator, and it does not consider the question of result type inference. Possibly as a consequence of these omissions, the same criticisms can still be leveled today (a) at many discussions of the algebra in the literature, (b) at today's SQL products, and (c) to a slightly lesser extent, at the SQL standard as well.

Additional commentary on this paper appears in Chapter 8, especially in Section 8.4.

7.2 Hugh Darwen (writing as Andrew Warden): "Adventures in Relationland," in C. J. Date, *Relational Database Writings 1985–1989.* Reading, Mass.: Addison-Wesley (1990).

A series of short papers that examine various aspects of the relational model and relational DBMSs in an original, entertaining, and informative style.

7.3 Hugh Darwen: "Valid Time and Transaction Time Proposals: Language Design Aspects," in Opher Etzion, Sushil Jajodia, and Suryanaryan Sripada (eds.), *Temporal Databases: Research and Practice.* New York, N.Y.: Springer-Verlag (1998).

7.4 Hugh Darwen and C. J. Date: "Into the Great Divide," in C. J. Date and Hugh Darwen, *Relational Database Writings 1989–1991.* Reading, Mass.: Addison-Wesley (1992).

This paper analyzes both (a) Codd's original divide as defined in reference [7.1] and (b) a generalization of that operator due to Hall, Hitchcock, and Todd [7.10] that—unlike Codd's original divide—allowed any relation to be divided by any relation (Codd's original divide was defined only for the case where the heading of the divisor was a subset of the heading of the dividend). The paper shows that both operators get into difficulties over empty relations, with the result that neither of them quite solves the problem it was originally intended for (i.e., neither of them is quite the counterpart of the universal quantifier it was meant to be). Revised versions of both operators (the "Small Divide" and the "Great Divide," respectively) are proposed to overcome these problems. *Note:* As the **Tutorial D** syntax for these two operators indicates, they really are two different operators; that is, the Great Divide is (unfortunately) not quite an upward-compatible extension of the Small Divide. The paper also suggests that the revised operators no longer merit the name "divide"! In connection with this last point, see Exercise 7.7.

For purposes of reference, we give here a definition of Codd's original divide. Let relations A and B have headings $\{X,Y\}$ and $\{Y\}$, respectively (where X and Y can be composite). Then the expression A DIVIDEBY B gives a relation with heading $\{X\}$ and body consisting of all tuples $\{X\,x\}$ such that a tuple $\{X\,x,Y\,y\}$ appears in A for *all* tuples $\{Y\,y\}$ appearing in B. In other words, loosely speaking, the result consists of those X values from A whose corresponding Y values (in A) include *all* Y values from B.

7.5 C. J. Date: "Quota Queries" (in three parts), in C. J. Date, Hugh Darwen, and David McGoveran, *Relational Database Writings 1994–1997.* Reading, Mass.: Addison-Wesley (1998).

A *quota query* is a query that specifies a desired limit on the cardinality of the result—for example, the query "Get the three heaviest parts." This paper discusses one approach to formulating such queries. Using that approach, "Get the three heaviest parts" can be formulated thus:

```
P QUOTA ( 3, DESC WEIGHT )
```

This expression is defined to be shorthand for the following:

```
( ( EXTEND P
    ADD COUNT ( ( P RENAME WEIGHT AS WT ) WHERE WT > WEIGHT )
    AS #_HEAVIER )
WHERE #_HEAVIER < 3 ) { ALL BUT #_HEAVIER }
```

(where the names WT and #_HEAVIER are arbitrary; given our usual sample data, the result consists of parts P2, P3, and P6). The paper analyzes the quota query requirement in depth and proposes several shorthands for dealing with it and related matters. *Note:* An alternative approach to formulating quota queries, involving a new relational operator called RANK, is described in reference [3.3].

7.6 R. C. Goldstein and A. J. Strnad: "The MacAIMS Data Management System," Proc. 1970 ACM SICFIDET Workshop on Data Description and Access (November 1970).

See the annotation to reference [7.7].

7.7 A. J. Strnad: "The Relational Approach to the Management of Data Bases," Proc. IFIP Congress, Ljubljana, Yugoslavia (August 1971).

We mention MacAIMS [7.6, 7.7] primarily for reasons of historical interest; it seems to have been the earliest example of a system supporting *n*-ary relations and an algebraic language. The interesting thing about it is that it was developed in parallel with, and at least partly independently of, Codd's work on the relational model. Unlike Codd's work, however, the MacAIMS effort seems not to have led to any significant follow-on activities.

7.8 M. G. Notley: "The Peterlee IS/1 System," IBM UK Scientific Centre Report UKSC-0018 (March 1972).

See the annotation to reference [7.9].

7.9 S. J. P. Todd: "The Peterlee Relational Test Vehicle—A System Overview," *IBM Sys. J. 15,* No. 4 (1976).

The Peterlee Relational Test Vehicle PRTV was an experimental system developed at the IBM UK Scientific Centre in Peterlee, England. It was based on an earlier prototype—possibly the very first implementation of Codd's ideas—called IS/1 [7.8]. It supported *n*-ary relations and a version of the algebra called ISBL (Information System Base Language), which was based on proposals documented in reference [7.10]. The ideas discussed in the present chapter regarding relation type inference can be traced back to ISBL, as well as the proposals of reference [7.10]. Significant aspects of PRTV included the following:

- It supported RENAME, EXTEND, and SUMMARIZE.
- It incorporated some sophisticated expression transformation techniques (see Chapter 18).
- It included a *lazy evaluation* feature, which was important both for optimization and for view support (see the discussion of WITH in the body of this chapter).
- It allowed users to define their own operators.

7.10 P. A. V. Hall, P. Hitchcock, and S. J. P. Todd: "An Algebra of Relations for Machine Computation," Conf. Record of the 2nd ACM Symposium on Principles of Programming Languages, Palo Alto, Calif. (January 1975).

7.11 Anthony Klug: "Equivalence of Relational Algebra and Relational Calculus Query Languages Having Aggregate Functions," *JACM 29,* No. 3 (July 1982).

Defines extensions to both the original relational algebra and the original relational calculus (see Chapter 8) to support aggregate operators, and demonstrates the equivalence of the two extended formalisms.

Relational Calculus

8.1 INTRODUCTION

Relational calculus is an alternative to relational algebra. The main difference between the two is as follows: Whereas the algebra provides a set of explicit operators—join, union, project, and so on—that can be used to tell the system how to *construct* some desired relation from certain given relations, the calculus, by contrast, merely provides a notation for stating the *definition* of that desired relation in terms of those given relations. For example, consider the query "Get supplier numbers and cities for suppliers who supply part P2." An algebraic formulation of that query might specify operations as follows (we deliberately do not use the formal syntax of Chapter 7):

1. Join suppliers and shipments over S#.

2. Restrict the result of that join to tuples for part P2.

3. Project the result of that restriction over S# and CITY.

A calculus formulation, by contrast, might state simply:

Get S# and CITY for suppliers such that there exists a shipment SP with the same S# value and with P# value P2.

In this latter formulation, the user has merely stated the defining characteristics of the desired result, and has left it to the system to decide exactly what joins, restrictions, and so on, must be executed, in what sequence, in order to construct that result. Thus, we might say that—at least superficially—the calculus formulation is *descriptive,* while the algebraic one is *prescriptive:* The calculus simply describes what the problem *is,* the algebra prescribes a procedure for *solving* that problem. Or, very informally: The algebra is procedural (admittedly high-level, but still procedural); the calculus is nonprocedural.

However, we stress the point that the foregoing differences *are* only superficial. The fact is, *the algebra and the calculus are logically equivalent:* For every algebraic expression there is an equivalent calculus one, for every calculus expression there is an equivalent algebraic one. There is a one-to-one correspondence between the two. Thus, the differences are really just a matter of *style:* The calculus is arguably closer to natural language, the algebra is perhaps more like a programming language. But, to repeat, such differences are more apparent than real; in particular, neither approach is truly more nonprocedural than the other. We will examine this question of equivalence in detail in Section 8.4.

Relational calculus is based on a branch of mathematical logic called **predicate** calculus. The idea of using predicate calculus as the basis for a query language appears to have originated in a paper by Kuhns [8.6]. The concept of a specifically *relational* calculus—that is, an applied form of predicate calculus specifically tailored to relational databases—was first proposed by Codd in reference [6.1]; a language explicitly based on that calculus called "Data Sublanguage ALPHA" was also presented by Codd in another paper, reference [8.1]. ALPHA itself was never implemented, but a language called QUEL [8.5, 8.10–8.12]—which certainly was implemented and for some time was a serious competitor to SQL—was very similar to it; indeed, QUEL was much influenced by ALPHA.

A fundamental feature of the calculus is the **range variable**. Briefly, a range variable is a variable that "ranges over" some specified relation (i.e., it is a variable whose permitted values are tuples of that relation). Thus, if range variable V ranges over relation r, then, at any given time, the expression "V" denotes some tuple of r. For example, the query "Get supplier numbers for suppliers in London" might be expressed in QUEL as follows:

```
RANGE OF SX IS S ;
RETRIEVE ( SX.S# ) WHERE SX.CITY = "London" ;
```

The sole range variable here is SX, and it ranges over the relation that is the current value of relvar S (the RANGE statement is a *definition* of that range variable). The RETRIEVE statement can thus be paraphrased: "For every possible value of variable SX, retrieve the S# component of that value, if and only if the CITY component of that value is London."

Because of its reliance on range variables whose values are tuples (and to distinguish it from the *domain* calculus—see the next paragraph), the original relational calculus has come to be known as the **tuple** calculus. The tuple calculus is described in detail in Section 8.2. *Note:* For simplicity, we adopt the convention throughout this book that the terms *calculus* and *relational calculus,* without a "tuple" or "domain" qualifier, refer to the tuple calculus specifically (where it makes any difference).

Subsequently, Lacroix and Pirotte [8.7] proposed an alternative version of the calculus called the **domain** calculus, in which the range variables range over domains (i.e., types) instead of relations. (The terminology is illogical: If the domain calculus is so called for the reason just stated—which it is—then the tuple calculus ought by rights to be called the *relation* calculus.) Various domain calculus languages have been proposed in the literature; probably the best known is Query-By-Example, QBE [8.14] (though QBE is really something of a hybrid—it incorporates elements of the tuple calculus as well). Several commercial QBE or "QBE-like" implementations exist. We sketch the domain calculus in Section 8.7, and discuss QBE briefly in Section 8.8.

Note: For space reasons, we omit discussion of calculus analogs of certain topics from Chapter 7 (e.g., grouping and ungrouping). We also omit consideration of calculus versions of the relational update operators. You can find a discussion of such matters in reference [3.3].

8.2 TUPLE CALCULUS

As with our discussions of the algebra in Chapter 7, we first introduce a concrete syntax— patterned after, though deliberately not quite identical to, the calculus version of **Tutorial D** defined in Appendix A of reference [3.3]—and then go on to discuss semantics. The subsection immediately following discusses syntax, the remaining subsections consider semantics.

Syntax

Note: Many of the syntax rules given in prose form in this subsection will not make much sense until you have studied some of the semantic material that comes later. However, we gather them all here for purposes of subsequent reference.

It is convenient to begin by repeating the syntax of *<relation exp>*s from Chapter 7:

```
<relation exp>
    ::=    RELATION { <tuple exp commalist> }
         | <relvar name>
         | <relation op inv>
         | <with exp>
         | <introduced name>
         | ( <relation exp> )
```

In other words, the syntax of *<relation exp>*s is the same as before; however, one of the most important cases, *<relation op inv>,* which is the only one we discuss in this chapter in any detail, now has a very different definition, as we will see.

```
<range var def>
    ::=    RANGEVAR <range var name>
           RANGES OVER <relation exp commalist> ;
```

A *<range var name>* can be used as a *<tuple exp>*,[1] but only in certain contexts—namely:

- Preceding the dot qualifier in a *<range attribute ref>*
- Immediately following the quantifier in a *<quantified bool exp>*
- As an operand within a *<bool exp>*
- As a *<proto tuple>* or as an *<exp>* (or an operand within an *<exp>*) within a *<proto tuple>*

```
<range attribute ref>
    ::=    <range var name> . <attribute name>
                        [ AS <attribute name> ]
```

A *<range attribute ref>* can be used as an *<exp>*, but only in certain contexts—namely:

- As an operand within a *<bool exp>*
- As a *<proto tuple>* or as an *<exp>* (or an operand within an *<exp>*) within a *<proto tuple>*

```
<bool exp>
    ::=    ... all the usual possibilities, together with:
        | <quantified bool exp>
```

References to range variables within a *<bool exp>* can be free within that *<bool exp>* only if both of the following are true:

- The *<bool exp>* appears immediately within a *<relation op inv>* (i.e., the *<bool exp>* immediately follows the keyword WHERE).
- A reference (necessarily free) to that very same range variable appears immediately within the *<proto tuple>* immediately contained within that very same *<relation op inv>* (i.e., the *<proto tuple>* immediately precedes the keyword WHERE).

Terminology: In the context of the relational calculus (either version), *<bool exp>*s are often called **well-formed formulas** or WFFs (pronounced "weffs"). We will use this term ourselves in much of what follows.

```
<quantified bool exp>
    ::=    <quantifier> <range var name> ( <bool exp> )

<quantifier>
    ::=    EXISTS | FORALL

<relation op inv>
    ::=    <proto tuple> [ WHERE <bool exp> ]
```

As in the algebra of Chapter 7, a *<relation op inv>* is one form of *<relation exp>*, but as noted earlier we are giving it a different definition here.

```
<proto tuple>
    ::=    ... see the body of the text
```

---

[1] We do not spell out the details of *<tuple exp>*s, trusting that examples will be sufficient to give the general idea; for reasons that are unimportant here, however, we do not use exactly the same syntax as we did in previous chapters.

All references to range variables appearing immediately within a *<proto tuple>* must be free within that *<proto tuple>*. *Note:* "Proto tuple" stands for "prototype tuple"; the term is apt but not standard.

Range Variables

Here are some sample range variable definitions (expressed as usual in terms of suppliers and parts):

```
RANGEVAR SX  RANGES OVER S ;
RANGEVAR SY  RANGES OVER S ;
RANGEVAR SPX RANGES OVER SP ;
RANGEVAR SPY RANGES OVER SP ;
RANGEVAR PX  RANGES OVER P ;

RANGEVAR SU RANGES OVER
      ( SX WHERE SX.CITY = 'London' ) ,
      ( SX WHERE EXISTS SPX ( SPX.S# = SX.S# AND
                              SPX.P# = P# ('P1') ) ) ;
```

Range variable SU in this last example is defined to range over the *union* of the set of supplier tuples for suppliers who are located in London and the set of supplier tuples for suppliers who supply part P1. Observe that the definition of range variable SU makes use of the range variables SX and SPX. Note too that in such "union-style" definitions, the relations to be "unioned" must (of course) all be of the same type.

Note: Range variables are not variables in the usual programming language sense, they are variables in the sense of logic. In fact, they are analogous, somewhat, to the *parameters* to predicates as discussed in Chapter 3; the difference is that the parameters of Chapter 3 stand for values from the applicable domain (whatever that might be), whereas range variables in the tuple calculus stand specifically for tuples.

Throughout the rest of this chapter, we will assume that the range variable definitions shown in this subsection are in effect. We note that in a real language there would have to be some rules regarding the *scope* of such definitions. We ignore such matters in the present chapter (except in SQL contexts).

Free and Bound Variable References

Every reference to a range variable is either **free** or **bound** (within some context—in particular, within some WFF). We explain this notion in purely syntactic terms in this subsection, then go on to discuss its semantic significance in subsequent subsections.

Let *V* be a range variable and let *p* and *q* be WFFs. Then:

- References to *V* in NOT *p* are free or bound within that WFF according as they are free or bound in *p*. References to *V* in *p* AND *q* and *p* OR *q* are free or bound in those WFFs according as they are free or bound in *p* or *q*, as applicable.

- References to *V* that are free in *p* are bound in EXISTS *V* (*p*) and FORALL *V* (*p*). Other references to range variables in *p* are free or bound in EXISTS *V* (*p*) and FORALL *V* (*p*) according as they are free or bound in *p*.

For completeness, we need to add the following:

- The sole reference to *V* in the *<range var name>* *V* is free within that *<range var name>*.

- The sole reference to *V* in the *<range attribute ref>* *V.A* is free within that *<range attribute ref>*.

- If a reference to *V* is free in some expression *exp,* that reference is also free in any expression *exp'* that immediately contains *exp* as a subexpression, unless *exp'* introduces a quantifier that makes that reference bound instead.

Here are some examples of WFFs containing range variable references:

- *Simple comparisons:*

```
SX.S# = S# ('S1')

SX.S# = SPX.S#

SPX.P# ≠ PX.P#
```

All references to SX, PX, and SPX are free in these examples.

- *Boolean combinations of simple comparisons:*

```
PX.WEIGHT < WEIGHT ( 15.5 ) AND PX.CITY = 'Oslo'

NOT ( SX.CITY = 'London' )

SX.S# = SPX.S# AND SPX.P# ≠ PX.P#

PX.COLOR = COLOR ('Red') OR PX.CITY = 'London'
```

Again, all references to SX, PX, and SPX here are free.

- *Quantified WFFs:*

```
EXISTS SPX ( SPX.S# = SX.S# AND SPX.P# = P# ('P2') )

FORALL PX ( PX.COLOR = COLOR ('Red') )
```

The references to SPX and PX in these two examples are bound, the reference to SX is free. See the subsection "Quantifiers" immediately following.

Quantifiers

There are two quantifiers, EXISTS and FORALL; EXISTS is the **existential** quantifier, FORALL is the **universal** quantifier.[2] Basically, if *p* is a WFF in which *V* is free, then

```
EXISTS V ( p )
```

and

```
FORALL V ( p )
```

are both valid WFFs, and *V* is bound in both of them. The first means: **There exists at least one value** of *V* that makes *p* true. The second means: **For all values** of *V*, *p* is true. For

---

[2] The term *quantifier* derives from the verb to *quantify,* which means, loosely, "to say how many." The symbols ∃ ("backward E") and ∀ ("upside-down A") are often used in place of EXISTS and FORALL, respectively.

example, suppose the variable *V* ranges over the set "Members of the U.S. Senate in 2003," and suppose *p* is the WFF "*V* is female" (we are not trying to use our formal syntax here!). Then EXISTS *V* (*p*) and FORALL *V* (*p*) are both valid WFFs, and they evaluate to TRUE and FALSE, respectively.

Look again at the EXISTS example from the end of the previous subsection:

```
EXISTS SPX ( SPX.S# = SX.S# AND SPX.P# = P# ('P2') )
```

It follows from the foregoing that we can read this WFF as follows:

> *There exists a tuple SPX, say, in the current value of relvar SP such that the S# value in that tuple SPX is equal to the value of SX.S#—whatever that might be— and the P# value in that tuple SPX is P2.*

Each reference to SPX here is bound. The single reference to SX is free.

We define EXISTS formally as **an iterated OR**. In other words, if (a) *r* is a relation with tuples *t1, t2, ..., tm,* (b) *V* is a range variable that ranges over *r,* and (c) *p*(*V*) is a WFF in which *V* occurs as a free variable, then the WFF

```
EXISTS V ( p ( V ) )
```

is defined to be equivalent to the WFF

```
FALSE OR p ( t1 ) OR ... OR p ( tm )
```

Observe in particular that this expression evaluates to FALSE if *r* is empty (equivalently, if *m* is zero).

By way of example, suppose relation *r* contains just the following tuples (we depart here from our usual syntax for simplicity):

```
( 1, 2, 3 )
( 1, 2, 4 )
( 1, 3, 4 )
```

Suppose the three attributes, in left-to-right order as shown, are called *A, B,* and *C,* respectively, and every attribute is of type INTEGER. Then the following WFFs have the indicated values:

```
EXISTS V ( V.C > 1 )            :   TRUE
EXISTS V ( V.B > 3 )            :   FALSE
EXISTS V ( V.A > 1 OR V.C = 4 ) :   TRUE
```

We turn now to FORALL. Here to repeat is the FORALL example from the end of the previous subsection:

```
FORALL PX ( PX.COLOR = COLOR ('Red') )
```

We can read this WFF as follows:

> *For all tuples PX, say, in the current value of relvar P, the COLOR value in that tuple PX is Red.*

The two references to PX here are both bound.

Just as we define EXISTS as an iterated OR, so we define FORALL as **an iterated AND**. In other words, if *r*, *V*, and *p(V)* are as before (in our discussion of EXISTS), then the WFF

```
FORALL V ( p ( V ) )
```

is defined to be equivalent to the WFF

```
TRUE AND p ( t1 ) AND ... AND p ( tm )
```

Observe in particular that this expression evaluates to TRUE if *r* is empty (equivalently, if *m* is zero).

By way of example, let relation *r* be as for our EXISTS examples. Then the following WFFs have the indicated values:

```
FORALL V ( V.A > 1 )                 :   FALSE
FORALL V ( V.B > 1 )                 :   TRUE
FORALL V ( V.A = 1 AND V.C > 2 )     :   TRUE
```

Note: We support both quantifiers purely for convenience—it is not logically necessary to support both, because each can be defined in terms of the other. To be specific, the equivalence

```
FORALL V ( p )   ≡   NOT EXISTS V ( NOT p )
```

(loosely, "all *V*'s satisfy *p*" is equivalent to "no *V*'s do not satisfy *p*") shows that any WFF involving FORALL can always be replaced by an equivalent WFF involving EXISTS instead, and *vice versa*. For example, the (true) statement "For all integers *x*, there exists an integer *y* such that *y* > *x*" (i.e., every integer has a greater integer) is equivalent to the statement "There does not exist an integer *x* such that there does not exist an integer *y* such that *y* > *x*" (i.e., there is no greatest integer). However, some problems are more naturally formulated in terms of FORALL and others in terms of EXISTS; to be more specific, if one of the quantifiers is not available, we will sometimes find ourselves having to use double negation (as the foregoing example illustrates), and double negation is always tricky. In practice, therefore, it is desirable to support both.

Free and Bound Variable References Revisited

Suppose *x* ranges over the set of all integers, and consider the WFF:

```
EXISTS x ( x > 3 )
```

Observe now that *x* here is a kind of *dummy*—it serves only to link the boolean expression inside the parentheses to the quantifier outside. The WFF simply states that there exists some integer, *x* say, that is greater than three. *Note, therefore, that the meaning of this WFF would remain totally unchanged if all references to* x *were replaced by references to some other variable* y. In other words, the WFF

```
EXISTS y ( y > 3 )
```

is semantically identical to the one shown previously.

Now consider the WFF:

```
EXISTS x ( x > 3 ) AND x < 0
```

Here there are three references to *x, denoting two different variables.* The first two references are bound, and could be replaced by references to some other variable *y* without changing the overall meaning. The third reference is free, and *cannot* be replaced with impunity. Thus, of the following two WFFs, the first is equivalent to the one just shown and the second is not:

```
EXISTS y ( y > 3 ) AND x < 0
EXISTS y ( y > 3 ) AND y < 0
```

Note, moreover, that the truth value of the original WFF cannot be determined without knowing the value denoted by the free variable reference *x.* By contrast, a WFF in which all variable references are bound evaluates to TRUE or FALSE, unequivocally. *More terminology:* A WFF in which all variable references are bound is called a **closed WFF**, while a WFF that contains at least one free variable reference is an **open WFF**. In other words, to use the terminology introduced in Chapter 3, a closed WFF is a *proposition,* and an open WFF is a *predicate* that is not a proposition. (Incidentally, note that a proposition is indeed a predicate—it is that degenerate special case in which the set of parameters is empty.)

Relational Operations

The name *<relation op inv>* is perhaps not very apt in a calculus context—*<relation def>* might be more appropriate—but we use it for consistency with Chapter 7. Here to remind you is the syntax:

```
<relation op inv>
    ::=    <proto tuple> [ WHERE <bool exp> ]
<proto tuple>
    ::=    ... see the body of the text
```

We remind you also of the following syntax rules, now slightly simplified:

- All references to range variables in the proto tuple must be free within that proto tuple.

- A reference to a range variable in the WHERE clause can be free only if a reference to that very same range variable (necessarily free) appears in the corresponding proto tuple.

For example, the following is a legal *<relation op inv>* ("Get supplier numbers for suppliers in London"):

```
SX.S# WHERE SX.CITY = 'London'
```

The reference to SX in the proto tuple here is free. The reference to SX in the WHERE clause is also free—a state of affairs that is legal because a reference (necessarily free) to the very same range variable also appears in the proto tuple.

Here is another example ("Get supplier names for suppliers who supply part P2"—see the discussion of EXISTS in the "Quantifiers" subsection earlier in this section):

```
SX.SNAME WHERE EXISTS SPX ( SPX.S# = SX.S# AND
                            SPX.P# = P# ('P2') )
```

The references to SX are all free; the references to SPX (in the WHERE clause) are all bound, as they must be, because there are no references to that same range variable in the proto tuple.

Intuitively, a given *<relation op inv>* evaluates to a relation containing every possible value of the *<proto tuple>* for which the *<bool exp>* specified in the WHERE clause evaluates to TRUE (and omitting the WHERE clause is equivalent to specifying WHERE TRUE). To be more specific:

■ First of all, a proto tuple is a commalist of items enclosed in braces (but the braces can be omitted if the commalist contains just one item), in which each item is either a range attribute reference—possibly including an AS clause to introduce a new attribute name—or a simple range variable name. (There are other possibilities, but we limit our attention until further notice to these two possibilities only.) However:

   a. A range variable name in this context is basically just shorthand for a commalist of range attribute references, one such for each attribute of the relation the range variable ranges over.

   b. A range attribute reference without an AS clause is basically just shorthand for one that includes such a clause in which the new attribute name is the same as the old one.

Without loss of generality, therefore, we can regard a proto tuple as a commalist in braces of range attribute references of the form *Vi.Aj* AS *Bj*. Note that the *Vi*'s will probably not all be distinct, and the *Aj*'s need not be, but the *Bj*'s must be.

■ Let the distinct range variables mentioned in the proto tuple be *V1, V2, ..., Vm*. Let the relations over which these variables range be *r1, r2, ..., rm*, respectively. Let the corresponding relations after application of the attribute renamings specified in the AS clauses be *r1', r2', ..., rm'*, respectively. Let *r'* be the Cartesian product of *r1', r2', ..., rm'*.

■ Let *r* be that restriction of *r'* that satisfies the WFF in the WHERE clause. *Note:* We assume for the sake of this explanation that the renamings in the previous step are applied to attributes mentioned in the WHERE clause also—for otherwise the WFF in that WHERE clause might not make sense. In fact, however, our concrete syntax does not rely on this assumption but instead relies on dot qualification to handle any necessary "disambiguation," as we will see in the next section.

■ The overall value of the *<relation op inv>* is defined to be the projection of *r* over all of the *Bj*'s.

For some examples, see the section immediately following.

8.3 EXAMPLES

We present a few examples of the use of the calculus in formulating queries. As an exercise, you might like to try giving algebraic solutions as well, for "compare and contrast" purposes. In some cases, the examples are repeats of examples from Chapter 7 (and are so indicated).

8.3.1 Get supplier numbers and status for suppliers in Paris with status > 20:

```
{ SX.S#, SX.STATUS }
WHERE SX.CITY = 'Paris' AND SX.STATUS > 20
```

8.3.2 Get all pairs of supplier numbers such that the suppliers concerned are colocated (i.e., located in the same city) (Example 7.5.5):

```
{ SX.S# AS SA, SY.S# AS SB }
              WHERE SX.CITY = SY.CITY AND SX.S# < SY.S#
```

Note that the AS clauses in the proto tuple give names to attributes of the *result;* those names are thus not available for use in the WHERE clause, which is why the second comparison in that WHERE clause takes the form SX.S# < SY.S#, not SA < SB.

8.3.3 Get full supplier information for suppliers who supply part P2 (modified version of Example 7.5.1):

```
SX WHERE EXISTS SPX ( SPX.S# = SX.S# AND SPX.P# = P# ('P2') )
```

Note the use of a range variable name in the proto tuple here. The overall expression is shorthand for the following:

```
{ SX.S#, SX.SNAME, SX.STATUS, SX.CITY }
   WHERE EXISTS SPX ( SPX.S# = SX.S# AND SPX.P# = P# ('P2') )
```

8.3.4 Get supplier names for suppliers who supply at least one red part (Example 7.5.2):

```
SX.SNAME
WHERE EXISTS SPX ( SX.S# = SPX.S# AND
                   EXISTS PX ( PX.P# = SPX.P# AND
                               PX.COLOR = COLOR ('Red') ) )
```

Or equivalently (but in **prenex normal form**, in which all quantifiers appear at the front of the WFF):

```
SX.SNAME
WHERE EXISTS SPX ( EXISTS PX ( SX.S# = SPX.S# AND
                               SPX.P# = PX.P# AND
                               PX.COLOR = COLOR ('Red') ) )
```

Prenex normal form is not inherently more or less correct than any other form, but with a little practice it does tend to become the most natural formulation in many cases. Furthermore, it raises the possibility of reducing the number of parentheses, as follows. The WFF

```
Q1 V1 ( Q2 V2 ( wff ) )
```

(where each of *Q1* and *Q2* is either EXISTS or FORALL) can optionally, and unambiguously, be abbreviated to just:

```
Q1 V1 Q2 V2 ( wff )
```

Thus we can simplify the calculus expression shown above to just:

```
SX.SNAME
WHERE EXISTS SPX EXISTS PX ( SX.S# = SPX.S# AND
                             SPX.P# = PX.P# AND
                             PX.COLOR = COLOR ('Red') )
```

For clarity, however, we will continue to show all parentheses explicitly in this section.

8.3.5 Get supplier names for suppliers who supply at least one part supplied by supplier S2:

```
SX.SNAME
WHERE EXISTS SPX ( EXISTS SPY ( SX.S# = SPX.S# AND
                                SPX.P# = SPY.P# AND
                                SPY.S# = S# ('S2') ) )
```

8.3.6 Get supplier names for suppliers who supply all parts (Example 7.5.3):

```
SX.SNAME WHERE FORALL PX ( EXISTS SPX ( SPX.S# = SX.S# AND
                                        SPX.P# = PX.P# ) )
```

Or equivalently, but without using FORALL:

```
SX.SNAME WHERE NOT EXISTS PX ( NOT EXISTS SPX
                               ( SPX.S# = SX.S# AND
                                 SPX.P# = PX.P# ) )
```

8.3.7 Get supplier names for suppliers who do not supply part P2 (Example 7.5.6):

```
SX.SNAME WHERE NOT EXISTS SPX
              ( SPX.S# = SX.S# AND SPX.P# = P# ('P2') )
```

Notice how readily this solution is derived from the solution to Example 8.3.3.

8.3.8 Get supplier numbers for suppliers who supply at least all those parts supplied by supplier S2 (Example 7.5.4):

```
SX.S# WHERE FORALL SPX ( SPX.S# ≠ S# ('S2') OR
                         EXISTS SPY ( SPY.S# = SX.S# AND
                                      SPY.P# = SPX.P# ) )
```

Paraphrasing: "Get supplier numbers for suppliers SX such that, for all shipments SPX, either that shipment is not from supplier S2, or if it is, then there exists a shipment SPY of the SPX part from supplier SX." We introduce another syntactic shorthand to help with queries such as this one—namely, an explicit syntactic form for the **logical implication** operator. If *p* and *q* are WFFs, then the logical implication expression

```
IF p THEN q END IF
```

is also a WFF, with semantics identical to those of the WFF

```
( NOT p ) OR q
```

The example can thus be reformulated as follows:

```
SX.S# WHERE FORALL SPX ( IF SPX.S# = S# ('S2') THEN
                            EXISTS SPY ( SPY.S# = SX.S# AND
                                         SPY.P# = SPX.P# )
                         END IF )
```

Paraphrasing: "Get supplier numbers for suppliers SX such that, for all shipments SPX, if that shipment SPX is from supplier S2, then there exists a shipment SPY of the SPX part from supplier SX."

8.3.9 Get part numbers for parts that either weigh more than 16 pounds or are supplied by supplier S2, or both:

```
RANGEVAR PU RANGES OVER
         ( PX.P# WHERE PX.WEIGHT > WEIGHT ( 16.0 ) ),
         ( SPX.P# WHERE SPX.S# = S# ('S2') ) ;
PU.P#
```

The relational algebra analog here would involve an explicit union.

For interest, we show an alternative formulation of this query. However, this second formulation relies (as the first did not) on the fact that every part number in relvar SP also appears in relvar P:

```
PX.P# WHERE PX.WEIGHT > WEIGHT ( 16.0 )
      OR    EXISTS SPX ( SPX.P# = PX.P# AND
                         SPX.S# = S# ('S2') )
```

8.4 CALCULUS *VS.* ALGEBRA

We claimed in the introduction to this chapter that the algebra and the calculus are fundamentally equivalent. We now examine that claim in more detail. First, Codd showed in reference [7.1] that the algebra is at least as powerful as the calculus. He did this by giving an algorithm—"Codd's reduction algorithm"—by which an arbitrary expression of the calculus could be reduced to a semantically equivalent expression of the algebra. We do not present Codd's algorithm in detail here, but content ourselves with a reasonably complex example that illustrates in broad terms how it works.[3]

As a basis for our example we use, not the familiar suppliers-and-parts database, but the extended suppliers-parts-projects version from the exercises in Chapter 4 and elsewhere. For convenience we show in Fig. 8.1 a set of sample values for that database (repeated from Fig. 4.5).

---

[3] Actually, the algorithm presented in reference [7.1] had a slight flaw in it [8.2]. Furthermore, the version of the calculus defined in that paper did not include a full counterpart to the union operator, so in fact Codd's calculus was strictly less powerful than Codd's algebra. The claim that the algebra and the calculus, enhanced to include a full union counterpart, are equivalent is nevertheless true, however, as several writers have demonstrated; see, for example, Klug [7.11].

S	S#	SNAME	STATUS	CITY
	S1	Smith	20	London
	S2	Jones	10	Paris
	S3	Blake	30	Paris
	S4	Clark	20	London
	S5	Adams	30	Athens

P	P#	PNAME	COLOR	WEIGHT	CITY
	P1	Nut	Red	12.0	London
	P2	Bolt	Green	17.0	Paris
	P3	Screw	Blue	17.0	Oslo
	P4	Screw	Red	14.0	London
	P5	Cam	Blue	12.0	Paris
	P6	Cog	Red	19.0	London

J	J#	JNAME	CITY
	J1	Sorter	Paris
	J2	Display	Rome
	J3	OCR	Athens
	J4	Console	Athens
	J5	RAID	London
	J6	EDS	Oslo
	J7	Tape	London

SPJ	S#	P#	J#	QTY
	S1	P1	J1	200
	S1	P1	J4	700
	S2	P3	J1	400
	S2	P3	J2	200
	S2	P3	J3	200
	S2	P3	J4	500
	S2	P3	J5	600
	S2	P3	J6	400
	S2	P3	J7	800
	S2	P5	J2	100
	S3	P3	J1	200
	S3	P4	J2	500
	S4	P6	J3	300
	S4	P6	J7	300
	S5	P2	J2	200
	S5	P2	J4	100
	S5	P5	J5	500
	S5	P5	J7	100
	S5	P6	J2	200
	S5	P1	J4	100
	S5	P3	J4	200
	S5	P4	J4	800
	S5	P5	J4	400
	S5	P6	J4	500

Fig. 8.1   The suppliers-parts-projects database (sample values)

Now consider the query "Get names and cities for suppliers who supply at least one Athens project with at least 50 of every part." A calculus expression for this query is:

```
{ SX.SNAME, SX.CITY } WHERE EXISTS JX FORALL PX EXISTS SPJX
                            ( JX.CITY = 'Athens' AND
                              JX.J# = SPJX.J# AND
                              PX.P# = SPJX.P# AND
                              SX.S# = SPJX.S# AND
                              SPJX.QTY ≥ QTY ( 50 ) )
```

where SX, PX, JX, and SPJX are range variables ranging over S, P, J, and SPJ, respectively. We now show how this expression can be evaluated to yield the desired result.

Step 1: For each range variable, retrieve the range (i.e., the set of possible values for that variable), restricted if possible. By "restricted if possible," we mean that there might be a simple restriction condition—see Chapter 7 for a definition of this term—embedded within the WHERE clause that can be used right away to eliminate certain tuples from all further consideration. In the case at hand, the sets of tuples retrieved are as follows:

SX	: All tuples of S	5 tuples
PX	: All tuples of P	6 tuples
JX	: Tuples of J where CITY = 'Athens'	2 tuples
SPJX	: Tuples of SPJ where QTY ≥ QTY(50)	24 tuples

Step 2: Construct the Cartesian product of the ranges retrieved in Step 1, to yield:

S#	SN	STATUS	CITY	P#	PN	COLOR	WEIGHT	CITY	J#	JN	CITY	S#	P#	J#	QTY
S1	Sm	20	Lon	P1	Nt	Red	12.0	Lon	J3	OR	Ath	S1	P1	J1	200
S1	Sm	20	Lon	P1	Nt	Red	12.0	Lon	J3	OR	Ath	S1	P1	J4	700
..	..	..	...	..	..	...	..	...	..	..	...	..	..	..	...
..	..	..	...	..	..	...	..	...	..	..	...	..	..	..	...
..	..	..	...	..	..	...	..	...	..	..	...	..	..	..	...

(etc.). The complete product contains 5 * 6 * 2 * 24 = 1440 tuples. *Note:* We have made a number of obvious abbreviations here in the interest of space. Also, we have not bothered to rename attributes (as we really ought to have done, to avoid ambiguity), but instead are relying on ordinal position to show (e.g.) which "S#" comes from S and which from SPJ. This trick is adopted purely to shorten the exposition.

Step 3: Restrict the Cartesian product constructed in Step 2 in accordance with the "join portion" of the WHERE clause. In the example, that portion is:

```
JX.J# = SPJX.J# AND PX.P# = SPJX.P# AND SX.S# = SPJX.S#
```

We therefore eliminate tuples from the product for which the supplier S# value is not equal to the shipment S# value or the part P# value is not equal to the shipment P# value or the project J# value is not equal to the shipment J# value, to yield a subset of the Cartesian product consisting (as it happens) of just ten tuples:

S#	SN	STATUS	CITY	P#	PN	COLOR	WEIGHT	CITY	J#	JN	CITY	S#	P#	J#	QTY
S1	Sm	20	Lon	P1	Nt	Red	12.0	Lon	J4	Cn	Ath	S1	P1	J4	700
S2	Jo	10	Par	P3	Sc	Blue	17.0	Osl	J3	OR	Ath	S2	P3	J3	200
S2	Jo	10	Par	P3	Sc	Blue	17.0	Osl	J4	Cn	Ath	S2	P3	J4	200
S4	Cl	20	Lon	P6	Cg	Red	19.0	Lon	J3	OR	Ath	S4	P6	J3	300
S5	Ad	30	Ath	P2	Bt	Green	17.0	Par	J4	Cn	Ath	S5	P2	J4	100
S5	Ad	30	Ath	P1	Nt	Red	12.0	Lon	J4	Cn	Ath	S5	P1	J4	100
S5	Ad	30	Ath	P3	Sc	Blue	17.0	Osl	J4	Cn	Ath	S5	P3	J4	200
S5	Ad	30	Ath	P4	Sc	Red	14.0	Lon	J4	Cn	Ath	S5	P4	J4	800
S5	Ad	30	Ath	P5	Cm	Blue	12.0	Par	J4	Cn	Ath	S5	P5	J4	400
S5	Ad	30	Ath	P6	Cg	Red	19.0	Lon	J4	Cn	Ath	S5	P6	J4	500

(This relation is the pertinent equijoin.)

Step 4: Apply the quantifiers from right to left, as follows:

- For the quantifier "EXISTS *V*" (where *V* is a range variable that ranges over some relation *r*), *project* the current intermediate result to eliminate all attributes of relation *r*.

- For the quantifier "FORALL *V*," *divide* the current intermediate result by the "restricted range" relation associated with *V* as retrieved in Step 1. This operation will also have the effect of eliminating all attributes of relation *r*. *Note:* "Divide" here means Codd's original divide operation (see the annotation to reference [7.4]).

In the example, the quantifiers are:

```
EXISTS JX FORALL PX EXISTS SPJX
```

We thus proceed as follows:

- *(EXISTS SPJX)* Project away the attributes of SPJ—*viz.*, SPJ.S#, SPJ.P#, SPJ.J#, and SPJ.QTY. *Result:*

S#	SN	STATUS	CITY	P#	PN	COLOR	WEIGHT	CITY	J#	JN	CITY
S1	Sm	20	Lon	P1	Nt	Red	12.0	Lon	J4	Cn	Ath
S2	Jo	10	Par	P3	Sc	Blue	17.0	Osl	J3	OR	Ath
S2	Jo	10	Par	P3	Sc	Blue	17.0	Osl	J4	Cn	Ath
S4	Cl	20	Lon	P6	Cg	Red	19.0	Lon	J3	OR	Ath
S5	Ad	30	Ath	P2	Bt	Green	17.0	Par	J4	Cn	Ath
S5	Ad	30	Ath	P1	Nt	Red	12.0	Lon	J4	Cn	Ath
S5	Ad	30	Ath	P3	Sc	Blue	17.0	Osl	J4	Cn	Ath
S5	Ad	30	Ath	P4	Sc	Red	14.0	Lon	J4	Cn	Ath
S5	Ad	30	Ath	P5	Cm	Blue	12.0	Par	J4	Cn	Ath
S5	Ad	30	Ath	P6	Cg	Red	19.0	Lon	J4	Cn	Ath

- *(FORALL PX)* Divide by P. *Result:*

S#	SNAME	STATUS	CITY	J#	JNAME	CITY
S5	Adams	30	Athens	J4	Console	Athens

(We now have room to show the result without any abbreviations.)

- *(EXISTS JX)* Project away the attributes of *J*—*viz.*, J.J#, J.JNAME, and J.CITY. *Result:*

S#	SNAME	STATUS	CITY
S5	Adams	30	Athens

Step 5: Project the result of Step 4 in accordance with the specifications in the proto tuple. In our example, the proto tuple is:

```
{ SX.SNAME, SX.CITY }
```

Hence the final result is just:

SNAME	CITY
Adams	Athens

It follows from all of the foregoing that the original calculus expression is semantically equivalent to a certain nested algebraic expression: to be precise, a projection of a projection of a division of a projection of a restriction of a product of four restrictions (!).

This concludes the example. Of course, many improvements to the algorithm are possible (see Chapter 18, in particular reference [18.4], for some ideas for such improvements), and many details have been glossed over in our explanation; nevertheless, the example should be adequate to give the general idea of how the reduction works.

Incidentally, we are now able to explain one of the reasons (not the only one) why Codd defined precisely the eight algebraic operators he did: Those eight operators provide a convenient **target language** as a vehicle for a possible implementation of the calculus. In other words, given a language such as QUEL that is founded on the calculus, one possible approach to implementing that language would be to take the query as submitted by the user—which is basically just a calculus expression—and apply the reduction algorithm to it, thereby obtaining an equivalent algebraic expression. That algebraic expression consists of a set of algebraic operators, which are inherently implementable by definition. (The next step is to go on to *optimize* that algebraic expression—see Chapter 18.)

Another point to note is that Codd's eight algebraic operators also provide a *yardstick* for measuring the expressive power of any given database language. We mentioned this issue briefly in Chapter 7, at the end of Section 7.6; we now examine it in a little more depth.

First, a language is said to be **relationally complete** if it is at least as powerful as the calculus—that is, if any relation definable by some expression of the calculus is also definable by some expression of the language in question [7.1]. (In Chapter 7 we said that "relationally complete" meant as powerful as the *algebra,* not the calculus, but it comes to the same thing, as we will see in a moment. Note that it follows immediately from the existence of Codd's reduction algorithm that the algebra is relationally complete.)

Relational completeness can be regarded as a basic measure of expressive power for database languages in general. In particular, since the calculus and the algebra are both relationally complete, they both provide a basis for designing languages that provide this power of expressiveness *without having to resort to explicit iteration*—a particularly important consideration in the case of a language that is intended for end users, though it is significant for application programmers as well.

Next, since the algebra is relationally complete, it follows that, to show that any given language L is also complete, it is sufficient to show (a) that L includes analogs of each of the eight algebraic operators—indeed, it is sufficient to show that it includes analogs of the five *primitive* algebraic operators—and (b) that the operands of any operator in L can be represented by arbitrary L expressions (of the appropriate type). SQL is an example of a language that can be shown to be relationally complete in this manner (see Exercise 8.9), and QUEL is another. Indeed, it is often easier in practice to show that a given language has equivalents of the algebraic operators than it is to show that it has equivalents of the expressions of the calculus, which is why we typically define relational completeness in algebraic rather than calculus terms.

Incidentally, please understand that relational completeness does not necessarily imply any other kind of completeness. For example, it is desirable that a language provide "computational completeness" also—that is, it should be capable of computing all computable functions. Computational completeness was one of the motivations for the EXTEND and SUMMARIZE operators that we added to the original algebra in Chapter 7. In the next section, we will consider calculus analogs of those operators.

To return to the question of the equivalence of the algebra and the calculus: We have shown by example that any calculus expression can be reduced to an algebraic equivalent, and hence that the algebra is at least as powerful as the calculus. Conversely, it is possible to show that any algebraic expression can be reduced to a calculus equivalent, and hence that the calculus is at least as powerful as the algebra; for proof, see, for example, Ullman [8.13]. It follows that the two are logically equivalent.

8.5   COMPUTATIONAL CAPABILITIES

We did not call the point out explicitly earlier, but in fact the calculus as we have defined it already includes analogs of the algebraic EXTEND and SUMMARIZE operators, because:

- One possible form of proto tuple is a *<tuple selector inv>* ("tuple selector invocation"), and the components of a *<tuple selector inv>* can be arbitrary expressions.

- The comparands in a comparison in a *<bool exp>* can also be arbitrary expressions.

- As we saw in Chapter 7, the first or only argument to an *<agg op inv>* ("aggregate operator invocation") is a *<relation exp>*.

It is not worth going into all of the applicable syntactic and semantic details here. We content ourselves with giving a few examples (and those examples themselves are slightly simplified in certain respects).

8.5.1 Get the part number and the weight in grams for each part with weight > 10,000 grams:

```
{ PX.P#, PX.WEIGHT * 454 AS GMWT }
                  WHERE PX.WEIGHT * 454 > WEIGHT ( 10000.0 )
```

Observe that (as in Example 8.3.2) the AS specification in the proto tuple gives a name to an attribute of the *result*. That name is thus not available for use in the WHERE clause, which is why the subexpression PX.WEIGHT * 454 appears twice.

8.5.2 Get all suppliers and tag each one with the literal value "Supplier":

```
{ SX, 'Supplier' AS TAG }
```

8.5.3 For each shipment, get full shipment details, including total shipment weight:

```
{ SPX, PX.WEIGHT * SPX.QTY AS SHIPWT } WHERE PX.P# = SPX.P#
```

8.5.4 For each part, get the part number and the total shipment quantity:

```
{ PX.P#, SUM ( SPX WHERE SPX.P# = PX.P#, QTY ) AS TOTQTY }
```

8.5.5 Get the total shipment quantity:

```
SUM ( SPX, QTY ) AS GRANDTOTAL
```

8.5.6 For each supplier, get the supplier number and the total number of parts supplied:

```
{ SX.S#, COUNT ( SPX WHERE SPX.S# = SX.S# ) AS #_OF_PARTS }
```

8.5.7 Get part cities that store more than five red parts:

```
RANGEVAR PY RANGES OVER P ;
PX.CITY WHERE COUNT ( PY WHERE PY.CITY = PX.CITY
                         AND    PY.COLOR = COLOR ('Red') ) > 5
```

8.6 SQL FACILITIES

We said in Section 8.4 that a given relational language could be based on either the relational algebra or the relational calculus. So which is SQL based on? The answer, regrettably, is partly both and partly neither . . . When it was first designed, SQL was specifically intended to be different from both the algebra and the calculus [4.9]; indeed, such a goal was the prime motivation for the introduction of the "IN *<subquery>*" construct (see Example 8.6.10 later in this section). As time went by, however, it turned out that certain features of both the algebra and the calculus were needed after all, and the language grew to accommodate them.[4] The situation today is thus that some aspects of SQL are "algebra-like," some are "calculus-like," and some are neither. This state of affairs explains why we said in Chapter 7 that we would defer discussion of the SQL data manipulation facilities to the present chapter. We leave it as an exercise to figure out which portions of SQL are based on the algebra, which on the calculus, and which on neither.

An SQL query is formulated as a *<table exp>* of potentially considerable complexity. We do not get into all of that complexity here; rather, we simply present a set of examples, in the hope that those examples will highlight some of the most important features. The examples are based on the SQL definitions for the suppliers-and-parts database shown in Chapter 4 (Fig. 4.1).

8.6.1 Get color and city for "nonParis" parts with weight greater than 10 pounds:

```
SELECT  PX.COLOR, PX.CITY
FROM    P AS PX
WHERE   PX.CITY <> 'Paris'
AND     PX.WEIGHT > WEIGHT ( 10.0 ) ;
```

Points arising:

1. Recall from Chapter 5 that "<>" is the SQL syntax for *not equals. Less than or equals* and *greater than or equals* are written "<=" and ">=", respectively.

2. The specification P AS PX in the FROM clause effectively constitutes the definition of a (tuple-calculus-style) range variable called PX, with range the current value of table P. The *name*—not the variable!—PX is said to be a **correlation name**, and its scope is, loosely, the table expression in which its definition appears, excluding any inner expression in which another range variable is defined with the same name (see, e.g., Example 8.6.12).

---

[4] One consequence of that growth is that—as noted in the annotation to reference [4.19], *q.v.*—the entire "IN *<subquery>*" construct could now be removed from the language with no loss of functionality! This fact is ironic, since it was that construct that the "Structured" in the original name "Structured Query Language" referred to; indeed, it was that construct that was the original justification for adopting SQL rather than the algebra or the calculus in the first place.

3. SQL also allows *implicit* range variables. Thus, the query at hand might alternatively be expressed as follows:

```
SELECT   P.COLOR, P.CITY
FROM     P
WHERE    P.CITY <> 'Paris'
AND      P.WEIGHT > WEIGHT ( 10.0 ) ;
```

The basic idea is to allow a table *name* to be used to denote an implicit range variable that ranges over the table with that name, provided no ambiguity results. In the example, the FROM clause FROM P can be regarded as shorthand for a FROM clause that reads FROM P AS P. In other words, it has to be clearly understood that the qualifying name P in (e.g.) the expression P.CITY in the SELECT and WHERE clauses here does *not* stand for table P—it stands for a *range variable* called P that ranges over the table with the same name.

4. As noted in Chapter 4, we could have used unqualified column names throughout in this example, thereby writing:

```
SELECT   COLOR, CITY
FROM     P
WHERE    CITY <> 'Paris'
AND      WEIGHT > WEIGHT ( 10.0 ) ;
```

The broad rule is that unqualified names are acceptable provided they cause no ambiguity. In our examples, however, we will usually (but not invariably!) include all qualifiers, even when they are technically redundant. Unfortunately, however, there are certain contexts in which column names are explicitly required *not* to be qualified! The ORDER BY clause is a case in point[5]—see the example immediately following.

5. The **ORDER BY** clause, mentioned in connection with DECLARE CURSOR in Chapter 4, can also be used in interactive SQL queries. For example:

```
SELECT   P.COLOR, P.CITY
FROM     P
WHERE    P.CITY <> 'Paris'
AND      P.WEIGHT > WEIGHT ( 10.0 )
ORDER    BY CITY DESC ;        /* note unqualified column name */
```

6. We remind you of the "SELECT *" shorthand, also mentioned in Chapter 4. For example:

```
SELECT   *
FROM     P
WHERE    P.CITY <> 'Paris'
AND      P.WEIGHT > WEIGHT ( 10.0 ) ;
```

The star in "SELECT *" is shorthand for a commalist of all column names in the table(s) referenced in the FROM clause, in the left-to-right order in which those column(s) are defined within those table(s). The star notation is convenient for interactive queries, since it saves keystrokes. However, it is potentially dangerous in embedded SQL—that is, SQL embedded in an application program—because the meaning of the "*" might change (e.g., if a column is added to or dropped from some table, via ALTER TABLE).

---

[5] Except as noted in Chapter 4, Section 4.6.

7. *(Much more important than the previous points!)* Note that, given our usual sample data, the query under discussion will return four rows, not two, even though three of those four rows are identical. SQL does not eliminate redundant duplicate rows from a query result unless the user explicitly requests it to do so via the keyword **DISTINCT**, as here:

```
SELECT DISTINCT P.COLOR, P.CITY
FROM    P
WHERE   P.CITY <> 'Paris'
AND     P.WEIGHT > WEIGHT ( 10.0 ) ;
```

This query will return just two rows.

It follows from the foregoing that (as in fact we already know from Chapter 6) the fundamental data object in SQL is not a relation—it is, rather, a table, and SQL-style tables contain (in general) not sets but *bags* of rows (and SQL thus violates *The Information Principle*). One important consequence is that the fundamental operators in SQL are not true relational operators but bag analogs of those operators. Another is that results and theorems that hold in the relational model—regarding the transformation of expressions, for example [6.6]—do not necessarily hold in SQL.

8.6.2 For all parts, get the part number and the weight of that part in grams (simplified version of Example 8.5.1):

```
SELECT P.P#, P.WEIGHT * 454 AS GMWT
FROM   P ;
```

The specification AS GMWT introduces an appropriate result column name for the "computed column." The two columns of the result table are thus called P# and GMWT, respectively. If the AS clause had been omitted, the corresponding result column would effectively have been unnamed. Observe, therefore, that SQL does not actually require the user to provide a result column name in such circumstances, but we will always do so in our examples.

8.6.3 Get all combinations of supplier and part information such that the supplier and part in question are colocated.

SQL provides many different ways of formulating this query. We give three of the simplest here:

1. ```
   SELECT S.*, P.P#, P.PNAME, P.COLOR, P.WEIGHT
   FROM   S, P
   WHERE  S.CITY = P.CITY ;
   ```
2. `S JOIN P USING CITY ;`
3. `S NATURAL JOIN P ;`

The result in each case is the **natural join** of tables S and P (on cities).[6]

The first of the foregoing formulations—which is the only one that would have been valid in SQL as originally defined (explicit JOIN support was added in SQL:1992)—merits further discussion. Conceptually, we can think of that version of the query as being implemented as follows:

---

[6] SQL:2003 is likely to require the second and third formulations to include a "SELECT * FROM" prefix.
   ```

- First, the FROM clause is executed, to yield the **Cartesian product** S TIMES SP. (Strictly, we should worry here about renaming columns before we compute the product; we ignore this issue for simplicity. Also, in the spirit of Section 7.7, we take the Cartesian product of a single table *t* to be just *t* itself.)

- Next, the WHERE clause is executed, to yield a **restriction** of that product in which the two CITY values in each row are equal (in other words, we have now computed the *equijoin* of suppliers and parts over cities).

- Finally, the SELECT clause is executed, to yield a **projection** of that restriction over the columns specified in the SELECT clause. The final result is the natural join.

Loosely speaking, therefore, FROM in SQL corresponds to Cartesian product, WHERE to restrict, and SELECT to project, and the SQL SELECT - FROM - WHERE represents a projection of a restriction of a product (though the "projection" in question does not necessarily eliminate duplicates, as we know).

8.6.4 Get all pairs of city names such that a supplier located in the first city supplies a part stored in the second city:

```
SELECT DISTINCT S.CITY AS SCITY, P.CITY AS PCITY
FROM   S JOIN SP USING S# JOIN P USING P# ;
```

Notice that the following is *not* correct (why not?). *Answer:* Because it includes CITY as a joining column in the second join.

```
SELECT DISTINCT S.CITY AS SCITY, P.CITY AS PCITY
FROM   S NATURAL JOIN SP NATURAL JOIN P ;
```

8.6.5 Get all pairs of supplier numbers such that the suppliers concerned are colocated (Example 8.3.2):

```
SELECT A.S# AS SA, B.S# AS SB
FROM   S AS A, S AS B
WHERE  A.CITY = B.CITY
AND    A.S# < B.S# ;
```

Explicit range variables are clearly required in this example. Note that the introduced column names SA and SB refer to columns of the *result table,* and so cannot be used in the WHERE clause.

8.6.6 Get the total number of suppliers:

```
SELECT COUNT(*) AS N
FROM   S ;
```

The result here is a table with one column, called N, and one row, containing the value 5. SQL supports the usual aggregate operators **COUNT, SUM, AVG, MAX, MIN, EVERY,** and **ANY,**[7] but there are a few SQL-specific points the user needs to be aware of:

---

[7] EVERY is the SQL analog of our ALL (the spelling ALL is *not* supported). ANY can be spelled SOME. Also, several further aggregate operators were added by the "online analytical processing" amendment, SQL/OLAP (see Chapter 22).

- In general, the argument can optionally be preceded by the keyword DISTINCT—as in, for example, SUM (DISTINCT QTY)—to indicate that duplicates are to be eliminated before the aggregation is done. For MAX, MIN, EVERY, and ANY, however, DISTINCT has no effect and should not be specified.

- The special operator COUNT(*)—DISTINCT not allowed—is provided to count all rows in a table without any duplicate elimination.

- Any nulls in the argument column (see Chapter 19) are eliminated before the aggregation is done, regardless of whether DISTINCT is specified—except in the case of COUNT(*), where nulls behave as if they were values.

- After nulls if any have been eliminated, if what is left is an empty set, COUNT returns zero; the other operators all return null. *Note:* This result is logically correct for COUNT but not for the other operators. For example, EVERY ought logically to return TRUE when applied to an empty set, as we saw in Section 8.2.

8.6.7 Get the maximum and minimum quantity for part P2:

```
SELECT MAX ( SP.QTY ) AS MAXQ, MIN ( SP.QTY ) AS MINQ
FROM    SP
WHERE   SP.P# = P# ('P2') ;
```

Observe that the FROM and WHERE clauses here both effectively provide part of the argument to the two aggregate operator invocations, and should therefore logically appear within the argument-enclosing parentheses. Nevertheless, the query is indeed written as shown. This unorthodox approach to syntax has significant negative repercussions on the structure, usability, and orthogonality[8] of the SQL language. For instance, one immediate consequence is that aggregate operator invocations cannot be nested, with the result that a query such as "Get the average of total part quantities" cannot be formulated without cumbersome circumlocutions. To be specific, the following query is illegal:

```
SELECT AVG ( SUM ( SP.QTY ) )              /* warning! illegal! */
FROM    SP ;
```

Instead, it has to be formulated something like this:

```
SELECT AVG ( X )
FROM ( SELECT SUM ( SP.QTY ) AS X
       FROM    SP
       GROUP  BY SP.S# ) AS POINTLESS ;
```

See the example immediately following for an explanation of GROUP BY, and several subsequent examples for an explanation of subqueries like the one in the FROM clause here. *Note:* The specification AS *POINTLESS* is pointless but is required by SQL's syntax rules. See reference [4.20] for further discussion.

8.6.8 For each part supplied, get the part number and the total shipment quantity
(modified version of Example 8.5.4):

---

[8] **Orthogonality** means *independence*. A language is orthogonal if independent concepts are kept independent, not mixed together in confusing ways. Orthogonality is desirable because the less orthogonal a language is, the more complicated it is and—paradoxically but simultaneously—the less powerful it is.

```
SELECT SP.P#, SUM ( SP.QTY ) AS TOTQTY
FROM   SP
GROUP  BY SP.P# ;
```

The foregoing is the SQL analog of the relational algebra expression

```
SUMMARIZE SP BY { P# } ADD SUM ( QTY ) AS TOTQTY
```

or the tuple calculus expression

```
( SPX.P#, SUM ( SPY WHERE SPY.P# = SPX.P#, QTY ) AS TOTQTY )
```

Observe in particular that if the GROUP BY clause is specified, expressions in the SELECT clause must be **single-valued per group**.

Here is an alternative (and in some ways preferable) formulation of the same query:

```
SELECT P.P#, ( SELECT SUM ( SP.QTY )
               FROM   SP
               WHERE  SP.P# = P.P# ) AS TOTQTY
FROM   P ;
```

The ability to use a subquery in this way allows us to obtain a result that includes rows for parts that are not supplied at all, which the previous formulation, using GROUP BY, did not. (The TOTQTY value for such parts will unfortunately be given as null, however, not zero.)

8.6.9 Get part numbers for parts supplied by more than one supplier:

```
SELECT SP.P#
FROM   SP
GROUP  BY SP.P#
HAVING COUNT ( SP.S# ) > 1 ;
```

The HAVING clause is to groups what the WHERE clause is to rows; in other words, HAVING is used to eliminate groups, just as WHERE is used to eliminate rows. Expressions in a HAVING clause must be single-valued per group.

8.6.10 Get supplier names for suppliers who supply part P2 (Example 7.5.1):

```
SELECT DISTINCT S.SNAME
FROM   S
WHERE  S.S# IN
     ( SELECT SP.S#
       FROM   SP
       WHERE  SP.P# = P# ('P2') ) ;
```

Explanation: This example makes use of a subquery in the WHERE clause. Loosely speaking, a subquery is a SELECT - FROM - WHERE - GROUP BY - HAVING expression that is nested inside another such expression. Subqueries are used among other things to represent the set of values to be searched via an **IN condition**, as the example illustrates. The system evaluates the overall query by evaluating the subquery first (at least conceptually). That subquery returns the set of supplier *numbers* for suppliers who supply part P2: namely, the set {S1,S2,S3,S4}. The original expression is thus equivalent to the following simpler one:

```
SELECT DISTINCT S.SNAME
FROM    S
WHERE   S.S# IN ( S#('S1)', S#('S2'), S#('S3'), S#('S4') ) ;
```

By the way, it is worth pointing out that the original problem ("Get supplier names for suppliers who supply part P2") can equally well be formulated by means of a *join*—for example, as follows:

```
SELECT DISTINCT S.SNAME
FROM    S, SP
WHERE   S.S# = SP.S#
AND     SP.P# = P# ('P2') ;
```

8.6.11 Get supplier names for suppliers who supply at least one red part (Example 8.3.4):

```
SELECT DISTINCT S.SNAME
FROM    S
WHERE   S.S# IN
        ( SELECT SP.S#
          FROM    SP
          WHERE   SP.P# IN
                ( SELECT P.P#
                  FROM    P
                  WHERE   P.COLOR = COLOR ('Red') ) ) ;
```

Subqueries can be nested to any depth. *Exercise:* Give some equivalent join formulations of this query.

8.6.12 Get supplier numbers for suppliers with status less than the current maximum status in the S table:

```
SELECT S.S#
FROM    S
WHERE   S.STATUS <
        ( SELECT MAX ( S.STATUS )
          FROM    S ) ;
```

This example involves *two distinct implicit range variables,* both denoted by the same symbol "S" and both ranging over the same table S.

8.6.13 Get supplier names for suppliers who supply part P2. *Note:* This example is the same as Example 8.6.10; we show a different solution, in order to introduce another SQL feature.

```
SELECT DISTINCT S.SNAME
FROM    S
WHERE   EXISTS
        ( SELECT *
          FROM    SP
          WHERE   SP.S# = S.S#
          AND     SP.P# = P# ('P2') ) ;
```

Explanation: The SQL expression "EXISTS (SELECT. . . FROM . . .)" evaluates to TRUE if and only if the result of evaluating the "SELECT . . . FROM . . ." is not empty. In other words, the SQL EXISTS operator corresponds to the *existential quantifier* of the tuple calculus (more or less—but see reference [19.6]). *Note:* SQL refers to the subquery in this particular example as a **correlated** subquery, since it includes references to a range variable (namely, the implicit range variable S) that is defined in the outer query. Another example of a correlated subquery appeared in the second solution to Example 8.6.8, earlier.

8.6.14 Get supplier names for suppliers who do not supply part P2 (Example 8.3.7):

```
SELECT  DISTINCT S.SNAME
FROM    S
WHERE   NOT EXISTS
      ( SELECT *
        FROM    SP
        WHERE   SP.S# = S.S#
        AND     SP.P# = P# ('P2') ) ;
```

Alternatively:

```
SELECT  DISTINCT S.SNAME
FROM    S
WHERE   S.S# NOT IN
      ( SELECT SP.S#
        FROM    SP
        WHERE   SP.P# = P# ('P2') ) ;
```

8.6.15 Get supplier names for suppliers who supply all parts (Example 8.3.6):

```
SELECT  DISTINCT S.SNAME
FROM    S
WHERE   NOT EXISTS
      ( SELECT *
        FROM    P
        WHERE   NOT EXISTS
            ( SELECT *
              FROM    SP
              WHERE   SP.S# = S.S#
              AND     SP.P# = P.P# ) ) ;
```

SQL does not include any direct support for the universal quantifier FORALL; hence, "FORALL-queries" typically have to be expressed in terms of EXISTS and double negation, as in this example.

By the way, it is worth pointing out that expressions such as the one just shown, daunting though they might appear at first glance, are easily constructed by a user who is familiar with relational calculus, as explained in reference [8.4]. Alternatively, if they are still thought too daunting, then there are several "workaround" approaches that can be used that avoid the need for negated quantifiers. In the example, for instance, we might write:

```
SELECT  DISTINCT S.SNAME
FROM    S
WHERE   ( SELECT COUNT ( SP.P# )
          FROM    SP
          WHERE   SP.S# = S.S# )
      = ( SELECT COUNT ( P.P# )
          FROM    P ) ;
```

("Get names of suppliers where the count of the parts they supply is equal to the count of all parts"). Observe, however, that this latter formulation relies, as the NOT EXISTS formulation did not, on the fact that every shipment part number is the number of some existing part. In other words, the two formulations are equivalent, and the second is correct, only because a certain integrity constraint is in effect (see the next chapter).

Note: What we would really like to do in the foregoing example is compare two *tables,* thereby expressing the query as follows:

```
SELECT  DISTINCT S.SNAME              /* warning! illegal! */
FROM    S
WHERE   ( SELECT SP.P#
            FROM    SP
            WHERE   SP.S# = S.S# )
    =   ( SELECT P.P#
            FROM    P ) ;
```

SQL does not directly support table comparisons, however, and so we have to resort to the trick of comparing cardinalities instead (relying on our own external knowledge that if the cardinalities are equal then the tables must be equal too, in the case at hand). See Exercise 8.11.

8.6.16 Get part numbers for parts that either weigh more than 16 pounds or are supplied by supplier S2, or both (Example 8.3.9):

```
SELECT  P.P#
FROM    P
WHERE   P.WEIGHT > WEIGHT ( 16.0 )

UNION

SELECT  SP.P#
FROM    SP
WHERE   SP.S# = S# ('S2') ;
```

Redundant duplicate rows are always eliminated from the result of an unqualified **UNION**, **INTERSECT**, or **EXCEPT** (EXCEPT is the SQL analog of our MINUS). However, SQL also provides the qualified variants **UNION ALL**, **INTERSECT ALL**, and **EXCEPT ALL**, where duplicates if any are retained. We deliberately omit examples of these variants.

8.6.17 Get the part number and the weight in grams for each part with weight > 10,000 grams (Example 8.5.1):

```
SELECT  P.P#, P.WEIGHT * 454 AS GMWT
FROM    P
WHERE   P.WEIGHT * 454 > WEIGHT ( 10000.0 ) ;
```

Recall now the WITH clause, which we introduced in Chapter 5 and used in connection with the relational algebra in Chapter 7.[9] The purpose of WITH is, loosely, to introduce names for expressions. SQL also has a WITH clause, though its use is limited to table expressions only. In the example, we can use such a clause to avoid having to write the expression P.WEIGHT * 454 out twice:

```
WITH T1 AS ( SELECT P.P#, P.WEIGHT * 454 AS GMWT
               FROM    P )
     SELECT T1.P#, T1.GMWT
     FROM    T1
     WHERE   T1.GMWT > WEIGHT ( 10000.0 ) ;
```

Note, incidentally, that entries in a WITH clause—what we called *<name intro>*s in the previous chapter—take the form *<name>* AS (*<exp>*) in SQL, whereas in **Tutorial D**

---

[9] It can be used in connection with the relational calculus too, of course.

they take the form *<exp>* AS *<name>*. We remark in passing that WITH is important in formulating the SQL analog of the algebraic TCLOSE operator. We omit the details here, but an example can be found in the online answer to Exercise 4.6.

This brings us to the end of our list of SQL retrieval examples. The list is rather long; nevertheless, there are many SQL features we have not even mentioned. The fact is, SQL is an extremely *redundant* language [4.19], in the sense that it almost always provides numerous different ways of formulating the same query, and space simply does not permit us to describe all possible formulations and all possible options, even for the comparatively small set of examples we have discussed in this section. See Appendix B for further details.

8.7   DOMAIN CALCULUS

We turn now to the domain calculus. As indicated in Section 8.1, the domain calculus differs from the tuple calculus in that its range variables range over domains (types) instead of relations. From a syntactic standpoint, the most immediately obvious difference between the domain and the tuple calculus is that the former supports an additional form of *<bool exp>*, which we will call a **membership condition**. Such a condition takes the form:

```
R { <pair commalist> }
```

where *R* is a relvar name and each *<pair>* takes the form *A x*, where *A* is the name of an attribute of *R* and *x* is either a range variable name or a selector invocation (often a literal). The overall condition evaluates to TRUE if and only if there exists a tuple in the relation denoted by *R* such that, for every specified *<pair> A x*, the comparison *A = x* evaluates to TRUE for that tuple. For example, the expression

```
SP { S# S#('S1'), P# P#('P1') }
```

is a membership condition that evaluates to TRUE if and only if there currently exists a shipment tuple with S# value S1 and P# value P1. Likewise, the membership condition

```
SP { S# SX, P# PX }
```

evaluates to TRUE if and only if there currently exists a shipment tuple with S# value equal to the current value of range variable SX (whatever that might be) and P# value equal to the current value of range variable PX (again, whatever that might be).

For the remainder of this section we assume the existence of range variables as follows:

Domain:	*Range variables:*
S#	SX, SY, ...
P#	PX, PY, ...
NAME	NAMEX, NAMEY, ...
COLOR	COLORX, COLORY, ...
WEIGHT	WEIGHTX, WEIGHTY, ...
QTY	QTYX, QTYY, ...
CHAR	CITYX, CITYY, ...
INTEGER	STATUSX, STATUSY, ...

Here then are some examples of domain calculus expressions:

```
SX

SX WHERE S { S# SX }

SX WHERE S { S# SX, CITY 'London' }

{ SX, CITYX } WHERE S { S# SX, CITY CITYX }
              AND     SP { S# SX, P# P#('P2') }

{ SX, PX } WHERE S { S# SX, CITY CITYX }
           AND    P { P# PX, CITY CITYY }
           AND    CITYX ≠ CITYY
```

Loosely speaking, the first of these expressions denotes the set of all supplier numbers; the second denotes the set of all supplier numbers in relvar S; the third denotes that subset of those supplier numbers for which the city is London. The next is a domain calculus representation of the query "Get supplier numbers and cities for suppliers who supply part P2" (note that the tuple calculus version of this query required an existential quantifier). The last is a domain calculus representation of the query "Get supplier-number/part-number pairs such that the supplier and part are not colocated."

We give domain calculus versions of some of the examples from Section 8.3 (some of them modified slightly here).

8.7.1 Get supplier numbers for suppliers in Paris with status > 20 (simplified version of Example 8.3.1):

```
SX WHERE EXISTS STATUSX
        ( STATUSX > 20 AND
          S { S# SX, STATUS STATUSX, CITY 'Paris' } )
```

This first example is somewhat clumsier than its tuple calculus counterpart (observe in particular that an explicit quantifier is still needed). On the other hand, there are also cases where the reverse is true; see especially some of the more complex examples later in this section.

8.7.2 Get all pairs of supplier numbers such that the suppliers concerned are colocated (Example 8.3.2):

```
{ SX AS SA, SY AS SB } WHERE EXISTS CITYZ
                             ( S { S# SX, CITY CITYZ } AND
                               S { S# SY, CITY CITYZ } AND
                               SX < SY )
```

8.7.3 Get supplier names for suppliers who supply at least one red part (Example 8.3.4):

```
NAMEX WHERE EXISTS SX EXISTS PX
           ( S { S# SX, SNAME NAMEX }
         AND SP { S# SX, P# PX }
         AND P { P# PX, COLOR COLOR('Red') } )
```

8.7.4 Get supplier names for suppliers who supply at least one part supplied by supplier S2 (Example 8.3.5):

```
NAMEX WHERE EXISTS SX EXISTS PX
         ( S { S# SX, SNAME NAMEX }
           AND SP { S# SX, P# PX }
           AND SP { S# S#('S2'), P# PX } )
```

8.7.5 Get supplier names for suppliers who supply all parts (Example 8.3.6):

```
NAMEX WHERE EXISTS SX ( S { S# SX, SNAME NAMEX }
          AND FORALL PX ( IF P { P# PX }
                          THEN SP { S# SX, P# PX }
                          END IF )
```

8.7.6 Get supplier names for suppliers who do not supply part P2 (Example 8.3.7):

```
NAMEX WHERE EXISTS SX ( S { S# SX, SNAME NAMEX }
                 AND NOT SP { S# SX, P# P#('P2') } )
```

8.7.7 Get supplier numbers for suppliers who supply at least all those parts supplied by supplier S2 (Example 8.3.8):

```
SX WHERE FORALL PX ( IF SP { S# S#('S2'), P# PX }
                     THEN SP { S# SX, P# PX }
                     END IF )
```

8.7.8 Get part numbers for parts that either weigh more than 16 pounds or are supplied by supplier S2, or both (Example 8.3.9):

```
PX WHERE EXISTS WEIGHTX
       ( P { P# PX, WEIGHT WEIGHTX }
         AND WEIGHTX > WEIGHT ( 16.0 ) )
     OR SP { S# S#('S2'), P# PX }
```

The domain calculus, like the tuple calculus, is formally equivalent to the relational algebra (and so it is relationally complete). For proof see, for example, Ullman [8.13].

8.8 QUERY-BY-EXAMPLE

The best-known example of a language based on the domain calculus is **Query-By-Example**, QBE [8.14]. (Actually QBE incorporates aspects of both the domain and the tuple calculus, but the emphasis is on the former.) Its syntax, which is attractive and intuitively very simple, is based on the idea of *making entries in blank tables*. For example, a QBE formulation of the query "Get supplier names for suppliers who supply at least one part supplied by supplier S2" might look like this:

S	S#	SNAME
	_SX	P._NX

SP	S#	P#
	_SX	_PX

SP	S#	P#
	S2	_PX

Explanation: The user asks the system to display three blank tables on the screen, one for suppliers and two for shipments, and makes entries in them as shown. Entries beginning with a leading underscore are *example elements* (i.e., domain calculus range variables); other entries are literal values. The user is asking the system to *present* ("P.") supplier names (_NX) such that, if the supplier number is _SX, then supplier _SX supplies some part _PX, and part _PX in turn is supplied by supplier S2. If you compare this QBE formulation with a tuple or domain calculus equivalent (see Examples 8.3.5 and 8.7.4), you will see that it differs from those other formulations in that it involves no explicit quantification[10]—another reason why QBE is intuitively easy to understand. It is worth comparing the QBE version with an SQL formulation, too (exercise for the reader).

We now present a series of examples in order to illustrate some of the major features of QBE. As an exercise, you might like to try comparing and contrasting these QBE examples with their pure domain calculus counterparts.

8.8.1 Get supplier numbers for suppliers in Paris with status > 20 (Example 8.7.1):

S	S#	SNAME	STATUS	CITY
	P.		> 20	Paris

Note how easy it is to express the ">" and "=" comparisons. Note too that there is no need to specify an example element explicitly if it is not referenced anywhere else (though an explicit example element, as in P._SX, would not be wrong). Note finally that character string values such as Paris can be specified without being enclosed in quotes (it would not be wrong to supply the quotes, however, and sometimes they are required—e.g., if the string includes any spaces).

It is also possible to specify "P." against the entire row—for example, as follows:

S	S#	SNAME	STATUS	CITY
P.			> 20	Paris

This example is equivalent to specifying "P." in every column position in the row, thus:

S	S#	SNAME	STATUS	CITY
	P.	P.	P. >20	P.Paris

One last point arising from this example: The system will provide facilities to allow blank tables to be edited on the screen by the addition or removal of columns and rows and by the widening and narrowing of columns. Tables can thus be tailored to fit the requirements of whatever operation the user is trying to formulate; in particular, columns that are not needed for the operation in question can be eliminated. For example, in the first QBE formulation of the example under discussion, the SNAME column could have been eliminated, to yield:

S	S#	STATUS	CITY
	P.	> 20	Paris

---

[10] An analogous remark applies to QUEL, incidentally (see, e.g., reference [8.5]).

In what follows, therefore, we will often omit columns that are not needed for the query under consideration.

8.8.2 Get part numbers for all parts supplied, with redundant duplicates eliminated:

SP	S#	P#	QTY
UNQ.		P.	

UNQ. stands for *unique* (it corresponds to DISTINCT in SQL).

8.8.3 Get supplier numbers and status for suppliers in Paris, in ascending supplier number order within descending status order:

S	S#	STATUS	CITY
	P.AO(2).	P.DO(1).	Paris

"AO." stands for ascending order, "DO." for descending order. The integers in parentheses indicate the major-to-minor sequence for ordering columns; in the example, STATUS is the major column and S# the minor column.

8.8.4 Get supplier numbers and status for suppliers who either are located in Paris or have status > 20, or both (modified version of Example 8.8.1).

Conditions specified within a single row are considered to be "ANDed" together (see, e.g., Example 8.8.1). To "OR" two conditions, they must be specified in different rows, as here:

S	S#	STATUS	CITY
	P.		Paris
	P.	> 20	

Another approach to this query makes use of what is known as a *condition box,* thus:

S	S#	STATUS	CITY
	P.	_ST	_SC

CONDITIONS
_SC = Paris OR _ST > 20

In general, a condition box allows the specification of conditions that are too complex to be expressed within a single column of a blank table—for example, comparisons involving two distinct columns, or comparisons involving an aggregate operator.

8.8.5 Get parts whose weight is in the range 16 to 19 inclusive:

P	P#	WEIGHT	WEIGHT
	P.	>= 16.0	<= 19.0

8.8.6 For all parts, get the part number and the weight of the part in grams (Example 8.6.2):

P	P#	WEIGHT	GMWT
	P.	_PW	P. _PW * 454

8.8.7 Get supplier names for suppliers who supply part P2 (Example 7.5.1):

S	S#	SNAME
	_SX	P.

SP	S#	P#
	_SX	P2

The row in table SP here is implicitly existentially quantified. The query can be paraphrased:

> Get supplier names for suppliers SX such that there exists a shipment showing supplier SX supplying part P2.

QBE thus does implicitly support EXISTS (and note that the implicit range variable ranges over a relation, not a domain, which is why we said earlier that QBE involves some aspects of the tuple calculus). However, it does not support NOT EXISTS.[11] As a consequence, certain queries—for example, "Get supplier names for suppliers who supply all parts" (Example 8.7.5)—cannot be expressed in QBE, and QBE is not relationally complete.

8.8.8 Get all supplier-number/part-number pairs such that the supplier and part concerned are "colocated" (modified version of Example 8.6.3):

S	S#	CITY
	_SX	_CX

P	P#	CITY
	_PX	_CX

P.	_SX	_PX

Three blank tables are needed for this query, one each for S and P (only relevant columns shown) and one for the result. Notice how example elements are specified to link these three tables together. The entire query can be paraphrased:

> Get supplier-number/part-number pairs, SX and PX say, such that SX and PX are both located in the same city CX.

8.8.9 Get all pairs of supplier numbers such that the suppliers concerned are colocated (Example 8.6.5):

S	S#	CITY
	_SX	_CZ
	_SY	_CZ

P.	_SX	_SY

---

[11] At least, not properly; it does support it partially. Originally, in fact, it supported it "completely," but the support was always troublesome. The basic problem was that there was no way to specify the order in which the various implicit quantifiers were to be applied, and unfortunately the order is significant when any NOTs are involved. As a result, certain QBE expressions were ambiguous. A detailed discussion of this point can be found in reference [8.3]. See also Exercise 8.2.

A condition box could be used if desired to specify the additional condition _SX < _SY.

8.8.10 Get the total quantity of part P2 supplied:

SP	S#	P#	QTY	
		P2	_QX	P.SUM._QX

QBE supports the usual aggregate operators.

8.8.11 For each part supplied, get the part number and the total shipment quantity (Example 8.6.8):

SP	S#	P#	QTY	
		G.P.	_QY	P.SUM._QY

"G." causes grouping (it corresponds to GROUP BY in SQL).

8.8.12 Get part numbers for all parts supplied by more than one supplier:

SP	S#	P#	CONDITIONS
	_SX	G.P.	CNT._SX >1

8.8.13 Get part numbers for parts that either weigh more than 16 pounds or are supplied by supplier S2, or both (Example 8.7.8):

P	P#	WEIGHT
	_PX	> 16.0

SP	S#	P#
	S2	_PY

P.	_PX
P.	_PY

8.8.14 Insert part P7 (city Athens, weight 24, name and color at present unknown) into table P:

P	P#	PNAME	COLOR	WEIGHT	CITY
I.	P7			24.0	Athens

Note that "I." applies to the entire row and so appears beneath the table name. *Note:* Of course, inserting new tuples is not a relational calculus (or relational algebra) operation at all; it is an update operation, not a read-only one. We include the example here for completeness. Analogous remarks apply to the next three examples also.

8.8.15 Delete all shipments with quantity greater than 300:

SP	S#	P#	QTY
D.			> 300

The "D." appears beneath the table name.

8.8.16 Change the color of part P2 to yellow, increase the weight by 5, and set the city to Oslo:

P	P#	PNAME	COLOR	WEIGHT	WEIGHT	CITY
	P2		U.Yellow	_WT	U._WT + 5	U.Oslo

8.8.17 Set the shipment quantity to five for all suppliers in London:

SP	S#	QTY
	_SX	U.5

S	S#	CITY
	_SX	London

8.9 SUMMARY

We have described the **relational calculus**, an alternative to the relational algebra. Superficially, the two look very different—the calculus is **descriptive** where the algebra is **prescriptive**—but at a deep level they are the same, because any expression of the calculus can be converted into a semantically equivalent expression of the algebra and *vice versa.*

The calculus comes in two versions, **tuple** calculus and **domain** calculus. The key difference between them is that the range variables of the tuple calculus range over relations, while the range variables of the domain calculus range over domains.

An expression of the tuple calculus consists of a **proto tuple** and an optional WHERE clause containing a boolean expression or **WFF** ("well-formed formula"). That WFF is allowed to contain **quantifiers** (EXISTS and FORALL), **free** and **bound variable references,** boolean operators (AND, OR, NOT, etc.), and so on. Every free variable mentioned in the WFF must also be mentioned in the proto tuple. *Note:* We did not explicitly discuss the point in the body of the chapter, but expressions of the calculus are intended to serve essentially the same purposes as expressions of the algebra (see Chapter 7, Section 7.6).

We showed by example how Codd's **reduction algorithm** can be used to convert an arbitrary expression of the calculus to an equivalent expression of the algebra, thus paving the way for a possible implementation strategy for the calculus. And we mentioned once again the issue of **relational completeness**, and discussed briefly what is involved in proving that some given language is complete in this sense.

We also considered the question of including **computational** capabilities (analogous to the capabilities provided by EXTEND and SUMMARIZE in the algebra) in the tuple calculus. Then we presented an overview of the relevant features of **SQL**. SQL is a kind of hybrid of the algebra and the tuple calculus; for example, it explicitly supports both the JOIN and UNION operators of the algebra and the range variables and the existential quantifier of the calculus.

An SQL query consists of a **table expression**—frequently just a single **select expression**, but various kinds of explicit **join** expressions are also supported, and join expressions and select expressions can be combined in various ways using the **UNION, INTERSECT,** and **EXCEPT** operators. We also mentioned the use of **ORDER BY** to impose an order on the table resulting from a table expression (of any kind). Regarding **select expressions** in particular, we described:

- The basic **SELECT clause** itself, including the use of **DISTINCT**, the use of computational expressions, the introduction of result column names, and the "SELECT *" shorthand
- The **FROM clause**, including the use of **range variables**
- The **WHERE clause**, including the use of the **EXISTS** operator
- The **GROUP BY** and **HAVING clauses**, including the use of the **aggregate operators** COUNT, SUM, AVG, and so on
- The use of **subqueries** in (e.g.) the SELECT, FROM, and WHERE clauses[12]

We also gave a **conceptual evaluation algorithm** (i.e., a basis for a formal definition) for an SQL select expression. In outline, that algorithm involves (a) forming the Cartesian product of the tables specified in the FROM clause, (b) restricting that product in accordance with the boolean expression specified in the WHERE clause, and finally (c) projecting that restriction over the columns specified in the SELECT clause. However, we hasten to add that this outline is extremely incomplete; see reference [4.20] for a more detailed explanation.

Next, we presented a brief introduction to the **domain** calculus, and claimed without attempting to prove as much that it too was relationally complete. Thus, the tuple calculus, the domain calculus, and the algebra are all equivalent to one another. Finally, we sketched the facilities of **Query-By-Example,** which is probably the best-known commercial implementation of the ideas of the domain calculus.

EXERCISES

8.1   Let $p(x)$ and q be arbitrary WFFs in which x does and does not appear, respectively, as a free variable. Which of the following statements are valid? *Note:* The symbol $\Rightarrow$ means *implies;* the symbol $\equiv$ means *is equivalent to.* Note too that $A \Rightarrow B$ and $B \Rightarrow A$ are together the same as $A \equiv B$.

a. `EXISTS x ( q )  ≡  q`

b. `FORALL x ( q )  ≡  q`

c. `EXISTS x ( p(x) AND q )  ≡  EXISTS x ( p(x) ) AND q`

d. `FORALL x ( p(x) AND q )  ≡  FORALL x ( p(x) ) AND q`

e. `FORALL x ( p(x) )  ⇒  EXISTS x ( p(x) )`

f. `EXISTS x ( TRUE )  ≡  TRUE`

g. `FORALL x ( FALSE )  ≡  FALSE`

---

[12] We now observe, however, that—speaking a trifle loosely—subqueries in the FROM clause are treated as *table* expressions, subqueries in the SELECT clause are treated as *scalar* expressions, and subqueries in the WHERE clause are treated as either table expressions or scalar expressions, depending on context (!).

8.2 Let $p(x,y)$ be an arbitrary WFF with free variables x and y. Which of the following statements are valid?

a. `EXISTS x EXISTS y ( p(x,y) )  ≡  EXISTS y EXISTS x ( p(x,y) )`

b. `FORALL x FORALL y ( p(x,y) )  ≡  FORALL y FORALL x ( p(x,y) )`

c. `FORALL x ( p(x,y) )  ≡  NOT EXISTS x ( NOT p(x,y) )`

d. `EXISTS x ( p(x,y) )  ≡  NOT FORALL x ( NOT p(x,y) )`

e. `EXISTS x FORALL y ( p(x,y) )  ≡  FORALL y EXISTS x ( p(x,y) )`

f. `EXISTS y FORALL x ( p(x,y) )  ⇒  FORALL x EXISTS y ( p(x,y) )`

8.3 Let $p(x)$ and $q(y)$ be arbitrary WFFs with free variables x and y, respectively. Which of the following statements are valid?

a. `EXISTS x ( p(x) ) AND EXISTS y ( q(y) )  ≡`
   `EXISTS x EXISTS y ( p(x) AND q(y) )`

b. `EXISTS x ( IF p(x) THEN q(x) END IF )  ≡`
   `IF FORALL x ( p(x) ) THEN EXISTS x ( q(x) ) END IF`

8.4 Consider once again the query "Get supplier numbers for suppliers who supply at least all those parts supplied by supplier S2." A possible tuple calculus formulation is:

```
SX.S# WHERE FORALL SPY ( IF SPY.S# = S# ('S2') THEN
                              EXISTS SPZ ( SPZ.S# = SX.S# AND
                                           SPZ.P# = SPY.P# )
                         END IF )
```

(SPZ here is another range variable that ranges over shipments.) What will this query return if supplier S2 currently supplies no parts at all? What difference would it make if we replaced SX by SPX throughout?

8.5 Here is a sample query against the suppliers-parts-projects database (the usual conventions apply regarding range variable names):

```
{ PX.PNAME, PX.CITY } WHERE FORALL SX FORALL JX EXISTS SPJX
                            ( SX.CITY = 'London' AND
                              JX.CITY = 'Paris' AND
                              SPJX.S# = SX.S# AND
                              SPJX.P# = PX.P# AND
                              SPJX.J# = JX.J# AND
                              SPJX.QTY < QTY ( 500 ) )
```

a. Translate this query into natural language.

b. Play DBMS and "execute" Codd's reduction algorithm on this query. Can you see any improvements that might be made to that algorithm?

8.6 Give a tuple calculus formulation of the query "Get the three heaviest parts."

8.7 Consider the bill-of-materials relvar PART_STRUCTURE of Chapter 4, Exercise 4.6. The well-known **part explosion** query "Get part numbers for all parts that are components, at any level, of some given part, say part P1"—the result of which, PART_BILL say, is certainly a relation that can be derived from PART_STRUCTURE—cannot be formulated as a single expression of the original relational algebra, nor of the calculus as described in this chapter. In other words, PART_BILL is a derivable relation that nevertheless cannot be derived by means of a single expression of the original algebra or calculus. Why is this?

8.8 Suppose the suppliers relvar S were to be replaced by a set of relvars LS, PS, AS, and so on (one for each distinct supplier city; the LS relvar, for example, contains just the supplier tuples for the suppliers in London). Suppose too that we are unaware of exactly what supplier cities exist, and are therefore unaware of exactly how many such relvars there are. Consider the query "Is supplier S1 represented in the database?" Can this query be expressed in the calculus (or the algebra)? Justify your answer.

8.9   Show that SQL is relationally complete.

8.10   Does SQL have equivalents of the relational EXTEND and SUMMARIZE operators?

8.11   Does SQL have equivalents of the relational comparison operators?

8.12   Give as many different SQL formulations as you can think of for the query "Get supplier names for suppliers who supply part P2."

Query Exercises

The remaining exercises are all based on the suppliers-parts-projects database. In each case you are asked to write an expression for the indicated query. (By way of an interesting variation, you might like to try looking at some of the online answers first and stating what the given expression means in natural language.)

8.13   Give tuple calculus solutions to Exercises 7.13–7.50.

8.14   Give SQL solutions to Exercises 7.13–7.50.

8.15   Give domain calculus solutions to Exercises 7.13–7.50.

8.16   Give QBE solutions to Exercises 7.13–7.50.

REFERENCES AND BIBLIOGRAPHY

8.1 E. F. Codd: "A Data Base Sublanguage Founded on the Relational Calculus," Proc. 1971 ACM SIGFIDET Workshop on Data Description, Access and Control, San Diego, Calif. (November 1971).

8.2 C. J. Date: "A Note on the Relational Calculus," *ACM SIGMOD Record 18,* No. 4 (December 1989). Republished as "An Anomaly in Codd's Reduction Algorithm" in C. J. Date and Hugh Darwen, *Relational Database Writings 1989–1991*. Reading, Mass.: Addison-Wesley (1992).

8.3 C. J. Date: "Why Quantifier Order Is Important," in C. J. Date and Hugh Darwen, *Relational Database Writings 1989–1991*. Reading, Mass.: Addison-Wesley (1992).

8.4 C. J. Date: "Relational Calculus as an Aid to Effective Query Formulation," in C. J. Date and Hugh Darwen, *Relational Database Writings 1989–1991*. Reading, Mass.: Addison-Wesley (1992).

> Just about every product on the market currently supports SQL, not the relational calculus (nor the relational algebra). This paper nevertheless advocates, and illustrates, the idea of using relational calculus as an intermediate step in the construction of SQL queries.

8.5 G. D. Held, M. R. Stonebraker, and E. Wong: "INGRES—A Relational Data Base System," Proc. NCC *44,* Anaheim, Calif. Montvale, N.J.: AFIPS Press (May 1975).

> There were two major relational prototypes under development in the mid to late 1970s: System R at IBM, and Ingres (originally INGRES, all uppercase) at the University of California at Berkeley. Both of those projects became extremely influential in the research world, and both subsequently led to commercial systems, including DB2 in the case of System R and the commercial Ingres product in the case of Ingres. *Note:* The Ingres prototype is sometimes referred to as "University Ingres" [8.11] in order to distinguish it from "Commercial Ingres," the commercial version of the system. A tutorial overview of the commercial version can be found in reference [1.5].

Ingres was not originally an SQL system; instead, it supported a language called QUEL ("Query Language"), which in many respects was technically superior to SQL. Indeed, QUEL still forms the basis of a certain amount of current research, and examples expressed in QUEL still appear in the research literature from time to time. This paper, which was the first to describe the Ingres prototype, includes a preliminary definition of QUEL. See also references [8.10–8.12].

8.6 J. L. Kuhns: "Answering Questions by Computer: A Logical Study," Report RM-5428-PR, Rand Corp., Santa Monica, Calif. (1967).

8.7 M. Lacroix and A. Pirotte: "Domain-Oriented Relational Languages," Proc. 3rd Int. Conf. on Very Large Data Bases, Tokyo, Japan (October 1977).

8.8 T. H. Merrett: "The Extended Relational Algebra, A Basis for Query Languages," in B. Shneiderman (ed.), *Databases: Improving Usability and Responsiveness*. New York, N.Y.: Academic Press (1978).

The extended relational algebra of this paper's title includes certain quantifiers—not just EXISTS and FORALL as described in this chapter, but quantifiers of the form *the number of* and *the proportion of* (e.g., at least three of, not more than half of, an odd number of, etc.).

8.9 M. Negri, G. Pelagatti, and L. Sbattella: "Formal Semantics of SQL Queries," *ACM TODS 16,* No. 3 (September 1991).

To quote from the abstract: "The semantics of SQL queries are formally defined by stating a set of rules that determine a syntax-driven translation of an SQL query to a formal model called Extended Three-Valued Predicate Calculus (E3VPC), which is largely based on well-known mathematical concepts. Rules for transforming a general E3VPC expression to a canonical form are also given; [in addition,] problems like equivalence analysis of SQL queries are completely solved." We note, however, that the paper addresses only SQL as defined by the very first (1986) version of the standard. *Note:* For an explanation of the terms *three-valued* and *canonical form,* see Chapters 19 and 18, respectively.

8.10 Michael Stonebraker (ed.): *The INGRES Papers: The Anatomy of a Relational Database Management System*. Reading, Mass.: Addison-Wesley (1986).

A collection of papers from the University Ingres project, edited and annotated by one of the original Ingres designers.

8.11 Michael Stonebraker, Eugene Wong, Peter Kreps, and Gerald Held: "The Design and Implementation of INGRES," *ACM TODS 1,* No. 3 (September 1976). Republished in reference [8.10].

A detailed description of the University Ingres prototype.

8.12 Michael Stonebraker: "Retrospection on a Data Base System," *ACM TODS 5,* No. 2 (June 1980). Republished in reference [8.10].

An account of the history of the Ingres prototype project (to January 1979). The emphasis is on mistakes and lessons learned rather than on successes.

8.13 Jeffrey D. Ullman: *Principles of Database and Knowledge-Base Systems: Volume I.* Rockville, Md.: Computer Science Press (1988).

Ullman's book includes a more formal treatment of relational calculus and related matters than the present book does. In particular, it discusses the concept of **safety** of calculus expressions. This topic is of concern if we adopt a slightly different version of the calculus, one in which range variables are not defined by separate statements but instead are bound to their range by means of explicit expressions within the WHERE clause. In such a version of the calculus, the query (e.g.) "Get suppliers in London" might look something like this:

```
X WHERE X ∈ S AND X.CITY = 'London'
```

One problem (not the only one) with this version of the calculus is that it would apparently permit a query such as

```
X WHERE NOT ( X ∈ S )
```

Such an expression is said to be "unsafe," because it does not return a finite result (the set of all things that are not tuples of S is infinite). As a consequence, certain rules must be imposed to guarantee that all legal expressions are safe. Such rules are described in Ullman's book (for both tuple and domain calculus). We note that Codd's original calculus did implicitly include such rules.

8.14 Moshé M. Zloof: "Query-By-Example," Proc. NCC *44,* Anaheim, Calif. (May 1975). Montvale, N.J.: AFIPS Press (1977).

Zloof was the original inventor and designer of QBE. This paper was the first of many by Zloof on the subject.

CHAPTER 9

Integrity

9.1 INTRODUCTION

The integrity part of the relational model is the part that has changed the most over the years (perhaps we should say *evolved* rather than *changed*). The original emphasis was on primary and foreign keys specifically ("keys" for short). Gradually, however, the importance—indeed, the *crucial* importance—of integrity constraints in general began to be better understood and more widely appreciated; at the same time, certain awkward questions regarding keys in particular began to be raised. The structure of this chapter reflects this shift in emphasis, inasmuch as it deals with integrity constraints in general first, at some considerable length, and then goes on to discuss keys (which do continue to be of major pragmatic importance) subsequently.

Loosely, then, an **integrity constraint** is a boolean expression that is associated with some database and is required to evaluate at all times to TRUE. Such a constraint can be regarded as the formal expression of some "business rule" [9.15]—though business rules in turn, which we assume for the sake of this chapter are always expressed in natural language, are also sometimes referred to as integrity constraints. Be that as it may, here are a few examples, all based on the suppliers-and-parts database:

1. Every supplier status value is in the range 1 to 100 inclusive.
2. Every supplier in London has status 20.
3. If there are any parts at all, at least one of them is blue.
4. No two distinct suppliers have the same supplier number.
5. Every shipment involves an existing supplier.
6. No supplier with status less than 20 supplies any part in a quantity greater than 500.

We will be making extensive use of these examples throughout this chapter.

Clearly, constraints must be formally declared to the DBMS, and the DBMS must then enforce them. Declaring them is simply a matter of using the relevant features of the database language; enforcing them is a matter of the DBMS monitoring updates that might violate the constraints and rejecting those that do. Here is a formal declaration of the first of our examples in **Tutorial D**:

```
CONSTRAINT SC1
    IS_EMPTY ( S WHERE STATUS < 1 OR STATUS > 100 ) ;
```

To enforce this constraint, the DBMS will have to monitor all operations that attempt to insert a new supplier or change an existing supplier's status [9.5].

Of course, when a constraint is initially declared, the system must check that the database currently satisfies it. If it does not, the constraint must be rejected; otherwise, it is accepted—that is, saved in the system catalog—and enforced from that point forward. By the way, note the constraint *name* SC1 ("suppliers constraint one") in the example. Assuming this constraint is accepted by the DBMS, it will be registered in the catalog under that name, and that name will then appear in diagnostic messages produced by the system in response to attempts to violate it.

Here are two more possible formulations of Example 1, now using a calculus-based version of **Tutorial D** (SX here is a range variable ranging over suppliers):

```
CONSTRAINT SC1
    NOT EXISTS SX ( SX.STATUS < 1 OR SX.STATUS > 100 ) ;

CONSTRAINT SC1
    FORALL SX ( SX.STATUS ≥ 1 AND SX.STATUS ≤ 100 ) ;
```

All three formulations are equivalent, of course. In this chapter, however, we use the calculus rather than the algebra as the basis for most of our discussions, for reasons that should become clear as we proceed. As an exercise, you might like to try giving algebraic versions of our calculus-based examples.

Of course, we also need a way of getting rid of existing constraints if they are no longer needed:

```
DROP CONSTRAINT <constraint name> ;
```

9.2   A CLOSER LOOK

Integrity constraints in general are constraints on the values some variable or combination of variables is permitted to assume.[1] Thus, the fact that a given variable is of some given type represents an *a priori* constraint on the variable in question (the values that can be assumed by that variable must obviously be values of that type). And it follows immediately—indeed, it is just a special case—that the fact that each attribute of a given relvar is of some given type represents an *a priori* constraint on the relvar in question. For example, relvar S (suppliers) is constrained to contain values that are relations in which every S# value is a supplier number (a value of type S#), every SNAME value is a name (a value of type NAME), and so on.

However, these simple *a priori* constraints are certainly not the only ones possible; in fact, none of the six examples in Section 9.1 was an *a priori* constraint in this sense. Consider Example 1 once again:

1. Every supplier status value is in the range 1 to 100 inclusive.

Here is a slightly more precise way of saying the same thing:

If *s* is a supplier, then *s* has a status value in the range 1 to 100 inclusive.

And here is a more precise (or more formal) way still:[2]

```
FORALL s# ∈ S#, sn ∈ NAME, st ∈ INTEGER, sc ∈ CHAR
  ( IF { S# s#, SNAME sn, STATUS st, CITY sc } ∈ S
    THEN st ≥ 1 AND st ≤ 100 )
```

This formal expression can be read as follows (in rather stilted English):

For all supplier numbers *s#*, all names *sn,* all integers *st,* and all character strings *sc,* if a tuple with S# *s#*, SNAME *sn,* STATUS *st,* and CITY *sc* appears in the suppliers relvar, then *st* is greater than or equal to 1 and less than or equal to 100.

Perhaps you can now see why we gave that alternative natural language version of Example 1 a few moments back. The fact is, that alternative version, the corresponding formal expression, and the stilted English analog all have a certain overall "shape" (as it were) that looks something like this:

IF *a certain tuple appears in a certain relvar,* **THEN** *that tuple satisfies a certain condition.*

---

[1] As this remark indicates, integrity constraints do apply (at least in principle) to variables of all kinds. For obvious reasons, however, our main focus in this book is on relation variables specifically.

[2] Please note that the syntax used in these formal examples is not **Tutorial D** (**Tutorial D** versions of the examples are given later). Nor is it exactly the syntax we defined for relational calculus in Chapter 8, though it is close (especially to the domain version).

This "shape" is an example of a **logical implication** (sometimes called a *material* implication). We have met this construct before, in Chapter 8; it takes the general form

```
IF p THEN q
```

where *p* and *q* are boolean expressions, called the **antecedent** and the **consequent**, respectively. The overall expression—that is, the implication—is false if *p* is true and *q* is false, and true otherwise; in other words, IF *p* THEN *q* is itself a boolean expression, and it is logically equivalent to (NOT *p*) OR *q*.

By the way, note how the foregoing shape tacitly includes the necessary FORALL quantification—"IF a certain tuple appears" means, tacitly, "FORALL tuples that do appear."

We now proceed to analyze Examples 2–6 similarly (omitting the stilted English formulations, however). *Note:* The formulations that follow are not unique, nor are they necessarily the simplest ones possible, but they are at least correct. Note too that each example does illustrate at least one new point.

2. Every supplier in London has status 20.

```
FORALL s# ∈ S#, sn ∈ NAME, st ∈ INTEGER, sc ∈ CHAR
  ( IF { S# s#, SNAME sn, STATUS st, CITY sc } ∈ S
    THEN ( IF sc = 'London'
             THEN st = 20 ) )
```

In this example, the consequent of the implication is itself an implication.

3. If there are any parts at all, at least one of them is blue.

```
IF
EXISTS p# ∈ P#, pn ∈ NAME, pl ∈ COLOR, pw ∈ WEIGHT, pc ∈ CHAR
  ( { P# p#, PNAME pn, COLOR pl, WEIGHT pw, CITY pc } ∈ P )
THEN
EXISTS p# ∈ P#, pn ∈ NAME, pl ∈ COLOR, pw ∈ WEIGHT, pc ∈ CHAR
  ( { P# p#, PNAME pn, COLOR pl, WEIGHT pw, CITY pc } ∈ P
    AND pl = COLOR ('Blue') )
```

Note that we cannot just say "at least one part is blue"—we have to worry about the case where there are no parts at all. *Note:* Although it might not be obvious, this example does conform to the same general shape as the previous two. Here is an alternative formulation that makes the point clear:

```
FORALL p# ∈ P#, pn ∈ NAME, pl ∈ COLOR, pw ∈ WEIGHT, pc ∈ CHAR
  ( IF { P# p#, PNAME pn, COLOR pl, WEIGHT pw, CITY pc } ∈ P
    THEN EXISTS q# ∈ P#, qn ∈ NAME, ql ∈ COLOR,
                         qw ∈ WEIGHT, qc ∈ CHAR
           ( { P# q#, PNAME qn, COLOR ql,
                       WEIGHT qw, CITY qc } ∈ P
             AND ql = COLOR ('Blue') ) )
```

4. No two distinct suppliers have the same supplier number.

```
FORALL x# ∈ S#, xn ∈ NAME, xt ∈ INTEGER, xc ∈ CHAR,
       y# ∈ S#, yn ∈ NAME, yt ∈ INTEGER, yc ∈ CHAR
  ( IF { S# x#, SNAME xn, STATUS xt, CITY xc } ∈ S AND
       { S# y#, SNAME yn, STATUS yt, CITY yc } ∈ S
    THEN ( IF x# = y#
             THEN xn = yn AND xt = yt AND xc = yc ) )
```

This expression is just a formal statement of the fact that {S#} is a candidate key—or a superkey, at any rate—for suppliers; thus, key constraints are just a special case of constraints in general. The **Tutorial D** syntax KEY {S#} might be regarded as shorthand for the foregoing more longwinded expression. (Note the braces, incidentally: Keys are always *sets* of attributes—even if the set in question contains just a single attribute—and so we always show key attributes enclosed in braces, at least in formal contexts.) *Note:* Both candidate keys and superkeys are discussed in detail in Section 9.10.

By the way, observe that this example takes the overall shape:

> **IF** *certain tuples appear in a certain relvar,* **THEN** *those tuples satisfy a certain condition.*

Compare Examples 2 and 3, which both take the same shape as Example 1 (as does Example 5, as we will see in a moment). By contrast, Example 6 takes the overall shape:

> **IF** *certain tuples appear in certain relvars,* **THEN** *those tuples satisfy a certain condition.*

This latter shape is the one that applies to integrity constraints in general (the first two can be regarded as special cases of this most general case).

5. Every shipment involves an existing supplier.

```
FORALL s# ∈ S#, p# ∈ P#, q ∈ QTY
  ( IF { S# s#, P# p#, QTY q } ∈ SP
    THEN EXISTS sn ∈ NAME, st ∈ INTEGER, sc ∈ CHAR
               ( { S# s#, SNAME sn, STATUS st, CITY sc } ∈ S ) )
```

This expression is a formal statement of the fact that {S#} is a foreign key for shipments, matching the candidate key {S#} for suppliers; thus, foreign key constraints too are just a special case of constraints in general (again, see Section 9.10 for further discussion). Note that this example involves two distinct relvars, SP and S, while Examples 1–4 all involve just one.[3]

6. No supplier with status less than 20 supplies any part in a quantity greater than 500.

```
FORALL s# ∈ S#, sn ∈ NAME, st ∈ INTEGER, sc ∈ CHAR,
       p# ∈ P#, q ∈ QTY
  ( IF { S# s#, SNAME sn, STATUS st, CITY sc } ∈ S AND
       { S# s#, P# p#, QTY q } ∈ SP
    THEN st ≥ 20 OR q ≤ QTY ( 500 ) )
```

This example also involves two distinct relvars, but it is not a foreign key constraint.

Tutorial D Examples

We close this section with (calculus-based) **Tutorial D** versions of Examples 2–6. We adopt our usual conventions regarding range variable names.

2. Every supplier in London has status 20.

```
CONSTRAINT SC2
    FORALL SX ( IF SX.CITY = 'London'
                THEN SX.STATUS = 20 END IF ) ;
```

---

[3] The previous edition of this book used the terms *relvar constraint* for a constraint involving exactly one relvar and *database constraint* for a constraint involving more than one. As we will see in Section 9.9, however, the importance of this distinction is more a matter of pragma than it is of logic, and we will have little to say about it in what follows.

Note that logical implications (IF/THEN expressions) include an "END IF" terminator in **Tutorial D**.

3. If there are any parts at all, at least one of them is blue.

```
CONSTRAINT PC3
    IF EXISTS PX ( TRUE )
    THEN EXISTS PX ( PX.COLOR = COLOR ('Blue') ) END IF ;
```

4. No two distinct suppliers have the same supplier number.

```
CONSTRAINT SC4
    FORALL SX FORALL SY ( IF    SX.S#     = SY.S#
                          THEN SX.SNAME  = SY.SNAME
                          AND   SX.STATUS = SY.STATUS
                          AND   SX.CITY   = SY.CITY
                          END IF ) ;
```

5. Every shipment involves an existing supplier.

```
CONSTRAINT SSP5
    FORALL SPX EXISTS SX ( SX.S# = SPX.S# ) ;
```

6. No supplier with status less than 20 supplies any part in a quantity greater than 500.

```
CONSTRAINT SSP6
    FORALL SX FORALL SPX
        ( IF SX.S# = SPX.S#
          THEN SX.STATUS ≥ 20 OR SPX.QTY ≤ 500 END IF ) ;
```

9.3 PREDICATES AND PROPOSITIONS

Consider once again the formal version of Example 1 ("every supplier status value is in the range 1 to 100 inclusive"):

```
FORALL s# ∈ S#, sn ∈ NAME, st ∈ INTEGER, sc ∈ CHAR
  ( IF { S# s#, SNAME sn, STATUS st, CITY sc } ∈ S
    THEN st ≥ 1 AND st ≤ 100 )
```

This formal version is a boolean expression. Note, however, that it involves a *variable:* namely, the suppliers relvar S.[4] Thus, *we cannot say what the value of the expression is—* that is, we cannot say what truth value it yields—*until we substitute a value for that variable* (indeed, different substitutions will yield different truth values, in general). In other words, the expression is a **predicate**, and the variable S is a **parameter** to that predicate; and when we want to "instantiate" that predicate—which is to say, when we want to check the constraint—we provide as **argument** the relation that is the current value of relvar S (relvar S being the sole parameter), and the expression can then be evaluated.

Now, when we do instantiate that predicate—in effect replacing the sole parameter by some argument—we wind up with a truth-valued expression that involves no variables at all, only values. Analogous remarks apply to constraints involving two, three, four, or any number of relvars; in all cases, when we want to evaluate the expression (i.e., when we want to check the constraint), we replace each parameter by the relation that is the current value of the applicable relvar, and what we wind up with is a truth-valued expression that

---

[4] It also involves several *range* variables, but as we saw in Chapter 8 range variables are not variables in the programming language sense—and we take the term *variable* throughout this chapter to mean a variable in the programming language sense specifically (barring explicit statements to the contrary).

involves no variables at all, or in other words a **proposition**. A proposition is either true or false, unequivocally (it can be thought of as a degenerate predicate—i.e., a predicate for which the set of parameters is empty, as we saw in the previous chapter). Here are a few simple examples:

- The sun is a star.
- The moon is a star.
- The sun is further away from us than the moon.
- George W. Bush won the U.S. presidential election in the year 2000.

Deciding which of these propositions are true and which false is left as an exercise. Do please note, however, that not all propositions are true; to think otherwise is a very common mistake.

The message of this section is this: A constraint as formally stated is a predicate. However, when that constraint is checked, arguments are substituted for the parameters and the predicate is thereby reduced to a proposition—and that proposition is then required to evaluate to TRUE.

9.4 RELVAR PREDICATES AND DATABASE PREDICATES

Of course, any given relvar will be subject to many constraints, in general. Let R be a relvar. Then the **relvar predicate** for R is the logical AND or *conjunction* of all of the constraints that apply to—in other words, mention—relvar R. Now, there is a small possibility of confusion here: Each individual constraint is a predicate in its own right, as we already know; however, **the** relvar predicate for R is the conjunction of *all* of the individual predicates that apply to R. For example, if we assume for simplicity that the six constraints of Section 9.1 are the only constraints that apply to the suppliers-and-parts database (apart from *a priori* ones), then the relvar predicate for suppliers is the conjunction of Numbers 1, 2, 4, 5, and 6, and the relvar predicate for shipments is the conjunction of Numbers 5 and 6. Observe that these two relvar predicates "overlap," in a sense, inasmuch as they have certain constituent constraints in common.[5]

Now let R be a relvar, and let RP be the relvar predicate for R. Clearly, then, R must never be allowed to have a value that, when it is substituted for R in RP (and when any other necessary substitutions of arguments for parameters have also been made in RP), causes RP to evaluate to FALSE. Thus, we can now introduce **The Golden Rule** (first version):

> *No update operation must ever assign to any relvar a value that causes its relvar predicate to evaluate to FALSE.*

---

[5] The previous edition of this book defined the relvar predicate for relvar R to be the conjunction of all *relvar* constraints that applied to R (where, as stated in Section 9.2, a relvar constraint is a constraint that mentions just one relvar). Following reference [3.3], however, we now define it to be the conjunction of *all* constraints, not just all *relvar* constraints, that apply to R. Apologies to anyone who might find this shift in terminology confusing.

Now let *D* be a database,[6] and let *D* contain relvars *R1, R2, ...Rn* (only). Let the relvar predicates for those relvars be *RP1, RP2, ..., RPn,* respectively. Then the **database predicate** for *D, DP* say, is the conjunction of all of those relvar predicates:

```
DP  ≡  RP1 AND RP2 AND ... AND RPn
```

And here is the extended (more general, and in fact final) version of **The Golden Rule**:

> *No update operation must ever assign to any database a value that causes its database predicate to evaluate to FALSE.*

Of course, a database predicate will evaluate to FALSE if and only if at least one of its constituent relvar predicates does so too. And a relvar predicate will evaluate to FALSE if and only if at least one of its constituent constraints does so too. *Note:* As we have seen, two distinct relvar predicates *RPi* and *RPj* (*i* ≠ *j*) might have certain constituent constraints in common. It follows that the very same constraint might appear many times over in the database predicate *DP*. From a logical point of view, there is no harm in this state of affairs, because if *c* is a constraint, then *c* AND *c* is logically equivalent to just *c*. Thus, although it is obviously desirable in such a situation that the system evaluate *c* once and not twice, the issue is one of implementation, not of the model.

9.5   CHECKING THE CONSTRAINTS

This section addresses two topics, one to do with implementation and one to do with the model, and both to do with the question of actually checking the constraints as declared. First, the implementation issue. Consider Example 1 once again, which as we know effectively states that if a certain tuple appears in relvar S, then that tuple has to satisfy a certain condition (*viz.,* "status in the range 1 to 100"). Observe in particular that the constraint talks about tuples *in the relvar.* Apparently, therefore, if we try to insert a new supplier tuple with status (say) 200, the sequence of events has to be:

1. Insert the new tuple.
2. Check the constraint.
3. Undo the update (because the check fails).

But this is absurd! Clearly, we would like to catch the error before the insert is done in the first place. So what the implementation clearly has to do is use the formal expression of the constraint to *infer* the appropriate check(s) to be performed on tuples presented for insertion before the insert is actually done.

In principle, that inference process is fairly straightforward. To be specific, if the database predicate includes a constraint of the form

```
IF { S# s#, SNAME sn, STATUS st, CITY sc } ∈ S
THEN ...
```

---

[6] *D* is a variable, of course (see the annotation to reference [3.3]), and therefore subject to integrity constraints.

—that is, if the antecedent in some implication within the overall predicate is of the form "Some tuple appears in S"—then the consequent in that implication is essentially a constraint on tuples that are presented for insertion into relvar S. *Note:* As an aside, we remark that if the database is designed in accordance with *The Principle of Orthogonal Design* (see Chapter 13)—and assuming the DBMS is aware of the pertinent constraints—then any given tuple will have to be checked against at most one relvar predicate, because it will be a plausible INSERT candidate for at most one relvar.

Now we turn to the model issue (which is more fundamental, of course). Consider **The Golden Rule** once again:

> *No update operation must ever assign to any database a value that causes its database predicate to evaluate to FALSE.*

Although we did not make the point explicitly in Section 9.4, you might have realized that this rule as stated implies that *all constraint checking is immediate.* Why? Because it talks in terms of *update operations* and not in terms of transactions (see next paragraph). In effect, therefore, **The Golden Rule** requires integrity constraints to be satisfied *at statement boundaries,*[7] and there is no notion of "deferred" or COMMIT-time integrity checking at all.

Now, you might already be aware that the position just articulated—that all checking must be immediate—is a very unorthodox one; most of the literature (including earlier editions of this book) argues, or simply assumes, that "the unit of integrity" is the *transaction* and that at least some checking has to be deferred until end-of-transaction (i.e., COMMIT time). However, there are good reasons why transactions are inadequate as that "unit of integrity" and *statements* have to be that unit instead. Unfortunately, it is not possible to explain those reasons properly without first going into a certain amount of background regarding the transaction concept in general. We therefore defer detailed discussion to Chapter 16; prior to that chapter, we merely assume, without attempting to justify our position further, that immediate checking is the logically correct thing to do. (However, one important argument in favor of our position can be found in the annotation to reference [9.16] at the end of the chapter.)

9.6 INTERNAL *VS.* EXTERNAL PREDICATES

We have seen that each relvar has a relvar predicate and that the overall database has a database predicate. Of course, the predicates in question are all ones that are "understood by the system": They are *stated formally* (they are part of the database definition, in fact), and they are *enforced* by the system, too. For such reasons, it is convenient to refer to the predicates in question, on occasion, as **internal** predicates specifically—principally

---

[7] We really need to be a bit more precise here, but making matters more precise depends in part on the particular language we happen to be dealing with. For present purposes, suffice it to say that constraints must be satisfied at the end of each and every statement that contains no other statement syntactically nested inside itself. Or, loosely: *Constraints must be satisfied at semicolons.*

because relvars and databases also have **external** predicates, which we now proceed to discuss.[8]

The first and most significant point is that, while internal predicates are a formal construct, external predicates are an informal construct merely. Internal predicates are (loosely) *what the data means to the system;* external predicates, by contrast, are what the data means to the *user.* Of course, users have to understand the internal predicates as well as the external ones, but, to repeat, the system has to understand—indeed, *can* only understand—the internal ones. In fact, we might say, loosely, that a given internal predicate is *the system's approximation to* the corresponding external predicate.

Let us concentrate on relvars specifically, until further notice. As just indicated, then, the external predicate for a given relvar is basically what that relvar means to the user. In the case of the suppliers relvar S, for example, the external predicate might look something like this:

The supplier with the specified supplier number (S#) is under contract, has the specified name (SNAME) and the specified status (STATUS), and is located in the specified city (CITY). Moreover, the status value is in the range 1 to 100 inclusive, and must be 20 if the city is London. Also, no two distinct suppliers have the same supplier number.

For the sake of the discussion that follows, however, let us replace this predicate by the following simpler one:

Supplier S# is under contract, is named SNAME, has status STATUS, and is located in CITY.

(After all, the external predicate is only informal, so we are at liberty to make it as simple or as complex as we please—within reason, of course.)

Now, note that the foregoing statement is indeed a predicate: It has four parameters (S#, SNAME, STATUS, and CITY) corresponding to the four attributes of the relvar,[9] and when arguments of the appropriate types are substituted for those parameters, we obtain a proposition (i.e., something that is categorically either true or false). Thus, each tuple appearing in relvar S at any given time can be regarded as denoting such a proposition, obtained by instantiating that predicate. And—very important!—those particular propositions (i.e., the ones currently represented by tuples of S) are ones that are understood by convention to be true at that time. For example, if the tuple

```
{ S# S#('S1'), SNAME NAME('Smith'), STATUS 20, CITY 'London' }
```

does indeed appear in relvar S at some given time, then we are to understand that it is a "true fact" that there does exist at that time a supplier under contract with supplier number S1, named Smith, with status 20, and located in London. More generally:

---

[8] They were discussed previously in Chapters 3 and 6, but there they were called just predicates. In fact, we have been using the term *predicate* throughout this book so far, tacitly, to mean an external predicate specifically. The only major exception was in the discussion of the restrict operation in Chapter 7, where we said a restriction condition is a predicate; so it is, but it is not an external one.

[9] The term *parameter* is being used here in a sense slightly different from the sense in which it was used in Sections 9.3 and 9.4. In those sections, parameters (and corresponding arguments) denoted whole relations; now they denote individual attribute values.

```
IF ( s ∈ S ) = TRUE THEN XPS ( s ) = TRUE
```

Here:

- *s* is a tuple of the form

  ```
  { S# s#, SNAME sn, STATUS st, CITY sc }
  ```

  (where *s#* is a value of type S#, *sn* is a value of type NAME, *st* is a value of type INTEGER, and *sc* is a value of type CITY).

- *XPS* is the external predicate for suppliers.

- *XPS(s)* is the proposition obtained by instantiating *XPS* with argument values S# = *s#*, SNAME = *sn*, STATUS = *st*, and CITY = *sc*.

As noted in Chapter 6, however, we go a step further with external predicates than we do with internal ones. To be specific, we adopt the **Closed World Assumption**, which states that if an otherwise valid tuple does *not* appear in the relvar at some given time, then the corresponding proposition is understood by convention to be one that is false at that time. For example, if the tuple

```
{ S# S#('S6'), SNAME NAME('Lopez'), STATUS 30, CITY 'Madrid' }
```

does not appear in relvar S at some given time, then we are to understand that it is not the case that there exists at that time a supplier under contract with supplier number S6, named Lopez, with status 30, and located in Madrid. More generally:

```
IF ( s ∈ S ) = FALSE THEN XPS ( s ) = FALSE
```

Or more succinctly:

```
IF NOT ( s ∈ S ) THEN NOT XPS ( s )
```

Putting the foregoing together, we have simply:

```
s ∈ S  ≡  XPS ( s )
```

In other words, a given tuple appears in a given relvar at a given time if and only if that tuple makes that relvar's external predicate evaluate to TRUE at that time. It follows that a given relvar contains *all* and *only* the tuples that correspond to true instantiations of that relvar's external predicate at the time in question.

9.7 CORRECTNESS *VS.* CONSISTENCY

By definition, external predicates, and the propositions obtained by instantiating such predicates, are not (and in fact cannot be) understood by the system. For example, the system cannot know what it means for a "supplier" to "be located" somewhere, or what it means for a "supplier" to "have a status" (etc.). All such issues are matters of *interpretation*—they make sense to the user but not to the system. By way of a more specific example, if the supplier number S1 and the city name London happen to appear together in some tuple, then the user can interpret that fact to mean that supplier S1 is located in London,[10] but (to repeat) there is no way the system can do anything analogous.

What is more, even if the system could know what it means for a supplier to be located somewhere, it still could not know *a priori* whether what the user tells it is true! If the user asserts to the system—typically by executing an INSERT statement—that supplier S1 is located in London, there is no way for the system to know whether that assertion is true. All the system can do is make sure it does not lead to any constraint violations (i.e., it does not cause any internal predicate to evaluate to FALSE). Assuming it does not, then the system must accept the assertion *and treat it as true from that point forward* (at least until the user tells the system—typically by executing a DELETE statement—that it is not true any more).

By the way, the foregoing shows clearly why the Closed World Assumption does not apply to internal predicates. To be specific, a tuple might satisfy the internal predicate for a given relvar and yet validly not appear in that relvar, because it does not correspond to a true proposition in the real world.

We can summarize this discussion by saying that, informally, the external predicate for a given relvar is the **intended interpretation** for that relvar. As such, it is important to the user, but not to the system. We can also say, again informally, that the external predicate for a given relvar is the **criterion for acceptability of updates** on the relvar in question—that is, it dictates, at least in principle, whether a requested INSERT, DELETE, or UPDATE operation on that relvar can be allowed to succeed. Ideally, therefore, the system would know the external predicate for every relvar, so that it could deal correctly with all possible attempts to update that relvar. As we have seen, however, this goal is unachievable; the system *cannot* know the external predicate for any given relvar. *But it does know a good approximation:* It knows the corresponding *internal* predicate—and that is what it will enforce. Thus, the *pragmatic* "criterion for acceptability of updates" (as opposed to the ideal one) is the internal predicate, not the external one. Another way of saying the same thing is as follows:

The system cannot enforce truth, only consistency.

That is, the system cannot guarantee that the database contains only true propositions—all it can do is guarantee that it does not contain anything that causes any integrity constraint to be violated (i.e., it does not contain any inconsistencies). Sadly, truth and consistency are not the same thing! Indeed, we can observe that:

- If the database contains only true propositions, then it is consistent, but the converse is not necessarily so.

- If the database is inconsistent, then it contains at least one false proposition, but the converse is not necessarily so.

---

[10] Or that supplier S1 *used to be* located in London, or that supplier S1 *has an office* in London, or that supplier S1 *does not* have an office in London, or any of an infinite number of other possible interpretations (corresponding to an infinite number of possible external predicates).

More succinctly: **Correct** implies **consistent** (but not the other way around), and **inconsistent** implies **incorrect** (but not the other way around)—where by *correct* we mean the database is correct if and only if it fully reflects the true state of affairs in the real world.

9.8   INTEGRITY AND VIEWS

It is important to understand that almost all of our discussions in this chapter so far apply to relvars in general, not just to base ones; in particular, they apply to *views* (which are *virtual* relvars). Thus, views too are subject to constraints, and they have relvar predicates, both internal and external. For example, suppose we define a view by projecting the suppliers relvar over attributes S#, SNAME, and STATUS (thereby effectively removing attribute CITY). Then the external predicate for that view looks something like this:

> *There exists some city CITY such that supplier S# is under contract, is named SNAME, has status STATUS, and is located in CITY.*

Observe that, as required, this predicate does have three parameters, not four, corresponding to the three attributes of the view (CITY is now no longer a parameter but a bound variable instead, thanks to the fact that it is quantified by the phrase "there exists some city"). Another, perhaps clearer, way of making the same point is to observe that the predicate as stated is logically equivalent to this one:

> *Supplier S# is under contract, is named SNAME, has status STATUS, and is located in some city.*

This version of the predicate very clearly has just three parameters.

What about the internal predicate? Here again are our usual six examples:

1. Every supplier status value is in the range 1 to 100 inclusive.
2. Every supplier in London has status 20.
3. If there are any parts at all, at least one of them is blue.
4. No two distinct suppliers have the same supplier number.
5. Every shipment involves an existing supplier.
6. No supplier with status less than 20 supplies any part in a quantity greater than 500.

Suppose the view under discussion (the projection of suppliers over S#, SNAME, and STATUS) is called SST. Then Example 3 is clearly irrelevant as far as view SST is concerned, since it has to do with parts, not suppliers. As for the others, each of them does also apply to view SST, but in a slightly modified form. Here, for example, is the modified form of Example 5:

```
FORALL s# ∈ S#, p# ∈ P#, q ∈ QTY
  ( IF { S# s#, P# p#, QTY q } ∈ SP
    THEN EXISTS sn ∈ NAME, st ∈ INTEGER
           ( { S# s#, SNAME sn, STATUS st } ∈ SST ) )
```

The changes are in the third and fourth lines: All references to CITY have been dropped, and the reference to S has been replaced by a reference to SST. Note that we can regard this constraint for SST as being derived from the corresponding constraint for S, just as relvar SST itself is derived from relvar S[11] (and as the external predicate for SST is derived from the external predicate for S, come to that).

Analogous remarks apply directly to Examples 1, 2, 4, and 6. Example 2 is slightly tricky, though, inasmuch as it involves the introduction of an EXISTS corresponding to the attribute that has been projected away:

```
FORALL s# ∈ S#, sn ∈ NAME, st ∈ INTEGER
  ( IF { S# s#, SNAME sn, STATUS st } ∈ SST
    THEN EXISTS sc ∈ CHAR
      ( { S# s#, SNAME sn, STATUS st, CITY sc } ∈ S AND
        ( IF sc = 'London'
          THEN st = 20 ) )
```

Again, however, we can regard this constraint as being derived from the corresponding constraint for S.

9.9 A CONSTRAINT CLASSIFICATION SCHEME

In this section, we briefly sketch a classification scheme for constraints (essentially the scheme adopted in reference [3.3]). Briefly, we divide constraints into four broad categories: database, relvar, attribute, and type constraints. In outline:

- A database constraint is a constraint on the values a given database is permitted to assume.

- A relvar constraint is a constraint on the values a given relvar is permitted to assume.

- An attribute constraint is a constraint on the values a given attribute is permitted to assume.

- A type constraint is, precisely, a definition of the set of values that constitute a given type.

It suits our purposes better to explain them in reverse order, however.

Type Constraints

Type constraints have not been mentioned in this chapter at all prior to this point. However, they were discussed in some detail in Chapter 5, and so the following is just to remind you of what we said in that chapter. First, a type constraint is, precisely, a specification of the values that make up the type in question. Here is an example (repeated from Chapter 5):

```
TYPE WEIGHT POSSREP { D DECIMAL (5,1)
                          CONSTRAINT D > 0.0 AND D < 5000.0 } ;
```

---

[11] Note too that the derived constraint is effectively a foreign key constraint from a base relvar to a view! See Section 9.10.

Meaning: Legal values of type WEIGHT are precisely those that can possibly be represented by decimal numbers of five digits precision with one digit after the decimal point, where the decimal number in question is greater than zero and less than 5,000.

Now, it should be clear that, ultimately, the only way *any* expression can yield a value of type WEIGHT is by means of some WEIGHT selector invocation. Hence, the only way any such expression can violate the WEIGHT type constraint is if the selector invocation in question does so. It follows that *type constraints can always be thought of, at least conceptually, as being checked during the execution of some selector invocation.* For example, consider the following selector invocation for type WEIGHT:

```
WEIGHT ( 7500.0 )
```

This expression will raise an exception at run time ("WEIGHT type constraint violation: value out of range").

As a consequence of the foregoing, we can say that type constraints are always checked immediately, and hence in particular that no relvar can ever acquire a value for any attribute in any tuple that is not of the appropriate type (in a system that supports type constraints properly, of course!).

Since type constraints are essentially just a specification of the values that make up the type in question, in **Tutorial D** we bundle such constraints with the definition of the applicable type, and we identify them by means of the applicable type name. It follows that a type constraint can be dropped only by dropping the type itself.

Attribute Constraints

Attribute constraints are basically what we called *a priori* constraints in Section 9.2; in other words, an attribute constraint is basically just a declaration to the effect that a specified attribute of a specified relvar is of a specified type. For example, consider the suppliers relvar definition once again:

```
VAR S BASE RELATION
    { S#     S#,
      SNAME  NAME,
      STATUS INTEGER,
      CITY   CHAR } ... ;
```

In this relvar, values of attributes S#, SNAME, STATUS, and CITY are constrained to be of types S#, NAME, INTEGER, and CHAR, respectively. In other words, attribute constraints are part of the definition of the attribute in question, and they can be identified by means of the corresponding attribute name. It follows that an attribute constraint can be dropped only by dropping the attribute itself (which in practice will usually mean dropping the containing relvar). *Note:* In principle, any attempt to introduce an attribute value into the database (via an INSERT or UPDATE operation) that is not a value of the relevant type will simply be rejected. In practice, however, such a situation should never arise, as long as the system in fact enforces type constraints as described in the previous subsection.

Relvar and Database Constraints

Relvar and database constraints are what we have been concentrating on throughout the bulk of this chapter so far; the difference between them is that a relvar constraint involves exactly one relvar, while a database constraint involves two or more relvars. As noted in Section 9.2, however, the difference is not very important from a theoretical point of view (though it might be useful from a pragmatic one).

One point we have not touched on so far, however, is that some relvar or database constraints can be *transition* constraints. A **transition constraint** is a constraint on the legal transitions that a given variable—in particular, a given relvar or a given database—can make from one value to another;[12] for example, a person's marital status can change from "never married" to "married," but not the other way around. Provided we have a way to refer within a single expression to both (a) the value of the variable in question before an arbitrary update and (b) the value of that same variable after that same update, then we have the means to formulate any desired transition constraint. Here is an example ("no supplier's status should ever decrease"):

```
CONSTRAINT TRC1
    FORALL SX' FORALL SX ( SX'.S# ≠ SX.S# OR
                           SX'.STATUS ≤ SX.STATUS ) ;
```

Explanation: We introduce the convention that a primed range variable name, such as SX' in the example, is understood to refer to the corresponding relvar as it was *prior to the update under consideration*. The constraint in the example can thus be understood as follows: If SX' is a supplier tuple before the update, then there does not exist a supplier tuple SX after the update with the same supplier number as SX' and with a status value smaller than that in SX'.

Observe that Constraint TRC1 is a *relvar* transition constraint (it applies to just a single relvar, relvar S). Here by contrast is a *database* transition constraint ("the total quantity of any given part, taken over all suppliers, should never decrease"):

```
CONSTRAINT TRC2
    FORALL PX
        SUM ( SPX' WHERE SPX'.P# = PX.P#, QTY ) ≤
        SUM ( SPX  WHERE SPX .P# = PX.P#, QTY ) ;
```

The concept of transition constraints does not apply to type or attribute constraints.

9.10 KEYS

As noted in Section 9.1, the relational model has always stressed the concept of keys, though as we have seen they are really just a special case—albeit a pragmatically important one—of a more general phenomenon. In this section, we consider keys specifically.

---

[12] Constraints that are not transition constraints are sometimes called *state* constraints.

Candidate Keys

Let R be a relvar. By definition, the set of all attributes of R has the *uniqueness* property—meaning that, at any given time, no two tuples in the value of R at that time are duplicates of one another. In practice, it is often the case that some proper subset of the set of all attributes of R also has the uniqueness property; in the case of the suppliers relvar S, for example, the subset containing just attribute S# has that property. Such considerations provide the intuition behind the following definition:[13]

- Let K be a set of attributes of relvar R. Then K is a **candidate key** for R if and only if it has both of the following properties:

  a. **Uniqueness:** No legal value of R ever contains two distinct tuples with the same value for K.

  b. **Irreducibility:** No proper subset of K has the uniqueness property.

Every relvar has at least one candidate key. The uniqueness property of such keys is self-explanatory. As for the irreducibility property, the point is that if we were to specify a "candidate key" that was *not* irreducible, the system would not be aware of the true state of affairs, and would thus not be able to enforce the associated integrity constraint properly. For example, suppose we were to define the combination {S#,CITY}—instead of just {S#} alone—as a candidate key for suppliers. Then the system would not enforce the constraint that supplier numbers are "globally" unique; instead, it would enforce only the weaker constraint that supplier numbers are "locally" unique within city. For this reason among others, we require candidate keys not to include any attributes that are irrelevant for unique identification purposes.[14]

We remark that irreducibility in the foregoing sense is referred to as *minimality* in much of the literature (including earlier editions of this book). However, "minimality" is really not the *mot juste,* because to say that candidate key *K1* is "minimal" does not mean that another candidate key *K2* cannot be found that has fewer components; it is entirely possible that, for example, *K1* has four components and *K2* only two. We will stay with the term *irreducible.*

In **Tutorial D**, we use the syntax

```
KEY { <attribute name commalist> }
```

within a relvar definition to specify a candidate key for the relvar in question. Here are some examples:

---

[13] Note that the definition applies to relation variables specifically; an analogous notion can be defined for relation values also [3.3], but relvars are the important case. Note too that we are relying once again on the notion of tuple equality (in the definition of the uniqueness property, to be specific).

[14] Another good reason why candidate keys are required to be irreducible is the following: Any foreign key that referenced a "reducible" candidate key (if such a thing were possible) would be "reducible" too, and the relvar containing it would thus almost certainly be in violation of the principles of further normalization as discussed in Chapter 12.

```
VAR S BASE RELATION
     { S#      S#,
       SNAME   NAME,
       STATUS  INTEGER,
       CITY    CHAR }
     KEY { S# } ;
```

Note: In previous chapters, we have shown this definition with a PRIMARY KEY clause, not an unqualified KEY clause. See the subsection "Primary and Alternate Keys" later in this section for further discussion and explanation.

```
VAR SP BASE RELATION
     { S#      S#,
       P#      P#,
       QTY     QTY }
     KEY { S#, P# } ... ;
```

This example shows a relvar with a **composite** candidate key (i.e., one involving two or more attributes). A **simple** candidate key is one that is not composite.

```
VAR ELEMENT BASE RELATION { NAME     NAME,
                            SYMBOL   CHAR,
                            ATOMIC#  INTEGER }
                 KEY { NAME }
                 KEY { SYMBOL }
                 KEY { ATOMIC# } ;
```

This example shows a relvar with several distinct candidate keys, all of which are simple.

```
VAR MARRIAGE BASE RELATION { HUSBAND              NAME,
                             WIFE                 NAME,
                             DATE /* of marriage */ DATE }
/* assume no polyandry, no polygyny, and no husband and */
/* wife marry each other more than once ...             */
                 KEY { HUSBAND, DATE }
                 KEY { DATE, WIFE }
                 KEY { WIFE, HUSBAND } ;
```

This example shows a relvar with several distinct candidate keys, all of which are composite. Note too the overlap among those keys.

Of course, as pointed out in Section 9.2, a candidate key definition is really just shorthand for a certain relvar constraint. The shorthand is useful for a variety of reasons, one of which is simply that candidate keys are important from a pragmatic point of view. In particular, they provide the basic **tuple-level addressing mechanism** in the relational model; that is, the only system-guaranteed way of pinpointing some specific tuple is by means of some candidate key value. For example, the expression

```
S WHERE S# = S# ('S3')
```

is guaranteed to yield at most one tuple (more precisely, it yields a relation containing at most one tuple). By contrast, the expression

```
S WHERE CITY = 'Paris'
```

yields (a relation containing) an unpredictable number of tuples, in general. It follows that *candidate keys are just as fundamental to the successful operation of a relational system as main memory addresses are to the successful operation of the underlying machine.* As a consequence:

1. "Relvars" that do not have a candidate key—that is, "relvars" that permit duplicate tuples—are bound to display strange and anomalous behavior on occasion.

2. A system that has no knowledge of candidate keys is bound to display behavior on occasion that is not "truly relational," even if the relvars it deals with are indeed true relvars and never contain duplicate tuples.

The behavior referred to here as "strange and anomalous" and "not truly relational" has to do with such matters as *view updating* and *optimization* (see Chapters 10 and 18, respectively).

A few final points to close this subsection:

■ It is not just base relvars that have candidate keys!—*all* relvars do, including views in particular. In the case of views in particular, however, whether such keys can or must be declared will depend, in part, on whether the system knows how to perform **candidate key inference** [3.3].

■ A superset of a candidate key is a **superkey** (for example, the set of attributes {S#,CITY} is a superkey for relvar S). A superkey has the uniqueness property but not necessarily the irreducibility property. Of course, a candidate key is a special case of a superkey.

■ If *SK* is a superkey for relvar *R* and *A* is an attribute of *R,* then the **functional dependency** *SK → A* necessarily holds in *R.* In fact, we can *define* a superkey to be a subset *SK* of the attributes of *R* such that the functional dependency *SK → A* holds for all attributes *A* of *R. Note:* The important concept of functional dependency is discussed in depth in Chapter 11.

■ Finally, please note that the logical notion of a candidate key should not be confused with the physical notion of a "unique index" (even though the latter is very often used to implement the former). In other words, there is no implication that there must be an index (or any other special physical access path, come to that) on a candidate key. In practice, there probably will be such an access path, but whether there is or not is beyond the scope of the relational model as such.

Primary Keys and Alternate Keys

As we have seen, it is possible for a given relvar to have two or more candidate keys. In such a case, the relational model has historically required (for base relvars, at least) that exactly one of those keys be chosen as the **primary** key, and the others are then called **alternate** keys. In the ELEMENT example, for instance, we might choose {SYMBOL} as the primary key; {NAME} and {ATOMIC#} would then be alternate keys. And in the case where there is only one candidate key anyway, the relational model has again historically required that that candidate key be considered the primary key for the base relvar in question. Hence every base relvar has always had a primary key.

Now, choosing one candidate key as primary (when there is a choice) might be a good idea in many cases—possibly even in most cases—but it cannot be justified in *all* cases, unequivocally. Detailed arguments in support of this position are given in reference [9.14]; here we just note one such, which is that the choice is not dictated by logic but instead is essentially arbitrary. (To quote Codd [9.9]: "The normal basis [for making the choice] is simplicity, but this aspect is outside the scope of the relational model.") In our own examples, we will sometimes specify a primary key and sometimes not. We will, however, always specify at least one *candidate* key.

Foreign Keys

Loosely speaking, a *foreign key* is a set of attributes of some relvar *R2* whose values are required to match values of some candidate key of some relvar *R1*. For example, consider the set of attributes {S#} of relvar SP. It should be clear that a given value for {S#} can be allowed to appear in relvar SP only if that same value also appears as a value of the sole candidate key {S#} for relvar S (we cannot have a shipment for a nonexistent supplier). Likewise, a given value for the set of attributes {P#} can be allowed to appear in relvar SP only if the same value also appears as a value of the sole candidate key {P#} for relvar P (we cannot have a shipment for a nonexistent part, either). These examples serve to motivate the following definition:[15]

- Let *R2* be a relvar. Then a **foreign key** in *R2* is a set of attributes of *R2,* say *FK,* such that:

    a. There exists a relvar *R1* (*R1* and *R2* not necessarily distinct) with a candidate key *CK.*

    b. It is possible to rename some subset of the attributes of *FK,* such that *FK* becomes *FK'* (say) and *FK'* and *CK* are of the same (tuple) type.

    c. For all time, each value of *FK* in the current value of *R2* yields a value for *FK'* that is identical to the value of *CK* in some tuple in the current value of *R1.*

    Points arising:

    1. It will rarely be necessary in practice to perform any actual renaming; that is, the subset of attributes of *FK* requiring renaming will usually be empty (an example of where it is not is discussed under point 7). For simplicity, therefore, we will assume from this point forward that *FK* and *FK'* are identical, barring explicit statements to the contrary.

    2. Note that while every value of *FK* must appear as a value of *CK,* the converse is *not* a requirement; that is, *R1* might contain a *CK* value that does not currently appear as an *FK* value in *R2.* In the case of suppliers and parts, for example (sample values as shown in Fig. 3.8 on the inside back cover), supplier number S5 appears in relvar S but not in relvar SP, because supplier S5 does not currently supply any parts.

    3. *FK* is **simple** or **composite** according as *CK* is simple or composite.

---

[15] Note that the definition relies yet again on the notion of tuple equality.

4. An *FK* value represents a **reference** to the tuple containing the matching *CK* value (the **referenced tuple**). The constraint that values of *FK* must match values of *CK* is known as a **referential constraint**. Relvar *R2* is the **referencing** relvar and relvar *R1* is the **referenced** relvar. The problem of ensuring that the database does not include any invalid foreign key values is the **referential integrity** problem (see point 12).

5. Consider suppliers and parts once again. We can represent the referential constraints on that database by means of the following **referential diagram**:

$$S \longleftarrow SP \longrightarrow P$$

Each arrow means there is a foreign key in the relvar from which the arrow emerges that refers to some candidate key in the relvar to which the arrow points. *Note:* For clarity, it is sometimes a good idea to label each arrow in a referential diagram with the name(s) of the attribute(s) that constitute the relevant foreign key.[16] For instance:

$$S \overset{S\#}{\longleftarrow} SP \overset{P\#}{\longrightarrow} P$$

In this book, however, we will show such labels only when omitting them might lead to confusion or ambiguity.

6. A given relvar can be both referenced and referencing, as in the case of R2 here:

$$R3 \longrightarrow R2 \longrightarrow R1$$

More generally, let relvars Rn, R(n–1), ..., R2, R1 be such that there is a referential constraint from Rn to R(n–1), a referential constraint from R(n–1) to R(n–2), ..., and a referential constraint from R2 to R1:

$$R n \longrightarrow R(n-1) \longrightarrow R(n-2) \longrightarrow \ldots \longrightarrow R2 \longrightarrow R1$$

Then the chain of arrows from Rn to R1 represents a **referential path** from Rn to R1.

7. Note that relvars *R1* and *R2* in the foreign key definition are not necessarily distinct. That is, a relvar might include a foreign key whose values are required to match the values of some candidate key in that same relvar. By way of example, consider the following relvar definition (we will explain the syntax in a few moments, but in any case it should be fairly self-explanatory):

```
VAR EMP BASE RELATION
      { EMP# EMP#, ..., MGR_EMP# EMP#, ... }
   KEY { EMP# }
   FOREIGN KEY { RENAME MGR_EMP# AS EMP# } REFERENCES EMP ;
```

Here attribute MGR_EMP# represents the employee number of the manager of the employee identified by EMP#; for example, the EMP tuple for employee E4 might include a MGR_EMP# value of E3, which represents a reference to the EMP tuple for employee E3. (As promised under point 1, we have here an example in which some explicit attribute renaming is required.) A relvar such as EMP is sometimes said to be **self-referencing**. *Exercise:* Invent some sample data for relvar EMP.

8. Self-referencing relvars actually represent a special case of a more general situation: namely, there can exist **referential cycles**. Relvars Rn, R(n–1), R(n–2), ..., R2, R1 form such a cycle if Rn includes a foreign key referring to R(n–1), R(n–1) includes a

---

[16] Alternatively (and perhaps preferably), we could *name* the foreign keys and then use those names to label the arrows.

foreign key referring to R(n–2), ..., and so on, and finally R1 includes a foreign key referring back to Rn again. More succinctly, a referential cycle exists if there is a referential path from some relvar Rn to itself:

$$Rn \longrightarrow R(n-1) \longrightarrow R(n-2) \longrightarrow \cdots \longrightarrow R2 \longrightarrow R1 \longrightarrow Rn$$

9. Foreign-to-candidate-key matches are sometimes said to be the "glue" that holds the database together. Another way of saying the same thing is that such matches represent certain *relationships*. Note carefully, however, that not all such relationships are represented by keys in this way. For example, there is a relationship ("colocation") between suppliers and parts, represented by the CITY attributes of relvars S and P; a given supplier and a given part are colocated if they are located in the same city. However, this relationship is not represented by keys.

10. Historically, the foreign key concept has been defined for base relvars only, a fact that raises some questions in itself (see the discussion of *The Interchangeability Principle* in Chapter 10, Section 10.2). We do not impose such a restriction here; however, we do limit our discussions to base relvars only (where it makes any difference), for reasons of simplicity.

11. The relational model originally required that foreign keys reference, very specifically, *primary* keys, not just candidate keys (see, e.g., reference [9.9] once again). We reject that limitation as unnecessary and undesirable in general, though it might often constitute good discipline in practice [9.14].

12. Along with the foreign key concept, the relational model includes the following rule (the *referential integrity* rule):

   ■ **Referential integrity:** The database must not contain any unmatched foreign key values.[17]

The term *unmatched foreign key value* here means a foreign key value in some referencing relvar for which there does not exist a matching value of the relevant candidate key in the relevant referenced relvar. In other words, the constraint says simply: If *B* references *A,* then *A* must exist.

Here then is the syntax for defining a foreign key:

```
FOREIGN KEY { <item commalist> } REFERENCES <relvar name>
```

This clause appears within a referencing relvar definition; the *<relvar name>* identifies the referenced relvar, and each *<item>* is either an *<attribute name>* of the referencing relvar or an expression of the form

```
RENAME <attribute name> AS <attribute name>
```

---

[17] Observe that the referential integrity rule can be regarded as a "metaconstraint": It implies that any given database must be subject to certain *specific* constraints that are peculiar to the database in question and together guarantee that referential integrity is not violated by that particular database. We note in passing that the relational model is usually considered to include another such "metaconstraint," the *entity integrity* rule. We defer discussion of that rule to Chapter 19.

(see the self-referencing relvar EMP under point 7 for an example of the RENAME case). Examples have already been given at many earlier points in this book (see, e.g., Fig. 3.9 in Chapter 3). Of course, as pointed out in Section 9.2, a foreign key definition is really just shorthand for a certain database constraint (or a certain relvar constraint, in the case of a self-referencing relvar)—*unless* the foreign key definition is extended to include certain "referential actions," in which case it becomes more than just an integrity constraint *per se.* See the subsection "Referential Actions" immediately following.

Referential Actions

Consider the following **Tutorial D** statement:

```
DELETE S WHERE S# = S# ('S1') ;
```

Assume this DELETE does exactly what it says—that is, it deletes the supplier tuple for supplier S1, no more and no less. Assume too that (a) the database does include some shipments for supplier S1 and (b) the application does not delete those shipments. When the system checks the referential constraint from shipments to suppliers, then, it will find a violation, and an exception will be raised.

However, an alternative approach is possible, one that might be preferable in some cases, and that is for the system to perform an appropriate *compensating action* that will guarantee that the overall result does still satisfy the constraint. In the example, the obvious compensating action would be for the system to delete the shipments for supplier S1 "automatically." We can achieve this effect by extending the foreign key definition as indicated here:

```
VAR SP BASE RELATION { ... } ...
    FOREIGN KEY { S# } REFERENCES S
                       ON DELETE CASCADE ;
```

The specification ON DELETE CASCADE defines a *delete rule* for this particular foreign key, and the specification CASCADE is the *referential action* for that delete rule. The meaning of these specifications is that a DELETE operation on the suppliers relvar will "cascade" to delete matching tuples (if any) in the shipments relvar as well.

Another common referential action is RESTRICT (nothing to do with the *restrict* operator of the relational algebra). In the case at hand, RESTRICT would mean that DELETE operations are "restricted" to the case where there are no matching shipments (they are rejected otherwise). Omitting a referential action for a particular foreign key is equivalent to specifying NO ACTION, which means what it says: The DELETE is performed exactly as requested, no more and no less. (If NO ACTION is specified in the case at hand, and a supplier that has matching shipments is deleted, we will subsequently get a referential integrity violation, so the net effect is very similar to that of RESTRICT.) Points arising:

1. DELETE is not the only operation for which referential actions make sense. For example, what should happen if we try to update the supplier number for a supplier for which there exists at least one matching shipment? Clearly, we need an *update rule* as well as a delete rule. In general, there are the same possibilities for UPDATE as there are for DELETE:

- CASCADE: The UPDATE cascades to update the foreign key in those matching shipments also.
- RESTRICT: The UPDATE is restricted to the case where there are no such matching shipments (it is rejected otherwise).
- NO ACTION: The UPDATE is performed exactly as requested (but a referential integrity violation might subsequently occur).

2. Of course, CASCADE, RESTRICT, and NO ACTION are not the only possible referential actions—they are merely ones that are commonly required in practice. In principle, however, there could be an arbitrary number of possible responses to (for example) an attempt to delete a particular supplier. Here are some examples:

- The attempt could be rejected out of hand for some reason.
- Information could be written to some archive database.
- The shipments for the supplier in question could be transferred to some other supplier.

It will never be feasible to provide declarative syntax for all conceivable responses. In general, therefore, it should be possible to specify a referential action consisting of an arbitrary user-defined procedure (see the next section). What is more, (a) the execution of that procedure must be considered part of the execution of the statement that caused the integrity check to be done; (b) that integrity check must be performed again after that procedure has executed (the procedure must obviously not leave the database in a state that violates the constraint).

3. Let R2 and R1 be, respectively, a referencing relvar and the corresponding referenced relvar:

$$R2 \longrightarrow R1$$

Let the applicable delete rule specify CASCADE. Then a DELETE on a given tuple of R1 will imply a DELETE on certain tuples of relvar R2 (in general). Now suppose relvar R2 in turn is referenced by some other relvar R3:

$$R3 \longrightarrow R2 \longrightarrow R1$$

Then the effect of the implied DELETE on tuples of R2 is exactly as if an attempt had been made to delete those tuples directly; that is, it depends on the delete rule specified for the referential constraint from R3 to R2. If that implied DELETE fails (because of the delete rule from R3 to R2 or for any other reason), then the entire operation fails and the database remains unchanged. And so on, recursively, to any number of levels.

Analogous remarks apply to the cascade update rule also, *mutatis mutandis,* if the foreign key in relvar R2 has any attributes in common with the candidate key of that relvar that is referenced by the foreign key in R3.

4. It follows from the foregoing that, from a logical point of view, database updates are always atomic (all or nothing), even if under the covers they involve several updates on several relvars because of, for example, a cascade referential action.

9.11   TRIGGERS (A DIGRESSION)

It should be clear from everything we have said in this chapter so far that we are specifically concerned with *declarative* integrity support. And although the situation has improved in recent years, the fact is that few products if any provided much in the way of such support when they first appeared. As a consequence, integrity constraints were often implemented procedurally, using **triggered procedures,** which are precompiled procedures that are stored along with (possibly in) the database and invoked automatically whenever some specified event occurs. For example, we might implement Example 1 ("status values must be in the range 1 to 100 inclusive") by means of a triggered procedure that (a) is invoked whenever a tuple is inserted into relvar S, (b) examines that newly inserted tuple, and (c) deletes it again if the status value is out of range. In this section, we take a brief look at triggered procedures, on the grounds that they are of considerable pragmatic importance. Please note immediately, however, that:

1. Precisely because they are procedures, triggered procedures are *not* the recommended way to implement integrity constraints. Procedures are harder for humans to understand and harder for the system to optimize. Note too that declarative constraints are checked on all relevant updates, whereas triggered procedures are executed only when the specified event—for example, inserting a tuple into relvar S—occurs.[18]

2. The applicability of triggered procedures is not limited to the integrity problem that is the topic of the present chapter. Indeed, given the remarks under point 1, it is the fact that they can serve other useful purposes that is their true *raison d'être*. Examples of those "other useful purposes" include:

   a. Alerting the user if some exception occurs (e.g., issuing a warning if the quantity on hand of some part goes below the danger level)

   b. Debugging (e.g., monitoring references to, and/or state changes in, designated variables)

   c. Auditing (e.g., tracking who performed what updates to which relvars when)

   d. Performance measurement (e.g., timing or tracing specified database events)

   e. Carrying out compensating actions (e.g., cascading the deletion of a supplier tuple to delete the corresponding shipment tuples as well)[19]

   and so on. This section is thus, as its title indicates, something of a digression.

   Consider the following example. (The example is based on SQL, not **Tutorial D**, because reference [3.3] does not prescribe—nor does it proscribe—any triggered procedure support; in fact, it is based on a commercial product, not the SQL standard, because

---

[18] Note that declarative constraint specifications do not explicitly tell the DBMS when the integrity checks are to be done. Nor do we want them to: first, because it would require extra work on the part of the user declaring the constraints if they did; second, because the user might get it wrong. Rather, we want the system to decide for itself when to do the checks (see the annotation to reference [9.5]).

[19] Indeed, cascade delete is a simple example of a triggered procedure. Note, however, that it is declaratively specified! We do not mean to suggest that referential actions are a bad idea just because they are "triggered."

the SQL standard does not support the particular feature illustrated.) Suppose we have a view called LONDON_SUPPLIER, defined as follows:

```
CREATE VIEW LONDON_SUPPLIER
    AS SELECT S#, SNAME, STATUS
       FROM   S
       WHERE  CITY = 'London' ;
```

Normally, if the user tries to insert a row into this view, SQL will actually insert a row into the underlying base table S with CITY value whatever the default is for the CITY column (see Chapter 10). Assuming that default is not London, the net effect is that the new row will not appear in the view! Let us therefore create a triggered procedure as follows:

```
CREATE TRIGGER LONDON_SUPPLIER_INSERT
       INSTEAD OF INSERT ON LONDON_SUPPLIER
       REFERENCING NEW ROW AS R
       FOR EACH ROW
       INSERT INTO S ( S#, SNAME, STATUS, CITY )
               VALUES ( R.S#, R.SNAME, R.STATUS, 'London' ) ;
```

Inserting a row into the view will now cause a row to be inserted into the underlying base table with CITY value equal to London instead of the default value (and the new row will now appear in the view, presumably as required).

Here are some points that arise from this example. *Note:* These points are not meant to be specific to SQL, despite the fact that our example was based on SQL (SQL specifics are given in the next section).

1. In general, CREATE TRIGGER specifies, among other things, an *event,* a *condition,* and an *action:*

   - The **event** is an operation on the database ("INSERT ON LONDON_SUPPLIER" in the example).

   - The **condition** is a boolean expression that has to evaluate to TRUE in order for the action to be executed (if no condition is specified explicitly, as in the example, then the default is just TRUE).

   - The **action** is the triggered procedure proper ("INSERT INTO S . . ." in the example.)

   The event and condition together are sometimes called the *triggering event.* The combination of all three (event, condition, and action) is usually called just a **trigger**. For obvious reasons, triggers are also known as *event-condition-action rules* (*ECA rules* for short).

2. Possible events include INSERT, DELETE, UPDATE (possibly attribute-specific), reaching end-of-transaction (COMMIT), reaching a specified time of day, exceeding a specified elapsed time, violating a specified constraint, and so on.

3. In general, the action can be performed BEFORE, AFTER, or INSTEAD OF the specified event (where such choices make sense).

4. In general, the action can be performed FOR EACH ROW or FOR EACH STATEMENT (where such a choice makes sense).

5. In general, there will be a way for the action to refer to the data as it is both before and after the specified event has occurred (where such a facility makes sense).

6. A database that has associated triggers is sometimes called an *active database*.

We close this section by noting that while triggers obviously have their uses, they do need to be used with caution, and they probably should not be used at all if there is an alternative way of solving the problem at hand. Here are some reasons why the use of triggers can be problematic in practice:

- If the same event causes several distinct triggers to "fire" (to use the jargon), then the sequence in which they do so might be both important and undefined.

- Trigger T1 could cause trigger T2 to fire, which could cause trigger T3 to fire, and so on (a *trigger chain*).

- Trigger T might even cause itself to fire again, recursively.

- Given the presence of triggers, the effect of a "simple" INSERT, DELETE, or UPDATE might be radically different from what the user expects (especially if INSTEAD OF is specified, as in our example).

Taking these points together, it should be clear that the overall effects of a given collection of triggers might be quite difficult to understand. Declarative solutions, when available, are always to be preferred to procedural ones.

9.12   SQL FACILITIES

We begin by considering SQL's support—or lack of support, rather, for the most part—for the constraint classification scheme described in Section 9.9.

- SQL does not support *type constraints* at all, except for those primitive constraints that are a direct consequence of the applicable physical representation. As we saw in Chapter 5, for example, we can say that values of type WEIGHT must be representable as DECIMAL(5,1) numbers, but we cannot say that those numbers must be greater than zero and less than 5,000.

- SQL does support *attribute constraints* (of course).

- SQL does not support *relvar constraints* as such. It does support *base table* constraints, but (a) such constraints specifically apply to base tables only, not to tables in general (in particular, not to views), and (b) they are not limited to mentioning just one such table but instead can be arbitrarily complex.

- SQL does not support *database constraints* as such. It does support *general* constraints, which it calls *assertions,* but such constraints are not required to mention at least two tables. (In fact, SQL's base table constraints and general constraints are logically interchangeable, except for the quirk noted at the very end of the subsection "Base Table Constraints" immediately following.)

SQL also has no direct support for transition constraints, though such constraints can be implemented procedurally via triggers. It also has no explicit concept of a relvar (or table) predicate, a point that will turn out to be significant in the next chapter.

Base Table Constraints

SQL base table constraints are specified on either CREATE TABLE or ALTER TABLE. Each such constraint is a candidate key constraint, a foreign key constraint, or a check constraint. We discuss each in turn. *Note:* Definitions of any of these constraints can optionally be preceded by the specification CONSTRAINT *<constraint name>*, thereby providing a name for the constraint. We ignore this option for brevity (though we note that it is probably a good idea to name all constraints in practice). We also ignore certain shorthands—for example, the ability to define a candidate key "inline" as part of a column definition—for the same reason.

Candidate keys: An SQL candidate key definition takes one of the following two forms:

```
PRIMARY KEY ( <column name commalist> )

UNIQUE ( <column name commalist> )
```

The *<column name commalist>* must not be empty in either case.[20] A given base table can have at most one PRIMARY KEY specification but any number of UNIQUE specifications. In the case of PRIMARY KEY, each specified column is additionally assumed to be NOT NULL, even if NOT NULL is not specified explicitly (see the discussion of check constraints below).

Foreign keys: An SQL foreign key definition takes the form

```
FOREIGN KEY ( <column name commalist> )
  REFERENCES <base table name> [ ( <column name commalist> ) ]
[ ON DELETE <referential action> ]
[ ON UPDATE <referential action> ]
```

where *<referential action>* is NO ACTION (the default), RESTRICT, CASCADE, SET DEFAULT, or SET NULL.[21] We defer discussion of SET DEFAULT and SET NULL to Chapter 19; the other options are as described in Section 9.10. The second *<column name commalist>* is required if the foreign key references a candidate key that is not a primary key. *Note:* The foreign-to-candidate-key matching is done on the basis not of column names but of column *position* (left to right) within the commalists.

Check constraints: An SQL check constraint takes the form:

```
CHECK ( <bool exp> )
```

---

[20] See Exercise 9.10.

[21] We observe in passing that support for certain of the *<referential action>*s (CASCADE in particular) implies that, under the covers at least, the system has to support some kind of multiple relational assignment!—despite the fact that no such operator is supported by SQL as such.

Let *CC* be a check constraint for base table *T*. Then *T* is considered to violate *CC* if and only if it currently contains at least one row—see the final paragraph in this subsection—and the current value of *T* makes the *<bool exp>* for *CC* evaluate to FALSE. *Note:* In general, SQL *<bool exp>*s can be arbitrarily complex; even in the context at hand, they are explicitly *not* limited to referring just to base table *T*, but can instead refer to any accessible portion of the database.

Here then is a CREATE TABLE example that illustrates base table constraints of all three kinds:

```
CREATE TABLE SP
     ( S# S# NOT NULL, P# P# NOT NULL, QTY QTY NOT NULL,
       PRIMARY KEY ( S#, P# ),
       FOREIGN KEY ( S# ) REFERENCES S
                          ON DELETE CASCADE
                          ON UPDATE CASCADE,
       FOREIGN KEY ( P# ) REFERENCES P
                          ON DELETE CASCADE
                          ON UPDATE CASCADE,
       CHECK ( QTY ≥ QTY ( 0 ) AND QTY ≤ QTY ( 5000 ) ) ) ;
```

We are assuming here that S# and P# have been explicitly defined to be the primary keys for tables S and P, respectively. Also, we have made use of the shorthand by which a check constraint of the form

```
CHECK ( <column name> IS NOT NULL )
```

can be replaced by a simple NOT NULL specification in the definition of the column in question. In the example, we have thus replaced three slightly cumbersome check constraints by three NOT NULL specifications.

We close this subsection by repeating the point that an SQL base table constraint is *always* considered to be satisfied if the base table in question happens to be empty—even if the constraint is of the form (say) "1 = 2" (or even, come to that, if it is of the form "this table must not be empty"!).

Assertions

We now turn to SQL's general constraints or *assertions*. Such constraints are defined by means of CREATE ASSERTION—syntax:

```
CREATE ASSERTION <constraint name>
     CHECK ( <bool exp> ) ;
```

And here is the syntax of DROP ASSERTION:

```
DROP ASSERTION <constraint name> ;
```

Note that, unlike most other forms of the SQL DROP operator (e.g., DROP TYPE, DROP TABLE, DROP VIEW), DROP ASSERTION does not offer a RESTRICT *vs.* CASCADE option.

Here are the six examples from Section 9.1, expressed in the form of SQL assertions. By way of an exercise, you might like to try formulating these examples as base table constraints instead.

1. Every supplier status value is in the range 1 to 100 inclusive.

```
CREATE ASSERTION SC1 CHECK
    ( NOT EXISTS ( SELECT * FROM S
                   WHERE  S.STATUS < 0
                   OR     S.STATUS > 100 ) ) ;
```

2. Every supplier in London has status 20.

```
CREATE ASSERTION SC2 CHECK
    ( NOT EXISTS ( SELECT * FROM S
                   WHERE  S.CITY = 'London'
                   AND    S.STATUS ≠ 20 ) ) ;
```

3. If there are any parts at all, at least one of them is blue.

```
CREATE ASSERTION PC3 CHECK
    ( NOT EXISTS ( SELECT * FROM P )
      OR  EXISTS ( SELECT * FROM P
                   WHERE  P.COLOR = COLOR ('Blue') ) ) ;
```

4. No two distinct suppliers have the same supplier number.

```
CREATE ASSERTION SC4 CHECK
    ( UNIQUE ( SELECT S.S# FROM S ) ) ;
```

UNIQUE here is an SQL operator that takes a table as argument and returns TRUE if that table contains no duplicate rows and FALSE otherwise.

5. Every shipment involves an existing supplier.

```
CREATE ASSERTION SSP5 CHECK
    ( NOT EXISTS
        ( SELECT * FROM SP
          WHERE  NOT EXISTS
               ( SELECT * FROM S
                 WHERE  S.S# = SP.S# ) ) ) ;
```

6. No supplier with status less than 20 supplies any part in a quantity greater than 500.

```
CREATE ASSERTION SSP6 CHECK
    ( NOT EXISTS ( SELECT * FROM S, SP
                   WHERE  S.STATUS < 20
                   AND    S.S# = SP.S#
                   AND    SP.QTY > QTY ( 500 ) ) ) ;
```

We briefly consider one further example. Recall this view definition from the previous section:

```
CREATE VIEW LONDON_SUPPLIER
    AS SELECT S#, SNAME, STATUS
       FROM   S
       WHERE  CITY = 'London' ;
```

We already know that we cannot include a specification of the form

```
UNIQUE ( S# )
```

in this view definition. Strangely, however, we *can* specify a general constraint of the following form:

```
CREATE ASSERTION LSK CHECK
    ( UNIQUE ( SELECT S# FROM LONDON_SUPPLIER ) ) ;
```

Deferred Checking

SQL's constraints also differ from ours with respect to when the checking is done. In our scheme, all constraints are checked immediately. In SQL, by contrast, they can be defined to be DEFERRABLE or NOT DEFERRABLE;[22] if a given constraint is DEFERRABLE, it can further be defined to be INITIALLY DEFERRED or INITIALLY IMMEDIATE, which defines its state at the beginning of each transaction. NOT DEFERRABLE constraints are always checked immediately, but DEFERRABLE constraints can be dynamically switched on and off by means of the statement

```
SET CONSTRAINTS <constraint name commalist> <option> ;
```

where *<option>* is either IMMEDIATE or DEFERRED. Here is an example:

```
SET CONSTRAINTS SSP5, SSP6 DEFERRED ;
```

DEFERRABLE constraints are checked only when they are in the IMMEDIATE state. Setting a DEFERRABLE constraint into the IMMEDIATE state causes that constraint to be immediately checked; if the check fails, the SET IMMEDIATE fails. COMMIT forces a SET IMMEDIATE for all DEFERRABLE constraints; if any integrity check then fails, the transaction is rolled back.

Triggers

The SQL CREATE TRIGGER statement looks like this:

```
CREATE TRIGGER <trigger name>
      <before or after> <event> ON <base table name>
    [ REFERENCING <naming commalist> ]
    [ FOR EACH <row or statement> ]
    [ WHEN ( <bool exp> ) ] <action> ;
```

Explanation:

1. The *<before or after>* specification is either BEFORE or AFTER (the SQL standard does not support INSTEAD OF, though some products do).

2. The *<event>* is INSERT, DELETE, or UPDATE. UPDATE can be further qualified by the specification OF *<column name commalist>*.

3. Each *<naming>* is one of the following:

```
OLD ROW    AS <name>
NEW ROW    AS <name>
OLD TABLE AS <name>
NEW TABLE AS <name>
```

4. The *<row or statement>* specification is either ROW or STATEMENT (STATEMENT is the default). ROW means the trigger fires for each individual row affected by the triggering statement; STATEMENT means the trigger fires just once for the statement taken as a whole.

---

[22] Certain constraints are required to be NOT DEFERRABLE, however. For example, if *FK* is a foreign key, then the candidate key constraint for the matching candidate key must be NOT DEFERRABLE.

5. If a WHEN clause is specified, it means the *<action>* is to be executed only if the *<bool exp>* evaluates to TRUE.

6. The *<action>* is a single SQL statement (that single statement can be *compound,* however, meaning, loosely, that it can consist of a sequence of statements bracketed by BEGIN and END delimiters).

Finally, here is the syntax of DROP TRIGGER:

```
DROP TRIGGER <trigger name> ;
```

Like DROP ASSERTION, DROP TRIGGER does not offer a RESTRICT *vs.* CASCADE option.

9.13   SUMMARY

In this chapter we have discussed the crucial concept of **integrity**. The integrity problem is the problem of ensuring that the data in the database is *correct* (or as correct as possible, at any rate; sadly, the best we can really do is ensure that the data is *consistent*). Naturally, we are interested in **declarative** solutions to that problem.

We began by showing that integrity constraints take the general form:

> *IF certain tuples appear in certain relvars, **THEN** those tuples satisfy a certain condition.*

(Type constraints are a little different—see subsequent discussion.) We gave a syntax for stating such constraints, based on the calculus version of **Tutorial D**, and pointed out that that syntax did not include any way for the user to tell the DBMS when to do the checking; rather, we want the DBMS to determine for itself when to do that checking. And we claimed (without yet justifying our position, however) that all constraint checking must be **immediate**.

Next, we explained that a constraint as stated is a **predicate**, but when it is checked (i.e., when current relation values are substituted for the relvars mentioned in that predicate) it becomes a **proposition**. The logical AND of all predicates that apply to a given relvar is the **relvar predicate** for that relvar, and the logical AND of all relvar predicates that apply to a given database is the **database predicate** for that database. And **The Golden Rule** states:

> *No update operation must ever assign to any database a value that causes its database predicate to evaluate to FALSE.*

Next, we distinguished between **internal** and **external** predicates. Internal predicates are formal: They are understood by the system, and they are checked by the DBMS (the relvar and database predicates referred to in the previous paragraph are internal predicates). External predicates, by contrast, are only informal: They are understood by the user but not by the system. The **Closed World Assumption** applies to external predicates but not to internal ones.

Incidentally, as you might have realized by now, what is usually called "integrity" in database contexts really means **semantics**: It is the integrity constraints (in particular, the relvar and database predicates) that represent the **meaning** of the data. And that is one reason why, as we claimed in the introduction to this chapter, integrity is *crucially important*.

We also pointed out that, *pace* conventional wisdom, everything to do with integrity applies to all relvars, not just to base ones (in particular, it applies to views)—though the constraints that apply to a given view can be derived from those that apply to the relvars from which the view in question is derived, of course.

We went on to divide integrity constraints into four categories:

- A **type** constraint specifies the legal values for a given type (or domain), and is checked during invocations of the corresponding selector.

- An **attribute** constraint specifies the legal values for a given attribute, and cannot possibly be violated if type constraints are checked.

- A **relvar** constraint specifies the legal values for a given relvar, and is checked when the relvar in question is updated.

- A **database** constraint specifies the legal values for a given database, and is checked when the database in question is updated.

We pointed out, however, that the distinction between relvar and database constraints is more one of pragma than it is of logic. We also briefly discussed **transition** constraints.

Next, we discussed the pragmatically important special cases of **candidate**, **primary**, **alternate**, and **foreign** keys. Candidate keys satisfy the **uniqueness** and **irreducibility** properties, and every relvar has at least one (no exceptions!). The constraint that values of a given foreign key must match values of the corresponding candidate key is a **referential constraint**; we explored several implications of the referential integrity idea, including in particular the notion of **referential actions** (especially **CASCADE**). This latter discussion led us to a brief digression into the realm of **triggers**.

We concluded our discussions with a look at the relevant aspects of SQL. SQL's type constraints are very weak; essentially, they are limited to saying that the type in question must have a certain physical representation. SQL's base table constraints (which include special-case support for keys) and general constraints ("assertions") include analogs of our relvar and database constraints (excluding transition constraints), but they are not nearly as carefully classified (in fact, they are almost interchangeable, and it is not at all clear why the language includes both). SQL also supports **deferred checking**. Finally, we briefly sketched SQL's support for triggers.

EXERCISES

9.1 Which operations can cause the constraints in Examples 1–6 from Section 9.1 to be violated?

9.2 Give algebraic **Tutorial D** formulations of Examples 1–6 from Section 9.1. Which do you prefer, the calculus formulations or the algebraic ones? Why?

9.3 Using the calculus-based **Tutorial D** syntax from Section 9.2, write integrity constraints for the following "business rules" on the suppliers-parts-projects database:

a. The only legal cities are London, Paris, Rome, Athens, Oslo, Stockholm, Madrid, and Amsterdam.

b. The only legal supplier numbers are ones that can be represented by a character string of at least two characters, of which the first is an "S" and the remainder denote a decimal integer in the range 0 to 9999.

c. All red parts must weigh less than 50 pounds.

d. No two projects can be located in the same city.

e. At most one supplier can be located in Athens at any one time.

f. No shipment can have a quantity more than double the average of all such quantities.

g. The highest-status supplier must not be located in the same city as the lowest-status supplier.

h. Every project must be located in a city in which there is at least one supplier.

i. Every project must be located in a city in which there is at least one supplier of that project.

j. There must exist at least one red part.

k. The average supplier status must be greater than 19.

l. Every London supplier must supply part P2.

m. At least one red part must weigh less than 50 pounds.

n. Suppliers in London must supply more different kinds of parts than suppliers in Paris.

o. Suppliers in London must supply more parts in total than suppliers in Paris.

p. No shipment quantity can be reduced (in a single update) to less than half its current value.

q. Suppliers in Athens can move only to London or Paris, and suppliers in London can move only to Paris.

9.4 For each of your answers to Exercise 9.3, (a) state whether the constraint is a relvar constraint or a database constraint; (b) state the operations that might cause the constraint to be violated.

9.5 Using the sample suppliers-parts-projects data values from Fig. 4.5 (see the inside back cover), say what the effect of each of the following operations is:

a. UPDATE project J7, setting CITY to New York.

b. UPDATE part P5, setting P# to P4.

c. UPDATE supplier S5, setting S# to S8, if the applicable referential action is RESTRICT.

d. DELETE supplier S3, if the applicable referential action is CASCADE.

e. DELETE part P2, if the applicable referential action is RESTRICT.

f. DELETE project J4, if the applicable referential action is CASCADE.

g. UPDATE shipment S1-P1-J1, setting S# to S2.

h. UPDATE shipment S5-P5-J5, setting J# to J7.

i. UPDATE shipment S5-P5-J5, setting J# to J8.

j. INSERT shipment S5-P6-J7.

k. INSERT shipment S4-P7-J6.

l. INSERT shipment S1-P2-*jjj* (where *jjj* stands for a default project number).

9.6 The body of the chapter discussed foreign key delete and update rules, but it did not mention any foreign key "insert rule." Why not?

9.7 An education database contains information about an in-house company education training scheme. For each training course, the database contains details of all prerequisite courses for that course and all offerings for that course; for each offering, it contains details of all teachers and all student enrollments for that offering. The database also contains information about employees. The relevant relvars are as follows, in outline:

```
COURSE       { COURSE#, TITLE }
PREREQ       { SUP_COURSE#, SUB_COURSE# }
OFFERING     { COURSE#, OFF#, OFFDATE, LOCATION }
TEACHER      { COURSE#, OFF#, EMP# }
ENROLLMENT   { COURSE#, OFF#, EMP#, GRADE }
EMPLOYEE     { EMP#, ENAME, JOB }
```

The meaning of the PREREQ relvar is that the superior course (SUP_COURSE#) has the subordinate course (SUB_COURSE#) as an immediate prerequisite; the others should be self-explanatory. Draw a referential diagram for this database. Also give the corresponding database definition (i.e., write an appropriate set of type and relvar definitions).

9.8 The following two relvars represent a database containing information about departments and employees:

```
DEPT   { DEPT#, ..., MGR_EMP#, ... }
EMP    { EMP#, ..., DEPT#, ... }
```

Every department has a manager (MGR_EMP#); every employee has a department (DEPT#). Again, draw a referential diagram and write a database definition for this database.

9.9 The following two relvars represent a database containing information about employees and programmers:

```
EMP    { EMP#, ..., JOB, ... }
PGMR   { EMP#, ..., LANG, ... }
```

Every programmer is an employee, but the converse is not the case. Once again, draw a referential diagram and write a suitable database definition.

9.10 Candidate keys are defined to be *sets* of attributes. What happens if the set in question is empty (i.e., contains no attributes)? Can you think of any uses for such an "empty" (or "nullary") candidate key?

9.11 Let *R* be a relvar of degree *n*. What is the maximum number of candidate keys *R* might possess?

9.12 Let *A* and *B* be two relvars. State the candidate key(s) for each of the following:

a. `A WHERE ...`
b. `A {...}`
c. `A TIMES B`
d. `A UNION B`
e. `A INTERSECT B`
f. `A MINUS B`
g. `A JOIN B`
h. `EXTEND A ADD exp AS Z`
i. `SUMMARIZE A PER B ADD exp AS Z`
j. `A SEMIJOIN B`
k. `A SEMIMINUS B`

Assume in each case that *A* and *B* meet the requirements for the operation in question (e.g., they are of the same type, in the case of UNION).

9.13 Repeat Exercise 9.10, replacing the word *candidate* by the word *foreign* (twice).

9.14 Give SQL solutions to Exercise 9.3.

9.15 Give SQL database definitions for Exercises 9.7–9.9.

9.16   We have seen that every relvar (and in fact every relation) corresponds to some predicate. Is the converse true?

9.17   In a footnote in Section 9.7, we said that if the values S1 and London appeared together in some tuple, then it might mean (among many other possible interpretations) that supplier S1 does not have an office in London. Actually, this particular interpretation is extremely unlikely. Why? *Hint:* Remember the Closed World Assumption.

REFERENCES AND BIBLIOGRAPHY

9.1 Alexander Aiken, Joseph M. Hellerstein, and Jennifer Widom: "Static Analysis Techniques for Predicting the Behavior of Active Database Rules," *ACM TODS 20,* No. 1 (March 1995).

This paper continues the work of references [9.2] and [9.5], *q.v.,* on "expert database systems" (here called *active* database systems). In particular, it describes the rule system of the IBM Starburst prototype (see references [18.21], [18.48], [26.19], [26.23], and [26.29, 26.30], as well as reference [9.25]).

9.2 Elena Baralis and Jennifer Widom: "An Algebraic Approach to Static Analysis of Active Database Rules," *ACM TODS 25,* No. 3 (September 2000). An earlier version of this paper, "An Algebraic Approach to Rule Analysis in Expert Database Systems," appeared in Proc. 20th Int. Conf. on Very Large Data Bases, Santiago, Chile (September 1994).

The "rules" of the title here are essentially *triggers*. One problem with such rules is that (as noted in Section 9.11) their behavior is inherently difficult to predict or understand. This paper presents methods for determining prior to execution time whether a given set of rules possesses the properties of termination and confluence. *Termination* means the rule processing is guaranteed not to go on forever. *Confluence* means the final database state is independent of the order in which the rules are executed.

9.3 Philip A. Bernstein, Barbara T. Blaustein, and Edmund M. Clarke: "Fast Maintenance of Semantic Integrity Assertions Using Redundant Aggregate Data," Proc. 6th Int. Conf. on Very Large Data Bases, Montreal, Canada (October 1980).

Presents an efficient method of enforcement for integrity constraints of a certain special kind. An example is "Every value in set *A* must be less than every value in set *B*." The enforcement technique is based on the observation that (e.g.) the constraint just given is logically equivalent to the constraint "The *maximum* value in *A* must be less than the *minimum* value in *B*." By recognizing this class of constraint and automatically keeping the relevant maximum and minimum values in hidden variables, the system can reduce the number of comparisons involved in enforcing the constraint on a given update from something on the order of the cardinality of either *A* or *B* (depending which set the update applies to) to *one*—at the cost, of course, of having to maintain the hidden variables.

9.4 O. Peter Buneman and Erik K. Clemons: "Efficiently Monitoring Relational Databases," *ACM TODS 4,* No. 3 (September 1979).

This paper is concerned with the efficient implementation of triggers (here called *alerters*)—in particular, with the problem of deciding when the trigger condition is satisfied, without necessarily evaluating that condition. It gives a method (an *avoidance* algorithm) for detecting updates that cannot possibly satisfy a given trigger condition; it also discusses a technique for reducing the processing overhead in the case where the avoidance algorithm fails, by evaluating the trigger condition for some small subset (a *filter*) of the total set of relevant tuples.

9.5 Stefano Ceri and Jennifer Widom: "Deriving Production Rules for Constraint Maintenance," Proc. 16th Int. Conf. on Very Large Data Bases, Brisbane, Australia (August 1990).

> Describes an SQL-based language for defining constraints and gives an algorithm by which the system can identify all of the operations that might violate a given constraint. (A preliminary outline of such an algorithm was previously given in reference [9.12].) The paper also addresses questions of optimization and correctness.

9.6 Stefano Ceri, Roberta J. Cochrane, and Jennifer Widom: "Practical Applications of Triggers and Constraints: Successes and Lingering Issues," Proc. 26th Int. Conf. on Very Large Data Bases, Cairo, Egypt (September 2000).

> A quote from the abstract: "[A] significant portion of . . . trigger applications are in fact nothing more than *constraint-maintainers* for various classes of integrity constraints." The paper goes on to suggest that many triggers, including those "constraint-maintainers" in particular, could in fact be generated automatically from declarative specifications.

9.7 Stefano Ceri, Piero Fraternali, Stefano Paraboschi, and Letizia Tanca: "Automatic Generation of Production Rules for Integrity Maintenance," *ACM TODS 19,* No. 3 (September 1994).

> This paper, which builds on the work of reference [9.5], introduces the possibility of *automatically repairing* damage done by a constraint violation. Constraints are compiled into *production rules* with the following components:
>
> 1. A list of operations that can violate the constraint
>
> 2. A boolean expression that will evaluate to TRUE if the constraint is violated (basically just the negation of the original constraint)
>
> 3. An SQL repair procedure
>
> The paper also includes a good survey of related work.

9.8 Roberta Cochrane, Hamid Pirahesh, and Nelson Mattos: "Integrating Triggers and Declarative Constraints in SQL Database Systems," Proc. 22nd Int. Conf. on Very Large Data Bases, Mumbai (Bombay), India (September 1996).

> To quote: "The semantics of the interaction of triggers and declarative constraints must be carefully defined to avoid inconsistent execution and to provide users [with] a comprehensive model for understanding such interactions. This [paper] defines such a model." The model in question became the basis for the relevant aspects of SQL:1999.

9.9 E. F. Codd: "Domains, Keys, and Referential Integrity in Relational Databases," *InfoDB 3,* No. 1 (Spring 1988).

> A discussion of the domain, primary key, and foreign key concepts. The paper is obviously authoritative, since Codd was the inventor of all three concepts; in this writer's opinion, however, it still leaves too many issues unresolved or unexplained. Incidentally, it gives the following argument in favor of the discipline of requiring one candidate key to be selected as primary: "Failure to support this discipline is something like trying to use a computer with an addressing scheme . . . that changes radix whenever a particular kind of event occurs (for example, encountering an address that happens to be a prime number)." But if we accept this argument, why not take it to its logical conclusion and use an identical addressing scheme for *everything*? Is it not awkward to have to "address" suppliers by supplier number and parts by part number?—not to mention shipments, which involve "addresses" that are *composite*. (In fact, there is much to be said for this idea of a globally uniform addressing scheme. See the discussion of *surrogates* in the annotation to reference [14.21] in Chapter 14.)

9.10 C. J. Date: "Referential Integrity," Proc. 7th Int. Conf. on Very Large Data Bases, Cannes, France (September 1981). Republished in revised form in *Relational Database: Selected Writings.* Reading, Mass.: Addison-Wesley (1986).

> The paper that introduced the referential actions (principally CASCADE and RESTRICT) discussed in Section 9.10 of the present chapter. The main difference between the original (VLDB 1981) version of the paper and the revised version is that the original version, following reference [14.7], permitted a given foreign key to reference any number of relvars, whereas—for reasons explained in detail in reference [9.11]—the revised version backed off from that excessively general position.

9.11 C. J. Date: "Referential Integrity and Foreign Keys" (in two parts), in *Relational Database Writings 1985–1989.* Reading, Mass.: Addison-Wesley (1990).

> Part I of this paper discusses the history of the referential integrity concept and offers a preferred set of basic definitions (with rationale). Part II provides further arguments in favor of those preferred definitions and gives some specific practical recommendations; in particular, it discusses problems caused by (a) overlapping foreign keys, (b) composite foreign key values that are partly null, and (c) *conterminous* referential paths (i.e., distinct referential paths that have the same start point and the same end point). *Note:* Certain of the positions of this paper are slightly (but not very seriously) undermined by the arguments of reference [9.14].

9.12 C. J. Date: "A Contribution to the Study of Database Integrity," in *Relational Database Writings 1985–1989.* Reading, Mass.: Addison-Wesley (1990).

> To quote from the abstract: "This paper attempts to impose some structure on the [integrity] problem by (a) proposing a classification scheme for integrity constraints, (b) using that scheme to clarify the principal underlying concepts of data integrity, (c) sketching an approach to a concrete language for formulating integrity constraints, and (d) pinpointing some specific areas for further research." Portions of the present chapter are based on this earlier paper, but the classification scheme itself should be regarded as superseded by the revised version described in Section 9.9 of the present chapter.

9.13 C. J. Date: "Integrity," Chapter 11 of reference [4.21].

> IBM's DB2 product does provide declarative primary and foreign key support (in fact, it was one of the first to do so, perhaps *the* first). As this reference explains, however, that support does suffer from certain implementation restrictions, the general purpose of which is *to guarantee predictable behavior.* We give a simple example here. Suppose relvar R currently contains just two tuples, with primary key values 1 and 2, respectively, and consider the update request "Double every primary key value in R." The correct result is that the tuples should now have primary key values 2 and 4, respectively. If the system updates the "2" first (replacing it by "4") and then updates the "1" second (replacing it by "2"), the request will succeed. If, on the other hand, the system updates—or, rather, tries to update—the "1" first (replacing it by "2"), it will run into a uniqueness violation, and the request will fail (the database will remain unchanged). In other words, *the result of the request is unpredictable.* In order to avoid such unpredictability, DB2 simply outlaws situations in which it might otherwise occur. Unfortunately, however, some of the resulting restrictions are quite severe [9.20].
>
> Note that, as the foregoing example suggests, DB2 typically does do "inflight checking"—that is, it applies integrity checks to each individual tuple *as it updates that tuple.* Such inflight checking is logically incorrect, however (see the subsection "Updating Relvars" in Chapter 6, Section 6.5); it is done for performance reasons.

9.14 C. J. Date: "The Primacy of Primary Keys: An Investigation," in *Relational Database Writings 1991–1994.* Reading, Mass.: Addison-Wesley (1995).

Presents arguments in support of the position that sometimes it is not a good idea to make one candidate key "more equal than others."

9.15 C. J. Date: *WHAT Not HOW: The Business Rules Approach to Application Development.* Reading, Mass.: Addison-Wesley (2000).

A very informal (and technically undemanding) introduction to "business rules." See also references [9.21] and [9.22].

9.16 C. J. Date: "Constraints and Predicates: A Brief Tutorial" (in three parts), *http://www.dbdebunk .com* (May 2001).

The present chapter is heavily based on this tutorial. The following edited (and abridged) version of the paper's concluding section is relevant, too:

> We have seen that a database is a collection of true propositions. In fact, a database, together with the operators that apply to the propositions in that database, is a **logical system**. And by "logical system" here, we mean a formal system—like euclidean geometry, for example—that has *axioms* ("given truths") and *rules of inference* by which we can prove *theorems* ("derived truths") from those axioms. Indeed, it was Codd's very great insight, when he first invented the relational model back in 1969, that a database is not really just a collection of *data* (despite the name); rather, it is a collection of *facts,* or what the logicians call true propositions. Those propositions— the given ones, which is to say the ones represented in the base relvars—are the axioms of the logical system under discussion. And the inference rules are essentially the rules by which new propositions are derived from the given ones; in other words, they are the rules that tell us how to apply the operators of the relational algebra. Thus, when the system evaluates some relational expression (in particular, when it responds to some query), it is really deriving new truths from given ones; in effect, it is proving a theorem!
>
> Once we recognize the truth of the foregoing, we see that the whole apparatus of formal logic becomes available for use in attacking "the database problem." In other words, questions such as
>
> - What should the database look like to the user?
> - What should the query language look like?
> - How should results be presented to the user?
> - How can we best implement queries (or, more generally, evaluate database expressions)?
> - How should we design the database in the first place?
>
> (not to mention the question of what integrity constraints should look like) all become, in effect, questions in logic that are susceptible to logical treatment and can be given logical answers.
>
> Of course, it goes without saying that the relational model supports the foregoing perception of what databases are all about very directly—which is why, in this writer's opinion, the relational model is rock solid, and "right," and will endure.
>
> Finally, given that a database together with the relational operators is indeed a logical system, we can now see the **absolutely vital importance** of integrity constraints. If the database is in violation of some integrity constraint, then the logical system we are talking about is inconsistent. And we can get *absolutely any answer at all* from an inconsistent system! Suppose the system in question is such that it

implies that both *p* and NOT *p* are true (there is the inconsistency), where *p* is some proposition. Now let *q* be some arbitrary proposition. Then:

- From the truth of *p*, we can infer the truth of *p* OR *q*.
- From the truth of *p* OR *q* and the truth of NOT *p*, we can infer the truth of *q*.

But *q* was arbitrary! It follows that any proposition whatsoever can be shown to be true in an inconsistent system.

9.17 M. M. Hammer and S. K. Sarin: "Efficient Monitoring of Database Assertions," Proc. 1978 ACM SIGMOD Int. Conf. on Management of Data, Austin, Texas (May/June 1978).

An algorithm is sketched for generating integrity-checking procedures that are more efficient than the obvious "brute force" method of simply evaluating constraints after an update has been performed. The checks are incorporated into application object code at compile time. In some cases it is possible to detect that no run-time checks are needed at all. Even when they are needed, it is frequently possible to reduce the number of database accesses significantly in a variety of ways.

9.18 Bruce M. Horowitz: "A Run-Time Execution Model for Referential Integrity Maintenance," Proc. 8th IEEE Int. Conf. on Data Engineering, Phoenix, Ariz. (February 1992).

It is well known that certain combinations of

1. Referential structures (i.e., collections of relvars that are interrelated via referential constraints)
2. Foreign key delete and update rules
3. Actual data values in the database

can together lead to certain conflict situations and can potentially cause unpredictable behavior on the part of the implementation (see, e.g., reference [9.11] for further explanation). There are three broad approaches to dealing with this problem:

a. Leave it to the user.
b. Have the system detect and reject attempts to define structures that might potentially lead to conflicts at run time.
c. Have the system detect and reject *actual* conflicts at run time.

Option *a* is a nonstarter and option *b* tends to be excessively cautious [9.13,9.20]; Horowitz therefore proposes option *c*. The paper gives a set of rules for such run-time actions and proves their correctness. Note, however, that the question of performance overhead of such run-time checking is not considered.

Horowitz was an active member of the committee that defined SQL:1992, and the referential integrity portions of the SQL standard effectively imply that the proposals of this paper must be supported.

9.19 Victor M. Markowitz: "Referential Integrity Revisited: An Object-Oriented Perspective," Proc. 16th Int. Conf. on Very Large Data Bases, Brisbane, Australia (August 1990).

The "object-oriented perspective" of this paper's title reflects the author's opening assertion that "referential integrity underlies the relational representation of object-oriented structures." The paper is not, however, really about objects in the object-oriented sense at all. Rather, it presents an algorithm that, starting from an entity/relationship diagram (see Chapter 14), will generate a relational database definition in which certain of the problem situations identified in reference [9.11] (e.g., overlapping keys) are guaranteed not to occur.

The paper also discusses three commercial products (DB2, Sybase, and Ingres, as of around 1990) from a referential integrity viewpoint. DB2, which provides *declarative* support, is shown to be unduly restrictive; Sybase and Ingres, which provide *procedural* support (via "triggers" and "rules," respectively), are shown to be less restrictive than DB2 but cumbersome and difficult to use (though the Ingres support is said to be "technically superior" to that of Sybase).

9.20 Victor M. Markowitz: "Safe Referential Integrity Structures in Relational Databases," Proc. 17th Int. Conf. on Very Large Data Bases, Barcelona, Spain (September 1991).

Proposes two formal "safeness conditions" that guarantee that certain of the problem situations discussed in (e.g.) references [9.11] and [9.18] cannot occur. The paper also considers what is involved in satisfying those conditions in DB2, Sybase, and Ingres (again, as of around 1990). Regarding DB2, it is shown that some of the implementation restrictions imposed in the interests of safety [9.13] are logically unnecessary, while at the same time others are inadequate (i.e., DB2 still permits certain unsafe situations). Regarding Sybase and Ingres, it is claimed that the procedural support found in those products does not provide for the detection of unsafe—or even incorrect!—referential specifications.

9.21 Ronald G. Ross: *The Business Rule Book: Classifying, Defining, and Modeling Rules* (Version 3.0). Boston, Mass.: Database Research Group (1994).

See the annotation to reference [9.22].

9.22 Ronald G. Ross: *Business Rule Concepts*. Houston, Tex.: Business Rule Solutions Inc. (1998).

A groundswell of support for "business rules" has been building in the commercial world over the last few years; some industry figures have begun to suggest that they might be a better basis for designing and building databases and database applications (better, that is, than more established techniques such as entity/relationship modeling, object modeling, semantic modeling, and others). And we agree, because business rules are essentially nothing more than a more user-friendly (i.e., less academic and less formal) way of talking about predicates, propositions, and all of the other aspects of integrity discussed in the present chapter. Ross is one of the foremost advocates of the business rules approach, and his books are recommended to the serious practitioner. Reference [9.21] is comprehensive; reference [9.22] is a short tutorial. *Note:* Another book by Ross, *Principles of the Business Rule Approach* (Addison-Wesley, 2003), was published just as the present book was going to press.

9.23 M. R. Stonebraker and E. Wong: "Access Control in a Relational Data Base Management System by Query Modification," Proc. ACM Nat. Conf., San Diego, Calif. (November 1974).

The University Ingres prototype [8.11] pioneered an interesting approach to integrity constraints (and security constraints—see Chapter 17), based on *request modification*. Integrity constraints were defined by means of the DEFINE INTEGRITY statement—syntax:

```
DEFINE INTEGRITY ON <relvar name> IS <bool exp>
```

For example:

```
DEFINE INTEGRITY ON S IS S.STATUS > 0
```

Suppose user U attempts the following QUEL REPLACE operation:

```
REPLACE S ( STATUS = S.STATUS - 10 )
WHERE    S.CITY = "London"
```

Then Ingres automatically modifies the REPLACE to:

```
REPLACE S ( STATUS = S.STATUS - 10 )
WHERE    S.CITY = "London"
AND      ( S.STATUS - 10 ) > 0
```

Obviously, this modified operation cannot possibly violate the integrity constraint.

One disadvantage of this approach is that not all constraints can be enforced in this simple way; as a matter of fact, QUEL supported only constraints in which the boolean expression was a simple restriction condition. However, even that limited support represented more than was found in most systems at the time.

9.24 A. Walker and S. C. Salveter: "Automatic Modification of Transactions to Preserve Data Base Integrity Without Undoing Updates," State University of New York, Stony Brook, N.Y.: Technical Report 81/026 (June 1981).

Describes a technique for automatically modifying any "transaction template" (i.e., transaction source code) into a corresponding *safe* template—safe, in the sense that no transaction conforming to that modified template can possibly violate any declared integrity constraints. The method works by adding queries and tests to the original template to ensure before any updating is done that no constraints will be violated. At run time, if any of those tests fails, the transaction is rejected and an error message is generated.

9.25 Jennifer Widom and Stefano Ceri (eds.): *Active Database Systems: Triggers and Rules for Advanced Database Processing*. San Francisco, Calif.: Morgan Kaufmann (1996).

A useful compendium of research and tutorial papers on "active database systems" (i.e., database systems that automatically carry out specified actions in response to specified events—in other words, database systems with triggers). Descriptions are included of several prototype systems, including in particular Starburst from IBM Research (see references [18.21], [18.48], [26.19], [26.23], and [26.29, 26.30]) and Postgres from the University of California at Berkeley (see references [26.36], [26.40], and [26.42, 26.43]). The book also summarizes the relevant aspects of SQL:1992, an early version of SQL:1999, and certain commercial products (Oracle, Informix, and Ingres among them). An extensive bibliography is included.

Views

10.1 INTRODUCTION

As we saw in Chapter 3, a view in the relational model is essentially just a named expression of the relational algebra (or something with the expressive power of the relational algebra). Here is a **Tutorial D** example:

```
VAR GOOD_SUPPLIER VIEW
    ( S WHERE STATUS > 15 ) { S#, STATUS, CITY } ;
```

When this statement is executed, the specified algebraic expression—which is the **view-defining** expression—is not evaluated but is merely "remembered" by the system (actually by saving it in the catalog, under the specified name GOOD_SUPPLIER). To the user, however, it is now as if there really were a relvar in the database called GOOD_SUPPLIER, with tuples and attributes as indicated in the unshaded portions of Fig. 10.1 (we assume our usual sample data values). In other words, the name GOOD_SUPPLIER denotes a **derived** (and **virtual**) relvar, whose value at any given time is the relation that would result if the view-defining expression were actually evaluated at that time.

GOOD_SUPPLIER	S#	SNAME	STATUS	CITY
	S1	Smith	20	London
	S2	Jones	10	Paris
	S3	Blake	30	Paris
	S4	Clark	20	London
	S5	Adams	30	Athens

Fig. 10.1   GOOD_SUPPLIER as a view of base relvar S (unshaded portions)

We also saw in Chapter 3 that a view such as GOOD_SUPPLIER is effectively just a *window* into the underlying data: Any updates to that underlying data will immediately and automatically be visible through that window (as long as they lie within the scope of the view); likewise, any updates to the view will immediately and automatically be applied to the underlying data, and hence be visible through the window.[1]

Now, depending on circumstances, the user might or might not realize that GOOD_SUPPLIER really is a view; some users might be aware of that fact and might understand that there is a real (base) relvar underneath, others might genuinely believe that GOOD_SUPPLIER is a real (base) relvar in its own right. Either way, it makes little difference: The point is, users can operate on GOOD_SUPPLIER just as if it *were* a real or base relvar. For example, here is a query against GOOD_SUPPLIER:

```
GOOD_SUPPLIER WHERE CITY ≠ 'London'
```

Given the sample data of Fig. 10.1, the result is:

S#	STATUS	CITY
S3	30	Paris
S5	30	Athens

This query certainly looks just like a regular query on a regular relvar. And, as we saw in Chapter 3, the system handles such a query by converting it into an equivalent query on the underlying base relvar (or base relvars, plural). It does this by effectively replacing each appearance in the query of the *name* of the view by the expression that *defines* the view. In the example, this **substitution procedure** gives

```
( ( S WHERE STATUS > 15 ) { S#, STATUS, CITY } )
                          WHERE CITY ≠ 'London'
```

which is readily seen to be equivalent to the simpler form

```
( S WHERE STATUS > 15 AND CITY ≠ 'London' )
                          { S#, STATUS, CITY }
```

And this query produces the result shown earlier.

---

[1] Actually they might *not* be visible in SQL!—see the discussion of WITH CHECK OPTION in Section 10.6.

Incidentally, it is worth pointing out that the substitution process just outlined—that is, the process of substituting the view-defining expression for the view name—*works precisely because of relational closure.* Closure implies, among many other things, that wherever a simple relvar name *R* can appear within an expression, a relational expression of arbitrary complexity can appear instead (just as long as it evaluates to a relation of the same type as *R*). In other words, views work precisely because of the fact that relations are closed under the relational algebra—yet another illustration of the fundamental importance of the closure property.

Update operations are treated in a similar manner. For example, the operation

```
UPDATE GOOD_SUPPLIER WHERE CITY = 'Paris'
     { STATUS := STATUS + 10 } ;
```

is effectively converted into

```
UPDATE S WHERE STATUS > 15 AND CITY = 'Paris'
     { STATUS := STATUS + 10 } ;
```

INSERT and DELETE operations are handled analogously.

Further Examples

Here are some more examples, illustrating a variety of points:

1. ```
VAR REDPART VIEW
     (P WHERE COLOR = COLOR ('Red')) { ALL BUT COLOR }
                                         RENAME WEIGHT AS WT ;
```

   View REDPART is a projection of a restriction (plus an attribute renaming) of the parts relvar. It has attributes P#, PNAME, WT, and CITY, and contains tuples for red parts only.

2. ```
VAR PQ VIEW
     SUMMARIZE SP PER P { P# } ADD SUM ( QTY ) AS TOTQTY ;
```

   View PQ is a kind of *statistical summary* or *compression* of the underlying data.

3. ```
VAR CITY_PAIR VIEW
     ((S RENAME CITY AS SCITY) JOIN SP JOIN
       (P RENAME CITY AS PCITY)) { SCITY, PCITY } ;
```

   View CITY_PAIR joins suppliers, parts, and shipments over supplier numbers and part numbers and then projects the result over SNAME and PNAME. Loosely speaking, a pair of city names (*x,y*) appears in the result if and only if a supplier located in city *x* supplies a part stored in city *y*. For example, supplier S1 supplies part P1; supplier S1 is located in London and part P1 is stored in London; so the pair (London, London) appears in the view.

4. ```
VAR HEAVY_REDPART VIEW
     REDPART WHERE WT > WEIGHT ( 12.0 ) ;
```

   This example shows one view defined in terms of another.

Defining and Dropping Views

Here then is the **Tutorial D** syntax for defining a view:

```
VAR <relvar name> VIEW <relation exp>
                  <candidate key def list> ;
```

The *<candidate key def list>* is allowed to be empty (equivalently, the specification can be omitted) because the system should be able to *infer* candidate keys for views [3.3]. In the case of GOOD_SUPPLIER, for example, the system should be aware that the sole candidate key is {S#}, inherited from the underlying base relvar S.

We remark that, in terms of the ANSI/SPARC terminology of Chapter 2, view definitions combine the *external schema* function and the *external/conceptual mapping* function, because they specify both (a) what the external object (i.e., the view) looks like and (b) how that object maps to the conceptual level (i.e., to the underlying base relvar(s)). *Note:* Some view definitions specify, not the external/conceptual mapping as such, but rather an *external/external* mapping. View HEAVY_REDPART from the previous subsection is a case in point.

The syntax for dropping a view is:

```
DROP VAR <relvar name> ;
```

where, of course, the *<relvar name>* refers to a view specifically. Now, in Chapter 6 we assumed that an attempt to drop a base relvar would fail if any view definition currently referred to that base relvar. Analogously, we assume that an attempt to drop a view will also fail if some other view definition currently refers to that view. Alternatively (and by analogy with referential constraints), we might consider extending the view definition statement to include some kind of RESTRICT *vs.* CASCADE option; RESTRICT would mean that an attempt to drop any relvar referenced in the view definition should fail, CASCADE would mean that such an attempt should succeed and should cascade to drop the referencing view as well. *Note:* SQL does support such an option, but puts it on the DROP statement instead of on the view definition. There is no default—the required option must be stated explicitly (see Section 10.6).

10.2 WHAT ARE VIEWS FOR?

There are many reasons why view support is desirable. Here are some of them:

■ *Views provide a shorthand or "macro" capability.*

Consider the query "Get cities that store parts that are available from some supplier in London." Given view CITY_PAIR from the subsection "Further Examples" in the previous section, the following formulation suffices:

```
( CITY_PAIR WHERE SCITY = 'London' ) { PCITY }
```

Without the view, by contrast, the query is much more complex:

```
( ( ( S RENAME CITY AS SCITY ) JOIN SP JOIN
    ( P RENAME CITY AS PCITY ) )
  WHERE SCITY = 'London' ) { PCITY }
```

While the user *could* use this second formulation directly (security constraints permitting), the first is obviously simpler. Of course, the first is really just shorthand for the second; the system's view-processing mechanism will effectively expand the first formulation into the second before it is executed.

There is a strong analogy here with *macros* in a programming language system. In principle, a user in a programming language system could write out the expanded form of a given macro directly in his or her source code—but it is much more convenient, for a variety of well-understood reasons, not to do so, but rather to use the macro shorthand and let the system's macro processor do the expansion on the user's behalf. Analogous remarks apply to views. Thus, views in a database system play a role somewhat analogous to that of macros in a programming language system, and the well-known advantages and benefits of macros apply directly to views as well, *mutatis mutandis.* Note in particular that (as with macros) no run-time performance overhead attaches to the use of views—there is only a small overhead at view-processing time (analogous to macro-expansion time).

■ *Views allow the same data to be seen by different users in different ways at the same time.*

Views effectively allow users to focus on, and perhaps logically restructure, just that portion of the database that is of concern to them and to ignore the rest. This consideration is obviously important when there are many different users, with many different requirements, all interacting simultaneously with a single integrated database.

■ *Views provide automatic security for hidden data.*

"Hidden data" refers to data not visible through some given view (e.g., supplier names, in the case of view GOOD_SUPPLIER from the previous section). Such data is clearly secure from access—retrieval access, at least—through that particular view. Thus, forcing users to access the database through views constitutes a simple but effective *security* mechanism. We will have more to say on this particular use of views in Chapter 17.

■ *Views can provide logical data independence.*

This is one of the most important points of all. See the subsection immediately following.

Logical Data Independence

We remind you that logical data independence can be defined as *the immunity of users and user programs to changes in the logical structure of the database* (where by *logical structure* we mean the conceptual or "community logical" level—see Chapter 2). And, of course, views are the means by which logical data independence is achieved in a relational system. There are two aspects to such logical data independence: **growth** and **restructuring**. (We discuss *growth* here mainly for completeness; it is important, but it has little to do with views as such.)

■ *Growth*

As the database grows to incorporate new kinds of information, the definition of the database must obviously grow accordingly. There are two possible kinds of growth that can occur:

1. The expansion of an existing base relvar to include a new attribute, corresponding to the addition of new information concerning some existing kind of object (for example, the addition of a DISCOUNT attribute to the suppliers base relvar)

2. The inclusion of a new base relvar, corresponding to the addition of a new kind of object (for example, the addition of project information to the suppliers-and-parts database)

Neither of these changes should have any effect on existing users or user programs at all, at least in principle (but see Example 8.6.1, point 6, in Chapter 8 for a warning regarding the use of "SELECT *" in SQL in this connection).

■ *Restructuring*

Occasionally it might become necessary to restructure the database in some way such that, although the overall information content remains the same, the *logical placement* of information changes—that is, the allocation of attributes to base relvars is altered in some way. We consider just one simple example here. Suppose that for some reason (the precise reason is not important for present purposes) we wish to replace base relvar S by the following two base relvars:

```
VAR SNC BASE RELATION { S# S#, SNAME NAME, CITY CHAR }
    KEY { S# } ;

VAR ST BASE RELATION { S# S#, STATUS INTEGER }
    KEY { S# } ;
```

The crucial point to note here is that *the old relvar S is the join of the two new relvars SNC and ST* (and SNC and ST are both *projections* of that old relvar S). So we create a *view* that is exactly that join, and we name it S:

```
VAR S VIEW
    SNC JOIN ST ;
```

Any expression that previously referred to base relvar S will now refer to view S instead. Hence—*provided the system supports data manipulation operations on views correctly*—users and user programs will indeed be logically immune to this particular restructuring of the database.[2]

---

[2] In principle! Sadly, today's SQL products (and the SQL standard) do *not* support data manipulation operations on views correctly, for the most part, and hence do not provide the desired degree of immunity to changes like the one in the example. To be more specific, most SQL products—not all—do support view retrievals correctly and thus do provide full logical data independence for retrieval operations; to this writer's knowledge, however, no SQL product supports view updates correctly (and the standard certainly does not), and so no SQL product currently provides full logical data independence for update operations. *Note:* A product that does support view updates correctly (not an SQL product, though) is described in reference [20.1].

As an aside, we remark that the replacement of the original suppliers relvar S by its two projections SNC and ST is not a totally trivial matter. In particular, observe that something must be done about the shipments relvar SP, since that relvar has a foreign key that references the original suppliers relvar. See Exercise 10.14 at the end of the chapter.

To revert to the main thread of the discussion: Of course, it does not follow from the SNC-ST example that logical data independence can be achieved in the face of *all possible* restructurings. The critical issue is whether there exists an unambiguous mapping from the restructured version of the database back to the previous version (i.e., whether the restructuring is reversible), or in other words whether the two versions are **information-equivalent**. If not, logical data independence is clearly not achievable.

Two Important Principles

The foregoing discussion of logical data independence raises another point. The fact is, views really serve two rather different purposes:

- A user who actually defines a view *V* is, obviously, aware of the corresponding view-defining expression *X;* that user can use the name *V* wherever the expression *X* is intended, but (as we have already seen) such uses are basically just shorthand.

- A user who is merely informed that view *V* exists and is available for use, on the other hand, is typically *not* aware of the view-defining expression *X* (to that user, in fact, view *V* should "look and feel" exactly like a base relvar).

Following on from the foregoing, we now stress the point that the question as to which relvars are base and which derived is to a large extent arbitrary anyway! Take the case of relvars S, SNC, and ST from the "restructuring" discussion in the previous subsection. It should be clear that we could *either*

a. Define S to be a base relvar and SNC and ST to be projection views of that base relvar

or

b. Define SNC and ST to be base relvars and S to be a join view of those two base relvars[3]

It follows that there must be no arbitrary and unnecessary distinctions between base and derived relvars. We refer to this fact as ***The Principle of Interchangeability*** (of base and derived relvars). Note in particular that this principle implies that we *must* be able to update views—the updatability of the database must not depend on the essentially arbitrary decision as to which relvars we decide should be base ones and which we decide should be views. See Section 10.4 for further discussion.

Let us agree for the moment to refer to the set of all base relvars as "the real database." But a typical user interacts (in general) not with that real database *per se* but with

---

[3] The discussion of *nonloss decomposition* in Chapter 12, Section 12.2, is pertinent here.

what might be called an "expressible" database, consisting (again in general) of some mixture of base relvars and views. Now, we can assume that none of the relvars in that expressible database can be derived from the rest, because such a relvar could be dropped without loss of information. Hence, *from the user's point of view,* those relvars are all base relvars, by definition! Certainly they are all independent of one another (i.e., all autonomous, to use the terminology of Chapter 3). And likewise for the database itself—that is, the choice of which database is the "real" one is arbitrary too, just as long as the choices are all information-equivalent. We refer to this fact as ***The Principle of Database Relativity.***

10.3 VIEW RETRIEVALS

We have already explained in outline how a retrieval operation on a view is converted into an equivalent operation on the underlying base relvar(s). We now make our explanation slightly more formal, as follows.

First of all, we remind you that (as noted in Chapter 6, at the end of Section 6.4) any given relational expression can be regarded as a relation-valued **function**: Given values for the various relvars mentioned in the expression (representing the arguments to this particular invocation of the function), the expression yields a result that is another relation value. Now let *D* be a database—which for present purposes we regard as just a set of base relvars—and let *V* be a view on *D* (that is, a view whose defining expression *X* is some function on *D*):

$$V \ = \ X \ (\ D \ )$$

Now let *RO* be a retrieval operation on *V; RO* is another relation-valued function, and the result of the retrieval is:

$$RO \ (\ V \ ) \ = \ RO \ (\ X \ (\ D \ ) \ )$$

Thus, the result of the retrieval is defined to be equal to the result of applying *X* to *D*—that is, **materializing** a copy of the relation that is the current value of view *V,* and then applying *RO* to that materialized copy. Now, it is almost certainly more efficient in practice to use the **substitution** procedure discussed in Section 10.1 instead (and we can now see that that procedure is equivalent to forming the function *C*(. . .) that is the *composition RO(X(. . .))* of the functions *X* and *RO,* in that order, and then applying *C* directly to *D*). Nevertheless, it is convenient, at least conceptually, to define the semantics of view retrieval in terms of materialization rather than substitution; in other words, substitution is valid as long as it is guaranteed to produce the same result as would be produced if materialization were used instead (and of course it *is* so guaranteed).

Now, you should already be familiar with the foregoing explanation, at least in principle, thanks to our earlier discussions. We spell it out explicitly here nevertheless, for the following reasons:

- First, it lays the groundwork for a similar but more searching discussion of update operations in the next section.

- Second, it makes it clear that materialization is a perfectly legitimate view implementation technique (albeit one that is likely to be rather inefficient)—at least for retrieval operations. But it cannot be used for update operations, of course, because the whole point of updating a view is precisely that updates should really be applied to the underlying data, not just to some temporary materialized copy of that data (again, see the next section).

- Third, although the substitution procedure is quite straightforward and works perfectly well in theory in 100 percent of cases, the sad fact is that (at the time of writing) there are some SQL products for which it does *not* work in practice!—that is, there are some SQL products in which some retrievals on some views fail in surprising ways. It also does not work for versions of the SQL standard prior to SQL:1992. And the reason for the failures is precisely that the products in question, and those earlier versions of the SQL standard, do not fully support the relational closure property. See Exercise 10.15, part *a*, at the end of the chapter.

10.4   VIEW UPDATES

Views are *relvars* and hence (like all variables) updatable by definition. Historically, however, view updating has not been regarded, or treated, as a straightforward matter. The problem can be stated thus: Given a particular update on a particular view, what updates need to be applied to what underlying base relvar(s) in order to implement the original view update? More precisely, let *D* be a database, and let *V* be a view on *D* (that is, a view whose definition *X* is a function on *D*):

```
V  =  X ( D )
```

(as in Section 10.3). Now let *UO* be an update operation on *V; UO* can be regarded as an operation that has the effect of changing its argument, yielding:

```
UO ( V )  =  UO ( X ( D ) )
```

The problem of view update is then the problem of finding an update operation *UO'* on *D* such that

```
UO ( X ( D ) )  =  X ( UO' ( D ) )
```

because, of course, *D* is the only thing that "really exists" (views are virtual), and so updates cannot be directly implemented in terms of views *per se*.

Now, the view update problem has been the subject of considerable research over the years, and many different approaches have been proposed to its solution; see, for example, references [10.4], [10.7–10.10], [10.12], and in particular Codd's proposals for RM/V2 [6.2]. In this chapter we describe a more recent approach [10.6, 10.11], one that is less *ad hoc* (more systematic) than previous proposals but does have the virtue of being upward-compatible with the best aspects of those previous proposals. It also has the virtue of treating as updatable a much wider class of views than earlier approaches do; in fact, it treats *all* views as updatable, barring integrity constraint violations.

The Golden Rule Revisited

Recall the first (simpler) version of **The Golden Rule** from the previous chapter:

> *No update operation must ever assign to any relvar a value that causes its relvar predicate to evaluate to FALSE.*

Or (a little loosely):

> *No relvar must ever be allowed to violate its own predicate.*

(Throughout this chapter, we use the term *relvar predicate* to mean the applicable *internal* predicate specifically, and we use the unqualified term *predicate* to mean such a relvar predicate specifically. In fact, we adopt the same convention throughout the remainder of this book, barring explicit statements to the contrary.)

When we introduced this rule, we stressed the point that it applied to *all* relvars, derived as well as base; in particular, we showed that views have predicates too (as indeed they must, by virtue of *The Principle of Interchangeability*). Thus, the system needs to know those predicates in order to perform view updating correctly. So what does the predicate for a view look like? Clearly, what we need is a set of **predicate inference rules**, such that if we know the predicate(s) for the input(s) to any relational operation, we can infer the predicate for the output from that operation. Given such a set of rules, we will be able to infer the predicate for an arbitrary view from the predicate(s) for the base relvar(s) in terms of which that view is directly or indirectly defined. (Of course, the predicates for those base relvars are already known: They are the logical AND of whatever constraints have been declared for the base relvar in question.)

It is in fact very easy to find such a set of rules—they follow directly from the definitions of the relational operators. For example, if A and B are two relvars of the same type and their predicates are PA and PB, respectively, and if view C is defined as A INTERSECT B, then the predicate PC for that view is obviously (PA) AND (PB). For consider:

- Tuple t will appear in C if and only if it appears in both A and B.
- If tuple t appears in A, then $PA(t)$ must be true (using "$PA(t)$" to mean the proposition that results from instantiating PA with t's attribute values as arguments).
- Likewise, if tuple t appears in B, then $PB(t)$ must also be true.
- Hence $PA(t)$ AND $PB(t)$ must be true, and predicate PC is thus (as claimed) the AND of PA and PB.

We will consider the other relational operators later in this section.

Derived relvars thus automatically "inherit" certain constraints from the relvars from which they are derived. Note, however, that it is possible that a given derived relvar will be subject to certain additional constraints, over and above the inherited ones [3.3]. Thus, it is desirable to be able to state constraints explicitly for derived relvars (an example might be a candidate key constraint for a view), and **Tutorial D** does in fact support such a possibility. For simplicity, however, we will mostly ignore that possibility in what follows.

Toward a View-Updating Mechanism

There are a number of further principles that must be satisfied by any systematic approach to the view-updating problem (**The Golden Rule** is the overriding one, but it is not the only one):

1. View updatability is a semantic issue, not a syntactic one—that is, it must not depend on the particular syntactic form in which the view definition in question happens to be stated. For example, the following two definitions are semantically equivalent:

```
VAR V VIEW
    S WHERE STATUS > 25 OR CITY  = 'Paris' ;

VAR V VIEW
  ( S WHERE STATUS > 25 ) UNION ( S WHERE CITY = 'Paris' ) ;
```

   Obviously, these two views should either both be updatable or both not be (in fact, of course, they should both be updatable). By contrast, the SQL standard, and most of today's SQL products, adopt the *ad hoc* position that the first is updatable and the second is not (see Section 10.6).

2. It follows from the previous point that the view-updating mechanism must work correctly in the special case when the "view" is in fact a base relvar—because any base relvar *B* is semantically indistinguishable from a view *V* that is defined as *B* UNION *B*, or *B* INTERSECT *B*, or *B* WHERE TRUE, or any of several other expressions that are identically equivalent to *B*. Thus, for example, the rules for updating a union view, when applied to the view *V* = *B* UNION *B*, must yield exactly the same result as if the update in question had been applied directly to the base relvar *B*. In other words, the topic of this section, though advertised as view updating, is really relvar updating in general; we will be describing a theory of updating that works for *all* relvars, not just for views.

3. The updating rules must preserve symmetry where applicable. For example, the delete rule for an intersection view *V* = *A* INTERSECT *B* must not arbitrarily cause a tuple to be deleted from *A* and not *B*, even though such a one-sided delete would certainly have the effect of deleting the tuple from the view. Instead, the tuple must be deleted from both *A* and *B*. (In other words, there should be *no ambiguity*—there should always be exactly one way of implementing a given update, a way that works in all cases. In particular, there should be no logical difference between a view defined as *A* INTERSECT *B* and one defined as *B* INTERSECT *A*.)

4. The updating rules must take into account any applicable triggered actions, including in particular referential actions such as cascade delete.

5. For reasons of simplicity among others, it is desirable to regard UPDATE as shorthand for a DELETE-INSERT sequence (i.e., just as syntactic sugar), and we will so regard it. This simplification is acceptable *provided* it is understood that:

   - No predicate checking is done "in the middle of" any given update; that is, the expansion of UPDATE is DELETE-INSERT-*check,* not DELETE-*check*-INSERT-*check.* The reason is that the DELETE might temporarily violate the predicate while the UPDATE overall does not. For example, suppose relvar *R* contains exactly 10 tuples, and consider the effect of an UPDATE on some tuple of *R* if *R*'s predicate says that *R* must contain at least 10 tuples.

- Triggers likewise never fire "in the middle of" any given update (in fact they fire at the end, immediately prior to the predicate checking).

- The shorthand requires some slight refinement in the case of projection views (see later in this section).

6. All updates on views must be implemented by the same kind of updates on the underlying relvars. That is, INSERTs map to INSERTs and DELETEs to DELETEs (we can ignore UPDATEs, thanks to the previous point). For suppose, contrariwise, that there is some kind of view—say a union view—for which (say) INSERTs map to DELETEs. Then it must follow that INSERTs *on a base relvar* must also sometimes map to DELETEs! This conclusion follows because (as already observed under Principle 2) base relvar *B* is semantically identical to the union view *V* = *B* UNION *B*. An analogous argument applies to every other kind of view also (restriction, projection, intersection, etc.). The idea that an INSERT on a base relvar might really be a DELETE we take to be self-evidently absurd; hence our position that (to repeat) INSERTs map to INSERTs and DELETEs to DELETEs.

7. In general, the updating rules when applied to a given view *V* will specify the operations to be applied to the relvar(s) in terms of which *V* is defined. And those rules must work correctly even when those underlying relvars are themselves views in turn. In other words, the rules must be capable of *recursive application*. Of course, if an attempt to update an underlying relvar fails for some reason, the original update will fail also; that is, updates on views are all or nothing, just as updates on base relvars are.

8. The rules cannot assume the database is well designed (e.g., they cannot assume it is fully normalized—see Chapters 12 and 13). However, they might on occasion produce a slightly surprising result if the database is *not* well designed, a fact that can be seen in itself as an additional argument in support of good design. We will give an example of such a "slightly surprising" result in the next subsection.

9. There should be no *prima facie* reason for permitting some updates but not others (e.g., DELETEs but not INSERTs) on a given view.

10. INSERT and DELETE should be inverses of each other, to the fullest extent possible.

We remind you of one other important point. As explained in Chapter 6, relational operations—relational updates in particular—are always set-level (a set containing a single tuple is merely a special case). What is more, multi-tuple updates are sometimes *required;* that is, some updates cannot be simulated by a series of single-tuple operations. And this remark is true of both base relvars and views, in general. For reasons of simplicity, we will for the most part present our updating rules in terms of single-tuple operations, but do not lose sight of the fact that considering single-tuple operations only is a simplification, and indeed an oversimplification in some respects.

We now consider the operators of the relational algebra one by one. We begin with the union, intersection, and difference operators; that is, we assume we are dealing with a view whose defining expression is of the form *A* UNION *B* or *A* INTERSECT *B* or *A* MINUS *B,* as applicable, where *A* and *B* are in turn relational expressions (i.e., they do not necessarily denote base relvars). The relations denoted by *A* and *B* must be of the same relation type. The corresponding predicates are *PA* and *PB,* respectively.

Note: Several of the rules and examples discussed in what follows refer to the possibility of *side effects.* Now, it is well known that side effects are usually undesirable; however, side effects might be unavoidable if *A* and *B* happen to represent overlapping subsets of the same underlying relvar, as will often be the case with union, intersection, and difference views. What is more, the side effects in question are (for once) desirable, not undesirable.

Union

Here then is the insert rule for *A* UNION *B:*

- **INSERT:** The new tuple must satisfy *PA* or *PB* or both. If it satisfies *PA,* it is inserted into *A;* note that this INSERT might have the side effect of inserting the tuple into *B* also. If it satisfies *PB,* it is inserted into *B,* unless it was inserted into *B* already as a side effect of inserting it into *A.*

Explanation: The new tuple must satisfy at least one of *PA* and *PB,* because otherwise it would not qualify for inclusion in *A* UNION *B*—that is, it would not satisfy the predicate (*PA*) OR (*PB*) for *A* UNION *B.* (We assume too—though in fact the assumption is not strictly necessary—that the new tuple must not currently appear in either *A* or *B,* because otherwise we would be trying to insert a tuple that already exists.) Assuming the foregoing requirements are satisfied, the new tuple is inserted into whichever of *A* or *B* it logically belongs to—possibly both.

Note: The specific procedural manner in which the foregoing rule is stated ("insert into *A,* then insert into *B*") should be understood purely as a pedagogic device; it does not mean that the DBMS must actually perform the INSERTs in sequence as stated. Indeed, the principle of symmetry—Principle 3 from the immediately preceding subsection—implies as much, because neither *A* nor *B* has precedence over the other. Analogous remarks apply to many of the other rules to be discussed in this section.

Examples: Let view UV be defined as follows:

```
VAR UV VIEW
   ( S WHERE STATUS > 25 ) UNION ( S WHERE CITY = 'Paris' ) ;
```

Fig. 10.2 shows a possible value for this view, corresponding to our usual sample data values.

- Let the tuple to be inserted be (S6,Smith,50,Rome).[4] This tuple satisfies the predicate for S WHERE STATUS > 25 but not the predicate for S WHERE CITY = 'Paris'. It is therefore inserted into S WHERE STATUS > 25. Because of the rules regarding INSERT on a restriction (which are straightforward—see later in this section), the

---

[4] We adopt this simplified notation for tuples throughout this section for readability reasons.

UV	S#	SNAME	STATUS	CITY
	S2	Jones	10	Paris
	S3	Blake	30	Paris
	S5	Adams	30	Athens

Fig. 10.2 View UV (sample values)

effect is to insert the new tuple into the suppliers base relvar, and hence to make the tuple appear in the view as desired.

- Now let the tuple to be inserted be (S7,Jones,50,Paris). This tuple satisfies the predicate for S WHERE STATUS > 25 *and* the predicate for S WHERE CITY = 'Paris'. It is therefore logically inserted into both of these two restrictions. However, inserting it into either has the side effect of inserting it into the other anyway, so there is no need to perform the second INSERT explicitly.

Now suppose SA and SB are two distinct base relvars, SA representing suppliers with status > 25 and SB representing suppliers in Paris (see Fig. 10.3); suppose also that view UV is defined as SA UNION SB, and consider again the two sample INSERTs previously discussed. Inserting the tuple (S6,Smith,50,Rome) into view UV will cause that tuple to be inserted into base relvar SA, presumably as required. However, inserting the tuple (S7,Jones,50,Paris) into view UV will cause that tuple to be inserted into both base relvars! This result is logically correct, although arguably counterintuitive (it is an example of what we called a "slightly surprising" result in the previous subsection). *It is our position that such surprises can occur only if the database is badly designed.* In particular, it is our position that a design that permits the very same tuple to appear in—that is, to satisfy the predicate for—two distinct base relvars, as in this example, is by definition a bad design. This perhaps controversial position is elaborated on in Chapter 13, Section 13.6.

We turn now to the delete rule for *A* UNION *B:*

- **DELETE:** If the tuple to be deleted appears in *A*, it is deleted from *A* (note that this DELETE might have the side effect of deleting the tuple from *B* also). If it (still) appears in *B*, it is deleted from *B*.

Examples to illustrate this rule are left as an exercise. Note that deleting a tuple from *A* or *B* might cause a cascade delete or some other triggered action to be performed.

SA					SB				
	S#	SNAME	STATUS	CITY		S#	SNAME	STATUS	CITY
	S3	Blake	30	Paris		S2	Jones	10	Paris
	S5	Adams	30	Athens		S3	Blake	30	Paris

Fig. 10.3 Base relvars SA and SB (sample values)

Finally, the update rule:

- **UPDATE:** The tuple to be updated must be such that the updated version satisfies *PA* or *PB* or both. If the tuple to be updated appears in *A*, it is deleted from *A* without performing any triggered actions (cascade delete, etc.) that such a DELETE would normally cause, and likewise without checking the predicate for *A*. Note that this DELETE might have the side effect of deleting the tuple from *B* also. If the tuple (still) appears in *B*, it is deleted from *B* (again without performing any triggered actions or predicate checks). Next, if the updated version of the tuple satisfies *PA*, it is inserted into *A* (note that this INSERT might have the side effect of inserting the tuple into *B* also). Finally, if the updated version satisfies *PB*, it is inserted into *B*, unless it was inserted into *B* already as a side effect of inserting it into *A*.

This update rule essentially consists of the delete rule followed by the insert rule, except that as indicated no triggered actions or predicate checks are performed after the DELETE (any triggered actions associated with the UPDATE are conceptually performed after all deletions and insertions have been done, just prior to the predicate checks).

It is worth pointing out that one important consequence of treating UPDATEs in this fashion is that a given UPDATE can cause a tuple to "migrate" from one relvar to another, loosely speaking. Given the database of Fig. 10.3, for example, updating the tuple (S5,Adams,30,Athens) in view UV to (S5,Adams,15,Paris) will delete the old tuple for S5 from SA and insert the new tuple for S5 into SB.

Intersect

Here now are the rules for updating *A* INTERSECT *B*. This time we simply state the rules without further discussion (they follow the same general pattern as the union rules), except to note that the predicate for *A* INTERSECT *B* is (*PA*) AND (*PB*). Examples to illustrate the various cases are left as an exercise.

- **INSERT:** The new tuple must satisfy both *PA* and *PB*. If it does not currently appear in *A*, it is inserted into *A* (note that this INSERT might have the side effect of inserting the tuple into *B* also). If it (still) does not appear in *B*, it is inserted into *B*.

- **DELETE:** The tuple to be deleted is deleted from *A* (note that this DELETE might have the side effect of deleting the tuple from *B* also). If it (still) appears in *B*, it is deleted from *B*.

- **UPDATE:** The tuple to be updated must be such that the updated version satisfies both *PA* and *PB*. The tuple is deleted from *A* without performing any triggered actions or predicate checks (note that this DELETE might have the side effect of deleting it from *B* also); if it (still) appears in *B*, it is deleted from *B*, again without performing any triggered actions or predicate checks. Next, if the updated version of the tuple does not currently appear in *A*, it is inserted into *A* (note that this INSERT might have the side effect of inserting the tuple into *B* also). If it (still) does not appear in *B*, it is inserted into *B*.

Difference

Here are the rules for updating *A* MINUS *B* (the predicate is (*PA*) AND NOT (*PB*)):

- **INSERT:** The new tuple must satisfy *PA* and not *PB*. It is inserted into *A*.
- **DELETE:** The tuple to be deleted is deleted from *A*.
- **UPDATE:** The tuple to be updated must be such that the updated version satisfies *PA* and not *PB*. The tuple is deleted from *A* without performing any triggered actions or predicate checks; the updated version is then inserted into *A*.

Restrict

Let the defining expression for view *V* be *A* WHERE *p,* and let the predicate for *A* be *PA.* Then the predicate for *V* is (*PA*) AND (*p*). For example, the predicate for the restriction S WHERE CITY = 'London' is (PS) AND (CITY = 'London'), where PS is the predicate for suppliers. Here then are the rules for updating *A* WHERE *p:*

- **INSERT:** The new tuple must satisfy both *PA* and *p*. It is inserted into *A*.
- **DELETE:** The tuple to be deleted is deleted from *A*.
- **UPDATE:** The tuple to be updated must be such that the updated version satisfies both *PA* and *p*. The tuple is deleted from *A* without performing any triggered actions or predicate checks. The updated version is then inserted into *A*.

    Examples: Let view LS be defined as:

```
VAR LS VIEW
    S WHERE CITY = 'London' ;
```

Fig. 10.4 shows a sample value for this view.

- An attempt to insert the tuple (S6,Green,20,London) into LS will succeed. The new tuple will be inserted into relvar S, and will therefore effectively be inserted into view LS as well.

- An attempt to insert the tuple (S1,Green,20,London) into LS will fail, because it violates the predicate for relvar S (and hence for LS too)—specifically, it violates the uniqueness constraint on candidate key {S#}.

- An attempt to insert the tuple (S6,Green,20,Athens) into LS will fail, because it violates the constraint CITY = 'London'.

- An attempt to delete the LS tuple (S1,Smith,20,London) will succeed. The tuple will be deleted from relvar S, and will therefore effectively be deleted from view LS as well.

LS	S#	SNAME	STATUS	CITY
	S1	Smith	20	London
	S4	Clark	20	London

Fig. 10.4 View LS (sample values)

- An attempt to update the LS tuple (S1,Smith,20,London) to (S6,Green,20,London) will succeed. An attempt to update that same tuple (S1,Smith,20,London) to either (S2,Smith,20,London) or (S1,Smith,20,Athens) will fail (why, exactly, in each case?).

Project

Again we begin with a discussion of the relevant predicate. Let the attributes of A (with predicate PA) be partitioned into two disjoint groups, X and Y say. Regard each of X and Y as a single *composite* attribute, and consider the projection of A over X, $A\{X\}$. Let (x) be a tuple of that projection. Then it should be clear that the predicate for that projection is basically "For all such x, there exists some y from the domain of Y values such that the tuple (x,y) satisfies PA." For example, consider the projection of relvar S over S#, SNAME, and CITY. Every tuple (s,n,c) appearing in that projection is such that there exists a status value t such that the tuple (s,n,t,c) satisfies the predicate for relvar S.

Here then are the rules for updating $A\{X\}$:

- **INSERT:** Let the tuple to be inserted be (x). Let the default value of Y be y (it is an error if no such default value exists—i.e., if Y has "defaults not allowed"). The tuple (x,y) (which must satisfy PA) is inserted into A.

    Note: Candidate key attributes will usually, though not invariably, have no default (see Chapter 19). As a consequence, a projection that does not include all candidate keys of the underlying relvar will usually not permit INSERTs.

- **DELETE:** All tuples of A with the same X value as the tuple to be deleted from $A\{X\}$ are deleted from A.

    Note: In practice, it will usually be desirable that X include at least one candidate key of A, so that the tuple to be deleted from $A\{X\}$ corresponds to exactly one tuple of A. However, there is no logical reason to make this a hard requirement. Analogous remarks apply in the case of UPDATE also—see the paragraphs immediately following.

- **UPDATE:** Let the tuple to be updated be (x) and let the updated version be (x'). Let a be a tuple of A with the same X value x, and let the value of Y in a be y. All such tuples a are deleted from A without performing any triggered actions or predicate checks. Then, for each such value y, the tuple (x',y)—which must satisfy PA—is inserted into A.

    Note: It is here that the "slight refinement" regarding projection mentioned in Principle 5 in the subsection "Toward a View-Updating Mechanism" (near the beginning of the present section) shows itself. Specifically, observe that the final "insert" step in the update rule reinstates the previous Y value in each inserted tuple: It does *not* replace it by the applicable default value, as a stand-alone INSERT would.

    Examples: Let view SC be defined as:

```
SC { S#, CITY }
```

Fig. 10.5 shows a sample value for this view.

	S#	CITY
SC	S1	London
	S2	Paris
	S3	Paris
	S4	London
	S5	Athens

Fig. 10.5   View SC (sample values)

- An attempt to insert the tuple (S6,Athens) into SC will succeed, and will have the effect of inserting the tuple (S6,*n*,*t*,London) into relvar S, where *n* and *t* are the default values for attributes SNAME and STATUS, respectively.

- An attempt to insert the tuple (S1,Athens) into SC will fail, because it violates the predicate for relvar S (and hence for SC too)—specifically, it violates the uniqueness constraint on candidate key {S#}.

- An attempt to delete the tuple (S1,London) from SC will succeed. The tuple for S1 will be deleted from relvar S.

- An attempt to update the SC tuple (S1,London) to (S1,Athens) will succeed; the effect will be to update the tuple (S1,Smith,20,London) in relvar S to (S1,Smith, 20,Athens)—*not* to (S1,*n*,*t*,Athens), please observe, where *n* and *t* are the applicable defaults.

- An attempt to update that same SC tuple (S1,London) to (S2,London) will fail (why, exactly?).

Consideration of the case in which the projection does not include a candidate key of the underlying relvar (e.g., the projection of relvar S over STATUS and CITY) is left as an exercise.

Extend

Let the defining expression for view *V* be

```
EXTEND A ADD exp AS X
```

(where as usual the predicate for *A* is *PA*). Then the predicate *PE* for *V* is:

```
PA ( a ) AND e.X = exp ( a )
```

Here *e* is a tuple of *V* and *a* is the tuple that remains when *e*'s *X* component is removed (i.e., *a* is the projection of *e* over all attributes of *A*). In (stilted) natural language:

> Every tuple *e* in the extension is such that (1) the tuple *a* that is derived from *e* by projecting away the *X* component satisfies *PA,* and (2) that *X* component has a value equal to the result of applying the expression *exp* to that tuple *a*.

VPX	P#	PNAME	COLOR	WEIGHT	CITY	GMWT
	P1	Nut	Red	12.0	London	5448.0
	P2	Bolt	Green	17.0	Paris	7718.0
	P3	Screw	Blue	17.0	Oslo	7718.0
	P4	Screw	Red	14.0	London	6356.0
	P5	Cam	Blue	12.0	Paris	5448.0
	P6	Cog	Red	19.0	London	8626.0

Fig. 10.6 View VPX (sample values)

Here then are the update rules:

- **INSERT:** Let the tuple to be inserted be *e; e* must satisfy *PE*. The tuple *a* that is derived from *e* by projecting away the *X* component is inserted into *A*.

- **DELETE:** Let the tuple to be deleted be *e*. The tuple *a* that is derived from *e* by projecting away the *X* component is deleted from *A*.

- **UPDATE:** Let the tuple to be updated be *e* and let the updated version be *e'; e'* must satisfy *PE*. The tuple *a* that is derived from *e* by projecting away the *X* component is deleted from *A* without performing any triggered actions or predicate checks. The tuple *a'* that is derived from *e'* by projecting away the *X* component is inserted into *A*.

Examples: Let view VPX be defined as:

```
EXTEND P ADD ( WEIGHT * 454 ) AS GMWT
```

Fig. 10.6 shows a sample value for this view.

- An attempt to insert the tuple (P7,Cog,Red,12,Paris,5448) will succeed, and will have the effect of inserting the tuple (P7,Cog,Red,12,Paris) into relvar P.

- An attempt to insert the tuple (P7,Cog,Red,12,Paris,5449) will fail (why?).

- An attempt to insert the tuple (P1,Cog,Red,12,Paris,5448) will fail (why?).

- An attempt to delete the tuple for P1 will succeed, and will have the effect of deleting the tuple for P1 from relvar P.

- An attempt to update the tuple for P1 to (P1,Nut,Red,10,Paris,4540) will succeed; the effect will be to update the tuple (P1,Nut,Red,12,London) in relvar P to (P1,Nut, Red,10,Paris).

- An attempt to update that same tuple to one for P2 (with all other values unchanged) or to one in which the GMWT value is not equal to 454 times the WEIGHT value will fail (in each case, why?).

Join

Most previous treatments of the view update problem—including those in the first few editions of this book and other books by this author—have argued that the updatability or otherwise of a given join depends, at least in part, on whether the join is one-to-one, one-to-many, or many-to-many. In contrast to those previous treatments, we now believe joins are *always* updatable. Moreover, the rules are identical in all three cases, and are essentially quite straightforward. What makes this claim plausible, startling though it might seem at first sight, is the perspective on the problem afforded by adoption of **The Golden Rule**, as we now explain.

Broadly speaking, the goal of view support has always been to make views look as much like base relvars as possible. However:

- It is usually assumed (implicitly) that it is always possible to update an individual tuple of a base relvar independently of all other tuples in that base relvar.

- At the same time, it is realized (explicitly) that it is *not* always possible to update an individual tuple of a view independently of all other tuples in that view.

For example, Codd shows in reference [12.2] that it is not possible to delete just one tuple from a certain join, because the effect would be to leave a relation that "is not the join of any two relations whatsoever" (which means the result could not possibly satisfy the predicate for the view). And the approach to such view updates historically has always been to reject them altogether, on the grounds that it is impossible to make them look completely like base relvar updates.

Our approach is rather different. To be specific, we recognize that even with a base relvar it is not always possible to update individual tuples independently of all the rest. Typically, therefore, we accept those view updates that have historically been rejected, interpreting them in an obvious and logically correct way to apply to the underlying relvar(s); we accept them, moreover, in full recognition of the fact that updating those underlying relvars might have side effects on the view—*side effects that are, however, required in order to avoid the possibility that the view might violate its own predicate.*

With that preamble out of the way, let us now get down to specifics. In what follows, we first define our terms. Then we present the rules for updating join views. Then we consider the implications of those rules for each of the three cases (one-to-one, one-to-many, many-to-many) in turn.

Consider the join $J = A$ JOIN B, where (as in Chapter 7, Section 7.4) A, B, and J have headings $\{X,Y\}$, $\{Y,Z\}$, and $\{X,Y,Z\}$, respectively. Let the predicates for A and B be PA and PB, respectively. Then the predicate PJ for J is

```
PA ( a ) AND PB ( b )
```

where for a given tuple j of the join, a is "the A portion" of j (i.e., the tuple that is derived from j by projecting away the Z component) and b is "the B portion" of j (i.e., the tuple that is derived from j by projecting away the X component). In other words, every tuple in the join is such that the A portion satisfies PA and the B portion satisfies PB. For example, the predicate for the join of relvars S and SP over S# is as follows:

Every tuple (s,n,t,c,p,q) in the join is such that the tuple (s,n,t,c) satisfies the predicate for S and the tuple (s,p,q) satisfies the predicate for SP.

Here then are the update rules:

- **INSERT:** The new tuple *j* must satisfy *PJ*. If the *A* portion of *j* does not appear in *A*, it is inserted into *A*.[5] If the *B* portion of *j* does not appear in *B*, it is inserted into *B*.

- **DELETE:** The *A* portion of the tuple to be deleted is deleted from *A* and the *B* portion is deleted from *B*.

- **UPDATE:** The tuple to be updated must be such that the updated version satisfies *PJ*. The *A* portion is deleted from *A*, without performing any triggered actions or predicate checks, and the *B* portion is deleted from *B*, again without performing any triggered actions or predicate checks. Then, if the *A* portion of the updated version of the tuple does not appear in *A*, it is inserted into *A;* if the *B* portion does not appear in *B*, it is inserted into *B*.

Let us now examine the implications of these rules for the three different cases.

Case 1 (one-to-one): Note first that the term *one-to-one* here would more accurately be *(zero-or-one)-to-(zero-or-one)*. In other words, there is an integrity constraint in effect that ensures that for each tuple of *A* there is at most one matching tuple in *B* and *vice versa*—implying, incidentally, that the set of attributes *Y* over which the join is performed must be a superkey for both *A* and *B*.
   Examples:

- For a first example, you are invited to consider the effect of the foregoing rules on the join of the suppliers relvar S to itself over supplier numbers (only).

- By way of a second example, suppose we have another base relvar SR with attributes S# and REST, where S# identifies a supplier and REST identifies that supplier's favorite restaurant. Assume that not all suppliers in S appear in SR. Consider the effect of the join update rules on S JOIN SR. What difference would it make if some supplier could appear in SR and not in S?

Case 2 (one-to-many): The term *one-to-many* here would more accurately be *(zero-or-one)-to-(zero-or-more);* in other words, there is an integrity constraint in effect that ensures that for each tuple of *B* there is at most one matching tuple in *A*. Typically, what this means is that the set of attributes *Y* over which the join is performed includes a subset *K,* say, such that *K* is a candidate key for *A* and a matching foreign key for *B*. *Note:* If the foregoing is in fact the case, we can replace the phrase "zero-or-one" by "exactly one."
   Examples: Let view SSP be defined as

```
S JOIN SP
```

(this is a foreign-to-matching-candidate-key join). Sample values are shown in Fig. 10.7.

- An attempt to insert the tuple (S4,Clark,20,London,P6,100) into SSP will succeed, and will have the effect of inserting the tuple (S4,P6,100) into relvar SP (thereby adding a tuple to the view).

---

[5] Note that this INSERT might have the side effect of inserting the *B* portion into *B* also, as in the case of the union, intersection, and difference views discussed earlier. Analogous remarks apply to the delete and update rules also; for brevity, we do not bother to spell out this possibility in detail in every case.

SSP	S#	SNAME	STATUS	CITY	P#	QTY
	S1	Smith	20	London	P1	300
	S1	Smith	20	London	P2	200
	S1	Smith	20	London	P3	400
	S1	Smith	20	London	P4	200
	S1	Smith	20	London	P5	100
	S1	Smith	20	London	P6	100
	S2	Jones	10	Paris	P1	300
	S2	Jones	10	Paris	P2	400
	S3	Blake	30	Paris	P2	200
	S4	Clark	20	London	P2	200
	S4	Clark	20	London	P4	300
	S4	Clark	20	London	P5	400

Fig. 10.7   View SSP (sample values)

- An attempt to insert the tuple (S5,Adams,30,Athens,P6,100) into SSP will succeed, and will have the effect of inserting the tuple (S5,P6,100) into relvar SP (thereby adding a tuple to the view).

- An attempt to insert the tuple (S6,Green,20,London,P6,100) into SSP will succeed, and will have the effect of inserting the tuple (S6,Green,20,London) into relvar S and the tuple (S6,P6,100) into relvar SP (thereby adding a tuple to the view).

  Note: Suppose for the moment that it is possible for SP tuples to exist without a corresponding S tuple. Suppose, moreover, that relvar SP already includes some tuples with supplier number S6, but not one with supplier number S6 and part number P1. Then the INSERT in the example just discussed will have the effect of inserting some additional tuples into the view: namely, the tuples obtained by joining the tuple (S6,Green,20,London) with each of those previously existing SP tuples for supplier S6.

- An attempt to insert the tuple (S4,Clark,20,Athens,P6,100) into SSP will fail (why?).

- An attempt to insert the tuple (S1,Smith,20,London,P1,400) into SSP will fail (why?).

- An attempt to delete the tuple (S3,Blake,30,Paris,P2,200) from SSP will succeed, and will have the effect of deleting the tuple (S3,Blake,30,Paris) from relvar S and the tuple (S3,P2,200) from relvar SP.

- An attempt to delete the tuple (S1,Smith,20,London,P1,300) from SSP will "succeed"—see the note immediately following—and will have the effect of deleting the tuple (S1,Smith,20,London) from relvar S and the tuple (S1,P1,300) from relvar SP.

  Note: Actually the overall effect of this attempted DELETE will depend on the foreign key delete rule from shipments to suppliers. If the rule specifies NO ACTION or RESTRICT, the overall operation will fail. If it specifies CASCADE, it will have the side effect of deleting all other SP tuples (and hence SSP tuples) for supplier S1 as well.

- An attempt to update the SSP tuple (S1,Smith,20,London,P1,300) to (S1,Smith,20, London,P1,400) will succeed, and will have the effect of updating the SP tuple (S1,P1,300) to (S1,P1,400).

- An attempt to update the SSP tuple (S1,Smith,20,London,P1,300) to (S1,Smith,20, Athens,P1,400) will succeed, and will have the effect of updating the S tuple (S1,Smith,20,London) to (S1,Smith,20,Athens) and the SP tuple (S1,P1,300) to (S1,P1,400).

- An attempt to update the SSP tuple (S1,Smith,20,London,P1,300) to (S6,Smith,20, London,P1,300) will "succeed"—see the note immediately following—and will have the effect of updating the S tuple (S1,Smith,20,London) to (S6,Smith,20,London) and the SP tuple (S1,P1,300) to (S6,P1,300).

    Note: Actually the overall effect of this attempted update will depend on the foreign key update rule from shipments to suppliers. The details are left as an exercise.

Case 3 (many-to-many): The term *many-to-many* here would more accurately be *(zero-or-more)-to-(zero-or-more);* in other words, there is no integrity constraint in effect to ensure that we are really dealing with a Case 1 or Case 2 situation instead.

Examples: Suppose we have a view defined as

```
S JOIN P
```

(join of S and P over CITY—a many-to-many join). Sample values are shown in Fig. 10.8.

- Inserting the tuple (S7,Bruce,15,Oslo,P8,Wheel,White,25) will succeed, and will have the effect of inserting the tuple (S7,Bruce,15,Oslo) into relvar S and the tuple (P8,Wheel,White,25,Oslo) into relvar P (thereby adding the specified tuple to the view).

- Inserting the tuple (S1,Smith,20,London,P7,Washer,Red,5) will succeed, and will have the effect of inserting the tuple (P7,Washer,Red,5,London) into relvar P (thereby adding *two* tuples to the view—the tuple (S1,Smith,20,London,P7,Washer,Red,5), as specified, and also the tuple (S4,Clark,20,London,P7,Washer,Red,5)).

- Inserting the tuple (S6,Green,20,London,P7,Washer,Red,5) will succeed, and will have the effect of inserting the tuple (S6,Green,20,London) into relvar S and the tuple (P7,Washer,Red,5,London) into relvar P (thereby adding *six* tuples to the view).

S#	SNAME	STATUS	CITY	P#	PNAME	COLOR	WEIGHT
S1	Smith	20	London	P1	Nut	Red	12.0
S1	Smith	20	London	P4	Screw	Red	14.0
S1	Smith	20	London	P6	Cog	Red	19.0
S2	Jones	10	Paris	P2	Bolt	Green	17.0
S2	Jones	10	Paris	P5	Cam	Blue	12.0
S3	Blake	30	Paris	P2	Bolt	Green	17.0
S3	Blake	30	Paris	P5	Cam	Blue	12.0
S4	Clark	20	London	P1	Nut	Red	12.0
S4	Clark	20	London	P4	Screw	Red	14.0
S4	Clark	20	London	P6	Cog	Red	19.0

Fig. 10.8 The join of S and P over CITY

- Deleting the tuple (S1,Smith,20,London,P1,Nut,Red,12) will succeed, and will have the effect of deleting the tuple (S1,Smith,20,London) from relvar S and the tuple (P1,Nut,Red,12,London) from relvar P (thereby deleting *four* tuples from the view).

Further examples are left as an exercise.

Other Operators

We consider the remaining operators of the algebra only briefly. Note first that θ-join, semijoin, semidifference, and divide are not primitive, so the rules for these operators can be derived from the rules for the operators in terms of which they are defined. As for the rest:

- *Rename:* Trivial.

- *Cartesian product:* As noted in Chapter 7, Section 7.4, Cartesian product is a special case of natural join (*A* JOIN *B* degenerates to *A* TIMES *B* if *A* and *B* have no attributes in common). As a consequence, the rules for *A* TIMES *B* are just a special case of the rules for *A* JOIN *B* (as are the rules for *A* INTERSECT *B* also, of course).

- *Summarize:* Summarize is also not primitive—it is defined in terms of extend, and so the updating rules can be derived from those for extend. *Note:* It is true that most updates on most SUMMARIZE views will fail in practice. However, the failures occur not because such views are *inherently* nonupdatable, but rather because attempts to update them usually fall foul of some integrity constraint. For example, let the view-defining expression be:

```
SUMMARIZE SP BY { S# } ADD SUM ( QTY ) AS TOTQTY
```

Then an attempt to delete, say, the tuple for supplier S1 will succeed. However, an attempt to update, say, the tuple (S4,900) to (S4,800) will fail, because it violates the constraint that the TOTQTY value must be equal to the sum of all applicable individual QTY values. An attempt to insert the tuple (S5,0) will also fail, but for a different reason (why, exactly?).

- *Group and ungroup:* Remarks analogous to those for summarize apply here also [3.3].

- *Tclose:* Somewhat analogous remarks apply once again.

10.5 SNAPSHOTS (A DIGRESSION)

In this section we digress briefly to discuss **snapshots** [10.1]. Snapshots do have some points in common with views, but they are not the same thing. Like views, snapshots are derived relvars; unlike views, however, they are real, not virtual—that is, they are represented not just by their definition in terms of other relvars, but also (at least conceptually) by their own separately materialized copy of the data. For example:

```
VAR P2SC SNAPSHOT
    ( ( S JOIN SP ) WHERE P# = P# ('P2') ) { S#, CITY }
    REFRESH EVERY DAY ;
```

Defining a snapshot is much like executing a query, except that:

1. The result of the query is kept in the database under the specified name (P2SC in the example) as a *read-only relvar* (read-only, that is, apart from the periodic refresh—see point 2).

2. Periodically (EVERY DAY in the example) the snapshot is **refreshed**—that is, its current value is discarded, the query is executed again, and the result of that new execution becomes the new snapshot value.

Thus, snapshot P2SC represents the relevant data as it was at most 24 hours ago. (So what is the predicate?)

The rationale for snapshots is that many applications—perhaps even most—can tolerate, or might even require, data "as of" some particular point in time. Reporting and accounting applications are a case in point; such applications typically require the data to be frozen at an appropriate moment (e.g., the end of an accounting period), and snapshots allow such freezing to occur without preventing other transactions from performing updates on the data in question (that is, on "the real data"). Similarly, it might be desirable to freeze large amounts of data for a complex query or read-only application, again without locking out updates. *Note:* This idea becomes particularly attractive in a distributed database or decision support environment—see Chapters 21 and 22, respectively. We remark that snapshots represent an important special case of *controlled redundancy* (see Chapter 1), and "snapshot refresh" is the corresponding *update propagation* process (again, see Chapter 1).

In general, then, a snapshot definition might look something like this:

```
VAR <relvar name> SNAPSHOT <relation exp>
    <candidate key def list>
    REFRESH EVERY <now and then> ;
```

where *<now and then>* might be, for example, MONTH or WEEK or DAY or HOUR or *n* MINUTES or MONDAY or WEEKDAY. Note in particular that a specification of the form REFRESH [ON] EVERY UPDATE might be used to keep the snapshot permanently in synch with the relvar(s) from which it is derived.

Here is the syntax of the corresponding DROP:

```
DROP VAR <relvar name> ;
```

where the *<relvar name>* refers to a snapshot specifically. *Note:* We assume that an attempt to drop a snapshot will fail if some other relvar definition currently refers to it. Alternatively, we might consider extending the snapshot definition to include some kind of "RESTRICT *vs.* CASCADE" option once again. We do not consider this latter possibility further here.

A note on terminology: At the time of writing, snapshots have come to be known—almost exclusively, in fact—not as snapshots at all but rather as **materialized views**[6] (see the "References and Bibliography" section in Chapter 22). However, this terminology is

---

[6] Some writers—not all—reserve the term *materialized view* to mean a snapshot that is guaranteed to be always up to date (i.e., one for which REFRESH ON EVERY UPDATE applies).

unfortunate in the extreme, and in this writer's opinion should be resisted, firmly. Snapshots are *not* views. The whole point about views is that they are *not* materialized, at least as far as the model is concerned. (Whether they are in fact materialized under the covers is an implementation issue and has nothing to do with the model.) As far as the model is concerned, in other words, *materialized view* is a contradiction in terms—and yet (all too predictably) *materialized view* has become so ubiquitous that the unqualified term *view* has come to mean, almost always, a "materialized view" specifically! And so we no longer have a good term to use when we want to refer to a view in the original sense. Certainly we run a severe risk of being misunderstood when we use the unqualified term *view* for that purpose. In this book, however, we choose to take that risk; to be specific, we will not use the term *materialized view* at all (except when quoting from other sources), keeping the term *snapshot* for the concept in question, and we will always use the unqualified term *view* in its original relational sense.

10.6   SQL FACILITIES

In this section we summarize SQL's support for views (only—SQL does not support snapshots at the time of writing). First, the syntax of CREATE VIEW (omitting a variety of options and alternatives in the interest of brevity, such as the ability to define a view to be "of" some structured type) is as follows:

```
CREATE VIEW <view name> AS <table exp>
    [ WITH [ <qualifier> ] CHECK OPTION ] ;
```

Explanation:

1. The *<table exp>* is the view-defining expression.

2. WITH CHECK OPTION, if specified, means that INSERTs and UPDATEs on the view will be rejected if they violate any integrity constraint implied by the view-defining expression. Observe, therefore, that such operations will fail *only* if WITH CHECK OPTION is specified—by default, they will *not* fail. You will realize from Section 10.4 that we regard such behavior as logically incorrect; we would therefore strongly recommend that WITH CHECK OPTION *always* be specified in practice[7] [10.5].

3. The *<qualifier>* is either CASCADED or LOCAL, and CASCADED is the default (and indeed the only sensible option, as explained in detail in reference [4.20]; we omit further discussion of LOCAL for this reason).

Here are SQL analogs of the view definitions from Section 10.1:

1. ```
CREATE VIEW GOOD_SUPPLIER
    AS SELECT S.S#, S.STATUS, S.CITY
       FROM   S
       WHERE S.STATUS > 15
    WITH CHECK OPTION ;
```

---

[7] If the view is updatable, that is. As we will see later, views in SQL are often *not* updatable, and WITH CHECK OPTION is illegal if the view is not updatable according to SQL.
```

2. CREATE VIEW REDPART
```
   AS SELECT P.P#, P.PNAME, P.WEIGHT AS WT, P.CITY
      FROM   P
      WHERE  P.COLOR = 'Red'
   WITH CHECK OPTION ;
```

3. CREATE VIEW PQ
```
   AS SELECT P.P#, ( SELECT SUM ( SP.QTY )
                     FROM    SP
                     WHERE   SP.P# = P.P# ) AS TOTQTY
      FROM    P ;
```

SQL does not regard this view as updatable, so WITH CHECK OPTION must be omitted.

4. CREATE VIEW CITY_PAIR
```
   AS SELECT DISTINCT S.CITY AS SCITY, P.CITY AS PCITY
      FROM    S, SP, P
      WHERE   S.S# = SP.S#
      AND     SP.P# = P.P# ;
```

Again SQL does not regard this view as updatable, so WITH CHECK OPTION must be omitted.

5. CREATE VIEW HEAVY_REDPART
```
   AS SELECT RP.P#, RP.PNAME, RP.WT, RP.CITY
      FROM    REDPART AS RP
      WHERE   RP.WT > 12.0
   WITH CHECK OPTION ;
```

An existing view can be dropped by means of DROP VIEW—syntax:

```
DROP VIEW <view name> <behavior> ;
```

where (as usual) *<behavior>* is either RESTRICT or CASCADE. If RESTRICT is specified and the view is currently in use anywhere (e.g., in another view definition or in an integrity constraint), the DROP will fail; if CASCADE is specified, the DROP will succeed, and will cause an implicit DROP . . . CASCADE for everything currently using the view.

View Retrievals

As indicated in Section 10.3, all retrievals against all views are guaranteed to work correctly in the current version of the SQL standard. The same is unfortunately not true for certain current products, nor for versions of the standard prior to SQL:1992.

View Updates

SQL's support for view updating is limited. It is also *extremely* difficult to understand!—in fact, the standard is even more impenetrable in this area than it usually is.[8] Here is a typical excerpt from that standard (edited just slightly here):

> [The] *<query expression>* QE1 is *updatable* if and only if for every *<query expression>* or *<query specification>* QE2 that is simply contained in *QE1*:

---

[8] To quote reference [10.11]: "The SQL standard has been and continues to be a barrier to developing (let alone implementing) approaches for general view updating."

    a. *QE1* contains *QE2* without an intervening *<non join query expression>* that specifies UNION DISTINCT, EXCEPT ALL, or EXCEPT DISTINCT.[9]

    b. If *QE1* simply contains a *<non join query expression>* *NJQE* that specifies UNION ALL, then:

        i. *NJQE* immediately contains a *<query expression>* *LO* and a *<query term>* *RO* such that no leaf generally underlying table of *LO* is also a leaf generally underlying table of *RO*.

        ii. For every column of *NJQE*, the underlying columns in the tables identified by *LO* and *RO*, respectively, are either both updatable or not updatable.

    c. *QE1* contains *QE2* without an intervening *<non join query term>* that specifies INTERSECT.

    d. *QE2* is updatable.

Note that (a) the foregoing is just one of the many rules that have to be taken in combination in order to determine whether a given view is updatable; (b) the rules in question are not all given in one place but are scattered over many different parts of the document; and (c) all of those rules rely on a variety of additional concepts and constructs—for example, updatable columns, leaf generally underlying tables, *<non join query term>*s—that are in turn defined in still further parts of the document.

Because of such considerations, we do not even attempt to give a precise characterization here of just which views are updatable in SQL. Loosely speaking, however, we can say that SQL regards the following views as updatable:

1. Views defined as a restriction and/or projection of a single base table

2. Views defined as a one-to-one or one-to-many join of two base tables (in the one-to-many case, only the "many" side is updatable)[10]

3. Views defined as a UNION ALL or INTERSECT of two distinct base tables

4. Certain combinations of Cases 1–3

What is more, even these limited cases are treated incorrectly, thanks to SQL's lack of understanding of predicates, and in particular to the fact that SQL permits duplicate rows. And the picture is complicated still further by the fact that SQL identifies four distinct cases; to be specific, a given view can be *updatable, potentially updatable, simply updatable,* or *insertable into*[11] (where "updatable" refers to UPDATE and DELETE and

---

[9] We did not mention the point in Chapter 8, but SQL:1999 added the ability to specify an explicit DISTINCT qualifier as an alternative to ALL on UNION, INTERSECT, and EXCEPT. Analogously, an explicit ALL qualifier can be specified as an alternative to DISTINCT on SELECT as well. Note, however, that DISTINCT is the default for UNION, INTERSECT, and EXCEPT, while ALL is the default for SELECT.

[10] In connection with one-to-one joins, we remark on the following oddity. SQL quite correctly requires updates on such joins to be all or nothing. But this requirement (like the requirement that updates in general are all or nothing, even if they involve referential actions such as cascade delete) implies that, under the covers at least, the system has to support some kind of multiple relational assignment—despite the fact that SQL includes no explicit support for any such operator.

[11] The standard defines these terms formally but gives no insight into their intuitive meaning or why they were chosen. Note the violation of Principles 9 and 10 from the subsection "Toward a View-Updating Mechanism" in Section 10.4.

"insertable into" refers to INSERT, and a view cannot be insertable into unless it is updatable).

Regarding Case 1, however, we can be a little more precise. To be specific, an SQL view is certainly updatable if the following eight conditions are all satisfied:

1. The view-defining table expression is a simple select expression (that is, it does not contain any of the keywords JOIN, UNION, INTERSECT, or EXCEPT).

2. The SELECT clause of that select expression does not contain the DISTINCT keyword.

3. Every select item in that SELECT clause (after any necessary expansion of "asterisk-style" select items) consists of a possibly qualified column name (optionally accompanied by an AS clause), representing a simple reference to a column of the underlying table (see condition 5), and no such column reference appears more than once.

4. The FROM clause of that select expression contains exactly one table reference.

5. That table reference identifies either a base table or a view that satisfies conditions 1–8. *Note:* The table identified by that table reference is said to be *the underlying table* for the updatable view in question (see condition 3).

6. That select expression does not include a WHERE clause that includes a subquery that includes a FROM clause that includes a reference to the same table as is referenced in the FROM clause mentioned in condition 4.

7. That select expression does not include a GROUP BY clause.

8. That select expression does not include a HAVING clause.

10.7   SUMMARY

A **view** is essentially a named relational expression; it can be regarded as a **derived, virtual relvar**. Operations against a view are normally implemented by a process of **substitution**—that is, references to the *name* of the view are replaced by the expression that *defines* the view—and this substitution process works precisely because of **closure**. For **retrieval** operations, the substitution process works 100 percent of the time (at least in theory, though not necessarily in practice). For **update** operations, it also works 100 percent of the time (again in theory, though definitely not in practice); in the case of some views, however (e.g., views defined in terms of summarize), updates will usually fail because of some integrity constraint violation. We presented an extensive set of **principles** that the updating scheme must satisfy, and we showed in detail how the updating scheme worked for views defined in terms of the **union, intersection, difference, restrict, project, join,** and **extend** operators. For each of these operators, we explained the corresponding **predicate inference rules**.

We also examined the question of views and **logical data independence**. There are two aspects to such independence, **growth** and **restructuring**. Other benefits of views include (a) their ability to hide data and thus to provide a certain measure of **security**, and (b) their ability to act as a shorthand and thus to make life easier for the user. We went on to explain two important principles, ***The Principle of Interchangeability*** (which implies among other things that we must be able to update views) and ***The Principle of Database Relativity***.

We also digressed for a few moments to give a brief discussion of **snapshots** (also known as *materialized views,* though this term is deprecated). Finally, we sketched the relevant aspects of SQL.

EXERCISES

10.1   Define a view for suppliers in London.

10.2   Define a view consisting of supplier numbers and part numbers for suppliers and parts that are not colocated.

10.3   Define relvar SP of the suppliers-and-parts database as a view of relvar SPJ of the suppliers-parts-projects database.

10.4   Define a view over the suppliers-parts-projects database consisting of all projects (project number and city attributes only) that are supplied by supplier S1 and use part P1.

10.5   Given the view definition—

```
VAR HEAVYWEIGHT VIEW
   ( ( P RENAME ( WEIGHT AS WT, COLOR AS COL ) )
       WHERE WT > WEIGHT ( 14.0 ) ) { P#, WT, COL } ;
```

—show the converted form after the substitution procedure has been applied for each of the following expressions and statements:

```
a. HEAVYWEIGHT WHERE COL = COLOR ('Green')

b. ( EXTEND HEAVYWEIGHT ADD ( WT + WEIGHT ( 5.3 ) ) AS WTP )
                                                    { P#, WTP }

c. INSERT HEAVYWEIGHT
   RELATION { TUPLE { P#  P# ('P99'),
                      WT  WEIGHT ( 12.0 ),
                      COL COLOR ('Purple') } } ;

d. DELETE HEAVYWEIGHT WHERE WT < WEIGHT ( 10.0 ) ;

e. UPDATE HEAVYWEIGHT WHERE WT = WEIGHT ( 18.0 )
       { COL := 'White' } ;
```

10.6   Suppose the HEAVYWEIGHT view definition from Exercise 10.5 is revised as follows:

```
VAR HEAVYWEIGHT VIEW
   ( ( ( EXTEND P ADD ( WEIGHT * 454 ) AS WT )
       RENAME COLOR AS COL ) WHERE WT > WEIGHT ( 6356.0 ) )
                                        { P#, WT, COL } ;
```

(i.e., attribute WT now denotes weights in grams rather than pounds). Now repeat Exercise 10.5.

10.7   Give calculus-based analogs of the algebraic view definitions in Section 10.1.

10.8   ORDER BY makes no sense in a view definition (despite the fact that at least one well-known product permits it!). Why not?

10.9   In Chapter 9 we suggested that it might sometimes be desirable to be able to declare candidate keys—or possibly a primary key—for a view. Why might such a facility be desirable?

10.10   What extensions are needed to the system catalog to support views? What about snapshots?

10.11 Suppose a given base relvar *R* is replaced by two restrictions *A* and *B* such that *A* UNION *B* is always equal to *R* and *A* INTERSECT *B* is always empty. Is logical data independence achievable?

10.12 If *A* and *B* are of the same relation type, *A* INTERSECT *B* is equivalent to *A* JOIN *B* (this join is one-to-one, but not *strictly* so, because there might exist tuples in *A* without counterparts in *B* and *vice versa*). Are the updatability rules given in Section 10.4 for intersection and join views consistent with this equivalence?

10.13 *A* INTERSECT *B* is also equivalent to *A* MINUS (*A* MINUS *B*) and to *B* MINUS (*B* MINUS *A*). Are the updatability rules given in Section 10.4 for intersection and difference views consistent with these equivalences?

10.14 One of the principles we laid down in Section 10.4 was that INSERT and DELETE should be inverses of each other, to the fullest extent possible. Do the rules given in that section for updating union, intersection, and difference views abide by this principle?

10.15 In Section 10.2 (in our discussion of logical data independence), we discussed the possibility of restructuring the suppliers-and-parts database by replacing base relvar S by two of its projections SNC and ST. We also observed that such a restructuring was not a totally trivial matter. What are the implications?

10.16 Investigate any SQL product that might be available to you. (a) Can you find any examples of view retrievals that fail in that product? (b) What are the rules regarding view updates in that product? Note that they are probably somewhat different from those given for SQL:1999 in Section 10.6.

10.17 Consider the suppliers-and-parts database, but ignore the parts relvar for simplicity. Here in outline are two possible designs for suppliers and shipments:

```
a.  S   { S#, SNAME, STATUS, CITY }
    SP  { S#, P#, QTY }

b.  SSP { S#, SNAME, STATUS, CITY, P#, QTY }
    XSS { S#, SNAME, STATUS, CITY }
```

Design *a* is as usual. In Design *b*, by contrast, relvar SSP contains a tuple for every shipment, giving the applicable part number and quantity and full supplier details, and relvar XSS contains supplier details for suppliers who supply no parts at all. (Note that the two designs are information-equivalent and that the two designs therefore illustrate *The Principle of Interchangeability*.) Write view definitions to express Design *b* as views over Design *a* and *vice versa*. Also, show the applicable *database constraints* for each design (see Chapter 9 if you need to refresh your memory regarding database constraints). Does either design have any obvious advantages over the other? If so, what are they?

10.18 Give SQL solutions to Exercises 10.1–10.4.

10.19 The algorithm given in Section 10.4 for updating join views in particular is sometimes criticized on the grounds that (e.g.) deleting a tuple from the join of suppliers and shipments should surely be understood to mean that the corresponding shipment, only, is to be deleted from relvar SP—that is, the supplier should not be deleted from relvar S. Discuss.

10.20 As the final (important!) exercise in this part of the book, revisit the definition of the relational model given at the end of Section 3.2 in Chapter 3, and make sure you understand it thoroughly.

REFERENCES AND BIBLIOGRAPHY

10.1 Michel Adiba: "Derived Relations: A Unified Mechanism for Views, Snapshots, and Distributed Data," Proc. 1981 Int. Conf. on Very Large Data Bases, Cannes, France (September 1981). See also the earlier version, "Database Snapshots," by Michel E. Adiba and Bruce G. Lindsay, IBM Research Report RJ2772 (March 7, 1980).

> The paper that first proposed the snapshot concept. Semantics and implementation are both discussed. Regarding implementation, note in particular that various kinds of "differential refresh" or *incremental maintenance* are possible under the covers—it is not always necessary for the system to reexecute the original query in its entirety at refresh time.

10.2 H. W. Buff: "Why Codd's Rule No. 6 Must Be Reformulated," *ACM SIGMOD Record 17,* No. 4 (December 1988).

> In 1985, Codd published a set of 12 rules to be used as "part of a test to determine whether a product that is claimed to be fully relational is actually so" [10.3]. His Rule No. 6 required that "all views that are theoretically updatable" in fact be updatable by the system. In this short paper, Buff criticizes that rule and claims that the general view-updatability problem is undecidable—that is, no general algorithm exists to determine the updatability or otherwise of an arbitrary view. (According to McGoveran [10.11], this paper "has been the dominant and most serious barrier to investigation of the problem of updating views.") But any real relational implementation will be subject to a variety of finite limits (e.g., on the maximum length of an expression), with the consequence that Buff's results do not apply to that particular system. To quote McGoveran again: "Buff [does not consider] those limited implementations of the relational algebra [that] are necessary to reduce the relational model to practice on physical computers; instead, his paper considers solely the pure mathematics for abstract, theoretical algorithms" [10.11].

10.3 E. F. Codd: "Is Your DBMS Really Relational?" and "Does Your DBMS Run by the Rules?" *Computerworld* (October 14 and 21, 1985).

10.4 Donald D. Chamberlin, James N. Gray, and Irving L. Traiger: "Views, Authorization, and Locking in a Relational Data Base System," Proc. NCC *44,* Anaheim, Calif. Montvale, N.J.: AFIPS Press (May 1975).

> Includes a brief rationale for the approach adopted to view updating in System R (and hence in SQL/DS, DB2, the SQL standard, etc.). See also reference [10.12], which performs the same function for University Ingres.

10.5 Hugh Darwen: "Without Check Option," in C. J. Date and Hugh Darwen, *Relational Database Writings 1989–1991.* Reading, Mass.: Addison-Wesley (1992).

10.6 C. J. Date and David McGoveran: "Updating Union, Intersection, and Difference Views" and "Updating Joins and Other Views," in C. J. Date, *Relational Database Writings 1991–1994.* Reading, Mass.: Addison-Wesley (1995).

> These two papers present an informal introduction to the view updating scheme described in some detail in Section 10.4. One of the authors (McGoveran) has prepared a formal description of the scheme and is pursuing a U.S. patent claim based on that description [10.11].

10.7 Umeshwar Dayal and Philip A. Bernstein: "On the Correct Translation of Update Operations on Relational Views," *ACM TODS 7,* No. 3 (September 1982).

> An early formal treatment of the view update problem (for restriction, projection, and join views only). Predicates are not considered.

10.8 Antonio L. Furtado and Marco A. Casanova: "Updating Relational Views," in reference [18.1].

> There are two broad approaches to the view update problem. One—the only one discussed in any detail in this chapter—attempts to provide a general mechanism that works regardless of the specific database involved; it is driven purely by the definitions of the views in question

(i.e., by system-understood semantics). The other, less ambitious, approach requires the DBA to specify, for each view, exactly what updates are allowed and what their semantics are, by (in effect) writing the procedural code to implement those updates in terms of the underlying base relvars. This paper surveys work on each of the two approaches as of 1985. An extensive set of references to earlier work is included.

10.9 Nathan Goodman: "View Update Is Practical," *InfoDB 5,* No. 2 (Summer 1990).

A very informal discussion of the problem of view updating. Here is a slightly paraphrased excerpt from the introduction: "Dayal and Bernstein [10.7] have proved that essentially no interesting views can be updated; Buff [10.2] has proved that no algorithm exists that can decide whether an arbitrary view is updatable. There seems little reason for hope. [However,] nothing could be further from the truth. The fact is, view update is both possible and practical." And the paper goes on to give a variety of *ad hoc* view update techniques. The crucial notion of predicates is not mentioned, however.

10.10 Arthur M. Keller: "Algorithms for Translating View Updates to Database Updates for Views Involving Selections, Projections, and Joins," Proc. 4th ACM SIGACT-SIGMOD Symposium on Principles of Database Systems, Portland, Ore. (March 1985).

Proposes a set of five criteria that should be satisfied by view-updating algorithms—no side effects, one-step changes only, no unnecessary changes, no simpler replacements possible, and no DELETE-INSERT pairs instead of UPDATEs—and presents algorithms that satisfy those criteria. Among other things, the algorithms permit the implementation of one kind of update by another; for example, a DELETE on a view might translate into an UPDATE on the underlying base relvar (e.g., a supplier could be deleted from the "London suppliers" view by changing the CITY value to Paris). As another example (beyond the scope of Keller's paper, however), a DELETE on *V* (where *V = A* MINUS *B*) might be implemented by means of an INSERT on *B* instead of a DELETE on *A*. Note that we explicitly rejected such possibilities in the body of this chapter, by virtue of our Principle 6.

10.11 David O. McGoveran: "Accessing and Updating Views and Relations in a Relational Database," U.S. Patent Application 10/114,609 (April 2, 2002).

10.12 M. R. Stonebraker: "Implementation of Views and Integrity Constraints by Query Modification," Proc. ACM SIGMOD Int. Conf. on Management of Data, San Jose, Calif. (May 1975).

See the annotation to reference [10.4].

PART **III**

DATABASE DESIGN

This part of the book is concerned with the general subject of database design (more specifically, *relational* database design). The database design problem can be stated very simply: Given some body of data to be represented in a database, how do we decide on a suitable logical structure for that data?—in other words, how do we decide what relvars should exist and what attributes they should have? The practical significance of this problem is obvious.

Before we start getting into details, a number of preliminary remarks are in order:

■ First, note that we are concerned here with *logical* (or *conceptual*) design only, not physical design. Now, we are not suggesting that physical design is not important—on the contrary, physical design is very important. However:

a. Physical design can be treated as a separate, follow-on activity. In other words, the "right" way to do database design is to do a clean logical (i.e., relational) design first, and then, as a separate and subsequent step, to map that logical design into whatever physical structures the target DBMS happens to support. In other words, as noted in Chapter 2, the physical design should be derived from the logical design, not the other way around.[1]

b. Physical design, by definition, tends to be somewhat DBMS-specific, and as a topic is thus not appropriate for a general textbook such as this one. Logical design, by contrast, is or should be quite DBMS-independent, and there are some solid theoretical principles that can be applied to the problem—and such principles definitely do have a place in a book of this nature.

Unfortunately we live in an imperfect world, and in practice it might be the case that design decisions made at the physical level will have an impact back on the logical level (precisely because, as noted several times in this book already, today's DBMS products typically support only rather simple mappings between the logical and physical levels). In other words, several iterations might have to be made over the

---

[1] Ideally, in fact, the system should be able to derive the physical design automatically, without the need for human involvement in the process at all. While this goal might sound utopian, Appendix A describes an approach to implementation that brings it into the realm of possibility.

"logical-then-physical" design cycle, and compromises might have to be made. Nevertheless, we stand by our original contention that the right way to do database design is to get the logical design right first, without paying any attention whatsoever at that stage to physical—that is, performance—considerations. Thus, this part of the book is primarily concerned with what is involved in "getting the logical design right first."

- Although (as already stated) we are interested mainly in *relational* design, it is our firm belief that the ideas to be discussed are relevant to the design of nonrelational databases also. In other words, we believe the right way to do database design in a nonrelational system is to do a clean relational design first, and then, as a separate and subsequent step, to map that relational design into whatever nonrelational structures (e.g., hierarchies) the target DBMS happens to support.

- Having said all of the above, we must now also say that database design is still very much an art, not a science. There are (to repeat) some scientific principles that can be brought to bear on the problem, and those principles are the subject of the next three chapters; however, there are many, many design issues that those principles simply do not address at all. As a consequence, numerous database theoreticians and practitioners have proposed design methodologies[2]—some of them fairly rigorous, others less so, but all of them *ad hoc* to a degree—that can be used as an attack on what at the time of writing is still a rather intractable problem: *viz.*, the problem of finding "the" logical design that is incontestably the right one. Since those methodologies *are* mostly *ad hoc* to some degree, there can be few objective criteria for preferring any given approach over all the rest; nevertheless, we present in Chapter 14 a well-known approach that does at least have the merit of being widely used in practice. We also briefly consider a number of other commercially supported approaches in that chapter.

- We should also state explicitly a couple of assumptions that underlie most of the discussions in this part of the book:

  a. Database design is not just a question of getting the data structures right; data integrity is a—perhaps *the*—key ingredient too. This remark will be repeated and amplified at many points in the chapters that follow.

  b. We will be concerned for the most part with what might be termed *application-independent* design. In other words, we are primarily concerned with what the data *is,* rather than how it will be *used.* Application independence in this sense is desirable for the very good reason that it is normally (perhaps always) the case that not all uses to which the data will be put are known at design time; thus, we want a design that will be robust, in the sense that it will not be invalidated by the advent of application requirements that were not foreseen at the time of the original design. To put this another way (and to use the terminology of Chapter 2),

---

[2] The term *methodology* originally meant *the study of methods,* but has come to mean "a system of methods and rules applicable to research or work in a given science or art" (*Chambers Twentieth Century Dictionary*).

what we are trying to do, primarily, *is get the conceptual schema right;* i.e., we are interested in producing a hardware-independent, operating-system-independent, DBMS-independent, language-independent, user-independent (and so on) abstract logical design. In particular, we are not interested in making compromises for performance reasons, as already explained.

■ We have said that the problem of database design is the problem of deciding what relvars should exist and what attributes they should have. In fact, of course, it involves the problem of deciding what *domains* or *types* should be defined too. We will have little to say on this topic, however, since little relevant work seems to have been done on it at the time of writing (references [14.12] and [14.44] are exceptions).

The structure of this part is as follows. Chapter 11 lays some theoretical groundwork. Chapters 12 and 13 are concerned with the ideas of *further normalization,* which build directly on that groundwork to give formal meaning to informal claims to the effect that certain designs are "better" than others in certain ways. Chapter 14 then discusses *semantic modeling;* in particular, it explains the concepts of "entity/relationship" modeling, and shows how those concepts can be used to tackle the design problem from the top down (starting with real-world entities and ending up with a formal relational design).

Functional Dependencies

11.1   INTRODUCTION

In this chapter, we examine a concept that has been characterized (by Hugh Darwen, in a private communication) as "not quite fundamental, but very nearly so"—*viz.*, the concept of **functional dependence**. This concept turns out to be crucially important to a number of issues to be discussed in later chapters, including in particular the database design theory described in Chapter 12. Please note immediately, however, that its usefulness is not limited to that purpose alone; indeed, this chapter could well have been included in Part II of this book instead of Part III.

A functional dependency (FD for short) is basically *a many-to-one relationship* from one set of attributes to another within a given relvar. In the case of the shipments relvar SP, for example, there is a functional dependency from the set of attributes {S#,P#} to the set of attributes {QTY}. What this means is that within any relation that is a legal value for that relvar:

1. For any given value for the pair of attributes S# and P#, there is just one corresponding value of attribute QTY.[1]

2. However, any number of distinct values of the pair of attributes S# and P# can have the same corresponding value for attribute QTY (in general).

Observe that our usual sample SP value (see Fig. 3.8 on the inside back cover) does satisfy both of these properties; observe too that once again we have a concept whose definition relies on the concept of tuple equality.

In Section 11.2, we define the notion of functional dependence more precisely, distinguishing carefully between those FDs that happen to be satisfied by a given relvar at some particular time and those that are satisfied by that relvar at *all* times. As already mentioned, it turns out that FDs provide a basis for a scientific attack on a number of practical problems. And the reason they do so is because they possess a rich set of interesting formal properties, which make it possible to treat the problems in question in a formal and rigorous manner. Sections 11.3–11.6 explore some of those formal properties in detail and explain some of their practical consequences. Finally, Section 11.7 presents a brief summary.

Note: This is the most formal chapter in the book, and you might like to skip portions of it on a first reading. Indeed, most of what you need in order to understand the material of the next three chapters is covered in Sections 11.2 and 11.3; you might therefore prefer to give the remaining sections a "once over lightly" reading for now, and come back to them later when you have assimilated the material of the next three chapters.

A small point regarding terminology: The terms *functional dependence* and *functional dependency* are used interchangeably in the literature. Normal English usage would suggest that the term *dependence* be used for the FD concept *per se* and would reserve the term *dependency* for "the thing that depends." But we very frequently need to refer to FDs in the plural, and "dependencies" seems to trip off the tongue more readily than "dependences"; hence our use of both terms.

11.2 BASIC DEFINITIONS

In order to illustrate the ideas of the present section, we make use of a slightly revised version of the shipments relvar, one that includes, in addition to the usual attributes S#, P#, and QTY, an attribute CITY, representing the city for the relevant supplier. We will refer to this revised relvar as SCP to avoid confusion. A sample value is shown in Fig. 11.1.

Now, it is very important in this area—as in so many others!—to distinguish clearly between (a) the value of a given relvar at a given point in time and (b) the set of all possible values that the given relvar might assume at different times. In what follows, we first define

---

[1] Note that this rather formal statement is true precisely because a certain "business rule" is in effect (see Chapter 9)—namely, that there is at most one shipment at any given time for a given supplier and a given part. Loosely speaking, in other words, FDs are a matter of *semantics* (what the data means), not a fluke arising from the particular values that happen to appear in the database at some particular point in time.

SCP	S#	CITY	P#	QTY
	S1	London	P1	100
	S1	London	P2	100
	S2	Paris	P1	200
	S2	Paris	P2	200
	S3	Paris	P2	300
	S4	London	P2	400
	S4	London	P4	400
	S4	London	P5	400

Fig. 11.1   Sample value for relvar SCP

the concept of functional dependence as it applies to Case *a,* and then extend it to apply to Case *b.* Here then is the definition for Case *a:*

- **Functional dependence**, Case *a:* Let *r* be a relation, and let *X* and *Y* be arbitrary subsets of the set of attributes of *r.* Then we say that *Y* is functionally dependent on *X*—in symbols,

  $X \rightarrow Y$

  (read "*X* **functionally determines** *Y*," or simply "*X* arrow *Y*")—if and only if each *X* value in *r* has associated with it precisely one *Y* value in *r.* In other words, whenever two tuples of *r* agree on their *X* value, they also agree on their *Y* value.

  For example, the relation shown in Fig. 11.1 satisfies the FD

  `{ S# } → { CITY }`

because all tuples of that relation with a given S# value also have the same CITY value. Indeed, it also satisfies several more FDs, the following among them:

```
{ S#, P# } → { QTY }
{ S#, P# } → { CITY }
{ S#, P# } → { CITY, QTY }
{ S#, P# } → { S# }
{ S#, P# } → { S#, P#, CITY, QTY }
{ S# }     → { QTY }
{ QTY }    → { S# }
```

(*Exercise:* Check these.)

The left and right sides of an FD are called the **determinant** and the **dependent**, respectively. As the definition indicates, the determinant and dependent are both *sets* of attributes. When such a set contains just one attribute, however—that is, when it is a *singleton set*—we often drop the set braces and write just, for example:

`S# → CITY`

As already explained, the foregoing definitions apply to Case *a*—that is, to individual relation values. However, when we consider relation variables (i.e., relvars)—in particular, when we consider *base* relvars—we are usually interested not so much in the FDs that happen to hold for the particular value that the relvar happens to have at some particular time, but rather in those FDs that hold for *all possible values* of that relvar. In the case of SCP, for example, the FD

```
S# → CITY
```

holds for all possible values of SCP, because at any given time a given supplier has precisely one corresponding city, and so any two tuples appearing in SCP at the same time with the same supplier number must necessarily have the same city as well. Indeed, the fact that this FD holds "for all time" (i.e., for all possible values of SCP) is an *integrity constraint* on relvar SCP—it places limits on the values that relvar SCP can legitimately have. Here is a formulation of that constraint using the calculus-based **Tutorial D** syntax from Chapter 9:

```
CONSTRAINT S#_CITY_FD
    FORALL SCPX FORALL SCPY
      ( IF SCPX.S# = SCPY.S#
        THEN SCPX.CITY = SCPY.CITY END IF ) ;
```

(SCPX and SCPY are range variables ranging over SCP.) The syntax S# → CITY can be regarded as shorthand for this longer formulation. *Exercise:* Give an algebraic version of this constraint.

Here then is the Case *b* definition of functional dependence (the extensions over the Case *a* definition are shown in **boldface**):

- **Functional dependence**, Case *b:* Let *R* be a relation **variable**, and let *X* and *Y* be arbitrary subsets of the set of attributes of *R*. Then we say that *Y* is functionally dependent on—in symbols,

  $X \rightarrow Y$

  (read "*X* functionally determines *Y*," or simply "*X* arrow *Y*")—if and only if, **in every possible legal value of R**, each *X* value has associated with it precisely one *Y* value. In other words, **in every possible legal value of R**, whenever two tuples agree on their *X* value, they also agree on their *Y* value.

Henceforth, we will use the term *functional dependence* in this latter, more demanding, and *time-independent* sense, barring explicit statements to the contrary.

Here then are some (time-independent) FDs that apply to relvar SCP:

```
{ S#, P# } → QTY
{ S#, P# } → CITY
{ S#, P# } → { CITY, QTY }
{ S#, P# } → S#
{ S#, P# } → { S#, P#, CITY, QTY }
{ S# }     → CITY
```

Note in particular that the following FDs, which do happen to hold for the relation value shown in Fig. 11.1, do not hold "for all time" for relvar SCP:

```
S#  → QTY
QTY → S#
```

In other words, the statement that (e.g.) "every shipment for a given supplier involves the same quantity" does happen to be true for the particular SCP relation value shown in Fig. 11.1, but it is not true for all possible legal values of the SCP relvar.

We now observe that if X is a candidate key for relvar R, then all attributes Y of relvar R must be functionally dependent on X. (We mentioned this important fact in passing in Chapter 9, Section 9.10. It follows from the definition of candidate key.) For the parts relvar P, for example, we necessarily have:

```
P# → { P#, PNAME, COLOR, WEIGHT, CITY }
```

In fact, if relvar R satisfies the FD $A \rightarrow B$ and A is *not* a candidate key,[2] then R will necessarily involve some **redundancy**. In the case of relvar SCP, for example, the FD S# $\rightarrow$ CITY implies that the fact that a given supplier is located in a given city will appear many times in that relvar, in general (see Fig. 11.1 for an illustration of this point). We will take up this question of redundancy and discuss it in detail in the next chapter.

Now, even if we restrict our attention to FDs that hold for all time, the complete set of FDs for a given relvar can still be very large, as the SCP example suggests. (*Exercise:* State the complete set of FDs satisfied by relvar SCP.) What we would like is to find some way of reducing that set to a manageable size—and, indeed, most of the remainder of this chapter is concerned with exactly this issue.

Why is this objective desirable? One reason is that (as already stated) FDs represent certain integrity constraints, and we would thus like the DBMS to enforce them. Given a particular set S of FDs, therefore, it is desirable to find some other set T that is (ideally) much smaller than S and has the property that every FD in S is implied by the FDs in T. If such a set T can be found, it is sufficient that the DBMS enforce just the FDs in T, and the FDs in S will then be enforced automatically. The problem of finding such a set T is thus of considerable practical interest.

11.3 TRIVIAL AND NONTRIVIAL DEPENDENCIES

Note: In the remainder of this chapter, we will occasionally abbreviate "functional dependency" to just "dependency." Similarly for "functionally dependent on," "functionally determines," and so on.

One obvious way to reduce the size of the set of FDs we need to deal with is to eliminate the *trivial* dependencies. A dependency is **trivial** if it cannot possibly fail to be satisfied. Just one of the FDs shown for relvar SCP in the previous section was trivial in this sense—*viz.*, the FD:

```
{ S#, P# } → S#
```

In fact, an FD is trivial if and only if the right side is a subset (not necessarily a proper subset) of the left side.

---

[2] And if the FD is not trivial (see Section 11.3) and A is not a superkey (see Section 11.5) and R contains at least two tuples (!).

As the name implies, trivial dependencies are not very interesting in practice; we are usually more interested in practice in **nontrivial** dependencies (which are, of course, precisely the ones that are not trivial), because they are the ones that correspond to "genuine" integrity constraints. When we are dealing with the formal theory, however, we have to account for *all* dependencies, trivial ones as well as nontrivial.

11.4   CLOSURE OF A SET OF DEPENDENCIES

We have already suggested that some FDs might imply others. As a simple example, the FD

```
{ S#, P# }  →  { CITY, QTY }
```

implies both of the following:

```
{ S#, P# }  →  CITY
{ S#, P# }  →  QTY
```

As a more complex example, suppose we have a relvar R with attributes A, B, and C, such that the FDs $A \rightarrow B$ and $B \rightarrow C$ both hold for R. Then it is easy to see that the FD $A \rightarrow C$ also holds for R. The FD $A \rightarrow C$ here is an example of a **transitive** FD—C is said to depend on A *transitively,* via B.

The set of all FDs that are implied by a given set S of FDs is called the **closure** of S, written S^+ (nothing to do with closure in the relational algebra sense, please note). Clearly we need an algorithm that will allow us to compute S^+ from S. The first attack on this problem appeared in a paper by Armstrong [11.2], which gave a set of **inference rules** (more usually called **Armstrong's axioms**) by which new FDs can be inferred from given ones. Those rules can be stated in a variety of equivalent ways, of which one of the simplest is as follows. Let A, B, and C be arbitrary subsets of the set of attributes of the given relvar R, and let us agree to write (e.g.) AB to mean the union of A and B. Then we have:

1. **Reflexivity:** If B is a subset of A, then $A \rightarrow B$.

2. **Augmentation:** If $A \rightarrow B$, then $AC \rightarrow BC$.

3. **Transitivity:** If $A \rightarrow B$ and $B \rightarrow C$, then $A \rightarrow C$.

Each of these three rules can be directly proved from the definition of functional dependency (the first is just the definition of a trivial dependency, of course). Moreover, the rules are **complete**, in the sense that, given a set S of FDs, all FDs implied by S can be derived from S using the rules. They are also **sound**, in the sense that no additional FDs (i.e., FDs not implied by S) can be so derived. In other words, the rules can be used to derive precisely the closure S^+.

Several further rules can be derived from the three already given, the following among them. These additional rules can be used to simplify the practical task of computing S^+ from S. (In what follows, D is another arbitrary subset of the set of attributes of R.)

4. **Self-determination:** $A \rightarrow A$.

5. **Decomposition:** If $A \rightarrow BC$, then $A \rightarrow B$ and $A \rightarrow C$.

6. **Union:** If $A \rightarrow B$ and $A \rightarrow C$, then $A \rightarrow BC$.

7. **Composition:** If $A \rightarrow B$ and $C \rightarrow D$, then $AC \rightarrow BD$.

And in reference [11.7], Darwen proves the following rule, which he calls the *General Unification Theorem:*

8. If $A \rightarrow B$ and $C \rightarrow D$, then $A \cup (C - B) \rightarrow BD$

(where "$\cup$" is union and "$-$" is set difference). The name "General Unification Theorem" refers to the fact that several of the earlier rules can be seen as special cases [11.7].

    Example: Suppose we are given a relvar R with attributes $A, B, C, D, E, F,$ and the FDs:

```
A   → BC
B   → E
CD  → EF
```

Observe that we are extending our notation slightly, though not incompatibly, by writing, for example, BC for the set consisting of attributes B and C (previously BC would have meant the *union* of B and $C,$ where B and C were *sets* of attributes). *Note:* If you would prefer a more concrete example, take A as employee number, B as department number, C as manager's employee number, D as project number for a project directed by that manager (unique within manager), E as department name, and F as percentage of time spent by the specified manager on the specified project.

    We now show that the FD $AD \rightarrow F$ holds for R and is thus a member of the closure of the given set:

1. $A \rightarrow BC$ (given)
2. $A \rightarrow C$ (1, decomposition)
3. $AD \rightarrow CD$ (2, augmentation)
4. $CD \rightarrow EF$ (given)
5. $AD \rightarrow EF$ (3 and 4, transitivity)
6. $AD \rightarrow F$ (5, decomposition)

11.5 CLOSURE OF A SET OF ATTRIBUTES

In principle, we can compute the closure S^+ of a given set S of FDs by means of an algorithm that says "Repeatedly apply the rules from the previous section until they stop producing new FDs." In practice, there is little need to compute the closure *per se* (which is just as well, because the algorithm just mentioned is hardly very efficient). In this section, however, we will show how to compute a certain subset of the closure: namely, that subset consisting of all FDs with a certain (specified) set Z of attributes as the left side. More precisely, we will show how, given a relvar R, a set Z of attributes of R, and a set S of FDs that hold for R, we can determine the set of all attributes of R that are functionally dependent

```
CLOSURE[Z,S] := Z ;
do "forever" ;
   for each FD X → Y in S
      do ;
         if X ⊆ CLOSURE[Z,S]
         then CLOSURE[Z,S] := CLOSURE[Z,S] ∪ Y ;
      end
   if CLOSURE[Z,S] did not change on this iteration
   then leave the loop ;          /* computation complete */
end ;
```

Fig. 11.2   Computing the closure Z^+ of Z under S

on Z—**the closure Z^+ of Z under S**.[3] A simple algorithm for computing that closure is given in pseudocode in Fig. 11.2. *Exercise:* Prove that algorithm is correct.

Example: Suppose we are given a relvar *R* with attributes *A, B, C, D, E, F,* and FDs:

$$
\begin{aligned}
A \;&\to\; BC \\
E \;&\to\; CF \\
B \;&\to\; E \\
CD \;&\to\; EF
\end{aligned}
$$

We now compute the closure $\{A,B\}^+$ of the set of attributes $\{A,B\}$ under this set of FDs.

1. We initialize the result CLOSURE[Z,S] to {A,B}.

2. We now go round the inner loop four times, once for each of the given FDs. On the first iteration (for the FD $A \to BC$), we find that the left side is indeed a subset of CLOSURE[Z,S] as computed so far, so we add attributes (*B* and) *C* to the result. CLOSURE[Z,S] is now the set {A,B,C}.

3. On the second iteration (for the FD $E \to CF$), we find that the left side is *not* a subset of the result as computed so far, which thus remains unchanged.

4. On the third iteration (for the FD $B \to E$), we add *E* to CLOSURE[Z,S], which now has the value {A,B,C,E}.

5. On the fourth iteration (for the FD $CD \to EF$), CLOSURE[Z,S] remains unchanged.

6. Now we go round the inner loop four times again. On the first iteration, the result does not change; on the second, it expands to {A,B,C,E,F}; on the third and fourth, it does not change.

7. Now we go round the inner loop four times again. CLOSURE[Z,S] does not change, and so the whole process terminates, with $\{A,B\}^+ = \{A,B,C,E,F\}$.

Note that if (as stated) Z is a set of attributes of relvar *R* and S is a set of FDs that hold for *R*, then the set of FDs that hold for *R* with Z as the left side is the set consisting of all FDs of the form $Z \to Z'$, where Z' is some subset of the closure Z^+ of Z under S. The

---

[3] Note that we now have two kinds of closure: closure of a set of FDs, and closure of a set of attributes under a set of FDs. Note too that we use the same "superscript plus" notation for both of them. We trust that this dual usage on our part will not prove confusing.

closure S^+ of the original set S of FDs is then the union of all such sets of FDs, taken over all possible attribute sets Z.

An important corollary of all of the foregoing is as follows: Given a set S of FDs, we can easily tell whether a specific FD $X \rightarrow Y$ follows from S, because that FD will follow if and only if Y is a subset of the closure X^+ of X under S. In other words, we now have a simple way of determining whether a given FD $X \rightarrow Y$ is in the closure S^+ of S, without actually having to compute that closure S^+.

Another important corollary is the following. Recall from Chapter 9 that a superkey for a relvar R is a set of attributes of R that includes some candidate key of R as a subset (not necessarily a proper subset). Now, it follows immediately from the definition that the superkeys for a given relvar R are precisely those subsets K of the attributes of R such that the FD

$$K \rightarrow A$$

holds true for every attribute A of R. In other words, K is a superkey if and only if the closure K^+ of K—under the given set of FDs—is precisely the set of all attributes of R (and K is a *candidate* key if and only if it is an irreducible superkey).

11.6   IRREDUCIBLE SETS OF DEPENDENCIES

Let $S1$ and $S2$ be two sets of FDs. If every FD implied by $S1$ is implied by $S2$—that is, if $S1^+$ is a subset of $S2^+$—we say that $S2$ is a **cover** for $S1$.[4] What this means is that if the DBMS enforces the FDs in $S2$, then it will automatically be enforcing the FDs in $S1$.

Next, if $S2$ is a cover for $S1$ and $S1$ is a cover for $S2$—that is, if $S1^+ = S2^+$—we say that $S1$ and $S2$ are **equivalent**. Clearly, if $S1$ and $S2$ are equivalent, then if the DBMS enforces the FDs in $S2$ it will automatically be enforcing the FDs in $S1$, and *vice versa*.

Now we define a set S of FDs to be **irreducible**[5] if and only if it satisfies the following three properties:

1. The right side (the dependent) of every FD in S involves just one attribute (i.e., it is a singleton set).

2. The left side (the determinant) of every FD in S is irreducible in turn—meaning that no attribute can be discarded from the determinant without changing the closure S^+ (i.e., without converting S into some set not equivalent to S). We call such an FD **left-irreducible**.

3. No FD in S can be discarded from S without changing the closure S^+ (i.e., without converting S into some set not equivalent to S).

With regard to points 2 and 3 here, by the way, note carefully that it is not necessary to know exactly what the closure S^+ is in order to tell whether it will be changed if something is discarded. For example, consider the familiar parts relvar P. The following FDs (among others) hold for that relvar:

---

[4] Some writers use the term *cover* to mean what we will be calling (in just a moment) an *equivalent* set.

[5] Usually called *minimal* in the literature.

```
P#  →  PNAME
P#  →  COLOR
P#  →  WEIGHT
P#  →  CITY
```

This set of FDs is easily seen to be irreducible: The right side is a single attribute in each case, the left side is obviously irreducible in turn, and none of the FDs can be discarded without changing the closure (i.e., without *losing some information*). By contrast, the following sets of FDs are not irreducible:

1.
```
P#  →  { PNAME, COLOR}
P#  →  WEIGHT
P#  →  CITY
```
   The right side of the first FD here is not a singleton set

2.
```
{ P#, PNAME }  →  COLOR
P#  →  PNAME
P#  →  WEIGHT
P#  →  CITY
```
   The first FD here can be simplified by dropping PNAME from the left side without changing the closure (i.e., it is not left-irreducible)

3.
```
P#  →  P#
P#  →  PNAME
P#  →  COLOR
P#  →  WEIGHT
P#  →  CITY
```
   The first FD here can be discarded without changing the closure

We now claim that for every set of FDs there exists at least one equivalent set that is irreducible. In fact, this is easy to see. Let the original set of FDs be S. Thanks to the decomposition rule, we can assume without loss of generality that every FD in S has a singleton right side. Next, for each FD f in S we examine each attribute A in the left side of f; if deleting A from the left side of f has no effect on the closure S^+, we delete A from the left side of f. Then, for each FD f remaining in S, if deleting f from S has no effect on the closure S^+, we delete f from S. The final set S is irreducible and is equivalent to the original set S.

Example: Suppose we are given a relvar R with attributes A, B, C, D, and FDs:

```
A   → BC
B   → C
A   → B
AB  → C
AC  → D
```

We now compute an irreducible set of FDs that is equivalent to this given set:

1. The first step is to rewrite the FDs such that each has a singleton right side:

```
A   → B
A   → C
B   → C
A   → B
AB  → C
AC  → D
```

We observe immediately that the FD $A \rightarrow B$ occurs twice, so one occurrence can be eliminated.

2. Next, attribute *C* can be eliminated from the left side of the FD *AC* → *D*, because we have *A* → *C*, so *A* → *AC* by augmentation, and we are given *AC* → *D*, so *A* → *D* by transitivity; thus the *C* on the left side of *AC* → *D* is redundant.

3. Next, we observe that the FD *AB* → *C* can be eliminated, because again we have *A* → *C*, so *AB* → *CB* by augmentation, so *AB* → *C* by decomposition.

4. Finally, the FD *A* → *C* is implied by the FDs *A* → *B* and *B* → *C*, so it can also be eliminated. We are left with:

```
A → B
B → C
A → D
```

This set is irreducible.

A set *I* of FDs that is irreducible and equivalent to some other set *S* of FDs is said to be an **irreducible equivalent** of *S*. Thus, given some particular set *S* of FDs that need to be enforced, it is sufficient for the system to find and enforce the FDs in an irreducible equivalent *I* instead (and, to repeat, there is no need to compute the closure *S*⁺ in order to compute an irreducible equivalent *I*). We should make it clear, however, that a given set of FDs does not necessarily have a unique irreducible equivalent (see Exercise 11.12).

11.7 SUMMARY

A **functional dependency** (FD) is a many-to-one relationship between two sets of attributes of a given relvar (it is a particularly common and important kind of integrity constraint). More precisely, given a relvar *R*, the FD *A* → *B* (where *A* and *B* are subsets of the set of attributes of *R*) is said to hold for *R* if and only if, whenever two tuples of *R* have the same value for *A*, they also have the same value for *B*. Every relvar necessarily satisfies certain **trivial** FDs; an FD is trivial if and only if the right side (the **dependent**) is a subset of the left side (the **determinant**).

Certain FDs imply others. Given a set *S* of FDs, the **closure** *S*⁺ of that set is the set of all FDs implied by the FDs in *S*. *S*⁺ is necessarily a superset of *S*. **Armstrong's inference rules** provide a **sound** and **complete** basis for computing *S*⁺ from *S* (usually, however, we do not actually need to perform that computation). Several other useful rules can easily be derived from Armstrong's rules.

Given a subset *Z* of the set of attributes of relvar *R* and a set *S* of FDs that hold for *R*, the **closure** *Z*⁺ of *Z* under *S* is the set of all attributes *A* of *R* such that the FD *Z* → *A* is a member of *S*⁺. If *Z*⁺ consists of all attributes of *R*, *Z* is said to be a **superkey** for *R* (and a **candidate key** is an irreducible superkey). We gave a simple algorithm for computing *Z*⁺ from *Z* and *S*, and hence a simple way of determining whether a given FD *X* → *Y* is a member of *S*⁺ (*X* → *Y* is a member of *S*⁺ if and only if *Y* is a subset of *X*⁺).

Two sets of FDs *S1* and *S2* are **equivalent** if and only if they are **covers** for each other, implying that *S1*⁺ = *S2*⁺. Every set of FDs is equivalent to at least one **irreducible** set. A set of FDs is irreducible if (a) every FD in the set has a singleton right side, (b) no FD in the set can be discarded without changing the closure of the set, and (c) no attribute can be discarded from the left side of any FD in the set without changing the closure of the set. If *I* is an irreducible set equivalent to *S,* enforcing the FDs in *I* will automatically enforce the FDs in *S.*

In conclusion, we note that many of the foregoing ideas can be extended to apply to integrity constraints in general, not just to FDs. For example, it is true in general that:

1. Certain constraints are trivial.

2. Certain constraints imply others.

3. The set of all constraints implied by a given set can be regarded as the closure of the given set.

4. The question of whether a specific constraint is in a certain closure—that is, whether the specific constraint is implied by certain given constraints—is an interesting practical problem.

5. The question of finding an irreducible equivalent for a given set of constraints is an interesting practical problem.

What makes FDs in particular much more tractable than integrity constraints in general is the existence of a sound and complete set of inference rules for FDs. The "References and Bibliography" sections in this chapter and Chapter 13 give references to publications describing several other specific kinds of constraints—*MVDs, JDs,* and *INDs*—for which such sets of inference rules also exist. In this book, however, we choose not to give those other kinds of constraints so extensive and so formal a treatment as the one we have just given FDs.

EXERCISES

11.1   (a) Let *R* be a relvar of degree *n.* What is the maximum number of functional dependencies *R* can possibly satisfy (trivial as well as nontrivial)? (b) Given that *A* and *B* in the FD *A* → *B* are both *sets* of attributes, what happens if either is the *empty* set?

11.2   What does it mean to say that Armstrong's inference rules are sound? Complete?

11.3   Prove the *reflexivity, augmentation,* and *transitivity* rules, assuming only the basic definition of functional dependence.

11.4   Prove that the three rules of the previous exercise imply the *self-determination, decomposition, union,* and *composition* rules.

11.5   Prove Darwen's "General Unification Theorem." Which of the rules of the previous two exercises did you use? Which rules can be derived as special cases of the theorem?

11.6   Define (a) the closure of a set of FDs; (b) the closure of a set of attributes under a set of FDs.

11.7   List the FDs satisfied by the shipments relvar SP.

11.8   Relvar $R\{A,B,C,D,E,F,G\}$ satisfies the following FDs:

$$
\begin{aligned}
A &\rightarrow B \\
BC &\rightarrow DE \\
AEF &\rightarrow G
\end{aligned}
$$

Compute the closure $\{A,C\}^{+}$ under this set of FDs. Is the FD $ACF \rightarrow DG$ implied by this set?

11.9   What does it mean to say that two sets *S1* and *S2* of FDs are equivalent?

11.10 What does it mean to say that a set of FDs is irreducible?

11.11 Here are two sets of FDs for a relvar $R\{A,B,C,D,E\}$. Are they equivalent?

1. $A \rightarrow B$ $AB \rightarrow C$ $D \rightarrow AC$ $D \rightarrow E$
2. $A \rightarrow BC$ $D \rightarrow AE$

11.12 Relvar $R\{A,B,C,D,E,F\}$ satisfies the following FDs:

$$
\begin{aligned}
AB &\rightarrow C \\
C &\rightarrow A \\
BC &\rightarrow D \\
ACD &\rightarrow B \\
BE &\rightarrow C \\
CE &\rightarrow FA \\
CF &\rightarrow BD \\
D &\rightarrow EF
\end{aligned}
$$

Find an irreducible equivalent for this set of FDs.

11.13 A relvar TIMETABLE is defined with the following attributes:

- D Day of the week (1 to 5)
- P Period within day (1 to 6)
- C Classroom number
- T Teacher name
- L Lesson name

Tuple (d,p,c,t,l) appears in this relvar if and only if at time (d,p) lesson l is taught by teacher t in classroom c (using the simplified notation for tuples introduced in Section 10.4). You can assume that lessons are one period in duration and that every lesson has a name that is unique with respect to all lessons taught in the week. What functional dependencies hold in this relvar? What are the candidate keys?

11.14 A relvar NADDR is defined with attributes NAME (unique), STREET, CITY, STATE, and ZIP. Assume that (a) for any given zip code, there is just one city and state; (b) for any given street, city, and state, there is just one zip code. Give an irreducible set of FDs for this relvar. What are the candidate keys?

11.15 Do the assumptions of the previous exercise hold in practice?

11.16 Let relvar R have attributes A, B, C, D, E, F, G, H, I, and J, and suppose it satisfies the following FDs:

$$
\begin{aligned}
ABD &\rightarrow E \\
AB &\rightarrow G \\
B &\rightarrow F \\
C &\rightarrow J \\
CJ &\rightarrow I \\
G &\rightarrow H
\end{aligned}
$$

Is this an irreducible set? What are the candidate keys?

REFERENCES AND BIBLIOGRAPHY

As noted in Section 11.1, this is the most formal chapter in the book; it thus seemed appropriate to include references [11.1], [11.3], and [11.10] here, since each is a book that offers a formal treatment of a variety of aspects of database theory (not just functional dependencies as such).

11.1 Serge Abiteboul, Richard Hull, and Victor Vianu: *Foundations of Databases*. Reading, Mass.: Addison-Wesley (1995).

11.2 W. W. Armstrong: "Dependency Structures of Data Base Relationships," Proc. IFIP Congress, Stockholm, Sweden (1974).

> The paper that first formalized the theory of FDs (it is the source of Armstrong's axioms). The paper also gives a precise characterization of candidate keys.

11.3 Paolo Atzeni and Valeria De Antonellis: *Relational Database Theory.* Redwood City, Calif.: Benjamin/Cummings (1993).

11.4 Marco A. Casanova, Ronald Fagin, and Christos H. Papadimitriou: "Inclusion Dependencies and Their Interaction with Functional Dependencies," Proc. 1st ACM SIGACT-SIGMOD Symposium on Principles of Database Systems, Los Angeles, Calif. (March 1982).

> **Inclusion dependencies** (INDs) can be regarded as a generalization of referential constraints. For example, the IND
>
> SP.S# ➞ S.S#
>
> (not the notation used in the paper) states that the set of values appearing in attribute S# of relvar SP must be a subset of the set of values appearing in attribute S# of relvar S. This particular example in fact *is* a referential constraint; in general, however, there is no requirement for an IND that the left side be a foreign key or the right side a candidate key. *Note:* INDs do have some points in common with FDs, since both represent many-to-one relationships; however, INDs usually span relvars, while FDs do not.
>
> The paper provides a sound and complete set of inference rules for INDs, which we may state (a little loosely) as follows:
>
> 1. $A \rightarrow A$.
> 2. If $AB \rightarrow CD$, then $A \rightarrow C$ and $B \rightarrow D$.
> 3. If $A \rightarrow B$ and $B \rightarrow C$, then $A \rightarrow C$.

11.5 R. G. Casey and C. Delobel: "Decomposition of a Data Base and the Theory of Boolean Switching Functions," *IBM J. R&D 17,* No. 5 (September 1973).

> This paper shows that for any given relvar, the set of FDs (called *functional relations* in this paper) satisfied by that relvar can be represented by a "boolean switching function." Moreover, that function is unique in the following sense: The original FDs can be specified in many superficially different (but actually equivalent) ways, each giving rise to a superficially different boolean function—but all such functions can be reduced by the laws of boolean algebra to the same "canonical form" (see Chapter 18). The problem of *nonloss-decomposing* the original relvar (see Chapter 12) is then shown to be logically equivalent to the well-understood boolean algebra problem of finding "a covering set of prime implicants" for the boolean function corresponding to that relvar together with its FDs. Hence the original problem can be transformed into an equivalent problem in boolean algebra, and well-known techniques can be brought to bear on it.
>
> This paper was the first of several to draw parallels between dependency theory and other disciplines. See, for example, reference [11.8] and several of the references in Chapter 13.

11.6 E. F. Codd: "Further Normalization of the Data Base Relational Model," in Randall J. Rustin (ed.), *Data Base Systems, Courant Computer Science Symposia Series 6.* Englewood Cliffs, N.J.: Prentice-Hall (1972).

> The paper was the first to describe the concept of functional dependence (apart from an early IBM internal memo, also by Codd). The "further normalization" of the title refers to the specific database design discipline discussed in Chapter 12; the purpose of the paper was, very

specifically, to show the applicability of the ideas of functional dependence to the database design problem. (Indeed, FDs represented the first scientific attack on that problem.) As noted in Section 11.1, however, the functional dependency idea has since shown itself to be of much wider applicability (see, e.g., reference [11.7]).

11.7 Hugh Darwen: "The Role of Functional Dependence in Query Decomposition," in C. J. Date and Hugh Darwen, *Relational Database Writings 1989–1991*. Reading, Mass.: Addison-Wesley (1992).

This paper gives a set of inference rules by which FDs holding for an arbitrary derived relvar can be inferred from those holding for the relvar(s) from which the relvar in question is derived. The set of FDs thus inferred can then be inspected to determine candidate keys for the derived relvar, thus providing the *candidate key* inference rules mentioned in passing (very briefly) in Chapters 9 and 10. The paper shows how these various rules can be used to provide significant improvements in DBMS performance, functionality, and usability. *Note:* Such rules are used in the SQL:1999 standard (a) to extend, slightly, the range of views the standard regards as updatable—see Chapter 10—and (b) to extend also the standard's understanding of what it means for an expression (e.g., in the SELECT clause) to be "single-valued per group." As an illustration of this latter point, consider the following query:

```
SELECT  S.S#, S.CITY, SUM ( SP.QTY ) AS TQ
FROM    S, SP
WHERE   S.S# = SP.S#
GROUP   BY S.S# ;
```

This query was invalid in SQL:1992 because S.CITY is mentioned in the SELECT clause and not in the GROUP BY clause, but is valid in SQL:1999 because SQL now understands that relvar S satisfies the FD S# → CITY.

11.8 R. Fagin: "Functional Dependencies in a Relational Database and Propositional Logic," *IBM J. R&D 21*, No. 6 (November 1977).

Shows that Armstrong's axioms [11.2] are strictly equivalent to the system of implicational statements in propositional logic. In other words, the paper defines a mapping between FDs and propositional statements, and then shows that a given FD *f* is a consequence of a given set *S* of FDs if and only if the proposition corresponding to *f* is a logical consequence of the set of propositions corresponding to *S*.

11.9 Claudio L. Lucchesi and Sylvia L. Osborn: "Candidate Keys for Relations," *J. Comp. and Sys. Sciences 17*, No. 2 (1978).

Presents an algorithm for finding all candidate keys for a given relvar, given the set of FDs that hold in that relvar.

11.10 David Maier: *The Theory of Relational Databases*. Rockville, Md.: Computer Science Press (1983).

Further Normalization I: 1NF, 2NF, 3NF, BCNF

12.1 INTRODUCTION

Throughout this book so far we have made use of the suppliers-and-parts database as a running example, with logical design as follows (in outline):

```
S   { S#, SNAME, STATUS, CITY }
    PRIMARY KEY { S# }

P   { P#, PNAME, COLOR, WEIGHT, CITY }
    PRIMARY KEY { P# }

SP  { S#, P#, QTY }
    PRIMARY KEY { S#, P# }
    FOREIGN KEY { S# } REFERENCES S
    FOREIGN KEY { P# } REFERENCES P
```

Note: As these definitions suggest, we assume in this chapter (until further notice) that relvars always have a primary key specifically.

Now, this design does have a feeling of rightness about it: It is "obvious" that three relvars S, P, and SP are necessary, and it is also "obvious" that the supplier CITY attribute belongs in relvar S, the part COLOR attribute belongs in relvar P, the shipment QTY attribute belongs in relvar SP, and so on. But what is it that tells us these things are so? Some insight into this question can be gained by seeing what happens if we change the design in some way. Suppose, for example, that we move the supplier CITY attribute out of the suppliers relvar and into the shipments relvar (intuitively the wrong place for it, since "supplier city" obviously concerns suppliers, not shipments). Fig. 12.1, a variation on Fig. 11.1 from Chapter 11, shows a sample value for this revised shipments relvar. *Note:* In order to avoid confusion with our usual shipments relvar SP, we will refer to this revised version as SCP, as we did in Chapter 11.

A glance at Fig. 12.1 is sufficient to show what is wrong with this design: **redundancy**. To be specific, every SCP tuple for supplier S1 tells us S1 is located in London, every SCP tuple for supplier S2 tells us S2 is located in Paris, and so on. More generally, the fact that a given supplier is located in a given city is stated as many times as there are shipments for that supplier. This redundancy in turn leads to several further problems. For example, after an update, supplier S1 might be shown as being located in London according to one tuple and in Amsterdam according to another.[1] So perhaps a good design principle is "one fact in one place" (i.e., avoid redundancy). *The subject of further normalization is essentially just a formalization of simple ideas like this one*—a formalization, however, that does have very practical application to the problem of database design.

Of course, relation values are always normalized as far as the relational model is concerned, as we saw in Chapter 6. As for relation variables (relvars), we can say that

SCP	S#	CITY	P#	QTY
	S1	London	P1	300
	S1	London	P2	200
	S1	London	P3	400
	S1	London	P4	200
	S1	London	P5	100
	S1	London	P6	100
	S2	Paris	P1	300
	S2	Paris	P2	400
	S3	Paris	P2	200
	S4	London	P2	200
	S4	London	P4	300
	S4	London	P5	400

Fig. 12.1   Sample value for relvar SCP

---

[1] Throughout this chapter and the next, it is necessary to assume (realistically enough!) that relvar predicates are not being fully enforced—for if they were, problems such as this one could not possibly arise (it would not be possible to update the city for supplier S1 in some tuples and not in others). In fact, one way to think about the normalization discipline is as follows: It helps us structure the database in such a way as to make more single-tuple updates logically acceptable than would otherwise be the case (i.e., if the design were not fully normalized). This goal is achieved because the predicates are simpler if the design is fully normalized than they would be otherwise.

they are normalized too as long as their legal values are normalized relations; thus, relvars are always normalized too as far as the relational model is concerned. Equivalently, we can say that relvars (and relations) are always in **first normal form** (abbreviated 1NF). In other words, "normalized" and "1NF" mean *exactly the same thing*—though you should be aware that the term *normalized* is often used to mean one of the higher levels of normalization (typically *third* normal form, 3NF); this latter usage is sloppy but very common.

Now, a given relvar might be normalized in the foregoing sense and yet still possess certain undesirable properties. Relvar SCP is a case in point (see Fig. 12.1). The principles of further normalization allow us to recognize such cases and to replace the relvars in question by ones that are more desirable in some way. In the case of relvar SCP, for example, those principles would tell us precisely what is wrong with that relvar, and they would tell us how to replace it by two "more desirable" relvars, one with attributes S# and CITY and the other with attributes S#, P#, and QTY.

Normal Forms

The process of further normalization—hereinafter abbreviated to just *normalization*—is built around the concept of **normal forms**. A relvar is said to be in a particular normal form if it satisfies a certain prescribed set of conditions. For example, a relvar is said to be in second normal form (2NF) if and only if it is in 1NF and also satisfies another condition, to be discussed in Section 12.3.

Many normal forms have been defined (see Fig. 12.2). The first three (1NF, 2NF, 3NF) were defined by Codd in reference [11.6]. As Fig. 12.2 suggests, all normalized relvars are in 1NF; some 1NF relvars are also in 2NF; and some 2NF relvars are also in 3NF. The motivation behind Codd's definitions was that 2NF was more desirable (in a sense to be explained) than 1NF, and 3NF in turn was more desirable than 2NF. Thus, the database designer should generally aim for a design involving relvars in 3NF, not ones that are merely in 2NF or 1NF.

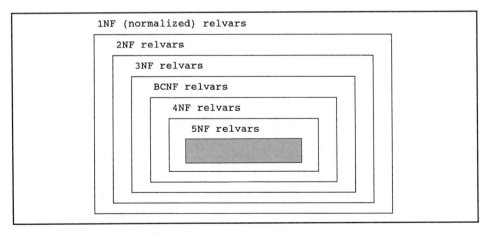

Fig. 12.2   Levels of normalization

Reference [11.6] also introduced the idea of a procedure, the **normalization proce-dure**, by which a relvar that happens to be in some given normal form, say 2NF, can be replaced by a set of relvars in some more desirable form, say 3NF. (The procedure as originally defined only went as far as 3NF, but it was subsequently extended all the way to 5NF, as we will see in the next chapter.) We can characterize that procedure as *the suc-cessive reduction of a given collection of relvars to some more desirable form.* Note that the procedure is **reversible**; that is, it is always possible to take the output from the pro-cedure (say the set of 3NF relvars) and map it back to the input (say the original 2NF rel-var). Reversibility is important, because it means the normalization process is **nonloss** or **information-preserving**.

To return to the topic of normal forms *per se:* Codd's original definition of 3NF as given in reference [11.6] turned out to suffer from certain inadequacies, as we will see in Section 12.5. A revised and stronger definition, due to Boyce and Codd, was given in ref-erence [12.2]—stronger, in the sense that any relvar that was in 3NF by the new definition was certainly in 3NF by the old, but a relvar could be in 3NF by the old definition and not by the new. The new 3NF is now usually referred to as **Boyce/Codd** normal form (BCNF) in order to distinguish it from the old form.

Subsequently, Fagin [13.14] defined a new "**fourth**" normal form (4NF—"fourth" because at that time BCNF was still being called "third"). And in reference [13.15] Fagin defined yet another normal form, which he called **projection-join** normal form (PJ/NF, also known as "**fifth**" normal form or 5NF). As Fig. 12.2 shows, some BCNF relvars are also in 4NF, and some 4NF relvars are also in 5NF.

By now you might well be wondering whether there is any end to this progression, and whether there might be a 6NF, a 7NF, and so on *ad infinitum.* Although this is a good question to ask, we are obviously not yet in a position to give it detailed consideration. We content ourselves with the rather equivocal statement that there are indeed additional nor-mal forms not shown in Fig. 12.2, but 5NF is the "final" normal form in a special (but important) sense. We will return to this question in Chapter 13.

Structure of the Chapter

The aim of this chapter is to examine the concepts of further normalization, up to and including Boyce/Codd normal form (we leave the others to Chapter 13). The plan of the chapter is as follows. Following this lengthy introduction, Section 12.2 discusses the basic concept of *nonloss decomposition,* and demonstrates the crucial importance of functional dependence to this concept (indeed, functional dependence forms the basis for Codd's original three normal forms, as well as for BCNF). Section 12.3 then describes the original three normal forms, showing by example how a given relvar can be carried through the normalization procedure as far as 3NF. Section 12.4 digresses slightly to consider the question of *alternative decompositions*—that is, the question of choosing the "best" decomposition of a given relvar, when there is a choice. Next, Section 12.5 discusses BCNF. Finally, Section 12.6 provides a summary and offers a few concluding remarks.

Caveat: You are warned that we make little attempt at rigor in what follows; rather, we rely to a considerable extent on plain intuition. Indeed, part of the point is that concepts such as nonloss decomposition, BCNF, and so on, despite the somewhat esoteric terminology, are essentially very simple and commonsense ideas. Most of the references treat the material in a much more formal and rigorous manner. A good tutorial can be found in reference [12.5].

Two final introductory remarks:

1. As already suggested, the general idea of normalization is that the database designer should aim for relvars in the "ultimate" normal form (5NF). However, this recommendation should not be construed as law; occasionally—*very* occasionally!—there might be good reasons for flouting the principles of normalization (see, e.g., Exercise 12.7 at the end of the chapter). Indeed, this is as good a place as any to make the point that database design can be an extremely complex task. Normalization is a useful aid in the process, but it is not a panacea; thus, anyone designing a database is certainly advised to be familiar with normalization principles, but we do not claim that the design process should be based on those principles alone. Chapter 14 discusses a number of other aspects of design that have little or nothing to do with normalization as such.

2. As already indicated, we will be using the normalization procedure as a basis for introducing and discussing the various normal forms. However, we do not mean to suggest that database design is actually done by applying that procedure in practice; in fact, it probably is not—it is much more likely that some top-down scheme will be used instead (see Chapter 14). The ideas of normalization can then be used to *verify* that the resulting design does not unintentionally violate any of the normalization principles. Nevertheless, the normalization procedure does provide a convenient framework in which to describe those principles. For the purposes of this chapter, therefore, we adopt the useful fiction that we are indeed carrying out the design process by applying that procedure.

12.2 NONLOSS DECOMPOSITION AND FUNCTIONAL DEPENDENCIES

Before we can get into the specifics of the normalization procedure, we need to examine one crucial aspect of that procedure more closely: namely, the concept of **nonloss** (also called **lossless**) **decomposition**. We have seen that the normalization procedure involves decomposing a given relvar into other relvars, and moreover that the decomposition is required to be reversible, so that no information is lost in the process; in other words, the only decompositions we are interested in are ones that are indeed nonloss. As we will see, the question of whether a given decomposition is nonloss is intimately bound up with the concept of functional dependence.

	S	S#	STATUS	CITY
		S3	30	Paris
		S5	30	Athens

(a)	SST	S#	STATUS		SC	S#	CITY
		S3	30			S3	Paris
		S5	30			S5	Athens

(b)	SST	S#	STATUS		STC	STATUS	CITY
		S3	30			30	Paris
		S5	30			30	Athens

Fig. 12.3   Sample value for relvar S and two corresponding decompositions

By way of example, consider the familiar suppliers relvar S, with attributes S#, STATUS, and CITY (for simplicity, we ignore attribute SNAME until further notice). Fig. 12.3 shows a sample value for this relvar and—in the parts of the figure labeled *a* and *b*—two possible decompositions corresponding to that sample value.

Examining the two decompositions, we observe that:

1. In Case *a,* no information is lost; the SST and SC values still tell us that supplier S3 has status 30 and city Paris, and supplier S5 has status 30 and city Athens. In other words, this first decomposition is indeed nonloss.

2. In Case *b,* by contrast, information definitely is lost; we can still tell that both suppliers have status 30, but we cannot tell which supplier has which city. In other words, the second decomposition is not nonloss but **lossy**.

What exactly is it here that makes the first decomposition nonloss and the other lossy? Well, observe first that the process we have been referring to as "decomposition" is actually a process of *projection;* SST, SC, and STC in the figure are each projections of the original relvar S. So the decomposition operator in the normalization procedure is **projection**. *Note:* As in Part II of this book, we often say things like "SST is a projection of relvar S" when what we should more correctly be saying is "SST is a relvar whose value at any given time is a projection of the relation that is the value of relvar S at that time." We hope these shorthands will not cause any confusion.

Observe next that when we say in Case *a* that no information is lost, what we mean, more precisely, is that *if we join SST and SC back together again, we get back to the original S.* In Case *b,* by contrast, if we join SST and SC together again, we do *not* get back the original S, and so we have lost information.[2] In other words, "reversibility" means, pre-

---

[2] To be more specific, we get back all of the tuples in the original S, together with some additional "spurious" tuples; we can never get back anything *less* than the original S. (*Exercise:* Prove this statement.) Since we have no way in general of knowing which tuples in the result are spurious and which genuine, we have indeed lost information.

cisely, that *the original relvar is equal to the join of its projections*. Thus, just as the decomposition operator for normalization purposes is projection, so the *re*composition operator is **join**.

So the interesting question is this: If *R1* and *R2* are both projections of some relvar *R*, and *R1* and *R2* between them include all of the attributes of *R*, what conditions must be satisfied in order to guarantee that joining *R1* and *R2* back together takes us back to the original *R?* And this is where functional dependencies come in. Returning to our example, observe that relvar S satisfies the irreducible set of FDs:

```
S# → STATUS
S# → CITY
```

Given the fact that it satisfies these FDs, it surely cannot be coincidence that relvar S is equal to the join of its projections on {S#,STATUS} and {S#,CITY}—and of course it is not. In fact, we have the following theorem (due to Heath [12.4]):

- **Heath's theorem:** Let $R\{A,B,C\}$ be a relvar, where *A*, *B*, and *C* are sets of attributes. If *R* satisfies the FD $A \rightarrow B$, then *R* is equal to the join of its projections on $\{A,B\}$ and $\{A,C\}$.

Taking *A* as S#, *B* as STATUS, and *C* as CITY, this theorem confirms what we have already observed: namely, that relvar S can be nonloss-decomposed into its projections on {S#,STATUS} and {S#,CITY}. At the same time, we also know that relvar S *cannot* be nonloss-decomposed into its projections on {S#,STATUS} and {STATUS,CITY}. Heath's theorem does not explain why this is so;[3] intuitively, however, we can see that the problem is that *one of the FDs is lost in this latter decomposition*. Specifically, the FD S# → STATUS is still represented (by the projection on {S#,STATUS}), but the FD S# → CITY has been lost.

To sum up, then, we can say that the decomposition of relvar *R* into projections *R1*, *R2*, ..., *Rn* is **nonloss** if *R* is equal to the join of *R1*, *R2*, ..., *Rn*. *Note:* In practice we would probably want to impose the additional requirement that *R1*, *R2*, ..., *Rn* are all needed in the join, in order to guarantee that certain redundancies that might otherwise occur are avoided. For example, we probably would not want to consider the decomposition of relvar S into its projections on (say) {S#}, {S#,STATUS}, and {S#,CITY} as a nonloss decomposition, yet S is certainly equal to the join of those three projections. For simplicity, let us agree from this point forward that this additional requirement is always in force, barring explicit statements to the contrary.

More on Functional Dependencies

We conclude this section with a few additional remarks concerning FDs.

1. **Irreducibility:** Recall from Chapter 11 that an FD is said to be **left-irreducible** if its left side is "not too big." For example, consider relvar SCP once again from Section 12.1. That relvar satisfies the FD

---

[3] It does not do so because it is of the form "if . . . then . . . ," not "if *and only if* . . . then . . . " (see Exercise 12.1 at the end of the chapter). We will be discussing a stronger form of Heath's theorem in Chapter 13, Section 13.2.

```
{ S#, P# } → CITY
```

However, attribute P# on the left side here is redundant for functional dependency purposes; that is, we also have the FD

```
S# → CITY
```

(CITY is also functionally dependent on S# alone). This latter FD is left-irreducible, but the previous one is not; equivalently, CITY is **irreducibly dependent** on S#, but not irreducibly dependent on {S#,P#}.[4] Left-irreducible FDs and irreducible dependencies will turn out to be important in the definition of the second and third normal forms (see Section 12.3).

2. **FD diagrams:** Let *R* be a relvar and let *I* be some irreducible set of FDs that apply to *R* (again, refer to Chapter 11 if you need to refresh your memory regarding irreducible sets of FDs). It is convenient to represent the set *I* by means of a *functional dependency diagram* (FD diagram). FD diagrams for relvars S, SP, and P—which should be self-explanatory—are given in Fig. 12.4. We will make frequent use of such diagrams throughout the rest of this chapter.

   Now, you will observe that every arrow in Fig. 12.4 is an *arrow out of a candidate key* (actually the primary key) of the relevant relvar. By definition, there will always be arrows out of each candidate key,[5] because, for one value of each candidate key, there is always one value of everything else; those arrows can never be eliminated. *It is if there are any other arrows that difficulties arise.* Thus, the normalization procedure can be characterized, very informally, as a procedure for eliminating arrows that are not arrows out of candidate keys.

3. **FDs are a semantic notion:** As noted in Chapter 11, FDs are really a special kind of integrity constraint. As such, they are definitely a *semantic* notion (in fact, they are

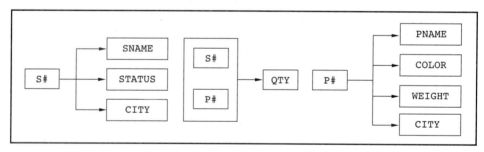

Fig. 12.4   FD diagrams for relvars S, SP, and P

---

[4] *Left-irreducible FD* and *irreducibly dependent* are our preferred terms for what are more usually called "**full** FD" and "**fully** dependent" in the literature (and were so called in the first few editions of this book). These latter terms have the merit of brevity but are less descriptive and less apt.

[5] More precisely, there will always be arrows out of *superkeys*. If the set *I* of FDs is irreducible as stated, however, all FDs (or "arrows") in *I* will be left-irreducible.

part of the relvar predicate). Recognizing the FDs is part of the process of understanding what the data *means;* the fact that relvar S satisfies the FD S# → CITY, for example, means that each supplier is located in precisely one city. To look at this another way:

- There is a constraint in the real world that the database represents: namely, that each supplier is located in precisely one city.

- Since it is part of the semantics of the situation, that constraint must somehow be observed in the database.

- The way to ensure that it is so observed is to specify it in the database definition, so that the DBMS can enforce it.

- The way to specify it in the database definition is to declare the FD.

And we will see later that the concepts of normalization lead to a very simple means of declaring FDs.

12.3   FIRST, SECOND, AND THIRD NORMAL FORMS

Caveat: Throughout this section, we assume for simplicity that each relvar has exactly one candidate key, which we further assume is the primary key. These assumptions are reflected in our definitions, which (we repeat) are not very rigorous. The case of a relvar having more than one candidate key is discussed in Section 12.5.

We are now in a position to describe Codd's original three normal forms. We present a preliminary, very informal, definition of 3NF first in order to give some idea of what we are aiming for. We then consider the process of reducing an arbitrary relvar to an equivalent collection of 3NF relvars, giving somewhat more precise definitions as we go. However, we note at the outset that 1NF, 2NF, and 3NF are not very significant in themselves except as stepping-stones to BCNF (and beyond).

Here then is our preliminary 3NF definition:

- **Third normal form** *(very informal definition):* A relvar is in 3NF if and only if the nonkey attributes (if any) are both:

   a. Mutually independent

   b. Irreducibly dependent on the primary key

   We explain the terms *nonkey attribute* and *mutually independent* (loosely) as follows:

- A *nonkey attribute* is any attribute that does not participate in the primary key of the relvar concerned.

- Two or more attributes are *mutually independent* if none of them is functionally dependent on any combination of the others. Such independence implies that each attribute can be updated independently of the rest.

By way of example, the parts relvar P is in 3NF according to the foregoing definition: Attributes PNAME, COLOR, WEIGHT, and CITY are all independent of one another (it is possible to change, e.g., the color of a part without simultaneously having to change its weight), and they are all irreducibly dependent on the primary key {P#}.

The foregoing informal definition of 3NF can be interpreted, even more informally, as follows:

■ **Third normal form** *(even more informal definition):* A relvar is in third normal form (3NF) if and only if, for all time, each tuple consists of a primary key value that identifies some entity, together with a set of zero or more mutually independent attribute values that describe that entity in some way.

Again, relvar P fits the definition: Each tuple of P consists of a primary key value (a part number) that identifies some part in the real world, together with four additional values (part name, part color, part weight, part city), each of which serves to describe that part, and each of which is independent of all of the others.

Now we turn to the normalization procedure. We begin with a definition of first normal form:

■ **First normal form:** A relvar is in 1NF if and only if, in every legal value of that relvar, every tuple contains exactly one value for each attribute.

This definition merely states that relvars are always in 1NF, which is of course correct. However, a relvar that is *only* in first normal form—that is, a 1NF relvar that is not also in 2NF, and therefore not in 3NF either—has a structure that is undesirable for a number of reasons. To illustrate the point, let us suppose that information concerning suppliers and shipments, rather than being split into the two relvars S and SP, is lumped together into a single relvar as follows:

```
FIRST { S#, STATUS, CITY, P#, QTY }
    PRIMARY KEY { S#, P# }
```

This relvar is an extended version of SCP from Section 12.1. The attributes have their usual meanings, except that for the sake of the example we introduce an additional constraint:

```
CITY → STATUS
```

(STATUS is functionally dependent on CITY; the meaning of this constraint is that a supplier's status is determined by the location of that supplier—e.g., all London suppliers *must* have a status of 20). Also, we ignore SNAME again, for simplicity. The primary key of FIRST is the combination {S#,P#}; the FD diagram is shown in Fig. 12.5.

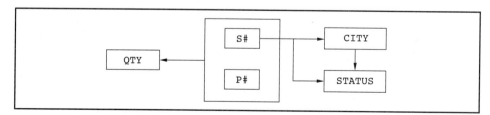

Fig. 12.5   FDs for relvar FIRST

Observe that this FD diagram is, informally, "more complex" than the FD diagram for a 3NF relvar. As indicated in the previous section, a 3NF diagram has arrows out of candidate keys only, whereas a non3NF diagram such as that for FIRST has arrows out of candidate keys *together with certain additional arrows*—and it is those additional arrows that cause the trouble. In fact, relvar FIRST violates both conditions *a* and *b* in our preliminary 3NF definition: The nonkey attributes are not all mutually independent, because STATUS depends on CITY (one additional arrow), and they are not all irreducibly dependent on the primary key, because STATUS and CITY are each dependent on S# alone (two more additional arrows).

As a basis for illustrating some of the difficulties that arise from those additional arrows, Fig. 12.6 shows a sample value for relvar FIRST. The attribute values are basically as usual, except that the status of supplier S3 has been changed from 30 to 10 to be consistent with the new constraint that CITY determines STATUS. The redundancies are obvious. For example, every tuple for supplier S1 shows the city as London; likewise, every tuple for city London shows the status as 20.

The redundancies in relvar FIRST lead to a variety of what (for historical reasons) are usually called **update anomalies**—that is, difficulties with the update operations INSERT, DELETE, and UPDATE. To fix our ideas, we concentrate first on the supplier-city redundancy, corresponding to the FD S# → CITY. Problems occur with each of the three update operations:

- **INSERT:** We cannot insert the fact that a particular supplier is located in a particular city until that supplier supplies at least one part. Indeed, Fig. 12.6 does not show that supplier S5 is located in Athens. The reason is that, until S5 supplies some part, we have no appropriate primary key value. (As in Chapter 10, Section 10.4, we assume throughout this chapter—reasonably enough—that primary key attributes have no default value. See Chapter 19 for further discussion.)

- **DELETE:** If we delete the sole FIRST tuple for a particular supplier, we delete not only the shipment connecting that supplier to a particular part but also the information that the supplier is located in a particular city. For example, if we delete the

FIRST	S#	STATUS	CITY	P#	QTY
	S1	20	London	P1	300
	S1	20	London	P2	200
	S1	20	London	P3	400
	S1	20	London	P4	200
	S1	20	London	P5	100
	S1	20	London	P6	100
	S2	10	Paris	P1	300
	S2	10	Paris	P2	400
	S3	10	Paris	P2	200
	S4	20	London	P2	200
	S4	20	London	P4	300
	S4	20	London	P5	400

Fig. 12.6 Sample value for relvar FIRST

FIRST tuple with S# value S3 and P# value P2, we lose the information that S3 is located in Paris. (The INSERT and DELETE problems are really two sides of the same coin.)

Note: The real problem here is that relvar FIRST contains too much information all bundled together; hence, when we delete a tuple, *we delete too much.* To be more precise, relvar FIRST contains information regarding shipments *and* information regarding suppliers, and so deleting a shipment causes supplier information to be deleted as well. The solution to this problem is to "unbundle"—that is, to place shipment information in one relvar and supplier information in another (and this is exactly what we will do in just a moment). Thus, another informal way of characterizing the normalization procedure is as an *unbundling* procedure: Place logically separate information into separate relvars.

- **UPDATE:** The city value for a given supplier appears in FIRST many times, in general. This redundancy causes update problems. For example, if supplier S1 moves from London to Amsterdam, we are faced with *either* the problem of searching FIRST to find every tuple connecting S1 and London (and changing it) *or* the possibility of producing an inconsistent result (the city for S1 might be given as Amsterdam in one tuple and London in another).

The solution to these problems is, as already indicated, to replace relvar FIRST by the two relvars:

```
SECOND { S#, STATUS, CITY }
SP     { S#, P#, QTY }
```

The FD diagrams for these two relvars are given in Fig. 12.7; sample values are given in Fig. 12.8. Observe that information for supplier S5 has now been included (in relvar SECOND but not in relvar SP). In fact, relvar SP is now exactly our usual shipments relvar.

It should be clear that this revised structure overcomes all of the problems with update operations sketched earlier:

- **INSERT:** We can insert the information that S5 is located in Athens, even though S5 does not currently supply any parts, by simply inserting the appropriate tuple into SECOND.

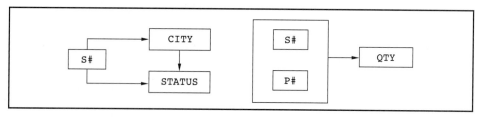

Fig. 12.7 FDs for relvars SECOND and SP

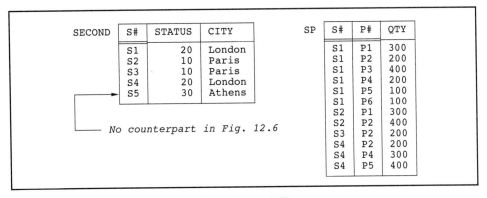

Fig. 12.8 Sample values for relvars SECOND and SP

- **DELETE:** We can delete the shipment connecting S3 and P2 by deleting the appropriate tuple from SP; we do not lose the information that S3 is located in Paris.

- **UPDATE:** In the revised structure, the city for a given supplier appears just once, not many times, because there is precisely one tuple for a given supplier in relvar SECOND (the primary key for that relvar is {S#}); in other words, the S#-CITY redundancy has been eliminated. Thus, we can change the city for S1 from London to Amsterdam by changing it once and for all in the relevant SECOND tuple.

Comparing Figs. 12.5 and 12.7, we see that the effect of the decomposition of FIRST into SECOND and SP has been to eliminate the dependencies that were not irreducible, and it is that elimination that has resolved the difficulties. Intuitively, we can say that in relvar FIRST the attribute CITY did not describe the entity identified by the primary key (i.e., a shipment); instead, it described the supplier involved in that shipment (and likewise for attribute STATUS). Mixing the two kinds of information in the same relvar was what caused the problems in the first place.

We now give a definition of second normal form:[6]

- **Second normal form** *(definition assuming only one candidate key, which we assume is the primary key):* A relvar is in 2NF if and only if it is in 1NF and every nonkey attribute is irreducibly dependent on the primary key.

Relvars SECOND and SP are both in 2NF (the primary keys are {S#} and the combination {S#,P#}, respectively). Relvar FIRST is not in 2NF. A relvar that is in first normal form and not in second can always be reduced to an equivalent collection of 2NF relvars. The reduction process consists of replacing the 1NF relvar by suitable projections; the collection of projections so obtained is equivalent to the original relvar, in the sense that the original relvar can always be recovered by joining those projections back together

---

[6] Strictly speaking, 2NF can be defined only *with respect to a specified set of dependencies,* but it is usual to ignore this point in informal discussion. Analogous remarks apply to all of the normal forms other than first.

again. In our example, SECOND and SP are projections of FIRST,[7] and FIRST is the join of SECOND and SP over S#.

To summarize, the first step in the normalization procedure is to take projections to eliminate "nonirreducible" functional dependencies. Thus, given relvar *R* as follows—

```
R { A, B, C, D }
   PRIMARY KEY { A, B }
   /* assume A → D holds */
```

—the normalization discipline recommends replacing *R* by its two projections *R1* and *R2,* as follows:

```
R1 { A, D }
   PRIMARY KEY { A }

R2 { A, B, C }
   PRIMARY KEY { A, B }
   FOREIGN KEY { A } REFERENCES R1
```

R can be recovered by taking the foreign-to-matching-primary-key join of *R2* and *R1.*

To return to the example: The SECOND-SP structure still causes problems, however. Relvar SP is satisfactory; as a matter of fact, relvar SP is now in 3NF, and we will ignore it for the rest of this section. Relvar SECOND, on the other hand, still suffers from a lack of mutual independence among its nonkey attributes. The FD diagram for SECOND is still "more complex" than a 3NF diagram. To be specific, the dependency of STATUS on S#, though it is functional, and indeed irreducible, is **transitive** (via CITY): Each S# value determines a CITY value, and that CITY value in turn determines the STATUS value. More generally, whenever the FDs $A \rightarrow B$ and $B \rightarrow C$ both hold, then it is a logical consequence that the transitive FD $A \rightarrow C$ holds also, as explained in Chapter 11. And transitive dependencies lead, once again, to update anomalies (we concentrate now on the city-status redundancy, corresponding to the FD CITY $\rightarrow$ STATUS):

- **INSERT:** We cannot insert the fact that a particular city has a particular status—for example, we cannot state that any supplier in Rome must have a status of 50—until we have some supplier actually located in that city.

- **DELETE:** If we delete the sole SECOND tuple for a particular city, we delete not only the information for the supplier concerned but also the information that that city has that particular status. For example, if we delete the SECOND tuple for S5, we lose the information that the status for Athens is 30. (Again, the INSERT and DELETE problems are really two sides of the same coin.)

    Note: The problem is bundling again, of course: Relvar SECOND contains information regarding suppliers *and* information regarding cities. And again the solution is to "unbundle"—that is, to place supplier information in one relvar and city information in another.

---

[7] Except for the fact that SECOND can include tuples, such as the tuple for supplier S5 in Fig. 12.8, that have no counterpart in FIRST; in other words, the new structure can represent information that could not be represented in the previous one. In this sense, the new structure can be regarded as a slightly more faithful representation of the real world.

- **UPDATE:** The status for a given city appears in SECOND many times, in general (the relvar still contains some redundancy). Thus, if we need to change the status for London from 20 to 30, we are faced with *either* the problem of searching SECOND to find every tuple for London (and changing it) *or* the possibility of producing an inconsistent result (the status for London might be given as 20 in one tuple and 30 in another).

Again the solution to the problems is to replace the original relvar (SECOND, in this case) by two projections—namely, the projections:

```
SC { S#, CITY }
CS { CITY, STATUS }
```

The FD diagrams for these two relvars are given in Fig. 12.9; sample values are given in Fig. 12.10. Observe that status information for Rome has been included in relvar CS. The reduction is reversible once again, since SECOND is the join of SC and CS over CITY.

It should be clear, again, that this revised structure overcomes all of the problems with update operations sketched earlier. Detailed consideration of those problems is left as an exercise. Comparing Figs. 12.7 and 12.9, we see that the effect of the further decomposition is to eliminate the transitive dependence of STATUS on S#, and again it is that elimination that has resolved the difficulties. Intuitively, we can say that in relvar SECOND the attribute STATUS did not describe the entity identified by the primary key (i.e., a supplier); instead, it described the city in which that supplier happened to be located. Once again, mixing the two kinds of information in the same relvar was what caused the problems.

We now give a definition of third normal form:

- **Third normal form** *(definition assuming only one candidate key, which we further assume is the primary key):* A relvar is in 3NF if and only if it is in 2NF and every nonkey attribute is nontransitively dependent on the primary key.

Fig. 12.9   FDs for relvars SC and CS

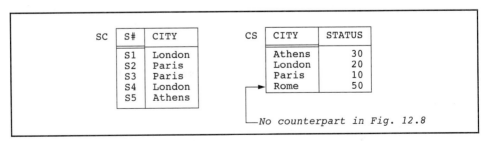

Fig. 12.10   Sample values for relvars SC and CS

(Note that "no transitive dependencies" implies no *mutual* dependencies, in the sense of that term explained near the beginning of this section.)

Relvars SC and CS are both in 3NF (the primary keys are {S#} and {CITY}, respectively). Relvar SECOND is not in 3NF. A relvar that is in second normal form and not in third can always be reduced to an equivalent collection of 3NF relvars. We have already indicated that the process is reversible, and hence that no information is lost in the reduction; however, the 3NF collection can contain information, such as the fact that the status for Rome is 50, that could not be represented in the original 2NF relvar.[8]

To summarize, the second step in the normalization procedure is to take projections to eliminate transitive dependencies. In other words, given relvar *R* as follows—

```
R { A, B, C }
   PRIMARY KEY { A }
   /* assume B → C holds */
```

—the normalization discipline recommends replacing *R* by its two projections *R1* and *R2*, as follows:

```
R1 { B, C }
   PRIMARY KEY { B }

R2 { A, B }
   PRIMARY KEY { A }
   FOREIGN KEY { B } REFERENCES R1
```

R can be recovered by taking the foreign-to-matching-primary-key join of *R2* and *R1*.

We conclude this section by stressing the point that the level of normalization of a given relvar is a matter of semantics, not merely a matter of the value that relvar happens to have at some particular time. In other words, it is not possible just to look at the value at a given time and to say whether the relvar is in (say) 3NF—it is also necessary to know the dependencies before such a judgment can be made. Note too that even knowing the dependencies, it is never possible to *prove* by examining a given value that the relvar is in 3NF. The best that can be done is to show that the value in question does not violate any of the dependencies; assuming it does not, then the value is *consistent with the hypothesis* that the relvar is in 3NF, but that fact does not guarantee that the hypothesis is valid.

12.4 DEPENDENCY PRESERVATION

It is frequently the case that a given relvar can be nonloss-decomposed in a variety of different ways. Consider the relvar SECOND from Section 12.3 once again, with FDs S# → CITY and CITY → STATUS and therefore also, by transitivity, S# → STATUS (refer to Fig. 12.11, in which the transitive FD is shown as a broken arrow). We showed in Section 12.3 that the update anomalies encountered with SECOND could be overcome by replacing it by its decomposition into the two 3NF projections:

```
SC { S#, CITY }
```

---

[8] It follows that, just as the SECOND-SP combination was a slightly better representation of the real world than the 1NF relvar FIRST, so the SC-CS combination is a slightly better representation than the 2NF relvar SECOND.

```
CS { CITY, STATUS }
```

Let us refer to this decomposition as Decomposition *A.* Here by contrast is an alternative decomposition (Decomposition *B*):

```
SC { S#, CITY }
SS { S#, STATUS }
```

(projection SC is the same in both cases). Decomposition *B* is also nonloss, and the two projections are again both in 3NF. But Decomposition *B* is less satisfactory than Decomposition *A* for a number of reasons. For example, it is still not possible in *B* to insert the information that a particular city has a particular status unless some supplier is located in that city.

Let us examine this example a little more closely. First, note that the projections in Decomposition *A* correspond to the *solid* arrows in Fig. 12.11, whereas one of the projections in Decomposition *B* corresponds to the *broken* arrow. In Decomposition *A,* in fact, the two projections are **independent** of one another, in the following sense: Updates can be made to either one without regard for the other.[9] Provided only that such an update is legal within the context of the projection concerned—which means only that it must not violate the primary key uniqueness constraint for that projection— then *the join of the two projections after the update will always be a valid SECOND* (i.e., the join cannot possibly violate the FD constraints on SECOND). In Decomposition *B,* by contrast, updates to either of the two projections must be monitored to ensure that the FD CITY → STATUS is not violated (if two suppliers have the same city, then they must have the same status; consider, for example, what is involved in Decomposition *B* in moving supplier S1 from London to Paris). In other words, the two projections are not independent of each other in Decomposition *B.*

The basic problem is that, in Decomposition *B,* the FD CITY → STATUS has become—to use the terminology of Chapter 9—a *database constraint* that spans two relvars (implying, incidentally, that in many of today's products it will have to be maintained by procedural code). In Decomposition *A,* by contrast, it is the *transitive* FD S# → STATUS that has become the database constraint, and that constraint will be enforced automatically if the two *relvar* constraints S# → CITY and CITY → STATUS are enforced. And enforcing these two latter constraints is very simple, of course, involving as it does nothing more than enforcing the corresponding primary key uniqueness constraints.

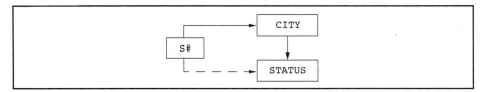

Fig. 12.11   FDs for relvar SECOND

---

[9] Except for the referential constraint from SC to CS.

The concept of independent projections thus provides a guideline for choosing a particular decomposition when there is more than one possibility. Specifically, a decomposition in which the projections are independent in the foregoing sense is generally preferable to one in which they are not. Rissanen shows in reference [12.6] that projections *R1* and *R2* of a relvar *R* are independent in the foregoing sense if and only if both of the following are true:

■ Every FD in *R* is a logical consequence of those in *R1* and *R2*.

■ The common attributes of *R1* and *R2* form a candidate key for at least one of the pair.

Consider Decompositions *A* and *B* as defined earlier. In *A* the two projections are independent, because their common attribute CITY constitutes the primary key for CS, and every FD in SECOND either appears in one of the two projections or is a logical consequence of those that do. In *B*, by contrast, the two projections are not independent, because the FD CITY → STATUS cannot be deduced from the FDs for those projections—although it is true that their common attribute, S#, does constitute a candidate key for both. *Note:* The third possibility, replacing SECOND by its two projections on {S#,STATUS} and {CITY,STATUS}, is not a valid decomposition, because it is not non-loss. *Exercise:* Prove this statement.

Reference [12.6] calls a relvar that cannot be decomposed into independent projections **atomic** (not a terribly good term). Note carefully, however, that the fact that some given relvar is not atomic in this sense should not necessarily be taken to mean that it should be decomposed into atomic components; for example, relvars S and P of the suppliers-and-parts database are not atomic, but there seems little point in decomposing them further. (Relvar SP, by contrast, *is* atomic.)

The idea that the normalization procedure should decompose relvars into projections that are independent in Rissanen's sense has come to be known as **dependency preservation**. We close this section by explaining this concept more precisely:

1. Suppose we are given some relvar *R*, which (after we have applied all steps of the normalization procedure) we replace by a set of projections *R1, R2, ..., Rn*.

2. Let the set of given FDs for the original relvar *R* be *S*, and let the sets of FDs that apply to relvars *R1, R2, ..., Rn* be *S1, S2, ..., Sn*, respectively.

3. Each FD in the set *Si* will refer to attributes of *Ri* only (*i* = 1, 2, ..., *n*). Enforcing the constraints (FDs) in any given set *Si* is thus a simple matter. But what we need to do is to enforce the constraints in the original set *S*. We would therefore like the decomposition into *R1, R2, ..., Rn* to be such that enforcing the constraints in *S1, S2, ..., Sn* individually is together equivalent to enforcing the constraints in the original set *S*—in other words, we would like the decomposition to be *dependency-preserving*.

4. Let *S'* be the union of *S1, S2, ..., Sn*. Note that it is *not* the case that *S'* = *S*, in general; in order for the decomposition to be dependency-preserving, however, it is sufficient that the *closures* of *S* and *S'* be equal (refer back to Chapter 11, Section 11.4, if you need to refresh your memory regarding the notion of the closure of a set of FDs).

5. There is no efficient way of computing the closure S^+ of a set of FDs, in general, so actually computing the two closures and testing them for equality is infeasible.

Nevertheless, there *is* an efficient way of testing whether a given decomposition is dependency-preserving. Details of the algorithm are beyond the scope of this chapter; see, for example, reference [8.13] for the specifics.

Here for purposes of future reference is a nine-step algorithm by which an arbitrary relvar *R* can be nonloss-decomposed, in a dependency-preserving way, into a set *D* of 3NF projections. Let the set of FDs satisfied by *R* be *S*. Then:

1. Initialize *D* to the empty set.
2. Let *I* be an irreducible cover for *S*.
3. Let *X* be a set of attributes appearing on the left side of some FD $X \rightarrow Y$ in *I*.
4. Let the complete set of FDs in *I* with left side *X* be $X \rightarrow Y1, X \rightarrow Y2, ..., X \rightarrow Yn$.
5. Let the union of *Y1, Y2, ..., Yn* be *Z*.
6. Replace *D* by the union of *D* and the projection of *R* over *X* and *Z*.
7. Repeat Steps 4 through 6 for each distinct *X*.
8. Let *A1, A2, ..., An* be those attributes of *R* (if any) still unaccounted for (i.e., still not included in any relvar in *D*); replace *D* by the union of *D* and the projection of *R* over *A1, A2, ..., An*.
9. If no relvar in *D* includes a candidate key of *R*, replace *D* by the union of *D* and the projection of *R* over some candidate key of *R*.

12.5 BOYCE/CODD NORMAL FORM

In this section we drop our assumption that every relvar has just one candidate key and consider what happens in the general case. The fact is, Codd's original definition of 3NF in reference [11.6] did not treat the general case satisfactorily. To be precise, it did not adequately deal with the case of a relvar that

1. Had two or more candidate keys, such that
2. The candidate keys were composite, and
3. They overlapped (i.e., had at least one attribute in common).

The original definition of 3NF was therefore subsequently replaced by a stronger definition, due to Boyce and Codd, that catered for this case also [12.2]. However, since that new definition actually defines a normal form that is strictly stronger than the old 3NF, it is better to use a different name for it, instead of just continuing to call it 3NF; hence the name *Boyce/Codd normal form* (BCNF).[10] *Note:* The combination of conditions 1, 2, and 3 might not occur very often in practice. For a relvar where it does not, 3NF and BCNF are equivalent.

In order to explain BCNF, we first remind you of the term *determinant*, introduced in Chapter 11 to refer to the left side of an FD. We also remind you of the term *trivial FD*,

---

[10] A definition of "third" normal form that was in fact equivalent to the BCNF definition was first given by Heath in 1971 [12.4]; "Heath normal form" might thus have been a more appropriate name.

which is an FD in which the left side is a superset of the right side. Now we can define BCNF:

- **Boyce/Codd normal form:** A relvar is in BCNF if and only if every nontrivial, left-irreducible FD has a candidate key as its determinant.

Or less formally:

- **Boyce/Codd normal form** *(informal definition):* A relvar is in BCNF if and only if every determinant is a candidate key.

In other words, the only arrows in the FD diagram are arrows out of candidate keys. We have already explained that there will always be arrows out of candidate keys; the BCNF definition says *there are no other arrows,* meaning there are no arrows that can be eliminated by the normalization procedure. *Note:* The difference between the two BCNF definitions is that we tacitly assume in the informal case (a) that determinants are "not too big" and (b) that all FDs are nontrivial. In the interest of simplicity, we will continue to make these same assumptions throughout the rest of this chapter, barring explicit statements to the contrary.

It is worth pointing out that the BCNF definition is conceptually simpler than the old 3NF definition, in that it makes no explicit reference to first and second normal forms as such, nor to the concept of transitive dependence. Furthermore, although (as already stated) BCNF is strictly stronger than 3NF, it is still the case that any given relvar can be nonloss-decomposed into an equivalent collection of BCNF relvars.

Before considering some examples involving more than one candidate key, let us convince ourselves that relvars FIRST and SECOND, which were not in 3NF, are not in BCNF either; also that relvars SP, SC, and CS, which were in 3NF, are also in BCNF. Relvar FIRST contains three determinants, {S#}, {CITY}, and {S#,P#}; of these, only {S#,P#} is a candidate key, so FIRST is not in BCNF. Similarly, SECOND is not in BCNF either, because the determinant {CITY} is not a candidate key. Relvars SP, SC, and CS, on the other hand, are each in BCNF, because in each case the sole candidate key is the only determinant in the relvar.

We now consider an example involving two disjoint—that is, nonoverlapping—candidate keys. Suppose in the usual suppliers relvar S{S#,SNAME,STATUS,CITY} that {S#} and {SNAME} are both candidate keys (i.e., for all time, it is the case that every supplier has a unique supplier number and also a unique supplier name). Assume, however (as elsewhere in this book), that attributes STATUS and CITY are mutually independent—that is, the FD CITY $\rightarrow$ STATUS, which we introduced purely for the purposes of Section 12.3, no longer holds. Then the FD diagram is as shown in Fig. 12.12.

Relvar S is in BCNF. Although the FD diagram does look "more complex" than a 3NF diagram, it is nevertheless still the case that the only determinants are candidate keys; that is, the only arrows are arrows out of candidate keys. So the message of this first example is just that having more than one candidate key is not necessarily bad.

Now we present some examples in which the candidate keys overlap. Two candidate keys overlap if they involve two or more attributes each and have at least one attribute in common. *Note:* In accordance with our discussions on this subject in Chapter 9, we will

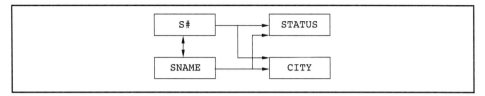

Fig. 12.12 FDs for relvar S if {SNAME} is a candidate key (and CITY → STATUS does not hold)

not attempt to choose one of the candidate keys as the primary key in any of the examples that follow. We will therefore also not mark any columns with double underlining in our figures in this section.

For our first example, we suppose again that supplier names are unique, and we consider the relvar:

```
SSP { S#, SNAME, P#, QTY }
```

The candidate keys are {S#,P#} and {SNAME,P#}. Is this relvar in BCNF? The answer is no, because it contains two determinants, S# and SNAME, that are not candidate keys for the relvar ({S#} and {SNAME} are both determinants because each determines the other). A sample value for this relvar is shown in Fig. 12.13.

As the figure shows, relvar SSP involves the same kind of redundancies as relvars FIRST and SECOND of Section 12.3 (and relvar SCP of Section 12.1) did, and hence suffers from the same kind of problems as those relvars did. For example, changing the name of supplier S1 from Smith to Robinson leads, once again, either to search problems or to possibly inconsistent results. Yet SSP *is* in 3NF by the old definition, because that definition did not require an attribute to be irreducibly dependent on each candidate key if it was itself a component of some candidate key of the relvar; thus, the fact that SNAME is not irreducibly dependent on {S#,P#} was ignored. *Note:* By "3NF" here we mean 3NF as originally defined by Codd in reference [11.6], not the simplified version as defined in Section 12.3.

The solution to the SSP problems is to break the relvar down into two projections, in this case the projections:

```
SS { S#, SNAME }
SP { S#, P#, QTY }
```

SSP	S#	SNAME	P#	QTY
	S1	Smith	P1	300
	S1	Smith	P2	200
	S1	Smith	P3	400
	S1	Smith	P4	200
	..	.....	..	...

Fig. 12.13 Sample value (partial) for relvar SSP

—or alternatively the projections

```
SS { S#, SNAME }
SP { SNAME, P#, QTY }
```

(there are two equally valid decompositions in this example). All of these projections are in BCNF.

At this point, we should probably stop for a moment and reflect on what is "really" going on here. The original design, consisting of the single relvar SSP, is *clearly* bad; the problems with it are intuitively obvious, and it is unlikely that any competent database designer would ever seriously propose it, even if he or she had no exposure to the ideas of BCNF and so on at all. Common sense would tell the designer that the SS-SP design is better. But what do we mean by "common sense"? What are the *principles* (inside the designer's brain) that the designer is applying when he or she chooses the SS-SP design over the SSP design?

The answer is, of course, that they are exactly the principles of functional dependency and Boyce/Codd normal form. In other words, those concepts (FD, BCNF, and all of the other formal ideas discussed in this chapter and the next) are nothing more nor less than *formalized common sense.* The whole point of normalization theory is to try to identify such commonsense principles and formalize them—which is not an easy thing to do! But if it can be done, then we can *mechanize* those principles; in other words, we can write a program and get the machine to do the work. Critics of normalization usually miss this point; they claim, quite rightly, that the ideas are all basically common sense, but they typically do not realize that it is a significant achievement to state what "common sense" means in a precise and formal way.

To return to the main thread of our discussion: As a second example of overlapping candidate keys—an example that we should warn you some people might consider pathological—we consider a relvar SJT with attributes S, J, and T, standing for student, subject, and teacher, respectively. The meaning of an SJT tuple (s,j,t)—simplified notation—is that student s is taught subject j by teacher t. The following constraints apply:

- For each subject, each student of that subject is taught by only one teacher.
- Each teacher teaches only one subject (but each subject is taught by several teachers).

A sample SJT value is given in Fig. 12.14.

What are the FDs for relvar SJT? From the first constraint, we have the FD $\{S,J\} \rightarrow$ T. From the second constraint, we have the FD $T \rightarrow J$. Finally, the fact that each subject is

SJT	S	J	T
	Smith	Math	Prof. White
	Smith	Physics	Prof. Green
	Jones	Math	Prof. White
	Jones	Physics	Prof. Brown

Fig. 12.14   Sample value for relvar SJT

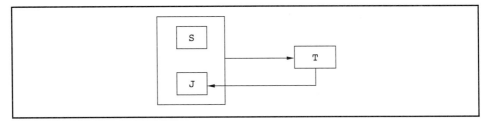

Fig. 12.15   FDs for relvar SJT

taught by several teachers tells us that the FD J → T does *not* hold. So the FD diagram is as shown in Fig. 12.15.

Again we have two overlapping candidate keys, {S,J} and {S,T}. Once again the relvar is in 3NF and not BCNF, and once again the relvar suffers from certain update anomalies; for example, if we wish to delete the information that Jones is studying physics, we cannot do so without at the same time losing the information that Professor Brown teaches physics. Such difficulties are caused by the fact that attribute T is a determinant but not a candidate key. Again we can get over the problems by replacing the original relvar by two BCNF projections, in this case the projections:

```
ST { S, T }
TJ { T, J }
```

It is left as an exercise to show the values of these two relvars corresponding to the data of Fig. 12.14, to draw a corresponding FD diagram, to prove that the two projections are indeed in BCNF (what are the candidate keys?), and to check that the decomposition does in fact avoid the anomalies.

There is another problem, however. The fact is, although the decomposition into ST and TJ does avoid certain anomalies, it unfortunately introduces others! The trouble is, the two projections are not *independent,* in Rissanen's sense (see Section 12.4). To be specific, the FD

```
{ S, J } → T
```

cannot be deduced from the FD

```
T → J
```

(which is the only FD represented in the two projections). As a result, the two projections cannot be independently updated. For example, an attempt to insert a tuple for Smith and Prof. Brown into relvar ST must be rejected, because Prof. Brown teaches physics and Smith is already being taught physics by Prof. Green; yet the system cannot detect this fact without examining relvar TJ. We are forced to the unpleasant conclusion that the twin objectives of (a) decomposing a relvar into *BCNF* components, and (b) decomposing it into *independent* components, can occasionally be in conflict—that is, it is not always possible to satisfy both of them at the same time.

To elaborate on the example for a moment longer: In fact, relvar SJT is *atomic* in Rissanen's sense (see Section 12.4), even though it is not in BCNF. Observe, therefore, that the fact that an atomic relvar cannot be decomposed into independent components does not mean it cannot be decomposed at all (where by "decomposed" we mean decomposed in a nonloss way). Intuitively speaking, therefore, *atomicity* is not a very good term, since it is neither necessary nor sufficient for good database design.

Our third and final example of overlapping candidate keys concerns a relvar EXAM with attributes S (student), J (subject), and P (position). The meaning of an EXAM tuple (s,j,p) is that student s was examined in subject j and achieved position p in the class list. For the purposes of the example, we assume that the following constraint holds:

■ There are no ties—that is, no two students obtained the same position in the same subject.

Then the FDs are as shown in Fig. 12.16.

Again we have two overlapping candidate keys, {S,J} and {J,P}, because (a) if we are given a student and a subject, then there is exactly one corresponding position, and equally (b) if we are given a subject and a position, there is exactly one corresponding student. However, the relvar is in BCNF, because those candidate keys are the only determinants, and update anomalies of the kind we have been discussing in this chapter do not occur with this relvar. (*Exercise:* Check this claim.) Thus, overlapping candidate keys do not *necessarily* lead to problems of the kind we have been discussing.

In conclusion, we see that the concept of BCNF eliminates certain additional problem cases that could occur under the old definition of 3NF. Also, BCNF is conceptually simpler than 3NF, in that it makes no overt reference to the concepts of 1NF, 2NF, primary key, or transitive dependence. What is more, the reference it does make to candidate keys could be replaced by a reference to the more fundamental notion of functional dependence (the definition given in reference [12.2] in fact makes this replacement). On the other hand, the concepts of primary key, transitive dependence, and so on are useful in practice, since they give some idea of the actual step-by-step process the designer might have to go through in order to reduce an arbitrary relvar to an equivalent collection of BCNF relvars.

For purposes of future reference, we close this section with a four-step algorithm by which an arbitrary relvar R can be nonloss-decomposed into a set D of BCNF projections (without necessarily preserving all dependencies, however):

1. Initialize D to contain just R.

2. For each nonBCNF relvar T in D, execute Steps 3 and 4.

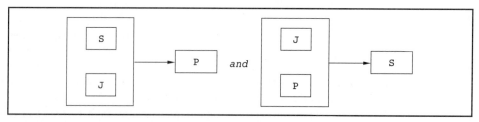

Fig. 12.16   FDs for relvar EXAM

3. Let $X \rightarrow Y$ be an FD for T that violates the requirements for BCNF.

4. Replace T in D by two of its projections: that over X and Y and that over all attributes except those in Y.

12.6   A NOTE ON RELATION-VALUED ATTRIBUTES

In Chapter 6, we saw that it is possible for a relation to include an attribute whose values are relations in turn (an example is shown in Fig. 12.17). As a result, relvars can have relation-valued attributes too. From the point of view of database design, however, such relvars are usually contraindicated, because they tend to be *asymmetric*[11]—not to mention the fact that their predicates tend to be rather complicated!—and such asymmetry can lead to various practical problems. In the case of Fig. 12.17, for example, suppliers and parts are treated asymmetrically. As a consequence, the (symmetric) queries

1. Get S# for suppliers who supply part P1

2. Get P# for parts supplied by supplier S1

have very different formulations:

1. (SPQ WHERE TUPLE { P# P# ('P1') } ∈ PQ { P# }) { S# }

2. ((SPQ WHERE S# = S# ('S1')) UNGROUP PQ) { P# }

(SPQ here is assumed to be a relvar whose values are relations of the form indicated by Fig. 12.17.) Note, incidentally, that not only do these two formulations differ considerably, but they are both much more complicated than their SP counterparts.

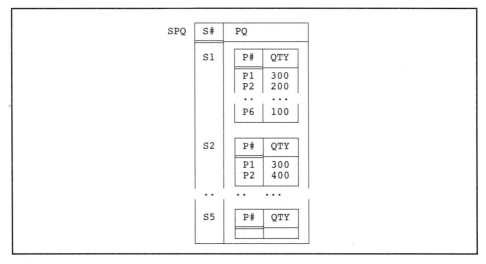

Fig. 12.17   A relation with a relation-valued attribute

---

[11] Historically, in fact, such relvars were not even legal—they were said to be *unnormalized*, meaning they were not even regarded as being in 1NF (see Chapter 6).

Matters are even worse for update operations. For example, consider the following two updates:

1. Create a new shipment for supplier S6, part P5, quantity 500.

2. Create a new shipment for supplier S2, part P5, quantity 500.

With our usual shipments relvar SP, there is no qualitative difference between these two updates—both involve the insertion of a single tuple into the relvar. With relvar SPQ, by contrast, the two updates differ in kind significantly (not to mention the fact that, again, they are both much more complicated than their SP counterpart):

```
1. INSERT SPQ RELATION
        { TUPLE { S# S# ('S6'),
                 PQ RELATION { TUPLE { P#  P# ('P5'),
                                      QTY QTY ( 500 ) } } } } ;
2. UPDATE SPQ WHERE S# = S# ('S2')
        { INSERT PQ RELATION { TUPLE { P#  P# ('P5'),
                                      QTY QTY ( 500 ) } } } ;
```

Relvars—at least, base relvars—without relation-valued attributes are thus usually to be preferred, because the fact that they have a simpler logical structure leads to corresponding simplifications in the operations we need to perform on them. Please understand, however, that this position should be seen as a guideline only, not as an inviolable law. In practice, there might well be cases where a relation-valued attribute does make sense, even for a base relvar. For example, Fig. 12.18 shows (part of) a possible value for

RVK	RVNAME	CK
	S	ATTRNAME
		S#
	SP	ATTRNAME
		S# P#
	MARRIAGE	ATTRNAME
		HUSBAND DATE
	MARRIAGE	ATTRNAME
		DATE WIFE
	MARRIAGE	ATTRNAME
		WIFE HUSBAND

Fig. 12.18   Sample value for catalog relvar RVK

a *catalog* relvar RVK that lists the relvars in the database and their candidate keys. Attribute CK in that relvar is relation-valued. It is also a component of the sole candidate key for RVK! A **Tutorial D** definition for RVK might thus look something like this:

```
VAR RVK BASE RELATION
     { RVNAME NAME, CK RELATION { ATTRNAME NAME } }
       KEY { RVNAME, CK } ;
```

Note: Exercise 12.3 at the end of the chapter asks you to consider what is involved in eliminating relation-valued attributes, if (as is usually the case) such elimination is considered desirable.[12]

12.7 SUMMARY

This brings us to the end of the first of our two chapters on further normalization. We have discussed the concepts of **first, second, third,** and **Boyce/Codd normal form.** The various normal forms (including those to be discussed in the next chapter) constitute *a total ordering,* in the sense that every relvar at a given level of normalization is automatically at all lower levels also, whereas the converse is not true—there exist relvars at each level that are not at any higher level. Furthermore, BCNF (and indeed 5NF) is always achievable; that is, any given relvar can always be replaced by an equivalent set of relvars in BCNF (or 5NF). And the purpose of such reduction is to **avoid redundancy,** and hence to avoid certain **update anomalies.**

The normalization process consists of replacing the given relvar by certain **projections,** in such a way that **joining** those projections back together again gives us back the original relvar; in other words, the process is **reversible** (equivalently, the decomposition is **nonloss**). We also saw the crucial role that **functional dependencies** play in the process; in fact, **Heath's theorem** tells us that if a certain FD is satisfied, then a certain decomposition is nonloss. This state of affairs can be seen as further confirmation of the claim made in Chapter 11 to the effect that FDs are "not quite fundamental, but very nearly so."

We also discussed Rissanen's concept of **independent projections,** and suggested that it is better to decompose into such projections rather than into projections that are not independent, when there is a choice. A decomposition into such independent projections is said to be **dependency-preserving.** Unfortunately, we also saw that the objectives of nonloss decomposition to BCNF and dependency preservation can sometimes be in conflict with one another.

---

[12] And is possible! Note that it is *not* possible in the case of RVK, at least not directly (i.e., without the introduction of some kind of CKNAME—"candidate key name"—attribute).

We conclude this chapter with a very elegant (and fully accurate) pair of definitions, due to Zaniolo [12.7], of the concepts of 3NF and BCNF. First, 3NF:

- **Third normal form** (*Zaniolo's definition*): Let R be a relvar, let X be any subset of the attributes of R, and let A be any single attribute of R. Then R is in 3NF if and only if, for every FD $X \rightarrow A$ in R, at least one of the following is true:

  1. X contains A (so the FD is trivial).
  2. X is a superkey.
  3. A is contained in a candidate key of R.

The definition of **Boyce/Codd normal form** is obtained from the 3NF definition by simply dropping possibility 3 (a fact that shows clearly that BCNF is strictly stronger than 3NF). In fact, possibility 3 is precisely the cause of the "inadequacy" in Codd's original 3NF definition that eventually led to the introduction of BCNF.

EXERCISES

12.1   Prove Heath's theorem. Is the converse of that theorem valid?

12.2   It is sometimes claimed that every binary relvar is necessarily in BCNF. Is this claim valid?

12.3   Fig. 12.19 shows the information to be recorded in a company personnel database, represented as it would be in a *hierarchic* system such as IMS. The figure is to be understood as follows:

- The company has a set of departments.
- Each department has a set of employees, a set of projects, and a set of offices.
- Each employee has a job history (set of jobs the employee has held).
- For each such job, the employee also has a salary history (set of salaries received while employed on that job).
- Each office has a set of phones.

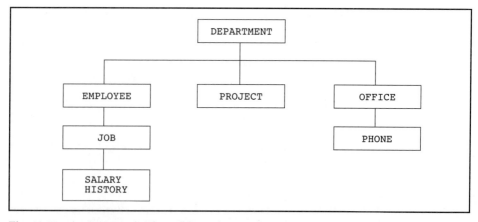

Fig. 12.19   A company database (hierarchic view)

The database is to contain the following information:

- For each department: department number (unique), budget, and the department manager's employee number (unique)
- For each employee: employee number (unique), current project number, office number, and phone number; also, title of each job the employee has held, plus date and salary for each distinct salary received in that job
- For each project: project number (unique) and budget
- For each office: office number (unique), floor area, and phone number (unique) for all phones in that office

Design an appropriate set of relvars to represent this information. State any assumptions you make regarding functional dependencies.

12.4   A database used in an order-entry system is to contain information about customers, items, and orders. The following information is to be included:

- For each customer:
  - Customer number (unique)
  - "Ship-to" addresses (several per customer)
  - Balance
  - Credit limit
  - Discount
- For each order:
  - Heading information:
    Customer number
    Ship-to address
    Date of order
  - Detail lines (several per order):
    Item number
    Quantity ordered
- For each item:
  - Item number (unique)
  - Manufacturing plants
  - Quantity on hand at each plant
  - Stock danger level for each plant
  - Item description

For internal processing reasons, a "quantity outstanding" value is associated with each detail line of each order; this value is initially set equal to the quantity of the item ordered and is progressively reduced to zero as partial shipments are made. Again, design a database for this data. As in the previous exercise, state any assumptions you make regarding dependencies.

12.5   Suppose that in Exercise 12.4 only a very small number of customers, say one percent or less, actually have more than one ship-to address. (This is typical of real-life situations, in which it is frequently the case that just a few exceptions—often rather important ones—fail to conform to some general pattern.) Can you see any drawbacks to your solution to Exercise 12.4? Can you think of any improvements?

12.6   *(Modified version of Exercise 11.13)* Relvar TIMETABLE has the following attributes:

D   Day of the week (1 to 5)
P   Period within day (1 to 6)
C   Classroom number
T   Teacher name
S   Student name
L   Lesson name

Tuple *(d,p,c,t,s,l)* appears in this relvar if and only if at time *(d,p)* student *s* is attending lesson *l,* which is being taught by teacher *t* in classroom *c.* You can assume that lessons are one period in duration and that every lesson has a name that is unique with respect to all lessons taught in the week. Reduce TIMETABLE to a more desirable structure.

12.7   *(Modified version of Exercise 11.14)* Relvar NADDR has attributes NAME (unique), STREET, CITY, STATE, and ZIP. Assume that (a) for any given zip code, there is just one city and state; (b) for any given street, city, and state, there is just one zip code. Is NADDR in BCNF? 3NF? 2NF? Can you think of a better design?

12.8   Let SPQ be a relvar whose values are relations of the form indicated by Fig. 12.17. State the external predicate for SPQ.

REFERENCES AND BIBLIOGRAPHY

In addition to the following, see also the references in Chapter 11, especially Codd's original paper on the first three normal forms [11.6].

12.1 Philip A. Bernstein: "Synthesizing Third Normal Form Relations from Functional Dependencies," *ACM TODS 1,* No. 4 (December 1976).

In this chapter we have discussed techniques for decomposing "large" relvars into "smaller" ones (i.e., ones of lower degree). In this paper, Bernstein considers the inverse problem of combining "small" relvars into "larger" ones (i.e., ones of higher degree). The problem is not actually characterized in this way in the paper; rather, it is described as the problem of *synthesizing* relvars given a set of attributes and a set of corresponding FDs, with the constraint that the synthesized relvars must be in 3NF. However, since attributes and FDs have no meaning outside the context of some containing relvar, it would be more accurate to regard the fundamental construct as a binary relvar (plus an FD), rather than as a pair of attributes (plus an FD).

Note: It would equally well be possible to regard the given set of attributes and FDs as defining a **universal relvar**—see, for example, reference [13.20]—that satisfies a given set of FDs, in which case the "synthesis" process can alternatively be perceived as a process of *decomposing* that universal relvar into 3NF projections. But we stay with the original "synthesis" interpretation for the purposes of the present discussion.

The synthesis process, then, is one of constructing *n*-ary relvars from binary relvars, given a set of FDs that apply to those binary relvars, and given the objective that all constructed relvars be in 3NF (BCNF had not been defined when this work was done). Algorithms are presented for performing this task.

One objection to the approach (recognized by Bernstein) is that the manipulations performed by the synthesis algorithm are purely syntactic in nature and take no account of semantics. For instance, given the FDs

$A \rightarrow B$ (for relvar $R\{A,B\}$)
$B \rightarrow C$ (for relvar $S\{B,C\}$)
$A \rightarrow C$ (for relvar $T\{A,C\}$)

the third might or might not be redundant (i.e., implied by the first and second), depending on the meanings of *R, S,* and *T*. As an example of where it is not so implied, take *A* as employee number, *B* as office number, *C* as department number; take *R* as "office of employee," *S* as "department owning office," *T* as "department of employee"; and consider the case of an employee working in an office belonging to a department not the employee's own. The synthesis algorithm simply assumes that, for example, the two *C* attributes are one and the same (in fact, it does not recognize relvar names at all); it thus relies on the existence of some external mechanism—in other words, human intervention—for avoiding semantically invalid manipulations. In the case at hand, it would be the responsibility of the person defining the original FDs to use distinct attribute names *C1* and *C2* (say) in the two relvars *S* and *T*.

12.2 E. F. Codd: "Recent Investigations into Relational Data Base Systems," Proc. IFIP Congress, Stockholm, Sweden (1974), and elsewhere.

This paper covers a mixed bag of topics. In particular, it gives "an improved definition of third normal form," where "third normal form" in fact refers to what is now known as BCNF. Other topics discussed include *views and view updating, data sublanguages, data exchange,* and *needed investigations* (all as of 1974).

12.3 C. J. Date: "A Normalization Problem," in *Relational Database Writings 1991–1994*. Reading, Mass.: Addison-Wesley (1995).

To quote the abstract, this paper "examines a simple problem of normalization and uses it to make some observations on the subject of database design and explicit integrity constraint declaration." The problem involves a simple airline application and the following FDs:

```
{ FLIGHT } → DESTINATION
{ FLIGHT } → HOUR
{ DAY, FLIGHT } → GATE
{ DAY, FLIGHT } → PILOT
{ DAY, HOUR, GATE } → DESTINATION
{ DAY, HOUR, GATE } → FLIGHT
{ DAY, HOUR, GATE } → PILOT
{ DAY, HOUR, PILOT } → DESTINATION
{ DAY, HOUR, PILOT } → FLIGHT
{ DAY, HOUR, PILOT } → GATE
```

Among other things, this example serves as a good illustration of the point that the "right" database design can rarely be decided on the basis of normalization principles alone.

12.4 I. J. Heath: "Unacceptable File Operations in a Relational Database," Proc. 1971 ACM SIGFIDET Workshop on Data Description, Access, and Control, San Diego, Calif. (November 1971).

This paper gives a definition of "3NF" that was in fact the first published definition of *BCNF*. It also includes a proof of what we referred to in Section 12.2 as *Heath's theorem*. Note that the three steps in the normalization procedure as discussed in the body of this chapter are all applications of that theorem.

12.5 William Kent: "A Simple Guide to Five Normal Forms in Relational Database Theory," *CACM 26*, No. 2 (February 1983).

The source of the following intuitively attractive characterization of "3NF" (more accurately, BCNF): *Each attribute must represent a fact about the key, the whole key, and nothing but the key* (slightly paraphrased).

12.6 Jorma Rissanen: "Independent Components of Relations," *ACM TODS 2,* No. 4 (December 1977).

12.7 Carlo Zaniolo: "A New Normal Form for the Design of Relational Database Schemata," *ACM TODS 7,* No. 3 (September 1982).

The source of the elegant definitions of 3NF and BCNF discussed in Section 12.7. However, the principal purpose of the paper is to define another normal form, *elementary key normal form* (EKNF), which lies between 3NF and BCNF and "captures the salient qualities of both" while avoiding the problems of both (namely, that 3NF is "too forgiving" and BCNF is "prone to computational complexity"). The paper also shows that Bernstein's algorithm [12.1] in fact generates relvars that are in EKNF, not just 3NF.

CHAPTER **13**

Further Normalization II: Higher Normal Forms

13.1 INTRODUCTION

In the previous chapter we discussed the ideas of further normalization up to and including Boyce/Codd normal form, BCNF (which is as far as the functional dependency concept can carry us). Now we complete our discussions by examining *fourth* and *fifth* normal forms (4NF and 5NF). As we will see, the definition of fourth normal form makes use of a new kind of dependency, called a *multi-valued* dependency (MVD); MVDs are a generalization of FDs. Likewise, the definition of fifth normal form makes use of another new kind of dependency, called a *join* dependency (JD); JDs in turn are a generalization of MVDs. Section 13.2 discusses MVDs and 4NF, Section 13.3 discusses JDs and 5NF (and explains why 5NF is, in a certain special sense, "the final normal form"). Note, however, that our discussions of MVDs and JDs are deliberately less formal and complete than our discussions of FDs in Chapter 11—we leave the formal treatment to the research papers (see the "References and Bibliography" section).

Section 13.4 then reviews the entire normalization procedure and makes some additional comments on it. Next, Section 13.5 briefly discusses the notion of *de*normalization. Section 13.6 then describes another important, and related, design principle called *orthogonal design*. Finally, Section 13.7 briefly examines some recent developments and possible directions for future research in the normalization field, and Section 13.8 presents a summary.

13.2 MULTI-VALUED DEPENDENCIES AND FOURTH NORMAL FORM

Suppose we are given a relvar HCTX—H for hierarchic—containing information about courses, teachers, and texts, in which the attributes corresponding to teachers and texts are *relation-valued* (see Fig. 13.1 for a sample HCTX value). As you can see, each HCTX tuple consists of a course name, plus a relation containing teacher names, plus a relation containing text names (two such tuples are shown in the figure). The intended meaning of such a tuple is that the specified course can be taught by any of the specified teachers and uses all of the specified texts as references. We assume that, for a given course *c,* there can be any number *m* of corresponding teachers and any number *n* of corresponding texts ($m > 0$, $n > 0$). Moreover, we also assume—perhaps not very realistically!—that teachers and texts are quite independent of one another; that is, no matter who actually teaches any particular offering of a given course, the same texts are used. Finally, we also assume that a given teacher or a given text can be associated with any number of courses.

Now suppose that (as in Chapter 12, Section 12.6) we want to eliminate the relation-valued attributes. One way to do this—probably not the best way, though, a point we will come back to at the end of this section—is simply to replace relvar HCTX by a relvar CTX with three *scalar* attributes COURSE, TEACHER, and TEXT, as indicated in Fig. 13.2. As you can see from the figure, each HCTX tuple gives rise to $m * n$ CTX tuples, where *m* and *n* are the cardinalities of the TEACHERS and TEXTS relations in that HCTX tuple. Note that the resulting relvar CTX is "all key" (the sole candidate key for

HCTX	COURSE	TEACHERS		TEXTS	
	Physics	TEACHER		TEXT	
		Prof. Green Prof. Brown		Basic Mechanics Principles of Optics	
	Math	TEACHER		TEXT	
		Prof. Green		Basic Mechanics Vector Analysis Trigonometry	

Fig. 13.1 Sample value for relvar HCTX

```
CTX   COURSE    TEACHER        TEXT
      Physics   Prof. Green    Basic Mechanics
      Physics   Prof. Green    Principles of Optics
      Physics   Prof. Brown    Basic Mechanics
      Physics   Prof. Brown    Principles of Optics
      Math      Prof. Green    Basic Mechanics
      Math      Prof. Green    Vector Analysis
      Math      Prof. Green    Trigonometry
```

Fig. 13.2   Value for relvar CTX corresponding to the HCTX value in Fig. 13.1

HCTX, by contrast, was just {COURSE}). *Exercise:* Give a relational expression by which CTX can be derived from HCTX.

The meaning of relvar CTX is basically as follows: A tuple (c,t,x)—simplified notation—appears in CTX if and only if course c can be taught by teacher t and uses text x as a reference. Observe that, for a given course, all possible combinations of teacher and text appear; that is, CTX satisfies the (relvar) constraint

if   tuples $(c,t1,x1)$ and $(c,t2,x2)$ both appear

then tuples $(c,t1,x2)$ and $(c,t2,x1)$ both appear also

Now, it should be apparent that relvar CTX involves a good deal of *redundancy,* leading as usual to certain *update anomalies.* For example, to add the information that the physics course can be taught by a new teacher, it is necessary to insert two separate tuples, one for each of the two texts. Can we avoid such problems? Well, it is easy to see that the problems in question are caused by the fact that teachers and texts are *completely independent of one another.* It is also easy to see that matters would be improved if CTX were decomposed into its two projections—let us call them CT and CX—on {COURSE, TEACHER} and {COURSE,TEXT}, respectively (see Fig. 13.3).

To add the information that the physics course can be taught by a new teacher, all we have to do given the design of Fig. 13.3 is insert a single tuple into relvar CT. (Note too that relvar CTX can be recovered by joining CT and CX back together again, so the decomposition is nonloss.) Thus, it does seem reasonable to suggest that there should be a way of further normalizing a relvar like CTX.

```
CT                            CX
COURSE    TEACHER             COURSE    TEXT
Physics   Prof. Green         Physics   Basic Mechanics
Physics   Prof. Brown         Physics   Principles of Optics
Math      Prof. Green         Math      Basic Mechanics
                              Math      Vector Analysis
                              Math      Trigonometry
```

Fig. 13.3   Values for relvars CT and CX corresponding to the CTX value in Fig. 13.2

Now, you might be thinking that the redundancy in CTX was unnecessary in the first place, and hence that the corresponding update anomalies were unnecessary too. More specifically, you might suggest that CTX need not include all possible teacher/text combinations for a given course; for example, two tuples are obviously sufficient to show that the physics course has two teachers and two texts. The problem is, *which* two tuples? Any particular choice leads to a relvar having a very unobvious interpretation and very strange update behavior. (Try stating the predicate for such a relvar!—i.e., try stating the criteria for deciding whether or not some given update is acceptable on that relvar.)

Informally, therefore, it is obvious that the design of CTX is bad and the decomposition into CT and CX is better. The trouble is, however, these facts are not *formally* obvious. Observe in particular that CTX satisfies no functional dependencies at all (apart from trivial ones such as COURSE → COURSE); in fact, CTX is in BCNF,[1] since as already noted it is all key—any "all key" relvar must necessarily be in BCNF. (Note, incidentally, that the two projections CT and CX are also all key and hence in BCNF.) The ideas of the previous chapter are therefore of no help with the problem at hand.

The existence of "problem" BCNF relvars like CTX was recognized very early on, and the way to deal with them was also understood, at least intuitively. However, it was not until 1977 that these intuitive ideas were put on a sound theoretical footing by Fagin's introduction of the notion of *multi-valued dependencies,* MVDs [13.14]. Multi-valued dependencies are a generalization of functional dependencies—meaning every FD is an MVD, but the converse is not true (i.e., there exist MVDs that are not FDs). In the case of relvar CTX, two MVDs hold:

```
COURSE  →→  TEACHER
COURSE  →→  TEXT
```

(note the double arrows; $A \rightarrow\rightarrow B$ is read as "*B* is **multi-dependent** on *A,*" or, equivalently, "*A* **multi-determines** *B*"). Let us concentrate on the MVD COURSE $\rightarrow\rightarrow$ TEACHER. Intuitively, what this MVD means is that, although a course does not have a *unique* corresponding teacher (i.e., the *functional* dependence COURSE → TEACHER does not hold), each course nevertheless does have a well-defined set of corresponding teachers. By "well-defined" here we mean, more precisely, that for a given course *c* and a given text *x,* the set of teachers *t* matching the pair (*c,x*) in CTX depends on the value *c* alone—it makes no difference which particular value of *x* we choose. The MVD COURSE $\rightarrow\rightarrow$ TEXT is interpreted analogously.

Here then is the formal definition:

- **Multi-valued dependence:** Let *R* be a relvar, and let *A, B,* and *C* be subsets of the attributes of *R*. Then we say that *B* is **multi-dependent** on *A*—in symbols,

  $A \rightarrow\rightarrow B$

  (read "*A* multi-determines *B*," or simply "*A* double arrow *B*")—if and only if, in every legal value of *R*, the set of *B* values matching a given *AC* value pair depends only on the *A* value and is independent of the *C* value.

---

[1] HCTX is in BCNF, too; as a matter of fact, it is also in 4NF and 5NF (see the definitions later in this chapter).

It is easy to show (see Fagin [13.14]) that, given the relvar $R\{A,B,C\}$, the MVD $A \twoheadrightarrow B$ holds if and only if the MVD $A \twoheadrightarrow C$ also holds. MVDs always go together in pairs in this way. For this reason it is usual to represent them both in one statement, thus:

    A $\twoheadrightarrow$ B | C

For example:

    COURSE $\twoheadrightarrow$ TEACHER | TEXT

Now, we stated earlier that multi-valued dependencies are a generalization of functional dependencies, in the sense that every FD is an MVD. More precisely, an FD is an MVD in which the set of dependent values matching a given determinant value is always a singleton set. Thus, if $A \rightarrow B$, then certainly $A \twoheadrightarrow B$.

Returning to our original CTX problem, we can now see that the trouble with relvars such as CTX is that they involve MVDs that are not FDs. (In case it is not obvious, we point out that it is precisely the existence of those MVDs that leads to, e.g., the need to insert two tuples to add one new physics teacher; both tuples are needed in order to maintain the integrity constraint that is represented by the MVD.) The two projections CT and CX do not involve any such MVDs, which is why they represent an improvement over the original design. We would therefore like to replace CTX by those two projections, and a theorem proved by Fagin in reference [13.14] allows us to make exactly that replacement:

- **Theorem** (Fagin): Let $R\{A,B,C\}$ be a relvar, where A, B, and C are sets of attributes. Then R is equal to the join of its projections on $\{A,B\}$ and $\{A,C\}$ if and only if R satisfies the MVDs $A \twoheadrightarrow B \mid C$.

(Notice that this is a stronger version of Heath's theorem [12.4] as stated in Chapter 12.) Following Fagin [13.14], we can now define *fourth normal form* (so called because—as noted in Chapter 12—BCNF was still being called *third* normal form at the time):

- **Fourth normal form:** Relvar R is in 4NF if and only if, whenever there exist subsets A and B of the attributes of R such that the nontrivial MVD $A \twoheadrightarrow B$ is satisfied, then all attributes of R are also *functionally* dependent on A. *Note:* The MVD $A \twoheadrightarrow B$ is **trivial** if either A is a superset of B or the union AB of A and B is the entire heading.

In other words, the only nontrivial dependencies (FDs or MVDs) in R are of the form $K \rightarrow X$ (i.e., a *functional* dependency from some superkey K to some other attribute X). Equivalently: R is in 4NF if and only if it is in BCNF and all MVDs in R are in fact "FDs out of keys." Note in particular, therefore, that 4NF implies BCNF.

Relvar CTX is not in 4NF, since it involves an MVD that is not an FD at all, let alone an FD "out of a key." The two projections CT and CX are both in 4NF, however. Thus, 4NF is an improvement over BCNF, in that it eliminates another form of undesirable dependency. What is more, Fagin shows in reference [13.14] that 4NF is always achievable; that is, any relvar can be nonloss-decomposed into an equivalent collection of 4NF relvars—though our discussion of the SJT example in Chapter 12, Section 12.5, shows that in some cases it might not be desirable to carry the decomposition that far (or even as far as BCNF).

As an aside, we remark that Rissanen's work on independent projections [12.6], though couched in terms of FDs, is applicable to MVDs also. Recall that a relvar $R\{A,B,C\}$ satisfying the FDs $A \rightarrow B$ and $B \rightarrow C$ is better decomposed into its projections on $\{A,B\}$ and $\{B,C\}$ rather than into those on $\{A,B\}$ and $\{A,C\}$. The same holds true if we replace the FDs $A \rightarrow B$ and $B \rightarrow C$ by the MVDs $A \rightarrow\rightarrow B$ and $B \rightarrow\rightarrow C$, respectively.

We conclude this section by returning, as promised, to the question of eliminating relation-valued attributes (RVAs for short). The point is this: If we start with a relvar like HCTX that involves two or more independent RVAs, then, instead of simply replacing those RVAs by scalar attributes (as we did earlier in this section) and then performing nonloss decomposition on the result, *it is better to separate the RVAs first.* In the case of HCTX, for example, it is better to replace the relvar by its two projections HCT {COURSE,TEACHERS} and HCX {COURSE,TEXTS} (where TEACHERS and TEXTS are still RVAs). The RVAs in those two projections can then be replaced by scalar attributes and the results reduced to BCNF (actually 4NF) in the usual way if necessary, and the "problem" BCNF relvar CTX will simply never arise. But the theory of MVDs and 4NF gives us a formal basis for what would otherwise be a mere rule of thumb.

13.3   JOIN DEPENDENCIES AND FIFTH NORMAL FORM

So far in this chapter (and throughout the previous chapter) we have tacitly assumed that the sole operation necessary or available in the normalization process is the replacement of a relvar in a nonloss way by *exactly two* of its projections. This assumption has successfully carried us as far as 4NF. It comes perhaps as a surprise, therefore, to discover that there exist relvars that cannot be nonloss-decomposed into two projections but *can* be nonloss-decomposed into three or more. To coin an ugly but convenient term, we will say a relvar (or a relation) is "*n*-decomposable" if it can be nonloss-decomposed into *n* projections but not into *m*, where $1 < m$ and $m < n$. *Note:* The phenomenon of *n*-decomposability for $n > 2$ was first noted by Aho, Beeri, and Ullman [13.1]. The particular case $n = 3$ was also studied by Nicolas [13.26].

Consider relvar SPJ from the suppliers-parts-projects database (but ignore attribute QTY for simplicity); a sample value is shown at the top of Fig. 13.4. That relvar is all key and involves no nontrivial FDs or MVDs at all, and is therefore in 4NF. Note too that Fig. 13.4 also shows:

a.   The three binary projections SP, PJ, and JS corresponding to the SPJ relation value shown at the top of the figure

b.   The effect of joining the SP and PJ projections (over P#)

c.   The effect of joining that result and the JS projection (over J# and S#)

Observe that the result of the first join is to produce a copy of the original SPJ relation plus one additional ("spurious") tuple, and the effect of the second join is then to eliminate that additional tuple, thereby getting us back to the original SPJ relation. In other words, that original SPJ relation is 3-decomposable. *Note:* The net result is the same whatever pair of projections we choose for the first join, though the intermediate result is different in each case. *Exercise:* Check this claim.

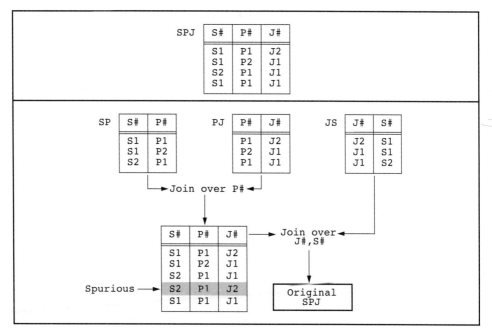

Fig. 13.4   Relation SPJ is the join of all three of its binary projections but not of any two

Now, the example of Fig. 13.4 is expressed in terms of relations, not relvars. However, the 3-decomposability of SPJ could be a more fundamental, time-independent property—that is, a property satisfied by all legal values of the relvar—*if* the relvar satisfies a certain time-independent integrity constraint. To understand what that constraint must be, observe first that the statement "SPJ is equal to the join of its three projections SP, PJ, and JS" is precisely equivalent to the following statement:

if the pair	*(s1,p1)*	appears in SP
and the pair	*(p1,j1)*	appears in PJ
and the pair	*(j1,s1)*	appears in JS
then the triple	*(s1,p1,j1)*	appears in SPJ

because the triple *(s1,p1,j1)* obviously appears in the join of SP, PJ, and JS. (*Note:* The converse of this statement—that if *(s1,p1,j1)* appears in SPJ then *(s1,p1)* appears in projection SP, etc.—is clearly true for any degree-3 relation SPJ.) Since *(s1,p1)* appears in SP if and only if *(s1,p1,j2)* appears in SPJ for some *j2*, and similarly for *(p1,j1)* and *(j1,s1)*, we can rewrite the foregoing statement as a constraint on SPJ:

if	*(s1,p1,j2)*, *(s2,p1,j1)*, and *(s1,p2,j1)* appear in SPJ
then	*(s1,p1,j1)* appears in SPJ also

And if *this* statement is true for all time—that is, for all possible values of relvar SPJ—then we do have a time-independent constraint on the relvar (albeit a rather bizarre one). Notice the **cyclic nature** of that constraint ("if *s1* is linked to *p1* and *p1* is linked to *j1* and *j1* is linked back to *s1* again, then *s1* and *p1* and *j1* must all coexist in the same tuple"). *A relvar will be n-decomposable for some n > 2 if and only if it satisfies some such (n-way) cyclic constraint.*

Suppose then for the remainder of this section that relvar SPJ does in fact satisfy that time-independent constraint (the sample values in Fig. 13.4 are consistent with this hypothesis). For brevity, let us agree to refer to that constraint as *Constraint 3D* (3D for 3-decomposable). What does Constraint 3D mean in real-world terms? Let us try to make it a little more concrete by giving an example. The constraint says that, in the portion of the real world that relvar SPJ is supposed to represent, it is a fact that *if* (for example)

a. Smith supplies monkey wrenches, and

b. Monkey wrenches are used in the Manhattan project, and

c. The Manhattan project is supplied by Smith,

then

d. Smith supplies monkey wrenches to the Manhattan project.

Note that (as pointed out in Chapter 1, Section 1.3), *a, b,* and *c* together normally do *not* imply *d;* indeed, exactly this example was held up in Chapter 1 as an illustration of "the connection trap." In the case at hand, however, we are saying *there is no trap*— because there is an additional real-world constraint in effect (Constraint 3D) that makes the inference of *d* from *a, b,* and *c* valid in this particular case.

To return to the main topic of discussion: Because Constraint 3D is satisfied if and only if the relvar concerned is equal to the join of certain of its projections, we refer to that constraint as a *join dependency* (JD). A JD is a constraint on the relvar concerned, just as an MVD or an FD is a constraint on the relvar concerned. Here is the definition:

- **Join dependency:** Let *R* be a relvar, and let *A, B, ..., Z* be subsets of the attributes of *R*. Then we say that *R* satisfies the JD

  ```
  * { A, B, ..., Z }
  ```

  (pronounced "star *A, B, ..., Z*") if and only if every legal value of *R* is equal to the join of its projections on *A, B, ..., Z*.

For example, if we agree to use SP to mean the subset {S#,P#} of the set of attributes of SPJ, and similarly for PJ and JS, then we can say that—given Constraint 3D—relvar SPJ satisfies the JD ∗ {SP,PJ,JS}.

By way of another example, consider the usual suppliers relvar S. If we agree to use SN to refer to the subset {S#,SNAME} of the set of attributes of S, and similarly for ST and SC, then we can say that relvar S satisfies the join dependency ∗ {SN,ST,SC}.

We have seen, then, that relvar SPJ, with its JD ∗ {SP,PJ,JS}, can be 3-decomposed. The question is, *should* it be? And the answer is "Probably yes." Relvar SPJ (with its JD) suffers from a number of update anomalies, anomalies that disappear when it is 3-decomposed. Examples of such anomalies are illustrated in Fig. 13.5. Consideration of what happens after 3-decomposition is left as an exercise.

SPJ	S#	P#	J#
	S1	P1	J2
	S1	P2	J1

- If (S2,P1,J1) is inserted, (S1,P1,J1) must also be inserted.
- Yet converse is not true.

SPJ	S#	P#	J#
	S1	P1	J2
	S1	P2	J1
	S2	P1	J1
	S1	P1	J1

- Can delete (S2,P1,J1) without side effects.
- If (S1,P1,J1) is deleted, another tuple must also be deleted (which?).

Fig. 13.5   Sample update anomalies in SPJ

Fagin's theorem, discussed in Section 13.2, to the effect that $R\{A,B,C\}$ can be nonloss-decomposed into its projections on $\{A,B\}$ and $\{A,C\}$ if and only if the MVDs $A \twoheadrightarrow B$ and $A \twoheadrightarrow C$ hold in R, can now be restated as follows:

- $R\{A,B,C\}$ satisfies the JD $*\{AB,AC\}$ if and only if it satisfies the MVDs $A \twoheadrightarrow B \mid C$.

Since this theorem can be taken as a *definition* of multi-valued dependency, it follows that an MVD is just a special case of a JD, or (equivalently) that JDs are a generalization of MVDs. Formally, we have:

$$A \twoheadrightarrow B \mid C \equiv *\{ AB, AC \}$$

Note: It is immediate from the definition of join dependency that JDs are **the most general form of dependency possible** (using, of course, the term *dependency* in a very special sense!). That is, there does not exist a still higher form of dependency such that JDs are merely a special case of that higher form—as long as we restrict our attention to dependencies that deal with a relvar being decomposed via projection and recomposed via join. (However, if we permit other decomposition and recomposition operators, then other types of dependencies might come into play. We consider this possibility briefly in Section 13.7.)

Returning now to our example, we can see that the problem with relvar SPJ is that it involves a JD that is not an MVD, and hence not an FD either. (*Exercise: Why* is this a problem, exactly?) We have also seen that it is possible, and probably desirable, to decompose such a relvar into smaller components: namely, into the projections specified by the join dependency. That decomposition process can be repeated until all resulting relvars are in *fifth normal form*, which we now define:

- **Fifth normal form:** A relvar R is in 5NF—also called **projection-join normal form** (PJ/NF)—if and only if every nontrivial join dependency that is satisfied by R is implied by the candidate key(s) of R, where:

    a. The join dependency $*\{ A, B, ..., Z \}$ on R is **trivial** if and only if at least one of A, B, ..., Z is the set of all attributes of R.

b. The join dependency ∗ { *A, B, ..., Z* } on *R* is **implied by the candidate key(s)** of *R* if and only if each of *A, B, ..., Z* is a superkey for *R*.

Relvar SPJ is not in 5NF; it satisfies a certain join dependency, Constraint 3D, that is certainly not implied by its sole candidate key (that key being the combination of all of its attributes). To state this differently, relvar SPJ is not in 5NF, because (a) it *can* be 3-decomposed and (b) that 3-decomposability is not implied by the fact that the combination {S#,P#,J#} is a candidate key. By contrast, after 3-decomposition, the three projections SP, PJ, and JS are each in 5NF, since they do not involve any nontrivial JDs at all.

Note that any relvar in 5NF is automatically in 4NF also, because as we have seen an MVD is a special case of a JD. What is more, Fagin shows in reference [13.15] that any MVD that is implied by a candidate key must in fact be an FD in which that candidate key is the determinant. Fagin also shows in that same paper that any given relvar can be nonloss-decomposed into an equivalent collection of 5NF relvars; that is, 5NF is always achievable.

Let us take a closer look at the question of what it means for a JD to be implied by candidate keys. Consider our familiar suppliers relvar S once again. That relvar satisfies several join dependencies—this one, for example:

```
∗ { { S#, SNAME, STATUS }, { S#, CITY } }
```

That is, relvar S is equal to the join of its projections on {S#,SNAME,STATUS} and {S#,CITY}, and hence can be nonloss-decomposed into those projections. (This fact does not mean it *should* be so decomposed, only that it *could* be.) This JD is implied by the fact that {S#} is a candidate key; in fact, it is implied by Heath's theorem [12.4].

Suppose now (as we did in Chapter 12, Section 12.5) that relvar S has a second candidate key, {SNAME}. Then here is another JD that is satisfied by that relvar:

```
∗ { { S#, SNAME }, { S#, STATUS }, { SNAME, CITY } }
```

This JD is implied by the fact that {S#} and {SNAME} are *both* candidate keys.

Both of these examples illustrate the fact that the JD ∗ {*A, B, ..., Z*} is implied by candidate keys if and only if each of *A, B, ..., Z* is a superkey for the relvar in question. Thus, given a relvar *R,* we can tell if *R* is in 5NF as long as we know all candidate keys *and all JDs* in *R.* However, discovering all of those JDs might itself be a nontrivial exercise. That is, whereas it is relatively easy to identify FDs and MVDs (because they have a fairly straightforward real-world interpretation), the same cannot be said for JDs—JDs, that is, that are not MVDs and therefore not FDs—because the intuitive meaning of JDs might not be obvious. Hence, the process of determining when a given relvar is in 4NF but not 5NF, and so could probably be decomposed to advantage, is still somewhat unclear. Experience suggests that such relvars are likely to be rare in practice.

In conclusion, we note that it follows from the definition that 5NF is the **ultimate normal form** with respect to projection and join (which accounts for its alternative name, *projection-join* normal form). That is, a relvar in 5NF is **guaranteed to be free of anomalies** that can be removed by taking projections. (Of course, this remark does not mean it is free of anomalies; it just means, to repeat, that it is free of anomalies that can be removed by taking projections.) For if a relvar is in 5NF, the only join dependencies are those that are implied by candidate keys, and so the only valid decompositions are ones that are based on those candidate keys (each projection in such a decomposition will consist of one or more of those candidate keys, plus zero or more additional attributes). For example, the suppliers relvar S is in 5NF. It *can* be further decomposed in several nonloss ways, as we saw earlier, but every projection in any such decomposition will still include a candidate key of the original relvar, and hence there does not seem to be any particular advantage in that further decomposition.

13.4   THE NORMALIZATION PROCEDURE SUMMARIZED

Up to this point in this chapter (and throughout the previous chapter), we have been concerned with the technique of *nonloss decomposition* as an aid to database design. The basic idea is as follows: Given some 1NF relvar *R* and some set of FDs, MVDs, and JDs that apply to *R*, we systematically reduce *R* to a collection of "smaller" (i.e., lower-degree) relvars that are equivalent to *R* in a certain well-defined sense but are also in some way more desirable.[2] Each step of the reduction process consists of taking projections of the relvars resulting from the preceding step. The given constraints are used at each step to guide the choice of which projections to take next. The overall process can be stated informally as a set of rules, thus:

1. Take projections of the original 1NF relvar to eliminate FDs that are not irreducible. This step will produce a collection of 2NF relvars.

2. Take projections of those 2NF relvars to eliminate transitive FDs. This step will produce a collection of 3NF relvars.

3. Take projections of those 3NF relvars to eliminate remaining FDs in which the determinant is not a candidate key. This step will produce a collection of BCNF relvars. *Note:* Rules 1–3 can be condensed into the single guideline "Take projections of the original relvar to eliminate FDs in which the determinant is not a candidate key."

4. Take projections of those BCNF relvars to eliminate MVDs that are not also FDs. This step will produce a collection of 4NF relvars. *Note:* In practice it is usual—by "separating independent RVAs," as explained in Section 13.2—to eliminate such MVDs before applying Rules 1–3 above.

5. Take projections of those 4NF relvars to eliminate JDs that are not implied by the candidate keys—though perhaps we should add "if you can find them." This step will produce a collection of relvars in 5NF.

Several points arise from the foregoing summary:

1. First of all, the process of taking projections at each step must be done in a nonloss way, and preferably in a dependency-preserving way as well.

---

[2] If *R* includes any RVAs (which it might), we assume it does so intentionally. RVAs that are not wanted can be eliminated as explained in Section 13.2.

2. Observe that (as was first noted by Fagin in reference [13.15]) there is a very attractive parallelism among the definitions of BCNF, 4NF, and 5NF:

   - A relvar *R* is in BCNF if and only if every FD satisfied by *R* is implied by the candidate keys of *R*.

   - A relvar *R* is in 4NF if and only if every MVD satisfied by *R* is implied by the candidate keys of *R*.

   - A relvar *R* is in 5NF if and only if every JD satisfied by *R* is implied by the candidate keys of *R*.

   The update anomalies discussed in Chapter 12 and in earlier sections of the present chapter are precisely anomalies that are caused by FDs or MVDs or JDs that are not implied by candidate keys. (The FDs, MVDs, and JDs we are referring to here are all assumed to be nontrivial ones.)

3. The overall objectives of the normalization process are as follows:

   - To eliminate certain kinds of redundancy

   - To avoid certain update anomalies

   - To produce a design that is a "good" representation of the real world—one that is intuitively easy to understand and a good base for future growth

   - To simplify the enforcement of certain integrity constraints

   We elaborate a little on the last item in this list. The general point is that (as we already know from discussions elsewhere in this book) *some integrity constraints imply others.* As a trivial example, the constraint that salaries must be greater than $10,000 certainly implies the constraint that they must be greater than zero. Now, if constraint *A* implies constraint *B,* then enforcing *A* will enforce *B* automatically (it will not even be necessary to state *B* explicitly, except perhaps in the form of a comment). And normalization to 5NF gives us a simple way of enforcing certain important and commonly occurring constraints; basically, all we need do is enforce uniqueness of candidate keys, and then all JDs (and all MVDs and all FDs) will be enforced automatically—because, of course, all of those JDs (and MVDs and FDs) will be implied by those candidate keys.

4. Once again, we stress the point that the normalization guidelines are only guidelines, and occasionally there might be good reasons for not normalizing "all the way." The classic example of a case where complete normalization *might* not be a good idea is provided by the name and address relvar NADDR (see Exercise 12.7 in Chapter 12)—though, to be frank, that example is not very convincing. As a general rule, not normalizing all the way is usually a bad idea.

5. We also repeat the point from Chapter 12 that the notions of dependency and further normalization are semantic in nature; in other words, they are concerned with what the data means. By contrast, the relational algebra and relational calculus, and languages such as SQL that are based on such formalisms, are concerned only with actual data values; they do not and cannot require any particular level of normalization other than first. The further normalization guidelines should be regarded primarily as a discipline to help the database designer (and hence the user)—a discipline by

which the designer can capture a part, albeit a small part, of the semantics of the real world in a simple and straightforward manner.

6. Following on from the previous point: The ideas of normalization are useful in database design, but they are not a panacea. Here are some of the reasons why not (this list is amplified in reference [13.9]):

   ■ It is true that normalization can help to enforce certain integrity constraints very simply, but (as we know from Chapter 9) JDs, MVDs, and FDs are not the only kinds of constraints that can arise in practice.

   ■ The decomposition might not be unique (usually, in fact, there will be many ways of reducing a given collection of relvars to 5NF), and there are few objective criteria by which to choose among alternative decompositions.

   ■ The BCNF and dependency preservation objectives can be in conflict, as explained in Section 12.5 ("the SJT problem").

   ■ The normalization procedure eliminates redundancies by taking projections, but not all redundancies can be eliminated in this manner ("the CTXD problem"—see the annotation to reference [13.14]).

We should also mention the fact that good top-down design methodologies tend to generate fully normalized designs anyway (see Chapter 14).

13.5 A NOTE ON DENORMALIZATION

Up to this point in this chapter (and throughout the previous chapter), we have generally assumed that full normalization all the way to 5NF is desirable. In practice, however, it is often claimed that "denormalization" is necessary to achieve good performance. The argument goes something like this:

1. Full normalization means lots of logically separate relvars (and we assume here that the relvars in question are base relvars specifically).

2. Lots of logically separate relvars means lots of physically separate stored files.

3. Lots of physically separate stored files means lots of I/O.

Strictly speaking, this argument is invalid, because (as explained elsewhere in this book) the relational model nowhere stipulates that base relvars must map one for one to stored files. *Denormalization, if necessary, should be done at the level of stored files, not at the level of base relvars.*[3] But the argument is valid, somewhat, for today's SQL products, precisely because of the inadequate degree of separation between those two levels found in those products. In this section, therefore, we take a closer look at the notion of "denormalization." *Note:* The discussion that follows is based on material from reference [13.6].

---

[3] This remark is not really accurate; denormalization is an operation on relvars, not stored files, and so it cannot be applied "at the level of stored files." But it is not unreasonable to assume that some analog of denormalization can be carried out at the level of stored files.

What *Is* Denormalization?

To review briefly, **normalizing** a relvar *R* means replacing *R* by a set of projections *R1, R2, ..., Rn,* such that *R* is equal to the join of *R1, R2, ..., Rn;* the objective is to *reduce redundancy,* by making sure that each of the projections *R1, R2, ..., Rn* is at the highest possible level of normalization.

In order to define denormalization, then, let *R1, R2, ..., Rn* be a set of relvars. Then **denormalizing** those relvars means replacing them by their join *R,* such that for all *i* (*i* = 1, 2, ..., *n*) projecting *R* over the attributes of *Ri* is guaranteed to yield *Ri* again. The objective is to *increase redundancy,* by ensuring that *R* is at a lower level of normalization than the relvars *R1, R2, ..., Rn.* More specifically, the objective is to reduce the number of joins that need to be done at run time by (in effect) doing some of those joins ahead of time, as part of the database design.

By way of an example, we might consider denormalizing parts and shipments to produce a relvar PSQ as indicated in Fig. 13.6.[4] Observe that relvar PSQ is in 1NF and not in 2NF.

Some Problems

The concept of denormalization suffers from a number of well-known problems. One obvious one is that once we start denormalizing, it is not clear where we should stop. With normalization, there are clear logical reasons for continuing until we reach the highest possible normal form; do we then conclude that with denormalization we should proceed until we reach the *lowest* possible normal form? Surely not; yet there are no established *logical* criteria for deciding exactly where to stop. In choosing to denormalize, in other words, we are backing off from a position that does at least have some solid science and theory behind it, and replacing it by one that is purely pragmatic in nature, and subjective.

The second obvious point is that there are redundancy and update problems, precisely because we are dealing once again with relvars that are less than fully normalized. We have already discussed these problems at length. What is less obvious, however, is that there can be retrieval problems too; that is, denormalization can actually make certain queries harder

PSQ	P#	PNAME	COLOR	WEIGHT	CITY	S#	QTY
	P1	Nut	Red	12.0	London	S1	300
	P1	Nut	Red	12.0	London	S2	300
	P2	Bolt	Green	17.0	Paris	S1	200
	..	.....	.....	......	......	..	...
	P6	Cog	Red	19.0	London	S1	100

Fig. 13.6   Denormalizing parts and shipments

---

[4] There is a problem with denormalizing *suppliers* and shipments, given our usual sample data, because supplier S5 is lost in the join. For such reasons, some people might argue that we should use "outer" joins in the denormalization process. But outer joins have problems of their own, as we will see in Chapter 19.

to express. For example, consider the query "For each part color, get the average weight." Given our usual normalized design, a suitable formulation is:

```
SUMMARIZE P BY { COLOR } ADD AVG ( WEIGHT ) AS AVWT
```

Given the denormalized design of Fig. 13.6, however, the formulation is a little trickier (not to mention the fact that it relies on the strong and generally invalid assumption that every part does have at least one shipment):

```
SUMMARIZE PSQ { P#, COLOR, WEIGHT } BY { COLOR }
                        ADD AVG ( WEIGHT ) AS AVWT
```

(Note that the latter formulation is likely to perform worse, too.) In other words, the common perception that denormalization is good for retrieval but bad for update is incorrect, in general, for both usability and performance reasons.

A third, and major, problem is as follows (and this point applies to "proper" denormalization—i.e., denormalization that is done at the level of stored files—as well as to the kind of denormalization that sometimes has to be done in today's SQL products): When we say that denormalization is good for performance, what we really mean is that it is good for the performance of *specific applications*. Any given physical design is, of necessity, good for some applications but bad for others (in terms of performance, that is). For example, assume that each base relvar does map to one physically stored file, and assume too that each stored file consists of a physically contiguous collection of stored records, one for each tuple in the corresponding relvar. Then:

- Suppose we represent the join of suppliers, shipments, and parts as one base relvar and hence one stored file. Then the query "Get supplier details for suppliers who supply red parts" will presumably perform well against this physical structure.

- However, the query "Get supplier details for London suppliers" will perform worse against this physical structure than it would if we had stayed with three base relvars and mapped them to three physically separate stored files. The reason is that, with the latter design, all supplier stored records will be physically contiguous, whereas in the former design they will be physically spread over a wider area, and will therefore require more I/O. Analogous remarks apply to any query that accesses suppliers only, or parts only, or shipments only, instead of performing some kind of join.

13.6   ORTHOGONAL DESIGN (A DIGRESSION)

In this section, following reference [13.12], we briefly examine another database design principle, one that is not part of further normalization *per se* but is closely related to it (and, like further normalization, is at least scientific). It is called *The Principle of Orthogonal Design*. Consider Fig. 13.7, which shows an obviously bad but possible design for suppliers; relvar SA in that design corresponds to suppliers who are located in Paris, while relvar SB corresponds to suppliers who are either not located in Paris or have status greater than 30 (i.e., these are the relvar predicates, loosely speaking). As the figure indicates, the design leads to certain redundancies; to be specific, the tuple for supplier S3

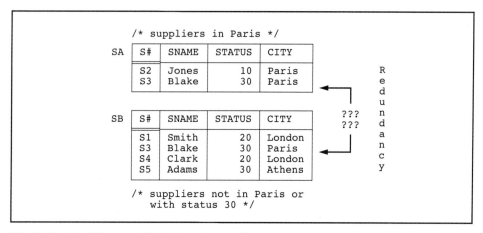

Fig. 13.7   A bad but possible design for suppliers

appears twice, once in each relvar. And those redundancies in turn lead to update anomalies once again.

Note, incidentally, that the tuple for supplier S3 *must* appear in both places. For suppose, contrariwise, that it were to appear in (say) SB but not SA. Applying the Closed World Assumption to SA would then tell us that it is not the case that supplier S3 is located in Paris. However, SB tells us that it *is* the case that supplier S3 is located in Paris. In other words, we would have a contradiction on our hands, and the database would be inconsistent.

The problem with the design of Fig. 13.7 is obvious, of course: It is precisely the fact that it is possible for the very same tuple to appear in two distinct relvars. In other words, the two relvars have *overlapping meanings,* in the sense that it is possible for the very same tuple to satisfy the predicates for both. So an obvious rule is:

- **The Principle of Orthogonal Design** *(initial version):* Within a given database, no two distinct base relvars should have overlapping meanings.

Points arising:

1. Recall from Chapter 10 that, from the user's point of view, *all* relvars are base relvars (apart from views that are defined as mere shorthands). In other words, the principle applies to the design of all "expressible" databases, not just to the "real" database— *The Principle of Database Relativity* at work once again. (Of course, analogous remarks apply to the principles of normalization also.)

2. Note that two relvars cannot possibly have overlapping meanings unless they are of the same type (i.e., unless they have the same heading).

3. Adherence to the principle implies that (e.g.) when we insert a tuple, we can regard the operation as inserting a tuple *into the database,* rather than into some specific relvar—because there will be at most one relvar whose predicate the new tuple satisfies.

We elaborate briefly on this last point. Of course, it is true that when we insert a tuple, we do typically specify the name of the relvar *R* into which that tuple is to be inserted. But this observation does not invalidate the argument. In fact, that name *R* is really just *shorthand for the corresponding predicate, PR* say; we are really saying "INSERT tuple *t*—and by the way, *t* is required to satisfy predicate *PR*." Furthermore, *R* might be a view, perhaps defined by means of an expression of the form *A* UNION *B*— and, as we saw in Chapter 10, it is very desirable that the system know whether the new tuple is to go into *A* or *B* or both.

As a matter of fact, remarks analogous to the foregoing apply to *all* operations, not just to INSERTs; in all cases, relvar names are really just shorthand for relvar predicates. *The point cannot be emphasized too strongly that it is predicates, not names, that represent data semantics.*

Now, we have not yet finished with the orthogonal design principle—there is an important refinement that needs to be addressed. Consider Fig. 13.8, which shows another obviously bad but possible design for suppliers. Here the two relvars *per se* do not have overlapping meanings, but their projections on {S#,SNAME} clearly do. As a consequence, an attempt to insert, say, the tuple (S6,Lopez) into a view defined as the union of those two projections will cause the tuple (S6,Lopez,*t*) to be inserted into SX and the tuple (S6,Lopez,*c*) to be inserted into SY (where *t* and *c* are the applicable default values). Clearly, we need to extend the orthogonal design principle to take care of problems like that of Fig. 13.8:

- ■ **The Principle of Orthogonal Design** *(final version):* Let *A* and *B* be distinct base relvars. Then there must not exist nonloss decompositions of *A* and *B* into *A1, A2, ..., Am* and *B1, B2, ..., Bn* (respectively) such that some projection *Ai* in the set *A1, A2, ..., Am* and some projection *Bj* in the set *B1, B2, ..., Bn* have overlapping meanings.

Points arising:

1. The term *nonloss decomposition* here means exactly what it always means—*viz.,* decomposition of a given relvar into a set of projections such that:

   - ■ The given relvar can be reconstructed by joining the projections back together again.

   - ■ None of those projections is redundant in that reconstruction process. (Strictly speaking, this second condition is not necessary in order for the decomposition to be nonloss, but it is usually desirable, as we saw in Chapter 12.)

SX	S#	SNAME	STATUS		SY	S#	SNAME	CITY
	S1	Smith	20			S1	Smith	London
	S2	Jones	10			S2	Jones	Paris
	S3	Blake	30			S3	Blake	Paris
	S4	Clark	20			S4	Clark	London
	S5	Adams	30			S5	Adams	Athens

Fig. 13.8 Another bad but possible design for suppliers

2. This version of the principle subsumes the original version, because one nonloss decomposition that is always available for relvar *R* is the identity projection (i.e., the projection of *R* over all attributes).

Further Observations

We offer a few additional remarks concerning the orthogonal design principle.

1. First of all, the term *orthogonality* derives from the fact that what the design principle effectively says is that base relvars should have mutually independent meanings. The principle is common sense, of course, but *formalized* common sense (like the principles of normalization).

2. Suppose we start with the usual suppliers relvar S, but decide for design purposes to break that relvar down into a set of restrictions. Then the orthogonal design principle tells us that the restrictions in that breakdown should all be disjoint, in the sense that no supplier tuple can ever appear in more than one of them. (Also, of course, the union of those restrictions must give us back the original relvar.) We refer to such a breakdown as an **orthogonal decomposition**.

3. The overall objective of orthogonal design is to reduce redundancy and thereby to avoid update anomalies (again like normalization). In fact, it complements normalization, in the sense that—loosely speaking—normalization reduces redundancy *within* relvars, while orthogonality reduces redundancy *across* relvars.

4. Orthogonality might be common sense, but it is often flouted in practice (indeed, such flouting is sometimes even recommended). Designs like the following one, from a financial database, are all too common:

```
ACTIVITIES_2001 { ENTRY#, DESCRIPTION, AMOUNT, NEW_BAL }
ACTIVITIES_2002 { ENTRY#, DESCRIPTION, AMOUNT, NEW_BAL }
ACTIVITIES_2003 { ENTRY#, DESCRIPTION, AMOUNT, NEW_BAL }
ACTIVITIES_2004 { ENTRY#, DESCRIPTION, AMOUNT, NEW_BAL }
ACTIVITIES_2005 { ENTRY#, DESCRIPTION, AMOUNT, NEW_BAL }
```

In fact, encoding meaning into names—of relvars or anything else—violates *The Information Principle,* which says (just to remind you) that all information in the database must be cast explicitly in terms of values, and in no other way.

5. If *A* and *B* are base relvars of the same type, adherence to the orthogonal design principle implies that:

```
A UNION B     : Is always a disjoint union
A INTERSECT B : Is always empty
A MINUS B     : Is always equal to A
```

13.7   OTHER NORMAL FORMS

Back to normalization *per se.* Recall from the introduction to Chapter 12 that there do exist other normal forms, over and above those discussed in that chapter and this one so far. The fact is, the theory of normalization and related topics—now usually known as **dependency theory**—has grown into a considerable field in its own right, with a very extensive literature. Research in the area continues; in fact, it flourished for several years (though more recently it might have tapered off somewhat). It is beyond the scope of this chapter to discuss that research in any depth; a good survey of the field, as of the mid 1980s, can be found in reference [13.18], and more recent surveys can be found in references [11.1] and [11.3]. Here we just mention a few specific issues:

1. **Domain-key normal form:** Domain-key normal form (DK/NF) was proposed by Fagin in reference [13.16]. DK/NF—unlike the normal forms we have been discussing—is not defined in terms of FDs, MVDs, or JDs at all. Instead, a relvar *R* is said to be in DK/NF if and only if every constraint on *R* is a logical consequence of the *domain constraints* and *key constraints* that apply to *R,* where:

   - A **domain constraint** is a constraint to the effect that values of a given attribute are taken from some prescribed domain. (Note therefore that, to use the terminology of Chapter 9, such a constraint is really an *attribute* constraint, not a type constraint, even though domains are types.)

   - A **key constraint** is a constraint to the effect that a certain set of attributes constitutes a candidate key.

   Enforcing constraints on a DK/NF relvar is thus conceptually simple, since it is sufficient to enforce just the "domain" (attribute) and key constraints and all other constraints will then be enforced automatically. Note too that "all other constraints" here means more than just FDs, MVDs, and JDs; in fact, it means the entire relvar predicate.

   Fagin shows in reference [13.16] that any DK/NF relvar is necessarily in 5NF (and hence in 4NF, etc.), and indeed in (3,3)NF also (see point 2). However, DK/NF is not always achievable, nor has the question "Exactly when *can* it be achieved?" been answered.

2. **"Restriction-union" normal form:** Consider the suppliers relvar S once again. Normalization theory as we have described it tells us that relvar S is in a "good" normal form; indeed, it is in 5NF, and is therefore guaranteed to be free of anomalies that can be eliminated by taking projections. But why keep all suppliers in a single relvar? What about a design in which London suppliers are kept in one relvar (LS, say), Paris suppliers in another (PS, say), and so on? In other words, what about the possibility of decomposing the original suppliers relvar via **restriction** instead of projection? Would the resulting structure be a good design or a bad one? (In fact it would almost certainly be bad—see Exercise 8.8 in Chapter 8—but the point is that classical normalization theory as such has absolutely nothing to say in answer to such questions.)

   Another direction for normalization research therefore consists of examining the implications of decomposing relvars by some operation other than projection. In the example, the decomposition operator is, as already mentioned, (disjoint) *restriction;* the corresponding recomposition operator is (disjoint) **union.** Thus, it might be possible to construct a "restriction-union" normalization theory, analogous but orthogonal once again to the projection-join normalization theory we have been discussing.[5] To

---

[5] Indeed, Fagin [13.15] originally called 5NF *projection-join* normal form precisely because it was *the* normal form with respect to the projection and join operators.

this writer's knowledge no such theory has ever been worked out in detail, but some initial ideas can be found in a paper by Smith [13.32], where a new normal form called "**(3,3)NF**" is defined. (3,3)NF implies BCNF; however, a (3,3)NF relvar need not be in 4NF, nor need a 4NF relvar be in (3,3)NF, so that (as already suggested) reduction to (3,3)NF is orthogonal to reduction to 4NF (and 5NF). Further ideas on this topic appear in references [13.15] and [13.23]. *The Principle of Orthogonal Design* is relevant, too [13.12] (and orthogonal design can thus be thought of as a kind of normalization after all).

3. **Sixth normal form:** Fifth normal form is the final normal form as far as classical projection and join are concerned. In Chapter 23, however, we will see that it is possible, and desirable, to define (a) generalized versions of those operators, and hence (b) a generalized form of join dependency, and hence (c) a new (sixth) normal form, 6NF. Note that it is reasonable to use the name "sixth normal form," because 6NF (unlike the normal forms discussed under points 1 and 2) really does represent another step along the road from 1NF to 2NF to . . . to 5NF. What is more, all 6NF relvars are necessarily in 5NF. See Chapter 23 for further explanation.

13.8   SUMMARY

In this chapter we have completed our discussion (begun in Chapter 12) of **further normalization**. We have discussed **multi-valued dependencies** (MVDs), which are a generalization of functional dependencies, and **join dependencies** (JDs), which are a generalization of multi-valued dependencies. To simplify considerably:

- A relvar $R\{A,B,C\}$ satisfies the MVDs $A \rightarrow\rightarrow B \mid C$ if and only if the set of B values matching a given AC value pair depends only on the A value, and similarly for the set of C values matching a given AB pair. Such a relvar can be nonloss-decomposed into its projections on $\{A,B\}$ and $\{A,C\}$; in fact, the existence of the MVDs is a necessary and sufficient condition for that decomposition to be nonloss (Fagin's theorem).

- A relvar satisfies the JD $* \{A, B, ..., Z\}$ if and only if it is equal to the join of its projections on $A, B, ..., Z$. Such a relvar can (obviously) be nonloss-decomposed into those projections.

A relvar is in 4NF if the only nontrivial MVDs it satisfies are in fact FDs out of superkeys. A relvar is in 5NF—also called **projection-join** normal form, PJ/NF—if and only if the only nontrivial JDs it satisfies are in fact FDs out of superkeys (i.e., if the JD is $* \{A, B, ..., Z\}$, then each of $A, B, ..., Z$ is a superkey). 5NF, which is always achievable, is the *ultimate normal form* with respect to projection and join.

We also summarized the **normalization procedure**, presenting it as an informal sequence of steps (but we remind you that database design is typically not done by following that procedure anyway). We then described *The Principle of Orthogonal Design:* Loosely, no two relvars should have projections with overlapping meanings. Finally, we briefly mentioned some *additional normal forms.*

In conclusion, we should perhaps point out that research into issues such as those we have been discussing is very much a worthwhile activity. The reason is that the field of further normalization, or rather **dependency theory** as it is now more usually called, does represent a small piece of science in a field (database design) that is regrettably still far too much of an artistic endeavor—that is, it is still far too subjective and lacking in solid principles and guidelines. Thus, any further successes in dependency theory research are very much to be welcomed.

EXERCISES

13.1 Relvars CTX and SPJ as discussed in the body of the chapter—see Figs. 13.2 and 13.4 for some sample values—satisfied a certain MVD and a certain JD, respectively, that was not implied by the candidate keys of the relvar in question. Express that MVD and that JD as integrity constraints, using the **Tutorial D** syntax of Chapter 9. Give both calculus and algebraic versions.

13.2 Let C be a certain club, and let relvar $R\{A,B\}$ be such that the tuple (a,b) appears in R if and only if a and b are both members of C. What FDs, MVDs, and JDs does R satisfy? What normal form is it in?

13.3 A database is to contain information concerning sales representatives, sales areas, and products. Each representative is responsible for sales in one or more areas; each area has one or more responsible representatives. Similarly, each representative is responsible for sales of one or more products, and each product has one or more responsible representatives. Every product is sold in every area; however, no two representatives sell the same product in the same area. Every representative sells the same set of products in every area for which that representative is responsible. Design a suitable set of relvars for this data.

13.4 In Chapter 12, Section 12.5, we gave an algorithm for nonloss decomposition of an arbitrary relvar R into a set of BCNF relvars. Revise that algorithm so that it yields 4NF relvars instead.

13.5 *(Modified version of Exercise 13.3)* A database is to contain information concerning sales representatives, sales areas, and products. Each representative is responsible for sales in one or more areas; each area has one or more responsible representatives. Similarly, each representative is responsible for sales of one or more products, and each product has one or more responsible representatives. Finally, each product is sold in one or more areas, and each area has one or more products sold in it. Moreover, if representative R is responsible for area A, and product P is sold in area A, and representative R is responsible for product P, then R sells P in A. Design a suitable set of relvars for this data.

13.6 Suppose we represent suppliers by the following two relvars SX and SY (as in Fig. 13.8 in Section 13.6):

```
SX { S#, SNAME, STATUS }
SY { S#, SNAME, CITY }
```

Does this design conform to the normalization guidelines described in this chapter and its predecessor? Justify your answer.

REFERENCES AND BIBLIOGRAPHY

13.1 A. V. Aho, C. Beeri, and J. D. Ullman: "The Theory of Joins in Relational Databases," *ACM TODS 4,* No. 3 (September 1979).

The paper that first pointed out that relvars could exist that were not equal to the join of any two of their projections, but were equal to the join of three or more. The major objective of the paper was to present an algorithm, now generally called the **chase**, for determining whether or not a given JD is a logical consequence of a given set of FDs (an example of the **implication problem**—see reference [13.18]). This problem is equivalent to the problem of determining whether a given decomposition is nonloss, given a certain set of FDs. The paper also discusses the question of extending the algorithm to deal with the case where the given dependencies are not FDs but MVDs.

13.2 Catriel Beeri, Ronald Fagin, and John H. Howard: "A Complete Axiomatization for Functional and Multi-Valued Dependencies," Proc. 1977 ACM SIGMOD Int. Conf. on Management of Data, Toronto, Canada (August 1977).

Extends the work of Armstrong [11.2] to include MVDs as well as FDs. In particular, it gives the following set of sound and complete inference rules for MVDs:

1. **Complementation:** If A, B, and C together include all attributes of the relvar and A is a superset of $B \cap C$, then $A \rightarrow\!\!\!\rightarrow B$ if and only if $A \rightarrow\!\!\!\rightarrow C$.

2. **Reflexivity:** If B is a subset of A, then $A \rightarrow\!\!\!\rightarrow B$.

3. **Augmentation:** If $A \rightarrow\!\!\!\rightarrow B$ and C is a subset of D, then $AD \rightarrow\!\!\!\rightarrow BC$.

4. **Transitivity:** If $A \rightarrow\!\!\!\rightarrow B$ and $B \rightarrow\!\!\!\rightarrow C$, then $A \rightarrow\!\!\!\rightarrow C - B$.

The following additional (and useful) inference rules can be derived from the first four:

5. **Pseudotransitivity:** If $A \rightarrow\!\!\!\rightarrow B$ and $BC \rightarrow\!\!\!\rightarrow D$, then $AC \rightarrow\!\!\!\rightarrow D - BC$.

6. **Union:** If $A \rightarrow\!\!\!\rightarrow B$ and $A \rightarrow\!\!\!\rightarrow C$, then $A \rightarrow\!\!\!\rightarrow BC$.

7. **Decomposition:** If $A \rightarrow\!\!\!\rightarrow BC$, then $A \rightarrow\!\!\!\rightarrow B \cap C$, $A \rightarrow\!\!\!\rightarrow B - C$, and $A \rightarrow\!\!\!\rightarrow C - B$.

The paper then goes on to give two rules involving a mixture of MVDs and FDs:

8. **Replication:** If $A \rightarrow B$, then $A \rightarrow\!\!\!\rightarrow B$.

9. **Coalescence:** If $A \rightarrow\!\!\!\rightarrow B$ and $C \rightarrow D$ and D is a subset of B and $B \cap C$ is empty, then $A \rightarrow D$.

Armstrong's rules [11.2] plus rules 1–4 and 8–9 above form a sound and complete set of inference rules for FDs and MVDs taken together.

The paper also derives one more useful rule relating FDs and MVDs:

10. If $A \rightarrow\!\!\!\rightarrow B$ and $AB \rightarrow C$, then $A \rightarrow C - B$.

13.3 Volkert Brosda and Gottfried Vossen: "Update and Retrieval Through a Universal Schema Interface," *ACM TODS 13,* No. 4 (December 1988).

Earlier attempts at providing a "universal relation" interface (see reference [13.20]) dealt with retrieval operations only. This paper proposes an approach for dealing with update operations also.

13.4 C. Robert Carlson and Robert S. Kaplan: "A Generalized Access Path Model and Its Application to a Relational Data Base System," Proc. 1976 ACM SIGMOD Int. Conf. on Management of Data, Washington, D.C. (June 1976).

See the annotation to reference [13.20].

13.5 C. J. Date: "Will the Real Fourth Normal Form Please Stand Up?" in C. J. Date and Hugh Darwen, *Relational Database Writings 1989–1991*. Reading, Mass.: Addison-Wesley (1992).

> To paraphrase from the abstract: "There are several distinct notions in the database design world all laying claim to the title of *fourth normal form* (4NF). The purpose of this paper is to try to set the record straight." Perhaps we should add that the notion referred to as 4NF in the body of this chapter is the only true 4NF . . . Accept no substitutes!

13.6 C. J. Date: "The Normal Is So . . . Interesting" (in two parts), *DBP&D 10,* Nos. 11–12 (November–December 1997).

> The denormalization discussion in Section 13.5 is taken from this paper. The following additional points are worth making:
>
> - Even in a read-only database, it is still necessary to state the integrity constraints, since they define the meaning of the data, and (as noted in Section 13.4) *not* denormalizing provides a simple way of stating certain important constraints. And if the database is not read-only, then not denormalizing provides a simple way of *enforcing* those constraints also.
>
> - Denormalization implies increased redundancy—but (contrary to popular opinion) increased redundancy does not necessarily imply denormalization! Many writers have fallen into this trap, and many continue to do so.
>
> - As a general rule, denormalization—denormalization at the logical level, that is—should be tried as a performance tactic only as a last resort ("only if all else fails," to quote reference [4.17]).

13.7 C. J. Date: "The Final Normal Form!" (in two parts), *DBP&D 11,* Nos. 1–2 (January–February 1998).

> A tutorial on JDs and 5NF. The title could be the subject of dispute (see Chapter 23).

13.8 C. J. Date: "What's Normal, Anyway?" *DBP&D 11,* No. 3 (March 1998).

> A survey of certain "pathological" normalization examples.

13.9 C. J. Date: "Normalization Is No Panacea," *DBP&D 11,* No. 4 (April 1998).

> A survey of some database design issues *not* helped by the theory of normalization. The paper is not meant as an attack.

13.10 C. J. Date: "Principles of Normalization," *http://www.BRCommunity.com* (February 2003); *http://www.dbdebunk.com* (March 2003).

> A brief tutorial. For reference purposes, we summarize the principles here:
>
> 1. A non5NF relvar should be decomposed into a set of 5NF projections.
> 2. The original relvar should be reconstructable by joining the projections back together again.
> 3. The decomposition process should preserve dependencies.
> 4. Every projection should be needed in the reconstruction process.
> 5. *(Not as firm as the first four)* Stop normalizing as soon as all relvars are in 5NF.

13.11 C. J. Date and Ronald Fagin: "Simple Conditions for Guaranteeing Higher Normal Forms in Relational Databases," in C. J. Date and Hugh Darwen, *Relational Database Writings 1989–1991*. Reading, Mass.: Addison-Wesley (1992). Also published in *ACM TODS 17,* No. 3 (September 1992).

> Shows that if (a) relvar R is in 3NF and (b) all candidate keys of R are simple, then R is automatically in 5NF. In other words, there is no need to worry in the case of such a relvar about the

comparatively complicated topics—MVDs, JDs, 4NF, and 5NF—discussed in the body of this chapter. *Note:* The paper also proves that if (a) *R* is in BCNF and (b) at least one of its candidate keys is simple, then *R* is automatically in 4NF, but not necessarily 5NF.

13.12 C. J. Date and David McGovern: "A New Database Design Principle," in C. J. Date, *Relational Database Writings 1991–1994.* Reading, Mass.: Addison-Wesley (1995).

13.13 C. Delobel and D. S. Parker: "Functional and Multi-valued Dependencies in a Relational Database and the Theory of Boolean Switching Functions," Tech. Report No. 142, Dept. Maths. Appl. et Informatique, Univ. de Grenoble, France (November 1978).

Extends the results of reference [11.5] to include MVDs as well as FDs.

13.14 Ronald Fagin: "Multi-valued Dependencies and a New Normal Form for Relational Databases," *ACM TODS 2,* No. 3 (September 1977).

The source of the MVD and 4NF concepts. *Note:* The paper also discusses *embedded* multi-valued dependencies. Suppose we extend relvar CTX from Section 13.2 to include an additional attribute DAYS, representing the number of days spent with the indicated text by the indicated teacher on the indicated course. Let us refer to this relvar as CTXD. Here is a sample value:

CTXD	COURSE	TEACHER	TEXT	DAYS
	Physics	Prof. Green	*Basic Mechanics*	5
	Physics	Prof. Green	*Principles of Optics*	5
	Physics	Prof. Brown	*Basic Mechanics*	6
	Physics	Prof. Brown	*Principles of Optics*	4
	Math	Prof. Green	*Basic Mechanics*	3
	Math	Prof. Green	*Vector Analysis*	3
	Math	Prof. Green	*Trigonometry*	4

The combination {COURSE,TEACHER,TEXT} is the sole candidate key, and we have the FD:

```
{ COURSE, TEACHER, TEXT } → DAYS
```

Observe that the relvar *is* in fourth normal form; it does not involve any MVDs that are not also FDs. However, it does include two **embedded** MVDs (of TEACHER on COURSE and TEXT on COURSE). The embedded MVD of *B* on *A* is said to hold in relvar *R* if the "regular" MVD $A \rightarrow\rightarrow B$ holds in some projection of *R*. A regular MVD is a special case of an embedded MVD, but not all embedded MVDs are regular MVDs.

As the example illustrates, embedded MVDs imply redundancy, just like regular MVDs; however, that redundancy cannot (in general) be eliminated by taking projections. For example, relvar CTXD cannot be nonloss-decomposed into projections at all (in fact, it is in fifth normal form as well as fourth), because DAYS depends on all three of COURSE, TEACHER, and TEXT and so cannot appear in a relvar with anything less than all three. Instead, therefore, the two embedded MVDs would have to be stated as additional, explicit constraints on the relvar. The details are left as an exercise.

13.15 Ronald Fagin: "Normal Forms and Relational Database Operators," Proc. 1979 ACM SIGMOD Int. Conf. on Management of Data, Boston, Mass. (May/June 1979).

This is the paper that introduced the concept of projection-join normal form (PJ/NF, or 5NF). However, it is also much more than that. It can be regarded as the definitive statement of what might be called "classical" normalization theory—that is, the theory of nonloss decomposition based on projection as the decomposition operator and natural join as the corresponding recomposition operator.

13.16 Ronald Fagin: "A Normal Form for Relational Databases That Is Based on Domains and Keys," *ACM TODS 6,* No. 3 (September 1981).

13.17 Ronald Fagin: "Acyclic Database Schemes (of Various Degrees): A Painless Introduction," IBM Research Report RJ3800 (April 1983). Republished in G. Ausiello and M. Protasi (eds.), *Proc. CAAP83 8th Colloquium on Trees in Algebra and Programming* (Springer-Verlag *Lecture Notes in Computer Science 159*). New York, N.Y.: Springer-Verlag (1983).

> Section 13.3 of the present chapter showed how a certain ternary relvar SPJ that satisfied a certain cyclic constraint could be nonloss-decomposed into its three binary projections. The resulting database structure (i.e., schema, called *scheme* in this paper) is said to be **cyclic**, because each of the three relvars has an attribute in common with each of the other two. (If the structure is depicted as a "hypergraph," in which edges represent individual relvars and the node that is the intersection of two edges corresponds precisely to the attributes in common to those two edges, then it should be clear why the term *cyclic* is used.) By contrast, most structures that arise in practice are acyclic. Acyclic structures enjoy a number of formal properties that do not apply to cyclic structures. In this paper, Fagin presents and explains a list of such properties.
>
> A helpful way to think about acyclicity is the following: Just as the theory of normalization can help in determining when *a single relvar* should be restructured in some way, so the theory of acyclicity can help in determining when a *set* of relvars should be restructured in some way.

13.18 R. Fagin and M. Y. Vardi: "The Theory of Data Dependencies—A Survey," IBM Research Report RJ4321 (June 1984). Republished in *Mathematics of Information Processing: Proc. Symposia in Applied Mathematics 34,* American Mathematical Society (1986).

> Provides a brief history of the subject of dependency theory as of the mid 1980s (note that "dependency" here does *not* refer to FDs only). In particular, the paper summarizes the major achievements in three specific areas within the overall field, and in so doing provides a good selected list of relevant references. The three areas are (1) the implication problem, (2) the "universal relation" model, and (3) acyclic schemas. The **implication problem** is the problem of determining, given a set of dependencies *D* and some specific dependency *d,* whether *d* is a logical consequence of *D*. The **universal relation model** and **acyclic schemas** (also known as acyclic *schemes*) are discussed briefly in the annotation to references [13.20] and [13.17], respectively.

13.19 Ronald Fagin, Alberto O. Mendelzon, and Jeffrey D. Ullman: "A Simplified Universal Relation Assumption and Its Properties," *ACM TODS 7,* No. 3 (September 1982).

> Conjectures that the real world can always be represented by means of a "universal relation" [13.20]—or universal relvar, rather—that satisfies precisely one join dependency plus a set of functional dependencies, and explores some of the consequences of that conjecture.

13.20 W. Kent: "Consequences of Assuming a Universal Relation," *ACM TODS 6,* No. 4 (December 1981).

> The concept of the **universal relation** manifests itself in several different ways. First of all, the normalization discipline described in this and the previous chapter tacitly assumed that it is possible to define an initial universal relation—or, more correctly, a universal *relvar*—that includes all of the attributes relevant to the database under consideration, and then showed how that relvar can be replaced by successively "smaller" (lower-degree) projections until some "good" structure is reached. But is that initial assumption realistic or justifiable? Reference [13.20] suggests not, on both practical and theoretical grounds. Reference [13.33] is a reply to reference [13.20], and reference [13.21] is a reply to that reply.

The second, and more pragmatically significant, manifestation of the universal relvar concept is as a *user interface*. The basic idea here is quite straightforward, and indeed (from an intuitive standpoint) quite appealing: Users should be able to frame their database requests, not in terms of relvars and joins among those relvars, but rather in terms of attributes alone. For example:

```
STATUS WHERE COLOR = COLOR ('Red')
```

("Get status for suppliers who supply some red part"). At this point the idea forks into two more or less distinct interpretations:

1. One possibility is that the system should somehow determine for itself what logical access paths to follow—in particular, what joins to perform—in order to answer the query. This is the approach suggested in reference [13.4] (which seems to have been the first paper to discuss the possibility of a "universal relation" interface, though it did not use that term). This approach is critically dependent on proper naming of attributes. Thus, for example, the two supplier number attributes (in relvars S and SP, respectively) *must* be given the same name; conversely, the supplier city and part city attributes (in relvars S and P, respectively) must *not* be given the same name. If either of these two rules is violated, there will be certain queries that the system will be unable to handle properly.

2. The other, less ambitious, approach is simply to regard all queries as being formulated in terms of a *predefined* set of joins—in effect, a predefined view consisting of "the" join of all relvars in the database.

While there is no question that either approach would greatly simplify the expression of many queries arising in practice—and indeed some such approach is essential to the support of any natural language front end—it is also clear that the system must support the ability to specify (logical) access paths explicitly as well, in general. To see that this must be so, consider the query:

```
STATUS WHERE COLOR ≠ COLOR ('Red')
```

Does this query mean "Get status of suppliers who supply a part that is not red" or "Get status of suppliers who do not supply a red part"? Whichever it is, there has to be some way of formulating the other. (Come to that, the previous example is also susceptible to an alternative interpretation: "Get status for suppliers who supply *only* red parts.") And here is a third example: "Get pairs of suppliers who are colocated." Here again it is clear that an explicit join will be necessary (because the problem involves a join of relvar S with itself, loosely speaking).

13.21 William Kent: "The Universal Relation Revisited," *ACM TODS 8*, No. 4 (December 1983).

13.22 Henry F. Korth *et al.*: "System/U: A Database System Based on the Universal Relation Assumption," *ACM TODS 9*, No. 3 (September 1984).

Describes the theory, DDL, DML, and implementation of an experimental "universal relation" system built at Stanford University.

13.23 David Maier and Jeffrey D. Ullman: "Fragments of Relations," Proc. 1983 SIGMOD Int. Conf. on Management of Data, San Jose, Calif. (May 1983).

13.24 David Maier, Jeffrey D. Ullman, and Moshe Y. Vardi: "On the Foundations of the Universal Relation Model," *ACM TODS 9*, No. 2 (June 1984). An earlier version of this paper, under the title "The Revenge of the JD," appeared in Proc. 2nd ACM SIGACT-SIGMOD Symposium on Principles of Database Systems, Atlanta, Ga. (March 1983).

13.25 David Maier and Jeffrey D. Ullman: "Maximal Objects and the Semantics of Universal Relation Databases," *ACM TODS 8*, No. 1 (March 1983).

Maximal objects represent an approach to the ambiguity problem that arises in "universal relation" systems when the underlying structure is not acyclic (see reference [13.17]). A maximal object corresponds to a predeclared subset of the totality of attributes for which the underlying structure *is* acyclic. Such objects are then used to guide the interpretation of queries that would otherwise be ambiguous.

13.26 J.-M. Nicolas: "Mutual Dependencies and Some Results on Undecomposable Relations," Proc. 4th Int. Conf. on Very Large Data Bases, Berlin, Federal German Republic (September 1978).

Introduces the concept of "mutual dependency." A mutual dependency is actually just a JD that is not an MVD or FD and happens to involve exactly three projections (like the "Constraint 3D" example in Section 13.3). It has nothing to do with the concept of mutual dependence discussed in Chapter 12.

13.27 Sylvia L. Osborn: "Towards a Universal Relation Interface," Proc. 5th Int. Conf. on Very Large Data Bases, Rio de Janeiro, Brazil (October 1979).

The proposals of this paper assume that if there are two or more sequences of joins in a "universal relation" system that will generate a candidate answer to a given query, then the desired response is the union of all such candidates. Algorithms are given for generating all such sequences of joins.

13.28 D. Stott Parker and Claude Delobel: "Algorithmic Applications for a New Result on Multivalued Dependencies," Proc. 5th Int. Conf. on Very Large Data Bases, Rio de Janeiro, Brazil (October 1979).

Applies the results of reference [13.13] to various problems, such as that of testing for a nonloss decomposition.

13.29 Y. Sagiv, C. Delobel, D. S. Parker, and R. Fagin: "An Equivalence Between Relational Database Dependencies and a Subclass of Propositional Logic," *JACM 28,* No. 3 (June 1981).

Combines references [11.8] and [13.30].

13.30 Y. Sagiv and R. Fagin: "An Equivalence Between Relational Database Dependencies and a Subclass of Propositional Logic," IBM Research Report RJ2500 (March 1979).

Extends the results of reference [11.8] to include MVDs as well as FDs.

13.31 E. Sciore: "A Complete Axiomatization of Full Join Dependencies," *JACM 29,* No. 2 (April 1982).

Extends the work of reference [13.2] to include JDs as well as FDs and MVDs.

13.32 J. M. Smith: "A Normal Form for Abstract Syntax," Proc. 4th Int. Conf. on Very Large Data Bases, Berlin, Federal German Republic (September 1978).

13.33 Jeffrey D. Ullman: "On Kent's 'Consequences of Assuming a Universal Relation,'" *ACM TODS 8,* No. 4 (December 1983).

13.34 Jeffrey D. Ullman: "The U.R. Strikes Back," Proc. 1st ACM SIGACT-SIGMOD Symposium on Principles of Database Systems, Los Angeles, Calif. (March 1982).

CHAPTER **14**

Semantic Modeling

14.1 INTRODUCTION

Semantic modeling has been a subject of research ever since the late 1970s. The general motivation for that research—that is, the problem the researchers have been trying to solve—is this: Database systems typically have only a very limited understanding of what the data in the database *means;* they typically "understand" certain simple data values, and perhaps certain simple constraints that apply to those values, but very little else (any more sophisticated interpretation is left to the human user). And it would be nice if systems could understand a little more,[1] so that they could respond a little more intelligently to user interactions, and perhaps support more sophisticated (higher-level) user interfaces. For example, it would be nice if the system understood that part weights and shipment

---

[1] Needless to say, it is our position that a system that supported predicates as discussed in Chapter 9 *would* "understand a little more"; in other words, we would argue that such predicate support is the right and proper foundation for semantic modeling. Sadly, however, most semantic modeling schemes are not based on any such solid foundation but are instead quite *ad hoc* (the proposals of references [14.22–14.24] are an exception). This state of affairs might be about to change, though, thanks to the increasing awareness in the commercial world of the importance of *business rules* [9.21, 9.22]; the external predicates of Chapter 9 are basically just "business rules" in this sense [14.14].

quantities, though obviously both numeric, are different in kind—that is, *semantically* different—so that (e.g.) a request to join parts and shipments on the basis of matching weights and quantities could at least be questioned, if not rejected out of hand.

Of course, the notion of types (or domains) is relevant to this particular example—which serves to illustrate the important point that current data models are not totally devoid of semantic features. For instance, domains, candidate keys, and foreign keys are all semantic features of the relational model as originally defined. To put it another way, the various "extended" data models that have been developed over the years to address the semantics issue are only slightly more semantic than earlier models; to paraphrase Codd [14.7], capturing the meaning of the data is a never-ending task, and we can expect (or hope!) to see continuing developments in this area as our understanding continues to evolve. The term *semantic model,* often used to refer to one or other of the "extended" models, is thus not particularly apt, because it suggests that the model in question has somehow managed to capture *all* of the semantics of the situation under consideration. On the other hand, **semantic modeling** *is* an appropriate label for the overall activity of attempting to represent meaning. In this chapter we first present a short introduction to some of the ideas underlying that activity; we then examine one particular approach, the *entity/relationship* approach (which is the one most commonly used in practice), in some depth.

We remark that semantic modeling is known by many names, including *data* modeling, *entity/relationship* modeling, *entity* modeling, and *object* modeling. We prefer *semantic* modeling (sometimes *conceptual* modeling) for the following reasons:

- We dislike *data modeling* because (a) it clashes with the previously established use of the term *data model* to mean a formal system like the relational model, and (b) it tends to reinforce the popular misconception that a data model (in our preferred sense) involves data structure *only.* (Recall from Chapter 1, Section 1.3, that the term *data model* is used in the literature with two quite different meanings. The first is as a model of *data in general;* the relational model is a data model in this sense. The second is as a model of the persistent data of *some given enterprise in particular.* We do not use the term in this latter sense ourselves in this book, but you should be aware that many writers do.)

- We also dislike *entity/relationship modeling* because it tends to suggest that there is just one specific approach to the problem, whereas many different approaches are possible, both in principle and in practice. However, the term *entity/relationship modeling* is well established, and indeed very popular and commonly encountered.

- We have no deep objections to *entity modeling,* except that it seems a little more specific as a label than *semantic modeling,* and might thus suggest an emphasis that is not intended or appropriate.

- As for *object modeling,* the problem here is that the term *object* is clearly a synonym for *entity* in this context, whereas it is used with a completely different meaning in other contexts (in other *database* contexts in particular—see Chapter 25). Indeed, it seems to us that it is exactly the fact that the term has two different meanings that is responsible for what we have elsewhere termed **The First Great Blunder**. See Chapter 26 for further elaboration of this point.

To get back to the main thread of the discussion, our reason for including this material in this part of the book is as follows: *Semantic modeling ideas can be useful as an aid in the process of database design, even in the absence of direct DBMS support for those ideas*. In other words, just as the ideas of the original relational model were used as a primitive database design aid well before there were any commercial implementations of that model, so the ideas of some "extended" model might be useful as a design aid even if there are no commercial implementations of those ideas. At the time of writing, in fact, it is probably fair to say that the *major* impact of semantic modeling ideas has been in the area of database design; several design methodologies have been proposed that are based on one semantic modeling approach or another. For this reason, the major emphasis of this chapter is on the application of semantic modeling ideas to the issue of database design specifically.

The plan of the chapter is as follows. Following this introductory section, Section 14.2 explains in general terms what is involved in semantic modeling. Section 14.3 then introduces the best known of the extended models, Chen's *entity/relationship* (E/R) model, and Sections 14.4 and 14.5 consider the application of that model to database design. (Other models are discussed briefly in the annotation to some of the references in the "References and Bibliography" section.) Finally, Section 14.6 offers a brief analysis of certain aspects of the E/R model, and Section 14.7 gives a summary.

14.2   THE OVERALL APPROACH

We can characterize the overall approach to the semantic modeling problem in terms of four steps, as follows:

1. First, we attempt to identify a set of *semantic* concepts that seem to be useful in talking informally about the real world. For example:

   ■ We might agree that the world is made up of **entities**. (Despite the fact that we cannot state with any precision exactly what an entity is, the concept does seem to be useful in talking about the world, at least intuitively.)

   ■ We might agree further that entities can usefully be classified into **entity types**. For example, we might agree that every employee is an **instance** of the generic EMPLOYEE entity **type**. The advantage of such classification is that entities of a given type will have certain **properties** in common—for example, all employees have a salary—and hence that it can lead to some (fairly obvious) *economies of representation*. In relational terms, for example, the commonality can be factored out into a relvar heading.

   ■ We might agree still further that every entity has a special property that serves to *identify* that entity—that is, every entity has an **identity**.

   ■ We might also agree that any entity can be related to other entities by means of **relationships**.

And so on. But note carefully that all of these terms (*entity instance, entity type, property, relationship,* etc.) are *not* precisely or formally defined—they are "real-world concepts," not formal ones. Step 1 is not a formal step. Steps 2–4, by contrast, are formal.

2. Next, we try to devise a set of corresponding *symbolic* (i.e., formal) **objects** that can be used to represent the foregoing semantic concepts. (*Note:* We are not using the term *object* here in any loaded sense!) For example, the *extended relational model* RM/T [14.7] provides some special kinds of relations called *E-* and *P-relations.* Roughly speaking, E-relations represent entities and P-relations represent properties; however, E- and P-relations have formal definitions, whereas (as already explained) entities and properties do not.

3. We also devise a set of formal, general **integrity rules** (or "metaconstraints," to use the terminology of Chapter 9) to go along with those formal objects. For example, RM/T includes a rule called *property integrity,* which says that every entry in a P-relation must have a corresponding entry in an E-relation (to reflect the fact that every property must be a property of some entity in the database).

4. Finally, we also develop a set of formal **operators** for manipulating those formal objects. For example, RM/T provides a *PROPERTY* operator, which can be used to join together an E-relation and all of its corresponding P-relations, regardless of how many there are and what their names are, thus allowing us to collect together all of the properties for an arbitrary entity.

The objects, rules, and operators of Steps 2–4 together constitute an extended data model ("extended," that is, if those constructs are truly a superset of those of one of the "basic" models—e.g., the relational model—but there is not really a clear distinction in this context between what is extended and what is basic). In particular, please note carefully that *the rules and operators are just as much part of the model as the objects are* (just as they are in the relational model, of course). On the other hand, it is probably fair to say that the operators are less important than the objects and rules from the point of view of database design;[2] the emphasis in the rest of this chapter is therefore on objects and rules rather than on operators, though we will offer a few comments regarding operators on occasion.

To return to Step 1: That step, to repeat, involves an attempt to identify a set of semantic concepts that seem to be useful in talking about the world. A few such concepts—entity, property, relationship, subtype—are shown in Fig. 14.1, along with informal definitions and a few examples. Note that the examples are deliberately chosen to illustrate the point that the very same object in the real world might legitimately be regarded as an entity by some people, as a property by others, and as a relationship by still others. (This observation shows why it is impossible to give terms such as *entity* a precise definition, by the way.) It is a goal of semantic modeling—by no means fully achieved as yet—to support such *flexibility of interpretation.*

---

[2] Except inasmuch as the operators are needed to formulate the rules.

Concept	Informal definition	Examples
ENTITY	A distinguishable object	Supplier, Part, Shipment Employee, Department Person Composition, Concerto Orchestra, Conductor Purchase order, Order line
PROPERTY	A piece of information that describes an entity	Supplier number Shipment quantity Employee department Person height Concerto type Purchase order date
RELATIONSHIP	An entity that serves to interconnect two or more other entities	Shipment (supplier-part) Assignment (employee- department) Recording (composition- orchestra- conductor)
SUBTYPE	Entity type Y is a subtype of entity type X if and only if every Y is necessarily an X	Employee is a subtype of Person Concerto is a subtype of Composition

Fig. 14.1   Some useful semantic concepts

By the way, note that there are likely to be clashes between (a) terms such as those illustrated in Fig. 14.1 that are used at the semantic level and (b) terms used in some underlying formalism such as the relational model. For example, many semantic modeling schemes use the term *attribute* in place of our *property*—but it does not necessarily follow that such an attribute is the same thing as, or maps to, an attribute at the relational level. As another (important!) example, the *entity type* concept as used in (e.g.) the E/R model is not at all the same thing as the *type* concept discussed in Chapter 5. To be more specific, such entity types will probably map to *relvars* in a relational design, so they certainly do not correspond to relational *attribute* types (domains). But they do not fully correspond to *relation* types either, because:

1. Some *base* relation types will probably correspond to relationship types, not entity types, at the semantic level.

2. Some *derived* relation types might not correspond to anything at all at the semantic level (though others might).

Confusion over levels—in particular, confusion arising from such terminological conflicts—has led to some expensive mistakes in the past, and continues to do so to this day (see Chapter 26, Section 26.2).

One final remark to close this section: We pointed out in Chapter 1 that relationships are best regarded as entities in their own right and that we would generally treat them as such in this book. And we pointed out in Chapter 3 that one advantage of the relational model was precisely that it represented all entities, including relationships, in the same uniform way: namely, by means of tuples in relations. Nevertheless, the relationship concept (like the entity concept) does seem to be *intuitively* useful in talking about the world; moreover, the approach to database design to be discussed in Sections 14.3–14.5 does rely heavily on the "entity *vs.* relationship" distinction. We therefore adopt the relationship terminology for the purposes of the next few sections. However, we will have more to say on this issue in Section 14.6.

14.3   THE E/R MODEL

As indicated in Section 14.1, one of the best-known semantic modeling approaches—certainly one of the most widely used—is the so-called **entity/relationship** (E/R) approach, based on the *entity/relationship model* introduced by Chen in 1976 [14.6], and refined in various ways by Chen and numerous others since that time (see, e.g., references [14.18] and [14.45–14.47]). The bulk of this chapter is therefore devoted to a discussion of the E/R approach. (We must stress, however, that the E/R model is very far from being the only "extended" model—many, many others have been proposed. See, for example, references [14.6], [14.18], [14.30], [14.37], and especially [14.24] for introductions to several others; see also references [14.27] and [14.36] for tutorial surveys of the field.)

The E/R model includes analogs of all of the semantic objects listed in Fig. 14.1. We will examine them one by one. First, however, we should note that reference [14.6] not only introduced the E/R model *per se,* it also introduced a corresponding **diagramming technique** ("E/R diagrams"). We will discuss E/R diagrams in some detail in the next section, but a simple example of such a diagram, based on a figure from reference [14.6], is shown in Fig. 14.2, and you might find it helpful to study that example in conjunction with the discussions of the present section. The example represents the data for a simple manufacturing company (it is an extended, though still incomplete, version of the E/R diagram given for the company KnowWare Inc. in Fig. 1.6 in Chapter 1).

Note: Most of the ideas to be discussed in the following subsections will be fairly familiar to anyone who knows the relational model. However, there are certain differences in terminology, as you will see.

Entities

Reference [14.6] begins by defining an **entity** as "a thing which can be distinctly identified." It then goes on to classify entities into **regular entities** and **weak entities**. A weak entity is an entity that is existence-dependent on some other entity, in the sense that it can-

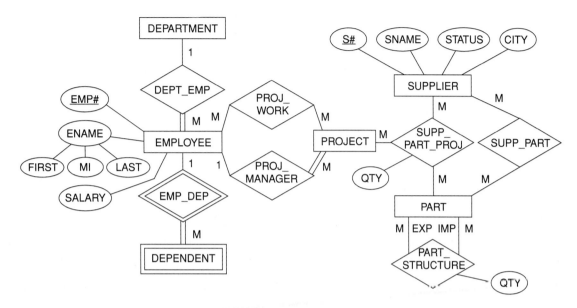

Fig. 14.2 Entity/relationship diagram (example, incomplete)

not exist if that other entity does not also exist. For example, referring to Fig. 14.2, an employee's dependents might be weak entities—they cannot exist (as far as the database is concerned) if the relevant employee does not exist. In particular, if a given employee is deleted, all dependents of that employee must be deleted too. A regular entity, by contrast, is an entity that is not weak; for example, employees might be regular entities. *Note:* Some writers use the term *strong entity* in place of *regular entity.*

Properties

Entities—also relationships, *q.v.*—have **properties**. All entities or relationships of a given type have certain kinds of properties in common; for example, all employees have an employee number, a name, a salary, and so on. (*Note:* We deliberately do not mention "department number" as an employee property here. See the discussion of relationships in the next subsection.) Each kind of property draws its values from a corresponding **value set** (in other words, a type or domain). Furthermore, properties can be:

- **Simple** or **composite:** For example, the composite property "employee name" might be made up of the simple properties "first name," "middle initial," and "last name."

- **Key** (i.e., unique, possibly within some context): For example, a dependent's name might be unique within the context of a given employee.

- **Single-** or **multi-valued** (in other words, repeating groups[3] are permitted, loosely speaking): All properties shown in Fig. 14.2 are single-valued, but if, for example, a given supplier could have several distinct supplier locations, then "supplier city" might be a multi-valued property.

- **Missing** (e.g., "unknown" or "not applicable"): This concept is not illustrated in Fig. 14.2; see Chapter 19 for a detailed discussion.

- **Base** or **derived:** For example, "total quantity" for a given part might be derived as the sum of the individual shipment quantities for that part (again, this concept is not illustrated in Fig. 14.2).

Note: Some writers use the term *attribute* in place of *property* in an E/R context.

Relationships

Reference [14.6] defines a **relationship** as "an association among entities." For example, there is a relationship called DEPT_EMP between departments and employees, representing the fact that certain departments are staffed by certain employees. As with entities (see Chapter 1), it is necessary in principle to distinguish between relationship *types* and relationship *instances,* but it is common to ignore such refinements in informal discourse, and we will often do so ourselves in what follows.

The entities involved in a given relationship are said to be the **participants** in that relationship. The number of participants in a given relationship is called the **degree** of that relationship. (Note, therefore, that this term does not mean the same here as it does in the relational model.)

Let R be a relationship type that involves entity type E as a participant. If every instance of E participates in at least one instance of R, then the participation of E in R is said to be **total**; otherwise, it is said to be **partial**. For example, if every employee must belong to a department, then the participation of employees in DEPT_EMP is total; if it is possible for a given department to have no employees, then the participation of departments in DEPT_EMP is partial.

An E/R relationship can be **one-to-one**, **one-to-many** (also known as **many-to-one**), or **many-to-many** (we assume for simplicity that all relationships are binary, i.e., degree two; extending the concepts, and the terminology, to relationships of higher degree is essentially straightforward). Now, if you are familiar with the relational model, you might be tempted to think of the many-to-many case as the only one that is a genuine relationship, since that case is the only one that demands representation by means of a separate relvar (one-to-one and one-to-many relationships can always be represented by means of a foreign key in one of the participant relvars). However, there are good reasons to treat the one-to-one and one-to-many cases just like the many-to-many case, at least if there is any possibility that they could ever evolve and become many-to-many over time. Only if there is no such possibility is it safe to treat them differently. Of course, sometimes there *is* no

---

[3] See Section 6.4, subsection "Relation-Valued Attributes," if you are not familiar with this term.

such possibility; for example, it will always be true that a circle has exactly one point as its center.

Entity Subtypes and Supertypes

Note: The ideas discussed in this subsection were not included in the original E/R model [14.6] but were added later. See, for example, reference [14.46].

Any given entity is of at least one entity type, but an entity can be of several types simultaneously. For example, if some employees are programmers (and all programmers are employees), then we might say that entity type PROGRAMMER is a **subtype** of entity type EMPLOYEE (or, equivalently, that entity type EMPLOYEE is a **supertype** of entity type PROGRAMMER). All properties of employees apply automatically to programmers, but the converse is not true; for example, programmers might have a property "programming language skill" that does not apply to employees in general. Likewise, programmers automatically participate in all relationships in which employees participate, but the converse is not true; for example, programmers might belong to some professional computer society, while employees in general do not. We say that properties and relationships that apply to the supertype are **inherited** by the subtype.

Note further that some programmers might be application programmers and others might be system programmers; thus, we might say that entity types APPLICATION_PROGRAMMER and SYSTEM_PROGRAMMER are both subtypes of the PROGRAMMER supertype (and so on). In other words, an entity subtype is still an entity type, and it can have subtypes of its own. A given entity type and its immediate subtypes, their immediate subtypes, and so on together constitute an **entity type hierarchy** (see Fig. 14.3). Points arising:

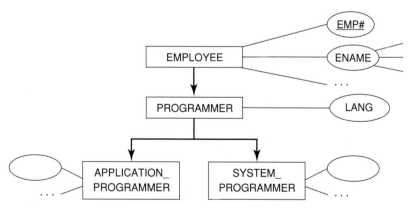

Fig. 14.3 Example of an entity type hierarchy

1. We will discuss type hierarchies and type inheritance in depth in Chapter 20. We should immediately warn you, however, that in that chapter we will use the term *type* to mean exactly what it meant in Chapter 5—it will *not* mean an "entity type" in the sense of this chapter.

2. If you happen to be familiar with IMS (or some other database system that supports a hierarchic data structure), you should note that type hierarchies are not like IMS-style hierarchies. In Fig. 14.3, for example, there is no suggestion that for one EMPLOYEE there are many corresponding PROGRAMMERs (as there would be if the figure was meant to represent an IMS-style hierarchy); on the contrary, for one instance of EMPLOYEE there is *at most one* corresponding PROGRAMMER, representing that same EMPLOYEE in his or her PROGRAMMER role.

This brings us to the end of our brief discussion of the major structural features of the E/R model. Now we turn our attention to E/R diagrams.

14.4   E/R DIAGRAMS

As explained in the previous section, reference [14.6] not only introduced the E/R model *per se,* it also introduced the concept of **entity/relationship diagrams** (E/R diagrams). E/R diagrams constitute a technique for representing the logical structure of a database in a pictorial manner. As such, they provide a simple and readily understood means of communicating the salient features of the design of any given database; indeed, the popularity of the E/R model as an approach to database design can probably be attributed more to the existence of the E/R diagramming technique than to any other cause ("a picture is worth a thousand words"?). We describe the rules for constructing an E/R diagram in terms of the examples already given in Figs. 14.2 and 14.3.

Note: Like the E/R model itself, the E/R diagramming technique has evolved somewhat over time. The version we describe here differs in certain important respects from the one originally described in reference [14.6].

Entities

Each entity type is shown as a rectangle containing the name of the entity type in question. For a weak entity type, the border of the rectangle is doubled.

Examples (see Fig. 14.2):

- Regular entities:
  DEPARTMENT
  EMPLOYEE
  SUPPLIER
  PART
  PROJECT
- Weak entity:
  DEPENDENT

Properties

Properties are shown as ellipses containing the name of the property in question and attached to the relevant entity or relationship by means of a solid line. The ellipse border is dotted or dashed if the property is derived and doubled if it is multi-valued. If the property is composite, its component properties are shown as further ellipses, connected to the ellipse for the composite property in question by means of further solid lines. Key properties are underlined. The value sets corresponding to properties are not shown.

Examples (see Fig. 14.2):

- For EMPLOYEE:
  EMP# (key)
  ENAME (composite, consisting of FIRST, MI, and LAST)
  SALARY
- For SUPPLIER:
  S# (key)
  SNAME
  STATUS
  CITY
- For SUPP_PART_PROJ:
  QTY
- For PART_STRUCTURE:
  QTY

All other properties are omitted from Fig. 14.2 for reasons of space.

Relationships

Each relationship type is shown as a diamond containing the name of the relationship type in question. The diamond border is doubled if the relationship in question is that between a weak entity type and the entity type on which its existence depends. The participants in each relationship are connected to the relevant relationship by means of solid lines; each such line is labeled "1" or "M" to indicate whether the relationship is one-to-one, many-to-one, or many-to-many. The line is doubled if the participation is total.

Examples (see Fig. 14.2):

- DEPT_EMP (one-to-many relationship between DEPARTMENT and EMPLOYEE)
- EMP_DEP (one-to-many relationship between EMPLOYEE and DEPENDENT, a weak entity type)
- PROJ_WORK and PROJ_MANAGER (many-to-many relationship and one-to-many relationship, respectively, between EMPLOYEE and PROJECT)
- SUPP_PART_PROJ (many-to-many-to-many relationship involving SUPPLIER, PART, and PROJECT)

- SUPP_PART (many-to-many relationship between SUPPLIER and PART)
- PART_STRUCTURE (many-to-many relationship between PART and PART)

Observe in the last example here that the two lines from PART to PART_
STRUCTURE are distinguished by labeling them with two distinct **role** names (EXP and
IMP, for "part explosion" and "part implosion," respectively). PART_STRUCTURE is an
example of what is sometimes called a **recursive relationship**.

Entity Subtypes and Supertypes

Let entity type *Y* be a subtype of entity type *X*. Then we draw a solid line from the *X* rectangle to the *Y* rectangle, marked with an arrowhead at the *Y* end. The line denotes what is
sometimes called "the **isa** relationship" (because every *Y* "is a" *X*—equivalently, the set of
all *Y*'s is a subset of the set of all *X*'s).

Examples (see Fig. 14.3):

- PROGRAMMER is a subtype of EMPLOYEE.
- APPLICATION_PROGRAMMER and SYSTEM_PROGRAMMER are subtypes of
  PROGRAMMER.

14.5   DATABASE DESIGN WITH THE E/R MODEL

In a sense, an E/R diagram constructed in accordance with the rules sketched in the previous section *is* a database design. If we attempt to map such a design into the formalisms of
a specific DBMS,[4] however, we will soon discover that the E/R diagram is still very
imprecise in certain respects and leaves a number of details unspecified (especially details
of integrity constraints). To illustrate the point, we consider what is involved in mapping
the design of Fig. 14.2 into a relational database definition.

Regular Entities

To repeat, the regular entities in Fig. 14.2 are as follows:

```
DEPARTMENT
EMPLOYEE
SUPPLIER
PART
PROJECT
```

Each regular entity type maps into a base relvar. The database will thus contain five
base relvars, say DEPT, EMP, S, P, and J, corresponding to these five entity types. Furthermore, each of those five base relvars will have a candidate key—represented by attributes
DEPT#, EMP#, S#, P#, and J#, say—corresponding to the "keys" identified in the E/R
diagram. For definiteness, let us agree, not just here but throughout this section, to give
every relvar a *primary* key specifically; then the definition of the DEPT relvar (for example) might start out looking something like this:

---

[4] Many tools are available to help in that mapping process (e.g., by using the E/R diagram to generate
SQL CREATE TABLE statements and the like).

```
VAR DEPT BASE RELATION
      { DEPT# ...,  ... }
      PRIMARY KEY { DEPT# } ;
```

The other four relvars are left as an exercise. *Note:* The types or "value sets" need to be pinned down too, of course. We omit detailed discussion of this aspect here, since as already mentioned value sets are not shown in the E/R diagram.

Many-to-Many Relationships

The many-to-many (or many-to-many-to-many, etc.) relationships in the example are as follows:

```
PROJ_WORK (involving employees and projects)
SUPP_PART (involving suppliers and parts)
SUPP_PART_PROJ (involving suppliers, parts, and projects)
PART_STRUCTURE (involving parts and parts)
```

Each such relationship also maps into a base relvar. We therefore introduce four more base relvars corresponding to these four relationships. Let us focus on the SUPP_PART relationship; the relvar for that relationship is SP (the usual shipments relvar). We defer for a moment the question of the primary key for this relvar, and concentrate instead on the matter of the foreign keys that are necessary in order to identify the participants in the relationship:

```
VAR SP BASE RELATION SP
      { S# ... , P# ... , ... }
        .....
      FOREIGN KEY { S# } REFERENCES S
      FOREIGN KEY { P# } REFERENCES P ;
```

Clearly, the relvar must include two foreign keys (S# and P#) corresponding to the two participants (suppliers and parts), and those foreign keys must reference the corresponding participant relvars S and P. Furthermore, an appropriate set of foreign key rules—that is, a delete rule and an update rule—must be specified for each of those foreign keys, perhaps as follows. *Note:* The specific rules shown are only by way of illustration (they are not the only possible ones). More important, note that whatever rules do apply are not derivable from or specified by the E/R diagram.

```
VAR SP BASE RELATION SP
      { S# ... , P# ... , ... }
        .....
      FOREIGN KEY { S# } REFERENCES S
                ON DELETE RESTRICT
                ON UPDATE CASCADE
      FOREIGN KEY { P# } REFERENCES P
                ON DELETE RESTRICT
                ON UPDATE CASCADE ;
```

What about the primary key for this relvar? One possibility would be to take the combination of the participant-identifying foreign keys (S# and P#, in the case of SP)—*if* (a) that combination has a unique value for each instance of the relationship (which might or might not be the case, but usually is), and *if* (b) the designer has no objection to composite primary keys (which might or might not be the case). Alternatively, a new noncomposite *surrogate* attribute, "shipment number" say, could be introduced to serve as the primary key (see references [14.11] and [14.21]). For the sake of the example, we will go with the first of these two possibilities, and so add the clause

```
PRIMARY KEY { S#, P# }
```

to the definition of base relvar SP.

Consideration of the PROJ_WORK, PART_STRUCTURE, and SUPP_PART_ PROJ relationships is left as an exercise.

Many-to-One Relationships

There are three many-to-one relationships in the example:

```
PROJ_MANAGER (from projects to managers)
DEPT_EMP (from employees to departments)
EMP_DEP (from dependents to employees)
```

Of these three, the last involves a weak entity type (DEPENDENT), while the other two involve only regular entity types. We will discuss the weak entity case in just a moment; for now, let us concentrate on the other two cases. Consider the DEPT_EMP example. This example does not cause the introduction of any new relvars;[5] instead, we simply introduce a foreign key in the relvar on the "many" side of the relationship (EMP) that references the relvar on the "one" side (DEPT), thus:

```
VAR EMP BASE RELATION
      { EMP# ..., DEPT# ..., ... }
      PRIMARY KEY { EMP# }
      FOREIGN KEY ( DEPT# ) REFERENCES DEPT
               ON DELETE ...
               ON UPDATE ... ;
```

The delete and update rule possibilities here are exactly the same as those for a foreign key that represents a participant in a many-to-many relationship (in general). Observe again that they are not specified by the E/R diagram.

Note: For the sake of the present exposition, we assume that one-to-one relationships (which in any case are not all that common in practice) are treated in exactly the same way as many-to-one relationships. Reference [14.8] contains an extended discussion of the special problems of the one-to-one case.

Weak Entities

The relationship from a weak entity type to the entity type on which it depends is a many-to-one relationship, as indicated in the previous subsection. However, the delete and update rules for that relationship *must* be as follows:

```
ON DELETE CASCADE
ON UPDATE CASCADE
```

---

[5] Though it could; as mentioned in Section 14.3, there are sometimes good reasons to treat a many-to-one relationship as if it were in fact many-to-many. Part IV of reference [19.19] discusses this issue further.

These specifications together capture and reflect the necessary existence dependence. Here is an example:

```
VAR DEPENDENT BASE RELATION
   { EMP# ..., ... }
   .....
   FOREIGN KEY ( EMP# ) REFERENCES EMP
           ON DELETE CASCADE
           ON UPDATE CASCADE ;
```

What is the primary key for such a relvar? As with the case of many-to-many relationships, it turns out we have a choice. One possibility is to take the combination of the foreign key and the weak entity "key" from the E/R diagram—*if* (once again) the database designer has no objection to composite primary keys. Alternatively, we could introduce a new noncomposite surrogate attribute to serve as the primary key (again, see references [14.11] and [14.21]). For the sake of the example again, we will go with the first of the two possibilities, and so add the clause

```
PRIMARY KEY { EMP#, DEP_NAME }
```

(where DEP_NAME is the name of the employee's dependent) to the definition of base relvar DEPENDENT.

Properties

Each property shown in the E/R diagram maps into an attribute in the appropriate relvar—except that, if the property is multi-valued, we would normally create a new relvar for it since (as discussed in Chapter 12, Section 12.6) relation-valued attributes are usually contraindicated. Value sets map into types in the obvious way (in fact, of course, value sets *are* types). These mappings are trivial and need no further discussion here. Note, however, that deciding what value sets we need in the first place might not be quite so easy!

Entity Subtypes and Supertypes

Since Fig. 14.2 does not involve any supertypes and subtypes, let us switch to the example of Fig. 14.3, which does. Let us concentrate for the moment on entity types EMPLOYEE and PROGRAMMER. Assume for simplicity that programmers have just one programming language skill (i.e., the property LANG is single-valued). Then:[6]

- The supertype EMPLOYEE maps into a base relvar, EMP say, as previously discussed.

- The subtype PROGRAMMER maps into another base relvar, PGMR say, with primary key the same as that of the supertype relvar and with other attributes corresponding to the properties that apply only to employees who are programmers (i.e., just LANG, in the example):

---

[6] Observe in particular that what we do *not* do in what follows is map employees and programmers into some kind of "supertable" and "subtable" constructs. There is a conceptual difficulty, or trap, here: Just because entity type *Y* is a subtype of entity type *X* in the E/R diagram, it does not follow that the relational analog of *Y* is a "sub" *anything* of the relational analog of *X*—and indeed it is not. See reference [14.13] for further discussion.

```
VAR PGMR BASE RELATION
   { EMP# ..., LANG ... }
   PRIMARY KEY { EMP# } ... ;
```

Furthermore, the PGMR primary key is also a *foreign* key, referring back to the EMP relvar. We therefore need to extend the definition accordingly (note the delete and update rules in particular):

```
VAR PGMR BASE RELATION
   { EMP# ..., LANG ... }
   PRIMARY KEY { EMP# }
   FOREIGN KEY { EMP# } REFERENCES EMP
         ON DELETE CASCADE
         ON UPDATE CASCADE ;
```

- We also need a *view,* EMP_PGMR say, that is the join of the supertype and subtype relvars:

```
VAR EMP_PGMR VIEW
    EMP JOIN PGMR ;
```

Note that this join is (zero-or-one)-to-one—it is a join over a candidate key and a matching foreign key, and that foreign key is itself a candidate key. The view thus contains just those employees who are programmers, loosely speaking.

Given this design:

- We can access properties that apply to all employees (e.g., for retrieval purposes, or to refer to them in some integrity constraint) by using base relvar EMP.
- We can access properties that apply just to programmers by using base relvar PGMR.
- We can access *all* properties that apply to programmers by using view EMP_PGMR.
- We can insert employees who are not programmers by using base relvar EMP.
- We can insert employees who are programmers by using view EMP_PGMR.
- We can delete employees, programmers or otherwise, by using base relvar EMP or (for programmers only) view EMP_PGMR.
- We can update properties that apply to all employees by using base relvar EMP or (for programmers only) view EMP_PGMR.
- We can update properties that apply just to programmers by using base relvar PGMR.
- We can make an existing nonprogrammer into a programmer by inserting the employee into either base relvar PGMR or view EMP_PGMR.
- We can make an existing programmer into a nonprogrammer by deleting the programmer from base relvar PGMR.

Consideration of the remaining entity types in Fig. 14.3 (APPLICATION_PROGRAMMER and SYSTEM_PROGRAMMER) is left as an exercise.

14.6   A BRIEF ANALYSIS

In this section we briefly examine certain aspects of the E/R model in a little more depth. The discussions that follow are taken in part from an extended examination of the same topics by the present writer in reference [14.9]. Additional analysis and commentary can be found in the annotation to many of the references in the "References and Bibliography" section at the end of the chapter.

The E/R Model as a Foundation for the Relational Model?

We begin by considering the E/R approach from a slightly different perspective. It is probably obvious to you that the ideas of the E/R approach, or something very close to those ideas, must have been the *informal* underpinnings in Codd's mind when he first developed the *formal* relational model. As explained in Section 14.2, the overall approach to developing an "extended" model involves four broad steps, as follows:

1. Identify useful semantic concepts.
2. Devise formal objects.
3. Devise formal integrity rules ("metaconstraints").
4. Devise formal operators.

But these same four steps are applicable to the design of the relational model also (and indeed to any formal data model), not just to "extended" models such as the E/R model. In other words, in order for Codd to have constructed the (formal) relational model in the first place, he must have had some (informal) "useful semantic concepts" in his mind, and those concepts must basically have been those of the E/R model, or something very like them. Indeed, Codd's own writings support this contention. In his very first paper on the relational model (the 1969 version of reference [6.1]), we find the following:

> The set of entities of a given entity type can be viewed as a relation, and we shall call such a relation an *entity type relation* . . . The remaining relations . . . are between entity types and are . . . called *inter-entity relations* . . . An essential property of every inter-entity relation is that [it includes at least two foreign keys that] either refer to distinct entity types or refer to a common entity type serving distinct roles.

Here Codd is clearly proposing that relations be used to represent both "entities" and "relationships." But—and it is a very big but—the point is that *relations are formal objects, and the relational model is a formal system.* The essence of Codd's contribution was that he found a good *formal* model for certain aspects of the real world.

In contrast to the foregoing, the entity/relationship model is *not* (or, at least, not primarily) a formal model. Instead, it consists primarily of a set of *in*formal concepts, corresponding to Step 1 (only) of the four steps under discussion. (Furthermore, what formal aspects it does possess do not seem to be significantly different from the corresponding aspects of the relational model—see the further discussion of this point in the next subsection.) And while it is unquestionably useful to have an armory of "Step 1" concepts at one's disposal for database design purposes among others, the fact remains that database designs cannot be completed without the formal objects and rules of Steps 2 and 3, and numerous other tasks cannot be carried out at all without the formal operators of Step 4.

Please understand that the foregoing remarks are not intended to suggest that the E/R model is not useful. It is. But it is not the whole story. Moreover, it is a little strange to realize that the first published description of the *in*formal E/R model appeared several years after the first published description of the *formal* relational model, given that—as we have seen—the latter was originally, and explicitly, based on some rather E/R-like ideas.

Is the E/R Model a Data Model?

In light of the foregoing discussions, it is not even clear that the E/R "model" is truly a data model at all, at least in the sense in which we have been using that term in this book so far (i.e., as a formal system involving structural, integrity, and manipulative aspects). Certainly the term *E/R modeling* is usually taken to mean the process of deciding the *structure* (only) of the database, although we did briefly consider certain integrity aspects also—mostly having to do with keys—in our discussions in Sections 14.3–14.5.[7] However, a charitable reading of reference [14.6] would suggest that the E/R model is indeed a data model, but one that is essentially just *a thin layer on top of the relational model* (it is certainly not a candidate for replacing the relational model, as some have suggested). We justify this claim as follows:

- First, the fundamental E/R data object—the fundamental *formal* object, that is, as opposed to the informal objects "entity," "relationship," and so on—is the *n*-ary relation.

- The E/R operators are basically the operators of the relational algebra. (Actually, reference [14.6] is not very clear on this point, but it seems to propose a set of operators that are strictly less powerful than those of the relational algebra; for example, there is apparently no union and no explicit join.)

- It is in the area of integrity that the E/R model has some (minor) functionality that the relational model does not: The E/R model includes a set of *built-in* integrity rules, corresponding to some but not all of the foreign key delete and update rules discussed in this book. Thus, where a "pure" relational system would require the user to formulate certain delete and update rules explicitly, an E/R system would require only that the user state that a given relvar represents a certain kind of relationship, and certain delete and update rules would then be understood.

Entities *vs.* Relationships

We have indicated several times already in this book that "relationships" are best regarded merely as a special kind of entity. By contrast, it is a *sine qua non* of the E/R approach

---

[7] In fact, there is a major weakness right here: The E/R model is *completely incapable* of dealing with integrity constraints or "business rules," except for a few special cases (admittedly important ones). Here is a typical quote: "Declarative rules are too complex to be captured as part of the business model and must be defined separately by the analyst/developer" [14.32]. And yet there is a very strong argument that database design should be, precisely, a process of pinning down the applicable constraints (see references [9.21, 9.22] and [14.22–14.24]).

that the two concepts be distinguished somehow. In this writer's opinion, any approach that insists on making such a distinction is seriously flawed, because (as indicated in Section 14.2) the very same object can quite legitimately be regarded as an entity by some users and a relationship by others. Consider the case of a marriage, for example:

- From one perspective, a marriage is clearly a relationship between two people (sample query: "Who was Elizabeth Taylor married to in 1975?").

- From another perspective, a marriage is equally clearly an entity in its own right (sample query: "How many marriages have been performed in this church since April?").

If the design methodology insists on distinguishing between entities and relationships, then (at best) the two interpretations will be treated asymmetrically (i.e., "entity" queries and "relationship" queries will take different forms); at worst, one interpretation will not be supported at all (i.e., one class of query will be impossible to formulate).

As a further illustration of the point, consider the following statement from a tutorial on the E/R approach in reference [14.22]:

> It is common *initially* to represent some relationships as attributes [*meaning, specifically, foreign keys*] during conceptual schema design and then to convert these attributes into relationships as the design progresses and is better understood.

But what happens if an attribute becomes a foreign key at some later time?—that is, if the database evolves after it has already been in existence for some time? If we take this argument to its logical conclusion, database designs should involve only relationships, no attributes at all. (In fact, there is some merit to this latter position. See the annotation to reference [14.23] at the end of the chapter.)

A Final Observation

There are many other semantic modeling schemes in addition to the specific one, E/R modeling, that we have been describing in this chapter. However, most of those schemes do bear a strong family resemblance to one another; in particular, most of them can be characterized as simply providing a graphical notation for representing certain foreign key constraints, plus a few other bits and pieces. Such graphical representations can be useful in a "big picture" kind of way, but they are far too simplistic to do the whole design job.[8] In particular, as noted earlier, they typically cannot deal with general integrity constraints. For example, how would you represent a general join dependency in an E/R diagram?

---

[8] It is a sad comment on the state of the IT field that simple solutions are popular even when they are *too* simple. On such matters, we agree with Einstein, who once said: "Everything should be made as simple as possible—*but no simpler.*"

14.7 SUMMARY

We opened this chapter by presenting a brief introduction to the general idea of **semantic modeling**. There are four broad steps involved, of which the first is informal and the rest are formal:

1. Identify useful semantic concepts.
2. Devise corresponding symbolic objects.
3. Devise corresponding integrity rules ("metaconstraints").
4. Devise corresponding operators.

Some useful semantic concepts are **entity**, **property**, **relationship**, and **subtype**. *Note:* We also stressed the points that (a) there will very likely be **terminological conflicts** between the (informal) semantic modeling level and the underlying (formal) support system level, and (b) such conflicts can cause confusion! *Caveat lector.*

The ultimate objective of semantic modeling research is to make database systems a little more intelligent. A more immediate objective is to provide a basis for a systematic attack on the problem of **database design**. We described in some detail the application of one particular "semantic" model, Chen's **entity/relationship (E/R) model**, to the design problem. We remind you that the original E/R paper [14.6] actually contained two distinct, and more or less independent, proposals: It proposed the E/R model *per se,* and it also proposed the **E/R diagramming technique**. And we claimed in Section 14.4 that the popularity of the E/R model can probably be attributed more to the existence of that diagramming technique than to any other cause. But it is not necessary to adopt all of the ideas of the *model* in order to use the *diagrams;* it is quite possible to use E/R diagrams as a basis for *any* design methodology—perhaps an RM/T-based methodology, for example [14.7]. Arguments regarding the relative suitability of E/R modeling and some other approach as a basis for database design often seem to miss this point.

Let us also contrast the ideas of semantic modeling (and of the E/R model in particular) with the normalization discipline as described in Chapters 12 and 13. The normalization discipline involves reducing large relvars to smaller ones; it assumes that we have some small number of large relvars as input, and it processes that input to produce a large number of small relvars as output—that is, it maps large relvars into small ones (we are speaking very loosely here!). But the normalization discipline has absolutely nothing to say about how we arrive at those large relvars in the first place. Top-down methodologies such as the one described in the present chapter, by contrast, address exactly that problem: They map the real world into large relvars. In other words, the two approaches (top-down design and normalization) *complement each other.* The overall design procedure might thus go something like this:

1. Use the E/R approach—or something analogous[9]—to generate "large" relvars representing regular entities, weak entities, and so on.

[9] Our own preferred approach would be (a) to write down the external predicates that describe the enterprise and then (b) to map those predicates straightforwardly into internal predicates as described in Chapter 9.

2. Use the ideas of further normalization to break those "large" relvars down into "small" ones.

However, you will have realized from the quality of the discussions in the body of this chapter that semantic modeling in general is not nearly as rigorous or clear-cut as the further normalization discipline discussed in Chapters 12 and 13. The reason for this state of affairs is that (as indicated in the introduction to this part of the book) database design is still very much a subjective exercise, not an objective one; there is comparatively little by way of really solid principles that can be brought to bear on the problem (the few principles that do exist being, basically, the principles discussed in the previous two chapters). The ideas of the present chapter can be regarded as more in the way of rules of thumb, albeit ones that do seem to work reasonably well in practical situations.

There is one final point that is worth calling out explicitly. Although the whole field is still somewhat subjective, there is one specific area in which semantic modeling ideas can be very relevant and useful today: namely, the **data dictionary** area. The data dictionary can be regarded in some respects as "the database designer's database"; it is after all a database in which database design decisions are recorded, among other things [14.2]. The study of semantic modeling can thus be useful in the design of the dictionary system, because it identifies the kinds of objects the dictionary itself needs to support and "understand"—for example, entity categories (such as the E/R model's regular and weak entities), integrity rules (such as the E/R model's notion of total *vs.* partial participation in a relationship), entity supertypes and subtypes, and so forth.

EXERCISES

14.1 What do you understand by the term "semantic modeling"?

14.2 Identify the four broad steps involved in defining an "extended" model such as the E/R model.

14.3 Explain the following E/R concepts in your own words:

entity	relationship
inheritance	supertype, subtype
key property	type hierarchy
property	value set
regular entity	weak entity

14.4 Suppose the E/R diagram for suppliers and parts specifies that the participation of parts in shipments is "total" (i.e., every part must be supplied by at least one supplier). How can this constraint be specified in (a) **Tutorial D**, (b) SQL?

14.5 Give examples of:

a. A many-to-many relationship in which one of the participants is a weak entity

b. A many-to-many relationship in which one of the participants is another relationship

c. A many-to-many relationship that has a subtype

d. A subtype that has an associated weak entity that does not apply to the supertype

14.6 Draw an E/R diagram for the education database from Exercise 9.7 in Chapter 9.

14.7 Draw an E/R diagram for the company personnel database from Exercise 12.3 in Chapter 12. Use that diagram to derive an appropriate set of base relvar definitions.

14.8 Draw an E/R diagram for the order-entry database from Exercise 12.4 in Chapter 12. Use that diagram to derive an appropriate set of base relvar definitions.

14.9 Draw an E/R diagram for the sales database from Exercise 13.3 in Chapter 13. Use that diagram to derive an appropriate set of base relvar definitions.

14.10 Draw an E/R diagram for the revised sales database from Exercise 13.5 in Chapter 13. Use that diagram to derive an appropriate set of base relvar definitions.

REFERENCES AND BIBLIOGRAPHY

The length of the following list of references is due, in large part, to the number of competing design methodologies currently to be found in the database world, both in industry and in academia. There is very little consensus in this field; the E/R scheme discussed in the body of the chapter is certainly the most widely used approach, but not everyone agrees with it (or likes it). In fact, the point should be made that the best-*known* approaches are not necessarily the *best* approaches. We remark too that certain of the commercially available products are more than just database design tools, in that they can be used to generate entire applications—front-end screens, application logic, triggers, and so on, as well as database definitions (schemas) in particular. (In this connection, see Ross's books on business rules [9.21, 9.22], also reference [9.15].) Some other references that are relevant to the material of the present chapter are the ISO report on the conceptual schema [2.3] and Kent's book *Data and Reality* [2.4].

14.1 J. R. Abrial: "Data Semantics," in J. W. Klimbie and K. L. Koffeman (eds.), *Data Base Management*. Amsterdam, Netherlands: North-Holland/New York, N.Y.: Elsevier Science (1974).

> One of the very earliest papers on semantic modeling. The following quote nicely captures the general flavor of the paper (some might say of the subject as a whole): "Hint for the reader: If you are looking for a definition of the term *semantics,* stop reading because there is no such definition in this paper."

14.2 Philip A. Bernstein: "The Repository: A Modern Vision," *DBP&D 9,* No. 12 (December 1996).

> The term *repository* seems to be supplanting the older term *dictionary;* thus, a repository system is a DBMS that is specialized to the management of metadata—metadata not just for DBMSs but for all kinds of software tools: "tools for the design, development, and deployment of software, as well as tools for managing electronic designs, mechanical designs, websites, and many other kinds of formal documents related to engineering activities," to quote Bernstein. The paper is a tutorial on repository concepts.

14.3 Michael Blaha and William Premerlani: *Object-Oriented Modeling and Design for Database Applications*. Upper Saddle River, N.J.: Prentice Hall (1998).

> Describes a design methodology called Object Modeling Technique (OMT) in depth. OMT can be regarded as a variation on the E/R model—its *objects* are basically E/R's *entities*—but it covers much more than just database design specifically. See also the annotation to reference [14.37].

14.4 Grady Booch: *Object-Oriented Design with Applications.* Redwood City, Calif.: Benjamin/Cummings (1991).

See the annotation to reference [14.37].

14.5 Grady Booch, James Rumbaugh, and Ivar Jacobson: *The Unified Modeling Language User Guide.* Reading, Mass.: Addison-Wesley (1999).

See the annotation to reference [14.37]. *Note:* Two related books are available from the same authors (in different permutations): *The Unified Modeling Language Reference Manual* (Rumbaugh, Jacobson, Booch) and *The Unified Software Development Process* (Jacobson, Booch, Rumbaugh), both also published by Addison-Wesley in 1999.

14.6 Peter Pin-Shan Chen: "The Entity-Relationship Model—Toward a Unified View of Data," *ACM TODS 1,* No. 1 (March 1976). Republished in Michael Stonebraker (ed.), *Readings in Database Systems.* San Mateo, Calif.: Morgan Kaufmann (1988).

The paper that introduced the E/R model and E/R diagrams. As mentioned in the body of this chapter, the model has been revised and refined considerably over time; certainly the explanations and definitions given in this first paper were quite imprecise, so such refinements were needed. (One of the criticisms of the E/R model has always been that the terms do not seem to have a single, well-defined meaning but are instead interpreted in many different ways. Of course, it is true that the whole database field is bedeviled by inaccurate and conflicting terminology, but this particular area is worse than most.) To illustrate:

- As stated in Section 14.3, an entity is defined as "a thing which can be distinctly identified" and a relationship as "an association among entities." So is a relationship an entity? A relationship is clearly "a thing which can be distinctly identified," but later sections of the paper seem to reserve the term *entity* to mean something that is definitely *not* a relationship. Presumably this latter is the intended interpretation, for otherwise why the term *entity/relationship* model? But the paper really is not clear.

- Entities and relationships can have *attributes* (we used the term *property* in the body of the chapter). Again, the paper is ambivalent as to the meaning of the term—at first it defines an attribute to be a property that is not the primary key, nor any component thereof (contrast the relational definition), but later it uses the term in the relational sense.

- The primary key for a relationship is assumed to be the combination of the foreign keys that identify the entities involved in the relationship (the term *foreign key* is not used, however). But this assumption is appropriate only for many-to-many relationships, and not always then. For example, consider a relvar SPD {S#,P#,DATE,QTY}, which represents shipments of certain parts by certain suppliers on certain dates; assume that the same supplier can ship the same part more than once, but not more than once on the same date. Then the primary key (or, at least, the sole candidate key) is the combination {S#,P#,DATE}; yet we might choose to regard suppliers and parts as entities but dates not.

14.7 E. F. Codd: "Extending the Database Relational Model to Capture More Meaning," *ACM TODS 4,* No. 4 (December 1979).

In this paper, Codd introduced an extended version of the relational model, which he called RM/T. RM/T addresses some of the same issues as the E/R model does but is rather more carefully defined. Some immediate differences between the two are as follows. First, RM/T makes no unnecessary distinctions between entities and relationships (a relationship is regarded merely as a special kind of entity). Second, the structural and integrity aspects of RM/T are more extensive, and more precisely defined, than those of the E/R model. Third, RM/T includes its own special operators, over and above those of the relational model *per se* (though much work remains to be done in this last area).

In outline, RM/T works as follows:

- Entities ("relationships" included) are represented by *E-* and *P-relvars*,[10] both of which are special forms of the general *n*-ary relvar. E-relvars are used to record the fact that certain entities exist, and P-relvars are used to record certain properties of those entities.

- A variety of relationships can exist among entities; for example, entity types *A* and *B* might be linked in an **association** (RM/T's term for a many-to-many relationship), or entity type *Y* might be a **subtype** of entity type *X*. RM/T includes a formal **catalog** structure by which such relationships can be made known to the system; the system is thus capable of enforcing the various **integrity constraints** that are implied by the existence of such relationships.

- A number of high-level **operators** are provided to facilitate the manipulation of the various RM/T objects (E-relvars, P-relvars, catalog relvars, etc.).

Like the E/R model, RM/T includes analogs of all of the constructs (entity, property, relationship, subtype) listed in Fig. 14.1. Specifically, it provides an **entity classification scheme**, which in many respects constitutes the most significant aspect—or, at least, the most immediately visible aspect—of the entire model. According to that scheme, entities are divided into three categories, called *kernels, characteristics,* and *associations,* as follows:

- **Kernels:** Kernel entities are entities that have *independent existence;* they are "what the database is really all about." In other words, kernels are entities that are neither characteristic nor associative (see the next two bullet items).

- **Characteristics:** A characteristic entity is an entity whose primary purpose is to describe or "characterize" some other entity. Characteristics are *existence-dependent* on the entity they describe. The entity described can be kernel, characteristic, or associative.

- **Associations:** An associative entity is an entity that represents a *many-to-many* (or many-to-many-to-many, etc.) *relationship* among two or more other entities. The entities associated can each be kernel, characteristic, or associative.

In addition:

- Entities (regardless of their classification) can also have **properties**.

- In particular, any entity (again, regardless of its classification) can have a property that **designates** some other related entity. A designation represents a many-to-one relationship between two entities. *Note:* Designations were not discussed in the original RM/T paper but were added later.

- Entity **supertypes** and **subtypes** are supported. If *Y* is a subtype of *X,* then *Y* is a kernel, a characteristic, or an association depending on whether *X* is a kernel, a characteristic, or an association.

We can relate the foregoing concepts to their E/R analogs, somewhat loosely, as follows: A kernel corresponds to an E/R "regular entity"; a characteristic corresponds to an E/R "weak entity," and an association corresponds to an E/R "relationship" (many-to-many variety only).

In addition to those aspects already discussed, RM/T also includes some proposals for supporting (a) *surrogates* (see reference [14.21]), (b) the *time* dimension (see Chapter 23), and (c) various kinds of *data aggregation* (see references [14.40, 14.41]).

14.8 C. J. Date: "A Note on One-to-One Relationships," in *Relational Database Writings 1985–1989.* Reading, Mass.: Addison-Wesley (1990).

---

[10] The paper calls them E- and P-*relations*.

An extensive discussion of the problem of one-to-one relationships, which turn out to be rather more complicated than they might appear at first sight.

14.9 C. J. Date: "Entity/Relationship Modeling and the Relational Model," in C. J. Date and Hugh Darwen, *Relational Database Writings 1989–1991*. Reading, Mass.: Addison-Wesley (1992).

14.10 C. J. Date: "Don't Encode Information into Primary Keys!", in C. J. Date and Hugh Darwen, *Relational Database Writings 1989–1991*. Reading, Mass.: Addison-Wesley (1992).

Presents a series of informal arguments against what are sometimes called "intelligent keys." See also reference [14.11] for some related recommendations regarding foreign keys.

14.11 C. J. Date: "Composite Keys," in C. J. Date and Hugh Darwen, *Relational Database Writings 1989–1991*. Reading, Mass.: Addison-Wesley (1992).

To quote from the abstract: "Arguments for and against the inclusion of composite [keys] in the design of a relational database are summarized and some . . . recommendations offered." In particular, the paper shows that surrogate keys [14.21] are not *always* a good idea.

14.12 C. J. Date: "A Database Design Dilemma?", *http://www.dbpd.com* (January 1999).

On the face of it, a given entity type—employees, say—could be represented in a relational system either by an employees *type* or by an employees *relvar.* This short paper (which is based on Appendix C of reference [3.3]) gives some guidance on how to choose between the two possibilities.

14.13 C. J. Date: "Subtables and Supertables," Appendix E of reference [3.3].

It is often thought that entity type inheritance should be dealt with in a relational context by means of what are called "subtables and supertables"—the entity subtype mapping to a "subtable" and the entity supertype mapping to a "supertable." For example, the SQL standard supports such an approach (see Chapter 26), and so do certain products. Reference [14.13] argues against this idea, strongly.

14.14 C. J. Date: "Twelve Rules for Business Rules," *http://www.versata.com* (May 1, 2000).

Proposes a set of rules, or *prescriptions,* that a "good" business rule system ought to abide by.

14.15 C. J. Date: "Models, Models, Everywhere, Nor Any Time to Think," *http://www.dbdebunk .com* (November 2000).

The term *model* is grotesquely overused (not to say abused) in the IT world, especially in the database community. This paper was written to alert people to some of the worst excesses in this regard and to try to persuade them to think twice (at least!) before using the term themselves.

14.16 C. J. Date: "Basic Concepts in UML: A Request for Clarification," *http://www.dbdebunk.com* (December 2000/January 2001).

This two-part paper is an examination and seriously critical analysis of the Unified Modeling Language, UML, with particular reference to the Object Constraint Language, OCL. Part I is primarily concerned with "the OCL book" [14.49]; Part II looks at "the UML book" [14.5].

14.17 Debabrata Dey, Veda C. Storey, and Terence M. Barron: "Improving Database Design Through the Analysis of Relationships," *ACM TODS 24,* No. 4 (December 1999).

14.18 Ramez Elmasri and Shamkant B. Navathe: *Fundamentals of Database Systems* (3d ed.). Redwood City, Calif.: Benjamin/Cummings (2000).

This general textbook on database management includes two full chapters on the use of E/R techniques for database design.

14.19 David W. Embley: *Object Database Development: Concepts and Principles*. Reading, Mass.: Addison-Wesley (1998).

> Presents a design methodology based on OSM (Object-oriented Systems Model). Parts of OSM resemble ORM [14.22–14.24].

14.20 Candace C. Fleming and Barbara von Hallé: *Handbook of Relational Database Design*. Reading, Mass.: Addison-Wesley (1989).

> A practical guide to database design in a relational system, with specific examples based on IBM's DB2 product and the Teradata (now NCR) DBC/1012 product. Both logical and physical design issues are addressed. Be warned, however, that the book uses the term *logical design* to mean what we would call "relational design," and the term *relational design* to include at least some aspects of what we would call "physical design" (!).

14.21 P. Hall, J. Owlett, and S. J. P. Todd: "Relations and Entities," in G. M. Nijssen (ed.), *Modelling in Data Base Management Systems*. Amsterdam, Netherlands: North-Holland/New York, N.Y.: Elsevier Science (1975).

> The first paper to treat the concept of **surrogate keys** in detail (the concept was later incorporated into RM/T [14.7]). Surrogate keys are keys in the usual relational sense but have the following specific properties:
>
> - They always involve exactly one attribute.
>
> - Their values serve *solely* as surrogates (hence the name) for the entities they stand for. In other words, such values serve merely to represent the fact that the corresponding entities exist—they carry absolutely no additional information or meaning, nor any other baggage of any kind.
>
> - When a new entity is inserted into the database, it is given a surrogate key value that has never been used before and will never be used again, even if the entity in question is subsequently deleted.
>
> Ideally, surrogate key values would be system-generated, but whether they are system- or user-generated has nothing to do with the basic idea of surrogate keys as such.
>
> It is worth emphasizing that surrogates are not, as some writers seem to think, the same thing as tuple IDs (or row IDs). For one thing, to state the obvious, tuple IDs identify tuples and surrogates identify entities, and there is certainly nothing like a one-to-one correspondence between tuples and entities. (Think of derived tuples in particular—e.g., tuples in the result of some arbitrary query. In fact, it is not at all clear that derived tuples will have tuple IDs anyway.) Furthermore, tuple IDs have performance connotations, while surrogates do not; access to a tuple via its tuple ID is usually assumed to be fast (we are assuming here that base tuples, at least, map fairly directly to physical storage, as is indeed the case in most of today's products). Also, tuple IDs are usually concealed from the user, while surrogates must not be (because of *The Information Principle*); in other words, it is not possible to store a tuple ID as an attribute value, while it certainly is possible to store a surrogate as an attribute value.
>
> In a nutshell: Surrogates are a model concept; tuple IDs are an implementation concept.

14.22 Terry Halpin: *Information Modeling and Relational Databases: From Conceptual Analysis to Logical Design*. San Francisco, Calif.: Morgan Kaufmann (2001).

> A detailed treatment of ORM (see the annotation to the next two references below). Among many other things, the book discusses the relationships between (a) ORM and E/R modeling and (b) ORM and UML. *Note:* The book is a major revision and expansion of an earlier book by the same author, *Conceptual Schema and Relational Database Design* (2d edition), published by Prentice Hall of Australia Pty., Ltd. (1995).

14.23 Terry Halpin: "Business Rules and Object-Role Modeling," *DBP&D 9,* No. 10 (October 1996).

An excellent introduction to **object-role modeling**, ORM [14.22]. Halpin begins by observing that "[unlike] E/R modeling, which has dozens of different dialects, ORM has only a few dialects with only minor differences." (*Note:* One of those dialects is NIAM [14.34].) ORM is also known as *fact-based* modeling, because what the designer does is write down—either in natural language or in a special graphical notation—a series of *elementary facts* (or fact *types,* rather) that together characterize the enterprise to be modeled. Examples of such fact types might be:

- Each Employee has at most one Empname.
- Each Employee reports to at most one Employee.
- If Employee *e1* reports to Employee *e2,* then it cannot be that Employee *e2* reports to Employee *e1.*
- No Employee can direct and assess the same Project.

As you can see, fact types are really *external predicates,* or in other words *business rules;* as the title of Halpin's paper suggests, ORM is very much in the spirit of the approach to database design that is preferred by the business rules advocates, and indeed by the present writer. In general, facts specify *roles* played by *objects* in relationships (hence the name "object-role modeling"). Note that (a) "objects" here really means entities, not objects in the special sense described in Part VI of this book, and (b) relationships are not necessarily binary. However, facts are *elementary*—they cannot be decomposed into smaller facts. *Note:* The idea that the database should contain only elementary (or *irreducible*) facts at the conceptual level was proposed earlier by Hall, Owlett, and Todd in reference [14.21].

Observe that ORM has no concept of "attributes." As a consequence, ORM designs are conceptually simpler and more robust than their E/R counterparts, as the paper shows (in this connection, see also the annotation to reference [14.24]). However, attributes can and do appear in E/R or SQL designs that are generated (automatically) from an ORM design.

ORM also emphasizes the use of "sample facts" (i.e., sample fact *instances*—what we would call *propositions*) as a way of allowing the end user to validate the design. The claim is that such an approach is straightforward with fact-based modeling, much less so with E/R modeling.

Now, there are many logically equivalent ways of describing a given enterprise, and hence many logically equivalent ORM schemas. ORM therefore includes a set of *transformation rules* that allow logically equivalent schemas to be transformed into one another, thus allowing an ORM tool to perform some optimization on the design as specified by the human designer. It is also possible, as previously mentioned, to generate an E/R or SQL schema from an ORM schema, and to reverse-engineer an ORM schema from an existing E/R or SQL schema. Depending on the target DBMS, a generated SQL schema can include SQL-style declarative constraints, or those constraints can be implemented via triggers or stored procedures. Regarding constraints, incidentally, note that, unlike the E/R model, ORM *by definition* includes "a rich language for expressing constraints." (However, Halpin does admit in reference [14.24] that not all business rules can be expressed in the ORM *graphical* notation—text is still needed for this purpose.)

Finally, an ORM schema can be regarded as a high-level, abstract view of the database; in fact, we would argue that it is rather close to a pure, perhaps somewhat disciplined, *relational* view. As such, it can serve as a basis for direct query formulation. See the annotation to reference [14.24] immediately following.

14.24 Terry Halpin: "Conceptual Queries," *Data Base Newsletter 26,* No. 2 (March/April 1998).

To quote the abstract: "Formulating nontrivial queries in relational languages such as SQL or QBE can prove daunting to end users. *ConQuer,* a new conceptual query language based on object-role modeling (ORM), enables users to pose queries in a readily understandable way . . . This article highlights the advantages of [such a language] over traditional query languages for specifying queries and business rules." Among other things, the article discusses a ConQuer query somewhat along the following lines:

```
✓ Employee
     +— drives Car
     +— works for ✓ Branch
```

("Get employee and branch for employees who drive cars"). If employees can drive any number of cars but work for just one branch, the underlying SQL design will involve two tables, and the generated SQL code will look something like this:

```
SELECT DISTINCT X1.EMP#, X1.BRANCH#
FROM    EMPLOYEE AS X1, DRIVES AS X2
WHERE   X1.EMP# = X2.EMP# ;
```

Now suppose it becomes possible for employees to work for several branches at the same time. Then the underlying SQL design will have to change to involve three tables instead of two, and the generated SQL code will have to change as well:

```
SELECT DISTINCT X1.EMP#, X3.BRANCH#
FROM    EMPLOYEE AS X1, DRIVES AS X2, WORKS_FOR AS X3
WHERE   X1.EMP# = X2.EMP# AND X1.EMP# = X3.EMP# ;
```

The ConQuer formulation remains unchanged, however.

As the foregoing example illustrates, a language like ConQuer can be regarded as providing a particularly strong form of logical data independence. In order to explain this remark, however, we first need to say a little more regarding the ANSI/SPARC architecture. We said in Chapter 2 that logical data independence meant independence of changes to the conceptual schema—but the whole point of the foregoing example is that changes to the conceptual schema do not occur! The trouble is, today's SQL products do not properly support a conceptual schema, they support an *SQL* schema instead. And that SQL schema can be regarded as lying at an intermediate level between the true conceptual level and the internal or physical level. If an ORM tool allows us to define a true conceptual schema and then map it to an SQL schema, then ConQuer can provide independence of changes to that SQL schema (by making appropriate changes to the mapping, of course).

It is not clear from the paper what limits there might be on ConQuer's expressive power. Halpin does not address this question directly; however, he does say (a little worryingly) that "the language should ideally allow you to formulate any question relevant to your application; in practice, something less than this ideal is acceptable" (slightly reworded). He also states that ConQuer's "most powerful feature . . . is its ability to perform *correlations* of arbitrary complexity," and gives the following as an example:

```
✓ Employee1
     +— lives in City1
     +— was born in Country1
     +— supervises Employee2
          +— lives in City1
          +— was born in Country2 <> Country1
```

("Get employees who supervise an employee living in the same city as the supervisor but born in a different country from the supervisor"). As Halpin says: Try this in SQL!

Finally, regarding ConQuer and business rules, Halpin has this to say: "Although ORM's graphical notation can capture more business rules than [E/R approaches], it still needs to be supplemented by a textual language [for expressing certain constraints]. Research is currently under way to adapt ConQuer for this purpose."

14.25 M. M. Hammer and D. J. McLeod: "The Semantic Data Model: A Modelling Mechanism for Database Applications," Proc. 1978 ACM SIGMOD Int. Conf. on Management of Data, Austin, Tex. (May/June 1978).

The Semantic Data Model (SDM) constitutes another proposal for a database design formalism. Like the E/R model, it concentrates on structural and (to some extent) integrity aspects, and has little or nothing to say regarding manipulative aspects. See also references [14.26] and [14.29].

14.26 Michael Hammer and Dennis McLeod: "Database Description with SDM: A Semantic Database Model," *ACM TODS 6,* No. 3 (September 1981).

See the annotation to reference [14.25].

14.27 Richard Hull and Roger King: "Semantic Database Modeling: Survey, Applications, and Research Issues," *ACM Comp. Surv. 19,* No. 3 (September 1987).

A comprehensive tutorial on the semantic modeling field and related matters as of the late 1980s. This paper is a good place to start a deeper investigation into the issues and research problems surrounding semantic modeling activities. See also reference [14.36].

14.28 Ivar Jacobson, Magnus Christerson, Patrick Jonsson, and Gunnar Övergaard: *Object-Oriented Software Engineering* (revised printing). Reading, Mass.: Addison-Wesley (1994).

Describes a design methodology called Object-Oriented Software Engineering (OOSE). Like OMT [14.3], the database portions, at least, of OOSE can be regarded as a variation on the E/R model (as with OMT, OOSE's *objects* are basically E/R's *entities*). The following quote is worthy of note: "Most of the methods used in the industry today, for both information and technical system development, are based on a functional and/or data-driven decomposition of the system. These approaches differ in many ways from the approach taken by object-oriented methods where data and functions are highly integrated." It seems to us that here the authors put their collective finger on a significant mismatch between object and database thinking. Databases—at least, general-purpose, shared databases, which are the primary focus of the database community at large—are *supposed* to be divorced from "functions"; they are *supposed* to be designed separately from the applications that use them. Thus, it seems to us that the term *database* as used in the object community really means a database that is *application-specific,* not one that is shared and general-purpose (in this connection, see the discussion of object databases in Chapter 25). See also the annotation to references [14.5], [14.16], and [14.37].

14.29 D. Jagannathan *et al.*: "SIM: A Database System Based on the Semantic Data Model," Proc. 1988 ACM SIGMOD Int. Conf. on Management of Data, Chicago, Ill. (June 1988).

Describes a commercial DBMS product based on "a semantic data model similar to" the Semantic Data Model proposed by Hammer and McLeod in reference [14.25].

14.30 Warren Keuffel: "Battle of the Modeling Techniques: A Look at the Three Most Popular Modeling Notations for Distilling the Essence of Data," *DBMS 9,* No. 9 (August 1996).

The "three most popular modeling notations" are said to be E/R modeling; Nijssen's Natural-language Information Analysis Method, NIAM [14.34]; and Semantic Object Modeling, SOM. Keuffel asserts that E/R modeling is the "grandfather" of the other two, but he is critical of its lack of a formal foundation; as he says, entities, relationships, and attributes (i.e., properties) are all "described without reference to how they are discovered." NIAM is much more rigorous; when its rules are followed faithfully, the resulting conceptual designs "possess much more integrity" than designs produced using other methodologies, although "some developers find the rigor of NIAM too confining" (!). As for SOM, it "resembles E/R modeling . . . with [its similarly] vaguely articulated definitions of entities, attributes, and relationships"; it differs from E/R modeling, however, in that it supports *group attributes* (i.e., repeating groups, in effect), which allow one "object" (i.e., entity) to contain others. (E/R modeling allows entities to contain repeating groups of *attributes* but not of other *entities*.)

14.31 Heikki Mannila and Kari-Jouko Räihä: *The Design of Relational Databases.* Reading, Mass.: Addison-Wesley (1992).

To quote from the preface, this book is "a graduate level textbook and reference on the design of relational databases." It covers both dependency theory and normalization on the one hand and the E/R approach on the other, in each case from a fairly formal perspective. The following (incomplete) list of chapter titles gives some idea of the book's scope:

- Design Principles
- Integrity Constraints and Dependencies
- Properties of Relational Schemas
- Axiomatizations for Dependencies
- Algorithms for Design Problems
- Mappings Between E/R Diagrams and Relational Database Schemas
- Schema Transformations
- Use of Example Databases in Design

 The techniques described in the book have been implemented by the authors in the form of a commercially available tool called Design By Example.

14.32 Terry Moriarty: *Enterprise View* (regular column), *DBP&D 10,* No. 8 (August 1997).

Describes a commercial application design and development tool called Usoft (*http://www .usoft.com*) that allows business rules to be defined using an SQL-like syntax and uses those rules to generate the application (including the database definition).

14.33 G. M. Nijssen, D. J. Duke, and S. M. Twine: "The Entity-Relationship Data Model Considered Harmful," Proc. 6th Symposium on Empirical Foundations of Information and Software Sciences, Atlanta, Ga. (October 1988).

"The E/R model considered harmful?" Well, it does seem that it has a lot to answer for, including:

- Confusion over the distinction between types and relvars (see the discussion of **The First Great Blunder** in Chapter 26)
- The strange business of "subtables and supertables" (see reference [14.13], also Chapter 26)
- A widespread failure to appreciate *The Principle of Database Relativity* (see Chapter 10)
- A widespread perception that there is or should be a distinction between entities and relationships, as discussed in the present chapter

 Reference [14.33] adds to the foregoing litany. To be more specific, it claims that the E/R model:

- Provides too many overlapping ways of representing data structure, thereby complicating the design process unduly.
- Provides no guidance on how to choose between alternative representations, and in fact can require existing designs to be changed unnecessarily if circumstances change.

- Provides too few ways of representing data integrity, thereby making certain aspects of the design process impossible ("[it is true that] constraints can be formally expressed in a more general notation [such as] predicate logic, [but] saying that this is a reasonable excuse for omitting [constraints] from the data model itself is like saying that a programming language is adequate [even though] it forces you to call assembly language routines to implement all those things you can't express in the language itself!").

- Contrary to popular opinion, does not serve as a good vehicle for communication between end users and database professionals.

- Violates *The Conceptualization Principle:* "A conceptual schema should . . . include [only] conceptually relevant aspects, both static and dynamic, of the universe of discourse, thus excluding all aspects of (external or internal) data representation, physical data organization and access, [and] all aspects of particular external user representation such as message formats, data structures, etc." [2.3]. In fact, the authors suggest that the E/R model is "essentially just a reincarnation" of the old CODASYL network model. "Could this strong bias toward implementation structures be the major reason that the E/R model has received such wide acceptance in the professional [database] community?"

The paper also identifies numerous additional weaknesses of the E/R model at the detail level. It then proposes the alternative methodology NIAM [14.34] as a way forward. In particular, it stresses the point that NIAM does not include the unnecessary E/R distinction between attributes and relationships.

14.34 T. W. Olle, H. G. Sol, and A. A. Verrijn-Stuart (eds.): *Information Systems Design Methodologies: A Comparative Review.* Amsterdam, Netherlands: North-Holland/New York, N.Y.: Elsevier Science (1982).

The proceedings of an IFIP Working Group 8.1 conference. Some 13 different methodologies are described and applied to a standard benchmark problem. One of the methodologies included is NIAM (see reference [14.33]); the paper in question must be one of the earliest on the NIAM approach. The book also includes reviews of some of the proposed approaches, again including NIAM in particular.

14.35 M. P. Papazoglou: "Unraveling the Semantics of Conceptual Schemas," *CACM 38,* No. 9 (September 1995).

This paper proposes an approach to what might be called *metadata queries*—that is, queries regarding the meaning (as opposed to the values) of the data in the database, or in other words queries regarding the conceptual schema itself. An example of such a query might be "What is a permanent employee?"

14.36 Joan Peckham and Fred Maryanski: "Semantic Data Models," *ACM Comp. Surv. 20,* No. 3 (September 1988).

A tutorial survey (see also reference [14.27]).

14.37 Paul Reed: "The Unified Modeling Language Takes Shape," *DBMS 11,* No. 8 (July 1998).

The Unified Modeling Language, UML, is yet another graphical notation to support the task of application design and development (in other words, it lets you develop applications, at least in part, by drawing pictures). It can also be used to develop SQL schemas. *Note:* When it first appeared, UML was expected to become commercially significant very quickly, partly because it was adopted as a standard by the Object Management Group, OMG (it does have a strong object flavor overall). But it now seems that its overall level of acceptance is rather less than was originally anticipated, though it is true that it is supported by a number of commercial products.

Be that as it may, UML supports the modeling of both data and processes (it goes beyond E/R modeling in this regard), but it does not seem to have much to say concerning integrity constraints. (The section of reference [14.37] titled "From Models to Code: Business Rules" does not mention the term *declarative* at all! Rather, it concentrates on the generation of *procedural application code* to implement "processes." Here is a direct quote: "The UML formalizes what object practitioners have known for years: Real-world objects are best modeled as self-contained entities that contain both data and functionality." And elsewhere: "It is evident from a historical perspective that the formal separation of data and function has rendered much of our software development efforts fragile at best." These remarks might be valid from an application perspective, but it is not at all clear that they are valid from a database perspective. See, e.g., reference [25.25].)

UML grew out of earlier work by Booch on "Booch method" [14.4], Rumbaugh on OMT [14.3], and Jacobson on OOSE [14.28]. See also references [14.5] and [14.16].

14.38 H. A. Schmid and J. R. Swenson: "On the Semantics of the Relational Data Base Model," Proc. 1975 ACM SIGMOD Int. Conf. on Management of Data, San Jose, Calif. (May 1975).

This paper proposed a "basic semantic model" that predated Chen's work on the E/R model [14.6] but in fact was very similar to that model (except in terminology—Schmid and Swenson used *independent object, dependent object,* and *association* in place of Chen's terms *regular entity, weak entity,* and *relationship,* respectively).

14.39 J. F. Sowa: *Conceptual Structures: Information Processing in Mind and Machine.* Reading, Mass.: Addison-Wesley (1984).

This book is not about database systems specifically but rather about the general problem of knowledge representation and processing. However, parts of it are directly relevant to the topic of the present chapter. (The remarks that follow are based on a live presentation by Sowa in or around 1990 on the application of "conceptual structures" to semantic modeling.) A major problem with E/R diagrams and similar formalisms is that they are strictly less powerful than formal logic. As a consequence, they are completely incapable of dealing with certain important design features—in particular, anything involving explicit quantification, which includes almost all integrity constraints—that formal logic *can* handle. (The quantifiers were invented by Frege in 1879, which makes E/R diagrams "a pre-1879 kind of logic"!) But formal logic tends to be hard to read; as Sowa says, "predicate calculus is the assembly language of knowledge representation." *Conceptual graphs* are a readable, rigorous, graphical notation that can represent the whole of logic. They are therefore (Sowa claims) much better suited to the activity of semantic modeling than are E/R diagrams and the like.

14.40 J. M. Smith and D. C. P. Smith: "Database Abstractions: Aggregation," *CACM 20,* No. 6 (June 1977).

See reference [14.41] immediately following.

14.41 J. M. Smith and D. C. P. Smith: "Database Abstractions: Aggregation and Generalization," *ACM TODS 2,* No. 2 (June 1977).

The proposals of these two papers [14.40, 14.41] had a significant influence on RM/T [14.7], especially in the area of entity subtypes and supertypes.

14.42 Veda C. Storey: "Understanding Semantic Relationships," *The VLDB Journal 2,* No. 4 (October 1993).

To quote from the abstract: "Semantic data models have been developed [in the database community] using abstractions such as [subtyping], aggregation, and association. Besides these well-known relationships, a number of additional semantic relationships have been identified by researchers in other disciplines such as linguistics, logic, and cognitive psychology. This article explores some of [these latter] relationships and discusses . . . their impact on database design."

14.43 B. Sundgren: "The Infological Approach to Data Bases," in J. W. Klimbie and K. L. Koffeman (eds.), *Data Base Management*. Amsterdam, Netherlands: North-Holland/New York, N.Y.: Elsevier Science (1974).

The "infological approach" was one of the earliest semantic modeling schemes to be developed. It was successfully used for database design for many years in Scandinavia.

14.44 Dan Tasker: *Fourth Generation Data: A Guide to Data Analysis for New and Old Systems.* Sydney, Australia: Prentice Hall of Australia Pty., Ltd. (1989).

A practical guide to database design, with the emphasis on "individual data items" (on *types*, in effect). Data items are divided into three basic kinds: label, quantity, and description. *Label* items stand for entities; in relational terms, they correspond to keys. *Quantity* items represent amounts or measures or positions on a scale (possibly a timeline scale), and are subject to the usual arithmetic manipulations. *Description* items are all of the rest. (Of course, there is much more to the classification scheme than this brief sketch can suggest.) The book goes on to deal with each kind in considerable detail. The discussions are not always "relationally pure"—for example, Tasker's use of the term *domain* does not fully coincide with the relational use of that good term—but the book does contain a good deal of sound advice.

14.45 Toby J. Teorey and James P. Fry: *Design of Database Structures.* Englewood Cliffs, N.J.: Prentice Hall (1982).

A textbook on all aspects of database design. The book is divided into five parts: Introduction, Conceptual Design, Implementation Design (i.e., mapping the conceptual design to constructs that a specific DBMS can understand), Physical Design, and Special Design Issues.

14.46 Toby J. Teorey, Dongqing Yang, and James P. Fry: "A Logical Design Methodology for Relational Databases Using the Extended Entity-Relationship Model," *ACM Comp. Surv. 18,* No. 2 (June 1986).

The "extended E/R model" of this paper's title adds support for entity type hierarchies, nulls (see Chapter 19), and relationships involving more than two participants.

14.47 Toby J. Teorey: *Database Modeling and Design: The Entity-Relationship Approach* (3rd edition). San Francisco, Calif.: Morgan Kaufmann (1998).

A more recent textbook on the application of E/R and "extended" E/R concepts [14.46] to database design.

14.48 Yair Wand, Veda C. Storey, and Ron Weber: "An Ontological Analysis of the Relationship Construct in Conceptual Modeling," *ACM TODS 24,* No. 4 (December 1999).

14.49 Jos Warmer and Anneke Kleppe: *The Object Constraint Language: Precise Modeling with UML.* Reading, Mass.: Addison-Wesley (1999).

See the annotation to reference [14.16].

PART IV

TRANSACTION MANAGEMENT

This part of the book consists of two chapters. The topics of those chapters, recovery and concurrency, are very much interrelated, both of them being aspects of the broader topic of *transaction management;* for pedagogic reasons, however, it is desirable to treat them separately as far as possible.

Recovery and concurrency—or, rather, recovery and concurrency *controls*—are both concerned with the general business of **data protection**: that is, protecting the data in the database (also results, to some extent) against loss or damage. In particular, they are concerned with problems such as the following:

- The system might crash in the middle of executing some program, thereby leaving the database in an unknown state.

- Or two programs executing at the same time ("concurrently") might interfere with each other and hence produce incorrect results, either inside the database or in the outside world.

Chapter 15 deals with recovery and Chapter 16 with concurrency.

Recovery

15.1   INTRODUCTION

As noted in the introduction to this part of the book, the topics of recovery and concurrency are very much intertwined. From a pedagogic point of view, however, it is desirable to keep them separate as much as possible; thus, our primary focus in this chapter is on recovery specifically, and we leave concurrency to Chapter 16 (though references to concurrency will inevitably creep into this chapter from time to time, especially in Section 15.4).

Recovery in a database system means, primarily, recovering the database itself: that is, restoring the database to a correct state after some failure has rendered the current state incorrect, or at least suspect. (We will elaborate on what we mean by "a correct state of the database" in the next section.) And the underlying principle on which such recovery is based is quite simple, and can be summed up in one word: **redundancy**. (Redundancy, that is, at the physical level; we do not want such redundancy to show through to the logical level, naturally, for reasons discussed in detail elsewhere in this book.) In other words, the way to make sure the database is recoverable is to make sure that any piece of information it contains can be reconstructed from some other information stored, redundantly, somewhere else in the system.

Before going any further, we should make it clear that the ideas of recovery (indeed, the ideas of transaction processing in general) are largely independent of whether the underlying system is relational or otherwise—though it is true that most of the theoretical work on transaction processing has historically been done, and continues to be done, in a relational context specifically. We should also make it clear that this is an enormous subject!—all we can hope to do here is introduce some of the most important ideas. See the "References and Bibliography" section for some suggestions for further reading. Reference [15.12] is particularly recommended.

The plan of the chapter is as follows. Following this introductory section, Sections 15.2 and 15.3 explain the fundamental notion of a *transaction* and the associated idea of *transaction recovery* (i.e., recovering after some individual transaction has failed). Section 15.4 then goes on to expand the foregoing ideas into the broader realm of *system* recovery (i.e., recovering after some kind of system crash has caused all current transactions to fail simultaneously). Section 15.5 takes a slight detour into the question of *media* recovery (i.e., recovering after the database has been physically damaged in some way—e.g., by a head crash on the disk). Section 15.6 then introduces the crucially important concept of *two-phase commit,* and Section 15.7 discusses *savepoints.* Section 15.8 describes the relevant facilities of SQL. Finally, Section 15.9 presents a summary and a few concluding remarks.

One last preliminary note: We assume throughout this chapter that we are in a "large" (shared, multi-user) database environment. "Small" (nonshared, single-user) DBMSs typically provide little or no recovery support; instead, recovery in such a system is typically regarded as the user's responsibility, implying that the user has to make periodic backup copies of the database and redo work manually if a failure occurs.

15.2   TRANSACTIONS

A transaction is a **logical unit of work**; it begins with the execution of a BEGIN TRANSACTION operation, and ends with the execution of a COMMIT or ROLLBACK operation. Consider Fig. 15.1, which shows pseudocode for a transaction whose purpose is to transfer the sum of $100 from account 123 to account 456. As you can see, what is presumably intended to be a single atomic operation—"transfer money from one account to another"—in fact involves two separate updates on the database. Moreover, the database is in an incorrect state between those two updates, in the sense that it does not reflect a valid state of affairs in the real world; clearly, a real-world transfer from one account to another must not affect the total number of dollars in the accounts concerned, but in the example the sum of $100 temporarily goes missing (as it were) between the two updates. Thus, the logical unit of work that is a transaction does not necessarily involve just a single database operation. Rather, it involves a *sequence* of several such operations, in general, and the

```
      BEGIN TRANSACTION ;

      UPDATE ACC 123 { BALANCE := BALANCE - $100 } ;
      IF any error occurred THEN GO TO UNDO ; END IF ;

      UPDATE ACC 456 { BALANCE := BALANCE + $100 } ;
      IF any error occurred THEN GO TO UNDO ; END IF ;

      COMMIT ;                          /* successful termination  */
      GO TO FINISH ;

UNDO :
      ROLLBACK ;                        /* unsuccessful termination */

FINISH :
      RETURN ;
```

Fig. 15.1   A sample transaction (pseudocode)

purpose of that sequence is to transform a correct state of the database into another such state, without necessarily preserving correctness at all intermediate points.

Now, it is clear that what must not be allowed to happen in the example is for one of the updates to be executed and the other not, because that would leave the database in an incorrect state. Ideally, we would like an ironclad guarantee that both updates will be executed. Unfortunately, it is impossible to provide any such guarantee—there is always a chance that things will go wrong, and go wrong moreover at the worst possible moment. For example, a system crash might occur between the two updates, or an arithmetic overflow might occur on the second of them, and so on.[1] But a system that supports **transaction management** does provide the next best thing to such a guarantee. Specifically, it guarantees that if the transaction executes some updates and then a failure occurs before the transaction reaches its planned termination, *then those updates will be undone*. Thus, the transaction *either* executes in its entirety *or* is totally canceled (i.e., made as if it never executed at all). In this way, a sequence of operations that is fundamentally not atomic can be made to look as if it were atomic from an external point of view.

The system component that provides this atomicity (or semblance of atomicity) is known as the **transaction manager**—also known as the **transaction processing monitor** or **TP monitor**—and the COMMIT and ROLLBACK operations are the key to the way it works:

- The COMMIT operation signals *successful* end-of-transaction: It tells the transaction manager that a logical unit of work has been successfully completed, the database should now be in a correct state again, and all of the updates made by that unit of work can be "committed" (i.e., recorded in the database).

- By contrast, the ROLLBACK operation signals *unsuccessful* end-of-transaction: It tells the transaction manager that something has gone wrong, the database might

---

[1] System crash, which affects all transactions running at the time, is also known as a *global* or *system* failure, and a failure such as overflow that affects just one transaction is also known as a *local* failure. See Sections 15.4 and 15.3, respectively.

be in an incorrect state, and all of the updates made by the logical unit of work so far must be "rolled back" (i.e., undone).

In the example, therefore, if we get through the two updates successfully, we issue a COMMIT to record those updates "permanently" (or "persistently") in the database. If anything goes wrong, however—that is, if either update raises an error condition—we issue a ROLLBACK instead, to undo all updates made so far.

We use the simple example of Fig. 15.1 to make a number of further important points:

- *Implicit ROLLBACK:* The example includes explicit tests for errors and issues an explicit ROLLBACK if an error is detected. But we cannot assume, nor would we want to assume, that transactions always include explicit tests for all possible errors. Therefore, the system will issue an *implicit* ROLLBACK for any transaction that fails for any reason to reach its planned termination (where "planned termination" means either an explicit COMMIT or an explicit ROLLBACK).

- *Message handling:* A typical transaction will not only update the database (or try to), it will also send some kind of message back to the end user indicating what has happened. In the example, we might send the message "Transfer done" if the COMMIT is reached, or the message "Error—transfer not done" otherwise. Message handling, in turn, has additional implications for recovery. See reference [15.12] for further discussion.

- *Recovery log:* You might be wondering how it is possible to undo an update. The answer is that the system maintains a **log** or **journal** on tape or (more commonly) disk, on which details of all updates—in particular, values of updated objects (e.g., tuples) before and after each update, sometimes called *before and after images*—are recorded. Thus, if it becomes necessary to undo some particular update, the system can use the corresponding log record to restore the updated object to its previous value. *Note:* Actually this explanation is somewhat oversimplified. In practice, the log will consist of two portions, an *active* or online portion and an *archive* or offline portion. The online portion is the portion used during normal system operation to record details of updates as they are performed, and is normally kept on disk. When the online portion becomes full, its contents are transferred to the offline portion, which (because it is always processed sequentially) can be kept on tape.

- *Statement atomicity:* The system must guarantee that individual statements—individual statement *executions,* that is—are atomic. This consideration becomes particularly significant in a relational system, where statements are set-level and typically operate on many tuples at a time; it must not be possible for such a statement to fail in the middle and leave the database in an incorrect state (e.g., with some tuples updated and some not). In other words, if an error does occur in the middle of such a statement, then the database must remain totally unchanged. Moreover, as explained in Chapters 9 and 10, the same is true even if the statement causes additional updates to occur under the covers (e.g., because of a cascade delete rule, or because a join view is being updated).

- *Program execution is a sequence of transactions:* Note carefully that COMMIT and ROLLBACK terminate the *transaction,* not the application program. In general, a

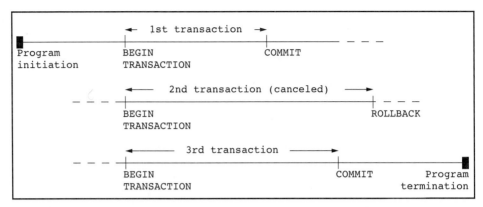

Fig. 15.2   Program execution is a sequence of transactions

single program execution will consist of a *sequence* of several transactions running one after another, as illustrated in Fig. 15.2.

■ *No nested transactions:* We assume until further notice that an application program can execute a BEGIN TRANSACTION statement only when it has no transaction currently in progress. In other words, no transaction has other transactions nested inside itself. Please note, however, that we will revisit this assumption in the next chapter.

■ *Correctness:* By definition, the database is always at least in a *consistent* state—where, following Chapter 9 (and indeed following the literature in general), we take *consistent* to mean, precisely, "not violating any known integrity constraint." Note too that consistency in that sense is *enforced by the DBMS.* It follows that transactions always transform a consistent state into a consistent state, again by definition. But consistency alone is not enough; we want *correctness,* not mere consistency! In the case of the transaction in Fig. 15.1, for example, we want the total number of dollars in accounts 123 and 456 taken together not to change. However, it would be unreasonable to declare an integrity constraint to that effect (why?), and so we cannot expect the DBMS to enforce the requirement; indeed, we already know from Chapter 9 that consistency does not imply correctness. Sadly, therefore, all we can do—and all the DBMS can do—is simply *assume* that transactions are correct, in the sense that they faithfully reflect just those real-world operations they are supposed to. More precisely, we assume that if *T* is a transaction that transforms the database from state *D1* to state *D2,* and if *D1* is correct, then *D2* is correct as well.[2] However, to say it again, this desirable property *cannot be enforced by the system* ("the system cannot enforce truth, only consistency," as we put it in Chapter 9).

---

[2] Note carefully too that this statement is supposed to apply to *all possible* correct states *D1.* Clearly, *T* might in fact not "faithfully reflect the real-world operations it is supposed to" and yet might still produce a correct state *D2* from *some specific* state *D1*—but that would not be good enough; we want correctness to be a guarantee, not a matter of mere happenstance.

■ *Multiple assignment:* Recall from Chapter 5 that, following reference [3.3], we require support for a multiple form of assignment, which allows any number of individual assignments (i.e., updates) to be performed "simultaneously." For example, we could replace the two separate UPDATEs in Fig. 15.1 by the following single statement (note the comma separator):

```
UPDATE ACC 123 { BALANCE := BALANCE - $100 } ,
UPDATE ACC 456 { BALANCE := BALANCE + $100 } ;
```

The transaction would now involve just a single updating operation; its effect on the database would therefore be atomic by definition, and—at least in this particular example—the BEGIN TRANSACTION, COMMIT, and ROLLBACK statements would no longer be necessary. As noted in Chapter 5, however, current products do not support multiple assignment (at least, not fully); for pragmatic reasons, therefore, we ignore the possibility of multiple assignment for the rest of this chapter. (In fact, of course, multiple assignment was not even considered as a possibility when the original theoretical work was done on transactions. See Section 16.10 for further discussion.)

15.3   TRANSACTION RECOVERY

A transaction begins by executing a BEGIN TRANSACTION operation and ends by executing either a COMMIT or a ROLLBACK operation. COMMIT establishes a **commit point** (also known, especially in older systems, as a **synchpoint**). A commit point thus corresponds to the (successful) end of a logical unit of work, and hence to a point at which the database is supposed to be in a correct state. ROLLBACK, by contrast, rolls the database back to the state it was in at BEGIN TRANSACTION, which effectively means back to the previous commit point. *Note:* The phrase "the previous commit point" is still accurate, even in the case of the first transaction in the program, if we agree to think of the first BEGIN TRANSACTION in the program as tacitly establishing an initial "commit point." Note too that in this context the term *database* should be understood to mean just that portion of the total database being accessed by the transaction under consideration; other transactions might be executing in parallel with that transaction and making changes to their own portions, and so "the total database" might in fact not be in a fully correct state at a commit point. As explained in Section 15.1, however, in this chapter we are ignoring the possibility of concurrent transactions as much as possible. This simplification does not materially affect the issue under discussion.

When a commit point is established:

1. As explained in Section 15.2, all database updates made by the executing program since the previous commit point are committed; that is, they are made permanent, in the sense that they are guaranteed to be recorded in the database. Prior to the commit point, all such updates must be regarded as *tentative only*—tentative in the sense that

they might subsequently be undone. Once committed, an update is guaranteed never to be undone[3] (this is the definition of "committed").

2. All database positioning is lost and all tuple locks are released. "Database positioning" here refers to the idea that at any given time an executing program will typically have addressability to certain tuples in the database (e.g., via certain *cursors* in the case of SQL, as explained in Chapter 4); this addressability is lost at a commit point. "Tuple locks" are explained in the next chapter. *Note:* Some systems do provide an option by which the program in fact might be able to retain addressability to certain tuples (and therefore retain certain tuple locks) from one transaction to the next; in fact, such an option was added to the SQL standard in 1999. See Section 15.8 for further discussion.

Note: Point 2 here—excluding the remark about possibly retaining some addressability and hence possibly retaining certain tuple locks—also applies if a transaction terminates with ROLLBACK instead of COMMIT. Point 1, of course, does not.

It follows from the foregoing that transactions are not only the unit of work but also the unit of **recovery**. For if a transaction successfully commits, then the system will guarantee that its updates will be permanently recorded in the database, even if the system crashes the very next moment. It is quite possible, for instance, that the system might crash after the COMMIT has been honored but before the updates have been physically written to the database—they might still be waiting in a main-memory buffer[4] and so lost at the time of the crash. Even if that happens, the system's restart procedure will still record those updates in the database; it is able to discover the values to be written by examining the relevant records in the log. (It follows that the log must be physically written before COMMIT processing can complete—the **write-ahead log rule**.) Thus, the restart procedure will recover any transactions that completed successfully but did not manage to get their updates physically written prior to the crash; hence, as stated earlier, transactions are indeed the unit of recovery. *Note:* In the next chapter we will see they are the unit of *concurrency* also.

There are a few implementation issues we need to discuss at this point. Intuitively, it should be clear that implementation will be simplest if both of the following are true:

- Database updates are kept in buffers in main memory and not physically written to disk until the transaction commits. That way, if the transaction terminates unsuccessfully, there will be no need to undo any disk updates.

- Database updates *are* physically written to disk as part of the process of honoring the transaction's COMMIT request. That way, if the system subsequently crashes, we can be sure there will be no need to redo any disk updates.

---

[3] Other than by explicit user action, that is. (Actually a committed update might be undone by implicit system action as well, if transactions can be nested [15.15], but we are ignoring this latter possibility until further notice.)

[4] *Buffers* are staging areas in main memory for data that is to be transferred (in either direction) between the physical database and some executing transaction.

In practice, however, neither of these properties will hold (in general). First, the buffers might simply not be big enough, implying that updates for transaction *A* might have to be written to disk prior to *A*'s COMMIT—perhaps to make space available for transaction *B*'s updates (*B* is said to **steal** buffer space from *A* in such a situation). Second, physically writing, or **forcing**, updates to the disk at COMMIT time could be very inefficient; for example, if 100 consecutive transactions all update the very same object, then forcing would mean 100 physical writes are done when one would suffice. For such reasons, real transaction managers typically employ what is called *a steal/no-force policy,* a fact that complicates implementation considerably as you might imagine. Further details are beyond the scope of this book.

Now, we said earlier that the write-ahead log rule meant that the log must be physically written before COMMIT processing can complete. That statement is true, of course, but now we can elaborate on it and make it more precise:

- The log record for a given database update must be physically written to the log before that update is physically written to the database.

- All other log records for a given transaction must be physically written to the log before the COMMIT log record for that transaction is physically written to the log.

- COMMIT processing for a given transaction must not complete until the COMMIT log record for that transaction is physically written to the log.[5]

The ACID Properties

Following reference [15.14], we can summarize this section and the previous one by saying that transactions possess (or are supposed to possess!) what are usually called "the ACID properties" of *atomicity, correctness,*[6] *isolation,* and *durability.* In brief:

- **Atomicity:** Transactions are atomic (all or nothing).

- **Correctness:** Transactions transform a correct state of the database into another correct state, without necessarily preserving correctness at all intermediate points.

- **Isolation:** Transactions are isolated from one another. That is, even though in general there will be many transactions running concurrently, any given transaction's updates are concealed from all the rest, until that transaction commits. Another way of saying the same thing is that, for any two distinct transactions *A* and *B, A* might see *B*'s updates (after *B* has committed) or *B* might see *A*'s updates (after *A* has committed), but not both.

---

[5] Some systems force the COMMIT log record to the disk as soon as the COMMIT request is received, others wait until (e.g.) the buffer is full before forcing it to the disk. This latter technique is called *group commit,* on the grounds that it typically causes several transactions to commit at the same time; it reduces the amount of I/O but delays the termination of some transactions.

[6] The term *consistency* is used in place of *correctness* in most of the literature (in reference [15.14] in particular), but we have already given our reasons for preferring the latter term.

- **Durability:** Once a transaction commits, its updates persist in the database, even if there is a subsequent system crash.

We will have quite a lot more to say regarding these properties in the next chapter.

15.4 SYSTEM RECOVERY

The system must be prepared to recover, not only from purely local failures such as an overflow exception within an individual transaction, but also from "global" failures such as a power outage. A local failure, by definition, affects only the transaction in which the failure has actually occurred; such failures have already been discussed in Sections 15.2 and 15.3. A global failure, by contrast, affects all of the transactions in progress at the time of the failure and hence has significant system-wide implications. In this section and the next, we briefly consider what is involved in recovering from a global failure. Such failures fall into two broad categories:

- **System failures** (e.g., power outage), which affect all transactions currently in progress but do not physically damage the database. A system failure is sometimes called a *soft crash*.
- **Media failures** (e.g., head crash on the disk), which do cause damage to the database or some portion thereof, and affect at least those transactions currently using that portion. A media failure is sometimes called a *hard crash*.

System failures are discussed in this section, media failures are discussed in Section 15.5.

The key point regarding system failure is that *the contents of main memory are lost* (in particular, the database buffers are lost). The precise state of any transaction that was in progress at the time of the failure is therefore no longer known; such a transaction can therefore never be successfully completed, and so must be *undone*—that is, rolled back—when the system restarts. Furthermore, it might also be necessary (as suggested in Section 15.3) to *redo* certain transactions at restart time that did successfully complete prior to the crash but did not manage to get their updates transferred from the buffers in main memory to the physical database.

The obvious question thus arises: How does the system know at restart time which transactions to undo and which to redo? The answer is as follows. At certain prescribed intervals—typically whenever some prescribed number of records have been written to the log—the system automatically *takes a checkpoint*. Taking a checkpoint involves (a) forcing the contents of the main-memory buffers out to the physical database, and (b) forcing a special **checkpoint record** out to the physical log. The checkpoint record contains a list of all transactions that were in progress at the time the checkpoint was taken. To see how this information is used, consider Fig. 15.3, which is read as follows (time in the figure flows from left to right):

- A system failure has occurred at time *tf*.
- The most recent checkpoint prior to time *tf* was taken at time *tc*.
- Transactions of type *T1* completed (successfully) prior to time *tc*.

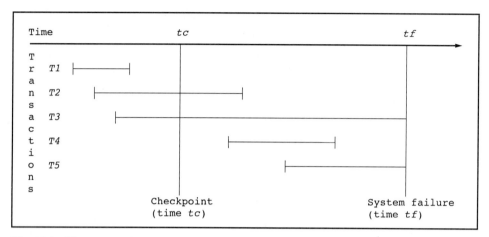

Fig. 15.3 Five transaction categories

- Transactions of type *T2* started prior to time *tc* and completed (successfully) after time *tc* and before time *tf.*

- Transactions of type *T3* also started prior to time *tc* but did not complete by time *tf.*

- Transactions of type *T4* started after time *tc* and completed (successfully) before time *tf.*

- Finally, transactions of type *T5* also started after time *tc* but did not complete by time *tf.*

It should be clear that when the system is restarted, transactions of types *T3* and *T5* must be undone, and transactions of types *T2* and *T4* must be redone. Note, however, that transactions of type *T1* do not enter into the restart process at all, because their updates were forced to the database at time *tc* as part of the checkpoint process. Note too that transactions that completed unsuccessfully (i.e., with a rollback) before time *tf* also do not enter into the restart process at all (why not?).

At restart time, therefore, the system first goes through the following procedure in order to identify all transactions of types *T2–T5:*

1. Start with two lists of transactions, the UNDO list and the REDO list.

2. Set the UNDO list equal to the list of all transactions given in the most recent checkpoint record and the REDO list to empty.

3. Search forward through the log, starting from the checkpoint record.

4. If a BEGIN TRANSACTION log record is found for transaction *T,* add *T* to the UNDO list.

5. If a COMMIT log record is found for transaction *T,* move *T* from the UNDO list to the REDO list.

6. When the end of the log is reached, the UNDO and REDO lists identify, respectively, transactions of types *T3* and *T5* and transactions of types *T2* and *T4.*

The system now works backward through the log, undoing the transactions in the UNDO list; then it works forward again, redoing the transactions in the REDO list. *Note:* Restoring the database to a correct state by redoing work is sometimes called *forward recovery.* Similarly, restoring it to a correct state by undoing work is sometimes called *backward* recovery. Note that forward recovery redoes updates in the order in which they were originally done, while backward recovery undoes updates in the reverse of that order.

Finally, when all such recovery activity is complete, then (and only then) the system is ready to accept new work.

ARIES

Of course, the foregoing description of the system recovery procedure is very much simplified.[7] Observe in particular that it shows "undo" operations being done before "redo" operations. Early systems did work that way, but for efficiency reasons modern systems typically do things the other way around; in fact, most systems today use a scheme called ARIES [15.20], or something very close to that scheme, which does indeed do redo operations first. ARIES operates in three broad phases:

1. *Analysis:* Build the REDO and UNDO lists.
2. *Redo:* Start from a position in the log determined in the analysis phase and restore the database to the state it was in at the time of the crash.
3. *Undo:* Undo the effects of transactions that failed to commit.

Note that "redo before undo" implies redoing work for transactions that failed to commit, work that will subsequently be undone again. Partly for this reason, the ARIES redo phase is often said to be *repeating history* [15.21]. Note too that ARIES logs the operations it performs during the undo phase, so that if the system crashes again during the restart procedure—an all-too-likely eventuality—then updates that have already been undone will not be undone again on the next restart.

The name ARIES stands for "Algorithms for Recovery and Isolation Exploiting Semantics."

15.5 MEDIA RECOVERY

Note: Media recovery is somewhat different in kind from transaction and system recovery. We cover it here for completeness.

To repeat from Section 15.4, a media failure is a failure—such as a disk head crash or a disk controller failure—in which some portion of the database has been physically destroyed. Recovery from such a failure basically involves reloading or *restoring* the

---

[7] Among other things, it assumes recovery is possible! If transactions never run concurrently, then they are recoverable (fairly obviously); however, the possibility of concurrent execution introduces certain complicating factors, and we must be careful not to let them do anything to undermine recoverability. We will revisit this issue in the next chapter.

database from a backup copy or *dump,* and then using the log—both active and archive portions, in general—to redo all transactions that completed since that backup copy was taken (forward recovery). There is no need to undo transactions that were still in progress at the time of the failure, since by definition all updates of such transactions have been "undone" (actually lost) anyway.

The need to be able to perform media recovery implies the need for a *dump/restore* (or *unload/reload*) *utility.* The dump portion of that utility is used to make backup copies of the database on demand. Such copies can be kept on tape or other archival storage; it is not necessary that they be on direct access media. After a media failure, the restore portion of the utility is used to rebuild the database from a specified backup copy.

15.6 TWO-PHASE COMMIT

Note: You might want to skip this section on a first reading.

In this section we briefly discuss a very important elaboration on the basic commit/ rollback concept called **two-phase commit**. Two-phase commit is important whenever a given transaction can interact with several independent "resource managers," each managing its own set of recoverable resources and maintaining its own recovery log.[8] For example, consider a transaction running on an IBM mainframe that updates both an IMS database and a DB2 database (such a transaction is perfectly legal, by the way). If the transaction completes successfully, then *all* of its updates, to both IMS data and DB2 data, must be committed; conversely, if it fails, then *all* of its updates must be rolled back. In other words, it must not be possible for the IMS updates to be committed and the DB2 updates rolled back, or *vice versa*—for then the transaction would no longer be atomic (all or nothing).

It follows that it does not make sense for the transaction to issue, say, a COMMIT to IMS and a ROLLBACK to DB2; and even if it issued the same instruction to both, the system could still crash between the two, with unfortunate results. Instead, therefore, the transaction issues a single "global" or **system-wide** COMMIT (or ROLLBACK). That COMMIT or ROLLBACK is handled by a system component called the **coordinator**, whose task it is to guarantee that both resource managers (i.e., IMS and DB2, in the example) commit or roll back the updates they are responsible for *in unison*—and furthermore to provide that guarantee *even if the system fails in the middle of the process.* And it is the two-phase commit protocol that enables the coordinator to provide such a guarantee.

Here is how it works. Assume for simplicity that the transaction has completed its database processing successfully, so that the system-wide instruction it issues is COMMIT, not ROLLBACK. On receiving that COMMIT request, the coordinator goes through the following two-phase process:

---

[8] In particular, it is important in the context of distributed database systems, and for that reason is discussed in more detail in Chapter 21.

- *Prepare:* First, it instructs all resource managers to get ready to "go either way" on the transaction. In practice, this means that each **participant** in the process—that is, each resource manager involved—must force all log records for local resources used by the transaction out to its own physical log (i.e., out to nonvolatile storage; whatever happens thereafter, the resource manager will now have a permanent record of the work it did on behalf of the transaction, and so will be able to commit its updates or roll them back, as necessary). Assuming the forced write is successful, the resource manager now replies "OK" to the coordinator; otherwise, it replies "Not OK."

- *Commit:* When the coordinator has received replies from all participants, it forces a record to its own physical log, recording its decision regarding the transaction. If all replies were "OK," that decision is "commit"; if any reply was "Not OK," the decision is "rollback." Either way, the coordinator then informs each participant of its decision, and *each participant must then commit or roll back the transaction locally, as instructed.* Note that each participant *must* do what it is told by the coordinator in Phase 2—that is the protocol. Note too that it is the appearance of the decision record in the coordinator's physical log that marks the transition from Phase 1 to Phase 2.

If the system fails at some point during the foregoing process, the restart procedure will look for the decision record in the coordinator's log. If it finds it, then the two-phase commit process can pick up where it left off. If it does not find it, then it assumes that the decision was "rollback," and again the process can complete appropriately. *Note:* It is worth pointing out that if the coordinator and the participants are executing on different machines, as they might be in a distributed system (see Chapter 21), then a failure on the part of the coordinator might keep some participant waiting a long time for the coordinator's decision—and, as long as it *is* waiting, any updates made by the transaction via that participant must be kept hidden from other transactions (i.e., those updates will probably have to be kept *locked,* as discussed in the next chapter).

We remark that the data communications manager (DC manager—see Chapter 2) can be regarded as a resource manager in the foregoing sense. That is, messages too can be regarded as a recoverable resource, just like databases, and the DC manager needs to be able to participate in the two-phase commit process. For further discussion of this point, and of the whole idea of two-phase commit in general, see reference [15.12].

15.7 SAVEPOINTS (A DIGRESSION)

We have seen that transactions as usually understood cannot be nested inside one another. Is there nevertheless some way of allowing transactions to be broken down into smaller "subtransactions"? The answer is a limited *yes*—it might be possible for a transaction to establish intermediate **savepoints** while it is executing, and subsequently to roll back to a previously established savepoint, if required, instead of having to roll back all the way to the beginning. In fact, a savepoint mechanism along such lines was included in several early systems, including Ingres—the commercial product, not the prototype—and System

R, and such a facility was added to the SQL standard in 1999. Note, however, that establishing a savepoint is not the same as performing a COMMIT; updates made by the transaction are still not visible to other transactions until the given transaction successfully executes a COMMIT. See Section 15.8 immediately following for further discussion.

15.8   SQL FACILITIES

SQL's support for transactions, and hence for transaction-based recovery, follows the general pattern described in the foregoing sections. First of all, most executable SQL statements are guaranteed to be atomic (the only exceptions are CALL and RETURN). Second, as we saw in Chapter 4, SQL provides direct analogs of BEGIN TRANSACTION, COMMIT, and ROLLBACK, called START TRANSACTION, COMMIT WORK, and ROLLBACK WORK, respectively. Here is the syntax for START TRANSACTION:

```
START TRANSACTION <option commalist> ;
```

The *<option commalist>* specifies an *access mode,* an *isolation level,* or both (a third option, having to do with *diagnostics area size,* is beyond the scope of this book):

- The **access mode** is either READ ONLY or READ WRITE. If neither is specified, READ WRITE is assumed, unless READ UNCOMMITTED isolation level is specified, in which case READ ONLY is assumed. If READ WRITE is specified, the isolation level must not be READ UNCOMMITTED.

- The **isolation level** takes the form ISOLATION LEVEL *<isolation>,* where *<isolation>* is READ UNCOMMITTED, READ COMMITTED, REPEATABLE READ, or SERIALIZABLE. For further explanation, see Chapter 16.

  The syntax for COMMIT and ROLLBACK is:

```
COMMIT [ WORK ] [ AND [ NO ] CHAIN ] ;
ROLLBACK [ WORK ] [ AND [ NO ] CHAIN ] ;
```

WORK is a noiseword. AND CHAIN causes a START TRANSACTION (with the same *<option commalist>* as the previous one) to be executed automatically after the COMMIT; AND NO CHAIN is the default. A CLOSE is executed automatically for every open cursor (thereby causing all database positioning to be lost), except—for COMMIT only—for cursors declared WITH HOLD. *Note:* We did not discuss it in Chapter 4, but WITH HOLD is an option on a cursor declaration. A cursor declared WITH HOLD is not automatically closed at COMMIT but is left open, positioned such that the next FETCH will move it to the next row in sequence; the possibly complex repositioning code that might otherwise be needed on the next OPEN is thus not required.

SQL also supports savepoints. The statement

```
SAVEPOINT <savepoint name> ;
```

creates a savepoint with the specified user-chosen name (which is local to the transaction). The statement

```
ROLLBACK TO <savepoint name> ;
```

undoes all updates done since the specified savepoint. And the statement

```
RELEASE <savepoint name> ;
```

drops the specified savepoint, meaning it is no longer possible to execute a ROLLBACK to that savepoint. All savepoints are automatically dropped at transaction termination.

15.9 SUMMARY

In this chapter we have presented a necessarily brief introduction to the topic of **transaction management**. A transaction is a **logical unit of work**, also a **unit of recovery** (and a unit of concurrency—see Chapter 16). Transactions possess the **ACID properties** of **atomicity**, **correctness** (more usually called *consistency* in the literature), **isolation**, and **durability**. **Transaction management** is the task of supervising the execution of transactions in such a way that they can be guaranteed to possess these important properties (except for correctness!). In fact, the overall purpose of the system might well be defined as **the reliable execution of transactions**.

Transactions are initiated by **BEGIN TRANSACTION** and are terminated by either **COMMIT** (*successful* termination) or **ROLLBACK** (*unsuccessful* termination). COMMIT establishes a **commit point** (updates are recorded in the database); ROLLBACK rolls the database back to the previous commit point (updates are undone). If a transaction does not reach its planned termination, the system automatically executes a ROLLBACK for it (**transaction recovery**). In order to be able to undo and redo updates, the system maintains a recovery **log**. Moreover, the log records for a given transaction must be written to the physical log before COMMIT processing for that transaction can complete (the **write-ahead log rule**).

If a system crash occurs, the system must (a) **redo** all work done by transactions that completed successfully prior to the crash and (b) **undo** all work done by transactions that started but did not complete prior to the crash. This **system recovery** activity is carried out as part of the system's **restart** procedure (sometimes known as the *restart/recovery* procedure). The system discovers what work has to be redone and what undone by examining the most recent **checkpoint record**. Checkpoint records are written to the log at prescribed intervals.

The system also provides **media recovery** by restoring the database from a previous **dump** and then—using the log—redoing the work completed since that dump was taken. Dump/restore **utilities** are needed to support media recovery.

Systems that permit transactions to interact with two or more distinct **resource managers**—for example, two different DBMSs, or a DBMS and a DC manager—must use a protocol called **two-phase commit** (or some variant thereof) if they are to maintain the transaction atomicity property. The two phases are (a) the **prepare** phase, in which the **coordinator** instructs all **participants** to "get ready to go either way," and (b) the **commit** phase, in which—assuming all participants responded satisfactorily during the prepare phase—the coordinator then instructs all participants to perform the actual commit (or the actual rollback otherwise).

We concluded with a brief mention of **savepoints** and a survey of the recovery features of SQL; in particular, we described SQL's **START TRANSACTION** statement, which allows the user to specify the transaction **access mode** and **isolation level**.

One last point: We have tacitly been assuming an application programming environment throughout this chapter. However, all of the concepts discussed apply equally to the end-user environment as well (though they might be somewhat more concealed at that level). For example, most SQL products allow the end user to enter SQL statements interactively from a terminal. Usually each such interactive SQL statement is treated as a transaction in its own right; the system will typically issue an automatic COMMIT on the user's behalf after the SQL statement has executed (or an automatic ROLLBACK if it failed). However, some systems do allow the user to inhibit those automatic COMMITs and hence to execute a whole series of SQL statements (followed by an explicit COMMIT or ROLLBACK) as a single transaction. The practice is not generally recommended, however, since it might cause portions of the database to remain locked, and therefore inaccessible to other users, for excessive periods of time (see Chapter 16). In such an environment, moreover, it is possible for end users to *deadlock* with one another, which is another good argument for prohibiting the practice (again, see Chapter 16).

EXERCISES

15.1 Systems do not allow a given transaction to commit changes to databases (or relvars or any other unit of data) on an individual basis, that is, without simultaneously committing changes to all other databases (or relvars or . . .). Why not?

15.2 Transactions usually cannot be nested inside one another. Why not?

15.3 State the write-ahead log rule. Why is the rule necessary?

15.4 What are the recovery implications of (a) physically writing database buffers at COMMIT; (b) never physically writing database buffers prior to COMMIT?

15.5 State the two-phase commit protocol, and discuss the implications of a failure on the part of (a) the coordinator and (b) some participant during each of the two phases.

15.6 Using the suppliers-and-parts database, write an SQL program to read and print all parts in part number order, deleting every tenth one as you go, and beginning a new transaction after every tenth row. You can assume the foreign key delete rule from parts to shipments specifies CASCADE (in other words, you can ignore shipments for the purposes of this exercise). *Note:* We specifically ask for an *SQL* solution here so that you can use the SQL cursor mechanism in your answer.

REFERENCES AND BIBLIOGRAPHY

15.1 Philip A. Bernstein: "Transaction Processing Monitors," *CACM 33,* No. 11 (November 1990).

As we saw in the body of the chapter, *TP monitor* is another name for the transaction manager. This article serves as a good informal introduction to the structure and functionality of TP monitors. To quote: "A *TP system* is an integrated set of products that . . . include both hardware, such as processors, memories, disks, and communications controllers, and software, such as operating systems, database management systems, computer networks, and TP monitors. Much of the integration of these products is provided by TP monitors."

15.2 Philip A. Bernstein, Vassos Hadzilacos, and Nathan Goodman: *Concurrency Control and Recovery in Database Systems.* Reading, Mass.: Addison-Wesley (1987).

A textbook, covering (as the title indicates) not just recovery but the whole of transaction management, from a much more formal perspective than the present chapter.

15.3 A. Bilris *et al.*: "ASSET: A System for Supporting Extended Transactions," Proc. 1994 ACM SIGMOD Int. Conf. on Management of Data, Minneapolis, Minn. (May 1994).

The basic transaction notions as described in the body of this chapter and the next are widely regarded as being too rigid for certain newer kinds of applications (especially highly interactive applications), and a variety of "extended transaction models" have therefore been proposed to address this issue (see reference [15.16]). At the time of writing, however, none of those proposals has been clearly shown to be superior to all of the rest; as a consequence, "database vendors [have been reluctant] to incorporate any one model into a product."

The focus of ASSET is rather different. Instead of proposing yet another new transaction model, it provides a set of primitive operators—including the usual COMMIT and so forth, but also certain new ones—that can be used "to define customized transaction models suitable for specific applications." In particular, the paper shows how ASSET can be used to specify "nested transactions, split transactions, sagas, and other extended transaction models described in the literature."

15.4 L. A. Bjork: "Recovery Scenario for a DB/DC System," Proc. ACM National Conf., Atlanta, Ga. (August 1973).

This paper and its companion paper by Davies [15.7] represent probably the earliest theoretical work in the area of recovery.

15.5 R. A. Crus: "Data Recovery in IBM DATABASE 2," *IBM Sys. J. 23,* No. 2 (1984).

Describes the DB2 recovery mechanism (as implemented in the first release of the product) in detail, and in so doing provides a good description of recovery techniques in general. In particular, the paper explains how DB2 recovers from a system crash during the recovery process itself, while some transaction is in the middle of a rollback. This problem requires special care to ensure that uncommitted updates from the transaction being rolled back are in fact undone (the opposite of the lost update problem, in a sense—see Chapter 16).

15.6 C. J. Date: "Distributed Database: A Closer Look," in C. J. Date and Hugh Darwen, *Relational Database Writings 1989–1991.* Reading, Mass.: Addison-Wesley (1992).

Section 15.6 of the present chapter describes what might be called the *basic* two-phase commit protocol. Several improvements on that basic protocol are possible. For example, if participant *P* responds to the coordinator *C* in Phase 1 that it did no updates for the transaction under consideration (i.e., it was *read-only*), then *C* can simply ignore *P* in Phase 2; moreover, if *all* participants respond *read-only* in Phase 1, then Phase 2 can be omitted entirely (see Chapter 21 for further discussion).

Other improvements and refinements are possible. This paper includes a tutorial description of some of them. Specifically, it discusses the *presumed commit* and *presumed rollback* protocols (improved versions of the basic protocol), the *tree of processes* model (when a participant needs to serve as the coordinator for certain portions of a transaction), and what happens if a *communication failure* occurs during the acknowledgment process from a participant to the coordinator. *Note:* Although the discussions are presented in the context of a distributed system, most of the concepts are actually of wider applicability. Again, see Chapter 21, and in particular reference [21.13], for an extended discussion of some of these issues.

15.7 C. T. Davies, Jr.: "Recovery Semantics for a DB/DC System," Proc. ACM National Conf., Atlanta, Ga. (August 1973).

See the annotation to reference [15.8].

15.8 C. T. Davies, Jr.: "Data Processing Spheres of Control," *IBM Sys. J. 17,* No. 2 (1978).

Spheres of control were the first attempt to investigate and formalize what later became the discipline of transaction management. A sphere of control is an abstraction that represents a piece of work that can be viewed from the outside as atomic. Unlike transactions as supported in most systems today, however, spheres of control can be nested inside one another, to arbitrary depth.

15.9 Hector Garcia-Molina and Kenneth Salem: "Sagas," Proc. 1987 ACM SIGMOD Int. Conf. on Management of Data, San Francisco, Calif. (May 1987).

A major problem with transactions as described in the body of this chapter is that they are tacitly assumed to be very short in duration (milliseconds or even microseconds). If a transaction lasts a long time (hours, days, weeks), then (a) if it has to be rolled back, a very great deal of work has to be undone, and (b) even if it succeeds, it still has to hold on to system resources (database data, etc.) for an inordinately long time, thereby locking other users out (see Chapter 16). Unfortunately, many real-world transactions tend to be long in duration, especially in some of the newer application areas such as hardware and software engineering. **Sagas** are an attack on this problem. A saga is a sequence of "short" transactions with the property that the system guarantees that *either* (a) all the transactions in the sequence execute successfully *or* (b) certain *compensating transactions* [15.17] are executed in order to cancel the effects of successfully completed transactions in an overall incomplete execution of the saga (thereby making it as if the saga had never executed in the first place). In a banking system, for example, we might have the transaction "Add $100 to account *A*"; the compensating transaction would obviously be "Subtract $100 from account *A*." An extension to the COMMIT statement allows the user to inform the system of the compensating transaction to be run should it later be necessary to cancel the effects of the now completed transaction. Note that a compensating transaction should ideally never terminate with rollback!

15.10 James Gray: "Notes on Data Base Operating Systems," in R. Bayer, R. M. Graham, and G. Seegmuller (eds.), *Operating Systems: An Advanced Course* (Springer-Verlag *Lecture Notes in Computer Science 60*). New York, N.Y.: Springer-Verlag (1978). Also available as IBM Research Report RJ 2188 (February 1978).

One of the earliest—certainly one of the most approachable—sources for material on transaction management. It contains the first generally available description of the two-phase commit protocol. It is obviously not as comprehensive as the more recent reference [15.12], but it is nevertheless still recommended.

15.11 Jim Gray: "The Transaction Concept: Virtues and Limitations," Proc. 7th Int. Conf. on Very Large Data Bases, Cannes, France (September 1981).

A concise statement of various transaction-related concepts and problems, including a variety of implementation issues.

15.12 Jim Gray and Andreas Reuter: *Transaction Processing: Concepts and Techniques.* San Mateo, Calif.: Morgan Kaufmann (1993).

If any computer science text ever deserved the epithet "instant classic," it is surely this one. Its size might be a little daunting at first, but the authors display an enviable lightness of touch that makes even the driest aspects of the subject enjoyable reading. In their preface, they state their intent as being "to help . . . solve real problems"; the book is "pragmatic, covering basic transaction issues in considerable detail"; and the presentation "is full of code fragments showing . . . basic algorithms and data structures" and is not "encyclopedic." Despite this last claim, the book is (not surprisingly) comprehensive, and has become the standard work. Strongly recommended.

15.13 Jim Gray *et al.*: "The Recovery Manager of the System R Data Manager," *ACM Comp. Surv. 13,* No. 2 (June 1981).

References [15.13] and [15.19] are both concerned with the recovery features of System R (which was something of a pioneer in this field). Reference [15.13] provides an overview of the entire recovery subsystem; reference [15.19] describes a specific aspect, called the *shadow page* mechanism, in detail.

15.14 Theo Härder and Andreas Reuter: "Principles of Transaction-Oriented Database Recovery," *ACM Comp. Surv. 15,* No. 4 (December 1983).

The source of the ACID acronym, this paper gives a very clear tutorial presentation of the principles of recovery. It also provides a terminological framework for describing a wide variety of recovery schemes and logging techniques in a uniform way, and classifies and describes a number of existing systems in accordance with that framework. The paper includes some interesting empirical figures regarding frequency of occurrence and typical "acceptable" recovery times for the three kinds of failures (local, system, media) in a typical large system:

Type of failure	Frequency of occurrence	Recovery time
Local	10–100 per minute	Same as transaction execution time
System	Several per week	Few minutes
Media	Once or twice per year	1–2 hours

15.15 Theo Härder and Kurt Rothermel: "Concepts for Transaction Recovery in Nested Transactions," Proc. 1987 ACM SIGMOD Int. Conf. on Management of Data, San Francisco, Calif. (May 1987).

Proposes a scheme in which any transaction can have lower-level subtransactions (where a subtransaction is a transaction in its own right and can have "subsubtransactions," and so on). A transaction that is not a subtransaction of any other transaction is called a *top-level* transaction and is supposed to satisfy the usual ACID properties; however, a transaction that *is* a subtransaction of some other transaction is required to satisfy only the atomicity and isolation properties. See Section 16.10 for further discussion.

15.16 Henry F. Korth: "The Double Life of the Transaction Abstraction: Fundamental Principle and Evolving System Concept" (invited talk), Proc. 21st Int. Conf. on Very Large Data Bases, Zurich, Switzerland (September 1995).

A good brief overview of ways in which the transaction concept needs to evolve in order to support new application requirements.

15.17 Henry F. Korth, Eliezer Levy, and Abraham Silberschatz: "A Formal Approach to Recovery by Compensating Transactions," Proc. 16th Int. Conf. on Very Large Data Bases, Brisbane, Australia (August 1990).

Formalizes the notion of **compensating transactions**, which are used in sagas [15.9] and elsewhere for "undoing" committed (as well as uncommitted) transactions.

15.18 David Lomet and Mark R. Tuttle: "Redo Recovery After System Crashes," Proc. 21st Int. Conf. on Very Large Data Bases, Zurich, Switzerland (September 1995).

> A precise and careful analysis of redo recovery (i.e., forward recovery). "[Although] redo recovery is just one form of recovery, it is . . . important [because it is a crucial part of the overall recovery process and] must solve the hardest [problems]." The authors claim their analysis leads to a better understanding of existing implementations and the potential for significantly improved recovery systems.

15.19 Raymond A. Lorie: "Physical Integrity in a Large Segmented Database," *ACM TODS 2,* No. 1 (March 1977).

> As explained in the annotation to reference [15.13], this paper is concerned with a specific aspect of the System R recovery subsystem, called the **shadow page** mechanism. (Note, incidentally, that the term *integrity* as used in the title of this paper has little to do with the notion of integrity as discussed in Chapter 9.) The basic idea is simple: When an uncommitted update is written to the database, the system does not overwrite the existing page but stores a new page somewhere else on the disk. The old page is then the "shadow" for the new one. Committing the update involves adjusting various pointers to point to the new page and discarding the shadow; rolling back the update, on the other hand, involves reinstating the shadow page and discarding the new one.
>
> Although conceptually simple, the shadow page scheme suffers from the serious drawback that it destroys any physical clustering that might previously have existed in the data. For this reason the scheme was not picked up for use in DB2 [15.5], though it was used in SQL/DS [4.14].

15.20 C. Mohan, Don Haderle, Bruce Lindsay, Hamid Pirahesh, and Peter Schwartz: "ARIES: A Transaction Recovery Method Supporting Fine-Granularity Locking and Partial Rollbacks Using Write Ahead Logging," *ACM TODS 17,* No. 1 (March 1992).

> The original ARIES paper. At the time this paper was published, ARIES had been implemented "to varying degrees" in several commercial and experimental systems, including in particular DB2. Here is a pertinent quote: "Solutions to [the transaction management problem] may be judged using several metrics: degree of concurrency supported within a page and across pages, complexity of the resulting logic, space overhead on nonvolatile storage and in memory for data and the log, overhead in terms of the number of synchronous and asynchronous I/O's required during restart/recovery and normal processing, kinds of functionality supported (partial transaction rollbacks, etc.), amount of processing performed during restart/recovery, degree of concurrent processing supported during restart/recovery, extent of system-induced transaction rollbacks caused by deadlocks, restrictions placed on stored data (e.g., requiring unique keys for all records, restricting maximum size of objects to the page size, etc.), ability to support novel lock modes that allow the concurrent execution—based on commutativity and other properties—of operations like increment/decrement on the same data by different transactions, and so on. [ARIES] fares very well with respect to all of these metrics."
>
> Since ARIES was first designed, numerous refinements and specialized versions have been developed and described in the literature: ARIES/CSA (for client/server systems), ARIES/IM (for index management), ARIES/KVL (for "key value locking" on indexes), ARIES/NT (for nested transactions), and so on. See reference [15.21].

15.21 C. Mohan: "Repeating History Beyond ARIES," Proc. 25th Int. Conf. on Very Large Data Bases, Edinburgh, Scotland (September 1999).

Concurrency

16.1 INTRODUCTION

The term **concurrency** refers to the fact that DBMSs typically allow many transactions to access the same database at the same time. In such a system, some kind of control mechanism is clearly needed to ensure that concurrent transactions do not interfere with each other. (Examples of the kinds of interference that can occur in the absence of such controls are given in Section 16.2.) In this chapter, we examine this issue in depth. The structure of the chapter is as follows:

- As just indicated, Section 16.2 explains some of the problems that can arise if proper controls are not provided.

- Section 16.3 introduces the conventional mechanism for dealing with such problems, *locking*. (Locking is not the only possible mechanism, but it is far and away the one most commonly encountered in practice. Several others are described in the annotation to the references at the end of the chapter.)

- Section 16.4 then shows how locking can be used to solve the problems described in Section 16.2.

- Locking unfortunately introduces problems of its own, one of the best known of which is *deadlock*. Section 16.5 discusses this issue.

- Section 16.6 describes the concept of *serializability,* which is generally recognized as the formal criterion of correctness in this area.

- Section 16.7 discusses the effects of concurrency on the topic of the previous chapter, *recovery.*

- Sections 16.8 and 16.9 then go on to consider two significant refinements to the basic locking idea, *levels of isolation* and *intent locking.*

- Section 16.10 offers some fresh and slightly skeptical observations on the question of the so-called *ACID properties* of transactions.

- Section 16.11 describes the relevant facilities of SQL.

- Finally, Section 16.12 presents a summary.

We close this introductory section with a couple of general observations. First, the ideas of concurrency, like those of recovery, are largely independent of whether the underlying system is relational or otherwise (though it is significant that—as with recovery—most of the early theoretical work in the area was done in a relational context specifically, "for definiteness" [16.6]). Second, concurrency, like recovery, is a very large subject, and all we can hope to do in this chapter is introduce some of the most important and basic ideas. Certain more advanced aspects of the subject are discussed briefly in the annotation to some of the references at the end of the chapter.

16.2   THREE CONCURRENCY PROBLEMS

We begin by considering some of the problems that any concurrency control mechanism must address. There are essentially three ways in which things can go wrong: three ways, that is, in which a transaction, though correct in itself in the sense explained in Chapter 15, can nevertheless produce the wrong answer if some other transaction interferes with it in some way. Note carefully that—in accordance with our usual assumption—the interfering transaction will also be correct in itself; it is the uncontrolled interleaving of operations from the two individually correct transactions that produces the overall incorrect result. The three problems are:

- The *lost update* problem
- The *uncommitted dependency* problem

- The *inconsistent analysis* problem

We examine each in turn.

The Lost Update Problem

Consider the situation illustrated in Fig. 16.1. That figure is meant to be read as follows: Transaction *A* retrieves some tuple *t* at time *t1;* transaction *B* retrieves that same tuple *t* at time *t2;* transaction *A* updates the tuple (on the basis of the values seen at time *t1*) at time *t3;* and transaction *B* updates the same tuple (on the basis of the values seen at time *t2,* which are the same as those seen at time *t1*) at time *t4*. Transaction *A*'s update is lost at time *t4,* because transaction *B* overwrites it without even looking at it. *Note:* Once again we adopt the convenient fiction, here and throughout this chapter, that it makes sense to talk in terms of "updating a tuple."

Transaction A	*Time*	*Transaction B*
—		—
—		—
RETRIEVE t	t1	—
—		—
—	t2	RETRIEVE t
—		—
UPDATE t	t3	—
—		—
—	t4	UPDATE t
—		—

Fig. 16.1   Transaction *A* loses an update at time *t4*

The Uncommitted Dependency Problem

The uncommitted dependency problem arises if one transaction is allowed to retrieve—or, worse, update—a tuple that has been updated by another transaction but not yet committed by that other transaction. For if it has not yet been committed, there is always a possibility that it never will be committed but will be rolled back instead, in which case the first transaction will have seen some data that now no longer exists (and in a sense never did exist). Consider Figs. 16.2 and 16.3 (overleaf).

In the first example (Fig. 16.2), transaction *A* sees an uncommitted update—also called an uncommitted change—at time *t2*. That update is then undone at time *t3*. Transaction *A* is therefore operating on a false assumption: namely, the assumption that tuple *t* has the value seen at time *t2,* whereas in fact it has whatever value it had prior to time *t1*. As a result, transaction *A* might well produce an incorrect result. Note, by the way, that the rollback of transaction *B* might be due to no fault of *B*'s; it might, for example, be the

Transaction A	Time	Transaction B
—		—
—		—
—	*t1*	UPDATE *t*
—		—
RETRIEVE *t*	*t2*	—
—		—
—	*t3*	ROLLBACK
—		

Fig. 16.2   Transaction *A* becomes dependent on an uncommitted change at time *t2*

Transaction A	Time	Transaction B
—		—
—		—
—	*t1*	UPDATE *t*
—		—
UPDATE *t*	*t2*	—
—		—
—	*t3*	ROLLBACK
—		

Fig. 16.3   Transaction *A* updates an uncommitted change at time *t2*, and loses that update at time *t3*

result of a system crash. (And transaction *A* might already have terminated by that time, in which case the crash would not cause a rollback to be issued for *A* also.)

The second example (Fig. 16.3) is even worse. Not only does transaction *A* become dependent on an uncommitted change at time *t2*, but it actually loses an update at time *t3*—because the rollback at time *t3* causes tuple *t* to be restored to its value prior to time *t1*. This is another version of the lost update problem.

The Inconsistent Analysis Problem

Consider Fig. 16.4, which shows two transactions *A* and *B* operating on account (ACC) tuples: Transaction *A* is summing account balances, transaction *B* is transferring an amount 10 from account 3 to account 1. The result produced by *A*, 110, is obviously incorrect; if *A* were to go on to write that result back into the database, it would actually leave the database in an inconsistent state.[1] In effect, *A* has seen an inconsistent state of the database and has therefore performed an inconsistent analysis. Note the difference between

---

[1] Regarding this possibility (i.e., writing the result back into the database), it is naturally necessary to assume there is no integrity constraint in place to prevent such a write.

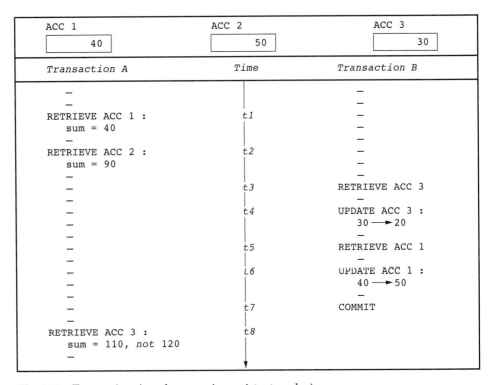

Fig. 16.4 Transaction *A* performs an inconsistent analysis

this example and the previous one: There is no question here of *A* being dependent on an uncommitted change, since *B* commits all of its updates before *A* sees ACC 3. *Note:* We observe in passing that the term *inconsistent analysis* ought by rights to be "*incorrect* analysis." However, we stay with the former term for historical reasons.

A Closer Look

Note: You might want to skip this subsection on a first reading.

Let us take a slightly closer look at the foregoing problems. Clearly, the operations that are of primary interest from a concurrency point of view are database retrievals and database updates; in other words, we can regard a transaction as consisting of a sequence of such operations *only* (apart from the necessary BEGIN TRANSACTION and COMMIT or ROLLBACK operations, of course). Let us agree to refer to those operations as simply *reads* and *writes,* respectively. Then it is clear that if *A* and *B* are concurrent transactions, problems can occur if *A* and *B* want to read or write the same database object, say tuple *t*. There are four possibilities:

- **RR:** *A* and *B* both want to read *t*. Reads cannot interfere with each other, so there is no problem in this case.

- **RW:** *A* reads *t* and then *B* wants to write *t*. If *B* is allowed to perform its write, then (as we saw in Fig. 16.4) the inconsistent analysis problem can arise; thus, we can say that inconsistent analysis is caused by a **RW conflict**. *Note:* If *B* does perform its write and *A* then reads *t* again, it will see a value different from what it saw before, a state of affairs referred to (somewhat inaptly) as **nonrepeatable read**; thus, nonrepeatable reads too are caused by RW conflicts.

- **WR:** *A* writes *t* and then *B* wants to read *t*. If *B* is allowed to perform its read, then (as we saw in Fig. 16.2, except that here we are reversing the roles of *A* and *B*) the uncommitted dependency problem can arise; thus, we can say that uncommitted dependencies are caused by **WR conflicts**. *Note: B's* read, if it is allowed, is said to be a **dirty read**.

- **WW:** *A* writes *t* and then *B* wants to write *t*. If *B* is allowed to perform its write, then (as we saw in Fig. 16.1 and, in effect, in Fig. 16.3 also) the lost update problem can arise; thus, we can say that lost updates are caused by **WW conflicts**. *Note: B's* write, if it is allowed, is said to be a **dirty write**.

16.3   LOCKING

As mentioned in Section 16.1, the problems of Section 16.2 can all be solved by means of a concurrency control mechanism called **locking**. The basic idea is simple: When some transaction *A* needs an assurance that some object it is interested in—typically a database tuple—will not change in some manner while its back is turned (as it were), it **acquires a lock** on that object. The effect of acquiring the lock is to "lock other transactions out of" the object in question, loosely speaking, and thus in particular to prevent them from changing it. Transaction *A* is thus able to continue its processing in the certain knowledge that the object in question will remain in a stable state for as long as that transaction *A* wishes it to.

We now proceed to give a more detailed explanation of the way locking works.

1. First, we assume the system supports two kinds of locks, **exclusive locks** (X locks) and **shared locks** (S locks), defined as indicated in the next two paragraphs. *Note:* X and S locks are sometimes called **write locks** and **read locks**, respectively. We assume until further notice that X and S locks are the only kinds available; see Section 16.9 for a discussion of other possibilities. We also assume until further notice that tuples are the only kinds of things that can be locked; again, see Section 16.9 for a discussion of other possibilities.

2. If transaction *A* holds an exclusive (X) lock on tuple *t,* then a request from some distinct transaction *B* for a lock of either type on *t* cannot be immediately granted.

3. If transaction *A* holds a shared (S) lock on tuple *t,* then:

   - A request from some distinct transaction *B* for an X lock on *t* cannot be immediately granted.

   - A request from some distinct transaction *B* for an S lock on *t* can and will be immediately granted (that is, *B* will now also hold an S lock on *t*).

	X	S	–
X	N	N	Y
S	N	Y	Y
–	Y	Y	Y

Fig. 16.5   Compatibility matrix for lock types X and S

These rules can be conveniently summarized by means of a **lock type compatibility matrix** (Fig. 16.5). That matrix is interpreted as follows: Consider some tuple *t;* suppose transaction *A* currently holds a lock on *t* as indicated by the entries in the column headings (dash = no lock); and suppose some distinct transaction *B* issues a request for a lock on *t* as indicated by the entries down the left side (for completeness we again include the "no lock" case). An "N" indicates a **conflict** (*B*'s request cannot be immediately granted), a "Y" indicates **compatibility** (*B*'s request can and will be immediately granted). The matrix is obviously symmetric.

Next, we introduce a **data access protocol** or **locking protocol** that makes use of X and S locks as just defined to guarantee that problems such as those described in Section 16.2 cannot occur:

1. A transaction that wishes to retrieve a tuple must first acquire an S lock on that tuple.

2. A transaction that wishes to update a tuple must first acquire an X lock on that tuple. Alternatively, if it already holds an S lock on the tuple, as it will in a RETRIEVE-UPDATE sequence, then it must *promote* or *upgrade* that S lock to X level.

    Note: We interrupt ourselves at this point to explain that requests for locks are usually *implicit*—a "tuple retrieve" operation implicitly requests an S lock on the relevant tuple, and a "tuple update" operation implicitly requests an X lock (or implicitly requests promotion of an existing S lock to X level) on the relevant tuple. Also, we take the term *update,* as always, to include INSERTs and DELETEs as well as UPDATEs *per se,* but the rules require some refinement to take care of INSERTs and DELETEs. We omit the details here.

3. If a lock request from transaction *B* cannot be immediately granted because it conflicts with a lock already held by transaction *A, B* goes into a **wait state**. *B* will wait until the lock request can be granted, which at the earliest will not be until *A*'s lock is released. *Note:* We say "at the earliest" because when *A*'s lock is released, another request for a lock on the pertinent tuple can be granted, but it might not be granted to *B*—there might be other transactions waiting by then. Of course, the system must guarantee that *B* does not wait forever (a possibility referred to as **livelock** or **starvation**). A simple way of providing such a guarantee is to service lock requests on a first-come/first-served basis.

4. X locks are released at end-of-transaction (COMMIT or ROLLBACK). S locks are normally released at that time also (at least, we will assume so until we get to Section 16.8).

The foregoing protocol is called **strict two-phase locking**. We will discuss it in more detail—in particular, we will explain why it has that name—in Section 16.6.

16.4 THE THREE CONCURRENCY PROBLEMS REVISITED

Now we are in a position to see how the strict two-phase locking protocol solves the three problems described in Section 16.2. Again we consider them one at a time.

The Lost Update Problem

Fig. 16.6 is a modified version of Fig. 16.1, showing what would happen to the interleaved execution of that figure under the strict two-phase locking protocol. Transaction *A*'s UPDATE at time *t3* is not accepted, because it is an implicit request for an X lock on *t,* and such a request conflicts with the S lock already held by transaction *B; so A* goes into a wait state. For analogous reasons, *B* goes into a wait state at time *t4*. Now both transactions are unable to proceed, so there is no question of any update being lost. We have thus solved the lost update problem by reducing it to another problem!—but at least we have solved the original problem. The new problem is called *deadlock*. It is discussed in Section 16.5.

Transaction A	Time	Transaction B
—		—
—		—
RETRIEVE *t*	*t1*	—
(acquire S lock on *t*)		—
—		—
—	*t2*	RETRIEVE *t*
—		(acquire S lock on *t*)
—		—
UPDATE *t*	*t3*	—
(request X lock on *t*)		—
wait		—
wait	*t4*	UPDATE *t*
wait		(request X lock on *t*)
wait		wait
wait		wait
wait		wait

Fig. 16.6 No update is lost, but deadlock occurs at time *t4*

The Uncommitted Dependency Problem

Figs. 16.7 and 16.8 are, respectively, modified versions of Figs. 16.2 and 16.3, showing what would happen to the interleaved executions of those figures under the strict two-phase locking protocol. Transaction *A*'s operation at time *t2* (RETRIEVE in Fig. 16.7, UPDATE in Fig. 16.8) is not accepted in either case, because it is an implicit request for a

Transaction A	Time	Transaction B
—		—
—		—
—	*t1*	UPDATE *t*
—		(acquire X lock on *t*)
—		—
RETRIEVE *t*	*t2*	—
(request S lock on *t*)		—
wait		—
wait	*t3*	COMMIT / ROLLBACK
wait		(release X lock on *t*)
resume : RETRIEVE *t*	*t4*	
(acquire S lock on *t*)		
—		

Fig. 16.7 Transaction *A* is prevented from seeing an uncommitted change at time *t2*

Transaction A	Time	Transaction B
—		—
—		—
—	*t1*	UPDATE *t*
—		(acquire X lock on *t*)
—		—
UPDATE *t*	*t2*	—
(request X lock on *t*)		—
wait		—
wait	*t3*	COMMIT / ROLLBACK
wait		(release X lock on *t*)
resume : UPDATE *t*	*t4*	
(acquire X lock on *t*)		
—		

Fig. 16.8 Transaction *A* is prevented from updating an uncommitted change at time *t2*

lock on *t,* and such a request conflicts with the X lock already held by *B;* so *A* goes into a wait state. It remains in that wait state until *B* reaches its termination (either COMMIT or ROLLBACK), when *B*'s lock is released and *A* is able to proceed; and at that point *A* sees a *committed* value (either the pre-*B* value, if *B* is rolled back, or the post-*B* value otherwise). Either way, *A* is no longer dependent on an uncommitted update, and so we have solved the original problem.

The Inconsistent Analysis Problem

Fig. 16.9 is a modified version of Fig. 16.4, showing what would happen to the interleaved execution of that figure under the strict two-phase locking protocol. Transaction *B*'s

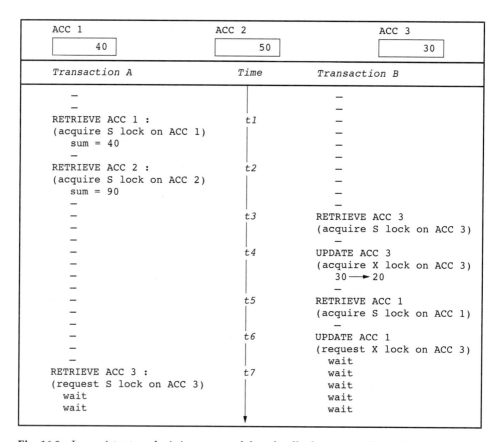

Fig. 16.9   Inconsistent analysis is prevented, but deadlock occurs at time *t7*

UPDATE at time *t6* is not accepted, because it is an implicit request for an X lock on ACC 1, and such a request conflicts with the S lock already held by *A;* so *B* goes into a wait state. Likewise, transaction *A*'s RETRIEVE at time *t7* is also not accepted, because it is an implicit request for an S lock on ACC 3, and such a request conflicts with the X lock already held by *B;* so *A* goes into a wait state also. Again, therefore, we have solved the original problem (the inconsistent analysis problem, in this case) by forcing a deadlock. Again, deadlock is discussed in Section 16.5.

16.5   DEADLOCK

We have now seen how locking—more precisely, the strict two-phase locking protocol—can be used to solve the three basic concurrency problems. Unfortunately, however, we have also seen that locking can introduce problems of its own, principally the problem of *deadlock.* Two examples of deadlock were given in the previous section. Fig. 16.10 shows

Transaction A	Time	Transaction B
—		—
—		—
LOCK *r1* EXCLUSIVE	*t1*	—
—		—
—	*t2*	LOCK *r2* EXCLUSIVE
—		—
—		—
LOCK *r2* EXCLUSIVE	*t3*	—
wait		—
wait	*t4*	LOCK *r1* EXCLUSIVE
wait		wait
wait		wait

Fig. 16.10   An example of deadlock

a slightly more general version of the problem; *r1* and *r2* in that figure are intended to represent any lockable resources, not necessarily just database tuples (see Section 16.9), and the "LOCK . . . EXCLUSIVE" statements are intended to represent any operations that request X locks, either explicitly or implicitly.

In general, then, **deadlock** is a situation in which two or more transactions are in a simultaneous wait state, each of them waiting for one of the others to release a lock before it can proceed.[2] Fig. 16.10 shows a deadlock involving two transactions, but deadlocks involving three, four, or more transactions are also possible, at least in principle. However, experiments with System R suggest that deadlocks almost never do involve more than two transactions in practice [16.9].

If a deadlock occurs, it is desirable that the system detect it and break it. Detecting the deadlock involves detecting a cycle in the **Wait-For Graph** (i.e., the graph of "who is waiting for whom"—see Exercise 16.4). Breaking the deadlock involves choosing one of the deadlocked transactions (i.e., one of the transactions in the cycle in the graph) as the **victim** and rolling it back, thereby releasing its locks and so allowing some other transaction to proceed. *Note:* In practice, not all systems do in fact detect deadlocks; some just use a timeout mechanism and simply assume that a transaction that has done no work for some prescribed period of time is deadlocked.

Observe, incidentally, that the victim has "failed" and been rolled back *through no fault of its own.* Some systems automatically restart such a transaction from the beginning, on the assumption that the conditions that caused the deadlock in the first place will probably not arise again. Other systems merely send a "deadlock victim" exception code back to the application; it is then up to the application to deal with the situation in some graceful manner. The first of these two approaches is clearly preferable from the application programmer's point of view. But even if the programmer does sometimes have to get involved, it is *always* desirable to conceal the problem from the end user, for obvious reasons.

---

[2] Deadlock is also referred to in the literature, somewhat colorfully, as *deadly embrace.*

Deadlock Avoidance

Instead of allowing deadlocks to occur and dealing with them when they do (which is what most systems do), it would be possible to avoid them entirely by modifying the locking protocol in various ways. We briefly consider one possible approach here. The approach in question (which was first proposed in the context of a distributed system [16.19], but could be used in a centralized system as well) comes in two versions, called *Wait-Die* and *Wound-Wait*. It works as follows:

- Every transaction is *timestamped* with its start time (which must be unique).

- When transaction *A* requests a lock on a tuple that is already locked by transaction *B*, then:

    - *Wait-Die:* *A* waits if it is older than *B;* otherwise, it "dies"—that is, *A* is rolled back and restarted.

    - *Wound-Wait:* *A* waits if it is younger than *B;* otherwise, it "wounds" *B*—that is, *B* is rolled back and restarted.

- If a transaction has to be restarted, it retains its original timestamp.

Note that the first component of the name (Wait or Wound) indicates in each case what happens if *A* is *older* than *B*. As you can see, Wait-Die means all waits consist of older transactions waiting for younger ones, Wound-Wait means all waits consist of younger transactions waiting for older ones. Whichever version is in effect, it is easy to see that deadlock cannot occur. It is also easy to see that every transaction is guaranteed to reach its proper conclusion eventually—that is, livelock cannot occur (no transaction will wait forever), and no transaction will be restarted over and over again forever either. The main drawback to the approach (either version) is that it does too many rollbacks.

16.6   SERIALIZABILITY

We have now laid the groundwork for explaining the crucial notion of *serializability.* Serializability is the generally accepted "criterion for correctness" for the interleaved execution of a set of transactions; that is, such an execution is considered to be correct if and only if it is serializable.[3] A given execution of a given set of transactions is **serializable**— and therefore correct—if and only if it is equivalent to (i.e., guaranteed to produce the same result as) some serial execution of the same transactions, where:

- A *serial execution* is one in which the transactions are run one at a time in some sequence.

- *Guaranteed* means that the given execution and the serial one always produce the same result as each other, no matter what the initial state of the database might be.

---

[3] Actually two kinds of serializability are defined in the literature, *conflict* serializability and *view* serializability. View serializability is of little practical interest, however, and it is usual to take the term *serializability* to mean conflict serializability specifically. See, for example, reference [16.21] for further discussion.

We justify this definition as follows:

1. Individual transactions are assumed to be correct; that is, they are assumed to transform a correct state of the database into another correct state, as discussed in Chapter 15.

2. Running the transactions one at a time in any serial order is therefore also correct ("any" serial order because individual transactions are assumed to be independent of one another).

3. It is thus reasonable to define an interleaved execution to be correct if and only if it is equivalent to some serial execution (i.e., if and only if it is serializable). Note that "only if"! The point is, a given interleaved execution might be nonserializable and yet still produce a result that happens to be correct, given some specific initial state of the database—see Exercise 16.3—but that would not be good enough; we want correctness to be *guaranteed* (i.e., independent of particular database states), not a matter of mere happenstance.

Referring back to the examples of Section 16.2 (Figs. 16.1–16.4), we can see that the problem in every case was precisely that the interleaved execution was not serializable—that is, it was never equivalent to running either *A*-then-*B* or *B*-then-*A*. And a study of Section 16.4 shows that the effect of the strict two-phase locking protocol is precisely to *force* serializability in every case. In Figs. 16.7 and 16.8, the interleaved execution is equivalent to *B*-then-*A*. In Figs. 16.6 and 16.9, a deadlock occurs, implying that one of the two transactions will be rolled back (and presumably run again later). If *A* is the one rolled back, then the interleaved execution again becomes equivalent to *B*-then-*A*.

Terminology: Given a set of transactions, any execution of those transactions, interleaved or otherwise, is called a **schedule**. Executing the transactions one at a time, with no interleaving, constitutes a **serial** schedule; a schedule that is not serial is an **interleaved** schedule (or simply a *nonserial* schedule). Two schedules are said to be **equivalent** if and only if, no matter what the initial state of the database, they are guaranteed to produce the same result as each other. Thus, a schedule is serializable, and correct, if and only if it is equivalent to some serial schedule.

Note that two different serial schedules involving the same transactions might well produce different results, and hence that two different interleaved schedules involving those same transactions might also produce different results, and yet both be correct. For example, suppose transaction *A* is of the form "Add 1 to *x*" and transaction *B* is of the form "Double *x*" (where *x* is some item in the database). Suppose also that the initial value of *x* is 10. Then the serial schedule *A*-then-*B* gives *x* = 22, whereas the serial schedule *B*-then-*A* gives *x* = 21. These two results are equally correct, and any schedule that is guaranteed to be equivalent to either *A*-then-*B* or *B*-then-*A* is likewise correct.

The concept of serializability was first introduced (although not by that name) by Eswaran *et al.* in reference [16.6]. That same paper also proved an important theorem, called the **two-phase locking theorem**, which we can state as follows:[4]

> *If all transactions obey the two-phase locking protocol, then all possible interleaved schedules are serializable.*

---

[4] Two-phase locking has nothing to do with two-phase commit—they just have similar names.

The **two-phase locking protocol,** in turn, is as follows:

- Before operating on any object (e.g., a database tuple), a transaction must acquire a lock on that object.

- After releasing a lock, a transaction must never go on to acquire any more locks.

A transaction that obeys this protocol thus has two phases, a lock acquisition or "growing" phase and a lock releasing or "shrinking" phase. *Note:* In practice, the shrinking phase is often compressed into the single operation of COMMIT or ROLLBACK at end-of-transaction (a point we will come back to in Sections 16.7 and 16.8); if it is, then the protocol becomes the "strict" version described in Section 16.3.

The notion of serializability is a great aid to clear thinking in this potentially confusing area, and we therefore offer a few additional observations on it here. Let *I* be an interleaved schedule involving some set of transactions *T1, T2, ..., Tn.* If *I* is serializable, then there exists at least one serial schedule *S* involving *T1, T2, ..., Tn* such that *I* is equivalent to *S. S* is said to be a **serialization** of *I.*

Now let *Ti* and *Tj* be any two distinct transactions in the set *T1, T2, ..., Tn.* Let *Ti* precede *Tj* in the serialization *S.* In the interleaved schedule *I,* then, the effect must be as if *Ti* really did execute before *Tj.* In other words, an informal but very helpful characterization of serializability is that if *A* and *B* are any two transactions involved in some serializable schedule, then either *A* logically precedes *B* or *B* logically precedes *A* in that schedule; that is, **either B can see A's output or A can see B's.** (If *A* produces *x, y, ..., z* as output and *B* sees any of *x, y, ..., z* as input, then *B* sees them *either* all as they are after being output by *A or* all as they were before being output by *A*—not a mixture of the two.) Conversely, if the effect is not as if either *A* ran before *B* or *B* ran before *A,* then the schedule is not serializable and not correct.

Finally, we stress the point that if some transaction *A* is not two-phase (i.e., does not obey the two-phase locking protocol), then it is **always** possible to construct some other transaction *B* that can run interleaved with *A* in such a way as to produce an overall schedule that is not serializable and not correct. Now, in the interest of reducing resource contention and thereby improving performance and throughput, real-world systems typically do allow the construction of transactions that are not two-phase—that is, transactions that "release locks early" (prior to COMMIT) and then go on to acquire more locks. However, it should be clear that such transactions are a risky proposition; at best, allowing a given transaction *A* not to be two-phase amounts to a gamble that no interfering transaction *B* will ever coexist in the system with *A* (for if it does, then the system overall has the potential to produce wrong answers).

16.7   RECOVERY REVISITED

Given a serial schedule, individual transactions are obviously *recoverable*—such a transaction can always be undone and/or redone as necessary, using the techniques described in the previous chapter. However, it is not as obvious that transactions are still recoverable if

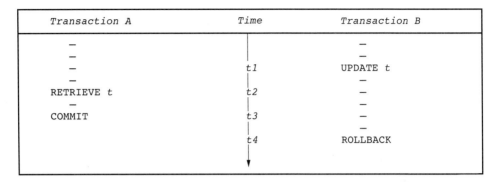

Transaction A	*Time*	*Transaction B*
—		—
—		—
—	*t1*	UPDATE *t*
—		—
RETRIEVE *t*	*t2*	—
—		—
COMMIT	*t3*	—
	t4	ROLLBACK

Fig. 16.11 An unrecoverable schedule

they are allowed to run interleaved. In fact, the uncommitted dependency problem discussed in Section 16.2 can cause recoverability problems, as we now show.

Assume for the moment that—as in Section 16.2—no locking protocol is in effect, and hence in particular that transactions never have to wait to acquire a lock. Now consider Fig. 16.11, which is a modified version of Fig. 16.2 (the difference is that transaction A now commits before transaction B rolls back). The problem here is that, in order to honor B's ROLLBACK request and make it as if B never executed, we need to roll A back too, because A has seen one of B's updates. But rolling back A is impossible, because A has already committed. Thus, the schedule shown in the figure is *unrecoverable*.

A sufficient condition for a schedule to be **recoverable** is as follows [15.2]:

If A sees any of B's updates, then A must not commit before B terminates.

Clearly, we want our concurrency control mechanism—that is, our locking protocol, if locking is what we are using—to guarantee that all schedules are recoverable in this sense.

However, the foregoing is not the end of the story. Suppose now that we do have a locking protocol in place, and the protocol in question is *the nonstrict form* of two-phase locking, according to which a transaction can release locks before it terminates. Now consider Fig. 16.12, which is a modified version of Fig. 16.11 (the differences are that transaction A now does not commit before transaction B's termination, but transaction B releases its lock on t "early"). As in Fig. 16.11, in order to honor B's ROLLBACK request and make it as if B never executed, we need to roll A back too, because A has seen one of B's updates. What is more, we *can* roll A back too, because A has not yet committed. But *cascading rollbacks* in this way is almost certainly undesirable; in particular, it is clear that if we permit the rollback of one transaction to cascade and cause the rollback of another, then we need to be prepared to deal with such "cascade chains" of arbitrary length. In other words, the trouble with the schedule shown in the figure is that it is not *cascade-free*.

A sufficient condition for a schedule to be **cascade-free** is as follows [15.2]:

If A sees any of B's updates, then A must not do so before B terminates.

Transaction A	Time	Transaction B
—		—
—		—
—	t1	UPDATE t
—		(acquire X lock on t)
—		—
RETRIEVE t	t2	—
(request S lock on t)		—
wait		—
wait		—
wait	t3	(release lock on t)
wait		—
resume : RETRIEVE t	t4	—
(acquire S lock on t)		—
—		—
(forced rollback)	t5	ROLLBACK

Fig. 16.12   A schedule involving cascaded rollback

Strict two-phase locking will guarantee that all schedules are cascade-free, which is why that protocol is the one used in the vast majority of systems.[5] Also, it is easy to see that a cascade-free schedule must necessarily also be a recoverable schedule, as we defined that term previously.

16.8   ISOLATION LEVELS

Serializability guarantees *isolation* in the ACID sense. One direct and very desirable consequence is that if all schedules are serializable, then the application programmer writing the code for a given transaction *A* need pay absolutely no attention at all to the fact that some other transaction *B* might be executing in the system at the same time. However, it can be argued that the protocols used to guarantee serializability reduce the degree of concurrency or overall system throughput to unacceptable levels. In practice, therefore, systems usually support a variety of *levels* of "isolation" (in quotes because any level lower than the maximum means the transaction is not truly isolated from others after all, as we will soon see).

The **isolation level** that applies to a given transaction might be defined as the *degree of interference* the transaction in question is prepared to tolerate on the part of concurrent transactions. Now, if serializability is to be guaranteed, the only amount of interference that can possibly be tolerated is obviously none at all! In other words, the isolation level should be the maximum possible—for otherwise correctness, recoverability, and cascade-

---

[5] Actually, strict two-phase locking is slightly *too* strict; there is no need to keep S locks until end-of-transaction, just as long as transactions are still two-phase.

free schedules can no longer be guaranteed, in general. But the fact remains that, as already stated, systems typically do support levels that are less than the maximum, and in this section we briefly examine this issue.

At least five different isolation levels can be defined, though reference [16.10], the SQL standard, and DB2 each support just four. Generally speaking, the higher the isolation level, the less the interference (and the lower the concurrency); the lower the isolation level, the more the interference (and the higher the concurrency). By way of illustration, we consider two of the levels supported by DB2, *cursor stability* and *repeatable read*. **Repeatable read** (RR) is the maximum level; if all transactions operate at this level, all schedules are serializable. Under **cursor stability** (CS), by contrast, if a transaction *A*

- Obtains addressability to some tuple t,[6] and thus
- Acquires a lock on t, and then
- Relinquishes its addressability to t without updating it, and so
- Does not promote its lock to X level, then
- That lock can be released without having to wait for end-of-transaction.

But note that some other transaction *B* can now update *t* and commit the change. If transaction *A* subsequently comes back and looks at *t* again—note the violation of the two-phase locking protocol here!—it will see that change, and so might in effect see an inconsistent state of the database. Under repeatable read (RR), by contrast, *all* tuple locks (not just X locks) are held until end-of-transaction, and the problem just mentioned therefore cannot occur.

Points arising:

1. The foregoing problem is *not* the only problem that can occur under CS—it just happens to be the easiest to explain. But it unfortunately suggests that RR is needed only in the comparatively unlikely case that a given transaction needs to look at the same tuple twice. On the contrary, there are arguments to suggest that RR is *always* a better choice than CS; a transaction running under CS is not two-phase, and so (as explained in the previous section) serializability can no longer be guaranteed. The counterargument is that CS gives more concurrency than RR (probably but not necessarily).

2. The fact that serializability cannot be guaranteed under CS seems not to be very well understood in practice. The following is therefore worth repeating: *If transaction* T *operates at less than the maximum isolation level, then we can no longer guarantee that* T *if running concurrently with other transactions will transform a correct state of the database into another correct state.*

3. An implementation that supports any isolation level lower than the maximum will normally provide some explicit concurrency control facilities—typically explicit LOCK statements—in order to allow users to write their applications in such a way

---

[6] It does this by setting a *cursor* to point to the tuple, as explained in Chapter 4—hence the name "cursor stability." In the interest of accuracy, we should mention that the lock *T1* acquires on *t* in DB2 is actually an "update" (U) lock, not an S lock (see reference [4.21]).

as to guarantee safety in the absence of such a guarantee from the system itself. For example, DB2 provides an explicit LOCK TABLE statement, which allows users operating at a level less than the maximum to acquire explicit locks, over and above the ones that DB2 acquires automatically to enforce that level. (We remark in passing that the SQL standard includes no such explicit concurrency control mechanisms. See Section 16.11.)

By the way, please note that the foregoing characterization of RR as the maximum isolation level refers to repeatable read as implemented in DB2. Unfortunately, the SQL standard uses the same term *repeatable read* to mean an isolation level that is strictly lower than the maximum level (again, see Section 16.11).

Phantoms

One special problem that can occur if transactions operate at less than the maximum isolation level is the so-called *phantom* problem. Consider the following example (it is very contrived, but it suffices to illustrate the idea):

- First, suppose transaction *A* is computing the average account balance for all accounts held by customer Joe. Suppose there are currently three such accounts, each with a balance of $100. Transaction *A* thus scans the three accounts, acquiring shared locks on them as it proceeds, and obtains a result ($100).

- However, now suppose a concurrent transaction *B* is executing, the effect of which is to add another account to the database for customer Joe, with balance $200. Assume for definiteness that the new account is added after *A* has computed its $100 average. Assume too that after adding the new account, *B* immediately commits (releasing the exclusive lock it will have held on the new account).

- Now suppose *A* decides to scan the accounts for customer Joe again, counting them and summing their balances and then dividing the sum by the count (perhaps it wants to see if the average really is equal to the sum divided by the count). This time, it sees *four* accounts instead of three, and it obtains a result of $125 instead of $100!

Now, both transactions have followed strict two-phase locking here, and yet something has still gone wrong; to be specific, transaction *A* has seen something that did not exist the first time around—a **phantom**. As a consequence, serializability has been violated (the interleaved execution is clearly equivalent to neither *A*-then-*B* nor *B*-then-*A*).

Note carefully, however, that the problem here has nothing to do with two-phase locking *per se*. Rather, the problem is that transaction *A* did not lock what it logically needed to lock; instead of locking customer Joe's three accounts as such, it really needed to lock *the set of accounts held by Joe,* or in other words the *predicate* "account holder = Joe" (see references [16.6] and [16.13]).[7] If it could have done that, then transaction *B* would have had to wait when it tried to add its new account (because *B* would certainly request a lock on that new account, and that lock would conflict with the lock held by *A*).

---

[7] We might also say that *A* needed to lock the *nonexistence* of any other accounts belonging to Joe.

Although for reasons discussed in reference [15.12] most systems today do not support predicate locking as such, they do still generally manage to prevent "phantoms" from occurring by locking the *access path* used to get to the data under consideration. In the case of the accounts held by Joe, for example, if that access path happens to be an index on customer name, then the system can lock the entry in that index for customer Joe. Such a lock will prevent the creation of phantoms, because such creation would require the access path—the index entry, in this example—to be updated, and would thus require an X lock to be obtained on that access path. See reference [15.12] for further discussion.

16.9 INTENT LOCKING

Up to this point we have been assuming for the most part that the unit for locking purposes is the individual tuple. In principle, however, there is no reason why locks should not be applied to larger or smaller units of data—for example, an entire relvar, or even the entire database, or (going to the opposite extreme) a specific component within a specific tuple. We speak of **locking granularity** [16.10, 16.11]. As usual, there is a trade-off: The finer the granularity, the greater the concurrency; the coarser, the fewer the locks that need to be set and tested and the lower the overhead. For example, if a transaction has an X lock on an entire relvar, there is no need to set X locks on individual tuples within that relvar; on the other hand, no concurrent transaction will be able to obtain any locks on that relvar, or on tuples within that relvar, at all.

Suppose some transaction T does in fact request an X lock on some relvar R. On receipt of T's request, the system must be able to tell whether any other transaction already has a lock on any tuple of R—for if it does, then T's request cannot be granted at this time. How can the system detect such a conflict? It is obviously undesirable to have to examine every tuple in R to see whether any of them is currently locked by any other transaction, or to have to examine every existing lock to see whether any of them is for a tuple in R. Instead, therefore, we introduce another protocol, the **intent locking protocol**, according to which no transaction is allowed to acquire a lock on a tuple before first acquiring a lock—probably an *intent* lock (see the next paragraph)—on the relvar that contains it. Conflict detection in the example then becomes a comparatively simple matter of seeing whether any transaction has a conflicting lock *at the relvar level.*

Now, we have effectively suggested already that X and S locks make sense for whole relvars as well as for individual tuples. Following references [16.10, 16.11], we now introduce three additional kinds of locks, called **intent locks**, that also make sense for relvars, but not for individual tuples: **intent shared** (IS) locks, **intent exclusive** (IX) locks, and **shared intent exclusive** (SIX) locks. These new kinds of locks can be defined informally as follows. (We suppose that transaction T has requested a lock of the indicated type on relvar R; for completeness, we include definitions for types X and S as well.)

- *Intent shared (IS):* T intends to set S locks on individual tuples in R, in order to guarantee the stability of those tuples while they are being processed.

- *Intent exclusive (IX):* Same as IS, *plus* T might update individual tuples in R and will therefore set X locks on those tuples.

- *Shared (S): T* can tolerate concurrent readers, but not concurrent updaters, in *R* (*T* itself will not update any tuples in *R*).
- *Shared intent exclusive (SIX):* Combines S and IX; that is, *T* can tolerate concurrent readers, but not concurrent updaters, in *R, plus T* might update individual tuples in *R* and will therefore set X locks on those tuples.
- *Exclusive (X): T* cannot tolerate any concurrent access to *R* at all (*T* itself might or might not update individual tuples in *R*).

The formal definitions of these five lock types are given by an extended version of the lock type compatibility matrix first discussed in Section 16.3. See Fig. 16.13.

	X	SIX	IX	S	IS	–
X	N	N	N	N	N	Y
SIX	N	N	N	N	Y	Y
IX	N	N	Y	N	Y	Y
S	N	N	N	Y	Y	Y
IS	N	Y	Y	Y	Y	Y
–	Y	Y	Y	Y	Y	Y

Fig. 16.13   Compatibility matrix extended to include intent locks

Here now is a more precise statement of the intent locking protocol:

1. Before a given transaction can acquire an S lock on a given tuple, it must first acquire an IS or stronger lock (see later) on the relvar containing that tuple.
2. Before a given transaction can acquire an X lock on a given tuple, it must first acquire an IX or stronger lock (see later) on the relvar containing that tuple.

(Note, however, that this is still not a complete definition. See the annotation to reference [16.10].)

The notion touched on in the foregoing protocol of *relative lock strength* can be explained as follows. Refer to the **precedence graph** in Fig. 16.14. We say that lock type *L2* is stronger—that is, higher in the graph—than lock type *L1* if and only if, whenever there is an "N" (conflict) in *L1*'s column in the compatibility matrix for a given row, there is also an "N" in *L2*'s column for that same row (see Fig. 16.13). Note that a lock request that fails for a given lock type will certainly fail for a stronger lock type (and this fact implies that it is always safe to use a lock type that is stronger than strictly necessary). Note too that neither of S and IX is stronger than the other.

It is worth pointing out that, in practice, the relvar locks required by the intent locking protocol will usually be acquired implicitly. For a read-only transaction, for example, the system will probably acquire an IS lock implicitly on every relvar the transaction accesses. For an update transaction, it will probably acquire IX locks instead. But the system will probably also have to provide an explicit LOCK statement of some kind in

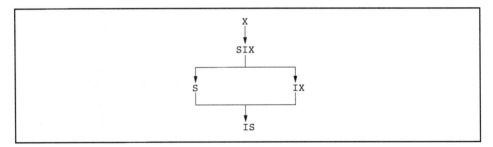

Fig. 16.14   Lock type precedence graph

order to allow transactions to acquire S, X, or SIX locks at the relvar level if they want them. Such a statement is supported by DB2, for example (for S and X locks only, not SIX locks).

We close this section with a remark on **lock escalation**, which is implemented in many systems and represents an attempt to balance the conflicting requirements of high concurrency and low lock management overhead. The basic idea is that when some pre-scribed threshold is reached, the system automatically replaces a collection of locks of fine granularity by a single lock of coarser granularity: for example, by trading in a set of individual tuple-level S locks and converting the IS lock on the containing relvar to an S lock. This technique seems to work well in practice [16.9].

16.10   DROPPING ACID

We promised in Chapter 15 that we would have more to say in this chapter regarding the ACID properties of transactions; in fact, we have some rather unorthodox opinions to offer on this topic, as will soon be clear.

Recall first that ACID is an acronym for *atomicity - correctness - isolation - durability.* Just to review briefly:

- *Atomicity:* Any given transaction is all or nothing.
- *Correctness* (usually called *consistency* in the literature): Any given transaction trans-forms a correct state of the database into another correct state, without necessarily preserving correctness at all intermediate points.
- *Isolation:* Any given transaction's updates are concealed from all other transactions, until the given transaction commits.
- *Durability:* Once a given transaction commits, its updates survive in the database, even if there is a subsequent system crash.

So ACID is a nice acronym—but do the concepts it represents really stand up to close examination? In this section, we present some evidence to suggest that the answer to this question is, in general, *no.*

Immediate Constraint Checking

We begin with what might look like a digression: a justification for our position, first articulated in Chapter 9, that all checking of integrity constraints must be done immediately (i.e., at end-of-statement), not deferred to end-of-transaction. We have at least four reasons for adopting this position, which we now proceed to explain.

1. As we know, a database can be regarded as a collection of propositions (assumed by convention to be true ones). And if that collection is ever allowed to include any inconsistencies, *then all bets are off.* We can never trust the answers we get from an inconsistent database; in fact, we can get *absolutely any answer whatsoever* from such a database (a proof of this fact appears in the annotation to reference [9.16] in Chapter 9). While the isolation or "I" property of transactions might mean that no more than one transaction will ever see any particular inconsistency, the fact remains that that particular transaction does see the inconsistency and can therefore produce wrong answers. Indeed, it is precisely because inconsistencies cannot be tolerated, not even if they are never visible to more than one transaction at a time, that the constraints need to be enforced in the first place.

2. In any case, it cannot be guaranteed that a given inconsistency (assuming such a thing is permitted) *will* be seen by just one transaction. Only if they follow certain protocols—certain *unenforced* (and in fact unenforceable) protocols—can transactions truly be guaranteed to be isolated from one another. For example, if transaction *A* sees an inconsistent state of the database and so writes inconsistent data to some file *F*, and transaction *B* then reads that same information from file *F*, then *A* and *B* are not really isolated from each other (regardless of whether they run concurrently or otherwise).[8] In other words, the "I" property of transactions is suspect, to say the least.

3. The previous edition of this book stated that relvar constraints were checked immediately but database constraints were checked at end-of-transaction (a position that many writers concur with, though they usually use different terminology). But *The Principle of Interchangeability* (of base and derived relvars—see Chapter 9) implies that the very same real-world constraint might be a relvar constraint with one design for the database and a database constraint with another! Since relvar constraints must *obviously* be checked immediately, it follows that database constraints must be checked immediately too.

4. The ability to perform "semantic optimization" requires the database to be consistent *at all times,* not just at transaction boundaries. *Note:* Semantic optimization is a technique for using integrity constraints to simplify queries in order to improve performance. Clearly, if the constraints are not satisfied, then the simplifications will be invalid. For further discussion, see Chapter 18.

Of course, the "conventional wisdom" is that database constraint checks, at least, surely *have* to be deferred. As a trivial example, suppose the suppliers-and-parts database is subject to the constraint "Supplier S1 and part P1 are in the same city." If supplier S1

---

[8] In fact the problem arises even if *A* does not see an inconsistent state of the database; it is still possible that *A* might write inconsistent data to some file that is subsequently read by *B*.

moves, say from London to Paris, then part P1 must move from London to Paris as well. The conventional solution to this problem is to wrap the two updates up into a single transaction, like this:

```
BEGIN TRANSACTION ;
UPDATE S WHERE S# = S# ('S1') { CITY := 'Paris' } ;
UPDATE P WHERE P# = P# ('P1') { CITY := 'Paris' } ;
COMMIT ;
```

In this conventional solution, the constraint is checked at COMMIT, and the database is inconsistent between the two UPDATE operations. Note in particular that if the transaction performing the UPDATEs were to ask the question "Are supplier S1 and part P1 in the same city?" between the two UPDATE operations, it would get the answer *no*.

Recall, however, that we require support for a *multiple assignment* operator, which lets us carry out several assignments as a single operation (i.e., within a single statement), without any integrity checking being done until all of the assignments in question have been executed. Recall too that INSERT, DELETE, and UPDATE are just shorthand for certain assignment operations. In the example, therefore, we should be able to perform the desired updating as a single operation, thus:

```
UPDATE S WHERE S# = S# ('S1') { CITY := 'Paris' } ,
UPDATE P WHERE P# = P# ('P1') { CITY := 'Paris' } ;
```

Now no integrity checking is done until both UPDATEs have been done (i.e., "until we reach the semicolon"). Note too that there is now no way for the transaction to see an inconsistent state of the database between the two UPDATEs, because the notion of "between the two UPDATEs" now has no meaning.

It follows from this example that if multiple assignment were supported, there would be no need for deferred checking in the traditional sense (i.e., checking that is deferred to end-of-transaction).

Now we turn to the ACID properties *per se*. However, it suits our purposes better to discuss them in the order C-I-D-A.

Correctness

We have already given our reasons (in Chapter 15) for preferring the term *correctness* here over the more usual *consistency*. In fact, however, the literature usually seems to equate the two concepts. Here, for example, is a quote from the glossary in the book by Gray and Reuter [15.12]:

> **Consistent**. Correct.

And the same book defines the consistency property of transactions thus:

> **Consistency**. A transaction is a correct transformation of the state. The actions taken as a group do not violate any of the integrity constraints associated with the state. This requires that the transaction be a correct program [*sic*].

But if integrity constraints are always checked immediately, the database is *always* consistent—not necessarily correct!—and transactions always transform a consistent state of the database into another consistent state *a fortiori*.

So if the C in ACID stands for consistency, then in a sense the property is trivial;[9] and if it stands for correctness, then it is unenforceable. Either way, therefore, the property is essentially meaningless, at least from a formal standpoint. As already indicated, our own preference would be to say that the C stands for correctness; then we can go on to regard "the correctness property" not really as a property as such, but rather as a desideratum.

Isolation

We turn now to the isolation property. As already explained earlier in this section, in the subsection "Immediate Constraint Checking," this property too is somewhat suspect. It is at least true that if every transaction behaves as if it were the only transaction in the system, then a proper concurrency control mechanism will guarantee isolation (and serializability). However, "behaving as if it were the only transaction in the system" implies among other things that the transaction in question must:

- Make no attempt, intentional or otherwise, to communicate with other transactions, concurrent or otherwise
- Make no attempt even to recognize the possibility (by specifying an isolation level lower than the maximum) that other transactions might exist in the system

So the isolation property too is really more of a desideratum than an ironclad guarantee. What is more, real-world systems typically provide explicit mechanisms—namely, isolation levels lower than the maximum—whose effect is precisely to undermine isolation.

Durability

We turn now to the durability property. This property is reasonable, thanks to the system's recovery mechanism, *as long as there is no transaction nesting*—and indeed we have assumed that such is the case, prior to this point. Suppose, however, that transaction nesting is supported. To be specific, suppose transaction *B* is nested inside transaction *A,* and the following sequence of events occurs:

```
BEGIN TRANSACTION (transaction A) ;
   ...
   BEGIN TRANSACTION (transaction B) ;
   transaction B updates tuple t ;
   COMMIT (transaction B) ;
   ...
ROLLBACK (transaction A) ;
```

If *A*'s ROLLBACK is honored, then *B* is effectively rolled back too (because *B* is really part of *A*), and *B*'s effects on the database are thus not "durable"; in fact, *A*'s ROLLBACK causes tuple *t* to be restored to its pre-*A* value. In other words, the durability property can

---

[9] As a matter of fact, it would be trivial even if constraints are not checked immediately—the transaction would still be rolled back, and thus in effect have never executed, if it violated any constraint. In other words, it would still be the case that transactions have a lasting effect on the database only if they do not violate any constraints.

no longer be guaranteed, at least not for a transaction like *B* in the example that is nested inside some other transaction.

Now, many writers (beginning with Davies in reference [15.8]) have in fact proposed the ability to nest transactions in the manner suggested by the foregoing example. Reference [15.15] claims that such support is desirable for at least three reasons: intra-transaction parallelism, intra-transaction recovery control, and system modularity. As the example indicates, in a system with such support, COMMIT by an inner transaction commits that transaction's updates, *but only to the next outer level.* In effect, the outer transaction has veto power over the inner transaction's COMMIT—if the outer transaction does a rollback, the inner transaction is rolled back too. In the example, *B*'s COMMIT is a COMMIT to *A* only, not to the outside world, and indeed that COMMIT is subsequently revoked (rolled back).

Note: We remark that nested transactions can be thought of as a generalization of *savepoints*. Savepoints allow a transaction to be structured as a linear *sequence* of actions that are executed one at a time (and rollback can occur at any time to the start of any earlier action in the sequence). Nesting, by contrast, allows a transaction to be structured, recursively, as a *hierarchy* of actions that are executed concurrently. In other words:

- BEGIN TRANSACTION is extended to support "subtransactions" (i.e., if BEGIN TRANSACTION is issued when a transaction is already running, it starts a *child* transaction).

- COMMIT "commits" but only within the *parent scope* (if this transaction is a child).

- ROLLBACK undoes work, but only back to the start of this particular transaction (including child, grandchild, etc., transactions but *not* including the parent transaction, if any).

To revert to the main thread of our discussion, we now see that the durability property of transactions applies only at the outermost level[10] (in other words, to transactions not nested inside any other transaction). Thus we see that that property too is less than 100 percent guaranteed, in general.

Atomicity

Finally, we turn to the atomicity property. Like the durability property, this property is guaranteed by the system's recovery mechanism (even with nested transactions). Our objections here are a little different. To be specific, we simply observe that if the system supported multiple assignment, there would be no need for transactions as such to have the atomicity property; rather, it would be sufficient for *statements* to do so. What is more, it is *necessary* for statements to do so, too, for reasons already discussed in detail elsewhere.[11]

---

[10] Reference [15.15] says the same is true for the consistency property as well, because like most of the rest of the literature it assumes that the outermost transaction is not required to preserve consistency at intermediate points. However, we reject this position for reasons already explained.

[11] We remind you in passing that most statements in the SQL standard in particular do have the atomicity property.

Concluding Remarks

We can summarize this section by means of the following somewhat rhetorical questions:

- *Is the transaction a unit of work?* Yes, but only if multiple assignment is not supported.
- *Is it a unit of recovery?* Same answer.
- *Is it a unit of concurrency?* Same answer.
- *Is it a unit of integrity?* Yes, but only if "all constraint checking immediate" is not supported.

Note: We answer the questions the way we do despite various remarks made in earlier chapters (and in earlier editions of the book) that adhere more to "the conventional wisdom" in this area.

Overall, then, we conclude that the transaction concept is important more from a pragmatic point of view than it is from a theoretical one. Please understand that this conclusion is not meant to be disparaging! We have nothing but respect for the many elegant and useful results obtained from over 25 years of transaction management research. We are merely observing that we now have a better understanding of some of the assumptions on which that research has been based—a better understanding of the crucial role of integrity constraints in particular, plus a recognition of the need to support multiple assignment as a primitive operator. Indeed, it would be surprising if a change in assumptions did not lead to a change in conclusions.

16.11   SQL FACILITIES

The SQL standard does not provide any explicit locking facilities; in fact, it does not mention locking, as such, at all.[12] However, it does require the implementation to provide the usual guarantees regarding interference, or rather lack thereof, among concurrently executing transactions. Most importantly, it requires that updates made by a given transaction *T1* not be visible to any distinct transaction *T2* until and unless transaction *T1* commits. *Note:* The foregoing assumes that all transactions execute at isolation level READ COMMITTED, REPEATABLE READ, or SERIALIZABLE (see the next paragraph). Special considerations apply to transactions executing at the READ UNCOMMITTED level, which (a) are allowed to perform "dirty reads" but (b) are required to be READ ONLY (if READ WRITE were permitted, recoverability could no longer be guaranteed).

Recall now from Chapter 15 that SQL isolation levels are specified on START TRANSACTION. There are four possibilities—**SERIALIZABLE, REPEATABLE READ, READ COMMITTED,** and **READ UNCOMMITTED**.[13] The default is SERIALIZABLE;

---

[12] The omission is deliberate—the idea is that the system should be free to use any concurrency control mechanism it likes, just as long as it implements the desired functionality.

[13] SERIALIZABLE is not a good keyword here, since it is *schedules* that are supposed to be serializable, not *transactions*. A better term might be just TWO PHASE, meaning the transaction will obey (or will be forced to obey) the two-phase locking protocol.

Isolation level	Dirty read	Nonrepeatable read	Phantom
READ UNCOMMITTED	Y	Y	Y
READ COMMITTED	N	Y	Y
REPEATABLE READ	N	N	Y
SERIALIZABLE	N	N	N

Fig. 16.15   SQL isolation levels

if any of the other three is specified, the implementation is free to assign some higher level, where "higher" is defined in terms of the ordering SERIALIZABLE > REPEATABLE READ > READ COMMITTED > READ UNCOMMITTED.

If all transactions execute at isolation level SERIALIZABLE (the default), then the interleaved execution of any set of concurrent transactions is guaranteed to be serializable. However, if any transaction executes at a lesser isolation level, then serializability can be violated in a variety of different ways. The standard defines three kinds of violations—*dirty read, nonrepeatable read,* and *phantoms* (the first two of these were explained in Section 16.2 and the third was explained in Section 16.8)—and the various isolation levels are defined in terms of the violations they permit.[14] They are summarized in Fig. 16.15 ("Y" means the violation can occur, "N" means it cannot).

We close this section by reminding you that the REPEATABLE READ of the SQL standard and the "repeatable read" (RR) of DB2 are not the same thing. In fact, DB2's RR is the same as the standard's SERIALIZABLE.

16.12   SUMMARY

We have examined the question of **concurrency control**. We began by looking at three problems that can arise in an interleaved execution of concurrent transactions if no such control is in place: the **lost update** problem, the **uncommitted dependency** problem, and the **inconsistent analysis** problem. All of these problems arise from schedules that are not **serializable**—that is, not equivalent to some serial schedule involving the same transactions.

The most widespread technique for dealing with such problems is **locking**. There are two basic types of locks, **shared** (S) and **exclusive** (X). If a transaction has an S lock on an object, other transactions can also acquire an S lock on that object, but not an X lock; if a transaction has an X lock on an object, no other transaction can acquire a lock on the object at all, of either type. Then we introduce a protocol for the use of these locks to ensure that the lost update and other problems cannot occur: Acquire an S lock on everything retrieved, acquire an X lock on everything updated, and keep all locks until end-of-transaction. This protocol guarantees serializability.

---

[14] But see references [16.2] and [16.14].

The protocol just described is a strict form of the **two-phase locking protocol**. It can be shown that if all transactions obey this protocol, then all schedules are serializable—the **two-phase locking theorem**. A serializable schedule implies that if *A* and *B* are any two transactions involved in that schedule, then either *A* can see *B*'s output or *B* can see *A*'s. The two-phase locking also guarantees **recoverability** and **cascade-free schedules**; unfortunately, it can also lead to **deadlocks**. Deadlocks can be resolved by choosing one of the deadlocked transactions as the victim and rolling it back (thereby releasing all of its locks).

Anything less than full serializability cannot be guaranteed to be safe (in general). However, systems typically allow transactions to operate at a **level of isolation** that is indeed unsafe, with the aim of reducing resource contention and increasing transaction throughput. We described one such "unsafe" level, **cursor stability** (this is the DB2 term; the SQL standard term is READ COMMITTED).

Next we briefly considered the question of **lock granularity** and the associated idea of **intent locking**. Basically, before a transaction can acquire a lock of any kind on some object, say a database tuple, it must first acquire an appropriate intent lock (at least) on the "parent" of that object (e.g., the containing relvar, in the case of a tuple). In practice, such intent locks will usually be acquired implicitly, just as S and X locks on tuples are usually acquired implicitly. However, **explicit LOCK statements** of some kind should be provided in order to allow a transaction to acquire stronger locks than the ones acquired implicitly (though the SQL standard provides no such mechanism).

Next, we took another look at the so-called **ACID properties** of transactions, concluding that matters are not nearly as clear-cut in this area as is commonly supposed. Finally, we outlined SQL's concurrency control support. Basically, SQL does not provide any explicit locking capabilities at all; however, it does support various isolation levels—**SERIALIZABLE**, **REPEATABLE READ**, **READ COMMITTED**, and **READ UNCOMMITTED**, which the DBMS will probably implement by means of locking behind the scenes.

EXERCISES

16.1   Explain *serializability* in your own words.

16.2   State (a) the two-phase locking protocol; (b) the two-phase locking theorem. Explain exactly how two-phase locking deals with RW, WR, and WW conflicts.

16.3   Let transactions *T1, T2,* and *T3* be defined to perform the following operations:

   T1 : Add one to *A*
   T2 : Double *A*
   T3 : Display *A* on the screen and then set *A* to one

(where *A* is some numeric item in the database).

   a. Suppose transactions *T1, T2, T3* are allowed to execute concurrently. If *A* has initial value zero, how many possible correct results are there? Enumerate them.

b. Suppose the internal structure of *T1*, *T2*, *T3* is as indicated in the following pseudocode. If the transactions execute *without* any locking, how many possible schedules are there?

T1	T2	T3

R1: RETRIEVE A
        INTO a1 ;
    a1 := a1 + 1 ;
U1: UPDATE A
        FROM a1 ;
	R2: RETRIEVE A
	        INTO a2 ;
	    a2 := a2 * 2 ;
	U2: UPDATE A
	        FROM a2 ;
		R3: RETRIEVE A
		        INTO a3 ;
		    display a3 ;
		U3: UPDATE A
		        FROM 1 ;

c. If again *A* has initial value zero, are there any interleaved schedules that in fact produce a correct result and yet are not serializable?

d. Are there any schedules that are in fact serializable but could not be produced if all three transactions obeyed the two-phase locking protocol?

16.4 The following represents the sequence of events in a schedule involving transactions *T1*, *T2*, ..., *T12*. *A*, *B*, ..., *H* are items in the database.

```
time t0    ..........
time t1 (T1)    : RETRIEVE A ;
time t2 (T2)    : RETRIEVE B ;
    ...     (T1)    : RETRIEVE C ;
    ...     (T4)    : RETRIEVE D ;
    ...     (T5)    : RETRIEVE A ;
    ...     (T2)    : RETRIEVE E ;
    ...     (T2)    : UPDATE E ;
    ...     (T3)    : RETRIEVE F ;
    ...     (T2)    : RETRIEVE F ;
    ...     (T5)    : UPDATE A ;
    ...     (T1)    : COMMIT ;
    ...     (T6)    : RETRIEVE A ;
    ...     (T5)    : ROLLBACK ;
    ...     (T6)    : RETRIEVE C ;
    ...     (T6)    : UPDATE C ;
    ...     (T7)    : RETRIEVE G ;
    ...     (T8)    : RETRIEVE H ;
    ...     (T9)    : RETRIEVE G ;
    ...     (T9)    : UPDATE G ;
    ...     (T8)    : RETRIEVE E ;
    ...     (T7)    : COMMIT ;
    ...     (T9)    : RETRIEVE H ;
    ...     (T3)    : RETRIEVE G ;
    ...     (T10)   : RETRIEVE A ;
    ...     (T9)    : UPDATE H ;
    ...     (T6)    : COMMIT ;
    ...     (T11)   : RETRIEVE C ;
    ...     (T12)   : RETRIEVE D ;
    ...     (T12)   : RETRIEVE C ;
    ...     (T2)    : UPDATE F ;
    ...     (T11)   : UPDATE C ;
    ...     (T12)   : RETRIEVE A ;
    ...     (T10)   : UPDATE A ;
    ...     (T12)   : UPDATE D ;
    ...     (T4)    : RETRIEVE G ;
time t36    ..........
```

Assume that RETRIEVE *i* (if successful) acquires an S lock on *i*, and UPDATE *i* (if successful) promotes that lock to X level. Assume also that all locks are held until end-of-transaction. Draw a *Wait-For Graph* (showing who is waiting for whom) representing the state of affairs at time *t36*. Are there any deadlocks at that time?

16.5   Consider the concurrency problems illustrated in Figs. 16.1–16.4 once again. What would happen in each case if all transactions were executing under isolation level CS instead of RR? *Note:* CS and RR here refer to DB2's isolation levels as described in Section 16.8.

16.6   Give both informal and formal definitions of lock types X, S, IX, IS, and SIX.

16.7   Define the notion of relative lock strength and give the corresponding precedence graph.

16.8   Define the intent locking protocol in its most general form. What is the purpose of that protocol?

16.9   SQL defines three concurrency problems: *dirty read, nonrepeatable read,* and *phantoms.* How do these relate to the three concurrency problems identified in Section 16.2?

16.10   Sketch an implementation mechanism for the multi-version concurrency control protocols described briefly in the annotation to reference [16.1].

REFERENCES AND BIBLIOGRAPHY

In addition to the following, see also references [15.2], [15.10], and (especially) [15.12] in Chapter 15.

16.1   R. Bayer, M. Heller, and A. Reiser: "Parallelism and Recovery in Database Systems," *ACM TODS 5,* No. 2 (June 1980).

As noted in Chapter 15, newer application areas (e.g., hardware and software engineering) often involve complex processing requirements for which the classical transaction management controls as described in the body of this chapter and its predecessor are not well suited. The basic problem is that complex transactions might last for hours or days, instead of for just a few milliseconds at most as in traditional systems. As a consequence:

1. Rolling back a transaction all the way to the beginning might cause the loss of an unacceptably large amount of work.

2. The use of conventional locking might cause unacceptably long delays waiting for locks to be released.

The present paper is one of several to address such concerns (others include references [16.8], [16.12], [16.15], and [16.20]). It proposes a concurrency control technique called **multi-version locking** (also known as **multi-version read**, and now implemented in some commercial products). The biggest advantage of the technique is that read operations never have to wait—any number of readers *and one writer* can operate on the same logical object simultaneously. To be more specific:

- Reads are never delayed (as just stated).
- Reads never delay updates.
- It is never necessary to roll back a read-only transaction.
- Deadlock is possible only between update transactions.

These advantages are particularly significant in distributed systems—see Chapter 21—where updates can take a long time and read-only queries might thus be unduly delayed (and *vice versa*). The basic idea is as follows:

- If transaction *B* asks to read an object that transaction *A* currently has update access to, transaction *B* is given access to a *previously committed* version of that object (such a version must exist anyway in the system somewhere—probably in the log—for recovery purposes).
- If transaction *B* asks to update an object that transaction *A* currently has read access to, transaction *B* is given access to that object, while transaction *A* retains access to its own version of the object (which is now really the previous version).

- If transaction *B* asks to update an object that transaction *A* currently has update access to, transaction *B* goes into a wait state[15] (deadlock, and hence forced rollback, are thus still possible, as noted earlier).

Of course, the approach includes appropriate controls to ensure that each transaction always sees a consistent state of the database.

16.2 Hal Berenson *et al.*: "A Critique of ANSI SQL Isolation Levels," Proc. 1995 ACM SIGMOD Int. Conf. on Management of Data, San Jose, Calif. (May 1995).

This paper criticizes the attempt on the part of "ANSI SQL" [*sic*] to characterize isolation levels in terms of serializability violations (see Section 16.11): "[The] definitions fail to properly characterize several popular isolation levels, including the standard locking implementations of the levels covered." The paper goes on to point out in particular that the standard fails to prohibit "dirty writes" (see Section 16.2).

It does seem to be true that the standard does not prohibit dirty writes explicitly. What it actually says is the following (slightly reworded here):

- "The execution of concurrent transactions at isolation level SERIALIZABLE is guaranteed to be serializable." Thus, if all transactions operate at isolation level SERIALIZABLE, the implementation is *required* to prohibit dirty writes, since dirty writes would certainly violate serializability.

- "The four isolation levels guarantee that . . . no updates will be lost." This claim is just wishful thinking—the definitions of the four isolation levels by themselves do *not* provide any such guarantee—but it does indicate that the standard definers *intended* to prohibit dirty writes.

- "Changes made by one transaction cannot be perceived by other transactions [except those with isolation level READ UNCOMMITTED] until the original transaction [commits]." The question here is, what exactly does *perceived* mean? Would it be possible for a transaction to update a piece of "dirty data" without "perceiving" it?

See also reference [16.14].

16.3 Philip A. Bernstein and Nathan Goodman: "Timestamp-Based Algorithms for Concurrency Control in Distributed Database Systems," Proc. 6th Int. Conf. on Very Large Data Bases, Montreal, Canada (October 1980).

Discusses a collection of approaches to concurrency control based not on locking but on **timestamping**. The basic idea is that if transaction *A* starts execution before transaction *B,* then the system should behave as if *A* actually executed in its entirety before *B* started (as in a genuine serial schedule). It follows that:

1. *A* must never be allowed to see any of *B*'s updates.

2. *A* must never be allowed to update anything *B* has already seen.

These two requirements can be enforced as follows: For any given database request, the system compares the timestamp of the requesting transaction with the timestamp of the transaction that last retrieved or updated the requested tuple; if there is a conflict, then the requesting transaction can simply be restarted with a new timestamp (as in the so-called *optimistic* methods [16.16]).

---

[15] In other words, WW conflicts can still occur, and we assume here that locking is used to resolve them. Other techniques (e.g., timestamping [16.3]) might perhaps be used instead.

As the title of the paper suggests, timestamping was originally introduced in the context of a distributed system (where it was felt that locking imposed intolerable overheads, because of the messages needed to test and set locks, etc.). It is almost certainly not appropriate in a non-distributed system. Indeed, there is considerable skepticism as to its practicality in distributed systems also. One obvious problem is that each tuple has to carry the timestamp of the transaction that last *retrieved* it (as well as the timestamp of the transaction that last updated it), which implies that every read becomes a write! Another problem is that *B* must not see any of *A*'s updates until *A* commits, implying that (in effect) *A*'s updates are "locked exclusive" until commit anyway. In fact, reference [15.12] claims that timestamping schemes are really just a degenerate case of optimistic concurrency control schemes [16.16], which in turn suffer from problems of their own.

Note: A notion much discussed in the literature, "Thomas's write rule" [16.22], is effectively a refinement on the foregoing scheme; it is based on the idea that certain updates can be skipped because they are already obsolete (the user-level request is honored but no physical update is done).

16.4 M. W. Blasgen, J. N. Gray, M. Mitoma, and T. G. Price: "The Convoy Phenomenon," *ACM Operating Systems Review 13,* No. 2 (April 1979).

The **convoy phenomenon** is a problem encountered with high-traffic locks, such as the lock needed to write a record to the log, in systems with *preemptive scheduling.* ("Scheduling" here refers to the problem of allocating machine cycles to transactions, not to the interleaving of database operations from different transactions as discussed in the body of this chapter.) The problem is as follows. If a transaction *T* is holding a high-traffic lock and is preempted by the system scheduler—that is, forced into a wait state, perhaps because its timeslice has expired—then a *convoy* of transactions will form, all waiting for their turn at the high-traffic lock. When *T* comes out of its wait state, it will soon release the lock, but (precisely because the lock is high-traffic) it will probably rejoin the convoy before the next transaction has finished with the resource, will therefore not be able to continue processing, and so will go into a wait state again.

The root of the problem is that the scheduler is usually part of the underlying operating system, not the DBMS, and is therefore based on different design assumptions. As the authors observe, a convoy, once established, tends to be stable; the system is in a state of "lock thrashing," most of the machine cycles are devoted to process switching, and not much useful work is being done. A suggested solution—barring the possibility of replacing the scheduler—is to grant the lock not on a first-come/first-served basis but instead in random order.

16.5 Stephen Blott and Henry F. Korth: "An Almost-Serial Protocol for Transaction Execution in Main-Memory Database Systems," Proc. 28th Int. Conf. on Very Large Data Bases, Hong Kong (August 2002).

Proposes a serializability mechanism for main-memory systems that avoids the use of locks entirely.

16.6 K. P. Eswaran, J. N. Gray, R. A. Lorie, and I. L. Traiger: "The Notions of Consistency and Predicate Locks in a Data Base System," *CACM 19,* No. 11 (November 1976).

The paper that first put the subject of concurrency control on a sound theoretical footing.

16.7 Peter Franaszek and John T. Robinson: "Limitations on Concurrency in Transaction Processing," *ACM TODS 10,* No. 1 (March 1985).

See the annotation to reference [16.16].

16.8 Peter A. Franaszek, John T. Robinson, and Alexander Thomasian: "Concurrency Control for High Contention Environments," *ACM TODS 17,* No. 2 (June 1992).

This paper claims that, for a variety of reasons, future transaction processing systems are likely to involve a significantly greater degree of concurrency than the systems of today, and that there is therefore likely to be substantially more data contention in such systems. The authors then present "a number of [nonlocking] concurrency control concepts and transaction scheduling techniques that are applicable to high-contention environments" that—it is claimed, on the basis of experiments with simulation models—"can offer substantial benefits" in such environments.

16.9 J. N. Gray: "Experience with the System R Lock Manager," IBM San Jose Research Laboratory internal memo (Spring 1980).

This reference is really just a set of notes, not a finished paper, and its findings might be a little out of date by now. Nevertheless, it does contain some interesting claims, the following among them:

- Locking imposes about ten percent overhead on online transactions, about one percent on batch transactions.
- It is desirable to support a variety of lock granularities.
- Automatic lock escalation works well.
- Repeatable read (RR) is more efficient, as well as safer, than cursor stability (CS).
- Deadlocks are rare in practice and never involve more than two transactions.
- Almost all deadlocks (97 percent) could be avoided by supporting *U locks,* as DB2 does but System R did not.

Note: U locks are defined to be compatible with S locks but not with other U locks, and certainly not with X locks. For further details, see reference [4.21].

16.10 J. N. Gray, R. A. Lorie, and G. R. Putzolu: "Granularity of Locks in a Large Shared Data Base," Proc. 1st Int. Conf. on Very Large Data Bases, Framingham, Mass. (September 1975).

The paper that introduced the concept of intent locking. As explained in Section 16.9, the term *granularity* refers to the size of the objects that can be locked. Since different transactions obviously have different characteristics and different requirements, it is desirable that the system provide a range of different locking granularities (as indeed many systems do). This paper presents an implementation mechanism for such a multi-granularity system, based on intent locking.

We elaborate here on the **intent locking protocol**, since the explanations given in the body of the chapter were deliberately somewhat simplified. First of all, the lockable object types need not be limited to just relvars and tuples, as we were assuming previously. Second, those lockable object types need not even form a strict hierarchy; the presence of indexes and other access structures means they should be regarded rather as a *directed acyclic graph*. For example, the suppliers-and-parts database might contain both (a stored form of) the parts relvar P and an index, XP say, on the P# attribute of that stored relvar. To get to the tuples of relvar P, we must start with the overall database, and then *either* go straight to the stored relvar and do a sequential scan *or* go to index XP and thence to the required P tuples. So the tuples of P have two "parents" in the graph, P and XP, both of which have the database as a "parent" in turn.

We can now state the protocol in its most general form:

- Acquiring an X lock on a given object implicitly acquires an X lock on all children of that object.
- Acquiring an S or SIX lock on a given object implicitly acquires an S lock on all children of that object.

■ Before a transaction can acquire an S or IS lock on a given object, it must first acquire an IS (or stronger) lock on at least one parent of that object.

■ Before a transaction can acquire an X, IX, or SIX lock on a given object, it must first acquire an IX (or stronger) lock on all parents of that object.

■ Before a transaction can release a lock on a given object, it must first release all locks it holds on all children of that object.

In practice, the protocol does not impose as much run-time overhead as might be thought, because at any given moment the transaction will probably already have most of the locks it needs. For example, an IX lock (say) will probably be acquired on the entire database just once, when the program starts execution. That lock will then be held throughout all transactions executed during the lifetime of the program.

16.11 J. N. Gray, R. A. Lorie, G. R. Putzolu, and I. L. Traiger: "Granularity of Locks and Degrees of Consistency in a Shared Data Base," in G. M. Nijssen (ed.), *Proc. IFIP TC-2 Working Conf. on Modelling in Data Base Management Systems.* Amsterdam, Netherlands: North-Holland/New York, N.Y.: Elsevier Science (1976).

The paper that introduced the concept of isolation levels (under the name *degrees of consistency*[16]).

16.12 Theo Härder and Kurt Rothermel: "Concurrency Control Issues in Nested Transactions," *The VLDB Journal 2,* No. 1 (January 1993).

As noted in the "References and Bibliography" section in Chapter 15, several writers have suggested the idea of *nested transactions*. This paper proposes a set of locking protocols for such transactions.

16.13 J. R. Jordan, J. Banerjee, and R. B. Batman: "Precision Locks," Proc. 1981 ACM SIGMOD Int. Conf. on Management of Data, Ann Arbor, Mich. (April/May 1981).

Precision locking is a tuple-level locking scheme that guarantees that only those tuples that need to be locked (in order to achieve serializability) are actually locked, phantoms included. It is in fact a form of *predicate* locking (see Section 16.8, also reference [16.6]). It works by (a) checking update requests to see whether a tuple to be inserted or deleted satisfies an earlier retrieval request by some concurrent transaction and (b) checking retrieval requests to see whether a tuple that has already been inserted or deleted by some concurrent transaction satisfies the retrieval request in question. Not only is the scheme quite elegant, the authors claim that it actually performs better than conventional techniques (which typically lock too much anyway).

16.14 Tim Kempster, Colin Stirling, and Peter Thanisch: "Diluting ACID," *ACM SIGMOD Record 28,* No. 4 (December 1999).

This paper might better be titled "*Concentrating* ACID"! Among other things, it claims that conventional concurrency control mechanisms preclude certain serializable schedules ("isolation is really a sufficient but not necessary condition for serializability"). Like the SQL standard and reference [16.2], it defines isolation levels in terms of serializability violations; however, its definitions are more refined than, and admit more serializable schedules than, those previous attempts. The paper also demonstrates a flaw (having to do with phantoms) in reference [16.2].

---

[16] Not the happiest of names! Data is either consistent or it is not. The notion that there might be "degrees" of consistency thus sounds like it might be subject to some dispute. In fact, it seems likely that the theory behind "degrees of consistency" was developed before we had a clear notion of the fundamental importance of data integrity (or "consistency").

16.15 Henry F. Korth and Greg Speegle: "Formal Aspects of Concurrency Control in Long-Duration Transaction Systems Using the NT/PV Model," *ACM TODS 19,* No. 3 (September 1994).

As noted elsewhere (see, e.g., references [15.3], [15.9], [15.16], and [15.17]), serializability is often considered too demanding a condition to impose on certain kinds of transaction processing systems, especially in newer application areas that involve human interaction and hence transactions of long duration. This paper presents a new transaction model called NT/PV ("nested transactions with predicates and views") that addresses such concerns. Among other things, (a) it shows that the standard model of transactions with serializability is a special case, (b) it defines "new and more useful correctness classes," and (c) it claims that the new model provides "an appropriate framework for solving long-duration transaction problems."

16.16 H. T. Kung and John T. Robinson: "On Optimistic Methods for Concurrency Control," *ACM TODS 6,* No. 2 (June 1981).

Locking schemes can be described as *pessimistic,* inasmuch as they make the worst-case assumption that every piece of data accessed by a given transaction might be needed by some concurrent transaction and had therefore better be locked. By contrast, **optimistic** schemes— also known as *certification* or *validation* schemes—make the opposite assumption that conflicts are likely to be quite rare in practice. Thus, they operate by allowing transactions to run to completion completely unhindered, and then checking at commit time to see whether a conflict did in fact occur. If it did, the offending transaction is simply started again from the beginning. No updates are ever written to the database prior to successful completion of commit processing, so such restarts do not require any updates to be undone.

A subsequent paper [16.7] showed that, under certain assumptions, optimistic methods enjoy certain inherent advantages over traditional locking methods in terms of the expected level of concurrency (i.e., number of simultaneous transactions) they can support, suggesting that optimistic methods might become the technique of choice in systems with large numbers of parallel processors. (By contrast, reference [15.12] claims that optimistic methods in general are actually worse than locking in "hotspot" situations—where a *hotspot* is a data item that is updated very frequently, by many distinct transactions. See the annotation to reference [16.17] for a discussion of a technique that works well on hotspots.)

16.17 Patrick E. O'Neil: "The Escrow Transactional Method," *ACM TODS 11,* No. 4 (December 1986).

Consider the following simple example. Suppose the database contains a data item *TC* representing "total cash on hand," and suppose almost every transaction in the system updates *TC,* decrementing it by some amount (corresponding to some cash withdrawal, say). Then *TC* is an example of a "hotspot," that is, an item in the database that is accessed by a significant percentage of the transactions running in the system. Under traditional locking, a hotspot can very quickly become a bottleneck (to mix metaphors horribly). But using traditional locking on a data item like *TC* is really overkill. If *TC* initially has a value of 10 million dollars, and each individual transaction decrements it (on average) by only 10 dollars, then we could run 1,000,000 such transactions, *and furthermore apply the 1,000,000 corresponding decrements in any order,* before running into trouble. There is thus no need to apply a traditional lock to *TC* at all; instead, all that is necessary is to make sure that the current value is large enough to permit the required decrement, and then do the update. (If the transaction subsequently fails, the amount of the decrement must be added back in again, of course.)

The **escrow** method applies to situations such as the one just described—that is, situations in which the updates are of a certain special form, instead of being completely arbitrary. The system must provide a special new kind of update statement (e.g., "decrement by *x,* if and only if the current value is greater than *y*"). It can then perform the update by placing the decrement amount *x* "in escrow," taking it out of escrow at end-of-transaction (and committing the change if end-of-transaction is COMMIT, or adding the amount back into the original total if end-of-transaction is ROLLBACK).

The paper describes a number of cases in which the escrow method can be used. One example of a commercial product that supports the technique is the Fast Path version of IMS, from IBM. We remark that the technique might be regarded as a special case of optimistic concurrency control [16.16]. Note, however, that the "special-case" aspect—the provision of the special update statements—is critical.

16.18 Christos Papadimitriou: *The Theory of Database Concurrency Control.* Rockville, Md.: Computer Science Press (1986).

A textbook, with emphasis on formal theory.

16.19 Daniel J. Rosencrantz, Richard E. Stearns, and Philip M. Lewis II: "System Level Concurrency Control for Distributed Database Systems," *ACM TODS 3,* No. 2 (June 1978).

16.20 Kenneth Salem, Hector Garcia-Molina, and Jeannie Shands: "Altruistic Locking," *ACM TODS 19,* No. 1 (March 1994).

Proposes an extension to two-phase locking according to which a transaction *A* that has finished with some locked piece of data but cannot unlock it (because of the two-phase locking protocol) can nevertheless "donate" the data back to the system, thereby allowing some other transaction *B* to acquire a lock on it. *B* is then said to be "in the wake of" *A*. Protocols are defined to prevent, for example, a transaction from seeing any updates by transactions in its wake. Altruistic locking (the term derives from the fact that "donating" data benefits other transactions, not the donor transaction) is shown to provide more concurrency than conventional two-phase locking, especially when some of the transactions are of long duration.

16.21 Abraham Silberschatz, Henry F. Korth, and S. Sudarshan: *Database System Concepts* (4th ed.). New York, N.Y.: McGraw-Hill (2002).

This general textbook on database management includes a strong treatment of transaction management issues (recovery as well as concurrency).

16.22 Robert H. Thomas: "A Majority Consensus Approach to Concurrency Control for Multiple Copy Databases," *ACM TODS 4,* No. 2 (June 1979).

See the annotation to reference [16.3].

16.23 Alexander Thomasian: "Concurrency Control: Methods, Performance, and Analysis," *ACM Comp. Surv. 30,* No. 1 (March 1998).

A detailed investigation into the performance of a wide variety of concurrency control algorithms.

PART V

FURTHER TOPICS

We claimed in Part II of this book that the relational model is the foundation for modern database technology, and so it is. However, it is *only* the foundation: There is a lot more to database technology than just the relational model as described in Part II, and database students and professionals need to be familiar with many additional concepts and facilities in order to be fully "database aware" (as indeed should be obvious from our discussions in Parts III and IV). We now turn our attention to a miscellaneous collection of further important topics. The topics to be covered, in sequence, are as follows:

- Security (Chapter 17)
- Optimization (Chapter 18)
- Missing information (Chapter 19)
- Type inheritance (Chapter 20)
- Distributed databases (Chapter 21)
- Decision support (Chapter 22)
- Temporal databases (Chapter 23)
- Logic-based databases (Chapter 24)

Actually the foregoing sequence is a little arbitrary, but the chapters have been written on the assumption that they will be read (possibly selectively) in order as written.

Security

17.1 INTRODUCTION

Data security is often mentioned in the same breath as data integrity, but the two are really quite distinct; security has to do with the protection of data against unauthorized access, while integrity has to do with data correctness.[1] To put it a little glibly:

- Security means protecting the data against unauthorized users.
- Integrity means protecting the data against *authorized* users (!).

In other words, security means making sure users are allowed to do the things they are trying to do; integrity means making sure the things they are trying to do are correct.

There are some similarities too, of course: In both cases, the system needs to be aware of certain constraints that users must not violate; in both cases those constraints must be specified, declaratively, in some suitable language and must be kept in the system catalog; and in both cases the system must monitor user operations in order to ensure that the constraints in question are enforced. In this chapter, we examine security in particular (integrity has already been discussed at length in Chapter 9). *Note:* The main reason we so

---

[1] See Chapter 9 for an explanation of why "correctness" ought really to be in quotes here.

clearly separate our own discussions of the two topics is that we regard integrity as absolutely fundamental but security as more of a secondary issue, albeit one of major pragmatic importance (especially in these days of widespread Internet access, electronic commerce, and similar considerations).

There are many aspects to the security problem. Here are some of them:

- Legal, social, and ethical aspects (for example, does the person making the request, say for a customer's credit rating, have a legal right to the requested information?)

- Physical controls (for example, is the computer or terminal room locked or otherwise guarded?)

- Policy questions (for example, how does the enterprise owning the system decide who should be allowed access to what?)

- Operational problems (for example, if a password scheme is used, how are the passwords themselves kept secret, and how often are they changed?)

- Hardware controls (for example, does the server provide any security features, such as storage protection keys or a protected operation mode?)

- Operating system support (for example, does the underlying operating system erase the contents of main memory and disk files when they are finished with—and what about the recovery log?)

and finally

- Issues that are the specific concern of the database system itself (for example, does that system have a concept of data ownership?)

For obvious reasons, we limit our attention in this chapter to issues in this last category only, for the most part.

Now, modern DBMSs typically support either or both of two broad approaches to data security, *discretionary* control and *mandatory* control. In both cases, the unit of data or "data object" that might need to be protected can range all the way from an entire database, on the one hand, to a specific component of a specific tuple on the other. How the two approaches differ is indicated by the following brief outline:

- In the case of **discretionary** control, a given user will typically have different access rights (also known as **privileges**) on different objects; further, there are few inherent limitations regarding which users can have which rights on which objects (for example, user U1 might be able to see *A* but not *B,* while user U2 might be able to see *B* but not *A*). Discretionary schemes are thus very flexible.

- In the case of **mandatory** control, by contrast, each data object is labeled with a certain **classification** level, and each user is given a certain **clearance** level. A given data object can then be accessed only by users with the appropriate clearance. Mandatory schemes thus tend to be hierarchic in nature and hence comparatively rigid (if user U1 can see *A* but not *B,* then the classification of *B* must be higher than that of *A,* and so no user U2 can see *B* but not *A*).

We discuss discretionary schemes in Section 17.2 and mandatory schemes in Section 17.3.

Now, regardless of whether we are dealing with a discretionary scheme or a mandatory one, all decisions as to which users are allowed to perform which operations on which objects are policy decisions, not technical ones. They are thus clearly outside the jurisdiction of the DBMS as such; all the DBMS can do is enforce those decisions once they are made. It follows that:

- The results of those policy decisions (a) must be made known to the system (this is done by declaring **security constraints** in some appropriate language) and (b) must be remembered by the system (this is done by saving those constraints in the catalog).

- There must be a means of checking a given access request against the applicable constraints in the catalog. (By "access request" here we mean the combination of *requested operation* plus *requested object* plus *requesting user,* in general.) That checking is done by the DBMS's **security subsystem**, also known as the **authorization** subsystem.

- In order to decide which constraints are applicable to a given access request, the system must be able to recognize the *source* of that request—that is, it must be able to recognize the *requesting user*. For that reason, when users sign on to the system, they are typically required to supply, not only their user ID (to say who they are), but also a **password** (to prove they are who they say they are). The password is supposedly known only to the system and to legitimate users of the user ID concerned. The password-checking process—that is, the process of checking that users are who they say they are—is called **authentication**. *Note:* We remark in passing that other authentication techniques are now available that are much more sophisticated than simple password checking, involving as they do a variety of biometric devices: fingerprint readers, retinal scanners, hand geometry imagers, voice verifiers, signature recognizers, and so on. Such devices can all effectively be used to check "personal characteristics no one can steal" [17.6].

With regard to user IDs, incidentally, note that any number of distinct users might be able to share the same ID. In this way, the system can support **user groups**—also known as *roles*—and can thus provide a way of allowing (say) everyone in the accounting department to share the same privileges on the same objects. The operations of adding individual users to or removing individual users from a given group can then be performed independently of the operation of specifying which privileges on which objects apply to that group. In this connection, we draw your attention to reference [17.11], which describes a system in which user groups can be *nested.* To quote: "The ability to classify users into a hierarchy of groups provides a powerful tool for administrating [*sic*] large systems with thousands of users and objects." Note, however, that the obvious place to keep a record of which users are in which groups is once again the catalog (or perhaps the database itself), and those records themselves must of course be subject to suitable security controls.

17.2 DISCRETIONARY ACCESS CONTROL

To repeat from the previous section, most DBMSs support either discretionary control or mandatory control or both. In fact it would be more accurate to say that most systems support discretionary control, and some systems support mandatory control as well; discretionary control is thus more likely to be encountered in practice, and so we deal with it first.

As already noted, we need a language in which to define (discretionary) security constraints. In practice, however, it is easier to state what is *allowed* rather than what is not allowed; security languages therefore typically support the definition, not of security constraints as such, but rather of **authorities**, which are effectively the opposite of security constraints (if something is authorized, it is not constrained). We therefore begin by briefly describing a hypothetical language for defining authorities.[2] Here first is a simple example:

```
AUTHORITY SA3
   GRANT RETRIEVE { S#, SNAME, CITY }, DELETE
   ON    S
   TO    Jim, Fred, Mary ;
```

This example is intended to illustrate the point that (in general) authorities have four components, as follows:

1. A **name** (SA3—"suppliers authority three"—in the example)
2. A set of **privileges**, specified by means of the GRANT clause
3. The **relvar** to which the authority applies, specified by means of the ON clause
4. A set of "**users**" (more accurately, *user IDs*) who are to be granted the specified privileges on the specified relvar, specified by means of the TO clause

Here then is the general syntax:

```
AUTHORITY <authority name>
   GRANT  <privilege commalist>
   ON     <relvar name>
   TO     <user ID commalist> ;
```

Explanation: The *<authority name>, <relvar name>,* and *<user ID commalist>* are self-explanatory (except that we regard ALL, meaning all known users, as a legal "user ID" in this context). Each *<privilege>* is one of the following:

```
RETRIEVE [ { <attribute name commalist> } ]
INSERT   [ { <attribute name commalist> } ]
DELETE
UPDATE   [ { <attribute name commalist> } ]
ALL
```

RETRIEVE (unqualified), INSERT (unqualified), DELETE, and UPDATE (unqualified) are self-explanatory (well, perhaps not quite; the RETRIEVE privilege is also needed just to *mention* the relevant object—e.g., in a view definition or an integrity constraint—as well as for retrieval *per se*). If a commalist of attribute names is specified with

---

[2] **Tutorial D** as currently defined [3.3] deliberately does not include any authority definition facilities, but the hypothetical language of the present section can be regarded as being in the spirit of **Tutorial D**.

RETRIEVE, then the privilege applies only to the attributes specified; INSERT and UPDATE with a commalist of attribute names are defined analogously. The specification ALL is shorthand for all privileges: RETRIEVE (all attributes), INSERT (all attributes), DELETE, and UPDATE (all attributes). *Note:* For simplicity, we ignore the question of whether any special privileges are required in order to perform general relational assignments. Also, we deliberately limit our attention to data manipulation operations; in practice, however, there would be many other operations that we would also want to be subject to authorization checking, such as the operations of defining and dropping relvars—and the operations of defining and dropping authorities themselves, come to that. We omit detailed consideration of such operations here for space reasons.

What should happen if some user attempts some operation on some object for which that user is not authorized? The simplest option is obviously just to reject the attempt (and to provide a suitable error message, of course); such a response will surely be the one most commonly required in practice, so we might as well make it the default. In more sensitive situations, however, some other action might be more appropriate; for example, it might be necessary to terminate the program or lock the user's keyboard. It might also be desirable to record such attempts in a special log ("threat monitoring"), in order to permit subsequent analysis of attempted security breaches and also to serve in itself as a deterrent against illegal infiltration (see the discussion of *audit trails* at the end of this section).

Of course, we also need a way of dropping authorities:

```
DROP AUTHORITY <authority name> ;
```

For simplicity, we assume that dropping a given relvar will automatically drop any authorities that apply to that relvar.

Here are some further examples of authorities, most of them fairly self-explanatory.

1. ```
   AUTHORITY EX1
        GRANT RETRIEVE { P#, PNAME, WEIGHT }
        ON     P
        TO     Jacques, Anne, Charley ;
   ```

   Users Jacques, Anne, and Charley can see a "vertical subset" of base relvar P. The example is thus an example of a **value-independent** authority.

2. ```
   AUTHORITY EX2
        GRANT RETRIEVE, DELETE, UPDATE { SNAME, STATUS }
        ON     LS
        TO     Dan, Misha ;
   ```

   Relvar LS here is the "London suppliers" view from Fig. 10.4 in Chapter 10. Users Dan and Misha can thus see a "horizontal subset" of base relvar S. This example is an example of a **value-dependent** authority. Note too that although users Dan and Misha can DELETE certain supplier tuples (via view LS), they cannot INSERT them, and they cannot UPDATE attributes S# or CITY.

3. ```
   VAR SSPPO VIEW
        ( S JOIN SP JOIN ( P WHERE CITY = 'Oslo' ) { P# } )
                                          { ALL BUT P#, QTY } ;

   AUTHORITY EX3
        GRANT RETRIEVE
        ON     SSPPO
        TO     Lars ;
   ```
   ```

This is another value-dependent example: User Lars can retrieve supplier information, but only for suppliers who supply some part stored in Oslo.

4. `VAR SSQ VIEW`
```
      SUMMARIZE SP PER S { S# } ADD SUM ( QTY ) AS SQ ;

   AUTHORITY EX4
      GRANT RETRIEVE
      ON    SSQ
      TO    Fidel ;
```

User Fidel can see total shipment quantities per supplier, but not individual shipment quantities. User Fidel thus sees a **statistical summary** of the underlying base data.

5. `AUTHORITY EX5`
```
      GRANT RETRIEVE, UPDATE { STATUS }
      ON    S
      WHEN  DAY () IN { 'Mon', 'Tue', 'Wed', 'Thu', 'Fri' }
            AND NOW () ≥ TIME '09:00:00'
            AND NOW () ≤ TIME '17:00:00'
      TO    ACCOUNTING ;
```

Here we are extending our AUTHORITY syntax to include a WHEN clause to specify certain "context controls"; we are also assuming that the system provides two niladic operators—that is, operators that take no explicit operands—called DAY() and NOW(), with the obvious interpretations. Authority EX5 guarantees that supplier status values can be changed by the user ACCOUNTING (presumably meaning anyone in the accounting department) only on a weekday, and only during working hours. This is thus an example of what is sometimes called a **context-dependent** authority, because a given access request will or will not be allowed depending on the context— here the combination of day of the week and time of day—in which it is issued.

Other examples of built-in operators that the system probably ought to support anyway and could be useful for context-dependent authorities include:

```
TODAY()    :  Value = the current date
USER()     :  Value = the ID of the current user
TERMINAL() :  Value = the ID of the originating terminal
                      for the current request
```

By now you have probably realized that, conceptually speaking, authorities are all "ORed" together. In other words, a given access request (meaning, to repeat, the combination of requested operation plus requested object plus requesting user) is acceptable if and only if at least one authority permits it. Note, however, that if, for example, (a) one authority lets user Nancy retrieve part colors and (b) another lets her retrieve part weights, it does *not* follow that she can retrieve part colors and weights together (a separate authority would be required for the combination).

Finally, we have implied, but never quite said as much, that users can do only the things they are explicitly allowed to do by the defined authorities. Anything not explicitly authorized is implicitly outlawed!

Request Modification

In order to illustrate some of the ideas introduced in this section so far, we now briefly describe the security aspects of the University Ingres prototype and its query language

QUEL, since they adopt an interesting approach to the problem. Basically, any given QUEL request is automatically modified before execution in such a way that it cannot possibly violate any security constraints. For example, suppose user U is allowed to retrieve parts stored in London only:

```
DEFINE PERMIT RETRIEVE ON P TO U
       WHERE  P.CITY = "London"
```

(see later for details of the DEFINE PERMIT operation). Now suppose user U issues the QUEL request:

```
RETRIEVE ( P.P#, P.WEIGHT )
WHERE        P.COLOR = "Red"
```

Using the specified "permit" for the combination of relvar P and user U as stored in the catalog, the system automatically modifies this request so that it looks like this:

```
RETRIEVE ( P.P#, P.WEIGHT )
WHERE        P.COLOR = "Red"
AND          P.CITY  = "London"
```

And this modified request cannot possibly violate the security constraint. Note, incidentally, that the modification process is "silent": User U is not informed that the system has in fact executed a statement that is somewhat different from his or her original request, because that fact in itself might be sensitive (user U might not even be allowed to know there are any non-London parts).

The process of **request modification** just outlined is actually identical to the technique used for the implementation of views [10.12] and also (in the case of the Ingres prototype specifically) integrity constraints [9.23]. So one advantage of the scheme is that it is very easy to implement—much of the necessary code exists in the system already. Another is that it is comparatively efficient—the security enforcement overhead occurs at compile time instead of run time, at least in part. Yet another advantage is that some of the awkwardnesses that can occur with the approach described earlier when a given user needs different privileges over different portions of the same relvar do not arise (see Section 17.6 for a specific illustration of this point).

One *dis*advantage is that not all security constraints can be handled in this simple fashion. As a trivial counterexample, suppose user U is not allowed to access relvar P at all. Then no simple "modified" form of the original RETRIEVE can preserve the illusion that relvar P does not exist. Instead, an explicit error message along the lines of "You are not allowed to access this relvar" must necessarily be produced. Or the system could simply lie and say "No such relvar exists." Or, better yet, it could say "*Either* no such relvar exists *or* you are not allowed to access it."

Here then is the syntax of DEFINE PERMIT:

```
DEFINE  PERMIT <operation name commalist>
        ON      <relvar name> [ ( <attribute name commalist> ) ]
        TO      <user ID>
    [ AT       <terminal ID commalist> ]
    [ FROM     <time> TO <time> ]
    [ ON       <day>  TO <day>  ]
    [ WHERE    <bool exp> ]
```

This statement is conceptually similar to our AUTHORITY statement, except that it supports a WHERE clause (the AT, FROM, and ON clauses are all subsumed by our WHEN clause). Here is an example:

```
DEFINE PERMIT RETRIEVE, APPEND, REPLACE
        ON      S ( S#, CITY )
        TO      Joe
        AT      TTA4
        FROM    9:00 TO 17:00
        ON      Sat TO Sun
        WHERE   S.STATUS < 50
        AND     S.S# = SP.P#
        AND     SP.P# = P.P#
        AND     P.COLOR = "Red"
```

Note: APPEND and REPLACE are the QUEL analogs of our INSERT and UPDATE, respectively.

Audit Trails

It is important not to assume that the security system is perfect. A would-be infiltrator who is sufficiently determined will usually find a way of breaking through the controls, especially if the payoff for doing so is high. In situations where the data is sufficiently sensitive, therefore, or where the processing performed on the data is sufficiently critical, an **audit trail** becomes a necessity. If, for example, data discrepancies lead to a suspicion that the database has been tampered with, the audit trail can be used to examine what has been going on and to verify that matters are under control (or to help pinpoint the wrongdoer if not).

An audit trail is essentially a special file or database in which the system automatically keeps track of all operations performed by users on the regular data. In some systems, the audit trail might be physically integrated with the recovery log (see Chapter 15), in others the two might be distinct; either way, users should be able to interrogate the audit trail using their regular query language (provided they are authorized to do so, of course!). A typical audit trail record might contain the following information:

- Request (source text)
- Terminal from which the operation was invoked
- User who invoked the operation
- Date and time of the operation
- Relvar(s), tuple(s), attribute(s) affected
- Before images (old values)
- After images (new values)

As mentioned earlier, the very fact that an audit trail is being maintained might be sufficient in itself to deter a would-be infiltrator in some cases.

17.3 MANDATORY ACCESS CONTROL

Mandatory controls are applicable to databases in which the data has a rather static and rigid classification structure, as might be the case in (e.g.) certain military or government environments. As explained briefly in Section 17.1, the basic idea is that each data object has a **classification level** (e.g., top secret, secret, confidential, etc.), and each user has a **clearance level** (with the same possibilities as for the classification levels). The levels are assumed to form a strict ordering (e.g., top secret > secret > confidential, etc.). The following simple rules, due to Bell and La Padula [17.3], are then imposed:

1. User i can retrieve object j only if the clearance level of i is greater than or equal to the classification level of j (the "simple security property").

2. User i can update object j only if the clearance level of i is equal to the classification level of j (the "star property").

The first rule here is obvious enough, but the second requires a word of explanation. Observe first that another way of stating that second rule is to say that, by definition, anything written by user i automatically acquires a classification level equal to i's clearance level. Such a rule is necessary in order to prevent a user with, for example, "secret" classification from copying secret data to a file of lower classification, thereby subverting the intent of the classification scheme. *Note:* From the point of view of pure "write" (INSERT) operations only, it would be sufficient for the second rule to say that the clearance level of i must be *less than or* equal to the classification level of j, and the rule is often stated in this form in the literature. But then users would be able to write things they could not read! (On second thought, some people do have difficulty reading their own writing . . . Perhaps the weaker form is not so unrealistic after all.)

Mandatory controls began to receive a lot of attention in the database world in the early 1990s, because that was when the U.S. Department of Defense (DoD) began to require any system it purchased to support such controls and DBMS vendors therefore began to implement them. The controls in question are documented in two DoD publications known informally as the *Orange Book* [17.21] and the *Lavender Book* [17.22], respectively; the Orange Book defines a set of security requirements for any "Trusted Computing Base" (TCB), and the Lavender Book defines an "interpretation" of the TCB requirements for database systems specifically.

The mandatory controls defined in the Orange and Lavender books in fact form part of a more general overall security classification scheme, which we summarize here for purposes of reference. First of all, four **security classes** A, B, C, and D are defined; class D is the least secure, class C is the next least, and so on. Class D is said to provide *minimal* protection, class C *discretionary* protection, class B *mandatory* protection, and class A *verified* protection. We elaborate briefly on classes C, B, and A.

- **Discretionary protection:** Class C is divided into two subclasses C1 and C2 (where C1 is *less* secure than C2). Each supports discretionary controls, meaning that access is subject to the discretion of the data *owner* (effectively as described in Section 17.2). In addition:

1. Class C1 distinguishes between ownership and access—that is, it supports the concept of shared data, while allowing users to have private data of their own as well.

2. Class C2 additionally requires accountability support through sign-on procedures, auditing, and resource isolation.

- **Mandatory protection:** Class B is the class that deals with mandatory controls. It is further divided into subclasses B1, B2, and B3 (where B1 is the *least* secure of the three and B3 is the most), as follows:

1. Class B1 requires "labeled security protection" (i.e., it requires each data object to be labeled with its classification level—secret, confidential, etc.). It also requires an informal statement of the security policy in effect.

2. Class B2 additionally requires a *formal* statement of the same thing. It also requires that *covert channels* be identified and eliminated. Examples of covert channels might be (a) the possibility of inferring the answer to an illegal query from the answer to a legal one (see Section 17.4) or (b) the possibility of deducing sensitive information from the time it takes to perform some legal computation (see the annotation to reference [17.14]).

3. Class B3 specifically requires audit and recovery support, as well as a designated *security administrator.*

- **Verified protection:** Class A, the most secure, requires a mathematical proof that the security mechanism is consistent and is adequate to support the specified security policy (!).

Several commercial DBMS products provide mandatory controls at the B1 level. They also typically provide discretionary controls at the C2 level. *Terminology:* DBMSs that support mandatory controls are sometimes called *multi-level secure systems* [17.15, 17.18, 17.23] (see the subsection "Multi-level Security" immediately following). The term *trusted system* is also used with much the same meaning [17.19, 17.21, 17.22].

Multi-level Security

Suppose we want to apply the ideas of mandatory access control to the suppliers relvar S. For definiteness and simplicity, suppose the unit of data we wish to control access to is the individual tuple within that relvar. Then each tuple needs to be labeled with its classification level, perhaps as shown in Fig. 17.1 (4 = top secret, 3 = secret, 2 = confidential, etc.).

Now suppose users U3 and U2 have clearance levels 3 (secret) and 2 (confidential), respectively. Then U3 and U2 will see relvar S differently! A request to retrieve all suppliers will return four tuples (for S1, S2, S3, and S5) if issued by U3, but just two tuples (for S1 and S3) if issued by U2. Moreover, neither user will see the tuple for S4.

One way to think about the foregoing is in terms of request modification once again. Consider the following query ("Get suppliers in London"):

```
S WHERE CITY = 'London'
```

S	S#	SNAME	STATUS	CITY	LEVEL
	S1	Smith	20	London	2
	S2	Jones	10	Paris	3
	S3	Blake	30	Paris	2
	S4	Clark	20	London	4
	S5	Adams	30	Athens	3

Fig. 17.1 Relvar S with classification levels (example)

The system will modify this request so that it looks like this:

```
S WHERE CITY = 'London' AND LEVEL ≤ user clearance
```

Analogous considerations apply to update operations. For example, user U3 is not aware that the tuple for S4 exists. To that user, therefore, the following INSERT seems reasonable:

```
INSERT S RELATION { TUPLE { S#     S# ('S4'),
                            SNAME  NAME ('Baker'),
                            STATUS 25,
                            CITY   'Rome' } } ;
```

The system must not reject this INSERT, because to do so would effectively tell user U3 that supplier S4 does exist after all. So it accepts it, but modifies it to:

```
INSERT S RELATION { TUPLE { S#     S# ('S4'),
                            SNAME  NAME ('Baker'),
                            STATUS 25,
                            CITY   'Rome',
                            LEVEL  3 } } ;
```

Observe, therefore, that the primary key for suppliers is not just {S#}, it is the combination {S#,LEVEL}. *Note:* We are assuming here for simplicity that there is just one candidate key, which we can therefore regard, harmlessly, as the *primary* key.

More terminology: The suppliers relvar is an example of a *multi-level relvar.* The fact that "the same" data looks different to different users is called *polyinstantiation.* Following the INSERT just discussed, for example, a request to retrieve supplier S4 returns one result to a user U4 with top secret clearance, another to user U3 (with secret clearance), and yet another to user U2 (with confidential clearance).

DELETE and UPDATE are treated analogously; we omit the details here, but several of the references at the end of the chapter discuss such issues in depth. A question: Do you think the ideas discussed in this subsection constitute a violation of *The Information Principle?* Justify your answer!

17.4 STATISTICAL DATABASES

In the present context, a **statistical database** is a database that permits queries that derive aggregated information—for example, sums or averages—but not queries that derive individual information. For example, the query "What is the average employee salary?" might be permitted, while the query "What is the salary of employee Mary?" would not be.

The problem with such databases is that sometimes it is possible to make inferences from legal queries to deduce the answers to illegal ones. As reference [17.8] puts it: "Summaries contain vestiges of the original information; a snooper might be able to (re)construct this information by processing enough summaries. This is called *deduction of confidential information by inference.*" We remark that this problem is likely to become more and more significant as the use of *data warehouses* increases (see Chapter 22).

Here is a detailed example. Suppose the database contains just one relvar, STATS (see Fig. 17.2). Assume for simplicity that all attributes contain either character strings or numbers. Suppose further that some user U is authorized to perform statistical queries (only) and is intent on discovering Alf's salary. Suppose finally that U knows that Alf is a programmer and is male. Now consider the following queries:[3]

1. ```
   WITH ( STATS WHERE SEX = 'M' AND
          OCCUPATION = 'Programmer' ) AS X :
   COUNT ( X )
   ```

Result: 1.

2. ```
   WITH ( STATS WHERE SEX = 'M' AND
          OCCUPATION = 'Programmer' ) AS X :
   SUM ( X, SALARY )
   ```

Result: 50K.

The security of the database has clearly been compromised, even though user U has issued only legitimate statistical queries. As the example illustrates, if the user can find a boolean expression that identifies some individual, then information regarding that individual is no longer secure. This fact suggests that the system should refuse to respond to a query for which the cardinality of the set to be summarized is less than some lower bound

NAME	SEX	CHILDREN	OCCUPATION	SALARY	TAX	AUDITS
Alf	M	3	Programmer	50K	10K	3
Bea	F	2	Physician	130K	10K	0
Cyn	F	0	Programmer	56K	18K	1
Dee	F	2	Builder	60K	12K	1
Ern	M	2	Clerk	44K	4K	0
Fay	F	1	Artist	30K	0K	0
Guy	M	0	Lawyer	190K	0K	0
Hal	M	3	Homemaker	44K	2K	0
Ivy	F	4	Programmer	64K	10K	1
Joy	F	1	Programmer	60K	20K	1

Fig. 17.2   Relvar STATS (sample value)

---

[3] To save writing, the queries in this section are all expressed in an abbreviated form of **Tutorial D**. The expression COUNT(X) in Query 1, for example, should more properly be EXTEND TABLE_DEE ADD COUNT(X) AS RESULT1 (say).

b. It also suggests that the system should refuse to respond if that cardinality is greater than the upper bound $n - b$ (where n is the cardinality of the containing relation), because the foregoing result could equally well be obtained as follows:

```
3. COUNT ( STATS )
```

Result: 12.

```
4. WITH ( STATS WHERE NOT ( SEX = 'M' AND
             OCCUPATION = 'Programmer' ) ) AS X :
   COUNT ( X )
```

Result: 11; 12 − 11 = 1.

```
5. SUM ( STATS, SALARY )
```

Result: 728K.

```
6. WITH ( STATS WHERE NOT ( SEX = 'M' AND
             OCCUPATION = 'Programmer' ) ) AS X :
   SUM ( X, SALARY )
```

Result: 678K; 728K − 678K = 50K.

Unfortunately, it is easy to show that simply restricting queries to those for which the set to be summarized has cardinality c in the range $b \le c \le n - b$ is inadequate to avoid compromise, in general. Consider Fig. 17.2 again, and suppose $b = 2$; queries will be answered only if c is in the range $2 \le c \le 8$. The boolean expression

```
SEX = 'M' AND OCCUPATION = 'Programmer'
```

is thus no longer admissible. But consider the following queries:

```
7. WITH ( STATS WHERE SEX = 'M' ) AS X :
   COUNT ( X )
```

Result: 4.

```
8. WITH ( STATS WHERE SEX = 'M' AND NOT
                        ( OCCUPATION = 'Programmer' ) ) AS X :
   COUNT ( X )
```

Result: 3.

From Queries 7 and 8, user U can deduce that there exists exactly one male programmer, who must therefore be Alf (since U already knows this description fits Alf). Alf's salary can thus be discovered as follows:

```
9. WITH ( STATS WHERE SEX = 'M' ) AS X :
   SUM ( X, SALARY )
```

Result: 328K.

```
10. WITH ( STATS WHERE SEX = 'M' AND NOT
                         ( OCCUPATION = 'Programmer' ) ) :
    SUM ( X, SALARY )
```

Result: 278K; 328K − 278K = 50K.

The boolean expression SEX = 'M' AND OCCUPATION = 'Programmer' is called an **individual tracker** for Alf [17.8], because it enables the user to track down information concerning the individual Alf. In general, if the user knows a boolean expression *BE* that identifies some specific individual *I,* and if *BE* can be expressed in the form *BE1* AND *BE2,* then the boolean expression *BE1* AND NOT *BE2* is a tracker for *I* (provided that *BE1* and *BE1* AND NOT *BE2* are both admissible—that is, they both identify result sets with cardinality c in the range $b \leq c \leq n - b$). The reason is that the set identified by *BE* is identical to the difference between the set identified by *BE1* and the set identified by *BE1* AND NOT *BE2:*

```
{ x : BE }  ≡  { x : BE1 AND BE2 }
            ≡  {x : BE1 } MINUS { x : BE1 AND NOT BE2 }
```

See Fig. 17.3.

Reference [17.8] generalizes the foregoing ideas and shows that, for *almost any* statistical database, a **general tracker** (as opposed to a set of individual trackers) can always be found. A general tracker is a boolean expression that can be used to find the answer to *any* inadmissible query—that is, any query involving an inadmissible expression. (By contrast, an individual tracker works only for queries involving some *specific* inadmissible expression.) In fact, any expression with result cardinality c in the range $2b \leq c \leq n - 2b$ is a general tracker (b must be less than $n/4$, which it typically will be in any realistic situation). Once such a tracker is found, a query involving an inadmissible expression *BE* can be answered as illustrated by the following example. (For definiteness we consider the case where the result set cardinality corresponding to *BE* is less than b. The case where it is instead greater than $n - b$ is handled analogously.) Note that it follows from the definition that *T* is a general tracker if and only if NOT *T* is also a general tracker.

Example: Assume again that $b = 2$; then a general tracker is any expression with result set cardinality c in the range $4 \leq c \leq 6$. Suppose again that user U knows that Alf is a male programmer—that is, the inadmissible boolean expression *BE* is (as before)

```
SEX = 'M' AND OCCUPATION = 'Programmer'
```

—and suppose that U wishes to discover Alf's salary. We will use a general tracker twice, first to ascertain that *BE* in fact identifies Alf uniquely (Steps 2–4), and then to determine Alf's salary (Steps 5–7).

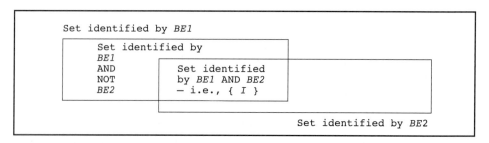

Fig. 17.3   The individual tracker *BE1* AND NOT *BE2*

Step 1: Make a guess at a tracker, *T*. As our guess we choose *T* to be the expression:

```
AUDITS = 0
```

Step 2: Get the total number of individuals in the database, using the expressions *T* and NOT *T*:

```
WITH ( STATS WHERE AUDITS = 0 ) AS X :
COUNT ( X )
```

Result: 5.

```
WITH ( STATS WHERE NOT ( AUDITS = 0 ) ) AS X :
COUNT ( X )
```

Result: 5; 5 + 5 = 10.

It can now easily be seen that our guess *T* is indeed a general tracker.

Step 3: Get the result of adding (a) the number of individuals in the database plus (b) the number satisfying the inadmissible expression *BE,* using the expressions *BE* OR *T* and *BE* OR NOT *T*:

```
WITH ( STATS WHERE ( SEX = 'M' AND
                     OCCUPATION = 'Programmer' )
               OR AUDITS = 0 ) AS X :
COUNT ( X )
```

Result: 6.

```
WITH ( STATS WHERE ( SEX = 'M' AND
                     OCCUPATION = 'Programmer' )
               OR NOT ( AUDITS = 0 ) ) AS X :
COUNT ( X )
```

Result: 5; 6 + 5 = 11.

Step 4: From the results so far, we have that the number of individuals satisfying *BE* is one (result of Step 3 minus result of Step 2); that is, *BE* designates Alf uniquely.

Now we repeat (in Steps 5 and 6) the queries of Steps 2 and 3, but using SUM instead of COUNT.

Step 5: Get the total salary of individuals in the database, using the expressions *T* and NOT *T*:

```
WITH ( STATS WHERE AUDITS = 0 ) AS X :
SUM ( X, SALARY )
```

Result: 438K.

```
WITH ( STATS WHERE NOT ( AUDITS = 0 ) ) AS X :
SUM ( X, SALARY )
```

Result: 290K; 438K + 290K = 728K.

Step 6: Get the sum of Alf's salary and the total salary, using the expressions *BE* OR *T* and *BE* OR NOT *T*:

```
WITH ( STATS WHERE ( SEX = 'M' AND
                     OCCUPATION = 'Programmer' )
                  OR AUDITS = 0 ) AS X :
SUM ( X, SALARY )
```

Result: 488K.

```
WITH ( STATS WHERE ( SEX = 'M' AND
                     OCCUPATION = 'Programmer' )
                  OR NOT ( AUDITS = 0 ) ) AS X :
SUM ( X, SALARY )
```

Result: 290K; 488K + 290K = 778K.

Step 7: Get Alf's salary by subtracting the total salary (found in Step 5) from the result of Step 6.

Result: 50K.

Fig. 17.4 illustrates the general tracker:

```
{ x : BE }  ≡  ( { x : BE OR T } UNION { x : BE OR NOT T } )
                          MINUS { x : T OR NOT T }
```

If the initial guess was wrong (i.e., *T* turns out not to be a general tracker), then one or both of the expressions (*BE* OR *T*) and (*BE* OR NOT *T*) might be inadmissible. For example, if the result set cardinalities for *BE* and *T* are *p* and *q,* respectively, where $p < b$ and $b \leq q < 2b,$ then it is possible that the result set cardinality for (*BE* OR NOT *T*) is greater than $n - b.$ In such a situation it is necessary to make another guess at a tracker and try again. Reference [17.8] suggests that the process of finding a general tracker is not difficult in practice. In our particular example, the initial guess is a general tracker (its result set cardinality is 5), and the queries in Step 3 are both admissible.

To sum up: A general tracker "almost always" exists, and is usually both easy to find and easy to use; in fact, it is often possible to find a tracker quickly just by guessing [17.8]. Even in those cases where a general tracker does not exist, reference [17.8] shows that specific trackers can usually be found for specific queries. It is hard to escape the conclusion that security in a statistical database is a real problem.

So what can be done? Several suggestions have appeared in the literature, but none of them seems totally satisfactory. For example, one possibility is "data swapping"—that is, swapping attribute values among tuples in such a way that overall statistical accuracy is maintained, so that even if a specific value (say a specific salary) is identified there is no

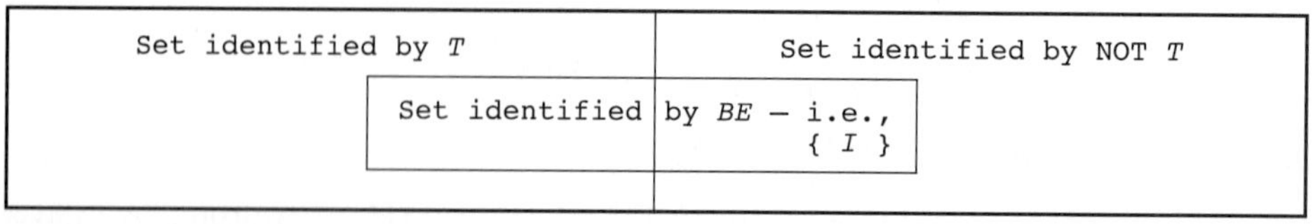

Fig. 17.4   The general tracker *T*

way of knowing which particular individual that value belongs to. The difficulty with this approach lies in finding sets of entries whose values can be swapped in such a fashion. Similar limitations apply to most other suggested solutions. For the present, therefore, it seems hard to disagree with the conclusions of reference [17.8]: "Compromise is straightforward and cheap. The requirement of complete secrecy of confidential information is not consistent with the requirement of producing exact statistical measures for arbitrary subsets of the population. At least one of these requirements must be relaxed before assurances of secrecy can be believed."

17.5 DATA ENCRYPTION

We have assumed so far in this chapter that any would-be infiltrator will be using the normal system facilities to access the database. We now turn our attention to the case of a "user" who attempts to *bypass* the system (e.g., by physically removing a disk or tapping into a communication line). The most effective countermeasure against such threats is **data encryption**: that is, storing and transmitting sensitive data in encrypted form.

In order to discuss some of the concepts of data encryption, we need to introduce some more terminology. The original (unencrypted) data is called the **plaintext**. The plaintext is **encrypted** by subjecting it to an **encryption algorithm**, whose inputs are the plaintext and an **encryption key**; the output from this algorithm—the encrypted form of the plaintext—is called the **ciphertext**. The details of the encryption algorithm are made public, or at least are not specially concealed, but the encryption key is kept secret. The ciphertext, which should be unintelligible to anyone not holding the encryption key, is what is stored in the database or transmitted down the communication line.

Example: Let the plaintext be the string

```
AS KINGFISHERS CATCH FIRE
```

(we assume for simplicity that the only data characters we have to deal with are uppercase letters and blanks). Let the encryption key be the string

```
ELIOT
```

and let the encryption algorithm be as follows:

1. Divide the plaintext into blocks of length equal to that of the encryption key:

   ```
   A S + K I   N G F I S   H E R S +   C A T C H   + F I R E
   ```

   (blanks now shown explicitly as "+").

2. Replace each character of the plaintext by an integer in the range 00–26, using blank = 00, A = 01, ..., Z = 26:

   ```
   0119001109  1407060919  0805181900  0301200308  0006091805
   ```

3. Repeat Step 2 for the encryption key:

   ```
   0512091520
   ```

4. For each block of the plaintext, replace each character by the sum modulo 27 of its integer encoding and the integer encoding of the corresponding character of the encryption key:

0119001109	1407060919	0805181900	0301200308	0006091805
0512091520	0512091520	0512091520	0512091520	0512091520
0604092602	1919152412	1317000720	0813021801	0518180625

5. Replace each integer encoding in the result of Step 4 by its character equivalent:

    F D I Z B   S S O X L   M Q + G T   H M B R A   E R R F Y

The decryption procedure for this example is straightforward, *given the key*. (*Exercise:* Decrypt the ciphertext just shown.) The question is, how difficult is it for a would-be infiltrator to determine the key without prior knowledge, given matching plaintexts and ciphertexts? In our simple example, the answer is, fairly obviously, "not very"; but, equally obviously, much more sophisticated schemes can easily be devised. Ideally the scheme employed should be such that the work involved in breaking it far outweighs any potential advantage to be gained in doing so. (In fact, a remark along the same general lines applies to all aspects of security: The aim should always be to make the cost of breaking the system significantly greater than the potential payoff.) The accepted ultimate objective for such schemes is that the *inventor* of the scheme, holding matching plaintext and ciphertext, should be unable to determine the key, and hence unable to decipher another piece of ciphertext.

The Data Encryption Standard

The foregoing example made use of a **substitution** procedure: An encryption key was used to determine, for each character of the plaintext, a ciphertext character to be *substituted* for that character. Substitution is one of the two basic approaches to encryption as traditionally practiced; the other is **permutation**, in which plaintext characters are simply rearranged into some different sequence. Neither of these approaches is particularly secure in itself, but algorithms that combine the two can provide quite a high degree of security. One such algorithm is the **Data Encryption Standard** (DES), which was developed by IBM and adopted as a U.S. federal standard in 1977 [17.20].

To use the DES, plaintext is divided into 64-bit blocks and each block is encrypted using a 64-bit key (actually the key consists of 56 data bits plus 8 parity bits, so there are not 2^{64} but only 2^{56} possible keys). A block is encrypted by applying an initial permutation to it, then subjecting the permuted block to a sequence of 16 complex substitution steps, and finally applying another permutation, the inverse of the initial permutation, to the result of the last of those steps. The substitution at the *i*th step is not controlled directly by the original encryption key *K* but by a key *Ki* that is computed from the values *K* and *i*. For details, see reference [17.20].

The DES has the property that the decryption algorithm is identical to the encryption algorithm, except that the *Ki*'s are applied in reverse order.

As computers have grown in speed and capacity, however, the DES has increasingly been criticized for its reliance on comparatively small (56-bit) keys. In 2000, therefore, the U.S. federal government adopted a new standard, the **Advanced Encryption Standard** (AES), based on the so-called *Rijndael algorithm* [17.5], which uses keys of 128, 192, or 256 bits. Even 128-bit keys mean the new standard is considerably more secure than the old one; according to reference [26.34], if "we could build a computer fast enough to crack DES in one second, then that computer would compute for about 149 trillion years to crack a 128-bit AES key" (slightly reworded). For further details, see reference [17.5].

Public-Key Encryption

We have already indicated that the DES might not be truly secure; the AES is better, but many people nevertheless feel that such schemes might be broken by brute force, if by no more intelligent means. Many people also feel that the various **public-key** encryption schemes render such approaches technologically obsolete anyway. In a public-key scheme, both the encryption algorithm *and the encryption key* are made freely available; thus, anyone can convert plaintext into ciphertext. But the corresponding **decryption key** is kept secret (public-key schemes involve *two* keys, one for encryption and one for decryption). Furthermore, the decryption key cannot feasibly be deduced from the encryption key; thus, even the person performing the original encryption cannot perform the corresponding decryption if not authorized to do so.

The original idea of public-key encryption is due to Diffie and Hellman [17.9]. We describe the best-known specific approach—due to Rivest, Shamir, and Adleman [17.17]—to show how such a scheme typically works in practice. Their approach (now usually referred to as *the RSA scheme,* from the initials of its inventors) is based on the following two facts:

1. There is a known fast algorithm for determining whether a given number is prime.

2. There is no known fast algorithm for finding the prime factors of a given composite (i.e., nonprime) number.

Reference [17.12] gives an example in which determining (on a typical machine of the time) whether a given number of 130 digits was prime took about seven minutes, whereas finding the two prime factors (on the same machine) of a number obtained by multiplying two primes of 63 digits each would take about *40 quadrillion years* (one quadrillion = 1,000,000,000,000,000).[4]

The RSA scheme works as follows:

1. Choose, randomly, two distinct large primes p and q, and compute the product $r = p * q$.

2. Choose, randomly, a large integer e that is relatively prime to—that is, has no factors other than unity in common with—the product $(p-1) * (q-1)$. The integer e is the

---

[4] Even so, there are questions about the security of the RSA scheme. Reference [17.12] appeared in 1977. In 1990, Lenstra and Manasse successfully factored a 155-digit number [17.24]; they estimated that the amount of computation involved, which was spread over some 1,000 computers, was equivalent to executing a million instructions a second on a single machine for a period of 273 years. The 155-digit number in question was the ninth Fermat number $2^{512} + 1$ (note that $512 = 2^9$). See also reference [17.14], which reports on a completely different—and successful!—approach to breaking RSA encryption.

encryption key. *Note:* Choosing *e* is straightforward; for example, any prime greater than both *p* and *q* will do.

3. Take the decryption key *d* to be the unique "multiplicative inverse" of *e* modulo (*p*–1) * (*q*–1); that is,

```
d * e = 1 modulo (p-1) * (q-1)
```

The algorithm for computing *d* given *e, p,* and *q* is straightforward and is given in reference [17.17].

4. Publish the integers *r* and *e* but not *d*.

5. To encrypt a piece of plaintext *P* (which we assume for simplicity to be an integer less than *r*), replace it by the ciphertext *C*, computed as follows:

```
C = Pe modulo r
```

6. To decrypt a piece of ciphertext *C*, replace it by the plaintext *P*, computed as follows:

```
P = Cd modulo r
```

Reference [17.17] proves that this scheme works—that is, that decryption of *C* using *d* does in fact recover the original *P*. However, computation of *d* knowing only *r* and *e* (and not *p* or *q*) is infeasible, as claimed earlier. Hence, anyone can encrypt plaintext, but only authorized users (holding *d*) can decrypt ciphertext.

We give a trivial example to illustrate the foregoing procedure. For obvious reasons we restrict ourselves to very small numbers throughout.

Example: Let *p* = 3, *q* = 5; then *r* = 15, and the product (*p*–1) * (*q*–1) = 8. Let *e* = 11 (a prime greater than both *p* and *q*). To compute *d*, we have

```
d * 11 = 1 modulo 8
```

whence *d* = 3.

Now let the plaintext *P* consist of the integer 13. Then the ciphertext *C* is given by:

```
C = Pe modulo r
  = 1311 modulo 15
  = 1,792,160,394,037 modulo 15
  = 7
```

Now the original plaintext *P* is given by:

```
P = Cd modulo r
  = 73 modulo 15
  = 343 modulo 15
  = 13
```

Because *e* and *d* are inverses of each other, public-key schemes also permit encrypted messages to be "**signed**" in such a way that the recipient can be certain the message originated with the person it purports to have done (i.e., "signatures" cannot be forged). Suppose *A* and *B* are two users who wish to communicate with each other using a public-key scheme. Then *A* and *B* will each publish an encryption algorithm (including in each case the corresponding encryption key), but will keep the decryption algorithm and key secret, even from each other. Let the encryption algorithms be ECA and ECB (for encrypting messages to be sent to *A* and *B*, respectively), and let the corresponding decryption algorithms be DCA and DCB, respectively. ECA and DCA are inverses of each other, as are ECB and DCB.

Now suppose *A* wishes to send a piece of plaintext *P* to *B*. Instead of simply computing ECB(*P*) and transmitting the result, *A* first applies the *decryption* algorithm DCA to *P*, then encrypts the result and transmits that as the ciphertext *C:*

```
C = ECB ( DCA ( P ) )
```

Upon receipt of *C,* user *B* applies the decryption algorithm DCB and then the *encryption* algorithm ECA, producing the final result *P:*

```
ECA ( DCB ( C ) )
    = ECA ( DCB ( ECB ( DCA ( P ) ) ) )
    = ECA ( DCA ( P ) )          /* because DCB and ECB cancel */
    = P                          /* because ECA and DCA cancel */
```

Now *B* knows the message did indeed come from *A,* because ECA will produce *P* only if the algorithm DCA was used in the encryption process, and that algorithm is known only to *A.* No one, *not even B,* can forge *A*'s signature.

17.6 SQL FACILITIES

SQL supports discretionary access control only. Two more or less independent SQL features are involved: the **view mechanism,** which can be used to hide sensitive data from unauthorized users, and the **authorization subsystem** itself, which allows users having specific privileges selectively and dynamically to grant those privileges to other users, and subsequently to revoke those privileges, if desired. Both features are discussed in what follows.

Views and Security

To illustrate the use of views for security purposes in SQL, we first give SQL analogs of the view examples (Examples 2–4) from Section 17.2.

```
2. CREATE VIEW LS AS
           SELECT S.S#, S.SNAME, S.STATUS, S.CITY
           FROM   S
           WHERE  S.CITY = 'London' ;
```

The view defines the data over which authorization is to be granted. The granting itself is done by means of the GRANT statement—for example:

```
GRANT SELECT, DELETE, UPDATE ( SNAME, STATUS )
ON     LS
TO     Dan, Misha ;
```

Note that, perhaps because they are defined by means of a special GRANT statement and not by some hypothetical "CREATE AUTHORITY" statement, authorities are *unnamed* in SQL. (Integrity constraints, by contrast, do have names, as we saw in Chapter 9.)

3. ```
CREATE VIEW SSPPO AS
       SELECT S.S#, S.SNAME, S.STATUS, S.CITY
       FROM   S
       WHERE EXISTS
            (SELECT * FROM SP
              WHERE EXISTS
                   (SELECT * FROM P
                     WHERE S.S# = SP.S#
                     AND   SP.P# = P.P#
                     AND   P.CITY = 'Oslo')) ;
```

Corresponding GRANT:

```
GRANT SELECT ON SSPPO TO Lars ;
```

4. ```
CREATE VIEW SSQ AS
       SELECT S.S#, (SELECT SUM (SP.QTY)
                      FROM   SP
                      WHERE SP.S# = S.S#) AS SQ
       FROM   S ;
```

Corresponding GRANT:

```
GRANT SELECT ON SSQ TO Fidel ;
```

Example 5 from Section 17.2 involved a *context-dependent* authority. SQL supports a variety of niladic built-in operators—CURRENT_USER, CURRENT_DATE, CURRENT_ TIME, and so on—that can be used among other things to define context-dependent views; however, it does not support an analog of the DAY() operator we used in our original Example 5. We therefore simplify the example somewhat here:

```
CREATE VIEW S_NINE_TO_FIVE AS
       SELECT S.S#, S.SNAME, S.STATUS, S.CITY
       FROM   S
       WHERE  CURRENT_TIME ≥ TIME '09:00:00'
       AND    CURRENT_TIME ≤ TIME '17:00:00' ;
```

Corresponding GRANT:

```
GRANT SELECT, UPDATE ( STATUS )
ON     S_NINE_TO_FIVE
TO     ACCOUNTING ;
```

Note, however, that S_NINE_TO_FIVE is rather an odd kind of view!—its value changes over time, even if the underlying data does not. (What is the corresponding predicate?) Furthermore, a view whose definition involves the built-in operator CURRENT_ USER might even (in fact, probably will) have different values for different users. Such views are really different in kind from views as normally understood—in effect, they are *parameterized.* It might be preferable, at least conceptually, to allow users to define their own (potentially parameterized) relation-valued *functions,* and then treat views like S_NINE_TO_FIVE as just special cases of such functions.

Be that as it may, the foregoing examples illustrate the point that the view mechanism provides an important measure of security "for free" ("for free" because the mechanism is included in the system for other purposes anyway). What is more, many authorization checks, even value-dependent ones, can be done at compile time instead of run time, a significant performance benefit. However, the view-based approach to security does suffer from some slight awkwardness on occasion—in particular, if some user needs different privileges over different subsets of the same table at the same time. For example, consider the structure of an application that is allowed to scan and display all London parts and is also allowed to update some of them (just the red ones, say) during that scan.

GRANT and REVOKE

The view mechanism allows the database to be conceptually divided into pieces in various ways so that sensitive information can be hidden from unauthorized users. But it does not allow for the specification of the operations that *authorized* users are allowed to execute against those pieces; instead, as we have already seen in the examples in the previous subsection, that task is performed by the **GRANT** statement, which we now discuss in more detail (we omit discussion of some of that statement's more esoteric aspects, however).

First of all, the creator of any object is automatically granted all privileges that make sense for that object. For example, the creator of a base table *T* is automatically granted the SELECT, INSERT, DELETE, UPDATE, REFERENCES, and TRIGGER[5] privileges on *T* (we will explain these privileges in just a moment). Furthermore, these privileges are granted "with grant authority" in each case, which means that the user holding the privilege can grant it to other users.

Here then is the syntax of the GRANT statement:

```
GRANT <privilege commalist>
      ON <object>
      TO <user ID commalist>
    [ WITH GRANT OPTION ] ;
```

Explanation:

1. The legal *<privilege>*s are USAGE, UNDER, SELECT, INSERT, DELETE, UPDATE, REFERENCES, TRIGGER, and EXECUTE. The SELECT, INSERT, UPDATE, and REFERENCES privileges can all be column-specific. *Note:* ALL PRIVILEGES can also be specified, but the semantics are not straightforward (see reference [4.20]).

   - USAGE is needed on a given user-defined type in order to use that type.

   - UNDER is needed (a) on a given user-defined type in order to create a subtype of that type and (b) on a given table in order to create a subtable of that table (see Chapters 20 and 26, respectively).

   - SELECT, INSERT, DELETE, and UPDATE are self-explanatory.

   - REFERENCES is needed on a given table in order to refer to that table in an integrity constraint (any constraint, that is, not necessarily a referential constraint specifically).

   - TRIGGER is needed on a given base table in order to create a trigger on that table.

   - EXECUTE is needed on a given SQL routine in order to invoke that routine.

---

[5] Presumably the UNDER privilege too (where that privilege makes sense), but the standard makes no mention of it.

2. The legal *<object>*s are TYPE *<type name>*, TABLE *<table name>*, and (for EXECUTE) something called a *<specific routine designator>*, details of which are beyond the scope of this book. *Note:* In this context—unlike most others in SQL— the keyword TABLE (which is in fact optional) includes views as well as base tables.

3. The *<user ID commalist>* can be replaced by the special keyword PUBLIC, meaning all users known to the system. *Note:* SQL also supports user-defined **roles**; an example might be ACCOUNTING, meaning everyone in the accounting department. Once created, a role can be granted privileges, just as if it were a regular user ID. Furthermore, roles themselves can be granted, like privileges, either to a user ID or to another role. In other words, roles are SQL's mechanism for supporting user groups (see Section 17.1).

4. WITH GRANT OPTION, if specified, means that the specified users are granted the specified privileges on the specified object **with grant authority**—meaning, as already indicated, that they can go on to grant those privileges on that object to some other user(s). Of course, WITH GRANT OPTION can be specified only if the user issuing the GRANT statement has the necessary grant authority in the first place.

Next, if user *A* grants some privilege to some other user *B,* user *A* can subsequently *revoke* that privilege from user *B*. Revoking privileges is done by means of the **REVOKE** statement—syntax:

```
REVOKE [ GRANT OPTION FOR ] <privilege commalist>
                    ON <object>
                    FROM <user ID commalist>
                    <behavior> ;
```

Here (a) GRANT OPTION FOR means that grant authority (only) is to be revoked; (b) *<privilege commalist>*, *<object>*, and *<user ID commalist>* are as for GRANT; and (c) *<behavior>* is either RESTRICT or CASCADE (as usual). Examples:

1. `REVOKE SELECT ON S FROM Jacques, Anne, Charley RESTRICT ;`

2. `REVOKE SELECT, DELETE, UPDATE ( SNAME, STATUS )`
   `        ON LS FROM Dan, Misha CASCADE ;`

3. `REVOKE SELECT ON SSPPO FROM Lars RESTRICT ;`

4. `REVOKE SELECT ON SSQ FROM Fidel RESTRICT ;`

Now, regarding RESTRICT *vs.* CASCADE: Suppose *p* is some privilege on some object, and user *A* grants *p* to user *B,* who in turn grants it to user *C*. What should happen if *A* now revokes *p* from *B*? Suppose for a moment that the REVOKE succeeds. Then the privilege *p* held by *C* would be "abandoned"—it would be derived from a user, *B,* who no longer holds it. The purpose of the RESTRICT *vs.* CASCADE option is to avoid the possibility of abandoned privileges. To be specific, RESTRICT causes the REVOKE to fail if it would lead to any abandoned privileges; CASCADE causes such privileges to be revoked as well.

Finally, dropping a type, table, column, or routine automatically revokes all privileges on the dropped object from all users.

17.7 SUMMARY

We have discussed various aspects of the database **security** problem. We began by contrasting security and *integrity:* Security means ensuring users are allowed to do the things they are trying to do; integrity means ensuring the things they are trying to do are "correct." Security, in other words, means *protecting data against unauthorized access.*

Security is enforced by the DBMS's **security subsystem**, which checks all access requests against the **security constraints** (or *authorities,* more likely) stored in the system catalog. First we considered **discretionary** schemes, in which access to a given object is at the discretion of the object's owner. Each authority in a discretionary scheme has a **name**, a set of **privileges** (RETRIEVE, INSERT, etc.), a corresponding **relvar** (i.e., the data to which the authority applies), and a set of **users**. Such authorities can be used to provide **value-dependent**, **value-independent**, **statistical summary**, and **context-dependent** controls. An **audit trail** can be used to record attempted security breaches. We took a brief look at an implementation technique for discretionary schemes known as **request modification** (a technique that was pioneered by the Ingres prototype in connection with the QUEL language).

Next we discussed **mandatory** controls, in which each object has a **classification** level and each user has a **clearance** level. We explained the rules for access under such a scheme. We also summarized the security classification scheme defined by the U.S. Department of Defense in the Orange and Lavender books, and briefly discussed the ideas of **multi-level relvars** and **polyinstantiation**.

Next we discussed the special problems of **statistical databases**. A statistical database is a database that contains a lot of individually sensitive items of information but is supposed to supply only statistical summary information to its users. We saw that the security of such databases is easily compromised by means of **trackers**—a fact that should be the cause for some alarm, given the increasing level of interest in data warehouse systems (see Chapter 22).

We then examined **data encryption**, touching on the basic ideas of **substitution** and **permutation**, explaining what the **Data Encryption Standard** (DES) and **Advanced Encryption Standard** (AES) are, and describing in outline how the **public-key** schemes work. In particular, we gave a simple example of the **RSA** prime number scheme. We also discussed the concept of **digital signatures**.

We also briefly described the security features of SQL—in particular, the use of **views** to hide information, and the use of **GRANT** and **REVOKE** to control which users have which privileges over which objects (primarily base tables and views).

In conclusion, the point is worth emphasizing that it is no good the DBMS providing an extensive set of security controls if it is possible to bypass those controls in some way. In DB2, for example, the database is physically stored as operating system files; thus, DB2's security mechanism would be almost useless if it were possible to access those files from a conventional program using conventional operating system services. For this reason, DB2 works in harmony with its various companion systems—the underlying operating system in particular—to guarantee that the total system is secure. The details are beyond the scope of this chapter, but the message should be clear.

EXERCISES

17.1   Let base relvar STATS be as in Section 17.4:

```
STATS { NAME, SEX, CHILDREN, OCCUPATION, SALARY, TAX, AUDITS }
        KEY { NAME }
```

Using the hypothetical language introduced in Section 17.2, define authorities as necessary to give:

a. User Ford RETRIEVE privileges over the entire relvar

b. User Smith INSERT and DELETE privileges over the entire relvar

c. Each user RETRIEVE privileges over that user's own tuple (only)

d. User Nash RETRIEVE privileges over the entire relvar and UPDATE privileges over the SALARY and TAX attributes (only)

e. User Todd RETRIEVE privileges over the NAME, SALARY, and TAX attributes (only)

f. User Ward RETRIEVE privileges as for Todd and UPDATE privileges over the SALARY and TAX attributes (only)

g. User Pope full privileges (RETRIEVE, INSERT, DELETE, UPDATE) over tuples for preachers (only)

h. User Jones DELETE privileges over tuples for people in a nonspecialist occupation, where a *nonspecialist occupation* is defined as one belonging to more than ten people

i. User King RETRIEVE privileges for maximum and minimum salaries per occupation

17.2   Consider what is involved in extending the syntax of AUTHORITY definitions to include control over operations such as defining and dropping base relvars, defining and dropping views, defining and dropping authorities, and so on.

17.3   Consider Fig. 17.2 once again. Suppose we know that Hal is a homemaker with at least two children. Write a sequence of statistical queries that will reveal Hal's tax figure, using an individual tracker. Assume as in Section 17.4 that the system will not respond to queries with a result set cardinality less than 2 or greater than 8.

17.4   Repeat Exercise 17.3, but use a general tracker instead of an individual tracker.

17.5   Decrypt the following ciphertext, which was produced in a manner similar to that used in the "AS KINGFISHERS CATCH FIRE" example in Section 17.5, but using a different five-character encryption key:

```
F N W A L
J P V J C
F P E X E
A B W N E
A Y E I P
S U S V D
```

17.6   Work through the RSA public-key encryption scheme with $p = 7$, $q = 5$, and $e = 17$ for plaintext $P = 3$.

17.7   Can you think of any implementation problems or other disadvantages that might be caused by encryption?

17.8   Give SQL solutions to Exercise 17.1.

17.9   Write SQL statements to drop the privileges granted in your solution to the previous exercise.

REFERENCES AND BIBLIOGRAPHY

17.1 Rakesh Agrawal, Jerry Kiernan, Ramakrishnan Srikant, and Yirong Xu: "Hippocratic Databases," Proc. 28th Int. Conf. on Very Large Data Bases, Hong Kong (August 2002).

To quote the abstract: "[We] argue that future database systems must include responsibility for the privacy of data they manage as a founding tenet . . . We enunciate . . . key privacy principles for . . . database systems."

17.2 Rakesh Agrawal and Jerry Kiernan: "Watermarking Relational Databases," Proc. 28th Int. Conf. on Very Large Data Bases, Hong Kong (August 2002).

Proposes a scheme for "watermarking" data so that pirate copies (in effect, copyright violations) can be detected.

17.3 D. E. Bell and L. J. La Padula: "Secure Computer Systems: Mathematical Foundations and Model," MITRE Technical Report M74-244 (May 1974).

17.4 Luc Bouganim and Philippe Pucheral: "Chip-Secured Data Access: Confidential Data on Untrusted Servers," Proc. 28th Int. Conf. on Very Large Data Bases, Hong Kong (August 2002).

To quote the abstract: "[This scheme] enforces data confidentiality and controls personal privileges [via] a client-based security component acting as a mediator between a client and an encrypted database. This component is embedded in a smartcard to prevent [tampering]." The scheme overcomes the classical problem with encrypted databases, which is that data typically has to be in plaintext format in the indexes.

17.5 J. Daemen and V. Rijnen: "The Block Cipher Rijndael," in J.-J. Quisquater and B. Schneier (eds.), *Smart Card Research and Applications* (Springer-Verlag *Lecture Notes in Computer Science 1820*). New York, N.Y.: Springer-Verlag (2000).

17.6 James Daly: "Fingerprinting a Computer Security Code," *Computerworld* (July 27, 1992).

17.7 Dorothy E. Denning: *Cryptography and Data Security*. Reading, Mass.: Addison-Wesley (1983).

17.8 Dorothy E. Denning and Peter J. Denning: "Data Security," *ACM Comp. Surv. 11,* No. 3 (September 1979).

A good early tutorial, covering discretionary access controls, mandatory access controls (here called *flow* controls), data encryption, and *inference* controls (the special problem of statistical databases).

17.9 W. Diffie and M. E. Hellman: "New Directions in Cryptography," *IEEE Transactions on Information Theory* IT-22 (November 1976).

17.10 Ronald Fagin: "On an Authorization Mechanism," *ACM TODS 3,* No. 3 (September 1978).

An extended corrigendum to reference [17.13], *q.v.* Under certain circumstances the mechanism of reference [17.13] would revoke a privilege that ought not to be revoked. This paper corrects that flaw.

17.11 Roberto Gagliardi, George Lapis, and Bruce Lindsay: "A Flexible and Efficient Database Authorization Facility," IBM Research Report RJ6826 (May 11, 1989).

17.12 Martin Gardner: "A New Kind of Cipher That Would Take Millions of Years to Break," *Scientific American 237,* No. 2 (August 1977).

A good informal introduction to the work on public-key encryption. The title might be an overclaim [17.14,17.24].

17.13 Patricia P. Griffiths and Bradford W. Wade: "An Authorization Mechanism for a Relational Data Base System," *ACM TODS 1,* No. 3 (September 1976).

Describes the GRANT and REVOKE mechanism originally proposed for System R. The scheme now included in the SQL standard is based on that mechanism, though significantly different (and much more complex) at the detail level.

17.14 Nigel Hawkes: "Breaking into the Internet," *London Times* (March 18, 1996).

Describes how a computer expert broke the RSA scheme by measuring how long it took for the system to decrypt messages—"the electronic equivalent of guessing the combination of a lock by watching someone turn the dials and seeing how long each took."

17.15 Sushil Jajodia and Ravi Sandhu: "Toward a Multi-Level Secure Relational Data Model," Proc. 1991 ACM SIGMOD Int. Conf. on Management of Data, Denver, Colo. (June 1991).

As explained in Section 17.3, "multi-level" in a security context refers to a system that supports mandatory access controls. This paper suggests that much of the current activity in the field is *ad hoc,* since there is very little consensus on basic concepts, and proposes a start at formalizing the principles of multi-level systems.

17.16 Abraham Lempel: "Cryptology in Transition," *ACM Comp. Surv. 11,* No. 4: Special Issue on Cryptology (December 1979).

A good early tutorial on encryption and related matters.

17.17 R. L. Rivest, A. Shamir, and L. Adleman: "A Method for Obtaining Digital Signatures and Public Key Cryptosystems," *CACM 21,* No. 2 (February 1978).

17.18 Ken Smith and Marianne Winslett: "Entity Modeling in the MLS Relational Model," Proc. 18th Int. Conf. on Very Large Data Bases, Vancouver, Canada (August 1992).

"MLS" in the title of this paper stands for "multi-level secure" [17.15]. This paper focuses on the *meaning* of MLS databases, and proposes a new BELIEVED BY clause on retrieval and update operations to direct those operations to the particular state of the database understood or "believed by" a specific user. This approach is claimed to solve a number of problems with prior approaches. See also reference [17.23].

17.19 Bhavani Thuraisingham: "Current Status of R&D in Trusted Database Management Systems," *ACM SIGMOD Record 21,* No. 3 (September 1992).

A brief survey and extensive set of references on "trusted" or multi-level systems (as of the early 1990s).

17.20 U.S. Department of Commerce/National Bureau of Standards: *Data Encryption Standard.* Federal Information Processing Standards Publication 46 (January 15, 1977).

The official DES definition. The encryption/decryption algorithm (see Section 17.5) is suitable for implementation on a hardware chip, which means that devices that incorporate it can operate at a high data rate. A number of such devices are commercially available.

17.21 U.S. Department of Defense: *Trusted Computer System Evaluation Criteria* (the "Orange Book"), Document No. DoD 5200-28-STD. DoD National Computer Security Center (December 1985).

17.22 U.S. National Computer Security Center: *Trusted Database Management System Interpretation of Trusted Computer System Evaluation Criteria* (the "Lavender Book"), Document No. NCSC-TG-201, Version 1 (April 1991).

17.23 Marianne Winslett, Kenneth Smith, and Xiaolei Qian: "Formal Query Languages for Secure Relational Databases," *ACM TODS 19,* No. 4 (December 1994).

Continues the work of reference [17.18].

17.24 Ron Wolf: "How Safe Is Computer Data? A Lot of Factors Govern the Answer," *San Jose Mercury News* (July 5, 1990).

CHAPTER **18**

Optimization

18.1 INTRODUCTION

Optimization represents both a challenge and an opportunity for relational systems: a challenge, because optimization is *required* if the system is to achieve acceptable performance; an opportunity, because it is precisely one of the strengths of such systems that relational expressions are at a sufficiently high semantic level that optimization is feasible in the first place. In a nonrelational system, by contrast, where user requests are expressed at a lower semantic level, any "optimization" has to be done manually by the human user ("optimization" in quotes, because the term is usually taken to mean *automatic* optimization); in other words, it is the *user* in such a system who decides what low-level operations are needed and what sequence they need to be executed in. And if the user makes a bad decision, there is nothing the system can do to improve matters. Note too the implication that the user must have some programming expertise; this fact by itself puts the system out of reach for many who could otherwise benefit from it.

The advantage of automatic optimization is not just that users do not have to worry about how best to state their queries (i.e., how to phrase their requests in order to get the

531

best performance). The fact is, there is a real possibility that the optimizer might actually do better than a human user. There are several reasons for this state of affairs, the following among them:

1. A good optimizer will have a wealth of information available to it that human users typically do not have. To be specific, it will know certain statistical information (cardinality information and the like), such as:

   - The number of distinct values of each type
   - The number of tuples currently appearing in each base relvar
   - The number of distinct values currently appearing in each attribute in each base relvar
   - The number of times each such value occurs in each such attribute

   and so on. (All of this information will typically be kept in the system catalog—see Section 18.5.) As a result, the optimizer should be able to make a more accurate assessment of the efficiency of any given strategy for implementing a particular request, and thus be more likely to choose the most efficient implementation.

2. Furthermore, if the database statistics change over time, then a different choice of strategy might become desirable; in other words, reoptimization might be required. In a relational system, reoptimization is trivial—it simply involves a reprocessing of the original relational request by the system optimizer. In a nonrelational system, by contrast, reoptimization involves rewriting the program, and very likely will not be done at all.

3. Next, the optimizer is a *program,* and therefore by definition much more patient than a typical human user. The optimizer is quite capable of considering literally hundreds of different implementation strategies for a given request, whereas it is extremely unlikely that a human user would ever consider more than three or four (at least in any depth).

4. Last, the optimizer can be regarded in a sense as embodying the skills and services of "the best" human programmers. As a consequence, it has the effect of making those skills and services available to everybody—which means it is making an otherwise scarce set of resources available to a wide range of users, in an efficient and cost-effective manner.

All of the above should serve as evidence in support of the claim made at the beginning of this section to the effect that optimizability—that is, the fact that relational requests are optimizable—is in fact a strength of relational systems.

The overall purpose of the optimizer, then, is to choose an efficient strategy for evaluating a given relational expression. In this chapter we briefly describe some of the fundamental principles and techniques involved in that process. Following an introductory motivating example in Section 18.2, Section 18.3 gives an overview of how optimizers work, and Section 18.4 then elaborates on one very important aspect of the process, *expression transformation* (also known as *query rewrite*). Section 18.5 discusses the question of *database statistics*. Next, Section 18.6 describes one specific approach to optimization, called *query decomposition,* in some detail. Section 18.7 then addresses the question of how the relational operators (join and so on) are actually implemented, and briefly considers the use of the statistics discussed in Section 18.5 to perform cost estimation. Finally, Section 18.8 presents a summary of the entire chapter.

One final introductory remark: It is usual to refer to this topic as *query* optimization specifically. This term is slightly misleading, however, inasmuch as the expression to be optimized—the "query"—might have arisen in some context other than interactive interrogation of the database (in particular, it might be part of an update operation instead of a query *per se*). What is more, the term *optimization* itself is somewhat of an overclaim, since there is usually no guarantee that the implementation strategy chosen is truly optimal in any measurable sense; it might in fact be so, but usually all that is known for sure is that the "optimized" strategy is an *improvement* on the original unoptimized version. (In certain cases, however, it might be possible to claim legitimately that the chosen strategy is indeed optimal in a very specific sense; see, for example, reference [18.30]. See also Appendix A.)

18.2 A MOTIVATING EXAMPLE

We begin with a simple example—an elaboration of one already discussed briefly in Chapter 7, Section 7.6—that gives some idea of the dramatic improvements that are possible. The query is "Get names of suppliers who supply part P2." An algebraic formulation of this query is:

```
( ( SP JOIN S ) WHERE P# = P# ('P2') ) { SNAME }
```

Suppose the database contains 100 suppliers and 10,000 shipments, of which only 50 are for part P2. Assume for simplicity that relvars S and SP are represented directly on the disk as two separate stored files, with one stored record per tuple. Then, if the system were simply to evaluate the expression as stated—that is, without any optimization at all—the sequence of events would be as follows:

1. *Join SP and S (over S#):* This step involves reading the 10,000 shipments; reading each of the 100 suppliers 10,000 times (once for each of the 10,000 shipments); constructing an intermediate result consisting of 10,000 joined tuples; and writing those 10,000 joined tuples back out to the disk. (For the sake of the example, we assume there is no room for this intermediate result in main memory.)

2. *Restrict the result of Step 1 to just the tuples for part P2:* This step involves reading the 10,000 joined tuples back into memory again, but produces a result consisting of only 50 tuples, which we assume is small enough to be kept in main memory.

3. *Project the result of Step 2 over SNAME:* This step produces the desired final result (50 tuples at most, which can stay in main memory).

The following procedure is equivalent to the one just described, in the sense that it necessarily produces the same final result, but is clearly much more efficient:

1. *Restrict SP to just the tuples for part P2:* This step involves reading 10,000 tuples but produces a result consisting of only 50 tuples, which we assume will be kept in main memory.

2. *Join the result of Step 1 to S (over S#):* This step involves reading the 100 suppliers (once only, not once per P2 shipment) and produces a result of 50 tuples again (still in main memory).

3. *Project the result of Step 2 over SNAME* (same as Step 3 before): The desired final result (50 tuples at most) stays in main memory.

The first of these two procedures involves a total of 1,030,000 tuple I/O's, whereas the second involves only 10,100. It is clear, therefore, that if we take "number of tuple I/O's" as our performance measure, then the second procedure is a little over 100 times better than the first. It is also clear that we would like the implementation to use the second procedure rather than the first! *Note:* In practice, it is *page* I/O's that matter, not tuple I/O's, so let us assume for simplicity that each stored tuple occupies its own page.

So we see that a very simple change in the execution algorithm—doing a restriction and then a join, instead of a join and then a restriction—has produced a dramatic (hundredfold) improvement in performance. And the improvement would be more dramatic still if shipments were *indexed* or *hashed* on P#—the number of shipment tuples read in Step 1 would be reduced from 10,000 to just 50, and the new procedure would then be nearly 7,000 times better than the original. Likewise, if suppliers were also indexed or hashed on S#, the number of supplier tuples read in Step 2 would be reduced from 100 to 50, so that the procedure would now be over 10,000 times better than the original. What this means is, if the original unoptimized query took three hours to run, the final version will run in a fraction over *one second.* And of course numerous further improvements are possible.

The foregoing example, simple though it is, should be sufficient to show the need for optimization and the kinds of improvement that are possible. In the next section, we will present an overview of a systematic approach to the optimization task; in particular, we will show how the overall problem can be divided into a series of more or less independent subproblems. That overview provides a convenient framework within which individual optimization strategies and techniques such as those discussed in subsequent sections can be explained and understood.

18.3   AN OVERVIEW OF QUERY PROCESSING

We can identify four broad stages in query processing, as follows (refer to Fig. 18.1):

1. Cast the query into internal form.

2. Convert to canonical form.

3. Choose candidate low-level procedures.

4. Generate query plans and choose the cheapest.

We now proceed to amplify each stage.

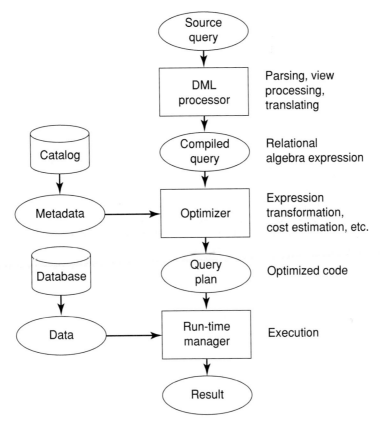

Fig. 18.1 Query processing overview

Stage 1: Cast the Query into Internal Form

The first stage involves the conversion of the original query into some internal representation that is more suitable for machine manipulation, thus eliminating purely external considerations (such as quirks of the concrete syntax of the query language under consideration) and paving the way for subsequent stages in the overall process. *Note:* View processing—that is, the process of replacing references to views by the applicable view-defining expressions—is also performed during this stage.

An obvious question is: What formalism should the internal representation be based on? Whatever formalism is chosen, it must be rich enough to represent all possible queries in the external query language. It should also be as neutral as possible, in the sense that it should not prejudice subsequent choices. The internal form typically chosen is some kind of **abstract syntax tree** or **query tree**. For example, Fig. 18.2 shows a possible query tree representation for the example from Section 18.2 ("Get names of suppliers who supply part P2").

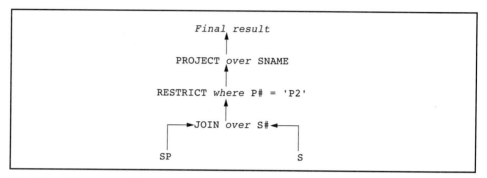

Fig. 18.2   "Get names of suppliers who supply part P2" (query tree)

For our purposes, however, it is more convenient to assume that the internal representation is one of the formalisms we are already familiar with: namely, the relational algebra or the relational calculus. A query tree such as that of Fig. 18.2 can be regarded as just an alternative, encoded representation of some expression in one of those two formalisms. To fix our ideas, we assume here that the formalism is the algebra specifically. Thus, we will assume henceforth that the internal representation of the query of Fig. 18.2 is precisely the algebraic expression shown earlier:[1]

```
( ( SP JOIN S ) WHERE P# = P# ('P2') ) { SNAME }
```

Stage 2: Convert to Canonical Form

In this stage, the optimizer performs a number of optimizations that are "guaranteed to be good," regardless of the actual data values and physical access paths that exist in the stored database. The point is, relational languages typically allow all but the simplest of queries to be expressed in a variety of ways that are at least superficially distinct. In SQL, for example, even a query as simple as "Get names of suppliers who supply part P2" can be expressed in literally dozens of different ways[2]—not counting trivial variations like replacing $A = B$ by $B = A$ or p AND q by q AND p. And the performance of a query really ought not to depend on the particular way the user chose to write it. The next step in processing the query is therefore to convert the internal representation into some equivalent *canonical form* (see the next paragraph), with the objective of eliminating such superficial distinctions and—more important—finding a representation that is more efficient than the original in some way.

---

[1] In fact, mapping the original query into a relational algebra equivalent is exactly what some commercial SQL optimizers do.

[2] We observe, however, that the SQL language is exceptionally prone to this problem (see Exercise 8.12 in Chapter 8, also reference [4.19]). Other languages (e.g., the algebra or the calculus) typically do not provide quite so many different ways of doing the same thing. This unnecessary "flexibility" on the part of SQL actually makes life harder for the *implementer*—not to mention the user—because it makes the optimizer's job much more difficult.

A note regarding "canonical form": The notion of **canonical form** is central to many branches of mathematics and related disciplines. It can be defined as follows. Given a set Q of objects (say queries) and a notion of equivalence among those objects (say the notion that queries $q1$ and $q2$ are equivalent if and only if they are guaranteed to produce the same result), subset C of Q is said to be a **set of canonical forms** for Q under the stated definition of equivalence if and only if every object q in Q is equivalent to just one object c in C. The object c is said to be the *canonical form* for the object q. All "interesting" properties that apply to the object q also apply to its canonical form c; thus, it is sufficient to study just the small set C, not the large set Q, in order to prove a variety of "interesting" results.

To revert to the main thread of our discussion: In order to transform the output from Stage 1 into some equivalent but more efficient form, the optimizer makes use of certain **transformation rules** or **laws**. Here is an example of such a law: The expression

```
( A JOIN B ) WHERE restriction on A
```

can be transformed into the equivalent but more efficient expression

```
( A WHERE restriction on A ) JOIN B
```

We have already discussed this transformation briefly in Chapter 7, Section 7.6; in fact, it was the one we were using in our introductory example in Section 18.2, and that example showed clearly why such a transformation is desirable. Many more such laws are discussed in Section 18.4.

Stage 3: Choose Candidate Low-Level Procedures

Having converted the internal representation of the query into some more desirable form, the optimizer must then decide how to execute the transformed query represented by that converted form. At this stage considerations such as the existence of indexes or other physical access paths, distribution of data values, physical clustering of stored data, and so on, come into play (note that we paid no heed to such matters in Stages 1 and 2).

The basic strategy is to consider the query expression as specifying a series of "low-level" operations,[3] with certain interdependencies among them. An example of such an interdependency is the following: The code to perform a projection will typically require its input tuples to be sorted into some sequence, to allow it to perform duplicate elimination, which means that the immediately preceding operation in the series must produce its output tuples in that same sequence.

Now, for each possible low-level operation (and probably for various common combinations of such operations also), the optimizer will have available to it a set of predefined **implementation procedures**. For example, there will be a set of procedures for implementing the restriction operation: one for the case where the restriction is an equality comparison, one where the restriction attribute is indexed, one where it is hashed, and

---

[3] Level is clearly a relative concept! The operators referred to as "low-level" in this context are basically the operators of the relational algebra (join, restrict, summarize, etc.), which are more usually regarded as *high*-level.

so on. Examples of such procedures are given in Section 18.7 (see also references [18.7, 18.12]).

Each procedure will also have a (parameterized) **cost formula** associated with it, indicating the cost—typically in terms of disk I/O's, though some systems take CPU[4] utilization and other factors into account also—of executing that procedure. These cost formulas are used in Stage 4 (see the next subsection). References [18.7–18.12] discuss and analyze the cost formulas for a number of different implementation procedures under a variety of different assumptions. See also Section 18.7.

Next, therefore, using information from the catalog regarding the current state of the database (existence of indexes, current cardinalities, etc.), together with the pertinent interdependency information, the optimizer will choose one or more candidate procedures for implementing each of the low-level operations in the query expression. This process is sometimes referred to as **access path selection** (see reference [18.33]). *Note:* Actually, reference [18.33]) uses the term *access path selection* to cover both Stage 3 and Stage 4, not just Stage 3. Indeed, it might be difficult in practice to make a clean separation between the two—Stage 3 does flow more or less seamlessly into Stage 4.

Stage 4: Generate Query Plans and Choose the Cheapest

The final stage in the optimization process involves the construction of a set of candidate **query plans**, followed by a choice of the best (i.e., cheapest) of those plans. Each query plan is built by combining a set of candidate implementation procedures, one such procedure for each of the low-level operations in the query. Note that there will normally be many possible plans—probably embarrassingly many—for any given query. In practice, in fact, it might not be a good idea to generate all possible plans, since there will be combinatorially many of them, and the task of choosing the cheapest might well become prohibitively expensive in itself; some heuristic technique for keeping the generated set within reasonable bounds is highly desirable, if not essential (but see reference [18.53]). "Keeping the set within bounds" is usually referred to as *reducing the search space,* because it can be regarded as reducing the range ("space") of possibilities to be examined ("searched") by the optimizer to manageable proportions.

Choosing the cheapest plan obviously requires a method for assigning a cost to any given plan. Basically, the cost for a given plan is just the sum of the costs of the individual procedures that make up that plan, so what the optimizer has to do is evaluate the cost formulas for those individual procedures. The problem is, those cost formulas will depend on the size of the relation(s) to be processed; since all but the simplest queries involve the generation of intermediate results during execution (at least conceptually), the optimizer might therefore have to estimate the size of those intermediate results in order to evaluate the formulas. Unfortunately, those sizes tend to be highly dependent on actual data values. As a consequence, accurate cost estimation can be a difficult problem. References [18.2, 18.3] discuss some approaches to that problem and give references to other research in the area.

---

[4] CPU stands for central processing unit.

18.4 EXPRESSION TRANSFORMATION

In this section we describe some transformation laws or rules that might be useful in Stage 2 of the optimization process. Producing examples to illustrate the rules and deciding exactly why they might be useful are both left (in part) as exercises.

Of course, you should understand that, given a particular expression to transform, the application of one rule might generate an expression that can then be transformed in accordance with some other rule. For example, it is unlikely that the original query will have been directly expressed in such a way as to require two successive projections—see the second rule in the subsection "Restrictions and Projections" immediately following— but such an expression might arise internally as the result of applying certain other transformations. (An important case in point is provided by *view processing;* consider, for example, the query "Get all cities in view V," where view V is defined as the projection of suppliers on S# and CITY.) In other words, starting from the original expression, the optimizer will apply its transformation rules repeatedly until it finally arrives at an expression that it judges—according to some built in set of heuristics—to be "optimal" for the query under consideration.

Restrictions and Projections

Here first are some transformation rules involving restrictions and projections only:

1. A sequence of restrictions on the same relation can be transformed into a single ("ANDed") restriction on that relation. For example, the expression

   ```
   ( A WHERE p1 ) WHERE p2
   ```

   is equivalent to the expression

   ```
   A WHERE p1 AND p2
   ```

   This transformation is desirable because the original formulation implies two passes over *A,* while the transformed version requires just one.

2. In a sequence of projections against the same relation, all but the last can be ignored. For example, the expression

   ```
   ( A { acl1 } ) { acl2 }
   ```

   (where *acl1* and *acl2* are commalists of attribute names) is equivalent to the expression

   ```
   A { acl2 }
   ```

   Of course, *acl2* must be a subset of *acl1* for the original expression to make sense in the first place.

3. A restriction of a projection can be transformed into a projection of a restriction. For example, the expression

   ```
   ( A { acl } ) WHERE p
   ```

   is equivalent to the expression

   ```
   ( A WHERE p ) { acl }
   ```

It is generally a good idea to do restrictions before projections, because the effect of the restriction will be to reduce the size of the input to the projection, and hence to reduce the amount of data that might need to be sorted for duplicate elimination purposes.

Distributivity

The transformation rule used in the example in Section 18.2 (transforming a join followed by a restriction into a restriction followed by a join) is actually a special case of a more general law called the *distributive* law. In general, the monadic operator *f* is said to **distribute** over the dyadic operator $\bigcirc$ if and only if

$$f \ (\ A \ \bigcirc \ B \ ) \ \equiv \ f \ (\ A \ ) \ \bigcirc \ f \ (\ B \ )$$

for all *A* and *B*. In ordinary arithmetic, for example, SQRT (square root, assumed nonnegative) distributes over multiplication, because

$$\text{SQRT} \ (\ A \ \ast \ B \ ) \ \equiv \ \text{SQRT} \ (\ A \ ) \ \ast \ \text{SQRT} \ (\ B \ )$$

for all *A* and *B*. Thus, an arithmetic expression optimizer can always replace either of these expressions by the other when doing arithmetic expression transformation. As a counterexample, SQRT does not distribute over addition, because the square root of $A + B$ is not equal to the sum of the square roots of *A* and *B,* in general.

In relational algebra, restriction distributes over union, intersection, and difference. It also distributes over join, if and only if the restriction condition consists, at its most complex, of two simple restriction conditions[5] ANDed together, one for each of the two join operands. In the case of the example in Section 18.2, this requirement was indeed satisfied—in fact, the condition was a simple restriction condition on just one of the operands—and so we could use the distributive law to replace the overall expression by a more efficient equivalent. The net effect was that we were able to "do the restriction early." Doing restrictions early is usually a good idea, because it serves to reduce the number of tuples to be scanned in the next operation in sequence, and probably reduces the number of tuples in the output from that next operation too.

Here are a couple more specific cases of the distributive law, this time involving projection. First, projection distributes over union and intersection but not difference:

```
( A UNION B ) { acl }  ≡  A   { acl } UNION B { acl }

( A INTERSECT B ) { acl }  ≡  A { acl } INTERSECT B { acl }
```

A and *B* here must be of the same type, of course.

Second, projection also distributes over join, as long as the projection retains all of the join attributes, thus:

```
( A JOIN B ) { acl }  ≡  ( A { acl1 } ) JOIN ( B { acl2 } )
```

Here *acl1* is the union of the join attributes and those attributes of *acl* that appear in *A* only, and *acl2* is the union of the join attributes and those attributes of *acl* that appear in *B* only.

---

[5] See Chapter 7, Section 7.4, subsection "Restrict," for an explanation of the term *simple restriction condition*.

These laws can be used to "do projections early," which again is usually a good idea for reasons similar to those given previously for restrictions.

Commutativity and Associativity

Two more important general laws are the laws of *commutativity* and *associativity*. First, the dyadic operator $\bigcirc$ is said to be **commutative** if and only if

    A ○ B   ≡   B ○ A

for all *A* and *B*. In arithmetic, for example, multiplication and addition are commutative, but division and subtraction are not. In relational algebra, union, intersection, and join are all commutative, but difference and division are not. So, for example, if a query involves a join of two relations *A* and *B*, the commutative law means it makes no logical difference which of *A* and *B* is taken as the "outer" relation and which the "inner." The system is therefore free to choose (say) the smaller relation as the "outer" one in computing the join (see Section 18.7).

Turning to associativity: The dyadic operator $\bigcirc$ is said to be **associative** if and only if

    A ○ (B ○ C)   ≡   (A ○ B) ○ C

for all *A, B, C*. In arithmetic, multiplication and addition are associative, but division and subtraction are not. In relational algebra, union, intersection, and join are all associative, but difference and division are not. So, for example, if a query involves a join of three relations *A, B,* and *C,* the associative and commutative laws together mean it makes no logical difference in which order the relations are joined. The system is thus free to decide which of the various possible sequences is most efficient.

Idempotence and Absorption

Another important general law is the law of *idempotence*. The dyadic operator $\bigcirc$ is said to be **idempotent** if and only if

    A ○ A   ≡   A

for all *A*. As might be expected, the idempotence property can also be useful in expression transformation. In relational algebra, union, intersection, and join are all idempotent, but difference and division are not.

Union and intersection also satisfy the following useful **absorption** laws:

    A UNION (A INTERSECT B)   ≡   A
    A INTERSECT (A UNION B)   ≡   A

Computational Expressions

It is not just relational expressions that are subject to transformation laws. For instance, we have already indicated that certain transformations are valid for arithmetic expressions. Here is a specific example: The expression

    A * B + A * C

can be transformed into

```
A * ( B + C )
```

by virtue of the fact that "*" distributes over "+". A relational optimizer needs to know about such transformations because it will encounter such expressions in the context of the extend and summarize operators.

Note, incidentally, that this example illustrates a slightly more general form of distributivity. Earlier, we defined distributivity in terms of a *monadic* operator distributing over a *dyadic* operator; in the case at hand, however, "*" and "+" are both *dyadic* operators. In general, the dyadic operator δ is said to **distribute** over the dyadic operator $\bigcirc$ if and only if

```
A δ ( B ○ C )  ≡  ( A δ B ) ○ ( A δ C )
```

for all *A, B, C* (in the arithmetic example, take δ as "*" and $\bigcirc$ as "+").

Boolean Expressions

We turn now to *boolean* expressions. Suppose *A* and *B* are attributes of two distinct relations. Then the boolean expression

```
A > B AND B > 3
```

is clearly equivalent to (and can therefore be transformed into) the following:

```
A > B AND B > 3 AND A > 3
```

The equivalence is based on the fact that the comparison operator ">" is **transitive**. Note that this transformation is certainly worth making, because it enables the system to perform an additional restriction (on *A*) before doing the greater-than join implied by the comparison "*A > B*". To repeat a point made earlier, doing restrictions early is generally a good idea; having the system **infer** additional "early" restrictions, as here, is also a good idea. *Note:* This technique is implemented in several commercial products, including, for example, DB2 (where it is called "predicate transitive closure") and Ingres.

Here is another example: The expression

```
A > B OR ( C = D AND E < F )
```

can be transformed into

```
( A > B OR C = D ) AND ( A > B OR E < F )
```

by virtue of the fact that OR distributes over AND. This example illustrates another general law—*viz.*, any boolean expression can be transformed into an equivalent expression in what is called **conjunctive normal form** (CNF). A CNF expression is an expression of the form

```
C1 AND C2 AND ... AND Cn
```

where each of *C1, C2, ..., Cn* is, in turn, a boolean expression (called a **conjunct**) that involves no ANDs. The advantage of CNF is that a CNF expression is true only if every conjunct is true; equivalently, it is false if any conjunct is false. Since AND is commutative (*A* AND *B* is the same as *B* AND *A*), the optimizer can evaluate the individual conjuncts in any order it likes; in particular, it can do them in order of increasing difficulty (easiest first). As soon as it finds one that is false, the whole process can stop. Furthermore, in a parallel-processing system, it might even be possible to evaluate all of the conjuncts in parallel [18.56–18.58]. Again, as soon as one is found that is false, the whole process can stop.

It follows from this subsection and its predecessor that the optimizer needs to know how general properties such as distributivity apply not only to relational operators such as join, but also to comparison operators such as ">", boolean operators such as AND and OR, arithmetic operators such as "+", and so on.

Semantic Transformations

Consider the following expression:

```
( SP JOIN S ) { P# }
```

The join here is a *foreign-to-matching-candidate-key join;* it matches a foreign key in SP with a corresponding candidate key in S. It follows that every SP tuple does join to some S tuple, and every SP tuple therefore does contribute a P# value to the overall result. In other words, there is no need to do the join!—the expression can be simplified to just:

```
SP { P# }
```

Note carefully, however, that this transformation is valid *only* because of the semantics of the situation. In general, each of the operands in a join will include some tuples that have no counterpart in the other (and hence some tuples that do not contribute to the overall result), and transformations such as the one just illustrated will not be valid. In the case at hand, however, every tuple of SP does have a counterpart in S, because of the integrity constraint (actually a referential constraint) that says every shipment must have a supplier, and so the transformation is valid after all.

A transformation that is valid only because a certain integrity constraint is in effect is called a **semantic transformation** [18.25], and the resulting optimization is called a **semantic optimization**. Semantic optimization can be defined as the process of transforming a specified query into another, qualitatively different, query that is nevertheless guaranteed to produce the same result as the original one, thanks to the fact that the data is guaranteed to satisfy a certain integrity constraint.

It is important to understand that, in principle, *any integrity constraint whatsoever* can be used in semantic optimization (the technique is not limited to referential constraints as in the example). For instance, suppose the suppliers-and-parts database is subject to the constraint "All red parts are stored in London," and consider the query:

> *Get suppliers who supply only red parts and are located in the same city as at least one of the parts they supply.*

This is a fairly complex query! By virtue of the integrity constraint, however, it can be transformed into the much simpler form:

> *Get London suppliers who supply only red parts.*

Note: As far as this writer is aware, few commercial products currently do much by way of semantic optimization. In principle, however, such optimization could provide significant performance improvements—much greater improvements, very likely, than are obtained by any of today's more traditional optimization techniques. For further discussion of the semantic optimization idea, see references [18.13], [18.26–18.28], and (especially) [18.25].

Concluding Remarks

In closing this section, we emphasize the fundamental importance of the relational *closure* property to everything we have been discussing. Closure means we can write nested expressions, which means in turn that a single query can be represented by a single expression instead of a multi-statement procedure; thus, no flow analysis is necessary. Also, those nested expressions are recursively defined in terms of subexpressions, which permits the optimizer to adopt a variety of divide-and-conquer evaluation tactics (see Section 18.6). What is more, the various general laws—distributivity and so on—would not even begin to make sense in the absence of closure.

18.5   DATABASE STATISTICS

Stages 3 and 4 of the overall optimization process, the "access path selection" stages, make use of the *database statistics* stored in the catalog (see Section 18.7 for more details on how those statistics are used). For purposes of illustration, we summarize in this section, with little further comment, some of the major statistics maintained by two commercial products, DB2 and Ingres. Here first are some of the principal statistics kept by DB2:[6]

- For each base table:
  - Cardinality
  - Number of pages occupied by this table
  - Fraction of "table space" occupied by this table
- For each column of each base table:
  - Number of distinct values in this column
  - Second highest value in this column
  - Second lowest value in this column
  - For indexed columns only, the ten most frequently occurring values in this column and the number of times they occur

---

[6] Since they are SQL systems, DB2 and Ingres use the terms *table* and *column* in place of *relvar* and *attribute;* in this section, therefore, so do we. Also, note that both products effectively assume that base tables map directly to stored tables.

- For each index:
    - An indication of whether this is a "clustering index" (i.e., an index that is used to cluster logically related data physically on the disk)
    - If it is, the fraction of the indexed table that is still in clustering sequence
    - Number of leaf pages in this index
    - Number of levels in this index

Note: The foregoing statistics are not updated "in real time" (i.e., every time the database is updated), because of the overhead such an approach would entail. Instead, they are updated, selectively, by means of a special system utility called RUNSTATS, which is executed on demand by the DBA (e.g., after a database reorganization). An analogous remark applies to most other commercial products (though not all), including in particular Ingres (see the next paragraph), where the utility is called OPTIMIZEDB.

Here then are some of the principal Ingres statistics. *Note:* In Ingres, an index is regarded as just a special kind of stored table; thus, the statistics shown here for base tables and columns can be kept for indexes too.

- For each base table:
    - Cardinality
    - Number of primary pages for this table
    - Number of overflow pages for this table
- For each column of each base table:
    - Number of distinct values in this column
    - Maximum, minimum, and average value for this column
    - Actual values in this column and the number of times they occur

18.6 A DIVIDE-AND-CONQUER STRATEGY

As mentioned at the end of Section 18.4, relational expressions are recursively defined in terms of subexpressions, and this fact allows the optimizer to adopt a variety of divide-and-conquer strategies. Note that such strategies are likely to be especially attractive in a parallel-processing environment—in particular, in a distributed system—where different portions of the query can be executed in parallel on different processors [18.56–18.58]. In this section we examine one such strategy, called **query decomposition**, which was pioneered by the Ingres prototype [18.34, 18.35].

The basic idea behind query decomposition is to break down a query involving many range variables[7] into a sequence of smaller queries involving (typically) one or two such variables each, using *detachment* and *tuple substitution* to achieve the desired decomposition:

---

[7] Recall that the Ingres query language QUEL is calculus-based.

- **Detachment** is the process of removing a component of the query that has just one variable in common with the rest of the query.

- **Tuple substitution** is the process of substituting for one of the variables in the query a tuple at a time.

Detachment is always applied in preference to tuple substitution as long as there is a choice. Eventually, however, the query will have been decomposed via detachment into a set of smaller queries that cannot be decomposed any further using that technique, and tuple substitution must then be brought into play.

We give a single example (based on one from reference [18.34]). The query is "Get names of London suppliers who supply some red part weighing less than 25 pounds in a quantity greater than 200." Here is a QUEL formulation of this query ("Query Q0"):

```
Q0: RETRIEVE ( S.SNAME ) WHERE S.CITY    = "London"
                         AND   S.S#       = SP.S#
                         AND   SP.QTY     > 200
                         AND   SP.P#      = P.P#
                         AND   P.COLOR    = "Red"
                         AND   P.WEIGHT   < 25.0
```

The (implicit) range variables here are S, P, and SP, each ranging over the base relvar with the same name.

Now, if we examine this query, we can see immediately from the last two comparisons that the only parts we are interested in are ones that are red and weigh less than 25 pounds. So we can detach the "one-variable query" (actually a projection of a restriction) involving the variable P:

```
D1: RETRIEVE INTO P' ( P.P# ) WHERE P.COLOR  = "Red"
                              AND   P.WEIGHT < 25.0
```

This one-variable query is detachable because it has just one variable (P itself) in common with the rest of the query. Since it links up to the rest of the original query via the attribute P# (in the comparison SP.P# = P.P#), attribute P# is what must appear in the "proto tuple" (see Chapter 8) in the detached version; that is, the detached query must retrieve exactly the part numbers of red parts weighing less than 25 pounds. We save that detached query as a query, Query D1, that retrieves its result into a temporary relvar P' (the effect of the INTO clause is to cause a new relvar P', with sole attribute P#, to be defined automatically to hold the result of executing the RETRIEVE). Finally, we replace references to P in the reduced version of Query Q0 by references to P'. Let us refer to this new reduced version as Query Q1:

```
Q1: RETRIEVE ( S.SNAME ) WHERE S.CITY = "London"
                         AND   S.S#   = SP.S#
                         AND   SP.QTY > 200
                         AND   SP.P#  = P'.P#
```

We now perform a similar process of detachment on Query Q1, detaching the one-variable query involving variable SP as Query D2 and leaving a modified version of Q1 (Query Q2):

```
D2: RETRIEVE INTO SP' ( SP.S#, SP.P# ) WHERE SP.QTY > 200

Q2: RETRIEVE ( S.SNAME ) WHERE S.CITY = "London"
                        AND    S.S#   = SP'.S#
                        AND    SP'.P# = P'.P#
```

Next we detach the one-variable query involving S:

```
D3: RETRIEVE INTO S' ( S.S#, S.SNAME ) WHERE S.CITY = "London"

Q3: RETRIEVE ( S'.SNAME ) WHERE S'.S#  = SP'.S#
                         AND    SP'.P# = P'.P#
```

Finally, we detach the two-variable query involving SP' and P':

```
D4: RETRIEVE INTO SP'' ( SP'.S# ) WHERE SP'.P# = P'.P#

Q4: RETRIEVE ( S'.SNAME ) WHERE S'.S# = SP''.S#
```

Thus, the original query Q0 has been decomposed into three one-variable queries D1, D2, and D3 (each of which is a projection of a restriction) and two two-variable queries D4 and Q4 (each of which is a projection of a join). We can represent the situation at this point by means of the tree structure shown in Fig. 18.3. That figure can be read as follows:

- Queries D1, D2, and D3 take as input relvars P, SP, and S (more precisely, the relations that are the current values of relvars P, SP, and S), respectively, and produce as output P', SP', and S', respectively.

- Query D4 then takes as input P' and SP' and produces as output SP''.

- Finally, Query Q4 takes as input S' and SP'' and produces as output the overall required result.

Observe now that Queries D1, D2, and D3 are completely independent of one another and can be processed in any order (possibly even in parallel). Likewise, Queries D3 and D4 can be processed in either order once Queries D1 and D2 have been processed. However, Queries D4 and Q4 cannot be decomposed any further and must be processed by tuple substitution (which really just means *brute force, index lookup,* or *hash lookup*—see Section 18.7). For example, consider Query Q4. With our usual sample data, the set of

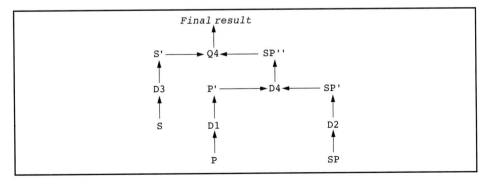

Fig. 18.3   Decomposition tree for Query Q0

supplier numbers in attribute SP".S# will be the set {S1,S2,S4}. Each of these three values will be substituted for SP".S# in turn. Query Q4 will therefore be evaluated as if it had been written as follows:

```
RETRIEVE ( S'.SNAME ) WHERE S'.S# = "S1"
                      OR    S'.S# = "S2"
                      OR    S'.S# = "S4"
```

Reference [18.34] gives algorithms for breaking the original query down into smaller queries and choosing variables for tuple substitution. It is in that latter choice that much of the actual optimization resides; reference [18.34] includes heuristics for making the cost estimates that drive the choice (Ingres will usually—but not always—choose the relation with the smallest cardinality as the one to do the substitution on). The principal objectives of the optimization process as a whole are to avoid having to build Cartesian products and to keep the number of tuples to be scanned to a minimum at each stage.

Reference [18.34] does not discuss the optimization of one-variable queries. However, information regarding that level of optimization is given in the Ingres overview paper [8.11]. Basically, it is similar to the analogous function in other systems, involving as it does the use of statistical information kept in the catalog and the choice of a particular access path (e.g., a hash or index) for scanning the data as stored. Reference [18.35] presents experimental evidence—measurements from a benchmark set of queries—that suggests that the Ingres optimization techniques sketched in this section are basically sound and in practice quite effective. Some specific conclusions from that paper are the following:

1. Detachment is the best first move.

2. If tuple substitution *must* be done first, then the best choice of variable to be substituted for is a join variable.

3. Once tuple substitution has been applied to one variable in a two-variable query, it is an excellent tactic to build an index or hash "on the fly," if necessary, on the join attribute in the other relation (Ingres in fact often applies this tactic).

18.7 IMPLEMENTING THE RELATIONAL OPERATORS

We now present a short description of some straightforward methods for implementing certain of the relational operators, join in particular. Our primary reason for including this material is simply to remove any remaining air of mystery that might possibly still surround the optimization process. The methods to be discussed correspond to what we called "low-level procedures" in Section 18.3. *Note:* More sophisticated techniques are described in the annotation to some of the references at the end of the chapter. See also Appendix A.

We assume for simplicity that tuples and relations are physically stored as such. The operators we consider are project, join, and summarize—where we take "summarize" to include both of the following cases:

1. The PER operand specifies no attributes at all ("PER TABLE_DEE").

2. The PER operand specifies at least one attribute.

Case 1 is straightforward: Basically, it involves scanning the entire relation over which the summarizing is to be done—except that, if the attribute to be aggregated happens to be indexed, it might be possible to compute the result directly from the index, without having to access the relation itself at all. For example, the expression

```
SUMMARIZE SP ADD SUM ( QTY ) AS TQ
```

can be evaluated by scanning the QTY index (assuming such an index exists) without touching the shipments *per se* at all. An analogous remark applies if SUM is replaced by COUNT or AVG (for COUNT, any index will do). As for MAX and MIN, the result can be found *in a single access* to the last index entry (for MAX) or the first (for MIN), assuming again that an index exists for the relevant attribute.

For the rest of this section we take "summarize" to mean Case 2 specifically. Here is an example of Case 2:

```
SUMMARIZE SP PER P { P# } ADD SUM ( QTY ) AS TOTQTY
```

From the user's point of view, project, join, and summarize (Case 2) are very different from one another. From an implementation point of view, however, they do have certain similarities, because in every case the system needs to group tuples on the basis of common values for specified attributes. In the case of projection, such grouping allows the system to eliminate duplicates; in the case of join, it allows it to find matching tuples; and in the case of summarize, it allows it to compute the individual aggregate values for each group. There are several techniques for performing such grouping:

1. Brute force
2. Index lookup
3. Hash lookup
4. Merge
5. Hash
6. Combinations of 1–5

Figs. 18.4–18.8 give pseudocode procedures for the case of join specifically (project and summarize are left as an exercise). The notation used in those figures is as follows: R and S are the relations to be joined; C is their (possibly composite) common attribute. We assume it is possible to access the tuples of each of R and S one at a time in some sequence, and we denote those tuples, in that sequence, by $R[1]$, $R[2]$, ..., $R[m]$ and $S[1]$, $S[2]$, ..., $S[n]$, respectively. We use the expression $R[i] * S[j]$ to denote the joined tuple formed from the tuples $R[i]$ and $S[j]$. Finally, we refer to R and S as the outer and inner relation, respectively (because they control the outer and inner loop, respectively).

Brute Force

Brute force is what might be termed "the plain case," in which all possible tuple combinations are inspected (i.e., every tuple of R is examined in conjunction with every tuple of S, as indicated in Fig. 18.4). *Note:* Brute force is often referred to as "nested loops" in the literature, but this name is misleading because nested loops are in fact involved in all of the algorithms.

```
do i := 1 to m ;                              /* outer loop */
   do j := 1 to n ;                           /* inner loop */
      if R[i].C = S[j].C then
         add joined tuple R[i] * S[j] to result ;
   end ;
end ;
```

Fig. 18.4 Brute force

Let us examine the costs associated with the brute-force approach. *Note:* We limit our attention here to I/O costs only, although other costs (e.g., CPU costs) might also be important in practice.

First of all, the approach clearly requires a total of $m + (m * n)$ tuple reads. But what about tuple writes?—that is, what is the cardinality of the joined result? (The number of tuple writes will be equal to that cardinality if the result is written back out to the disk.)

- In the common special case of a many-to-one join (in particular, a foreign-to-matching-candidate-key join), the cardinality of the result is clearly equal to the cardinality, m or n, of whichever of R and S represents the foreign-key side of the join.

- Now consider the more general case of a many-to-many join. Let dCR be the number of distinct values of the join attribute C in relation R, and let dCS be defined analogously. If we assume *uniform value distributions* (so that any given value of C in relation R is as likely to occur as any other), then for a given tuple of R there will be n/dCS tuples of S with the same value for C as that tuple; hence, the total number of tuples in the join (i.e., the cardinality of the result) will be $(m * n)/dCS$. Or, if we start by considering a given tuple of S instead of R, the total number will be $(n * m)/dCR$; the two estimates will differ if $dCR \neq dCS$ (i.e., if there are some values of C that occur in R but not in S or *vice versa*), in which case the lower estimate is the one to use.

In practice, as stated in Section 18.2, it is *page* I/O's that matter, not tuple I/O's. Suppose, therefore, that the tuples of R and S are stored pR to a page and pS to a page, respectively (so that the two relations occupy m/pR pages and n/pS pages, respectively). Then it is easy to see that the procedure of Fig. 18.4 will involve $(m/pR) + (m * n)/pS$ page reads. Alternatively, if we interchange the roles of R and S (making S the outer relation and R the inner), the number of page reads will be $(n/pS) + (n * m)/pR$.

By way of example, suppose $m = 100$, $n = 10,000$, $pR = 1$, $pS = 10$. Then the two formulas evaluate to 100,100 and 1,001,000 page reads, respectively. *Conclusion:* It is desirable in the brute-force approach for the smaller relation of the two to be chosen as the outer relation (where *smaller* means "smaller number of pages").

We conclude this brief discussion of the brute-force technique by observing that it should be regarded as a worst-case procedure; it assumes that relation S is neither indexed nor hashed on the join attribute C. Experiments by Bitton *et al.* [18.6] indicate that, if that assumption is in fact valid, matters will usually be improved by constructing an index or hash on the fly and then proceeding with an index- or hash-lookup join (see the next two subsections). Reference [18.35] supports this idea, as mentioned at the end of the previous section.

Index Lookup

We now consider the case in which there is an index X on attribute C of the inner relation S (refer to Fig. 18.5). The advantage of this technique over brute force is that for a given tuple of the outer relation R we can go "directly" to the matching tuples of the inner relation S. The total number of tuple reads on relations R and S is thus simply the cardinality of the joined result; making the worst-case assumption that every tuple read on S is in fact a separate page read, the total number of page reads is thus $(m/pR) + ((m * n)/dCS)$.

```
/* assume index X on S.C */

do i := 1 to m ;                            /* outer loop */
   /* let there be k index entries X[1], ..., X[k] with    */
   /* indexed attribute value = R[i].C                     */
   do j := 1 to k ;                         /* inner loop */
      /* let tuple of S indexed by X[j] be S[j] */
      add joined tuple R[i] * S[j] to result ;
   end ;
end ;
```

Fig. 18.5   Index lookup

If relation S happens to be stored in sequence by values of the join attribute C, however, the page-read figure reduces to $(m/pR) + ((m * n)/dCS)/pS$. Taking the same sample values as before ($m = 100$, $n = 10,000$, $pR = 1$, $pS = 10$), and assuming $dCS = 100$, the two formulas evaluate to 10,100 and 1,100, respectively. The difference between these two figures clearly points up the importance of keeping stored relations in a "good" physical sequence [18.7].

However, we must include the overhead for accessing the index X itself. The worst-case assumption is that each tuple of R requires an "out of the blue" index lookup to find the matching tuples of S, which implies reading one page from each level of the index. For an index of x levels, this will add an extra $m * x$ page reads to the overall page-read figure. In practice, x will typically be 3 or less (moreover, the top level of the index will very likely reside in main memory throughout processing, thereby reducing the page-read figure still further).

Hash Lookup

Hash lookup is similar to index lookup, except that the "fast access path" to the inner relation S on the join attribute $S.C$ is a hash instead of an index (refer to Fig. 18.6). Derivation of cost estimates for this case is left as an exercise.

```
/* assume hash table H on S.C */

do i := 1 to m ;                                      /* outer loop */
   k := hash (R[i].C) ;
   /* let there be h tuples S[1], ..., S[h] stored at H[k] */
   do j := 1 to h ;                                   /* inner loop */
      if S[j].C = R[i].C then
      add joined tuple R[i] * S[j] to result ;
   end ;
end ;
```

Fig. 18.6   Hash lookup

Merge

The merge technique assumes that the two relations R and S are both physically stored in sequence by values of the join attribute C. If such is in fact the case, the two relations can be scanned in physical sequence, the two scans can be synchronized, and the entire join can be done in a single pass over the data (at least, this claim is true if the join is one-to-many; it might not be quite true for the many-to-many case). Such a technique is unquestionably optimal under our stated assumptions, because every page is accessed just once (refer to Fig. 18.7). In other words, the number of page reads is just $(m/pR) + (n/pS)$. It follows that:

- Physical clustering of logically related data is one of the most critical performance factors of all; that is, it is highly desirable that data be clustered in such a way as to match the joins that are most important to the enterprise [18.7].

- In the absence of such clustering, it is often a good idea to sort either or both relations at run time and then do a merge join anyway (of course, the effect of such sorting is precisely to produce the desired clustering dynamically). This technique is referred to, logically enough, as **sort/merge** [18.8].

```
/* assume R and S are both sorted on attribute C ; */
/* following code assumes join is many-to-many ;   */
/* simpler many-to-one case is left as an exercise */

r := 1 ;
s := 1 ;
do while r ≤ m and s ≤ n ;                         /* outer loop */
   v := R[r].C ;
   do j := s by 1 while S[j].C < v ;
   end ;
   s := j ;
   do j := s by 1 while S[j].C = v ;    /* main inner loop */
      do i := r by 1 while R[i].C = v ;
         add joined tuple R[i] * S[j] to result ;
      end ;
   end ;
   s := j ;
   do i := r by 1 while R[i].C = v ;
   end ;
   r := i ;
end ;
```

Fig. 18.7   Merge (many-to-many case)

Hash

Like the merge technique just discussed, the hash technique requires a single pass over each of the two relations (refer to Fig. 18.8). The first pass builds a hash table for relation S on values of the join attribute $S.C$; the entries in that table contain the join-attribute value—possibly other attribute values also—and a pointer to the corresponding tuple on the disk. The second pass then scans relation R and applies the same hash function to the join attribute $R.C$. When an R tuple collides in the hash table with one or more S tuples, the algorithm checks to see that the values of $R.C$ and $S.C$ are indeed equal, and if so generates the appropriate joined tuple(s). The great advantage of this technique over the merge technique is that relations R and S do not need to be stored in any particular order, and no sorting is necessary.

As with the hash-lookup technique, we leave the derivation of cost estimates for this approach as an exercise.

```
/* build hash table H on S.C */

do j := 1 to n ;
    k := hash (S[j].C) ;
    add S[j] to hash table entry H[k] ;
end ;

/* now do hash lookup on R */
```

Fig. 18.8   Hash

18.8   SUMMARY

Optimization represents both a challenge and an opportunity for relational systems. In fact, optimizability is a strength of such systems, for several reasons; a relational system with a good optimizer might well outperform a nonrelational system. Our introductory example gave some idea of the kind of improvement that might be achievable (a factor of over 10,000 to 1 in that particular case). The four broad stages of optimization are:

1. Cast the query into some **internal form** (typically a **query tree** or **abstract syntax tree**, but such representations can be thought of as just an internal form of the relational algebra or relational calculus).

2. Convert to **canonical form**, using various **laws of transformation.**

3. Choose candidate **low-level procedures** for implementing the various operations in the canonical representation of the query.

4. Generate **query plans** and choose the cheapest, using **cost formulas** and knowledge of **database statistics.**

Next, we discussed the general **distributive, commutative,** and **associative** laws and their applicability to relational operators such as join (also their applicability to **arithmetic, logical,** and **comparison** operators), and we mentioned the **idempotence** and

absorption laws. We also discussed some specific transformations for the **restriction** and **projection** operators. Then we introduced the important idea of **semantic** transformations—that is, transformations based on the system's knowledge of **integrity constraints**.

By way of illustration, we sketched some of the database statistics maintained by the **DB2** and **Ingres** products. Then we described a divide-and-conquer strategy called **query decomposition** (which was introduced with the Ingres prototype), and we mentioned that such strategies might be very attractive in a parallel-processing or distributed environment.

Finally, we examined certain **implementation techniques** for certain of the relational operators, especially **join**. We presented pseudocode algorithms for five join techniques—**brute force**, **index lookup**, **hash lookup**, **merge** (including **sort/merge**), and **hash**—and briefly considered the costs associated with these techniques.

We should not close this section without mentioning the fact that many of today's products do unfortunately include certain **optimization inhibitors,** which users should at least be aware of (even though there is little they can do about them, in most cases). An optimization inhibitor is a feature of the system in question that prevents the optimizer from doing as good a job as it might do otherwise (i.e., in the absence of that feature). The inhibitors in question include *duplicate rows* (see reference [6.6]), *three-valued logic* (see Chapter 19), and *SQL's implementation of three-valued logic* (see references [19.6] and [19.10]).

One last point: In this chapter, we have discussed optimization as conventionally understood and conventionally implemented; in other words, we have described "the conventional wisdom." More recently, however, a radically new approach to DBMS implementation has emerged, an approach that has the effect of invalidating many of the assumptions underlying that conventional wisdom. As a consequence, many aspects of the overall optimization process can be simplified (even eliminated entirely, in some cases), including:

- The use of *cost-based access path selection* (Stages 3 and 4 of the process)
- The use of *indexes* and other conventional access paths
- The choice between *compiling* and *interpreting* database requests
- The algorithms for *implementing the relational operators*

and many others. See Appendix A for further discussion.

EXERCISES

18.1   Some of the following pairs of expressions on the suppliers-parts-projects database are equivalent and some not. Which ones are?

```
a1.  S JOIN ( ( P JOIN J ) WHERE CITY = 'London' )

a2.  ( P WHERE CITY = 'London' ) JOIN ( J JOIN S )

b1.  ( S MINUS ( ( S JOIN SPJ ) WHERE P# = P# ('P2') )
                { S#, SNAME, STATUS, CITY } ) { S#, CITY }

b2.  S { S#, CITY } MINUS
        ( S { S#, CITY } JOIN
            ( SPJ WHERE P# = P# ('P2') ) ) { S#, CITY }
```

```
c1.  ( S { CITY } MINUS P { CITY } ) MINUS J { CITY }

c2.  ( S { CITY } MINUS J { CITY } )
         MINUS ( P { CITY } MINUS J { CITY } )

d1.  ( J { CITY } INTERSECT P { CITY } ) UNION S { CITY }

d2.  J { CITY } INTERSECT ( S { CITY } UNION P { CITY } )

e1.  ( ( SPJ WHERE S# = S# ('S1') )
                        UNION ( SPJ WHERE P# = P# ('P1') ) )
     INTERSECT
     ( ( SPJ WHERE J# = J# ('J1') )
                        UNION ( SPJ WHERE S# = S# ('S1') ) )

e2.  ( SPJ WHERE S# = S# ('S1') ) UNION
     ( ( SPJ WHERE P# = P# ('P1') ) INTERSECT
     ( SPJ WHERE J# = J# ('J1') ) )

f1.  ( S WHERE CITY = 'London' ) UNION ( S WHERE STATUS > 10 )

f2.  S WHERE CITY = 'London' AND STATUS > 10

g1.  ( S { S# } INTERSECT ( SPJ WHERE J# = J# ('J1') ) { S# } )
         UNION ( S WHERE CITY = 'London' ) { S# }

g2.  S { S# } INTERSECT ( ( SPJ WHERE J# = J# ('J1') ) { S# }
                   UNION ( S WHERE CITY = 'London' ) { S# } )

h1.  ( SPJ WHERE J# = J# ('J1') ) { S# }
         MINUS ( SPJ WHERE P# = P# ('P1') ) { S# }

h2.  ( ( SPJ WHERE J# = J# ('J1') )
         MINUS ( SPJ WHERE P# = P# ('P1') ) ) { S# }

i1.  S JOIN ( P { CITY } MINUS J { CITY } )

i2.  ( S JOIN P { CITY } ) MINUS ( S JOIN J { CITY } )
```

18.2   Show that join, union, and intersection are commutative and difference is not.

18.3   Show that join, union, and intersection are associative and difference is not.

18.4   Show that (a) union distributes over intersection; (b) intersection distributes over union.

18.5   Prove the absorption laws.

18.6   Show that (a) restriction is unconditionally distributive over union, intersection, and difference, and conditionally distributive over join; (b) projection is unconditionally distributive over union and intersection, is conditionally distributive over join, and is not distributive over difference. State the relevant conditions in the conditional cases.

18.7   Extend the transformation rules of Section 18.4 to take account of extend and summarize.

18.8   Can you find any useful transformation rules for the relational division operation?

18.9   Give an appropriate set of transformation rules for conditional expressions involving AND, OR, and NOT. An example of such a rule would be "commutativity of AND"—that is, *A* AND *B* is the same as *B* AND *A*.

18.10   Extend your answer to the previous exercise to include boolean expressions involving the quantifiers EXISTS and FORALL. An example of such a rule would be the rule given in Chapter 8 (Section 8.2) that allows an expression involving a FORALL to be converted into one involving a negated EXISTS instead.

18.11   Here is a list of integrity constraints for the suppliers-parts-projects database (extracted from the exercises in Chapter 9):

■ The only legal cities are London, Paris, Rome, Athens, Oslo, Stockholm, Madrid, and Amsterdam.

- No two projects can be located in the same city.
- At most one supplier can be located in Athens at any one time.
- No shipment can have a quantity more than double the average of all such quantities.
- The highest-status supplier must not be located in the same city as the lowest-status supplier.
- Every project must be located in a city in which there is at least one supplier of that project.
- There must exist at least one red part.
- The average supplier status must be greater than 19.
- Every London supplier must supply part P2.
- At least one red part must weigh less than 50 pounds.
- Suppliers in London must supply more different kinds of parts than suppliers in Paris.
- Suppliers in London must supply more parts in total than suppliers in Paris.

And here are some sample queries against that database:

- a. Get suppliers who do not supply part P2.
- b. Get suppliers who do not supply any project in the same city as the supplier.
- c. Get suppliers such that no supplier supplies fewer kinds of parts.
- d. Get Oslo suppliers who supply at least two distinct Paris parts to at least two distinct Stockholm projects.
- e. Get pairs of colocated suppliers who supply pairs of colocated parts.
- f. Get pairs of colocated suppliers who supply pairs of colocated projects.
- g. Get parts supplied to at least one project only by suppliers not in the same city as that project.
- h. Get suppliers such that no supplier supplies more kinds of parts.

Use the integrity constraints to transform these queries into simpler forms (still in natural language, however; you are not asked to answer this exercise *formally*).

18.12   Investigate any DBMS that might be available to you. What expression transformations does that system perform? Does it perform any semantic transformations?

18.13   Try the following experiment: Take a simple query, say "Get names of suppliers who supply part P2," and state that query in as many different ways as you can think of in whatever query language is available to you (probably SQL). Create and populate a suitable test database, run the different versions of the query, and measure the execution times. If those times vary significantly, you have empirical evidence that the optimizer is not doing a very good job of expression transformation. Repeat the experiment with several different queries. If possible, repeat it with several different DBMSs also. *Note:* Of course, the different versions of the query should all give the same result. If not, you have probably made a mistake—or it might be an optimizer bug; if so, report it to the vendor!

18.14   Investigate any DBMS that might be available to you. What database statistics does that system maintain? How are they updated—in real time, or via some utility? If the latter, what is the utility called? How frequently is it run? How selective is it, in terms of the specific statistics that it can update on any specific execution?

18.15   We saw in Section 18.5 that among the database statistics maintained by DB2 are the second highest and second lowest value for each column of each base table. Why the *second* highest and lowest, do you think?

18.16 Several commercial products allow the user to provide hints to the optimizer. In DB2, for example, the specification OPTIMIZE FOR n ROWS on an SQL cursor declaration means the user expects to retrieve no more than n rows via the cursor in question (i.e., to execute FETCH against that cursor no more than n times). Such a specification can sometimes cause the optimizer to choose an access path that is more efficient, at least for the case where the user does in fact execute the FETCH no more than n times. Do you think such hints are a good idea? Justify your answer.

18.17 Devise a set of implementation procedures for the restriction and projection operations (along the lines of the procedures sketched for join in Section 18.7). Derive an appropriate set of cost formulas for those procedures. Assume that page I/O's are the only quantity of interest; that is, do not attempt to include CPU or other costs in your formulas. State and justify any other assumptions you make.

18.18 Read Appendix A and discuss.

REFERENCES AND BIBLIOGRAPHY

The field of optimization is huge, and growing all the time; the following list represents a relatively small selection from the vast literature on this subject. It is divided into groups, as follows:

- References [18.1–18.6] provide introductions to, or overviews of, the general optimization problem.

- References [18.7–18.14] are concerned with the efficient implementation of specific relational operations, such as join or summarize.

- References [18.15–18.32] describe a variety of techniques based on expression transformation, as discussed in Section 18.4 (in particular, references [18.25–18.28] consider *semantic* transformations).

- References [18.33–18.43] discuss the techniques used in System R, DB2, and Ingres, and the general problem of optimizing queries involving SQL-style nested subqueries.

- References [18.44–18.62] address a miscellaneous set of techniques, tricks, directions for future research, and so forth (in particular, references [18.55–18.58] consider the impact on optimization of parallel-processing techniques).

Note: Publications on optimization in distributed database and decision support systems are deliberately excluded. See Chapters 21 and 22, respectively.

18.1 Won Kim, David S. Reiner, and Don S. Batory (eds.): *Query Processing in Database Systems.* New York, N.Y.: Springer-Verlag (1985).

This book is an anthology of papers on the general topic of query processing (not just optimization). It consists of an introductory survey paper by Jarke, Koch, and Schmidt (similar but not identical to reference [18.2]), followed by groups of papers that discuss query processing in a variety of contexts: distributed databases, heterogeneous systems, view updating (reference [10.8] is the sole paper in this section), nontraditional applications (e.g., CAD/CAM), multi-statement optimization (see reference [18.47]), database machines, and physical database design.

18.2 Matthias Jarke and Jürgen Koch: "Query Optimization in Database Systems," *ACM Comp. Surv. 16,* No. 2 (June 1984).

An excellent early tutorial. The paper gives a general framework for query processing, much like the one in Section 18.3 of the present chapter, but based on the relational calculus rather than the algebra. It then discusses a large number of optimization techniques within that framework: syntactic and semantic transformations, low-level operation implementation, and algorithms for generating query plans and choosing among them. An extensive set of syntactic transformation rules for calculus expressions is given. A lengthy bibliography (not annotated) is also included; note, however, that the number of papers on the subject published since 1984 is probably an order of magnitude greater than the number prior to that time.

The paper also briefly discusses certain other related issues: the optimization of higher-level query languages (i.e., languages that are more powerful than the algebra or calculus), optimization in a distributed-database environment, and the role of database machines with respect to optimization.

18.3 Götz Graefe: "Query Evaluation Techniques for Large Databases," *ACM Comp. Surv. 25,* No. 2 (June 1993).

Another excellent tutorial, more recent than reference [18.2], with an extensive bibliography. To quote the abstract: "This survey provides a foundation for the design and implementation of query execution facilities . . . It describes a wide array of practical query evaluation techniques . . . including iterative execution of complex query evaluation plans, the duality of sort- and hash-based set-matching algorithms, types of parallel query execution and their implementation, and special operators for emerging database application domains." Recommended.

18.4 Frank P. Palermo: "A Data Base Search Problem," in Julius T. Tou (ed.), *Information Systems: COINS IV.* New York, N.Y.: Plenum Press (1974).

One of the very earliest papers on optimization (in fact, a classic). Starting from an arbitrary expression of the relational calculus, the paper first uses Codd's reduction algorithm to reduce that expression to an equivalent algebraic expression (see Chapter 8), and then introduces a number of improvements on that algorithm, among them the following:

- No tuple is ever retrieved more than once.

- Unnecessary values are discarded from a tuple as soon as that tuple is retrieved—"unnecessary values" being either values of attributes not referenced in the query or values used solely for restriction purposes. This process is equivalent to projecting the relation over the "necessary" attributes, and thus not only reduces the space required for each tuple but also reduces the number of tuples that need to be retained (in general).

- The method used to build up the result is based on a least-growth principle, so that result tends to grow slowly. This technique has the effect of reducing both the number of comparisons involved and the amount of intermediate storage required.

- An efficient technique is employed in the construction of joins, involving (a) the dynamic factoring out of values used in join terms (such as S.S# = SP.S#) into *semijoins,* which are effectively a kind of dynamically constructed secondary index—note that Palermo's semijoins are not the same thing as the semijoins of Chapter 7, *q.v.*—and (b) the use of an internal representation of each join called an *indirect join,* which makes use of internal tuple IDs to identify the tuples that participate in the join. These techniques are designed to reduce the amount of scanning needed in the construction of the join, by ensuring for each join term that the tuples concerned are logically ordered on the values of the join attributes. They also permit the dynamic determination of the best sequence in which to access the required relations.

18.5 Meikel Poess and Chris Floyd: "New TPC Benchmarks for Decision Support and Web Commerce," *ACM SIGMOD Record 29,* No. 4 (December 2000).

TPC stands for the *Transaction Processing Council,* which is an independent body that has produced several industry-standard benchmarks over the years. *TPC-C* (which is modeled after an order/entry system) is a benchmark for measuring OLTP performance. *TPC-H* and *TPC-R* are decision support benchmarks; they are designed to measure performance on *ad hoc* queries (*TPC-H*) and planned reports (*TPC-R*), respectively. *TPC-W* is designed to measure performance in an e-commerce environment. See *http://www.tpc.org* for further information, including numerous actual benchmark results.

18.6 Dina Bitton, David J. DeWitt, and Carolyn Turbyfill: "Benchmarking Database Systems: A Systematic Approach," Proc. 9th Int. Conf. on Very Large Data Bases, Florence, Italy (October/November 1983).

The first paper to describe what is now usually called "the Wisconsin benchmark" (since it was developed by the authors of the paper at the University of Wisconsin). The benchmark defines a set of relations with precisely specified attribute values, and then measures the performance of certain precisely specified algebraic operations on those relations (for example, various projections, involving different degrees of duplication in the attributes over which the projections are taken). It thus represents a systematic test of the effectiveness of the optimizer on those fundamental operations.

18.7 M. W. Blasgen and K. P. Eswaran: "Storage and Access in Relational Databases," *IBM Sys. J. 16,* No. 4 (1977).

Several techniques for handling queries involving restriction, projection, and join operations are compared on the basis of their cost in disk I/O. The techniques in question are basically those implemented in System R [18.33].

18.8 T. H. Merrett: "Why Sort/Merge Gives the Best Implementation of the Natural Join," *ACM SIGMOD Record 13,* No. 2 (January 1983).

Presents a set of intuitive arguments to support the position statement of the title. The argument is essentially that:

a. The join operation itself will be most efficient if the two relations are each sorted on values of the join attribute (because in that case, as we saw in Section 18.7, merge is the obvious technique, and each data page will be retrieved exactly once, which is clearly optimal).

b. The cost of sorting the relations into that desired sequence, on a large enough machine, is likely to be less than the cost of any scheme for getting around the fact that they are not so sorted.

   However, the author does admit that there could be some exceptions to his somewhat contentious position. For instance, one of the relations might be sufficiently small—that is, it might be the result of a previous restriction operation—that direct access to the other relation via an index or a hash could be more efficient than sorting it. References [18.9–18.11] give further examples of cases where sort/merge might not be the best technique in practice.

18.9 Giovanni Maria Sacco: "Fragmentation: A Technique for Efficient Query Processing," *ACM TODS 11,* No. 2 (June 1986).

Presents a divide-and-conquer method for performing joins by recursively splitting the relations to be joined into disjoint restrictions ("fragments") and performing a series of sequential scans on those fragments. Unlike sort/merge, the technique does not require the relations to be sorted first. The paper shows that the fragmentation technique always performs better than sort/merge in the case where sort/merge requires both relations to be sorted first, and usually performs better in the case where sort/merge requires just one relation (the larger) to be sorted first. The author claims that the technique can also be applied to other operations, such as intersection and difference.

18.10 Leonard D. Shapiro: "Join Processing in Database Systems with Large Main Memories," *ACM TODS 11,* No. 3 (September 1986).

Presents three hash join algorithms, one of which is "especially efficient when the main memory available is a significant fraction of the size of one of the relations to be joined." The algorithms work by splitting the relations into disjoint partitions (i.e., restrictions) that can be processed in main memory. The author contends that hash methods are destined to become the technique of choice, given the rate at which main-memory costs are decreasing.

18.11 M. Negri and G. Pelagatti: "Distributive Join: A New Algorithm for Joining Relations," *ACM TODS 16,* No. 4 (December 1991).

Another divide-and-conquer join method. "[The method] is based on the idea that . . . it is not necessary to sort both relations completely . . . It is sufficient to sort one completely and the other only partially, thus avoiding part of the sort effort." The partial sort breaks down the affected relation into a sequence of unsorted partitions *P1, P2, ..., Pn* (somewhat as in Sacco's method [18.9], except that Sacco uses hashing instead of sorting), with the property that $MAX(Pi) < MIN(P(i+1))$ for $i = 1, 2, ..., n-1$. The paper claims that this method performs better than sort/merge.

18.12 Götz Graefe and Richard L. Cole: "Fast Algorithms for Universal Quantification in Large Databases," *ACM TODS 20,* No. 2 (June 1995).

The universal quantifier FORALL is not directly supported in SQL and is therefore not directly implemented in current commercial DBMSs either, yet it is extremely important in formulating a wide class of queries. This paper describes and compares "three known algorithms and one recently proposed algorithm for relational division, [which is] the algebra operator that embodies universal quantification," and shows that the new algorithm runs "as fast as hash (semi-)join evaluates existential quantification over the same relations" (slightly reworded). The authors conclude among other things that FORALL should be directly supported in the user language because most optimizers "do not recognize the rather indirect formulations available in SQL."

18.13 David Simmen, Eugene Shekita, and Timothy Malkemus: "Fundamental Techniques for Order Optimization," Proc. 1996 ACM SIGMOD Int. Conf. on Management of Data, Montreal, Canada (June 1996).

Presents techniques for optimizing or avoiding sorts. The techniques, which rely in part on the work of Darwen [11.7], have been implemented in DB2.

18.14 Gurmeet Singh Manku, Sridhar Rajagopalan, and Bruce G. Lindsay: "Approximate Medians and Other Quantiles in One Pass and with Limited Memory," Proc. 1998 ACM SIGMOD Int. Conf. on Management of Data, Seattle, Wash. (June 1998).

18.15 César A. Galindo-Legaria and Milind M. Joshi: "Orthogonal Optimization of Subqueries and Aggregation," Proc. 2001 ACM SIGMOD Int. Conf. on Management of Data, Santa Barbara, Calif. (May 2001).

18.16 James Miles Smith and Philip Yen-Tang Chang: "Optimizing the Performance of a Relational Algebra Database Interface," *CACM 18,* No. 10 (October 1975).

Describes the algorithms used in the "Smart Query Interface for a Relational Algebra" (SQUIRAL). The techniques used include the following:

- Transforming the original algebraic expression into an equivalent but more efficient sequence of operations, along the lines discussed in Section 18.4

- Assigning distinct operations in the transformed expression to distinct processes and exploiting concurrency and pipelining among them
- Coordinating the sort orders of the temporary relations passed between those processes
- Exploiting indexes and attempting to localize page references

This paper and reference [18.17] were probably the first to discuss expression transformations.

18.17 P. A. V. Hall: "Optimisation of a Single Relational Expression in a Relational Data Base System," *IBM J. R&D 20,* No. 3 (May 1976).

This paper describes some of the optimizing techniques used in the system PRTV [7.9]. Like SQUIRAL [18.16], PRTV begins by transforming the given algebraic expression into some more efficient form before evaluating it. A feature of PRTV is that the system does not automatically evaluate each expression as soon as it receives it; rather, it defers actual evaluation until the last possible moment (see the discussion of step-at-a-time query formulation in Chapter 7, Section 7.5). Thus, the "single relational expression" of the paper's title might actually represent an entire sequence of user operations. The optimizations described resemble those of SQUIRAL but go further in some respects. They include the following (in order of application).

- Performing restrictions as early as possible
- Combining sequences of projections into a single projection
- Eliminating redundant operations
- Simplifying expressions involving empty relations and trivial conditions
- Factoring out common subexpressions

The paper concludes with some experimental results and some suggestions for further investigations.

18.18 Matthias Jarke and Jürgen Koch: "Range Nesting: A Fast Method to Evaluate Quantified Queries," Proc. 1983 ACM SIGMOD Int. Conf. on Management of Data, San Jose, Calif. (May 1983).

Defines a version of the relational calculus that permits some additional transformation rules to be applied, and presents algorithms for evaluating expressions of that calculus. (Actually, the version in question is quite close to the tuple calculus as presented in Chapter 8.) The paper describes the optimization of a certain class of expressions of the revised calculus, called "perfect nested expressions." Methods are given for converting apparently complex queries—in particular, certain queries involving FORALL—into perfect expressions. The authors show that a large subset of the queries that arise in practice correspond to perfect expressions.

18.19 Surajit Chaudhuri and Kyuseok Shim: "Including Group-By in Query Optimization," Proc. 20th Int. Conf. on Very Large Data Bases, Santiago, Chile (September 1994).

18.20 A. Makinouchi, M. Tezuka, H. Kitakami, and S. Adachi: "The Optimization Strategy for Query Evaluation in RDB/V1," Proc. 7th Int. Conf. on Very Large Data Bases, Cannes, France (September 1981).

RDB/V1 was the prototype forerunner of the Fujitsu product AIM/RDB. This paper describes the optimization techniques used in that prototype and briefly compares them with the techniques used in the Ingres and System R prototypes. One particular technique seems to be novel: the use of dynamically obtained MAX and MIN values to induce additional restrictions. This technique has the effect of simplifying the process of choosing a join order and improving the performance of the joins themselves. As a simple example of the latter point, suppose suppliers and parts are to be joined over cities. First, the suppliers are sorted on CITY; during the sort, the maximum and minimum values, HIGH and LOW say, of S.CITY are determined. Then the restriction

```
LOW ≤ P.CITY AND P.CITY ≤ HIGH
```

can be used to reduce the number of parts that need to be inspected in building the join.

18.21 Hamid Pirahesh, Joseph M. Hellerstein, and Waqar Hasan: "Extensible Rule Based Query Rewrite Optimization in Starburst," Proc. 1992 ACM SIGMOD Int. Conf. on Management of Data, San Diego, Calif. (June 1992).

As noted in Section 18.1, "query rewrite" is expression transformation by another name. The authors claim that, rather surprisingly, commercial products do little in the way of such transformation (at least as of 1992). Be that as it may, the paper describes the expression transformation mechanism of the IBM Starburst prototype (see references [18.48], [26.19], [26.23], and [26.29, 26.30]). Suitably qualified users can add new transformation rules to the system at any time (hence the "extensible" of the paper's title).

18.22 Inderpal Singh Mumick, Sheldon J. Finkelstein, Hamid Pirahesh, and Raghu Ramakrishnan: "Magic Is Relevant," Proc. 1990 ACM SIGMOD Int. Conf. on Management of Data, Atlantic City, N.J. (May 1990).

The infelicitous term *magic* refers to an optimization technique originally developed for use with queries—especially ones involving recursion—expressed in Datalog (see Chapter 24). The present paper extends the approach to conventional relational systems, claiming on the basis of experimental measurements that it is often more effective than traditional optimization techniques (note that the query does not have to be recursive for the approach to be applicable). The basic idea is to decompose the given query into a number of smaller queries that define a set of "auxiliary relations" (somewhat as in the query decomposition approach discussed in Section 18.6), in such a way as to filter out tuples that are irrelevant to the problem at hand. The following example (expressed in relational calculus) is based on one given in the paper. The original query is:

```
{ EX.ENAME }
    WHERE EX.JOB = 'Clerk' AND
          EX.SAL > AVG ( EY WHERE EY.DEPT# = EX.DEPT#, SAL )
```

("Get names of clerks whose salary is greater than the average for their department"). If this expression is evaluated as written, the system will scan the employees tuple by tuple and hence compute the average salary for any department that employs more than one clerk several times. A traditional optimizer might therefore break down the query into the following two smaller queries:

```
WITH { EX.DEPT#,
       AVG ( EY WHERE
             EY.DEPT# = EX.DEPT#, SAL ) AS ASAL } AS T1 :

{ EMP.ENAME } WHERE EMP.JOB = 'Clerk' AND
                    EXISTS T1 ( EMP.DEPT# = T1.DEPT# AND
                                EMP.SALARY > T1.ASAL )
```

Now no department's average will be computed more than once, but some *irrelevant* averages will be computed—namely, those for departments that do not employ clerks.

The "magic" approach avoids both the repeated computations of the first approach and the irrelevant computations of the second, at the cost of generating extra "auxiliary" relations:

```
/* first auxiliary relation : name, department, and salary  */
/* for clerks                                               */
WITH ( { EMP.ENAME, EMP.DEPT#, EMP.SAL }
       WHERE EMP.JOB = 'Clerk' ) AS T1 :
```

```
/* second auxiliary relation : departments employing clerks */
WITH { T1.DEPT# } AS T2 :

/* third auxiliary relation : departments employing clerks  */
/* and corresponding average salaries                       */
WITH ( { T2.DEPT#,
         AVG ( EMP WHERE
               EMP.DEPT# = T2.DEPT#, SAL ) AS ASAL } ) AS T3 :

/* result relation */
{ T1.ENAME } WHERE EXISTS T3 ( T1.DEPT# = T3.DEPT# AND
                               T1.SAL > T3.ASAL )
```

The "magic" consists in determining exactly which auxiliary relations are needed.

See references [18.23, 18.24] immediately following and the "References and Bibliography" section in Chapter 24 for further references to "magic."

18.23 Inderpal Singh Mumick and Hamid Pirahesh: "Implementation of Magic in Starburst," Proc. 1994 ACM SIGMOD Int. Conf. on Management of Data, Minneapolis, Minn. (May 1994).

18.24 Inderpal Singh Mumick, Sheldon J. Finkelstein, Hamid Pirahesh, and Raghu Ramakrishnan: "Magic Conditions," *ACM TODS 21*, No. 1 (March 1996).

18.25 Jonathan J. King: "QUIST: A System for Semantic Query Optimization in Relational Databases," Proc. 7th Int. Conf. on Very Large Data Bases, Cannes, France (September 1981).

The paper that introduced the idea of semantic optimization (see Section 18.4). It describes a prototype implementation called QUIST ("QUery Improvement through Semantic Transformation").

18.26 Sreekumar T. Shenoy and Z. Meral Ozsoyoglu: "A System for Semantic Query Optimization," Proc. 1987 ACM SIGMOD Int. Conf. on Management of Data, San Francisco, Calif. (May/June 1987).

Extends the work of King [18.25] by introducing a scheme that dynamically selects, from a potentially very large set of integrity constraints, just those that are likely to be useful in transforming a given query. The integrity constraints considered are of two basic kinds, called *implication constraints* and *subset constraints* in the paper. Such constraints are used to transform queries by eliminating redundant restrictions and joins and introducing additional restrictions on indexed attributes. Cases in which the query can be answered from the constraints alone are also handled efficiently.

18.27 Michael Siegel, Edward Sciore, and Sharon Salveter: "A Method for Automatic Rule Derivation to Support Semantic Query Optimization," *ACM TODS 17*, No. 4 (December 1992).

As explained in Section 18.4, semantic optimization makes use of integrity constraints to transform queries. However, there are several problems associated with this idea:

- How does the optimizer know which transformations will be effective (i.e., will make the query more efficient)?

- Some integrity constraints are not very useful for optimization purposes. For example, the constraint that part weights must be greater than zero, though important for integrity purposes, is essentially useless for optimization. How does the optimizer distinguish between useful and useless constraints?

- Some conditions might be valid for some states of the database—even for most states—and hence be useful for optimization purposes, and yet not strictly be integrity constraints as such. An example might be the condition "employee age is less than or equal to 50"; though not an integrity constraint *per se* (employees can be older than 50), it might well be the case that no current employee is in fact older than 50.

This paper describes the architecture for a system that addresses the foregoing issues.

18.28 Upen S. Chakravarthy, John Grant, and Jack Minker: "Logic Based Approach to Semantic Query Optimization," *ACM TODS 15,* No. 2 (June 1990).

To quote from the abstract: "In several previous papers [the authors have] described and proved the correctness of a method for semantic query optimization . . . This paper consolidates the major results of those papers, emphasizing the techniques and their applicability for optimizing relational queries. Additionally, [it shows] how this method subsumes and generalizes earlier work on semantic query optimization. [It also indicates] how semantic query optimization techniques can be extended to [recursive queries] and integrity constraints that contain disjunction, negation, and recursion."

18.29 Qi Cheng *et al.*: "Implementation of Two Semantic Query Optimization Techniques in DB2 Universal Database," Proc. 25th Int. Conf. on Very Large Data Bases, Edinburgh, Scotland (September 1999).

18.30 A. V. Aho, Y. Sagiv, and J. D. Ullman: "Efficient Optimization of a Class of Relational Expressions," *ACM TODS 4,* No. 4 (December 1979).

The relational expressions referred to in the title of this paper involve only equality restrictions ("selections"), projections, and natural joins: so-called *SPJ-expressions*. SPJ-expressions correspond to calculus queries in which the *<bool exp>* in the WHERE clause involves only equality comparisons, ANDs, and existential quantifiers. The paper introduces *tableaus* as a means of symbolically representing SPJ-expressions. A **tableau** is a rectangular array, in which columns correspond to attributes and rows to conditions: specifically, to *membership conditions,* which state that a certain (sub)tuple exists in a certain relation. Rows are logically connected by the appearance of common symbols in the rows concerned. For example, the tableau

```
S#      STATUS   CITY     P#    COLOR
        f1
b1      f1       London                 — suppliers
b1                         b2           — shipments
                           b2    Red    — parts
```

represents the query "Get status (*f1*) of suppliers (*b1*) in London who supply some red part (*b2*)." The top row of the tableau lists all attributes mentioned in the query, the next row is the "summary" row (corresponding to the proto tuple in a calculus query or the final projection in an algebraic query), and the remaining rows (as already stated) represent membership conditions. We have tagged those rows in the example to indicate the relevant relations (or relvars, rather). Notice that the "*b*"s refer to bound variables and the "*f*"s to free variables; the summary row contains only "*f*"s.

Tableaus represent another candidate for a canonical formalism for queries (see Section 18.3), except that they are not general enough to represent all possible relational expressions. (In fact, they can be regarded as a syntactic variation on Query-By-Example, one that is however strictly less powerful than QBE.) The paper gives algorithms for reducing any tableau to another, semantically equivalent tableau in which the number of rows is reduced to a minimum. Since the number of rows (not counting the top two, which are special) is one more than the number of joins in the corresponding SPJ-expression, the converted tableau represents an optimal form of the query—optimal, in the very specific sense that the number of joins is minimized. (In the example, however, the number of joins is already the minimum possible for the query, and such optimization has no effect.) The minimal tableau can then be converted if desired into some other representation for subsequent additional optimization.

The idea of minimizing the number of joins has applicability to queries formulated in terms of join views (in particular, queries formulated in terms of a "universal relation"—see the "References and Bibliography" section in Chapter 13). For example, suppose the user is presented with a view V that is defined as the join of suppliers and shipments over S#, and the user issues the query:

```
V { P# }
```

A straightforward view-processing algorithm would convert this query into the following:

```
( SP JOIN S ) { P# }
```

As pointed out in Section 18.4, however, the following query produces the same result, and does not involve a join (i.e., the number of joins has been minimized):

```
SP { P# }
```

Note therefore that, since the algorithms for tableau reduction given in the paper take into account any explicitly stated functional dependencies among the attributes, those algorithms provide a limited example of a *semantic* optimization technique.

18.31 Y. Sagiv and M. Yannakakis: "Equivalences Among Relational Expressions with the Union and Difference Operators," *JACM 27,* No. 4 (October 1980).

Extends the ideas of reference [18.30] to include queries that make use of union and difference operations.

18.32 Alon Y. Levy, Inderpal Singh Mumick, and Yehoshua Sagiv: "Query Optimization by Predicate Move-Around," Proc. 20th Int. Conf. on Very Large Data Bases, Santiago, Chile (September 1994).

18.33 P. Griffiths Selinger *et al.*: "Access Path Selection in a Relational Database System," Proc. 1979 ACM SIGMOD Int. Conf.on Management of Data, Boston, Mass. (May/June 1979).

This seminal paper discusses the optimization techniques used in System R. A query in System R is an SQL statement and thus consists of a set of "SELECT - FROM - WHERE" blocks (*query blocks*), some of which might be nested inside others. The System R optimizer first decides on an order in which to execute those query blocks; it then seeks to minimize the total cost of the query by choosing the cheapest implementation for each individual block. Note that this strategy (choosing block order first, then optimizing individual blocks) means that certain possible query plans will never be considered; in effect, it amounts to a technique for "reducing the search space" (see the remarks on this subject near the end of Section 18.3). *Note:* In the case of nested blocks, the optimizer effectively just follows the nested order as specified by the user—that is, the innermost block will be executed first, loosely speaking. See references [18.37–18.43] for criticism and further discussion of this strategy.

For a given query block, there are basically two cases to consider (the first of which can be regarded as a special case of the second):

1. For a block that involves just a restriction and/or projection of a single relation, the optimizer uses statistical information from the catalog, together with formulas (given in the paper) for estimating intermediate result sizes and low-level operation costs, to choose a strategy for performing that restriction and/or projection.

2. For a block that involves two or more relations to be joined together, with (probably) local restrictions and/or projections as well, the optimizer (a) treats each individual relation as in

Case 1 and (b) decides on a sequence for performing the joins. The two operations *a* and *b* are not independent of one another; for example, a given strategy—using a certain index, say—for accessing an individual relation *A* might well be chosen precisely because it produces tuples of *A* in the order in which they are needed to perform a subsequent join of *A* with some other relation *B*.

Joins are implemented by sort/merge, index lookup, or brute force. The paper stresses the point that, in evaluating (for example) the nested join (*A* JOIN *B*) JOIN *C*, it is not necessary to compute the join of *A* and *B* in its entirety before computing the join of the result and *C;* on the contrary, as soon as any tuple of *A* JOIN *B* has been produced, it can immediately be passed to the process that joins such tuples with tuples of *C*. Thus, it might never be necessary to materialize the relation "*A* JOIN *B*" in its entirety at all. (This general *pipelining* idea was discussed briefly in Chapter 3, Section 3.2. See also references [18.16] and [18.58].)

The paper also includes a few observations on the cost of optimization. For a join of two relations, the cost is said to be approximately equal to the cost of between 5 and 20 database retrievals, a negligible overhead if the optimized query will subsequently be executed a large number of times. (Note that System R is a compiling system—in fact, it pioneered the compiling approach—and hence an SQL statement might be optimized once and then executed many times, perhaps many thousands of times.) Optimization of complex queries is said to require "only a few thousand bytes of storage and a few tenths of a second" on an IBM System 370 Model 158. "Joins of eight tables have been optimized in a few seconds."

18.34 Eugene Wong and Karel Youssefi: "Decomposition—A Strategy for Query Processing," *ACM TODS 1,* No. 3 (September 1976).

18.35 Karel Youssefi and Eugene Wong: "Query Processing in a Relational Database Management System," Proc. 5th Int. Conf. on Very Large Data Bases, Rio de Janeiro, Brazil (September 1979).

18.36 Lawrence A. Rowe and Michael Stonebraker: "The Commercial Ingres Epilogue," in reference [8.10].

"Commercial Ingres" is the product that grew out of the "University Ingres" prototype. Some of the differences between the University and Commercial Ingres optimizers are as follows:

1. The University optimizer used "incremental planning"—that is, it decided what to do first, did it, decided what to do next on the basis of the size of the result of the previous step, and so on. The Commercial optimizer decides on a complete plan before beginning execution, based on estimates of intermediate result sizes.

2. The University optimizer handled two-variable (i.e., join) queries by tuple substitution, as explained in Section 18.6. The Commercial optimizer supports a variety of preferred techniques for handling such queries, including in particular the sort/merge technique described in Section 18.7.

3. The Commercial optimizer uses a much more sophisticated set of statistics than the University optimizer.

4. The University optimizer did incremental planning, as noted under point 1. The Commercial optimizer does a more exhaustive search. However, the search process stops if the time spent on optimization exceeds the current best estimate of the time required to execute the query (for otherwise the overhead of doing the optimization might well outweigh the advantages).

5. The Commercial optimizer considers all possible index combinations, all possible join sequences, and "all available join methods—sort/merge, partial sort/merge, hash lookup, ISAM lookup, B-tree lookup, and brute force" (see Section 18.7).

18.37 Won Kim: "On Optimizing an SQL-Like Nested Query," *ACM TODS 7,* No. 3 (September 1982).

See the annotation to reference [18.41].

18.38 Werner Kiessling: "On Semantic Reefs and Efficient Processing of Correlation Queries with Aggregates," Proc. 11th Int. Conf. on Very Large Data Bases, Stockholm, Sweden (August 1985).

See the annotation to reference [18.41].

18.39 Richard A. Ganski and Harry K. T. Wong: "Optimization of Nested SQL Queries Revisited," Proc. 1987 ACM SIGMOD Int. Conf. on Management of Data, San Francisco, Calif. (May 1987).

See the annotation to reference [18.41].

18.40 Günter von Bültzingsloewen: "Translating and Optimizing SQL Queries Having Aggregates," Proc. 13th Int. Conf. on Very Large Data Bases, Brighton, UK (September 1987).

See the annotation to reference [18.41].

18.41 M. Muralikrishna: "Improved Unnesting Algorithms for Join Aggregate SQL Queries," Proc. 18th Int. Conf. on Very Large Data Bases, Vancouver, Canada (August 1992).

The SQL language includes the concept of a "nested subquery"—that is, a SELECT - FROM - WHERE block that is nested inside another such block, loosely speaking (see Chapter 8). This construct has caused implementers much grief. Consider the following SQL query ("Get names of suppliers who supply part P2"), which we will refer to as Query Q1:

```
SELECT  S.SNAME
FROM    S
WHERE   S.S# IN
      ( SELECT  SP.S#
        FROM    SP
        WHERE   SP.P# = P# ('P2') ) ;
```

In System R [18.33], this query is implemented by (a) evaluating the inner block first to yield a temporary table, T say, containing supplier *numbers* for the required suppliers, and then (b) searching table S one row at a time, and, for each such row, searching table T to see if it contains the corresponding supplier number. This strategy is likely to be quite inefficient (especially as table T will not be indexed).

Now consider the following query (Query Q2):

```
SELECT  S.SNAME
FROM    S, SP
WHERE   S.S# = SP.S#
AND     SP.P# = P# ('P2') ;
```

This query is readily seen to be semantically identical to the previous one, but System R will now consider additional implementation strategies for it. In particular, if tables S and SP happen to be physically stored in supplier number sequence, it will use a merge join, which will be very efficient. And given that (a) the two queries are logically equivalent but (b) the second is more immediately susceptible to efficient implementation, the possibility of transforming queries of type Q1 into queries of type Q2 seems worth exploring. That possibility is the subject of references [18.37–18.43].

Kim [18.37] was the first to address the problem. Five types of nested queries were identified and corresponding transformation algorithms described. Kim's paper included some experimental measurements that showed that the proposed algorithms improved the performance of nested queries by (typically) one to two orders of magnitude.

Subsequently, Kiessling [18.38] showed that Kim's algorithms did not work correctly if a nested subquery (at any level) included a COUNT operator in its SELECT list (it did not properly handle the case where the COUNT argument evaluated to an empty set). The "semantic reefs" of the paper's title referred to the SQL awkwardnesses and complexities that users have to navigate around in order to get correct answers to such queries. Furthermore, Kiessling also showed that Kim's algorithm was not easy to fix ("there seems to be no uniform way to do these transformations efficiently and correctly under all circumstances").

The paper by Ganski and Wong [18.39] provides a fix to the problem identified by Kiessling, by using an *outer join* (see Chapter 19) instead of the regular inner join in the transformed version of the query. (The fix is not totally satisfactory, in the present writer's opinion, because it introduces an undesirable ordering dependence among the operators in the transformed query.) The paper also identifies a further bug in Kim's original paper, which it fixes in the same way. However, the transformations in this paper contain additional bugs of their own, some having to do with the problem of duplicate rows (a notorious "semantic reef") and others with the flawed behavior of the SQL EXISTS quantifier (see Chapter 19).

The paper by von Bültzingsloewen [18.40] represents an attempt to put the entire topic on a theoretically sound footing (the basic problem being that, as several writers have observed, the behavior—both syntactic and semantic—of SQL-style nesting and aggregation is not well understood). It defines extended versions of both the relational calculus and the relational algebra (the extensions having to do with aggregates and nulls), and proves the equivalence of those two extended formalisms (using, incidentally, a new method of proof that seems more elegant than those previously published). It then defines the semantics of SQL by mapping SQL into the extended calculus just defined. However, it should be noted that:

1. The dialect of SQL discussed, though closer to the dialect typically supported in commercial products than that of references [18.37–18.39], is still not fully orthodox: It does not include UNION, it does not directly support operators of the form "=ALL" or ">ALL" (see Appendix B), and its treatment of *unknown* truth values—see Chapter 19—is different from (actually better than) that of conventional SQL.

2. The paper omits consideration of matters having to do with duplicate elimination "for technical simplification." But the implications of this omission are not clear, given that (as already indicated) the possibility of duplicates has significant consequences for the validity or otherwise of certain transformations [6.6].

Finally, Muralikrishna [18.41] claims that Kim's original algorithm [18.37], though incorrect, can still be more efficient than "the general strategy" of reference [18.39] in some cases, and therefore proposes an alternative correction to Kim's algorithm. It also provides some additional improvements.

18.42 Lars Baekgaard and Leo Mark: "Incremental Computation of Nested Relational Query Expressions," *ACM TODS 20,* No. 2 (June 1995).

Another paper on the optimization of queries involving SQL-style subqueries, especially *correlated* ones. The strategy is (1) to convert the original query into an unnested equivalent and then (2) to evaluate the unnested version incrementally. "To support step (1), we have developed a very concise algebra-to-algebra transformation algorithm . . . The [transformed] expression makes intensive use of the [MINUS] operator. To support step (2), we present and analyze an efficient algorithm for incrementally evaluating [MINUS operations]." The term *incremental computation* refers to the idea that evaluation of a given query can make use of previously computed results.

18.43 Jun Rao and Kenneth A. Ross: "Using Invariants: A New Strategy for Correlated Queries," Proc. 1998 ACM SIGMOD Int. Conf. on Management of Data, Seattle, Wash. (June 1998).

Yet another paper on the optimization of queries involving SQL-style subqueries.

18.44 David H. D. Warren: "Efficient Processing of Interactive Relational Database Queries Expressed in Logic," Proc. 7th Int. Conf. on Very Large Data Bases, Cannes, France (September 1981).

Presents a view of query optimization from a rather different perspective: namely, that of formal logic. The paper reports on techniques used in an experimental database system based on Prolog. The techniques are apparently very similar to those of System R, although they were arrived at quite independently and with somewhat different objectives. The paper suggests that, in contrast to conventional query languages such as QUEL and SQL, logic-based languages such as Prolog permit queries to be expressed in such a manner as to highlight:

- What the essential components of the query are: namely, the logic goals
- What it is that interrelates those components: namely, the logic variables
- What the crucial implementation problem is: namely, the sequence in which to try to satisfy the goals

As a consequence, it is suggested that such a language is very convenient as a base for optimization. Indeed, it could be regarded as yet another candidate for the internal representation of queries originally expressed in some other language (see Section 18.3).

18.45 Yannis E. Ioannidis and Eugene Wong: "Query Optimization by Simulated Annealing," Proc. 1987 ACM SIGMOD Int. Conf. on Management of Data, San Francisco, Calif. (May 1987).

The number of possible query plans grows exponentially with the number of relations involved in the query. In conventional commercial applications, the number of relations in a query tends to be small and so the number of candidate plans (the "search space") usually stays within reasonable bounds. In newer applications, however, the number of relations in a query can easily become quite large (see Chapter 22). Furthermore, such applications are also likely to need "global" (i.e., multi-query) optimization [18.47] and recursive query support, both of which also have the potential for increasing the search space significantly. Exhaustive search rapidly becomes out of the question in such an environment; some effective technique of reducing the search space becomes imperative.

The present paper gives references to previous work on the problems of optimization for large numbers of relations and multi-query optimization, but claims that no previous algorithms have been published for recursive-query optimization. It then presents an algorithm that it claims is suitable whenever the search space is large, and in particular shows how to apply that algorithm to the recursive case. The algorithm (called *simulated annealing* because it models the annealing process by which crystals are grown by first heating the containing fluid and then allowing it to cool gradually) is a probabilistic, hill-climbing algorithm that has successfully been applied to optimization problems in other contexts.

18.46 Arun Swami and Anoop Gupta: "Optimization of Large Join Queries," Proc. 1988 ACM SIGMOD Int. Conf. on Management of Data, Chicago, Ill. (June 1988).

The general problem of determining the optimal join order in queries involving large numbers of relations (as arise in connection with, e.g., deductive database systems—see Chapter 24) is combinatorially hard. This paper presents a comparative analysis of a number of algorithms that address this problem: perturbation walk, quasi-random sampling, iterative improvement, sequence heuristic, and simulated annealing [18.45] (the names add a pleasing element of poetry to a subject that might otherwise be thought a trifle prosaic). According to that analysis, iterative improvement is superior to all of the other algorithms; in particular, simulated annealing is not useful "by itself" for large join queries.

18.47 Timos K. Sellis: "Multiple-Query Optimization," *ACM TODS 13,* No. 1 (March 1988).

Classical optimization research has focused on the problem of optimizing individual relational expressions in isolation. In future, however, the ability to optimize several distinct queries as a unit is likely to become important. One reason for this state of affairs is that what starts out as a single query at some higher level of the system might give rise to several queries at the relational level. For example, the natural language query "Is Mike well paid?" might require the execution of three separate relational queries:

- "Does Mike earn more than $75,000?"
- "Does Mike earn more than $60,000 and have less than five years of experience?"
- "Does Mike earn more than $45,000 and have less than three years of experience?"

This example illustrates the point that sets of related queries are likely to share some common subexpressions, and hence lend themselves to global optimization.

The paper considers queries involving conjunctions of restrictions and/or equijoins only. Some encouraging experimental results are included, and directions are identified for future research.

18.48 Guy M. Lohman: "Grammar-Like Functional Rules for Representing Query Optimization Alternatives," Proc. 1988 ACM SIGMOD Int. Conf. on Management of Data, Chicago, Ill. (June 1988).

In some respects, a relational optimizer can be regarded as an expert system; however, the rules that drive the optimization process have historically been embedded in procedural code, not separately and declaratively stated. As a consequence, extending the optimizer to incorporate new optimization techniques has not been easy. Future database systems (see Chapter 26) will exacerbate this problem, because there will be a clear need for individual installations to extend the optimizer to incorporate, for example, support for specific user-defined data types. Several researchers have therefore proposed structuring the optimizer as a conventional expert system, with explicitly stated declarative rules.

However, this idea suffers from certain performance problems. In particular, a large number of rules might be applicable at any given stage during query processing, and determining the appropriate one might involve complex computation. The present paper describes an alternative approach (implemented in the Starburst prototype—see reference [18.21], also references [26.19], [26.23], and [26.29, 26.30]), in which the rules are stated in the form of production rules in a grammar somewhat like the grammars used to describe formal languages. The rules, called STARs (STrategy Alternative Rules), permit the recursive construction of query plans from other plans and "low-level plan operators" (LOLEPOPs), which are basic operations on relations such as join, sort, and so on. LOLEPOPs come in various *flavors;* for example, the join LOLEPOP has a sort/merge flavor, a hash flavor, and so on.

The paper claims that the foregoing approach has several advantages: The rules (STARs) are readily understandable by people who need to define new ones, the process of determining which rule to apply in any given situation is simpler and more efficient than the more traditional expert-system approach, and the extensibility objective is met.

18.49 Ryohei Nakano: "Translation with Optimization from Relational Calculus to Relational Algebra Having Aggregate Functions," *ACM TODS 15,* No. 4 (December 1990).

As explained in Chapter 8 (Section 8.4), queries in a calculus-based language can be implemented by (a) translating the query under consideration into an equivalent algebraic expression, then (b) optimizing that algebraic expression, and finally (c) implementing that optimized expression. In this paper, Nakano proposes a scheme for combining steps *a* and *b* into a single step, thereby translating a given calculus expression directly into an *optimal* algebraic equivalent. This scheme is claimed to be "more effective and more promising . . . because it seems quite difficult to optimize complicated algebraic expressions." The translation process makes use of certain *heuristic* transformations, incorporating human knowledge regarding the equivalence of certain calculus and algebraic expressions.

18.50 Kyu-Young Whang and Ravi Krishnamurthy: "Query Optimization in a Memory-Resident Domain Relational Calculus Database System," *ACM TODS 15,* No. 1 (March 1990).

The most expensive aspect of query processing (in the specific main-memory environment assumed by this paper) is shown to be the evaluation of boolean expressions. Optimization in that environment is thus aimed at minimizing the number of such evaluations.

18.51 Johann Christoph Freytag and Nathan Goodman: "On the Translation of Relational Queries into Iterative Programs," *ACM TODS 14,* No. 1 (March 1989).

Presents methods for compiling relational expressions directly into executable code in a language such as C or Pascal. Note that this approach differs from the approach discussed in the body of the chapter, where the optimizer effectively combines *prewritten* (parameterized) code fragments to build the query plan.

18.52 Kiyoshi Ono and Guy M. Lohman: "Measuring the Complexity of Join Enumeration in Query Optimization," *Proc.* 16th Int. Conf. on Very Large Data Bases, Brisbane, Australia (August 1990).

Given that join is basically a dyadic operation, the optimizer has to break down a join involving *n* relations (*n* > 2) into a sequence of dyadic joins. Most optimizers do this in a strictly nested fashion; that is, they choose a pair of relations to join first, then a third to join to the result of joining the first two, and so on. In other words, an expression such as *A* JOIN *B* JOIN *C* JOIN *D* might be treated as, say, ((*D* JOIN *B*) JOIN *C*) JOIN *A,* but never as, say, (*A* JOIN *D*) JOIN (*B* JOIN *C*). Further, traditional optimizers are usually designed to avoid Cartesian products if at all possible. Both of these tactics can be seen as ways of "reducing the search space" (though heuristics for choosing the sequence of joins are still needed, of course).

The present paper describes the relevant aspects of the optimizer in the IBM Starburst prototype (see references [18.21], [18.48], [26.19], [26.23], and [26.29, 26.30]). It argues that both of the foregoing tactics can be inappropriate in certain situations, and hence that what is needed is an *adaptable* optimizer that can use, or be instructed to use, different tactics for different queries.

18.53 Bennet Vance and David Maier: "Rapid Bushy Join-Order Optimization with Cartesian Products," *Proc.* 1996 ACM SIGMOD Int. Conf. on Management of Data, Montreal, Canada (June 1996).

As noted in the annotation to reference [18.52], optimizers tend to "reduce the search space" by (among other things) avoiding plans that involve Cartesian products. This paper shows that searching the entire space "is more affordable than has been previously recognized" and that avoiding Cartesian products is not necessarily beneficial (in this connection, see the discussion of "star join" in Chapter 22). According to the authors, the paper's main contributions are in (a) fully separating join-order enumeration from predicate analysis and (b) presenting "novel implementation techniques" for addressing the join-order enumeration problem.

18.54 Yannis E. Ioannidis, Raymond T. Ng, Kyuseok Shim, and Timos K. Sellis: "Parametric Query Optimization," *Proc.* 18th Int. Conf. on Very Large Data Bases, Vancouver, Canada (August 1992).

Consider the following query:

```
EMP WHERE SALARY > salary
```

(where *salary* is a run-time parameter). Suppose there is an index on SALARY. Then:

- If *salary* is $10,000 per month, then the best way to implement the query is to use the index (because presumably most employees will not qualify).

- If *salary* is $1,000 per month, then the best way to implement the query is by a sequential scan (because presumably most employees *will* qualify).

This example illustrates the point that some optimization decisions are best made at run time, even in a compiling system. The present paper explores the possibility of generating *sets* of query plans at compile time (each plan being "optimal" for some subset of the set of all possible values of the run-time parameters), and then choosing the appropriate plan at run time when the actual parameter values are known. It considers one specific run-time parameter in particular, the amount of buffer space available to the query in main memory. Experimental results show that the approach described imposes very little time overhead on the optimization process and sacrifices very little in terms of quality of the generated plans; accordingly, it is claimed that the approach can significantly improve query performance. "The savings in execution cost of using a plan that is specifically tailored to actual parameter values . . . could be enormous."

18.55 Navin Kabra and David J. DeWitt: "Efficient Mid-Query Re-Optimization of Sub-Optimal Query Execution Plans," Proc. 1998 ACM SIGMOD Int. Conf. on Management of Data, Seattle, Wash. (June 1998).

18.56 Jim Gray: "Parallel Database Systems 101," Proc. 1995 ACM SIGMOD Int. Conf. on Management of Data, San Jose, Calif. (May 1995).

This is not a research paper but an extended abstract for a tutorial presentation. The basic idea behind parallel systems in general is to break a large problem into a lot of smaller ones that can be solved simultaneously, thereby improving performance (throughput and response time). Relational database systems in particular are highly amenable to parallelization because of the nature of the relational model: It is conceptually easy (a) to break relations down into subrelations in a variety of ways and (b) to break relational expressions down into subexpressions, again in a variety of ways. In the spirit of the title of this reference, we offer a few words on certain important parallel-database-system concepts.

First of all, the architecture of the underlying hardware will itself presumably involve some kind of parallelism. There are three principal architectures, each involving several processing units, several disk drives, and an interconnection network of some kind:

- *Shared memory:* The network allows all of the processors to access the same memory.

- *Shared disk:* Each processor has its own memory, but the network allows all of the processors to access all of the disks.

- *Shared nothing:* Each processor has its own memory and disks, but the network allows the processors to communicate with each other.

In practice, shared nothing is usually the architecture of choice, at least for large systems (the other two approaches quickly run into problems of *interference* as more and more processors are added). To be specific, shared nothing provides both linear **speed-up** (increasing hardware by a given factor improves response time by the same factor) and linear **scale-up** (increasing both hardware and data volume by the same factor keeps response time constant). *Note:* "Scale-up" is also known as **scalability**.

There are also several approaches to *data partitioning* (i.e., breaking a relation *r* into partitions or subrelations and assigning those partitions to *n* different processors):

- *Range partitioning:* Relation *r* is divided into disjoint partitions 1, 2, ..., *n* on the basis of values of some subset *s* of the attributes of *r* (conceptually, *r* is sorted on *s* and the result divided into *n* equal-size partitions). Partition *i* is then assigned to processor *i*. This approach is good for queries involving equality or range restrictions on *s*.

- *Hash partitioning:* Each tuple t of r is assigned to processor $i = h(t)$, where h is some hash function. This approach is good for queries involving an equality restriction on the hashed attribute(s), also for queries that involve sequential access to the entire relation r.

- *Round-robin partitioning:* Conceptually, r is sorted in some way; the ith tuple in the sorted result is then assigned to processor i modulo n. This approach is good for queries that involve sequential access to the entire relation r.

  Parallelism can apply to the execution of an individual operation (*intraoperation* parallelism), to the execution of distinct operations within the same query (*interoperation* or *intraquery* parallelism), and to the execution of distinct queries (*interquery* parallelism). Reference [18.3] includes a tutorial on all of these possibilities, and references [18.57, 18.58] discuss some specific techniques and algorithms. We remark that a parallel version of *hash join* (see Section 18.7) is particularly effective and widely used in practice.

18.57 Dina Bitton, Haran Boral, David J. DeWitt, and W. Kevin Wilkinson: "Parallel Algorithms for the Execution of Relational Database Operations," *ACM TODS 8,* No. 3 (September 1983).

  Presents algorithms for implementing sort, projection, join, aggregation, and update operations in a multi-processor environment. The paper gives general cost formulas that take into account I/O, message, and processor costs, and can be adjusted to different multi-processor architectures.

18.58 Waqar Hasan and Rajeev Motwani: "Optimization Algorithms for Exploiting the Parallelism-Communication Tradeoff in Pipelined Parallelism," Proc. 20th Int. Conf. on Very Large Data Bases, Santiago, Chile (September 1994).

18.59 Donald Kossmann and Konrad Stocker: "Iterative Dynamic Programming: A New Class of Optimization Algorithms," *ACM TODS 25,* No. 1 (March 2000).

18.60 Parke Godfrey, Jarek Gryz, and Calisto Zuzarte: "Exploiting Constraint-Like Data Characterizations in Query Optimization," Proc. 2001 ACM SIGMOD Int. Conf. on Management of Data, Santa Barbara, Calif. (May 2001).

18.61 Alin Deutsch, Lucian Poppa, and Val Tannen: "Physical Data Independence, Constraints, and Optimization with Universal Plans," Proc. 25th Int. Conf. on Very Large Data Bases, Edinburgh, Scotland (September 1999).

18.62 Michael Stillger, Guy Lohman, Volker Markl, and Mohtar Kandil: "LEO—DB2's LEarning Optimizer," Proc. 27th Int. Conf. on Very Large Data Bases, Rome, Italy (September 2001).

CHAPTER 19

Missing Information

19.1   INTRODUCTION

Information is often missing in the real world; examples such as "date of birth unknown," "speaker to be announced," "present address not known," and so on, are common and familiar to all of us. Clearly, therefore, we need some way of dealing with such missing information inside our database systems. And the approach to this problem most commonly adopted in practice—in SQL in particular, and hence in most commercial products—is based on *nulls* and *three-valued logic* (3VL). For example, we might not know the weight of some part, say part P7, and so we might say, loosely, that the weight of that part "is null"—meaning, more precisely, that (a) we do know the part exists, and of course (b) we also know it has a weight, but (c) to repeat, we do not know what that weight is.

To pursue this example a little further, consider the tuple that represents part P7 in the database. Obviously we cannot put a genuine WEIGHT value in that tuple. What we do instead, therefore, is *mark* or *flag* the WEIGHT position in that tuple as "null," and then we interpret that mark or flag to mean, precisely, that we do not know what the genuine value is. Now, we might think, informally, of that WEIGHT position as "containing a null," or of that WEIGHT value as "being null," and indeed we often talk in such terms in practice. But it should be clear that such talk *is* only informal, and indeed not very accurate; to say that the WEIGHT component of some tuple "is null" is really to say that *the tuple contains no WEIGHT value at all.* That is why the expression "null value," which is heard very frequently, is deprecated: The whole point about nulls (or a large part of the point, at any rate) is precisely that they are not values—they are, to repeat, marks or flags.

Now, we will see in the next section that any scalar comparison in which one of the comparands is null evaluates to the *unknown* truth value, instead of to *true* or *false*.[1] The justification for this state of affairs is the intended interpretation of null as "value unknown": If the value of *A* is unknown, then obviously it is unknown whether, for example, *A > B,* **regardless of the value of *B*** (even—perhaps especially—if the value of *B* is unknown as well). Note in particular, therefore, that two nulls are not considered to be equal to one another; that is, the comparison *A = B* evaluates to *unknown,* not *true,* if *A* and *B* are both null. (They are not considered to be unequal, either; that is, the comparison *A ≠ B* evaluates to *unknown* as well.) Hence the term *three-valued logic:* The concept of nulls, at least as that term is usually understood, inevitably leads us into a logic in which there are three truth values (*true, false,* and *unknown*).

Before we go any further, we should make it very clear that in our opinion (and in that of many other writers too, we hasten to add), nulls and 3VL are and always were a serious mistake and have no place in the relational model. For example, to say that a certain part tuple contains no WEIGHT value is to say, by definition, that the tuple in question is not a part tuple after all; equivalently, it is to say that the tuple in question is not an instantiation of the applicable predicate. In fact, the "tuple" in question is simply not a tuple!—as can easily be seen by reference to the definition of the term *tuple* in Chapter 6. The truth is, the very act of trying to state precisely what the nulls scheme is all about is (or should be) sufficient to show why the idea is not exactly coherent. As a consequence, it is hard to explain it coherently, too. To quote reference [11.10]: "It all makes sense if you squint a little and don't think too hard."

Be that as it may, it would not be appropriate to exclude a discussion of nulls and 3VL entirely from a book of this nature; hence the present chapter.

The plan of the chapter, then, is as follows. Following this introduction, in Section 19.2 we suspend disbelief for a while and describe as best we can the basic ideas behind nulls and 3VL, without offering much in the way of criticism of those ideas. (It is obviously not possible to criticize the ideas properly or fairly without first explaining what those ideas *are.*) Then in Section 19.3 we discuss some of the more important consequences of those ideas, in an attempt to justify our own position that nulls are a mistake. Section 19.4 considers the implications of nulls for primary and foreign keys. Section 19.5 digresses to consider an operation commonly encountered in the context of nulls and 3VL, called *outer join.* Section 19.6 very briefly considers an alternative approach to missing information, using *special values.* Section 19.7 sketches the relevant aspects of SQL. Finally, Section 19.8 presents a summary.

---

[1] Elsewhere in this book we set truth values in all uppercase. In this chapter, by contrast, we set them in lowercase italics (mainly for consistency with other publications by this author on the same topic).

One last preliminary remark: There are many reasons why we might be unable to put a genuine data value in some position within some tuple—"value unknown" is only one such reason. Others include "value not applicable," "value does not exist," "value undefined," "value not supplied," and so on [19.5].[2] Indeed, in reference [6.2] Codd proposes that the relational model should be extended to include not one but two nulls, one meaning "value unknown" and the other "value not applicable," and further proposes that DBMSs should therefore deal in terms of not three- but *four*-valued logic. We have argued against such a proposal elsewhere [19.5]; in this chapter we limit our attention to a single kind of null only, the value-unknown null, which for definiteness we will henceforward often—but not invariably—refer to as **UNK** (for unknown).

19.2   AN OVERVIEW OF THE 3VL APPROACH

In this section we briefly describe the principal components of the 3VL approach to missing information. We begin by considering (in the two subsections immediately following) the effect of nulls—meaning UNKs specifically—on boolean expressions.

Boolean Operators

We have already said that any scalar comparison in which either of the comparands is UNK evaluates to the *unknown* truth value, instead of *true* or *false,* and hence that we are dealing with three-valued logic (3VL). *Unknown* (which we will henceforward often—but not invariably—abbreviate to just *unk*) is "the third truth value." Here then are the 3VL truth tables for AND, OR, and NOT (t = *true, f* = *false, u* = *unk*):

AND	t	u	f		OR	t	u	f		NOT	
t	t	u	f		t	t	t	t		t	f
u	u	u	f		u	t	u	u		u	u
f	f	f	f		f	t	u	f		f	t

For example, suppose A = 3, B = 4, and C is UNK. Then the following expressions have the indicated truth values:

```
A > B AND B > C  :  false
A > B OR  B > C  :  unk
A < B OR  B < C  :  true
NOT ( A = C )    :  unk
```

---

[2] We remark, however, that there is no missing information, as such, in these other cases. For example, if we say that the commission for employee Joe is "not applicable," we are saying, quite explicitly, that the property of earning a commission does not apply to Joe; no information is missing here. (It is still the case, however, that if, for example, Joe's "employee tuple" "contains" a not-applicable null in the commission position, then that tuple is not an employee tuple—that is, it is not an instantiation of the "employee" predicate; in fact, it is not a tuple at all.)

AND, OR, and NOT are not the only boolean operators we need, however [19.11]; another important one is MAYBE [19.5], with truth table as follows:

```
MAYBE   |
--------+----
   t    |  f
   u    |  t
   f    |  f
```

To see why MAYBE is desirable, consider the query "Get employees who *may* be— but are not definitely known to be—programmers born before January 18, 1971, with a salary less than $50,000." With the MAYBE operator, the query can be stated quite succinctly as follows:[3]

```
EMP WHERE MAYBE ( JOB = 'Programmer' AND
                  DOB < DATE ('1971-1-18') AND
                  SALARY < 50000.00 )
```

(We have assumed that attributes JOB, DOB, and SALARY of relvar EMP are of types CHAR, DATE, and RATIONAL, respectively.) Without the MAYBE operator, however, the query has to look something like this:

```
EMP WHERE     ( JOB = 'Programmer'
                OR IS_UNK ( JOB ) )
      AND     ( DOB < DATE ('1971-1-18')
                OR IS_UNK ( DOB ) )
      AND     ( SALARY < 50000.00
                OR IS_UNK ( SALARY ) )
      AND NOT ( JOB = 'Programmer' AND
                DOB < DATE ('1971-1-18') AND
                SALARY < 50000.00 )
```

We have assumed the existence of another truth-valued operator called **IS_UNK**, which takes a single scalar operand and returns *true* if that operand evaluates to UNK and *false* otherwise. (As an aside, we note that a version of IS_UNK would be needed for nonscalars too. We make no attempt to define such a thing here, however, because the complexities involved are too daunting, and we do not really believe in 3VL support anyway.)

Incidentally, the foregoing should not be construed to mean that MAYBE is the *only* new boolean operator needed for 3VL. In practice, for example, a TRUE_OR_MAYBE operator (returning *true* if its operand evaluates to *true* or *unk, false* otherwise) might be useful [19.5]. See the annotation to reference [19.11] in the "References and Bibliography" section.

Quantifiers

Despite the fact that we use the algebra rather than the calculus as a basis for most of our examples, we do need to consider the implications of 3VL for EXISTS and FORALL. As explained in Chapter 8, we define these quantifiers as iterated OR and AND, respectively.

---

[3] It is necessary to pretend for the sake of examples in this chapter that **Tutorial D** includes support for UNKs and 3VL. In fact, of course, it does not.

In other words, if (a) *r* is a relation with tuples *t1, t2, ..., tm,* (b) *V* is a range variable that ranges over *r,* and (c) *p(V)* is a boolean expression in which *V* occurs as a free variable, then the expression

```
EXISTS V ( p ( V ) )
```

is defined to be equivalent to:

```
false OR p ( t1 ) OR ... OR p ( tm )
```

Likewise, the expression

```
FORALL V ( p ( V ) )
```

is defined to be equivalent to

```
true AND p ( t1 ) AND ... AND p ( tm )
```

So what happens if *p(ti)* evaluates to *unk* for some *i?* By way of example, let relation *r* contain exactly the following tuples:

```
(  1,   2,   3  )
(  1,   2,   UNK )
( UNK, UNK, UNK )
```

For simplicity, assume that the three attributes, in left-to-right order as shown, are called *A, B,* and *C,* respectively, and every attribute is of type INTEGER. Then the following expressions have the indicated values:

```
EXISTS V ( V.C > 1 )              :  true
EXISTS V ( V.B > 2 )              :  unk
EXISTS V ( MAYBE ( V.A > 3 ) )    :  true
EXISTS V ( IS_UNK ( V.C ) )       :  true

FORALL V ( V.A > 1 )              :  false
FORALL V ( V.B > 1 )              :  unk
FORALL V ( MAYBE ( V.C > 1 ) )    :  false
```

Other Scalar Operators

Consider the numeric expression

```
WEIGHT * 454
```

where WEIGHT represents the weight of some part. What if the weight in question happens to be UNK?—what then is the value of the expression? The answer is that it too must be considered to be UNK. In general, in fact, *any* numeric expression is considered to evaluate to UNK if any of the operands of that expression is itself UNK. Thus, for example, if WEIGHT happens to be UNK, then all of the following expressions also evaluate to UNK:

```
WEIGHT + 454      454 + WEIGHT       + WEIGHT
WEIGHT - 454      454 - WEIGHT       - WEIGHT
WEIGHT * 454      454 * WEIGHT
WEIGHT / 454      454 / WEIGHT
```

Note: Perhaps we should point out right away that the foregoing treatment of numeric expressions does give rise to certain anomalies. For example, the expression WEIGHT – WEIGHT, which should clearly yield zero, actually yields UNK, and the expression WEIGHT / 0, which should clearly raise a "zero divide" error, also yields UNK (assuming in both cases that WEIGHT is UNK in the first place). We ignore such anomalies until further notice.

Analogous considerations apply to all other scalar types and operators, except for (a) the boolean operators (see the two previous subsections), (b) the operator IS_UNK discussed earlier, and (c) the operator IF_UNK discussed in the next paragraph. Thus, for example, the character-string expression *A* || *B* returns UNK if *A* is UNK or *B* is UNK or both. (Again there are certain anomalous cases, details of which we omit here.)

The **IF_UNK** operator takes two scalar operands and returns the value of the first operand unless that operand evaluates to UNK, in which case it returns the value of the second operand instead (in other words, the operator effectively provides a way to convert an UNK to some nonUNK value). For example, suppose UNKs are permitted for the suppliers CITY attribute. Then the expression

```
EXTEND S ADD IF_UNK ( CITY, 'City unknown' ) AS SCITY
```

yields a result in which the SCITY value is "City unknown" for any supplier whose city is given as UNK in S.

Note, incidentally, that IF_UNK can be defined in terms of IS_UNK. To be specific, the expression

```
IF_UNK ( exp1, exp2 )
```

(where expressions *exp1* and *exp2* must be of the same type) is defined to be equivalent to the expression

```
IF IS_UNK ( exp1 ) THEN exp2 ELSE exp1 END IF
```

UNK Is Not *unk*

It is important to understand that UNK (the value-unknown null) and *unk* (the *unknown* truth value) are not the same thing.[4] Indeed, this state of affairs is an immediate consequence of the fact that *unk* is a value (a truth value, to be precise), whereas UNK is not a value at all. But let us be a little more specific. Suppose *X* is a variable of type BOOLEAN. Then *X* must have one of the values *true, false,* or *unk*. Thus, the statement "*X* is *unk*" means, precisely, that the value of *X* is **known to be** *unk*. By contrast, the statement "*X* is UNK" means that the value of *X* is **not known**.

Can a Type Contain an UNK?

It is also an immediate consequence of the fact that UNK is not a value that no type can contain an UNK (types are sets of *values*). Indeed, if it were possible for a given type to

---

[4] SQL thinks they are, though (see Section 19.7).

contain an UNK, then type constraint checks for that type would never fail! However, since types in fact cannot contain UNKs, a "relation" that includes an UNK—whatever else it might be—is in fact *not a relation at all,* neither by the definition we gave in Chapter 6, nor by Codd's original definition as given in reference [6.1]. We will return to this important point later.

Relational Operators

Now we turn our attention to the effect of UNKs on the operators of the relational algebra. For simplicity we limit ourselves to the operators product, restrict, project, union, and difference (the effect of UNKs on the other operators can be determined from their effect on these five).

First of all, **product** is unaffected.

Second, the **restriction** operation is (slightly) redefined to return a relation whose body contains only those tuples for which the restriction condition evaluates to *true,* that is, not to *false* and not to *unk. Note:* We were tacitly assuming this redefinition in our MAYBE example in the subsection "Boolean Operators" earlier in this section.

Next, **projection**. Projection involves the elimination of redundant duplicate tuples. Now, in conventional two-valued logic (2VL), two tuples *t1* and *t2* are duplicates of each other if and only if they are in fact the same tuple—that is, if and only if they have the same attributes *A1, A2, ..., An* and, for all *i* (*i* = 1, 2, ..., *n*), the value of *Ai* in *t1* is equal to the value of *Ai* in *t2*. But in 3VL some of those attribute values might be UNK, and UNK (as we have seen) is not equal to *anything,* not even itself. Are we then forced to conclude that a tuple that contains an UNK can never be a duplicate of anything, not even of itself?

According to Codd, the answer to this question is *no:* Two UNKs, even though they are not equal to one another, are still considered to be "duplicates" of each other for purposes of duplicate tuple elimination [14.7].[5] The apparent contradiction is explained away as follows:

> [Equality testing] for duplicate removal is ... at a lower level of detail than equality testing in the evaluation of retrieval conditions. Hence, it is possible to adopt a different rule.

We leave it to you to judge whether this rationale is reasonable; however, let us accept it for now, and hence accept the following definition:

- Two tuples *t1* and *t2* are **duplicates** of each other if and only if they have the same attributes *A1, A2, ..., An* and, for all *i* (*i* = 1, 2, ..., *n*), either the value of *Ai* in *t1* is equal to the value of *Ai* in *t2,* or *Ai* in *t1* and *Ai* in *t2* are both UNK.

With this extended definition of "duplicate tuples," the original definition of projection applies unchanged. Note, however, that it is now no longer the case that the following statements are equivalent:

---

[5] Reference [14.7] was the first of Codd's papers to discuss missing information in any detail (although that issue was not the paper's primary focus—see Chapter 14). Among other things, the paper proposes "maybe" versions of the θ-join, θ-select (i.e., restrict), and divide operators (see Exercise 19.4), and "outer" versions of the union, intersection, difference, θ-join, and natural join operators (see Section 19.5).

- *t1 = t2*
- *t1* and *t2* are duplicates of each other

Union likewise involves the elimination of redundant duplicate tuples, and the same definition of duplicate tuples applies. Thus, we define the union of two relations *r1* and *r2* (of the same type) to be that relation *r* (again of the same type) whose body consists of all possible tuples *t* such that *t* is a duplicate of some tuple of *r1* or of some tuple of *r2* (or both).

Finally—even though it does not involve any duplicate elimination as such—**difference** is defined analogously; that is, a tuple *t* appears in *r1* MINUS *r2* if and only if it is a duplicate of some tuple of *r1* and not a duplicate of any tuple of *r2*. (As for **intersect**, of course it is not primitive, but for completeness we note that it is also defined analogously; that is, a tuple *t* appears in *r1* INTERSECT *r2* if and only if it is a duplicate of some tuple of *r1* and of some tuple of *r2*.)

Update Operators

There are two general points to make under this heading:

1. If attribute *A* of relvar *R* permits UNKs and an attempt is made via INSERT to place a tuple in *R* for which no *A* value is specified, the system will automatically place an UNK in the *A* position in that tuple. (Of course, we are assuming here that no non-UNK default value has been defined for *A*.) If attribute *A* of relvar *R* does not permit UNKs, an attempt to place a tuple in *R* via either INSERT or UPDATE in which the *A* position is UNK is an error.

2. An attempt via either INSERT or UPDATE to place a duplicate tuple in *R* is an error, as usual. The definition of "duplicate tuples" here is as in the previous subsection.

Integrity Constraints

As explained in Chapter 9, an integrity constraint can be regarded, loosely, as a boolean expression that must not evaluate to *false*. Note, therefore, that the constraint is not considered to be violated if it evaluates to *unk* (in fact, we were tacitly assuming as much in our remarks earlier in this section regarding type constraints). Technically, we should say in such a case that it is *not known* whether the constraint is violated, but, just as *unk* is regarded as *false* for the purposes of a WHERE clause, so it is regarded as *true* for the purposes of an integrity constraint (speaking somewhat loosely in both cases).

19.3   SOME CONSEQUENCES OF THE FOREGOING SCHEME

The 3VL approach as described in the previous section has a number of logical consequences, not all of which are immediately obvious. In this section we point out some of those consequences and discuss their significance.

Expression Transformations

First, we observe that several expressions that always evaluate to *true* in 2VL do not necessarily always evaluate to *true* in 3VL. Here are some examples, with commentary. Please note that the list is nowhere near exhaustive.

- *The comparison x = x does not necessarily give true.*

  In 2VL, any value *x* is always equal to itself. In 3VL, however, *x* is not equal to itself if it happens to be UNK.

- *The boolean expression p OR NOT (p) does not necessarily give true.*

  In 2VL, the expression *p* OR NOT(*p*), where *p* in turn is some boolean expression, always evaluates to *true*. In 3VL, however, if *p* happens to evaluate to *unk,* the overall expression evaluates to *unk* OR NOT(*unk*), that is, to *unk* OR *unk,* which reduces to *unk,* not *true*. This fact accounts for a well-known counterintuitive property of 3VL, which we illustrate as follows: If we execute the query "Get all suppliers in London," followed by the query "Get all suppliers not in London," and take the union of the two results, we do not necessarily get all suppliers. Instead, we need to include "all suppliers who *may* be in London." (In other words, an expression that does always evaluate to *true* in 3VL—that is, the 3VL analog of the 2VL expression *p* OR NOT(*p*)—is *p* OR NOT(*p*) OR MAYBE(*p*).)

    It is worth examining the foregoing example a little more closely. The key point is this: While the two cases "city is London" and "city is not London" are mutually exclusive and exhaust the full range of possibilities in the real world, the database does *not* contain the real world—instead, it contains only **knowledge about** the real world. And there are three possible cases, not two, concerning knowledge about the real world; in the example, the three cases are "city is known to be London," "city is known not to be London," and "city is not known." Furthermore, of course (as reference [19.6] puts it), we obviously cannot ask the system questions about the real world, we can only ask it questions about its *knowledge* of the real world as represented by the data in the database. The counterintuitive nature of the example thus derives from a confusion over realms: The user is thinking in terms of the realm that is the real world, but the system is operating in terms of the realm that is *its knowledge about* that real world. (It seems to this writer, however, that such a confusion over realms is a trap very easily fallen into. Note that *every single query* mentioned in previous chapters in this book—in examples, exercises, and so on—has been stated in "real world" terms, not "knowledge about the real world" terms. And this book is certainly not unusual in this regard.)

- *The expression r JOIN r does not necessarily give r.*

  In 2VL, forming the join of a relation *r* with itself always yields the original relation *r* (i.e., join is *idempotent*). In 3VL, however, a tuple with an UNK in any position will not join to itself, because—according to reference [14.7]—join, unlike union, is based on "retrieval-style" equality testing, not "duplicate-style" equality testing (?).

- *INTERSECT is no longer a special case of JOIN.*

  This fact is a consequence of the fact that (again) join is based on retrieval-style equality testing, while intersection is based on duplicate-style equality testing.

- *$A = B$ and $B = C$ together do not imply $A = C$.*

  An extended illustration of this point is given in the subsection "The Departments-and-Employees Example," to follow in a moment.

To sum up, many equivalences that are valid in 2VL break down in 3VL. One very serious consequence of such breakdowns is as follows. In general, simple equivalences such as *r* JOIN *r* ≡ *r* lie at the heart of the various *transformation laws* that are used to convert queries into some more efficient form, as explained in Chapter 18. Furthermore, those laws are used not only by the *system* (when doing optimization), but also by *users* (when trying to decide the "best" way to state a given query). And if the equivalences are not valid, then the laws are not valid. And if the laws are not valid, then the transformations are not valid. And if the transformations are not valid, then we will get *wrong answers* out of the system.

The Departments-and-Employees Example

In order to illustrate the problem of incorrect transformations, we discuss a specific example in some detail. (The example is taken from reference [19.9]; for reasons that are unimportant here, it is based on relational calculus instead of relational algebra.) Consider the simple departments-and-employees database shown in Fig. 19.1, and the expression

```
DEPT.DEPT# = EMP.DEPT# AND EMP.DEPT# = DEPT# ('D1')
```

(which might be part of a query, for example); DEPT and EMP here are implicit range variables. For the only tuples that exist in the database, this expression evaluates to *unk* AND *unk*, that is, to *unk*. However, a "good" optimizer will observe that the expression is of the form $a = b$ AND $b = c$, will therefore infer that $a = c$, and hence will append an additional restriction term $a = c$ to the original expression (as discussed in Chapter 18, Section 18.4), yielding:

```
DEPT.DEPT# = EMP.DEPT# AND EMP.DEPT# = DEPT# ('D1')
               AND DEPT.DEPT# = DEPT# ('D1')
```

This modified expression now evaluates to *unk* AND *unk* AND *false*, that is, to *false*, for the only two tuples in the database. It follows, therefore, that the query (e.g.)

```
EMP.EMP# WHERE EXISTS DEPT ( NOT
( DEPT.DEPT# = EMP.DEPT# AND EMP.DEPT# = DEPT# ('D1') ) )
```

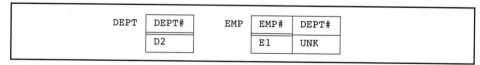

Fig. 19.1   The departments-and-employees database

will return employee E1 if "optimized" in the foregoing sense and will not do so otherwise (in fact, of course, the "optimization" is not valid). Thus we see that certain optimizations that are perfectly valid, and useful, under conventional 2VL are no longer valid under 3VL.

Note the implications of the foregoing for extending a 2VL system to support 3VL: At best, such an extension is likely to require some reengineering of the existing system, since portions of the existing optimizer code are likely to be invalidated; at worst, it will introduce bugs. More generally, note the implications for extending a system that supports *n*-valued logic to support (*n*+1)-valued logic instead, for any *n* greater than one; analogous difficulties will arise for every discrete value of *n*.

The Interpretation Issue

Now let us examine the departments-and-employees example a little more carefully. Since employee E1 does have *some* corresponding department in the real world, the UNK does stand for some real value, say *d*. Now, either *d* is D1 or it is not. If it is, then the original expression

```
DEPT.DEPT# = EMP.DEPT# AND EMP.DEPT# = DEPT# ('D1')
```

evaluates (for the given data) to *false,* because the first term evaluates to *false.* Alternatively, if *d* is not D1, then the expression also evaluates (for the given data) to *false,* because the second term evaluates to *false.* In other words, the original expression is always *false* in the real world, *regardless of what real value the UNK stands for.* Thus, the result that is correct according to three-valued logic and the result that is correct in the real world are not the same! In other words, three-valued logic does not behave in accordance with the way the real world behaves; that is, 3VL does not seem to have a sensible *interpretation* in terms of how the real world works.

Note: This question of interpretation is very far from being the only problem arising from nulls and 3VL (see references [19.1–19.11] for an extensive discussion of many others). It is not even the most fundamental (see the next subsection). However, it is perhaps the one of greatest pragmatic significance; in this writer's opinion, in fact, it is a showstopper.

Predicates Again

Suppose the relation that is the current value of the EMP relvar contains just two tuples, (E2,D2) and (E1,UNK). The first corresponds to the proposition "There is an employee identified as E2 in the department identified as D2." The second corresponds to the proposition "There is an employee identified as E1." (Remember that to say that a tuple "contains an UNK" is really to say that the tuple in fact contains nothing at all in the applicable position; thus, the tuple (E1,UNK)—setting aside for the moment the question of whether it is even a tuple at all—should effectively be considered as being of the form just (E1).) In other words, the two tuples are instantiations of *two different predicates,* and the "relation" is not a relation at all but instead a kind of union (not a relational union!) of two different relations with, in particular, two different headings.

Now, it might be suggested that the situation can be rescued by asserting that there really is just one predicate after all, one that involves an OR—perhaps as follows:

*There is an employee identified as E# in the department identified as D# **OR** there is an employee identified as E#.*

Observe, however, that now, thanks to the Closed World Assumption, the relation will have to contain a tuple of the form (E*i*,UNK) for every employee E*i*! Generalizing this rescue attempt to a relation that "contains UNKs" in several different attributes is almost too horrible to contemplate. (And in any case the "relation" that results will still not be a relation—see the next paragraph.)

To put the foregoing another way: If the value of a given attribute within a given tuple within a given relation "is UNK," then (to repeat) that attribute position in fact contains nothing at all . . . which implies that the "attribute" is not an attribute, the "tuple" is not a tuple, the "relation" is not a relation, and the foundation for what we are doing (whatever else it might be) is no longer mathematical relation theory. In other words, UNKs and 3VL *undermine the entire foundation of the relational model.*

19.4 NULLS AND KEYS

Note: We now drop the term UNK (for the most part) and revert for historical reasons to the more traditional "nulls" terminology.

Despite the message of the previous section, the fact is that nulls and 3VL are supported in most products at the time of writing. Furthermore, such support has important implications for keys in particular. In this section, therefore, we explore those implications briefly.

Primary Keys

As explained in Section 9.10, the relational model has historically required—in the case of base relvars, at least—that, out of the set of candidate keys for the relvar in question, exactly one be chosen as the *primary* key. The other candidate keys, if any, are then said to be *alternate* keys. And then, along with the primary key concept, the model has historically included the following "metaconstraint" or rule (the *entity integrity* rule):

- **Entity integrity:** No component of the primary key of any base relvar is allowed to accept nulls.

The rationale for this rule goes something like this: (a) Tuples in base relations represent entities in the real world; (b) entities in the real world are identifiable by definition; (c) therefore their counterparts in the database must be identifiable too; (d) primary key values serve as those identifiers in the database; (e) therefore primary key values must not be "missing." Points arising:

1. First of all, it is often thought that the entity integrity rule says something along the lines of "Primary key values must be unique," but it does not. (It is true that primary key values must be unique, but that requirement is implied by the basic definition of the primary key concept *per se*.)

2. Next, note that the rule applies explicitly to *primary* keys; by implication, therefore, *alternate* keys can apparently allow nulls. But if *AK* is an alternate key that allows nulls, then *AK* could not have been chosen as the primary key, because of the entity integrity rule—so in what sense exactly was *AK* a "candidate" key in the first place? Alternatively, if we have to say that alternate keys cannot allow nulls either, then the entity integrity rule applies to *all candidate keys,* not just to the primary key. Either way, there seems to be something wrong with the rule as stated.

3. Finally, note that the entity integrity rule applies only to *base relvars;* other relvars can apparently have a primary key that does allow nulls. As a trivial and obvious example, consider the projection of a relvar *R* over any attribute *A* that allows nulls. The rule thus violates *The Principle of Interchangeability* (of base and derived relvars). In our opinion, this would be a strong argument for rejecting it even if it did not involve nulls (a concept we reject anyway).

Now, suppose we agreed to drop the whole idea of nulls and used *special values*[6] instead to represent missing information (just as we do in the real world, in fact—see Section 19.6, later). Then we might want to retain a modified version of the entity integrity rule—"No component of the primary key of any base relvar is allowed to accept such special values"—as a *guideline,* but *not* as an inviolable law (much as the ideas of further normalization serve as guidelines, but not as inviolable laws). Fig. 19.2 gives an example of a base relvar called SURVEY for which we might want to violate that guideline; it represents the results of a salary survey, showing the average, maximum, and minimum salary by birth year for a certain sample population (BIRTHYEAR is the primary key). And the tuple with the special BIRTHYEAR value "????" represents people who declined to answer the question "When were you born?"

SURVEY	BIRTHYEAR	AVGSAL	MAXSAL	MINSAL
	1960	85K	130K	33K
	1961	82K	125K	32K
	1962	77K	99K	32K
	1963	78K	97K	35K
	....	...	...	...
	1970	29K	35K	12K
	????	56K	117K	20K

Fig. 19.2   Base relvar SURVEY (sample value)

---

[6] Often inappropriately called *default* values [19.12].

Foreign Keys

Consider the departments-and-employees database of Fig. 19.1 once again. You might not have noticed at the time, but we deliberately did not say that attribute DEPT# of relvar EMP in that figure was a foreign key. But now suppose it is. Then it is clear that the referential integrity rule needs some refinement, because foreign keys must now apparently be allowed to accept nulls, and nulls in a foreign key position obviously violate the rule as originally stated in Chapter 9:[7]

- **Referential integrity** (*original version*): The database must not contain any unmatched foreign key values.

Actually, we can keep the rule as stated, as long as we extend the definition of the term *unmatched foreign key value* appropriately. To be specific, we now define an unmatched foreign key value to be a *nonnull* foreign key value in some referencing relvar for which there does not exist a matching value of the relevant candidate key in the relevant referenced relvar. Points arising:

1. Whether or not any given foreign key allows nulls will have to be specified as part of the database definition. (In fact, of course, the same is true for attributes in general, regardless of whether they are part of some foreign key.)

2. The possibility that foreign keys might allow nulls raises the possibility of another referential action, SET NULL, that might be specified in a foreign key delete or update rule. For example:

```
VAR SP BASE RELATION { ... } ...
    FOREIGN KEY { S# } REFERENCES S
                       ON DELETE SET NULL
                       ON UPDATE SET NULL ;
```

With these specifications, a DELETE operation on the suppliers relvar will set the foreign key to null in all matching shipments and then delete the applicable suppliers; likewise, an UPDATE operation on attribute S# in the suppliers relvar will set the foreign key to null in all matching shipments and then update the applicable suppliers. *Note:* SET NULL can be specified only for a foreign key that allows nulls in the first place, naturally.

3. Last, and most important, we observe that the apparent "need" to allow nulls in foreign keys can be avoided by appropriate database design [19.19]. Consider departments and employees once again, for example. If it is really possible for the department number to be unknown for certain employees, then (as suggested near the end of the previous section) it would clearly be better not to include DEPT# in the EMP relvar at all, but rather to have a separate relvar ED (say), with attributes EMP# and DEPT#, to represent the fact that a specified employee is in a specified department. Then the fact that a certain employee has an unknown department can be represented by simply not including a tuple for that employee in relvar ED.

---

[7] Note that such nulls would be in violation of that rule even if there were a tuple in the relevant referenced relvar in which the relevant candidate key was null!

19.5 OUTER JOIN (A DIGRESSION)

In this section we digress briefly to discuss an operation known as **outer join** (see references [19.3, 19.4], [19.7], and [19.14–19.16]). Outer join is an extended form of the regular or *inner* join operation. It differs from the inner join in that tuples in one relation having no counterpart in the other appear in the result with nulls in the other attribute positions, instead of simply being ignored as they normally are. It is not a primitive operation; for example, the following expression could be used to construct the outer join of suppliers and shipments on supplier numbers (assuming for the sake of the example that "NULL" is a legal scalar expression):

```
( S JOIN SP )
  UNION
( EXTEND ( ( S { S# } MINUS SP { S# } ) JOIN S )
  ADD ( NULL AS P#, NULL AS QTY ) )
```

The result includes tuples for suppliers who supply no parts, extended with nulls in the P# and QTY positions.

Let us examine this example a little more closely. Refer to Fig. 19.3. In that figure, the top portion shows some sample data values for relvars S and SP, the middle portion shows the regular inner join, and the bottom portion shows the corresponding outer join. As the figure indicates, the inner join "loses information"—speaking *very* loosely!—for suppliers who supply no parts (supplier S5, in the example), whereas the outer join "preserves" such information; indeed, exactly that distinction is the whole point of outer join.

Now, the problem that outer join is intended to solve—that is, the fact that inner join sometimes "loses information"—is certainly an important problem. Some writers would therefore argue that the system should provide direct, explicit support for outer join, instead

S

S#	SNAME	STATUS	CITY
S2	Jones	10	Paris
S5	Adams	30	Athens

SP

S#	P#	QTY
S2	P1	300
S2	P2	400

Regular (inner) join:

S#	SNAME	STATUS	CITY	P#	QTY
S2	Jones	10	Paris	P1	300
S2	Jones	10	Paris	P2	400

"Loses" information for supplier S5

Outer join:

S#	SNAME	STATUS	CITY	P#	QTY
S2	Jones	10	Paris	P1	300
S2	Jones	10	Paris	P2	400
S5	Adams	30	Athens	UNK	UNK

"Preserves" information fo supplier S5

Fig. 19.3 Inner *vs.* outer join (example)

of requiring the user to indulge in circumlocutions to achieve the desired effect. Reference [6.2] in particular considers outer join to be an intrinsic part of the relational model. However, we do not endorse this position ourselves, for the following reasons among others:

- First of all, the operation involves nulls, and we are opposed to nulls anyway for numerous good reasons.

- Second, note that outer join comes in several varieties: left, right, and full outer *θ-join*, and left, right, and full outer *natural* join. (The left joins preserve information from the first operand, the right joins preserve information from the second operand, and the full joins do both; the example of Fig. 19.3 is a left join—a left outer natural join, to be precise.) Note further that there is no very straightforward way of deriving the outer natural joins from the outer θ-joins [19.7]. As a result, it is unclear as to exactly which outer joins need to be explicitly supported.

- Next, the outer join issue is far from being as trivial as the simple example of Fig. 19.3 might suggest. In fact, as reference [19.7] puts it, outer join suffers from a number of *Nasty Properties* that together imply that adding outer join support to existing languages—in particular, to SQL—is difficult to do gracefully. Several DBMS products have tried to solve this problem and dismally failed (i.e., they have tripped over those Nasty Properties). See reference [19.7] for an extensive discussion of this issue.

- Finally, *relation-valued attributes* provide an alternative approach to the problem anyway—an approach that does not involve nulls and does not involve outer join either, and is in fact, in this writer's opinion, an altogether more elegant solution (not to mention the fact that it is a *relational* solution and does not do violence to the relational model). Given the sample data values from the top of Fig. 19.3, for example, the expression

```
WITH ( S RENAME S# AS X ) AS Y :
      ( EXTEND Y ADD ( SP WHERE S# = X ) AS PQ ) RENAME X AS S#
```

yields the result shown in Fig. 19.4.

S#	SNAME	STATUS	CITY	PQ	
S2	Jones	10	Paris	**P#**	**QTY**
				P1	300
				P2	400
S5	Adams	30	Athens	**P#**	**QTY**

Fig. 19.4   Preserving information for supplier S5 (a better way)

Observe in particular that in Fig. 19.4 the empty set of parts supplied by supplier S5 is represented by an empty set, not (as in Fig. 19.3) by some strange "null." To represent an empty set by an empty set seems like an obviously good idea. In fact, *there would be no need for outer join at all* if relation-valued attributes were properly supported!

To pursue the point just a moment longer: How are we supposed to *interpret* the nulls that appear in the result of an outer join, anyway? What do they mean in the example of Fig. 19.3, for instance? They certainly do not mean either "value unknown" or "value does not apply"; in fact, the only interpretation that does make any logical sense is, precisely, "value is the empty set." See reference [19.7] for further discussion of this issue as well.

We close this section by remarking that it is also possible to define "outer" versions of certain other operations of the relational algebra—specifically, the union, intersection, and difference operations [14.7]—and reference [6.2] in particular considers at least one of these, *outer union,* to be an intrinsic part of the relational model. Such operations permit unions (etc.) to be performed between two relations even if those relations are not of the same type; they basically work by extending each operand to include those attributes that are peculiar to the other (so that the operands are now of the same type), putting nulls in every tuple for all such added attributes, and then performing a normal union or intersection or difference, as applicable.[8] We do not discuss these operations in detail, however, for the following reasons:

- Outer intersection is guaranteed to return an empty relation, except in the special case in which the original relations are of the same type in the first place, in which case it degenerates to the normal intersection.

- Outer difference is guaranteed to return its first (null-extended) operand, except in the special case in which the original relations are of the same type in the first place, in which case it degenerates to the normal difference.

- Outer union has *major* problems of interpretation (they are much worse than those arising with outer join, as reference [19.2] shows).

19.6   SPECIAL VALUES

We have seen that nulls wreck the relational model. In fact, it is worth pointing out that the relational model managed perfectly well without them for ten years!—the model was first defined in 1969 [6.1], and nulls were not added until 1979 [14.7].

Suppose, therefore, that (as suggested in Section 19.4) we agree to drop the whole idea of nulls, and use *special values* instead to represent missing information. Note that using special values is exactly what we do in the real world. In the real world, for example, we might use the special value "?" to denote the hours worked by a certain employee

---

[8] This explanation refers to the operations as originally defined in reference [14.7]; the definitions were changed somewhat in reference [6.2].

if the actual value is unknown for some reason.[9] Thus, the general idea is simply to use an appropriate special value, distinct from all regular values of the attribute in question, when no regular value can be used. Note that the special value must be a value of the applicable type; in the "hours worked" example, therefore, the type of the HOURS_WORKED attribute is not just integers, but integers plus whatever the special value is. (A nice analogy here: For many card games, the type TRUMPS contains five values, not four—"hearts," "clubs," "diamonds," "spades," and "no trumps.")

Now, we would be the first to admit that the foregoing scheme is not very elegant, but it does have the overwhelming advantage of *not undermining the logical foundations of the relational model.* In subsequent chapters, therefore, we will simply ignore the possibility of null support (except in certain SQL-specific contexts, where occasional references to nulls are unavoidable). See reference [19.12] for a detailed description of the special values scheme.

19.7 SQL FACILITIES

SQL's support for nulls and 3VL follows the broad outlines of the approach described in previous sections. Thus, for example, when SQL applies a WHERE clause to some table *T*, it eliminates all rows of *T* for which the expression in that WHERE clause evaluates to either *false* or *unk* (i.e., not to *true*). Likewise, when it applies a HAVING clause to some "grouped table" *G*, it eliminates all groups of *G* for which the expression in that HAVING clause evaluates either to *false* or *unk* (i.e., not to *true*).[10] In what follows, therefore, we merely draw your attention to certain 3VL features that are specific to SQL *per se,* instead of being an intrinsic part of the 3VL approach as previously discussed.

Note: The full implications and ramifications of SQL's null support are very complex; in fact, although we just said that SQL follows three-valued logic in broad outline, the truth is that it also manages to make a variety of mistakes in its support for that logic, as we will soon see. For additional information, we refer you to the official standard specification [4.23] or the detailed tutorial treatment in reference [4.20].

Data Types

As we saw in Chapter 4, SQL includes the built-in type BOOLEAN (it was added to the standard in 1999, though few products if any yet support it). The usual boolean operators AND, OR, and NOT are available, and boolean expressions can appear wherever scalar expressions in general can appear. As we know, however, there are now three truth values, not two (the corresponding literals are TRUE, FALSE, and UNKNOWN); this fact notwithstanding, type BOOLEAN includes just two values, not three—the *unknown* truth value is represented, quite incorrectly, by null! Here are some consequences of this fact:

---

[9] Observe that the one thing we do *not* do is use a null for this purpose. There is no such thing as a null in the real world [19.12].

[10] A *grouped table* in SQL is what is produced when a GROUP BY (possibly implicit) is executed. Such a table is reduced to a regular "ungrouped" table when the accompanying SELECT is executed.

- Assigning the value UNKNOWN to a variable B of type BOOLEAN will actually set that variable to null.

- After such an assignment, the comparison B = UNKNOWN will *not* give *true* (or TRUE, rather)—instead, it will give null.

- In fact, the comparison B = UNKNOWN will *always* give null, regardless of the value of B!—because it is logically equivalent to the comparison "B = NULL" (not meant to be valid syntax).

To understand the seriousness of such flaws, you might care to meditate on the analogy of a numeric type that uses null instead of zero to represent zero.

Now let *T* be either a nonscalar type or a structured type (and here it makes no difference whether we regard structured types as scalar or nonscalar). To fix our ideas, let *T* be a row type specifically, and let *V* be a variable of type *T*. Then there is clearly a logical difference between (a) *V* itself being null and (b) *V* having at least one component (i.e., field) that is null. In fact, *V* itself is not necessarily null even if all of its components are null![11]—though it is probably true (though the standard is unclear on the issue) that if *V* is null then all of its components are considered to be null as well. Thus, if *V* is not null but does contain at least one null component, the comparison *V* = *V* gives null, and yet the expression *V* IS NULL gives FALSE. In general, however, we can at least say that if ((*V* = *V*) IS NOT TRUE) IS TRUE is TRUE, then either *V* is null or it has a null component.

Base Tables

As explained in Chapter 6, Section 6.6, columns in base tables usually have an associated default value, and that default value is frequently defined, explicitly or implicitly, to be null. Furthermore, columns in base tables always *permit* nulls, unless there is an integrity constraint—usually just NOT NULL—for the column in question that expressly prohibits them.

It follows from the foregoing that if we are to be true to our own principles, we should really have specified NOT NULL, either explicitly or implicitly, for every base table column in every SQL example at every prior point in this book. At least we will do so in our SQL examples from this point forward. Note, however, that NOT NULL is assumed implicitly for any column mentioned in a PRIMARY KEY specification.

Table Expressions

Recall from Section 8.6 that explicit JOIN support was added to the SQL standard in 1992. If the keyword JOIN is prefixed with LEFT, RIGHT, or FULL (optionally followed by the noiseword OUTER in each case), then the join in question is an *outer* join. Here are some examples:

---

[11] Actually SQL gets this one wrong too—see the discussion of IS [NOT] NULL in the subsection "Boolean Expressions" later in this section.

```
S LEFT JOIN SP ON S.S# = SP.S#

S LEFT JOIN SP USING ( S# )

S LEFT NATURAL JOIN SP
```

These three expressions are effectively all equivalent, except that the first produces a table with two identical columns both called S# and the second and third produce a table with just one such column.

SQL also supports an approximation to outer union, which it calls *union join* (added in SQL:1992, to be deleted in SQL:2003). The details are beyond the scope of this book.

Boolean Expressions

SQL boolean expressions are, not surprisingly, extensively affected by nulls and 3VL. We content ourselves here with examining a few important special cases:

- *Tests for null:* SQL provides two special comparison operators, IS NULL and IS NOT NULL, to test for the presence or absence of nulls. The syntax is:

  ```
  <row value constructor> IS [ NOT ] NULL
  ```

  If the *<row value constructor>* "constructs" a row of degree one, then SQL treats it as if it actually denoted the value contained in that row instead of denoting the row as such; otherwise, it treats it as denoting the row. In the latter case, however, it regards the row as (a) null if and only if every component is null and (b) nonnull if and only if every component is nonnull! One consequence of this mistake is that if r is a row with two components, $c1$ and $c2$ say, then the expressions r IS NOT NULL and NOT (r IS NULL) are not equivalent; the first is equivalent to $c1$ IS NOT NULL AND $c2$ IS NOT NULL, while the second is equivalent to $c1$ IS NOT NULL OR $c2$ IS NOT NULL. Another consequence is that if r includes some null and some nonnull components, then r itself is apparently neither null nor nonnull.

- *Tests for true, false, unknown:* If p is a boolean expression in parentheses (actually the parentheses are sometimes unnecessary, but they are never wrong), then the following are also boolean expressions:

  ```
  p IS [ NOT ] TRUE
  p IS [ NOT ] FALSE
  p IS [ NOT ] UNKNOWN
  ```

  The meanings of these expressions are as indicated by the following truth table:

p	*true*	*false*	*unk*
p IS TRUE	*true*	*false*	*false*
p IS NOT TRUE	*false*	*true*	*true*
p IS FALSE	*false*	*true*	*false*
p IS NOT FALSE	*true*	*false*	*true*
p IS UNKNOWN	*false*	*false*	*true*
p IS NOT UNKNOWN	*true*	*true*	*false*

Observe, therefore, that the expressions p IS NOT TRUE and NOT p are not equivalent. *Note:* The expression p IS UNKNOWN corresponds to our MAYBE(p). Given that SQL uses null to represent *unk*, it is also equivalent to p IS NULL.

- *EXISTS conditions:* The SQL EXISTS operator is not the same as the existential quantifier of 3VL, because it always evaluates to *true* or *false,* never to *unk,* even when *unk* is the logically correct answer. To be specific, it returns *false* if its argument table is empty, and *true* otherwise (thus, it sometimes returns *true* when *unk* is the logically correct answer). See reference [19.6] for further discussion.

- *UNIQUE conditions:* UNIQUE conditions are, loosely, tests to check that a specified table contains no duplicate rows (!). To be more precise, the expression UNIQUE (*<table exp>*) returns *true* if the table denoted by the *<table exp>* contains no two distinct rows, *r1* and *r2* say, such that the comparison *r1 = r2* gives *true,* and *false* otherwise. Like EXISTS, therefore, UNIQUE sometimes returns *true* when *unk* is the logically correct answer.

- *DISTINCT conditions:* DISTINCT conditions are, loosely, tests to check whether two rows are duplicates of each other. Let the rows in question be *Left* and *Right; Left* and *Right* must be of the same degree, *n* say. Let the *i*th components of *Left* and *Right* be *Li* and *Ri,* respectively (*i* = 1, 2, ..., *n*); *Li* and *Ri* must be such that the comparison *Li = Ri* is valid. Then the expression

```
Left IS DISTINCT FROM Right
```

returns *false* if, for all *i,* either (a) "*Li = Ri*" is *true* or (b) *Li* and *Ri* are both null; otherwise, it returns *true.*

Other Scalar Expressions

Again we content ourselves with examining a few important special cases:

- *"Literals":* The keyword NULL can sometimes be used as a kind of literal representation of null (e.g., in an INSERT statement), but not in all contexts; as the standard puts it, "the keyword NULL . . . can be used to denote the null value . . . in certain contexts, [but not] everywhere that a literal is permitted" [4.23]. Note in particular that it is not possible to use the keyword NULL to denote an operand of a simple comparison—for example, "WHERE X = NULL" is illegal (the correct form is WHERE X IS NULL, of course).

- *COALESCE:* COALESCE is the SQL analog of our IF_UNK operator. More precisely, the expression COALESCE (*x,y,* ..., *z*) returns null if *x, y,* ..., *z* all evaluate to null; otherwise, it returns the value of its first nonnull operand.

- *Aggregate operators:* The SQL aggregate operators (SUM, AVG, etc.) do not behave in accordance with the rules for scalar operators explained in Section 19.2, but instead simply ignore any nulls in their argument (except for COUNT(*), where nulls are treated as if they were regular values). Also, if the argument to such an operator happens to evaluate to an empty set, COUNT returns zero; the other operators all return null. (As noted in Chapter 8, this latter behavior is logically incorrect, but it is the way SQL is defined.)

- *"Scalar subqueries":* If a scalar expression is in fact a table expression enclosed in parentheses—for example, (SELECT S.CITY FROM S WHERE S.S# = S#('S1'))— then normally that table expression is required to evaluate to a table containing exactly one column and exactly one row. The value of the scalar expression is then taken to be, precisely, the single scalar value contained within that table. But if the table expression evaluates to a one-column table that contains no rows at all, then SQL defines the value of the scalar expression to be null.

Keys

The interactions between nulls and keys in SQL can be summarized as follows:

- *Candidate keys:* Let *C* be a column that is a component of some candidate key *K* of some base table. As noted earlier in this section, if *K* is a primary key, SQL will not allow *C* to contain any nulls (in other words, it enforces the entity integrity rule). If *K* is not a primary key, however, SQL will allow *C* to contain *any number* of nulls (just as long as no two distinct rows contain the same value for *K,* of course).

  In connection with the foregoing, you might like to meditate on the following slightly edited extract from reference [4.20]: "Let *k2* be a new value for *K* that some user is attempting to introduce via an INSERT or UPDATE operation . . . That INSERT or UPDATE will be rejected if *k2* is the same as some value for *K, k1* say, that already exists in the table . . . What then does it mean for the two values *k1* and *k2* to be the same? It turns out that *no two* of the following three statements are equivalent:

  1. *k1* and *k2* are the same for the purposes of comparison.
  2. *k1* and *k2* are the same for the purposes of candidate key uniqueness.
  3. *k1* and *k2* are the same for the purposes of duplicate elimination.

  Number 1 is defined in accordance with the rules of 3VL; Number 2 is defined in accordance with the rules for the UNIQUE condition; and Number 3 is defined in accordance with the definition of duplicates in Section 19.2. In particular, if *k1* and *k2* are both null, then Number 1 gives *unk,* Number 2 gives *false,* and Number 3 gives *true.*"

- *Foreign keys:* The rules defining what it means in the presence of nulls for a given foreign key value to match some corresponding candidate key value are quite complex. We omit the details here. *Note:* Nulls also have implications for the referential actions (CASCADE, SET NULL, etc.) specified in the ON DELETE and ON UPDATE clauses. (SET DEFAULT is also supported, with the obvious interpretation.) Once again, the details are quite complex, and beyond the scope of the present text; see reference [4.20] for further discussion.

Embedded SQL

- *Indicator variables:* Consider the following example (repeated from Chapter 4) of an embedded SQL "singleton SELECT":

```
EXEC SQL SELECT STATUS, CITY
         INTO   :RANK, :TOWN
         FROM   S
         WHERE  S# = S# ( :GIVENS# ) ;
```

Suppose there is a possibility that STATUS might be null for some supplier. Then the SELECT statement just shown will fail if the STATUS selected is null (SQLSTATE will be set to the exception value 22002). In general, if it is possible that some item in the SELECT clause might be null, the user should specify an *indicator variable* in addition to the ordinary target variable, as here:

```
EXEC SQL SELECT STATUS, CITY
         INTO   :RANK INDICATOR :RANKIND, :TOWN
         FROM   S
         WHERE  S# = S# ( :GIVENS# ) ;
IF RANKIND = -1 THEN /* STATUS was null */ ... ; END IF ;
```

If the item to be retrieved is null and an indicator variable has been specified, then that indicator variable will be set to the value –1. The effect on the ordinary target variable is implementation-dependent.

■ *Ordering:* The ORDER BY clause is used to impose an ordering on the rows resulting from the evaluation of the table expression in a cursor definition. (It can also be used in interactive queries, of course.) The question arises: What is the relative ordering for two scalar values *A* and *B* if *A* is null or *B* is null or both? The SQL answer is as follows:

1. For ordering purposes, all nulls are considered to be equal to one another.

2. For ordering purposes, null is considered *either* to be greater than all nonnull values *or* less than all nonnull values (it is implementation-defined which).

19.8 SUMMARY

We have discussed the problem of **missing information** and a currently fashionable—though very bad—approach to that problem based on **nulls** and **three-valued logic** (3VL). We stressed the point that null is not a value, though it is common to speak as if it were (saying, e.g., that some particular attribute value within some particular tuple "is null"). A comparison in which a comparand is null evaluates to "the third truth value" *unknown* (abbreviated *unk*), which is why the logic is three-valued. We also mentioned that, at least conceptually, there can be many different kinds of nulls, and introduced **UNK** as a convenient (and explicit) shorthand for the value-unknown kind.

We then explored the implications of UNKs and 3VL for the boolean operators **AND**, **OR**, and **NOT** (and **MAYBE**); the quantifiers **EXISTS** and **FORALL**; other **scalar** operators; the **relational** operators; and the **update** operators INSERT and UPDATE. We introduced the operators **IS_UNK** (which tests for UNK) and **IF_UNK** (which converts UNK into a nonUNK value). We discussed the question of **duplicates** in the presence of UNKs, and pointed out also that UNK and *unk* are not the same thing.

Next, we examined some consequences of the foregoing ideas. First, we explained that **certain equivalences break down** in 3VL—equivalences, that is, that are valid in 2VL but not in 3VL. As a result, both users and optimizers are likely to **make mistakes in transforming expressions**. And even if such mistakes are not made, 3VL suffers from the very serious ("showstopper") problem that **it does not match reality**—that is, results that are correct according to 3VL are sometimes incorrect in the real world.

We then went on to describe the implications of nulls for **primary** and **foreign keys** (mentioning the **entity integrity rule** and the revised **referential integrity rule** in particular). Then we digressed to explain **outer join**. We do not advocate direct support for that operation ourselves (at least, not as it is commonly understood), because we believe there are better solutions to the problem that outer join is intended to solve—in particular, we prefer a solution that makes use of **relation-valued attributes**. We briefly mentioned the possibility of other "outer" operations, in particular **outer union**.

Next we examined the question of **SQL support** for the foregoing ideas. SQL's treatment of missing information is broadly based on 3VL, but it does manage to include a large number of additional complications, most of them beyond the scope of the present book. Indeed, SQL manages to introduce a number of **additional flaws**, over and above the flaws that are inherent to 3VL *per se* [19.6, 19.10]. What is more, those additional flaws serve as an additional **inhibitor to optimization** (as mentioned in Section 18.8 in Chapter 18).

We close with the following observations.

- You will appreciate that we have merely scratched the surface of the problems that can arise from nulls and 3VL. However, we have tried to cover enough ground to make it clear that the "benefits" of the 3VL approach are more than a little doubtful.

- We should also make it clear that, even if you are not convinced regarding the problems of 3VL *per se*, it would still be advisable to avoid the corresponding features of SQL, because of the additional flaws already mentioned.

- Our recommendation to DBMS users would thus be to ignore the vendor's 3VL support entirely, and to use a disciplined special values scheme instead (thereby staying firmly in two-valued logic). Such a scheme is described in detail in reference [19.12].

- Finally, we repeat the following fundamental point from Section 19.3: If—speaking *very* loosely—the value of a given attribute within a given tuple within a given relation "is null," then that attribute position in fact contains nothing at all . . . which implies that the "attribute" is not an attribute, the "tuple" is not a tuple, the "relation" is not a relation, and the foundation for what we are doing (whatever else it might be) is no longer mathematical relation theory.

EXERCISES

19.1   If A = 6, B = 5, C = 4, and D is UNK, state the truth values of the following expressions:

a. `A = B OR ( B > C AND A > D )`

b. `A > B AND ( B < C OR IS_UNK ( A - D ) )`

c. `A < C OR B < C OR NOT ( A = C )`

d. `B < D OR B = D OR B > D`

e. `MAYBE ( A > B AND B > C )`

f. `MAYBE ( IS_UNK ( D ) )`

g. `MAYBE ( IS_UNK ( A + B ) )`

h. `IF_UNK ( D, A ) > B AND IF_UNK ( C, D ) < B`

19.2   Let relation *r* contain exactly the following tuples:

```
(   6,    5,    4   )
( UNK,    5,    4   )
(   6,  UNK,    4   )
( UNK,  UNK,    4   )
( UNK,  UNK,  UNK   )
```

Assume as in the body of the chapter that the three attributes, in left-to-right order as shown, are called *A*, *B*, and *C*, respectively, and every attribute is of type INTEGER. If *V* is a range variable that ranges over *r*, state the truth values of the following expressions:

a. `EXISTS V ( V.B > 5 )`

b. `EXISTS V ( V.B > 2 AND V.C > 5 )`

c. `EXISTS V ( MAYBE ( V.C > 3 ) )`

d. `EXISTS V ( MAYBE ( IS_UNK ( V.C ) ) )`

e. `FORALL V ( V.A > 1 )`

f. `FORALL V ( V.B > 1 OR IS_UNK ( V.B ) )`

g. `FORALL V ( MAYBE ( V.A > V.B ) )`

19.3   Strictly speaking, the IS_UNK operator is unnecessary. Why?

19.4   In reference [14.7], Codd proposes "maybe" versions of some (not all) of the relational algebra operators. For example, *maybe-restrict* differs from the normal restrict in that it returns a relation whose body contains just those tuples for which the restriction condition evaluates to *unk* instead of *true*. However, such operators are strictly unnecessary. Why?

19.5   In two-valued logic (2VL), there are exactly two truth values, *true* and *false*. As a consequence, there are exactly four possible *monadic* (single-operand) logical operators: one that maps both *true* and *false* into *true*, one that maps them both into *false*, one (NOT) that maps *true* into *false* and *vice versa*, and one that leaves them both unchanged. And there are exactly 16 possible dyadic (two-operand) operators, as indicated by the following table:

A	B																
t	*t*	*t*	*t*	*t*	*t*	*t*	*t*	*t*	*t*	*f*	*f*	*f*	*f*	*f*	*f*	*f*	*f*
t	*f*	*t*	*t*	*t*	*t*	*f*	*f*	*f*	*f*	*t*	*t*	*t*	*t*	*f*	*f*	*f*	*f*
t	*t*	*t*	*t*	*f*	*f*	*t*	*t*	*f*	*f*	*t*	*t*	*f*	*f*	*t*	*t*	*f*	*f*
t	*f*	*t*	*f*	*t*	*f*	*t*	*f*	*t*	*f*	*t*	*f*	*t*	*f*	*t*	*f*	*t*	*f*

Prove that in 2VL all four monadic operators and all 16 dyadic operators can be formulated in terms of suitable combinations of NOT and either AND or OR (and hence that it is not necessary to support all 20 operators explicitly).

19.6   How many logical operators are there in 3VL? What about 4VL? More generally, what about *n*VL?

19.7   The truth table for the 2VL operator NOR (also known as the *Sheffer stroke* and usually written as a single vertical bar, "|") is as follows:

	t	*f*
t	*f*	*f*
f	*f*	*t*

As the truth table suggests, *p*|*q* is equivalent to NOT *p* AND NOT *q* (it can be thought of as "neither nor"—"neither the first operand nor the first operand is *true*"). Show that the 20 2VL operators can all be formulated in terms of this operator. *Note:* NOR is thus a "generating" operator for the whole of 2VL. Can you find an operator that performs an analogous function for 3VL? 4VL? nVL?

19.8   (Taken from reference [19.5].) Fig. 19.5 represents some sample values for a slight variation on the usual suppliers-and-parts database (the variation is that relvar SP includes a new *shipment number* attribute SHIP#, and attribute P# in that relvar now has "UNKs allowed"; relvar P is irrelevant to the exercise and has been omitted). Consider the relational calculus query

```
S WHERE NOT EXISTS SP ( SP.S# = S.S# AND
                        SP.P# = P# ('P2') )
```

(where S and SP are implicit range variables). Which of the following (if any) is a correct interpretation of this query?

a. Get suppliers who do not supply P2.

b. Get suppliers who are not known to supply P2.

c. Get suppliers who are known not to supply P2.

d. Get suppliers who are either known not or not known to supply P2.

S					SP			
S#	SNAME	STATUS	CITY		SHIP#	S#	P#	QTY
S1	Smith	20	London		SHIP1	S1	P1	300
S2	Jones	10	Paris		SHIP2	S2	P2	200
S3	Blake	30	Paris		SHIP3	S3	UNK	400
S4	Clark	20	London					

Fig. 19.5   A variation on suppliers and parts

19.9   Design a physical representation scheme for SQL base tables in which columns are permitted to contain nulls.

19.10   Define the SQL EXISTS, UNIQUE, and IS DISTINCT FROM operators. Are any of these operators primitive, in the sense that they cannot be expressed in terms of other operators? Is there an IS NOT DISTINCT FROM operator? Give an example of a query involving (a) EXISTS, (b) UNIQUE, that produces the "wrong" answer.

REFERENCES AND BIBLIOGRAPHY

19.1 E. F. Codd and C. J. Date: "Much Ado About Nothing," in C. J. Date, *Relational Database Writings 1991–1994.* Reading, Mass.: Addison-Wesley (1995).

Codd is probably the foremost advocate of nulls and 3VL as a basis for dealing with missing information (an odd state of affairs, given that nulls violate Codd's own *Information Principle!*). This article contains the text of a debate between Codd and the present writer on the subject. It includes the following delightful remark: "Database management would be easier if missing values didn't exist" (Codd).

19.2 Hugh Darwen: "Into the Unknown," in C. J. Date, *Relational Database Writings 1985–1989.* Reading, Mass.: Addison-Wesley (1990).

Raises a number of additional questions concerning nulls and 3VL, of which the following is perhaps the most searching: If (as stated in Chapter 6, Section 6.4) TABLE_DEE corresponds to *true* and TABLE_DUM corresponds to *false,* and TABLE_DEE and TABLE_DUM are the only possible relations of degree zero, then **what corresponds to *unk*?**

19.3 Hugh Darwen: "Outer Join with No Nulls and Fewer Tears," in C. J. Date and Hugh Darwen, *Relational Database Writings 1989–1991.* Reading, Mass.: Addison-Wesley (1992).

Proposes a simple outer join variant that does not involve nulls and does solve many of the problems that outer join is supposed to solve. See also reference [3.3].

19.4 C. J. Date: "The Outer Join," in *Relational Database: Selected Writings.* Reading, Mass.: Addison-Wesley (1986).

Analyzes outer joins in depth and shows how they could be supported in a language like SQL.

19.5 C. J. Date: "NOT Is Not "Not"! (Notes on Three-Valued Logic and Related Matters)," in *Relational Database Writings 1985–1989.* Reading, Mass.: Addison-Wesley (1990).

Let X be a variable of type BOOLEAN. In a 3VL system, then, X must have one of the values *true, false,* or *unk.* Thus, the statement "X is not *true*" means that the value of X is either *unk* or *false.* By contrast, the statement "X is NOT *true*" means that the value of X is *false* (see the truth table for NOT). Thus the NOT of 3VL is not the not of natural language . . . This fact has already caused several people (including the designers of the SQL standard) to stumble, and will doubtless do so again.

19.6 C. J. Date: "EXISTS Is Not 'Exists'! (Some Logical Flaws in SQL)," in *Relational Database Writings 1985–1989.* Reading, Mass.: Addison-Wesley (1990).

19.7 C. J. Date: "Watch Out for Outer Join," in C. J. Date and Hugh Darwen, *Relational Database Writings 1989–1991.* Reading, Mass.: Addison-Wesley (1992).

Section 19.5 of the present chapter mentioned the fact that outer join suffers from a number of "Nasty Properties." This paper summarizes those properties as follows:

1. Outer θ-join is not a restriction of Cartesian product.

2. Restriction does not distribute over outer θ-join.

3. "$A \leq B$" is not the same as "$A < B$ OR $A = B$" (in the context of outer join).

4. The θ-comparison operators are not transitive (in 3VL).

5. Outer natural join is not a projection of outer equijoin.

   The paper goes on to consider what is involved in adding outer join support to the SQL SELECT - FROM - WHERE construct. It shows that the foregoing Nasty Properties imply that:

1. Extending the WHERE clause does not work.

2. ANDing outer joins and restrictions does not work.

3. Expressing the join condition in the WHERE clause does not work.

4. Outer joins of more than two relations cannot be formulated without nested expressions.

5. Extending the SELECT clause (alone) does not work.

The paper also shows how several products have fallen foul of such considerations.

19.8 C. J. Date: "Composite Foreign Keys and Nulls," in C. J. Date and Hugh Darwen, *Relational Database Writings 1989–1991.* Reading, Mass.: Addison-Wesley (1992).

Discusses this question: Should composite foreign key values be allowed to be wholly or partly null?

19.9 C. J. Date: "Three-Valued Logic and the Real World," in C. J. Date and Hugh Darwen, *Relational Database Writings 1989–1991*. Reading, Mass.: Addison-Wesley (1992).

19.10 C. J. Date: "Oh No Not Nulls Again," in C. J. Date and Hugh Darwen, *Relational Database Writings 1989–1991*. Reading, Mass.: Addison-Wesley (1992).

This paper tells you more than you probably wanted to know about nulls.

19.11 C. J. Date: "A Note on the Logical Operators of SQL," in *Relational Database Writings 1991–1994*. Reading, Mass.: Addison-Wesley (1995).

Since 3VL has three truth values *true, false,* and *unk* (here abbreviated to *t, f,* and *u,* respectively), there are 3 * 3 * 3 = 27 possible monadic 3VL operators, because each of the three possible inputs *t, f,* and *u* can map to each of the three possible outputs *t, f,* and *u*. And there are 3^9 = 19,683 possible dyadic 3VL operators, as the following table suggests:

```
      t      u      f
t | t/u/f  t/u/f  t/u/f
u | t/u/f  t/u/f  t/u/f
f | t/u/f  t/u/f  t/u/f
```

More generally, in fact, *n*-valued logic involves *n to the power n* monadic operators and *n to the power n²* dyadic operators:

	Monadic operators	Dyadic operators
2VL	4	16
3VL	27	19,683
4VL	256	4,294,967,296
...	....	....
nVL	(n)**(n)	(n)**(n²)

For any *n*VL with *n* > 2, then, the following questions arise:

- What is a suitable set of *primitive* operators? (E.g., either of the sets {NOT,AND} or {NOT,OR} is a suitable primitive set for 2VL.)
- What is a suitable set of *useful* operators? (E.g., the set {NOT,AND,OR} is a suitable useful set for 2VL.)

Reference [19.11] shows that the SQL standard (under a *very* charitable interpretation) does at least support, directly or indirectly, all of the 19,710 3VL operators.

19.12 C. J. Date: "Faults and Defaults" (in five parts), in C. J. Date, Hugh Darwen, and David McGoveran, *Relational Database Writings 1994–1997*. Reading, Mass.: Addison-Wesley (1998).

Describes a systematic approach to the missing information problem that is based on special values and 2VL instead of nulls and 3VL. The paper argues strongly that special values are what we use in the real world, and hence that it would be desirable for our database systems to behave in this respect in the same way as the real world does.

19.13 Debabrata Dey and Sumit Sarkar: "A Probabilistic Relational Model and Algebra," *ACM TODS 21,* No. 3 (September 1996).

Proposes an approach to "uncertainty in data values" based on probability theory instead of nulls and 3VL. The "probabilistic relational model" is a compatible extension of the conventional relational model.

19.14 César A. Galindo-Legaria: "Outerjoins as Disjunctions," Proc. 1994 ACM SIGMOD Int. Conf. on Management of Data, Minneapolis, Minn. (May 1994).

Outer join is not in general an associative operator [19.4]. This paper characterizes precisely those outer joins that are and are not associative and proposes implementation strategies for each case.

19.15 César Galindo-Legaria and Arnon Rosenthal: "Outerjoin Simplification and Reordering for Query Optimization," *ACM TODS 22,* No. 1 (March 1997).

Presents "a complete set of transformation rules" for expressions involving outer joins.

19.16 Piyush Goel and Bala Iyer: "SQL Query Optimization: Reordering for a General Class of Queries," Proc. 1996 ACM SIGMOD Int. Conf. on Management of Data, Montreal, Canada (June 1996).

Like reference [19.15], this paper is concerned with transforming expressions involving outer joins: "[We] propose a method to reorder [an] SQL query containing joins, outer joins, and . . . aggregations . . . [We] identify a powerful primitive needed [to assist in such reordering, which we call] *generalized selection.*"

19.17 I. J. Heath: IBM internal memo (April 1971).

The paper that introduced the term (and the concept) *outer join.*

19.18 Ken-Chih Liu and Rajshekhar Sunderraman: "Indefinite and Maybe Information in Relational Databases," *ACM TODS 15,* No. 1 (March 1990).

Contains a set of formal proposals for extending the relational model to deal with *maybe information* (e.g., "part P7 may be black") and *indefinite* or *disjunctive information* (e.g., "part P8 or part P9 is red"). *I-tables* are introduced as a means of representing normal (definite) information, maybe information, and indefinite information. The restrict, project, product, union, intersect, and difference operators are extended to operate on I-tables.

19.19 David McGoveran: "Nothing from Nothing" (in four parts), in C. J. Date, Hugh Darwen, and David McGoveran, *Relational Database Writings 1994–1997.* Reading, Mass.: Addison-Wesley (1998).

Part I of this four-part paper explains the crucial role of logic in database systems. Part II shows why that logic must be two-valued logic (2VL) specifically, and why attempts to use three-valued logic (3VL) are misguided. Part III examines the problems that 3VL is supposed to solve. Finally, Part IV describes a set of pragmatic solutions to those problems that do not involve 3VL.

19.20 Nicholas Rescher: *Many-Valued Logic.* New York, N.Y.: McGraw-Hill (1969).

The standard text.

Type Inheritance

20.1   INTRODUCTION

Note: This chapter relies heavily on material first discussed in Chapter 5. If you originally gave that chapter a "once over lightly" reading, therefore, you might want to go back and revisit it now before studying the present chapter in any depth.

We touched on the idea of subtypes and supertypes—more specifically, *entity* subtypes and supertypes—in Chapter 14, where we observed that (e.g.) if some employees are programmers and all programmers are employees, then we might regard entity type PROGRAMMER as a *subtype* of entity type EMPLOYEE, and entity type EMPLOYEE as a *supertype* of entity type PROGRAMMER. However, we did also say in that chapter that an "entity type" was not a type in any very formal sense of the term (partly because the term *entity* itself is not very formally defined). In this chapter, we will examine subtypes and supertypes in depth, but we will use the term *type* in the more formal and precise sense of Chapter 5. Let us begin, therefore, by defining the term carefully:

- A **type** is *a named set of values* (i.e., all possible values of the type in question), along with an associated set of *operators* that can be applied to values and variables of the type in question.

Furthermore:

- Any given type can be either system- or user-defined.
- Part of the definition of any given type is a specification of the set of all legal values of that type (that specification is the applicable *type constraint,* as described in Chapters 5 and 9).
- Such values can be of arbitrary complexity.
- The physical representation of such values is always hidden from the user; that is, *types* are distinguished from (physical) *representations*. However, each type has at least one *possible* representation that is explicitly exposed to the user by means of suitable THE_ operators (or something logically equivalent).
- Values and variables of a given type can be operated upon *solely* by means of the operators defined for the type in question.
- In addition to the THE_ operators already mentioned, those operators include:
  - At least one *selector* operator (more precisely, one such operator for each exposed possible representation), which allows every value of the type in question to be "selected," or specified, via an appropriate selector invocation
  - An *equality* operator, which allows two values of the type in question to be tested to see if they are in fact the same value
  - An *assignment* operator, which allows a value of the type in question to be assigned to a variable that has been declared to be of the type in question

And to the foregoing we now add:

- Some types are **subtypes** of other **supertypes**. If *B* is a subtype of *A,* then operators and type constraints that apply to *A* apply to—that is, "are inherited by"—*B* also, but *B* has operators and type constraints of its own that do not apply to *A*. (We will make these statements much more precise later.)

By way of example, suppose we have two types ELLIPSE and CIRCLE, with the obvious interpretations. Then we might say that type CIRCLE is a subtype of type ELLIPSE (and type ELLIPSE is a supertype of type CIRCLE), by which we mean that:

- Every circle is an ellipse (i.e., the set of all circles is a subset of the set of all ellipses), but the converse is not true.
- Therefore, every operator that applies to ellipses in general applies to circles in particular (because circles *are* ellipses), but the converse is not true. For example, the

operator THE_CTR ("the center of") might apply to ellipses and therefore to circles too, but the operator THE_R ("the radius of") might apply to circles only.

■ Moreover, any constraint that applies to ellipses in general applies to circles in particular (again, because circles are ellipses), but the converse is not true. For example, if ellipses are subject to the constraint $a \geq b$ (where a and b are the major and minor semiaxis, respectively), then this same constraint must be satisfied by circles too. For circles, of course, a and b coincide in the radius r, and the constraint is satisfied trivially; in fact, the constraint $a = b$ is, precisely, a constraint that applies to circles in particular but not to ellipses in general. *Note:* Here and throughout this chapter we use the unqualified term *constraint* to mean a type constraint specifically. We also use the terms *radius* and *semiaxis,* loosely, to mean what would more properly be called the corresponding radius or semiaxis *length.*

In sum: Type CIRCLE inherits operators and constraints from type ELLIPSE, but also has operators and constraints of its own that do not apply to type ELLIPSE. Observe, therefore, that the subtype has a *sub*set of the values but a *super*set of the properties—a fact that can sometimes cause confusion! (Here and throughout this chapter we use the term *properties* as a convenient shorthand for "operators and constraints.")

Why Type Inheritance?

Why is this topic worth investigating? There seem to be at least two answers to this question:

■ The ideas of subtyping and inheritance do seem to arise naturally in the real world; it is not at all unusual to encounter situations in which all values of a given type have certain properties in common, while some subset of those values have additional special properties of their own. Thus, subtyping and inheritance look as if they might be useful tools for "modeling reality" (or *semantic modeling,* as we called it in Chapter 14).

■ Second, if we can recognize such patterns—patterns of subtyping and inheritance, that is—and build intelligence regarding them into our application and system software, we might be able to achieve certain practical economies. For example, a program that works for ellipses might work for circles too, even if it was originally written with no thought for circles at all (perhaps type CIRCLE had not been defined at the time the program was written): the so-called **code reuse** benefit.

Despite these potential advantages, however, we now observe that there does not seem to be any consensus on a formal, rigorous, and abstract *model* of type inheritance. To quote reference [20.13]:

> The basic idea of inheritance is quite simple . . . [and yet, despite] its central role in current . . . systems, inheritance is still quite a controversial mechanism . . . [A] comprehensive view of inheritance is still missing.

The discussions in this chapter are based on a model developed by the present writer in conjunction with Hugh Darwen and described in detail in reference [3.3].[1] Be aware, therefore, that other writers and other texts use terms such as *subtype* and *inheritance* in ways that differ from ours. *Caveat lector.*

Some Preliminaries

There are a number of preliminaries we need to get out of the way before we can get down to a proper discussion of inheritance *per se.* Those preliminaries are the subject of this subsection.

- *Values are typed*

  To repeat from Chapter 5, if *v* is a value, then *v* can be thought of as carrying around with it a kind of flag that announces "I am an integer" or "I am a supplier number" or "I am a circle" (etc.). Now, without inheritance, every value is of exactly one type. With inheritance, however, a value can be of several types simultaneously; for example, a given value might be of types ELLIPSE and CIRCLE at the same time.

- *Variables are typed*

  Every variable has exactly one **declared** type. For example, we might declare a variable as follows:

  ```
  VAR E ELLIPSE ;
  ```

  The declared type of variable E here is ELLIPSE. Now, without inheritance, all possible values of a given variable are of exactly one type: namely, the applicable declared type. With inheritance, however, a given variable might have a value that is of several types simultaneously; for example, the current value of variable E might be an ellipse that is in fact a circle, and hence be of types ELLIPSE and CIRCLE at the same time.

- *Single vs. multiple inheritance*

  There are two broad "flavors" of type inheritance, single and multiple. Loosely speaking, **single** inheritance means each subtype has just one supertype and inherits properties from just that one supertype; **multiple** inheritance means a subtype can have any number of supertypes and inherits properties from all of them. Obviously, the former is a special case of the latter. Even single inheritance is fairly complicated, however (surprisingly so, in fact); in this chapter, therefore, we limit our attention to single inheritance only, and we take the unqualified term *inheritance* to mean *single* inheritance specifically. See reference [3.3] for a detailed treatment of both kinds of inheritance, multiple as well as single.

---

[1] As that reference makes clear, we do *not* want our model to be seen as just another academic exercise. Rather, we offer it for consideration by the community at large as a contender for filling the gap alluded to—that is, as a candidate for the role of an inheritance model that can provide that missing "comprehensive view of inheritance."

- *Scalar, tuple, and relation inheritance*

  Clearly, inheritance has implications for nonscalar values as well as scalar values,[2] since, ultimately, nonscalar values are built out of scalar values. In particular, it has implications for tuple and relation values specifically. Even scalar inheritance is fairly complicated, however (again, surprisingly so); in this chapter, therefore, we limit our attention to scalar inheritance only, and we take the unqualified terms *type, value, variable, operator,* and *expression* to refer to *scalar* types, values, variables, operators, and expressions specifically. See reference [3.3] for a detailed treatment of all kinds of inheritance, tuple and relation as well as scalar.

- *Structural vs. behavioral inheritance*

  Recall that scalar values can have an internal—that is, physical—representation or structure of arbitrary complexity; for example, ellipses and circles, which as we already know can legitimately be regarded as scalar values in suitable circumstances, certainly might have an internal structure that is quite complicated. However, that internal structure is always *hidden from the user.* It follows that when we talk of inheritance (at least so far as our model is concerned), we do not mean inheritance of structure, because from the user's point of view there *is* no structure to inherit! In other words, we are interested in what is sometimes called **behavioral** inheritance, not **structural** inheritance (where "behavior" refers to operators—though we remind you that in our model, at least, constraints are inherited too). *Note:* We do not preclude structural inheritance; it is just that we see it as an implementation issue merely, not relevant to the model.

- *"Subtables and supertables"*

  By now it should be clear to you that our inheritance model is concerned with what in relational terms might be called *domain* inheritance (recall that domains and types are the same thing). When asked about the possibility of inheritance in a relational context, however, most people immediately assume it is some kind of *table* inheritance that is under discussion. For example, SQL includes support for something it calls "subtables and supertables," according to which some table *B* might inherit all of the columns of some other table *A* and then add some more of its own (see Chapter 26). However, it is our position that the "subtables and supertables" idea is a totally separate phenomenon, one that might possibly be interesting—though we are skeptical [14.13]—but has nothing to do with type inheritance *per se.*

One last preliminary remark: The subject of type inheritance really has to do with *data in general*—it is not limited to just *database* data in particular. For simplicity, therefore, most examples in this chapter are expressed in terms of local data (ordinary program variables, etc.) instead of database data.

---

[2] Recall that *scalar* means there are no user-visible components. Do not be misled by the fact that scalar types have possible representations that do in turn have user-visible components, as explained in Chapter 5; those components are components of the possible representation, not components of the type—despite the fact that we sometimes refer to them, sloppily, as if they were indeed components of the type.

20.2 TYPE HIERARCHIES

We now introduce a running example that we will use throughout the rest of the chapter. The example involves a set of geometric types—PLANE_FIGURE, ELLIPSE, CIRCLE, POLYGON, and so on—arranged into what is called a **type hierarchy** (see Fig. 20.1). Here in outline are **Tutorial D** definitions for some of those geometric types (note the type constraints in particular):

```
TYPE PLANE_FIGURE ... ;

TYPE ELLIPSE
    IS PLANE_FIGURE
        POSSREP { A LENGTH, B LENGTH, CTR POINT
                CONSTRAINT A ≥ B } ;

TYPE CIRCLE
    IS ELLIPSE
        CONSTRAINT THE_A ( ELLIPSE ) = THE_B ( ELLIPSE )
        POSSREP { R  = THE_A ( ELLIPSE ) ,
                CTR = THE_CTR ( ELLIPSE ) } ;
```

Let us take a closer look at these definitions. First of all, we are assuming for simplicity that ellipses are always oriented such that their major axis *a* is horizontal and their minor axis *b* vertical; we are also assuming that the major semiaxis *a* is always greater than or equal to the minor semiaxis *b* (in other words, ellipses are "short and fat," not "tall and thin"). Thus, ellipses might possibly be represented by their semiaxes *a* and *b* (and their center). By contrast, circles might possibly be represented by their radius *r* (and their center).

Next, observe that:

- Type PLANE_FIGURE has no declared possible representation at all; in fact, we will see later in this chapter that PLANE_FIGURE is really a *union type*. (Actually it is a special kind of union type called a *dummy* type. A detailed discussion of dummy types is beyond the scope of this chapter, however; see reference [3.3] for further explanation.)

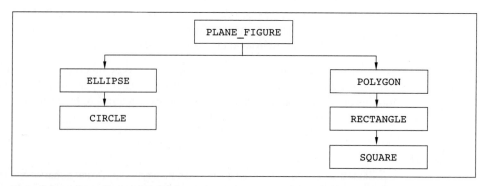

Fig. 20.1 A sample type hierarchy

- For type ELLIPSE, we have specified that every ellipse is a plane figure; we have also specified the {*a,b,ctr*} possible representation in the usual way, with a constraint to the effect that $a \geq b$. *Note:* For completeness, we ought really to add a constraint to the effect that *b* is greater than zero. We omit this constraint for brevity.

- For type CIRCLE, by contrast, we have specified that every circle is an ellipse, and we have also specified a constraint to the effect that $a = b$. Within that constraint, moreover, we have specified the {*r,ctr*} possible representation for circles, and we have also indicated how that possible representation is related to that for ellipses. Observe how the supertype name can be used in the context of such a constraint to denote an arbitrary value of the supertype in question.

Now the system knows, for example, that CIRCLE is a subtype of ELLIPSE, and hence that operators (and constraints) that apply to ellipses in general apply to circles in particular. Here in outline are definitions for some of those operators:

```
OPERATOR AREA ( E ELLIPSE ) RETURNS AREA ;
   /* "area of" — note that AREA is the name of both */
   /* the operator per se and the type of the result */ ... ;
END OPERATOR ;

OPERATOR THE_A ( E ELLIPSE ) RETURNS LENGTH ;
   /* "the a¯ semiaxis of" */ ... ;
END OPERATOR ;

OPERATOR THE_B ( E ELLIPSE ) RETURNS LENGTH ;
   /* "the b¯ semiaxis of" */ ... ;
END OPERATOR ;

OPERATOR THE_CTR ( E ELLIPSE ) RETURNS POINT ;
   /* "the center of" */ ... ;
END OPERATOR ;

OPERATOR THE_R ( C CIRCLE ) RETURNS LENGTH ;
   /* "the radius of" */ ... ;
END OPERATOR ;
```

All of these operators except THE_R apply to values of type ELLIPSE and hence *a fortiori* to values of type CIRCLE as well; THE_R, by contrast, applies to values of type CIRCLE only.

Terminology

There are unfortunately several more definitions and terms we need to introduce before we can proceed much further. The concepts are mostly straightforward, however.

1. A supertype of a supertype is a supertype; for example, POLYGON is a supertype of SQUARE.

2. Every type is a supertype of itself; for example, ELLIPSE is a supertype of ELLIPSE.

3. If *A* is a supertype of *B* and *A* and *B* are distinct, then *A* is a **proper** supertype of *B;* for example, POLYGON is a proper supertype of SQUARE. And if *A* is a proper supertype of *B,* then *A* must also be a proper super*set* of *B*—that is, there must be at least one value of type *A* that is not a value of type *B*.

Analogous remarks apply to subtypes, of course. Thus:

4. A subtype of a subtype is a subtype; for example, SQUARE is a subtype of POLYGON.

5. Every type is a subtype of itself; for example, ELLIPSE is a subtype of ELLIPSE.

6. If *B* is a subtype of *A* and *B* and *A* are distinct, then *B* is a **proper** subtype of *A;* that is, SQUARE is a proper subtype of POLYGON. And if *B* is a proper subtype of *A,* then *B* must also be a proper sub*set* of *A.*

Moreover:

7. If *A* is a supertype of *B* and there is no type *C* that is both a proper subtype of *A* and a proper supertype of *B,* then *A* is an **immediate** supertype of *B,* and *B* is an **immediate** subtype of *A;* for example, RECTANGLE is an immediate supertype of SQUARE, and SQUARE is an immediate subtype of RECTANGLE. Note, therefore, that in our **Tutorial D** syntax the keyword IS means, quite specifically, "is an *immediate* subtype of."

8. A **root** type is a type with no proper supertype; for example, PLANE_FIGURE is a root type. *Note:* We do not assume there is just one root type. If there are two or more, however, we can always invent some kind of "system" type that is an immediate supertype for all of them, so there is no loss of generality in assuming just one.

9. A **leaf** type is a type with no proper subtype; for example, CIRCLE is a leaf type. *Note:* This definition is slightly simplified, but it is adequate for present purposes (it needs a tiny extension to deal properly with multiple inheritance [3.3]).

10. Every proper subtype has exactly one immediate supertype. *Note:* Here we are just making explicit our assumption that we are dealing with single inheritance only. As already noted, the effects of relaxing this assumption are explored in detail in reference [3.3].

11. As long as (a) there is at least one type and (b) there are no *cycles*—that is, there is no sequence of types *T1, T2, T3, ..., Tn* such that *T1* is an immediate subtype of *T2, T2* is an immediate subtype of *T3, ...,* and *Tn* is an immediate subtype of *T1*—then at least one type *must* be a root type. *Note:* In fact, there *cannot* be any cycles (why not?).

The Disjointness Assumption

We make one further simplifying assumption, as follows: If *T1* and *T2* are distinct root types or distinct immediate subtypes of the same supertype (implying in particular that neither is a subtype of the other), then we assume they are **disjoint**—that is, no value is of both type *T1* and type *T2.* For example, no value is both an ellipse and a polygon.

The following further points are immediate consequences of this assumption:

12. Distinct type hierarchies are disjoint.

13. Distinct leaf types are disjoint.

14. Every value has exactly one **most specific** type. For example, a given value might be "just an ellipse" and not a circle, meaning its most specific type is ELLIPSE (in the

real world, some ellipses are not circles). In fact, to say that the most specific type of some value *v* is *T* is to say, precisely, that the set of types possessed by *v* is the set of all supertypes of *T* (a set that includes *T* itself, by definition).

One reason the disjointness assumption is desirable is that it avoids certain ambiguities that might otherwise occur. For example, suppose some value *v* could be of two types *T1* and *T2,* neither of which is a subtype of the other. Suppose further that an operator named *Op* has been defined for type *T1* and another operator with the same name *Op* has been defined for type *T2* (in other words, *Op* is *overloaded*—see Section 20.3). Then an invocation of *Op* with argument *v* would be ambiguous.

Note: The disjointness assumption is reasonable as long as we limit our attention to single inheritance only, but it does need to be relaxed for multiple inheritance. See reference [3.3] for a detailed discussion.

A Note on Physical Representation

Although we are primarily concerned with a *model* of inheritance, not with implementation matters, there are certain implementation issues that you do need to understand to some extent in order to understand the overall concept of inheritance properly—and now we come to one such:

15. The fact that *B* is a subtype of *A* does not imply that the hidden physical representation of *B* values is the same as that of *A* values.[3] For example, ellipses might physically be represented by their center and semiaxes, while circles might physically be represented by their center and radius (though there is no requirement, in general, that a physical representation be the same as any of the declared possible ones). This point will turn out to be important in several of the sections that follow.

20.3 POLYMORPHISM AND SUBSTITUTABILITY

In this section we discuss two crucial concepts, *polymorphism* and *substitutability,* that together provide the basis for achieving the code reuse benefit mentioned briefly in Section 20.1. We note immediately that these two concepts are really just different ways of looking at the same thing. Be that as it may, we begin with polymorphism.

Polymorphism

The very notion of inheritance implies that if *T'* is a subtype of *T,* then all operators that apply to values of type *T* apply to values of type *T'* as well. For example, if AREA(*e*) is

---

[3] In fact, there is no logical reason why all values of the *same* type have to have the same physical representation. For example, some points might be physically represented by Cartesian coordinates and some by polar coordinates; some temperatures might be physically represented in Celsius and some in Fahrenheit; some integers might be physically represented in decimal and some in binary; and so on. Of course, the system will have to know how to convert between physical representations in such cases in order to be able to implement assignments, comparisons, and so on properly.

legal, where *e* is an ellipse, then AREA(*c*), where *c* is a circle, must be legal as well. Note, therefore, that we need to be very careful over the logical difference between the **parameters** in terms of which a given operator is defined, with their *declared* types, and the corresponding **arguments** to a given invocation of that operator, with their *most specific* types. For example, the operator AREA is defined in terms of a parameter of declared type ELLIPSE—see Section 20.2—but the most specific type of the argument in the invocation AREA(*c*) is CIRCLE.

Recall now that ellipses and circles, at least as we defined them in Section 20.2, have different possible representations:

```
TYPE ELLIPSE ...
    POSSREP { A ..., B ..., CTR ... } ;

TYPE CIRCLE ...
    POSSREP { R ..., CTR ... } ;
```

It is conceivable, therefore, that two different versions of the AREA operator might exist under the covers, one that makes use of the ELLIPSE possible representation and one that makes use of the CIRCLE possible representation. To repeat, it is *conceivable*—but it is not *necessary*. For example, the code for ellipses might look like this:

```
OPERATOR AREA ( E ELLIPSE ) RETURNS AREA ;
    RETURN ( 3.14159 * THE_A ( E ) * THE_B ( E ) ) ;
END OPERATOR ;
```

(The area of an ellipse is π*ab*.) And this code obviously works correctly if it is invoked with a circle instead of a more general ellipse since, for a circle, THE_A and THE_B both return the radius *r*. However, the person responsible for defining type CIRCLE might prefer, for a variety of reasons, to implement a distinct version of AREA that is specific to circles and invokes THE_R instead of THE_A and THE_B. *Note:* In fact, it might be desirable for reasons of efficiency to implement two versions of the operator anyway, even if the possible representations are the same. Consider polygons and rectangles, for example. The algorithm that computes the area of a general polygon will certainly work for a rectangle, but for rectangles a more efficient algorithm—multiply the height by the width—is available.

Note, however, that the code for ellipses will certainly not work for circles if it is written in terms of the *physical* ELLIPSE representation instead of a possible one and the physical representations for types ELLIPSE and CIRCLE differ. The practice of implementing operators in terms of physical representations is generally not a good idea. Code defensively![4]

Anyway, if AREA is *not* reimplemented for type CIRCLE, then we get *code reuse* (for the AREA implementation code, that is). *Note:* We will encounter a more important kind of reuse in the next subsection.

From the point of view of the model, of course, it makes no difference how many versions of AREA exist under the covers: As far as the user is concerned, there is just one

---

[4] In fact, our own recommendation would be that access to physical representations be limited just to the code that implements those operators—selectors, THE_ operators, and so forth—*that are prescribed by the model.* (What is more, many of those operators are likely in practice to have system-provided implementations anyway.)

AREA operator, which works for ellipses and therefore for circles too, by definition. From the point of view of the model, in other words, AREA is **polymorphic**, meaning it can take arguments of different types on different invocations. Observe, therefore, that such polymorphism is a logical consequence of inheritance: If we have inheritance, we *must* have polymorphism—otherwise, we do not have inheritance!

Now, polymorphism *per se* is not a new idea, as you might have already realized (in fact, we discussed it briefly in Chapter 5). SQL, for example, already has polymorphic operators ("=", "+", "||", and many others), and in fact so do most other languages. Some languages even permit users to define their own polymorphic operators; PL/I provides such a facility, for example, under the name "GENERIC functions." However, there is no inheritance, as such, involved in any of these examples—they are all examples of what is called **overloading** polymorphism. The kind of polymorphism exhibited by the AREA operator, by contrast, is called **inclusion** polymorphism, on the grounds that the relationship between (say) circles and ellipses is basically that of *set inclusion* [20.4]. For obvious reasons, we take the unqualified term *polymorphism* in the remainder of this chapter to mean inclusion polymorphism specifically, barring explicit statements to the contrary.

Note: A helpful way of thinking about the difference between overloading and inclusion polymorphism is as follows:

- *Overloading* polymorphism means there are several distinct operators with the same name (and the user does need to know that the operators in question are in fact distinct, with distinct—though preferably similar—semantics). For example, "+" is overloaded in most languages: There is one "+" operator for adding integers, another "+" operator for adding rationals, and so on.

- *Inclusion* polymorphism means there is just one operator, with possibly several distinct implementation versions under the covers (but the user does not need to know whether or not there are in fact several implementation versions—to the user, to say it again, there is just one operator).

Programming with Polymorphism

Consider the following example. Suppose we need to write a program to display some diagram, made up of squares, circles, ellipses, and so on. Without polymorphism, the code will look something like the following pseudocode:

```
FOR EACH x ∈ DIAGRAM
    CASE ;
        WHEN IS_SQUARE ( x ) THEN CALL DISPLAY_SQUARE ... ;
        WHEN IS_CIRCLE ( x ) THEN CALL DISPLAY_CIRCLE ... ;
        .....
    END CASE ;
```

(We are assuming the existence of operators IS_SQUARE, IS_CIRCLE, and so forth, which can be used to test whether a given value is of the specified type. See Section 20.6.) With polymorphism, by contrast, the code is much simpler and much more succinct:

```
FOR EACH x ∈ DIAGRAM CALL DISPLAY ( x ) ;
```

Explanation: DISPLAY here is a polymorphic operator. The implementation version of DISPLAY that works for values of type *T* will be specified when type *T* is defined and will be made known to the system at that time. At run time, then, when the system encounters the DISPLAY invocation with argument *x,* it will have to determine the most specific type of *x* and then invoke the version of DISPLAY appropriate to that type—a process known as **run-time binding.**[5] In other words, polymorphism effectively means that CASE expressions and CASE statements that otherwise would have had to appear in the user's source code are *moved under the covers:* The system effectively performs those CASE operations on the user's behalf.

Note the implications of the foregoing for program maintenance in particular. Suppose, for example, that a new type TRIANGLE is defined as another immediate subtype of POLYGON, and hence that the diagram to be displayed can now additionally include triangles. Without polymorphism, every program that contains a CASE expression or statement like the one in the example will now have to be modified to include code of the form:

```
WHEN IS_TRIANGLE ( x ) THEN CALL DISPLAY_TRIANGLE ... ;
```

With polymorphism, however, no such source code modifications are necessary.

Because of examples like the foregoing, polymorphism is sometimes characterized, a little colorfully, as implying that "old code can invoke new code"; that is, a program *P* can effectively invoke some version of some operator that did not even exist (the version, that is) at the time *P* was written. So here we have another—and more important—example of *code reuse:* The very same program *P* might be usable on data that is of a type *T* that, to repeat, did not even exist at the time *P* was written.

Substitutability

As already mentioned, the concept of substitutability is really just the concept of polymorphism looked at from a slightly different point of view. We have seen, for example, that if AREA(*e*) is legal, where *e* is an ellipse, then AREA(*c*), where *c* is a circle, must be legal too. In other words, wherever the system expects an ellipse, we can always substitute a circle instead. More generally, wherever the system expects a value of type *T,* we can always substitute a value of type *T'* instead, where *T'* is a subtype of *T*—*The Principle of Value Substitutability*.

Note in particular that this principle implies that if some relation *r* has an attribute *A* of declared type ELLIPSE, some of the *A* values in *r* might be of type CIRCLE instead of just type ELLIPSE. Likewise, if some type *T* has a possible representation that involves a component *C* of declared type ELLIPSE, then for some values *v* of type *T* the operator invocation THE_*C*(*v*) might return a value of type CIRCLE instead of just type ELLIPSE.

Finally, we observe that, since it is really just polymorphism in another guise, substitutability too is a logical consequence of inheritance: If we have inheritance, we *must* have substitutability; otherwise, we do not have inheritance.

---

[5] Run-time binding is an implementation issue, of course, not a model issue. It is another of those implementation issues that you do have to appreciate to some extent in order to understand the overall concept of inheritance properly.

20.4 VARIABLES AND ASSIGNMENTS

Suppose we have two variables E and C of declared types ELLIPSE and CIRCLE, respectively:

```
VAR E ELLIPSE ;
VAR C CIRCLE ;
```

Let us initialize C to some circle—say (just to be definite) the circle with radius three and center the origin:

```
C  :=  CIRCLE ( LENGTH ( 3.0 ), POINT ( 0.0, 0.0 ) ) ;
```

The expression on the right side here is a selector invocation for type CIRCLE. Recall from Chapter 5 that for every declared possible representation there is a corresponding selector operator with the same name and with parameters corresponding to the components of the possible representation in question. The purpose of a selector is to allow the user to specify or "select" a value of the type in question by supplying a value for each component of the possible representation in question. *Note:* For simplicity, we assume here and throughout this chapter that the Cartesian possible representation for points is called POINT, instead of (as in Chapter 5) CARTESIAN. The second argument to the CIRCLE selector in the example is thus an invocation of that Cartesian selector for points.

Now consider the following assignment:

```
E  :=  C ;
```

Normally—that is, in the absence of subtyping and inheritance—the assignment operation requires the value denoted by the expression on the right side to be of the same type (namely, the *declared* type) as the variable on the left side. However, *The Principle of Value Substitutability* implies that wherever the system expects a value of type ELLIPSE we can always substitute a value of type CIRCLE, so the assignment is legal as shown (in fact, assignment is a polymorphic operator). And the effect is to copy the circle value from variable C into variable E; thus, the value of variable E after the assignment is of type CIRCLE, not just type ELLIPSE. In other words:

- **Values retain their most specific type on assignment to variables of less specific declared type.** Type conversion does *not* occur on such assignment (in the example, the circle is *not* converted to become "just an ellipse").[6] Note that we do not want any such conversion to be done, because it would cause the value's most specific behavior to be lost; in the case at hand, for example, it would mean that after the assignment we would not be able to obtain the radius of the circle value in variable E. (See the subsection "TREAT DOWN" later in this section for a discussion of what is involved in obtaining that radius.)

- It follows that *substitutability implies that a variable of declared type T can have a value whose most specific type is **any subtype** of T*. Note, therefore, that we must now

---

[6] In fact, a moment's reflection shows that the very idea of such a conversion is nonsense—for if it were possible, it would mean some value could have two most specific types at the same time.

be very careful over the logical difference between the *declared* type of a given variable and the *most specific* type of the current value of that variable. We will come back to this important point in the next subsection.

To continue with the example, suppose we now have another variable A, of declared type AREA:

```
VAR A AREA ;
```

Consider the following assignment:

```
A  :=  AREA ( E ) :
```

What happens here is the following:

- First, the system performs compile-time type checking on the expression AREA(E). That check succeeds, because E is of declared type ELLIPSE and the single parameter to the AREA operator is of declared type ELLIPSE also, as we saw in Section 20.2.

- Second, the system discovers at run time that the current most specific type of (the value in) E is CIRCLE, and therefore invokes the version of AREA that applies to circles; in other words, it performs the run-time binding process discussed in the previous section.

Of course, the fact that it is the circle version of AREA that is invoked, not the ELLIPSE version, should be of no concern to the user—to the user, to say it one more time, there is just one AREA operator.

Variables

We have seen that the current value v of a variable V of declared type T can have any subtype of T as its most specific type. It follows that we can model V as an *ordered triple* of the form $<DT,MST,v>$, where:

- DT is the declared type for variable V.
- MST is the current most specific type for variable V (meaning the most specific type of the value that is the current value of variable V).
- v is a value of most specific type MST—namely, the current value of variable V.

We use the notation $DT(V)$, $MST(V)$, and $v(V)$ to refer to the DT, MST, and v components, respectively, of this model of variable V. Note that (a) $MST(V)$ is always a subtype—not necessarily a proper subtype—of $DT(V)$; (b) $MST(V)$ and $v(V)$ change with time, in general; (c) in fact, $MST(V)$ is implied by $v(V)$, because every value is of exactly one most specific type.

This model of a variable is useful in pinning down the precise semantics of various operations, including assignment operations in particular. Before we can elaborate on this point, however, we must explain that the notions of declared type and current most specific type can be extended in an obvious way to apply to arbitrary expressions as well as to simple variables. Let X be such an expression, and let $v(X)$ be the result of evaluating that expression. Then:

- *X* has a *declared type, DT(X)*—namely, the declared type of the operator *Op* that is invoked at the outermost level of *X*. *DT(X)* is known at compile time.

- *X* also has a *current most specific type, MST(X)*—namely, the type that is the most specific type of *v(X)*. *MST(X)* is not known until run time (in general).

Now we can explain assignment properly. Consider the assignment

```
V  :=  X ;
```

(where *V* is a variable and *X* is an expression). *DT(X)* must be a subtype of *DT(V)*, otherwise the assignment is illegal (this is a compile-time check). If the assignment is legal, its effect is to set *MST(V)* equal to *MST(X)* and *v(V)* equal to *v(X)*.

Incidentally, note that if the current most specific type of variable *V* is *T*, then every proper supertype of type *T* is also a "current type" of variable *V*. For example, if variable E (of declared type ELLIPSE) has a current value of most specific type CIRCLE, then CIRCLE, ELLIPSE, and PLANE_FIGURE are all "current types" of E. However, the phrase "the current type of *X*" is usually taken, at least informally, to mean *MST(X)* specifically.

Substitutability Revisited

Consider the following operator definition:

```
OPERATOR COPY ( E ELLIPSE ) RETURNS ELLIPSE ;
   RETURN ( E ) ;
END OPERATOR ;
```

Because of substitutability, the COPY operator can be invoked with an argument of most specific type either ELLIPSE or CIRCLE—and whichever it is, it will clearly return a result of that same most specific type. It follows that the notion of substitutability has the further implication that *if operator Op is defined to have a result of declared type T, then the actual result of an invocation of Op can be of **any subtype** of type T* (in general). In other words, just as (a) a reference to a variable of declared type *T* can in fact denote a value of any subtype of *T* (in general), so (b) an invocation of an operator with declared type *T* can in fact return a value of any subtype of *T* (again, in general).

TREAT DOWN

Here again is the example from the beginning of this section:

```
VAR E ELLIPSE ;
VAR C CIRCLE ;

C  :=  CIRCLE ( LENGTH ( 3.0 ), POINT ( 0.0, 0.0 ) ) ;
E  :=  C ;
```

MST(E) is now CIRCLE. So suppose we want to get the radius of the circle in question and assign it to some variable L. We might try the following:

```
VAR L LENGTH ;

L  :=  THE_R ( E ) ;          /* compile-time type error !!! */
```

As the comment indicates, however, this code fails on a compile-time type error. To be specific, it fails because the operator THE_R ("the radius of") appearing on the right side of the assignment requires an argument of type CIRCLE and the declared type of the variable E is ELLIPSE, not CIRCLE. Note that if the compile-time type check were not done, we would get a *run-time* type error instead—which is worse—if the value of E at run time were just an ellipse and not a circle. In the case at hand, we do know that the value at run time will be a circle; the trouble is, we know this, but the compiler does not.

To address such problems, we introduce a new operator, which we refer to informally as *TREAT DOWN*. The correct way to obtain the radius in the example is as follows:

```
L  :=  THE_R ( TREAT_DOWN_AS_CIRCLE ( E ) ) ;
```

The expression TREAT_DOWN_AS_CIRCLE(E) is defined to be of declared type CIRCLE, so the compile-time type checking now succeeds. Then at run time:

- If the current value of E is indeed of type CIRCLE, then the overall expression does correctly return the radius of that circle. More precisely, the TREAT DOWN invocation yields a result, Z say, with (a) declared type $DT(Z)$ equal to CIRCLE, because of the ". . ._AS_CIRCLE" specification; (b) current most specific type $MST(Z)$ equal to $MST(E)$, which is CIRCLE also in the example; and (c) current value $v(Z)$ equal to $v(E)$. Finally, (d) the expression "THE_R(Z)" is evaluated, to give the desired radius (which can then be assigned to L).

- However, if the current value of E is only of type ELLIPSE, not CIRCLE, then the TREAT DOWN fails on a *run-time* type error.

The general intent of TREAT DOWN is to ensure that run-time type errors can occur only in the context of a TREAT DOWN invocation.

Note: Suppose CIRCLE in turn has a proper subtype, O_CIRCLE say (where an "O-circle" is a circle that is centered on the origin):

```
TYPE O_CIRCLE
    IS CIRCLE
        CONSTRAINT THE_CTR ( CIRCLE ) = POINT ( 0.0, 0.0 )
        POSSREP { R = THE_R ( CIRCLE ) } ;
```

Then the current value of variable E at some given time might be of most specific type O_CIRCLE instead of just CIRCLE. If it is, then the TREAT DOWN invocation

```
TREAT_DOWN_AS_CIRCLE ( E )
```

will succeed, and will yield a result, Z say, with (a) $DT(Z)$ equal to CIRCLE, because of the ". . ._AS_CIRCLE" specification; (b) $MST(Z)$ equal to O_CIRCLE, because O_CIRCLE is the most specific type of E; and (c) $v(Z)$ equal to $v(E)$. In other words (loosely): TREAT DOWN always leaves the most specific type alone, it never "pushes it up" to make it less specific than it was before.

Here for future reference is a more formal statement of the semantics of the operator invocation TREAT_DOWN_AS_$T(X)$, where X is some expression. First, $MST(X)$ must be a subtype of T (this is a run-time check); assuming this condition is satisfied, the invocation returns a result Z with $DT(Z)$ equal to T, $MST(Z)$ equal to $MST(X)$, and $v(Z)$ equal to $v(X)$. *Note:* Reference [3.3] also defines a generalized form of TREAT DOWN that allows one operand to be "treated down" to the type of another, instead of to some explicitly named type.

20.5 SPECIALIZATION BY CONSTRAINT

Consider the following example of a selector invocation for type ELLIPSE:

```
ELLIPSE ( LENGTH ( 5.0 ), LENGTH ( 5.0 ), POINT ( ... ) )
```

This expression returns an ellipse with equal semiaxes. But in the real world an ellipse with equal semiaxes is in fact a circle; so does this expression return a result of most specific type CIRCLE, rather than most specific type ELLIPSE?

Much controversy has raged in the literature—and in fact still does [20.6]—over questions like this one. In our own model, we decided, after much careful thought, to insist that the expression *does* return a result of most specific type CIRCLE. More generally, if type T' is a subtype of type T, and a selector invocation for type T returns a value that satisfies the type constraint for type T', then (in our model) the result of that selector invocation is of type T'. Now, few if any of today's commercial products actually behave this way at the time of writing, but we regard this fact as a failing on the part of those products; reference [3.3] shows that, as a consequence of this failing, those systems are forced to support "noncircular circles," "nonsquare squares," and similar nonsenses—a criticism that does not apply to our approach. *Note:* See also the discussion **of The Second Great Blunder** in Chapter 26.

It follows from the foregoing that (at least in our model) no value of most specific type ELLIPSE ever has $a = b$; in other words, values of most specific type ELLIPSE correspond precisely to real-world ellipses that are not circles. By contrast, values of most specific type ELLIPSE in other inheritance models correspond to real-world ellipses that *might or might not* be circles. We thus feel our model is a little closer to being "a good model of reality."

Finally, the idea that, for example, an ellipse with $a = b$ must be of type CIRCLE is known as **specialization by constraint** [3.3]—though we should warn you that other writers use this term, or something very close to it, to mean something completely different (see, e.g., references [20.10, 20.14]).

THE_ Pseudovariables Revisited

Recall from Chapter 5 that THE_ pseudovariables provide a way of updating one component of a variable while leaving the other components unchanged ("components" here referring to components of some *possible* representation, not necessarily a *physical* representation). For example, let variable E be of declared type ELLIPSE, and let the current value of E be an ellipse with (say) a five and b three. Then the assignment

```
THE_B ( E )  :=  LENGTH ( 4.0 ) ;
```

updates the b semiaxis of E to four without changing its a semiaxis or its center.

Now, as also noted in Chapter 5, THE_ pseudovariables are logically unnecessary—they are really just shorthand. For example, the assignment just shown, which uses a THE_ pseudovariable, is equivalent to the following one, which does not:

```
E  :=  ELLIPSE ( THE_A ( E ), LENGTH ( 4.0 ), THE_CTR ( E ) ) ;
```

So consider the following assignment:

```
THE_B ( E )  :=  LENGTH ( 5.0 ) ;
```

By definition, this assignment is equivalent to the following one:

```
E  :=  ELLIPSE ( THE_A ( E ), LENGTH ( 5.0 ), THE_CTR ( E ) ) ;
```

Specialization by constraint therefore comes into play (because the expression on the right side returns an ellipse with $a = b$), and the net effect is that after the assignment *MST*(E) is CIRCLE, not ELLIPSE.

Next, consider the assignment:

```
THE_B ( E )  :=  LENGTH ( 4.0 ) ;
```

Now E contains an ellipse with a five and b four, and *MST*(E) becomes ELLIPSE once again—an effect that we refer to as **generalization** by constraint.

Note: Suppose (as we did near the end of Section 20.4) that type CIRCLE has a proper subtype O_CIRCLE (where an "O-circle" is a circle with center the origin):

```
TYPE O_CIRCLE
     IS CIRCLE
        CONSTRAINT THE_CTR ( CIRCLE ) = POINT ( 0.0, 0.0 )
        POSSREP { R = THE_R ( CIRCLE ) } ;
```

Then the current value of variable E at some given time might be of most specific type O_CIRCLE instead of just CIRCLE. Suppose it is, and consider the following sequence of assignments:[7]

```
THE_A ( E )  :=  LENGTH ( 7.0 ) ;
THE_B ( E )  :=  LENGTH ( 7.0 ) ;
```

After the first of these assignments, E contains "just an ellipse," thanks to generalization by constraint. After the second, however, it contains a circle again—but is it an O-circle specifically or "just a circle"? Obviously, we would like it to be an O-circle specifically. And indeed so it is, precisely because it satisfies the constraint for type O_CIRCLE (including the constraint inherited by that type from type CIRCLE).

Changing Types Sideways

Once again, let E be a variable of declared type ELLIPSE. We have seen how to change the type of E "down" (e.g., if its current most specific type is ELLIPSE, we have seen how to update it so that its current most specific type becomes CIRCLE); we have also seen how to change the type of E "up" (e.g., if its current most specific type is CIRCLE, we have seen how to update it so that its current most specific type becomes ELLIPSE). But

---

[7] If multiple assignment were supported, we would be able to perform the sequence as a single operation.

what about changing type "sideways"? Suppose we extend our running example such that type ELLIPSE has two immediate subtypes, CIRCLE and NONCIRCLE, with the obvious meanings.[8] Without going into too much detail, it should be clear that:

- If the current value of E is of type CIRCLE (so $a = b$), updating E such that $a > b$ will cause *MST*(E) to become NONCIRCLE.
- If the current value of E is of type NONCIRCLE (so $a > b$), updating E such that $a = b$ will cause *MST*(E) to become CIRCLE.

Thus, specialization by constraint takes care of "sideways" type changes too. *Note:* In case you were wondering, updating E such that $a < b$ is impossible (it violates the constraint on type ELLIPSE).

20.6 COMPARISONS

Suppose we have our usual two variables E and C of declared types ELLIPSE and CIRCLE, respectively, and we assign the current value of C to E:

```
E  :=  C ;
```

Then it is surely obvious that if we now perform the equality comparison

```
E  =  C
```

we ought to get the result TRUE—and so indeed we do. The general rule is as follows. Let X and Y be arbitrary expressions. Then the comparison $X = Y$ is legal if the declared types $DT(X)$ and $DT(Y)$ have a common supertype (a requirement that is certainly satisfied if either is a supertype of the other, of course), otherwise it is illegal (this is a compile-time check). If it is legal, it returns TRUE if the value $v(X)$ is equal to the value $v(Y)$ and FALSE otherwise. Incidentally, note that X and Y cannot possibly "compare equal" if their most specific types are different, because if $v(X)$ is equal to $v(Y)$, then $MST(X)$ must be equal to $MST(Y)$.

Effect on the Relational Algebra

As we know from Chapter 7, equality comparisons are involved, implicitly or explicitly, in many of the operations of the relational algebra.[9] And when supertypes and subtypes are involved, it turns out that certain of those operations exhibit behavior that might be thought (at least at first blush) a little counterintuitive. Consider the relations RX and RY shown in Fig. 20.2. Observe that the sole attribute A in RX is of declared type ELLIPSE and its counterpart A in RY is of declared type CIRCLE. We adopt the convention that values of the form E*i* in the figure are ellipses that are not circles and values of the form C*i* are circles. Most specific types are shown in lowercase italics.

---

[8] ELLIPSE now becomes a *union type,* incidentally. See Section 20.7.

[9] The comparisons in question are actually tuple comparisons, but for present purposes we can treat them as if they were simple scalar comparisons instead.

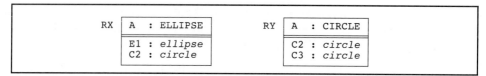

Fig. 20.2   Relations RX and RY

```
      RJ │ A   : ELLIPSE
         ├─────────────────
         │ C2  : circle
```

Fig. 20.3   The join RJ of relations RX and RY

Now consider the join of RX and RY, RJ say (see Fig. 20.3). Clearly, every A value in RJ will necessarily be of type CIRCLE (because any A value in RX whose most specific type is merely ELLIPSE cannot possibly "compare equal" to any A value in RY). Thus, it might be thought that the declared type of attribute A in RJ should be CIRCLE, not ELLIPSE. But consider the following:

- Since RX and RY each have A as their sole attribute, RX JOIN RY reduces to RX INTERSECT RY. In this case, therefore, the rule regarding the declared type of the result attribute for JOIN must obviously reduce to the analogous rule for INTERSECT.

- RX INTERSECT RY in turn is logically equivalent to RX MINUS (RX MINUS RY). Let the result of the second operand here—that is, RX MINUS RY—be RZ. Then it should be clear that:

  a. RZ will include some A values of most specific type ELLIPSE, in general, and so the declared type of attribute A in RZ must be ELLIPSE.

  b. The original expression thus reduces to RX MINUS RZ, where the declared type of attribute A in both RX and RZ is ELLIPSE, and hence yields a final result in which the declared type of attribute A must obviously be ELLIPSE once again.

- It follows that the declared type of the result attribute for RX INTERSECT RY, and therefore for RX JOIN RY as well, must be ELLIPSE, not CIRCLE—even though (to repeat) every *value* of that attribute must in fact be of type CIRCLE!

Now we turn to the relational difference operator, MINUS. First, consider RX MINUS RY. It should be clear that some A values in the result of this operation will be of type ELLIPSE, not CIRCLE, and so the declared type of A in that result must be of type ELLIPSE. But what about RY MINUS RX? Clearly, every A value in the result of this latter operation will be of type CIRCLE, and so again it might be thought that the declared type of A in that result should be CIRCLE, not ELLIPSE. However, observe that RX INTERSECT RY is logically equivalent, not only to RX MINUS (RX MINUS RY) as already discussed, but also to RY MINUS (RY MINUS RX); given this fact, it is easy to see that specifying the declared type of A in the result of RY MINUS RX to be CIRCLE leads to a contradiction. It follows that the declared type of the result attribute for RY MINUS RX must also be ELLIPSE, not CIRCLE, even though every *value* of that attribute will in fact be of type CIRCLE.

Finally, consider RX UNION RY. In this case it should be obvious that the result will include some A values of most specific type ELLIPSE, in general, and so the declared type of attribute A in that result must necessarily be ELLIPSE. Thus, the declared type of the result attribute for UNION must also be ELLIPSE (but this particular case—unlike the JOIN, INTERSECT, and MINUS cases—can hardly be said to be counterintuitive).

Here then is the general rule:

- Let *rx* and *ry* be relations with a common attribute *A,* and let the declared types of *A* in *rx* and *ry* be *DT(Ax)* and *DT(Ay)*, respectively. Consider the join of *rx* and *ry* (necessarily over *A,* at least in part). *DT(Ax)* and *DT(Ay)* must have a common supertype *T,* otherwise the join is illegal (this is a compile-time check). If the join is legal, the declared type of *A* in the result is the **most specific** of all such common supertypes *T.*

Analogous remarks apply to union, intersection, and difference: In every case, (a) corresponding attributes of the operands must be such that their declared types have a common supertype *T* and (b) the declared type of the corresponding attribute in the result is the most specific of all such common supertypes *T.*

Type Testing

In Section 20.3, we showed a code fragment that made use of operators of the form IS_SQUARE, IS_CIRCLE, and so on, for testing whether a specified value was of some specified type. It is time to take a closer look at such operators. First of all, we assume that defining a given type *T* causes automatic definition of a truth-valued operator of the form:

```
IS_T ( X )
```

This expression gives TRUE if the expression *X* is of type *T* and FALSE otherwise. For example, if C is a variable of declared type CIRCLE, then the expressions

```
IS_CIRCLE ( C )
IS_ELLIPSE ( C )
```

both give TRUE. And if E is a variable of declared type ELLIPSE but current most specific type some subtype of CIRCLE, the expression

```
IS_CIRCLE ( E )
```

gives TRUE also.

Type testing has implications for the relational operators, too. Consider the following example. Let relvar R have an attribute A of declared type ELLIPSE, and suppose we want to get those tuples of R where the A value is in fact a circle and the radius of that circle is greater than two. We might try the following:

```
R WHERE THE_R ( A ) > LENGTH ( 2.0 )
```

However, this expression will fail on a compile-time type error, because THE_R requires an argument of type CIRCLE and the declared type of A is ELLIPSE, not CIRCLE. (Of course, if the compile-time type check were not done, we would get a *run-time* type error instead as soon as we encountered a tuple in which the A value was just an ellipse and not a circle.) Clearly, what we need to do is eliminate the tuples in which the A value is just an ellipse before we even attempt to check the radius. And that is exactly what happens with the following formulation:

```
R : IS_CIRCLE ( A ) WHERE THE_R ( A ) > LENGTH ( 2.0 )
```

This expression is defined (loosely) to return those tuples in which the A value is a circle with radius greater than two. More precisely, it returns a relation with:

a. A heading the same as that of R, except that the declared type of attribute A in that result is CIRCLE instead of ELLIPSE

b. A body consisting of just those tuples of R in which the A value is of type CIRCLE and the radius for the circle in question is greater than two

In other words, we propose a new relational operator of the form

```
R : IS_T ( A )
```

where *R* is a relational expression and *A* is an attribute of the relation—*r,* say—denoted by that expression. The value of the overall expression is defined to be a relation with:

a. A heading the same as that of *r,* except that the declared type of attribute *A* in that heading is *T*

b. A body consisting of those tuples of *r* in which attribute *A* contains a value of type *T,* except that the declared type of attribute *A* in each of those tuples is *T*

Note: Reference [3.3] defines generalized forms of both of the operators introduced in this subsection—for example, a generalized form of IS_T that tests whether one operand is of the same type as another, instead of just testing whether it is of some explicitly named type.

20.7   OPERATORS, VERSIONS, AND SIGNATURES

Recall from Section 20.3 that a given operator can have many different implementation versions under the covers. That is, as we travel down the path from some supertype *T* to some subtype *T'* in the type hierarchy, we must (for a variety of reasons) at least be *allowed* to reimplement type *T* operators for type *T'*. By way of example, consider the following:

```
OPERATOR MOVE ( E ELLIPSE, R RECTANGLE ) RETURNS ELLIPSE
   VERSION ER_MOVE ;
   RETURN ( ELLIPSE ( THE_A ( E ), THE_B ( E ),
                               R_CTR ( R ) ) ) ;
END OPERATOR ;
```

Operator MOVE "moves" ellipse E, loosely speaking, so that it is centered on the center of rectangle R—or, more precisely, it returns an ellipse just like the argument ellipse corresponding to parameter E, except that it is centered on the center of the argument rectangle corresponding to parameter R. Note the VERSION specification in the second line, which introduces a distinguishing name, ER_MOVE, for this particular *version* of MOVE (we will define another version in just a moment). Note too that we have assumed the availability of an operator R_CTR that returns the center point of a specified rectangle.

Now we define another version of MOVE to move circles instead of ellipses:[10]

```
OPERATOR MOVE ( C CIRCLE, R RECTANGLE ) RETURNS CIRCLE
    VERSION CR_MOVE ;
    RETURN ( CIRCLE ( THE_R ( C ), R_CTR ( R ) ) ) ;
END OPERATOR ;
```

In like manner, we might define a version of MOVE for the case where the arguments are of most specific types ELLIPSE and SQUARE, respectively (ES_MOVE, say), and another for the case where the arguments are of most specific types CIRCLE and SQUARE, respectively (CS_MOVE, say).

Signatures

The term *signature* means, loosely, the combination of the name of some operator and the types of the operands to the operator in question. (We note in passing, however, that different writers and different languages ascribe slightly different meanings to the term. For example, the result type is sometimes regarded as part of the signature, and so too are operand and result names.) However, we have to be very careful once again over the logical differences between:

a. Arguments and parameters

b. Declared types and most specific types

c. Operators as perceived by the user and by the system (meaning in the latter case implementation versions of those operators that exist under the covers, as previously described)

In fact, we can distinguish—though the literature often does not!—at least three different kinds of signatures that are associated with any given operator *Op:* the unique *specification* signature, a set of *version* signatures, and a set of *invocation* signatures. To elaborate:

- The unique **specification signature** consists of the operator name *Op* together with the declared types, in order, of the parameters to *Op* as specified to the user by the *Op* definer. This signature corresponds to operator *Op* as perceived by the user. The specification signature for MOVE, for example, is just MOVE (ELLIPSE, RECTANGLE).

  Note: Reference [3.3] proposes that it be possible to separate the definition of the specification signature for a given operator from the definitions of *all* of the implementation versions of that operator. The basic idea is to support **union types** (also known as "abstract" or "noninstantiable" types, or sometimes just as "interfaces")— that is, types that are not the most specific type of any value at all. Such a type provides a way of specifying operators that apply to several different regular types, all of

---

[10] Actually there is little point in defining such a version in this particular example (why, exactly?).

them proper subtypes of the union type in question. Implementation versions of such an operator can then be defined for each of those regular subtypes. In terms of our running example, PLANE_FIGURE might well be a union type in this sense; the AREA operator specification signature might then be defined at the PLANE_FIGURE level, and explicit implementation versions then defined for type ELLIPSE, type POLYGON, and so on.

- Each implementation version of *Op* has its own **version signature**, consisting of the operator name *Op* together with the declared types, in order, of the parameters defined for that version. These signatures correspond to the various pieces of implementation code that implement *Op* under the covers. The version signature for the CR_MOVE version of MOVE, for example, is MOVE (CIRCLE, RECTANGLE).

- Each possible combination of most specific argument types has its own **invocation signature**, consisting of the operator name *Op* together with the most specific argument types, in order. These signatures correspond to various possible invocations of *Op* (the correspondence is one-to-many, of course—that is, one invocation signature can correspond to many actual invocations). For example, let E and R have most specific types CIRCLE and SQUARE, respectively. Then the invocation signature for the MOVE invocation MOVE(E,R) is MOVE (CIRCLE, SQUARE).

Different invocation signatures involving the same operator thus correspond, at least potentially, to different implementation versions of the operator under the covers. Thus, if several versions of the same operator do in fact exist under the covers, then which version is invoked on any given occasion will depend on which version signature is "the best match" for the applicable invocation signature. The process of deciding that best match—that is, the process of deciding which version to invoke—is the *run-time binding* process already discussed in Section 20.3.

Note, incidentally, that (a) *specification* signatures are truly a model concept; (b) *version* signatures are an implementation concept; (c) *invocation* signatures, though a model concept in a way, are really—like the concept of substitutability—just a logical consequence of the basic idea of type inheritance in the first place. Indeed, the fact that different invocation signatures are possible is really just part of the concept of substitutability.

Read-Only *vs.* Update Operators

Up to this point, our MOVE operator has been a read-only operator specifically. But suppose we were to make it an update operator instead:

```
OPERATOR MOVE ( E ELLIPSE, R RECTANGLE ) UPDATES E
   VERSION ER_MOVE ;
      THE_CTR ( E )  :=  R_CTR ( R ) ;
END OPERATOR ;
```

(We remind you that read-only and update operators are sometimes called *observers* and *mutators,* respectively. Refer to Chapter 5 if you need to refresh your memory on the difference between them.)

Observe now that an invocation of this version of MOVE *updates its first argument* (loosely, it "changes the center" of that argument). Observe further that the update works regardless of whether that first argument is of most specific type ELLIPSE or most specific type CIRCLE; in other words, an explicit implementation version for circles is no longer needed.[11] Thus, one advantage of update operators in general is that they might save us from having to write out certain implementation versions explicitly. Note the implications for program maintenance in particular; for example, what happens if we subsequently introduce O_CIRCLE as a subtype of CIRCLE? (*Answer:* Invoking MOVE with an argument variable of declared type ELLIPSE or CIRCLE but current most specific type O_CIRCLE will work just fine. However, invoking it with an argument variable of declared type O_CIRCLE will *not* work, in general.)

Changing Operator Semantics

The fact that it is always at least legal to reimplement operators as we go down the type hierarchy has one very important consequence: It opens up the possibility of *changing the semantics* of the operator in question. In the case of AREA, for example, it might be the case that the implementation for type CIRCLE actually returns the circumference of the circle in question, say, instead of the area. (Careful type design can help to alleviate this problem somewhat; for example, if operator AREA is defined to return a result of type AREA, obviously the implementation cannot return a result of type LENGTH instead. It can, however, still return the *wrong* area!)

Surprising as it might seem, it can even be claimed—in fact, it *has* been claimed—that changing semantics in this way can be desirable. For example, let type TOLL_HIGHWAY be a proper subtype of type HIGHWAY, and let TRAVEL_TIME be an operator that computes the time it takes to travel between two specified points on a specified highway. For a toll highway, the formula is $(d/s) + (n*t)$, where d = distance, s = speed, n = number of tollbooths, and t = time spent at each tollbooth. For a nontoll highway, by contrast, the formula is just d/s.

By way of a counterexample—that is, an example of a situation in which a semantic change is surely *un*desirable—consider ellipses and circles once again. Presumably we would like the AREA operator to be defined in such a way that a given circle has the same area, regardless of whether we consider it as a circle specifically or just as an ellipse. In other words, suppose the following sequence of events occurs:

1. We define type ELLIPSE and a corresponding version of the AREA operator. Assume for simplicity that the AREA code does not make use of the *physical* representation for ellipses.

2. We define type CIRCLE as a subtype of ELLIPSE but do not (yet) define a separate implementation version of AREA for circles.

3. We invoke AREA on some specific circle c to obtain a result, *a1* say. That invocation makes use of the ELLIPSE version of AREA (since that is the only version that currently exists).

4. We now define a separate implementation version of AREA for circles.

---

[11] As noted in Footnote 10, such a version was not really needed in the read-only case either—we introduced it purely for the sake of the example.

5. We invoke AREA again on the same specific circle *c* as before to obtain a result, *a2* say (and this time it is the CIRCLE version of AREA that is invoked).

At this point, surely we would require that *a2* = *a1*. However, this would-be requirement is not enforceable; that is, there is, as already noted, always the possibility that the version of AREA implemented for circles might return (say) the circumference instead of the area, or simply the wrong area.

Let us return to the TRAVEL_TIME example. The fact is, we find that example, and others like it, extremely unconvincing—unconvincing, that is, as an example of a situation in which changing the semantics of an operator might be thought desirable. For consider:

- If TOLL_HIGHWAY is truly a subtype of HIGHWAY, it means by definition that every individual toll highway is in fact a highway.

- Therefore, some highways (i.e., some values of type HIGHWAY) are indeed toll highways—they do indeed have tollbooths. So type HIGHWAY is not "highways with no tollbooths," it is "highways with *n* tollbooths" (where *n* might be zero).

- So the operator TRAVEL_TIME for type HIGHWAY is not "compute the travel time for a highway *with no* tollbooths," it is "compute the travel time *d/s* for a highway *ignoring* tollbooths."

- The operator TRAVEL_TIME for type TOLL_HIGHWAY, by contrast, is "compute the travel time *(d/s) + (n∗t)* for a highway *not* ignoring tollbooths." So in fact the two TRAVEL_TIMEs are logically different operators! Confusion arises because those two different operators have been given the same name; in fact, what we have here is *overloading* polymorphism, not *inclusion* polymorphism. (As an aside, we remark that further confusion arises in practice because, regrettably, many writers use the term *overloading* to refer to inclusion polymorphism anyway.)

To sum up: We still do not believe that changing semantics is ever a good idea. As we have seen, this requirement is not enforceable; however, we can certainly define our inheritance model—and we do—to say that if the semantics *are* changed, then **the implementation is in violation** (i.e., it is not an implementation of the model, and the consequences are unpredictable). Observe that our position on this matter (i.e., that such changes are illegal) does have the advantage that, regardless of whether any explicit specializations of a given operator *Op* are defined, the user perception remains the same: namely, (a) there exists an operator—a *single* operator—called *Op*, and (b) that operator *Op* applies to argument values of some specified type *T* and hence, by definition, to argument values of any proper subtype of *T*.

20.8   IS A CIRCLE AN ELLIPSE?

Are circles really ellipses? We have been assuming throughout this chapter so far—reasonably enough!—that they are, but we must now face up to the fact there is much debate in the literature on this apparently obvious point [20.6]. Consider our usual variables E and C of declared types ELLIPSE and CIRCLE, respectively. Suppose these variables have been initialized as follows:

```
E  :=  ELLIPSE ( LENGTH ( 5.0 ), LENGTH ( 3.0 ),
                           POINT ( 0.0, 0.0 ) ) ) ;
C  :=  CIRCLE  ( LENGTH ( 5.0 ), POINT ( 0.0, 0.0 ) ) ) ;
```

Note in particular that THE_A(C) and THE_B(C) both now have the value five.

Now, one operation we can certainly perform on E is "update the *a* semiaxis"—for example:

```
THE_A ( E )  :=  LENGTH ( 6.0 ) ;
```

But if we try to perform the analogous operation on C—

```
THE_A ( C )  :=  LENGTH ( 6.0 ) ;
```

—we get an error! What kind of error, exactly? Well, if the update were to be done, variable C would wind up containing a "circle" that violates the constraint on circles to the effect that *a* = *b;* to be specific, *a* would now be six, while *b* would presumably still be five (since we have not changed it). In other words, C would now contain a "noncircular circle," thereby violating the type constraint on type CIRCLE.

Since "noncircular circles" are an affront to logic and common sense, it seems reasonable to suggest that the update not be allowed in the first place. And the obvious way to achieve this effect is to reject such operations at compile time, by defining update of— that is, assignment to—the *a* or *b* semiaxis of a circle to be *syntactically* illegal. In other words, assignment to THE_A or THE_B does not apply to type CIRCLE, and the attempted update fails on a compile-time type error.

Note: In fact, it is obvious that such assignments must be syntactically illegal. Recall that assignment to a THE_ pseudovariable is really just shorthand. Thus, for example, the attempted assignment to THE_A(C), if it were legal, would have to be shorthand for something like this:

```
C  :=  CIRCLE ( ... ) ;
```

And the CIRCLE selector invocation on the right side here would have to include a THE_A argument of LENGTH(6.0). But the CIRCLE selector does not take a THE_A argument!— it takes a THE_R argument and a THE_CTR argument. So the original assignment must clearly be illegal.

What About Changing the Semantics?

Let us immediately head off a suggestion that might be made in an attempt to rescue the idea that assignment to THE_A or THE_B should be legal for circles after all. The suggestion is that assignment to (e.g.) THE_A should be *redefined*—in other words, a new version of the operator should be implemented—for a circle in such a way as to have the side effect of assignment to THE_B too, so that the circle still satisfies the constraint *a* = *b* after the update. We reject this suggestion for at least three reasons:

- First, the semantics of assignment to THE_A and THE_B are—very deliberately!— prescribed by our model and *must not* be changed in the manner suggested.

- Second, even if those semantics were not prescribed by the model, we have already argued that (a) changing the semantics of an operator in arbitrary ways is a bad idea in general and (b) changing the semantics of an operator in such a way as to cause side effects is an even worse one. It is a good general principle to insist that operators have exactly the requested effect, no more and no less.

- Third, and most important, the option of changing the semantics in the manner suggested is not always available, anyway. For example, let type ELLIPSE have another immediate subtype NONCIRCLE; let the constraint $a > b$ apply to noncircles; and consider an assignment to THE_A for a noncircle that, if accepted, would set a equal to b. What would be an appropriate semantic redefinition for that assignment? Exactly what side effect would be appropriate?

Does a Sensible Model Even Exist?

So we are left with the situation that assignment to THE_A or THE_B is an operation that applies to ellipses in general but not to circles in particular. But:

a. Type CIRCLE is supposed to be a subtype of type ELLIPSE.

b. To say that type CIRCLE is a subtype of type ELLIPSE is supposed to mean that operations that apply to ellipses in general apply to—in other words, are *inherited by*—circles in particular.

c. But now we are saying that the operation of assignment to THE_A or THE_B is *not* inherited after all.

So do we not have a contradiction on our hands? What is going on?

Before trying to answer these questions, we need to stress the seriousness of the problem. The foregoing argument looks like a real threadpuller. For if certain operators are *not* inherited by type CIRCLE from type ELLIPSE, in what sense exactly can we say that a circle is an ellipse? What does inheritance mean if some operators are in fact not inherited after all? Does a sensible inheritance model even exist? Are we chasing a chimera in trying to find one?

Note: Some writers have even seriously suggested that assignment to THE_A should work for both circles and ellipses (for a circle, it would update the radius), while assignment to THE_B should work for ellipses only, and so ELLIPSE should really be a subtype of CIRCLE! In other words, we have the type hierarchy upside down. A moment's thought suffices to show that this idea is a nonstarter, however; in particular, substitutability would break down (what is the radius of a general ellipse?).

It is precisely considerations such as the foregoing that have led some writers to conclude that there really is no such thing as a sensible inheritance model (see the annotation to reference [20.2]). Others have proposed inheritance models with features that are counterintuitive or clearly undesirable. For example, SQL permits "noncircular circles" and other such nonsenses, as we will see in Section 20.10. (In fact, SQL does not support type constraints at all, and it is that omission that allows such nonsenses to arise in the first place. Again, see Section 20.10.)

The Solution

To summarize the situation so far, we find ourselves faced with the following dilemma:

- If circles inherit the operators "assignment to THE_A and THE_B" from ellipses, then we get noncircular circles.

- The way to prevent noncircular circles is to support type constraints.

- But if we support type constraints, then the operators cannot be inherited.

- So there is no inheritance after all!

How can we resolve this dilemma?

The way out is—as so often—to recognize and act upon the fact that there is a major logical difference between values and variables. When we say "every circle is an ellipse," what we mean, more precisely, is that every circle *value* is an ellipse *value*. We certainly do not mean that every circle *variable* is an ellipse *variable* (a variable of declared type CIRCLE is *not* a variable of declared type ELLIPSE, and it cannot contain a value of most specific type ELLIPSE). In other words, **inheritance applies to values, not variables.** In the case of ellipses and circles, for example:

- As just noted, every circle value is an ellipse value.

- Therefore, all operations that apply to ellipse values apply to circle values too.

- But the one thing we cannot do to *any* value is change it!—if we could, it would be that value no longer. (Of course, we can "change the current value of" a variable, by updating that variable, but—to repeat—we cannot change the value as such.)

Now, the operations that apply to ellipse values are precisely all of the *read-only* operators defined for type ELLIPSE, while the operations that update ELLIPSE variables are, of course, the *update* operators defined for that type. Hence, our dictum that "inheritance applies to values, not variables" can be stated more precisely as follows:

- **Read-only operators are inherited by values, and hence *a fortiori* by current values of variables** (since read-only operators can obviously be applied—harmlessly—to those values that happen to be the current values of variables).

This more precise statement also serves to explain why the concepts of polymorphism and substitutability refer very specifically to *values,* not variables. For example (and just to remind you), substitutability says that wherever the system expects a **value** of type *T,* we can always substitute a **value** of type *T'* instead, where *T'* is a subtype of *T* (boldface added for emphasis). In fact, we specifically referred to this principle, when we first introduced it, as *The Principle of Value Substitutability* (again, note the emphasis).

What about update operators, then? By definition, such operators apply to variables, not values. So can we say that update operators that apply to variables of type ELLIPSE are inherited by variables of type CIRCLE?

Well, no, we cannot—not quite. For example, assignment to THE_CTR does apply to variables of both declared types, but (as we have seen) assignment to THE_A does not. Thus, inheritance of update operators has to be *conditional;* in fact, precisely which update operators are inherited must be specified explicitly. For example:

- Variables of declared type ELLIPSE have update operators MOVE (update version) and assignment to THE_A, THE_B, and THE_CTR.
- Variables of declared type CIRCLE have update operators MOVE (update version) and assignment to THE_CTR and THE_R but *not* to THE_A or THE_B.

Note: The MOVE operator was discussed in the previous section.

Of course, if an update operator *is* inherited, then we do have a kind of polymorphism and a kind of substitutability that apply to variables instead of values. For example, the update version of MOVE expects an argument that is a variable of declared type ELLIPSE, but we can invoke it with an argument that is a variable of declared type CIRCLE instead (though not with an argument that is a variable of declared type O_CIRCLE!). Thus, we can (and do) talk sensibly about another principle, *The Principle of **Variable** Substitutability*—but that principle is more restrictive than *The Principle of Value Substitutability* discussed previously.

20.9   SPECIALIZATION BY CONSTRAINT REVISITED

There is a small but significant postscript that needs to be added to the discussions of the foregoing sections. It has to do with examples like this one: "Let type CIRCLE have a proper subtype called COLORED_CIRCLE" (meaning that "colored circles" are supposed to be a special case of circles in general). Examples of this general nature are commonly cited in the literature. Yet we have to say that we find such examples extremely unconvincing—even misleading, in certain important respects. To be more specific, we suggest in the case at hand that it really does not make sense to think of colored circles as being somehow a special case of circles in general. After all, "colored circles" must by definition be *images,* on a display screen perhaps, whereas circles in general are not images but *geometric figures.* Thus, it seems more reasonable to regard COLORED_CIRCLE not as a subtype of CIRCLE, but rather as *a completely separate type.*[12] That separate type might well have a *possible representation* in which one component is of type CIRCLE and another is of type COLOR, but it is not—to repeat—a subtype of type CIRCLE.

Inheriting Possible Representations

A strong argument in support of the foregoing position is as follows. First, let us switch back for a moment to our more usual example of ellipses and circles. Here once again are the type definitions (in outline):

```
TYPE ELLIPSE ...
      POSSREP { A ..., B ..., CTR ... } ;

TYPE CIRCLE ...
      POSSREP { R ..., CTR ... } ;
```

---

[12] Indeed, COLORED_CIRCLE is a subtype of CIRCLE to exactly the same extent that it is a subtype of COLOR (which is to say, not at all).

Note in particular that ellipses and circles have different declared possible representations. However, the possible representation for ellipses is—necessarily, albeit implicitly—a possible representation for circles too, because circles *are* ellipses. That is, circles can certainly be "possibly represented" by their *a* and *b* semiaxes (and their center), even though in fact their *a* and *b* semiaxes are both the same. Of course, the converse is not true; that is, a possible representation for circles is not necessarily a possible representation for ellipses.

It follows that we might regard possible representations, like operators and constraints, as further "properties" that are inherited by circles from ellipses, or more generally by subtypes from supertypes.[13] But (reverting now to the case of circles and colored circles) it should be clear that the declared possible representation for type CIRCLE is *not* a possible representation for type COLORED_CIRCLE, because there is nothing in it that is capable of representing the color! This fact strongly suggests that colored circles are not circles in the same sense that, for example, circles are ellipses.

So What Do Subtypes Really Mean?

The next argument is related (somewhat) to the previous one, but is in fact stronger (*logically* stronger, that is). Here it is: *There is no way to obtain a colored circle from a circle via specialization by constraint.*

In order to explain this point, we go back once again to the case of ellipses and circles. Here again are the type definitions, now shown complete:

```
TYPE ELLIPSE
    IS PLANE_FIGURE
       POSSREP { A LENGTH, B LENGTH, CTR POINT
                CONSTRAINT A ≥ B } ;

TYPE CIRCLE
    IS ELLIPSE
       CONSTRAINT THE_A ( ELLIPSE ) = THE_B ( ELLIPSE )
       POSSREP { R  = THE_A ( ELLIPSE ) ,
                CTR = THE_CTR ( ELLIPSE ) } ;
```

As we know, thanks to specialization by constraint, the CONSTRAINT specification for type CIRCLE guarantees that an ellipse with $a = b$ will automatically be specialized to type CIRCLE. But—switching back to circles and colored circles—there is no CONSTRAINT specification we can write for type COLORED_CIRCLE that will analogously cause a circle to be specialized to type COLORED_CIRCLE; in other words, there is no type constraint we can write such that if it is satisfied by some given circle, it means the circle in question is really a colored circle.

Again, therefore, it seems much more reasonable to regard COLORED_CIRCLE and CIRCLE as completely different types, and to regard type COLORED_CIRCLE in

---

[13] We do not regard them in this way in our formal model—that is, we do not regard such inherited possible representations as *declared* ones—because to say they were declared ones would lead to a contradiction. To be specific, if we said that type CIRCLE inherits a possible representation from type ELLIPSE, then reference [3.3] would require assignment to THE_A or THE_B for a variable of declared type CIRCLE to be legal, and of course we know it is not. Thus, to say that type CIRCLE inherits a possible representation from type ELLIPSE is only a manner of speaking—it carries no formal weight.

particular as having a possible representation in which one component is of type CIRCLE and another is of type COLOR, thus:

```
TYPE COLORED_CIRCLE POSSREP { CIR CIRCLE, COL COLOR } ... ;
```

In fact, we are touching here on a much larger issue. The fact is, we believe that subtyping should *always* be via specialization by constraint! That is, we suggest that **if T' is a subtype of T, there should *always* be a type constraint such that, if it is satisfied by some given value of type T, then the value in question is really a value of type T'** (and should automatically be specialized to type T'). For let T and T' be types, and let T' be a subtype of T (in fact, we can assume without loss of generality that T' is an *immediate* subtype of T). Then:

- T and T' are both basically *sets* (named sets of values), and T' is a subset of T.

- Thus, T and T' both have *membership predicates:* predicates, that is, such that a value is a member of the set in question (and hence a value of the type in question) if and only if it satisfies the predicate in question. Let those predicates be P and P', respectively.

- Observe now that predicate P' is, by definition, a predicate that can evaluate to TRUE only for certain values that are in fact values of type T. Thus, it can in fact be formulated in terms of values of type T (rather than in terms of values of type T').

- And that predicate P', formulated in terms of values of type T, is precisely the type constraint that values of type T have to satisfy in order to be values of type T'. In other words, a value of type T is specialized to type T' precisely if it satisfies the constraint P'.

Thus, we claim that specialization by constraint is the *only* conceptually valid means of defining subtypes. As a consequence, we reject examples like the one suggesting that COLORED_CIRCLE might be a subtype of CIRCLE.

20.10 SQL FACILITIES

SQL's explicit inheritance support is limited to single inheritance (only) for "structured types" (only); it has no explicit inheritance support for generated types, no explicit support for multiple inheritance, and no inheritance support at all for built-in types or DISTINCT types.[14]

Here then is the syntax (slightly simplified) for defining a structured type:

```
CREATE TYPE <type name>
      [ UNDER <type name> ]
      [ AS <representation> ]
      [ [ NOT ] INSTANTIABLE ]
        NOT FINAL
      [ <method specification commalist> ] ;
```

---

[14] As these remarks are meant to suggest, SQL does have some *implicit* support for inheritance of generated types and for multiple inheritance (as do the proposals of reference [3.3] also, though these latter are more extensive). In this chapter, however, we are limiting our attention to single inheritance and scalar types only.

And here by way of example are possible SQL definitions for the types PLANE_ FIGURE, ELLIPSE, and CIRCLE:

```
CREATE TYPE PLANE_FIGURE
       NOT INSTANTIABLE
       NOT FINAL ;

CREATE TYPE ELLIPSE UNDER PLANE_FIGURE
   AS ( A LENGTH, B LENGTH, CTR POINT )
       INSTANTIABLE
       NOT FINAL ;

CREATE TYPE CIRCLE UNDER ELLIPSE
   AS ( R LENGTH )
       INSTANTIABLE
       NOT FINAL ;
```

Points arising (some repeated from Chapter 5):

1. NOT INSTANTIABLE means the type in question has no "instances," where the term *instance* means—presumably—a value whose most specific type is the type in question.[15] In other words, the type in question is what we have called a union type. INSTANTIABLE means the type in question does have at least one "instance"; that is, it is not a union type, and there does exist at least one value whose most specific type is the type in question. In our example, type PLANE_FIGURE is NOT INSTANTIABLE, while types ELLIPSE and CIRCLE are INSTANTIABLE (the default is INSTANTIABLE).

2. As noted in Chapter 5, NOT FINAL *must* be specified (though SQL:2003 will probably allow the alternative FINAL to be specified instead). NOT FINAL means the type in question is allowed to have proper subtypes; FINAL, if supported, would mean the opposite.

3. The UNDER specification identifies this type's immediate supertype (or *direct* supertype, in SQL terms), if any. Thus, for example, CIRCLE is a "direct subtype" of ELLIPSE, and properties that apply to ellipses in general are inherited, unconditionally, by circles in particular. Note, however, that:

   a. "Properties" here does not mean (as it does in our inheritance model) operators and constraints, it means operators and *structure* (or representation). In other words, SQL supports both behavioral inheritance and structural inheritance, because the internal structure of "structured types" is explicitly exposed to the user. See point 5.

   b. "Operators" here does not mean (as it does in our inheritance model) just read-only operators, it means *all* operators. In other words, SQL does not adequately distinguish between values and variables, and it requires unconditional inheritance of update operators as well as read-only ones—with the consequence that, for example, circles might not be circular, squares might not be square, and so on. (To pursue the point a moment longer: In our model, if some value v is of most specific type ELLIPSE, then it is definitely an ellipse that is not a circle, and if it is of most specific type CIRCLE, then it is definitely an ellipse that is a circle, in real-world terms. In SQL, by contrast, if v is of most specific type ELLIPSE, it might in fact

---

[15] Reference [4.23] defines an *instance* to be "a physical representation of a value" (?).

be a circle, and if it is of most specific type CIRCLE, it might in fact be an ellipse that is not a circle—again in real-world terms.)

   c. The operators in question fall into three categories: *functions, procedures,* and *methods.* As noted in Chapter 5, functions and procedures correspond roughly to our read-only and update operators, respectively; methods behave like functions, but are invoked using a different syntactic style. Also, functions and procedures are specified via separate CREATE FUNCTION and CREATE PROCEDURE statements, but methods are specified inline as part of the relevant CREATE TYPE statement, as the CREATE TYPE syntax indicates (we omitted method specifications from our examples for simplicity). Compile-time binding—that is, binding on the basis of declared types only—applies to functions and procedures; run-time binding applies to methods, but it is done on the basis of just one of the arguments involved (as is also the case, typically, in object systems—see Chapter 25).

4. The SQL term for *root type* is *maximal supertype;* thus, PLANE_FIGURE in our example is a maximal supertype. (Oddly, the SQL term for *leaf type* is not *minimal subtype* but *leaf type,* so CIRCLE in our example is a leaf type.)

5. The *<representation>*, if specified, consists of an *<attribute definition commalist>* enclosed in parentheses, where an *<attribute>* consists of an *<attribute name>* followed by a *<type name>*. Note, however, that such a *<representation>* is the actual *physical representation*—not a "possrep"—for values of the type in question (and so those physical representations are exposed to the user, as already noted under point 3). Observe in particular that it is not possible to specify two or more distinct *<representation>*s for the same type. *Note:* As mentioned in Chapter 5, however, the type designer can effectively conceal the fact that the *<representation>* is physical by a judicious choice and design of operators.

6. Each *<attribute>* has an *observer method* and a *mutator method,* which are provided automatically and together can be used to achieve functionality analogous, somewhat, to that of **Tutorial D**'s THE_ operators (see Chapter 5 for some examples). There are no automatically provided selector operators, but each type does have an automatically provided *constructor function* that when invoked returns that unique value of the type for which each and every attribute takes the applicable default value—which as we saw in Chapter 5 must be null for any attribute that is itself of a user-defined type in turn. Thus, for example, the expression

```
ELLIPSE ()
```

returns the "ellipse" with A and B both "the null length" and CTR "the null point" (not to be confused with the point whose X and Y components are both null, of course). And the expression

```
ELLIPSE () . A    ( LENGTH () . L ( 4.0 ) )
          . B    ( LENGTH () . L ( 3.0 ) )
          . CTR ( POINT ()   . X ( 0.0 ) . Y ( 0.0 ) )
```

returns the ellipse with *a* four, *b* three, and center the origin. (We have assumed that type LENGTH has a representation consisting of just one attribute, L, of type FLOAT.)

7. Observe that there is no way to specify the set of legal values of the type; in other words, there are no type constraints, except for the *a priori* ones that are implied by the physical representation. It follows *a fortiori* that SQL does not support much in the way of constraint inheritance!—as already noted under point 3.

8. Every structured type has an associated *reference type*. We do not discuss reference types in this chapter, however, except to note that, along with its support for reference types, SQL includes support for "subtables and supertables." We will examine these matters further in Chapter 26.

Now we proceed to examine SQL's type inheritance support in a little more detail. Note first that SQL does resemble our model (at least as that model applies to single inheritance only) insofar as it relies on the disjointness assumption and hence on the assumption that most specific types are unique. Also, SQL does support substitutability (though since it does not distinguish properly between values and variables, nor between read-only and update operators, it also does not distinguish properly between value and variable substitutability). It does not use the term *polymorphism*.

SQL supports counterparts to our TREAT DOWN and type testing operators. For example:

- The SQL analog of TREAT_DOWN_AS_CIRCLE (E) is TREAT (E AS CIRCLE).

- The SQL analog of IS_CIRCLE (E) is TYPE (E) IS OF (CIRCLE).

- The SQL analog of

```
R : IS_CIRCLE ( E )
```

is

```
SELECT TREAT ( E AS CIRCLE ) AS E, F, G, ..., H
FROM    R
WHERE   TYPE ( E ) IS OF ( CIRCLE )
```

(where F, G, ..., H are all of the attributes of R apart from E).

Now, since it does not support type constraints, SQL obviously does not support specialization or generalization by constraint either. Note, however, that this fact does not mean that the most specific type of a variable cannot change. For example:

```
DECLARE E ELLIPSE ;

SET E = CX ;
SET E = EX ;
```

CX and EX here are expressions that return values of most specific type CIRCLE and ELLIPSE, respectively. Thus, after the first assignment, the variable E (which has declared type ELLIPSE) has most specific type CIRCLE; after the second, it has most specific type ELLIPSE. Note carefully, however, that (to say it again) these effects are *not* obtained by specialization or generalization by constraint.

Finally, recall from Chapter 5 that a given structured type does not necessarily have an associated "=" operator—and even if it does, the semantics of that operator are completely user-defined. In fact, SQL does not even require the most specific types of the comparands to be the same in order for the comparison to give TRUE! It follows that if there are any structured types involved, there is no guarantee that SQL will support joins, unions, intersections, and differences properly. Note too that this criticism applies regardless of whether there is any type inheritance involved.

Inheritance or Delegation?

Now we need to confess that our discussions in this section so far might have been misleading in one important respect. The fact is, SQL's type inheritance mechanism—unlike our own inheritance model—is almost certainly *not* designed to support the idea that subtypes are obtained by constraining supertypes. Consider ellipses and circles once again:

```
CREATE TYPE ELLIPSE UNDER PLANE_FIGURE
   AS ( A LENGTH, B LENGTH, CTR POINT ) ... ;

CREATE TYPE CIRCLE UNDER ELLIPSE
   AS ( R LENGTH ) ... ;
```

With these definitions, type CIRCLE has attributes A, B, CTR (inherited from type ELLIPSE), and R (specified for type CIRCLE only). And if it is true that the specified attributes constitute the *physical* representation, then any given circle will be physically represented by a collection of four values, three of which will normally all be the same! For this reason, it is likely that the definition of type CIRCLE would actually *not* specify any *<representation>* of its own at all; instead, it would simply inherit the representation specified for type ELLIPSE. On the other hand, if the representation for type CIRCLE has no R ("radius") component, there will be no automatically provided observer and mutator methods for the radius. And then on the third hand . . . If the representation does have an R component, and we "mutate" it, we will wind up with a "noncircular circle"—that is, a "circle" for which the A, B, and R values are *not* all the same after all.

For one reason or another, therefore, it might be argued that "ellipses and circles" is not a good example to use as a basis for illustrating SQL's type inheritance functionality. Certainly it is true that SQL does not deal with that example very well. So let us switch to a different one:

```
CREATE TYPE CIRCLE
   AS ( R LENGTH, CTR POINT )
       INSTANTIABLE
       NOT FINAL ;

CREATE TYPE COLORED_CIRCLE UNDER CIRCLE
   AS ( COL COLOR )
       INSTANTIABLE
       NOT FINAL ;
```

This example is exactly the one we were deprecating earlier, in Section 20.9, where we claimed that "colored circles are not circles in the same sense that, for example, circles are ellipses." But if we are talking about inheriting, and possibly extending, *representations,* then the example makes a little more sense. Certainly it is reasonable to think of a colored circle as being represented by a radius, a center, and a color. Note further that if we say that type COLORED_CIRCLE is "UNDER" type CIRCLE, then it is also reasonable to think of operators that work for circles in general—for example, an operator to get the radius—as applying to colored circles in particular (colored circles can be *substituted* for circles). But the one thing that does not make sense is to think of colored circles being a "constrained form" of circles in general, or equivalently of colored circles being obtained from circles via specialization by constraint. In other words, the SQL inheritance mechanism seems to be designed, not for dealing with inheritance at all in the sense in which we defined that term earlier in this chapter, but rather for dealing with what some writers call *delegation.* Delegation means that the responsibility for implementing certain operators associated with the type is "delegated" to the type of some component of that type's representation (for example, "get the radius" for a colored circle is implemented by invoking "get the radius" on the corresponding circle component). And it might have been clearer to call the SQL mechanism a delegation mechanism in the first place, instead of pretending it had anything to do with subtypes.

20.11 SUMMARY

We have sketched the basic concepts of a **type inheritance model**. If type B is a subtype of type A (equivalently, if type A is a supertype of type B), then every value of type B is also a value of type A, and hence constraints and operators that apply to values of type A apply to values of type B also (but there will also be constraints and operators that apply to values of type B that do not apply to values that are only of type A). In fact, we can now be more specific and say that if B is a proper subtype of A, then:

- The set of B values is a proper subset of the set of A values.
- B has a proper superset of the constraints that apply to A.
- B has a proper superset of the read-only operators that apply to A.
- B has a proper subset of the update operators that apply to A (but it might have additional update operators of its own as well that do not apply to A).

We distinguished **single** *vs.* **multiple** inheritance (but discussed single inheritance only) and **scalar** *vs.* **tuple** *vs.* **relation** inheritance (but discussed scalar inheritance only),[16] and we introduced the concept of a **type hierarchy**. We also defined the terms *proper subtype* and *supertype,* *immediate* subtype and *supertype,* and *root* type and *leaf type,* and we stated a **disjointness assumption**: Types $T1$ and $T2$ are disjoint unless one is a subtype of the other. As a consequence of this assumption, every value has a unique **most specific type** (not necessarily a leaf type).

Next, we discussed the concepts of (inclusion) **polymorphism** and (value) **substitutability**, both of which are logical consequences of the basic notion of inheritance. We distinguished between **inclusion** polymorphism, which has to do with inheritance, and **overloading** polymorphism, which does not. And we showed how—thanks to **run-time binding**—inclusion polymorphism could lead to **code reuse**.

We then moved on to consider the effects of inheritance on **assignment** operations. The basic point is that type conversions do *not* occur—values retain their most specific

---

[16] We can at least say, however, that the ideas discussed in this chapter for single and scalar inheritance extend quite gracefully (and in fact surprisingly easily) to multiple, tuple, and relation inheritance, as is shown in reference [3.3].

type on assignment to variables of less specific declared type—and hence a variable of declared type T can have a value whose most specific type is any subtype of T. (Likewise, if operator Op is defined to have a result of declared type T, the actual result of an invocation of Op can be a value whose most specific type is any subtype of type T.) We therefore model a variable V—or, more generally, an arbitrary expression—as an ordered triple of the form $<DT,MST,v>$, where DT is the declared type, MST is the current most specific type, and v is the current value. We introduced the **TREAT DOWN** operator to allow us to operate in ways that would otherwise give rise to a compile-time type error on expressions whose most specific type at run time is some proper subtype of their declared type. (Run-time type errors can still occur, but only within the context of TREAT DOWN.)

Next we took a closer look at **selectors**. We saw that invoking a selector for type T will sometimes yield a result of some proper subtype of T (at least in our model, though not—typically—in today's commercial products): **specialization by constraint**. We then took a closer look at **THE_ pseudovariables**; since they are really just shorthand, both specialization and **generalization** by constraint can occur on assignment to a THE_ pseudovariable.

We then went on to discuss the effects of subtypes and supertypes on **equality comparisons** and certain relational operations (**join, union, intersection,** and **difference**). We also introduced a number of **type testing** operators (**IS_T** and so on). Then we considered the question of **read-only** *vs.* **update operators**, operator **versions**, and operator **signatures**, pointing out that the ability to define different versions of an operator opens the door to **changing the semantics** of the operator in question (but our model prohibits such changes).

Next, we examined the question "Are circles really ellipses?" That examination led us to the position that **inheritance applies to values, not variables**. More precisely, read-only operators (which apply to values) can be inherited 100 percent without any problem, but update operators (which apply to variables) can be inherited only **conditionally**. (Our model is at odds with most other approaches here. Those other approaches typically require update operators to be inherited unconditionally, but they then suffer from a variety of problems having to do with "noncircular circles" and the like.) It is our opinion that specialization by constraint is the *only* logically valid way of defining subtypes.

We also briefly discussed the concept of **delegation**, which is related to inheritance but logically distinct from it (it too has code reuse as a goal). And we sketched the SQL inheritance mechanism, concluding that the mechanism in question was really aimed at solving the delegation problem rather than the inheritance problem. We remind you that we will have more to say regarding SQL-style inheritance in Chapter 26.

EXERCISES

20.1 Explain the following in your own words:

code reuse	proper subtype
delegation	root type
generalization by constraint	run-time binding

immediate subtype	signature
inheritance	specialization by constraint
leaf type	substitutability
polymorphism	union type

20.2 Explain the TREAT DOWN operator.

20.3 Distinguish:

argument	*vs.*	parameter
declared type	*vs.*	current most specific type
inclusion polymorphism	*vs.*	overloading polymorphism
version signature	*vs.*	specification signature
	vs.	invocation signature
read-only operator	*vs.*	update operator
value	*vs.*	variable

(Regarding the last two of these, see also Exercise 5.2.)

20.4 With reference to the type hierarchy of Fig. 20.1, consider a value *e* of type ELLIPSE. The most specific type of *e* is either ELLIPSE or CIRCLE. What is the *least* specific type of *e?*

20.5 Any given type hierarchy includes several subhierarchies that can be regarded as type hierarchies in their own right. For example, the hierarchy obtained from that of Fig. 20.1 by deleting types PLANE_FIGURE, ELLIPSE, and CIRCLE (only) can be regarded as a type hierarchy in its own right, and so can the one obtained by deleting types CIRCLE, SQUARE, and RECTANGLE (only). On the other hand, the hierarchy obtained by deleting ELLIPSE (only) *cannot* be regarded as a type hierarchy in its own right (at least, not one that can be derived from that of Fig. 20.1), because type CIRCLE "loses some of its inheritance," as it were, in that hierarchy. How many distinct type hierarchies are there altogether in Fig. 20.1?

20.6 Using the syntax sketched in the chapter, give type definitions for types RECTANGLE and SQUARE. Assume for simplicity that all rectangles are centered on the origin, but do not assume that all sides are either vertical or horizontal.

20.7 Given your answer to Exercise 20.6, define an operator to rotate a specified rectangle through 90 degrees about its center. Also define an implementation version of that operator for squares.

20.8 Here is a repeat of an example from Section 20.6: "Relvar R has an attribute A of declared type ELLIPSE, and we want to query R to get those tuples where the A value is in fact a circle and the radius of that circle is greater than two." We gave the following formulation of this query in Section 20.6:

```
R : IS_CIRCLE ( A ) WHERE THE_R ( A ) > LENGTH ( 2.0 )
```

a. Why could we not simply express the type test in the WHERE clause?—for example:

```
R WHERE IS_CIRCLE ( A ) AND THE_R ( A ) > LENGTH ( 2.0 )
```

b. Another putative formulation is:

```
R WHERE CASE
          WHEN IS_CIRCLE ( A ) THEN
                THE_R ( TREAT_DOWN_AS_CIRCLE ( A ) )
                                    > LENGTH ( 2.0 )
          WHEN NOT ( IS_CIRCLE ( A ) ) THEN FALSE
        END CASE
```

Is this one valid? If not, why not?

20.9   Reference [3.3] proposes support for relational expressions of the form:

```
R TREAT_DOWN_AS_T ( A )
```

Here *R* is a relational expression, *A* is an attribute of the relation—*r*, say—denoted by that expression, and *T* is a type. The value of the overall expression is defined to be a relation with:

    a. A heading the same as that of *r*, except that the declared type of attribute *A* in that heading is *T*

    b. A body containing the same tuples as *r*, except that the *A* value in each of those tuples has been treated down to type *T*

Once again, however, this operator is just a shorthand—for what, exactly?

20.10   Expressions of the form *R*:IS_*T*(*A*) are also shorthand—for what, exactly?

20.11   SQL supports constructor functions instead of selectors. What is the difference?

20.12   Why do you think SQL fails to support type constraints? What about specialization by constraint?

REFERENCES AND BIBLIOGRAPHY

For interest, we state here without further elaboration the sole major changes required to our inheritance model as described in the body of the chapter in order to support multiple inheritance. First, we relax the disjointness assumption by requiring only that *root* types must be disjoint. Second, we replace the definition of "most specific type" by the following requirement: Every set of types *T1, T2, ..., Tn (n ≥ 0)* must have a common subtype *T'* such that a given value is of each of the types *T1, T2, ..., Tn* if and only if it is of type *T'*. See reference [3.3] for a detailed discussion of these points, also of the extensions required to support tuple and relation inheritance.

20.1 Alphora: *Dataphor™ Product Documentation.* Available from Alphora, 2474 North University Avenue, Provo, Utah 84604 (see also *http://www.alphora.com*).

    Dataphor is a commercial product that supports a large subset of the inheritance model as described in the body of this chapter (as well as a large subset of everything else proposed in *The Third Manifesto* [3.3]).

20.2 Malcolm Atkinson *et al.:* "The Object-Oriented Database System Manifesto," Proc. 1st Int. Conf. on Deductive and Object-Oriented Databases, Kyoto, Japan (1989). New York, N.Y.: Elsevier Science (1990).

    Regarding the lack of consensus (noted in Section 20.1) on a good inheritance model, the authors of this paper have the following to say: "[There] are at least four types of inheritance: *substitution* inheritance, *inclusion* inheritance, *constraint* inheritance, and *specialization* inheritance . . . Various degrees of these four types of inheritance are provided by existing systems and prototypes, and we do not prescribe a specific style of inheritance."

    Here are some more quotes that illustrate the same general point:

- Cleaveland [20.5] says: "[Inheritance can be] based on [a variety of] different criteria and there is no commonly accepted standard definition"—and proceeds to give eight possible interpretations. (Meyer [20.11] gives twelve.)

- Baclawski and Indurkhya [20.3] say: "[A] programming language [merely] provides a set of [inheritance] mechanisms. While these mechanisms certainly restrict what one can do in that language and what views of inheritance can be implemented . . . they do not by themselves validate some view of inheritance or other. Classes, specializations, generalizations, and inheritance are only concepts, and . . . they do not have a universal objective meaning . . . This [fact] implies that how inheritance is to be incorporated into a specific system is up to the designers of [that] system, and it constitutes a policy decision that must be implemented with the available mechanisms." In other words, there is no model!

However, we disagree with the foregoing conclusions, as this chapter makes clear.

Note: This reference appears again as reference [25.1] in Chapter 25, where further commentary on it can be found.

20.3 Kenneth Baclawski and Bipin Indurkhya: Technical Correspondence, *CACM 37,* No. 9 (September 1994).

20.4 Luca Cardelli and Peter Wegner: "On Understanding Types, Data Abstraction, and Polymorphism," *ACM Comp. Surv. 17,* No. 4 (December 1985).

20.5 J. Craig Cleaveland: *An Introduction to Data Types.* Reading, Mass.: Addison-Wesley (1986).

20.6 C. J. Date: "Is a Circle an Ellipse?" *http://www.dbdebunk.com* (July 2001).

There seems to be virtual unanimity in the industry that the answer to the question of this paper's title is *no.* The paper quotes some authorities on the issue and attempts to deconstruct their arguments. *Note:* When it was first published, this paper attracted a huge amount of online commentary and criticism, most of which can also be found on *http://www.dbdebunk.com.*

20.7 C. J. Date: "What Does Substitutability Really Mean?" *http://www.dbdebunk.com* (July 2002).

A careful analysis and criticism of reference [20.9].

20.8 You-Chin Fuh *et al.:* "Implementation of SQL3 Structured Types with Inheritance and Value Substitutability," Proc. 25th Int. Conf. on Very Large Data Bases, Edinburgh, Scotland (September 1999).

To quote from the abstract: "This paper presents the DB2 approach . . . First, values of structured types are represented in a self-descriptive manner and manipulated only through system-generated observer/mutator methods, minimizing the impact on the low-level storage manager. Second, the value-based semantics of mutators is implemented efficiently through a compile-time copy avoidance algorithm. Third, values of structured types are stored inline or out-of-line dynamically." *Note:* The expression "the value-based semantics of mutators" refers to the fact that SQL mutators are actually *read-only* operators (the desired "mutation" effect is achieved by invoking the mutator on the desired target, *T* say, and then assigning the result of that invocation back to *T*).

20.9 Barbara Liskov and Jeannette Wing: "A Behavioral Notion of Subtyping," *ACM TOPLAS (Transactions on Programming Languages and Systems) 16,* No. 6 (November 1994).

Substitutability is referred to as *the Liskov Substitution Principle* (LSP) in much of the literature. This paper is credited with being the source of that principle.

20.10 Nelson Mattos and Linda G. DeMichiel: "Recent Design Trade-Offs in SQL3," *ACM SIGMOD Record 23,* No. 4 (December 1994).

This paper gives the rationale for the decision on the part of the SQL language designers not to support type constraints (it is based on an argument given earlier by Zdonik and Maier in reference [20.14]). We disagree with that rationale, however. The fundamental problem with it is that it fails to distinguish properly between values and variables.

20.11 Bertrand Meyer: "The Many Faces of Inheritance: A Taxonomy of Taxonomy," *IEEE Computer 29,* No. 5 (May 1996).

20.12 James Rumbaugh: "A Matter of Intent: How to Define Subclasses," *Journal of Object-Oriented Programming* (September 1996).

As noted in Section 20.9, we take the view that specialization by constraint is the only logically valid way of defining subtypes. It is interesting to observe, therefore, that the object world takes exactly the opposite position!—or, at least, some occupants of that world do. To quote Rumbaugh: "Is SQUARE a subclass of RECTANGLE? . . . Stretching the *x*-dimension of a rectangle is a perfectly reasonable thing to do. But if you do it to a square, then the object is no longer a square. This is not necessarily a bad thing conceptually. When you stretch a square you *do* get a rectangle . . . But . . . most object-oriented languages do not want objects to change class . . . All of this suggests [a] design principle for classification systems: *A subclass should not be defined by constraining a superclass*" (italics in the original). *Note:* The object world often uses the term *class* to mean what we mean by the term *type* (see Chapter 25).

We find it striking that Rumbaugh apparently takes the position he does simply because object-oriented languages "do not want objects to change class." We would rather get the model right first before worrying about implementations. (In any case, we believe we do know how to implement specialization by constraint efficiently, and we have documented some of our ideas in this connection in reference [3.3].)

20.13 Andrew Taivalsaari: "On the Notion of Inheritance," *ACM Comp. Surv. 28,* No. 3 (September 1996).

20.14 Stanley B. Zdonik and David Maier: "Fundamentals of Object-Oriented Databases," in reference [25.42].

Distributed Databases

21.1 INTRODUCTION

We touched on the subject of distributed databases at the end of Chapter 2, where we said that (to quote) "full distributed database support implies that a single application should be able to operate "transparently" on data that is spread across a variety of different databases, managed by a variety of different DBMSs, running on a variety of different machines, supported by a variety of different operating systems, and connected by a variety of different communication networks—where "transparently" means the application operates from a logical point of view as if the data were all managed by a single DBMS running on a single machine." We are now in a position to examine these ideas in some detail. To be specific, in this chapter we will explain exactly what a distributed database is, why such databases are becoming increasingly important (think of the World Wide Web in particular—see Chapter 27), and what some of the technical problems are in this field.

Chapter 2 also briefly discussed **client/server** systems, which can be regarded as a simple special case of distributed systems in general. We will consider client/server systems specifically in Section 21.5.

The overall plan of the chapter is explained at the end of the next section.

21.2 SOME PRELIMINARIES

We begin with a working definition (necessarily a little imprecise at this stage):

- A distributed database system consists of a collection of *sites,* connected together via some kind of communications network, in which:

  a. Each site is a full database system site in its own right, but

  b. The sites have agreed to work together so that a user at any site can access data anywhere in the network exactly as if the data were all stored at the user's own site.

It follows that a "distributed database" is really a kind of *virtual* database, whose component parts are physically stored in a number of distinct "real" databases at a number of distinct sites (in effect, it is the logical union of those real databases). An example is shown in Fig. 21.1.

Note that, to repeat, *each site is a database system site in its own right.* In other words, each site has its own local "real" databases, its own local users, its own local DBMS and transaction management software (including its own local locking, logging, recovery, etc., software), and its own local data communications manager (DC manager). In particular, a given user can perform operations on data at that user's own local site exactly as if that site did not participate in the distributed system at all (at least, such a capability is an objective). The overall distributed system can thus be regarded as a kind of **partnership** among the individual local DBMSs at the individual local sites; a new software component at each site—logically an extension of the local DBMS—provides the necessary partnership functionality, and it is the combination of these new components together with the existing DBMSs that constitutes what is usually called the **distributed database management system**.

Incidentally, it is common to assume that the component sites are physically dispersed—possibly in fact geographically dispersed also, as suggested by Fig. 21.1—although actually it is sufficient that they be dispersed *logically.* Two "sites" might even coexist on the same physical machine (especially during initial system testing). In fact, the emphasis in distributed systems has shifted back and forth over time; the earliest research tended to assume geographic distribution, but most of the first few commercial installations involved *local* distribution instead, with (e.g.) several "sites" all in the same building and connected together by means of a local area network (LAN). More recently, however, the dramatic proliferation of wide area networks (WANs) has revived interest in the geographically distributed case. Either way, it makes little difference—essentially the same problems have to be solved (at least, this is true from a *database* perspective)—and so we can reasonably regard Fig. 21.1 as representing a typical system for the purposes of this chapter.

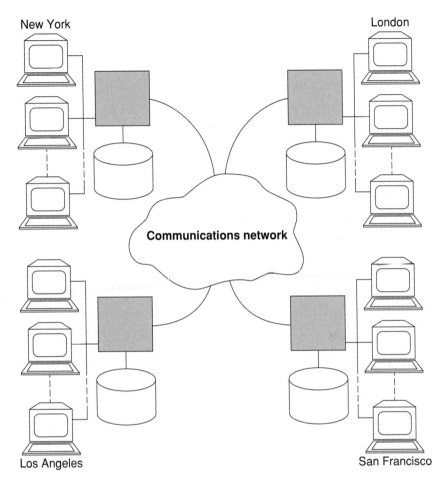

Fig. 21.1 A typical distributed database system

Note: In order to simplify the exposition, we will assume until further notice that the system is *homogeneous,* in the sense that each site is running a copy of the same DBMS: the **strict homogeneity assumption**. We will explore the possibility of relaxing this assumption in Section 21.6.

Advantages

Why are distributed databases desirable? The basic answer to this question is that enterprises are usually distributed already, at least logically (into divisions, departments, workgroups, etc.), and very likely physically too (into plants, factories, laboratories, etc.)—from which it follows that data is usually distributed already as well, because each organizational unit within the enterprise will naturally maintain data that is relevant to its own operation. The total information asset of the enterprise is thus splintered into what are sometimes called *islands of information.* And what a distributed system does is provide the necessary "bridges" to connect those islands together. In other words, it enables the structure of the database to mirror the structure of the enterprise—local data can be kept locally, where it most logically belongs—while at the same time remote data can be accessed when necessary.

An example will help clarify the foregoing. Consider Fig. 21.1 once again. For simplicity, suppose there are only two sites, Los Angeles and San Francisco, and suppose the system is a banking system, with account data for Los Angeles accounts kept in Los Angeles and account data for San Francisco accounts kept in San Francisco. Then the advantages are surely obvious: The distributed arrangement combines **efficiency of processing** (the data is kept close to the point where it is most frequently used) with **increased accessibility** (it is possible to access a Los Angeles account from San Francisco and *vice versa,* via the communications network).

Allowing the structure of the database to mirror the structure of the enterprise is, as just explained, probably the most significant benefit of distributed systems. Numerous additional benefits do also accrue, of course, but we will defer discussion of them to appropriate points later in the chapter. However, we should mention that there are some disadvantages too, of which the biggest is the fact that distributed systems are *complex,* at least from a technical point of view. Ideally, that complexity should be the implementer's problem, not the user's, but it is likely—to be pragmatic—that some aspects of it will show through to users, unless very careful precautions are taken.

Sample Systems

For purposes of subsequent reference, we briefly mention some of the better-known distributed DBMS implementations. First, prototypes. Out of numerous research systems, three of the best known are (a) *SDD-1,* which was built in the research division of Computer Corporation of America in the late 1970s and early 1980s [21.32]; (b) *R** ("R star"), a distributed version of the System R prototype, built at IBM Research in the early 1980s [21.37];[1] and (c) *Distributed Ingres,* a distributed version of the Ingres prototype, also built in the early 1980s at the University of California at Berkeley [21.34].

As for commercial implementations, most of today's SQL products offer some kind of distributed database support (with varying degrees of functionality). Some of the best known are (a) *Ingres/Star,* the distributed database component of Ingres; (b) the *distributed database option* of Oracle; and (c) the *distributed data facility* of DB2.

Note: Vendors have a habit of changing product names with great frequency, and we do not guarantee that the foregoing names (or possibly even products, in some cases) are still in current use. Also, the product and prototype lists are not meant to be exhaustive— they are just meant to identify systems that either have been particularly influential for one reason or another, or else have some special intrinsic interest. But it is at least worth pointing out that all of the systems mentioned, both prototypes and products, are relational sys-

---

[1] The star is the so-called *Kleene operator*—"R*" means "zero or more [System] R's."

tems specifically (at least, they all support SQL). In fact, there are several reasons why, for a distributed database system to be successful, that system *must* be relational; relational technology is a prerequisite to (effective) distributed technology [15.6]. We will see some of the reasons for this state of affairs as we proceed through the chapter.

A Fundamental Principle

Now we can state what might be regarded as **the fundamental principle of distributed database** [21.13]:

> *To the user, a distributed system should look exactly like a **non**distributed system.*

In other words, users in a distributed system should be able to behave exactly as if the system were not distributed. All of the problems of distributed systems are—or should be—internal or implementation-level problems, not external or user-level problems.

Note: The term *users* in the foregoing paragraph refers specifically to users (end users or application programmers) who are performing data *manipulation* operations; all such operations should remain logically unchanged. Data *definition* operations, by contrast, will require some extension in a distributed system—for example, so that a user (perhaps the DBA) at site X can specify that a given base relvar be divided into "fragments" that are to be stored at sites Y and Z (see the discussion of fragmentation in the next section).

The foregoing fundamental principle leads to certain subsidiary rules or objectives,[2] twelve in number, which will be discussed in the next section. For reference, we list those objectives here:

1. Local autonomy

2. No reliance on a central site

3. Continuous operation

4. Location independence

5. Fragmentation independence

6. Replication independence

7. Distributed query processing

8. Distributed transaction management

9. Hardware independence

10. Operating system independence

11. Network independence

12. DBMS independence

---

[2] *Rules* was the term used in the paper [21.13] in which they were first introduced (and the "fundamental principle" was referred to as *Rule Zero*). However, *objectives* is really a better term—*rules* is too dogmatic. We will stay with the milder term *objectives* in this chapter.

Please understand that these objectives are not all independent of one another, nor are they necessarily exhaustive, nor are they all equally significant (different users will attach different degrees of importance to different objectives in different environments; indeed, some of them might be totally inapplicable in some situations). However, the objectives are useful as a basis for understanding distributed technology in general and as a framework for characterizing the functionality of specific distributed systems. We will therefore use them as an organizing principle for the bulk of the chapter. Section 21.3 presents a brief discussion of each objective; Section 21.4 then homes in on certain specific issues in more detail. Section 21.5 (as previously mentioned) discusses client/server systems. Section 21.6 examines the specific objective of DBMS independence in depth. Finally, Section 21.7 addresses the question of SQL support, and Section 21.8 offers a summary and a few concluding remarks.

One final introductory point: It is desirable to distinguish true, generalized, distributed *database* systems from systems that merely provide some kind of *remote data access* (which is all that client/server systems really do, incidentally). In a remote data access system, the user might be able to operate on data at a remote site, or even on data at several remote sites simultaneously, but "the seams show"; that is, the user is definitely aware, to a greater or lesser extent, that the data is remote and has to behave accordingly. In a true distributed database system, by contrast, the seams are hidden. (Much of the rest of this chapter is concerned with what it means in this context to say that the seams are hidden.) Throughout what follows, we will use the term *distributed system* to refer to a true, generalized, distributed database system specifically (as opposed to a simple remote data access system), barring explicit statements to the contrary.

21.3   THE TWELVE OBJECTIVES

1. Local Autonomy

The sites in a distributed system should be **autonomous**. Local autonomy means that all operations at a given site are controlled by that site; no site *X* should depend on some other site *Y* for its successful operation—for otherwise the fact that site *Y* is down might mean that site *X* is unable to run even if there is nothing wrong with site *X* itself, obviously an undesirable state of affairs. Local autonomy also implies that local data is locally owned and managed, with local accountability; all data "really" belongs to some local database, even if it is accessible from other sites. Such matters as integrity, security, and physical storage representation of local data thus remain under the control and jurisdiction of the local site.

Actually, the local autonomy objective is not wholly achievable; it turns out there are some situations in which a given site *X must* relinquish a certain degree of control to some other site *Y*. The autonomy objective would thus more accurately be stated: Sites should be autonomous *to the maximum extent possible*. See the annotation to reference [21.13] for more specifics on this point.

2. No Reliance on a Central Site

Local autonomy implies that **all sites must be treated as equals**. In particular, therefore, there must not be any reliance on a central "master" site for some central service—for example, centralized query processing, centralized transaction management, or centralized naming services—such that the entire system is dependent on that central site. This second objective is thus in fact a corollary of the first (if the first is achieved, the second follows *a fortiori*). But "no reliance on a central site" is desirable in its own right, even if full local autonomy is not achieved, which is why we spell it out as a separate objective.

Reliance on a central site would be undesirable for at least the following two reasons: First, that central site might be a bottleneck; second, and more important, the system would be *vulnerable*—if the central site went down, the whole system would be down (the "single point of failure" problem).

3. Continuous Operation

An advantage of distributed systems in general is that they can provide greater *reliability* and greater *availability:*

- **Reliability** is the probability that the system is up and running at any given moment. Reliability is improved in distributed systems because such systems are not an all-or-nothing proposition—they can continue to operate (at a reduced level) in the face of failure of some individual component, such as an individual site.

- **Availability** is the probability that the system is up and running continuously throughout a specified period. Like reliability, availability is improved in a distributed system, partly for the same reason and partly because of the possibility of *data replication* (for further discussion, see Objective 6).

The foregoing discussions apply to the case where an **unplanned shutdown** (i.e., a failure of some kind) has occurred at some point within the system. Unplanned shutdowns are obviously undesirable, but hard to prevent entirely! **Planned** shutdowns, by contrast, should *never* be required; that is, it should never be necessary to shut the system down in order to perform a task such as adding a new site or upgrading the DBMS at an existing site to a new release level.

4. Location Independence

The basic idea of **location independence** (also known as location **transparency**) is simple: Users should not have to know where data is physically stored, but rather should be able to behave—at least from a logical standpoint—as if the data were all stored at their own local site. Location independence is desirable because it simplifies application programs and end-user activities; in particular, it allows data to migrate from site to site without invalidating any of those programs or activities. Such migratability is desirable because it allows data to be moved around the network in response to changing performance requirements.

Note: Doubtless you will have realized already that location independence is just an extension to the distributed case of the familiar concept of (physical) *data* independence. In fact—to jump ahead of ourselves for a moment—every objective in our list that has "independence" in its name can be regarded as an extension of data independence, as we will see. We will have a little more to say regarding location independence specifically in Section 21.4 (subsection "Catalog Management").

5. Fragmentation Independence

A system supports **data fragmentation** if a given base relvar can be divided into pieces or *fragments* for physical storage purposes, and distinct fragments can be stored at different sites. Fragmentation is desirable for performance reasons: Data can be stored at the location where it is most frequently used, so that most operations are local and network traffic is reduced. For example, consider a base relvar EMP ("employees"), with sample value as shown in the top portion of Fig. 21.2. In a system that supports fragmentation, we might define two fragments thus:

```
FRAGMENT EMP AS
     N_EMP AT SITE 'New York'  WHERE DEPT# = DEPT# ('D1')
                               OR     DEPT# = DEPT# ('D3') ,
     L_EMP AT SITE 'London'    WHERE DEPT# = DEPT# ('D2') ;
```

(refer to the lower portion of Fig. 21.2). *Note:* We are assuming that EMP tuples map to physical storage in some fairly direct manner, and that D1 and D3 are New York depart-

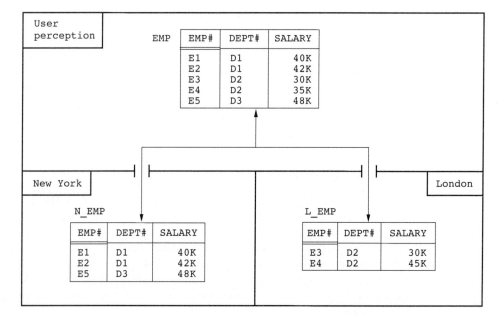

Fig. 21.2 An example of fragmentation

ments and D2 is a London department. Hence, tuples for New York employees are stored at the New York site and tuples for London employees are stored at the London site. Note the system's *internal fragment names* N_EMP and L_EMP.

There are basically two kinds of fragmentation, *horizontal* and *vertical,* corresponding to the relational operations of restriction and projection, respectively (Fig. 21.2 shows a horizontal fragmentation). More generally, a fragment can be derived by any arbitrary combination of restrictions and projections—arbitrary, that is, except that:

- In the case of restriction, the restrictions must constitute an *orthogonal* decomposition in the sense of Chapter 13.

- In the case of projection, the projections must constitute a *nonloss* decomposition in the sense of Chapters 12 and 13.

The net effect of these two rules is that all fragments of a given base relvar will be *independent,* in the sense that none of them can be derived—or, more generally, has a restriction or a projection that can be derived—from the others. *Note:* If we really do want to store the same piece of information in several different places, we can use the system's *replication* mechanism to achieve the desired effect. See the next subsection.

Reconstructing the original base relvar from the fragments is done via suitable join and union operations (join for vertical fragments, union for horizontal ones). In the case of union, incidentally, observe that no duplicate elimination will be required, thanks to the first of the foregoing rules (i.e., the union will be a *disjoint* union).

We elaborate briefly on the issue of vertical fragmentation. Since such a fragmentation must be nonloss, it is clear that fragmenting relvar EMP from Fig. 21.2 into its projections on, say, {EMP#,DEPT#} and {SALARY} would not be valid. In some systems, however, stored relvars are regarded as having a hidden, system-provided "tuple ID" (TID) attribute, where the TID for a given stored tuple is, loosely, the *address* of the tuple in question. That TID attribute is clearly a candidate key for the applicable relvar; thus, for example, if relvar EMP included such an attribute, it *could* validly be fragmented into its projections on {TID,EMP#,DEPT#} and {TID,SALARY}, since that fragmentation is clearly nonloss. Note too that the fact that the TID attributes are hidden does not violate *The Information Principle,* since fragmentation independence (which we will be discussing in just a moment) means that users are not aware of the fragmentation anyway.

Observe, incidentally, that ease of fragmentation and ease of reconstruction are two of the many reasons why distributed systems are relational; the relational model provides exactly the operations that are needed for these tasks [15.6].

Now we come to the main point: A system that supports data fragmentation should also support **fragmentation independence** (also known as fragmentation **transparency**)—that is, users should be able to behave, at least from a logical standpoint, as if the data were in fact not fragmented at all. Fragmentation independence (like location independence) is desirable because it simplifies application programs and end-user activities. In particular, it allows the data to be refragmented at any time (and fragments to be redistributed at any time) in response to changing performance requirements, without invalidating any of those programs or activities.

Fragmentation independence implies that users will be presented with a view of the data in which the fragments are logically recombined by means of suitable joins and unions. It is the responsibility of the optimizer to determine which fragments need to be physically accessed in order to satisfy any given user request. Given the fragmentation shown in Fig. 21.2, for example, if the user issues the query

```
EMP WHERE SALARY > 40K AND DEPT# = DEPT# ('D1')
```

the optimizer will know from the fragment definitions (which are stored in the catalog, of course) that the entire result can be obtained from the New York site—there is no need to access the London site at all.

Let us examine this example in a little more detail. First of all, relvar EMP as perceived by the user might be regarded, loosely, as a *view* of the underlying fragments N_EMP and L_EMP:

```
VAR EMP "VIEW"                              /* pseudocode */
    N_EMP UNION L_EMP ;
```

The optimizer thus transforms the user's original query into the following:

```
( N_EMP UNION L_EMP ) WHERE SALARY > 40K
                    AND DEPT# = DEPT# ('D1')
```

This expression can then be transformed further into:

```
( N_EMP WHERE SALARY > 40K AND DEPT# = DEPT# ('D1') )
  UNION
( L_EMP WHERE SALARY > 40K AND DEPT# = DEPT# ('D1') )
```

(because restriction distributes over union). Next, given the definition of fragment L_EMP in the catalog, the optimizer knows that the second of these two UNION operands is equivalent to:

```
EMP WHERE SALARY > 40K AND
        DEPT# = DEPT# ('D1') AND DEPT# = DEPT# ('D2')
```

This expression must evaluate to an empty relation, since the condition in the WHERE clause can never evaluate to TRUE. The original query can thus be simplified to just

```
N_EMP WHERE SALARY > 40K AND DEPT# = DEPT# ('D1')
```

Now the optimizer knows it need access only the New York site. *Exercise:* Consider what is involved on the part of the optimizer in dealing with the request:

```
EMP WHERE SALARY > 40K
```

As the foregoing discussion indicates, the problem of supporting operations on fragmented relvars has a lot in common with the problem of supporting operations on join and union views (in fact, the two problems are one and the same—they just manifest themselves at different points in the overall system architecture). In particular, the problem of *updating* fragmented relvars is the same as the problem of updating join and union views (see Chapter 10). It follows too that updating a given tuple—loosely speaking once again!—might cause that tuple to migrate from one fragment to another (and possibly even from one site to another), if the updated tuple no longer satisfies the predicate for the fragment it previously belonged to.

6. Replication Independence

A system supports **data replication** if a given base relvar—or, more generally, a given *fragment* of a given base relvar—can be represented in storage by many distinct copies or *replicas,* stored at many distinct sites. For example:

```
REPLICATE N_EMP AS
   LN_EMP AT SITE 'London' ;

REPLICATE L_EMP AS
   NL_EMP AT SITE 'New York' ;
```

(see Fig. 21.3). Note the system's *internal replica names* NL_EMP and LN_EMP.

Replication is desirable for at least two reasons: First, it can mean better performance (applications can operate on local copies instead of having to communicate with remote sites); second, it can also mean better availability (a given replicated object remains available for processing— at least for retrieval—as long as at least one copy remains available). The major *dis*advantage of replication is that when a given replicated object is updated, *all copies* of that object must be updated: the **update propagation** problem. We will have more to say regarding this problem in Section 21.4.

We remark in passing that replication in a distributed system represents a specific application of the idea of *controlled redundancy* as discussed in Chapter 1.

Now, replication, like fragmentation, ideally should be "transparent to the user." In other words, a system that supports data replication should also support **replication independence** (also known as replication **transparency**)—that is, users should be able to behave, at least from a logical standpoint, as if the data were in fact not replicated at all. Replication independence (like location independence and fragmentation independence) is desirable because it simplifies application programs and end-user activities; in particular, it allows replicas to be created and destroyed at any time in response to changing requirements, without invalidating any of those programs or activities.

New York				London			
N_EMP				L_EMP			

EMP#	DEPT#	SALARY		EMP#	DEPT#	SALARY
E1	D1	40K		E3	D2	30K
E2	D1	42K		E4	D2	35K
E5	D3	48K				

EMP#	DEPT#	SALARY		EMP#	DEPT#	SALARY
E3	D2	30K		E1	D1	40K
E4	D2	35K		E2	D1	42K
				E5	D3	48K

NL_EMP (L_EMP replica)   LN_EMP (N_EMP replica)

Fig. 21.3 An example of replication

Replication independence implies that it is the responsibility of the optimizer to determine which replicas physically need to be accessed in order to satisfy any given user request. We omit the specifics of this issue here.

We close this subsection by mentioning that many commercial products currently support a form of replication that does *not* include full replication independence (that is, it is *not* entirely "transparent to the user"). See the further remarks on this topic in Section 21.4 (subsection "Update Propagation").

7. Distributed Query Processing

There are two broad points to be made under this heading:

- First, consider the query "Get London suppliers of red parts." Suppose the user is at the New York site and the data is at the London site. Suppose too that there are n suppliers that satisfy the request. If the system is relational, the query will basically involve two messages: one to send the request from New York to London, and one to return the result set of n tuples from London to New York. If, on the other hand, the system is not relational but a record-at-a-time system, the query will basically involve $2n$ messages: n from New York to London requesting "the next" supplier, and n from London to New York to return that "next" supplier. The example thus illustrates the point that a relational distributed system is likely to outperform a nonrelational one by possibly orders of magnitude.

- Second, optimization is even more important in a distributed system than it is in a centralized one. The basic point is that in a query such as the one mentioned in the previous paragraph that involves several sites, there will be many possible ways of moving data around the system in order to satisfy the request, and it is crucially important that an efficient strategy be found. For instance, a request for (say) the union of a relation rx stored at site X and a relation ry stored at site Y could be carried out by moving rx to Y or by moving ry to X or by moving both to a third site Z (etc.). A compelling illustration of this point, involving the same query once again ("Get supplier numbers for London suppliers of red parts"), is presented in Section 21.4. To summarize the example briefly, six different strategies for processing the query are analyzed under a certain set of plausible assumptions, and the response time is shown to vary from a minimum of one tenth of a second to a maximum of nearly *six hours!* Optimization is thus clearly crucial, and this fact in turn can be seen as yet another reason why distributed systems are always relational (the point being that relational requests are optimizable, while nonrelational ones are not).

8. Distributed Transaction Management

There are two major aspects to transaction management, recovery and concurrency, and both require extended treatment in the distributed environment. In order to explain that extended treatment, it is first necessary to introduce a new term, *agent*. In a distributed system, a single transaction can involve the execution of code at many sites; in particular, it can involve updates at many sites. Each transaction is therefore said to consist of several

agents, where an agent is the process performed on behalf of a given transaction at a given site. And the system clearly needs to know when two agents are part of the same transaction; for example, two agents that are part of the same transaction must obviously not be allowed to deadlock with each other.

Turning now to recovery specifically: In order to ensure that a given transaction is atomic (all or nothing) in the distributed environment, the system must clearly ensure that the set of agents for that transaction either all commit in unison or all roll back in unison. This effect can be achieved by means of the **two-phase commit** protocol, already discussed, though not in the distributed context, in Chapter 15. We will have more to say regarding two-phase commit for a distributed system in Section 21.4.

As for concurrency: Concurrency control in most distributed systems is typically based on **locking**, just as it is in nondistributed systems. (Some products use *multi-version* controls instead [16.1], but conventional locking still seems to be the technique of choice in most systems.) We will discuss this topic also in a little more detail in Section 21.4.

9. Hardware Independence

There is really not much to be said on this topic—the heading says it all. Real-world computer installations typically involve a multiplicity of different machines—IBM machines, Fujitsu machines, HP machines, PCs and workstations of various kinds, and so on—and there is a real need to be able to integrate the data on all of those systems and present the user with a "single-system image" [21.9]. Thus, it is desirable to be able to run the same DBMS on different hardware platforms, and furthermore to have those different machines all participate as equal partners in a distributed system.

10. Operating System Independence

This objective is partly a corollary of the previous one, and also does not really require much discussion here. It is obviously desirable, not only to be able to run the same DBMS on different hardware platforms, but also to be able to run it on different operating system platforms as well—including different operating systems on the same hardware—and have (e.g.) an OS/390 version and a UNIX version and a Windows version all participate in the same distributed system.

11. Network Independence

Once again there is not much to say; if the system is to be able to support many disparate sites, with disparate hardware and disparate operating systems, it is obviously desirable to be able to support a variety of disparate communication networks also.

12. DBMS Independence

Under this heading, we consider what is involved in relaxing the strict homogeneity assumption. That assumption is arguably a little too strong: All that is really needed is that the DBMS instances at different sites *all support the same interface*—they do not necessarily all have to be copies of the same DBMS software. For example, if Ingres and Oracle both supported the official SQL standard, then it might be possible to get an Ingres site and an Oracle site to talk to each other in the context of a distributed system. In other words, it might be possible for the distributed system to be *hetero*geneous, at least to some degree.

Support for heterogeneity is definitely desirable. The fact is, real-world computer installations typically run not only many different machines and many different operating systems, they very often run different DBMSs as well; and it would be nice if those different DBMSs could all participate somehow in a distributed system. In other words, the ideal distributed system should provide **DBMS independence**.

This is such a large topic, however, and such an important one in practice, that we devote a separate section to it. See Section 21.6.

21.4 PROBLEMS OF DISTRIBUTED SYSTEMS

In this section, we elaborate a little on some of the problems that were mentioned only briefly in Section 21.3. The overriding problem is that communication networks—at least, "long haul" or wide area networks (WANs)—are *slow*. A typical WAN might have an effective data rate of some 5 to 10 thousand bytes per second; a typical disk drive, by contrast, might have a data rate of some 5 to 10 *million* bytes per second. (On the other hand, some local area networks do support data rates of the same order of magnitude as disk drives.) Thus, an overriding objective in distributed systems (at least in the WAN case, and to some extent in the LAN case also) is to *minimize network utilization*—that is, to minimize the number and volume of messages. This objective in turn gives rise to problems in a number of subsidiary areas, the following among them (this list is not meant to be exhaustive):

- Query processing
- Catalog management
- Update propagation
- Recovery
- Concurrency

Query Processing

The objective of minimizing network utilization implies that the query optimization process itself needs to be distributed, as well as the query execution process. In other words, the overall optimization process will typically consist of a **global** optimization step, followed by **local** optimization steps at each affected site. For example, suppose a query Q is submitted at site X, and suppose Q involves a join of a relation ry of 10 thousand tuples at site Y with a relation rz of 10 million tuples at site Z. The optimizer at site X will choose the global strategy for executing Q; and it is clearly desirable that it decide to move ry to Z and not rz to Y (or, depending on the cardinality of the result of the join, it might be better to move both *ry* and *rz* to *X*). Suppose it does decide to move *ry* to Z. Then the strategy for performing the actual join at site Z will be decided by the local optimizer at Z.

The following more detailed illustration of the foregoing point is based on an example given in an early paper by Rothnie and Goodman [21.31]. *Note:* The actual figures shown might be somewhat out of date by now, given subsequent hardware developments and typical modern database sizes, but the overall message is still valid.

- *Database* (suppliers-and-parts, simplified):

```
S  { S#, CITY }           10,000 stored tuples at site A
P  { P#, COLOR }         100,000 stored tuples at site B
SP { S#, P# }          1,000,000 stored tuples at site A
```

Assume every stored tuple is 25 bytes (200 bits) long.

- *Query* ("Get supplier numbers for London suppliers of red parts"):

```
( ( S JOIN SP JOIN P ) WHERE CITY = 'London' AND
                       COLOR = COLOR ('Red') ) { S# }
```

- *Estimated cardinalities of certain intermediate results:*

Number of red parts   —   10
Number of shipments by London suppliers =   100,000

- *Communication assumptions:*

Data rate   = 50,000 bits per second
Access delay = 0.1 second

We now briefly examine six possible strategies for processing this query, and for each strategy *i* calculate the total communication time T_i from the formula

```
( total access delay ) + ( total data volume / data rate )
```

which becomes, in seconds,

```
( number of messages / 10 ) + ( number of bits / 50000 )
```

1. Move parts to site A and process the query at A.

```
T1 = 0.1 + ( 100000 * 200 ) / 50000
   = 400 seconds approx. (6.67 minutes)
```

2. Move suppliers and shipments to site B and process the query at B.

```
T2 = 0.2 + ( ( 10000 + 1000000 ) * 200 ) / 50000
   = 4040 seconds approx. (1.12 hours)
```

3. Join suppliers and shipments at site A, restrict the result to London suppliers, and then, for each of those suppliers in turn, check site B to see whether the corresponding part is red. Each of these checks will involve two messages—a query and a response. The transmission time for these messages will be small compared with the access delay.

```
T3 = 20000 seconds approx. (5.56 hours)
```

4. Restrict parts at site B to those that are red, and then, for each of those parts in turn, check site A to see whether there exists a shipment relating the part to a London

supplier. Each of these checks will involve two messages; again, the transmission time for these messages will be small compared with the access delay.

```
T4  =   2 seconds approx.
```

5. Join suppliers and shipments at site A, restrict the result to London suppliers, project the result over S# and P#, and move the result to site B. Complete the processing at site B.

```
T5  =   0.1 + ( 100000 * 200 ) / 50000
    =   400 seconds approx. (6.67 minutes)
```

6. Restrict parts at site B to those that are red and move the result to site A. Complete the processing at site A.

```
T6  =   0.1 + ( 10 * 200 ) / 50000
    =   0.1 second approx.
```

Fig. 21.4 summarizes the foregoing results. Points arising:

Strategy	Technique	Communication time
1	Move P to A	6.67 mins
2	Move S and SP to B	1.12 hrs
3	For each London shipment, check if part is red	5.56 hrs
4	For each red part, check if a London supplier exists	2.00 secs
5	Move London shipments to B	6.67 mins
6	**Move red parts to A**	**0.10 secs** (best)

Fig. 21.4   Distributed query processing strategies (summary)

1. The overall variation in communication time is enormous (the slowest is *two million* times slower than the fastest).

2. Data rate and access delay are both important factors in choosing a strategy.

3. Computation and I/O times are likely to be negligible compared with communication time for the poor strategies. *Note:* Actually, for the better strategies this might or might not be the case [21.33]. It also might not be the case on a fast LAN.

In addition, some strategies permit parallel processing at the two sites; thus, the response time to the user might actually be less than in a centralized system. Note, however, that we have ignored the question of which site is to receive the final result.

Catalog Management

In a distributed system, the system catalog will include not only the usual catalog data regarding base relvars, views, integrity constraints, authorizations, and so on, but also all the necessary control information to enable the system to provide the desired location, fragmentation, and replication independence. The question arises: Where and how should the catalog itself be stored? Here are some possibilities:

1. *Centralized:* The total catalog is stored exactly once, at a single central site.

2. *Fully replicated:* The total catalog is stored in its entirety at every site.

3. *Partitioned:* Each site maintains its own catalog for objects stored at that site. The total catalog is the union of all of those disjoint local catalogs.

4. *Combination of Approaches 1 and 3:* Each site maintains its own local catalog, as in Approach 3; in addition, a single central site maintains a unified copy of all of those local catalogs, as in Approach 1.

Each of these approaches has its problems. Approach 1 obviously violates the objective of "no reliance on a central site." Approach 2 suffers from a severe loss of autonomy, in that every catalog update has to be propagated to every site. Approach 3 makes nonlocal operations very expensive (finding a remote object will require access to half the sites, on average). Approach 4 is more efficient than Approach 3 (finding a remote object requires only one remote catalog access), but violates the objective of "no reliance on a central site" again. In practice, therefore, systems typically do not use any of these four approaches! By way of example, we describe the approach used in R* [21.37].

In order to explain how the R* catalog is structured, it is first necessary to say something about R* **object naming**. Now, object naming is a significant issue for distributed systems in general; the possibility that two distinct sites *X* and *Y* might both have an object, say a base relvar, called *R* implies that some mechanism—typically qualification by site name—will be required in order to "disambiguate" (i.e., to guarantee system-wide name uniqueness). If dot-qualified names such as *X.R* and *Y.R* are exposed to the user, however, the location independence objective will clearly be violated. What is needed, therefore, is a means of mapping the names known to users to their corresponding system-known names.

Here then is the R* approach to this problem. First, R* distinguishes between an object's **printname**, which is the name by which the object is normally referenced by users (e.g., in an SQL SELECT statement), and its **system-wide name**, which is a globally unique internal identifier for the object. System-wide names have four components:

- *Creator ID* (the ID of the user who issued the CREATE operation that created the object in the first place)

- *Creator site ID* (the ID of the site at which the CREATE operation was executed)

- *Local name* (the unqualified name of the object)

- *Birth site ID* (the ID of the site at which the object was initially stored)

User IDs are unique within site and site IDs are globally unique. Thus, for example, the system-wide name

```
MARILYN @ NEWYORK . STATS @ LONDON
```

denotes an object—for definiteness, let us assume it is a base relvar—with local name STATS, created by the user called Marilyn at the New York site and initially stored at the London site.[3] This name is *guaranteed never to change,* even if the object subsequently migrates to another site (see later).

---

[3] Base relvars map directly to stored relvars in R*, as indeed they do in almost every system known to this writer. See Appendix A for some criticisms of this state of affairs.

As already indicated, users normally refer to objects by their *printname*. A printname consists of a simple unqualified name—either the "local name" component of the system-wide name (STATS in the foregoing example) or a **synonym** for that system-wide name, defined by means of the special R* statement CREATE SYNONYM. Here is an example:

```
CREATE SYNONYM MSTATS FOR MARILYN @ NEWYORK . STATS @ LONDON ;
```

Now the user can say either (e.g.)

```
SELECT ... FROM STATS ... ;
```

or

```
SELECT ... FROM MSTATS ... ;
```

In the first case (using the local name), the system infers the system-wide name by assuming all the obvious defaults: namely, that the object was created by this user, it was created at this site, and it was initially stored at this site. We note in passing that one consequence of these default assumptions is that old System R applications will run unchanged on R* (once the System R data has been redefined to R*, that is).

In the second case (using the synonym), the system determines the system-wide name by interrogating the relevant **synonym table**. Synonym tables can be thought of as the first component of the catalog; each site maintains a set of such tables for each user known at that site, mapping the synonyms known to that user to their corresponding system-wide names.

In addition to the synonym tables, each site maintains:

1. A catalog entry for every object *born* at that site

2. A catalog entry for every object *currently stored* at that site

Suppose the user issues a request referring to the synonym MSTATS. First, the system looks up the corresponding system-wide name in the appropriate synonym table (a purely local lookup). Now it knows the birthsite—London in the example—and so it can interrogate the London catalog (which we assume for generality to be a remote lookup, so this is the first remote access). The London catalog will contain an entry for the object, by virtue of point 1. If the object is still at London, it has now been found. However, if the object has migrated to (say) Los Angeles, then the catalog entry in London will say as much, and so the system can now interrogate the Los Angeles catalog (second remote access). And the Los Angeles catalog will contain an entry for the object, by virtue of point 2. So the object has been found in at most two remote accesses.

Furthermore, if the object migrates again, say to San Francisco, then the system will:

1. Insert a San Francisco catalog entry.

2. Delete the Los Angeles catalog entry.

3. Update the London catalog entry to point to San Francisco instead of Los Angeles.

The net effect is that the object can still be found in at most two remote accesses. And this is a completely distributed scheme—there is no central catalog site, and no single point of failure within the system.

We remark that the naming scheme used in the DB2 distributed data facility is similar but not identical to the one just described.

Update Propagation

The basic problem with data replication, as pointed out in Section 21.3, is that an update to any given logical object must be propagated to all stored copies of that object. A difficulty that arises immediately is that some site holding a copy of the object might be unavailable (because of a site or network failure) at the time of the update. The obvious strategy of propagating updates immediately to all copies is thus probably unacceptable, because it implies that the update—and therefore the transaction—will fail if any one of those copies is currently unavailable. In a sense, in fact, data is *less* available under this strategy than it would be in the nonreplicated case, thereby undermining one of the advantages claimed for replication in the previous section.

A common scheme for dealing with this problem (not the only one possible) is the so-called **primary copy** scheme, which works as follows:

- One copy of each replicated object is designated as the *primary* copy. The remainder are all secondary copies.

- Primary copies of different objects are at different sites (so this is a distributed scheme once again).

- Update operations are deemed to be logically complete as soon as the primary copy has been updated. The site holding that copy is then responsible for propagating the update to the secondary copies at some subsequent time. *Note:* That "subsequent time" must be prior to COMMIT, however, if the ACID properties of the transaction—see Chapters 15 and 16—are to be preserved. We will return to this issue in a few moments.

Of course, this scheme leads to several additional problems of its own, most of them beyond the scope of this book. Note too that it does represent a violation of the local autonomy objective, because a transaction might now fail because a remote (primary) copy of some object is unavailable—even if a local copy is available.

Now, we have said that the ACID requirements of transaction processing imply that all update propagation must be completed before the relevant transaction can complete ("synchronous replication"). However, several commercial products support a less ambitious form of replication, in which update propagation is done at some later time (possibly at some user-specified time), *not* necessarily within the scope of the relevant transaction ("asynchronous replication"). Indeed, the term *replication* has unfortunately been more or less usurped by those products, with the result that—in the commercial marketplace, at least—it is almost always taken to imply that update propagation is delayed past COMMIT (see, e.g., references [21.1], [21.16], and [21.18]). One problem with this delayed propagation approach is that the database can no longer be guaranteed to be consistent at all times;[4] indeed, the user might not even know whether it is consistent or not.

We close this subsection with a few further observations on the delayed propagation approach:

1. The concept of replication in a system with delayed update propagation can be thought of as an application of the idea of *snapshots* as discussed in Chapter 10. Indeed, it would have been better to use a different term for this kind of replication; then we could have kept the term *replica* to mean what it is usually understood to mean in ordinary discourse (namely, an exact copy). Note, however, that snapshots are supposed to be read-only (apart from the periodic refreshing), whereas some systems do allow users to update "replicas" directly—see, for example, reference [21.18]. Of course, this latter capability constitutes a violation of replication independence.

2. We do not mean to suggest that delayed propagation is a bad idea—it is clearly the right thing to do in appropriate circumstances, as we will see in Chapter 22, for example. The point is, however, that delayed propagation means the "replicas" are not true replicas (it is possible for a given data value at the logical level to be represented by two or more stored values at the physical level, and furthermore for those stored values to be different!), and the system is not a true distributed database system.

3. One reason (perhaps the major reason) why many products implement replication with delayed propagation is that the alternative—that is, updating all replicas prior to COMMIT—requires two-phase commit support (see the next subsection), which can be costly in performance. This state of affairs explains the articles sometimes encountered in the trade press with mystifying titles along the lines of "Replication *vs.* Two-Phase Commit"—mystifying, because on the surface they appear to be comparing the merits of two totally different things.

Recovery

As explained in Section 21.3, recovery in distributed systems is typically based on two-phase commit, or some variant thereof. Two-phase commit is required in *any* environment in which a single transaction can interact with several autonomous resource managers; however, it is particularly important in a distributed system, because the resource managers in question—that is, the local DBMSs—are operating at distinct sites and are hence *very* autonomous. Points arising:

1. The objective of "no reliance on a central site" dictates that the coordinator function must not be assigned to one distinguished site in the network, but instead must be performed by different sites for different transactions. Typically it is handled by the site at which the transaction in question is initiated; thus, each site must be capable of acting as the coordinator site for some transactions and as a participant site for others (in general).

---

[4] Of course, if all integrity checking is immediate (see Chapters 9 and 16), then such a state of affairs cannot arise. Even if such checking is deferred until COMMIT—a possibility we regard as logically incorrect, but one that is found in some systems—it still cannot arise. In a sense, therefore, delayed propagation can be regarded as "even more logically incorrect" than deferred checking (if it makes any sense to talk in terms of *degrees of correctness*).

2. The two-phase commit process requires the coordinator to communicate with every participant site—which means more messages and more overhead.

3. If site Y acts as a participant in a two-phase commit process coordinated by site X, then site Y *must* do what it is told by site X (commit or rollback, whichever applies): a loss of local autonomy, though perhaps a minor one.

Let us review the basic two-phase commit process as described in Chapter 15. Fig. 21.5 shows the interactions between the coordinator and a typical participant. We assume for generality that the coordinator and participant are at different sites; also, note that time in the figure runs from left to right (more or less!). We also assume for simplicity that the transaction has requested a COMMIT, not a ROLLBACK. On receiving that COMMIT request, the coordinator goes through the following two-phase process:

■ It instructs each participant to "get ready to go either way" on the transaction. Fig. 21.5 shows the "get ready" message being sent at time *t1* and being received by the participant at time *t2*. The participant now forces a log entry for the local agent out to its own physical log, and then replies "OK" to the coordinator (of course, if anything has gone wrong—in particular, if the local agent has failed), it replies "Not OK" instead. In the figure, that reply—which we assume for simplicity to be "OK"—is sent at time *t3* and is received by the coordinator at time *t4*. Note that (as already indicated) the participant now suffers a loss of autonomy: It *must* do what the coordinator subsequently tells it to do. Furthermore, any resources locked by the local agent *must remain locked* until the participant receives and acts on that decision from the coordinator.

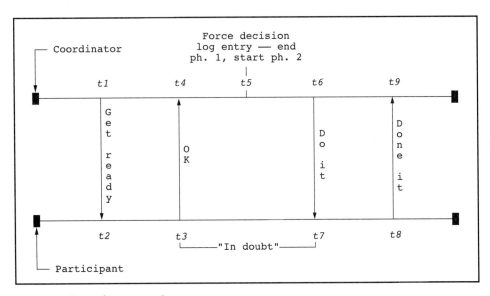

Fig. 21.5 Two-phase commit

- When the coordinator has received replies from all of the participants, it makes its decision (which will be *commit* if all of the replies were "OK" and *rollback* otherwise). It then forces an entry to its own physical log, recording that decision, at time *t5*. That time *t5* marks the transition from Phase 1 to Phase 2.

- We assume the decision was *commit*. The coordinator therefore instructs each participant to "do it" (i.e., perform commit processing for the local agent); Fig. 21.5 shows the "do it" message being sent at time *t6* and being received by the participant at time *t7*. The participant commits the local agent and sends an acknowledgment ("done it") back to the coordinator. In the figure, that acknowledgment is sent at time *t8* and is received by the coordinator at time *t9*.

- When all acknowledgments have been received by the coordinator, the entire process is complete.

In practice, the overall process is considerably more complicated than just indicated, because we have to worry about the possibility of site or network failures at any point. For example, suppose the coordinator site fails at some time *t* between times *t5* and *t6*. When the site recovers, then, the restart procedure will discover from the log that a certain transaction was in Phase 2 of the two-phase commit process and will continue the process of sending the "do it" messages to the participants. (Note that the participant is **"in doubt"** on the transaction in the period from *t3* to *t7;* if the coordinator does fail at time *t* as suggested, that "in doubt" period might be quite lengthy.)

Ideally, we would like the two-phase commit process to be resilient to *any conceivable* kind of failure. Unfortunately, it is easy to see that this objective is fundamentally unachievable—that is, there does not exist any finite protocol that will *guarantee* that all participants will commit successful transactions in unison and roll back unsuccessful ones in unison, in the face of arbitrary failures. For suppose, conversely, that such a protocol does exist. Let *n* be the minimum number of messages required by such a protocol. Suppose now that the last of these *n* messages is lost because of some failure. Then either that message was unnecessary, which is contrary to the assumption that *n* was minimal, or the protocol now does not work. Either way there is a contradiction, from which we deduce that no such protocol exists.

Despite this depressing fact, there are at least various enhancements that can be made to the basic algorithm with a view to improving performance:

- First of all (as noted in the annotation to reference [15.6]), if the agent at some particular participant site is read-only, that participant can reply "ignore me" in Phase 1, and the coordinator can indeed ignore that participant in Phase 2.

- Second (again, see the annotation to reference [15.6]), if *all* participants reply "ignore me" in Phase 1, Phase 2 can be skipped entirely.

- Third, there are two important variants on the basic scheme, called *presumed commit* and *presumed rollback,* which we describe in more detail in the paragraphs immediately following.

In essence, the presumed commit and presumed rollback schemes have the effect of reducing the number of messages involved in the success case (for presumed commit) or the failure case (for presumed rollback). In order to explain the two schemes, we note first that the basic mechanism as already described requires the coordinator to remember its decision until it has received an acknowledgment from every participant. The reason is that if a participant crashes while it is "in doubt," it will have to interrogate the coordinator on restart in order to discover what the coordinator's decision was. Once all acknowledgments have been received, however, the coordinator knows that all participants have done what they were told, and so it can "forget" the transaction.

We focus now on **presumed commit**. Under this scheme, participants are required to acknowledge "rollback" ("undo it") messages but not "commit" ("do it") messages, and the coordinator can forget the transaction as soon as it has broadcast its decision, *provided* that decision is "commit." If an in-doubt participant crashes, then on restart it will (as always) interrogate the coordinator. If the coordinator still remembers the transaction (i.e., the coordinator is still waiting for the participant's acknowledgment), then the decision must have been "rollback"; otherwise, it must have been "commit."

Presumed rollback is the opposite, of course: Participants are required to acknowledge "commit" messages but not "rollback" messages, and the coordinator can forget the transaction as soon as it has broadcast its decision, as long as that decision is "rollback." If an in-doubt participant crashes, then on restart it will interrogate the coordinator. If the coordinator still remembers the transaction (i.e., the coordinator is still waiting for the participant's acknowledgment), then the decision was "commit"; otherwise, it was "rollback."

Interestingly, and somewhat counterintuitively, presumed rollback seems to be preferable to presumed commit (we say "counterintuitively" because surely most transactions succeed, and presumed commit reduces the number of messages in the success case). The problem with presumed commit is as follows. Suppose the coordinator crashes in Phase 1 (i.e., before it has made its decision). On restart at the coordinator site, then, the transaction is rolled back (since it did not complete). Subsequently, some participant interrogates the coordinator, asking for its decision with respect to this transaction. The coordinator does not remember the transaction, and so presumes "commit"—which is incorrect.

In order to avoid such "false commits," the coordinator (if it is following presumed commit) must force a log entry to its own physical log at the start of Phase 1, giving a list of all participants in the transaction. (If the coordinator now crashes in Phase 1, then on restart it can broadcast "rollback" to all participants.) And this physical I/O to the coordinator log is on the critical path for *every transaction*. Thus, presumed commit is not quite as attractive as it might appear at first sight. In fact, it is probably fair to say that presumed rollback is the *de facto* standard in implemented systems at the time of writing.

Concurrency

As stated in Section 21.3, concurrency control in most distributed systems is based on locking, just as it is in most nondistributed systems. In a distributed system, however, requests to test, set, and release locks become *messages* (assuming that the object under consideration is at a remote site), and messages mean overhead. For example, consider a transaction T that needs to update an object for which there exist replicas at n remote sites. If each site is responsible for locks on objects stored at that site (as it will be under the local autonomy assumption), then a straightforward implementation will require at least $5n$ messages:

n lock requests
n lock grants
n update messages
n acknowledgments
n unlock requests

Of course, we can easily improve on the foregoing by "piggybacking" messages—for example, the lock request and update messages can be combined, and so can the lock grant and acknowledgment messages—but even so, the total time for the update could still be orders of magnitude greater than it would be in a centralized system.

The usual approach to this problem is to adopt the *primary copy* strategy already described in the subsection "Update Propagation." For a given object A, the site holding the primary copy of A will handle all locking operations involving A (remember that primary copies of different objects will be at different sites, in general). Under this strategy the set of all copies of an object can be considered as a single object for locking purposes, and the total number of messages will be reduced from $5n$ to $2n + 3$ (one lock request, one lock grant, n updates, n acknowledgments, and one unlock request). But notice once again that this solution entails a (severe) loss of autonomy—a transaction can now fail if a primary copy is unavailable, even if the transaction is read-only and a local copy is available. (Note that not only update operations, but also retrieval operations, need to lock the primary copy [15.6]. Thus, an unpleasant side-effect of the primary copy strategy is to reduce performance and availability for retrievals as well as for updates.)

Another problem with locking in a distributed system is that it can lead to **global deadlock,** or in other words a deadlock involving two or more sites. For example (refer to Fig. 21.6):

1. The agent of transaction $T2$ at site X is waiting for the agent of transaction $T1$ at site X to release a lock.

2. The agent of transaction $T1$ at site X is waiting for the agent of transaction $T1$ at site Y to complete.

3. The agent of transaction $T1$ at site Y is waiting for the agent of transaction $T2$ at site Y to release a lock.

4. The agent of transaction $T2$ at site Y is waiting for the agent of transaction $T2$ at site X to complete: *Deadlock!*

The problem with a deadlock such as this one is that *neither site can detect it using only information that is internal to that site.* In other words, there are no cycles in the local Wait-For Graphs, but a cycle will appear if those two local graphs are combined to form a global graph. It follows that global deadlock detection incurs further communication overhead, because it requires individual local graphs to be brought together somehow.

SITE X

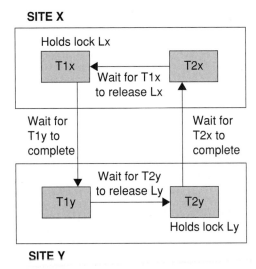

SITE Y

Fig. 21.6 An example of global deadlock

An elegant distributed scheme for detecting global deadlocks is described in the R* papers (see, e.g., reference [21.37]). *Note:* As pointed out in Chapter 16, not all systems do in fact detect deadlocks in practice—some just use a timeout mechanism instead. For reasons that should be obvious, this remark is particularly true of distributed systems.

21.5 CLIENT/SERVER SYSTEMS

As mentioned in Section 21.1, client/server systems can be regarded as a special case of distributed systems in general. More precisely, a client/server system is a distributed system in which (a) some sites are *client* sites and some are *server* sites, (b) all data resides at the server sites, (c) all applications execute at the client sites, and (d) "the seams show" (full location independence is not provided). Refer to Fig. 21.7 (a repeat of Fig. 2.6 from Chapter 2).

In the late 1980s and early to mid 1990s there was quite a lot of commercial interest in client/server systems and comparatively little in true general-purpose distributed systems. This picture has recently changed somewhat, as we will see in the next section, but client/server systems are still important; hence the present section.

First of all, then, recall that the term *client/server* refers primarily to an *architecture,* or logical division of responsibilities; the **client** is the application (also known as the *front end*), and the **server** is the DBMS (also known as the *back end*). Precisely because the overall system can be so neatly divided into two parts, however, the possibility arises of running the two on different machines. And this latter possibility is so attractive (for so

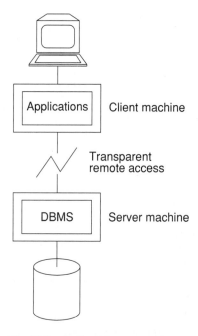

Fig. 21.7   A client/server system

many reasons—see Chapter 2) that the term *client/server* has come to apply almost exclusively to the case where client and server are indeed on different machines.[5] This usage is sloppy but common, and we adopt it ourselves in what follows.

We remind you also that several variations on the basic theme are possible:

- Several clients might be able to share the same server (indeed, this is the normal case).

- A single client might be able to access several servers. This latter possibility divides in turn into two cases:

  1. The client is limited to accessing just one server at a time—that is, each individual database request must be directed to just one server; it is not possible, within a single request, to combine data from two or more different servers. Furthermore, the user has to know which particular server stores which pieces of data.

  2. The client can access many servers simultaneously—that is, a single database request can combine data from several servers, which means that the servers look to the client as if they were really just one server, and the user does not have to know which servers store which pieces of data.

---

[5] For obvious reasons, the term *two-tier system* is also used with essentially the same meaning.

But Case 2 here is effectively a true distributed database system ("the seams are hidden"); it is not what is usually meant by the term *client/server,* and we ignore it from this point forward.

Client/Server Standards

There are several standards that are applicable to the world of client/server processing:

- First of all, certain client/server features are included in the *SQL* standard. We defer discussion of these features to Section 21.7.

- Next, there is the ISO **Remote Data Access** standard, RDA [21.23, 21.24]. The general intent of RDA is to define *formats and protocols* for client/server communication. It assumes that (a) the client expresses database requests in a standard form of SQL (basically a subset of the SQL standard) and (b) the server supports a standard catalog (also basically as defined in the SQL standard). It then defines specific representation formats for passing messages—SQL requests, data and results, and diagnostic information—between the client and the server.

- The third and last standard we mention here is IBM's **Distributed Relational Database Architecture** (DRDA) standard [21.22] (which is a *de facto* standard, not a *de jure* one). DRDA and RDA have similar objectives; however, DRDA differs from RDA in several important respects—in particular, it reflects its IBM origins. For example, DRDA does not assume that the client is using a standard version of SQL, but instead allows for arbitrary SQL dialects. One consequence is (possibly) better performance, since the client might be able to exploit certain server-specific features; on the other hand, portability suffers, precisely because those server-specific features are exposed to the client (i.e., the client has to know what kind of server it is talking to). In a similar vein, DRDA does not assume any particular catalog structure at the server. The DRDA formats and protocols are quite different from those of RDA (essentially, DRDA is based on IBM's own architectures and standards, while RDA is based on international, non-vendor-specific standards).

Further details of RDA and DRDA are beyond the scope of this book. See references [21.20] and [21.28] for some analysis and comparisons.

Client/Server Application Programming

We have said that a client/server system is a special case of distributed systems in general. As suggested in the introduction to this section, a client/server system can be thought of as a distributed system in which all requests originate at one site and all processing is performed at another (assuming for simplicity that there is just one client site and just one server site). *Note:* Under this simple definition, the client site is not really "a database system site in its own right" at all, and the system thus contravenes the definition of a general-purpose distributed database system given in Section 21.2. Of course, the client site might well have its own local databases, but those databases will not play a direct role in the client/server arrangement as such.

Be that as it may, the client/server approach does have certain implications for application programming (as indeed do distributed systems in general). One of the most important points has already been touched on in our discussion of Objective 7 (distributed query processing) in Section 21.3: namely, the fact that relational systems are, by definition and design, **set-level** systems. In a client/server system (and indeed in distributed systems in general), it is more important than ever that the application programmer not just "use the server like an access method" and write record-level code. Instead, as much functionality as possible should be bundled up into set-level requests—for otherwise performance will suffer, because of the number of messages involved. *Note:* In SQL terms, the foregoing implies *avoiding cursors* as much as possible—that is, avoiding FETCH loops and the CURRENT forms of DELETE and UPDATE (see Chapter 4).

The number of messages between client and server can be reduced still further if the system supports *stored procedures*. A **stored procedure** is basically a precompiled program that is stored at the server site (and is known to the server). It is invoked from the client by a **remote procedure call** (RPC). In particular, therefore, the performance penalty associated with record-level processing in a client/server system can be partly offset by creating a suitable stored procedure to do that processing directly at the server site.

Note: Although it is somewhat tangential to the topic of client/server processing as such, we should point out that improved performance is not the only advantage of stored procedures. Others include:

- Such procedures can be used to conceal a variety of DBMS- and/or database-specific details from the user, thereby providing a greater degree of data independence than might otherwise be the case.

- One stored procedure can be shared by many clients.

- Optimization can be done at the time the stored procedure is compiled instead of at run time. (This advantage applies only to systems that normally do optimization at run time.)

- Stored procedures can provide better security. For example, a given user might be authorized to invoke a given procedure but not to operate directly on the data accessed by that procedure.

One disadvantage is that different vendors provide very different facilities in this area—despite the fact that, as mentioned in Chapter 4, the SQL standard was extended in 1996 (via the addition of the "Persistent Stored Modules" feature, SQL/PSM) to include some support for stored procedures.

21.6   DBMS INDEPENDENCE

Now we return to our discussion of the twelve objectives for distributed database systems in general. The last of those objectives, you will recall, was *DBMS independence.* As explained in the brief discussion of this objective in Section 21.3, the strict homogeneity assumption is arguably too strong; all that is really needed is that the various DBMSs at different sites all support the same interface. As we put it in Section 21.3, if (e.g.) Ingres and Oracle both supported the official SQL standard—no more and no less!—then it might be possible to get them to behave as equal partners in a heterogeneous distributed system; indeed, such a possibility has always been one of the arguments in favor of the SQL standard in the first place, and we therefore examine it in detail. *Note:* We base our discussion on the specific products Ingres and Oracle merely to make matters a little more concrete. The concepts are generally applicable, of course.

Gateways

Suppose we have two sites X and Y running Ingres and Oracle, respectively, and suppose some user U at site X wishes to see a single distributed database that includes data from the Ingres database at site X and data from the Oracle database at site Y. By definition, user U is an Ingres user, and the distributed database must therefore be an Ingres database as far as that user is concerned. The onus is thus on Ingres, not Oracle, to provide the necessary support. What must that support consist of?

In principle, it is quite straightforward: Ingres must provide a special program—at one time called a **gateway**, now more usually called a **wrapper**, though neither term is very precisely defined—whose effect is "to make Oracle look like Ingres." Refer to Fig. 21.8.[6] The gateway might run at the Ingres site or the Oracle site or (as the figure suggests) at some special site of its own between the other two; no matter where it runs, however, it must clearly provide at least all of the functions in the following list. Observe that several of these functions present implementation problems of a very nontrivial nature. However, the RDA and DRDA standards discussed in Section 21.5 do address some of those problems, as does XML (see Chapter 27).

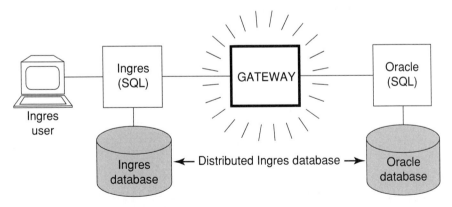

Fig. 21.8 A hypothetical Ingres-provided gateway to Oracle

---

[6] For obvious reasons, the term *three-tier system* is sometimes used to refer to the kind of arrangement illustrated in the figure (as well as to other software configurations similarly involving three components; see in particular the discussion of "middleware" in the next subsection).

- Implementing protocols for the exchange of information between Ingres and Oracle —which involves (among other things) mapping the message format in which SQL source statements are sent from Ingres to the format expected by Oracle, and mapping the message format in which results are sent from Oracle into the format expected by Ingres.

- Providing an "SQL server" capability for Oracle (analogous to the interactive SQL server functionality found in most SQL products already). In other words, the gateway must be able to execute arbitrary unplanned SQL statements on the Oracle database. In order to be able to provide this function, the gateway will have to make use of the *dynamic SQL* support or (more likely) a call-level interface such as *SQL/CLI* or *ODBC* or *JDBC* provided at the Oracle site (see Chapter 4). *Note:* Alternatively, the gateway might be able to make direct use of the interactive SQL processor already provided by Oracle.

- Mapping between the Oracle and Ingres data types. This problem includes a variety of subproblems having to do with such matters as processor differences (e.g., different machine word lengths), character code differences (character-string comparisons and ORDER BY requests can give unexpected results), floating-point format differences (a notorious problem area), differences in date and time support (no two DBMSs known to this writer currently provide identical support in this area)—not to mention differences in user-defined types. See reference [15.6] for further discussion of all of these issues.

- Mapping the Ingres dialect of SQL to the Oracle dialect—for in fact neither Ingres nor Oracle does support exactly the SQL standard, "no more and no less"; in fact, both support certain features that the other does not, and there are also some features that have identical syntax in the two products but different semantics. *Note:* In this connection, we should mention that some gateway products do provide a *passthrough* mechanism by which the user can formulate (e.g.) a query in the dialect of the target system and have it passed through the gateway unmodified for execution by that target system.

- Mapping Oracle feedback information (return codes, etc.) to Ingres format.

- Mapping the Oracle catalog to Ingres format, so that the Ingres site (and users at the Ingres site) can find out what the Oracle database contains.

- Dealing with a variety of **semantic mismatch** problems that are likely to occur across disparate systems (see, e.g., references [21.8], [21.11], [21.14], [21.36], and [21.38]). Examples include differences in naming (Ingres might use EMP# where Oracle uses EMPNO); differences in data types (Ingres might use character strings where Oracle uses numbers); differences in units (Ingres might use centimeters where Oracle uses inches); differences in the logical representation of information (Ingres might omit tuples where Oracle uses nulls); and much, much more.

- Serving as a participant in (the Ingres variant of) the two-phase commit protocol (assuming that Ingres transactions are to be allowed to perform updates on the Oracle database). Whether the gateway will actually be able to perform this function will depend on the facilities provided by the transaction manager at the Oracle site. It is worth pointing out that, at the time of writing, commercial transaction managers (with certain exceptions) typically do *not* provide what is necessary in this respect: namely, the ability for an application program to instruct the transaction manager to "prepare to terminate" (as opposed to instructing it to terminate—i.e., commit or roll-back—unconditionally).

- Ensuring that data at the Oracle site that Ingres requires to be locked is in fact locked as and when Ingres needs it to be. Again, whether the gateway will actually be able to perform this function will presumably depend on whether the locking architecture of Oracle matches that of Ingres or not.

So far we have discussed DBMS independence in the context of relational systems only. What about nonrelational systems—that is, what about the possibility of including a nonrelational site in an otherwise relational distributed system? For example, would it be possible to provide access to an IMS site from an Ingres or Oracle site? Again, such a feature would be very desirable in practice, given the enormous quantity of data that currently resides in IMS and other prerelational systems.[7] But can it be done?

If the question means "Can it be done at the 100 percent level?"—meaning "Can all nonrelational data be made accessible from a relational interface, and can all relational operations be performed on that data?"—then the answer is categorically *no*, for reasons explained in detail in reference [21.14]. But if the question means "Can some useful level of functionality be provided?", then the answer is obviously *yes*. This is not the place to go into details; see references [21.13, 21.14] for further discussion.

Data Access Middleware

Gateways as described in the previous subsection (sometimes called, more specifically, *point-to-point* gateways) do suffer from a number of obvious limitations. One is that they provide little location independence. Another is that the very same application might need to make use of several distinct gateways (say one for DB2, one for Oracle, and one for Informix), without any support for (e.g.) joins that span sites and so forth. As a consequence—and despite the many technical difficulties identified in the previous subsection—gateway-style products with ever more sophisticated functionality have appeared at frequent intervals over the past few years; in fact, the whole business of what has come to be called *middleware* (also known as *mediators*) is now a significant industry in its own right.

Perhaps unsurprisingly, the term *middleware* (like the term *wrapper*) is not very precisely defined—any piece of software whose general purpose is to paper over the differences among distinct systems that are supposed to work together somehow (for example, a TP monitor) might reasonably be regarded as "middleware" [21.3]. However, we focus here on what might be termed *data access* middleware. Examples of such products include Cohera from Cohera Inc., DataJoiner from IBM Corp., and OmniConnect and

---

[7] The conventional wisdom is that some 85% of business data still resides in such systems (i.e., prerelational database systems and even file systems), and there is little indication that that data will move into newer systems any time soon.

InfoHub from Sybase Inc. By way of illustration, we briefly describe the DataJoiner product [21.6].

There are several different ways to characterize DataJoiner (see Fig. 21.9). From the point of view of an individual client, it looks like a regular database server (i.e., a DBMS); it stores data, supports SQL queries, provides a catalog, does query optimization, and so forth (in fact, the heart of DataJoiner is the AIX version of IBM's DBMS product DB2). However, the data is stored, mostly, not at the DataJoiner site (though that capability is available), but rather at any number of other sites behind the scenes, under the control of a variety of other DBMSs, or even file managers such as VSAM. DataJoiner thus effectively provides the user with a virtual database that is the union of all of those "behind the scenes" databases and/or files; it allows queries[8] to span those databases and/or files, and uses its knowledge of the capabilities of the systems behind the scenes (and of network characteristics) to decide on "globally optimal" query plans. *Note:* DataJoiner also includes the ability to emulate certain DB2 SQL features on systems that do not support those features directly. An example might be the WITH HOLD option on a cursor declaration (see Chapter 15).

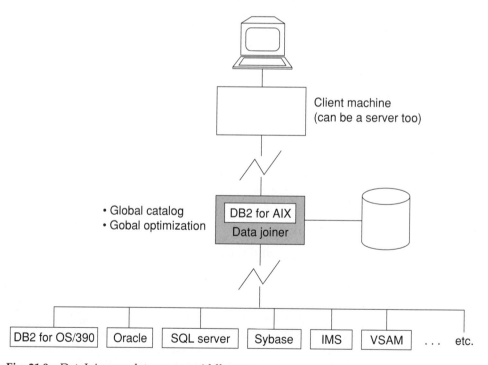

Fig. 21.9   DataJoiner as data access middleware

---

[8] Emphasis on "queries"; update capabilities are necessarily somewhat limited, especially—but not solely—when the system behind the scenes is, say, IMS or some other nonSQL system (again, see reference [21.14]).

Now, the system as described thus far is not a full distributed database system, because the various sites behind the scenes are unaware of one another's existence (i.e., they cannot be considered equal partners in a cooperative venture). However, when any new "behind the scenes" site is added, that new site can also behave as a client site and hence issue queries via DataJoiner that access any or all of the other sites. The overall system thus constitutes what is sometimes called a **federated** system, also known as a **multidatabase** system [21.17]. A federated system is a distributed system, usually heterogeneous, with close to full local autonomy; in such a system, purely local transactions are managed by the local DBMSs, though global transactions are a different matter [21.7].

Internally, DataJoiner includes a *driver* component—in effect a point-to-point gateway or wrapper in the sense of the previous subsection—for each of the "behind the scenes" systems. (Those drivers typically make use of ODBC to access the remote system.) It also maintains a *global catalog,* which is used among other things to tell it what to do when it encounters semantic mismatches among those systems.

We remark that products like DataJoiner can be useful to third-party software vendors, who can develop generic tools (e.g., report writers, statistical packages, and so on) without having to worry too much about the differences among the different DBMS products against which those tools are supposed to run. Finally, we note that IBM has recently incorporated DataJoiner technology into its DBMS product DB2; the intent is clearly to evolve DB2 to become the "only true interface"—at least, the only true IBM interface—to stored data in all of its forms (at the time of writing, it supports access to data stored in Informix, Oracle, SQL Server, and Sybase, among other systems). In other words, DB2, with DataJoiner technology, represents IBM's attack on what has become known as the **information integration** problem [21.9].

A Final Word

There are clear technical difficulties in trying to provide full DBMS independence, even when all of the participating DBMSs are SQL systems specifically. However, the potential payoff is huge, even if the solutions are less than perfect; for this reason, several data access middleware products already exist, and more are likely to appear in the near future. However, be warned that the solutions will necessarily be less than perfect—vendor claims to the contrary notwithstanding. *Caveat emptor.*

21.7 SQL FACILITIES

SQL currently provides no support at all for true distributed database systems.[9] Of course, no support is *required* in the area of data manipulation—the whole point of a distributed database (at least as far as the user is concerned) is that data manipulation operations

---

[9] Part 9 of the standard, SQL/MED (Management of External Data) [4.23], does provide support for *federated* systems, however. The details are beyond the scope of this book; a tutorial can be found in reference [26.32].

should remain unchanged. However, data definition operations such as FRAGMENT, REPLICATE, and so on, *are* required [15.6] but are not currently provided.

On the other hand, SQL does support certain client/server capabilities, including in particular **CONNECT** and **DISCONNECT** operations for making and breaking client/server connections. In fact, an SQL application *must* execute a CONNECT operation to connect to the server before it can issue any database requests at all (though that CONNECT might be implicit). Once the connection has been established, the application—that is, the client—can issue SQL requests in the usual way, and the necessary database processing will be carried out by the server.

SQL also allows a client that is already connected to one server to connect to another. Establishing that second connection causes the first to become **dormant**; subsequent SQL requests are processed by the second server, until such time as the client either (a) switches back to the previous server (via another new operation, **SET CONNECTION**) or (b) connects to yet another server, which causes the second connection to become dormant as well (and so on). At any given time, in other words, a given client can have one **active** connection and any number of **dormant** connections, and all database requests from that client are directed to, and processed by, the server on the active connection.

Note: The SQL standard also permits (but does not require) the implementation to support *multi-server transactions*. That is, the client might be able to switch from one server to another in the middle of a transaction, so that part of the transaction is executed on one server and part on another. Note in particular that if *update* transactions are permitted to span servers in this way, the implementation must presumably support some kind of two-phase commit in order to provide the transaction atomicity that the standard mandates.

Finally, every connection established by a given client (whether currently active or currently dormant) must eventually be broken via an appropriate DISCONNECT operation (though that DISCONNECT, like the corresponding CONNECT, might be implicit in simple cases).

For further information—in particular, for details of the SQL facilities for writing stored procedures—refer to the SQL standard itself [4.23, 4.24] or the tutorial treatment in reference [4.20].

21.8   SUMMARY

In this chapter, we have presented an introduction to distributed database systems. We used the "**twelve objectives**" for distributed database systems [21.13] as a basis for structuring the discussion, though we stress the point once again that not all of those objectives will be relevant in all situations. We also briefly examined certain technical problems arising in the areas of **query processing, catalog management, update propagation, recovery**, and **concurrency**. In particular, we discussed what is involved in trying to satisfy the **DBMS independence** objective (the discussion of **gateways, data access middleware**, and **federated systems** in Section 21.6). We also took a closer look at **client/server** processing, which can be regarded as an important special case of distributed processing in general. Finally, we summarized those aspects of SQL that are relevant to client/server processing, and we stressed the point that users should **avoid record-level code** (cursor operations, in SQL terms). We also briefly described the concept of **stored procedures** and **remote procedure calls**.

Note: One problem we did not discuss at all is the (physical) **database design** problem for distributed systems. In fact, even if we ignore the possibility of fragmentation and/or replication, the problem of deciding which data should be stored at which sites—the so-called **allocation problem**—is a notoriously difficult one [21.31]. Fragmentation and replication support only serve to complicate matters further.

Another point that is worthy of mention is that certain so-called *massively parallel* computer systems are beginning to make their presence felt in the marketplace (see the annotation to reference [18.56]). Such systems typically consist of a large number of separate processors connected by means of a high-speed bus; each processor has its own main memory and its own disk drives and runs its own copy of the DBMS software—and the complete database is spread across the complete set of disk drives. In other words, such a system essentially consists of "a distributed database system in a box"!—and all of the issues we have been discussing in the present chapter regarding (e.g.) query processing strategies, two-phase commit, global deadlock, and so on, are relevant.

By way of conclusion, we remark that the "twelve objectives" of distributed database (or possibly some subset of them that includes at least Objectives 4, 5, 6, and 8), taken together, seem to be equivalent to Codd's "distribution independence" rule for relational DBMSs [10.3]. For reference, we state that rule here:

- *Distribution independence* (Codd): A relational DBMS has distribution independence . . . [meaning the] DBMS has a data sublanguage that enables application programs and [end-user] activities to remain logically unimpaired:

  1. When data distribution is first introduced (if the originally installed DBMS manages nondistributed data only)

  2. When data is redistributed (if the DBMS manages distributed data)

Note finally that (as mentioned earlier in the chapter) Objectives 4–6 and 9–12—that is, all of the objectives that include the word *independence* in their name—can be regarded as extensions of the familiar notion of data independence, as that concept applies to the distributed environment. As such, they all translate into **protection for the application investment**.

EXERCISES

21.1 Explain in your own words location independence, fragmentation independence, and replication independence.

21.2 Why are distributed database systems almost invariably relational?

21.3 What are the advantages of distributed systems? What are the disadvantages?

21.4 Explain the following terms:

primary copy update strategy
primary copy locking strategy
global deadlock

two-phase commit

global optimization

21.5   Describe the R* naming scheme.

21.6   Successful implementation of a point-to-point gateway depends on reconciling the interface differences between the two DBMSs involved (among many other things). Take any two SQL systems you might be familiar with and identify as many interface differences between them as you can. Consider both syntactic and semantic differences.

21.7   Investigate any client/server system that might be available to you. Does that system support explicit CONNECT and DISCONNECT operations? Does it support SET CONNECTION or any other "connection-type" operations? Does it support multi-server transactions? Does it support two-phase commit? What formats and protocols does it use for client/server communication? What network environments does it support? What client and server hardware platforms does it support? What software platforms (operating systems, DBMSs) does it support?

21.8   Investigate any SQL DBMS that might be available to you. Does that DBMS support stored procedures? If so, how are they created? How are they invoked? What language are they written in? Do they support the whole of SQL? Do they support conditional branching (IF - THEN - ELSE)? Do they support loops? How do they return results to the client? Can one stored procedure invoke another? At a different site? Does the stored procedure execute as part of the invoking transaction?

REFERENCES AND BIBLIOGRAPHY

21.1 Todd Anderson, Yuri Breitbart, Henry F. Korth, and Avishai Wool: "Replication, Consistency, and Practicality: Are These Mutually Exclusive?" Proc. 1998 ACM SIGMOD Int. Conf. on Management of Data, Seattle, Wash. (June 1998).

This paper describes three schemes for asynchronous (here called *lazy*) replication schemes that guarantee transaction atomicity and global serializability without using two-phase commit, and reports on a simulation study of their comparative performance. Global locking as proposed in reference [21.18] is the first scheme; the other two—one of which is pessimistic and the other optimistic—make use of a *replication graph*. The paper concludes that the replication graph schemes typically outperform the locking scheme "usually by a huge margin."

21.2 David Bell and Jane Grimson: *Distributed Database Systems*. Reading, Mass.: Addison-Wesley (1992).

One of several textbooks on distributed systems (two others are references [21.10] and [21.29]). A notable feature of this particular book is the inclusion of an extended case study involving a health-care network. It is also a little more pragmatic in tone than the other two.

21.3 Philip A. Bernstein: "Middleware: A Model for Distributed System Services," *CACM 39,* No. 2 (February 1996).

"Various types of middleware are classified, their properties described, and their evolution explained, providing a conceptual model for understanding today's and tomorrow's distributed system software" (from the abstract).

21.4 Philip A. Bernstein *et al.*: "Query Processing in a System for Distributed Databases (SDD-1)," *ACM TODS 6,* No. 4 (December 1981).

See the annotation to reference [21.32].

21.5 Philip A. Bernstein, David W. Shipman, and James B. Rothnie, Jr: "Concurrency Control in a System for Distributed Databases (SDD-1)," *ACM TODS 5,* No. 1 (March 1980).

See the annotation to reference [21.32].

21.6 Charles J. Bontempo and C. M. Saracco: "Data Access Middleware: Seeking Out the Middle Ground," *InfoDB 9,* No. 4 (August 1995).

A useful tutorial, with the emphasis on IBM's DataJoiner (though other products are also mentioned).

21.7 Yuri Breitbart, Hector Garcia-Molina, and Avi Silberschatz: "Overview of Multi-Database Transaction Management," *The VLDB Journal 1,* No. 2 (October 1992).

21.8 M. W. Bright, A. R. Hurson, and S. Pakzad: "Automated Resolution of Semantic Heterogeneity in Multi-Databases," *ACM TODS 19,* No. 2 (June 1994).

21.9 Michael L. Brodie: "Data Management Challenges in Very Large Enterprises" (panel outline), Proc. 28th Int. Conf. on Very Large Data Bases, Hong Kong (August 2002).

Much of this panel was devoted to information integration issues: "A leading [problem is information] integration. Recent analyst studies conclude that over 40 percent of IT budgets [is] devoted to the integration of new and existing systems and databases . . . [There arc] massive integration challenges and costs."

21.10 Stefano Ceri and Giuseppe Pelagatti: *Distributed Databases: Principles and Systems.* New York, N.Y.: McGraw-Hill (1984).

21.11 William W. Cohen: "Integration of Heterogeneous Databases Without Common Domains Using Queries Based on Textual Similarity," Proc. 1998 ACM SIGMOD Int. Conf. on Management of Data, Seattle, Wash. (June 1998).

Describes an approach to what is sometimes called "the junk mail problem"—that is, recognizing when two distinct text strings, say "AT&T Bell Labs" and "AT&T Research," refer to the same object (a particular kind of semantic mismatch). The approach involves reasoning about the similarity of such strings "as measured using the vector space model commonly adopted in statistical information retrieval." According to the paper, the approach is much faster than "naïve inference methods," and in fact surprisingly accurate.

21.12 D. Daniels *et al.:* "An Introduction to Distributed Query Compilation in R*," in H.-J. Schneider (ed.), *Distributed Data Bases:* Proc. 2nd Int. Symposium on Distributed Data Bases (September 1982). New York, N.Y.: North-Holland (1982).

See the annotation to reference [21.37].

21.13 C. J. Date: "What Is a Distributed Database System?" in *Relational Database Writings 1985–1989.* Reading, Mass.: Addison-Wesley (1990).

The paper that introduced the "twelve objectives" for distributed systems (Section 21.3 is modeled fairly directly on this paper). As mentioned in the body of the chapter, the objective of *local autonomy* is not 100 percent achievable; there are certain situations that necessarily involve compromising on that objective somewhat. We summarize those situations here for purposes of reference:

- Individual fragments of a fragmented relvar cannot normally be accessed directly, not even from the site at which they are stored.

- Individual copies of a replicated relvar or fragment cannot normally be accessed directly, not even from the site at which they are stored.

- Let *P* be the primary copy of some replicated relvar or fragment *R,* and let *P* be stored at site *X;* then every site that accesses *R* is dependent on site *X,* even if another copy of *R* is in fact stored at the site in question.

- A relvar that participates in a multi-site integrity constraint cannot be accessed for update purposes within the local context of the site at which it is stored, but only within the context of the distributed database in which the constraint is defined.

- A site that is acting as a participant in a two-phase commit process must abide by the decision (i.e., commit or rollback) of the corresponding coordinator site.

See also reference [15.6], which is a sequel to this paper.

21.14 C. J. Date: "Why Is It So Difficult to Provide a Relational Interface to IMS?" in *Relational Database: Selected Writings.* Reading, Mass.: Addison-Wesley (1986).

The question "Can we provide a relational interface to IMS?" has two possible interpretations:

1. Can we build a relational DBMS using IMS as a storage manager?

2. Can we build a "wrapper" on top of IMS that makes existing IMS data look like relational data?

If the first is the intended interpretation, the answer is clearly *yes* (though there are many IMS features that would probably not be used); if the second is, the answer is *no* (at least at the 100 percent level), as this paper demonstrates.

21.15 R. Epstein, M. Stonebraker, and E. Wong: "Distributed Query Processing in a Relational Data Base System," Proc. 1978 ACM SIGMOD Int. Conf. on Management of Data, Austin, Tex. (May/June 1978).

See the annotation to reference [21.34].

21.16 Rob Goldring: "A Discussion of Relational Database Replication Technology," *InfoDB 8,* No. 1 (Spring 1994).

A good overview of asynchronous replication.

21.17 John Grant, Witold Litwin, Nick Roussopoulos, and Timos Sellis: "Query Languages for Relational Multi-Databases," *The VLDB Journal 2,* No. 2 (April 1993).

Proposes extensions to the relational algebra and relational calculus for dealing with multi-database systems. Issues of optimization are discussed, and it is shown that every multi-relational algebraic expression has a multi-relational calculus equivalent ("the converse of this theorem is an interesting research problem").

21.18 Jim Gray, Pat Helland, Patrick O'Neil, and Dennis Shasha: "The Dangers of Replication and a Solution," Proc. 1996 ACM SIGMOD Int. Conf. on Management of Data, Montreal, Canada (June 1996).

"Update anywhere-anytime-anyway transactional replication has unstable behavior as the workload scales up . . . A new algorithm is proposed that allows mobile (disconnected) applications to propose tentative update transactions that are later applied to a master copy" (from the abstract, slightly reworded).

21.19 Ramesh Gupta, Jayant Haritsa, and Krithi Ramamritham: "Revisiting Commit Processing in Distributed Database Systems," Proc. 1997 ACM SIGMOD Int. Conf. on Management of Data, Tucson, Ariz. (May 1997).

Proposes a new distributed commit protocol called OPT that (a) is easy to implement, (b) can coexist with traditional protocols, and (c) "provides the best transaction throughput performance for a variety of workloads and system configurations."

21.20 Richard D. Hackathorn: "Interoperability: DRDA or RDA?" *InfoDB 6,* No. 2 (Fall 1991).

21.21 Michael Hammer and David Shipman: "Reliability Mechanisms for SDD-1: A System for Distributed Databases," *ACM TODS 5,* No. 4 (December 1980).

See the annotation to reference [21.32].

21.22 IBM Corporation: *Distributed Relational Database Architecture Reference.* IBM Form No. SC26-4651.

> IBM's DRDA defines four levels of distributed database functionality, as follows: *remote request, remote unit of work, distributed unit of work,* and *distributed request.* Since these terms have become *de facto* standards in at least some portions of the industry, we briefly explain them here. *Note: Request* and *unit of work* are IBM's terms for *SQL statement* and *transaction,* respectively.
>
> **Remote request** means that an application at one site X can send an individual SQL statement to some remote site Y for execution. That request is executed *and committed* (or rolled back) entirely at site Y. The original application at site X can subsequently send another request to site Y (or possibly to another site Z), regardless of whether the first request was successful or unsuccessful.
>
> **Remote unit of work** (abbreviated RUW) means that an application at one site X can send all of the database requests in a given "unit of work" (i.e., transaction) to some remote site Y for execution. The database processing for the transaction is thus executed in its entirety at the remote site Y; however, the local site X decides whether the transaction is to be committed or rolled back. *Note:* RUW is effectively client/server processing with a single server.
>
> **Distributed unit of work** (abbreviated DUW) means that an application at one site X can send some or all of the database requests in a given unit of work (transaction) to one or more remote sites $Y, Z, ...,$ for execution. The database processing for the transaction is thus spread across several sites, in general; each individual request is still executed in its entirety at a single site, but different requests can be executed at different sites. However, site X is still the coordinating site, that is, the site that decides whether the transaction is to be committed or rolled back. *Note:* DUW is effectively client/server processing with many servers.
>
> Finally, **distributed request** is the only one of the four levels that approaches what is commonly regarded as true distributed database support. Distributed request means everything that distributed unit of work means, *plus* it permits individual database requests (SQL statements) to span several sites—for example, a request originating from site X might ask for a join or union to be performed between a relation at site Y and a relation at site Z. Note that it is only at this level that the system can be said to be providing genuine location independence; at all three previous levels, users do have to have some knowledge regarding the physical location of data.

21.23 International Organization for Standardization (ISO): *Information Processing Systems, Open Systems Interconnection, Remote Data Access Part 1: Generic Model, Service, and Protocol (Draft International Standard).* Document ISO DIS 9579-1 (March 1990).

21.24 International Organization for Standardization (ISO): *Information Processing Systems, Open Systems Interconnection, Remote Data Access Part 2: SQL Specialization (Draft International Standard).* Document ISO DIS 9579-2 (February 1990).

21.25 Donald Kossmann: "The State of the Art in Distributed Query Processing," *ACM Comp. Surv. 32,* No. 4 (December 2000).

21.26 B. G. Lindsay *et al.*: "Notes on Distributed Databases," IBM Research Report RJ2571 (July 1979).

> This paper (by some of the original members of the R* team) is divided into five chapters:

1. Replicated Data

2. Authorization and Views

3. Introduction to Distributed Transaction Management

4. Recovery Facilities

5. Transaction Initiation, Migration, and Termination

Chapter 1 discusses the update propagation problem. Chapter 2 is almost totally concerned with authorization in a *non*distributed system (in the style of System R), except for a few remarks at the end. Chapter 3 considers transaction initiation and termination, concurrency, and recovery, all rather briefly. Chapter 4 is devoted to the topic of recovery in the *non*distributed case (again). Finally, Chapter 5 discusses distributed transaction management in some detail; in particular, it gives a very careful presentation of two-phase commit.

21.27 C. Mohan and B. G. Lindsay: "Efficient Commit Protocols for the Tree of Processes Model of Distributed Transactions," Proc. 2nd ACM SIGACT-SIGOPS Symposium on Principles of Distributed Computing (1983).

See the annotation to reference [21.37].

21.28 Scott Newman and Jim Gray: "Which Way to Remote SQL?" *DBP&D 4,* No. 12 (December 1991).

21.29 M. Tamer Özsu and Patrick Valduriez: *Principles of Distributed Database Systems* (2d ed.). Englewood Cliffs, N.J.: Prentice-Hall (1999).

21.30 Martin Rennhackkamp: "Mobile Database Replication," *DBMS 10,* No. 11 (October 1997).

The combination of cheap, highly portable computers and wireless communication makes possible a new kind of distributed database system with its own special benefits but also its own special problems. In particular, data in such a system can be replicated at literally thousands of "sites"—but those sites are mobile, they are frequently offline, their operational characteristics are very different from those of more conventional sites (e.g., communication costs must take battery usage and connection time into account), and so on. Research into such systems is comparatively new (references [21.1] and [21.18] are relevant); this short article highlights some of the principal concepts and concerns.

21.31 James B. Rothnie, Jr., and Nathan Goodman: "A Survey of Research and Development in Distributed Database Management," Proc. 3rd Int. Conf. on Very Large Data Bases, Tokyo, Japan (October 1977).

A very useful early survey. The field is discussed under the following headings:

1. Synchronizing Update Transactions

2. Distributed Query Processing

3. Handling Component Failures

4. Directory Management

5. Database Design

The last of these refers to the *physical* design problem—what we called the *allocation* problem in Section 21.8.

21.32 J. B. Rothnie, Jr. *et al.*: "Introduction to a System for Distributed Databases (SDD-1)," *ACM TODS 5,* No. 1 (March 1980).

References [21.4, 21.5], [21.21], and [21.32] are all concerned with the early distributed prototype SDD-1, which ran on a collection of DEC PDP-10s interconnected via the Arpanet (see

Chapter 27, Section 27.2). It provided full location, fragmentation, and replication independence. We offer a few comments here on selected aspects of the system.

Query processing: The SDD-1 optimizer (see reference [21.4]) made extensive use of the *semijoin* operator as described in Chapter 7, Section 7.8. The advantage of using semijoins in distributed query processing is that they can have the effect of reducing the amount of data shipped across the network. For example, suppose the suppliers relvar S is stored at site A and the shipments relvar SP is stored at site B, and the query is just "Join suppliers and shipments." Instead of shipping the whole of relvar S to B (say), we can do the following:

- Compute the projection (TEMP1) of SP over S# at B
- Ship TEMP1 to A
- Compute the semijoin (TEMP2) of TEMP1 and S over S# at A
- Ship TEMP2 to B
- Compute the semijoin of TEMP2 and SP over S# at B

This procedure will obviously reduce the total amount of data movement across the network if and only if

```
size (TEMP1) + size (TEMP2) < size (S)
```

where the "size" of a relation is the cardinality of that relation multiplied by the width of an individual tuple (in bits, say). The optimizer thus clearly needs to be able to estimate the size of intermediate results such as TEMP1 and TEMP2.

Update propagation: The SDD-1 update propagation algorithm is "propagate immediately" (there is no notion of a primary copy).

Concurrency: Concurrency control is based on a technique called **timestamping**, instead of locking; the objective is to avoid the message overhead associated with locking, but the price seems to be that there is not in fact very much concurrency! The details are beyond the scope of this book (though the annotation to reference [16.3] does describe the basic idea very briefly); see reference [21.5] for more information.

Recovery: Recovery is based on a *four*-phase commit protocol; the intent is to make the process more resilient than the conventional two-phase commit protocol to a failure at the coordinator site, but unfortunately it also makes the process considerably more complex. The details are (again) beyond the scope of this book.

Catalog: The catalog is managed by treating it as if it were ordinary user data—it can be arbitrarily fragmented, and the fragments can be arbitrarily replicated and distributed, just like any other data. The advantages of this approach are obvious. The disadvantage is that since the system has no *a priori* knowledge of the location of any given piece of the catalog, it is necessary to maintain a higher-level catalog—the **directory locator**—to provide exactly that information! The directory locator is fully replicated (i.e., a copy is stored at every site).

21.33 P. G. Selinger and M. E. Adiba: "Access Path Selection in Distributed Data Base Management Systems," in S. M. Deen and P. Hammersley (eds.), Proc. Int. Conf. on Data Bases, Aberdeen, Scotland (July 1980). London, England: Heyden and Sons Ltd. (1980).

See the annotation to reference [21.37].

21.34 M. R. Stonebraker and E. J. Neuhold: "A Distributed Data Base Version of Ingres," Proc. 2nd Berkeley Conf. on Distributed Data Management and Computer Networks, Lawrence Berkeley Laboratory (May 1977).

References [21.15], [21.34], and [21.35] are all concerned with the Distributed Ingres prototype. Distributed Ingres consists of several copies of University Ingres, running on several interconnected DEC PDP-11s. It supports location independence (like SDD-1 and R*); it also supports data fragmentation (via restriction but not projection), with fragmentation independence, and data replication for such fragments, with replication independence. Unlike SDD-1 and R*, Distributed Ingres does not necessarily assume that the communication network is slow; on the contrary, it is designed to handle both "slow" (long haul) networks and local (i.e., comparatively fast) networks (the optimizer understands the difference between the two cases). The optimization algorithm is basically an extension of the Ingres decomposition strategy described in Chapter 18 of this book; it is described in detail in reference [21.15].

Distributed Ingres provides two update propagation algorithms: a "performance" algorithm, which works by updating a primary copy and then returning control to the transaction (leaving the propagated updates to be performed in parallel by a set of slave processes), and a "reliable" algorithm, which updates all copies immediately (see reference [21.35]). Concurrency control is based on locking in both cases. Recovery is based on two-phase commit, with improvements.

As for the catalog, Distributed Ingres uses a combination of full replication for certain portions of the catalog—basically the portions containing a logical description of the base relvars visible to the user and a description of how those relvars are fragmented—together with purely local catalog entries for other portions, such as the portions describing local indexes, local database statistics (used by the optimizer), and security and integrity constraints.

21.35 M. R. Stonebraker: "Concurrency Control and Consistency of Multiple Copies in Distributed Ingres," *IEEE Transactions on Software Engineering 5*, No. 3 (May 1979).

See the annotation to reference [21.34].

21.36 Wen-Syan Li and Chris Clifton: "Semantic Integration in Heterogeneous Databases Using Neural Networks," Proc. 20th Int. Conf. on Very Large Data Bases, Santiago, Chile (September 1994).

21.37 R. Williams *et al.*: "R*: An Overview of the Architecture," in P. Scheuermann (ed.), *Improving Database Usability and Responsiveness*. New York, N.Y.: Academic Press (1982). Also available as IBM Research Report RJ3325 (December 1981).

References [21.12], [21.27], [21.33], and [21.37] are all concerned with R*, the distributed version of the original System R prototype. R* provides location independence, but no fragmentation or replication, and therefore no fragmentation or replication independence either. The question of update propagation does not arise, for the same reason. Concurrency control is based on locking (note that there is only one copy of any object to be locked; the question of a primary copy also does not arise). Recovery is based on two-phase commit, with improvements.

21.38 Ling Ling Yan, Renée J. Miller, Laura M. Haas, and Ronald Fagin: "Data-Driven Understanding and Refinement of Schema Mappings," Proc. 2001 ACM SIGMOD Int. Conf. on Management of Data, Santa Barbara, Calif. (May 2001).

Decision Support

22.1 INTRODUCTION

Note: David McGoveran of Alternative Technologies was the original author of this chapter.

Decision support systems are systems that help in the analysis of business information. Their aim is to help management "spot trends, pinpoint problems, and make . . . intelligent decisions" [22.9]. The roots of such systems—operations research, behavioral and scientific theories of management, and statistical process control—can be traced back to the late 1940s and 1950s, well before computers became generally available. The basic idea was, and of course still is, to collect business *operational data* (see Chapter 1) and reduce it to a form that can be used to analyze the behavior of the business and modify that behavior in an intelligent manner. For obvious reasons, the extent to which the data was reduced in those early days was fairly minimal, however, typically involving little more than the generation of simple summary reports.

In the late 1960s and early 1970s, researchers at Harvard and MIT began promoting the use of computers to help in the decision-making process [22.26]. At first, such use was mostly limited to automating the task of report generation, although rudimentary analytical capabilities were sometimes provided as well [22.6–22.8]. Those early computer systems were initially known as *management decision systems;* later they also became known as *management information systems.* We prefer the more modern term *decision support systems,* however, since a good case can be made that *all* information systems—including, for example, OLTP systems (OLTP = online transaction processing)—can or should be regarded as "management information systems" (after all, they are all involved in, and affect, the management of the business). We will stay with the more modern term in what follows.

The 1970s also saw the development of several *query languages,* and a number of custom (in-house) decision support systems were built around such languages. They were implemented using report generators such as RPG or data retrieval products such as Focus, Datatrieve, and NOMAD. Those systems were the first to allow suitably skilled end users to access computer data stores directly; that is, they allowed such users to formulate business-related queries against those data stores and execute those queries directly, without having to wait for assistance from the IT department.

Of course, the data stores just mentioned were mostly just simple files—most business data at the time was kept in such files, or possibly in nonrelational databases (relational systems still lay in the realm of research). Even in the latter case, the data usually had to be extracted from the database and copied to files before it could be accessed by a decision support system. It was not until the early 1980s that relational databases began to be used in place of simple files for decision support purposes (in fact, decision support, *ad hoc* query, and reporting were among the earliest commercial uses of relational technology). And even though SQL products are now widely available, the idea of **extract processing**—that is, copying data from the operational environment to some other environment for subsequent processing—continues to be very important; it allows users to operate on the extracted data in whatever manner they desire, without interfering further with the operational environment. And the reason for performing such extracts is very often decision support.

It should be clear from the foregoing brief history that decision support is not really part of database technology *per se.* Rather, it is a *use* of that technology (albeit an important one)—or, to be more precise, it is several such uses, distinct but intertwined. The uses in question fall under the headings of *data warehouse, data mart, operational data store, online analytical processing (OLAP), multi-dimensional databases,* and *data mining,* among others. Of course, we will explain all of these concepts in the pages to come; however, we remark immediately that one thing they all have in common is that good logical design principles are rarely followed in any of them! The practice of decision support is, regrettably, not as scientific as it might be; often, in fact, it is quite *ad hoc.* In particular, it tends to be driven by physical considerations much more than by logical ones—indeed, it tends to blur the logical *vs.* physical distinction considerably. Partly for such reasons, in this chapter we use SQL, not **Tutorial D**, as the basis for our examples, and we use the "fuzzier" terminology of rows, columns, and tables in place of our preferred terminology of tuples, attributes, and relation values and variables (relvars). Also, we use the terms *logical schema* and *physical schema* as synonyms for what in Chapter 2 we called the *conceptual* schema and the *internal* schema, respectively.

The plan of the chapter is as follows. In Section 22.2 we discuss aspects of decision support that have motivated certain design practices that we believe are somewhat misguided. Section 22.3 describes our own preferred approach to dealing with those aspects. Section 22.4 then examines the issue of data preparation (i.e., the process of getting operational data into a form in which it can be useful for decision support purposes); it also briefly considers "operational data stores." Section 22.5 discusses data warehouses, data marts, and "dimensional schemas." Section 22.6 explores online analytical processing (OLAP) and multi-dimensional databases. Section 22.7 discusses data mining. Section 22.8 sketches the pertinent SQL facilities. Finally, Section 22.9 presents a summary.

22.2 ASPECTS OF DECISION SUPPORT

Decision support databases display a number of special characteristics, of which the overriding one is this: **The database is primarily** (though not totally) **read-only**. What updating there might be is limited, typically, to periodic *load* or *refresh* operations—and those operations in turn are dominated by INSERTs; DELETEs are done only very occasionally, UPDATEs almost never. (Updating is sometimes done on certain auxiliary work tables, but normal decision support processes as currently practiced almost never update the decision support database itself.)

The following further characteristics of decision support databases are also worthy of note (we will elaborate on them in Section 22.3). Note that the first three are logical in nature, while the last three are physical.

- Columns tend to be used in combination.

- Integrity in general is not a concern (the data is assumed to be correct when first loaded and is not subsequently updated).

- Keys often include a temporal component (indeed, proper temporal support in general—see Chapter 23—would be extremely useful but is rarely available).

- The database tends to be large, especially when (as is often the case) business transaction[1] details are accumulated over time.

- The database tends to be heavily indexed.

- The database often involves various kinds of controlled redundancy.

Decision support queries display special characteristics, too; in particular, they tend to be complicated. Here are some of the kinds of complexities that can arise:

- *Boolean expression complexity:* Decision support queries often involve complex expressions in the WHERE clause: expressions that are hard to write, hard to understand, and hard for the system to implement efficiently. A common problem is queries involving time (e.g., a query that asks for rows with a maximum timestamp value within a specified time interval). If any joins are involved, such queries

---

[1] Here and throughout this chapter we distinguish business transactions (e.g., product sales) from transactions in the sense of Part IV of this book by always using the "business" qualifier when it is a business transaction we mean (unless the context makes the meaning obvious).

quickly become very complex indeed, especially since proper temporal support is probably not available. The net result in such cases is typically poor performance, among other things.

- *Join complexity:* Decision support queries often require access to many kinds of facts. As a consequence, in a properly designed (i.e., fully normalized) database, such queries typically involve many joins. Unfortunately, conventional join implementation technology has never managed to keep up with the ever-growing demands of decision support queries.[2] Often, therefore, designers decide to "denormalize" the database by "prejoining" certain tables. As we saw in Chapter 13, however, this approach is rarely successful (it tends to cause as many problems as it solves). What is more, the desire to avoid explicit run-time joins can lead to further inefficiencies, with large amounts of data being retrieved that is not logically needed and join processing being done by the application instead of by the DBMS.

- *Function complexity:* Decision support queries often involve statistical and other mathematical functions. Until recently, few products supported such functions (though the situation is improving in this respect, somewhat). As a result, it is often necessary to break a query into a sequence of smaller ones, which are then executed interleaved with user-written procedures that compute the desired functions. This approach has the unfortunate consequence that large amounts of data might need to be retrieved; also, it makes the overall query much harder to write and understand.

- *Analytical complexity:* Business questions are rarely answered in a single query. Not only is it difficult for users to write queries of extreme complexity, but SQL product limitations can prevent such queries from being processed. One way to reduce the complexity of such queries is (again) to break them into a series of smaller ones, keeping intermediate results in auxiliary tables.

All of the foregoing characteristics, both those of decision support databases *per se* and those of the corresponding queries, lead to a strong emphasis on *designing for performance*—especially batch insert and *ad hoc* retrieval performance. Needless to say, it is our position that this emphasis should affect only physical design, not logical design (and we elaborate on this position in the next section). Unfortunately, however, as noted in Section 22.1, vendors and users of decision support systems often fail to distinguish adequately between logical and physical issues;[3] in fact, they often ignore logical design entirely. As a consequence, attempts to deal with all of the various characteristics discussed in the fore-

---

[2] The writer (McGoveran), working on early decision support systems in 1981, observed that a three-table join of tables of even moderate size could easily take many hours. Joins of four to six tables were generally considered too costly. Today, joins of six to ten very large tables are common, and the technology usually does well. However, it is still easy (and not unusual) to generate queries that join more tables than the technology can reasonably handle. Queries joining more than twelve tables can rapidly become an adventure—and yet the requirement for such queries is common! *Note:* See Appendix A for a description of a possible solution to this problem.

[3] Data warehouse and OLAP specialists tend to be especially guilty on this count; they often argue that relational design is simply "wrong" for decision support, claiming that the relational model is incapable of representing the data and must be circumvented. Such arguments almost always hinge on a failure to distinguish the relational model from its implementation.

going tend to be *ad hoc* and often lead to insurmountable difficulties in trying to balance correctness, maintainability, performance, scalability, and usability requirements.

22.3 DATABASE DESIGN FOR DECISION SUPPORT

As stated earlier in this book (see the introduction to Part III), it is our position that database design should always be done in two stages, logical then physical:

a. The logical design should be done first. In this stage, the focus is on *relational correctness:* Tables must represent proper relations, thereby guaranteeing that relational operations work as advertised and do not produce surprising results. Types (domains) are specified, columns defined on them, and dependencies among columns (FDs, etc.) identified. From this information, normalization can proceed and further integrity constraints defined as appropriate.

b. Second, the physical design should be derived from the logical design. In this stage, the focus is on *storage efficiency and performance.* In principle, any physical arrangement of the data is permissible, as long as there exists an information-preserving transformation, expressible in the relational algebra (see reference [2.5]), between the logical and physical schemas. Note in particular that the existence of such a transformation implies that there exist relational views of the physical schema that make it look like the logical schema and *vice versa.*

Of course, the logical schema might subsequently change (e.g., to accommodate new kinds of data or new—or newly discovered—dependencies), and such a change will naturally require a corresponding change to the physical schema as well. Such a possibility does not concern us here. What does concern us is the ability to make a change to the physical schema *without* having to make a corresponding change to the logical schema. For example, suppose joining tables SP (shipments) and P (parts) is the dominant access pattern. Then we might wish to "prejoin" the SP and P tables at the physical level, thereby reducing I/O and join costs. However, *the logical schema must remain unchanged* if physical data independence is to be achieved. (Of course, the query optimizer will need to be aware of the existence of the stored "prejoin," and use it appropriately, in order to obtain the desired performance benefits.) Furthermore, if the access pattern subsequently changes to one dominated by individual table accesses instead of joins, we should be able to change the physical schema again so that the SP and P tables are physically separated, again without any impact at the logical level.

It should be clear from the foregoing that the problem of providing physical data independence is basically the same as the problem of supporting views—except that, as with the fragment update problem discussed in Chapter 21, it manifests itself at a different point in the overall system architecture. In particular, we need to be able to update those views. To be specific, if (a) we think of the base tables at the logical level as views and the stored versions of those "views" at the physical level as base tables, then (b) the physical schema has to be such that the DBMS can implement updates on those "views" in terms of those "base tables."

Now, we saw in Chapter 10 that, in theory, *all* views are updatable. In theory, therefore, if the physical schema is derived from the logical schema in the manner described, maximum physical data independence will be achieved: Any update expressed in terms of the logical schema will be automatically translatable into one expressed in terms of the physical schema and *vice versa,* and changes to the physical schema will not in and of themselves require changes to the logical schema. Unfortunately, however, today's SQL products do not support view updating properly. As a consequence, the set of permissible physical schemas is considerably (and unnecessarily) limited in those products. *Note:* In practice, it might be possible to simulate the proper view updating mechanism by means of stored procedures, triggers, middleware, or some combination thereof. Such techniques are beyond the scope of this chapter, however.

Logical Design

The rules of logical design do not depend on the intended use of the database—the same rules apply, regardless of the kinds of applications intended. In particular, therefore, it should make no difference whether those applications are operational (OLTP) or decision support applications: Either way, the same design procedure should be followed. So let us revisit the three *logical* characteristics of decision support databases identified near the beginning of Section 22.2 and consider their implications for logical design.

- *Column combinations and fewer dependencies*

  Decision support queries—and updates, when applicable—often treat combinations of columns as a unit, meaning the component columns are never accessed individually (ADDRESS is an obvious example). Let us agree to refer to such a column combination as a *composite column.* From a logical design point of view, then, such composite columns behave as if they were in fact *not* composite! To be more specific, let *CC* be a composite column and let *C* be some other column of the same table. Then dependencies involving *C* and component(s) of *CC* reduce to dependencies involving *C* and *CC per se.* What is more, dependencies involving components of *CC* and no other columns are irrelevant and can simply be ignored. The net effect is that the total number of dependencies is reduced and the logical design becomes simpler, with fewer columns and possibly even fewer tables.

- *Integrity constraints in general*

  Since as already explained (a) decision support databases are primarily read-only and (b) data integrity is checked when the database is loaded (or refreshed), it is often assumed that there is no point in declaring integrity constraints in the logical schema. Such is not the case, however. While it is true (if the database genuinely is read-only) that the constraints can never be violated, the *semantic value* of those constraints should not be overlooked. As we saw in Chapter 9, constraints serve to define the formal meaning of the tables and the formal meaning of the overall database. Declaring the constraints thus provides a means of telling users what the data means, thereby helping them in their task of formulating queries. What is more, declaring the constraints can also provide crucial information to the optimizer (see the discussion of semantic optimization in Chapter 18).

Note: In some products, declaring certain constraints causes the automatic creation of indexes and/or other enforcement mechanisms, a fact that can significantly increase the cost of load and refresh operations. This fact in turn can serve to encourage designers to avoid constraint declarations. Once again, however, the problem derives from a confusion over logical *vs.* physical issues; it should be possible to specify integrity constraints declaratively at the *logical* level and to specify the corresponding enforcement mechanisms separately at the *physical* level. Unfortunately, however, today's products do not adequately differentiate between the two levels—and they scarcely recognize the semantic value of constraints at all.

- *Temporal keys*

Operational databases usually involve current data only. Decision support databases, by contrast, usually involve historical data and therefore tend to *timestamp* most or all of that data. As a result, keys in such databases often include timestamp columns. Consider our usual suppliers-and-parts database, for example. Suppose we need to extend that database to show, for each shipment, the particular month (1 to 12) in which that shipment occurred. Then the shipments table SP might look as shown in Fig. 22.1. Observe that the additional column MID ("month ID") is indeed part of the key of this extended version of table SP. Observe too that queries involving SP must now be formulated very carefully in order to access exactly the data required, no more and no less. We touched on such issues briefly in Section 22.2; Chapter 23 discusses them in depth.

Note: Adding timestamp columns might lead to the need for some redesign. For example, suppose, somewhat artificially, that the quantity of each shipment is determined by the month in which the shipment occurs (the sample data of Fig. 22.1 is consistent with this constraint). Then the revised version of table SP satisfies the functional dependency MID $\rightarrow$ QTY and is thus not in fifth—or even third—normal form;

SP	S#	P#	MID	QTY
	S1	P1	3	300
	S1	P1	5	100
	S1	P2	1	200
	S1	P3	7	400
	S1	P4	1	200
	S1	P5	5	100
	S1	P6	4	100
	S2	P1	3	300
	S2	P2	9	400
	S3	P2	6	200
	S3	P2	8	200
	S4	P2	1	200
	S4	P4	8	200
	S4	P5	7	400
	S4	P5	11	400

Fig. 22.1 Sample value for table SP, including month IDs

SP	S#	P#	MID
	S1	P1	3
	S1	P1	5
	S1	P2	1
	S1	P3	7
	S1	P4	1
	S1	P5	5
	S1	P6	4
	S2	P1	3
	S2	P2	9
	S3	P2	6
	S3	P2	8
	S4	P2	1
	S4	P4	8
	S4	P5	7
	S4	P5	11

MONTH_QTY	MID	QTY
	1	200
	2	600
	3	300
	4	100
	5	100
	6	200
	7	400
	8	200
	9	400
	10	100
	11	400
	12	50

Fig. 22.2   Normalized counterpart of Fig. 22.1

it should therefore be further normalized as indicated in Fig. 22.2. Unfortunately, decision support designers rarely bother to take such issues into account. Again, see Chapter 23 for further discussion.

Physical Design

We said in Section 22.2 that decision support databases tend to be large and heavily indexed, and tend to involve various kinds of controlled redundancy. In this subsection and the next two we briefly elaborate on these physical design issues.

First we consider **partitioning** (also known as *fragmentation*). Partitioning represents an attack on the database size problem; it divides a given table into a set of disjoint *partitions* or *fragments* for physical storage purposes (see the discussion of fragmentation in Chapter 21). Such partitioning can significantly improve the manageability and accessibility of the table in question. Typically, each partition is assigned its own more or less dedicated hardware resources (e.g., disk, CPU), thereby minimizing competition for such resources among partitions. Tables are partitioned horizontally[4] by means of a *partitioning function,* which takes values of selected columns (the *partition key*) as arguments and returns a partition number or address. Such functions typically support range, hash, and round-robin partitioning, among other kinds (see the annotation to reference [18.56] in Chapter 18).

Now we turn to **indexing**. Of course, it is well known that using the right kind of index can dramatically reduce I/O. Most early SQL products provided just one kind of index, the B-tree, but several other kinds have become available over the years, especially in connection with decision support databases; they include *bitmap, hash, multi-table, boolean,* and *functional* indexes, as well as B-tree indexes *per se.* We comment briefly on each.

---

[4] Vertical partitioning, though possibly advantageous, is not much used, since few products support it.

- *B-tree indexes:* B-tree indexes provide efficient access for range queries (unless the number of rows accessed becomes too large). Update of B-trees is relatively efficient.

- *Bitmap indexes:* Suppose the indexed table T contains n rows. Then a bitmap index on column C of table T keeps a vector of n bits for each possible value of C, setting the bit corresponding to row r if row r contains the applicable value in column C. Such indexes are efficient for queries involving sets of values, though they become less efficient when the sets become too large. Observe in particular that several relational operations (joins, unions, equality restrictions, etc.) can be performed entirely within the index(es) by means of simple boolean operations (AND, OR, NOT) on the bit vectors; access to the actual data is not needed at all until the final result set has to be retrieved. Update of bitmap indexes is relatively inefficient.

- *Hash indexes* (also known as *hash addressing* or just *hashing*): Hash indexes are efficient for accessing specific rows (not ranges). The computational cost is linear with the number of rows, as long as the hash function does not need to be extended to accommodate additional key values. Hashing can also be used to implement joins efficiently, as described in Chapter 18.

- *Multi-table indexes* (also known as *join indexes*): Essentially, a multi-table index entry contains pointers to rows in several tables instead of just to rows in one table. Such indexes can improve the performance of joins and the checking of multi-table (i.e., database) integrity constraints. See reference [22.33].

- *Boolean indexes* (also known as *expression indexes*): A boolean index indicates for which rows of a specified table a specified boolean expression involving columns of the table in question evaluates to TRUE. Such indexes are particularly useful when the relevant boolean expression is a common component of restriction conditions.

- *Functional indexes:* A functional index indexes the rows of a table not on the basis of values in those rows, but rather on the basis of the result of invoking some specified function on those values.

In addition to all of the foregoing, various kinds of *hybrid* indexes (combinations of those already mentioned) have been proposed. The value of such hybrids is hard to characterize in general terms. A huge number of *specialized* kinds of indexes have also been proposed (e.g., *R-trees,* which are intended for dealing with spatial data). We do not attempt the daunting task of describing all of these kinds of indexes in this book; see, for example, reference [26.37] for a comprehensive discussion.

Third, we consider the issue of **controlled redundancy**. Controlled redundancy is an important tool for reducing I/O and minimizing contention. As explained in Chapter 1, redundancy is controlled when it is managed by the DBMS and hidden from users. (Note that, by definition, redundancy that is properly controlled at the physical level is invisible at the logical level, so it has no effect on the correctness of that logical level.) There are two broad kinds of such redundancy:

- The first involves maintaining exact copies or *replicas* of the base data. *Note:* What might be regarded as a less ambitious form of replication, *copy management,* is also widely supported (see the next subsection).

- The second involves maintaining *derived data* in addition to the base data, most often in the form of *summary tables* and/or *calculated*—or *computed* or *derived*—columns.

We discuss each of these possibilities in a subsection of its own.

Replication

The basic concepts of replication were explained in Chapter 21, in Sections 21.3 and 21.4 (see especially the subsection "Update Propagation" in Section 21.4). Here we just repeat a few salient points from those discussions and make a few additional remarks. Recall first that replication can be either synchronous or asynchronous:

- In the *synchronous* case, if a given replica is updated, then all other replicas of the same piece of data are also updated within the same transaction, implying that (logically speaking) just one version of the data exists. Some products implement synchronous replication via (possibly hidden, system-managed) triggers. However, synchronous replication has the disadvantage that it imposes an overhead on all transactions that update any replica (there might be availability problems, too).

- In the *asynchronous* case, updates to one replica are propagated to the others at some later time, *not* within the same transaction. Asynchronous replication thus introduces a *time delay* or *latency* during which the replicas might not in fact be identical (and so the term *replicas* is no longer very appropriate, since we are no longer talking about exact copies). Most products implement asynchronous replication by reading the transaction log or a stable queue of updates that need to be propagated.

   The advantage of asynchronous replication is that the replication overhead is uncoupled from the updating transaction, which might be "mission-critical" and highly performance-sensitive. The disadvantage is that the data can become inconsistent (inconsistent as seen by the user, that is[5]); in other words, the redundancy can show through to the logical level—meaning, strictly speaking, that the term *controlled redundancy* is no longer appropriate.

   We elaborate briefly on the issue of consistency (or inconsistency, rather). The fact is, replicas can become inconsistent in ways that are hard (though not impossible) to avoid and hard to fix. In particular, conflicts can arise over the order in which updates are applied. For example, suppose transaction *A* inserts a row into replica *X* and transaction *B* then deletes that row, and suppose *Y* is a replica of *X*. If the updates are propagated to *Y* but arrive at *Y* in reverse order (e.g., because of routing delays), *B* finds no row to delete in *Y* and *A* then inserts it! The net effect is that *Y* contains the row while *X* does not. In general, conflict management and consistency enforcement across replicas are difficult problems. Further details are beyond the scope of this book.

As noted in Chapter 21, the term *replication* has come to mean, primarily—indeed, almost exclusively—*asynchronous* replication specifically, at least in the commercial world.

---

[5] See the remarks on this topic in the previous chapter.

The basic difference between replication as just described and **copy management** is as follows. With replication, updates to one replica are (eventually) propagated to all others in an "automatic" fashion. With copy management, by contrast, there is no such automatic propagation; instead, data copies are created and maintained by means of some batch or background process that is uncoupled in time from the updating transactions. Copy management is generally more efficient than replication, since large amounts of data can be copied at one time. The disadvantage is that most of the time the copies are not identical to the base data; indeed, users must generally be aware of when they have been synchronized. Copy management is usually simplified by requiring that updates be applied in accordance with some kind of "primary copy" scheme, as described in Chapter 21.

Derived Data

The other kind of redundancy we consider is derived data: to be specific, *calculated columns* and *summary tables*. These constructs are particularly important in the decision support context. They are used to hold precomputed data values (i.e., values that are computed from other data kept somewhere else in the database), thereby avoiding the need to recompute the values in question each time they are needed in some query.

- A **calculated column** is a column whose value in any given row is derived in some way from other values in the same row. (Alternatively, the calculated value might be derived from values in several rows, in the same table or in some other table(s). However, such an approach implies that updating one row could require many other rows to be updated as well; in particular, it could have a very negative effect on load and refresh operations.)

- A **summary table** is a table that holds aggregations (sums, averages, counts, etc.) of values in other tables. Such aggregations are often precalculated for several different groupings of the same detail data (see Section 22.6). *Note:* Summary tables are known by a variety of names, including *automatic summary tables* (ASTs), *materialized query tables* (MQTs), *snapshots,* and *"materialized views."* We have met the last two of these terms before—in Chapter 10, Section 10.5—where we were extremely critical of the term *materialized view* in particular. Be that as it may, the concept is now the subject of an extensive body of literature, and most of that literature usurps the term *view* to mean a "materialized view" specifically (see, e.g., references [22.3] and [22.4], among many others).

Calculated columns and summary tables are most often implemented via system-managed triggers, though they can also be implemented via user-written procedural code. The former approach allows consistency to be maintained between the base and derived data; the latter approach is more likely to expose inconsistencies to the user. Of course, if calculated columns and summary tables are truly to be instances of controlled redundancy, they need to be completely hidden from users, but with the latter approach to implementation they might not be.

Common Design Errors

In this subsection, we comment briefly on some design practices that are common in the decision support environment and yet we feel are not a good idea.

- *Duplicate rows:* Decision support designers often claim that their data simply has no unique identifier and that they therefore have to permit duplicates. References [6.3] and [6.6] explain in detail why duplicates are a mistake; here we just remark that the "requirement" typically arises because the physical schema is not derived from a logical schema (which was probably never created in the first place). We note too that in such a design the rows often have nonuniform meanings (especially if any nulls are present)—that is, they are not all instantiations of the same predicate (see Section 3.4 or Chapter 9). *Note:* Duplicates are sometimes even regarded as a positive feature, especially if the designer has an object-oriented background (see the very last paragraph of Section 25.2 in Chapter 25).

- *Denormalization and related practices:* In a misguided effort to eliminate joins and reduce I/O, designers often prejoin tables, introduce derived columns of various kinds, and so on. Such practices might be acceptable at the physical level, but not if they are detectable at the logical level.

- *Star schemas:* "Star schemas" (also known as *dimensional* schemas) are most often the result of an attempt to short-circuit proper design technique. There is little to be gained from such shortcuts. Often both performance and flexibility suffer as the database grows, and resolving such difficulties via physical redesign forces changes in applications as well (because star schemas are really *physical* schemas, even though they are exposed to applications).   The overall problem lies in the *ad hoc* nature of the design. *Note:* We will discuss star schemas in more detail in Section 22.5.

- *Nulls:* Designers often attempt to save space by permitting nulls in columns (this trick *might* work if the column in question is of some variable-length data type and the product in question represents nulls in such columns by empty strings at the physical level). Such attempts are generally a mistake, however. Not only is it possible (and desirable) to design in such a way as to avoid nulls in the first place [19.19], but the resulting schemas often provide better storage efficiency and better I/O performance.

- *Design of summary tables:* The question of logical design for summary tables is often ignored, leading to uncontrolled redundancy and difficulties in maintaining consistency. As a consequence, users can become confused as to the meaning of summary data and how to formulate queries involving it. To avoid such problems, all summary tables "at the same level of aggregation" (see Section 22.6) should be designed as if they constituted a database in their own right. Certain *cyclic update* problems can then be avoided by (a) prohibiting updates from spanning aggregation levels and (b) synchronizing the summary tables by always aggregating from the detail level up.

- *"Multiple navigation paths":* Decision support designers and users often speak, incorrectly, of there being a "multiplicity of navigational paths" to some desired data, meaning the same data can be reached via several different relational expressions. Sometimes the expressions in question are truly equivalent, as in the case of, for example, *A* JOIN (*B* JOIN *C*) and (*A* JOIN *B*) JOIN *C* (see Chapter 7); sometimes they are equivalent only because there is some integrity constraint in effect that makes them so (see Chapter 18); and sometimes they are not equivalent at all! As an example of the last case, suppose tables *A, B,* and *C* are such that *A* and *B* have a common column *KAB, B* and *C* have a common column *KBC,* and *A* and *C* have a common column *KAC;* then joining *A* and *B* over *KAB* and then joining the result to *C* over *KBC* is certainly not the same as joining *A* and *C* over *KAC.*

It is clear that users can become confused in such cases and be unsure as to which expression to use and whether or not there will be any difference in the result. Part of this problem can only be solved by proper user education, of course. Another part can be solved if the optimizer does its job properly. However, yet another part is due to designers allowing redundancies in the logical schema and/or letting users access the physical schema directly, and *that* part of the problem can only be solved by proper design practice.

In sum, we believe that many of the design difficulties allegedly arising from decision support requirements can be addressed by following a disciplined approach. Indeed, many of those difficulties are *caused* by not following such an approach (though it is only fair to add that they are often aggravated by problems with SQL).

22.4 DATA PREPARATION

Many of the issues surrounding decision support concern the tasks of obtaining and preparing the data in the first place. The data must be *extracted* (from various sources), *cleansed, transformed* and *consolidated, loaded* into the decision support database, and then periodically *refreshed.* Each of these operations involves its own special considerations.[6] We examine each in turn, then wrap up the section with a brief discussion of *operational data stores.*

Extract

Extract is the process of capturing data from operational databases and other sources. Many tools are available to help in this task, including system-provided utilities, custom extract programs, and commercial (general-purpose) extract products. The extract process tends to be I/O-intensive and thus can interfere with mission-critical operations; for this reason, it is often performed in parallel (i.e., as a set of parallel subprocesses) and at a physical level. Such "physical extracts" can cause problems for subsequent processing, however, because they can lose information—especially relationship information—that is represented in some physical manner (e.g., by pointers or physical contiguity). For this reason, extract programs sometimes provide a means of preserving such information by introducing sequential record numbers and replacing pointers by what are in effect foreign keys.

---

[6] We remark in passing that these operations could often benefit from the set-level capabilities of relational systems, though in practice they rarely do.

Cleansing

Few data sources control data quality adequately. As a result, data often requires **cleansing** (which is usually done in batch) before it can be entered into the decision support database. Typical cleansing operations include filling in missing values, correcting typographical and other data entry errors, establishing standard abbreviations and formats, replacing synonyms by standard identifiers, and so on. Data that is known to be in error and cannot be cleansed is rejected. *Note:* Information obtained during the cleansing process can sometimes be used to identify the cause of errors at the source and hence to improve data quality over time.

Transformation and Consolidation

Even after it has been cleansed, the data will probably still not be in the form the decision support system requires, and so will need to be **transformed** appropriately. Usually the required form will be a set of files, one for each table identified in the physical schema; as a result, transforming the data might involve splitting and/or combining source records along the lines discussed in Chapter 1 (Section 1.5). For performance reasons, transformation operations are often performed in parallel. They can be both I/O- and CPU-intensive. *Note:* Data errors that were not corrected during cleansing are sometimes found during the transformation process. As before, any such incorrect data is generally rejected. Also as before, information obtained as part of this process can sometimes be used to improve the quality of the data source.

Transformation is particularly important when several data sources need to be merged, a process called **consolidation**. In such a case, any implicit relationships among data from distinct sources need to be made explicit (by introducing explicit data values). In addition, dates and times associated with the business meaning of the data need to be maintained and correlated among sources, a process called "time synchronization" [*sic!*].

We remark in passing that time synchronization can be a difficult problem. For example, suppose we want to find average customer revenue per salesperson per quarter. Suppose customer *vs.* revenue data is maintained by fiscal quarter in an accounting database, while salesperson *vs.* customer data is maintained by calendar quarter in a sales database. Clearly, we need to merge data from the two databases. Consolidating the customer data is easy—it simply involves matching customer IDs. However, the time synchronization issue is much more difficult; we can find customer revenues per *fiscal* quarter (from the accounting database), but we cannot tell which salespersons were responsible for which customers at that time, and we cannot find customer revenues per *calendar* quarter at all.

Load

DBMS vendors have placed considerable importance on the efficiency of load operations. For present purposes, we consider "load operations" to include (a) moving the transformed and consolidated data into the decision support database, (b) checking it for consistency (i.e., integrity checking), and (c) building any necessary indexes. We comment briefly on each step.

a. *Moving the data:* Modern systems usually provide parallel load utilities. Sometimes they will preformat the data to the internal physical format required by the target DBMS prior to the actual load. An alternative technique that delivers much of the efficiency of preformatted loads is to load the data into work tables that mirror the target schema. The necessary integrity checking can be done on those work tables— see paragraph *b*—and set-level INSERTs can then be used to move the data from the work tables to the target tables.

b. *Integrity checking:* Most integrity checking on the data to be loaded can be done prior to the actual load without reference to data already in the database. However, certain constraints cannot be checked without examining the existing database; for example, a uniqueness constraint will generally have to be checked during the actual load (or in batch after the load is completed).

c. *Building indexes:* The presence of indexes can slow the load process dramatically, since most products update indexes as each row is inserted into the underlying table. For this reason, it is sometimes a good idea to drop indexes before the load and then to create them again subsequently. However, this approach is not worthwhile when the ratio of new data to existing data is small, because the cost of creating an index does not scale with the size of the table to be indexed. Also, creating a large index can be subject to unrecoverable allocation errors (and the larger the index the more likely such errors are to occur). *Note:* Most DBMS products support parallel index creation in an effort to speed the load and index build processes.

Refresh

Most decision support databases require periodic **refreshing** of the data in order to keep it reasonably current. Refresh generally involves a partial load, although some decision support applications require dropping everything in the database and completely reloading it. Refresh involves all of the problems associated with load, but might also need to be performed while users are accessing the database (implying further problems).

Operational Data Stores

An **operational data store** (ODS) is a "subject-oriented, integrated, volatile (i.e., updatable), current or near current collection of data" [22.20]. In other words, it is a special kind of database. The term *subject-oriented* means the data in question has to do with some specific subject area (e.g., customers or products). An operational data store can be used (a) as a staging area for the physical reorganization of extracted operational data, (b) to provide operational reports, and (c) to support operational decisions. It can also serve (d) as a point of consolidation, if operational data comes from several sources. ODSs thus serve many purposes. *Note:* Since they do not accumulate historical data, they do not grow very large (usually); on the other hand, they are typically subject to very frequent or even continuous refresh from operational data sources. Asynchronous replication from the operational data sources to the ODS is sometimes used for this purpose (in this way, the data can often be kept current to within a few minutes). Time synchronization problems—

see the earlier subsection "Transformation and Consolidation"—can be successfully addressed within an ODS, if refresh is frequent enough.

22.5   DATA WAREHOUSES AND DATA MARTS

Operational systems usually have strict performance requirements, predictable workloads, small units of work, and high utilization. By contrast, decision support systems typically have varying performance requirements, unpredictable workloads, large units of work, and erratic utilization. These differences can make it very difficult to combine operational and decision support processing within a single system—conflicts arise over capacity planning, resource management, and system performance tuning, among other things. For such reasons, operational system administrators are usually reluctant to allow decision support activities on their systems; hence the familiar dual-system approach.

Note: We remark as an aside that matters were not always thus; early decision support systems were indeed run on operational systems, but at low priority or during the so-called batch window. Given sufficient computing resources, there are several advantages to this arrangement, perhaps the most obvious of which is that it avoids all of the possibly expensive data copying, reformatting, and transfer (etc.) operations required by the dual-system approach. In fact, the value of integrating operational and decision support activities is becoming increasingly recognized (see reference [21.9]). Further details of such integration are beyond the scope of this chapter, however.

The previous paragraph notwithstanding, the fact remains that, at least at the time of writing, decision support data usually needs to be collected from a variety of operational systems (often disparate systems) and kept in a data store of its own on a separate platform. That separate data store is a *data warehouse*.

Data Warehouses

Like an operational data store (and like a data mart—see the next subsection), a data warehouse is a special kind of database. The term seems to have originated in the late 1980s [22.15, 22.18], though the concept is somewhat older. Reference [22.19] defines a data warehouse as "a subject-oriented, integrated, nonvolatile, time-variant data store in support of management's decisions" (where the term *nonvolatile* means that, once inserted, data cannot be changed, though it might be deleted). Data warehouses arose for two reasons: first, the need to provide a single, clean, consistent source of data for decision support purposes; second, the need to do so without impacting operational systems.

By definition, data warehouse workloads are decision support workloads and hence query-intensive (with occasional intensive batch insert activities); also, data warehouses themselves tend to be quite large (often many terabytes, and growing by as much as 50 percent a year or even more). As a result, performance tuning is hard, though not impossible. Scalability can be a problem, though. Contributors to that problem include (a) database design errors (discussed in the final subsection of Section 22.3); (b) inefficient use of relational operations (mentioned briefly in Section 22.2); (c) weaknesses in the DBMS implementation of the relational model; (d) a lack of scalability in the DBMS itself; and (e) architectural design errors that limit capacity and preclude platform scalability. Points *a* and *b* have already been discussed in this chapter, and point *c* was discussed at length in Part II and elsewhere; points *d* and *e* are beyond the scope of this book.

Data Marts

Data warehouses are generally meant to provide a single source of data for all decision support activities. However, when data warehouses became popular in the early 1990s, it was soon realized that extensive reporting and data analysis operations were often performed on a relatively small subset of the complete warehouse. Indeed, the same operations were often repeated on the same subset of the data every time it was refreshed. Moreover, some of those activities—for example, predictive analysis (forecasting), simulation, "what if" modeling of business data—involved the creation of new schemas and data, with subsequent updates to that new data.

Repeatedly executing such operations on the same subset of the complete warehouse is obviously not very efficient; the idea of building some kind of limited, special-purpose "warehouse" that is tailored to the purpose at hand thus seems like a good idea. In some cases, moreover, it might be possible to extract and prepare the required data directly from local sources, providing access to the data more quickly than if it had to be synchronized with all of the other data to be loaded into the full warehouse. Such considerations led to the concept of **data marts**.

Actually there is some controversy over the definition of the term *data mart*. For our purposes, we can define it as "a specialized, subject-oriented, integrated, volatile, time-variant data store in support of a specific subset of management's decisions." As you can see, the primary distinctions between a data mart and a data warehouse are that a data mart is *specialized* and *volatile*. By *specialized,* we mean it contains data to support a specific area (only) of business analysis; by *volatile,* we mean users can update the data, possibly even create new data (meaning new tables) for some purpose.

There are three main approaches to creating a data mart:

- The data can simply be extracted from the data warehouse, in effect following a divide-and-conquer approach to the overall decision support workload, in order to achieve better performance and scalability. Usually the extracted data is loaded into a database with a physical schema that closely resembles the applicable subset of that for the data warehouse; however, it might be possible to simplify it somewhat, thanks to the specialized nature of the data mart.

- Despite the fact that the data warehouse is meant to provide a "single point of control," a data mart might still be created independently (i.e., *not* via extract from the warehouse). Such an approach might be appropriate if the warehouse is inaccessible for some reason, say for financial, operational, or even political reasons (or the data warehouse might not exist yet—see the point immediately following).

- Some installations have followed a "data mart first" approach, in which data marts are created as needed, with the overall data warehouse eventually being created as a consolidation of the various data marts.

The last two approaches both suffer from possible semantic mismatch problems. Independent data marts are particularly susceptible to such problems, since there is no obvious way to check for semantic mismatches if databases are designed independently. Consolidation of data marts into a data warehouse generally fails unless a single logical schema for the data warehouse is constructed first and the schemas for the individual data marts then derived from that warehouse schema. (Of course, the warehouse schema can evolve—assuming good design practice is followed—to include the subject matter of each new data mart as it is needed.)

An important decision to be made in the design of any decision support database is the database **granularity**. The term *granularity* here refers to the lowest level of data aggregation that will be kept in the database. Now, most decision support applications require access to detail data sooner or later, so for the data warehouse the decision is easy. For a data mart, it can be more difficult. Extracting large amounts of detail data from the data warehouse and storing it in the data mart can be very inefficient if that level of detail is not needed very often. On the other hand, it is sometimes hard to state definitively just what the lowest level of aggregation needed actually is. In such cases, detail data can be accessed directly from the data warehouse if and when needed, with data that is somewhat aggregated being maintained in the data mart. At the same time, full aggregation of the data is generally not done, because the very many ways in which the data can be aggregated will generate very large amounts of summary data. This point is discussed in more detail in Section 22.6.

One further point: Because data mart users often employ certain analytical tools, the physical design is often dictated, in part, by the specific tools to be used (see the discussion of "ROLAP *vs.* MOLAP" in Section 22.6). This unfortunate circumstance can lead to "dimensional schemas" (discussed next), which do not abide by good relational design practice.

Dimensional Schemas

Suppose we wish to collect a history of business transactions for analysis purposes. As noted in Section 22.1, early decision support systems would typically keep that history as a simple file, which would then be accessed via sequential scan. As the data volume increases, however, it becomes more and more desirable to support direct access lookup to the file from a number of different perspectives. For example, it might be useful to be able to find all business transactions involving a particular product, or all occurring within a particular time interval, or all pertaining to a particular customer.

One method of organization that supported this type of access was called a "multi-catalog" database.[7] Continuing with our example, such a database would consist of a large central data file containing the business transaction data, together with three individual "catalog" files for products, time intervals, and customers, respectively. Such catalog files resemble indexes in that they contain pointers to records in the data file, but (a) entries can be placed in them explicitly by the user ("catalog maintenance"), and (b) they can contain

---

[7] Nothing to do with database catalogs in the modern sense of the term.

supplemental information (e.g., customer address) that can then be removed from the data file. Note that the catalog files are usually small compared to the data file.

This organization is more efficient in terms of both space and I/O than the original design (involving just a single data file). Note in particular that the product, time interval, and customer information in the central data file now reduces to just product, time interval, and customer *identifiers*.

When this approach is mimicked in a relational database, the catalog files and data file become tables (images of the corresponding files); the pointers in the catalog files become keys in the catalog-file image tables; and the identifiers in the data file become foreign keys in the data-file image table. Typically, those various keys are all indexed. In such an arrangement, the data-file image is called a **fact table**, and the catalog-file images are called **dimension tables**. The overall structure is referred to as a **dimensional schema** or—owing to the way it looks when drawn as an entity/relationship diagram, with the fact table being surrounded by and connected by "spokes" or "rays" to the dimension tables— a **star schema**. *Note:* The reason for the "dimensional" terminology is explained in Section 22.6.

By way of illustration, let us modify the suppliers-and-parts database once again, this time to show for each shipment the particular time interval in which that shipment occurred. We identify time intervals by a time interval identifier (TI#), and we introduce another table TI to relate those identifiers to the corresponding time intervals *per se*. Then the revised shipments table SP and the new time intervals table TI might look as shown in Fig. 22.3.[8] In star schema terminology, table SP is the fact table and table TI is a dimension table (so too are the suppliers table S and the parts table P—see Fig. 22.4). *Note:* We remind you once again that the general question of handling time interval data will be discussed in detail in Chapter 23.

SP	S#	P#	TI#	QTY		TI	TI#	FROM	TO
	S1	P1	TI3	300			TI1	*ta*	*tb*
	S1	P1	TI5	100			TI2	*tc*	*td*
	S1	P2	TI1	200			TI3	*te*	*tf*
	S1	P3	TI2	400			TI4	*tg*	*th*
	S1	P4	TI1	200			TI5	*ti*	*tj*
	S1	P5	TI5	100					
	S1	P6	TI4	100					
	S2	P1	TI3	300					
	S2	P2	TI4	400					
	S3	P2	TI1	200					
	S3	P2	TI3	200					
	S4	P2	TI1	200					
	S4	P4	TI3	200					
	S4	P5	TI2	400					
	S4	P5	TI1	400					

Fig. 22.3   Sample fact table (SP) and dimension table (TI)

---

[8] The FROM and TO columns in table TI contain data of some timestamp type. For simplicity, we do not show actual timestamp values in the figure, but instead represent them symbolically.

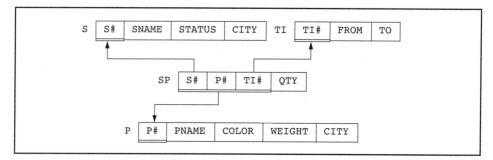

Fig. 22.4   Star schema for suppliers-and-parts (with time intervals)

Querying a star schema database typically involves using the dimension tables to find all foreign key combinations of interest, and then using those combinations to access the fact table. Assuming the dimension table accesses and subsequent fact table access are all bundled up into a single query, the best way to implement that query is usually by means of what is called a **star join**. "Star join" is a specific join implementation strategy; it differs from the usual strategies in that it deliberately begins by computing a Cartesian product—namely, the Cartesian product of the dimension tables. Now, we saw in Chapter 18 that query optimizers usually try to avoid computing Cartesian products; in the case at hand, however, forming the product of the much smaller dimension tables first and then using the result to perform index-based lookups on the fact table is almost always more efficient than any other strategy. Many commercial optimizers have been extended to support star joins.

Now, at this point you might be wondering what the difference is between a star schema and what we would regard as a proper relational design. In fact, a *simple* star schema like the one in Fig. 22.4 can look very similar (even identical) to a good relational design. Unfortunately, however, there are several problems with the star schema approach in general. Here are some of them:

1. First of all, it is *ad hoc*—it is based on intuition rather than principle. This lack of discipline makes it difficult to change the schema in a proper fashion when (for example) new types of data are added to the database or constraints change. In fact, star schemas are often constructed by simply editing a previous design, and that previous design in turn is often constructed by trial and error.

2. Star schemas are really physical, not logical, though they are usually talked about as if they were logical. The problem is that there is really no concept of logical design, as distinct from physical design, in the star schema approach.

3. The star schema approach does not always result in a legitimate physical design (i.e., one that preserves all of the information in a relationally correct logical design). This shortcoming becomes more apparent the more complex the schema becomes.

4. Because there is little discipline, designers often include several different types of facts in the fact table. As a consequence, the rows and columns of the fact table typically do not have a uniform interpretation. What is more, certain columns then typi-

cally apply only to certain types of facts, implying that the columns in question must permit nulls. As more and more types of facts are included, the table becomes more and more difficult to maintain and understand, and access becomes less and less efficient. For example, we might decide to modify the shipments table to track part purchases as well as part shipments. We will then need some kind of "flag" column to show which rows correspond to purchases and which to shipments. By contrast, a proper design would create a distinct fact table for each distinct type of fact.

5. Again because of the lack of discipline, the dimension tables too can become nonuniform. This error typically occurs when the fact table is used to maintain data pertaining to differing levels of aggregation. For example, we might mistakenly add rows to the shipments table that show the total part quantities for each day, each month, each quarter, each year, and even the grand total to date. Notice first that this change causes the time interval identifier (TI#) and quantity (QTY) columns in the table to have different meanings in different rows. Suppose now that the FROM and TO columns in the dimension table TI are each replaced by a combination of YEAR, MONTH, DAY, and other columns. Then those YEAR, MONTH, DAY, and other columns must now all permit nulls. Also, a flag column will probably be needed too, in order to indicate the type of the applicable time interval.

6. The dimension tables are often less than fully normalized.[9] The desire to avoid joins often leads designers to bundle distinct information together in those tables that would better be kept separate. In the extreme case, columns that simply happen to be accessed together are kept together in the same dimension table. It should be clear that following such an extreme, and nonrelational, "discipline" will almost certainly lead to uncontrolled—and possibly uncontrollable—redundancy.

We remark finally that a variant of the star schema is the **snowflake schema**, which normalizes the dimension tables. Again, the name is derived from the way the schema looks when drawn as an entity/relationship diagram. The terms *constellation schema* and *blizzard* (or *snowstorm*) *schema* have also been heard, with the obvious (?) meanings.

22.6 ONLINE ANALYTICAL PROCESSING

The term **OLAP** ("online analytical processing") was coined in a white paper written for Arbor Software Corp. in 1993 [22.11], though, as with the term *data warehouse,* the concept is much older. It can be defined as "the interactive process of creating, managing, analyzing, and reporting on data"—and it is usual to add that the data in question is perceived and manipulated as though it were stored in a "multi-dimensional array." However, we choose to explain the ideas in terms of conventional SQL-style tables first, before getting into the issue of multi-dimensional representation *per se.*

---

[9] In this connection, consider this advice from a book on data warehouses [22.24]: "[Resist] normalization . . . Efforts to normalize any of the tables in a dimensional database solely in order to save disk space [*sic!*] are a waste of time . . . The dimension tables must not be normalized . . . Normalized dimension tables destroy the ability to browse."

The first point is that analytical processing invariably requires some kind of *data aggregation,* usually in many different ways, or in other words according to many different groupings. In fact, it is precisely one of the problems of analytical processing that the number of possible groupings quickly becomes very large indeed, and yet users need to consider all of them (or most of them). Now, the SQL standard does support such aggregation, but any given SQL query produces just one table as its result, and—at least prior to SQL:1999—all rows in that result table are of the same form and have the same kind of interpretation.[10] Thus, to obtain *n* distinct groupings requires *n* distinct queries and produces *n* distinct result tables. For example, consider the following queries on the usual suppliers-and-parts database:

1. Get the total shipment quantity.
2. Get total shipment quantities by supplier.
3. Get total shipment quantities by part.
4. Get total shipment quantities by supplier and part.

(Of course, the "total" quantity for a given supplier and given part is just the *actual* quantity for that supplier and part. The example would be more realistic if we used the suppliers-parts-projects database instead. However, we stay with the simpler database here.)

Suppose now that there are just two parts, P1 and P2, and the shipments table looks like this:

SP

S#	P#	QTY
S1	P1	300
S1	P2	200
S2	P1	300
S2	P2	400
S3	P2	200
S4	P2	200

Here then are SQL formulations of the four queries and the corresponding results. *Note:* SQL:1999 allows—as SQL:1992 did not—(a) GROUP BY operands to be enclosed in parentheses and (b) a GROUP BY with no operands at all (this latter is equivalent to omitting the GROUP BY clause entirely).

1.
```
SELECT  SUM(QTY) AS TOTQTY
FROM    SP
GROUP   BY () ;
```

TOTQTY
1600

2.
```
SELECT  S#,
        SUM(QTY) AS TOTQTY
FROM    SP
GROUP   BY (S#) ;
```

S#	TOTQTY
S1	500
S2	700
S3	200
S4	200

---

[10] Unless that result table includes any nulls (see Chapter 19, Section 19.3, subsection "Predicates Again"). In fact, the SQL:1999 constructs to be described in this section can be characterized as "taking advantage of" this highly deprecated feature of SQL (?); in effect, they capitalize on the fact that distinct appearances of null can have distinct meanings, and thereby allow many distinct predicates to be bundled up into a single table (as we will see).

3. ```
SELECT P#,
        SUM(QTY) AS TOTQTY
FROM   SP
GROUP   BY (P#) ;
```

| P# | TOTQTY |
|----|--------|
| P1 | 600    |
| P2 | 1000   |

4. ```
SELECT  S#, P#,
        SUM(QTY) AS TOTQTY
FROM    SP
GROUP   BY (S#,P#) ;
```

S#	P#	TOTQTY
S1	P1	300
S1	P2	200
S2	P1	300
S2	P2	400
S3	P2	200
S4	P2	200

The drawbacks to this approach are obvious: Formulating so many similar but distinct queries is tedious for the user, and executing all of those queries (in particular, passing over the same data over and over again) is likely to be quite expensive in execution time. It thus seems worthwhile to try to find a way of requesting several levels of aggregation in a single query, thereby (a) making life easier for the user and (b) offering the implementation the opportunity to compute all of those aggregations more efficiently (i.e., in a single pass). Such considerations are the motivation behind the *GROUPING SETS, ROLLUP,* and *CUBE* options on the GROUP BY clause. *Note:* Such options have been supported in commercial products for several years. They were added to the SQL standard in 1999.

The **GROUPING SETS** option allows the user to specify exactly which particular groupings are required. For example, the following SQL statement represents a combination of Queries 2 and 3:

```
SELECT  S#, P#, SUM ( QTY ) AS TOTQTY
FROM    SP
GROUP   BY GROUPING SETS ( ( S# ), ( P# ) ) ;
```

The GROUP BY clause here is effectively asking the system to execute two queries, one in which the grouping is by S# and one in which it is by P#. *Note:* The inner parentheses are not actually required in this example (because each of the "grouping sets" involves just one column), but we show them for clarity.

Now, the idea of bundling several distinct queries into a single statement in such a manner might be unobjectionable in itself (though we have to say that we would prefer to see this very general issue attacked in a more general, systematic, and orthogonal way). Unfortunately, however, SQL goes on to bundle the *results* of those logically distinct queries into a single result table! In the example, that result table looks something like this:

S#	P#	TOTQTY
S1	null	500
S2	null	700
S3	null	200
S4	null	200
null	P1	600
null	P2	1000

Now, this result might perhaps be thought of as a *table* (an SQL-style table, at any rate), but it is hardly a *relation.* Note that the supplier rows (those with nulls in the P# position) and the part rows (those with nulls in the S# position) have very different interpretations, and the meaning of TOTQTY values varies according to whether they appear in a supplier row or a part row. So what is the predicate for this "relation"? (In fact, the result table in this example can be regarded as an "outer union"—an extremely bizarre form of outer union, too—of the results from Queries 2 and 3. It should be clear from Chapter 19 that, even in its least bizarre form, "outer union" is *not* a respectable relational operation.)

We remark too that the nulls in the result table constitute yet another kind of "missing information." They certainly do not mean either "value unknown" or "value not applicable," but exactly what they do mean is very unclear. *Note:* SQL does at least provide a way of distinguishing those new nulls from other kinds, but the details are tedious and effectively force the user into a kind of row-at-a-time thinking. You can get some idea of what is involved from the following example (which indicates what the GROUPING SETS example shown earlier might actually have to look like in practice):

```
SELECT CASE GROUPING ( S# )
            WHEN 1 THEN '??'
            ELSE S#
       AS S#,
       CASE GROUPING ( P# )
            WHEN 1 THEN '!!'
            ELSE P#
       AS P#,
       SUM ( QTY ) AS TOTQTY
FROM   SP
GROUP  BY GROUPING SETS ( ( S# ), ( P# ) ) ;
```

With this revised formulation, the nulls in column S# of the result will be replaced by a pair of question marks and the nulls in column P# will be replaced by a pair of exclamation points, thus:

S#	P#	TOTQTY
S1	!!	500
S2	!!	700
S3	!!	200
S4	!!	200
??	P1	600
??	P2	1000

Back to GROUP BY specifically. The other two GROUP BY options, ROLLUP and CUBE, are both shorthands for certain GROUPING SETS combinations. First, **ROLLUP.** Consider the following query:

```
SELECT S#, P#, SUM ( QTY ) AS TOTQTY
FROM   SP
GROUP  BY ROLLUP ( S#, P# ) ;
```

The GROUP BY clause here is logically equivalent to the following one:

```
GROUP  BY GROUPING SETS ( ( S#, P# ), ( S# ), ( ) )
```

In other words, the query is a bundled SQL formulation of Queries 4, 2, and 1. The result looks like this:

S#	P#	TOTQTY
S1	P1	300
S1	P2	200
S2	P1	300
S2	P2	400
S3	P2	200
S4	P2	200
S1	*null*	500
S2	*null*	700
S3	*null*	200
S4	*null*	200
null	*null*	1600

The term *ROLLUP* derives from the fact that (in the example) the quantities have been "rolled up" for each supplier (i.e., rolled up "along the supplier dimension"—see the subsection "Multi-dimensional Databases," later). In general, GROUP BY ROLLUP (*A, B, ..., Z*)—loosely, "roll up along the A dimension"—means "group by all of the following combinations":

```
( A, B, ..., Z )
( A, B, ... )
  .....
( A, B )
( A )
( )
```

Note that there are many distinct "rollups along the *A* dimension," in general (it depends what other columns are mentioned in the ROLLUP commalist). Note too that GROUP BY ROLLUP (*A, B*) and GROUP BY ROLLUP (*B, A*) have different meanings—that is, GROUP BY ROLLUP (*A, B*) is not symmetric in A and B.

Now we turn to **CUBE**. Consider the following query:

```
SELECT S#, P#, SUM ( QTY ) AS TOTQTY
FROM   SP
GROUP  BY CUBE ( S#, P# ) ;
```

The GROUP BY clause here is logically equivalent to the following one:

```
GROUP  BY GROUPING SETS ( ( S#, P# ), ( S# ), ( P# ), ( ) )
```

In other words, the query is a bundled SQL formulation of all four of our original Queries 4, 3, 2, and 1. The result looks like this:

S#	P#	TOTQTY
S1	P1	300
S1	P2	200
S2	P1	300
S2	P2	400
S3	P2	200
S4	P2	200
S1	*null*	500
S2	*null*	700
S3	*null*	200
S4	*null*	200
null	P1	600
null	P2	1000
null	*null*	1600

The unhelpful term *CUBE* derives from the fact that in OLAP (or at least multi-dimensional) terminology, data values can be perceived as being stored in the cells of a multi-dimensional array or *hypercube*. In the case at hand, (a) the data values are quantities; (b) the "cube" has just two dimensions, a suppliers dimension and a parts dimension (and so that "cube" is rather flat!); and of course (c) those two dimensions are of unequal sizes (so the "cube" is not even a square but rather a nonsquare rectangle). Anyway, GROUP BY CUBE (*A, B, ..., Z*) means "group by all possible subsets of the set { *A, B, ..., Z* }."

A given GROUP BY clause can include any mixture of GROUPING SETS, ROLLUP, and CUBE specifications.

Cross Tabulations

OLAP products often display query results not as SQL-style tables but as **cross tabulations** ("crosstabs" for short). Consider Query 4 once again ("Get total shipment quantities by supplier and part"). Here is a crosstab representation of the result of that query. Incidentally, note that we show the quantities of part P1 for suppliers S3 and S4 (correctly) as zero; SQL, by contrast, would say those quantities should be *null* (see Chapter 19). In fact, the *table* that SQL produces in response to Query 4 contains no rows for (S3,P1) or (S4,P1)!—as a consequence of which, producing the crosstab from that table is not entirely trivial.

	P1	P2
S1	300	200
S2	300	400
S3	0	200
S4	0	200

This crosstab is arguably a more compact and readable way of representing the Query 4 result. What is more, it does look a little like a relational table. However, observe that *the number of columns in that "table" depends on the actual data;* to be specific, there is one column for each kind of part (and so the structure of the crosstab and the meaning of the rows both depend on the actual data). Thus, a crosstab is not a relation but a *report:* to be more specific, a report that is formatted as a simple array. (A relation has a predicate that can be deduced from the predicates for the relations from which it is derived; by contrast, the "predicate" for a crosstab—if such a thing can even be said to exist, in general—cannot be derived from the predicates for the relations from which it is derived, since as we have just seen it depends on actual data *values*.)

Crosstabs like the one just shown are said to have two *dimensions,* in this case suppliers and parts. Dimensions are treated as though they were *independent variables;* the intersection "cells" then contain values of the corresponding *dependent* variable(s). See the subsection "Multi-dimensional Databases" for further explanation.

Here is another crosstab example, representing the result from the CUBE example shown earlier:

	P1	P2	Total
S1	300	200	500
S2	300	400	700
S3	0	200	200
S4	0	200	200
Total	600	1000	1600

The rightmost column contains row totals (i.e., totals for the indicated supplier across all parts), and the bottom row contains column totals (i.e., totals for the indicated part across all suppliers). The bottom right cell contains the grand total, which is the row total of all column totals and the column total of all row totals.

Multi-dimensional Databases

So far, we have been assuming that our OLAP data is stored in a conventional SQL database (although we have touched on the terminology and concepts of "multi-dimensional" databases a couple of times). In fact, we have tacitly been describing what is sometimes called *ROLAP* ("relational OLAP"). However, many people believe that *MOLAP* ("multi-dimensional OLAP") is a better way to go. In this subsection we take a closer look at MOLAP.

MOLAP involves a **multi-dimensional database**, which is a database in which the data is conceptually stored in the cells of a multi-dimensional array. (*Note:* We say "conceptually stored," but in fact the physical organization in MOLAP tends to be very close to the logical organization.) The supporting DBMS is called a *multi-dimensional DBMS*. As a simple example, the data might be represented as an array of three dimensions, corresponding to products, customers, and time intervals, respectively; each individual cell value might then represent the total quantity of the indicated product sold to the indicated customer in the indicated time interval. As already noted, the crosstabs of the previous subsection can also be regarded as such arrays.

Now, in a well-understood body of data, all relationships would be known, and the "variables" involved (not variables in the usual programming language sense) could then be classified, loosely, as either **dependent** or **independent**. In terms of the foregoing example, for instance, *product, customer,* and *time interval* would be the independent variables and *quantity* the sole dependent variable. More generally, independent variables are variables whose values together determine the values of dependent variables (much as, in relational terms, a candidate key is a set of columns whose values determine the values of other columns). The independent variables thus form the dimensions of the array by which the data is organized and form an *addressing scheme* for that array,[11] and dependent variable values—which constitute the actual data—can then be stored in the cells of that array. *Note:* The distinction between values of independent or "dimensional" variables and values of dependent or "nondimensional" variables is sometimes characterized as *location vs. content.*

Unfortunately, the foregoing characterization of multi-dimensional databases is somewhat too simplistic, because most bodies of data are *not* well understood. Indeed, it is for this very reason that we want to analyze the data in the first place: to obtain a better understanding. Often the lack of understanding is severe enough that we do not know ahead of time which variables are independent and which dependent—independent variables are often chosen based on current belief (i.e., *hypothesis*) and the resulting array then tested to see how well it works (see Section 22.7). Such an approach is clearly going to involve a lot of iteration and trial and error. For such reasons, the system will typically permit dimensional and nondimensional variables to be swapped, an operation known as *pivoting.* Other operations supported will include *array transpose* and *dimensional reordering.* There will also be a way to add dimensions.

By the way, it should be clear from the foregoing description that array cells will often be empty (and the more dimensions there are, the truer this statement will be). In other words, arrays will often be *sparse.* For example, suppose product *p* was not sold to customer *c* at all in time interval *t;* then cell [*c,p,t*] will be empty (or, at best, contain a zero). Multi-dimensional DBMSs support various techniques for storing sparse arrays in some more efficient (compressed) form.[12] More to the point, those empty cells correspond to "missing information," and systems therefore need to provide some computational support for them—and they do so, typically, in a manner similar to SQL (unfortunately). Note that the fact that a given cell is empty might mean the information is unknown, or has not been captured, or is not applicable, or a whole host of other things (see Chapter 19 once again).

The independent variables are often related in *hierarchies,* which determine ways in which dependent data can be aggregated. For example, there is a temporal hierarchy relating seconds to minutes to hours to days to weeks to months to years. As another example, there might be a hierarchy relating parts to assembly kits to components to boards to products. Often the same data can be aggregated in many different ways (i.e., the same independent variable can belong to many different hierarchies). The system will provide operators to "drill up" and "drill down" in such hierarchies; *drill up* means going from a lower level of aggregation to a higher, *drill down* means the opposite. Numerous other opera-

---

[11] Array cells are thus addressed symbolically instead of by the numeric subscripts more conventionally associated with arrays.

[12] Observe the contrast here with relational systems. In a proper relational analog of the example, we would not have a (*c,p,t*) row with an empty quantity "cell"—we would simply not have a (*c,p,t*) row. The concept of "sparse arrays" in the multi-dimensional sense (or "sparse tables," rather) thus does not arise, and there is no need for clever compression techniques to deal with them.

tions will also be provided for dealing with such hierarchies (e.g., an operation to rearrange the hierarchic levels).

Note: There is a subtle difference between "drill up" and "roll up," as follows: "Roll up" is the operation of *creating* the desired groupings and aggregations; "drill up" is the operation of *accessing* those aggregations. As for "drill down," an example might be: *Given the total shipment quantity, get the total quantities for each individual supplier.* Of course, the more detailed data must be available (or computable) in order for the system to be able to respond to such a request.

Multi-dimensional products generally also provide a variety of statistical and other mathematical functions to help in formulating and testing hypotheses (i.e., hypothesized relationships). Visualization and reporting tools are also provided to help in these tasks. Unfortunately, however, there is as yet no standard multi-dimensional query language, although research is under way to develop a calculus on which such a standard might be based [22.31]. There is also nothing analogous to normalization theory that could serve as a scientific basis for the design of multi-dimensional databases.

We close this section by noting that some products combine the ROLAP and MOLAP approaches: *HOLAP* ("hybrid OLAP"). There is considerable controversy over which of the three approaches is "best," and little can be said here to help resolve that controversy.[13] Generally speaking, however, MOLAP products provide faster computation but support smaller amounts of data than ROLAP products (becoming less efficient as the amount of data increases), while ROLAP products provide scalability, concurrency, and management features that are more mature than those of MOLAP products. In addition, the SQL standard has recently been extended to include numerous statistical and analytical functions (see Section 22.8), implying that ROLAP products can now provide considerably extended functionality as well.

22.7 DATA MINING

Data mining can be described as "exploratory data analysis." The aim is to look for interesting patterns in the data—patterns that can be used to set business strategy or identify unusual behavior (for example, a sudden increase in credit card activity could mean a card has been stolen). Data mining tools apply statistical techniques to large quantities of stored data in order to look for such patterns. *Note:* The word *large* needs to be emphasized here. Data mining databases are often *extremely* large, and it is important that algorithms be scalable.

---

[13] There is one thing that does need to be said, however, and that is the following. It is often claimed that "tables are flat" (i.e., two-dimensional) while "real data is multi-dimensional," and hence that relations are inadequate as a basis for OLAP. But to argue thus is to confuse tables and relations! As we saw in Chapter 6, tables are only *pictures* of relations, not relations as such. And while it is true that those pictures are two-dimensional, relations are not; rather, they are *n*-dimensional, where *n* is the degree. To be more precise, each tuple in a relation with *n* attributes represents a point in *n*-dimensional space, and the relation as a whole represents a set of such points.

Consider the—*not* very large!—SALES table shown in Fig. 22.5, which gives information regarding a certain retail business's sales transactions.[14] The business would like to perform *market basket analysis* on this data (where the term *market basket* refers to the set of products purchased in a single transaction), thereby discovering, for example, that a customer who buys shoes is likely to buy socks as well as part of the same transaction. This correlation between shoes and socks is an example of an **association rule**; it can be expressed (a little loosely) as follows:

```
FORALL tx ( Shoes ∈ tx ⇒ Socks ∈ tx )
```

Here "Shoes ∈ *tx*" is the rule *antecedent,* "Socks ∈ *tx*" is the *rule consequent,* and *tx* ranges over all sales transactions.

We introduce some terminology. The set of all sales transactions in the example is called the **population.** Any given association rule has a *support* level and a *confidence* level. The **support** is the percentage of the population that satisfies the rule; and if the percentage of the population in which the antecedent is satisfied is *s,* then the **confidence** is that percentage of *s* in which the consequent is also satisfied. (Note that the antecedent and consequent can each involve any number of different products, not necessarily just one.) By way of example, consider this rule:

```
FORALL tx ( Socks ∈ tx ⇒ Tie ∈ tx )
```

Given the sample data of Fig. 22.5, the population is the set of four transactions, the support is 50 percent, and the confidence is 66.67 percent.

More general association rules might be discovered from appropriate aggregations of the given data. For example, grouping by customer would enable us to test the validity of

SALES	TX#	CUST#	TIMESTAMP	PRODUCT
	TX1	C1	d1	Shoes
	TX1	C1	d1	Socks
	TX1	C1	d1	Tie
	TX2	C2	d2	Shoes
	TX2	C2	d2	Socks
	TX2	C2	d2	Tie
	TX2	C2	d2	Belt
	TX2	C2	d2	Shirt
	TX3	C3	d2	Shoes
	TX3	C3	d2	Tie
	TX4	C2	d3	Shoes
	TX4	C2	d3	Socks
	TX4	C2	d3	Belt

Fig. 22.5   The SALES table

[14] Note that (a) the key is {TX#,PRODUCT}; (b) the table satisfies the FDs TX# → CUST# and TX# → TIMESTAMP and is thus not in BCNF; (c) a version of the table in which column PRODUCT is relation-valued (and TX# is the key) *would* be in BCNF and might well be better suited to the kind of exploration involved in the case at hand (but it would probably not be suitable for other kinds).

rules such as "If a customer buys shoes, he or she is likely to buy socks as well, though not necessarily in the same transaction."

Other kinds of rules can also be defined. For example, a **sequence correlation** rule might be used to identify buying patterns over time ("If a customer buys shoes today, he or she is likely to buy socks within five days"); a **classification** rule might be used to help decide whether to grant a credit application ("If a customer has income over $75,000 a year, he or she is likely to be a good credit risk"); and so on. Like association rules, sequence correlation and classification rules also have a support level and a confidence level.

Data mining is a huge subject in its own right [22.2], and it is clearly not possible to go into very much detail here. We therefore content ourselves by concluding with a brief description of how data mining techniques might apply to an extended version of suppliers and parts. First (in the absence of other sources for the information), we might use *neural induction* to classify suppliers by their specialty (e.g., fasteners *vs.* engine parts), and *value prediction* to predict which suppliers are most likely to be able to supply which parts. We might then use *demographic clustering* to associate shipping charges with geographic location, thereby assigning suppliers to shipping regions. *Association discovery* might then be used to discover that certain parts are generally obtained together in a single shipment; *sequential pattern discovery* to discover that shipments of fasteners are generally followed by shipments of engine parts; and *similar time sequence discovery* to discover that there are seasonal quantity changes in shipments of certain parts (some of those changes occurring in the fall and some in the spring).

22.8 SQL FACILITIES

Certain OLAP facilities—essentially the GROUPING SETS, ROLLUP, and CUBE extensions to GROUP BY as described in Section 22.7—were included in the SQL:1999 standard as originally published, and many more were added the following year in the form of an "OLAP amendment" to that standard [22.21]. Full details of that amendment are far beyond the scope of this book, and we content ourselves with the following brief summary of the features included:

- New numeric functions (e.g., natural logarithm, exponentiate, power, square root, floor, ceiling)

- New aggregation operators (e.g., variance, standard deviation)

- Ranking functions (providing, e.g., the ability to derive the rank of parts within a hypothetical list ordered by weight)

- Cumulative and other kinds of "moving average" functions (involving a new WINDOW clause on the usual SQL SELECT - FROM - WHERE - GROUP BY - HAVING expressions)

- Distribution, inverse distribution, correlation, and other statistical functions applied to columns taken pairwise

22.9 SUMMARY

We have offered an overview of the use of database technology for the purpose of **decision support**. The basic idea is to collect operational data and reduce it to a form that can be used to help management understand and modify the behavior of the enterprise.

First we identified certain aspects of decision support systems that set them apart from operational systems. The key point is that the database is primarily (though not totally) **read-only**. Decision support databases tend to be very **large** and **heavily indexed** and to involve a lot of **controlled redundancy** (especially in the form of *replication* and precomputed *summary tables*); keys tend to involve a **temporal** component; and queries tend to be **complex**. As a consequence of such considerations, there is an emphasis on **designing for performance**; we understand this requirement, but believe it should not be allowed to interfere with good design discipline. The problem is that, in practice, decision support systems usually do not distinguish adequately between **logical** and **physical** considerations.

Next, we discussed what is involved in preparing operational data for decision support. We looked at the tasks of **extraction**, **cleansing**, **transformation**, **consolidation**, **load**, and **refresh**. We also briefly mentioned **operational data stores**, which can be used (among other things) as a staging area during the data preparation process. They can also be used to provide decision support services on current data.

We then considered **data warehouses** and **data marts**; a data mart can be regarded as a specialized data warehouse. We explained the basic idea of **star schemas**, in which data is organized as a large central **fact table** and several much smaller **dimension tables**. In simple situations a star schema is indistinguishable from a classical normalized schema; in practice, however, star schemas depart from classical design principles in a variety of ways, always for performance reasons. (The problem, again, is that star schemas are really more physical than logical in nature.) We also mentioned the join implementation strategy known as **star join** and a variant of the star schema called the **snowflake** schema.

Next we turned our attention to **OLAP**. We discussed the SQL **GROUPING SETS**, **ROLLUP**, and **CUBE** features (all of which are options on the GROUP BY clause and provide ways of requesting several distinct aggregations within a single SQL query). We noted that SQL—unfortunately, in our opinion—bundles the results of those distinct aggregations into a single "table" containing many nulls. We also suggested that, in practice, OLAP products might convert such "tables" into **crosstabs** (simple arrays) for display purposes. Then we took a look at **multi-dimensional databases**, in which the data is stored (conceptually) not in tables but in a multi-dimensional array or *hypercube*. The dimensions of such an array represent **independent variables** (at least hypothetically), and the cells contain values of the corresponding **dependent variables**. The independent variables are usually related in various **hierarchies**, which determine the ways in which the dependent data can sensibly be grouped and aggregated.

Next, we briefly considered **data mining**. The basic idea here is that decision support data is often not well understood, and we can use the power of the computer to help us discover patterns in that data and hence to understand it better. We briefly considered various kinds of *rules*—**association**, **classification**, and **sequence correlation** rules—and discussed the associated notions of **support** and **confidence** levels.

Finally, we very briefly sketched the facilities of the SQL:1999 **OLAP amendment**.

EXERCISES

22.1 What are some of the major points of difference between decision support and operational databases? Why do decision support and operational applications typically use different data stores?

22.2 Summarize the steps involved in preparing operational data for decision support.

22.3 Distinguish between *controlled* and *uncontrolled* redundancy. Give some examples. Why is controlled redundancy important in the context of decision support? What happens if the redundancy is uncontrolled instead?

22.4 Distinguish between *data warehouses* and *data marts*.

22.5 What do you understand by the term *star schema?*

22.6 Star schemas are usually not fully normalized. What is the justification for this state of affairs? Explain the methodology by which such schemas are designed.

22.7 Explain the difference between ROLAP and MOLAP.

22.8 How many ways could data be summarized if it is characterized by four dimensions, each of which belongs to a three-level aggregation hierarchy (e.g., city, county, state)?

22.9 Using the suppliers-parts-projects database, express the following as SQL queries:

a. Get the number of shipments and average shipment quantities for suppliers, parts, and projects considered pairwise (i.e., for each S#-P# pair, each P#-J# pair, and each J#-S# pair).

b. Get the maximum and minimum shipment quantities for each project, each project/part combination, and overall.

c. Get total shipment quantities rolled up "along the supplier dimension" and "along the part dimension" (there is a trap here!).

d. Get average shipment quantities by supplier, by part, by supplier/part combinations, and overall.

In each case, show the result SQL would produce given the sample data of Fig. 4.5 (see the inside back cover). Also show those results as crosstabs.

22.10 Near the beginning of Section 22.6, we showed a simple version of table SP containing just six rows. Suppose that table additionally included the following row (meaning—perhaps!—that supplier S5 exists but currently supplies no parts):

S5	*null*	*null*

Discuss the implications for all of the various SQL queries shown in Section 22.6.

22.11 Does the term *dimensional* mean the same thing in the phrases "dimensional schema" and "multi-dimensional database"? Explain your answer.

22.12 Consider the market basket analysis problem. Sketch an algorithm by which association rules having support and confidence levels greater than specified thresholds might be discovered. *Hint:* If some combination of products is "uninteresting" because it occurs in too few sales transactions, the same is true for all supersets of that combination of products.

REFERENCES AND BIBLIOGRAPHY

Note: The "views" mentioned in the titles of references [22.3–22.5], [22.10], [22.12], [22.16], [22.25], [22.28], [22.30], and [22.35] are not views but snapshots. Annotation to those references talks in terms of snapshots, not views.

22.1 Brad Adelberg, Hector Garcia-Molina, and Jennifer Widom: "The STRIP Rule System for Efficiently Maintaining Derived Data," Proc. 1997 ACM SIGMOD Int. Conf. on Management of Data, Tucson, Ariz. (May 1997).

> STRIP is an acronym for STanford Real-time Information Processor. It uses "rules" (here meaning what would more usually be called *triggers*) to update snapshots (here called *derived data*) whenever changes occur to the underlying base data. The problem with such systems in general is that if the base data changes very frequently, the computation overhead in executing the rules can be excessive. This paper describes the STRIP techniques for reducing that overhead.

22.2 Pieter Adriaans and Dolf Zantinge: *Data Mining*. Reading, Mass.: Addison-Wesley (1996).

> Although advertised as an executive-level overview, this book is actually a fairly detailed (and good) introduction to the subject.

22.3 Foto N. Afrati, Chen Li, and Jeffrey D. Ullman: "Generating Efficient Plans for Queries Using Views," Proc. 2001 ACM SIGMOD Int. Conf. on Management of Data, Santa Barbara, Calif. (May 2001).

22.4 D. Agrawal, A. El Abbadi, A. Singh, and T. Yurek: "Efficient View Maintenance at Data Warehouses," Proc. 1997 ACM SIGMOD Int. Conf. on Management of Data, Tucson, Ariz. (May 1997).

> As noted in the annotation to reference [22.12], snapshots can be maintained incrementally, and such incremental maintenance is desirable for performance reasons. However, incremental maintenance can lead to problems if the snapshots are derived from several distinct databases that are all being updated at the same time. This paper offers a solution to this problem.

22.5 Sanjay Agrawal, Surajit Chaudhuri, and Vivek Narasayya: "Automated Selection of Materialized Views and Indexes for SQL Databases," Proc. 26th Int. Conf. on Very Large Data Bases, Cairo, Egypt (September 2000).

22.6 S. Alter: *Decision Support Systems: Current Practice and Continuing Challenges.* Reading, Mass.: Addison-Wesley (1980).

22.7 J. L. Bennett (ed.): *Building Decision Support Systems.* Reading, Mass.: Addison-Wesley (1981).

22.8 R. H. Bonczek, C. W. Holsapple, and A. Whinston: *Foundations of Decision Support Systems.* Orlando, Fla.: Academic Press (1981).

> One of the first texts to promote a disciplined approach to decision support systems. The roles of modeling (in the general sense of empirical and mathematical modeling) and management science are emphasized.

22.9 Charles J. Bontempo and Cynthia Maro Saracco: *Database Management: Principles and Products.* Upper Saddle River, N.J.: Prentice Hall (1996).

22.10 Rada Chirkova, Alon Y. Halevy, and Dan Suciu: "A Formal Perspective on the View Selection Problem," Proc. 27th Int. Conf. on Very Large Data Bases, Rome, Italy (September 2001).

22.11 E. F. Codd, S. B. Codd, and C. T. Salley: "Providing OLAP (Online Analytical Processing) to User-Analysts: An IT Mandate," available from Arbor Software Corp. (1993).

The source of the term *OLAP* (though not the concept, as noted in Section 22.6). *Note:* Near the beginning, the paper states categorically that "The need which exists is NOT for yet another database technology, but rather for robust . . . analysis tools." It then goes on to describe, and argue for, yet another database technology!—with a new conceptual data representation, new operators (for update as well as retrieval), multi-user support (including security and concurrency features), new storage structures, and new optimization features: in other words, a new data model, and a new DBMS.

22.12 Latha S. Colby *et al.*: "Supporting Multiple View Maintenance Policies," Proc. 1997 ACM SIGMOD Int. Conf. on Management of Data, Tucson, Ariz. (May 1997).

There are three broad approaches to snapshot maintenance: *immediate* (every update to any underlying relvar immediately triggers a corresponding update to the snapshot), *deferred* (the snapshot is refreshed only when it is queried), and *periodic* (the snapshot is refreshed at specified intervals—e.g., every day). The purpose of snapshots in general is to improve query performance at the expense of update performance, and the three maintenance policies represent a spectrum of trade-offs between the two. This paper investigates issues relating to the support of different policies on different snapshots in the same system at the same time.

22.13 C. J. Date: "We Don't Need Composite Columns," in C. J. Date, Hugh Darwen, and David McGoveran, *Relational Database Writings 1994–1997.* Reading, Mass.: Addison-Wesley (1998).

Section 22.3 mentioned the concept of composite columns; this short paper examines that concept in some detail. The title refers to the fact that flawed attempts have been made in the past to introduce composite column support without basing it on user-defined type support. If proper user-defined type support is provided, composite columns "come out in the wash."

22.14 Barry Devlin: *Data Warehouse from Architecture to Implementation.* Reading, Mass.: Addison-Wesley (1997).

22.15 B. A. Devlin and P. T. Murphy: "An Architecture for a Business and Information System," *IBM Sys. J. 27,* No. 1 (1988).

The first published article to define and use the term *information warehouse.*

22.16 Jonathan Goldstein and Per-Åke Larson: "Optimizing Queries Using Materialized Views: A Practical, Scalable Solution," Proc. 2001 ACM SIGMOD Int. Conf. on Management of Data, Santa Barbara, Calif. (May 2001).

22.17 Jim Gray, Adam Bosworth, Andrew Layman, and Hamid Pirahesh: "Data Cube: A Relational Aggregation Operator Generalizing Group-By, Cross-Tab, and Sub-Totals," Proc. 12th IEEE Int. Conf. on Data Engineering, New Orleans, La. (February 1996).

The paper that first suggested adding options such as CUBE to the SQL GROUP BY clause.

22.18 W. H. Inmon: *Data Architecture: The Information Paradigm.* Wellesley, Mass.: QED Information Sciences (1988).

Discusses the genesis of the data warehouse concept and what a data warehouse would look like in practice. The term *data warehouse* first appeared in this book.

22.19 W. H. Inmon: *Building the Data Warehouse.* New York, N.Y.: John Wiley & Sons (1992).

The first book devoted to data warehouses. It defines the term and discusses the key problems involved in developing a data warehouse. It is concerned primarily with justifying the concept and with operational and physical design issues.

22.20 W. H. Inmon and R. D. Hackathorn: *Using the Data Warehouse.* New York, N.Y.: John Wiley & Sons (1994).

A discussion for users and administrators of the data warehouse. Like other books on the topic, it concentrates on physical issues. The operational data store concept is discussed in some detail.

22.21 International Organization for Standardization (ISO): *SQL/OLAP,* Document ISO/IEC 9075-1:1999/Amd.1:2000(E).

A tutorial on the material of this document can be found in reference [26.32].

22.22 P. G. W. Keen and M. S. Scott Morton: *Decision Support Systems: An Organizational Perspective.* Reading, Mass.: Addison-Wesley (1978).

This classic text is one of the earliest, if not *the* earliest, to address decision support explicitly. The orientation is behavioral and covers analysis, design, implementation, evaluation, and development of decision support systems.

22.23 Werner Kiessling: "Foundations of Preferences in Database Systems" and "Preference SQL—Design, Implementation, Experiences," Proc. 28th Int. Conf. on Very Large Data Bases, Hong Kong (August 2002).

Preferences allow the user to formulate "fuzzy queries" (e.g., "Find me a good Szechuan restaurant, not too expensive, downtown preferred").

22.24 Ralph Kimball: *The Data Warehouse Toolkit.* New York, N.Y.: John Wiley & Sons (1996).

A how-to book. As the subtitle "Practical Techniques for Building Dimensional Data Warehouses" suggests, the emphasis is on pragmatic issues, not theoretical ones. A tacit assumption throughout is that there is essentially no difference between the logical and physical levels of the system.

22.25 Yannis Kotidis and Nick Roussopoulos: "A Case for Dynamic View Management," *ACM TODS 26,* No. 4 (December 2001).

22.26 M. S. Scott Morton: "Management Decision Systems: Computer-Based Support for Decision Making," Harvard University, Division of Research, Graduate School of Business Administration (1971).

This is the classic article that introduced the concept of management decision systems, bringing decision support clearly into the realm of computer-based systems. A specific "management decision system" was built to coordinate production planning for laundry equipment. It was then subjected to scientific test, with marketing and production managers as users.

22.27 K. Parsaye and M. Chignell: *Intelligent Database Tools and Applications.* New York, N.Y.: John Wiley & Sons (1993).

This book appears to be the first to be devoted to the principles and techniques of data mining (though it refers to the subject as "intelligent databases").

22.28 Rachel Pottinger and Alon Levy: "A Scalable Algorithm for Answering Queries Using Views," Proc. 26th Int. Conf. on Very Large Data Bases, Cairo, Egypt (September 2000).

22.29 Dallan Quass and Jennifer Widom: "On-Line Warehouse View Maintenance," Proc. 1997 ACM SIGMOD Int. Conf. on Management of Data, Tucson, Ariz. (May 1997).

Presents an algorithm for snapshot maintenance that allows the maintenance transactions to run simultaneously with queries against the snapshots.

22.30 Kenneth Salem, Kevin Beyer, Bruce Lindsay, and Roberta Cochrane: "How to Roll a Join: Asynchronous Incremental View Maintenance," Proc. 2000 ACM SIGMOD Int. Conf. on Management of Data, Dallas, Tex. (May 2000).

22.31 Erik Thomsen: *OLAP Solutions: Building Multi-Dimensional Information Systems* (2d ed.). New York, N.Y.: John Wiley & Sons (2002).

One of the first books on OLAP and perhaps the most comprehensive. The focus is on understanding the concepts and methods of analysis using multi-dimensional systems. A serious attempt to inject some discipline into a confused subject.

22.32 R. Uthurusamy: "From Data Mining to Knowledge Discovery: Current Challenges and Future Directions," in U. M. Fayyad, G. Piatetsky-Shapiro, P. Smyth, and R. Uthurusamy (eds.): *Advances in Knowledge Discovery and Data Mining.* Cambridge, Mass.: AAAI Press/MIT Press (1996).

22.33 Patrick Valduriez: "Join Indices," *ACM TODS 12,* No. 2 (June 1987).

22.34 Markos Zaharioudakis *et al.*: "Answering Complex SQL Queries Using Automatic Summary Tables," Proc. 2000 ACM SIGMOD Int. Conf. on Management of Data, Dallas, Tex. (May 2000).

22.35 Yue Zhuge, Hector Garcia-Molina, Joachim Hammer, and Jennifer Widom: "View Maintenance in a Warehousing Environment," Proc. 1995 ACM SIGMOD Int. Conf. on Management of Data, San Jose, Calif. (May 1995).

When it is informed of an update to some underlying data, the data warehouse site might need to issue a query to the base data site before it can carry out the necessary snapshot maintenance, and the time lag between such a query and the original base data update can lead to anomalies. This paper presents an algorithm for dealing with such anomalies.

Temporal Databases

23.1 INTRODUCTION

A **temporal database** can be defined, loosely, as a database that contains historical data[1] as well as or instead of current data (data warehouses provide an obvious example—see Chapter 22). Conventional or *nontemporal* databases contain current data only; their currency is maintained by updating them as soon as the propositions they represent become untrue. Temporal databases, by contrast, are updated only rarely—possibly not at all, apart from the INSERTs that are needed to populate them in the first place. For example, consider the suppliers-and-parts database. Given our usual sample values, that database shows among other things that the status (i.e., the status "right now") for supplier S1 is 20. But a temporal version of that database might show not only that supplier S1's status is currently 20 but also that it has been 20 ever since July 1st last year, and perhaps that it was 15 from April 5th to June 30th last year, and so on.

---

[1] Temporal databases can contain data regarding the future as well as the past, and the term *historical* must be understood as including this possibility.

Temporal database research has been under way since at least the early 1980s, and it has involved a certain amount of investigation into the nature of time itself. Here are some of the questions that have been explored:

- Does time have a beginning or an end?
- Is time a continuum or is it divided into discrete quanta?
- How can we best characterize the important concept "now" (sometimes known as "*the moving point* now")?

However, such questions are not really database questions as such, and we therefore do not delve very deeply into them in this chapter; instead, we simply make reasonable assumptions as we proceed, and focus our interest on matters more directly relevant to our overall aim.

We referred a moment ago to the fact that data in general can be regarded as representing propositions. It follows that temporal data in particular can be regarded as representing *timestamped* propositions—by which we mean propositions that involve at least one argument of some timestamp type. For example, consider the following tuple:

S#	SINCE
S1	July 1, 2003

As you can see, this tuple has a supplier number attribute S# and a timestamp attribute SINCE, and the corresponding timestamped proposition is:

*Supplier S1 has been under contract **since** July 1, 2003.*

Of course, we are assuming that the proposition is an instantiation of a predicate[2] of the form: *Supplier S# has been under contract **since** date SINCE.* Now, we will explain in just a moment why we set the word *since* in boldface in this predicate (and in the sample instantiation). First, however, here is another example:

S#	FROM	TO
S1	May 1, 2002	April 30, 2003

This tuple has a supplier number attribute S# and *two* timestamp attributes FROM and TO, and the corresponding timestamped proposition is:

*Supplier S1 was under contract **during** the interval from May 1, 2002, to April 30, 2003.*

This time we are assuming that the proposition is an instantiation of a predicate of the form: *Supplier S# was under contract **during** the interval from date FROM to date TO.* Again, we will explain our use of boldface in just a moment.

As these two examples suggest, the notions of *since* and *during* are going to turn out to be extremely important (all-pervasive, in fact) in what follows. In order for them to be truly

---

[2] We use the unqualified term *predicate* throughout this chapter to mean what in Chapter 9 we called an *external* or user-understood predicate.

useful, however, we need to pin their meanings down very precisely (much more precisely than we do in normal discourse!). To be specific:

1. We take *since* to mean **ever since and not immediately before** the specified point in time. Thus, when we say that supplier S1 has been under contract since July 1, 2003, we mean that (a) supplier S1 has been under contract ever since July 1, 2003, up to and including the date today—whatever that date might happen to be—and furthermore that (b) supplier S1 was not under contract on June 30, 2003.

2. We take *during* to mean **throughout and not immediately before or immediately after** the specified interval. Thus, when we say that supplier S1 was under contract during the interval from May 1, 2002, to April 30, 2003, we mean that (a) supplier S1 was under contract throughout the interval from May 1, 2002, to April 30, 2003, inclusive,[3] and furthermore that (b) supplier S1 was not under contract on April 30, 2002, or May 1, 2003.

We used the boldface forms **since** and **during** in the propositions and predicates shown earlier in order to emphasize the fact that we were using the terms in the foregoing extremely precise senses. However, we will drop the boldface from this point forward.

Some Fundamental Assumptions

We have already mentioned both *intervals* and *points in time;* now it is time to explain them—or, at least, to explain some of the fundamental assumptions on which such notions rest. First of all, we assume that time itself can be thought of as a **timeline**, consisting of a finite sequence of discrete, indivisible *time quanta,* where a **time quantum** in turn is the smallest time unit the system is capable of representing. In other words, even if time in the real world is continuous and infinite, we represent it in our model as discrete and finite instead. *Note:* There is an obvious parallel here with the way our usual model of computation represents real numbers by rationals.

Next, we distinguish carefully between (a) time quanta as such, which as just explained are the smallest time units the system is capable of representing, and (b) the time units that are relevant for some particular purpose, which might be days or months or milliseconds (etc.). For example, in the examples discussed earlier regarding suppliers, we were clearly interested only in times that were accurate to the day. We call the time units that are relevant for some particular purpose **time points** (*points* for short), in order to stress the fact that *for that purpose* they too are considered to be indivisible. Now, we might say, *informally,* that a time point is "a section of the timeline," meaning the set of time quanta between one "boundary" quantum and the next (e.g., between midnight on one day and midnight on the next). We might therefore say, again informally, that time points have a duration (one day, in our example). *Formally,* however, time points are indeed points—they are indivisible, and the concept of duration strictly does not apply.

---

[3] Throughout this chapter we adopt what is called the closed-closed interpretation of intervals, according to which the interval from *b* to *e* is regarded as including both the "begin point" *b* and the "end point" *e*. We note without further comment that other interpretations can be found in the literature.

Note: The foregoing paragraph notwithstanding, we do occasionally make use of the term *granularity,* which refers informally to the "size" or duration of the applicable time points, or equivalently to the "size" or duration of the gap between adjacent points. Thus, we might say in our example that the granularity is one day, meaning that we are casting aside (in this context) our usual notion of a day being made up of hours, which are made up of minutes, and so on. Such notions can be expressed only by recourse to finer levels of granularity.

For a specific purpose, then, the timeline can be regarded as a finite sequence of time points (as opposed to time quanta); the sequence is chronological, of course. And since it is finite, it follows that:

- The sequence has a beginning and an end. In other words, there is a unique first point in the sequence that corresponds to **the beginning of time**, and a unique last point in the sequence that corresponds to **the end of time**.

- Every point in the sequence other than that corresponding to the beginning of time has a unique **predecessor** point, and every point in the sequence other than that corresponding to the end of time has a unique **successor** point.

- We define an **interval** to be a nonempty section of the timeline.[4] More precisely, the interval with **begin point *b*** and **end point *e*** can be thought of as **the subsequence of the timeline consisting of all points *p* such that $b \leq p \leq e$** (where "<" means "earlier than").

The Running Example

Until further notice we base our examples on a greatly simplified version of the suppliers-and-parts database that we refer to as "suppliers and shipments." To be specific:

1. We drop the parts relvar P entirely.

2. We simplify the suppliers relvar S by dropping all attributes except S#. The predicate for this revised—and dramatically simplified!—relvar is just:

   Supplier S# is currently under contract.

3. We drop attribute QTY from the shipments relvar SP, and interpret that revised relvar thus:

   Supplier S# is currently able *to supply part P#.*

   In other words, instead of representing *actual* shipments of parts by suppliers, this simplified version of relvar SP represents what might be called *potential* shipments—that is, the *ability* of certain suppliers to supply certain parts. *Note:* Despite this change in meaning, we still find it convenient to use the unqualified term *shipments* in what follows.

---

[4] If you happen to be familiar with SQL, we should warn you that intervals as defined here are nothing to do with intervals as understood in SQL—which are not intervals at all in the usual sense, but rather *durations* (e.g., "3 days").

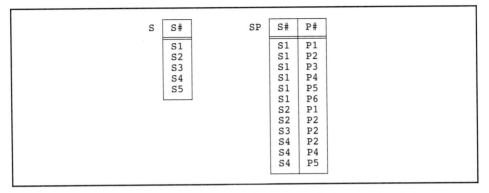

Fig. 23.1 Suppliers-and-shipments database (original version)—sample values

Fig. 23.1 shows a set of sample values for this simplified database. *Note:* The database is, of course, still a purely conventional one—it involves no temporal aspects at all as yet.

We now show some constraints and queries for this database. In the next section, we will see what happens to those constraints and queries when we extend the database to include various temporal features.

Constraints (original database): The only constraints we want to consider are as follows:

- {S#} and {S#,P#} are the primary keys for relvars S and SP, respectively.[5]
- {S#} is a foreign key in relvar SP that references the primary key of relvar S.

Queries (original database): We consider just two queries:

- *Query A:* Get supplier numbers for suppliers who are currently able to supply at least one part.

  ```
  SP { S# }
  ```

- *Query B:* Get supplier numbers for suppliers who are currently unable to supply any parts at all.

  ```
  S { S# } MINUS SP { S# }
  ```

Observe that Query A involves a simple projection and Query B involves the difference between two such projections. When we consider temporal versions of these queries in Section 23.5, we will find that they involve "temporal" (or at least generalized) versions of these two operators—and you will probably not be surprised to learn in that same section that similarly generalized versions of the other relational operators can be defined as well.

To close this rather lengthy introductory section, here is the plan for the rest of the chapter. First, Section 23.2 shows why temporal data seems to require special treatment.

---

[5] Throughout this chapter we assume that relvars have primary keys specifically, for definiteness. However, we do not bother to distinguish primary and alternate keys in **Tutorial D** relvar definitions but treat them all as just candidate keys.

Section 23.3 then explains what is involved in treating intervals as values in their own right, instead of as pairs of begin and end values; in particular, it introduces a variety of operators for dealing with such intervals. Section 23.4 discusses two extremely important relational operators called PACK and UNPACK. Section 23.5 then describes generalized versions of the familiar operators of the relational algebra; finally, Sections 23.6 and 23.7 discuss database design issues and integrity constraints, respectively.

23.2   WHAT IS THE PROBLEM?

The first step in converting the suppliers-and-shipments database to temporal form involves *semitemporalizing* (so to speak) relvars S and SP by adding a timestamp attribute, SINCE, to each and renaming them accordingly. See Fig. 23.2.

For simplicity, we do not show real timestamps in Fig. 23.2; instead, we use symbols of the form *d01, d02,* and so on, where the "*d*" can conveniently be pronounced "day," a convention to which we adhere throughout the chapter. (Most of our examples make use of time points that are days specifically; the applicable granularity in those examples is thus one day.) We assume that day 1 immediately precedes day 2, day 2 immediately precedes day 3, and so on; also, we drop insignificant leading zeros from expressions such as "day 1" (as you can see).

The predicates for relvars S_SINCE and SP_SINCE are:

- S_SINCE: *Supplier S# has been under contract since day SINCE.*
- SP_SINCE: *Supplier S# has been able to supply part P# since day SINCE.*

Constraints (semitemporal database): The primary and foreign keys for the semitemporal database of Fig. 23.2 are the same as they were for the original database of Fig. 23.1. Hence, the relvar definitions might look as follows:

S_SINCE			SP_SINCE		
S#	SINCE		S#	P#	SINCE
S1	d04		S1	P1	d04
S2	d07		S1	P2	d05
S3	d03		S1	P3	d09
S4	d04		S1	P4	d05
S5	d02		S1	P5	d04
			S1	P6	d06
			S2	P1	d08
			S2	P2	d09
			S3	P2	d08
			S4	P2	d06
			S4	P4	d04
			S4	P5	d05

Fig. 23.2   Suppliers-and-shipments database (semitemporal version) —sample values

```
VAR S_SINCE BASE RELATION { S# S#, SINCE DATE }
    KEY { S# } ;

VAR SP_SINCE BASE RELATION { S# S#, P# P#, SINCE DATE }
    KEY { S#, P# }
    FOREIGN KEY { S# } REFERENCES S_SINCE ;
```

Type DATE here represents *Gregorian dates*—by which we mean dates that are accurate to the day and are constrained by the rules of the Gregorian calendar (implying among other things that, e.g., "April 31, 2005" and "February 29, 2100" are not valid dates).

However, we need an additional constraint, over and above the foreign key constraint from SP_SINCE to S_SINCE, to express the fact that no supplier can supply any part before that supplier is under contract:

```
CONSTRAINT XST1    /* "extra semitemporal constraint no. 1" */
    IS_EMPTY ( ( ( S_SINCE   RENAME SINCE AS SS  ) JOIN
                 ( SP_SINCE RENAME SINCE AS SPS ) )
               WHERE SPS < SS ) ;
```

("if tuple *sp* in SP_SINCE references tuple *s* in S_SINCE, then the SINCE value in *sp* must not be less than that in *s*"). With this example we begin to see the problem: Given a "semitemporal" database like that of Fig. 23.2, we will probably need to state many constraints of the same general and rather cumbersome nature as Constraint XST1, and we will soon begin to wish we had some convenient shorthand for the purpose.

Queries (semitemporal database): We now consider semitemporal analogs of Queries A and B.

- *Query A:* Get supplier numbers for suppliers who are currently able to supply at least one part, showing in each case the date since when they have been able to do so.

If supplier S*x* is currently able to supply several different parts, then S*x* has been able to supply at least one part since the earliest SINCE date shown for S*x* in relvar SP_SINCE (e.g., if S*x* is S1, then the earliest SINCE date is *d04*). Hence:

```
SUMMARIZE SP BY { S# } ADD MIN ( SINCE ) AS SINCE
```

The result looks like this:

S#	SINCE
S1	*d04*
S2	*d08*
S3	*d08*
S4	*d04*

- *Query B:* Get supplier numbers for suppliers who are currently unable to supply any parts at all, showing in each case the date since when they have been unable to do so.

In our sample data there is just one supplier—namely, supplier S5—who is currently unable to supply any parts at all. However, we cannot discover the date since when S5 has been unable to supply any parts, because there is insufficient information in the database (to repeat, the database is only *semi*temporal). For example, suppose today is day 10. Then it might be the case that S5 was able to supply at least one part from as early as day

2, when S5 was placed under contract, right up to as late as day 9; or, going to the other extreme, it might be the case that S5 has never been able to supply anything at all.

In order to have any hope of answering Query B, we must complete the "temporalizing" of our database, or at least the SP portion of it; to be more precise, we must keep *historical records* in the database that show which suppliers were able to supply which parts when. See Fig. 23.3.

Comparing Fig. 23.3 with Fig. 23.2, we see that the SINCE attributes have become FROM attributes, and each relvar has acquired an additional timestamp attribute called TO (and we have replaced _SINCE by _FROM_TO in the relvar names accordingly). The FROM and TO attributes together express the notion of an interval of time during which some proposition was true. *Note:* We have assumed for definiteness that today is day 10, and so we have shown *d10* as the TO value for each tuple that pertains to the current state of affairs. However, that assumption might—and should!—immediately lead you to wonder what mechanism could cause all of those *d10*'s to be replaced by *d11*'s on the stroke of midnight, as it were, on day 10. Unfortunately, we will have to set this issue aside for the time being. We will return to it in Section 23.6.

Observe that, because we are now keeping historical records, there are more tuples than there were before; in fact, the fully temporal database of Fig. 23.3 includes all of the information from the semitemporal one of Fig. 23.2, except that, purely for the sake of the example, we have shown the TO value for two of supplier S4's shipments as a date prior to the current date (i.e., we have converted those two shipments from "current" to "historical" information). Fig. 23.3 also includes historical information concerning an earlier interval of time, from *d02* to *d04,* during which supplier S2 was previously under contract and able to supply certain parts. The predicates are as follows:

- S_FROM_TO: *Supplier S# was under contract during the interval from day FROM to day TO.*

S_FROM_TO

S#	FROM	TO
S1	d04	d10
S2	d02	d04
S2	d07	d10
S3	d03	d10
S4	d04	d10
S5	d02	d10

SP_FROM_TO

S#	P#	FROM	TO
S1	P1	d04	d10
S1	P2	d05	d10
S1	P3	d09	d10
S1	P4	d05	d10
S1	P5	d04	d10
S1	P6	d06	d10
S2	P1	d02	d04
S2	P1	d08	d10
S2	P2	d03	d03
S2	P2	d09	d10
S3	P2	d08	d10
S4	P2	d06	d09
S4	P4	d04	d08
S4	P5	d05	d10

Fig. 23.3   Suppliers-and-shipments database (first fully temporal version, using explicit FROM and TO attributes)—sample values

- SP_FROM_TO: *Supplier S# was able to supply part P# during the interval from day FROM to day TO.*

There are a few other points we need to make regarding the running example now it is fully temporalized. To be specific, we assume from this point forward (realistically enough) that:

1. No supplier can end one contract on one day and begin another on the very next day.

2. No supplier can be under two distinct contracts at the same time.

3. Supplier contracts can be open-ended—that is, a supplier can be currently under contract and the end date for that contract can be currently unknown.

Constraints (first fully temporal database): First of all, observe from the double underlining in Fig. 23.3 that we have included the FROM attribute in the primary key for both relvars. Indeed, the primary key for S_FROM_TO (for example) clearly cannot be just {S#}, because if it were we would not be able to deal with a supplier like supplier S2 who has been under contract during two or more separate intervals. A similar observation applies to SP_FROM_TO. *Note:* We could have included the TO attributes in the primary keys instead of the FROM attributes; in fact, relvars S_FROM_TO and SP_FROM_TO both have two candidate keys and are good examples of relvars for which there is no obvious reason to choose one of those candidate keys as primary [9.14]. We make the choices we do purely for reasons of definiteness.

Here then are **Tutorial D** definitions:

```
VAR S_FROM_TO
        BASE RELATION { S# S#, FROM DATE, TO DATE }
      KEY { S#, FROM }
      KEY { S#, TO } ;

VAR SP_FROM_TO
        BASE RELATION { S# S#, P# P#, FROM DATE, TO DATE }
      KEY { S#, P#, FROM }
      KEY { S#, P#, TO } ;
```

Next, we need to guard against the absurdity of a FROM-TO pair appearing in which the TO value is less than the FROM value:

```
CONSTRAINT S_FROM_TO_OK
    IS_EMPTY ( S_FROM_TO WHERE TO < FROM ) ;

CONSTRAINT SP_FROM_TO_OK
    IS_EMPTY ( SP_FROM_TO WHERE TO < FROM ) ;
```

However, the constraints we have discussed so far still do not capture everything we would like them to. Consider relvar S_FROM_TO, for example. Obviously, if there is a tuple for supplier S*x* in that relvar with FROM value *f* and TO value *t*, then we want there *not* to be a tuple for supplier S*x* in that same relvar indicating that S*x* was under contract on the day immediately before *f* or the day immediately after *t*. By way of example, consider supplier S1, for whom we have just one S_FROM_TO tuple, with FROM = *d04* and TO = *d10*. The fact that {S#,FROM} is a candidate key for this relvar is clearly insufficient to prevent the appearance of an additional "overlapping" S1 tuple with (say) FROM = *d02* and TO = *d06,* indicating among other things that S1 *was* under contract on the day immediately before day 4. Clearly, what we would like is for those two S1 tuples to be combined into a single tuple with FROM = *d02* and TO = *d10*.

Now, you might have guessed already that this idea of combining tuples is going to turn out to be very important. Indeed, *not* combining the two tuples in the foregoing example would be almost as bad as permitting duplicates! Duplicates amount to "saying the same thing twice." And those two tuples for supplier S1 with overlapping FROM-TO intervals do indeed "say the same thing twice"; to be specific, they both say supplier S1 was under contract on days 4, 5, and 6. Indeed, if those two tuples did both appear, then relvar S_FROM_TO would be in violation of its own predicate. We will revisit this issue and discuss it in detail in Section 23.7.

Next, the fact that {S#,FROM} is a candidate key for S_FROM_TO is also insufficient to prevent the appearance of an "abutting" S1 tuple with (say) FROM = *d02* and TO = *d03*, indicating again that S1 was under contract on the day immediately before day 4. As before, what we would like is for the two tuples in question to be combined into one—for otherwise, again, relvar S_FROM_TO would be in violation of its own predicate. Again, we will revisit this issue and discuss it in detail in Section 23.7.

Here then is a constraint that does prohibit such overlapping and abutting:

```
CONSTRAINT XFT1
    IS_EMPTY
        ( ( ( S_FROM_TO RENAME ( FROM AS F1, TO AS T1 ) ) JOIN
            ( S_FROM_TO RENAME ( FROM AS F2, TO AS T2 ) ) )
              WHERE ( T1 ≥ F2 AND T2 ≥ F1 ) ) OR
                   ( F2 = T1+1 OR F1 = T2+1 ) ) ;
```

Now we *really* begin to see the problem! This constraint is quite complex—not to mention the fact that we have taken the gross liberty of writing (e.g.) T1+1 to designate the immediate successor of the day denoted by T1, a point we will come back to in the next section. Moreover, given a fully temporal database like that of Fig. 23.3, we will probably have to state many constraints of the same general nature as Constraint XFT1, and again we will surely wish we had some good shorthand for the purpose. *Note:* In fact, there is yet another problem with Constraint XFT1 as stated: namely, what happens to the expression T1+1 if T1 happens to denote "the end of time"?

Next, note that the attribute combination {S#,FROM} in relvar SP_FROM_TO is *not* a foreign key from that relvar to relvar S_FROM_TO (even though it does involve the same attributes as the primary key of relvar S_FROM_TO). However, we certainly need to ensure that if a given supplier is represented in relvar SP_FROM_TO, then that same supplier is represented in relvar S_FROM_TO as well:

```
CONSTRAINT XFT2
    SP_FROM_TO { S# } ⊆ S_FROM_TO { S# } ;
```

This constraint is an example of an *inclusion dependency* [11.4]. Inclusion dependencies can be regarded as a generalization of referential constraints, as we know from Chapter 11. And it should be clear that any temporal database like that of Fig. 23.3 is likely to involve a large number of such dependencies, at least implicitly.

Constraint XFT2 is still not enough, however—we also need to ensure that if relvar SP_FROM_TO shows some supplier as being able to supply any parts at all during some interval of time, then relvar S_FROM_TO shows that same supplier as being under contract throughout that same interval of time:

```
CONSTRAINT XFT3
    COUNT ( SP_FROM_TO { ALL BUT P# } ) =
    COUNT ( ( ( SP_FROM_TO RENAME ( FROM AS SPF, TO AS SPT ) )
                                                    { ALL BUT P# }

              JOIN
                ( S_FROM_TO RENAME ( FROM AS SF, TO AS ST ) ) )
      WHERE SF ≤ SPF AND ST ≥ SPT ) ;
```

The intuition here is that if relvar SP_FROM_TO includes a tuple showing supplier S*x* as able to supply some specific part from day *spf* to day *spt,* then relvar S_FROM_TO must include a tuple showing supplier S*x* as being under contract throughout that same interval. (We are assuming here that *all* of the constraints discussed prior to this point are in effect!) We deliberately do not offer any further analysis of the constraint, but content ourselves with observing that once again it is quite complex, and once again we will probably have to state many constraints of the same general nature in a realistic database. Once again, therefore, we will surely wish we had some good shorthand available.

Queries (first fully temporal database): Here now are fully temporal analogs of Queries A and B:

- *Query A:* Get S#-FROM-TO triples for suppliers who have been able to supply at least one part during at least one interval of time, where FROM and TO together designate such an interval. Note that the result of the query might contain several tuples for the same supplier (but with different intervals, of course; moreover, those intervals will neither abut nor overlap).

- *Query B:* Get S#-FROM-TO triples for suppliers who have been unable to supply any parts at all during at least one interval of time, where FROM and TO together designate such an interval. (Again the result might contain several tuples for the same supplier.)

Well, you might like to take a little time to convince yourself that, like us, you would really prefer not even to attempt these queries! If you do make the attempt, however, the fact that they *can* be expressed, albeit exceedingly laboriously, should eventually emerge, but it will surely be obvious that some kind of shorthand would be highly desirable.

In a nutshell, then, the problem of temporal data is that it quickly leads to constraints and queries—not to mention updates, which are beyond the scope of this chapter—that are unreasonably complex to express: unreasonably complex, that is, unless the system provides some appropriate shorthands, which commercial DBMSs currently do not.

23.3   INTERVALS

We now embark on our development of such an appropriate set of shorthands. The first and most fundamental step is to treat intervals as values in their own right, instead of as pairs of separate begin and end values as we have been doing up to this point. For example, consider the interval from day 4 to day 10. In order to stress the fact that we are now treating this interval as a value in its own right, we will represent it, informally, by means of the abbreviated expression [*d04:d10*], instead of using circumlocutions such as "the interval from day 4 to day 10." To be specific:

- That value [*d04:d10*] is an *interval value,* or just an *interval* for short.
- The values *d04* and *d10* are the *begin point* and the *end point,* respectively, of that interval value.
- That interval value is of a certain *interval type.*
- That interval type is defined over a certain *point type.*

We will define all of these terms precisely in just a moment. First, however, we show what happens to our example database if we adopt this approach. See Fig. 23.4.

The predicates are as follows:

- S_DURING: *Supplier S# was under contract during the interval from the begin point of DURING to the end point of DURING.*
- SP_DURING: *Supplier S# was able to supply part P# during the interval from the begin point of DURING to the end point of DURING.*

Now for the formal definitions. First of all, a given type *T* can be used as a **point type** (and values of type *T* can be called **points**) if all of the following are defined for that type *T:*

- A **total ordering,** according to which the operator ">" is defined for every pair of values *v1* and *v2* of type *T;* if *v1* and *v2* are distinct, exactly one of the expressions "*v1 > v2*" and "*v2 > v1*" is true and the other is false. *Note:* As we know from Chapter 5, the "=" operator is certainly defined for *T.* Given that ">" is defined as well, therefore (and given also the availability of the boolean NOT operator), we can legiti-

S_DURING	
S#	DURING
S1	[*d04:d10*]
S2	[*d02:d04*]
S2	[*d07:d10*]
S3	[*d03:d10*]
S4	[*d04:d10*]
S5	[*d02:d10*]

SP_DURING		
S#	P#	DURING
S1	P1	[*d04:d10*]
S1	P2	[*d05:d10*]
S1	P3	[*d09:d10*]
S1	P4	[*d05:d10*]
S1	P5	[*d04:d10*]
S1	P6	[*d06:d10*]
S2	P1	[*d02:d04*]
S2	P1	[*d08:d10*]
S2	P2	[*d03:d03*]
S2	P2	[*d09:d10*]
S3	P2	[*d08:d10*]
S4	P2	[*d06:d09*]
S4	P4	[*d04:d08*]
S4	P5	[*d05:d10*]

Fig. 23.4 Suppliers-and-shipments database (second fully temporal version, using intervals)—sample values

mately assume that all of the usual comparison operators—"=", "≠", ">", "≥", "<", and "≤"—are in fact available for all pairs of values of type *T.*

- Niladic **FIRST_*T*** and **LAST_*T*** operators, which return the first and the last value of type *T,* respectively, according to the aforementioned total ordering.

- Monadic **NEXT_*T*** and **PRIOR_*T*** operators, which return the successor and the predecessor, respectively, of any given value of type *T,* according to the aforementioned total ordering. *Note:* NEXT_*T* is the **successor function** for type *T;* of course, NEXT_*T*(p) is undefined if p = LAST_*T*(). Likewise, PRIOR_*T*(p) is undefined if p = FIRST_*T*().

Next, we define the **INTERVAL type generator.**[6] If T is a point type, then INTERVAL_*T* is an **interval type**, obtained by invoking that type generator on type *T.* Like all type generators, INTERVAL has associated with it (a) a set of generic possible representations, (b) a set of generic operators, and (c) a set of generic constraints, all of which apply to every generated type obtained from it. To be more specific:

- We consider just one possible representation: Any value of type INTERVAL_*T*—that is, any **interval** of that type—can possibly be represented by a pair of values of type *T,* corresponding to the begin point and the end point, respectively, of the interval in question. Here is the syntax of the corresponding **selector** operator:

```
INTERVAL_T ( [ b : e ] )
```

Here b and e are expressions of type *T,* and the overall selector invocation returns the interval with begin and end points equal to the values denoted by those expressions.

- Here is the syntax of the corresponding "THE_ operators" **BEGIN** and **END**:

```
BEGIN ( i )
END ( i )
```

Here i is an expression of some interval type, and the two operator invocations return the begin point and the end point, respectively, of the interval denoted by that expression. *Note:* As just indicated, BEGIN and END are really "THE_" operators, and in **Tutorial D** we would normally refer to them as THE_BEGIN and THE_END. We use BEGIN and END instead, here and throughout this chapter, for consistency with other writings in this field.

- Other generic operators include ":="; a set of boolean operators, including "=" in particular, known collectively as *Allen's operators* (see later in this section); and a variety of other operators (again, see later in this section).

- We consider just one generic constraint: namely, the constraint that if i is an interval, then BEGIN(i) ≤ END(i). One consequence is that intervals are never empty—they always contain at least one point. Another is that explicit constraints "to guard against the absurdity of a FROM-TO pair appearing in which the TO value is less than the FROM value" (as we put it in the previous section) are no longer necessary.

---

[6] It is worth pointing out that the INTERVAL type generator is the only construct introduced in this chapter that is not just shorthand. Our approach to temporal databases—unlike some others that have been described in the literature—thus involves no changes at all to the classical relational model (although it does involve certain *generalizations,* as we will see in Sections 23.5 and 23.7).

Now, it should be clear that type DATE in particular satisfies the requirements of, and can thus be used as, a point type. Hence, INTERVAL_DATE is a valid interval type, and so the definitions for relvars S_DURING and SP_DURING might look like this:

```
VAR S_DURING BASE RELATION
    { S# S#, DURING INTERVAL_DATE }
    KEY { S#, DURING } ;

VAR SP_DURING BASE RELATION
    { S# S#, P# P#, DURING INTERVAL_DATE }
    KEY { S#, P#, DURING } ;
```

Note that these definitions are still very incomplete! We will come back and elaborate on them in Section 23.7. Observe, however, that we have now defined away the problem of having to make an arbitrary choice as to which of two candidate keys should be chosen as primary. As for the other constraints and the queries from Section 23.2, it should be clear that direct analogs of those constraints and queries can be formulated against the database of Fig. 23.4, thanks to the existence of the operators BEGIN and END. We do not show any such formulations, however, since it is precisely part of our goal to come up with a better way of expressing such constraints and queries.

To repeat, type DATE is a valid point type—but there is no requirement that point types have to be "datetime" types specifically, nor that intervals have to be "datetime" intervals specifically. In fact, while intervals are the fundamental abstraction we need for dealing with temporal data, it should be clear that the interval concept is actually of much wider applicability; that is, there are many other applications for intervals, applications in which the intervals are not necessarily temporal ones. Here are a few examples:

- Tax brackets are represented by taxable-income ranges—that is, intervals whose begin and end points (and all points in between) are money values.

- Machines are built to operate within certain temperature and voltage ranges—that is, intervals whose contained points are temperatures and voltages, respectively.

- Animals vary in the range of frequencies of light and sound waves to which their eyes and ears are receptive.

- Various natural phenomena occur and can be measured in ranges in depth of soil or sea or height above sea level.

Although our primary focus in this chapter is on temporal intervals specifically, many of our discussions are in fact relevant to intervals in general. Space does not permit much elaboration here, however, and we therefore content ourselves with a couple of examples of nontemporal interval types:

- INTERVAL_INTEGER

  The point type here is INTEGER; the successor function is "next integer" (i.e., "add one"), and values of this interval type are intervals of the form $[b:e]$, where b and e are values of type INTEGER and $b \le e$.

- INTERVAL_MONEY

  MONEY here is—let us assume—a type that represents monetary amounts measured in dollars and cents. The successor function is "add one cent." Values of this interval type are intervals of the form [*b*:*e*], where *b* and *e* are values of type MONEY and $b \leq e$.

Operators on Points and Intervals

We now proceed to define a number of useful operators on points and intervals (over and above those already discussed). Development of examples to illustrate the functionality of these operators is left as an exercise. *Terminology:* Let *T* be a point type, and let *p*, *p1*, and *p2* be values of type *T*; informally, we use the expressions *p*+1 and *p*−1 to denote *p*'s successor and predecessor, respectively. Further, let *i*, *i1*, and *i2* be intervals of type INTERVAL_*T*, and let *b*, *b1*, and *b2* be the begin points and *e*, *e1*, and *e2* the end points of *i*, *i1*, and *i2*, respectively; informally, we use the expressions [*b*:*e*], [*b1*:*e1*], and [*b2*:*e2*] to denote *i*, *i1*, and *i2*, respectively. Then:

- IS_NEXT_*T*(*p1*,*p2*) is true if and only if *p1* is the immediate successor of *p2*. IS_PRIOR_*T*(*p1*,*p2*) is true if and only if IS_NEXT_*T*(*p2*,*p1*) is true—that is, IS_PRIOR_*T*(*p1*,*p2*) ≡ IS_NEXT_*T*(*p2*,*p1*).

- MAX(*p1*,*p2*) returns *p2* if *p1* < *p2* is true and *p1* otherwise; MIN(*p1*,*p2*) returns *p1* if *p1* < *p2* is true and *p2* otherwise.

- *p* ∈ *i* is true if and only if $b \leq p$ and $p \leq e$ are both true—that is, *p* ∈ *i* ≡ ($b \leq p$ AND *p* ≤ *e*). Also, *i* ∋ *p* ≡ *p* ∈ *i*. *Note:* The symbols ∈ and ∋ can be read as "is contained in" and "contains," respectively.

- COUNT(i) returns a count of the number of distinct points *p* such that *p* ∈ *i*.

- If and only if COUNT(*i*) = 1, *i* is a *unit interval*. POINT FROM *i* returns the sole point *p* in the unit interval *i*.

- PRE(*i*) and POST(*i*) return *b*−1 and *e*+1, respectively. *Note:* PRE(*i*) and POST(*i*) are shorthand for PRIOR_*T*(BEGIN(*i*)) and NEXT_*T*(END(*i*)), respectively.

Next, a variety of operators can be defined for testing whether two intervals are equal, whether they overlap, and so on. The operators in question are known collectively as **Allen's operators**, most of them having first been proposed by Allen in reference [23.1]; however, we do not always follow Allen's nomenclature here. They are defined most succinctly in terms of equivalences, but you might like to try drawing some pictures in order to understand them at an intuitive level.

- *Equals (=): (i1 = i2) ≡ (b1 = b2 AND e1 = e2)*
- *Includes (⊇) and included in (⊆): (i1 ⊇ i2) ≡ (b1 ≤ b2 AND e1 ≥ e2); (i2 ⊆ i1) ≡ (i1 ⊇ i2)*
- *Properly includes (⊃) and properly included in (⊂): (i1 ⊃ i2) ≡ (i1 ⊇ i2 AND i1 ≠ i2); (i2 ⊂ i1) ≡ (i1 ⊃ i2)*
- *BEFORE and AFTER: (i1 BEFORE i2) ≡ (e1 < b2); (i1 AFTER i2) ≡ (i2 BEFORE i1)*
- *MEETS: (i1 MEETS i2) ≡ (b2 = e1+1 OR b1 = e2+1)*
- *OVERLAPS: (i1 OVERLAPS i2) ≡ (b1 ≤ e2 AND b2 ≤ e1)*

- *MERGES: (i1 MERGES i2) ≡ (i1 OVERLAPS i2 OR i1 MEETS i2)*
- *BEGINS: (i1 BEGINS i2) ≡ (b1 = b2 AND e1 ≤ e2)*
- *ENDS: (i1 ENDS i2) ≡ (e1 = e2 AND b1 ≥ b2)*

Finally, we define some useful dyadic operators on intervals that return intervals: namely, interval analogs of the familiar operators UNION, INTERSECT, and MINUS. Each takes two intervals of the same type as its operands and returns another interval of the same type as its result (and here we do give some examples).

- *UNION: i1* UNION *i2* returns [MIN(*b1,b2*):MAX(*e1,e2*)] if *i1* MERGES *i2* is true and is otherwise undefined. For example, the union of [*d04:d08*] and [*d06:d10*] is [*d04:d10*]; the union of [*d02:d03*] and [*d06:d10*] is undefined.
- *INTERSECT: i1* INTERSECT *i2* returns [MAX(*b1,b2*):MIN(*e1,e2*)] if *i1* OVERLAPS *i2* is true and is otherwise undefined. For example, the intersection of [*d04:d08*] and [*d06:d10*] is [*d06:d08*]; the intersection of [*d02:d03*] and [*d06:d10*] is undefined.
- *MINUS: i1* MINUS *i2* returns [*b1*:MIN(*b2*−1,*e1*)] if *b1* < *b2* and *e1* ≤ *e2* are both true; [MAX(*e2*+1,*b1*):*e1*] if *b1* ≥ *b2* and *e1* > *e2* are both true; and is otherwise undefined. For example, the difference between [*d04:d08*] and [*d06:d10*] (in that order) is [*d04:d05*]; the difference between [*d06:d10*] and [*d04:d08*] (in that order) is [*d09:d10*]; the difference between [*d02:d03*] and [*d06:d10*] (in either order) is undefined.

Sample Queries

We close this section with some sample queries to illustrate the use of some of the operators defined in the previous subsection. First, consider the query "Get supplier numbers for suppliers who were able to supply part P2 on day 8." Here is a possible formulation of that query on the database of Fig. 23.4:

```
( SP_DURING WHERE P# = P# ('P2')
         AND    d08 ∈ DURING ) { S# }
```

Explanation: The expression within the outer parentheses restricts the set of tuples currently appearing in relvar SP_DURING to just those for which the P# value is P2 and day 8 is contained in the interval that is the DURING value. That set of tuples is then projected over attribute S# to yield the desired result. *Note:* In practice, the expression "*d08*" here would have to be replaced by an appropriate DATE selector invocation.

By way of a second example, here is a possible formulation of the query "Get pairs of suppliers who were able to supply the same part at the same time":

```
WITH ( SP_DURING RENAME ( S# AS X#, DURING AS XD ) ) AS T1 ,
     ( SP_DURING RENAME ( S# AS Y#, DURING AS YD ) ) AS T2 ,
     ( T1 JOIN T2 ) AS T3 ,
     ( T3 WHERE XD OVERLAPS YD ) AS T4 ,
     ( T4 WHERE X# < Y# ) AS T5 :
  T5 { X#, Y# }
```

Explanation: T1 here is the relation that is the current value of relvar SP_DURING, except that attributes S# and DURING are renamed as X# and XD, respectively; relation T2 is the same, except that the new attribute names are Y# and YD instead. Relation T3 is the join of T1 and T2 over part numbers. Relation T4 is the restriction of T3 to just those tuples where the XD and YD intervals overlap (meaning the suppliers were not only able to supply the same part but in fact were able to supply the same part *at the same time,* as required). Relation T5 is the restriction of T4 to just those tuples where supplier number X# is less than supplier number Y# (compare Example 7.5.5 in Chapter 7). The final projection over X# and Y# produces the desired result.

As a third example, suppose we want to get, not just pairs of suppliers who were able to supply the same part at the same time, but also the parts and times in question. Here then is a possible formulation:

```
WITH ( SP_DURING RENAME ( S# AS X#, DURING AS XD ) ) AS T1 ,
     ( SP_DURING RENAME ( S# AS Y#, DURING AS YD ) ) AS T2 ,
     ( T1 JOIN T2 ) AS T3 ,
     ( T3 WHERE XD OVERLAPS YD ) AS T4 ,
     ( T4 WHERE X# < Y# ) AS T5 ,
     ( EXTEND T5 ADD ( XD INTERSECT YD ) AS DURING ) AS T6 :
T6 { X#, Y#, P#, DURING }
```

Explanation: Relations T1, T2, T3, T4, and T5 are exactly as in the previous example. The EXTEND then computes the relevant intervals, and the final projection produces the desired result.

23.4 PACKING AND UNPACKING RELATIONS

In this section we introduce two new (and extremely important) relational operators called PACK and UNPACK. As a stepping-stone on the way to those operators, however, we first need to digress briefly and discuss two simpler analogs of them called COLLAPSE and EXPAND, respectively. For pedagogic reasons, moreover, we discuss these latter operators in the inverse order.

EXPAND and COLLAPSE

EXPAND and COLLAPSE as we describe them here[7] both take as sole operand a unary relation in which the tuples contain intervals and produce another such relation as their result. For example, suppose relation *r* looks like this:

DURING
[*d06*:*d09*]
[*d04*:*d08*]
[*d05*:*d10*]
[*d01*:*d01*]

---

[7] More general versions of the operators are described in reference [23.4].

Then EXPAND *r* and COLLAPSE *r* produce results that look like this:

```
EXPAND  r                COLLAPSE  r

 DURING                    DURING

[d01:d01]                 [d01:d01]
[d04:d04]                 [d04:d10]
[d05:d05]
[d06:d06]
[d07:d07]
[d08:d08]
[d09:d09]
[d10:d10]
```

Explanation: Let unary relation *r* have DURING as its sole attribute, and let DURING be interval-valued. Then the *expanded* and *collapsed forms* of *r* are both unary relations of the same type as *r*:

- The **expanded** form is that relation *rx* that contains all and only those tuples that contain a unit interval of the form [*p*:*p*], where *p* is a point in some interval in some tuple in *r*.

- The **collapsed** form of *r* is that relation *rc* such that:

  a. Relations *r* and *rc* have the same expanded form.

  b. No two distinct tuples in *rc* contain intervals *i1* and *i2*, respectively, such that *i1* MERGES *i2* is true. Equivalently, no two distinct tuples in *rc* contain intervals *i1* and *i2*, respectively, such that *i1* UNION *i2* is defined. (It follows that *rc* can be computed from *r* by successively replacing pairs of tuples *t1* and *t2* in *r* by a tuple *t* containing the union of the intervals in *t1* and *t2* until no more such replacements are possible.)

We now take a closer look at these ideas. For simplicity, we assume for the rest of this subsection that the only relations we are dealing with are, precisely, unary relations in which the tuples contain intervals. Then we define the important notion of *equivalence* among such relations thus:

- Two relations *r1* and *r2* are **equivalent** if and only if the set of all points contained in intervals in tuples in *r1* is equal to the set of all points contained in intervals in tuples in *r2*.

Armed with this definition and the earlier definitions of expanded and collapsed form, it should be clear that:

- For any given relation *r*, a corresponding expanded form of *r* always exists.

- That expanded form is equivalent to *r*. In fact, we can say that two relations are equivalent if and only if they have the same expanded form.

- That expanded form is unique; to be precise, it is that unique equivalent relation for which the intervals are all of the minimum possible length (one).

- Intuitively, the expanded form of *r* allows us to focus on the information content of *r* at an atomic level, without having to worry about the many different ways in which that information might be bundled together into "clumps."

- If *r* is empty, the expanded form of *r* is empty too.

Likewise:

- For any given relation *r*, a corresponding collapsed form of *r* always exists.
- That collapsed form is equivalent to *r*. In fact, we can say that two relations are equivalent if and only if they have the same collapsed form.
- That collapsed form is unique; to be precise, it is that unique equivalent relation that has the minimum possible cardinality.
- Intuitively, the collapsed form of *r* allows us to focus on the information content of *r* in a compressed ("clumped") form, without having to worry about the possibility that distinct "clumps" might meet or overlap.
- If *r* is empty, the collapsed form of *r* is empty too.

By the way, do not make the mistake of thinking that EXPAND and COLLAPSE are inverses of each other. In fact, neither EXPAND (COLLAPSE *r*) nor COLLAPSE (EXPAND *r*) is identically equal to *r*, in general (though they are both *equivalent* to *r*, of course). Indeed, it is easy to see that the following identities hold:

- EXPAND (COLLAPSE *r*) ≡ EXPAND *r*
- COLLAPSE (EXPAND *r*) ≡ COLLAPSE *r*

It follows that the first operation in a collapse-then-expand or expand-then-collapse sequence on some relation *r* can simply be ignored, a fact that could be useful for optimization purposes (especially when that first operation is EXPAND).

Two final points to close this subsection:

- Reference [23.4] shows that EXPAND and COLLAPSE can both be defined in terms of operators already available in the relational algebra. In other words, they are both just shorthand.
- Reference [23.4] also shows that it is highly desirable to define versions of the EXPAND and COLLAPSE operators that work on *nullary* relations instead of unary ones. We omit the detailed analysis here, instead simply defining both EXPAND *r* and COLLAPSE *r* to return *r* if *r* is a nullary relation. We also define two nullary relations to be equivalent if and only if they are equal.

PACK and UNPACK

In their commonest form, PACK and UNPACK both take as sole operand an *n*-ary relation in which one of the attributes is interval-valued and produce another such relation as their result. For example, suppose relation *r* looks like this:

S#	DURING
S2	[d02:d04]
S2	[d03:d05]
S4	[d02:d05]
S4	[d04:d06]
S4	[d09:d10]

Then PACK *r* ON DURING and UNPACK *r* ON DURING produce results that look like this:

```
PACK r ON DURING               UNPACK r ON DURING
```

S#	DURING
S2	[d02:d05]
S4	[d02:d06]
S4	[d09:d10]

S#	DURING
S2	[d02:d02]
S2	[d03:d03]
S2	[d04:d04]
S2	[d05:d05]
S4	[d02:d02]
S4	[d03:d03]
S4	[d04:d04]
S4	[d05:d05]
S4	[d06:d06]
S4	[d09:d09]
S4	[d10:d10]

Observe that, informally, each of these results represents the same information as the original relation *r,* but:

- In the case of PACK, the information has been rearranged in such a way that no two DURING intervals for a given supplier either meet or overlap.

- In the case of UNPACK, the information has been rearranged in such a way that every DURING value (and hence every DURING interval for a given supplier, *a fortiori*) is a unit interval specifically.

The relevance of COLLAPSE and EXPAND to the PACK and UNPACK operations should be intuitively obvious. What is probably also obvious is that the original relation *r* and the corresponding packed and unpacked forms are all *equivalent* in a certain sense (we will make that sense precise at the end of this section).

We now concentrate on PACK specifically. Here first is a restatement of Query A in terms of the database of Fig. 23.4:

- *Query A:* Get S#-DURING pairs for suppliers who have been able to supply at least one part during at least one interval of time, where DURING designates such an interval.

Given the sample data of Fig. 23.4, the desired result looks like this:

S#	DURING
S1	[d04:d10]
S2	[d02:d04]
S2	[d08:d10]
S3	[d08:d10]
S4	[d04:d10]

This relation is *the packed form on DURING* of a certain projection of relvar SP: namely, the projection on S# and DURING. And we will eventually reach a point where we can obtain this result by means of a simple expression of the form

```
PACK T1 ON DURING
```

where T1 is the specified projection. However, we will build up to that point one small step at a time. The first step is:

```
WITH SP_DURING { S#, DURING } AS T1 :
```

This step yields the required projection (in effect, it just "projects away" part numbers, which are irrelevant to the query at hand). In terms of our usual sample data values, T1 looks like this:

S#	DURING
S1	[d04:d10]
S1	[d05:d10]
S1	[d09:d10]
S1	[d06:d10]
S2	[d02:d04]
S2	[d08:d10]
S2	[d03:d03]
S2	[d09:d10]
S3	[d08:d10]
S4	[d06:d09]
S4	[d04:d08]
S4	[d05:d10]

Observe that this relation contains redundant information; for example, we are told no fewer than three times that supplier S1 was able to supply something on day 6 (the desired result, by contrast, contains no such redundancy).

The next step is as follows:

```
WITH ( T1 GROUP { DURING } AS X ) AS T2 :
```

T2 looks like this:

S#	X
S1	**DURING** [d04:d10] [d05:d10] [d09:d10] [d06:d10]
S2	**DURING** [d02:d04] [d08:d10] [d03:d03] [d09:d10]
S3	**DURING** [d08:d10]
S4	**DURING** [d06:d09] [d04:d08] [d05:d10]

Attribute X of T2 is *relation-valued,* and so we can apply the COLLAPSE operator to the unary relations that are values of that attribute:

```
WITH ( EXTEND T2 ADD COLLAPSE ( X ) AS Y )
                          { ALL BUT X } AS T3 :
```

T3 looks like this (note that attribute X has been projected away, thanks to the specification "{ALL BUT X}"):

S#	Y
S1	DURING [*d04:d10*]
S2	DURING [*d02:d04*] [*d08:d10*]
S3	DURING [*d08:d10*]
S4	DURING [*d04:d10*]

Finally, we ungroup:

```
T3 UNGROUP Y
```

This expression yields the desired result. In other words, now showing all of the steps together (and simplifying slightly), that result is obtained by evaluating the following overall expression:

```
WITH SP_DURING { S#, DURING } AS T1 ,
     ( T1 GROUP { DURING } AS X ) AS T2 ,
     ( EXTEND T2 ADD COLLAPSE ( X ) AS Y ) { ALL BUT X } AS T3 :
T3 UNGROUP Y
```

Now we can define our PACK operator (which is shorthand, of course). The syntax is:

```
PACK r ON A
```

Here *r* is a relational expression and *A* is an interval attribute of the relation denoted by that expression. The semantics are defined by obvious generalization of the grouping, extension, projection, and ungrouping operations by which we obtained RESULT from T1:

```
PACK r ON A  ≡  WITH ( r GROUP { A } AS X ) AS R1 ,
                    ( EXTEND R1 ADD COLLAPSE ( X ) AS Y )
                                    { ALL BUT X } AS R2 :
                R2 UNGROUP Y
```

As suggested earlier, Query A can now be formulated thus:

```
PACK SP_DURING { S#, DURING } ON DURING
```

Note: It might help to point out explicitly that—as should be clear from the definition—packing a relation *on* some attribute *A* involves grouping that relation *by* all of its attributes apart from that attribute *A*. (Recall from Chapter 7 that, e.g., the expression "T1 GROUP {DURING} . . ." can be read as "group T1 *by* S#," S# being the sole attribute of T1 apart from the one mentioned in the GROUP specification.) However, note that, while *r* GROUP {*A*} . . . is guaranteed to return a result with exactly one tuple for each distinct value of *B* (where *B* is all of the attributes of *r* apart from *A*), PACK *r* ON *A* might return a result with several tuples for any given value of *B*. By way of illustration, refer to the PACK result for Query A, which has two tuples for supplier S4.

We turn now to UNPACK and Query B:

- *Query B:* Get S#-DURING pairs for suppliers who have been unable to supply any parts at all during at least one interval of time, where DURING designates such an interval.

Now, you can probably see that what we need to do here, in essence, is look for S#-DURING pairs that appear in or are implied by S_DURING and do *not* appear in and are *not* implied by SP_DURING. This brief characterization should be sufficient to suggest (correctly) that, again in essence, what we need to do is perform a couple of unpack operations, take the difference between the results, and then repack that difference. So let us first introduce the UNPACK operator:

```
UNPACK r ON A  ≡  WITH ( r GROUP { A } AS X ) AS R1 ,
                       ( EXTEND R1 ADD EXPAND ( X ) AS Y )
                                           { ALL BUT X } AS R2 :
               R2 UNGROUP Y
```

This definition is identical to that for PACK, except for the appearance of EXPAND rather than COLLAPSE in the second line. We call the result of the expression *the unpacked form of r on A.*

With regard to Query B, therefore, we can obtain the left operand we need (i.e., S#-DURING pairs that appear in or are implied by S_DURING) as follows:

```
UNPACK S_DURING { S#, DURING } ON DURING
```

Here is the expanded form of this expression:

```
WITH S_DURING { S#, DURING } AS T1 ,
   ( T1 GROUP { DURING } AS X ) AS T2 ,
   ( EXTEND T2 ADD EXPAND ( X ) AS Y ) { ALL BUT X } AS T3 :
T3 UNGROUP Y
```

Working through this expression in detail, step by step, is left as an exercise. Given the sample data of Fig. 23.4, however, the overall result—let us call it U1—looks like this:

S#	DURING
S1	[d04:d04]
S1	[d05:d05]
S1	[d06:d06]
S1	[d07:d07]
S1	[d08:d08]
S1	[d09:d09]
S1	[d10:d10]
S2	[d02:d02]
S2	[d03:d03]
S2	[d04:d04]
S2	[d07:d07]
S2	[d08:d08]
S2	[d09:d09]
S2	[d10:d10]
S3	[d03:d03]
S3	[d04:d04]
S3	[d05:d05]
S3	[d06:d06]
S3	[d07:d07]
S3	[d08:d08]
S3	[d09:d09]
S3	[d10:d10]
S4	[d04:d04]
S4	[d05:d05]
S4	[d06:d06]
S4	[d07:d07]
S4	[d08:d08]
S4	[d09:d09]
S4	[d10:d10]
S5	[d02:d02]
S5	[d03:d03]
S5	[d04:d04]
S5	[d05:d05]
S5	[d06:d06]
S5	[d07:d07]
S5	[d08:d08]
S5	[d09:d09]
S5	[d10:d10]

Of course, the right operand (i.e., S#-DURING pairs that appear in or are implied by SP_DURING) is obtained in like fashion:

```
UNPACK SP_DURING { S#, DURING } ON DURING
```

The result of this expression—let us call it U2—looks like this:

S#	DURING
S1	[d04:d04]
S1	[d05:d05]
S1	[d06:d06]
S1	[d07:d07]
S1	[d08:d08]
S1	[d09:d09]
S1	[d10:d10]
S2	[d02:d02]
S2	[d03:d03]
S2	[d04:d04]
S2	[d08:d08]
S2	[d09:d09]
S2	[d10:d10]
S3	[d08:d08]
S3	[d09:d09]
S3	[d10:d10]
S4	[d04:d04]
S4	[d05:d05]
S4	[d06:d06]
S4	[d07:d07]
S4	[d08:d08]
S4	[d09:d09]
S4	[d10:d10]

Now we can apply the difference operator:

```
U1 MINUS U2
```

The result of this expression, U3 say, looks like this:

S#	DURING
S2	[d07:d07]
S3	[d03:d03]
S3	[d04:d04]
S3	[d05:d05]
S3	[d06:d06]
S3	[d07:d07]
S5	[d02:d02]
S5	[d03:d03]
S5	[d04:d04]
S5	[d05:d05]
S5	[d06:d06]
S5	[d07:d07]
S5	[d08:d08]
S5	[d09:d09]
S5	[d10:d10]

Finally, we pack U3 to obtain the desired overall result:

```
PACK U3 ON DURING
```

The final result looks like this:

S#	DURING
S2	[d07:d07]
S3	[d03:d07]
S5	[d02:d10]

Here then is a formulation of Query B as a single expression:

```
PACK
   ( ( UNPACK S_DURING { S#, DURING } ON DURING )
     MINUS
     ( UNPACK SP_DURING { S#, DURING } ON DURING ) )
ON DURING
```

Observe that unpacking *r* on *A* (like packing *r* on *A*) involves grouping *r* by all of the attributes of *r* apart from *A*.

Like the operators COLLAPSE and EXPAND on which they are based, PACK and UNPACK are not inverses of each other. That is, neither UNPACK (PACK *r* ON *A*) ON *A* nor PACK (UNPACK *r* ON *A*) ON *A* is identically equal to *r*, in general (though they are both *equivalent* to *r*, in a sense still to be explained). Indeed, it is easy to see that the following identities hold:

- UNPACK *r* ON *A* ≡ UNPACK (PACK *r* ON *A*) ON *A*

- PACK *r* ON *A* ≡ PACK (UNPACK *r* ON *A*) ON *A*

It follows that the first operation in a pack-then-unpack or unpack-then-pack sequence on some given relation can simply be ignored, a fact that could be useful for optimization purposes (especially when that first operation is UNPACK).

Further Examples

We give some further examples of the use of PACK and UNPACK in formulating queries. We assume, reasonably enough, that the result is required in suitably packed form in each case.

Our first example is deliberately not a temporal one. Suppose we are given a relvar NHW, with attributes NAME, HEIGHT, and WEIGHT, giving the height and weight of certain persons. Consider the query "For each weight represented in NHW, get every range of heights such that for each such range *r* and for each height in *r* there is at least one person represented in NHW who is of that height and that weight." Here then is a possible formulation:

```
PACK
   ( ( EXTEND NHW { HEIGHT, WEIGHT }
       ADD INTERVAL_HEIGHT ( [ HEIGHT : HEIGHT ] ) AS HR )
     { WEIGHT, HR } )
ON HR
```

Explanation: We begin by projecting NHW over HEIGHT and WEIGHT, thereby obtaining all height-weight pairs in the original relation (i.e., all height-weight pairs such that there is at least one person of that height and weight). We then extend that projection by introducing another attribute, HR, whose value in any given tuple is a unit interval of the form [*h:h*], where *h* is the HEIGHT value in that same tuple (note the invocation of the interval selector INTERVAL_HEIGHT). We then project away the HEIGHT attribute and pack the result on HR. The final result is a relation with two attributes, WEIGHT and HR, and predicate as follows:

> *For all heights h in HR—but not for h = PRE(HR) or h = POST(HR)—there exists at least one person p such that p has weight WEIGHT and height h.*

By way of a second example, consider relvar SP_DURING once again. At any given time, if there are any shipments at all at that time, then there is some part number *pmax* such that no supplier is able to supply any part at that time with a part number greater than *pmax*. (Obviously we are assuming here that the operator ">" is defined for values of type P#.) So consider the query "For each part number that has ever been such a *pmax* value, get that part number together with the interval(s) during which it actually was that *pmax* value." Here is a possible formulation:

```
WITH ( UNPACK SP_DURING ON DURING ) AS SP_UNPACKED ,
     ( SUMMARIZE SP_UNPACKED
       BY { DURING }
       ADD MAX ( P# ) AS PMAX ) AS SUMMARY :
PACK SUMMARY ON DURING
```

Closing Remarks

There is much, much more to the PACK and UNPACK operators than we have room for in this chapter. Detailed discussions can be found in reference [23.4]; here we just list without proof or further commentary some of the most important points.

- Packing or unpacking a relation *r* on no attributes at all simply returns *r*.

- Unpacking a relation *r* on two or more attributes, all of which are interval-valued,[8] is straightforward; if the attributes in question are *A1, A2, ..., An* (in some order), then the result can be obtained by unpacking *r* on *A1*, then unpacking the result of that first unpacking on *A2*, ..., and finally unpacking the result of the penultimate unpacking on *An*.

- Packing a relation *r* on two or more attributes, all of which are interval-valued, is not nearly as straightforward. Loosely, however, we can say that if the attributes in question are *A1, A2, ..., An* (in that order), then the result can be obtained by (a) first *un*packing *r* on all of those attributes and then (b) packing the result of that unpacking on *A1*, packing the result of the first packing on *A2*, ..., and finally packing the result of the penultimate packing on *An*.

- Let *r1* and *r2* be relations of the same type, and let attributes *A1, A2, ..., An* of those two relations be interval-valued. Then *r1* and *r2* are *equivalent* (with respect to attributes *A1, A2, ..., An*) if and only if the results of UNPACK *r1* ON (*A1, A2, ..., An*) and UNPACK *r2* ON (*A1, A2, ..., An*) are equal.

---

[8] Note the implication that it is perfectly acceptable for a relation to have two or more interval-valued attributes.

23.5 GENERALIZING THE RELATIONAL OPERATORS

In the previous section we showed this formulation for Query B:

```
PACK
   ( ( UNPACK S_DURING { S#, DURING } ON DURING )
     MINUS
     ( UNPACK SP_DURING { S#, DURING } ON DURING ) )
ON DURING
```

Now, it turns out that expressions like this one, involving a couple of unpackings, followed by a regular relational operation, followed by a repacking, are needed so often in practice that the idea of defining a shorthand for them seems worthwhile (a further shorthand, that is!—they are basically just shorthand already, as we know). Certainly such a shorthand would save some writing. Moreover, it also offers the opportunity of improving performance: When long intervals of fine granularity are involved, the output from an unpack operation can be very large in comparison to the input; and if the system were actually to materialize the result of such an unpacking, the query might "execute forever" or run out of memory. By contrast, expressing the overall requirement as a single operation might allow the optimizer to choose a more efficient implementation, one that does not require materialization of unpacked intermediate results.

With the foregoing by way of motivation, we define the expression

```
USING ( ACL ) ◄ r1 MINUS r2 ►
```

to be shorthand for the following:

```
PACK
   ( ( UNPACK r1 ON ( ACL ) ) MINUS ( UNPACK r2 ON ( ACL ) ) )
ON ( ACL )
```

Here *r1* and *r2* are relational expressions denoting relations of the same type, and *ACL* is a commalist of attribute names in which every attribute mentioned (a) is of some interval type and (b) appears in both relations. Points arising:

1. Until further notice, we will refer to the operator just defined as "U_difference" (U for USING), or simply U_MINUS for short.

2. The parentheses surrounding the commalist of attribute names in the USING specification can be omitted if the commalist contains just one attribute name. *Note:* This remark applies to all of the "U_" shorthands we will be defining, and we will not bother to repeat it every time.

3. In every context discussed in this section in which a USING specification can appear, solid arrowheads ◄ and ► are used to delimit the expression to which the USING specification applies.

4. Unlike the regular MINUS operator, U_MINUS can produce a result whose cardinality is greater than that of its left operand! For example, let *r1* and *r2* be as follows:

r1

A
[d02:d04]

r2

A
[d03:d03]

Then USING A ◄ *r1* MINUS *r2* ► gives:

A
[d02:d02]
[d04:d04]

So much for U_MINUS. Now, it should be clear that we can define "U_" versions of *all* of the regular relational operators (and reference [23.4] in fact does so). For space reasons, however, we limit ourselves here to the most useful of those operators, which we take to be (in addition to U_MINUS) U_UNION, U_INTERSECT, U_JOIN, and U_project. U_UNION and U_INTERSECT follow the same general pattern as U_MINUS; that is, the expression

```
USING ( ACL ) ◄ r1 op r2 ►
```

(where *op* is either UNION or INTERSECT and *ACL, r1,* and *r2* are as for U_MINUS) is shorthand for:

```
PACK
    ( ( UNPACK r1 ON ( ACL ) ) op ( UNPACK r2 ON ( ACL ) ) )
ON ( ACL )
```

As an aside, we remark that there is actually no need to perform the preliminary UNPACKs in the case of U_UNION. That is, the U_UNION expansion can be further simplified to just:

```
PACK ( r1 UNION r2 ) ON ( ACL )
```

It is not hard to see why this simplification is possible, but you can try working through an example if you need to convince yourself it is valid. (In fact, similar simplifications are possible with several of the other "U_" operators as well, but the details are beyond the scope of this chapter.)

Also, just as U_MINUS, slightly counterintuitively, can increase the cardinality (loosely speaking), so U_UNION can decrease it; in fact, U_UNION can produce a result with cardinality less than that of either operand (exercise for the reader). Likewise, U_INTERSECT can produce a result with cardinality greater than that of either operand (another exercise).

We turn now to U_JOIN, and define the expression

```
USING ( ACL ) ◄ r1 JOIN r2 ►
```

to be shorthand for

```
PACK
    ( ( UNPACK r1 ON ( ACL ) ) JOIN ( UNPACK r2 ON ( ACL ) ) )
ON ( ACL )
```

Every attribute mentioned in *ACL* must be of some interval type and must appear in both *r1* and *r2* (and so the join is to be done on all of the attributes mentioned in *ACL,* as well as possibly others). *Note:* If *r1* and *r2* are of the same type, then U_JOIN degenerates to U_INTERSECT.

Here is an example to illustrate the use of U_JOIN. Suppose we have another relvar in the database, S_CITY_DURING, with attributes S#, CITY, and DURING, with candidate key {S#,DURING}, and with predicate as follows:

> *Supplier S# was located in city CITY during the interval from the begin point of DURING to the end point of DURING.*

Now consider the query "Get S#-CITY-P#-DURING tuples such that supplier S# was located in city CITY and was able to supply part P# throughout interval DURING, where DURING contains day 4." Here is a possible formulation of that query:

```
( USING DURING ◄ S_CITY_DURING JOIN SP_DURING ► )
                                    WHERE d04 ∈ DURING
```

Turning finally to U_projection, we define the expression

```
USING ( ACL ) ◄ R { BCL } ►
```

to be shorthand for

```
PACK ( ( UNPACK r ON ( ACL ) ) { BCL } ) ON ( ACL )
```

Every attribute mentioned in *ACL* must be of some interval type and must be mentioned in *BCL* (and hence *a fortiori* must be an attribute of *r*). By way of an example, recall Query A once again:

- *Query A:* Get S#-DURING pairs for suppliers who have been able to supply at least one part during at least one interval of time, where DURING designates such an interval.

Here is a "U_project" formulation for this query:

```
USING DURING ◄ SP_DURING { S#, DURING } ►
```

Since we already have the following as a "U_MINUS" formulation of Query B—

```
USING DURING ◄ S_DURING { S#, DURING }
                MINUS
                SP_DURING { S#, DURING } ►
```

—we have now achieved one of our original goals: namely, we have found a (much!) better way of formulating Queries A and B.

Relational Comparisons

Relational comparisons are strictly speaking not relational operations as such, because they return a truth value, not a relation. Nevertheless, we can subject them to the same kind of treatment we have been applying to the relational operators, and indeed it is desirable to do so. The point is, when the relations in question involve interval attributes, what we often want to do is compare certain *unpacked counterparts* of those relations, not those relations *per se*. To that end, we introduce, first, a "U_" counterpart to the regular "relation equality" comparison. To be specific, we define the expression

```
USING ( ACL ) ◄ r1 = r2 ►
```

to be shorthand for

```
( UNPACK r1 ON ( ACL ) ) = ( UNPACK r2 ON ( ACL ) )
```

Every attribute mentioned in *ACL* must be an interval attribute and must appear in both *r1* and *r2*. Note that the question of a final PACK step does not arise, because as already indicated the result of "=" is a truth value, not a relation.

By way of example, let *r1* and *r2* be as follows:

r1
A
[d01:d03]
[d02:d05]
[d04:d04]

r2
A
[d01:d02]
[d03:d05]

Then *r1* = *r2* gives FALSE, but USING A ◄ *r1* = *r2* ► gives TRUE.

We will refer to the foregoing operator as "U_=" for brevity (in fact, it is precisely the *equivalence* operator as defined for *n*-ary relations at the very end of the previous section). In the same kind of way, we can define "U_" analogs of all of the other relational comparison operators ($\neq$, $\subset$, $\subseteq$, $\supset$, and $\supseteq$). For example, if *r1* and *r2* are as for the "U_=" example, then USING A ◄ *r1* $\subseteq$ *r2* ► gives TRUE, but USING A ◄ *r1* $\subset$ *r2* ► gives FALSE.

The Regular Relational Operations Revisited

Consider the operator U_MINUS once again. Recall that we defined the expression

```
USING ( ACL ) ◄ r1 MINUS r2 ►
```

to be shorthand for

```
PACK
    ( ( UNPACK r1 ON ( ACL ) ) MINUS ( UNPACK r2 ON ( ACL ) ) )
ON ( ACL )
```

Suppose now that *ACL* is empty (i.e., specifies no attributes at all), thus:

```
USING ( ) ◄ r1 MINUS r2 ►
```

Then the expansion becomes

```
PACK
    ( ( UNPACK r1 ON ( ) ) MINUS ( UNPACK r2 ON ( ) ) )
ON ( )
```

Recall now from the previous section that UNPACK *r* ON () and PACK *r* ON () both reduce to just *r*. Thus, the entire expression reduces to just:

```
r1 MINUS r2
```

In other words, the regular relational MINUS is essentially just a special case of U_MINUS! Thus, if we redefine the syntax of the regular MINUS operator as follows—

```
[ USING ( ACL ) ] ◄ <relation exp> MINUS <relation exp> ►
```

—and allow the USING specification (and the solid arrowheads ◄ and ► enclosing the rest of the expression) to be omitted if and only if *ACL* is empty, then we no longer have any need to talk about a special "U_MINUS" operator at all—all MINUS invocations effectively become U_MINUS invocations, and we can generalize the meaning of MINUS accordingly.

Analogous remarks apply to all of the other relational operators, as well as to relational comparisons: In all cases, the regular operator is basically just that special case of the corresponding "U_" operator in which the USING specification mentions no attributes at all, and we can allow that specification (and the solid arrowheads enclosing the rest of the expression) to be omitted in that case. To put it another way, the "U_" operators are all just straightforward generalizations of their regular counterparts. Thus, we no longer need to talk explicitly about "U_" operators, as such, at all (and we no longer will, except occasionally for emphasis); instead, all we need to do is recognize that the regular operators permit but do not require an additional operand when they are applied to relations with interval attributes. *Please note carefully, therefore, that throughout the rest of this chapter we will take all references to relational operators, and all references to relational comparisons, to refer to the generalized versions as described in the present section* (barring explicit statements to the contrary). For clarity, however, we will occasionally make use of the explicit qualifiers *regular* (or *classical*) and *generalized,* as applicable, when referring to those operators and comparisons; as already noted, we will also sometimes use an explicit "U_" qualifier for the same reason.

23.6 DATABASE DESIGN

Special issues arise in connection with the design of temporal databases. In order to illustrate some of those issues, we revise our running example once again, as follows: First, we drop shipments entirely; second, we reinstate supplier name, status, and city information. And we present our preferred design for that revised database immediately:[9]

```
VAR S_SINCE BASE RELATION
   { S#      S#,        S#_SINCE      DATE,
     SNAME   NAME,      SNAME_SINCE   DATE,
     STATUS  INTEGER,   STATUS_SINCE  DATE,
     CITY    CHAR,      CITY_SINCE    DATE }
   KEY { S# } ;
```

```
VAR S_DURING                       VAR S_NAME_DURING
   BASE RELATION                      BASE RELATION
   { S#      S#,                      { S#      S#,
     DURING  INTERVAL_DATE }            SNAME   NAME,
   KEY { S#, DURING } ;                 DURING  INTERVAL_DATE }
                                      KEY { S#, DURING } ;
```

```
VAR S_STATUS_DURING                VAR S_CITY_DURING
   BASE RELATION                      BASE RELATION
   { S#      S#,                      { S#      S#,
     STATUS  INTEGER,                   CITY    CHAR,
     DURING  INTERVAL_DATE }            DURING  INTERVAL_DATE }
   KEY { S#, DURING } ;               KEY { S#, DURING } ;
```

---

[9] Note in particular in this design that relvar S_SINCE is not the same as relvar S_SINCE of Section 23.2.

The predicates are as follows:

- S_SINCE: *Supplier S# has been under contract since S#_SINCE, has been named SNAME since SNAME_SINCE, has had status STATUS since STATUS_SINCE, and has been located in city CITY since CITY_SINCE.*
- S_DURING: *Supplier S# was under contract during interval DURING.*
- S_NAME_DURING: *Supplier S# had name SNAME during interval DURING.*
- S_STATUS_DURING: *Supplier S# had status STATUS during interval DURING.*
- S_CITY_DURING: *Supplier S# was located in city CITY during interval DURING.*

Also, we need to add in the case of the four "during" predicates that *the day that is the end point of DURING is in the past* (see the subsection "The Moving Point *Now*" later in this section).

As you can see, our preferred design keeps *current* information in a "since relvar" and *historical* information in a set of "during relvars." We refer to that separation as **horizontal decomposition**. Furthermore, the historical information is kept in a set of several distinct relvars—one for each distinct supplier "property," loosely speaking—and we refer to *that* separation as **vertical decomposition**. We justify these decompositions in the subsections following.

Horizontal Decomposition

The main justification for horizontal decomposition is simply that there is a clear logical difference between historical and current information:

- For historical information, the begin and end times are both known.
- For current information, by contrast, the begin time is known but the end time is not.

In other words, the predicates are different, a fact that suggests very strongly that separating historical and current information into distinct relvars is the right thing to do. *Note:* Actually both of the foregoing statements are somewhat oversimplified, but they are accurate enough for present purposes.

Observe, however, that the "current" relvar S_SINCE has four "since" attributes, one for each of the "nonsince" attributes. By contrast, it has been suggested in the literature, under the rubric of *timestamping tuples,* that a single "since" attribute should suffice, thus:

```
S_SINCE { S#, SNAME, STATUS, CITY, SINCE }
```

If we try stating the predicate for this design, however, it is easy to see what is wrong with it:

Since day SINCE, all four of the following have been true:

a. *Supplier S# has been under contract.*

b. *Supplier S# has been named SNAME.*

c. *Supplier S# has had status STATUS.*

d. *Supplier S# has been located in city CITY.*

For example, suppose the relvar currently includes the following tuple:

S#	SNAME	STATUS	CITY	SINCE
S1	Smith	20	London	*d04*

Suppose too that today is day 10 and that, effective from today, the status of supplier S1 is to be changed to 30, and so we replace the tuple just shown by this one:

S#	SNAME	STATUS	CITY	SINCE
S1	Smith	30	London	*d10*

Now we have lost (among other things) the information that supplier S1 has been located in London since day 4. More generally, it should be clear that this design is incapable of representing any information about a current supplier that predates the time of the most recent update to that supplier (speaking somewhat loosely). Informally, the problem is that the timestamp attribute SINCE "timestamps too much"; in effect, it timestamps a combination of *four different propositions* (supplier is under contract, supplier has name, supplier has status, supplier has city), instead of just a single proposition. In our preferred design, by contrast, each proposition has its own timestamp.

Vertical Decomposition

Of course, even with the four separate "since" attributes, relvar S_SINCE is only *semi-temporal*, which is why we need the "during" relvars as well, in order to represent historical information. But why is vertical decomposition necessary for that historical information? In order to examine this question, suppose, contrariwise, that we had just one "during" relvar that looked like this:

```
S_DURING { S#, SNAME, STATUS, CITY, DURING }
```

Here is the predicate:

> *During interval DURING, all four of the following were true:*
> a. *Supplier S# was under contract.*
> b. *Supplier S# was named SNAME.*
> c. *Supplier S# had status STATUS.*
> d. *Supplier S# was located in city CITY.*

As with the version of relvar S_SINCE with just one "since" attribute in the previous subsection, it should be immediately clear from this predicate that the relvar is not very well designed. For suppose it currently includes the following tuple:

S#	SNAME	STATUS	CITY	DURING
S2	Jones	10	Paris	[*d02:d04*]

Suppose too that we now learn that (a) the status of supplier S2 was indeed 10 on days 2 and 3 but became 15 on day 4, and (b) supplier S2 was indeed in Paris on days 3 and 4 but should have been in London on day 2. Then we have to make a rather complicated set of updates to the relvar in order to reflect these real-world changes. To be specific, we have to replace the existing tuple by *three* tuples that look like this:

S#	SNAME	STATUS	CITY	DURING
S2	Jones	10	London	[*d02*:*d02*]

S#	SNAME	STATUS	CITY	DURING
S2	Jones	10	Paris	[*d03*:*d03*]

S#	SNAME	STATUS	CITY	DURING
S2	Jones	15	Paris	[*d04*:*d04*]

Observe now that we are taking two separate tuples instead of one to say that the status was 10 during the interval [*d02*:*d03*], and two separate tuples instead of one to say that the city was Paris during the interval [*d03*:*d04*].

As this example suggests, the task of updating relvar S_DURING to reflect real-world changes is, in general, not entirely straightforward. Again the problem is basically that the timestamp attribute (now DURING) "timestamps too much"; again, in fact, it timestamps a combination of four different propositions. The solution is to separate the four propositions out into four separate relvars, thus:

```
S_DURING          { S#, DURING }
                  KEY { S#, DURING }

S_NAME_DURING     { S#, SNAME, DURING }
                  KEY { S#, DURING }

S_STATUS_DURING   { S#, STATUS, DURING }
                  KEY { S#, DURING }

S_CITY_DURING     { S#, CITY, DURING }
                  KEY { S#, DURING }
```

Relvar S_DURING shows which suppliers were under contract when; relvar S_NAME_DURING shows which suppliers had which name when; relvar S_STATUS_DURING shows which suppliers had which status when; and relvar S_CITY_DURING shows which suppliers were located in which city when.

Sixth Normal Form

The foregoing vertical decomposition is very reminiscent, in both rationale and effect, of classical normalization, and it is worth taking a moment to examine the similarities in a little more depth. In fact, of course, vertical decomposition is exactly what classical normalization theory has always been concerned with; the decomposition operator in that theory is *projection* (which is a vertical decomposition operator by definition), and the corresponding recomposition operator is *join*. Indeed, as we saw in Chapter 13, the ultimate normal form with respect to classical normalization theory, fifth normal form or 5NF, is sometimes called *projection-join normal form* for these very reasons. *Note:* Since these remarks are concerned with classical normalization specifically, the references to projection and join must be understood to mean the classical versions of those operators, not the generalized versions introduced in Section 23.5.

Now, even before temporal data was studied, some researchers (see, e.g., reference [14.21]) argued in favor of decomposing relvars as far as possible, instead of just as far as classical normalization would require. The general idea was to reduce relvars to **irreducible components** [14.21], meaning no further nonloss decomposition was possible. In the case of a nontemporal relvar, the argument in favor of "decomposing all the way" is not very strong; but it is much stronger in the case of a relvar like S_DURING from the previous subsection (first version, with just one "during" attribute). A supplier's name, status, and city vary independently over time. Moreover, they probably vary at different rates as well. For example, it might be that a supplier's name hardly ever changes, while that same supplier's location changes occasionally and the corresponding status changes quite often. Besides, the name history, status history, and city history of a supplier are probably all more interesting and more digestible concepts than the concept of a combined "name-status-city" history; hence our proposed vertical decomposition.

Recall now that 5NF is based on what are called *join dependencies* (JDs). Just to remind you, relvar *R* satisfies the JD $* \{A,B, ...,Z\}$ (where *A*, *B*, ..., *Z* are subsets of the attributes of *R*) if and only if every legal value of *R* is equal to the join of its projections on *A*, *B*, ..., *Z*—that is, if and only if *R* can be nonloss-decomposed into those projections. Now, since we have generalized the definition of join, we can generalize the definition of JD accordingly—and then we can define a new ("sixth") normal form, based on that generalized JD notion. Here are the definitions:

- Let *R* be a relvar, let *A*, *B*, ..., *Z* be subsets of the attributes of *R*, and let *ACL* be a commalist of interval-valued attributes of *R*. Then we say that *R* satisfies the generalized **join dependency** (JD):

  ```
  USING ( ACL ) * { A, B, ..., Z }
  ```

  if and only if the expression

  ```
  USING ( ACL ) ◄ R = R' ►
  ```

  —where *R'* is the U_join of the U_projections of *R* on *A*, *B*, ..., *Z*, and the U_join and U_projections in question all involve a USING specification of the form USING (*ACL*)—is true for every legal value of *R*. *Note:* We are tacitly appealing here to the fact that U_join, like join, is associative, meaning we can speak unambiguously of "the" U_join of any number of relations. Note too that to say that the foregoing expression is true is to say that *R* and *R'* are *equivalent* (with respect to *ACL*)—see the discussion of this concept at the very end of Section 23.4.

- A relvar *R* is in **sixth normal form** (6NF) if and only if it satisfies no nontrivial join dependencies at all—where a join dependency is **trivial** if and only if at least one of the projections (possibly U_projections) involved is over all of the attributes of the relvar concerned.

It is immediate from this definition that every relvar that is in 6NF is also in 5NF. It is also immediate that a given relvar is in 6NF if and only if it is *irreducible* in the sense explained earlier.

Now, the version of relvar S_DURING that had attributes S#, SNAME, STATUS, CITY, and DURING is not in 6NF by this definition, because:

a. It satisfies the generalized join dependency USING DURING * {SND,STD,SCD} (where the name "SND" refers to the set of attributes {S#,SNAME,DURING}, and similarly for the names "STD" and "SCD").

b. That join dependency is definitely nontrivial.

We therefore recommend that it be decomposed into 6NF projections as discussed in the previous subsection.

Note: You might have noticed in the foregoing example that it would be sufficient to decompose into just three 6NF relvars, not four—relvar S_DURING, with attributes S# and DURING, is strictly unnecessary in the decomposition, since it is at all times equal to the (generalized) projection on S# and DURING of any of the other three relvars. Nevertheless, we still prefer to include S_DURING in our overall design, partly just for reasons of completeness, and partly because such inclusion avoids a certain degree of awkwardness and arbitrariness that would otherwise occur [23.4].

"The Moving Point *Now*"

We return briefly to the question of horizontal decomposition (i.e., the separation into "since" and "during" relvars). We obviously cannot have "since" relvars only, because such relvars are merely semitemporal and cannot represent historical information. However, we *could* have "during" relvars only—but only if we have no objection to our database telling lies, as we now explain.

Consider the case of a supplier whose contract has not yet terminated. Of course, it is possible that we know when that contract is supposed to terminate; more generally, however, all we can say is that the contract is *open-ended* (think of a typical employment contract, for example). In a "during" relvar, therefore, whatever we specify as the END (DURING) value for such a supplier is likely to be incorrect. Of course, we could, and probably would, adopt the convention that such END(DURING) values should be specified as the *last day* (i.e., the value returned by LAST_DATE()).[10] But note that this scheme means that if "the last day" appears in the result of a query, then the user will probably have to interpret that value as *until further notice,* not as the last day *per se.* In other words, to say that END(DURING) for such a supplier is "the last day" is almost certainly a lie.

Precisely in order to avoid having to tell such lies, some writers—see, for example, reference [23.2]—have proposed the use of a special "NOW marker" to denote what in Section 23.1 we called the moving point *now* (in other words, to stand for *until further notice*). The basic idea is to permit that special marker to appear wherever both (a) a value

---

[10] Of course, we can replace that artificial value by the true value when the true value later becomes known.

of the applicable point type is permitted and (b) the intended interpretation is indeed *until further notice.* Thus, for example, relvar S_DURING might include, say, a tuple for supplier S1 with a DURING value of [*d04*:NOW] instead of [*d04:d99*]. (We are assuming here that day 99 is the last day and that the particular appearance of *d99* shown is indeed meant to stand for *until further notice* and not for day 99 *per se.*)

In our opinion, however, the introduction of the NOW marker represents an incautious departure from sound relational principles. Noting that NOW is really a *variable,* we observe that the approach involves the very strange—we would say logically indefensible—notion of *values* (interval values, to be specific) that contain *variables.*[11] Here are some examples of the kinds of questions that arise from the concept of NOW that you might care to ponder over:

- Let *i* be the interval [NOW:*d14*], let *t* be a tuple containing *i,* and let today be day 10. Then tuple *t* can be thought of as a kind of shorthand for five separate tuples containing the unit intervals [*d10:d10*], [*d11:d11*], [*d12:d12*], [*d13:d13*], and [*d14:d14*], respectively. But when the clock reaches midnight on day 10, the first of these tuples is (in effect) automatically deleted! Likewise for day 11, day 12, and day 13 . . . and what exactly happens at midnight on day 14?
- What is the result of the comparison *d99* = NOW?
- What is the value of "NOW+1" or "NOW−1"?
- If *i1* and *i2* are the intervals [*d01*:NOW] and [*d06:d07*], respectively, do they meet or overlap?
- What is the result of unpacking a relation containing a tuple in which the interval attribute on which the unpacking is to be done has the value [*d04*:NOW]?
- What is the cardinality of the set {[*d01*:NOW],[*d01:d04*]}?

And so on (this is not an exhaustive list). We believe it is hard to give coherent answers to questions like these; clearly, we would prefer an approach that does not rely on any such suspect notions as NOW and values that contain variables. And it is precisely an argument in favor of horizontal decomposition that NOW is not needed.

23.7 INTEGRITY CONSTRAINTS

In this section we turn our attention to the question of the integrity constraints that apply to temporal data. In Section 23.2, we saw how difficult it was, in the absence of proper interval support, even to formulate such constraints correctly; now we will see how the concepts introduced in preceding sections can alleviate the problem.

For definiteness, we focus until further notice on relvar S_STATUS_DURING from the previous section, with definition as follows:

```
S_STATUS_DURING { S#, STATUS, DURING }
             KEY { S#, DURING }
```

---

[11] Indeed, NOW resembles NULL, inasmuch as NULL too leads to the notion of values that contain something that is not a value (see Chapter 19).

We now proceed to examine, in the next three subsections, three general problems that can occur with temporal relvars like this one. We refer to those problems as *the redundancy problem, the circumlocution problem,* and *the contradiction problem,* respectively.

The Redundancy Problem

The KEY constraint for relvar S_STATUS_DURING, though logically correct, is inadequate in a sense. To be specific, it fails to prevent the relvar from containing, for example, both of the following tuples at the same time:

S#	STATUS	DURING
S4	25	[d05:d06]

S#	STATUS	DURING
S4	25	[d06:d07]

As you can see, these two tuples display a certain **redundancy**, inasmuch as the status for supplier S4 on day 6 is effectively stated twice. Clearly, it would be better to replace them by the following single tuple:

S#	STATUS	DURING
S4	25	[d05:d07]

Observe now that if the two original tuples were the only tuples in some two-tuple relation and we packed that relation on DURING, we would wind up with a one-tuple relation containing the single tuple just shown. Loosely speaking, therefore, we might say the tuple just shown is a "packed" tuple, obtained by packing the two original tuples on attribute DURING (we say "loosely speaking" because packing really applies to relations, not tuples). So what we want to do is replace those two original tuples by that "packed" tuple. In fact, as pointed out in Section 23.2, *not* performing that replacement—that is, permitting both original tuples to appear—would be almost as bad as permitting duplicate tuples to appear (duplicate tuples, if allowed, would also constitute a kind of redundancy). Indeed, if both original tuples did appear, the relvar would be in violation of its own predicate! For example, the tuple on the right says among other things that supplier S4 did *not* have status 25 on the day immediately before day 6. But then the tuple on the left says among other things that supplier S4 *did* have status 25 on day 5, and of course day 5 is the day immediately before day 6.

The Circumlocution Problem

The KEY constraint for relvar S_STATUS_DURING is inadequate in another way also. To be specific, it fails to prevent the relvar from containing, for example, both of the following tuples at the same time:

S#	STATUS	DURING
S4	25	[d05:d05]

S#	STATUS	DURING
S4	25	[d06:d07]

Here there is no redundancy as such, but there is a certain **circumlocution**, inasmuch as we are taking two tuples to say what could be better said with just a single "packed" tuple (the same one as before, in fact):

S#	STATUS	DURING
S4	25	[d05:d07]

Indeed, not replacing the two original tuples by that "packed" tuple would mean, again, that the relvar would be in violation of its own predicate, as can easily be confirmed.

Fixing the Redundancy and Circumlocution Problems

It should be clear that, in order to avoid redundancies and circumlocutions like those we have been discussing, what we need to do is enforce a constraint—let us call it Constraint A—along the following lines:

> *Constraint A:* If at any given time relvar S_STATUS_DURING contains two distinct tuples that are identical except for their DURING values *i1* and *i2,* then *i1* MERGES *i2* must be false.

Recall that, loosely speaking, MERGES is the logical OR of OVERLAPS and MEETS: Replacing it by OVERLAPS in Constraint A gives the constraint we need to enforce in order to avoid the redundancy problem, and replacing it by MEETS gives the constraint we need to enforce in order to avoid the circumlocution problem.

It should be clear too that there is a very simple way to enforce Constraint A: namely, by keeping the relvar packed at all times on attribute DURING. Let us therefore invent a new PACKED ON constraint that can appear in a relvar definition, as here:

```
VAR S_STATUS_DURING BASE RELATION
   { S# S#, STATUS INTEGER, DURING INTERVAL_DATE }
   PACKED ON DURING
   KEY { S#, DURING } ;
```

PACKED ON DURING here is a constraint—a relvar constraint, in fact, in terms of the classification scheme described in Chapter 9—on relvar S_STATUS_DURING. It is interpreted as follows: Relvar S_STATUS_DURING must at all times be kept packed on DURING. This special syntax thus suffices to solve the redundancy and circumlocution problems; in other words, it solves the problem exemplified by the constraint we referred to as Constraint XFT1 in Section 23.2.

The Contradiction Problem

The PACKED ON and KEY constraints are still not fully adequate, even when taken together. To be specific, they fail to prevent the relvar from containing, for example, both of the following tuples at the same time:

S#	STATUS	DURING
S4	10	[d04:d06]

S#	STATUS	DURING
S4	25	[d05:d07]

Here supplier S4 is shown as having a status of both 10 and 25 on days 5 and 6—clearly an impossible state of affairs. In other words, we have a **contradiction** on our hands; in fact, the relvar is in violation of its own predicate once again, because each supplier is supposed to have exactly one status on any given day.

Fixing the Contradiction Problem

It should be clear that, in order to avoid contradictions like the one just discussed, what we need to do is enforce a constraint—let us call it Constraint B—along the following lines:

> *Constraint B:* If at any given time relvar S_STATUS_DURING contains two tuples that have the same S# value but differ on their STATUS value, then their DURING values *i1* and *i2* must be such that *i1* OVERLAPS *i2* is false.

Note carefully that—as we have already seen—Constraint B is obviously not enforced by the mere fact that the relvar is kept packed on DURING. Even more obviously, it is also not enforced by the mere fact that {S#,DURING} is a candidate key. But suppose the relvar were kept unpacked at all times on attribute DURING (we ignore for the moment the fact that this supposition is actually an impossibility, given that we have already stipulated that the relvar is to be kept packed on DURING). Then:

- All DURING values in that unpacked form would be unit intervals and would thus effectively correspond to individual time points.

- The sole candidate key for that unpacked form would thus still be {S#,DURING}, because any given supplier under contract at any given time has just one status at that time.

It follows that if we were to enforce the constraint that {S#,DURING} is a candidate key for the unpacked form UNPACK S_STATUS_DURING ON DURING, then we would be enforcing Constraint B *a fortiori*. Let us therefore invent a new WHEN/THEN constraint that can appear in a relvar definition wherever a simple KEY constraint can appear, as here:

```
VAR S_STATUS_DURING BASE RELATION
  { S# S#, STATUS INTEGER, DURING INTERVAL_DATE }
  PACKED ON DURING
  WHEN UNPACKED ON DURING THEN KEY { S#, DURING }
  KEY { S#, DURING } ;
```

WHEN UNPACKED ON DURING THEN KEY {S#,DURING} here is a constraint—a relvar constraint again, like the PACKED ON constraint discussed earlier—on relvar S_STATUS_DURING. It is interpreted as follows: Relvar S_STATUS_DURING must at all times be such that no two tuples in the result of the expression UNPACK S_STATUS_DURING ON DURING have the same value for the attribute combination {S#,DURING} (loosely, "{S#,DURING} is a candidate key for UNPACK S_STATUS_DURING ON DURING"). This special syntax thus suffices to solve the contradiction problem.

U_keys

There is much more that could be said about KEY, PACKED ON, and WHEN/THEN constraints [23.4]; for space reasons, however, we content ourselves with the following. First, we propose that the definition of any given relvar *R* be allowed to include a shorthand specification of the form:

```
USING ( ACL ) KEY { K }
```

ACL and *K* here are both commalists of attribute names, where every attribute mentioned in *ACL* must also be mentioned in *K* (and, as usual, the parentheses can be omitted if *ACL* contains just one attribute name). The specification is defined to be shorthand for the combination of the following three constraints:

```
PACKED ON ( ACL )
WHEN UNPACKED ON ( ACL ) THEN KEY { K }
KEY { K }
```

We refer to {*K*} as a "U_key" for short (but see later). Using this shorthand, the definition of relvar S_STATUS_DURING, for example, can be simplified to just:

```
VAR S_STATUS_DURING BASE RELATION
  { S# S#, STATUS INTEGER, DURING INTERVAL_DATE }
  USING DURING KEY { S#, DURING } ;
```

Suppose now that within the U_key specification for relvar *R* the commalist of attribute names *ACL* is empty, thus:

```
USING ( ) KEY { K }
```

By definition, this specification is shorthand for the combination of constraints:

```
PACKED ON ( )
WHEN UNPACKED ON ( ) THEN KEY { K }
KEY { K }
```

In other words:

1. Relvar *R* must be kept packed on no attributes at all. But packing a relation *r* on no attributes at all simply returns *r*, so the implicit PACKED ON specification has no effect.

2. Relvar *R* must be such that if it is unpacked on no attributes at all, then {*K*} is a candidate key for the result. But unpacking a relation *r* on no attributes at all simply returns *r*, so the implicit WHEN/THEN specification simply means that {*K*} is a candidate key for *R*, and the implicit KEY constraint is thus redundant.

It follows that we can take a regular KEY constraint of the form KEY {*K*} to be shorthand for a certain U_key constraint: namely, one of the form USING () KEY {*K*}. In other words, regular KEY constraints are essentially just a special case of our proposed new syntax! So if we redefine the syntax of a regular KEY constraint thus—

```
[ USING ( ACL ) ] KEY { K }
```

—and allow the USING specification to be omitted if and only if *ACL* is empty, then we have no need to talk about U_keys at all; all candidate keys effectively become U_keys, and we can generalize the meaning of "candidate key" (or just "key") accordingly. And so we will.

Without going into details, we claim that analogous generalizations apply to the *foreign* key concept as well. One consequence is that a specification of the form

```
USING DURING FOREIGN KEY { S#, DURING }
              REFERENCES S_DURING
```

(part of the definition of relvar S_STATUS_DURING) can be used to enforce the constraint that if relvar S_STATUS_DURING shows some supplier as having some status during some interval of time, then relvar S_DURING shows that same supplier as being under contract during that same interval of time. And a similar approach can be used to solve the problem exemplified by the constraint we referred to as Constraint XFT3 in Section 23.2—and so we have now achieved another of our original goals: namely, we have found a better way of formulating the constraints discussed in that earlier section.

The Nine Requirements

We close this section by observing that there is considerably more to the question of constraints on a temporal database than we have suggested so far. Reference [23.4] presents a careful and detailed analysis of the overall problem; to be specific, it considers, in very general terms, a set of nine requirements that we might want a typical temporal database like the suppliers-and-shipments database to satisfy. We list those requirements here:

- *Requirement R1:* If the database shows supplier Sx as being under contract on day d, then it must contain exactly one tuple that shows that fact.

- *Requirement R2:* If the database shows supplier Sx as being under contract on days d and $d+1$, then it must contain exactly one tuple that shows that fact.

- *Requirement R3:* If the database shows supplier Sx as being under contract on day d, then it must also show supplier Sx as having some status on day d.

- *Requirement R4:* If the database shows supplier Sx as having some status on day d, then it must contain exactly one tuple that shows that fact.

- *Requirement R5:* If the database shows supplier Sx as having the same status on days d and $d+1$, then it must contain exactly one tuple that shows that fact.

- *Requirement R6:* If the database shows supplier Sx as having some status on day d, then it must also show supplier Sx as being under contract on day d.

- *Requirement R7:* If the database shows supplier Sx as able to supply some specific part Py on day d, then it must contain exactly one tuple that shows that fact.

- *Requirement R8:* If the database shows supplier Sx as able to supply the same part Py on days d and $d+1$, then it must contain exactly one tuple that shows that fact.

- *Requirement R9:* If the database shows supplier Sx as able to supply some part Py on day d, then it must also show supplier Sx as being under contract on day d.

Reference [23.4] analyzes these nine requirements in depth and shows how they can be formulated in a relationally complete language like **Tutorial D**. We omit further discussion here.

23.8 SUMMARY

There is a growing requirement for databases (especially "data warehouses") to contain temporal data. Temporal data can be regarded as an encoded representation of **time-stamped propositions**. The propositions in question make use of the prepositions **since** (for current data) and **during** (for historical data), and we assigned very precise meanings to those two terms. To be specific, we take *since* to mean **ever since and not immediately before** the specified point in time, and *during* to mean **throughout and not immediately before or immediately after** the specified interval.

Next, we introduced a very simple running example (suppliers and shipments) and proceeded (a) to semitemporalize it by adding SINCE attributes and then (b) to temporalize it fully by adding FROM and TO attributes. And we saw that both of those designs led to considerable complexity in the formulation of constraints and queries. We therefore introduced the idea of dealing with **intervals** as values in their own right. To be specific, we defined the concept of a **point type** and an **INTERVAL type generator**, and we discussed the corresponding **interval selector** and **BEGIN** and **END** operators. We then went on to define many more operators for points and intervals, including **Allen's operators** and interval **UNION, INTERSECT,** and **MINUS** operators.

Next, we defined two extremely important relational operators called **PACK** and **UNPACK** (using two simpler operators on unary relations called **COLLAPSE** and **EXPAND** as a stepping-stone on the way). EXPAND and UNPACK allow us to focus on the information content of their relational argument at an atomic level, without having to worry about the many different ways in which that information might be bundled into "clumps." Similarly, COLLAPSE and PACK allow us to focus on the information content of their relational argument in a compressed ("clumped") form, without having to worry about the possibility that distinct "clumps" might meet or overlap. We showed how PACK and UNPACK can be used to simplify the formulation of temporal queries. We also used them as a basis for defining **generalized** or "U_" versions of the familiar relational operators (U_JOIN, U_MINUS, U_project, and so on). And we showed that those familiar relational operators are in fact all just special cases of the generalized versions.

Next, we examined certain **database design** issues and recommended (a) **horizontal decomposition** in order to separate current and historical information and (b) **vertical decomposition** in order to separate information regarding different "properties" of the same "entity" (speaking very loosely). In fact, we defined a new normal form, **6NF**.

Then we considered certain problems that temporal data might suffer from in the absence of appropriate integrity constraints—to be specific, the **redundancy, circumlocution,** and **contradiction** problems—and we showed how the **PACKED ON** and **WHEN/THEN** constraints could be used to address those problems. We defined a generalized version of the familiar KEY constraint called **U_key constraints**, and then showed that the familiar KEY constraint is in fact just a special case of the generalized version.

We close with two final remarks:

- We remind you that everything we have introduced in this chapter, apart from the INTERVAL type generator, is in the last analysis only shorthand for something that can already be expressed in the relational model.

- Our recommended design approach (horizontal decomposition in particular) does have the implication that queries—and updates too, if applicable—often span relvars and can thus be somewhat complicated. Reference [23.4] includes a series of proposals for further shorthands to alleviate these difficulties, too.

EXERCISES

23.1 What is a time quantum? What is a time point? What do you understand by the term *granularity?*

23.2 Define the terms *point type* and *interval type*.

23.3 List as many advantages as you can in favor of replacing FROM-TO attribute pairs by individual DURING attributes.

23.4 Let *i* be a value of type INTERVAL_INTEGER. Write an expression denoting the interval resulting from extending *i* by its own length in both directions (e.g., [5:7] becomes [2:10]). In what circumstances will evaluation of your expression fail at run time?

23.5 Again, let *i* be a value of type INTERVAL_INTEGER. Write an expression denoting the interval representing the middle third of *i*. You can assume that COUNT(*i*) is a multiple of three.

23.6 Let *i1, i2,* and *i3* be intervals such that there is a single interval *i4* consisting of every point *p* such that $p \in i1$ or $p \in i2$ or $p \in i3$. Write an expression that when evaluated yields *i4*.

23.7 If *a* and *b* are relations (or sets), then it is a fact that:

```
a INTERSECT b  ≡  a MINUS ( a MINUS b )
```

Is the same true if *a* and *b* are intervals?

23.8 Give examples of (a) a relation with two interval attributes (temporal or otherwise); (b) a relation with three; (c) a relation consisting of interval attributes only.

23.9 Consider a relation *r* with two distinct interval attributes A1 and A2. Prove or disprove the following assertions:

```
UNPACK (UNPACK r ON A1) ON A2  ≡  UNPACK (UNPACK r ON A2) ON A1

PACK (PACK r ON A1) ON A2      ≡  PACK (PACK r ON A2) ON A1
```

23.10 We are given the following relvars:

```
FEDERAL_GOVT { PRESIDENT, PARTY, DURING }
STATE_GOVT   { GOVERNOR, STATE, PARTY, DURING }
```

The semantics are meant to be self-explanatory (the two DURING attributes are each assumed to be of type INTERVAL_DATE; we ignore the fact that presidential and gubernatorial administrations are usually expressed in terms of years, not days). Now suppose we want to obtain a result looking like this:

```
RESULT { PRESIDENT, GOVERNOR, STATE, PARTY, DURING }
```

A tuple is to appear in this result if and only if the specified president and specified state governor both belong to the specified party and have overlapping periods of administration (and DURING specifies exactly the overlap in question). Write a suitable expression to obtain this result.

23.11   Can you think of an example of a relvar with an interval attribute that you would not want to keep in packed form?

23.12   Give a U_INTERSECT example in which the result has cardinality greater than that of either of the relations being "U_intersected."

23.13   Consider the operator U_JOIN. Assume for simplicity that the packing and unpacking is to be done on the basis of a single attribute *A*. Confirm that the following identity holds:

```
USING A ◄ r1 JOIN r2 ►
≡  WITH   ( r1 RENAME A AS X ) AS T1 ,
          ( r2 RENAME A AS Y ) AS T2 ,
          ( T1 JOIN T2 ) AS T3 ,
          ( T3 WHERE X OVERLAPS Y ) AS T4 ,
          ( EXTEND T4 ADD ( X INTERSECT Y ) AS A ) AS T5 ,
          T5 { ALL BUT X, Y } AS T6 :
     PACK T6 ON A
```

Confirm also that if *r1* and *r2* are both initially packed on *A*, then the final PACK step is unnecessary. *Note:* The INTERSECT operator in the EXTEND step here is the *interval* INTERSECT, not the relational one.

23.14   Define 6NF. Is it really fair to think of that normal form as "sixth" in the same kind of way that 5NF is fifth?

23.15   "The moving point *now*" is not a value but a variable. Discuss.

23.16   Given the design for shipments in Section 23.2, write **Tutorial D** expressions for the following queries:

a.   Get supplier numbers for suppliers who are currently able to supply at least two different parts, showing in each case the date since when they have been able to do so.

b.   Get supplier numbers for suppliers who are currently unable to supply at least two different parts, showing in each case the date since when they have been unable to do so.

23.17   Explain the redundancy, circumlocution, and contradiction problems in your own words.

23.18   Explain in your own words (a) PACKED ON constraints, (b) WHEN/THEN constraints, (c) U_key constraints. Explain how classical keys can be regarded as a special case of U_keys.

REFERENCES AND BIBLIOGRAPHY

Rather than giving what could easily be a very lengthy list of references here, we draw your attention to the extensive bibliography in reference [23.4], *q.v.*

23.1   J. F. Allen: "Maintaining Knowledge About Temporal Intervals," *CACM 16,* No. 11 (November 1983).

23.2   James Clifford, Curtis Dyreson, Tomás Isakowitz, Christian S. Jensen, and Richard T. Snodgrass: "On the Semantics of 'Now' in Databases," *ACM TODS 22,* No. 2 (June 1997).

23.3   Hugh Darwen and C. J. Date: "An Overview and Analysis of Proposals Based on the TSQL2 Approach" (to appear; tentative title). A preliminary draft is available on the website *http://www.thethirdmanifesto.com*.

Of previously published proposals for dealing with the temporal database problem, TSQL2 [23.5] is probably the best known, and several other proposals have been based on it. This paper provides an overview and critical analysis of such proposals, comparing and contrasting them with the approach espoused in the present chapter.

23.4 C. J. Date, Hugh Darwen, and Nikos A. Lorentzos: *Temporal Data and the Relational Model.* San Francisco, Calif.: Morgan Kaufmann (2003).

The present chapter is heavily based on this book, but the book goes into much more detail and covers many topics not even mentioned in the body of this chapter. Such additional topics include:

- Further query operators and shorthands
- Update operators and shorthands
- "Valid time *vs.* transaction time"
- Implementation and optimization
- Cyclic point types
- Granularity and scale
- Continuous point types

and much more. One point worth mentioning is that the inheritance model discussed in Chapter 20 of the present book turns out to be crucial to the granularity issue (it provides the key to the problem of having two distinct successor functions—e.g., "next day" and "next month"—over the same point type).

23.5 Richard T. Snodgrass (ed.): *The Temporal Query Language TSQL2.* Dordrecht, Netherlands: Kluwer Academic Pub. (1995). See also R. T. Snodgrass *et al.*: "TSQL2 Language Specification," *ACM SIGMOD Record 23,* No. 1 (March 1994).

See the annotation to reference [23.3].

CHAPTER **24**

Logic-Based Databases

24.1   INTRODUCTION

In the mid 1980s or so, a significant trend began to emerge in the database research community toward **database systems that are based on logic**. Expressions such as *logic database, inferential DBMS, expert DBMS, deductive DBMS, knowledge base, knowledge base management system (KBMS), logic as a data model, recursive query processing,* and so on, began to appear in the research literature. However, it is not always easy to relate such terms and the ideas they represent to familiar database terms and concepts, nor to understand the motivation underlying the research from a traditional database perspective; in other words, there is a clear need for an explanation of all of this activity in terms of conventional database ideas and principles. This chapter is an attempt to meet that need. Our aim is to explain what logic-based systems are all about from the viewpoint of someone who is familiar with traditional database technology but perhaps not so much with logic as such. As each new idea from logic is introduced, therefore, we will explain it in conventional database terms, where possible or appropriate. (Of course, we have discussed certain ideas from logic in this book already, especially in our description of relational calculus in Chapter 8. Relational calculus is directly based on logic. However, there is more to logic-based systems than just the relational calculus, as we will see.)

The structure of the chapter is as follows. Following this introductory section, Section 24.2 provides a brief overview of the subject, with a little history. Sections 24.3 and 24.4 then provide an elementary (and very much simplified) treatment of *propositional calculus* and *predicate calculus,* respectively. Next, Section 24.5 introduces the so-called *proof-theoretic* view of a database, and Section 24.6 builds on the ideas of that section to explain what is meant by the term *deductive DBMS*. Section 24.7 then discusses some approaches to the problem of *recursive query processing*. Finally, Section 24.8 offers a summary and a few concluding remarks.

24.2 OVERVIEW

Research on the relationship between database theory and logic goes back to the late 1970s, if not earlier—see, for example, references [24.3], [24.4], and [24.8]. However, the principal stimulus for the recent considerable expansion of interest in the subject seems to have been the publication in 1984 of a landmark paper by Reiter [24.10]. In that paper, Reiter characterized the traditional perception of database systems as **model-theoretic**—by which he meant, loosely, that:

  a. The database at any given time can be seen as a set of explicit (i.e., base) relations, each containing a set of explicit tuples.

  b. Executing a query can be regarded as evaluating some specified *formula* (i.e., boolean expression) over those explicit relations and tuples.

Note: We will define the term *model-theoretic* more precisely in Section 24.5.

Reiter then went on to argue that an alternative **proof-theoretic** view was possible, and indeed preferable in certain respects. In that alternative view (again loosely speaking):

  a. The database at any given time is seen as a set of *axioms* ("ground" axioms, corresponding to values in domains[1] and tuples in base relations, plus certain "deductive" axioms, to be discussed).

  b. Executing a query is regarded as proving that some specified formula is a logical consequence of those axioms—in other words, proving it is a *theorem.*

Note: We will define the term *proof-theoretic* more precisely in Section 24.5 also—though it might help to point out right away that the proof-theoretic view is very close to our own characterization of a database as *a collection of true propositions.*

An example is in order. Consider the following relational calculus query against the usual suppliers-and-parts database:

```
SPX WHERE SPX.QTY > 250
```

---

[1] For consistency with other writings in this field, we use the term *domain* rather than our preferred term *type* in this chapter.

(SPX here is a range variable ranging over shipments.) In the traditional—that is, model-theoretic—interpretation, we examine the shipment tuples one by one, evaluating the formula "QTY > 250" for each in turn; the query result then consists of just those shipment tuples for which the formula evaluates to TRUE. In the proof-theoretic interpretation, by contrast, we consider the shipment tuples (plus certain other items) as *axioms* of a certain **logical theory**; we then apply certain theorem-proving techniques to determine for which possible values of the range variable SPX the formula "SPX.QTY > 250" is a logical consequence of those axioms within that theory. The query result then consists of just those particular values of SPX.

Of course, this example is extremely simple: so simple, in fact, that you might be having difficulty in seeing what the difference between the two interpretations really is. The point is, however, that the reasoning mechanism employed in the attempted proof (in the proof-theoretic interpretation) can be much more sophisticated than our simple example is able to convey; indeed, it can handle certain problems that are beyond the capabilities of classical relational systems, as we will see. Furthermore, the proof-theoretic interpretation carries with it an attractive set of additional features [24,10]:

- *Representational uniformity:* It lets us define a database language in which values in domains, tuples in base relations, "deductive axioms," queries, and integrity constraints are all represented in essentially the same uniform way.

- *Operational uniformity:* It provides a basis for a unified attack on a variety of apparently distinct problems, including query optimization (especially semantic optimization), integrity constraint enforcement, database design (dependency theory), program correctness proofs, and other problems.

- *Semantic modeling:* It offers a solid foundation on which to build a variety of "semantic" extensions to the basic model.

- *Extended application:* Finally, it provides a basis for dealing with certain issues that classical approaches have traditionally had difficulty with—for example, *disjunctive information* (e.g., "Supplier S5 supplies either part P1 or part P2, but it is not known which").

Deductive Axioms

We offer a brief and preliminary explanation of the concept, already mentioned a couple of times, of a *deductive axiom.* Basically, a **deductive axiom**—also known as a **rule of inference**—is a rule by which, given certain facts, we are able to deduce or infer additional facts. For example, given the facts "Anne is the mother of Betty" and "Betty is the mother of Celia," there is an obvious deductive axiom that allows us to deduce that Anne is the grandmother of Celia. To jump ahead of ourselves for a moment, therefore, we might imagine a **deductive DBMS** in which the two given facts are represented as tuples in a relation, thus:

MOTHER_OF	MOTHER	DAUGHTER
	Anne	Betty
	Betty	Celia

These two facts represent **ground axioms** for the system. Let us suppose also that the deductive axiom has been formally stated to the system somehow—for example, as follows:

```
IF MOTHER_OF ( x, y ) AND MOTHER_OF ( y, z )
THEN GRANDMOTHER_OF ( x, z )
END IF
```

(hypothetical and simplified syntax). Now the system can apply the rule expressed in the deductive axiom to the data represented by the ground axioms, in a manner to be explained in Section 24.4, to deduce the result GRANDMOTHER_OF (Anne,Celia). Thus, users can ask queries such as "Who is the grandmother of Celia?" or "Who are the granddaughters of Anne?" (or, more precisely, "Who is Anne the grandmother of?").

Let us now try to relate the foregoing ideas to traditional database concepts. In traditional terms, the deductive axiom can be thought of as a *view definition*—for example:

```
VAR GRANDMOTHER_OF VIEW
   { MX.MOTHER AS GRANDMOTHER, MY.DAUGHTER AS GRANDDAUGHTER }
     WHERE MX.DAUGHTER = MY.MOTHER ;
```

(We deliberately use a relational calculus style here; MX and MY are range variables ranging over MOTHER_OF.) Queries such as the ones mentioned previously can now be framed in terms of this view:

```
GX.GRANDMOTHER WHERE GX.GRANDDAUGHTER = NAME ('Celia')

GX.GRANDDAUGHTER WHERE GX.GRANDMOTHER = NAME ('Anne')
```

(GX is a range variable ranging over GRANDMOTHER_OF.)

So far, therefore, all we have really done is presented a different syntax and different interpretation for material that is already familiar. However, we will see in later sections that there are in fact some significant differences, not illustrated by these simple examples, between logic-based systems and more traditional DBMSs.

24.3   PROPOSITIONAL CALCULUS

In this section and the next, we present a very brief introduction to some of the basic ideas of logic. The present section considers *propositional calculus* and the next considers *predicate calculus*. We remark immediately, however, that as far as we are concerned, propositional calculus is not all that important as an end in itself; the major aim of the present section is really just to pave the way for an understanding of the next one. The aim of the two sections taken together is to provide a basis on which to build in the rest of the chapter.

You are assumed to be familiar with the basic concepts of boolean algebra. For purposes of reference, we state certain laws of boolean algebra that we will be needing later on:

- *Distributive laws:*

```
f AND ( g OR  h )  ≡  ( f AND g )  OR  ( f AND h )
f OR  ( g AND h )  ≡  ( f OR  g )  AND ( f OR  h )
```

- *De Morgan's laws:*

```
NOT ( f AND g )  ≡  ( NOT f )  OR  ( NOT g )
NOT ( f OR  g )  ≡  ( NOT f )  AND ( NOT g )
```

Here *f, g,* and *h* are arbitrary boolean expressions.

Now we turn to logic *per se.* Logic can be defined as **a formal method of reasoning**. Because it is formal, it can be used to perform formal tasks, such as testing the validity of an argument by examining just the structure of that argument as a sequence of steps (i.e., without paying any attention to the meaning of those steps). In particular, because it is formal, it can be *mechanized*—that is, it can be programmed, and thus applied by the machine.

Propositional calculus and predicate calculus are two special cases of logic in general (in fact, the former is a subset of the latter). The term *calculus,* in turn is just a general term that refers to any system of symbolic computation; in the particular cases at hand, the kind of computation involved is the computation of the truth value—TRUE or FALSE—of certain formulas or expressions.

Terms

We begin by assuming that we have some collection of objects, called **constants**, about which we can make statements of various kinds. In database parlance, the *constants* are the values in the underlying domains, and a *statement* might be, for example, a boolean expression such as "3 > 2". We define a **term** as a statement that involves such constants[2] and:

a. Either does not involve any boolean operators (see the next subsection) or is enclosed in parentheses

b. Evaluates unequivocally to either TRUE or FALSE

For example, "Supplier S1 is located in London," "Supplier S2 is located in London," and "Supplier S1 supplies part P1" are all terms (they evaluate to TRUE, FALSE, and TRUE, respectively, given our usual sample data values). By contrast, "Supplier S1 supplies part *p*" (where *p* is a variable) and "Supplier S5 will supply part P1 at some time in the future" are not terms, because they do not evaluate to either TRUE or FALSE unequivocally.

Formulas

Next, we define the concept of a **formula**. Formulas of the propositional calculus—and, more generally, of the *predicate* calculus—are used in database systems in the formulation of queries (among many other things).

```
<formula>
    ::=     <term>
          | NOT <term>
          | <term> AND <formula>
          | <term> OR <formula>
          | <term> ⇒ <formula>

<term>
    ::=     <atomic formula>
          | ( <formula> )
```

---

[2] More accurately, *names* of such constants, or in other words literals. The distinction is blurred in much of the literature.

Formulas are evaluated in accordance with the truth values of their constituent terms and the usual truth tables for the boolean operators (AND, OR, etc.). Points arising:

1. An *<atomic formula>* is a boolean expression that involves no boolean operators and is not contained in parentheses.

2. The symbol "⇒" represents the boolean operator known as **logical implication**. The expression $f \Rightarrow g$ is defined to be logically equivalent to the expression (NOT f) OR g. *Note:* We used "IF . . . THEN . . . END IF" for this operator in Chapter 8 and other earlier chapters.

3. We adopt the usual precedence rules for the boolean operators (NOT, then AND, then OR, then ⇒) in order to reduce the number of parentheses needed to express a desired order of evaluation.

4. A **proposition** is just a *<formula>* as already defined (we use the term *formula* for consistency with the next section).

Rules of Inference

Now we come to the **rules of inference** for the propositional calculus. Many such rules exist. Each is a statement of the form

$$\models\ f \Rightarrow g$$

(where f and g are formulas, and the symbol $\models$ can be read as **it is always the case that**; note that we do need some such symbol in order to be able to make *metastatements*, i.e., statements about statements). Here are some examples of inference rules:

1. $\models$ (f AND g) ⇒ f
2. $\models f \Rightarrow$ (f OR g)
3. $\models$ (($f \Rightarrow g$) AND ($g \Rightarrow h$)) ⇒ ($f \Rightarrow h$)
4. $\models$ (f AND ($f \Rightarrow g$)) ⇒ g

Note: This one is particularly important. It is called the ***modus ponens*** rule. Informally, it says that if f is true and f implies g, then g must be true as well. For example, given the fact that formulas a and b are both true—

a. I have no money.

b. If I have no money then I will have to wash dishes.

—then we can infer that formula c is true as well:

c. I will have to wash dishes.

To continue with the inference rules:

5. $\models$ ($f \Rightarrow$ ($g \Rightarrow h$)) ⇒ ((f AND g) ⇒ h)
6. $\models$ ((f OR g) AND (NOT g OR h)) ⇒ (f OR h)

Note: This is another particularly important one. It is called the **resolution** rule. We will have more to say about it under "Proofs" immediately following, and again in Section 24.4.

Proofs

We now have the necessary apparatus for dealing with formal proofs (in the context of the propositional calculus). The problem of proof is the problem of determining whether some given formula *g* (the **conclusion**) is a logical consequence of some given set of formulas *f1, f2, ..., fn* (the **premises**[3])—in symbols:

```
f1, f2, ..., fn ⊢ g
```

(read as *g* **is deducible from** *f1, f2, ..., fn;* observe the use of another metalinguistic symbol, ⊢). The basic method of proceeding is known as **forward chaining**. Forward chaining consists of applying the rules of inference repeatedly to the premises, and to formulas deduced from those premises, and to formulas deduced from those formulas, and so on, until the conclusion is deduced; in other words, the process "chains forward" from the premises to the conclusion. However, there are several variations on this basic theme:

1. **Adopting a premise:** If *g* is of the form $p \Rightarrow q$, adopt *p* as an additional premise and show that *q* is deducible from the given premises plus *p*.

2. **Backward chaining:** Instead of trying to prove $p \Rightarrow q$, prove the **contrapositive** NOT $q \Rightarrow$ NOT *p*.

3. *Reductio ad absurdum:* Instead of trying to prove $p \Rightarrow q$ directly, assume that *p* and NOT *q* are both true and derive a contradiction.

4. **Resolution:** This method uses the resolution inference rule (Rule 6 in the list given earlier).

We discuss the resolution technique in some detail, since it is of wide applicability (in particular, it generalizes to the case of predicate calculus also, as we will see in Section 24.4).

Note first that the resolution rule is effectively a rule that allows us to *cancel subformulas*—that is, given the two formulas

```
f OR g          and          NOT g OR h
```

we can cancel *g* and NOT *g* to derive the simplified formula:

```
f OR h
```

In particular, given *f* OR *g* and NOT *g* (i.e., taking *h* as TRUE), we can derive *f*.

Observe, therefore, that the rule applies in general to a **conjunction** (AND) of two formulas, each of which is a **disjunction** (OR) of two formulas. In order to apply the resolution rule, therefore, we proceed as follows. (To make our discussion a little more concrete, we explain the process in terms of a specific example.) Suppose we wish to determine whether the following putative proof is in fact valid:

```
A ⇒ ( B ⇒ C ), NOT D OR A, B ⊢ D ⇒ C
```

---

[3] Also spelled **premisses** (singular *premiss*).

(where *A, B, C,* and *D* are formulas). We start by adopting the negation of the conclusion as an additional premise and then writing each premise on a separate line, as follows:

```
A ⇒ ( B ⇒ C )
NOT D OR A
B
NOT ( D ⇒ C )
```

These four lines are implicitly all "ANDed" together.

We now convert each individual line to **conjunctive normal form,** that is, a form consisting of one or more formulas all ANDed together, each individual formula containing (possibly) NOTs and ORs but no ANDs (see Chapter 18). Of course, the second and third lines are already in this form. In order to convert the other two lines, we first eliminate all appearances of "⇒" (using the definition of that operator in terms of NOT and OR); we then apply the distributive laws and De Morgan's laws as necessary (see the beginning of this section). We also drop redundant parentheses and pairs of adjacent NOTs (which cancel out). The four lines become:

```
NOT A OR NOT B OR C
NOT D OR A
B
D AND NOT C
```

Next, any line that includes any explicit ANDs we replace by a set of separate lines, one for each of the individual formulas ANDed together (dropping the ANDs in the process). In the example, this step applies to the fourth line only. The premises now look like this:

```
NOT A OR NOT B OR C
NOT D OR A
B
D
NOT C
```

Now we can start to apply the resolution rule. We choose a pair of lines that can be *resolved,* that is, a pair that contain some particular formula and the negation of that formula, respectively. Let us choose the first two lines, which contain NOT *A* and *A,* respectively, and resolve them, giving:

```
NOT D OR NOT B OR C
B
D
NOT C
```

Note: In general we also need to keep the two original lines, but in this particular example they will not be needed any more.

Now we apply the rule again, again choosing the first two lines (resolving NOT *B* and *B*), giving:

```
NOT D OR C
D
NOT C
```

We choose the first two lines again (NOT *D* and *D*):

```
C
NOT C
```

And once again (*C* and NOT *C*); the final result is the empty set of propositions (usually represented thus: []), which is interpreted by convention as a contradiction. By *reductio ad absurdum,* therefore, the desired result is proved.

24.4 PREDICATE CALCULUS

We now turn our attention to the *predicate* calculus. The big difference between propositional calculus and predicate calculus is that the latter allows formulas to contain variables[4] and quantifiers, which makes it much more powerful and of much wider applicability. For example, the statement "Supplier S1 supplies part *p*" and "Some supplier *s* supplies part *p*" are not legal formulas of the propositional calculus, but they are legal formulas of the predicate calculus. Hence, predicate calculus provides us with a basis for expressing queries such as "Which parts are supplied by supplier S1?" or "Get suppliers who supply some part" or even "Get suppliers who do not supply any parts at all."

Predicates

As explained in Chapter 3, a **predicate** is a *boolean function,* that is, a function that, given appropriate arguments for its parameters, returns either TRUE or FALSE. For example, "$>(x,y)$"—more conventionally written "$x > y$"—is a predicate with two parameters, *x* and *y;* it returns TRUE if the argument corresponding to *x* is greater than the argument corresponding to *y* and FALSE otherwise. A predicate that takes *n* arguments (i.e., equivalently, one that is defined in terms of *n* parameters) is called an *n*-place or *n*-adic predicate. A proposition (i.e., a formula in the sense of Section 24.3) can be regarded as a zero-place or niladic predicate—it has no parameters and evaluates to TRUE or FALSE, unequivocally.

It is convenient to assume that predicates corresponding to "=", ">", "≥", and so on, are built in (i.e., they are part of the formal system we are describing) and that expressions using them can be written in the conventional manner. However, users should be able to define their own predicates as well, of course. Indeed, that is the whole point: The fact is, in database terms, a user-defined predicate corresponds to a user-defined *relvar* (as we already know from earlier chapters). The suppliers relvar S, for example, can be regarded as a predicate with four parameters S#, SNAME, STATUS, and CITY. Furthermore, the expressions S(S1,Smith,20,London) and S(S6,White,45,Rome)—to adopt an obvious shorthand notation—represent "instances" or "instantiations" or "invocations" of that predicate that (given our usual sample set of values) evaluate to TRUE and FALSE, respectively. Informally, we can regard such predicates—together with any applicable *integrity constraints,* which are also predicates—as defining what the database "means," as explained in earlier parts of this book (in Chapter 9 in particular).

---

[4] More accurately, *names* of variables. The variables in question are *logic* variables, not programming language variables. You can think of them as range variables in the sense of Chapter 8.

Well-Formed Formulas

The next step is to extend the definition of *formula*. In order to avoid confusion with the formulas of the previous section (which are actually a special case), we now switch to the term *well-formed formula* (WFF, pronounced "weff") from Chapter 8. Here is a simplified syntax for WFFs:

```
<wff>
    ::=    <term>
         | NOT ( <wff> )
         | ( <wff> ) AND ( <wff> )
         | ( <wff> ) OR ( <wff> )
         | ( <wff> ) ⇒ ( <wff> )
         | EXISTS <var name> ( <wff> )
         | FORALL <var name> ( <wff> )

<term>
    ::= [ NOT ] <pred name> [ ( <argument commalist> ) ]
```

Points arising:

1. A *<term>* is simply a possibly negated "predicate instance" (if we think of a predicate as a boolean function, then a predicate instance is an invocation of that function). Each *<argument>* must be a constant, a variable name, or a function invocation, where each argument to a function invocation in turn is a constant or variable name or function invocation. The *<argument commalist>* and (optionally) the corresponding parentheses are omitted for a zero-place predicate. *Note:* Functions (over and above the boolean functions that are the predicates, that is) are permitted in order to allow WFFs to include computational expressions such as "$+(x,y)$"—more conventionally written "$x + y$"—and so forth.

2. As in Section 24.3, we adopt the usual precedence rules for the boolean operators (NOT, then AND, then OR, then ⇒) in order to reduce the number of parentheses needed to express a desired order of evaluation.

3. You are assumed to be familiar with the quantifiers EXISTS and FORALL. *Note:* We are concerned here only with the *first-order* predicate calculus, which basically means that (a) there are no "predicate variables" (i.e., variables whose permitted values are predicates), and hence that (b) predicates cannot themselves be subjected to quantification. See Exercise 8.8 in Chapter 8.

4. De Morgan's laws can be generalized to apply to quantified WFFs, as follows:

```
NOT ( FORALL x ( f ) )  ≡  EXISTS x ( NOT ( f ) )
NOT ( EXISTS x ( f ) )  ≡  FORALL x ( NOT ( f ) )
```

This point was also discussed in Chapter 8.

5. To repeat yet another point from Chapter 8: Within a given WFF, each reference to a variable is either free or bound. A reference is **bound** if and only if (a) it appears immediately following EXISTS or FORALL (i.e., it denotes the *quantified variable*) or (b) it lies within the scope of a quantifier and denotes the applicable quantified variable. A variable reference is **free** if and only if it is not bound.

6. A **closed WFF** is one that contains no free variable references (in fact, it is a proposition). An **open WFF** is a WFF that is not closed.

Interpretations and Models

What do WFFs *mean?* In order to provide a formal answer to this question, we introduce the notion of an **interpretation**. An interpretation of a set of WFFs is defined as follows:

- First, we specify a **universe of discourse** over which those WFFs are to be interpreted. In other words, we specify a *mapping* between (a) the permitted constants of the formal system (the domain values, in database terms) and (b) objects in "the real world." Each individual constant corresponds to precisely one object in the universe of discourse.

- Second, we specify a meaning for each predicate in terms of objects in the universe of discourse.

- Third, we also specify a meaning for each function in terms of objects in the universe of discourse.

Then the interpretation consists of the combination of the universe of discourse, plus the mapping of individual constants to objects in that universe, plus the defined meanings for the predicates and functions with respect to that universe.

By way of example, let the universe of discourse be the set of integers $\{0,1,2,3,4,5\}$; let constants such as "2" correspond to objects in that universe in the obvious way; and let the predicate "$x > y$" be defined to have the usual meaning. (We could also define functions such as "+", "−", etc., if desired.) Now we can assign truth values to WFFs such as the following, as indicated:

```
2 > 1                    :   TRUE
2 > 3                    :   FALSE
EXISTS x ( x > 2 )       :   TRUE
FORALL x ( x > 2 )       :   FALSE
```

Note, however, that other interpretations are possible. For example, we might specify the universe of discourse to be a set of security classification levels, as follows:

```
destroy before reading   (level 5)
destroy after reading    (level 4)
top secret               (level 3)
secret                   (level 2)
confidential             (level 1)
unclassified             (level 0)
```

The predicate ">" could now mean "more secure (i.e., higher classification) than."

Now, you will probably realize that the two possible interpretations just given are *isomorphic*—that is, it is possible to set up a one-to-one correspondence between them, and hence at a deep level the two interpretations are really one and the same. But it must be clearly understood that interpretations can exist that are genuinely different in kind. For example, we might once again take the universe of discourse to be the integers 0 to 5, but define the predicate ">" to mean *equality.* (Of course, we would probably cause a lot of confusion that way, but at least we would be within our rights to do so.) Now the first WFF in the list ("2 > 1") would evaluate to FALSE instead of TRUE.

Another point that must be clearly understood is that two interpretations might be genuinely different in the foregoing sense and yet give the same truth values for the given set of WFFs. This would be the case with the two different definitions of ">" in our example if the WFF "2 > 1" were omitted.

Note, incidentally, that all of the WFFs we have been discussing in this subsection so far have been *closed* WFFs. The reason is that, given an interpretation, it is always possible to assign a specific truth value to a closed WFF, but the truth value of an open WFF will depend on the values assigned to the free variables. For example, the open WFF

```
x > 3
```

evaluates, obviously enough, to TRUE if the value of *x* is greater than 3 and FALSE otherwise (whatever "greater than" and "3" mean in the interpretation).

Now we define a **model** of a set of (necessarily closed) WFFs to be an interpretation for which all WFFs in the set evaluate to TRUE. The two interpretations we gave for the four WFFs

```
2 > 1
2 > 3
EXISTS x ( x > 2 )
FORALL x ( x > 2 )
```

in terms of the integers 0 to 5 were not models for those WFFs, because some of the WFFs evaluated to FALSE under that interpretation. By contrast, the first interpretation (in which ">" was defined "properly") *would* have been a model for the set of WFFs:

```
2 > 1
3 > 2
EXISTS x ( x > 2 )
FORALL x ( x > 2 OR NOT ( x > 2 ) )
```

Note finally that, since a given set of WFFs can admit several interpretations in which all of the WFFs are true, it can therefore have several models (in general). Thus, a database can have several models (in general), since—in the model-theoretic view—a database *is* just a set of WFFs. See Section 24.5.

Clausal Form

Just as any propositional calculus formula can be converted to conjunctive normal form, so any predicate calculus WFF can be converted to **clausal form**, which can be regarded as an extended version of conjunctive normal form. One motivation for making such a conversion is that (again) it allows us to apply the resolution rule in constructing or verifying proofs, as we will see.

The conversion process proceeds as follows (in outline; for more details, see reference [24.6]). We illustrate the steps by applying them to the following WFF:

```
FORALL x ( p ( x ) AND EXISTS y ( FORALL z ( q ( y, z ) ) ) )
```

Here *p* and *q* are predicates and *x, y,* and *z* are variables.

1. Eliminate "⟹" symbols as in Section 24.3. In our example, this first transformation has no effect.

2. Use De Morgan's laws, plus the fact that two adjacent NOTs cancel out, to move NOTs so that they apply only to terms, not to general WFFs. (Again this particular transformation has no effect in our particular example.)

3. Convert the WFF to *prenex normal form* by moving all quantifiers to the front (systematically renaming variables if necessary):

   `FORALL x ( EXISTS y ( FORALL z ( p ( x ) AND q ( y, z ) ) ) )`

4. Note that an existentially quantified WFF such as

   `EXISTS v ( r ( v ) )`

   is equivalent to the WFF

   `r ( a )`

   for some unknown constant *a;* that is, the original WFF asserts that some such *a* certainly does exist, even if we do not know its value. Likewise, a WFF such as

   `FORALL u ( EXISTS v ( s ( u, v ) ) )`

   is equivalent to the WFF

   `FORALL u ( s ( u, f ( u ) ) )`

   for some unknown function *f* of the universally quantified variable *u*. The constant *a* and the function *f* in these examples are known, respectively, as a **Skolem constant** and a **Skolem function**, after the logician T. A. Skolem. (*Note:* A Skolem constant is really just a Skolem function with no arguments.) So the next step is to eliminate existential quantifiers by replacing the corresponding quantified variables by (arbitrary) Skolem functions of all universally quantified variables that precede the quantifier in question in the WFF:

   `FORALL x ( FORALL z ( p ( x ) AND q ( f ( x ), z ) ) )`

5. All variables are now universally quantified. We can therefore adopt a convention by which all variables are *implicitly* universally quantified and so drop the explicit quantifiers:

   `p ( x ) AND q ( f ( x ), z )`

6. Convert the WFF to conjunctive normal form, that is, to a set of clauses all ANDed together, each clause involving possibly NOTs and ORs but no ANDs. In our example, the WFF is already in this form.

7. Write each clause on a separate line and drop the ANDs:

   ```
   p ( x )
   q ( f ( x ), z )
   ```

   This is the clausal form equivalent of the original WFF.

Note: It follows from the foregoing procedure that the general form of a WFF in clausal form is a set of clauses, each on a line of its own, and each of the form

   `NOT A1 OR NOT A2 OR ... OR NOT Am OR B1 OR B2 OR ... OR Bn`

where the *A*'s and *B*'s are all nonnegated terms. We can rewrite such a clause, if we like, as:

   `A1 AND A2 AND ... AND Am  ⇒  B1 OR B2 OR ... OR Bn`

If there is at most one *B* ($n = 0$ or 1), the clause is called a **Horn clause**, after the logician Alfred Horn.

Using the Resolution Rule

Now we are in a position to see how a logic-based database system can deal with queries. We use the example from the end of Section 24.2. First, we have a predicate MOTHER_OF, which involves two parameters representing mother and daughter, respectively, and we are given the following two terms (predicate instances):

1. MOTHER_OF (Anne, Betty)
2. MOTHER_OF (Betty, Celia)

We are also given the following WFF (the "deductive axiom"):

3. MOTHER_OF (x, y) AND MOTHER_OF (y, z) ⇒
                              GRANDMOTHER_OF (x, z)

(note that this is a Horn clause). In order to simplify the application of the resolution rule, let us rewrite the clause to eliminate the "⇒" symbol:

4. NOT MOTHER_OF (x, y) OR NOT MOTHER_OF (y, z)
              OR GRANDMOTHER_OF (x, z)

We now proceed to prove that Anne is the grandmother of Celia—that is, we show how to answer the query "Is Anne Celia's grandmother?" We begin by negating the conclusion that is to be proved and adopting it as an additional premise:

5. NOT GRANDMOTHER_OF (Anne, Celia)

Now, to apply the resolution rule, we must systematically substitute values for variables in such a way that we can find two clauses that contain, respectively, a WFF and its negation. Such substitution is legitimate because the variables are all implicitly universally quantified, and hence individual (nonnegated) WFFs must be true for each and every legal combination of values of their variables. *Note:* The process of finding a set of substitutions that make two clauses resolvable in this manner is known as **unification**.

To see how the foregoing works in the case at hand, note first that lines 4 and 5 contain the terms GRANDMOTHER_OF (x,z) and NOT GRANDMOTHER_OF (Anne,Celia), respectively. So we substitute Anne for x and Celia for z in line 4 and resolve, to obtain:

6. NOT MOTHER_OF (Anne, y) OR NOT MOTHER_OF (y, Celia)

Line 2 contains MOTHER_OF (Betty,Celia). So we substitute Betty for y in line 6 and resolve, to obtain:

7. NOT MOTHER_OF (Anne, Betty)

Resolving line 7 and line 1, we obtain the empty set of clauses []: *Contradiction.* Hence the answer to the original query is "Yes, Anne is Celia's grandmother."

What about the query "Who are the granddaughters of Anne?" Observe first of all that the system does not know about granddaughters, it only knows about grandmothers. We could add another deductive axiom to the effect that z is the granddaughter of x if and only if x is the grandmother of z (no males are allowed in this database). Alternatively, we could rephrase the question as "Who is Anne the grandmother of?" Let us consider this latter formulation. The premises are (to repeat):

1. MOTHER_OF (Anne, Betty)
2. MOTHER_OF (Betty, Celia)
3. NOT MOTHER_OF (x, y) OR NOT MOTHER_OF (y, z)
                           OR GRANDMOTHER_OF (x, z)

We introduce a fourth premise, as follows:

4. NOT GRANDMOTHER_OF (Anne, r) OR RESULT (r)

Intuitively, this new premise states that either Anne is not the grandmother of anyone, or alternatively there is some person r who belongs in the result (because Anne *is* the grandmother of that person r). We wish to discover the identity of all such persons r. We proceed as follows.

First, substitute Anne for x and r for z and resolve lines 4 and 3, to obtain:

5. NOT MOTHER_OF (Anne, y) OR NOT MOTHER_OF (y, z)
                           OR RESULT (z)

Next, substitute Betty for y and resolve lines 5 and 1, to obtain:

6. NOT MOTHER_OF (Betty, z) OR RESULT (z)

Now substitute Celia for z and resolve lines 6 and 2, to obtain:

7. RESULT (Celia)

Hence Anne is the grandmother of Celia.

Note: If we had been given an additional term, as follows—

MOTHER_OF (Betty, Delia)

—then we could have substituted Delia for z in the final step (instead of Celia) and obtained:

RESULT (Delia)

The user expects to see both names in the result, of course. Thus, the system needs to apply the unification and resolution process exhaustively to generate *all possible* result values. Details of this refinement are beyond the scope of the present chapter.

24.5 A PROOF-THEORETIC VIEW OF DATABASES

As explained in Section 24.4, a *clause* is an expression of the form

$A1$ AND $A2$ AND ... AND Am $\Rightarrow$ $B1$ OR $B2$ OR ... OR Bn

where the A's and B's are all terms of the form:

r ($x1$, $x2$, ..., xt)

(Here r is a predicate and $x1$, $x2$, ..., xt are the arguments to that predicate.) Following reference [24.7], we now consider two important special cases of this general construct:

1. $m = 0$, $n = 1$

   In this case the clause can be simplified to just

   $\Rightarrow$ $B1$

or in other words (dropping the implication symbol) to just

```
r ( x1, x2, ..., xt )
```

for some predicate *r* and some set of arguments *x1, x2, ..., xt.* If the *x*'s are all constants, the clause represents a **ground axiom**—that is, it is a statement that is unequivocally true. In database terms, such a statement corresponds to a tuple of some relvar *R*.[5] The predicate *r* corresponds to the "meaning" of relvar *R,* as explained in Chapter 6 and elsewhere in this book. For example, in the suppliers-and-parts database, there is a relvar called SP, the meaning of which is that the indicated supplier (S#) supplies the indicated part (P#) in the indicated quantity (QTY). Note that this meaning corresponds to an **open WFF**, since it includes references to free variables (S#, P#, and QTY). By contrast, the tuple (S1,P1,300)—in which the arguments are all constants— is a ground axiom or **closed WFF** that asserts unequivocally that supplier S1 supplies part P1 in a quantity of 300.

2. $m > 0$, $n = 1$

In this case the clause takes the form

```
A1 AND A2 AND ... AND Am  ⇒  B
```

which can be regarded as a **deductive axiom**; it gives a (possibly incomplete) definition of the predicate on the right of the implication symbol in terms of those on the left (see the definition of the GRANDMOTHER_OF predicate earlier for an example).

Alternatively, such a clause might be regarded as defining an **integrity constraint**—a *relvar* constraint, as it happens, to use the terminology of Chapter 9. Suppose for the sake of the example that the suppliers relvar S has just two attributes, S# and CITY. Then the clause

```
S ( s, c1 ) AND S ( s, c2 )  ⇒  c1 = c2
```

expresses the constraint that CITY is functionally dependent on S#. Note the use of the built-in predicate "=" in this example.

As the foregoing discussions demonstrate, tuples in relations ("ground axioms"), derived relations ("deductive axioms"), and integrity constraints can all be regarded as special cases of the general *clause* construct. Let us now try to see how these ideas can lead to the "proof-theoretic" view of a database mentioned in Section 24.2.

First, the traditional view of a database can be regarded as **model**-theoretic. By "traditional view" here, we simply mean a view in which the database is perceived as consisting of a collection of explicitly named relvars, each consisting of a set of explicit tuples, together with an explicit set of integrity constraints. It is this perception that can be characterized as *model-theoretic,* as we now explain:

- The underlying domains contain values or constants that are supposed to stand for certain objects in the "real world" (more precisely, in some **interpretation**, in the sense of Section 24.4). They thus correspond to the universe of discourse.

---

[5] Or to a value in some domain.

- The relvars (more precisely, the relvar *headings*) represent a set of predicates or open WFFs that are to be interpreted over that universe. For example, the heading of relvar SP represents the predicate "Supplier S# supplies part P# in quantity QTY."

- Each tuple in a given relvar represents an instantiation of the corresponding predicate; that is, it represents a proposition (a closed WFF—it contains no variables) that is unequivocally true in the universe of discourse.

- The integrity constraints are open WFFs, interpreted over the same universe. Since the data does not (i.e., *must* not!) violate the constraints, these constraints necessarily evaluate to TRUE as well when current database values are substituted for their parameters.

- The tuples and the integrity constraints can together be regarded as the set of axioms defining a certain **logical theory** (loosely speaking, a "theory" in logic *is* a set of axioms). Since those axioms are all true in the interpretation, then by definition that interpretation is a **model** of that logical theory, in the sense of Section 24.4. Note that, as pointed out in that section, the model might not be unique—that is, a given database might have several possible interpretations, all of them equally valid from a logical standpoint.

In the model-theoretic view, therefore, the "meaning" of the database *is* the model, in the foregoing sense of the term *model*. And since there are many possible models, there are many possible meanings, at least in principle.[6] Furthermore, query processing in the model-theoretic view is essentially a process of evaluating a certain open WFF to discover which values of the free variables in that WFF cause the WFF to evaluate to TRUE within the model.

So much for the model-theoretic view. However, in order to be able to apply the rules of inference described in Sections 24.3 and 24.4, it is necessary to adopt a different perspective, one in which the database is explicitly regarded as a certain logical theory, that is, as a set of axioms. The "meaning" of the database then becomes, precisely, the collection of all true statements that can be deduced from those axioms—that is, it is the set of **theorems** that can be proved from those axioms. This is the **proof-theoretic** view. In this view, query evaluation becomes a theorem-proving process (conceptually speaking, at any rate; in the interest of efficiency, however, the system is likely to use more conventional query processing techniques, as we will see in Section 24.7).

Note: It follows from the foregoing paragraph that one difference between the model- and proof-theoretic views (intuitively speaking) is that, whereas a database can have many "meanings" in the model-theoretic view, it typically has precisely one "meaning" in the proof-theoretic view—except that (a) as pointed out earlier, that one meaning is really *the* canonical meaning in the model-theoretic case, and in any case (b) the remark to the effect that there is only one meaning in the proof-theoretic case ceases to be correct, in general, if the database includes any negative axioms [24.5, 24.6].

---

[6] However, if we assume that the database does not explicitly contain any negative information (e.g., a proposition of the form "NOT S#(S9)," meaning that S9 is not a supplier number), there will also be a "minimal" or *canonical* meaning, which is the intersection of all possible models [24.6]. In this case, moreover, that canonical meaning will be the same as the meaning ascribed to the database under the proof-theoretic view, to be explained in a few moments.

The axioms for a given database (proof-theoretic view) can be informally summarized as follows [24.10]:

1. Ground axioms, corresponding to the values in the domains and the tuples in the base relvars. These axioms constitute what is sometimes called the **extensional database** (as opposed to the *intensional* database—see the next section).

2. A "completion axiom" for each relvar, which states that failure of an otherwise valid tuple to appear in the relvar in question can be interpreted as meaning that the proposition corresponding to that tuple is false. (In fact, these completion axioms taken together constitute the **Closed World Assumption**, already discussed in Chapters 6 and 9.) For example, the fact that the suppliers relvar S does not include the tuple (S6,White,45,Rome) means the proposition "There exists a supplier S6 under contract named White with status 45 located in Rome" is false.

3. The "unique name" axiom, which states that every constant is distinguishable from all of the others (i.e., it has a unique name).

4. The "domain closure" axiom, which states that no constants exist other than those in the database domains.

5. A set of axioms (essentially standard) to define the built-in *equality* predicate. These axioms are needed because the completion, uniqueness, and domain closure axioms all make use of the equality predicate.

We conclude this section with a brief summary of the principal differences between the two perceptions (model-theoretic and proof-theoretic). First of all, it has to be said that from a purely pragmatic standpoint there might not be very much difference at all!—at least in terms of the DBMSs of today. However:

- The axioms for the proof-theoretic view (apart from the ground axioms) make explicit certain assumptions that are only implicit in the notion of interpretation in the model-theoretic view [24.10]. Stating assumptions explicitly is generally a good idea; furthermore, it is necessary to specify those additional axioms explicitly in order to be able to apply general proof techniques, such as the resolution method described in Sections 24.3 and 24.4.

- Note that the list of axioms makes no mention of integrity constraints. The reason for that omission is that (in the proof-theoretic view) adding such constraints converts the system into a "deductive" DBMS. See Section 24.6.

- The proof-theoretic view does enjoy a certain elegance that the model-theoretic view does not, inasmuch as it provides a uniform perception of several constructs that are usually thought of as more or less distinct: base data, queries, integrity constraints (the previous point notwithstanding), virtual data, and so on. As a consequence, the possibility arises of more uniform interfaces and more uniform implementations.

- The proof-theoretic view also provides a natural basis for treating certain problems that relational systems have traditionally always had difficulty with—**disjunctive information** (e.g., "Supplier S6 is located in either Paris or Rome"), the derivation of **negative information** (e.g., "Who is not a supplier?"), and **recursive queries** (see the next section)—though in this last case, at least, there is no reason in principle why a conventional relational system could not be extended to deal with such queries, and indeed several commercial products already have been.[7] We will have more to say regarding such matters in Sections 24.6 and 24.7.

■ Finally, to quote Reiter [24.10], the proof-theoretic view "provides a correct treatment of [extensions to] the relational model to incorporate more real-world semantics" (as noted in Section 24.2).

24.6 DEDUCTIVE DATABASE SYSTEMS

A **deductive DBMS** is a DBMS that supports the proof-theoretic view of a database, and in particular is capable of deducing or inferring additional facts from the given facts in the extensional database by applying specified **deductive axioms** or **rules of inference** to those given facts.[8] The deductive axioms, together with the integrity constraints (discussed later), form what is sometimes called the **intensional database**, and the extensional database and the intensional database together constitute what is usually called the *deductive database* (not a very good term, since it is the DBMS, not the database, that carries out the deductions).

As just indicated, the deductive axioms form one part of the intensional database. The other part consists of additional axioms that represent integrity constraints (i.e., rules whose primary purpose is to constrain updates, though actually such rules can also be used in the process of deducing additional facts from the given ones).

Let us see what our usual suppliers-and-parts database would look like in "deductive DBMS" form. First, there will be a set of ground axioms defining the legal domain values. *Note:* In what follows, for readability reasons, we adopt essentially the same conventions regarding the representation of values as we did in Fig. 3.8 (see the inside back cover) and elsewhere, thereby writing 300 as a convenient shorthand for QTY(300), and so on.

```
S# ( S1 )     NAME ( Smith )    INTEGER (  5 )    CHAR ( London )
S# ( S2 )     NAME ( Jones )    INTEGER ( 10 )    CHAR ( Paris  )
S# ( S3 )     NAME ( Blake )    INTEGER ( 15 )    CHAR ( Rome   )
S# ( S4 )     NAME ( Clark )    etc.              CHAR ( Athens )
S# ( S5 )     NAME ( Adams )                      etc.
S# ( S6 )     NAME ( White )
S# ( S7 )     NAME ( Nut   )
etc.          NAME ( Bolt  )
              NAME ( Screw )
              etc.
```

Next, there will be ground axioms for the tuples in the base relations:

```
S ( S1, Smith, 20, London )
S ( S2, Jones, 10, Paris  )
etc.
```

---

[7] So has the SQL standard [4.23]. See Exercise 4.6 in Chapter 4.

[8] In this connection, it is worth noting that Codd was claiming as far back as 1974 that one of the objectives of the relational model was precisely "to merge the fact retrieval and file management fields in preparation for the addition at a later time of inferential services in the commercial world" [12.2, 26.12].

```
P ( P1, Nut, Red, 12, London )
etc.

SP ( S1, P1, 300 )
etc.
```

Note: We are not seriously suggesting that the extensional database will be created by explicitly listing all of the ground axioms as just indicated; rather, traditional data definition and data entry methods will be used. In other words, deductive DBMSs will typically apply their deductions to conventional databases that already exist and have been constructed in the conventional manner. Note, however, that it now becomes more important than ever that the extensional database not violate any of the declared integrity constraints!—because a database that does violate any such constraints represents (in logical terms) an inconsistent set of axioms, and it is well known that *absolutely any proposition whatsoever* can be proved to be "true" from such a starting point (in other words, contradictions can be derived, as we showed in the annotation to reference [9.16]). For exactly the same reason, it is also important that the stated set of integrity constraints be consistent.

Now for the intensional database. Here are the attribute constraints:

```
S ( s, sn, st, sc )  ⇒  S# ( s ) AND
                         NAME ( sn ) AND
                         INTEGER ( st ) AND
                         CHAR ( sc )

P ( p, pn, pl, pw, pc )  ⇒  P# ( p ) AND
                            NAME ( pn ) AND
                            COLOR ( pl ) AND
                            WEIGHT ( pw ) AND
                            CHAR ( pc )
etc.
```

Candidate key constraints:

```
S ( s, sn1, st1, sc1 ) AND S ( s, sn2, st2, sc2 )
                 ⇒      sn1 = sn2 AND
                        st1 = st2 AND
                        sc1 = sc2
etc.
```

Foreign key constraints:

```
SP ( s, p, q )  ⇒  S ( s, sn, st, sc ) AND
                   P ( p, pn, pl, pw, pc )
```

And so on. *Note:* We assume for the sake of the exposition that variables appearing on the right of the implication symbol and not on the left (*sn, st,* etc., in the example) are existentially quantified. (All others are universally quantified, as explained in Section 24.4.) Technically, we need some Skolem functions; *sn,* for example, should really be replaced by (say) SN(*s*), where SN is a Skolem function.

Notice, incidentally, that most of the constraints shown in the example are not pure clauses in the sense of Section 24.5, because the right side is not just a disjunction of simple terms.

Now let us add some more deductive axioms:

```
S ( s, sn, st, sc ) AND st > 15
                ⇒   GOOD_SUPPLIER ( s, st, sc )
```

(compare the GOOD_SUPPLIER view definition in Chapter 10, Section 10.1).

```
S ( sx, sxn, sxt, sc ) AND S ( sy, syn, syt, sc )
                ⇒   SS_COLOCATED ( sx, sy )

S ( s, sn, st, c ) AND P ( p, pn, pl, pw, c )
                ⇒   SP_COLOCATED ( s, p )
```

And so on.

In order to make the example a little more interesting, let us now extend the database to include a "part structure" relvar, showing which parts *px* contain which parts *py* as immediate (i.e. first-level) components. First a constraint to show that *px* and *py* must both identify existing parts:

```
PART_STRUCTURE ( px, py )  ⇒  P ( px, xn, xl, xw, xc ) AND
                               P ( py, yn, yl, yw, yc )
```

Some data values:

```
PART_STRUCTURE ( P1, P2 )
PART_STRUCTURE ( P1, P3 )
PART_STRUCTURE ( P2, P3 )
PART_STRUCTURE ( P2, P4 )
(etc.)
```

(In practice PART_STRUCTURE would probably also have a "quantity" argument, showing how many *py*'s it takes to make a *px*, but we omit this refinement for simplicity.)

Now we add a pair of deductive axioms to explain what it means for part *px* to contain part *py* as a component (at any level):

```
PART_STRUCTURE ( px, py )  ⇒  COMPONENT_OF ( px, py )

PART_STRUCTURE ( px, pz )  AND COMPONENT_OF ( pz, py )
                           ⇒   COMPONENT_OF ( px, py )
```

In other words, part *py* is a component of part *px* (at some level) if it is either an immediate component of part *px* or an immediate component of some part *pz* that is in turn a component (at some level) of part *px*. Note that the second axiom here is recursive—it defines the COMPONENT_OF predicate in terms of itself. Now, relational systems did not originally allow view definitions (or queries or integrity constraints or . . .) to be recursive in such a manner; thus, this ability to support recursion is one of the most immediately obvious distinctions between deductive DBMSs and their classical relational counterparts—although, as mentioned in Section 24.5 (and as we saw in Chapter 7, in our discussion of the operator TCLOSE), there is no reason why classical relational systems should not be extended to support such recursion, and some already have been. We will have more to say regarding recursion in Section 24.7.

Datalog

From the foregoing discussion, it should be clear that one of the most directly visible portions of a deductive DBMS will be a language in which the deductive axioms (usually called **rules**) can be formulated. The best-known example of such a language is called (by analogy with Prolog) **Datalog** [24.5]. We present a brief discussion of Datalog in this subsection. *Note:* The emphasis in Datalog is on its descriptive power, not its computational power (as in fact was also the case with the original relational model [6.1]). The objective is to define a language that ultimately will have greater expressive power than conventional relational languages [24.5]. As a consequence, the stress in Datalog—indeed, the stress throughout logic-based systems in general—is very heavily on query, not update, though it is possible, and desirable, to extend the language to support update also (see later).

In its simplest form, Datalog supports the formulation of rules as simple Horn clauses without functions. In Section 24.4, we defined a Horn clause to be a WFF of either of the following two forms:

```
A1 AND A2 AND ... AND An
```

```
A1 AND A2 AND ... AND  An  ⇒  B
```

(where the *A*'s and *B* are nonnegated predicate instances involving only constants and variables). Following the style of Prolog, however, Datalog actually writes the second of these the other way around:

```
B  ⇐  A1 AND A2 AND ... AND An
```

For consistency with other publications in this area, therefore, we will do the same in what follows.

In such a clause, *B* is the **rule head** (or conclusion) and the *A*'s are the **rule body** (or premises or **goal**; each individual *A* is a **subgoal**). For brevity, the ANDs are often replaced by commas. A **Datalog program** is a set of such clauses separated in some conventional manner—for example, by semicolons (in this chapter, however, we will not use semicolons but instead will simply start each new clause on a new line). No meaning attaches to the order of the clauses within such a program.

Note that *the entire "deductive database"* can be regarded as a Datalog program in the foregoing sense. For example, we could take all of the axioms shown for suppliers and parts (the ground axioms, the integrity constraints, and the deductive axioms), write them all in Datalog style, and separate them by semicolons or by writing them on separate lines, and the result would be a Datalog program. As explained earlier, however, the extensional part of the database will typically *not* be specified in such a fashion, but rather in some more conventional manner. Thus, the primary aim of Datalog is to support the formulation of deductive axioms specifically. As already noted, that function can be regarded as an extension of the view definition mechanism found in conventional relational DBMSs today.

Datalog can also be used as a query language (again, much like Prolog). For example, suppose we have been given the following Datalog definition of GOOD_SUPPLIER:

```
GOOD_SUPPLIER ( s, st, sc )  ⇐  S ( s, sn, st, sc )
                                AND st > 15
```

Here then are some typical queries against GOOD_SUPPLIER:

1. Get all good suppliers:

```
?  ⇐  GOOD_SUPPLIER ( s, st, sc )
```

2. Get good suppliers in Paris:

    ```
    ?  ⇐  GOOD_SUPPLIER ( s, st, Paris )
    ```

3. Is supplier S1 a good supplier?

    ```
    ?  ⇐  GOOD_SUPPLIER ( S1, st, sc )
    ```

And so on. In other words, a query in Datalog consists of a special rule with a head of "?" and a body consisting of a single term that denotes the query result; the head "?" means (by convention) "Display."

It should be pointed out that, although it did support recursion, there are quite a few features of conventional relational languages that Datalog as originally defined did *not* support: simple computational operators ("+", "∗", etc.), aggregate operators (COUNT, SUM, etc.), set difference (because clauses cannot be negated), grouping and ungrouping, and so on. It also did not support attribute naming (the significance of a predicate argument depended on its ordinal position), nor did it provide full domain support (i.e., user-defined types in the sense of Chapter 5). As indicated earlier in this section, it also did not provide any update operations, nor (as a consequence of this latter fact) did it support the declarative specification of foreign key delete and update rules (ON DELETE CASCADE, etc.).

In order to address some of the foregoing shortcomings, a variety of extensions to basic Datalog have been proposed. Those extensions are intended to provide the following features, among others:

- *Negative premises*—for example:

    ```
    SS_COLOCATED ( sx, sy )  ⇐  S ( sx, sxn, sxt, sc ) AND
                                S ( sy, syn, syt, sc ) AND
                                NOT ( sx = sy )
    ```

- *Computational operators* (both built-in and user-defined)—for example:

    ```
    P_WT_IN_GRAMS ( p, pn, pl, pg, pc )  ⇐
                    P ( p, pn, pl, pw, pc ) AND pg = pw * 454
    ```

    In this example we have assumed that the built-in function "∗" can be written using conventional infix notation. A more orthodox logic representation of the term following the AND would be "=(pg,∗(pw,454))".

- *Grouping and aggregate operators* (somewhat along the lines of our relational SUMMARIZE operator—see Chapter 7): Such operators are necessary in order to address (for example) what is sometimes called the *gross requirements* problem, which is the problem of finding, not only which parts py are components of some part px at any level, but also *how many py's* (at all levels) it takes to make a px. (Naturally we are assuming here that relvar PART_STRUCTURE includes a QTY attribute.)

- *Update operations:* One approach to meeting this obvious requirement—not the only one—is based on the observations that in basic Datalog, (a) any predicate in a rule head must be nonnegated and (b) every tuple generated by the rule can be regarded as being "inserted" into the result. A possible extension would thus be to allow negated predicates in a rule head and to treat the negation as requesting the *deletion* (of pertinent tuples).

■ *NonHorn clauses in the rule body:* In other words, allow completely general WFFs in the definition of rules.

A survey of the foregoing extensions, with examples, can be found in the book by Gardarin and Valduriez [24.6], which also discusses a variety of Datalog implementation techniques.

24.7   RECURSIVE QUERY PROCESSING

As indicated in the previous section, one of the most notable features of deductive database systems is their support for recursion (recursive rule definitions, and hence recursive queries also). As a consequence of this fact, the past several years have seen a great deal of research into techniques for implementing such recursion, and we briefly discuss some of that research in this section.

By way of example, we repeat from Section 24.6 the recursive definition of COMPONENT_OF in terms of PART_STRUCTURE (for brevity, however, we now abbreviate PART_STRUCTURE to PS and COMPONENT_OF to COMP, and we show the definition in Datalog form):

```
COMP ( px, py )  ⇐  PS ( px, py )
COMP ( px, py )  ⇐  PS ( px, pz ) AND COMP ( pz, py )
```

Here is a typical recursive query against this database ("Explode part P1"):

```
?  ⇐  COMP ( P1, py )
```

To return to the definition for a moment: The second rule in that definition—that is, the recursive rule—is said to be **linearly** recursive, because the predicate in the rule head appears just once in the rule body. Here by contrast is a definition for COMP in which the second (recursive) rule is not linearly recursive in the same sense:

```
COMP ( px, py )  ⇐  PS ( px, py )
COMP ( px, py )  ⇐  COMP ( px, pz ) AND COMP ( pz, py )
```

However, there is a general feeling in the literature that linear recursion represents "the interesting case," in the sense that most recursions that arise in practice are naturally linear, and furthermore there are known efficient techniques for dealing with the linear case [24.11]. We therefore restrict our attention to linear recursion for the remainder of this section.

Note: For completeness, we should point out that it is necessary to generalize the definition of "recursive rule" (and of linear recursion) to deal with more complex cases such as the following:

```
P ( x, y )  ⇐  Q ( x, z ) AND R ( z, y )
Q ( x, y )  ⇐  P ( x, z ) AND S ( z, y )
```

For brevity, we ignore such refinements here. See reference [24.11] for a more detailed discussion.

As in classical (i.e., nonrecursive) query processing, the overall problem of implementing a given recursive query can be divided into two subproblems: namely, (a) transforming the original query into some equivalent but more efficient form and then (b) actually executing the result of that transformation. The literature contains descriptions of a variety of attacks on both of these problems. Here we briefly discuss some of the simpler techniques, showing their application to the query "Explode part P1" on the following sample data:

PS	PX	PY
	P1	P2
	P1	P3
	P2	P3
	P2	P4
	P3	P5
	P4	P5
	P5	P6

Unification and Resolution

One possible approach is to use the standard Prolog techniques of **unification** and **resolution** as described in Section 24.4. In the example, this approach works as follows. The first premises are the deductive axioms, which look like this (in conjunctive normal form):

1. NOT PS (*px, py*) OR COMP (*px, py*)
2. NOT PS (*px, pz*) OR NOT COMP (*pz, py*) OR COMP (*px, py*)

We construct another premise from the desired conclusion:

3. NOT COMP (P1, *py*) OR RESULT (*py*)

The ground axioms form the remaining premises. Consider, for example, the ground axiom:

4. PS (P1, P2)

Substituting P1 for *px* and P2 for *py* in line 1, we can resolve lines 1 and 4 to yield:

5. COMP (P1, P2)

Now substituting P2 for *py* in line 3 and resolving lines 3 and 5, we obtain:

6. RESULT (P2)

So P2 is a component of P1. An exactly analogous argument will show that P3 is also a component of P1. Now we have the additional axioms—or theorems, rather—COMP(P1,P2) and COMP(P1,P3); we can now apply the foregoing process recursively to determine the complete explosion. The details are left as an exercise.

In practice, however, unification and resolution can be quite costly in performance. It will thus usually be desirable to find some more efficient strategy. The remaining subsections discuss some possible approaches to this problem.

Naïve Evaluation

Naïve evaluation [24.20] is probably the simplest approach of all. As the name suggests, the algorithm is very simple-minded; it can most easily be explained (for our sample query) in terms of the following pseudocode:

```
COMP := PS ;
do until COMP reaches a "fixpoint" ;
   COMP := COMP UNION ( COMP ⋈ PS ) ;
end ;
DISPLAY := COMP WHERE PX = P# ('P1') ;
```

Relvars COMP and DISPLAY (like relvar PS) each have two attributes, PX and PY. Loosely speaking, the algorithm works by repeatedly forming an intermediate result consisting of the union of the join of PS and the previous intermediate result, until that intermediate result reaches a **fixpoint**—that is, until it ceases to grow. *Note:* The expression "COMP ⋈ PS" is shorthand for "join COMP and PS over COMP.PY and PS.PX and project the result over COMP.PX and PS.PY"; for brevity, we ignore the attribute renaming operations that our dialect of the algebra would require to make this operation work (see Chapter 7).

Let us step through the algorithm with our sample data. After the first iteration of the loop, the value of the expression COMP ⋈ PS is as shown here (on the left) and the resulting value of COMP is as shown on the right (with tuples added on this iteration flagged with an asterisk):

COMP ⋈ PS	PX	PY		COMP	PX	PY	
	P1	P3			P1	P2	
	P1	P4			P1	P3	
	P1	P5			P2	P3	
	P2	P5			P2	P4	
	P3	P6			P3	P5	
	P4	P6			P4	P5	
					P5	P6	
					P1	P4	*
					P1	P5	*
					P2	P5	*
					P3	P6	*
					P4	P6	*

After the second iteration, they look like this:

COMP ⋈ PS	PX	PY		COMP	PX	PY	
	P1	P3			P1	P2	
	P1	P4			P1	P3	
	P1	P5			P2	P3	
	P2	P5			P2	P4	
	P3	P6			P3	P5	
	P4	P6			P4	P5	
	P1	P6			P5	P6	
	P2	P6			P1	P4	
					P1	P5	
					P2	P5	
					P3	P6	
					P4	P6	
					P1	P6	*
					P2	P6	*

Note carefully that the computation of COMP ⋦ PS in this second step repeats the entire computation of COMP ⋦ PS from the first step but additionally computes some extra tuples (actually two extra tuples—(P1,P6) and (P2,P6)—in the case at hand). This is one reason why the naïve evaluation algorithm is not very intelligent.

After the third iteration, the value of COMP ⋦ PS (after more repeated computation) turns out to be the same as on the previous iteration; COMP has thus reached a fixpoint, and we exit from the loop. The final result is then computed as a restriction of COMP:

COMP

PX	PY
P1	P2
P1	P3
P1	P4
P1	P5
P1	P6

Another glaring inefficiency is now apparent: The algorithm has effectively computed the explosion for *every* part—in fact, it has computed the entire transitive closure of relation PS—and has then thrown everything away again except for the tuples actually required; in other words, again, a great deal of unnecessary work has been done.

We close this subsection by pointing out that the naïve evaluation technique can be regarded as an application of forward chaining: Starting from the extensional database (i.e., the actual data values), it applies the premises of the definition (i.e., the rule body) repeatedly until the desired result is obtained. In fact, the algorithm actually computes the *minimal model* for the Datalog program (see Sections 24.5 and 24.6).

Seminaïve Evaluation

The first obvious improvement to the naïve evaluation algorithm is to avoid repeating the computations of each step in the next step: **semi**naïve evaluation [24.23]. In other words, in each step we now compute just the new tuples that need to be appended on this particular iteration. Again we explain the idea in terms of the "Explode part P1" example. Pseudocode:

```
NEW   := PS ;
COMP := NEW ;
do until NEW is empty ;
    NEW  := ( NEW ⋦ PS ) MINUS COMP ;
    COMP := COMP UNION NEW ;
end ;
DISPLAY := COMP WHERE PX = P# ('P1') ;
```

Let us again step through the algorithm. On initial entry into the loop, NEW and COMP are both identical to PS:

NEW

PX	PY
P1	P2
P1	P3
P2	P3
P2	P4
P3	P5
P4	P5
P5	P6

COMP

PX	PY
P1	P2
P1	P3
P2	P3
P2	P4
P3	P5
P4	P5
P5	P6

At the end of the first iteration, they look like this:

NEW	PX	PY		COMP	PX	PY	
	P1	P4			P1	P2	
	P1	P5			P1	P3	
	P2	P5			P2	P3	
	P3	P6			P2	P4	
	P4	P6			P3	P5	
					P4	P5	
					P5	P6	
					P1	P4	*
					P1	P5	*
					P2	P5	*
					P3	P6	*
					P4	P6	*

COMP is the same as it was at this stage under naïve evaluation, and NEW is just the new tuples that were added to COMP on this iteration; note in particular that NEW does not include the tuple (P1,P3) (compare the naïve evaluation counterpart).

At the end of the next iteration we have:

NEW	PX	PY		COMP	PX	PY	
	P1	P6			P1	P2	
	P2	P6			P1	P3	
					P2	P3	
					P2	P4	
					P3	P5	
					P4	P5	
					P5	P6	
					P1	P4	
					P1	P5	
					P2	P5	
					P3	P6	
					P4	P6	
					P1	P6	*
					P2	P6	*

The next iteration makes NEW empty, and so we leave the loop.

Static Filtering

Static filtering is a refinement on the basic idea from classical optimization theory of performing restrictions as early as possible. It can be regarded as an application of backward chaining, in that it effectively uses information from the query (the conclusion) to modify the rules (the premises). It is also referred to as *reducing the set of relevant facts,* in that it (again) uses information from the query to eliminate useless tuples in the extensional database right at the outset [24.24]. The effect on our example can be explained in terms of the following pseudocode:

```
NEW  := PS WHERE PX = P# ('P1') ;
COMP := NEW ;
do until NEW is empty ;
   NEW  := ( NEW ⋈ PS ) MINUS COMP ;
   COMP := COMP UNION NEW ;
end ;
DISPLAY := COMP ;
```

Once again we step through the algorithm. On initial entry into the loop, NEW and COMP both look like this:

NEW	PX	PY
	P1	P2
	P1	P3

COMP	PX	PY
	P1	P2
	P1	P3

At the end of the first iteration, they look like this:

NEW	PX	PY
	P1	P4
	P1	P5

COMP	PX	PY	
	P1	P2	
	P1	P3	
	P1	P4	*
	P1	P5	*

At the end of the next iteration we have:

NEW	PX	PY
	P1	P6

COMP	PX	PY	
	P1	P2	
	P1	P3	
	P1	P4	
	P1	P5	
	P1	P6	*

The next iteration makes NEW empty, and so we leave the loop.

This concludes our brief introduction to recursive query processing strategies. Of course, many other approaches have been proposed in the literature, most of them much more sophisticated than the simple ones we have been discussing; however, there is insufficient space in a book of this nature to cover all of the background material that is needed for a proper understanding of those approaches. See, for example, references [24.11–24.25] for further discussion.

24.8 SUMMARY

This brings us to the end of our short introduction to the topic of databases that are based on logic. Although the ideas are still restricted for the most part to the research world, a few of them have begun to find their way into commercial relational products (this remark is especially true of some of the optimization techniques). Overall, the concept of logic-based databases does look interesting; several potential advantages were identified at various points in the preceding sections. One further advantage, not mentioned explicitly in the body of the chapter, is that logic could form the basis of a genuinely seamless integration between general-purpose programming languages and the database. In other words, instead of the "embedded data sublanguage" approach supported by SQL products today—an approach that is not particularly elegant, to say the least—the system could provide a single logic-based language in which "data is data," regardless of whether it is kept in a shared database or is local to the application. (Of course, there are a number of obstacles to be overcome before such a goal can be achieved, not the least of which is to demonstrate to the satisfaction of the IT community at large that logic is a suitable basis for a general-purpose programming language in the first place.)

Let us quickly review the major points of the material we have covered. We began with a brief tutorial on **propositional** and **predicate calculus**, introducing the following concepts among others:

- An **interpretation** of a set of WFFs is the combination of (a) a universe of discourse, (b) a mapping from individual constants appearing in those WFFs to objects in that universe, and (c) a set of defined meanings for the predicates and functions appearing in those WFFs.

- A **model** for a set of WFFs is an interpretation for which all WFFs in the set are true. A given set of WFFs can have any number of models (in general).

- A **proof** is the process of showing that some given WFF *g* (the **conclusion**) is a logical consequence of some given set of WFFs *f1, f2, ..., fn* (the **premises**). We discussed one proof method, known as **resolution and unification**, in some detail.

We then examined the **proof-theoretic** view of databases. In such a view, the database is regarded as consisting of the combination of an **extensional** database and an **intensional** database. The extensional database contains **ground axioms** (i.e., the base data, loosely speaking); the intensional database contains integrity constraints and **deductive axioms** (i.e., views, again loosely speaking). The "meaning" of the database then consists of the set of **theorems** that can be deduced from the axioms; executing a query becomes (at least conceptually) a **theorem-proving** process. A **deductive DBMS** is a DBMS that supports this proof-theoretic view. We briefly described **Datalog**, a user language for such a DBMS.

One immediately obvious distinction between Datalog and classical relational languages is that Datalog supports **recursive** axioms, and hence recursive queries—though there is no reason why the classical relational algebra and calculus should not be extended to do likewise (see the discussion of the TCLOSE operator in Chapter 7).[9] We discussed some simple techniques for evaluating such queries.

In conclusion: We opened this chapter by mentioning a number of terms—*logic database, inferential DBMS, deductive DBMS,* and so on—that are often met with in the research literature (and even in vendor advertising, to some extent). Let us therefore close it by providing some definitions for those terms. We warn you, however, that there is not always consensus on these matters, and different definitions can probably be found in the literature. Those given here are the ones preferred by the present writer.

---

[9] It is interesting to observe in this connection that relational DBMSs need to be able to perform recursive processing under the covers anyway, because the catalog will contain certain recursively structured information (view definitions expressed in terms of other view definitions are a case in point).

- *Recursive query processing:* This is an easy one. Recursive query processing refers to the evaluation, and in particular optimization, of queries whose definition is intrinsically recursive (see Section 24.7).

- *Knowledge base:* This term is sometimes used to mean what we called the intensional database in Section 24.6—that is, it consists of the *rules* (the integrity constraints and deductive axioms), as opposed to the base data, which constitutes the extensional database. But then other writers use *knowledge base* to mean the combination of both the intensional and extensional databases—except that, as reference [24.6] puts it, "a knowledge base often includes complex objects [as well as] classical relations" (see Part VI of this book for a discussion of "complex objects"). Then again, the term has another, more specific meaning altogether in natural language systems. It is probably best to avoid the term entirely.

- *Knowledge:* Another easy one! Knowledge is what is in the knowledge base . . . This definition thus reduces the problem of defining "knowledge" to a previously unsolved problem.

- *Knowledge base management system (KBMS):* The software that manages the knowledge base. The term is typically used as a synonym for *deductive DBMS* (see the next paragraph).

- *Deductive DBMS:* A DBMS that supports the proof-theoretic view of databases, and in particular is capable of deducing additional information from the extensional database by applying inferential (i.e., deductive) rules that are stored in the intensional database. A deductive DBMS will almost certainly support recursive rules and so perform recursive query processing.

- *Deductive database* (deprecated term): A database that is managed by a deductive DBMS.

- *Expert DBMS:* Synonym for *deductive DBMS.*

- *Expert database* (deprecated term): A database that is managed by an expert DBMS.

- *Inferential DBMS:* Synonym for *deductive DBMS.*

- *Logic-based system:* Synonym for *deductive DBMS.*

- *Logic database* (deprecated term): Synonym for *deductive database.*

- *Logic as a data model:* A data model consists of (at least) objects, integrity rules, and operators. In a deductive DBMS, the objects, integrity rules, and operators are all represented in the same uniform way (namely, as axioms in a logic language such as Datalog); indeed, as explained in Section 24.6, a database in such a system can be regarded, precisely, as a logic program containing axioms of all three kinds. In such a system, therefore, we might legitimately say that the abstract data model for the system *is* logic itself.

EXERCISES

24.1   Use the resolution method to see whether the following constitute valid proofs in the propositional calculus:

a. $A \Rightarrow B$, $C \Rightarrow B$, $D \Rightarrow$ (A OR C), D $\vdash$ B

b. ($A \Rightarrow B$) AND ($C \Rightarrow D$), ($B \Rightarrow E$ AND $D \Rightarrow F$),
   NOT (E AND F), $A \Rightarrow C$ $\vdash$ NOT A

c. (A OR B) $\Rightarrow D$, $D \Rightarrow$ NOT (E OR F), NOT (B AND C AND E)
   $\vdash$ NOT ($G \Rightarrow$ NOT (C AND H))

24.2   Convert the following WFFs to clausal form:

a. FORALL x (FORALL y
   (p (x, y) $\Rightarrow$ EXISTS z (q (x, z))))

b. EXISTS x (EXISTS y
   (p (x, y) $\Rightarrow$ FORALL z (q (x, z))))

c. EXISTS x (EXISTS y
   (p (x, y) $\Rightarrow$ EXISTS z (q (x, z))))

24.3   The following is a fairly standard example of a logic database:

```
MAN    ( Adam )
WOMAN  ( Eve )
MAN    ( Cain )
MAN    ( Abel )
MAN    ( Enoch )

PARENT ( Adam, Cain )
PARENT ( Adam, Abel )
PARENT ( Eve, Cain )
PARENT ( Eve, Abel )
PARENT ( Cain, Enoch )

FATHER ( x, y )   ⇐   PARENT ( x, y ) AND MAN ( x )
MOTHER ( x, y )   ⇐   PARENT ( x, y ) AND WOMAN ( x )

SIBLING ( x, y )  ⇐   PARENT ( z, x ) AND PARENT ( z, y )

BROTHER ( x, y )  ⇐   SIBLING ( x, y ) AND MAN ( x )

SISTER ( x, y )   ⇐   SIBLING ( x, y ) AND WOMAN ( x )

ANCESTOR ( x, y ) ⇐   PARENT ( x, y )
ANCESTOR ( x, y ) ⇐   PARENT ( x, z ) AND ANCESTOR ( z, y )
```

Use the resolution method to answer the following queries:

a. Who is the mother of Cain?

b. Who are Cain's siblings?

c. Who are Cain's brothers?

d. Who are Cain's sisters?

e. Who are Enoch's ancestors?

24.4   Explain the terms *interpretation* and *model* in your own words.

24.5   Write a set of Datalog axioms for the definitional portion (only) of the suppliers-parts-projects database.

24.6   Give Datalog solutions, where possible, to Exercises 7.13–7.50.

24.7   Give Datalog solutions, where possible, to Exercise 9.3.

24.8 Complete to your own satisfaction the explanation given in Section 24.7 of the unification and resolution implementation of the "Explode part P1" query.

REFERENCES AND BIBLIOGRAPHY

The field of logic-based systems has mushroomed over the past few years, and the following list represents only a tiny fraction of the literature currently available. It is partially arranged into groups, as follows:

- References [24.1–24.5] are books that either are devoted to the subject of logic in general (particularly in a computing and/or database context) or are collections of papers on logic-based databases specifically.

- References [24.6] and [24.7] are tutorials.

- References [24.9], [24.12–24.15], [24.25], and [24.27, 24.28] are concerned with the transitive closure operation and its implementation.

- References [24.16-24.19] describe an important recursive query processing technique called *magic sets* (and variations thereon). *Note:* In this connection, see also references [18.22–18.24].

The remaining references are included principally to show just how much investigation is going on in this field; they address a variety of aspects of the subject and are presented for the most part without further comment.

24.1 Robert R. Stoll: *Sets, Logic, and Axiomatic Theories.* San Francisco, Calif.: W. H. Freeman and Company (1961).

A good introduction to logic in general.

24.2 Peter M. D. Gray: *Logic, Algebra and Databases.* Chichester, England: Ellis Horwood Ltd. (1984).

Contains a good gentle introduction to propositional calculus and predicate calculus (among a number of other relevant topics) from a database point of view.

24.3 Hervé Gallaire and Jack Minker: *Logic and Data Bases.* New York, N.Y.: Plenum Publishing Corp. (1978).

One of the first, if not *the* first, collections of papers in the field.

24.4 Jack Minker (ed.): *Foundations of Deductive Databases and Logic Programming.* San Mateo, Calif.: Morgan Kaufmann (1988).

24.5 Jeffrey D. Ullman: *Database and Knowledge-Base Systems* (in two volumes). Rockville, Md.: Computer Science Press (1988, 1989).

Volume I of this two-volume work includes one (long) chapter (out of a total of 10) that is entirely devoted to the logic-based approach. That chapter (which is the origin of Datalog, incidentally) includes a discussion of the relationship between logic and relational algebra, and another on relational calculus—both domain and tuple versions—as a special case of the logic approach. Volume II includes five chapters (out of seven) on various aspects of logic-based databases.

24.6 Georges Gardarin and Patrick Valduriez: *Relational Databases and Knowledge Bases.* Reading, Mass.: Addison-Wesley (1989).

Contains a chapter on deductive systems that (although still tutorial in nature) goes into the underlying theory, optimization algorithms, and so on, in much more depth than the present chapter does.

24.7 Hervé Gallaire, Jack Minker, and Jean-Marie Nicolas: "Logic and Databases: A Deductive Approach," *ACM Comp. Surv. 16,* No. 2 (June 1984).

24.8 Veronica Dahl: "On Database Systems Development Through Logic," *ACM TODS 7,* No. 1 (March 1982).

> A good and clear description of the basic ideas underlying logic-based databases, with examples taken from a Prolog-based prototype implemented by Dahl in 1977.

24.9 Rakesh Agrawal: "Alpha: An Extension of Relational Algebra to Express a Class of Recursive Queries," *IEEE Transactions on Software Engineering 14,* No. 7 (July 1988).

> Proposes a new operator called *alpha* that supports the formulation of "a large class of recursive queries" (actually a superset of linear recursive queries) while staying within the framework of conventional relational algebra. The contention is that the *alpha* operator is sufficiently powerful to deal with most practical problems involving recursion, while at the same time being easier to implement efficiently than any completely general recursion mechanism would be. The paper gives several examples of the use of the proposed operator; in particular, it shows how the transitive closure and "gross requirements" problems (see reference [24.12] and Section 24.6, respectively) can both easily be handled.
>
> Reference [24.14] describes some related work on implementation. Reference [24.13] is also relevant.

24.10 Raymond Reiter: "Towards a Logical Reconstruction of Relational Database Theory," in Michael L. Brodie, John Mylopoulos, and Joachim W. Schmidt (eds.), *On Conceptual Modelling: Perspectives from Artificial Intelligence, Databases, and Programming Languages.* New York, N.Y.: Springer-Verlag (1984).

> As mentioned in Section 24.2, Reiter's work was by no means the first in this area—many researchers had investigated the relationship between logic and databases before (see, e.g., references [24.3], [24.4], and [24.8])—but it seems to have been Reiter's "logical reconstruction of relational theory" that spurred much of the subsequent activity and current high degree of interest in the field.

24.11 François Bancilhon and Raghu Ramakrishnan: "An Amateur's Introduction to Recursive Query Processing Strategies," Proc. 1986 ACM SIGMOD Int. Conf. on Management of Data, Washington, D.C. (May 1986). Republished in revised form in Michael Stonebraker (ed.), *Readings in Database Systems.* San Mateo, Calif.: Morgan Kaufmann (1988).

> An excellent overview. The paper starts by observing that there is both a positive and a negative side to all of the research on the recursive query implementation problem. The positive side is that numerous techniques have been identified that do at least solve the problem; the negative side is that it is not at all clear how to choose the technique that is most appropriate in a given situation (in particular, most of the techniques are presented in the literature with little or no discussion of performance characteristics). Then, after a section describing the basic ideas of logic databases, the paper goes on to describe a number of proposed algorithms: naïve evaluation, seminaïve evaluation, iterative query/subquery, recursive query/subquery, APEX, Prolog, Henschen/Naqvi, Aho-Ullman, Kifer-Lozinskii, counting, magic sets, and generalized magic sets. The paper compares these different approaches on the basis of application domain (i.e., the class of problems to which the algorithm can usefully be applied), performance, and ease of implementation. The paper also includes performance figures (with comparative analyses) from testing the various algorithms on a simple benchmark.

24.12 Yannis E. Ioannidis: "On the Computation of the Transitive Closure of Relational Operators," Proc. 12th Int. Conf. on Very Large Data Bases, Kyoto, Japan (August 1986).

Proposes a divide-and-conquer algorithm for implementing transitive closure. See also references [24.9], [24.13–24.15], and [24.27, 24.28].

24.13 H. V. Jagadish, Rakesh Agrawal, and Linda Ness: "A Study of Transitive Closure as a Recursion Mechanism," Proc. 1987 ACM SIGMOD Int. Conf. on Management of Data, San Francisco, Calif. (May 1987).

To quote from the abstract: "[This paper shows] that every linearly recursive query can be expressed as a transitive closure possibly preceded and followed by operations already available in relational algebra." The authors therefore suggest that providing an efficient implementation of transitive closure is sufficient as a basis for providing an efficient implementation of linear recursion in general, and hence for making deductive DBMSs efficient on a large class of recursive problems.

24.14 Rakesh Agrawal and H. Jagadish: "Direct Algorithms for Computing the Transitive Closure of Database Relations," Proc. 13th Int. Conf. on Very Large Data Bases, Brighton, UK (September 1987).

Proposes a set of transitive closure algorithms that "do not view the problem as one of evaluating a recursion, but rather obtain the closure from first principles" (hence the term *direct*). The paper includes a useful summary of earlier work on other direct algorithms.

24.15 Hongjun Lu: "New Strategies for Computing the Transitive Closure of a Database Relation," Proc. 13th Int. Conf. on Very Large Data Bases, Brighton, UK (September 1987).

More algorithms for transitive closure. Like reference [24.14], the paper also includes a useful survey of earlier approaches to the problem.

24.16 François Bancilhon, David Maier, Yehoshua Sagiv, and Jeffrey D. Ullman: "Magic Sets and Other Strange Ways to Implement Logic Programs," Proc. 5th ACM SIGMOD-SIGACT Symposium on Principles of Database Systems (1986).

The basic idea of "magic sets" is to introduce new transformation rules ("magic rules") into the optimization process dynamically. Those rules are used to replace the original query by a modified version that is more efficient, because it reduces the set of "relevant facts" (see Section 24.7). The details are a little complex, and beyond the scope of these notes; refer to the paper or to Bancilhon and Ramakrishnan's survey [24.11] or the books by Ullman [24.5] or Gardarin and Valduriez [24.6] for more explanation. We remark that numerous variations on the basic idea have subsequently been devised—see, for example, references [24.17–24.19]. See also references [18.22–18.24].

24.17 Catriel Beeri and Raghu Ramakrishnan: "On the Power of Magic," Proc. 6th ACM SIGMOD-SIGACT Symposium on Principles of Database Systems (1987).

24.18 Domenico Saccà and Carlo Zaniolo: "Magic Counting Methods," Proc. 1987 ACM SIGMOD Int. Conf. on Management of Data, San Francisco, Calif. (May 1987).

24.19 Georges Gardarin: "Magic Functions: A Technique to Optimize Extended Datalog Recursive Programs," Proc. 13th Int. Conf. on Very Large Data Bases, Brighton, UK (September 1987).

24.20 A. Aho and J. D. Ullman: "Universality of Data Retrieval Languages," Proc. 6th ACM Symposium on Principles of Programming Languages, San Antonio, Tex. (January 1979).

Given a sequence of relations $r, f(r), f(f(r)), \ldots$ (where f is some fixed function), the **least fixpoint** of the sequence is defined to be a relation $r*$ derived in accordance with the following naïve evaluation algorithm (see Section 24.7):

```
r* := r ;
do until r* stops growing ;
    r* := r* UNION f(r*) ;
end ;
```

This paper proposes the addition of a least fixpoint operator to the relational algebra.

24.21 Jeffrey D. Ullman: "Implementation of Logical Query Languages for Databases," *ACM TODS 10,* No. 3 (September 1985).

Describes an important class of implementation techniques for possibly recursive queries. The techniques are defined in terms of "capture rules" on "rule/goal trees," which are graphs that represent a query strategy in terms of clauses and predicates. The paper defines several such rules—one that corresponds to the application of relational algebra operators, two more that correspond to forward and backward chaining, respectively, and a "sideways" rule that allows results to be passed from one subgoal to another. Sideways information passing later became the basis for the so-called *magic set* techniques [24.16–24.19].

24.22 Shalom Tsur and Carlo Zaniolo: "LDL: A Logic-Based Data-Language," Proc. 12th Int. Conf. on Very Large Data Bases, Kyoto, Japan (August 1986).

LDL includes (1) a "set" type generator, (2) negation (based on set difference), (3) data definition operations, and (4) update operations. It is a pure logic language (there are no ordering dependencies among statements) and is compiled, not interpreted.

24.23 François Bancilhon: "Naïve Evaluation of Recursively Defined Relations," in Michael Brodie and John Mylopoulos (eds.), *On Knowledge Base Management Systems*: *Integrating Database and AI Systems.* New York, N.Y.: Springer-Verlag (1986).

24.24 Eliezer L. Lozinskii: "A Problem-Oriented Inferential Database System," *ACM TODS 11,* No. 3 (September 1986).

The source of the concept of "relevant facts." The paper describes a prototype system that makes use of the extensional database to curb the otherwise very fast expansion of the search space that inferential techniques typically give rise to.

24.25 Arnon Rosenthal *et al.*: "Traversal Recursion: A Practical Approach to Supporting Recursive Applications," Proc. 1986 ACM SIGMOD Int. Conf. on Management of Data, Washington, D.C. (June 1986).

24.26 Michael Kifer and Eliezer Lozinskii: "On Compile Time Query Optimization in Deductive Databases by Means of Static Filtering," *ACM TODS 15,* No. 3 (September 1990).

24.27 Rakesh Agrawal, Shaul Dar, and H. V. Jagadish: "Direct Transitive Closure Algorithms: Design and Performance Evaluation," *ACM TODS 15,* No. 3 (September 1990).

24.28 H. V. Jagadish: "A Compression Method to Materialize Transitive Closure," *ACM TODS 15,* No. 4 (December 1990).

Proposes an indexing technique that allows the transitive closure of a given relation to be stored in compressed form, such that testing to see whether a given tuple appears in the closure can be done via a single table lookup followed by an index comparison.

OBJECTS, RELATIONS, AND XML

Note: Like Chapter 20, the chapters in this part of the book rely heavily on material first discussed in Chapter 5. If you originally gave that chapter a "once over lightly" reading, you might want to go back and revisit it now (if you have not already done so) before studying these chapters in any depth.

Object technology is an important discipline in the field of software engineering in general. It is therefore natural to ask whether it might be relevant to the field of database management in particular, and if so what that relevance might be. While there is less agreement on these questions than there might be, some kind of consensus does seem to be emerging. When object database systems first appeared, some industry figures claimed they would take over the world, replacing relational systems entirely; other authorities felt they were suited only to certain very specific problems and would never capture more than a tiny fraction of the overall market. While this debate was raging, systems supporting a "third way" began to appear: systems, that is, that combined object and relational technologies in an attempt to get the best of both worlds. And it now looks as if those "other authorities" were right: Pure object systems might have a role to play, but it is a niche role, and relational systems will continue to dominate the market for the foreseeable future—not least because those "object/relational" systems are really just relational systems after all, as we will see.

More recently, one particular kind of object that has attracted a great deal of attention is *XML documents;* the problem of keeping such documents in a database and querying and updating them has rapidly become a problem of serious pragmatic significance. "XML databases"—that is, databases that contain XML documents and nothing else—are possible; however, it would clearly be preferable, if possible, to integrate XML documents with other kinds of data in either an object or a relational (or "object/relational") database.

The chapters in this part of the book examine such matters in depth. Chapter 25 considers pure object systems; Chapter 26 addresses object/relational systems; and Chapter 27 discusses XML.

Object Databases

25.1 INTRODUCTION

There was a great deal of interest in the late 1980s to mid 1990s in *object-oriented* database systems (**object systems** for short). Such systems were even regarded in some quarters as serious competitors to relational systems (or SQL systems, at any rate). Few agree with that position today; most IT people now feel that, while object systems might well have a role to play, that role is a comparatively limited one [25.33]. Nevertheless, such systems are still worth studying. In this chapter, therefore, we examine object systems in detail; we introduce and explain basic object concepts, analyze and criticize those concepts where appropriate, and offer some opinions regarding the suitability of incorporating such concepts into the database systems of the future.

Why was there so much interest in object systems in the first place? Well, it was certainly true at the time that SQL products were (and indeed still are) inadequate in a variety of ways. Some people even argued that the underlying theory—that is, the relational model—was and is inadequate too. And since some of the new features we seemed to need in DBMSs had existed for years in *object programming languages* such as C++ and Smalltalk, it was natural to investigate the idea of incorporating those features into database systems. And many researchers, and some vendors, did exactly that.

Object systems thus have their origins in object programming languages. And the basic idea is the same in both cases: namely, that users should not have to wrestle with machine-oriented constructs such as bits and bytes, or even fields and records, but rather should be able to deal with **objects**, and **operations** on those objects, that more closely resemble their counterparts in the real world. For example, instead of having to think in terms of a "DEPT tuple" plus a collection of corresponding "EMP tuples" that include "foreign key values" that "reference" the "primary key value" in that "DEPT tuple," the user should be able to think directly in terms of a *department object* that actually contains a corresponding set of *employee objects*. And instead of, for example, having to "insert" a "tuple" into the "EMP relvar" with an appropriate "foreign key value" that "references" the "primary key value" of some "tuple" in the "DEPT relvar," the user should be able to *hire* an employee object directly into the relevant department object. In other words, the fundamental idea is to **raise the level of abstraction**.

Now, raising the level of abstraction is unquestionably a worthy goal, and the object paradigm has been quite successful in meeting that goal in the programming languages arena. It therefore makes sense to ask whether the same paradigm can be applied success-fully in the database arena also. Indeed, the idea of dealing with a database that is made up of "complex objects" (e.g., department objects that "know what it means" to hire an employee or change their manager or cut their budget), instead of having to deal with "rel-vars" and "tuple inserts" and "foreign keys" (etc.) is obviously more attractive from the user's point of view—at least at first sight.

A word of caution is appropriate here, however. The point is, although the program-ming language and database management disciplines certainly have a lot in common, they do also differ in certain important respects. To be specific:

- An application program is intended, by definition, to solve some specific problem.

- By contrast, a database is intended, again by definition, to solve a variety of differ-ent problems (some of which might not even be known at the time the database is created).

In the application programming environment, therefore, embedding a lot of "intelligence" into complex objects is clearly a good idea: It reduces the amount of code that needs to be written to make use of those objects, it increases programmer productivity, it improves application maintainability, and so on. In the database environment, by contrast, embed-ding a lot of intelligence into the database might or might not be a good idea: It might sim-plify some problems, but it might at the same time make others more difficult or even impossible.

As an aside, we remark that exactly this argument was made against prerelational database systems like IMS back in the 1970s. A department object that contains a set of employee objects is conceptually very similar to an IMS hierarchy in which department "parent segments" have subordinate employee "child segments." Such a hierarchy is well suited to problems like "Get employees that work in the accounting department." It is not well suited to problems like "Get departments that employ MBAs" (intuitively, the hierar-chy is "the wrong way up" for this latter kind of problem). Thus, many of the arguments that were made against the hierarchic approach in the 1970s surface again, in a different guise, in the object context.

The foregoing arguments notwithstanding, many people felt that object systems represented "a great leap forward" in database technology. In particular, they claimed that object techniques were the approach of choice for "complex" application areas such as the following:

- Computer-aided design and manufacturing (CAD/CAM)
- Computer-integrated manufacturing (CIM)
- Computer-aided software engineering (CASE)
- Geographic information systems (GIS)
- Science and medicine
- Document storage and retrieval

and many others (note that these are all areas in which classical SQL products did tend to run into trouble). Certainly there have been numerous technical papers on such matters in the literature over the years, and there are now several commercial products available in the marketplace.

The aim of this chapter, then, is to explain what object database technology is all about—that is, to introduce the most important concepts of the object approach, and in particular to describe those concepts *from a database perspective* (much of the literature, by contrast, presents the ideas very much from a *programming* perspective instead). The structure of the chapter is as follows. In the next subsection, we present a motivating example (an example, that is, that classical SQL products do not handle very well, and hence one that object technology stands a good chance of doing better on). Next, Section 25.2 presents an overview of *objects, classes, messages,* and *methods,* and Section 25.3 then focuses on certain specific aspects of these concepts and discusses them in depth. Section 25.4 presents a "cradle-to-grave" example. Section 25.5 covers a few miscellaneous topics, and Section 25.6 presents a summary.

Two last preliminary remarks:

- Despite the fact that object systems were originally meant for "complex" applications such as CAD/CAM, for obvious reasons we base our examples on much simpler applications (departments and employees, etc.). Of course, this simplification in no way invalidates the presentation—and in any case, object databases, if they are to be worth their salt, should be able to handle simple applications too.
- Please note clearly that we are concerned in this chapter with object *database* systems specifically. We are not concerned with object programming or object programming languages, object analysis and design, "object modeling," graphical object interfaces, and so on. Most important, we make no claim that any criticisms we might have of objects in the database context are valid in any of these other contexts.

A Motivating Example

In this subsection we present a simple example, originally due to Stonebraker and elaborated by the present writer in reference [25.15], that illustrates some of the problems with classical SQL products. The database (which might be thought of as a grossly simplified approximation to a CAD/CAM database) concerns rectangles, all of which we assume for simplicity are "square on" to the *X* and *Y* axes—that is, all of their sides are either vertical or horizontal. Any individual rectangle can thus be uniquely identified by the coordinates $(x1,y1)$ and $(x2,y2)$ of its bottom left and top right corners, respectively (see Fig. 25.1). In SQL:

```
CREATE TABLE RECTANGLES
     ( X1 ... , Y1 ... , X2 ... , Y2 ... , ... ,
       PRIMARY KEY ( X1, Y1, X2, Y2 ) ) ;
```

Now consider the query "Get all rectangles that overlap the unit square $(0,0,1,1)$" (see Fig. 25.2). The "obvious" formulation of this query is:

```
SELECT ...
FROM    RECTANGLES
WHERE   ( X1 >= 0 AND X1 <= 1 AND Y1 >= 0 AND Y1 <= 1 )
                 /* bottom left corner inside unit square  */
OR      ( X2 >= 0 AND X2 <= 1 AND Y2 >= 0 AND Y2 <= 1 )
                 /* top right corner inside unit square     */
OR      ( X1 >= 0 AND X1 <= 1 AND Y2 >= 0 AND Y2 <= 1 )
                 /* top left corner inside unit square      */
OR      ( X2 >= 0 AND X2 <= 1 AND Y1 >= 0 AND Y1 <= 1 )
                 /* bottom right corner inside unit square */
OR      ( X1 <= 0 AND X2 >= 1 AND Y1 <= 0 AND Y2 >= 1 )
                 /* rectangle totally includes unit square */
OR      ( X1 <= 0 AND X2 >= 1 AND Y1 >= 0 AND Y1 <= 1 )
                 /* bottom edge crosses unit square         */
OR      ( X1 >= 0 AND X1 <= 1 AND Y1 <= 0 AND Y2 >= 1 )
                 /* left edge crosses unit square           */
OR      ( X2 >= 0 AND X2 <= 1 AND Y1 <= 0 AND Y2 >= 1 )
                 /* right edge crosses unit square          */
OR      ( X1 <= 0 AND X2 >= 1 AND Y2 >= 0 AND Y2 <= 1 ) ;
                 /* top edge crosses unit square            */
```

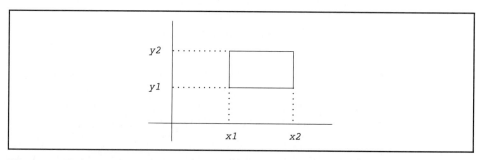

Fig. 25.1 The rectangle $(x1, y1, x2, y2)$

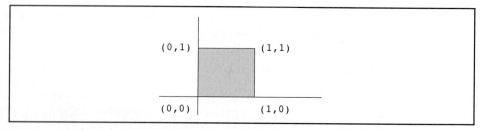

Fig. 25.2 The unit square $(0,0,1,1)$

(*Exercise:* Convince yourself that this formulation is correct.)

With a little further thought, however, it can be seen that the query can be more simply expressed thus:

```
SELECT  ...
FROM    RECTANGLES
WHERE   ( X1 <= 1 AND Y1 <= 1
                /* bottom left corner is "downwind" of (1,1) */
AND       X2 >= 0 AND Y2 >= 0 ) ;
                /* top right corner is "upwind" of (0,0)    */
```

(Exercise 25.3 at the end of the chapter asks you to convince yourself that this formulation is correct too.)

The question now is: Could the system optimizer transform the original long form of the query into the corresponding short form? In other words, suppose the user expresses the query in the "obvious"—and obviously inefficient—long form; would the optimizer be capable of reducing that query to the more efficient short form before executing it? Reference [25.15] gives evidence to suggest that the answer to this question is almost certainly *no,* at least as far as today's commercial optimizers are concerned.

In any case, although we just described the short form as "more efficient," performance on that short form will still be poor in many products, given the usual storage structures—for example, B-tree indexes—supported by those products. (On average, the system will examine 50 percent of the index entries for each of X1, Y1, X2, and Y2.) In other words, the problem is more than just one of good optimization.

We see, therefore, that classical SQL products are indeed inadequate in certain respects. To be specific, problems like the rectangles problem show clearly that certain "simple" user requests (a) are unreasonably difficult to express, and (b) execute with unacceptably poor performance, in those products. Such considerations provided much of the motivation behind the original interest in object systems.

Note: We will give a "good" solution to the rectangles problem in the next chapter (Section 26.1).[1]

25.2 OBJECTS, CLASSES, METHODS, AND MESSAGES

In this section, we introduce some of the principal concepts of the object approach: *objects* themselves (of course), *object classes, methods,* and *messages.* We also relate these concepts to more familiar concepts where appropriate. In fact, it is probably helpful to show a rough mapping of object terms to traditional terminology right at the outset (see Fig. 25.3).

Caveat: Before we start getting into details, we should warn you not to expect the kind of precision in the object world that you are (or should be) accustomed to in the relational world. Indeed, many object concepts—or the published definitions of those concepts, at any rate—are quite imprecise, and there is very little true consensus and much

---

[1] That solution involves a user-defined type. SQL did not support user-defined types when object systems first came on the market; now it does. In fact, SQL now includes several features that make it somewhat more "object-like"; however, we deliberately defer discussion of such features to the next chapter.

Object term	Traditional term
immutable object	value
mutable object	variable
object class	type
method	operator
message	operator invocation

Fig. 25.3   Object terminology (summary)

disagreement, even at the most basic level (as a careful comparative reading of, e.g., references [25.10], [25.39], and [25.42] will show). In particular, there is no abstract, formally defined "object data model," nor is there even consensus on an *in*formal model. (For such reasons we usually place phrases such as "the object model" in quotes in this chapter.) In fact, there seems, rather surprisingly, to be much confusion over levels of abstraction: specifically, over the crucial distinction between **model** and **implementation,** as we will see.

You should also be warned that, as a consequence of the foregoing state of affairs, the definitions and explanations presented in this chapter are not universally agreed upon and do not necessarily correspond 100 percent to the way any given system actually works. Indeed, just about every one of those definitions and explanations could be challenged by some other writer in this field, and probably will be.

An Overview of Object Technology

Question: What is an object? *Answer:* Everything!

It is a basic tenet of the object approach that "**everything is an object**" (sometimes "everything is a **first-class** object"). Some objects are **immutable**; examples might be integers (e.g., 3, 42) and character strings (e.g., "Mozart", "Hayduke Lives!"). Other objects are **mutable**; examples might be the department and employee objects mentioned near the beginning of Section 25.1. In traditional terminology, therefore, immutable objects correspond to *values* and mutable objects to *variables*[2]—where the values and variables in question can be of arbitrary complexity (i.e., they can make use of any or all of the usual programming language types and type generators: numbers, strings, lists, arrays, stacks, etc.). *Note:* In some systems the term *object* is reserved for the mutable case only, the term *value*—sometimes *literal* (!)—then being used for the immutable case. Even in those systems where the term *object* does strictly refer to both cases, you should be aware that it is common in informal contexts to take the term to mean a mutable object specifically, barring explicit statements to the contrary.

Every object has a *type* (the object term is *class*). Individual objects are sometimes referred to as object **instances** specifically (also just as *instances*), in order to distinguish them from the corresponding object type or class. Also, please note that we are using the term *type* here in its usual programming language sense (as in Chapter 5); in particular,

---

[2] Note, however, that the unqualified term *variable* is typically used in object contexts to mean, very specifically, a variable—either a local variable or an "instance variable"—that holds an *object ID* (see later in this section).

therefore, we take the term to include the set of *operators* (the object term is ***methods***) that can be applied to objects of the type in question. Read-only and update operators are called **observers** and **mutators**, respectively. *Note:* Actually, some object systems do distinguish between types and classes, and we will discuss such systems briefly in Section 25.3; prior to that point, however, we will use the terms interchangeably.

Objects are **encapsulated**. What this means is that the physical representation—that is, the internal structure—of such an object, say a DEPT ("department") object, is not visible to users of that object; instead, users know only that the object is capable of executing certain operations (methods). For example, the methods that apply to DEPT objects might be HIRE_EMP, FIRE_EMP, CUT_BUDGET, and so on. *Note carefully that such methods constitute the ONLY operations that can be applied to the objects in question.* The code that implements those methods *is* permitted to see the internal representation of the objects—to use the jargon, that code (but only that code) is allowed to "break encapsulation"[3]—but of course that code is likewise not visible to users.

Actually, it has to be said that there is much confusion in the object literature surrounding the notion of encapsulation. The position that seems to make the most sense, and the one we adopt in this book, is to say that an object is encapsulated if and only if it is **scalar** in the sense of Chapter 5 (meaning it has no user-visible components); hence, *encapsulated* and *scalar* mean exactly the same thing. Note, therefore, that certain "collection" objects—see Section 25.3—are definitely not scalar, and hence not encapsulated, by this definition. By contrast, some writers state categorically that *all* objects are encapsulated, a position that inevitably leads to certain contradictions. Others take the concept to mean that, in addition to the internal structure being hidden, *the corresponding methods are physically bundled with* (i.e., are physically part of) the object or object class in question. We feel this latter interpretation mixes model and implementation considerations; indeed, that confusion is another of the reasons why, as noted in Chapter 5, we prefer not to use the term *encapsulation* at all. In the present chapter, however, we do necessarily have to use it from time to time.

The advantage of encapsulation, then, is that it allows the internal representation of objects to be changed without requiring applications that use those objects to be rewritten (provided, of course, that any such change in internal representation is accompanied by a corresponding change to the code that implements the applicable methods). In other words, encapsulation implies **physical data independence**.

Now we need to explain that, while the foregoing characterization of encapsulation in terms of data independence makes sense from a database perspective, it is not the way the concept is usually described in the object literature. Instead, encapsulated objects are usually described as having a *private memory* and a *public interface:*

- The **private memory** consists of **instance variables** (also known as *members* or *attributes*), whose values represent the internal state of the object. Now, in a "pure" system, instance variables would be completely private and hidden from users, though

---

[3] As noted in Chapters 5 and 20, we would recommend a stronger discipline ourselves: Only those operators that are *prescribed by the model* (selectors and THE_ operators in particular) should be allowed to break encapsulation in this sense; all other operators should be implemented in terms of those prescribed operators. Code defensively! But since there is no consensus on an object model, there is no consensus in object systems on that notion of "prescribed operators" either.

as already indicated they are naturally visible to the code that implements the methods. However, many systems are *not* pure in this sense but do expose instance variables to users, a point we will come back to in the next subsection.

■ The **public interface** consists of interface definitions for the methods that apply to this object. Those interface definitions correspond to what in Chapter 20 we called *specification signatures*—except that (as explained in the next paragraph) object systems usually insist that such signatures be tied to just one specific "target" type or class, whereas we had no such notion in Chapter 20 (nor do we find it necessary, nor even desirable [3.3]). As already noted, the code that implements those methods, like the instance variables, is hidden from the user. *Note:* It would be more accurate to say that the public interface is not part of the object in question but is, rather, part of the corresponding "class-defining" object. The **class-defining object** or CDO for a given object is the object that defines the class of which the given object is an instance; in database terms, it is analogous to a *catalog entry* or *descriptor*. Clearly, the public interface for a given object is common to all objects of the class of which the given object is an instance, and it thus makes sense for it to be part of the CDO.

Methods are invoked by means of **messages**. A message is essentially just an *operator invocation,* in which one argument, the **target**, is distinguished and given special syntactic treatment. For example, the following might be a message to department D, asking it to hire employee E:

```
D HIRE_EMP ( E )
```

(hypothetical syntax; see the subsection "Class *vs.* Instance *vs.* Collection" in Section 25.3 for an explanation of the arguments D and E). The target here is the department object denoted by D. The analog of this message in a more conventional programming language —that is, one that treats all arguments equally—might look like this:[4]

```
HIRE_EMP ( D, E )
```

In practice, an object system will come equipped with several *built-in* classes and methods. In particular, the system will almost certainly provide classes such as INTEGER (with methods "=", "<", "+", "−", etc.), CHAR (with methods "=", "<", "||", SUBSTR, etc.), and so forth. Also, of course, the system will provide facilities for suitably skilled users to define and implement classes and methods of their own.

Instance Variables

We now briefly revisit the concept of instance variables. The fact is, a certain amount of confusion does surround this concept. As stated previously, instance variables would be hidden from the user in a pure system; unfortunately, however, most systems are not pure

---

[4] Treating one argument as special can make it easier for the system to perform the *run-time binding* process described in Chapter 20. However, it suffers from many disadvantages [3.3], not the least of which is that it can make it harder for the method implementer to write the implementation code. Another is that which argument is chosen as the target (in cases where there is a choice—i.e., whenever there are two or more arguments) is arbitrary.

in this sense. As a consequence, it is necessary in practice to distinguish between **public** and **private** instance variables; private ones truly are hidden, but public ones are not.

By way of example, suppose we have an object class of line segments, and suppose line segments are physically represented by their BEGIN and END points (we used a similar example in Chapter 5, as you might recall). Then the system will typically allow the user to write expressions of the form *ls*.BEGIN and *ls*.END to "get" the BEGIN and END points for a given line segment *ls*. Thus, BEGIN and END are *public* instance variables (note that, by definition, access to public instance variables must be via some special syntax—typically dot qualification, as our example suggests). And if the physical representation of line segments is now changed—say to the combination of MIDPOINT, LENGTH, and SLOPE—then any program that includes expressions such as *ls*.BEGIN and *ls*.END will now break. In other words, we have lost data independence.

Observe now that public instance variables are logically unnecessary. Suppose we define methods GET_BEGIN, GET_END, GET_MIDPOINT, GET_LENGTH, and GET_SLOPE for line segments. Then the user can "get" the begin point, the end point, the midpoint, and so on, for line segment *ls* by means of appropriate *method invocations:* GET_BEGIN(*ls*), GET_END(*ls*), GET_MIDPOINT(*ls*), and so on. And now it makes no difference what the physical representation of line segments is!—just as long as the various GET_ methods are implemented appropriately, and reimplemented appropriately if that physical representation changes. Furthermore, there would be nothing wrong in allowing the user to abbreviate, for example, GET_BEGIN(*ls*) to just *ls*.BEGIN **as a shorthand**; note that the availability of that shorthand would *not* make BEGIN into a public instance variable. Sadly, however, real systems do not usually operate in this manner; usually, public instance variables really do expose the physical representation (or part of it, at any rate, though there might be some additional instance variables that truly are private and hidden). In accordance with common practice, therefore, we will assume in what follows, until further notice, that objects typically do expose certain public instance variables, even though such exposure is logically unnecessary.

There is another point that needs to be made here. Suppose certain arguments—which the user might well think of, loosely, as "instance variable" arguments—happen to be required in order to create objects of some particular class.[5] Then it does *not* follow that those same "instance variables" can be used for arbitrary purposes. For example, suppose that in order to create a line segment we have to specify the applicable BEGIN and END points. Then it does not follow that (for example) we can get all line segments with a given BEGIN point; rather, such a request will be possible only if a suitable method has been defined.

Finally, note that some systems support a variation on private instance variables called **protected** instance variables. If objects of class *C* have a protected instance variable *P*, then *P* is visible to the code that implements the methods defined for class *C* (of course) *and* to the code that implements the methods defined for *any subclass* (at any level) of class *C*. See the end of Section 25.3 for a brief discussion of subclasses.

---

[5] The objects in question must necessarily be mutable ones, by the way (why?).

Object Identity

Every object has a unique *identifier* called its **object ID** or OID. Immutable objects like the integer 42 are *self-identifying;* that is, they serve as their own OIDs. By contrast, mutable objects have (conceptual) *addresses* as their OIDs, and those addresses can be used elsewhere in the database as (conceptual) *pointers* to the objects in question. While the actual values of such addresses will probably not be directly exposed to the user, they can nevertheless be assigned to program variables and to instance variables within other objects. See Sections 25.3 and 25.4 for further discussion.

   We remark in passing that it is sometimes claimed that it is an advantage of object systems that two distinct objects can be identical in all user-visible respects—that is, be duplicates of one another—and yet be regarded as distinct precisely because they have distinct OIDs. To this writer, however, this claim seems specious. For how can the *user* distinguish between two such objects, externally? See references [6.3], [6.6], and (especially) [25.17] for further discussion of this issue.

25.3   A CLOSER LOOK

We now take a closer look at some of the ideas introduced in the previous section. Suppose we wish to define two object classes, DEPT (departments) and EMP (employees). Suppose also that the user-defined classes MONEY and JOB have already been defined and the class CHAR is built in. Then the necessary class definitions for DEPT and EMP might look somewhat as follows (hypothetical syntax):

```
CLASS DEPT
   PUBLIC  ( DEPT#      CHAR,
             DNAME      CHAR,
             BUDGET     MONEY,
             MGR        OID ( EMP ),
             EMPS       OID ( SET ( OID ( EMP ) ) ) )
   METHODS ( HIRE_EMP ( OID ( EMP ) ) code ,
             FIRE_EMP ( OID ( EMP ) ) code , ... ) ... ;

CLASS EMP
   PUBLIC  ( EMP#       CHAR,
             ENAME      CHAR,
             SALARY     MONEY,
             POSITION   OID ( JOB ) )
   METHODS ( ... ) ... ;
```

Points arising:

1. We have chosen to represent departments and employees by means of a **containment hierarchy**, in which EMP objects are conceptually contained within DEPT objects. Thus, objects of class DEPT include a public instance variable called MGR, representing the given department's manager, and another one called EMPS, representing the given department's employees. More precisely, objects of class DEPT include a public instance variable called MGR whose value is *a pointer to* (i.e., the OID of) an employee, and another one called EMPS whose value is a pointer to a set of pointers to employees. We will elaborate on the containment hierarchy notion in a few moments.

2. For the sake of the example, we have chosen not to include an instance variable within objects of class EMP whose value is either a department OID or a DEPT# value (i.e., what might be called a "foreign key" instance variable). This decision is consistent with our decision to represent departments and employees by means of a containment hierarchy. However, it does mean there is no direct way to get from a given EMP object to the corresponding DEPT object. See Section 25.5, subsection "Relationships," for further discussion of this point.

3. Observe that each class definition includes definitions (coding details omitted) of the methods that apply to objects of the class in question. The *target class* for such methods is, of course, the class whose definition includes the definition of the method in question.[6]

Fig. 25.4 shows some sample object instances corresponding to the DEPT and EMP classes as just defined. Consider first the EMP object at the top of that figure (with OID *eee*), which contains:

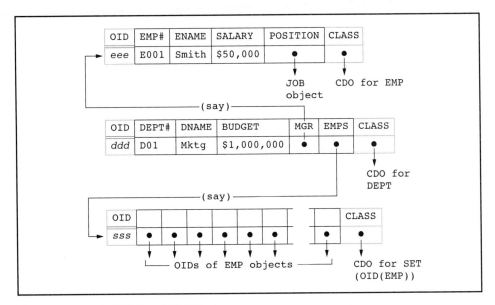

Fig. 25.4 Sample DEPT and EMP instances

---

[6] Note that our hypothetical syntax (undesirably, but quite typically) mixes model and implementation considerations. Note too that we have argued elsewhere [14.12] that departments and employees are bad examples of object classes anyway! Further discussion of this particular point would take us too far afield here, however.

- An immutable object "E001" of the built-in class CHAR in its public instance variable EMP#
- An immutable object "Smith" of the built-in class CHAR in its public instance variable ENAME
- An immutable object "$50,000" of the user-defined class MONEY in its public instance variable SALARY
- *The OID of* a mutable object of the user-defined class JOB in its public instance variable POSITION[7]

It also contains at least two additional private instance variables, one containing the OID *eee* of the EMP object itself, and one containing the OID of the class-defining object—that is, the CDO—for EMPs (so that the implementation can find descriptor information for this object). *Note:* These two OIDs might or might not be physically stored with the object. For instance, the value *eee* need not necessarily be stored as part of the relevant EMP object; it is necessary only that the implementation have some way of locating that EMP object given that value *eee* (i.e., some way of mapping that value *eee* to that EMP object's physical address). Conceptually, however, the user can always think of the OID as being part of the object as shown.

Now we turn to the DEPT object in the center of the figure, with OID *ddd*. That object contains:

- An immutable object "D01" of the built-in class CHAR in its public instance variable DEPT#
- An immutable object "Mktg" of the built-in class CHAR in its public instance variable DNAME
- An immutable object "$1,000,000" of the user-defined class MONEY in its public instance variable BUDGET
- The OID *eee* of a mutable object of the user-defined class EMP in its public instance variable MGR (this is the OID of the object that represents the department manager)
- The OID *sss* of a mutable object of the user-defined class SET(OID(EMP)) in its public instance variable EMPS
- Two private instance variables containing, respectively, the OID *ddd* of the DEPT object itself and the OID of the corresponding class-defining object

Finally, the object with OID *sss* contains a set of OIDs of individual (mutable) EMP objects, plus the usual private instance variables.

Now, Fig. 25.4 depicts the objects "as they really are"; in other words, the figure illustrates the *data structure* component of "the object model," and such figures must thus be clearly understood by users of that model. Object texts and presentations, however, typically do not show diagrams like that of Fig. 25.4; instead, they typically represent the situation as shown in Fig. 25.5 (which might be regarded as being at a higher level of abstraction and hence easier to understand).

---

[7] The other three public instance variables can also be regarded as containing OIDs, since immutable objects serve as their own OIDs.

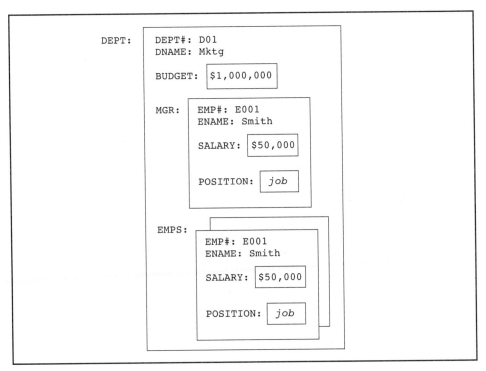

Fig. 25.5   Sample DEPT and EMP instances as a containment hierarchy

The representation shown in Fig. 25.5 is certainly more consistent with the containment hierarchy interpretation. However, it obscures the important fact that (as already explained) objects usually contain not other objects as such but rather *OIDs* of—that is, pointers to—other objects. For example, Fig. 25.5 clearly suggests that the DEPT object for department D01 includes the EMP object for employee E001 twice (implying among other things that employee E001 might be represented, inconsistently, as having two different salaries in its two different appearances). This sleight of hand is the source of much confusion, which is why we prefer pictures like that of Fig. 25.4.

As an aside, we note that real object class definitions often increase the confusion, because they often do not define instance variables as "OIDs" (as our hypothetical syntax does) but instead directly reflect the containment hierarchy interpretation. Thus, for example, instance variable EMPS in object class DEPT might be defined not as OID(SET (OID(EMP))) but just as SET(EMP). Though cumbersome, we prefer our style of definition, for clarity and accuracy.

It is worth pointing out too that all of the old criticisms of hierarchies in general as found in, for example, IMS apply to containment hierarchies in particular. Space does not permit detailed consideration of those criticisms here; suffice it to say that the overriding issue is **lack of symmetry**. In particular, hierarchies do not lend themselves well to the representation of many-to-many relationships. Consider suppliers and parts, for instance:

Do the suppliers contain the parts, or *vice versa?* Or both? What about suppliers, parts, and projects?

Actually matters are more confused than we have been pretending so far. On the one hand, it is claimed (as previously explained) that objects are *hierarchies,* which means they are subject to the usual criticisms of hierarchies, as already noted. On the other hand, however, it is clear from figures like Fig. 25.4 that objects are not really hierarchies at all but **tuples**—where the tuple components can be any of the following:

1. Immutable "subobjects" (i.e., self-identifying values such as integers or money amounts)

2. OIDs of mutable "subobjects" (i.e., pointers to other, possibly shared, mutable objects)

3. Sets, lists, arrays, . . . of 1, 2, or 3

plus certain hidden components. Note point 3 in particular: Object systems typically support several "collection" type generators—for example, SET, LIST, ARRAY, BAG, and so on (though usually not RELATION!)—and those generators can be combined in arbitrary ways. For example, an array of lists of bags of arrays of pointers to integer variables might constitute a single object in appropriate circumstances. See the subsection "Class *vs.* Instance *vs.* Collection," later in this section, for further discussion.

Object IDs Revisited

Relational DBMSs typically rely on user-defined, user-controlled keys—"user keys" for short—for entity identification and referencing purposes. (In fact, pointer-style OIDs are expressly prohibited in relational databases, as we know from Chapters 1 and 3; see also further discussion in Chapter 26.) It is well known, however, that user keys do suffer from a number of problems; references [14.11] and [14.21] discuss such problems in detail and argue that relational DBMSs should support *system*-defined keys ("surrogates") instead, at least as an option. And the argument in favor of OIDs in object systems is similar, somewhat, to the argument in favor of surrogates in relational systems. (Do not, however, make the mistake of equating the two: Surrogates are *regular values* and are visible to the user, while OIDs are *addresses*—at least conceptually—and are hidden from the user. See reference [25.17] for an extensive discussion of these distinctions and related issues.) Points arising:

1. First, note that OIDs do not avoid the need for user keys, as we will see in Section 25.4. To be more precise, user keys are still needed for interaction with the outside world, even if all object cross-referencing inside the database is done via OIDs.

2. What is the OID for a *derived* object?—for example, the "join" of a given EMP and the corresponding DEPT, or the "projection" of a given DEPT over BUDGET and MGR? (This question of *derived objects* is an important one, by the way, but we have to defer it for now. See Section 25.5.)

3. OIDs are the source of the often-heard criticisms to the effect that object systems look like "CODASYL warmed over"—where, as explained in Chapter 1, the term

CODASYL refers generically to certain network (i.e., prerelational) database systems such as IDMS. Certainly OIDs tend to lead to a rather low-level, pointer-chasing style of programming (see Section 25.4) that is very reminiscent of the old CODASYL style. Also, the fact that OIDs are pointers accounts for the claims, also sometimes heard, to the effect that:

- CODASYL systems are closer to object systems than relational systems are.

- Relational systems are *value-based* while object systems are *identity-based.*

Class *vs.* Instance *vs.* Collection

Object systems distinguish the concepts of *class, instance,* and *collection.* As already explained, a **class** is basically a data type[8]—possibly built-in, possibly user-defined—of arbitrary complexity. Every class understands a **NEW** message, which causes a new, mutable **instance** of the class to be created; the method invoked by the NEW message is called a **constructor function**. Here is an example (hypothetical syntax):

```
E  :=  EMP NEW ( 'E001', 'Smith', MONEY ( 50000 ), POS ) ;
```

Here POS is a program variable that contains the OID of some JOB object. The NEW method is invoked on the object class EMP; it creates a new object of that class, with instance variables initialized to the values specified, and returns that new object's OID. That OID is then assigned to the program variable E.

Next, because objects can be pointed to (via OIDs) by any number of other objects, they can effectively be *shared* by those other objects. In particular, they can belong to any number of **collection** objects simultaneously. To continue with the example:

```
CLASS EMP_COLL
    PUBLIC ( EMPS OID ( SET ( OID ( EMP ) ) ) ) ... ;

ALL_EMPS  :=  EMP_COLL NEW ( ) ;

ALL_EMPS ADD ( E ) ;
```

Explanation:

1. An object of class EMP_COLL contains a single public instance variable, called EMPS, whose value is a pointer (OID) to a mutable object whose value is a set of pointers (OIDs) to individual EMP objects.

2. ALL_EMPS is a program variable whose value is the OID of an object of class EMP_COLL. After the assignment operation, it contains the OID of such an object whose value in turn is the OID of an *empty* set of OIDs of EMP objects.

3. ADD is a method that is understood by objects of class EMP_COLL. In the example, that method is applied to the object of that class whose OID is given in the program variable ALL_EMPS; its effect is to add the OID of the EMP object whose

---

[8] As mentioned in Section 25.2, some systems use both "type" and "class," in which case "type" means *type* or *intension* and "class" means *extension* (i.e., a certain *collection*), or sometimes *implementation* (of the type in question). Then again, other systems use the terms the other way around . . . We will continue to take "class" to mean a type in the sense of Chapter 5.

OID is given in the program variable E to the (previously empty) set of OIDs whose OID is given in the EMP_COLL object whose OID is given in the program variable ALL_EMPS.

After the foregoing sequence of operations, we can say, loosely, that the variable ALL_EMPS denotes a collection of EMPs that currently contains just one EMP (*viz.,* employee E001). By the way, note the need to mention a user key in this latter sentence!

Naturally, we can have any number of distinct, and possibly overlapping, "sets of employees" at any given time:

```
PROGRAMMERS   :=  EMP_COLL NEW ( ) ;

PROGRAMMERS ADD ( E ) ;

    . . . . .

HIGHLY_PAID   :=  EMP_COLL NEW ( ) ;

HIGHLY_PAID ADD ( E ) ;
```

and so on. Contrast the state of affairs in SQL systems. For example, the SQL statement

```
CREATE TABLE EMP
      ( EMP# ....... NOT NULL,
        ENAME ...... NOT NULL,
        SALARY ..... NOT NULL,
        POSITION ... NOT NULL ) ... ;
```

creates a type *and* a collection simultaneously; the type is defined by the table heading, and the (initially empty) collection is the table body. Likewise, the SQL statement

```
INSERT INTO EMP ( ... ) VALUES ( ... ) ;
```

creates an individual EMP row—we assume for simplicity that the INSERT is indeed inserting just a single row—*and* adds it to the EMP collection simultaneously. In SQL, therefore:

1. There is no way for an individual EMP "object" to exist without being part of some "collection": in fact, exactly one "collection" (but see subsequent discussion, and note in any case that thinking of an EMP row as an "object" is somewhat suspect, as we will see in Chapter 26).

2. There is no direct way to create two distinct "collections" of the same "class" of EMP "objects" (but see subsequent discussion).

3. There is no direct way to share the same "object" across distinct "collections" of EMP "objects" (but see subsequent discussion).

At least, the foregoing are claims that are sometimes heard. But they do not stand up to close scrutiny. First, the *foreign key* mechanism can be used to achieve an analogous effect in each case; for example, we could define two more base tables called PROGRAMMERS and HIGHLY_PAID, each of them containing just the employee numbers for the relevant employees. Second (and much more important), the *view* mechanism can also be used to achieve a similar effect. For example, we could define PROGRAMMERS and HIGHLY_PAID as views of the EMP base table:

```
CREATE VIEW PROGRAMMERS
     AS SELECT EMP#, ENAME, SALARY, POSITION
        FROM    EMP
        WHERE   POSITION = 'Programmer' ;

CREATE VIEW HIGHLY_PAID
     AS SELECT EMP#, ENAME, SALARY, POSITION
        FROM    EMP
        WHERE   SALARY > some threshold ;
```

And now it is perfectly possible for the very same EMP "object" to belong to two or more "collections" simultaneously. What is more, membership in those collections that happen to be views is handled automatically by the system, not manually by the programmer.

We close this discussion by noting that there is an illuminating parallel between the mutable objects of object systems and the **explicit dynamic variables** of certain programming language systems (PL/I's BASED variables are a case in point). Like mutable objects of a given class, there can be any number of distinct explicit dynamic variables of a given type, the storage for which is allocated at run time by explicit program action. Furthermore, those distinct variables, again like individual mutable objects, *have no name,* and thus must be addressed via pointers. In PL/I, for example, we might write:

```
DCL XYZ INTEGER BASED ;          /* XYZ is a BASED variable */
DCL P POINTER ;                  /* P is a pointer variable */

ALLOCATE XYZ SET ( P ) ;         /* create a new XYZ instance */
                                 /* and set P to point to it  */

P -> XYZ = 3 ;                   /* assign the value 3 to the XYZ */
                                 /* instance pointed to by P      */
```

(and so on). This PL/I code bears a striking resemblance to the object code shown earlier; in particular, the declaration of the BASED variable is akin to the creation of an object class, and the ALLOCATE operation is akin to the creation of a NEW instance of that class. We can thus see that the reason OIDs are necessary in the object model is precisely because, in general, the objects they identify do not possess any other unique name—just like BASED variable instances in PL/I.

Class Hierarchies

No treatment of basic object concepts would be complete without some mention of **class hierarchies** (not to be confused with containment hierarchies). However, the "class hierarchy" concept in the object world is analogous to the type hierarchy concept, already discussed at length in Chapter 20; we therefore content ourselves here with a few brief definitions (paraphrased from Chapter 20, for the most part) and a few pertinent observations. *Note:* We remind you that there is little consensus—in the object world or anywhere else—on an abstract inheritance *model,* and different inheritance systems therefore differ from one another considerably at the detail level.

First of all, object class Y is said to be a **subclass** of object class X—equivalently, object class X is said to be a **superclass** of object class Y—if and only if every object of class Y is necessarily an object of class X ("Y **ISA** X"). Objects of class Y then **inherit** the public instance variables and methods that apply to class X.[9] Inheriting instance variables is called **structural** inheritance, inheriting methods is called **behavioral** inheritance. In a pure system, there is only behavioral inheritance, no structural inheritance—at least for scalar or fully encapsulated objects—because there is no structure to inherit (no structure visible to the user, that is). In practice, however, object systems are typically not pure and do support some degree of structural inheritance (meaning, to stress the point, inheritance of public instance variables). *Note:* If a subclass has additional public instance variables, over and above the ones it inherits from its (immediate) superclass, it is said to *extend* that superclass.

If class *Y* is a subclass of class *X,* the user can always use an object of class *Y* wherever an object of class *X* is permitted (e.g., as an argument to various methods)—this is the principle of **substitutability**—and thereby obtain **code reuse**. Because object systems often do not clearly distinguish between values and variables, however—that is, between immutable and mutable objects—they tend to run into trouble over the distinction between value and variable substitutability (see Chapter 20 for further discussion). Be that as it may, the ability to apply the same method to objects of class *X* and class *Y* is referred to as **polymorphism**.

The system will come equipped with certain built-in class hierarchies. In OPAL, for example (see Section 25.4), every class is considered to be a subclass at some level of the built-in class OBJECT (because "everything is an object"). Built-in subclasses of OBJECT include BOOLEAN, CHAR, INTEGER, COLLECTION, and so on; COLLECTION in turn has a subclass called BAG, and BAG has another called SET, and so on. (But surely COLLECTION, BAG, and SET are not classes as such but "class generators"—like RELATION in **Tutorial D**? There seems to be some confusion here.)

One important point is that object systems typically do not allow objects to change their class (see the annotation to reference [20.12]). As a consequence, object systems do not support specialization or generalization by constraint; hence, such systems cannot support what we would regard as a "good" model of inheritance. We will elaborate on this point in the next chapter (in Section 26.3).

Finally, some object systems do support some form of **multiple** inheritance in addition to single inheritance. However, no object system known to this writer supports tuple or relation inheritance (either single or multiple) in the sense of reference [3.3].

25.4   A CRADLE-TO-GRAVE EXAMPLE

We have now introduced the basic concepts of object systems. In this section we show how those concepts fit together by presenting a "cradle-to-grave" example—that is, we show how an object database can be defined, how it can be populated, and how retrieval and update operations can be performed on it. Our example is based on the GemStone product from GemStone Systems Inc. and its language OPAL [25.13]; OPAL in turn is based on Smalltalk [25.23]. *Note:* Smalltalk is one of the earliest and purest of the object

---

[9] They will probably inherit the private instance variables as well, but we regard such inheritance as an implementation matter, not part of the model.

languages, which is why we use it here, but it is only fair to mention that in products and applications it seems to have been largely supplanted by C++ and, increasingly, Java.

The example involves a simplified version of the education database from Exercise 9.7 in Chapter 9. The database contains information about an in-house company education training scheme. For each training course, the database contains details of all offerings of that course; for each offering it contains details of all student enrollments and all teachers for that offering. The database also contains information about employees. A relational version of the database looks (in outline) something like this:

```
COURSE     { COURSE#, TITLE }
OFFERING   { COURSE#, OFF#, OFFDATE, LOCATION }
TEACHER    { COURSE#, OFF#, EMP# }
ENROLLMENT { COURSE#, OFF#, EMP#, GRADE }
EMP        { EMP#, ENAME, SALARY, POSITION }
```

Fig. 25.6 is a referential diagram for this database.

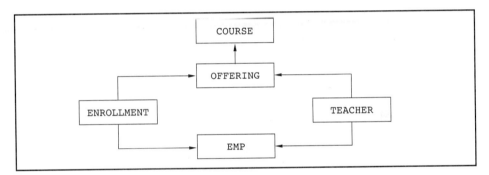

Fig. 25.6   Referential diagram for the education database

Data Definition

We now proceed to show a set of OPAL definitions for this database. Here first is the definition for an object class called EMP (the lines are numbered for purposes of subsequent reference):

```
1  OBJECT SUBCLASS : 'EMP'
2      INSTVARNAMES : #[ 'EMP#', 'ENAME', 'POSITION' ]
3      CONSTRAINTS  : #[ #[ #EMP#, STRING ] ,
4                         [ #ENAME, STRING ] ,
5                         [ #POSITION, STRING ] ] .
```

Explanation: Line 1 defines an object class called EMP, a subclass of the built-in class OBJECT. (In OPAL terms, line 1 is *sending a message* to the OBJECT object, asking it to invoke the SUBCLASS method; INSTVARNAMES and CONSTRAINTS specify arguments to that method invocation. Defining a new class—like everything else in OPAL—is thus done by sending a message to an object.) Line 2 states that objects of class EMP have three private instance variables called EMP#, ENAME, and POSITION, respectively, and lines 3–5 constrain those instance variables each to contain objects of class STRING. *Note:* Throughout this section we omit discussion of purely syntactic details (such as the ubiquitous "#" signs) that are irrelevant to our main purpose.

To repeat, instance variables EMP#, ENAME, and POSITION are *private* to class EMP; they can thus be accessed by name solely within the code that implements methods for that class. Here, for example, are definitions of methods to "get and set"—that is, retrieve and update—employee numbers (the symbol "^" can be read as "return"):

```
METHOD : EMP
   GET_EMP#
      ^EMP#
%

METHOD : EMP
   SET_EMP# : EMP#_PARM
      EMP#  :=  EMP#_PARM
%
```

We will have more to say regarding methods in the next subsection. Meanwhile, here is the definition of the COURSE class:

```
1   OBJECT SUBCLASS : 'COURSE'
2       INSTVARNAMES : #[ 'COURSE#', 'TITLE', 'OFFERINGS' ]
3       CONSTRAINTS  : #[ #[ #COURSE#, STRING ] ,
4                          [ #TITLE, STRING ] ,
5                          [ #OFFERINGS, OSET ] ] .
```

Explanation: Line 5 here specifies that the private instance variable OFFERINGS will contain *the OID of* an object of class OSET (a class we will define in a few moments). Informally, OFFERINGS will denote the set of all offerings for the course in question; in other words, we have chosen to model the course/offerings relationship as a containment hierarchy, in which offerings are conceptually contained within the corresponding course.

Next the OFFERING class:

```
1   OBJECT SUBCLASS : 'OFFERING'
2       INSTVARNAMES : #[ 'OFF#', 'ODATE', 'LOCATION',
3                          'ENROLLMENTS', 'TEACHERS' ]
4       CONSTRAINTS  : #[ #[ #OFF#, STRING ] ,
5                          [ #ODATE, DATETIME ] ,
6                          [ #LOCATION, STRING ] ,
7                          [ #ENROLLMENTS, NSET ] ,
8                          [ #TEACHERS, TSET ] ] .
```

Explanation: Line 7 specifies that the private instance variable ENROLLMENTS will contain the OID of an object of class NSET; informally, ENROLLMENTS will denote the set of all enrollments for the offering in question. Likewise, TEACHERS will denote the set of all teachers for the offering in question. Again, therefore, we are adopting a containment hierarchy representation. See later for the NSET and TSET definitions.

Next the ENROLLMENT class:

```
1   OBJECT SUBCLASS : 'ENROLLMENT'
2       INSTVARNAMES : #[ 'EMP', 'GRADE' ]
3       CONSTRAINTS  : #[ #[ #EMP, EMP ] ,
4                          [ #GRADE, STRING ] ] .
```

Explanation: The private instance variable EMP (line 3) will contain the OID of an object of class EMP, representing the individual employee to whom this enrollment pertains. *Note:* We have placed the EMP object "inside" the corresponding ENROLLMENT object in order to continue with the containment hierarchy representation. But notice the asymmetry: Enrollments are a many-to-many relationship, but the participants in that relationship, employees and offerings, are being treated quite differently.

Finally, teachers. For the sake of the example, we depart slightly from the original relational version of the database and treat teachers as a subclass of employees:

```
1   EMP SUBCLASS : 'TEACHER'
2         INSTVARNAMES  : #[ 'COURSES' ]
3         CONSTRAINTS   : #[ #[ #COURSES, CSET ] ] .
```

Explanation: Line 1 defines an object class called TEACHER, a subclass of the user-defined class EMP (in other words, TEACHER "ISA" EMP). Thus, each individual TEACHER object has private instance variables EMP#, ENAME, and POSITION (all inherited from EMP[10]), plus COURSES, which will contain the OID of an object of class CSET; that CSET object will denote the set of all courses this teacher can teach. Each TEACHER object also inherits all EMP methods.

As already noted, the foregoing class definitions assume the existence of several collection classes (ESET, CSET, OSET, NSET, and TSET). Here now are the definitions of those classes:

```
1   SET SUBCLASS    : 'ESET'
2         CONSTRAINTS : EMP .
```

Explanation: Line 1 defines an object class ESET, a subclass of the built-in class SET. Line 2 constrains objects of class ESET to be sets of OIDs of objects of class EMP. In general, there could be any number of objects of class ESET, but we will create just one (see the next subsection), which will be the set of OIDs of *all* EMP objects that currently exist in the database. Informally, that single ESET object can be regarded as the object counterpart of the EMP base relvar in the relational version of the database.

The CSET, OSET, NSET, and TSET definitions are analogous. In each of these cases, however, we will definitely have to create several objects of the relevant collection class, not just one; for example, there will be a separate OSET collection object for each individual COURSE object.

```
SET SUBCLASS    : 'CSET'
      CONSTRAINTS : COURSE .

SET SUBCLASS    : 'OSET'
      CONSTRAINTS : OFFERING .

SET SUBCLASS    : 'NSET'
      CONSTRAINTS : ENROLLMENT .

SET SUBCLASS    : 'TSET'
      CONSTRAINTS : TEACHER .
```

---

[10] Note that it is the *private* representation (i.e., the physical implementation) that is being inherited here.

Populating the Database

Now we consider what is involved in populating the database. We consider each of the five basic object classes (EMP, COURSE, etc.) in turn. First, employees. Recall that we intend to collect the OIDs of all currently existing EMP objects in an ESET object, so first we need to create that ESET object:

```
OID_OF_SET_OF_ALL_EMPS  :=  ESET NEW .
```

The expression on the right side of this assignment returns the OID of a new, empty instance of class ESET (i.e., an empty set of EMP OIDs); the OID of that new instance is then assigned to the program variable OID_OF_SET_OF_ALL_EMPS. *Very* informally, we will say that OID_OF_SET_OF_ALL_EMPS denotes "the set of all employees."

Now, every time we create a new EMP object we want the OID of that object to be inserted into the ESET object identified by the OID just saved in the variable OID_OF_SET_OF_ALL_EMPS. We therefore define a *method* for creating such an EMP object and inserting its OID into that ESET object. (Alternatively, we could write an application program to perform the same task.) Here is that method:

```
 1   METHOD : ESET                           " anonymous!      "
 2     ADD_EMP#  : EMP#_PARM                  " parameters      "
 3     ADD_ENAME : ENAME_PARM
 4     ADD_POS   : POS_PARM
 5     | EMP_OID |                            " local variable "
 6     EMP_OID := EMP NEW .                   " new employee    "
 7     EMP_OID SET_EMP#  : EMP#_PARM ;        " initialize      "
 8             SET_ENAME : ENAME_PARM ;
 9             SET_POS   : POS_PARM .
10     SELF ADD: EMP_OID .                    " insert          "
11   %
```

Explanation:

1. Line 1 defines the code that follows (up to the terminating percent sign in line 11) to be a method that applies to objects of class ESET. (In fact, *exactly one* object of class ESET will exist in the system at run time.)

2. Lines 2–4 define three parameters, with external names ADD_EMP#, ADD_ENAME, and ADD_POS. These names are used in messages that invoke the method. The corresponding internal names EMP#_PARM, ENAME_PARM, and POS_PARM are used in the code that implements the method.

3. Line 5 defines EMP_OID to be a local variable, and line 6 then assigns to that variable the OID of a new, uninitialized EMP instance.

4. Lines 7–9 send a message to that new EMP instance; the message specifies three methods to be invoked (SET_EMP#, SET_ENAME, and SET_POS) and passes one argument to each of them (EMP#_PARM to SET_EMP#, ENAME_PARM to SET_ENAME, and POS_PARM to SET_POS). *Note:* We are assuming here that methods SET_ENAME and SET_POS—analogous to the method SET_EMP# shown earlier—have also been defined already.

5. Line 10 sends a message to SELF, which is a special symbol that denotes the object to which the method being defined is currently being applied at run time (i.e., the current

target object). The message causes the built-in method ADD to be applied to that object (ADD is a method that is understood by all collections); the effect in the case at hand is to insert the OID of the object identified by EMP_OID into the object identified by SELF (which will be the ESET object containing the OIDs for all EMP objects that currently exist). *Note:* The reason the special variable SELF is required is that the parameter corresponding to the target object has no name of its own (see line 1).

6. Note that—as pointed out in the comment in line 1—the method being defined is likewise unnamed. In general, in fact, methods do not have names in OPAL, but instead are identified by their *signature* (defined in OPAL to be the combination of the name of the class to which they apply and the external names of their parameters). This convention can lead to awkward circumlocutions, as can be seen. Note too another slightly unfortunate implication: namely, that if two methods both apply to the same class and take the same parameters, those parameters must be given arbitrarily different external names in the two methods.

Now we have a method for inserting new EMPs into the database, but we still have not actually inserted any. So let us do so:

```
OID_OF_SET_OF_ALL_EMPS ADD_EMP#  : 'E009'
                       ADD_ENAME : 'Helms'
                       ADD_POS   : 'Janitor' .
```

This statement creates an EMP object for employee E009 and adds the OID of that EMP object to the set of OIDs of all currently existing EMP objects.

Note, incidentally, that the built-in NEW method must now never be used on class EMP other than as part of the method we have just defined—for otherwise we might create some dangling EMP objects, that is, employees who are not represented in the ESET object containing the OIDs for all EMP objects that currently exist. *Note:* We apologize for the burdensome repetition of awkward circumlocutions like "the method we have just defined" and "the ESET object containing the OIDs for all EMP objects that currently exist," but it is hard to talk concisely about things that have no name.

Now, employees really represent the simplest possible case, since they correspond to "regular entities" (to use the terminology of the E/R model), and moreover do not contain other objects embedded within themselves (apart from immutable ones). We now move on to consider the more complex case of *courses,* which—although still "regular entities"—do conceptually include other mutable objects embedded within them. In outline, the steps we must go through are as follows:

1. Apply the NEW method to class CSET to create an initially empty "set of all courses" (actually COURSE OIDs).

2. Define a method for creating a new COURSE object and adding its OID to "the set of all courses." That method will take a specified COURSE# and TITLE as arguments and will create a new COURSE object with the specified values. It will also apply the NEW method to class OSET to create an initially empty set of OFFERING OIDs, and will then place the OID of that empty set of offering OIDs into the OFFERINGS position within the new COURSE object.

3. Invoke the method just defined for each individual course in turn.

Next we turn to offerings. This time the steps are as follows:

1. Define a method for creating a new OFFERING object. That method will take a specified OFF#, ODATE, and LOCATION as arguments and create a new OFFERING object with those specified values. It will also:

   - Apply the NEW method to class NSET to create an initially empty set of EN-ROLLMENT OIDs, and then place the OID of that empty set into the ENROLL-MENTS position within the new OFFERING object.

   - Apply the NEW method to class TSET to create an initially empty set of TEACHER OIDs, and then place the OID of that empty set into the TEACHERS position within the new OFFERING object.

2. The method will also take a COURSE# value as argument and use that COURSE# value to:

   - Locate the corresponding COURSE object for the new OFFERING object (see the next subsection for an indication of how this might be done).[11]

   - Hence, locate "the set of all offerings" for that COURSE object.

   - Hence, add the OID of the new OFFERING object to the appropriate "set of all offerings."

   Note carefully, therefore, that (as mentioned earlier in this chapter) OIDs do not avoid the need for user keys such as COURSE#. Indeed, such keys are needed, not just to identify objects in the outside world, but also to serve as the basis for certain lookups inside the database.

3. Finally, invoke the method just defined for each individual offering in turn.

   Observe, incidentally, that (in keeping with our containment hierarchy design) we have chosen not to create a "set of *all* offerings." One implication of this omission is that any query that requires that set as its scope—for example, "Get all offerings in New York"—will involve a certain amount of procedural workaround code (see the next subsection).

   Next, enrollments. The difference in kind between the enrollments and offerings cases is that ENROLLMENT objects include an instance variable, EMP, whose value is the OID of the relevant EMP object. Hence the necessary sequence of steps is as follows:

1. Define a method for creating a new ENROLLMENT object. That method will take a specified COURSE#, OFF#, EMP#, and GRADE as arguments and create a new ENROLLMENT object with the specified GRADE value. It will then:

   - Use the COURSE# and OFF# values to locate the corresponding OFFERING object for the new ENROLLMENT object.

   - Hence, locate "the set of all enrollments" for that OFFERING object.

   - Hence, add the OID of the new ENROLLMENT object to the appropriate "set of all enrollments."

---

[11] Of course, the method must reject the attempt to create a new offering if the corresponding course cannot be found. We omit detailed consideration of such exception cases here and throughout these discussions.

It will also:

- Use the EMP# value to locate the relevant EMP object.
- Hence, place the OID of that EMP object in the EMP position within the new ENROLLMENT object.

2. Invoke the method just defined for each individual enrollment in turn.

Finally, teachers. The difference in kind between the teachers and offerings cases is that we have made TEACHER a subclass of EMP. Hence:

1. Define a method for creating a new TEACHER object. That method will take a specified COURSE#, OFF#, and EMP# as its arguments. It will then:

- Use the EMP# value to locate the relevant EMP object.
- Change the most specific class of that EMP object to TEACHER, since that employee is now additionally a teacher (just how that change of class is done is highly dependent on the particular system under consideration, however, and we omit further details here).

It will also:

- Use the COURSE# and OFF# values to locate the corresponding OFFERING object for the new TEACHER object.
- Hence, locate "the set of all teachers" for that OFFERING object.
- Hence, add the OID of the new TEACHER object to the appropriate "set of all teachers."

2. In addition, the set of courses this teacher can teach must be specified somehow and the COURSES instance variable set appropriately in the new TEACHER object. We omit the details of this step here.

3. Invoke the method just defined for each individual teacher in turn.

Retrieval Operations

Before getting into details of retrieval operations as such, we make the point (though it should already be obvious) that OPAL—like object languages in general—is essentially a record-level (or at least object-level) language, not a set-level language. Hence, most problems will require some programmer to write some procedural code. We consider a single example: the query "Get all New York offerings of course C001." We suppose for the sake of the example that we have a variable called OOSOAC whose value is the OID of "the set of all courses." Here then is the code:

```
1 | COURSE_C001 , C001_OFFS , C001_NY_OFFS |
2   COURSE_C001
3     :=  OOSOAC DETECT : [ :CX | ( CX GET_COURSE# ) = 'C001' ] .
4   C001_OFFS
5     :=  COURSE_C001 GET_OFFERINGS .
6   C001_NY_OFFS
7     :=  C001_OFFS SELECT :
8               [ :OX | ( OX GET_LOCATION ) = 'New York' ] .
9 ^ C001_NY_OFFS .
```

Explanation:

1. Line 1 declares three local variables: COURSE_C001, which will be used to hold the OID of course C001; C001_OFFS, which will be used to hold the OID of the set of OIDs of offerings of course C001; and C001_NY_OFFS, which will be used to hold the OID of the set of OIDs of the offerings actually required (i.e., the New York ones).

2. Lines 2–3 send a message to the (collection) object denoted by the variable OOSOAC. The message calls for the built-in method **DETECT** to be applied to that collection. The DETECT argument is an expression of the form:

   ```
   [ :x | p(x) ]
   ```

   Here $p(x)$ is a boolean expression involving the variable x, and x is effectively a range variable that ranges over the members of the collection to which the DETECT is applied (i.e., the set of COURSE objects, in the example). The result of the DETECT is the OID of the first object x encountered in that set for which $p(x)$ evaluates to TRUE—that is, it is the COURSE object for course C001, in the example.[12] The OID of that COURSE object is then assigned to the variable COURSE_C001. *Note:* It is also possible to specify an "escape" argument to DETECT to deal with the case in which $p(x)$ never evaluates to TRUE. We omit the details here.

3. Lines 4–5 assign the OID of "the set of all offerings" for course C001 to the variable C001_OFFS.

4. Lines 6–8 are rather similar to lines 2–3: The operation of the built-in method **SELECT** is the same as that of DETECT, except that it returns the OID of the set of OIDs of *all* objects x (instead of just the first such) for which $p(x)$ evaluates to TRUE. In the example, therefore, the effect is to assign the OID of the set of OIDs of New York offerings of course C001 to the variable C001_NY_OFFS.

5. Finally, line 9 returns that OID to the caller.

Points arising:

- First, note that the boolean expression $p(x)$ in SELECT and DETECT can involve (at its most complex) a set of simple scalar comparisons all ANDed together—that is, it is not an arbitrarily complex expression.

- The brackets surrounding the overall argument expression in SELECT and DETECT can be replaced by braces. If braces are used, OPAL will attempt to use an index (if one exists) in applying the method. If brackets are used, it will not.

- When we say that DETECT returns the OID of the "first" object encountered that makes $p(x)$ evaluate to TRUE, we mean the first according to whatever sequence OPAL uses to search the set (sets have no intrinsic ordering of their own). In our example it makes no difference, because the "first" object that makes the boolean expression evaluate to TRUE is in fact the only such.

---

[12] We assume throughout this example that methods such as GET_COURSE#—analogous to the method GET_EMP# shown earlier in this section—have already been defined.

- You might have noticed that we have been making considerable use of expressions such as "the DETECT method," whereas we said previously that methods in OPAL have no names. Indeed, DETECT and SELECT are not method names (and phraseology such as "the DETECT method" is strictly incorrect). Rather, they are *external parameter names* for certain built-in, unnamed methods. For brevity and simplicity, however, we will continue to talk as if DETECT and SELECT (and other similar items) were indeed method names.

- You might also have noticed that we have been using (many times!) the expression "the NEW method." This usage is in fact *not* incorrect: Methods that take no arguments other than the required target argument are an exception to the general OPAL rule that methods are unnamed.

Update Operations

The object analog of the relational INSERT operation has already been discussed in the previous subsection. The object analogs of UPDATE and DELETE are discussed in the remainder of this section.

- *Update:* Update operations are performed in essentially the same manner as retrieval operations, except that SET_ methods are used instead of GET_ methods.

- *Delete:* The built-in method REMOVE is used to delete objects (more precisely, it is used to remove the OID of a specified object from a specified collection). When an object reaches a point when there are no remaining pointers to it anywhere—that is, it can no longer be accessed at all—then OPAL deletes it automatically by means of a garbage-collection process. Here is an example:

```
E001   :=   OID_OF_SET_OF_ALL_EMPS
            DETECT : [ :EX | ( EX GET_EMP# ) = 'E001' ] .
OID_OF_SET_OF_ALL_EMPS REMOVE : E001 .
```

("remove employee E001 from the set of all employees").

But what if we want to enforce (say) an ON DELETE CASCADE rule?—for example, a rule to the effect that deleting an employee is to delete all enrollments for that employee as well? The answer, of course, is that we have to implement an appropriate method once again; in other words, we have to write some more procedural code.

Incidentally, it might be thought that the garbage-collection approach to deletion does at least implement a kind of ON DELETE RESTRICT rule, inasmuch as an object is not actually deleted as long as any pointers to that object exist. However, such is not necessarily the case. For example, OFFERING objects do not include the OID of the corresponding COURSE object, and hence offerings do not "restrict" DELETEs on courses. (In fact, containment hierarchies tacitly imply a kind of ON DELETE CASCADE rule, *unless* the user chooses either (a) to include the OID of the parent in the child or (b) to include the OID of the child in some other object elsewhere in the database, in which case the containment hierarchy interpretation no longer makes sense anyway. See the discussion of *inverse variables* in the next section.)

Note finally that REMOVE can be used to emulate a relational DROP operation—for example, to drop the ENROLLMENT class. The details are left as an exercise.

25.5   MISCELLANEOUS ISSUES

In this section we take a brief look at a somewhat mixed bag of issues—namely:

- *Ad hoc* query and related issues
- Integrity
- Relationships
- Database programming languages
- Performance considerations
- Is an object DBMS really a DBMS?

Ad Hoc Query and Related Issues

We did not call the point out explicitly before, but if it is really true that predefined methods are the only way to manipulate objects, then *ad hoc* query is impossible!—unless classes and methods are designed in accordance with a certain very specific discipline. For example, if the only methods defined for class DEPT are (as suggested in Section 25.2) HIRE_EMP, FIRE_EMP, and CUT_BUDGET, then even a query as simple as "Who is the manager of the programming department?" cannot be formulated.

For essentially the same reason, view definitions and declarative integrity constraints on objects are also impossible, in general—again, unless a certain specific discipline is followed.

Our own recommended solution to these problems (i.e., the "specific discipline" we have in mind) is as follows:

1. Define a set of operators ("THE_ operators") that expose *some possible representation* for the objects in question, as discussed in Chapter 5.

2. Embed the objects properly in a relational framework (this part of the solution is discussed in detail in the next chapter).

But object systems typically do *not* follow this discipline—not exactly. Instead:[13]

1. They typically define operators that expose, not some *possible* representation, but rather the *physical* representation (see the discussion of public instance variables in Section 25.2). To quote reference [25.31]: "All object DBMS products currently require that [instance variables mentioned] in . . . queries be public."

2. They typically support, not a relational framework, but rather a variety of other frameworks based on bags, arrays, and so on. In this connection, we remind you of our contention that classes—that is, types—plus relations are both necessary and sufficient at the logical level (see Chapter 3); as far as the core model is concerned, in fact, we believe that arrays and the rest are both unnecessary and undesirable. We

---

[13] We assume here that the object system in question does in fact support *ad hoc* query, as indeed most modern ones do. Early systems sometimes did not, however, partly for the reasons to be discussed later in this section.

conjecture that the emphasis on collections other than relations (and in fact the almost total rejection of relations) in and by object systems derives from a confusion over model *vs.* implementation issues once again.

There is another important question that arises in connection with *ad hoc* query: namely, *what class is the result*? For example, suppose we execute the query "Get name and salary for employees in the programming department" on the departments-and-employees database of Section 25.3. Presumably the result has (public) instance variables ENAME and SALARY. But there is no class in the database that has this structure. Do we therefore have to predefine such a class before we can ask the query? (Note the implications if we do: A class with n instance variables would require at least 2^n such predefined classes in order to support retrieval operations alone!) And whatever the result class is, what methods apply to it?

Analogous questions arise in connection with join operations (in particular, though not exclusively). For example, if we can join department and employee objects, then again what class is the result? What methods apply?

Possibly because such questions are hard to answer in a pure object context, some object systems support "path tracing" operations [25.38] instead of joins *per se*. Given the OPAL database of Section 25.4, for example, the following might be a valid path expression:

```
ENROLLMENT . OFFERING . COURSE
```

Meaning: "Access the unique COURSE object pointed to by the unique OFFERING object pointed to by the specified ENROLLMENT object."[14] A relational analog of this expression would typically involve two joins and a projection. In other words, path tracing implies access along *predefined paths* only (as in prerelational systems, in fact) to objects of *predefined classes* only (again as in prerelational systems).

Integrity

We claimed in Chapter 9 that integrity is absolutely fundamental. However, object systems, even ones that do support *ad hoc* query, usually do not support declarative integrity constraints; instead, they require such constraints to be enforced by means of procedural code (i.e., by methods, or possibly by application programs). For example, consider the following constraint (or "business rule") from Section 9.1: "No supplier with status less than 20 supplies any part in a quantity greater than 500." Procedural code to enforce this constraint will typically have to be included in at least all of the following methods:

- Method for creating a shipment
- Method for changing a shipment quantity
- Method for changing a supplier status
- Method for assigning a shipment to a different supplier

---

[14] Actually this example is not a valid path expression for the database as we have defined it, because the pointers point the wrong way! For example, OFFERINGs do not point to COURSEs but are pointed to by them.

Points arising:

1. We have obviously lost the possibility of the system determining for itself when to do the integrity checking.

2. How do we ensure that all necessary methods include all necessary enforcement code?

3. How do we prevent the user from (e.g.) bypassing the "create shipment" method and using the built-in method NEW directly on the shipment object class, thereby bypassing the integrity check?

4. If the constraint changes, how do we find all methods that need to be rewritten?

5. How do we ensure that the enforcement code is correct?

6. How do we do transition constraints?

7. How do we query the system to find all constraints that apply to a given object or combination of objects?

8. Will the constraints be enforced during load and other utility processing?

9. What about semantic optimization (i.e., using integrity constraints to simplify queries, as discussed in Chapter 18)?

10. What are the implications of all of the foregoing points for productivity, both during application creation and subsequent application maintenance?

Relationships

Object products and the object literature typically use the term *relationships* to mean, specifically, relationships that would be represented by *foreign keys* in a relational system. And they then typically provide special-case support for this special kind of integrity constraint, as follows. Consider departments and employees once again. In a relational system, employees would normally have a foreign key referencing departments, and that would be the end of the matter. In an object system, by contrast, there are at least these three possibilities:

1. Each employee can include a pointer (OID) to the corresponding department. This possibility is similar to the relational approach but *not* identical (OIDs and foreign keys are not the same thing).

2. Each department can include a set of pointers to the corresponding employees. This possibility corresponds to the containment hierarchy approach as described in Section 25.3.

3. Approaches 2 and 3 can be combined as indicated here:

```
CLASS EMP ...
      ( ... DEPT OID ( DEPT ) INVERSE DEPT.EMPS ) ... ;

CLASS DEPT ...
      ( ... EMPS
            OID ( SET ( OID ( EMP ) ) ) INVERSE EMP.DEPT ) ... ;
```

Note the INVERSE specifications on the instance variables EMP.DEPT and DEPT.EMPS. These two instance variables are said to be *inverses* of each other;

EMP.DEPT is a "reference" instance variable and DEPT.EMPS is a "reference-set" instance variable. (If they were both reference-set variables, the relationship would be many-to-many instead of one-to-many.)

Each of these possibilities requires some kind of referential integrity support, of course. We will discuss referential integrity in a few moments. First, however, there is an obvious question that needs to be asked: How do object systems deal with relationships that involve more than two classes—say that involving suppliers, parts, and projects? The best (i.e., most symmetric) answer to this question seems to require an "SPJ" class to be created, such that each individual SPJ object has an "inverse variables" relationship with the appropriate supplier, the appropriate part, and the appropriate project. But then—given that creating a new object class is apparently the best approach for relationships of degree more than two—the obvious question arises as to why relationships of degree two are not treated in the same way.

Also, regarding inverse variables specifically, why is it necessary to introduce the asymmetry, the directionality, and two different names for what is essentially one thing? For example, the object analogs of the two relational expressions

```
SP.P# WHERE SP.S# = S# ('S1')
SP.S# WHERE SP.P# = P# ('P1')
```

look something like this:

```
S.PARTS.P# WHERE S.S# = S# ('S1')
P.SUPPS.S# WHERE P.P# = P# ('P1')
```

(hypothetical syntax, deliberately chosen to highlight essential distinctions—for example, the use of two distinct relationship names, PARTS and SUPPS—and to avoid irrelevancies).

Referential integrity: As promised, we now take a slightly closer look at object support for referential integrity (which is frequently claimed as a strength of object systems, incidentally). Various levels of support are possible. The following taxonomy is based on one given by Cattell [25.10]:

- *No system support:* Referential integrity is the responsibility of user-written code (as it was in the original SQL standard, incidentally).
- *Pointer validation:* The system checks that all pointers are to existing objects of the right type; however, object deletion might not be allowed—instead, objects might be garbage-collected when there are no remaining pointers to them, as in OPAL. As explained in Section 25.4, this level of support is roughly equivalent (but only roughly) to (a) an ON DELETE CASCADE rule for nonshared subobjects within a containment hierarchy and (b) a kind of ON DELETE RESTRICT rule for other objects (but only if "the pointers point the right way").
- *System maintenance:* Here the system keeps all pointers up-to-date automatically (e.g., by setting pointers to deleted objects to *nil*). This level of support is somewhat akin to an ON DELETE SET NULL rule.
- *"Custom semantics":* ON DELETE CASCADE (outside of a containment hierarchy) might be an example of this case. Such possibilities are typically not supported by object systems directly but must rather be handled by user-written code.

Database Programming Languages

The OPAL examples in Section 25.4 illustrate the point that object systems typically do not employ the SQL-style "embedded data sublanguage" approach. Instead, the same **integrated language** is used for both database operations and nondatabase operations. To use the terminology of Chapter 2, the host language and the database language are *tightly coupled* in object systems (in fact, of course, they are one and the same).

Now, it is undeniable that there are advantages to such an approach (which is why we adopt it in **Tutorial D**). One important one is the improved type checking that becomes possible [25.2]. And reference [25.38] argues that the following is another:

> With a single unified language, there is no *impedance mismatch* between a procedural programming language and an embedded DML with declarative semantics.

The term ***impedance mismatch*** here refers to the difference between the record-at-a-time level of today's typical programming languages and the set-at-a-time level of database languages such as SQL. And it is true that this difference in level does give rise to practical problems in SQL products. However, the solution to those problems is *not* to bring the database language down to the record-at-a-time level (which is what object systems do)—it is to bring the programming language up to the set-at-a-time level instead. The fact that object languages are record-level (i.e., procedural) is a throwback to the days of prerelational systems such as IMS and IDMS.

To pursue the point just a moment longer: It is indeed the case that most object languages are procedural or "3GL" in nature. As a consequence, all of the relational set-level advantages are lost; in particular, the system's ability to optimize user requests is severely undermined, which means that—as in prerelational systems—performance is left in large part to human users (application programmers and/or the DBA). See the subsection "Performance Considerations" immediately following.

Performance Considerations

Raw performance is one of the biggest objectives of all for object systems. As reference [25.10] puts it, "an order-of-magnitude performance difference can effectively constitute a *functional* difference, because it is not possible to use the system at all if performance is too far below requirements." We agree with these remarks (which we have reworded just slightly here).

Many factors are relevant to the performance issue. Here are a few of them:[15]

- *Clustering:* As we saw in Chapter 18, physical clustering of logically related data on the disk is one of the most important performance factors of all. Object systems typically use logical information from the database definition (regarding class hierarchies, containment hierarchies, or other explicitly declared inter-object relationships) as a hint as to how the data should be physically clustered. Alternatively (and

---

[15] In addition to the factors listed, it could be argued that object systems achieve improved performance (to the extent they do) by "moving the user closer to the metal"—that is, by exposing pointers and other features that ought to be hidden in the implementation.

preferably), the DBA might be given some more explicit and direct control over the conceptual/internal mapping (to use the terminology of Chapter 2 again).

- *Caching:* Object systems are typically intended for use in a client/server environment. Fetching clustered (and hence—ideally—logically related) data as a unit from the server site and caching it for an extended period of time at the client site obviously make sense in such an environment.

- *Swizzling:* The term *swizzling* refers to the process of replacing OID-style pointers— which are typically logical disk addresses—by main-memory addresses when objects are read into memory (and *vice versa* when the objects are written back to the database, of course). The advantages for applications that process "complex objects" and thus require extensive pointer chasing are obvious.

- *Executing methods at the server:* Consider the query "Get all books with more than 20 chapters." In a classical SQL system, books might be represented as CLOBs or BLOBs (see Chapter 5), and the client application will have to retrieve each book in turn and scan it to see if it has more than 20 chapters. In an object system, by contrast, the "get chapter count" operator will be executed by the server, and only those books actually desired will be transmitted to the client. Executing methods at the server in this way thus reduces communication costs.[16]

  Note: The foregoing is not really an argument for objects, it is an argument for *stored procedures* (see Chapter 21). A classical SQL system with stored procedures will give the same performance benefits here as an object system with methods.

Reference [25.12] discusses a benchmark called OO1 for measuring system performance on a bill-of-materials database. The benchmark involves:

1. Random retrieval of 1,000 parts, applying a user-defined method to each
2. Random insertion of 1,000 parts, connecting each one to three others
3. Random part explosion (up to seven levels), applying a user-defined method to every part encountered, together with the corresponding implosion

According to reference [25.12], comparison of an (unspecified) object product with an (unspecified) SQL product showed a performance difference of up to two orders of magnitude in favor of the object system—especially on "warm" accesses (after the cache had been populated). However, reference [25.12] is also careful to say that:

> The differences . . . should *not* be attributed to a difference between the relational and object models . . . There is reason to believe that most of the differences can be attributed to [implementation matters].

This disclaimer is supported by the fact that the differences were much smaller when the database was "large" (i.e., when it was no longer possible to accommodate the entire database in the cache).

A similar but more extensive benchmark called OO7 is described in reference [25.9].

---

[16] Actually this claim is an oversimplification. Data-intensive methods like "get chapter count" are indeed better executed at the server, but others—for example, display-intensive ones—might better be executed at the client.

Is an Object DBMS Really a DBMS?

Note: The remarks in this subsection are taken for the most part from reference [25.16], which argues among other things that object and relational systems are more different than is usually realized. To quote:

> Object databases grew out of a desire on the part of object application programmers—for a variety of application-specific reasons—to keep their application-specific objects in persistent memory. That persistent memory might perhaps be regarded as a database, but the important point is that *it was indeed application-specific;* it was not a shared, general-purpose database, intended to be suitable for applications that might not have been foreseen at the time the database was defined. As a consequence, many features that database professionals regard as essential were simply not requirements in the object world, at least not originally. Thus, there was little perceived need for:
>
> 1. Data sharing across applications
>
> 2. Physical data independence
>
> 3. *Ad hoc* queries
>
> 4. Views and logical data independence
>
> 5. Application-independent, declarative integrity constraints
>
> 6. Data ownership and a flexible security mechanism
>
> 7. Concurrency control
>
> 8. A general-purpose catalog
>
> 9. Application-independent database design
>
>   These requirements all surfaced later, after the basic idea of storing objects in a database was first conceived, and thus all constitute add-on features to the original object model . . . One important consequence . . . is that there really is a **difference in kind** between an object DBMS and a relational DBMS. In fact, it could be argued that an object DBMS is not really a DBMS at all—at least, not in the same sense that a relational DBMS is a DBMS. For consider:
>
> ■ A relational DBMS comes *ready for use.* In other words, as soon as the system is installed, users . . . can start building databases, writing applications, running queries, and so on.
>
> ■ An object DBMS, by contrast, can be thought of as a kind of *DBMS construction kit.* When it is originally installed, it is *not* available for immediate use . . . Instead, it must first be *tailored* by suitably skilled technicians, who must define the necessary classes and methods, and so on (the system provides a set of building-blocks—class library maintenance tools, method compilers, etc.—for this purpose). Only when that tailoring activity is complete will the system be available for use by application programmers and end users; in other words, the result of that tailoring will indeed more closely resemble a DBMS in the more familiar sense of the term.
>
>   Note further that the resultant "tailored" DBMS will be *application-specific;* it might, for example, be suitable for CAD/CAM applications, but be essentially useless for, e.g., medical applications. In other words, it will still not be a general-purpose DBMS, in the same sense that a relational DBMS is a general-purpose DBMS.

Reference [25.16] also argues against the idea—often referred to as **persistence orthogonal to type** [25.2]—according to which the database is allowed to include (mutable) objects of arbitrary complexity:[17]

> The object model requires support for [a large number of] *type generators* . . . Examples include STRUCT (or TUPLE), LIST, ARRAY, SET, BAG, and so on . . . Along with object IDs, the availability of these type generators essentially means that *any data structure that can be created in an application program can be created as an object in an object database*—and further that the structure of such objects is *visible to the user.* For example, consider the object, EX say, that is (or rather denotes) the collection of employees in a given department. Then EX might be implemented either as a linked list or as an array, and users will have to know which it is (because the access operators will differ accordingly).

This *anything-goes* approach to what can be stored in the database is a major point of difference between the object and relational models, of course, and it deserves a little further discussion here. In essence:

- The object model says we can store anything we like—any data structure we can create with the usual programming language mechanisms.
- The relational model effectively says the same thing, but goes on to insist that whatever we do store be presented to the user in pure relational form.

More precisely, the relational model—quite rightly—says *nothing* about what can be physically stored . . . It therefore imposes no limits on what data structures are allowed at the physical level; the only requirement is that whatever structures *are* in fact physically stored must be mapped to relations at the logical level and hence be hidden from the user. Relational systems thus make a clear distinction between logical and physical (data model *vs.* implementation), while object systems do not. One consequence is that—contrary to conventional wisdom—object systems might very well provide less data independence than relational systems. For example, suppose the implementation in some object database of the object EX mentioned above (denoting the collection of employees in a given department) is changed from an array to a linked list. What are the implications for existing code that accesses that object EX?

25.6 SUMMARY

By way of summary, here is a list of the principal features of the object model as we have presented it, together with a subjective assessment as to which features are essential; which ones are "nice to have" but not essential; which are "nasty to have"; which are really orthogonal to the question of whether the system is an object system or some other kind; and so on. This analysis paves the way for our discussion of *object/relational* systems in Chapter 26.

- **Object classes** (i.e., *types*): Obviously essential (indeed, they are the most fundamental construct of all).

---

[17] See also reference [25.19].

- **Objects:** Objects themselves, both "mutable" and "immutable," are clearly essential—though we would prefer to call them simply *variables* and *values,* respectively.

- **Object IDs:** Unnecessary, and in fact undesirable (at the model level, that is), because they are basically just pointers. See reference [25.17] for an extended discussion of this issue.

- **Encapsulation:** As explained in Section 25.2, "encapsulated" just means *scalar,* and we would prefer to use that term (always remembering that some "objects" are not scalar anyway).

- **Instance variables:** First, *private* (also *protected*) instance variables are by definition merely implementation matters and hence not relevant to the definition of an abstract model, which is what we are concerned with here. Second, *public* instance variables do not exist in a pure object system and are thus also not relevant. We conclude that instance variables can be ignored; "objects" should be manipulable solely by "methods."

- **Containment hierarchy:** We explained in Section 25.3 that in our opinion containment hierarchies are misleading and in fact a misnomer, since they typically contain OIDs, not "objects." *Note:* A (nonencapsulated) hierarchy that really did include objects *per se* would be permissible, however, though usually contraindicated; it would be analogous, somewhat, to a relvar with relation-valued attributes.

- **Methods:** The concept is essential, though we would prefer to use the more conventional term *operators.* Bundling methods with classes is *not* essential, however, and leads to several problems [3.3]; we would prefer to define "classes" (types) and "methods" (operators) separately, as we did in Chapter 5, and thereby avoid the notion of "target objects" and the use of what are sometimes called "selfish methods."

  There are certain operators we would insist on, too: Selectors (which among other things effectively provide a way of writing literals of the relevant type), THE_ operators, assignment and equality comparison operators, and type testing operators (see Chapter 20). *Note:* We reject "constructor functions," however. Constructors construct *variables;* since the only kind of variable we want in the database is, specifically, the relvar, the only "constructor" we need is an operator that creates a relvar (CREATE TABLE or CREATE VIEW, in SQL terms). Selectors, by contrast, select *values.* Also, constructors return *pointers to* the constructed variables, while selectors return the selected values *per se.*

- **Messages:** Again, the concept is essential, though we would prefer to use the more conventional term *invocation* (and, again, avoid the notion that such invocations have to be directed at some "target object," but instead treat all arguments equally).

- **Class hierarchy** (and related notions—inheritance, substitutability, inclusion polymorphism, and so on): Desirable but orthogonal (we see class hierarchy support, if provided, as just part of support for classes *per se*).

- **Class *vs.* instance *vs.* collection:** The distinctions are essential, of course, but orthogonal (the *concepts* are distinct, and that is really all that needs to be said).

- **Relationships:** We have already argued in Chapter 14 (Section 14.6) that it is not a good idea to treat "relationships" as a formally distinct construct—especially if it is only binary relationships that receive such special treatment. We also do not think it is a good idea to treat the associated referential integrity constraints in some manner that is divorced from the treatment, if any, of integrity constraints in general.

- **Integrated database programming language:** Nice to have, but orthogonal. However, the languages actually supported in today's object systems are typically *procedural* (3GLs) and therefore—we would argue—nasty to have (in fact, a giant step backward).

And here is a list of features that "the object model" typically does not support or does not support well:

- ***Ad hoc* queries:** Early object systems typically did not support *ad hoc* queries at all. More recent systems do, but they do so, typically, either by breaking encapsulation or by imposing limits on the queries that can be asked (meaning in this latter case that the queries are not really *ad hoc* after all).

- **Views:** Typically not supported (for essentially the same reasons that *ad hoc* queries are typically not supported). *Note:* Some object systems do support "derived" or "virtual" instance variables (necessarily public ones); for example, the instance variable AGE might be derived by subtracting the value of the instance variable BIRTHDATE from the current date. However, such a capability falls far short of a full view mechanism—and in any case we have already rejected the notion of public instance variables.

- **Declarative integrity constraints:** Typically not supported (for essentially the same reasons that *ad hoc* queries and views are typically not supported). In fact, they are typically not supported even by systems that do support *ad hoc* queries.

- **Foreign keys:** The "object model" has several different mechanisms for dealing with referential integrity, none of which is quite the same as the relational model's more uniform foreign key mechanism. Such matters as ON DELETE RESTRICT and ON DELETE CASCADE are typically left to procedural code (probably methods, possibly application code).

- **Closure and completeness:** What are the object analogs of the relational closure and completeness properties?

- **Catalog:** Where is the catalog in an object system? What does it look like? Are there any standards? *Note:* These questions are rhetorical. What actually happens is that a catalog has to be built by the professional staff whose job it is to tailor the object DBMS for whatever application it has been installed for, as discussed at the end of Section 25.5. That catalog will then be application-specific, as will the overall tailored DBMS.

To summarize, then, the good (i.e., essential, fundamental) features of the "object model"—the ones we would really like to support—are as shown in the following table:

Feature	Preferred term	Remarks
object class	type	scalar & nonscalar; possibly user-defined
immutable object	value	scalar & nonscalar
mutable object	variable	scalar & nonscalar
method	operator	including selectors, THE_ ops, ":=", "=", & type test operators
message	operator invocation	no "target" operand

More succinctly, we might say that the sole good idea of object systems in general is **proper data type support**; everything else—including in particular the notion of *user-defined operators*—follows from that one idea.[18] But that idea is hardly new!

EXERCISES

25.1 Explain the following in your own words:

class	message
class hierarchy	method
class-defining object	object
constructor function	object ID
containment hierarchy	object instance
encapsulation	private instance variable
instance	protected instance variable
inverse variables	public instance variable

25.2 What are the advantages of OIDs? What are the disadvantages? How might OIDs be implemented?

25.3 In Section 25.2 we gave two SQL formulations of the query "Get all rectangles that overlap the unit square." Prove those two formulations are equivalent.

25.4 Investigate any object system that might be available to you. What programming language(s) does that system support? Does it support a query language? If so, what is it? In your opinion, is it more or less powerful than SQL? What does the catalog look like? How does the user interrogate the catalog? Is there any view support? If so, how extensive is it? (For example, what about view updating?) How is "missing information" handled?

25.5 Design an object version of the suppliers-and-parts database. *Note:* This design will be used as a basis for Exercises 25.6–25.8.

25.6 Write a set of OPAL data definition statements for your object version of suppliers and parts.

25.7 Sketch the details of the necessary "database-populating" methods for your object version of suppliers and parts.

25.8 Write OPAL code against your object version of suppliers and parts to (a) get all London suppliers; (b) get all red parts.

---

[18] Some might claim that type inheritance is a good idea, too. We agree, but stand by our position that support for inheritance is orthogonal to support for objects *per se*.

25.9   Consider the education database once again. Show what is involved in (a) deleting an enrollment; (b) deleting an employee; (c) deleting a course; (d) dropping the enrollments class; (e) dropping the employees class. You can assume that the OPAL-style garbage-collection process applies. State any assumptions you make regarding such matters as cascade delete and so on.

25.10   Suppose an object version of the suppliers-parts-projects database is to be represented by means of a single containment hierarchy. How many possible such hierarchies are there? Which one is best?

25.11   Consider a variation on the suppliers-parts-projects database in which, instead of recording that certain suppliers supply certain parts to certain projects, we wish to record only that (a) certain suppliers supply certain parts, (b) certain parts are supplied to certain projects, and (c) certain projects are supplied by certain suppliers. How many possible object designs are there now (with or without containment hierarchies)?

25.12   Consider the performance factors discussed briefly in Section 25.5. Are any of them truly object-specific? Justify your answer.

25.13   Object systems typically support integrity constraints in a *procedural* fashion, via methods; the main exception is that *referential* constraints are typically supported (at least in part) *declaratively*. What are the advantages of procedural support? Why do you think referential constraints are handled differently?

25.14   Explain the concept of *inverse variables*.

REFERENCES AND BIBLIOGRAPHY

References [25.5], [25.10], [25.23], and [25.31] are textbooks on object topics and related matters. References [25.29, 25.30] and [25.42] are collections of research papers. References [25.24], [25.35], and [25.38] are tutorials. References [25.4], [25.8], and [25.21] describe specific systems.

25.1 Malcolm Atkinson *et al.*: "The Object-Oriented Database System Manifesto," Proc. 1st Int. Conf. on Deductive and Object-Oriented Databases, Kyoto, Japan (1989). New York, N.Y.: Elsevier Science (1990).

One of the first attempts to lay down some rules as to what "the object model" should include. First, the writers propose the following as *mandatory* features—that is, features that must be supported if the DBMS in question is to deserve the label "object-oriented":

1. collections
2. object IDs
3. encapsulation
4. types or classes [*sic*]
5. inheritance
6. late binding
7. computational completeness

8. user-defined types
9. persistence
10. large databases
11. concurrency
12. recovery
13. *ad hoc* query

They also propose certain *optional* features, including multiple inheritance and compile-time type checking; certain *open* features, including "programming paradigm" (e.g., functional *vs.* imperative); and certain features on which the authors could reach no consensus, including—a little surprisingly, considering their importance—views and integrity constraints. *Note:* References [3.3] and [25.28] both comment on this paper. With respect to reference [3.3], however, we should explain that the commentary in question is based on the premise that the aim of the paper is to define features of a good, genuine, general-purpose DBMS. We do not deny that the features listed might be useful for a highly specialized DBMS that is tied to some specific application such as CAD/CAM, with no need for (say) integrity constraint support—but then we would question whether such a system is truly a DBMS, as that term is usually understood.

This reference also appears as reference [20.2] in Chapter 20, where further commentary on it can be found.

25.2 Malcolm P. Atkinson and O. Peter Buneman: "Types and Persistence in Database Programming Languages," *ACM Comp. Surv. 19,* No. 2 (June 1987).

One of the first papers—perhaps *the* first—to argue in favor of the position that persistence should be orthogonal to type. This paper is a good starting point for reading in the area of database programming languages in general (such languages being perceived by many people as the *sine qua non* of object systems; see, for example, references [25.10, 25.11]).

25.3 François Bancilhon: "A Logic-Programming/Object-Oriented Cocktail," *ACM SIGMOD Record 15,* No. 3 (September 1986).

To quote the introduction: "The object-oriented approach . . . seems to be particularly well fitted to [handling] new types of applications such as CAD, software [engineering], and [artificial intelligence]. However, the natural extension to relational database technology is . . . the logic-programming paradigm, [not] the object-oriented one. [This paper addresses the question of] whether the two paradigms are compatible." And it concludes, somewhat cautiously, that they are. *Note:* Reference [25.40] offers an opposing point of view.

25.4 J. Banerjee *et al.*: "Data Model Issues for Object-Oriented Applications," *ACM TOOIS (Transactions on Office Information Systems) 5,* No. 1 (March 1987). Republished in Michael Stonebraker (ed.), *Readings in Database Systems* (2d ed.). San Mateo, Calif.: Morgan Kaufmann (1994). Also republished in reference [25.42].

25.5 Douglas K. Barry: *The Object Database Handbook: How to Select, Implement, and Use Object-Oriented Databases.* New York, N.Y.: John Wiley & Sons (1996).

The principal thesis of this book is that we need an object system, not a relational one, if we have to deal with "complex data." Complex data is characterized as (a) ubiquitous, (b) often lacking unique identification (!), (c) involving numerous many-to-many relationships, and (d) often requiring the use of type codes "in the relational schema" (because of the lack of direct support for subtypes and supertypes in today's SQL products). *Note:* The author is executive director of the Object Data Management Group, ODMG [25.11].

25.6 David Beech: "A Foundation for Evolution from Relational to Object Databases," in J. W. Schmidt, S. Ceri, and M. Missikoff (eds.), *Extending Database Technology.* New York, N.Y.: Springer-Verlag (1988).

This is one of several papers to discuss the possibility of extending SQL to become some kind of "Object SQL" or "OSQL" (be aware, however, that those "Object SQLs" often do not look much like SQL *per se*). Reference [25.32] gives more detail on the proposals of this particular paper.

25.7 Anders Björnerstedt and Christer Hultén: "Version Control in an Object-Oriented Architecture," in reference [25.30].

Many applications need the concept of distinct **versions** of a given object; examples of such applications include software development, hardware design, document creation, and so forth. And some object systems support this concept directly (though in fact it is orthogonal to the question of whether we are dealing with an object system or some other kind). Such support typically includes:

- The ability to create a new version of a given object, typically by **checking out** a copy of the object and moving it from the database to the user's private workstation, where it can be kept and modified over a possibly extended period of time (e.g., hours or days)

- The ability to establish a given object version as the current database version, typically by **checking it in** and moving it from the user's workstation back to the database (which might in turn require some kind of mechanism for **merging** distinct versions)

- The ability to **delete** (and perhaps **archive**) obsolete versions

- The ability to interrogate the **version history** of a given object

Note that, as Fig. 25.7 suggests, version histories are not necessarily linear—version V.2 in that figure leads to two distinct versions V.3a and V.3b, which are subsequently merged into a single version V.4.

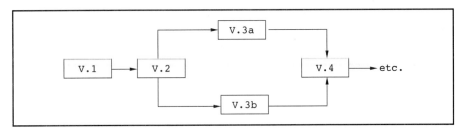

Fig. 25.7   Typical version history

Next, because objects are typically interrelated in various ways, the concept of versioning leads to the concept of *configurations*. A **configuration** is a collection of mutually consistent versions of interrelated objects. Configuration support typically includes:

- The ability to **copy** an object version from one configuration to another (e.g., from an "old" configuration to a "new" one)

- The ability to **move** an object version from one configuration to another (i.e., to add it to the "new" configuration and drop it from the "old" one)

Internally, such operations basically just involve a lot of pointer juggling—but there are major implications for language syntax and semantics in general, and *ad hoc* query in particular.

25.8 Paul Butterworth, Allen Otis, and Jacob Stein: "The GemStone Object Database Management System," *CACM 34,* No. 10 (October 1991).

25.9 Michael J. Carey, David J. DeWitt, and Jeffrey F. Naughton: "The OO7 Object-Oriented Database Benchmark," Proc. 1993 ACM SIGMOD Int. Conf. on Management of Data, Washington, D.C. (May 1993).

25.10 R. G. G. Cattell: *Object Data Management* (revised edition). Reading, Mass.: Addison-Wesley (1994).

The first book-length tutorial on the application of object technology to databases specifically. The following edited extract suggests that the field was still a long way from any kind of consensus in 1994 (and probably still is): "Programming languages may need new syntax . . . swizzling, replication, and new access methods also need further study . . . new end-user and application development tools [are] required . . . more powerful query language features [must be] developed . . . new research in concurrency control is needed . . . timestamps and object-based concurrency semantics need more exploration . . . performance models are needed . . .

new work in knowledge management needs to be integrated with object and data management capabilities . . . this [will lead to] a complex optimization problem [and] few researchers have [the necessary] expertise . . . federated [object] databases require more study."

25.11 R. G. G. Cattell and Douglas K. Barry (eds.): *The Object Data Standard: ODMG 3.0.* San Francisco, Calif.: Morgan Kaufmann (2000).

The term *ODMG* is used, loosely, to refer to the proposals of the Object Data Management Group, a consortium of representatives from "member companies [covering] almost the entire object DBMS industry." Those proposals consist of an *Object Model,* an *Object Definition Language* (ODL), an *Object Interchange Format* (OIF), an *Object Query Language* (OQL), and *bindings* of these facilities to C++, Smalltalk, and Java. (There is no "Object Manipulation Language" component; instead, object manipulation capabilities are provided by whatever language ODMG happens to be bound to.)

A detailed analysis and critique of Version 2.0 of the ODMG Object Model (which is actually not all that different from Version 3.0) can be found in Appendix I of reference [3.3]. See also reference [25.28].

25.12 R. G. G. Cattell and J. Skeen: "Object Operations Benchmark," *ACM TODS 17,* No. 1 (March 1992).

25.13 George Copeland and David Maier: "Making Smalltalk a Database System," Proc. 1984 ACM SIGMOD Int. Conf. on Management of Data, Boston, Mass. (June 1984). Republished in Michael Stonebraker (ed.), *Readings in Database Systems* (2d ed.). San Mateo, Calif.: Morgan Kaufmann (1994).

Describes some of the changes that were made to Smalltalk [25.23] in order to create GemStone and OPAL.

25.14 O. J. Dahl, B. Myhrhaug, and K. Nygaard: *The SIMULA 67 Common Base Language,* Pub. S-22, Norwegian Computing Center, Oslo, Norway (1970).

SIMULA 67 was a language designed expressly for writing simulation applications. Object programming languages grew out of such languages; in fact, SIMULA 67 was really the first object language.

25.15 C. J. Date: "An Optimization Problem," in C. J. Date and Hugh Darwen, *Relational Database Writings 1989–1991.* Reading, Mass.: Addison-Wesley (1992).

25.16 C. J. Date: "Why the 'Object Model' Is Not a Data Model," in C. J. Date, Hugh Darwen, and David McGoveran, *Relational Database Writings 1994–1997.* Reading, Mass.: Addison-Wesley (1998).

Argues that "the object model," whatever it might consist of, is "closer to the metal"—less abstract, and therefore less data-independent—than the relational model; in fact, it is really a model of *storage,* not a data model at all.

25.17 C. J. Date: "Object Identifiers *vs.* Relational Keys," in C. J. Date, Hugh Darwen, and David McGoveran, *Relational Database Writings 1994–1997.* Reading, Mass.: Addison-Wesley (1998).

Argues that OIDs have no place in the data model as seen by the user. *Note:* One important argument in support of this position but not included in the paper, having to do with inheritance, can be found in the next chapter (Section 26.6).

25.18 C. J. Date: "Encapsulation Is a Red Herring," *DBP&D 12,* No. 9 (September 1998).

In the body of this chapter, we said encapsulation implied data independence. However, we also said we would rather not use the term *encapsulation* anyway (preferring the term *scalar*). Part of the point is that "encapsulated objects" cannot provide any more data independence than *unencapsulated* relations can (at least in principle). For example, there is absolutely no reason why a base relvar representing points, with Cartesian coordinate attributes X and Y, should not be stored in terms of polar coordinates R and θ instead.

25.19 C. J. Date: "Persistence *Not* Orthogonal to Type," *http://www.dbpd.com* (October 1998).

Argues strongly (a) against the object dictum that "persistence [should be] orthogonal to type" [25.2], and thus, not incidentally, (b) in favor of *The Information Principle.*

25.20 C. J. Date: "Decent Exposure," *http://www.dbpd.com* (November 1998).

25.21 O. Deux *et al.*: "The O2 System," *CACM 34,* No. 10 (October 1991).

25.22 Fabrizio Ferrandina, Thorsten Meyer, Roberto Zicari, Guy Ferran, and Joëlle Madec: "Schema and Database Evolution in the O2 Object Database System," Proc. 21st Int. Conf. on Very Large Data Bases, Zurich, Switzerland (September 1995).

See the annotation to reference [25.34].

25.23 Adele Goldberg and David Robson: *Smalltalk-80: The Language and Its Implementation.* Reading, Mass.: Addison-Wesley (1983).

The definitive account of the pioneering efforts at the Xerox Palo Alto Research Center to design and build the Smalltalk-80 system. The first part of the book (out of four parts) is a detailed description of the Smalltalk-80 programming language, on which the OPAL language of GemStone is based.

25.24 Nathan Goodman: "Object-Oriented Database Systems," *InfoDB 4,* No. 3 (Fall 1989).

To quote: "At this stage it is futile to compare [the] relational and object [approaches]. We have to compare like to like: apples to apples, dreams to dreams, theory to theory, and mature products to mature products . . . [The] relational approach has been in existence for some time: It rests on a very solid theoretical foundation, and it is the basis for a large number of mature products. The object approach, by contrast, is new (at least in the database arena); it does not possess a theoretical foundation that can meaningfully be compared with the relational model, and the few products that exist can scarcely be described as mature. Thus, a great deal remains to be done before we can seriously begin to consider the question of whether object technology will ever represent a viable alternative to the relational approach." While some of these remarks are still applicable today, matters have crystallized somewhat since 1989; in many ways, in fact, relations *vs.* objects can be regarded as something of an apples-and-oranges comparison, as we will see in Chapter 26.

25.25 Nathan Goodman: "An Object-Oriented DBMS War Story: Developing a Genome Mapping Database in C++," in reference [25.29].

This paper supports several of the criticisms in the body of this chapter. To quote the abstract: "Contrary to conventional wisdom, our experience suggests that it is a mistake to make the database too smart by implementing complex programs as methods inside database objects. Our experience also indicates that C++ is a poor language for implementing databases, with problems related to the mechanics of defining attributes, the mechanics of referring to objects in a systematic way, the lack of a garbage collector, and subtle traps in the inheritance model. We also found that current C++-based DBMSs lack important database functions, and to compensate for this, we were forced to provide our own simple implementations of standard DBMS functions: transaction logging for roll-forward recovery, a multi-thread transaction monitor, a query language and query processor, and storage structures. In effect, we used the C++-based DBMS as an object-oriented storage manager, and built a data management system specialized for large-scale genome mapping on top of it."

25.26 H. V. Jagadish and Xiaolei Qian: "Integrity Maintenance in an Object-Oriented Database," Proc. 18th Int. Conf. on Very Large Data Bases, Vancouver, Canada (August 1992).

Proposes a declarative integrity mechanism for object systems, showing how a constraints compiler can incorporate the necessary integrity-checking code into methods for the appropriate object classes.

25.27 Michael Kifer, Won Kim, and Yehoshua Sagiv: "Querying Object-Oriented Databases," Proc. 1982 ACM SIGMOD Int. Conf. on Management of Data, San Diego, Calif. (June 1992).

Proposes another "Object SQL" called XSQL.

25.28 Won Kim: "Observations on the ODMG-93 Proposal for an Object-Oriented Database Language," *ACM SIGMOD Record 23,* No. 1 (March 1994).

25.29 Won Kim (ed.): *Modern Database Systems: The Object Model, Interoperability, and Beyond.* New York, N.Y.: ACM Press/Reading, Mass.: Addison-Wesley (1995).

25.30 Won Kim and Frederick H. Lochovsky: *Object-Oriented Concepts, Databases, and Applications.* Reading, Mass.: ACM Press/Addison-Wesley (1989).

25.31 Mary E. S. Loomis: *Object Databases: The Essentials.* Reading, Mass.: Addison-Wesley (1995).

25.32 Peter Lyngbaek *et al.*: "OSQL: A Language for Object Databases," Technical Report HPL-DTD-91-4, Hewlett-Packard Company (January 15, 1991).

See the annotation to reference [25.6].

25.33 Bertrand Meyer: "The Future of Object Technology," *IEEE Computer 31,* No. 1 (January 1998).

To quote: "The future of [object] databases is an interesting topic for speculation . . . Relational database vendors [have] managed since 1986 to stifle the growth of [object] databases through preemptive announcements . . . Ten years later, [object database] experts will still tell you that the offerings from the main relational vendors . . . are still far from the real thing . . . [The] market for [object] databases will continue to grow, but it will remain a fraction of the traditional database market."

25.34 John F. Roddick: "Schema Evolution in Database Systems—An Annotated Bibliography," *ACM SIGMOD Record 21,* No. 4 (December 1992).

Traditional database products typically support only rather simple changes to an existing schema (e.g., the addition of a new column to an existing base table, in SQL products). However, some applications require more sophisticated schema change support, and some object prototypes have investigated this problem in depth. Note that the problem is actually more complex in an object environment, because the schema is more complex.

The following taxonomy of possible schema changes is based on one given in a paper on the object prototype ORION [25.4]. We remark that several of them (which?) seem to betray some confusion over the model *vs.* implementation distinction.

- Changes to an object class
    1. Instance variable changes
        - Add instance variable
        - Delete instance variable
        - Rename instance variable
        - Change instance variable default value
        - Change instance variable data type
        - Change instance variable inheritance source

2. Method changes
   - Add method
   - Delete method
   - Rename method
   - Change method internal code
   - Change method inheritance source
- Changes to the class hierarchy (assuming multiple inheritance)
   - Add class *A* to superclass list for class *B*
   - Delete class *A* from superclass list for class *B*
- Changes to the overall schema
   - Add class (anywhere)
   - Delete class (anywhere)
   - Rename class
   - Partition class
   - Coalesce classes

It is not clear how much transparency can be achieved with respect to the foregoing changes, however, especially since views are typically not supported. In fact, the possibility of "schema evolution" implies a significant problem for object systems, owing to their 3GL nature. As reference [25.28] puts it: "If . . . indexes [are added or dropped] or the data is reorganized to be differently clustered, there is no way for [methods] to automatically take advantage of such changes."

Furthermore, schema evolution is also more of a *requirement* in object systems, because many of the decisions that would be DBA decisions—or even DBMS decisions!—in a relational system become application programmer decisions in an object system (see reference [25.35]). In particular, performance tuning can lead to schema redesign (again, see reference [25.35]).

25.35 C. M. Saracco: "Writing an Object DBMS Application" (in two parts), *InfoDB 7,* No. 4 (Winter 1993/94) and *InfoDB 8,* No. 1 (Spring 1994).

Gives some simple but complete (and informative) coding examples.

25.36 Gail M. Shaw and Stanley B. Zdonik: "A Query Algebra for Object-Oriented Databases," Proc. 6th IEEE Int. Conf. on Data Engineering (February 1990).

This paper serves to support this writer's contention that any "object algebra" will be inherently complex (because objects are complex). In particular, *equality* of arbitrarily nested hierarchic objects requires very careful treatment. The basic idea behind the specific proposals of this paper is that each algebraic operator produces a *relation,* in which each tuple contains OIDs for certain objects. In the case of join, for example, each tuple contains OIDs of objects that match one another under the joining condition. Those tuples do not inherit any methods from the component objects.

25.37 David W. Shipman: "The Functional Data Model and the Data Language DAPLEX," *ACM TODS 6,* No. 1 (March 1981). Republished in Michael Stonebraker (ed.), *Readings in Database Systems* (2d ed.). San Mateo, Calif.: Morgan Kaufmann (1994).

There have been several attempts over the years to construct systems based on functions instead of relations, and DAPLEX is one of the best known. The reason we mention it here is that the functional approaches share certain ideas with the object approach, including in particular a somewhat navigational (i.e., path-tracing) style of addressing objects that are functionally related to other objects (that are functionally related to other objects, etc.). Note, however, that a function in this context is typically not a true mathematical function as such; it might, for example, be multi-valued. In fact, considerable violence has to be done to the function concept in order to make it capable of all the things required of it in the "functional data model" context.

25.38 Jacob Stein and David Maier: "Concepts in Object-Oriented Data Management," *DBP&D 1,* No. 4 (April 1988).

A good early tutorial on object concepts, by two of the GemStone designers.

25.39 D. C. Tsichritzis and O. M. Nierstrasz: "Directions in OO Research," in reference [25.30].

This paper lends further weight to the contention of the present writer that object database technology is a long way from consensus: "There are disagreements on basic definitions; e.g., what is an object? . . . There is no reason to worry: Loose definitions are inevitable and sometimes welcome during a dynamic period of scientific discovery. They should and will become more rigorous during a period of consolidation that will inevitably follow." But object concepts have been around for nearly 40 years!—in fact, they predate the relational model.

25.40 Jeffrey D. Ullman: "A Comparison Between Deductive and Object-Oriented Database Systems," Proc. 2nd Int. Conf. on Deductive and Object-Oriented Databases, Munich, Germany (December 1991); C. Delobel, M. Kifer, and Y. Masunaga (eds.), *Lecture Notes in Computer Science 566.* New York, N.Y.: Springer-Verlag (1992).

Although we disagree with this paper on several points of detail, we do agree with its overall conclusion, which is that "deductive" (i.e., logic-based) database systems hold more promise for the long term than object systems do. Also, the paper has an important point to make regarding *optimizability*:

> [Suppose we were to define] an object class that behaves like binary relations, and . . . a *join* method for this class, so we can write an expression like R JOIN S JOIN T. It appears we could evaluate this expression as (R JOIN S) JOIN T or as R JOIN (S JOIN T). But can we? It was never stated what the *join* method means. Is it associative, for example? . . . The conclusion is that, if we want to program in an [object] way, and still program at the level of relations or higher, we need to give the system the information embodied in the . . . laws of relational algebra. That information cannot be deduced by the system, but must be built into it. Thus, . . . the only part of the query language that will be optimizable is the fixed set of methods for which . . . adequate semantics have been provided to the system.

25.41 Carlo Zaniolo: "The Database Language GEM," Proc. 1983 ACM SIGMOD Int. Conf. on Management of Data, San Jose, Calif. (May 1983). Republished in Michael Stonebraker (ed.), *Readings in Database Systems* (2d ed.). San Mateo, Calif.: Morgan Kaufmann (1994).

GEM stands for "General Entity Manipulator." It is effectively an extension to QUEL that supports relations with set-valued attributes and relations with alternative attributes (e.g., exempt EMPs might have a SALARY attribute, while nonexempt EMPs have HOURLY_WAGE and OVERTIME attributes). It also makes use of the object idea that objects conceptually contain other objects (instead of foreign keys that reference those other objects), and extends the familiar dot-qualification notation to provide a simple way of referring to attributes of such contained objects—in effect, by implicitly traversing certain predefined join paths. For example, the qualified name EMP.DEPT.BUDGET could be used to refer to the budget of the department of some given employee. Many systems have adopted and/or adapted this idea.

25.42 Stanley B. Zdonik and David Maier (eds.): *Readings in Object-Oriented Database Systems.* San Francisco, Calif.: Morgan Kaufmann (1990).

CHAPTER **26**

Object/Relational
Databases

26.1 INTRODUCTION

In the late 1990s, several vendors released "object/relational" DBMS products, also known as *universal servers*. Examples include the Universal Database version of DB2, the Universal Data Option for Informix Dynamic Server, and the Oracle Universal Server (other names are also used). The broad idea in every case was that the product should support both object and relational capabilities; in other words, the products in question represent attempts at a *rapprochement* between the two technologies.

Now, it is this writer's strong opinion that any such *rapprochement* should be firmly based on the relational model (which is after all the foundation of modern database technology in general, as explained in Part II of this book). Thus, what we want is for relational systems to evolve[1] to incorporate the features—at least, the good features—of objects (we surely do not want to discard relational systems entirely, nor do we want to have to deal with two separate systems, relational and object, existing side by side). And this opinion is shared by many other writers, including the authors of the "Third-Generation Database System Manifesto" [26.44] in particular, who state categorically that *third-generation DBMSs must subsume second-generation DBMSs.* (To elaborate briefly: "First-generation DBMSs" are the prerelational ones, like IMS; "second-generation DBMSs" are SQL systems; "third-generation DBMSs" are whatever comes next.) The opinion is apparently not shared, however, by some of the object vendors, nor by certain object writers. Here is a typical quote [26.7]:

> Computer science has seen many generations of data management, starting with indexed files, and later, network and hierarchical DBMSs . . . [and] more recently relational DBMSs . . . Now, we are on the verge of another generation of database systems . . . [that] provide *object management,* [supporting] much more complex kinds of data.

Here the writer is clearly suggesting that just as relational systems displaced the older hierarchic and network systems, so object systems will displace relational systems in turn.

The reason we disagree with this position is that **relational really is different** [26.17]. It is different because it is not *ad hoc.* The older, prerelational systems were *ad hoc;* they might have provided solutions to certain important problems of their day, but they did not rest on any solid theoretical foundation. Unfortunately, relational advocates (this writer included) did themselves a major disservice in the early days when they argued the relative merits of relational and prerelational systems; such arguments were necessary at the time, but they had the unlooked-for effect of reinforcing the idea that relational and prerelational DBMSs were essentially the same kind of thing. And this mistaken idea in turn supports the position that objects are to relations as relations were to hierarchies and networks.

So what about objects? Are they *ad hoc?* The following quote from "The Object-Oriented Database System Manifesto" [20.2, 25.1] is revealing in this regard: "With respect to the specification of the system, we are taking a Darwinian approach: We hope that, out of the set of experimental prototypes being built, a fit [object] model will emerge." In other words, the suggestion is apparently that we should write code and build systems *without* any predefined model and see what happens!

In what follows, therefore, we take it as axiomatic (as most of the major DBMS vendors do, in fact) that what we want to do is enhance relational systems to incorporate the good features of object technology. To repeat, we do not want to discard relational technology; it would be a great pity to walk away from almost 35 years of solid relational research and development.

Now, we argued in Chapter 25—see also the annotation to reference [26.31]—that object orientation involves just one good idea: namely, **proper data type support** (or two

---

[1] Note that we are definitely interested in evolution, not revolution. By contrast, consider this quote from reference [25.11]: "[Object DBMSs] are *a revolutionary rather than an evolutionary development*" (italics added). We do not think the marketplace in general is ready for revolution, nor do we think it need be or ought to be—which is one reason why *The Third Manifesto* [3.3] is very specifically evolutionary, not revolutionary, in nature.

good ideas, if you count type inheritance separately). So the question becomes: How can we incorporate proper data type support into the relational model? And the answer, of course, as you have doubtless already realized, is that the support is already there, in the shape of *domains*—which we prefer to call *types* anyway. In other words, we need do *nothing* to the relational model in order to achieve object functionality in relational systems: nothing, that is, except implement it, fully and properly, which today's SQL systems have so signally failed to do.[2]

Thus, we believe that a relational system that supported domains properly would be able to deal with all of those "problem" kinds of data that (it is sometimes claimed) object systems can handle and relational systems cannot: multi-media data, time-series data, biological data, financial data, engineering design data, office automation data, and so on. Accordingly, we also believe that a true object/relational system would be nothing more nor less than a true *relational* system—which is to say, a system that supports the relational model, with all that such support entails. Hence, DBMS vendors should be encouraged to do what they are in fact trying to do: namely, extend their systems to include proper type support. Indeed, an argument can be made that the whole reason object systems looked attractive when they first appeared is precisely because the SQL vendors did not support the relational model adequately. But this fact should not be seen as an argument for abandoning relational systems entirely (or at all!).

By way of example, we now take care of some unfinished business from Chapter 25 and show a good *relational* solution to the rectangles problem. (We give that solution in **Tutorial D**; producing an SQL analog is left as an exercise.) First, we define a rectangle *type:*

```
TYPE RECTANGLE POSSREP ( X1 RATIONAL, Y1 RATIONAL,
                         X2 RATIONAL, Y2 RATIONAL ) ... ;
```

We assume that rectangles are represented *physically* by means of one of those storage structures that are specifically intended to support spatial data efficiently—quadtrees, R-trees, and so on [26.37].

We also define an operator to test whether two given rectangles overlap:

```
OPERATOR OVERLAP ( R1 RECTANGLE, R2 RECTANGLE )
                                      RETURNS BOOLEAN ;
     RETURN ( THE_X1 ( R1 ) ≤ THE_X2 ( R2 ) AND
              THE_Y1 ( R1 ) ≤ THE_Y2 ( R2 ) AND
              THE_X2 ( R1 ) ≥ THE_X1 ( R2 ) AND
              THE_Y2 ( R1 ) ≥ THE_Y1 ( R2 ) ) ;
END OPERATOR ;
```

This operator implements the efficient "short" form of the overlaps test (refer to Chapter 25 if you need to refresh your memory regarding that short form) against the efficient (R-tree or whatever) storage structure.

---

[2] In particular, today's systems have given rise to the all too common misconception that relational systems can support only a limited number of very simple types. The following quotes are quite typical: "Relational . . . systems support a small, fixed collection of data types (e.g., integers, dates, strings)" [26.34]; "a relational DBMS can support only . . . its built-in types [basically just numbers, strings, dates, and times]" [25.31]; "*object/relational data models* extend the relational data model by providing a richer type system" [16.21]; and so on.

Now the user can create a base relvar with an attribute of type RECTANGLE:

```
VAR RECTANGLES BASE RELATION { R RECTANGLE, ... } KEY { R } ;
```

And the query "Get all rectangles that overlap the unit square" now becomes simply:

```
RECTANGLES
WHERE OVERLAP ( R, RECTANGLE ( 0.0, 0.0, 1.0, 1.0 ) )
```

This solution overcomes *all* of the drawbacks discussed in connection with this query in Chapter 25.

Now, the foregoing ideas are conceptually very simple and straightforward—to repeat, all we have to do is implement the relational model, and in particular let users define their own types—and yet (once again) confusion reigns . . . In fact, we observe at least two huge mistakes in existing commercial products, which we refer to as *The Two Great Blunders*.[3] Clearly, we need to discuss those mistakes and show in particular just why we regard them as blunders; thus, the plan of the remainder of the chapter is as follows. Sections 26.2 and 26.3 discuss *The Two Great Blunders*. Section 26.4 then considers certain aspects of the implementation of an object/relational system. Section 26.5 describes the benefits of a *genuine* object/relational system (i.e., one that does not commit either of the two blunders). Section 26.6 describes the pertinent SQL facilities. Section 26.7 offers a summary.

26.2 THE FIRST GREAT BLUNDER

We begin with a quote from *The Third Manifesto* [3.3]:

[Before] we can consider the question of [a *rapprochement* between] objects and relations in any detail, there is a crucial preliminary question that we need to address, and that is as follows:

> **What concept is it in the relational world that is the counterpart to the concept *object class* in the object world?**

The reason this question is so crucial is that *object class* really is the most fundamental concept of all in the object world—all other object concepts depend on it to a greater or lesser degree. And there are two equations that can be, and have been, proposed as answers to this question:

- domain = object class
- relvar = object class

We now proceed to argue, strongly, that the first of these equations is right and the second is wrong.

---

[3] One reviewer objected to the use of the word *blunder* here, observing correctly that it is not a term commonly found in textbooks. Well, we admit we chose it partly for its shock value. But if some system *X* is supposed to be an implementation of the relational model, and then—some 25 years after the relational model was first defined—somebody adds a "feature" to that system *X* that totally violates the prescriptions of that model, it seems quite reasonable to us to describe the introduction of that "feature" as a blunder.

In fact, the first equation is *obviously* right, since object classes and domains are both just types. Indeed, given that relvars are variables and classes are types, it should be immediately obvious too that the second equation is wrong (variables and types are not the same thing); for this very reason, reference [3.3] asserts categorically that **relvars are not domains**. Nevertheless, many people, and some products, have in fact embraced the second equation—a mistake that we refer to as **The First Great Blunder**. It is therefore instructive to take a very careful look at the second equation, and so we do. *Note:* Most of the rest of this section is taken more or less *verbatim* from reference [3.3].

Why might anyone commit such a blunder? Well, consider the following simple class definition, expressed in a hypothetical object language that is similar but deliberately not quite identical to that of Section 25.3:

```
CREATE OBJECT CLASS EMP
     ( EMP#      CHAR(5),
       ENAME     CHAR(20),
       SAL       NUMERIC,
       HOBBY     CHAR(20),
       WORKS_FOR CHAR(20) ) ... ;
```

(EMP#, ENAME, etc., here are *public instance variables*. We deliberately define them to be of simple built-in types instead of user-defined types; moreover, we will do the same throughout our examples in this chapter, for simplicity.) Now consider the following SQL "base relvar" definition:

```
CREATE TABLE EMP
     ( EMP#      CHAR(5)  NOT NULL,
       ENAME     CHAR(20) NOT NULL,
       SAL       NUMERIC  NOT NULL,
       HOBBY     CHAR(20) NOT NULL,
       WORKS_FOR CHAR(20) NOT NULL ) ... ;
```

These two definitions certainly look very similar, and the idea of equating them thus looks very tempting. And (as already indicated) certain systems, including some commercial products, have effectively done just that. So let us take a closer look. More precisely, let us take the CREATE TABLE statement just shown and consider a series of possible extensions to it that (some people would argue) serve to make it more "object-like." *Note:* The discussion that follows is based on a specific commercial product; in fact, it is based on an example in that product's own documentation. We do not identify that product here, however, since it is not our intent in this book to criticize or praise specific products. Rather, the criticisms we will be making later in this section apply, *mutatis mutandis,* to *any* system that espouses the "relvar = class" equation.

The first extension is to permit *composite* (i.e., tuple-valued) *attributes;* that is, we allow attribute values to be tuples from some other relvar, or possibly from the same relvar (?). In the example, we might replace the original CREATE TABLE statement by the following collection of statements (refer to Fig. 26.1):

```
CREATE TABLE EMP
     ( EMP#      CHAR(5)   NOT NULL,
       ENAME     CHAR(20)  NOT NULL,
       SAL       NUMERIC   NOT NULL,
       HOBBY     ACTIVITY  NOT NULL,
       WORKS_FOR COMPANY   NOT NULL ) ;
```

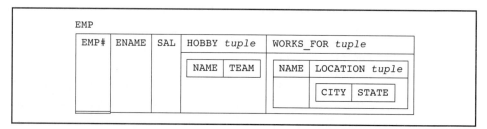

Fig. 26.1   Attributes containing (pointers to) tuples—deprecated

```
CREATE  TABLE  ACTIVITY
      ( NAME        CHAR(20)   NOT NULL,
        TEAM        INTEGER    NOT NULL ) ;

CREATE  TABLE  COMPANY
      ( NAME        CHAR(20)   NOT NULL,
        LOCATION    CITYSTATE  NOT NULL ) ;

CREATE  TABLE  CITYSTATE
      ( CITY        CHAR(20)   NOT NULL,
        STATE       CHAR(2)    NOT NULL ) ;
```

Explanation: Attribute HOBBY in relvar EMP is declared to be of type ACTIVITY. ACTIVITY in turn is a relvar of two attributes, NAME and TEAM, where TEAM gives the number of players in a team corresponding to NAME; for instance, a possible "activity" might be (Soccer,11). Each HOBBY value is thus actually a *pair* of values, a NAME value and a TEAM value (more precisely, it is a pair of values that currently appear as a tuple in relvar ACTIVITY). *Note:* Observe that we have already violated the *Third Manifesto* dictum that relvars are not domains—the "domain" for attribute HOBBY is defined to be the *relvar* ACTIVITY. See later in this section for further discussion of this point.

Similarly, attribute WORKS_FOR in relvar EMP is declared to be of type COMPANY, and COMPANY is also a relvar of two attributes, one of which is defined to be of type CITYSTATE, which is another two-attribute relvar, and so on. In other words, relvars ACTIVITY, COMPANY, and CITYSTATE are all considered to be *types* (domains) as well as relvars. The same is true for relvar EMP itself, of course.

This first extension is thus roughly analogous to allowing objects to contain other objects, thereby supporting the *containment hierarchy* concept (see Chapter 25).

As an aside, we remark that we have characterized this first extension as *attributes containing tuples* because that is the way advocates of the "relvar = class" equation themselves characterize it. It would be more accurate, however, to characterize it as "attributes containing *pointers to* tuples"—an issue we will examine more closely in a few moments, and more closely still in the next section. (In Fig. 26.1, therefore, we should really replace each of the three occurrences of the term *tuple* by the term *pointer to tuple*.)

Remarks analogous to those of the previous paragraph apply to the second extension also, which is to allow *relation-valued attributes;* that is, attribute values are allowed to be

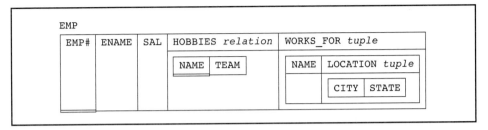

Fig. 26.2   Attributes containing sets of (pointers to) tuples—deprecated

sets of tuples from some other relvar, or possibly from the same relvar (?). For example, suppose employees can have an arbitrary number of hobbies, instead of just one (refer to Fig. 26.2):

```
CREATE TABLE EMP
     ( EMP#      CHAR(5)               NOT NULL,
       ENAME     CHAR(20)              NOT NULL,
       SAL       NUMERIC               NOT NULL,
       HOBBIES   SET OF ( ACTIVITY )   NOT NULL,
       WORKS_FOR COMPANY               NOT NULL ) ;
```

Explanation: The HOBBIES value within any given tuple of relvar EMP is now (conceptually) a set of zero or more (NAME,TEAM) pairs—that is, tuples—from relvar ACTIVITY. This second extension is thus roughly analogous to allowing objects to contain "collection" objects: a more complex version of the containment hierarchy. *Note:* We remark in passing that in the particular product on which our example is based, those collection objects can be sequences or bags as well as sets *per se.*

The third extension is to permit relvars to have associated *methods* (i.e., operators). For example:

```
CREATE TABLE EMP
     ( EMP#      CHAR(5)               NOT NULL,
       ENAME     CHAR(20)              NOT NULL,
       SAL       NUMERIC               NOT NULL,
       HOBBIES   SET OF ( ACTIVITY )   NOT NULL,
       WORKS_FOR COMPANY               NOT NULL )
METHOD RETIREMENT_BENEFITS ( ) : NUMERIC ;
```

Explanation: RETIREMENT_BENEFITS is a method that takes a given EMP tuple as its argument and produces a result of type NUMERIC.

The final definitional extension is to permit *subclasses*. For example (refer to Fig. 26.3):

```
CREATE TABLE PERSON
     ( SS#       CHAR(9)   NOT NULL,
       BIRTHDATE DATE      NOT NULL,
       ADDRESS   CHAR(50)  NOT NULL ) ;
```

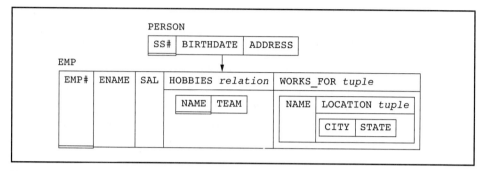

Fig. 26.3   Relvars as superclasses and subclasses—deprecated

```
CREATE  TABLE  EMP
    AS  SUBCLASS  OF  PERSON
      (  EMP#       CHAR(5)                  NOT  NULL,
         ENAME      CHAR(20)                 NOT  NULL,
         SAL        NUMERIC                  NOT  NULL,
         HOBBIES    SET  OF  (  ACTIVITY  )  NOT  NULL,
         WORKS_FOR  COMPANY                  NOT  NULL  )
METHOD  RETIREMENT_BENEFITS  (  )  :  NUMERIC  ;
```

Explanation: EMP now has three additional attributes (SS#, BIRTHDATE, and ADDRESS), inherited from PERSON (because each EMP instance "is a" PERSON instance as well, loosely speaking[4]). If PERSON had any methods, it would inherit those too. *Note:* PERSON and EMP here are examples of what are sometimes called *super-tables* and *subtables,* respectively. See reference [14.13], also Section 26.6, for further discussion—and criticism—of these concepts.

Along with the definitional extensions sketched in the foregoing, certain manipulative extensions are required too—for instance:

- *Path expressions* (e.g., EMP.WORKS_FOR.LOCATION.STATE). Note that such expressions can return scalars or tuples or relations, in general. Note further that in the latter two cases the components of those tuples or relations might themselves be tuples or relations in turn (and so on); for example, the expression EMP.HOBBIES .NAME returns a relation. Incidentally, note that these path expressions go *down* the containment hierarchy, whereas the path expressions discussed in Chapter 25 go *up.*

- *Tuple and relation literals* (possibly nested). For example:

```
( 'E001', 'Smith', $50000,
       ( ( 'Soccer', 11 ), ( 'Baseball', 9 ) ),
                          ( 'IBM', ( 'San Jose', 'CA' ) ) )
```

(not meant to be actual syntax).

---

[4] We apologize for our use of the fuzzy terminology of "instances" here, but if we tried to use the precise terminology of values and variables, the scheme we are trying (as fairly as we can) to describe would *obviously* make no sense.

- *Relational comparison operators* (e.g., SUBSET, SUBSETEQ, and so on). *Note:* The particular operators mentioned are taken from the particular product under discussion. In that product, SUBSET really means "*proper* subset," and SUBSETEQ means "subset" (!).

- *Operators for traversing the class hierarchy* (e.g., to retrieve EMP and PERSON information together). *Note:* Care is needed here, too. It might well be the case that a request to retrieve PERSON information together with associated EMP information yields a result that is not a relation—meaning that the vital relational property of *closure* has been violated, with potentially disastrous implications. (In this connection, reference [26.41]—which refers to such a result as a "jagged return"—merely observes blithely that "the client program must be prepared to deal with the complexity of a jagged return.")

- *The ability to invoke methods within, for example, SELECT and WHERE clauses (in SQL terms).*

- *The ability to access individual components within attribute values that happen to be tuples or relations.*

So much for a quick overview of how the "relvar = class" equation is realized in practice. So what is wrong with it?

Well, observe first of all that (as noted earlier) a relvar is a variable and a class is a type; so how can they possibly be the same? This first observation should be logically sufficient to stop the "relvar = class" idea dead in its tracks. However, there is more that can usefully be said, so let us agree to suspend disbelief a little longer . . . Here are some additional points to consider:

- The equation "relvar = class" implies the further equations "tuple = object" and "attribute = (public) instance variable." Thus, whereas (as we saw in Chapter 25) a true object class—at least, a scalar or "encapsulated" object class—has methods and no public instance variables, a relvar "object class" has public instance variables and only optionally has methods (it is definitely not "encapsulated"). So, again, how can the two notions possibly be the same?

- There is a major difference between the attribute definitions (e.g.) "SAL NUMERIC" and "WORKS_FOR COMPANY." NUMERIC is a true data type (equivalently, a true, albeit primitive, domain); it places a time-independent constraint on the values that can legally appear in attribute SAL. By contrast, COMPANY is *not* a true data type; the constraint it places on the values that can appear in attribute WORKS_FOR is *time-dependent* (it depends, obviously, on the current value of relvar COMPANY). In fact, as pointed out earlier, the relvar *vs.* domain distinction—or, if you prefer, the collection *vs.* class distinction—has been muddied here.

- We have seen that tuple "objects" are apparently allowed to contain other such "objects"; for example, EMP "objects" apparently contain COMPANY "objects." But they do not—not really; instead, they contain *pointers* to those "contained objects," and users must be absolutely clear on this point. For example, suppose the user updates some particular COMPANY tuple in some way (see Fig. 26.1). Then that update will immediately be visible in all EMP tuples that "contain" that COMPANY tuple.   *Note:* We are not saying this effect is undesirable, we are only saying it has to be explained to the user. But explaining it to the user amounts to telling the user that the "model" shown in Fig. 26.1 is incorrect—EMP tuples do not contain COMPANY tuples, they contain *pointers to* COMPANY tuples instead (as already stated).

Here are some further implications and questions arising from this same point:

a. Can we insert an EMP tuple and specify a value for the "contained" COMPANY tuple that does not currently exist in the COMPANY relvar? If the answer is *yes,* the fact that attribute WORKS_FOR is defined as being of type COMPANY does not mean very much, since it does not significantly constrain the INSERT operation in any way. If the answer is *no,* the INSERT operation becomes unnecessarily complex—the user has to specify, not just an existing company name (i.e., a foreign key value) as would be required in the analogous relational situation, but an entire existing COMPANY tuple. Moreover, specifying an entire COMPANY tuple means, at best, telling the system something it already knows; at worst, it means that if the user makes a mistake, the INSERT will fail when it could perfectly well have succeeded.

b. Suppose we want an ON DELETE RESTRICT rule for companies (i.e., an attempt to delete a company must fail if the company has any employees). Presumably this rule must be enforced by procedural code, say by some method *M* (note that relvar EMP has no foreign key to which a declarative version of the rule might be attached). Furthermore, regular SQL DELETE operations must now not be performed on relvar COMPANY other than within the code that implements that method *M*. How is this requirement enforced? Analogous remarks and questions apply to other foreign key rules, of course, such as ON DELETE CASCADE.

c. Note too that deleting an EMP tuple presumably will not cascade to delete the corresponding COMPANY tuple, despite the pretense that the EMP tuple contains that COMPANY tuple.

It follows from all of the foregoing that we are not exactly talking about the relational model any more. The fundamental data object is no longer a relation containing values, it is a "relation"—actually not a proper relation at all, as far as the relational model is concerned—containing values *and pointers.* In other words, **we have undermined the conceptual integrity of the relational model**. *Note:* The term *conceptual integrity* is due to Fred Brooks, who has this to say about it [26.3]: "[Conceptual] integrity is *the* most important consideration in system design. It is better to have a system omit certain anomalous features [and] to reflect one set of design ideas, than to have one that contains many good but independent and uncoordinated ideas" (italics in the original). And writing 20 years later, he adds: "A clean, elegant programming product must present . . . a coherent mental model . . . [Conceptual] integrity . . . is the most important factor in ease of use . . . **Today I am more convinced than ever**. Conceptual integrity *is* central to product quality" (boldface and italics in the original).

■ Suppose we define view V to be the projection of EMP over (say) just the attribute HOBBIES. V is a relvar too, of course, but a derived relvar instead of a base one. So if "relvar = class" is a correct equation, V is also a class. *What class is it?* Also, classes have methods; *what methods apply to V?*

Well, "class" EMP has just one method, RETIREMENT_BENEFITS, and that method clearly does not apply to "class" V. In fact, it hardly seems reasonable that *any* methods that applied to "class" EMP would apply to "class" V—and there certainly are no others. So it looks as if (in general) *no methods at all* apply to the result of a projection; that is, the result, whatever it is, is not really a class at all. (We might *say* it is a class, but that does not make it one!—it will have public instance variables and no methods, whereas we have already observed that a true "encapsulated" class has methods and no public instance variables.)

In fact, it is quite clear that when people equate relvars and classes, it is specifically base relvars they have in mind—they are forgetting about the derived ones. (Certainly the pointers discussed previously are pointers to tuples in base relvars, not derived ones.) But to distinguish between base and derived relvars in this way is a mistake of the highest order, because the question as to which relvars are base and which are derived is, in a very important sense, arbitrary (recall the discussion of *The Principle of Interchangeability* in Chapter 10).

■ Finally, *what domains are supported?* Those who advocate the "relvar = class" equation never seem to have much to say about domains, presumably because they cannot see how domains as such fit into their overall scheme. And yet domains are essential, as we know.

The overall message of the foregoing can be summarized as follows. Obviously, systems can be built that are based on the wrong equation "relvar = class"; indeed, some such systems already exist. Equally obviously, those systems (like a car with no oil in its engine, or a house that is built on sand) might even provide useful service, for a while—but they are doomed to eventual failure.

Where Did The First Great Blunder Come From?

It is interesting to speculate on the source of **The First Great Blunder**. It seems to us that it has its roots in the lack of consensus, noted in Chapter 25, on the meaning of certain terms in the object world. In particular, the term *object* itself does not have a universally accepted and agreed-upon meaning—which is precisely why we prefer not to use it ourselves.

The foregoing remarks notwithstanding, it is at least fairly clear that in object programming language circles, at any rate, the term *object* refers to what more traditionally would be called either a *value* or a *variable* (possibly both). Unfortunately, however, the term is used in other circles as well; in particular, it is used in certain *semantic modeling* circles, as part of various "object analysis and design" or "object modeling" techniques and methodologies—see, for example, reference [14.3]. And in those circles, it seems clear that the term does not mean a value or a variable, but rather what the database community would more usually call an *entity* (implying among other things, incidentally, that, unlike programming language objects, such objects are definitely not encapsulated). In other words, "object modeling" is really just "entity/relationship modeling" by another name; indeed, reference [14.3] more or less admits as much. As a consequence, things that are identified as "objects" in such methodologies are then (correctly) mapped to tuples in relvars instead of to values in domains. Hey presto!

26.3   THE SECOND GREAT BLUNDER

In this section, we examine **The Second Great Blunder**; as we will see, that second blunder is a logical consequence of the first, but it is also significant in its own right. In fact, it can be *committed* in its own right, too, even if **The First Great Blunder** is avoided; indeed, it *is* being committed by just about every object/relational product on the market, as well as by the SQL standard (see Section 26.6). The blunder consists of **mixing pointers and relations**.

We begin by revisiting the major features of the "relvar = class" approach as identified in the previous section. The fact is, some readers might possibly have found that section a little confusing, since some of the features we seemed to be objecting to were features we have argued in favor of at earlier points in the book (tuple- and relation-valued attributes might be a case in point). So let us clarify our position:

- *Tuple- and relation-valued attributes:* Indeed, we do not object to such attributes (how could we?). What we do object to is (a) the idea that such attributes must have, very specifically, values that currently appear in some other (base) relvar, and (b) the idea that such attributes really have values that are not tuples or relations *per se* but are, rather, **pointers** to tuples or relations—which means that we are not really talking about tuple- or relation-valued attributes at all. *Note:* In fact, the idea of pointers pointing to "tuples or relations"—meaning, specifically, tuple or relation *values*—makes no sense anyway, a point we will be discussing in detail in a few moments.

- *Associating operators ("methods") with relvars:* We have no objections to this idea, either—it is basically just the notion of triggers or stored procedures under another guise. But we do object to the idea that such operators must be associated with relvars (and only relvars), not with domains or types. We also object to the idea that they must be associated with *one specific* relvar (the notion of target arguments under another guise).

- *Subclasses and superclasses:* Now here we do object. In a system that equates relvars and classes, subclasses and superclasses become sub*tables* and super*tables*—and this notion is one we are highly skeptical of (see reference [14.13], also Section 26.6). We want proper type inheritance as described in Chapter 20.

- *Path expressions:* We would have no objections to path expressions that were merely syntactic shorthand for following certain associative references—for example, from a foreign key to a matching candidate key, as proposed in reference [26.15]. However, path expressions as discussed in Section 26.2 are, rather, shorthand for following certain *pointer chains,* and these we do object to (because we object to pointers in the first place, at the model level).

- *Tuple and relation literals:* These are essential—though they need to be generalized into tuple and relation *selectors* [3.3].

- *Relational comparison operators:* Also essential (though they ought to be done right).

- *Operators for traversing the class hierarchy:* If "class hierarchy" really means "relvar hierarchy," then (as noted in the previous section) we have major objections, because of the probable violation of the relational closure property (see, e.g., reference [26.41]). If it means "type hierarchy" in the sense of Chapter 20, then we have no objections (but it does not).

- *Invoking methods in, for example, SELECT and WHERE clauses:* Of course.

- *Accessing individual components within attribute values that happen to be tuples or relations:* Of course.

So now let us focus on the issue of mixing pointers and relations. The crux of our argument here is very simple. By definition, pointers point to *variables,* not *values* (because variables have addresses and values do not). By definition, therefore, if relvar *R1* is allowed to have an attribute whose values are pointers "into" relvar *R2,* then those pointers point to tuple *variables,* not to tuple *values.* **But there is no notion of a tuple variable in the relational model.** The relational model deals with relation values, which are (loosely speaking) sets of tuple values, which are in turn (again loosely speaking) sets of scalar values. It also deals with relation variables, which are variables whose values are relations. However, it does *not* deal with tuple variables (which are variables whose values are tuples) or scalar variables (which are variables whose values are scalars). The *only* kind of variable included in the relational model—and the only kind of variable permitted in a relational database—is, very specifically, the *relation* variable. *It follows that the idea of mixing pointers and relations constitutes a MAJOR departure from the relational model, introducing as it does an entirely new kind of variable* (thereby violating *The Information Principle,* in fact). As noted in the previous section, in fact, we would argue that it seriously undermines the conceptual integrity of the relational model.

Given the truth of the foregoing, it is sad to see that most (perhaps all) of the current crop of object/relational products—even those that do avoid **The First Great Blunder**—nevertheless seem to be mixing pointers and relations in exactly the manner discussed, and objected to, in the previous section. When Codd first defined the relational model, he very deliberately excluded pointers. To quote reference [6.2]:

> It is safe to assume that all kinds of users [including end users in particular] understand the act of comparing values, but that relatively few understand the complexities of pointers. The relational model is based on this fundamental principle . . . [The] manipulation of pointers is more bug-prone than is the act of comparing values, even if the user happens to understand the complexities of pointers.

To be specific, pointers lead to pointer chasing, and pointer chasing is notoriously error-prone. As noted in Chapter 25, it is precisely this aspect of object systems that gives rise to the criticisms, sometimes heard, to the effect that such systems "look like CODASYL warmed over."

Numerous detailed arguments in further support of the foregoing position can be found in references [25.19] and [26.15]. See also references [26.12–26.14] and [26.17], which discuss the related, and important, notion of *essentiality*.

Pointers and a Good Model of Inheritance Are Incompatible

Actually there is another powerful argument against supporting pointers, one that Codd could not possibly have been aware of when he was writing reference [6.2]. We illustrate that argument with a simple example. (We state the example in terms of ordinary program variables instead of database relations, in order to focus on the real issue without being distracted by irrelevancies.) Consider types ELLIPSE and CIRCLE once again. Let PTR_TO_ELLIPSE and PTR_TO_CIRCLE be associated pointer types; in other words, let values of types PTR_TO_ELLIPSE and PTR_TO_CIRCLE be (loosely speaking) "pointers to ellipses" and "pointers to circles," respectively. Finally, let ELLIPSE be a proper supertype of CIRCLE, and hence let PTR_TO_ELLIPSE be a proper supertype of PTR_TO_CIRCLE. Now consider the following code fragment:

```
VAR E  ELLIPSE ;
VAR XC PTR_TO_CIRCLE ;

E   :=  CIRCLE ( LENGTH ( 5.0 ), POINT ( 0.0, 0.0 ) ) ;

XC  :=  TREAT_DOWN_AS_PTR_TO_CIRCLE ( PTR_TO ( E ) ) ;

THE_A ( E )  :=  LENGTH ( 6.0 ) ;
```

Explanation:

1. The two variable declarations are self-explanatory.

2. After the first assignment (to E), variable E contains a circle of radius five.[5] Note the appeal to substitutability in this assignment; note too that the most specific type of E is now CIRCLE.

3. PTR_TO, which appears in the expression on the right side of the second assignment, is what is usually called the **referencing** operator: Given a variable *V*, it returns the address of—that is, a pointer to—that variable *V*. In the example, therefore, it returns a pointer value of type PTR_TO_ELLIPSE. However, since the variable that pointer value points to has most specific type CIRCLE, that pointer value is in fact of type PTR_TO_CIRCLE, not merely of type PTR_TO_ELLIPSE. So the TREAT DOWN succeeds, and the assignment thus places in variable XC a pointer to (= the address of) variable E.

4. The third assignment (to THE_A(E)) is the crucial one. What happens? It seems there are three possibilities, all of them bad:

   a. A run-time type error occurs, because assignment to THE_A is not supported for variables of most specific type CIRCLE. In other words, generalization by constraint is not supported—and hence specialization by constraint is not supported either, and the inheritance model is therefore bad (certainly it is not "a faithful model of reality"—see Chapter 20). In any case, run-time type errors are always undesirable.

---

[5] As in Chapter 20, we assume in this chapter that the Cartesian possible representation for points is called POINT instead of CARTESIAN. The second argument to the CIRCLE selector in the example is thus an invocation of that POINT selector.

b. The assignment "succeeds," but generalization by constraint does not occur. The effect is that variable E now contains a "noncircular circle" (its most specific type is still CIRCLE, but that "circle" has semiaxes of different lengths). Again, then, the inheritance model is bad (it is not a faithful model of reality), because generalization by constraint and specialization by constraint are not supported. What is more, not only does variable E now contain a "noncircular circle," but variable XC points to a "noncircular circle" as well. Furthermore, *type constraints cannot be supported!*—for if they were, then "noncircular circles" could not occur. In other words, what is arguably the most fundamental kind of integrity constraint of all cannot be supported: When we define a type, *we cannot specify what values are legal for that type.*

We note in passing that this case is SQL:1999! See Chapter 20 and Section 26.6.

c. The assignment succeeds and generalization by constraint does occur; that is, variable E now contains "just an ellipse," and its most specific type is ELLIPSE. But then the inheritance model is bad, because the variable XC, whose declared type is PTR_TO_CIRCLE, now contains a value of most specific type PTR_TO_ELLIPSE!—implying, again, that type constraints cannot be supported. *Note:* Since the idea of allowing a variable of some declared type *T* to contain a value of most specific type some proper supertype of *T* is a logical nonsense, it is more likely that the original assignment will either fail as under paragraph 1 or "succeed" without generalization by constraint as under paragraph 2. In other words, this third possibility is probably a nonstarter.

We conclude from this example that if pointers are supported, the inheritance model must be bad; in other words, *pointers and a good model of inheritance are incompatible.* Which seems like another very good reason for rejecting pointers.

Where Did The Second Great Blunder Come From?

It is hard to find any real justification in the literature for The Second Great Blunder (any technical justification, that is—but there is evidence that the justification is not technical at all but political). Given the fact that object systems and object languages do all include pointers in the form of object IDs, the idea of mixing pointers and relations almost certainly arises from a desire to make relational systems more "object-like." However, this "justification" merely pushes the problem off to another level; we have already made it abundantly clear that—in our opinion—object systems expose pointers to the user precisely because they fail to distinguish properly between model and implementation.

We can only conjecture, therefore, that the reason why the idea of mixing pointers and relations is being so widely promulgated is because too few people understand why pointers were excluded from relations in the first place. As Santayana has it: *Those who cannot remember the past are condemned to repeat it* (usually quoted in the form "Those who don't know history are doomed to repeat it"). On such matters we agree strongly with Maurice Wilkes, when he writes [26.46]:

> I would like to see computer science teaching set deliberately in a historical framework
> . . . Students need to understand how the present situation has come about, what was tried,
> what worked and what did not, and how improvements in hardware made progress possi-
> ble. The absence of this element in their training causes people to approach every problem
> from first principles. They are apt to propose solutions that have been found wanting in the
> past. Instead of standing on the shoulders of their precursors, they try to go it alone.

26.4 IMPLEMENTATION ISSUES

One important implication of proper data type support is that it allows third-party vendors
(as well as DBMS vendors themselves) to build and sell separate "type packages" that can
effectively be plugged into the DBMS. Examples include packages to support sophisticated text handling, financial time-series processing, geospatial (cartographic) data analysis, and so on. Such packages are variously referred to as *data blades* (Informix), *data car-
tridges* (Oracle), *relational extenders*[6] (IBM), *application packages* (this is the term used
in the SQL/MM standard [26.25]), and so on. In what follows, we will stay with the term
type packages.

Adding a new type package to the system is a nontrivial undertaking, however, and
providing the ability to do so has significant implications for the design and structure of the
DBMS itself. To see why in both cases, consider what happens if, for example, some query
includes references to data of some user-defined type or invocations of some user-defined
operator (or both):

- First of all, the query language compiler has to be able to parse and type-check that
  request, so it has to know something about those user-defined types and operators.

- Second, the optimizer has to be able to decide on an appropriate query plan for that
  request, so it too has to be aware of certain properties of those user-defined types and
  operators. In particular, it has to know how the data is physically stored (see the next
  point).

- Third, the component that manages physical storage has to support the newer storage
  structures—quadtrees, R-trees, and so on—mentioned in our discussion of the rectangles problem in Section 26.1. It might even have to support the ability for suitably
  skilled users to introduce new storage structures and access methods of their own
  [26.29, 26.43].

One important consequence of all of the foregoing is that the system needs to be *extensible*—extensible at several levels, in fact. We discuss each level briefly.

Parsing and Type Checking

In a conventional system, since the only available types and operators are all built in, information regarding them can be (and typically is) "hardwired" into the compiler. In a system

---

[6] An *exceedingly* inappropriate term, in our opinion.

in which users can define their own types and operators, by contrast, this "hardwired" approach is clearly not going to work. Instead, therefore, what has to happen is this:

■ Information regarding user-defined types and operators—and possibly built-in types and operators as well—is kept in the system catalog. This fact implies that the catalog itself needs to be redesigned (or at least extended); it also implies that introducing a new type package involves a lot of catalog updating. (In **Tutorial D** terms, that updating is performed under the covers as part of the process of executing the applicable TYPE and OPERATOR definitional statements.)

■ The compiler itself needs to be rewritten in order to access the catalog to obtain the necessary type and operator information. It can then use that information to carry out all of the compile-time type checking as described in Chapters 5 and 20.

Optimization

There are many, many issues involved here, and we can only scratch the surface of the problem in this book. However, we can at least point out what a few of the issues are:

■ *Expression transformation ("query rewrite"):* A conventional optimizer applies certain laws of transformation to rewrite queries, as we saw in Chapter 18. Historically, however, those laws of transformation have all been "hardwired" into the optimizer (because, again, the available data types and operators were all built in). In an object/relational system, by contrast, the relevant knowledge (at least insofar as it applies to user-defined types and operators specifically) needs to be kept in the catalog—implying more extensions to the catalog, and implying too that the optimizer itself needs to be rewritten. Here are some illustrations:

a. Given an expression such as NOT (STATUS > 20), a good conventional optimizer will transform it into STATUS ≤ 20 (because the second version can make use of an index on STATUS while the first cannot). For analogous reasons, there needs to be a way of informing the optimizer when one user-defined operator is the negation of another.

b. A good conventional optimizer will also know that, for example, the expressions STATUS > 20 and 20 < STATUS are logically equivalent. There needs to be a way of informing the optimizer when two user-defined operators are opposites in this sense.

c. A good conventional optimizer will also know that, for example, the operators "+" and "−" cancel out (i.e., are inverses); for example, the expression STATUS + 20 − 20 reduces to just STATUS. There needs to be a way of informing the optimizer when two user-defined operators are inverses in this sense.

■ *Selectivity:* Given a boolean expression such as STATUS > 20, optimizers typically make a guess at the *selectivity* of that expression (i.e., the percentage of tuples that make that expression evaluate to TRUE). For built-in data types and operators, again, that selectivity information can be "hardwired" into the optimizer; for user-defined types and operators, by contrast, there needs to be a way of providing the optimizer with some user-defined code to invoke in order to guess selectivities.

- *Cost formulas:* The optimizer needs to know how much it costs to execute a given user-defined operator. Given an expression such as *p* AND *q*, for example, where *p* is (say) an invocation of the AREA operator on some complicated polygon and *q* is a simple comparison like STATUS > 20, we would probably prefer the system to execute *q* first, so that *p* is executed only on tuples for which *q* evaluates to TRUE. Indeed, some of the classical expression-transformation heuristics, such as always doing restrictions before joins, are not necessarily valid for user-defined types and operators (see, e.g., references [26.10] and [26.24]).

- *Storage structures and access methods:* The optimizer clearly needs to be aware of the storage structures and access methods in effect (see the next subsection).

Storage Structures

It seems clear that object/relational systems are going to need more ways—possibly many more ways—of storing and accessing data at the physical level than (e.g.) SQL systems have traditionally provided. Here are some relevant considerations:

- *New storage structures:* As already noted, the system will probably need to support new "hardwired" storage structures (R-trees, etc.), and there might even need to be a way for suitably skilled users to introduce additional storage structures and access methods of their own.

- *Indexes on data of a user-defined type:* Traditional indexes are based on data of some built-in type and a built-in understanding of what the "<" operator means. In an object/relational system, it must be possible to build indexes on data of a user-defined type, based on the semantics of the applicable user-defined "<" operator (assuming such an operator has been defined in the first place, of course).

- *Indexes on operator results:* There would probably be little point in building an index directly over a set of data values of type POLYGON; most likely, all such an index would do would be to order the polygons by their internal byte string encodings. However, an index based on the *areas* of those polygons could be very useful. *Note:* We referred to such indexes as *functional* indexes in Chapter 22.

26.5 BENEFITS OF TRUE *RAPPROCHEMENT*

In reference [26.41], Stonebraker presents a "classification matrix" for DBMSs (see Fig. 26.4). *Quadrant 1* of that matrix represents applications that deal only with rather simple data and have no requirement for *ad hoc* query (a traditional word processor is a good example). Such applications are not really database applications at all, in the usual sense of that term; the "DBMS" that best serves their needs is just the built-in file manager provided as part of the underlying operating system.

Quadrant 2 represents applications that do have an *ad hoc* query requirement but still deal only with rather simple data. Most of today's business applications fall into this quadrant, and they are fairly well supported by traditional relational (or at least SQL) DBMSs.

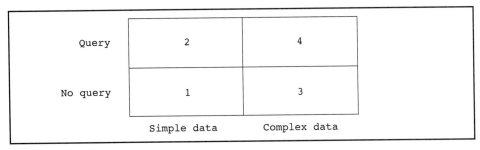

Fig. 26.4   Stonebraker's DBMS classification matrix

Quadrant 3 represents applications with complex data and processing requirements but no *ad hoc* query requirement. For example, CAD/CAM applications might fall into this quadrant. Current object DBMSs are primarily aimed at this segment of the market (traditional SQL products tend not to do a very good job on Quadrant 3 applications).

Finally, *Quadrant 4* represents applications with a need for both complex data and *ad hoc* queries against that data. Stonebraker gives an example of a database containing digitized 35-mm slides, with a typical query being "Get pictures of sunsets taken within 20 miles of Sacramento, California." He then goes on to give arguments in support of his position that (a) an object/relational DBMS is required for applications that fall into this quadrant, and (b) over the next few years, the majority of applications will fall into, or move over into, this quadrant. For example, even a simple human resources application might expand to include employee photographs, audio recordings (spoken messages), and the like.

In sum, Stonebraker is arguing (and we agree) that "object/relational systems are in everyone's future"; they are not just a passing fad, soon to be replaced by some other briefly fashionable idea. However, we should perhaps remind you that, as far as we are concerned, a true object/relational system is nothing more nor less than a true *relational* system. In particular, it is a system that does not commit either of **The Two Great Blunders**! Stonebraker does not quite seem to agree with our position here; at least, reference [26.41] never quite says as much, and indeed it implies that mixing pointers and relations is not only acceptable but desirable (in fact, required).

Be that as it may, we would argue that a *genuine* object/relational system would solve all of the problems that (we claimed in the previous chapter) are indeed problems of systems that are just plain object systems instead of object/relational ones. To be specific, such a system should be able to support all of the following without undue difficulty:

- *Ad hoc* query, view definition, and declarative integrity constraints
- Methods that span classes (there is no need for a distinguished target argument)
- Dynamically defined classes (for *ad hoc* query results)
- Dual-mode access (see Chapter 4; we did not stress the point in Chapter 25, but object systems typically do not support the dual-mode principle—instead, they use different languages for programmed and interactive access to the database)
- Transition constraints

- Semantic optimization
- Relationships of degree greater than two
- Foreign key rules (ON DELETE CASCADE, etc.)
- Optimizability

and so on. In addition:

- OIDs and pointer chasing are now totally "under the covers" and hidden from the user.
- "Difficult" object questions (e.g., what does it mean to join two objects?) go away.
- The benefits of encapsulation, such as they are, still apply, but to scalar values within relations, not to relations *per se.*
- Relational systems can now handle "complex" application areas such as CAD/CAM, as previously discussed.

And the approach is conceptually clean.

26.6   SQL FACILITIES

SQL:1999's object/relational features are the most obvious and extensive difference between it and its predecessor SQL:1992. We have already described and analyzed many of those features in earlier chapters. To be specific:

- In Chapter 5, we showed that SQL supports two different kinds of user-defined types, DISTINCT types and structured types. Both kinds can be used as a basis for (among other things) defining columns in base tables.
- In Chapter 6, we showed that SQL also allows structured types specifically to be used as the basis for defining what it calls "typed tables."
- In Chapter 20, we showed that SQL also supports a form of type inheritance, albeit for structured types only.

In addition to these features, however, SQL also supports (a) a *REF type generator*[7] and (b) *subtables and supertables.* Now, these additional constructs are very much intertwined with those just mentioned (especially with structured types). Just why they should be so intertwined is not at all clear—in principle, the concepts are quite orthogonal—but perhaps the point is not important, because in our opinion the additional constructs are not very useful anyway, as we now attempt to show.

REF Types

We begin with a simple example (irrelevant details omitted):

---

[7] REF here stands for *reference,* but REF types have nothing to do with either the REFERENCES privilege (see Chapter 17) or references in the sense of foreign keys. We remark in passing that REF types are scalar types, so we have here an example of a scalar type generator.

```
CREATE TYPE DEPT_TYPE
   AS ( DEPT#  CHAR(3),
        DNAME  CHAR(25),
        BUDGET MONEY ) ...
      REF IS SYSTEM GENERATED ;

CREATE TABLE DEPT OF DEPT_TYPE
      ( REF IS DEPT_ID SYSTEM GENERATED,
        PRIMARY KEY ( DEPT# ) ) ... ;
```

Explanation (partly repeated from Chapter 6):

1. Recall first from Chapter 5 that whenever we create a structured type *ST,* the system automatically generates an associated *reference type* ("REF type") called REF(*ST*); in the example, therefore, the reference type REF(DEPT_TYPE) is generated automatically. REF types can be used wherever a data type of any kind can be used; however, they can be generated only implicitly, as a side effect of creating a structured type.

2. Values of type REF(ST) are "references" to—in other words, *pointers to* or *addresses of*—rows within some base table[8] that has been defined to be "OF" type *ST* (see point 4). In the example, therefore, values of type REF(DEPT_TYPE) are pointers to rows within base table DEPT. (We are assuming here that DEPT is the *sole* table that has been defined to be "OF" type DEPT_TYPE, though this assumption would not always be valid.) *Note:* The structured type *ST* can be used in other contexts, of course—for example, as the declared type for some column or some local variable—but no REF(*ST*) values are associated with those other uses.

3. The specification REF IS SYSTEM GENERATED in a CREATE TYPE statement means that values of the associated REF type are provided by the system. (Other options—for example, REF IS USER GENERATED—are available, but the details are beyond the scope of this book.) *Note:* In fact, REF IS SYSTEM GENERATED is the default; in our example, therefore, we could have omitted that specification entirely from the definition of type DEPT_TYPE.

4. A base table can be defined (via CREATE TABLE) to be "OF" some structured type; such a table is said to be a *typed table* or *referenceable table.* The keyword OF here is not really very appropriate, however, because (as explained in Chapter 6) the table is *not* actually "of" the type in question, and neither are its rows. In fact, the table has one column for each attribute of the structured type in question, plus one additional column—namely, a column of the applicable REF type—though the syntax for defining that additional column is not the usual column definition syntax but instead looks like this:

```
REF IS <column name> SYSTEM GENERATED
```

This extra "self-referencing" column, which is first in the left-to-right ordering of columns in the table, is used to contain unique IDs ("references") for the rows of the base table in question (the specifications UNIQUE and NOT NULL are implied). The ID

---

[8] Or possibly some view. Details of the view case are beyond the scope of this book.

for a given row is assigned when the row is inserted, and remains associated with that row[9] until it is deleted.

5. A structured type is not regarded as encapsulated when it is used as the basis for defining a base table (although it *is* so regarded, more or less, in other contexts). In our example, therefore, base table DEPT has four columns DEPT_ID, DEPT#, DNAME, and BUDGET (in that order), instead of just two as it would have had if DEPT_TYPE were encapsulated.

6. The default for column DEPT_ID is NULL (as in fact it is for all columns that are defined to be of some REF type, though that default will not make much sense if the column in question is additionally specified to be NOT NULL).

Let us now extend the example to introduce an EMP base table, thus:[10]

```
CREATE TABLE EMP
      ( EMP#    CHAR(5)   NOT NULL,
        ENAME   CHAR(25) NOT NULL,
        SALARY  MONEY     NOT NULL,
        DEPT_ID REF ( DEPT_TYPE ) SCOPE DEPT
                REFERENCES ARE CHECKED
                ON DELETE CASCADE
                          NOT NULL,
        PRIMARY KEY ( EMP# ) ) ;
```

Normally, base table EMP would include a foreign key column DEPT# that refers to departments by department number. Here, however, we have a "reference" column DEPT_ID—not explicitly declared to be a foreign key column as such, please note—that refers to departments by their "references" instead. SCOPE DEPT specifies the applicable referenced table. REFERENCES ARE CHECKED means referential integrity is to be maintained (REFERENCES ARE NOT CHECKED would permit "dangling references"; it is not clear why it would ever be desirable to specify this option[11]). ON DELETE . . . specifies a delete rule, analogous to the usual foreign key delete rules (the same options are supported). There is no analogous ON UPDATE . . . specification.

Using References

We now consider a few sample queries and updates on the departments-and-employees database as just defined. Here first is an SQL formulation of the query "Get the department number for employee E1":

```
SELECT DEPT_ID -> DEPT# AS DEPT#
FROM    EMP
WHERE   EMP# = 'E1' ;
```

---

[9] There seems to be some circularity here: "That row" can only mean "the row that has the particular ID in question." In particular, note the value *vs.* variable confusion!—if "that row" is to have an address, then "that row" has to be a row *variable* (see Section 26.3).

[10] Note the NOT NULL specifications on the columns of table EMP. Specifying that the columns of table DEPT also have nulls not allowed is not so easy! The details are left as an exercise.

[11] And yet the REFERENCES . . . specification is likely to be deleted in SQL:2003, implying that (by default) REFERENCES ARE NOT CHECKED will *always* be specified.

Note the **dereferencing** operator "–>" in the SELECT clause (the expression DEPT_ID –> DEPT# yields the DEPT# value from the DEPT row that the DEPT_ID value in question points to).[12] Note too the need to specify an AS clause; if that clause had been omitted, the corresponding result column would effectively have been unnamed. Finally, note the counterintuitive nature of the FROM clause—the DEPT# value to be retrieved comes from DEPT, not EMP, but *DEPT_ID* values come from EMP, not DEPT.

Incidentally, we cannot resist the temptation to point out that this first query will probably perform worse than its conventional SQL counterpart (which would access just one table, not two). We make this observation because the usual argument in favor of "references" is that they are supposed to improve performance ("following a pointer is faster than doing a join"). Of course, to argue thus is to confuse logical and physical issues.

By way of a second example, suppose the original query had been "Get the *department* (instead of just the department number) for employee E1." Now the dereferencing operation looks rather different:

```
SELECT  DEREF ( DEPT_ID ) AS DEPT
FROM    EMP
WHERE   EMP# = 'E1' ;
```

Furthermore, the DEREF invocation here yields, not—as might have been expected—a DEPT *row* value, but an "encapsulated" (scalar) value instead. That value is of type DEPT_TYPE and thus has just three attributes, DEPT#, DNAME, and BUDGET (it does *not* include a DEPT_ID attribute).[13] *Note:* To repeat an observation we made in Chapter 6, if the declared type of some parameter *P* to some operator *Op* is DEPT_TYPE, we cannot pass a row from table DEPT as a corresponding argument to an invocation of that operator *Op*. We can now see, however, that we *can* pass DEREF(DEPT_ID) instead, if DEPT_ID contains a reference to a row of table DEPT.

Here is another example—"Get employee numbers for employees in department D1":

```
SELECT  EMP#
FROM    EMP
WHERE   DEPT_ID -> DEPT# = 'D1' ;
```

Note the dereferencing in the WHERE clause in this example.

Here now is an INSERT example (insertion of an employee):

```
INSERT INTO EMP ( EMP#, DEPT_ID )
       VALUES ( 'E5', ( SELECT DEPT_ID
                        FROM   DEPT
                        WHERE  DEPT# = 'D2' ) ) ;
```

---

[12] Most languages that support dereferencing support a *referencing* operator as well (see, e.g., the discussion of PTR_TO in Section 26.3), but SQL does not. Moreover, dereferencing usually returns a *variable*, but in SQL it returns a *value* instead.

[13] It follows from the semantics of DEREF that—although for most purposes columns DEPT#, DNAME, and BUDGET of table DEPT behave as regular columns—the system is also required to remember that those columns are derived from the structured type DEPT_TYPE. In other words, to use the terminology of types and headings from Chapter 6, we might say that table DEPT has a heading (and therefore type) with four components in some contexts but a heading (and therefore type) with just two components in others. Perhaps "typed tables" might better be called *schizophrenic* tables?

Now, apologists for the constructs we have been discussing (REF types and so forth) stress the point that there is no need for concern because "everything is really just shorthand." For example, the SQL expression

```
SELECT DEPT_ID -> DEPT# AS DEPT#
FROM    EMP
WHERE   EMP# = 'E1' ;
```

("Get the department number for employee E1," the first of our examples in this subsection) is claimed to be shorthand for the following:

```
SELECT ( SELECT DEPT#
         FROM    DEPT
         WHERE   DEPT.DEPT_ID = EMP.DEPT_ID ) AS DEPT#
FROM   EMP
WHERE  EMP# = 'E1' ;
```

In fact, however, the shorthand claim does not really stand up, because the new syntax—for dereferencing in particular—can be used only in conjunction with data that has been defined in a special new way, using a brand new type generator (REF). Moreover, those data definitions also make use of a lot of new syntax. Also, the functionality in question is provided in a highly unorthogonal manner (among other things, it applies only to tables that are defined in that special new way, not to all tables).

What is more, even if we accept the shorthand claim, we have to ask why the shorthands are provided anyway. What problem are they supposed to solve? Why is the support so unorthogonal? When are we supposed to do things the old-fashioned way, and when this strange new way? And so on (this is not an exhaustive list of questions). *Note:* In this connection, see reference [26.15] and the annotation to reference [26.21].

Subtables and Supertables

SQL allows base table *B* to be defined as a "subtable" of base table *A* only if *B* and *A* are both "typed tables" and the structured type *STB* on which *B* is defined is a subtype of the structured type *STA* on which *A* is defined. By way of example, consider the following structured type definitions:

```
CREATE TYPE EMP_TYPE                          /* employees   */
    AS ( EMP# ..., DEPT# ... ) ...
       REF IS SYSTEM GENERATED ;

CREATE TYPE PGMR_TYPE UNDER EMP_TYPE          /* programmers */
    AS ( LANG ... ) ;
```

Note that PGMR_TYPE has no REF IS . . . clause; instead, it effectively inherits such a clause from its immediate ("direct") supertype EMP_TYPE. In other words, a value of type REF(EMP_TYPE) can now refer to a row in a table that is defined to be of type PGMR_TYPE instead of type EMP_TYPE.

Now consider the following base table definitions:

```
CREATE TABLE EMP OF EMP_TYPE
       ( REF IS EMP_ID SYSTEM GENERATED,
         PRIMARY KEY ( EMP# ) ) ... ;

CREATE TABLE PGMR OF PGMR_TYPE UNDER EMP ;
```

Note the specification UNDER EMP on the definition of base table PGMR (note also the omission of the REF IS and PRIMARY KEY specifications for that base table). Base tables PGMR and EMP are said to be a **subtable** and the corresponding immediate ("direct") **supertable**, respectively; PGMR inherits the columns (etc.) of EMP and adds one extra column, LANG, of its own. The intuition behind the example is that nonprogrammers have a row in table EMP only, while programmers have a row in both tables—so every row in PGMR has a counterpart in EMP, but the converse is not true.

Data manipulation operations on these tables behave as follows:

- *SELECT:* SELECT on EMP behaves normally. SELECT on PGMR behaves as if PGMR actually contained the columns of EMP, as well as the column LANG.

- *INSERT:* INSERT into EMP behaves normally. INSERT into PGMR effectively causes new rows to appear in both EMP and PGMR.

- *DELETE:* DELETE from EMP causes rows to disappear from EMP and (when the rows in question happen to correspond to programmers) from PGMR too. DELETE from PGMR causes rows to disappear from both EMP and PGMR.

- *UPDATE:* Updating LANG, necessarily via PGMR, updates PGMR only; updating other columns, via either EMP or PGMR, updates both tables (conceptually).

Note the following implications in particular:

- Suppose some existing employee Joe becomes a programmer. If we simply try to insert a row for Joe into PGMR, the system will attempt to insert a row for Joe into EMP as well—an attempt that will fail, of course. Instead, we have to delete Joe's row from EMP and then insert an appropriate row into PGMR.

- Conversely, suppose some existing employee Joe ceases to be a programmer. This time, we have to delete Joe's row from either EMP or PGMR (whichever table we specify, the effect will be to delete it from both) and then insert an appropriate row into EMP.

As an aside, we note that SQL provides an ONLY feature that effectively allows us to operate on just those rows of a given table that have no counterpart in any subtable of the given table. For example, SELECT * FROM ONLY (EMP) retrieves only rows in EMP with no counterpart in PGMR; likewise, DELETE FROM ONLY (EMP) deletes only rows in EMP with no counterpart in PGMR, and similarly for UPDATE (there is no ONLY version of INSERT). We observe, however, that this ONLY feature is of no use for the problems described previously, in which some existing employee Joe becomes or ceases to be a programmer.

So what exactly do subtables and supertables as just described have to do with true type inheritance? As far as we can see, the answer is *nothing*. Tables are not types! Certainly there does not seem to be any substitutability—and we explained in Chapter 20 that if we do not have substitutability, then we do not have true type inheritance. Thus, if subtables and supertables have any advantages to offer, it is not at all clear why, in order to obtain those advantages, SQL should require that the subtable in question and its immediate ("direct") supertable be defined in terms of types that are, respectively, a subtype and its immediate ("direct") supertype.

More fundamentally, we need to ask what those advantages might be. What do subtables and supertables buy us? The answer seems to be "very little," at least at the level of the *model*.[14] It is true that certain *implementation* economies might be realized, if the subtable and its supertable are physically stored as a single table on the disk; but, of course, such considerations should not be allowed to have any effect on the model as such. In other words, not only is it unclear, as noted in the previous paragraph, as to why "sub and super" tables have to rely on "sub and super" structured types, it is also very unclear as to why the feature is supported at all.

SQL and The Two Great Blunders

How does the SQL functionality we have been describing relate to the goal of providing good object/relational support? Well, if SQL does not quite commit **The Two Great Blunders**, it certainly sails very close to the wind. And it has to be said that its justification for doing so is very unclear, at least to this writer; it seems to be little more than a vague idea that the features that give rise to the blunders somehow make SQL more "object-like" (well, perhaps they do).

Regarding **The First Great Blunder**, it seems likely that the idea of tying typed tables to structured types has something to do with the idea of equating tables and classes. To be more specific, it seems likely that if typed table *TT* is defined to be "of" structured type *ST*, then *TT* is supposed to contain what is sometimes called the "extent" of type *ST*—that is, the set of all currently existing "instances" of type *ST*.[15] Otherwise, why the tight connection between *TT* and *ST*?

That said, there are some problems. One is that it is possible to have two or more typed tables "of" the same structured type; the implications of such an arrangement are unclear (except that they almost certainly include a violation of *The Principle of Orthogonal Design*). Other problems are discussed in Section 6.6.

As for **The Second Great Blunder**, it should be clear that SQL does suffer from this (major!) defect, even if we agree that its "references" and related features are, as claimed, really just shorthand. As noted earlier, if rows can have "references" (addresses), then those rows are row *variables* by definition. In particular, SQL does suffer from the problem explained in Section 26.3, in the subsection "Pointers and a Good Model of Inheritance Are Incompatible." We omit the details here, since they are somewhat messy; suffice it to say that a REF value that is supposed to reference a row containing a circle might in fact reference a row containing a noncircular ellipse instead.

---

[14] You might be thinking the answer has something to do with the issue of *entity* subtypes and supertypes as discussed in Chapter 14. If so, then we remind you of our own preferred approach to that issue, which is based on the use of views. See the example at the very end of Section 14.5.

[15] That "extent" is not automatically maintained, however; rather, "instances" of type *ST* appear in and disappear from table *TT* only as a result of explicit updates on that table.

26.7 SUMMARY

We have briefly examined the field of **object/relational** systems. Such systems are, or should be, basically just *relational* systems that support the relational **domain** concept (i.e., types) properly—in other words, true relational systems, meaning in particular systems that allow users to define their own types. We need do nothing to the relational model in order to achieve object/relational functionality, except implement it.

We then examined **The Two Great Blunders**. The first is to equate object classes and relvars (an equation that is unfortunately all too attractive, at least on the surface). We speculated that the blunder arises from a confusion over two quite distinct interpretations of the term *object*. We described in detail what a system might look like that commits **The First Great Blunder**, and we explained some of the consequences of that mistake. One major consequence is that it seems to lead directly to committing **The Second Great Blunder** as well!—namely, mixing pointers and relations (though in fact this second blunder can be committed without the first, and just about every system on the market unfortunately seems to be committing it). It is our position that **The Second Great Blunder** *undermines the conceptual integrity of the relational model* in numerous ways (in fact, the first does too). In particular, it violates both *The Information Principle* and *The Principle of Interchangeability* (of base and derived relations).

Next, we briefly examined a few implementation issues. The overriding point is that adding a new "type package" affects at least the compiler, optimizer, and storage manager components of the system. As a consequence, an object/relational system cannot be implemented—at least, not well—by simply imposing a new layer of code (a "wrapper") over an existing relational system; rather, the system needs to be rebuilt from the ground up, in order to make each component individually extensible as needed.

We then took a look at Stonebraker's *DBMS classification matrix,* and briefly discussed the benefits that could accrue from a true *rapprochement* between object and relational technologies (where by "true" we mean among other things that the system in question does not commit either of **The Two Great Blunders**). Finally, we examined SQL's support for **REF types** and **subtables and supertables**.

EXERCISES

26.1 Define the term *object/relational*. What is "the object/relational model"?

26.2 The following is a variation on the code used in Section 26.3 to show that pointers and a good model of inheritance are incompatible:

```
VAR E   ELLIPSE ;
VAR XE PTR_TO_ELLIPSE ;
VAR XC PTR_TO_CIRCLE ;

E    :=   CIRCLE ( LENGTH ( 5.0 ), POINT ( 0.0, 0.0 ) ) ;
XE   :=   PTR_TO ( E ) ;
XC   :=   TREAT_DOWN_AS_PTR_TO_CIRCLE ( XE ) ;
THE_A ( DEREF ( XE ) ) :=  LENGTH ( 6.0 ) ;
```

What happens when this code is executed? *Note:* DEREF here is the conventional dereferencing operator, not the SQL operator of the same name (given the address of a variable, it returns that variable).

26.3 Following on from the previous question: Why does not an analogous problem arise with foreign keys in place of pointers? Or does it arise?

26.4 Do you think SQL's structured types are encapsulated? Justify your answer.

26.5 In SQL, does it make sense to declare a local variable to be of some REF type? If so, what are the implications?

26.6 Give an SQL version of the code shown in Exercise 26.2. *Note:* You will probably need access to the SQL standard or the documentation for an SQL product for this exercise.

26.7 Investigate any object/relational DBMS that might be available to you. Does that system commit either of **The Two Great Blunders**? If so, what justification does it offer for doing so?

26.8 Explain the concept of subtables and supertables (a) in general terms, (b) in SQL terms specifically.

REFERENCES AND BIBLIOGRAPHY

Several object/relational prototypes were built in the 1980s and 1990s. Two of the best known, and most influential, are *Postgres* from the University of California at Berkeley [26.36, 26.40, 26.42, 26.43] and *Starburst* from IBM Research [26.19, 26.23, 26.29, 26.30]. We remark that, at least in their original form, neither of these systems adhered to the equation *domain* = *class* that we claimed in the body of the chapter was "obviously correct."

26.1 David W. Adler: "IBM DB2 Spatial Extender—Spatial Data Within the RDBMS," Proc. 27th Int. Conf. on Very Large Data Bases, Rome, Italy (September 2001).

26.2 Christian Böhm, Stefan Berchtold, and Daniel A. Keim: "Searching in High-Dimensional Spaces—Index Structures for Improving the Performance of Multimedia Databases," *ACM Comp. Surv. 33,* No. 3 (September 2001).

26.3 Frederick P. Brooks, Jr.: *The Mythical Man-Month* (20th anniversary edition). Reading, Mass.: Addison-Wesley (1995).

26.4 Michael J. Carey, Nelson M. Mattos, and Anil K. Nori: "Object/Relational Database Systems: Principles, Products, and Challenges," Proc. 1997 ACM SIGMOD Int. Conf. on Management of Data, Tucson, Ariz. (May 1997).

To quote: "Abstract data types, user-defined functions, row types, references, inheritance, subtables, collections, triggers—just what is all this stuff, anyway?" A good question! There are eight features in the list (and there is a tacit assumption, or implication, that they are all SQL features specifically). Of those eight, we would argue that at least four are undesirable, two others are part of the same thing, and the other two are orthogonal to the question of whether the system is object/relational or otherwise.

26.5 Michael J. Carey *et al.*: "The BUCKY Object/Relational Benchmark," Proc. 1997 ACM SIGMOD Int. Conf. on Management of Data, Tucson, Ariz. (May 1997).

From the abstract: "BUCKY (Benchmark of Universal or Complex Kwery Ynterfaces [*sic*]) is a query-oriented benchmark that tests many of the key features offered by object/relational systems, including row types and inheritance, references and path expressions, sets of atomic values and of references, methods and late binding, and user-defined abstract data types and their methods." *Note:* Regarding this list of "key features," see the annotation to reference [26.4].

26.6 Michael Carey *et al.*: "O-O, What Have They Done to DB2?" Proc. 25th Int. Conf. on Very Large Data Bases, Edinburgh, Scotland (September 1999).

An overview of the object/relational features of DB2. See also references [26.1], [26.4], and [26.11].

26.7 R. G. G. Cattell: "What Are Next-Generation DB Systems?" *CACM 34,* No. 10 (October 1991).

26.8 Donald D. Chamberlin: "Relations and References—Another Point of View," *InfoDB 10,* No. 6 (April 1997).

See the annotation to reference [26.15].

26.9 Surajit Chaudhuri and Luis Gravano: "Optimizing Queries over Multi-media Repositories," Proc. 1996 ACM SIGMOD Int. Conf. on Management of Data, Montreal, Canada (June 1996).

The "multi-media repositories" of this paper's title represent one possible use for object/relational databases. Queries against multimedia data typically yield not just a set of resultant objects, but also a *grade of match* for each such object that indicates how well it satisfies the search condition (e.g., the "degree of redness" of an image). Such queries can specify a threshold on the grade of match and can also specify a *quota* [7.5]. The paper considers the optimization of such queries. See also reference [26.2].

26.10 Surajit Chaudhuri and Kyuseok Shim: "Optimization of Queries with User-Defined Predicates," *ACM TODS 24,* No. 2 (June 1999).

See also references [26.26] and [26.35].

26.11 Weidong Chen *et al.*: "High Level Indexing of User-Defined Types," Proc. 25th Int. Conf. on Very Large Data Bases, Edinburgh, Scotland (September 1999).

Explains some of the implementation techniques used in DB2.

26.12 E. F. Codd and C. J. Date: "Interactive Support for Nonprogrammers: The Relational and Network Approaches," in C. J. Date, *Relational Database: Selected Writings.* Reading, Mass.: Addison-Wesley (1986).

The paper that introduced the notion of *essentiality,* a concept that is critical to a proper understanding of data models (in both senses of that term!—see Chapter 1, Section 1.3). The relational model basically has just one essential data construct, the relation itself. The object model, by contrast, has many: sets, bags, lists, arrays, and so forth (not to mention object IDs). See references [26.13, 26.14] and [26.17] for further explanation.

26.13 C. J. Date: "Support for the Conceptual Schema: The Relational and Network Approaches," in *Relational Database Writings 1985–1989.* Reading, Mass.: Addison-Wesley (1990).

One argument against mixing pointers and relations [26.15] is the complexity that pointers cause. This paper includes an example that illustrates the point very clearly (see Figs. 26.5 and 26.6).

MAJOR_P#	MINOR_P#	QTY
P1	P2	2
P1	P4	4
P5	P3	1
P3	P6	3
P6	P1	9
P5	P6	8
P2	P4	3

Fig. 26.5 A bill-of-materials relation

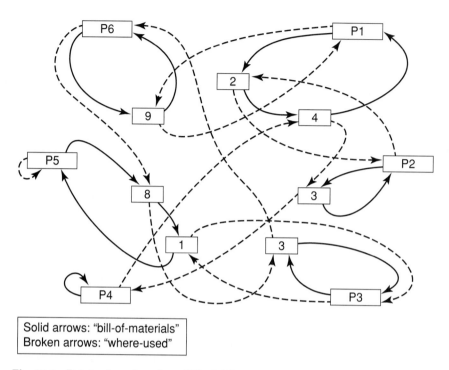

Fig. 26.6   Pointer-based analog of Fig. 26.5

26.14 C. J. Date: "Essentiality," in *Relational Database Writings 1991–1994*. Reading, Mass.: Addison-Wesley (1995).

26.15 C. J. Date: "Don't Mix Pointers and Relations!" and "Don't Mix Pointers and Relations— *Please!*" both in C. J. Date, Hugh Darwen, and David McGoveran, *Relational Database Writings 1994–1997*. Reading, Mass.: Addison-Wesley (1998).

The first of these two papers argues strongly against **The Second Great Blunder**. In reference [26.8], Chamberlin offers a rebuttal to some of the arguments of that first paper. The second paper was written as a direct response to Chamberlin's rebuttal.

26.16 C. J. Date: "Objects and Relations: Forty-Seven Points of Light," in C. J. Date, Hugh Darwen, and David McGoveran, *Relational Database Writings 1994–1997*. Reading, Mass.: Addison-Wesley (1998).

A blow-by-blow response to reference [26.27].

26.17 C. J. Date: "Relational Really Is Different," Chapter 10 of reference [6.9].

26.18 C. J. Date: "What Do You Mean, 'Post-Relational'?" *http://www.dbdebunk.com* (June 2000).

The term *post-relational* is sometimes encountered in the literature. It might or might not mean the same thing as *object/relational*.

26.19 Linda G. DeMichiel, Donald D. Chamberlin, Bruce G. Lindsay, Rakesh Agrawal, and Manish Arya: "Polyglot: Extensions to Relational Databases for Sharable Types and Functions in a Multi-language Environment," IBM Research Report RJ8888 (July 1992).

To quote from the abstract: "Polyglot is an extensible relational database type system that supports inheritance, encapsulation, and dynamic method dispatch." (*Dynamic method dispatch* is another term for *run-time binding*. To continue:) "[Polyglot] allows use from multiple application languages and permits objects to retain their behavior as they cross the boundary between database and application program. This paper describes the design of Polyglot, extensions to the SQL language to support the use of Polyglot types and methods, and the implementation of Polyglot in the Starburst relational [prototype]."

Polyglot is clearly addressing the kinds of issues that are the subject of the present chapter (as well as Chapters 5, 20, and 25). A couple of comments are relevant, however. First, the relational term *domain* is (surprisingly) never mentioned. Second, Polyglot provides the built-in type generators (the Polyglot term is *metatypes*) *base-type, tuple-type, rename-type, array-type,* and *language-type,* but (again surprisingly) not *relation-type*. However, the system is designed to allow the introduction of additional type generators.

26.20 David J. DeWitt, Navin Kabra, Jun Luo, Jignesh M. Patel, and Jie-Bing Yu: "Client-Server Paradise," Proc. 20th Int. Conf. on Very Large Data Bases, Santiago, Chile (September 1994).

Paradise—"Parallel Data Information System"—is an object/relational (originally "extended relational") prototype from the University of Wisconsin, "designed for handling GIS applications" (GIS = Geographic Information System). This paper describes the Paradise design and implementation.

26.21 Andrew Eisenberg and Jim Melton: "SQL:1999, Formerly Known as SQL3," *ACM SIGMOD Record 28,* No. 1 (March 1999).

An overview of the differences between SQL:1992 and SQL:1999. Incidentally, when this article first appeared, Hugh Darwen and the present author wrote to the *SIGMOD Record* editor as follows: "With reference to [the subject article]—in particular, with reference to the sections entitled 'Objects . . . Finally' and 'Using REF Types'—we have a question: What useful purpose is served by the features described in those sections? To be more specific, what useful functionality is provided that cannot be obtained via features already found in SQL:1992?" Our letter was not published.

26.22 Michael Godfrey, Tobias Mayr, Praveen Seshadri, and Thorsten von Eichen: "Secure and Portable Database Extensibility," Proc. 1998 ACM SIGMOD Int. Conf. on Management of Data, Seattle, Wash. (June 1998).

"Since user-defined operators are supplied by unknown or untrusted clients, the DBMS must be wary of operators that might crash the system, or modify its files or memory directly (circumventing the authorization mechanisms), or monopolize CPU, memory, or disk resources" (slightly reworded). Controls are obviously needed. This paper reports on investigations into this issue, using Java and the object/relational prototype PREDATOR [26.33]. It concludes, encouragingly, that a database system "can support secure and portable extensibility using Java, without unduly sacrificing performance."

26.23 Laura M. Haas, J. C. Freytag, G. M. Lohman, and Hamid Pirahesh: "Extensible Query Processing in Starburst," Proc. 1989 ACM SIGMOD Int. Conf. on Management of Data, Portland, Ore. (June 1989).

The aims of the Starburst project expanded somewhat after the original paper [26.29] was first written: "Starburst provides support for adding new storage methods for tables, new types of access methods and integrity constraints, new data types, functions, and new operations on tables." The system is divided into two major components, Core and Corona, corresponding to the RSS and RDS, respectively, in the original System R prototype (see references [4.2] and [4.3] for an explanation of these two System R components). Core supports the extensibility functions described in reference [26.29]. Corona supports the Starburst query language Hydrogen, which is a dialect of SQL that (a) eliminates most of the implementation restrictions of System R SQL, (b) is much more orthogonal than System R SQL, (c) supports recursive queries, and (d) is user-extensible. The paper includes an interesting discussion of "query rewrite"—that is, expression transformation rules (see Chapter 18). See also reference [18.48].

26.24 Joseph M. Hellerstein and Jeffrey F. Naughton: "Query Execution Techniques for Caching Expensive Methods," Proc. 1996 ACM SIGMOD Int. Conf. on Management of Data, Montreal, Canada (June 1996).

26.25 International Organization for Standardization (ISO): *Information Technology—Database Languages—SQL Multimedia and Application Packages,* Document ISO/IEC 13249:2000.

The official SQL/MM standard definition. Like the SQL standard on which it is based [4.23], it consists of an open-ended series of separate "Parts" (ISO/IEC 13249-1, -2, etc.). At the time of writing, the following Parts have been defined:

Part 1: Framework
Part 2: Full-Text
Part 3: Spatial
Part 4: *There is no Part 4*
Part 5: Still Image
Part 6: Data Mining

26.26 Michael Jaedicke and Bernhard Mitschang: "User-Defined Table Operators: Enhancing Extensibility for ORDBMS," Proc. 25th Int. Conf. on Very Large Data Bases, Edinburgh, Scotland (September 1999).

26.27 Won Kim: "On Marrying Relations and Objects: Relation-Centric and Object-Centric Perspectives," *Data Base Newsletter 22,* No. 6 (November/December 1994).

This paper argues *against* the position that equating relvars and classes is a serious mistake (**"The First Great Blunder"**). Reference [26.16] is a response to this paper.

26.28 Won Kim: "Bringing Object/Relational Down to Earth," *DBP&D 10,* No. 7 (July 1997).

In this article, Kim claims that "confusion is sure to reign" in the object/relational marketplace because, first, "an inordinate weight has been placed on the role of data type extensibility," and, second, "the measure of a product's object/relational completeness . . . is a potentially serious area of perplexity." He goes on to propose "a practical metric for object/relational completeness that can be used as a guideline for determining whether a product is truly [object/relational]." His scheme involves the following criteria:

1. data model
2. query language
3. mission-critical services
4. computational model
5. performance and scalability
6. database tools
7. harnessing the power

With respect to the first of these criteria (the crucial one!), Kim takes the position—very different from that of *The Third Manifesto* [3.3]—that the data model must be "the Core Object Model defined by the Object Management Group" (OMG), which "comprises the relational data model as well as the core object-oriented modeling concepts of object-oriented programming languages." According to Kim, it thus includes all of the following concepts: *class* (Kim adds "or type"), *instance, attribute, integrity constraints, object IDs, encapsulation, (multiple) class inheritance, (multiple) ADT inheritance, data of type reference, set-valued attributes, class attributes, class methods,* and more besides. Note that relations—which we regard as both crucial and fundamental—are never explicitly mentioned; Kim claims that the OMG Core Object Model includes the entire relational model in addition to everything in the foregoing list, but in fact it does not.

26.29 Bruce Lindsay, John McPherson, and Hamid Pirahesh: "A Data Management Extension Architecture," Proc. 1987 ACM SIGMOD Int. Conf. on Management of Data, San Francisco, Calif. (May 1987).

Describes the overall architecture of the Starburst prototype. Starburst "facilitates the implementation of data management extensions for relational database systems." Two kinds of extensions are described in this paper: user-defined storage structures and access methods, and user-defined triggers and integrity constraints (but surely *all* integrity constraints are user-defined?). However (to quote the paper), "there are, of course, other directions in which it is important to be able to extend [DBMSs, including] user-defined . . . data types [and] query evaluation techniques."

26.30 Guy M. Lohman *et al.*: "Extensions to Starburst: Objects, Types, Functions, and Rules," *CACM 34,* No. 10 (October 1991).

26.31 David Maier: "Comments on the Third-Generation Database System Manifesto," Tech. Report No. CS/E 91-012, Oregon Graduate Center, Beaverton, Ore. (April 1991).

Maier is highly critical of just about everything in reference [26.44]. We agree with some of his criticisms and disagree with others. However, we do find the following remarks interesting (they bear out our contention that objects involve just one good idea—*viz., proper data type support*): "Many of us in the object-oriented database field have struggled to distill out the essence of 'object-orientedness' for a database system . . . My own thinking about what was the most important [feature] of OODBs has changed over time. At first I thought it was inheritance and the message model. Later I came to think that object identity, support for complex state, and encapsulation of behavior were more important. Recently, after starting to hear from users of OODBMSs about what they most value about those systems, I think that *type extensibility* is the key. Identity, complex state, and encapsulation are still important, but [only] insomuch as they support the creation of new data types."

26.32 Jim Melton: *Advanced SQL:1999—Understanding Object-Relational and Other Advanced Features.* San Francisco, Calif.: Morgan Kaufmann (2003).

A tutorial on the SQL topics discussed in Section 26.6 and other "advanced" features of SQL:1999, including SQL/MED (see Chapter 21), SQL/OLAP (see Chapter 22), and the separate standard SQL/MM [26.25].

26.33 Jignesh Patel *et al.*: "Building a Scalable Geo-spatial DBMS: Technology, Implementation, and Evaluation," Proc. 1997 ACM SIGMOD Int. Conf. on Management of Data, Tucson, Ariz. (May 1997).

To quote the abstract: "This paper presents a number of new techniques for parallelizing geospatial database systems and discusses their implementation in the Paradise object/relational database system" (see reference [26.20]).

26.34 Raghu Ramakrishnan and Johannes Gehrke: *Database Management Systems* (3d ed.). Boston, Mass.: McGraw-Hill (2003).

26.35 Karthikeyan Ramasamy, Jignesh M. Patel, Jeffrey F. Naughton, and Raghav Kaushik: "Set Containment Joins: The Good, the Bad, and the Ugly," Proc. 26th Int. Conf. on Very Large Data Bases, Cairo, Egypt (September 2000).

26.36 Lawrence A. Rowe and Michael R. Stonebraker: "The Postgres Data Model," Proc. 13th Int. Conf. on Very Large Data Bases, Brighton, UK (September 1987).

26.37 Hanan Samet: *The Design and Analysis of Spatial Data Structures.* Reading, Mass.: Addison-Wesley (1990).

26.38 Cynthia Maro Saracco: *Universal Database Management: A Guide to Object/Relational Technology.* San Francisco, Calif.: Morgan Kaufmann (1999).

> A readable high-level overview. However, we note that Saracco embraces (as does Stonebraker, incidentally, in reference [26.41], *q.v.*) a very suspect form of inheritance, involving a version of the subtables and supertables idea—which we are skeptical about to begin with [14.13]—that is significantly different from the version included in SQL. To be specific, suppose table PGMR ("programmers") is defined to be a subtable of table EMP ("employees"). Then Saracco and Stonebraker regard EMP as containing rows only for employees who are not programmers, whereas SQL would regard it as containing rows for *all* employees, as we saw in Section 26.6.

26.39 Praveen Seshadri and Mark Paskin: "PREDATOR: An OR-DBMS with Enhanced Data Types," Proc. 1997 ACM SIGMOD Int. Conf. on Management of Data, Tucson, Ariz. (May 1997).

> To quote: "The basic idea in PREDATOR is to provide mechanisms for each data type to specify the semantics of its methods; these semantics are then used for query optimization."

26.40 Michael Stonebraker: "The Design of the Postgres Storage System," Proc. 13th Int. Conf. on Very Large Data Bases, Brighton, UK (September 1987).

26.41 Michael Stonebraker and Paul Brown (with Dorothy Moore): *Object/Relational DBMSs: Tracking the Next Great Wave* (2d ed.). San Francisco, Calif.: Morgan Kaufmann (1999).

> This book is a tutorial on object/relational systems. It is heavily—in fact, almost exclusively—based on the Universal Data Option for Informix's Dynamic Server product, which in turn was based on an earlier system called Illustra (a commercial product that Stonebraker himself was instrumental in developing). See reference [3.3] for an extended analysis and critique of this book; see also the annotation to reference [26.38].

26.42 Michael Stonebraker and Greg Kemnitz: "The Postgres Next Generation Database Management System," *CACM 34,* No. 10 (October 1991).

26.43 Michael Stonebraker and Lawrence A. Rowe: "The Design of Postgres," Proc. 1986 ACM SIGMOD Int. Conf. on Management of Data, Washington, D.C. (June 1986).

> The stated objectives of Postgres are:
>
> 1. To provide better support for complex objects
> 2. To provide user extensibility for data types, operators, and access methods
> 3. To provide active database facilities (alerters and triggers) and inferencing support
> 4. To simplify the DBMS code for crash recovery
> 5. To produce a design that can take advantage of optical disks, multiprocessor workstations, and custom designed VLSI chips
> 6. To make as few changes as possible (preferably none) to the relational model

26.44 Michael Stonebraker *et al.*: "Third-Generation Database System Manifesto," *ACM SIGMOD Record 19,* No. 3 (September 1990).

In part, this paper is a response to—in other words, a counterproposal to—"The Object-Oriented Database System Manifesto" [20.2, 25.1], which (among other things) essentially ignores the relational model entirely (!). A quote: "Second-generation systems made a major contribution in two areas, nonprocedural data access and data independence, and these advances must not be compromised by third-generation systems." The following features are claimed as essential requirements of a third-generation DBMS (we have paraphrased the original somewhat):

1. Provide traditional database services plus richer object structures and rules.

   - Rich type system
   - Inheritance
   - Functions and encapsulation
   - Optional system-assigned tuple IDs
   - Rules (e.g., integrity rules), not tied to specific objects

2. Subsume second-generation DBMSs.

   - Navigation only as a last resort
   - Intensional and extensional set definitions (meaning collections that are maintained automatically by the system and collections that are maintained manually by the user)
   - Updatable views
   - Clustering, indexes, and so on, hidden from the user

3. Support open systems.

   - Multiple language support
   - Persistence orthogonal to type
   - SQL (characterized as *intergalactic dataspeak*)
   - Queries and results must be the lowest level of client/server communication

See reference [3.3] for an extended analysis and critique of this paper, also reference [26.31].

26.45 Haixun Wang and Carlo Zaniolo: "Using SQL to Build New Aggregates and Extenders for Object-Relational Systems," Proc. 26th Int. Conf. on Very Large Data Bases, Cairo, Egypt (September 2000).

26.46 Maurice V. Wilkes: "Software and the Programmer," *CACM 34,* No. 5 (May 1991).

CHAPTER 27

The World Wide Web and XML

27.1 INTRODUCTION

Note: Nick Tindall of IBM was the original author of this chapter.

The World Wide Web and XML are hot topics; many books have been written about them already, and more are sure to come. Of course, the emphasis in this book is on database matters specifically, and we do not wish to dwell on details of the Web or XML except insofar as they relate to that primary concern. In the case of the Web, therefore, we give just enough background (in Section 27.2) to provide some context for the discussions in later sections. In the case of XML, however, there is rather more that needs to be said, and we devote three sections to it: Section 27.3 gives an overview, and Sections 27.4 and 27.5 cover XML data definition and XML data manipulation, respectively. Section 27.6 then examines the relationship between XML and databases. Of course, this latter topic is the main reason we include this chapter at all!—but we deliberately ignore it (for the most part) prior to Section 27.6. Finally, Section 27.7 describes the relevant SQL facilities, and Section 27.8 presents a summary.

27.2   THE WEB AND THE INTERNET

The terms *the Web* and *the Internet* are often used as if they were interchangeable, but strictly speaking they refer to different things. We can characterize the difference as follows: The Web is a gigantic *database* (though not one designed in accordance with conventional database principles); the Internet is an equally gigantic *network* over which that database is distributed. *Note:* As you probably know, web access is not the only service provided by the Internet—others include news readers, instant messaging, e-mail, ftp, telnet, and so on—but it is the one we are interested in here. It is not the purpose of this book to get into details of news readers, instant messaging, and the rest.

The Internet evolved from the Arpanet, which was a project in the late 1960s under the auspices of the U.S. Department of Defense Advanced Research Projects Agency, DARPA, to connect all of the various government and academic networks in the United States into a single coherent "supernetwork" with a common communications protocol called TCP/IP (Transmission Control Protocol/Internet Protocol). But the Internet as such (i.e., without the Web) was still not as integrated as it might be; users still had to use a variety of different mechanisms—ftp, gopher, archie, different kinds of e-mail, and so on—in order to access information. For example, if you wanted to pursue some reference you had found in some document, you would typically have to (a) use e-mail or a bulletin-board system to discover the name of the relevant file; (b) use telnet to log on to an archie server to search for the location of that file; (c) use ftp to log on to the system where that file was stored; (d) navigate to the relevant directory on that system; (e) copy the file to your own system; and finally (f) choose the proper program on your system to display it.

The Web was invented by Tim Berners-Lee in 1989–90 as a basis for addressing all of this complexity [27.2]. The central notion is that of **hypertext**, invented several years previously by Ted Nelson [27.19]. Hypertext is a way of structuring information that allows text documents to reference other documents and files, or components of other documents and files, by means of embedded **links**. Berners-Lee's great contribution was to implement the linking in a graphical browser that could integrate all of the different kinds of information in a single window; the net effect was that users could access and display anything they wanted by means of a single mouse click, instead of having to use all of the separate commands and procedures they had to use before. He achieved this remarkable simplification by defining:

- A mechanism, **Uniform Resource Locators** (URLs, later generalized to *Uniform Resource Identifiers* or URIs), for identifying and referencing documents and other resources
- A markup language, the **Hypertext Markup Language** (HTML), for creating documents that include instructions on how they are to be displayed
- A protocol, the **Hypertext Transfer Protocol** (HTTP), for transmitting such documents over the Internet

Note: We will have a little more to say in the next section regarding markup languages and HTML.

Now, we said earlier that the Web is a giant database. Users perceive that database, via a *web browser,* as being distributed over a set of *sites* ("websites"), each of which has its own *web server* and is identified by its own URL. Each site contains a set of web *pages,* and each page has an associated *root document* that specifies among other things how that page is to be displayed. Like all documents, that root document typically includes URL links to a variety of different kinds of information[1] (text, images, audio, video, and so forth), at a variety of different sites; to the user, however, it is perceived as one integrated whole—the user is probably aware of the URL for the original page at most and nothing more. But when the page is displayed, the links are displayed too, and if the user clicks on such a link, then the browser displays the corresponding information in the same window (or in some additional window).

Note: For some web pages, users can retrieve further information by filling out forms. *Search engines* provide an important special case. Typically, a search engine takes a specified search argument—for example, "Camelot"—and returns a list of websites containing pertinent information. To be able to do this kind of searching in a reasonable time, the search engine uses comprehensive indexes of the keywords that appear in the millions of documents stored on the Web. Those indexes are created and maintained by *web crawlers* that run continuously, retrieving web pages and recording their use of potential search arguments.

The information at a given site can be stored in operating system files; increasingly, however, it is stored in databases (SQL databases and others), and web servers thus need to be able to interact with DBMSs. Sections 27.6 and 27.7 give some idea as to what might be involved in such interactions.

27.3   AN OVERVIEW OF XML

The name "XML" stands for **Extensible**—not "eXtensible"!—**Markup Language**. An **XML document** is, loosely, a document created using XML facilities. Here is a simple example. Note the heavy use of angle brackets "<" and ">" (not to be confused with the angle brackets used elsewhere in this book in BNF grammars).

```
<?xml version="1.0"?>
<greeting kind="succinct">Hello, world.</greeting>
```

The first line here is an **XML declaration** (with certain optional features omitted); XML documents usually include such a declaration, though they are not required to. The second line is an XML **element**, consisting of a **start tag**, some **character data**, and an **end tag**. (More generally, a given element can contain character data or other elements or a mixture of both.) The character data is the string "Hello, world."; the start tag is the **markup** preceding that string, and the end tag is the markup following it. (The unqualified term *tag* is also used, informally, to refer to a start tag and its corresponding end tag taken together.) Tags are identified by whatever name they are given by the document definer,

---

[1] It might also directly *embed* such additional information.

and that name is also considered to identify the element **type**; in the example, therefore, the tag is a "greeting" tag and the element is a "greeting" element. The specification

```
kind="succinct"
```

within the start tag is an XML **attribute** (nothing to do with attributes in the relational sense). The attribute *name* is "kind"; the string "succinct" is its *value.*

As you can see from this rather trivial example, from one point of view an XML document is just a character string. That character string consists of *data* and *markup,* where the markup is *metadata* that describes the data.[2] Typically, XML documents are meant to be readable and understandable by both humans and machines; in particular, they are meant to be easy for application programs to process. *Note:* In connection with this last point, we observe that the markup makes it possible for application programs to tolerate a considerable degree of variation in data format. For example:

- Since elements include delimiting tags, distinct "instances" of "the same" element do not have to be of fixed size but can vary from document to document, or even within a single document.

- (More important!) New elements—that is, elements of some new type—can be added to an existing document at any time without affecting existing users (existing application programs in particular).

In other words, as long as producers and consumers of the data agree on how to interpret the markup, XML addresses some of the problems of *data interchange.* With more traditional fixed-format protocols, by contrast, such as Electronic Data Interchange (EDI), changes in data format require corresponding changes on the part of all producers and consumers of the data concerned.

Markup Languages

In order to appreciate some of the rationale behind XML, it is helpful to look at how it evolved from earlier markup languages. Markup languages were never meant to be like conventional programming languages; rather, their aim (at least, their original aim) was simply to allow the creation of text files that included formatting instructions—markup— that could be understood by the applicable word processor. The markup was expressed in binary in some cases and as regular text in others, but the language as such was always proprietary. For example, IBM used a proprietary text-based language called Script for formatting user manuals and the like. Here by way of example is an excerpt from a typical Script file:

```
.sp 2
.il 3m;You should specify the ;.us on;first;.us off; parameter
as PRIVATE.  This specification will allow the processor to
complete the conversion without further input.
.br
```

---

[2] Although data that is directly contained in the document must be character data specifically, the document can effectively contain, for example, images, video recordings, and other kinds of noncharacter data, thanks to the use of embedded links. Such links are considered part of the markup.

The markup here tells the formatter to space down two lines (".sp 2"), indent the first line of text by three em spaces (".il 3m"), underscore the word "first" (".us on" and ".us off"), and then break to a new line (".br").

Now, one problem with Script and similar languages was that the markup was quite procedural in nature—not to mention the fact that it controlled document formatting only, and further was appropriate only for certain kinds of devices (typically monochrome line printers). Precisely in order to remedy such deficiencies, three IBM researchers introduced the *Generalized Markup Language,* GML.[3] The key difference between GML and languages like Script is that the markup in GML is more descriptive, or declarative, than the rather procedural markup found in those earlier languages. Here again is our Script example, expressed now in GML:

```
<p>You should specify the <emp1>first</emp1> parameter as PRIVATE.
This specification allows the processor to complete the conversion
without further input.
```

The markup now simply tells the formatter that the text is a *paragraph* ("<p>"), instead of spelling out the detailed layout for such a paragraph ("space down two lines" and so forth). It also tells the formatter that "first" is to have *the first level of emphasis* ("<emp1>" and "</emp1>"), instead of stating specifically that it is to be underscored. *Note:* We have deliberately taken a few liberties with GML in our example; in particular, we have used angle brackets for tags, instead of the more usual colon characters (":"). These departures from usual practice are unimportant for present purposes.

GML markup is thus indeed more descriptive, but it is still focused on presentation or *text rendering* (though it does facilitate certain other tasks, such as counting the number of paragraphs). In particular, users are limited to just those tags that are built into the language. By contrast, *Standard GML* (SGML), an extended form of GML, allows users to define their own tags and give them whatever meaning they like.[4] Using this facility, we could extend our example to specify the structure of the data in fine detail—for example:

```
<paragraph>
  <sentence>
    <subject>You</subject>
    <verb> should specify</verb>
    <object> the <adjective><emp1>first</emp1></adjective>
            parameter</object>
    ...
  </sentence>
  <sentence>
    ...
  </sentence>
</paragraph>
```

Note: We draw your attention to the fact that the "object" element here contains both character-string data and another ("adjective") element.

---

[3] The fact that these initials correspond with those of its inventors Charles Goldfarb, Edward Mosher, and Raymond Lorie is not a coincidence.

[4] Here is an interesting quote in this connection: "Even in the smallest organization, most conflicts stem from a lack of clearly defined and shared meaning for the words we use" [27.4].

As you can see from this example, however, SGML is not really a markup language *per se* (and "SGML" is thus really a misnomer). Rather, it is a *meta*language—it provides rules by which users can define tailored markup languages of their own, with their own user-defined tags in particular.[5] HTML is one such language; that is, HTML is defined in terms of SGML, and it can be thought of as a particular *SGML application* (where by the term *SGML application* we mean a language defined by applying the rules of the SGML metalanguage, not an application program that uses SGML). Unfortunately, however, HTML does not preserve the purely descriptive nature of GML, but reintroduces specific formatting markup in addition to structural and semantic markup. In fact, some HTML tags provide all three kinds of information at once; for example, the HTML tag "<H1>" specifies both a *level 1 heading* (structure) and a *page title* (semantics), and it can optionally specify a *font* (formatting) as well.

The Development of XML

XML [27.25] was originally developed in 1996 by an SGML review board under the auspices of the World Wide Web Consortium, W3C (founded by Berners-Lee in 1994), with the aim of remedying certain problems with SGML and HTML. The problem with SGML was that it was just too large and complicated to support easily over the Web. As for HTML, the problems were twofold:

- As already explained, it failed to separate structural, semantic, and formatting metadata properly.

- What is more, it allowed documents to violate the rules for "well-formedness"—that is, it actually allowed them to disobey its own syntax rules![6] This problem arose because there were several browsers on the market at the time, all of them naturally competing with one another; and if the ill-formed document *D* could be successfully displayed by browser *A* and not by browser *B*, then that fact was perceived as a deficiency not in document *D*, but rather in browser *B*.

XML, like SGML before it, is really a metalanguage (and so "XML" too is a misnomer); in fact, XML is a proper subset of SGML. As the XML specification [27.25] puts it:

> The Extensible Markup Language (XML) is a subset of SGML . . . Its goal is to enable generic SGML to be served, received, and processed on the Web in the way that is now possible with HTML. XML has been designed for ease of implementation and for interoperability with both SGML and HTML.

XML reestablishes the descriptive nature of the markup (i.e., markup languages defined using XML involve descriptive markup only). Note carefully, however, that XML as such does not ascribe any particular meaning to the markup in question.

Despite its stated goal, XML has not yet significantly displaced HTML as the medium of choice for web pages (a browser that does not support XML will still usually display

---

[5] Actually the same is true of GML.

[6] Sad to say, there is a strong move afoot at the time of writing for XML to do the same thing.

web pages properly). On the other hand, XML use in other areas has been growing by leaps and bounds; for example, it is now being used for such diverse purposes as configuration files, data interchange formats for analysis tools, new messaging protocols between application programs in corporate networks, and data interchange between such programs. Largely as a consequence of this fact, there is an increasing need to be able to keep XML data in databases. Here by way of illustration are a couple of examples of situations in which we might wish to keep XML data in a database:

- Consider our usual parts relvar P. We might wish to extend that relvar to incorporate an additional DRAWING attribute (see Fig. 27.1), whose value within any given tuple is a line drawing of the part in question, expressed in a particular XML derivative—see the next subsection—called *Scalable Vector Graphics* (SVG). Observe that each such value is an entire SVG document, and the overall database might thus be thought of as an "object/relational" database in the sense of the previous chapter. *Note:* Actually it is not quite accurate to say that DRAWING values are line drawings as such; rather, they are XML documents that can be interpreted by some application program to produce such line drawings. Again, see Fig. 27.1.

- In like manner we might add a DESCRIPTION attribute to relvar P, whose value within any given tuple is an XML document describing the part in question and explaining the proper ways of using it.

Of course, XML can also be used to represent the kinds of data found in more traditional databases. For example, purchase orders, part catalogs, and inventory records can all be expressed in XML. Thus, a database—not a relational one, of course—might consist of XML documents *only*. We will discuss this possibility briefly in Section 27.6.

XML can also be used to represent relations, a fact that could be useful for importing data into or exporting data out of a relational database (again, see Section 27.6). For example, here is an XML representation of our usual parts relation (tuples for P1 and P2 only):

```
<?xml version="1.0"?>
<!-- This is an XML representation of the parts relation -->
<!-- of Fig. 3.8 (tuples for P1 and P2 only).  Note that -->
<!-- all data values are represented as simple character -->
<!-- strings.                                             -->
<PartsRelation>
  <PartTuple>
    <PNUM>P1</PNUM>
    <PNAME>Nut</PNAME>
    <COLOR>Red</COLOR>
    <WEIGHT>12.0</WEIGHT>
    <CITY>London</CITY>
  </PartTuple>
  <PartTuple>
    <PNUM>P2</PNUM>
    <PNAME>Bolt</PNAME>
    <COLOR>Green</COLOR>
    <WEIGHT>17.0</WEIGHT>
    <CITY>Paris</CITY>
  </PartTuple>
</PartsRelation>
```

P2	Bolt	Green	17.0	Paris	. .

```
<?xml version="1.0" encoding="utf-8"?>
<svg>
<g>
<g>
<path d="M48.888,0.361-0.144-0.2881-48-6,25.05610.288,0.576148.6-25.056L48.888,0.36z"/>
<path d="M194.184,25.4161-0.144-0.2881-48.6,24.98410.288,0.576148.6-24.984L194.184,25.416z"/>
<path d="M194.472,25.41610.144-0.2881-48.6-25.0561-0.288,0.576148.6,25.056L194.472,25.416z"/>
<path d="M48.888,50.410.144-0.2881-48.6-25.0561-0.288,0.576148.6,25.056L48.888,50.4z"/>
<path d="M145.944,0.36V0h-97.2v0.72h97.2V0.36z"/>
<path d="M146.016,50.4v-0.36h-97.2v0.72h97.2V50.4z"/>
<path d="M194.112,64.081-0.144-0.2881-48.6,24.98410.288,0.576148.6-24.984L194.112,64.08z"/>
<path d="M48.816,89.06410.144-0.288L0.36,63.721-0.288,0.576148.6,25.056L48.816,89.064z"/>
<path d="M145.944,89.064v-0.36h-97.2v0.72h97.2V89.064z"/>
<path d="M0.36,64.08h0.36V25.272H0V64.08H0.36z"/>
<path d="M145.944,88.992h0.36V50.256h-0.72v38.736H145.944z"/>
<path d="M194.328,64.152h0.36V25.344h-0.72v38.808H194.328z"/>
<path d="M48.456,89.064h0.36V50.256h-0.72v38.808H48.456z"/>
</g>
<path d="M50.976,211.824h0.36V89.352h-0.72v122.472H50.976z"/>
<path d="M142.416,199.152h0.36V89.208h-0.72v109.944H142.416z"/>
</g>
<path d="M143.424,232.1281-0.288-1.1521-0.576-1.0081-0.864-1.081-1.08-0.9361-1.296-0.7921-1.44-0.7921
. . ."/>
</g>
</svg>
```

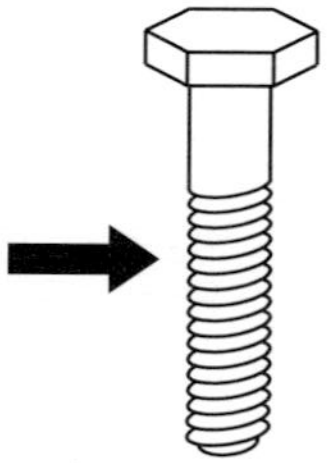

Fig. 27.1 Adding a DRAWING attribute value to the parts relvar (example)

Points arising:

- The specific layout shown—indentation and line breaks in particular—is included purely for readability. It is not a necessary part of XML documents. In fact, most business-related XML documents do not contain any such "white space" but consist of markup and data strung together without breaks of any kind.

- We have replaced the name P# by PNUM because "#" is not legal in XML tag names (and we will make analogous changes in all of our examples in this chapter, relational as well as XML ones, for consistency).

- As the opening **XML comments** indicate, all (relational) attribute values have been mapped into simple character strings.

- For simplicity, we have chosen to represent just the body of the relation and not the heading (and we will do the same in all subsequent examples in this chapter, where applicable).

- We remark that **empty elements** are permitted. For example, suppose some parts have no color, and we decide to use the empty string to denote the COLOR value for such a part. Then the specification <COLOR></COLOR>, or (more succinctly) just <COLOR/>, suffices.

  Note: As the term *empty element* suggests, XML regards such elements as containing nothing at all. However, it would be more logically correct to say they do contain something—namely, a string (albeit an empty one)—and the term *empty element* is thus another misnomer. What is more, we will see in Section 27.4, in the subsection "XML Schema," that "empty elements" can also have XML attributes.

- Finally, it has to be said that the XML document just shown is not a very faithful representation of a parts relation, because it imposes a top-to-bottom sequence on the tuples and a left-to-right sequence on the attributes of those tuples (actually lexical sequence in both cases). Indeed, XML documents always have an ordering to their elements[7] (the official term is ***document ordering***). We will have a little more to say on this issue in Section 27.6, in the subsection "Shred and Publish."

XML Document Structure

We have used the term *XML document* several times in this chapter already, but it should be clear by now that the term is a little sloppy: Documents are expressed not in XML *per se* but rather in some **XML derivative**—that is, in some markup language that has been defined using XML.[8] However, it is convenient to refer to all such documents generically as "XML documents," and we will continue to do so in what follows.

---

[7] XML attributes are unordered, however; thus, it might be preferable to represent PNUM, PNAME, COLOR, WEIGHT, and CITY by such attributes instead of by elements. See Section 27.4.

[8] The official term for "XML derivative" is *XML application*. We prefer our term, since it is less likely to be interpreted to mean an application program that uses XML.

Let *XD* be an XML derivative. Then the definer of *XD* will specify the meaning of the markup available in *XD* (at least informally), and operators can be defined and programs written for processing documents that use *XD*. Let *D* be such a document. Abstractly, then, *D* has a hierarchic structure, consisting of a **root node** and a sequence of **child nodes** (where each child node can have a sequence of child nodes of its own, and so on, and each child node has exactly one **parent** node). Fig. 27.2 shows the hierarchy for the PartsRelation document from the previous subsection. As you can see from that figure, each node represents an XML element, except for:

- The root or **document** node, which represents the entire document (note that it does *not* correspond to the document root element!).

- The leaf nodes, which represent character data. *Note:* Leaf nodes are also used to represent (a) XML attributes (but there are no attributes in the example) and (b) various items such as XML comments, white space, and so on (a few such nodes are shown in the figure).

The complete hierarchy is called the **information set** ("infoset") for the document in question, and an application programming interface (API) to that hierarchy is provided by an XML feature called the **Document Object Model**, DOM [27.24]. Using that API, an application program can retrieve, insert, delete, and change nodes (among other things).[9]

Clearly, many distinct XML documents might all conform to the same general hierarchic structure (i.e., their respective infosets might all have the same generic structure). For example, we might agree, at least for the sake of this discussion, that every book consists of a title, a preface (optional), a sequence of chapters, a sequence of appendixes (optional), and an index (optional); that every chapter consists of a title and a nonempty sequence of sections; that every section consists of a title and a nonempty sequence of paragraphs; and so on. At the same time, we can surely also agree that books differ in their *specific* structure, in that some have no preface, some have no appendixes, some have no index, different books have different numbers of chapters, and so on. Thus, if we represent each book by an XML document, then those documents will display considerable variation at the detail level—more variation, it might be thought, than is typically found among the tuples of a relation in the relational model. And since relations are usually thought of as being very tightly structured while XML documents appear to have a much looser structure,[10] relations are sometimes said to contain *structured data* and XML documents to contain *semi*structured data (or to be based on "**the semistructured data model**").

The foregoing argument does not really stand up to close scrutiny, however. The truth is that relations are no more and no less "structured" than XML documents are. (They do have a *different* structure, of course, but it is nevertheless the case that anything that can be represented as an XML document can equally well be represented relationally—possibly as a tuple, possibly as a set of tuples, possibly otherwise.) However, the term *semistructured* is much used in the industry, which is why we mention it here.

---

[9] It might help to point out that the infoset for a given document is very close to being a "possrep" for that document, in the sense of Chapter 5.

[10] Though not, of course, no structure at all. "Data" that is completely unstructured is, by definition, pure noise, and *unstructured data* is a contradiction in terms.

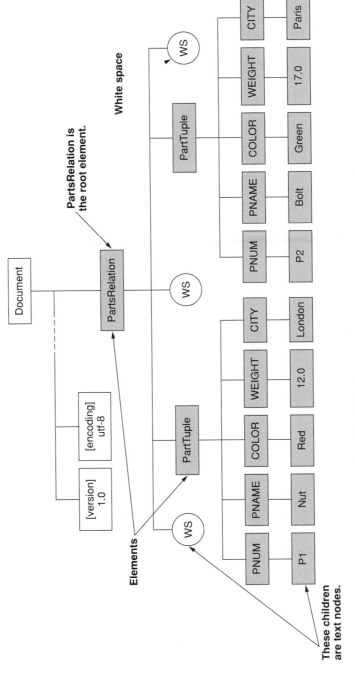

Fig. 27.2 PartsRelation document infoset (simplified)

Note: It is only fair to add that alternative justifications for the term can be found in the literature. For example:

- Reference [26.35] suggests that it derives from the fact that part of the data does have a fixed structure while the rest varies (for example, every book has a title, but not every book has an index).

- Reference [27.13] says it derives from the fact that the data does not have a conventional schema but is instead "schemaless" and "self-describing." Reference [27.17] says the same, but adds "object-like."

- Reference [27.23] says it derives from the fact that the data "may be irregular or incomplete, and [has a] structure [that] may change rapidly and unpredictably."

- Of course, what structure an XML document does possess is in large part at the discretion of the document designer;[11] in a sense, it is *imposed* on the data by the designer, and different designers are obviously at liberty to impose different structures, by dividing the data in different ways and choosing different tags. For example, a poem might be represented as a single monolithic chunk of text (<poem> . . . </poem>), or as a sequence of verses (<poem> <verse> . . . </verse> . . . </poem>), or in many other ways. And it might be argued that the term *semistructured* derives from such considerations.

It is our opinion, however, that none of these justifications stands up to careful analysis. In fact, we see no substantial difference between "the semistructured model" and the structural aspects of the old-fashioned **hierarchic** model as described (and criticized) in Chapter 13 of reference [1.5]. Which raises another point, of course: Data models in general, including the hierarchic model in particular, are supposed to include operators; but "the semistructured model" seems to be primarily, or even exclusively, concerned with data structure only.

One last point on this subject: It is often suggested in the literature that either the infoset—under the generic interpretation of that term [27.26]—or, more generally, "the semistructured model" is "the XML data model." But the picture is muddied considerably by the fact that every one of references [27.24], [27.28], and (jointly) [27.27] and [27.29], as well as reference [27.26] as such, defines its own "XML data model" (and some of those models have operators and some do not). Thus, it is not at all clear as to which of those models, if any, deserves to be called *the* XML data model.

XML Derivatives and Standards

XML as such was standardized only fairly recently (February 1998),[12] and the level of acceptance it has received in the short time since then is astonishing. At the time of writ-

---

[11] And/or the document *type* designer (see Section 27.4).

[12] Because W3C is a consortium of organizations as opposed to a formal standards body, the XML specification is not a standard as such but only a "recommendation." However, the distinction is unimportant in practice. We remark in passing that the XML specification is itself dependent on, and defined in terms of, the Unicode standard [27.22].

ing (early 2003), there are at least 200 different XML derivatives—some brand new, others reworkings of earlier HTML-based specifications. Here is a small sampling by way of illustration:

- *CML:* The Chemical Markup Language
- *ebXML:* A proposed replacement for EDI in business-to-business (B2B) communications
- *MathML:* The Mathematical Markup Language
- *PMML:* A data mining standard
- *WML:* The Wireless Markup Language
- *XMLife:* An insurance industry standard

There are also several application- and industry-wide specifications that rely on XML, such as:

- *SOAP:* Simple Object Access Protocol, one of the bases of Web Services, a new kind of programming in which applications are constructed by combining components that are discovered and accessed via the Web
- *XMI:* XML Metadata Interchange, a tool-to-tool communication standard

And there are many additional standards or potential standards that either augment or depend on the XML standard (refer to Fig. 27.3). Here are some of the most important:

- *Namespaces in XML:* A name qualification scheme that allows distinct XML vocabularies[13] to be used together without naming conflicts
- *XML Information Set:* An abstract model of the structure of XML documents (see the previous subsection)
- *XML Schema:* A language for constructing schemas that describe XML documents (see Section 27.4)
- *DOM:* Document Object Model, an object-oriented API for operating on XML infosets (see the previous subsection)
- *XPath:* XML Path Language, which provides a means ("path expressions") for addressing, and hence accessing, parts of an XML document (see Section 27.5)
- *XPointer:* XML Pointer Language, which is based on XPath but provides more extensive addressing facilities
- *XQuery:* XML Query, an XML query language (see Section 27.5)
- *XLink:* XML Linking Language, a language that allows elements to be inserted into XML documents in order to create and describe links between resources
- *XSL and XSLT:* XML stylesheet and stylesheet transformation languages that together allow—in fact, encourage—formatting information to be kept separate from descriptive markup

---

[13] See the subsection "Document Type Definitions" in Section 27.4 for an explanation of this term.

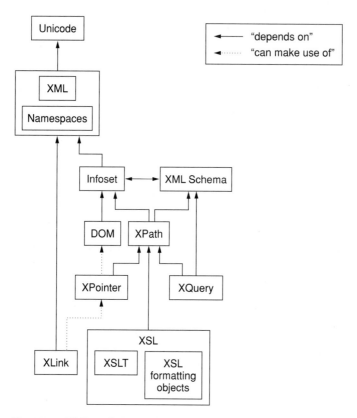

Fig. 27.3   XML and XML-related standards and specifications

27.4   XML DATA DEFINITION

Like conventional database data, a given XML document usually has some associated descriptor information. Such information can be specified by means of either (a) a *document type definition* (DTD), constructed using what we will call the **DTD definition language** [27.25],[14] or (b) an *XML schema,* constructed using a language called, somewhat confusingly, **XML Schema** [27.28]. We discuss both languages in the present section.

---

[14] The name *DTD definition language* stands for "Document Type Definition definition language" and might thus appear to involve some redundancy. But it does not—the two "definitions" refer to different things! See the further remarks on this subject in the subsection "XML Derivatives Revisited" at the very end of this section.

Document Type Definitions

The DTD definition language is defined in reference [27.25], which is the XML specification (in other words, DTDs are part of the XML standard *per se*). Among other things, that reference gives:

- The basic rules for defining and using markup languages based on XML (i.e., XML derivatives)—how to distinguish markup *vs.* character data, how to pair up start and end tags properly, how to specify comments, and so forth

- The rules for how a program designed to process XML documents (commonly called an **XML parser**) is supposed to present information to other programs

And (as already stated) it also gives the rules for defining DTDs.

To illustrate DTD functionality, we make use of a revised version of the PartsRelation example from Section 27.3. The major changes are as follows: We use XML attributes instead of elements to represent part colors and cities, and we allow an optional NOTE element to be included at certain places within the document. Thus, a typical PartsRelation document might now look like this:

```
<?xml version="1.0"?>
<!-- This is an XML representation of the parts relation   -->
<!-- of Fig. 3.8 (tuples for P1-P3 only; COLOR and CITY    -->
<!-- now represented by XML attributes instead of by XML   -->
<!-- elements).                                            -->
<!DOCTYPE ... >              <!-- See subsequent explanation -->
<PartsRelation>
  <NOTE>Revised version</NOTE>
  <PartTuple CITY="London">
    <PNUM>P1</PNUM>
    <PNAME>Nut</PNAME>
    <WEIGHT>12.0</WEIGHT>
    <NOTE>Part color is Red by default</NOTE>
  </PartTuple>
  <PartTuple COLOR="Green" CITY="Paris">
    <PNUM>P2</PNUM>
    <PNAME>Bolt</PNAME>
    <WEIGHT>17.0</WEIGHT>
  </PartTuple>
  <PartTuple CITY="Oslo" COLOR="Blue">
    <PNUM>P3</PNUM>
    <PNAME>Screw</PNAME>
    <WEIGHT>17.0</WEIGHT>
  </PartTuple>
</PartsRelation>
```

Documents of the general form just illustrated might have a DTD that looks like this (we have numbered the lines for purposes of subsequent reference):

```
1    <!ELEMENT PartsRelation (NOTE?, PartTuple*)>
2    <!ELEMENT NOTE (#PCDATA)>
3    <!ELEMENT PartTuple (PNUM, PNAME, WEIGHT, NOTE?)>
4    <!ATTLIST PartTuple
5       CITY  (London | Oslo | Paris) #REQUIRED
6       COLOR (Red | Green | Blue) "Red">
7    <!ELEMENT PNUM (#PCDATA)>
8    <!ELEMENT PNAME (#PCDATA)>
9    <!ELEMENT WEIGHT (#PCDATA)>
```

Explanation:

- *Line 1:* Every document that conforms to this DTD has exactly one root element, called PartsRelation. That root element contains a sequence of zero or more Part-Tuple elements, optionally preceded by a NOTE element. *Note:* The optionality is indicated by the question mark, and the "zero or more" by the asterisk.[15] Specifying a plus sign instead of an asterisk—that is, PartTuple+ instead of PartTuple∗—would mean "one or more" instead of "zero or more." Specifying neither would mean "exactly one."

  In general, DTDs can be either internal (i.e., directly included in the document they describe) or external (i.e., included in some other file):

- In the internal case, (a) the DTD precedes the root element, and (b) it must be enclosed in a pair of *delimiters*. The opening delimiter takes the form:

  ```
  <!DOCTYPE document type name [
  ```

  (where the document type name—PartsRelation, in the example—must be the same as the root element name). The closing delimiter takes the form:

  ```
  ]>
  ```

- In the external case, (a) the delimiter lines do not appear; (b) a *reference* to the DTD in question appears preceding the root element in every document that uses it (the external case thus makes it easier for several documents to share the same DTD). Such a reference might look like this:

  ```
  <!DOCTYPE PartsRelation SYSTEM "file:///c:/parts.dtd">
  ```

  (indicating that the DTD is to be found in a file called "parts.dtd"). Even in the external case, therefore, the document still has a <!DOCTYPE . . .> line, specifying among other things the document type name.

- *Line 2:* Every NOTE element contains "parsed character data" (#PCDATA), meaning, loosely, regular text without any markup. Lines 7, 8, and 9 are similar.

- *Line 3:* Every PartTuple element contains exactly one PNUM element, one PNAME element, and one WEIGHT element (in that order), optionally followed by a NOTE element.

- *Lines 4–6:* Every PartTuple start tag contains a CITY attribute and, optionally, a COLOR attribute (in either order if both are specified). The CITY attribute value must be London, Oslo, or Paris. The COLOR attribute value must be Red, Green, or Blue, and is assumed to be Red by default if the attribute is omitted.

  A couple of additional points:

- First, the set of all element type names and attribute names defined within a given DTD is said to be the corresponding *vocabulary*. There is no requirement that such names be unique to just one vocabulary (the namespace mechanism mentioned in the previous section can be used to resolve naming conflicts, if necessary).

---

[15] The asterisk is the Kleene operator, previously encountered in Chapter 21.

- Second, the XML specification defines two **levels of conformance** for XML documents, "well-formedness" and "validity." Given a particular "textual object"—in other words, a character string—it is the responsibility of the XML parser to determine whether that object meets either of the conformance requirements. The next two subsections elaborate.

Well-Formedness

A given textual object *X* is **well-formed** if and only if both of the following are true:

- *X* conforms to the generic grammar defined in reference [27.25] and satisfies a set of twelve rules also defined in that reference (details beyond the scope of this chapter).

- Every textual object *Y* referenced directly or indirectly from within *X* is well-formed in turn. *Note:* By "directly or indirectly" here, we mean *X* directly contains either a reference to *Y* or a reference to some other textual object *Z* that directly or indirectly contains a reference to *Y*.

These rules imply among other things that *X* must have exactly one root element, which can and usually does contain other elements; the start tag for each element must have a corresponding end tag with exactly the same name (and the matching is case-sensitive); elements must be properly nested; and so on. All of our examples of XML documents prior to this point have been well-formed in this sense (in fact, if a textual object is not well-formed, then by definition it is not an XML document). Here by way of contrast is a textual object that, for reasons as indicated in the comments, is not well-formed:

```
<!-- Warning!  This textual object is not well-formed (and -->
<!-- so is not an XML document at all, by definition).     -->
<PartsRelation>
  <PartTuple>
    <PNUM>P1</pnum>   <!-- End tag does not match start tag -->
    <PNAME>Nut        <!-- Missing end tag                  -->
  </PartTuple>
  </PartTuple>        <!-- Missing start tag                -->
</PartsRelation>
<PartsRelation>       <!-- More than one root element       -->
  ...
```

Validity

A given textual object *X* is **valid** if and only if it is well-formed *and* it conforms to some specified DTD. Here is an example of an XML document that is well-formed (by definition) but for reasons as indicated in the comments is nevertheless not valid:

```
<!DOCTYPE PartsRelation SYSTEM "file:///c:/parts.dtd">
<!-- Warning!  This document is well-formed (and is thus -->
<!-- an XML document), but it is not a valid PartsRelation -->
<!-- document because it does not conform to the DTD for   -->
<!-- such documents as given in the "parts.dtd" file.      -->
<partsRelation>                       <!-- Undefined element -->
  <PartTuple CITY="London">
    <PNAME>Nut</PNAME>      <!-- PNUM and PNAME elements ... -->
    <PNUM>P1</PNUM>         <!--          ... in wrong order -->
    <WEIGHT>12.0</WEIGHT>
  </PartTuple>
```

```
        <PartTuple>                      <!-- Missing CITY attribute -->
          <PNUM>P2</PNUM>
          <PNAME>Bolt</PNAME>
          <remarks>Best quality</remarks> <!-- Undefined element -->
        </PartTuple>                      <!-- Missing WEIGHT element -->
      </partsRelation>
```

Attributes of Type ID and IDREF

As you can see, DTDs do support certain kinds of integrity constraints (legal attribute values, etc.).[16] For the most part, however, those constraints are fairly weak in nature (especially for elements—as opposed to attributes—that directly contain actual data, for which essentially no constraints can be specified at all). But DTDs do also support certain **uniqueness** and **referential** constraints, thanks to the special attribute types *ID* and *IDREF*. For example, suppose we were to specify a DTD for an XML document corresponding not just to parts but to the whole suppliers-and-parts database. Then that DTD might include definitions as follows:

```
<!ATTLIST SupplierTuple SNUM ID #REQUIRED>
<!ATTLIST PartTuple PNUM ID #REQUIRED>
<!ATTLIST ShipmentTuple SNUM IDREF #REQUIRED>
<!ATTLIST ShipmentTuple PNUM IDREF #REQUIRED>
```

(Note in particular that PartTuple elements now have a PNUM attribute instead of a PNUM element.) If document *D* is valid according to this DTD, then:

- Every SupplierTuple element in *D* will have a unique SNUM value and every PartTuple element in *D* will have a unique PNUM value.

- Every ShipmentTuple element in *D* will have an SNUM value that appears as a value of some attribute of type ID somewhere in *D* and a PNUM value that appears as a value of some attribute of type ID somewhere in *D*.

In other words, attributes of type ID behave a little bit like primary keys, and attributes of type IDREF behave a little bit like foreign keys. However, the analogies are not very strong:

- There is no way to specify a "key" value that is anything but a simple character string.

- There is no way to specify a "key" value that involves more than one attribute. (In the example, note that we have *not* specified that ShipmentTuple elements have a unique SNUM/PNUM value.)

- In the example, SNUM values in SupplierTuple elements are not merely unique with respect to all such elements, they are unique with respect to all attributes of type ID in the entire document, and similarly for PNUM values in PartTuple elements. (In particular, therefore, no SNUM value is equal to any PNUM value.)

---

[16] The general question of integrity constraints in an XML context is explored in reference [27.8].

- Moreover, SNUM values in ShipmentTuple elements are not guaranteed to be equal to the SNUM value in some SupplierTuple element—they are merely guaranteed to be equal to the value of some attribute of type ID, somewhere in the document.

- Most important, referential constraint checking—such as it is—is performed only within the context of a single document. There is no cross-document checking.

Limitations of DTDs

We have seen that DTD support for integrity constraints is quite weak. In fact, many other problems with DTDs have also become apparent since they were first introduced. For example:

- They do not use XML syntax (i.e., they are not themselves XML documents), which means they cannot be processed by a regular XML parser. For instance, consider the element declaration:

```
<!ELEMENT PNUM (#PCDATA)>
```

This declaration looks a bit like an XML start tag, but it is not—"!ELEMENT" is not a legal XML element type name, and "PNUM" and "(#PCDATA)" are not legal XML attributes. Surely, if XML is really as versatile and powerful as it is claimed to be, it ought to be able to describe itself![17]

- They provide essentially no data type support (everything is just a character string).

- They typically require that elements of different types appear in some specific sequence, even when that sequence has no intrinsic meaning. For example, suppose PartsRelation documents have a DTD that includes the following specification:

```
<!ELEMENT PartTuple (PNUM, PNAME, COLOR, WEIGHT, CITY)>
```

Then the PNUM, PNAME, WEIGHT, COLOR, and CITY elements within a given PartTuple element must appear in exactly the specified order, even though that order has no meaning in relational terms. *Note:* In principle we could define a DTD that would allow the five elements to appear in arbitrary order, but only by writing out the 120 distinct possible orderings as explicit alternatives (!) and specifying that those 120 orderings are all equally acceptable.

This list of problems is not exhaustive.

Despite problems like those just listed, however, it is still the case that DTDs represent a well-established and important standard, and they are much used in practice. Moreover, real-world DTDs tend to be much more complicated and comprehensive than our simple examples might have suggested. For example, XML Schema, which we describe next, is defined by a DTD of over 400 lines (see *http://www.w3.org/2001/XMLSchema.dtd*).

---

[17] This statement is dreadfully loose, of course. More precisely, it ought to be possible to define an XML derivative *XD* such that documents that are valid according to *XD* are "document type definitions"—not DTDs as such, of course, since we have just seen that DTDs as such are *not* XML documents, but, rather, "document type definitions" that provide DTD-like functionality, and ideally more besides. In fact, XML Schema—see the next subsection—is exactly such an *XD*.

XML Schema

XML Schema [27.28] is itself an XML derivative (it is not defined as part of the XML specification *per se,* unlike the DTD definition language). Thus, the XML schema corresponding to a given XML document *D* is itself an XML document, *SD* say. There is no explicit, formally specified link between documents *D* and *SD,* but *D* can use the special attribute *schemaLocation* to provide "hints" regarding the location of *SD.*

Typically, an XML schema provides more extensive constraints than a DTD could on the XML document(s) it describes. By way of example, here is an XML Schema counterpart to the PartsRelation DTD shown in the subsection "Document Type Definitions" earlier in this section (the one in which COLOR and CITY are represented by XML attributes instead of elements):

```
<?xml version="1.0"?>
<!-- XML Schema schema for PartsRelation documents -->
<!DOCTYPE xsd:schema SYSTEM "http://www.w3.org/2001/XMLSchema.dtd">

<xsd:schema xmlns:xsd="http://www.w3.org/2001/XMLSchema">

  <xsd:element name="NOTE" type="xsd:string"/>

  <xsd:element name="PartsRelation">
    <xsd:complexType>
      <xsd:sequence>
        <xsd:element ref="NOTE" minOccurs="0"/>
        <xsd:element name="PartTuple" type="PartTupleType"
                     minOccurs="0" maxOccurs="unbounded"/>
      </xsd:sequence>
    </xsd:complexType>
  </xsd:element>

  <xsd:complexType name="PartTupleType">
    <xsd:sequence>
      <xsd:element name="PNUM" type="PartNum"/>
      <xsd:element name="PNAME" type="xsd:string"/>
      <xsd:element name="WEIGHT">
        <xsd:simpleType>
          <xsd:restriction base="xsd:decimal">
            <xsd:totalDigits value="5"/>
            <xsd:fractionDigits value="1" fixed="true"/>
            <xsd:minInclusive value="0.1"/>
          </xsd:restriction>
        </xsd:simpleType>
      </xsd:element>
      <xsd:element ref="NOTE" minOccurs="0"/>
    </xsd:sequence>
    <xsd:attribute name="CITY" type="City"/>
    <xsd:attribute name="COLOR" type="Color" default="Red"/>
  </xsd:complexType>

  <xsd:simpleType name="PartNum">
    <xsd:restriction base="xsd:string">
      <xsd:pattern value="P[0-9]{1,3}"/>
    </xsd:restriction>
  </xsd:simpleType>

  <xsd:simpleType name="Color">
    <xsd:restriction base="xsd:string">
      <xsd:enumeration value="Red"/>
      <xsd:enumeration value="Green"/>
      <xsd:enumeration value="Blue"/>
    </xsd:restriction>
  </xsd:simpleType>
```

```
<xsd:simpleType name="City">
  <xsd:restriction base="xsd:string">
    <xsd:enumeration value="London"/>
    <xsd:enumeration value="Oslo"/>
    <xsd:enumeration value="Paris"/>
  </xsd:restriction>
</xsd:simpleType>

</xsd:schema>
```

Now, the foregoing schema is clearly much longer and more complex than its DTD counterpart, even though for the most part it specifies just the same constraints as that DTD did. The big difference is that the schema additionally imposes certain **type** constraints on elements and attributes. XML Schema provides a set of built-in *primitive* types—boolean, decimal, string, and several others—as well as certain built-in *derived* types (integer, positiveInteger, negativeInteger, and so on), which are defined in terms of the primitive ones. It also allows users to define their own types in terms of the built-in ones. Types can be either *simple* or *complex;* the difference is that elements that are of a complex type can contain other elements nested inside themselves, while elements that are of a simple type cannot. We illustrate these ideas with reference to the PartsRelation schema, which constrains PartsRelation documents as follows:

1. The root (PartsRelation) element is defined to be of an unnamed complex type, values of which are defined inline to consist of an optional NOTE element, followed by a sequence of zero or more PartTuple elements, each of which is of type PartTupleType.

2. Elements that are of type PartTupleType are defined to consist of elements PNUM, PNAME, and WEIGHT, in that order, together with attributes CITY and COLOR, of which the latter is optional (if omitted, Red is assumed by default). Of these elements and attributes, PNAME is defined to be of type string; PNUM, CITY, and COLOR are defined to be of types PartNum, City, and Color, respectively (see points 4 and 5); and WEIGHT is defined to be of an unnamed type whose definition is given inline (see point 3).

3. The type of WEIGHT elements is defined to be a "restriction" of type decimal, with precision five, scale factor one, and minimum value 0.1—which is to say, legal values of elements of type WEIGHT are exactly 0.1, 0.2, ..., 9999.9.

4. Type PartNum (a restriction of type string) is defined by means of the *regular expression* P[0-9]{1,3}, which is interpreted to mean that legal values of type PartNum consist of an uppercase P followed by one, two, or three decimal digits. *Note:* The "regular expression" construct is borrowed from the Perl programming language.

5. Types Color and City (also restrictions of type string) are defined by enumeration.

Note: The foregoing discussion notwithstanding, it is important to understand that XML Schema "types" are not really types in the sense of Chapter 5. In particular, almost no associated operators are defined, as would be required for genuine types. In fact, XML Schema "type definitions" are really closer to the PICTURE specifications found in languages like COBOL and PL/I; that is, all they really do is define certain *character-string representations* for the "types" in question. Partly for such reasons, we have felt free to depart from our usual user-defined types (as shown in, e.g., Chapter 3) in the foregoing example.

Here then are some of the advantages of XML Schema over the DTD definition language as a vehicle for describing XML documents:

- XML schemas are themselves XML documents.

- XML Schema supports a more sophisticated type mechanism.

- XML Schema provides a simpler means (not illustrated in our example) for specifying that elements of different types directly contained in the same element can appear in any order.

- XML Schema supports *key* and *keyref* elements (also not illustrated in our example), which more closely resemble the relational key and foreign key constructs. Such keys can involve combinations of values from several levels of nesting within a given element, thus supporting among other things what used to be called "uniqueness within parent" (see Chapter 13 of reference [1.5]).

Of course, one disadvantage is that XML schemas are considerably more complex than a simple DTD.

We conclude our discussion of XML Schema with a few miscellaneous points:

- Checking a given XML document against an XML schema is called **schema validation** (as opposed to just plain *validation,* unqualified, which means checking it against a DTD).

- Since a schema is itself an XML document, it typically contains numerous XML elements. Note in particular, however, that many of those elements are *empty;* typically, in fact, we use an empty element whenever we want to specify an element that has attributes but no content, as here:

```
<xsd:element name="NOTE" type="xsd:string"/>
```

(see the PartsRelation example).

- Schemas also have their own DTD, identified by the specification:

```
<!DOCTYPE xsd:schema [ ... ]>
```

(again, see the PartsRelation example).

In closing this subsection, we stress the fact that we have hardly begun to get into all of the richness (and complexity) of XML Schema in its full generality. For further information, see reference [27.14] or, for the full story, the XML Schema specification [27.28].

XML Derivatives Revisited

Earlier in this chapter, we said that XML is a metalanguage; that is, it is a language that allows users to define tailored languages of their own, with their own user-defined tags in particular. We observe now that a given DTD or XML schema is, precisely, *the definition of such a tailored language*—that is, of such an "XML derivative," as we called it previously. In other words, a given DTD or XML schema is, precisely, a definition of the syntax rules that a conforming XML document is required to abide by.

It follows from the foregoing that XML is not just a metalanguage but, rather, what might be called a "metametalanguage." XML *per se* defines (among other things) the rules for constructing DTDs; and a DTD in turn is a metalanguage that defines the rules for constructing conforming documents. Note too that all of those rules are, primarily, *syntax* rules; neither XML in general nor a given DTD in particular ascribes any meaning to documents created in accordance with those rules.

27.5   XML DATA MANIPULATION

We turn now to the question of XML data manipulation languages. Many such languages have been proposed, but the one that looks set to become a standard is **XQuery** [27.29]. As we will see in just a moment, XQuery—which is still a work in progress at the time of writing—is based on several earlier languages, including in particular **XPath** [27.27]; in fact, XQuery fully subsumes XPath.

XQuery is read-only. Updating, if necessary, must be done either by means of DOM [27.24] or by means of some proprietary (vendor-specific) facilities—but of course both of these approaches have problems:

- The problem with DOM is that (as mentioned in Section 27.3) it is meant for programmers, not end users.

- The problem with proprietary facilities is precisely that they *are* proprietary and vary from vendor to vendor. (We will, however, illustrate the kind of functionality typically provided in Section 27.7.)

A vendor-independent language called XUpdate is currently under development [27.30], but it is in too preliminary a state at the time of writing to be discussed here. In what follows, therefore, we limit our attention to XQuery (and XPath) only.

XQuery is derived from an earlier language called Quilt [27.9], which was in turn influenced by SQL, OQL, and various older XML languages, including XQL, XML-QL, and Lorel (see reference [25.11] for a discussion of OQL, and references [27.5] and [25.18] for information regarding XQL, XML-QL, and Lorel). Now, the full XQuery language is quite large and complex, and it would not be appropriate in a book of this nature to try to cover it exhaustively. Instead, therefore, we simply show a series of examples, with commentary, that we feel should be sufficient to give an idea of the general power, scope, and nature of the language. Before we can do that, however, we need to explain that XQuery does not really operate on XML documents, as such, at all! The reason is as follows:

- XML documents are, by definition, essentially character strings that are (among other things) meant to be readable by humans.

- As a result, they include a variety of features—tags, line breaks, indentation, and so forth—that help with that readability objective but have nothing to do with the real information content of the document in question.

- And, of course, it is that information content that XQuery really needs to deal with.

Thus, XQuery is defined to operate not in terms of XML documents *per se* but rather in terms of XML documents that have been converted into a certain *abstract* ("parsed") *form.* The abstract form of any given XML document is said to be "an instance of the XQuery Data Model" [27.29]; it can be thought of as an infoset[18]—that is, a hierarchy— like the one shown in Fig. 27.2 (in the subsection "XML Document Structure" in Section 27.3). Note in particular, therefore, that the result of a query expressed in XQuery is an infoset, not an XML document. As reference [27.29] puts it, "transformation of a Data Model instance [back] into an XML document is currently an open issue." As a matter of fact, the result of evaluating an XQuery expression might not even be a proper infoset, because (as we will see later) it might not be well-formed.

XPath

XQuery relies heavily on XPath's **path expressions**, so we begin with a brief explanation of such expressions. Conceptually, such expressions bear a strong family resemblance to path expressions as described in Chapters 25 and 26. To be more specific, a path expression in XPath is an expression that, starting from some given source node or nodes within some given infoset, navigates along a specified path or paths within that infoset to find some desired target node or nodes. *Note:* The terms *source* and *target* are not official XPath terms.

Syntactically, then, an XPath path expression consists of a sequence of *steps,* where each step except the first is separated from the previous one by a slash character ("/") and the first is optionally preceded by either one or two such characters:

```
[ / | // ] step / step ... / step
```

An initial single slash means the navigation is to start at the root (i.e., the root is the source node); an initial double slash means it is to start at every node in turn (in effect, it causes the entire infoset to be navigated, in depth-first, left-to-right order, with every node in turn acting as the source node). If there are no initial slashes at all, the current node—that is, the one most recently accessed—acts as the source node.

Here are some simple examples, based on the PartsRelation document from the subsection "Document Type Definitions" in Section 27.4 (which, as you will recall, contains PartTuple elements for parts P1, P2, and P3):

- The expression

  ```
  /PartsRelation/PartTuple
  ```

  returns a sequence of nodes corresponding to those three PartTuple elements.

- The expression

  ```
  /PartTuple
  ```

  returns an empty sequence of nodes, because the root node has no PartTuple children. *Note:* The root node here is *not* the PartsRelation node but, rather, the overall docu-

---

[18] More precisely, the abstract form consists of an *augmented* infoset called the "Post Schema Validation Infoset" (PSVI), converted to XQuery Data Model form.

ment node (see the discussion of Fig. 27.2 in Section 27.3). The same remark applies to the previous example, of course, as well as to the next one.

- The expression

```
//PartTuple
```

returns the same result as the first example.

In general, each step in a given path expression is evaluated in the context of the result of the previous step (more precisely, if the result of that previous step is the sequence of nodes *SN*, then each node in *SN* in turn becomes the *context node* for the current step). Each step has three parts:

1. An *axis,* which specifies the direction in which navigation is to proceed; up (parent, ancestor), down (child, descendant), left (preceding, preceding-sibling), or right (following, following-sibling)

2. A *node test,* which specifies the kind(s) of node(s) that are of interest

3. Optionally, one or more *predicates,* which are used to eliminate unwanted nodes

Note: The specific axes "parent," "child," and so on, shown under the first point here do not exhaust the possibilities—they are merely mentioned by way of illustration. If no axis is specified, it defaults to "child" (i.e., the navigation process moves on to the children of the context node).

In order to explain in a little more detail how path expressions are evaluated, we consider the following slightly more complicated example:

```
/PartsRelation/PartTuple[WEIGHT="17.0"]
```

Explanation:

1. The initial "/" establishes the root node (i.e., the document node) as the context node for the step immediately following.

2. Path expressions can be (and usually are) written in *abbreviated form.* Thus, the expression "PartsRelation" in the example is an abbreviation for "child::PartsRelation" (where "child" is the axis and "PartsRelation" is the node test). The result of this step is thus the PartsRelation node that is the sole child of the root node.

3. Similarly, "PartTuple" is an abbreviation for "child::PartTuple"; it yields the sequence of three PartTuple nodes that are the children of the PartsRelation node.

4. Finally, the predicate

```
[WEIGHT="17.0"]
```

eliminates all PartTuple nodes except those whose WEIGHT children have a value of 17.0. *Note:* The expression "WEIGHT" is itself an abbreviation; the unabbreviated predicate is:

```
[child::WEIGHT="17.0"]
```

The final result is thus a sequence of two PartTuple nodes, corresponding to parts P2 and P3 (in that order).

We conclude our brief discussion of XPath with a remark on the crucial role played by the notion of *currency* in all of the foregoing. We have seen that each step in a given path expression is executed with respect to some context node, which acts as "the current node." Now, a very similar notion pervaded the access languages in those early "manual navigation" systems (especially hierarchic systems) that dominated the DBMS market-place before SQL systems appeared on the scene. And it was that notion that was the direct cause of much of the complexity—not to mention the coding errors—that such systems suffered from; indeed, it was one of the many great contributions of the relational model that it eliminated the notion of currency entirely. The wisdom of reintroducing such a notion (and making it such a key feature, moreover) thus surely deserves to be questioned.

XQuery

One problem with XPath is that it is fundamentally just an addressing mechanism; its path expressions can navigate to existing nodes in the hierarchy, but they cannot construct nodes that do not already exist. In other words, the XPath language is a little like a "relational" language—"relational" in quotes because, of course, relational languages are not navigational—that supports restrictions and projections but not joins.[19] This observation provides part of the motivation for XQuery; one of the major extensions provided by XQuery over XPath is precisely the ability to construct new nodes.

This ability is illustrated in our first example. Once again, suppose we have the XML document PartsRelation, exactly as in the preceding subsection. Suppose we also have analogously structured SuppliersRelation and ShipmentsRelation documents. Here then is an XQuery formulation of the query "For every shipment, get the supplier name, part name, and shipment quantity":

```
<Result>
  { for $spx in document("ShipmentsRelation.xml")
                //ShipmentTuple,
        $sx  in document("SuppliersRelation.xml")
                //SupplierTuple[SNUM = $spx/SNUM],
        $px  in document("PartsRelation.xml")
                //PartTuple[PNUM = $spx/PNUM]
    order by SNAME, PNAME
    return
      <ResultTuple>
        { $sx/SNAME, $px/PNAME, $spx/QTY }
      </ResultTuple> }
</Result>
```

Explanation:

1. The expression overall evaluates to ("constructs") a single Result element, containing a sequence of ResultTuple elements. As an aside, we note that if we were to delete the

---

[19] This statement is slightly oversimplified; XPath does effectively support a kind of Cartesian product operation (which is a degenerate case of join, of course). However, it does not support joins in any more general form.

enclosing Result tags, the expression that remained would still be a legal XQuery query, but it would return a result that was not well-formed.

2. A good way to explain the semantics of the expression overall (ignoring the enclosing Result tags) is in terms of the following relational calculus analog:

```
{ SX.SNAME, PX.PNAME, SPX.QTY } WHERE SX.SNUM = SPX.SNUM
                                  AND PX.PNUM = SPX.PNUM
```

This expression effectively asks for suppliers, parts, and shipments to be joined as specified, and then for the result of that join to be projected over SNAME, PNAME, and QTY. *Note:* We show no analog of the XQuery "order by" step, since "order by" is not a relational operation. Also, we adopt our usual conventions regarding range variable names (SX, PX, and SPX are range variables ranging over suppliers, parts, and shipments, respectively). Finally, we ignore the fact that the relational expression will automatically eliminate duplicate tuples, which the XQuery expression will not.

3. As the previous paragraph suggests, the XQuery variables $sx, $px, and $spx behave a little like range variables in relational calculus. However, the analogy is rather misleading; the XQuery formulation is not really much like the relational one, because it is quite procedural in nature, as you can see (in this connection, we draw your attention to the annotation to reference [27.3]). In fact, the XQuery formulation looks very much like the following *nested-loop* formulation (expressed here in pseudocode, and using "." instead of "/" as a separator):

```
do for each shipment $spx ;
   do for each supplier $sx where $sx.snum = $spx.snum ;
      do for each part $px where $px.pnum = $spx.pnum ;
         emit { $sx.SNAME, $px.PNAME, $spx.QTY } ;
      end do ;
   end do ;
end do ;
```

It follows that $sx, $px, and $spx really resemble loop control variables (in the conventional programming sense) much more than they do range variables. What is more, observe that we have to iterate over shipments specifically in the outermost loop; that is, we have to introduce the loop control variable $spx first, because the other two variables are defined in terms of it—a fact that could have some interesting implications for the optimizer. By contrast, the other two variables $sx and $px could be introduced in either order, though whether the order has any implications for the optimizer could also be an interesting question. It is at least relevant to observe that the order in which the variables are introduced does have an effect on the order in which result elements are produced (see the discussion of the *return* clause under point 7); thus, the XQuery analogs of the expressions *A* JOIN *B* and *B* JOIN *A* are not equivalent, in general.

As a consequence of such considerations, it could be argued that XQuery is really more of a programming language than it is an end-user query language.

4. Now we focus on the *for* clause in particular, and more specifically on the portion of that clause that precedes the first comma. The expression

```
document("ShipmentsRelation.xml")
```

returns the abstract ("parsed") version of the XML document that is contained in the file called ShipmentsRelation.xml, with the overall document node as the context node. The specification "//ShipmentTuple" indicates that we are interested in ShipmentTuple elements in that document. And the specification "for $spx in" indicates that the variable $spx is to take on as its value each of those shipment tuples in turn, in the order in which they appear in that document.

5. The next part of the *for* clause—

```
$sx in document("SuppliersRelation.xml")
        //SupplierTuple[SNUM = $spx/SNUM]
```

—is analogous, except that the variable $sx "ranges over" only those suppliers whose SNUM value is equal to that in the current value of $spx.

6. The last part of the *for* clause is analogous again.

7. The *return* clause is executed for every combination of values of the variables $sx, $px, and $spx, in the order in which those values are produced by the *for* clause. In the example, therefore, the *return* clause will produce ResultTuple elements in a sequence dictated by the rule that $px values change most rapidly, $sx values change next most rapidly, and $spx values change least rapidly of all.

8. The *order by* clause is more or less self-explanatory. Note, however, that it appears *before* the corresponding *return* clause. This placement allows the result to be ordered on the basis of values that do not actually appear in the result (as in, e.g., the SQL query SELECT CITY FROM P ORDER BY WEIGHT). Conceptually, however, it is still the case that the *return* clause needs to be executed first, because the ordering cannot be done until there is something to order.

Here now is a second example ("Get part numbers and total shipment quantity for parts supplied by two or more suppliers"):

```
for $pnum in
    distinct-values(document("ShipmentsRelation.xml")//PNUM)
let $spx := document("ShipmentsRelation.xml")
            //ShipmentTuple[PNUM = $pnum]
where count ( $spx ) > 1
order by PNUM
return
  <Result>
    { $pnum,
      <totqty> { sum ( $spx/qty ) } </totqty> }
  </Result>
```

1. This example shows a complete "FLWOR expression" (FLWOR = *for* + *let* + *where* + *order by* + *return;* it is pronounced "flower").

2. Note the use of "distinct-values" to eliminate duplicate part numbers in the *for* clause; $pnum ranges over just the *distinct* shipment part numbers.

3. The *let* clause differs from the *for* clause in that the specified variable does not *iterate* over the specified sequence of values—rather, it is *assigned* that sequence of values in its entirety. In the example, moreover, the *let* clause will be evaluated for each distinct shipment part number in turn, because it is effectively nested inside the *for* clause.

4. The *where* clause then causes the remainder of the expression to be evaluated only when the current sequence of shipments (i.e., the sequence of shipments with the cur-

rent part number) has length greater than one. XQuery supports the usual aggregate operators *count, sum, avg, max,* and *min.*

5. Again it has to be said that the overall expression looks quite procedural. Pseudocode analog:

```
do for each distinct shipment part number $pnum ;
   do for all shipments $spx where $spx.pnum = $pnum ;
      if ( count of such shipments $spx ) > 1 then
         emit { $pnum, sum ( $spx.qty ) } ;
      end if ;
   end do ;
end do ;
```

Relational counterpart:

```
{ SPX.PNUM, SUM ( SPY WHERE SPY.PNUM = SPX.PNUM, QTY ) }
            WHERE COUNT ( SPY WHERE SPY.PNUM = SPX.PNUM ) > 1
```

Now, our examples so far have perhaps been a little unrealistic, precisely because they are somewhat relational in flavor; in particular, they make little use of the hierarchic nature of XML documents in general. So consider the following redesign. First, let the PartsRelation document be exactly the same as before. In place of the SuppliersRelation and ShipmentsRelation documents, however, suppose we have a SuppliersOverShipments document, in which:

- The root element contains a sequence of Supplier elements.
- Each Supplier element contains SNUM, SNAME, STATUS, and CITY elements, followed by a sequence of Shipment elements.
- Each Shipment element contains a PNUM element and a QTY element.

Refer to Fig. 27.4.

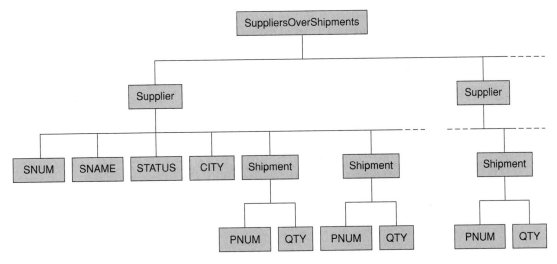

Fig. 27.4 Suppliers and shipments as a hierarchy

Now consider the queries "Get suppliers who supply part P2" and "Get parts supplied by supplier S2." Here are relational formulations:

```
SX WHERE EXISTS SPX ( SPX.SNUM = SX.SNUM AND SPX.PNUM = 'P2' )

PX WHERE EXISTS SPX ( SPX.PNUM = PX.PNUM AND SPX.SNUM = 'S2' )
```

Note: For simplicity, we assume that SNUM and PNUM values are simple character strings, not values of some user-defined type.

Here now is an XQuery formulation of the first query:

```
for $sx in document("SuppliersOverShipments.xml")//Supplier
where $sx//PNUM = "P2"
return
  <Result>
    { $sx//SNUM, $sx//SNAME, $sx//STATUS, $sx//CITY }
  </Result>
```

And here is an XQuery formulation of the second query:

```
let $sx := document("SuppliersOverShipments.xml")
              //Supplier[SNUM = "S2"]
return
  <Result>
    { document("PartsRelation.xml")
        //PartTuple[PNUM = $sx//PNUM] }
  </Result>
```

As you can see, the XQuery formulations are less symmetric than their relational analogs—as is only to be expected, because of the asymmetric (hierarchic) character of the XML design.

We close this section with a few miscellaneous remarks.

- Like SQL as originally formulated [4.9–4.11], XQuery has no explicit join support. In fact, reference [27.29] specifically states that "[FLWOR expressions are] useful for computing joins," implying, in effect, that the user has to spell out the sequence of steps involved in any such computation. However, it does include explicit union, intersect, and difference ("except") support, with duplicate elimination.

- XQuery also includes explicit support for the existential and universal quantifiers. Here are a couple of examples:

```
some $x in ( 2, 4, 8 ) satisfies $x < 7

every $x in ( 2, 4, 8 ) satisfies $x < 7
```

The first of these expressions evaluates to true and the second to false.

- As explained in Chapters 7 and 8, the relational model has an associated (and important) concept of *completeness.* There seems to be no analogous concept for XQuery, nor for XML in general.[20]

---

[20] Except perhaps for *flower power?* (Apologies, but the temptation was too great to resist.)

27.6   XML AND DATABASES

We are now (finally!) in a position to consider the implications of all of our discussions in this chapter so far for databases in particular. Clearly, there is a requirement to be able to store XML documents—perhaps we should say XML *data,* rather—in databases, and to be able to retrieve and update that data on demand. In fact, there is the inverse requirement too: namely, to be able to take "regular" or nonXML data—in particular, the result of some query—and convert it to XML form, so that it can (for example) be transmitted as an XML document to some consumer. We begin by concentrating on the first of these two requirements.

It should be apparent that there are basically three ways we might store an XML document in a database:

1. We might store the entire document as the value of some attribute within some tuple.

2. We might *shred* the document (technical term!) and represent various pieces of it as various attribute values within various tuples within various relations.

3. We might store the document not in a conventional database at all, but rather in a "native XML" database (i.e., one that contains XML documents as such instead of relations).

We consider each possibility in turn.

Documents as Attribute Values

We touched on this approach in the subsection "The Development of XML" in Section 27.3, when we mentioned the possibility of extending the parts relvar P to include DRAWING and DESCRIPTION attributes. Essentially, the idea here is as follows:

- First of all, we define a new data type, say XMLDOC, values of which are XML documents; then we can define specific attributes of specific relvars to be of that type. *Note:* As we have seen, XML as such is somewhat verbose; an XML document might easily be five or ten times the size of the raw data it represents, and processing it in source form might be quite inefficient. Storing such documents internally in some compressed form (perhaps parsed form) might thus be advantageous. However, such considerations have nothing to do with the model, of course.

- Tuples containing XMLDOC values can be inserted and deleted using the conventional relational INSERT and DELETE operators, and XMLDOC values within such tuples can be replaced in their entirety using the conventional relational UPDATE operator. Also, of course, XMLDOC values can participate in read-only operations in the conventional manner.

- Like all types, type XMLDOC will have a set of associated operators. The operators in question will presumably provide retrieval and update capabilities on XMLDOC-valued attributes at a more fine-grained level, supporting (e.g.) access to individual elements or XML attributes. In the case of retrieval, the operators will probably be very similar to those found in XQuery; they might even be invoked by means of an "escape" to XQuery, though native (direct) support would be more user-friendly. However, update operators should be supported as well.

- Operators should also be provided to check that a given XMLDOC value conforms to—that is, is valid according to—some specified DTD or some specified XML schema. (Of course, XMLDOC values will be *well-formed* by definition, but they still might not be *valid*.)

Note: This first approach, storing entire documents as attribute values, is sometimes referred to in the literature and current practice, informally, as *XML column.* Some of the factors that might make this approach an appropriate choice are:

- The documents already exist.
- They are usually operated on in their entirety instead of piecemeal.
- They are rarely updated.
- What searching is done is usually based on a small, known set of elements or attributes.
- Documents must be stored intact for audit purposes.

In a nutshell, this approach is appropriate for what are sometimes called *document-centric* applications [27.7]—that is, applications where the documents are mainly intended for eventual human consumption and consist primarily of natural language text.

Shred and Publish

The second approach does not involve any new data types. Instead, XML documents are *shredded* into pieces—individual XML elements and attributes, for example—and those pieces are then stored as values of various relational attributes in various places in the database.[21] Note, therefore, that in this case the database does not contain XML documents as such; the DBMS has no knowledge of such documents, and the fact that certain values in the database can be combined in certain ways to create such a document is understood by some application program (perhaps a web server), not by the DBMS.

Observe, however, that since that application program *can* create an XML document from regular database data, we have effectively met the second of our original objectives!—namely, we now have a means of taking the result of a query on regular (non-XML) data and converting it to XML form. Such a conversion is referred to as *publishing* (the data in question); thus, *publishing*, as the term is used in this context, is the opposite of shredding, in a sense. We remark in passing that the mapping rules governing such shredding and publishing are themselves typically kept in the form of XML documents.

Incidentally, the ability to publish nonXML data in XML form might also be regarded as the ability to support **XML views** of nonXML data. (More precisely, such publishing might be regarded as supporting XML views for *retrieval* purposes. *Updating*

---

[21] A degenerate special case of this approach is to store the entire document as a character string in a single attribute position within a single tuple. Also, note that this approach and the previous one are not mutually exclusive: Either might be appropriate, depending on what we subsequently want to do with the data. We might even use both approaches at the same time—perhaps even on the very same document.

such views, if allowed, will require support from the corresponding shredding function.) After all, there is no intrinsic reason why—to use the terminology of Chapter 2—the external and conceptual levels of the system need be based on the same data model; in fact, we mentioned the possibility in Chapter 3 of a system in which the conceptual view was relational while a given external view was hierarchic. The only hard requirement is that there must be a reversible mapping between the two.

There are some problems here, however, caused by what might be termed an *impedance mismatch*—see Chapter 25—between the relational model and "the XML model," which as we have seen is basically the old hierarchic model in another guise. One problem is that the child nodes of a given parent node in the hierarchic model form not a set but a *sequence* (i.e., they are ordered), whereas the tuples of a relation are not ordered. Given an XML document *D*, therefore, it is possible that certain aspects of *D* (informational or otherwise) might be lost when *D* is shredded and stored in a relational database. If they are, there can be no guarantee that publishing the data in XML form will reconstruct document *D* in its exact original form. In particular, white space will probably be different in the original and (re)published versions of *D*.

Note: The "shred and publish" approach is sometimes referred to, informally, as *XML collection*. Some of the factors that might make it an appropriate choice are:

- The data already exists in a relational database and must interact with corresponding data in XML documents.
- Only the character data portions of documents need be stored intact (the tags can be factored out into relational attribute names).
- Operations are frequently performed on individual elements or attributes.
- Updates are frequent, and update performance is important.
- Processing programs use existing relational interfaces.

In a nutshell, the "shred and publish" approach is appropriate for what are sometimes called *data-centric* applications [27.7]—that is, applications where the documents represent (typically) operational or decision support information, rather than natural language text.

XML Databases

The main reason we mention this third approach is just a desire for completeness. After all, we saw in Chapter 3 that the relational model is both necessary and sufficient to represent any data whatsoever. We also know there is a huge investment in terms of research, development, and commercial products in what might be called *relational infrastructure* (i.e., support for recovery, concurrency, security, and optimization—not to mention integrity!—and all of the other topics we have been discussing in this book). In our opinion, therefore, it would be unwise to embark on the development of a totally new kind of database technology when there does not seem to be any overwhelming reason to do so—not to mention the fact that any such technology would obviously suffer from problems similar to those that hierarchic database technology already suffers from (see, e.g., Chapter 13 of reference [1.5] or the annotation to references [27.3] and [27.6]).

27.7 SQL FACILITIES

The SQL standard has no XML support at the time of writing, but some such support is likely to be included, under the generic name *SQL/XML* [27.15], as Part 14 of the next version of the standard (probably in 2003). In this section, we offer a preview of that support; however, it goes without saying that everything we say here is subject to change until SQL/XML is formally ratified.

"XML Collection"

It follows from our discussions in the previous section that there are basically two ways in which XML data might be stored in an SQL database, "XML collection" and "XML column," and SQL/XML supports both. (For obvious reasons it does not support native XML databases as such.) In this subsection, we concentrate on the "XML collection" support.

We start by observing that it is somewhat strange that "XML collection" support should be included in the *SQL* standard at all!—since, as we saw in Section 27.6, it has nothing to do with the DBMS (it has to do rather with some application program, perhaps a web server, that runs on top of the DBMS). Be that as it may, the support in question consists essentially of:

- Rules for mapping SQL character sets, identifiers, data types,[22] and values to XML character sets, names, data types, and values
- Rules for mapping an SQL table or set of tables to *two* XML documents—one containing the data as such, the other a corresponding XML Schema schema

Taken together, these rules support the publishing of SQL data in XML form; equivalently, they support what in the previous section we called *XML views* of SQL data (though for retrieval only). In particular, therefore, they provide a basis for performing XQuery queries on such data. Note, however, that SQL/XML does *not* define any rules for the inverse process: namely, shredding XML data into SQL form (with the rather minor exception that it does include rules for mapping XML character sets and names to SQL character sets and identifiers).

By way of an example, consider the SQL analog of our usual parts relvar, table P. Here is a simplified SQL definition of that table:[23]

```
CREATE TABLE P
    ( PNUM    CHAR(6),
      PNAME   CHAR(20),
      COLOR   CHAR(6),
      WEIGHT  NUMERIC(5,1),
      CITY    CHAR(20) ) ;
```

---

[22] Structured types are not supported at the time of writing.

[23] The simplifications are as follows: We have omitted the PRIMARY KEY clause, since reference [27.15] is silent on the question of mapping keys to XML; we have avoided the use of user-defined types; and we have omitted the NOT NULL specifications.

Suppose the table contains just the usual rows for parts P1 and P2. Then mapping it to XML will produce a data document that looks like this:

```
<P>
  <row>
    <PNUM>P1</PNUM>
    <PNAME>Nut</PNAME>
    <COLOR>Red</COLOR>
    <WEIGHT>12.0</WEIGHT>
    <CITY>London</CITY>
  </row>
  <row>
    <PNUM>P2</PNUM>
    <PNAME>Bolt</PNAME>
    <COLOR>Green</COLOR>
    <WEIGHT>17.0</WEIGHT>
    <CITY>Paris</CITY>
  </row>
</P>
```

It will also produce a schema document that looks like this:

```
<xsd:schema xmlns:xsd="http://www.w3.org/2001/XMLSchema">

  <xsd:simpleType name="CHAR_6">
    <xsd:restriction base="xsd:string">
      <xsd:length value="6"/>
    </xsd:restriction>
  </xsd:simpleType>

  <xsd:simpleType name="CHAR_20">
    <xsd:restriction base="xsd:string">
      <xsd:length value="20"/>
    </xsd:restriction>
  </xsd:simpleType>

  <xsd:simpleType name="DECIMAL_5_1">
    <xsd:restriction base="xsd:decimal">
      <xsd:totalDigits value="5"/>
      <xsd:fractionDigits value="1"/>
    </xsd:restriction>
  </xsd:simpleType>

  <xsd:complexType name="RowType.P">
    <xsd:sequence>
      <xsd:element name="PNUM" type="CHAR_6"/>
      <xsd:element name="PNAME" type="CHAR_20"/>
      <xsd:element name="COLOR" type="CHAR_6"/>
      <xsd:element name="WEIGHT" type="DECIMAL_5_1"/>
      <xsd:element name="CITY" type="CHAR_20"/>
    </xsd:sequence>
  </xsd:complexType>

  <xsd:complexType name="TableType.P">
    <xsd:sequence>
      <xsd:element name="row" type="RowType.P"
                   minOccurs="0"
                   maxOccurs="unbounded"/>
    </xsd:sequence>
  </xsd:complexType>

  <xsd:element name="P" type="TableType.P"/>

</xsd:schema>
```

"XML Column"

We turn now to SQL's "XML column" support. SQL/XML introduces a new data type called simply XML (not XMLDOC as in Section 27.6), values of which are, essentially, XML documents or fragments thereof—where by the term *fragment* we mean, for example, an individual XML element or a sequence of such elements. Various operators are supported for deriving or "generating" values of type XML from conventional SQL data. Here is a simple example:

```
INSERT INTO RESULT ( XMLCOL)
      SELECT XMLGEN ( '<Result>
                          <SNAME>{SX.SNAME}</SNAME>
                          <PNAME>{PX.PNAME}</PNAME>
                          <QTY>{SPX.QTY}</QTY>
                       </Result>',
                       SX.SNAME, PX.PNAME, SPX.QTY ) AS Result
      FROM    S AS SX, P AS PX, SP AS SPX
      WHERE   SX.SNUM = SPX.SNUM
      AND     PX.PNUM = SPX.PNUM ;
```

We are assuming here that column XMLCOL of table RESULT is of type XML. The similarity between this example and the first XQuery example in Section 27.5 is not a coincidence. However, it does mean that XMLGEN is almost certain to change before SQL/XML is ratified, because it relies on another proposal, XQuery, that itself is still just "work in progress" at the time of writing.

  To repeat, then: SQL/XML introduces the new type XML; but it defines almost no operators on values of that type—not even equality![24] In fact, reference [27.15] says "If *V1* and *V2* are both of the XML type, then whether *V1* and *V2* are identical or not . . . is implementation-defined." However, this state of affairs is likely to be corrected by the time SQL/XML is formally ratified. And reference [27.11] suggests that the following might be added at that same time (or possibly some time later):

- Support for "escape" to XPath or XQuery
- The ability to test whether a specified value of type XML is a well-formed XML element, or is a valid XML document, or conforms to some specified XML schema, and so on.

Even with these enhancements, however, SQL/XML access to XML data will still mostly be read-only, and *native* access will still mostly be missing.

Proprietary Support

As noted in Section 27.5, some SQL products (e.g., DB2, Oracle) already include proprietary support for retrieving and updating XML data. It is not our aim to go into detail on specific products here, but we give some hypothetical examples in order to illustrate the

---

[24] It does define an operator called XMLSERIALIZE, which converts a value of type XML to character-string form. It also defines an operator called XMLPARSE for "going the other way"—that is, for converting a character-string representation of an XML document or document fragment to type XML. Between them, these two operators provide some support for shredding and publishing.

kind of functionality such products typically provide. Our examples are loosely based on IBM's "XML Extender" product for DB2, but we have simplified them considerably to eliminate aspects that are irrelevant to our main purpose.

The XML Extender product makes use of SQL's support for user-defined functions (see Chapter 5) to provide a set of what are in effect—from the user's point of view—*built-in* functions. The functions can be invoked from SQL, and they provide a variety of retrieval and update capabilities against XML data. The ones we illustrate are XMLFILE-TOCLOB, XMLCONTENT, XMLEXTRACTREAL, and XMLUPDATE (not their real names), and the capabilities they provide include the following:

- *Storing an XML document as an SQL column value*

  Example: The following UPDATE statement (a) uses the function XMLFILETOCLOB to convert the XML document in the external file BoltDrawing.svg to type CLOB, and then (b) stores that CLOB string as the value of column DRAWING in the row in table P for part P2:

  ```
  UPDATE P
  SET     DRAWING = XMLFILETOCLOB ( 'BoltDrawing.svq' )
  WHERE   PNUM = 'P2' ;
  ```

  Of course, we are assuming here that table P does include a DRAWING column, and that column is of type CLOB.

- *Retrieving such an SQL column value*

  Example: The following SELECT statement retrieves the CLOB value stored in the previous example and publishes it as an XML document to the external file Retrieved-BoltDrawing.svg:

  ```
  SELECT XMLCONTENT ( DRAWING, 'RetrievedBoltDrawing.svg' )
  FROM    P
  WHERE   PNUM = 'P2' ;
  ```

- *Retrieving a specified component of an XML document*

  Example: Suppose once again that the PartsRelation document is stored in a file called PartsRelation.xml. Then the following UPDATE statement (a) extracts the WEIGHT value for part P3 from that document and converts it to type REAL, and then (b) stores that value as the value of column WEIGHT in the row in table P for part P3:

  ```
  UPDATE P
  SET     WEIGHT = XMLEXTRACTREAL
                  ( 'PartsRelation.xml',
                    '//PartTuple[PNUM = "P3"]/WEIGHT' )
  WHERE   PNUM = 'P3' ;
  ```

  Note: We adopt the fiction here that column WEIGHT in table P is of type REAL instead of NUMERIC(5,1), because the XML Extender product does not currently support an "extract to NUMERIC" function. More important, note that XMLEX-TRACTREAL and the other "extract" functions can be used on XML documents stored in SQL columns, not just on XML documents stored in external files.

- *Updating a specified component of an XML document*

  Example: Suppose, somewhat unrealistically, that table SP includes a PARTDETAIL column, of type CLOB, whose value within any given row is an XML document describing the part in question. Then the following UPDATE statement sets the COLOR component of that XML document to Green for every part supplied by supplier S4:

```
UPDATE SP
SET    PARTDETAIL = XMLUPDATE
                  ( PARTDETAIL,
                    '//PartTuple/COLOR', 'Green' )
WHERE  SNUM = 'S4' ;
```

27.8   SUMMARY

We have examined the relationship between XML and databases. In order to set the scene for that examination, however, we had to begin by explaining a lot of background: first a little on the World Wide Web, and then a lot more on XML *per se*.

XML grew out of the earlier languages SGML and HTML; the name "XML" stands for "Extensible Markup Language," but (like SGML) XML is really a **metalanguage**, or even a "metametalanguage." A specific *application* of XML—that is, an **XML derivative**, as we called it earlier in this chapter—is a language for defining XML documents of some specific kind (e.g., PartsRelation documents). Originally, XML had nothing to do with databases; rather, the idea was simply to allow "generic SGML to be served, received, and processed on the Web in the way that is now possible with HTML" [27.25]. However, there is a clear need to be able to store XML data in databases and operate on it there, and this fact has led some people to advocate XML as (a basis for) a database technology as such.

An **XML document** consists primarily of a properly nested hierarchic arrangement of **elements**, each of which includes a pair of delimiting **tags**. A given element can include **character data**, nested elements, or a mixture of both. **Empty elements** are supported. A start tag can optionally include a nonempty set of **attributes**. We saw that an XML document might be used to represent a relation, but it necessarily imposes a top-to-bottom ordering on the tuples, and probably a left-to-right ordering on the attributes as well.

Any given XML document has an abstract structure called an **infoset** that can be operated on via an API called the **Document Object Model** and queried using **XQuery**. XML documents are also sometimes said to conform to **the semistructured data model**—though in fact XML documents are no more and no less structured than relations are; in fact, we see no substantial difference between the semistructured model and the old **hierarchic** model (at least in its structural aspects).

Any given XML document is **well-formed** by definition. It might also be **valid**, meaning it conforms to some specified **Document Type Definition** (DTD). The rules for writing DTDs are an intrinsic part of the XML standard (in fact, a given DTD *is* the definition of some XML derivative). However, DTDs suffer from a variety of problems; in particular, they support very little by way of integrity constraints. **XML Schema** is a metalanguage that supports the creation of XML schemas, which can be used to provide a tighter and more detailed description of XML documents (with respect to *data types* in particular, though the types in question are hardly true types in the sense of Chapter 5). The process of checking that a given XML document conforms to a specified XML schema is called **schema validation**.

Next, we took a look at **XQuery** and **XPath** (the second of which is a proper subset of the first), which provide read-only access to XML data—or, more precisely, to an abstract or parsed form of such data (i.e., an infoset, in effect). We did not attempt to define either of these languages in detail, but we did show a few examples in order to give some idea of what they can do. We discussed **path expressions**, which effectively allow the user to **navigate** along some specified path in the infoset to some desired target. We also pointed out the crucial role played by **currency** in such expressions, and questioned the desirability of such a feature (certainly it contributes to the overall procedural "look and feel" of both XPath and XQuery, an aspect of those languages that we were somewhat critical of). Then we observed that, in effect, XPath is just an **addressing scheme**—it can be used to navigate to existing nodes in the hierarchy, but it cannot construct new nodes (we need XQuery for that).

We then presented a series of XQuery examples, illustrating "**flower expressions**" ("FLWOR" = *for* + *let* + *where* + *order by* + *return*) in particular. We drew parallels between such expressions and (a) expressions of the relational calculus and (b) nested loops in a conventional programming language; we then claimed that the second of these parallels was closer than the first, and we mentioned a few questions regarding optimization. We noted the lack of any explicit join support (as in the original version of SQL).

Next, we described three ways in which we might store an XML document in a database:

1. **"XML column":** We might store the entire document as the value of some attribute within some tuple. This approach involves a **new data type,** say XMLDOC (with operators for dealing with values and variables of that type, of course).

2. **"XML collection":** We might **shred** the document and represent various pieces of it as various attribute values within various tuples within various relations. *Note:* The inverse of shredding—that is, converting nonXML data to XML form—is called **publishing**. Together, shredding and publishing can be regarded as providing **XML views** of nonXML data (publishing supports retrieval, shredding supports update).

3. We might store the document in a **native XML database** (i.e., a database that contains XML documents as such, instead of relations).

We explained some of the pros and cons of these various approaches.

Finally, we briefly discussed **SQL/XML** (which will probably be incorporated into the SQL standard in 2003). SQL/XML—somewhat inappropriately, in our opinion—supports the publication of SQL data in XML form. It also introduces a new data type called XML, values of which are XML documents or fragments, thereby allowing XML data to be stored in SQL columns, but it provides very few operators on such data. We closed with a brief discussion of **proprietary XML support**, based on the support provided for **DB2**.

EXERCISES

27.1 Explain the following terms in your own words:

attribute	SGML	website
element	tag	World Wide Web
HTML	URL	XML
HTTP	web browser	XML derivative
Internet	web crawler	XML Schema
markup	web page	XPath
search engine	web server	XQuery

27.2 How are XML, HTML, and SGML related?

27.3 Consider the list of contents at the front of this book. Show how you might represent that list of contents as an XML document. Include an internal DTD as part of your answer.

27.4 Revise your answer to Exercise 27.3 to make the DTD external. What are the advantages of an external DTD?

27.5 What does it mean to say that an XML document is (a) well-formed, (b) valid?

27.6 What is an empty element?

27.7 Do you think XML documents are containment hierarchies in the sense of Chapter 25?

27.8 In the subsection "Limitations of DTDs" in Section 27.4, we criticized DTDs on the grounds that they themselves were not expressed in XML ("Surely, if XML is really as versatile and powerful as it is claimed to be, it ought to be able to describe itself"). Does an analogous criticism apply to data definitions in SQL? Or in the relational model? Justify your answer.

27.9 Show the projects relation from Fig. 4.5 (see the inside back cover) as an XML document. Use XML elements, not attributes, to represent data values. To what extent can uniqueness constraints be enforced?

27.10 Repeat Exercise 27.9 but use XML attributes to represent data values. What are the advantages of using attributes? What are the disadvantages?

27.11 Suppose the answers to Exercises 27.9 and 27.10 are extended to include suppliers, parts, and shipments. To what extent can referential constraints be enforced?

For Exercises 27.12–27.14, you will probably need to refer to the official XML Schema documentation [27.28] or some similar reference source (the body of the chapter does not include sufficient detail to answer the exercises fully).

27.12 Create an XML schema for your answer to Exercise 27.3.

27.13 Consider the PartsRelation document from Section 27.3. Create an XML schema for documents of this form that does not impose an ordering on the elements of PartTuple.

27.14 We claimed in Section 27.4 that XML Schema data types are not really types as normally understood. Do you agree? Justify your answer.

27.15 What do you understand by the term *infoset?*

27.16 What is a path expression?

27.17 What is a "FLWOR expression"? What is the crucial difference between the *for* clause and the *let* clause? When should you use a predicate rather than a *where* clause (and *vice versa*)?

Exercises 27.18–27.21 refer to the PartsRelation document from Section 27.4. All results should be well-formed.

27.18 Write an XQuery expression to list all PartTuple elements that contain a NOTE element.

27.19 Write an XQuery expression to list all green parts, with each result PartTuple enclosed in a GreenPart element.

27.20 If the following XQuery expression is evaluated on a version of the PartsRelation document that represents all six parts P1–P6, what does it yield?

```
<Parts>
   { count(document("PartsRelation.xml")//PartTuple) }
</Parts>
```

27.21 Suppose we are given the SuppliersOverShipments document (see Fig. 27.4) as well as the PartsRelation document. Write an XQuery expression to list suppliers who supply at least one blue part.

27.22 If the SuppliersOverShipments document from Exercise 27.21 represents all of the suppliers and shipments from Fig. 3.8 (see the inside back cover), what does the following expression yield?

```
for $sx in document("SuppliersOverShipments.xml")/
             Supplier[CITY = 'London']
return
   <Result>
      { $sx/SNUM, $sx/SNAME, $sx/STATUS, $sx/CITY }
   </Result>
```

27.23 What is the semantic difference (if any) between the following two *return* clauses?

```
return <Result> { $a, $b } </Result>

return <Result> { $a } { $b } </Result>
```

27.24 How might we consider storing XML data in a database? What are the advantages and disadvantages of each approach?

27.25 Consider the functions described (briefly) in Section 27.6, subsection "Proprietary Support." Do you have any opinions regarding the design of those functions?

27.26 It is sometimes suggested that an XML document resembles a tuple, as that concept is understood in the relational database world. Discuss.

27.27 It is sometimes said that XML data is "schemaless." How would you go about querying data that has no schema? How would you design a query language for such data?

27.28 In Section 27.3, we said that what structure an XML document does possess is in large part imposed on the data by the document designer. Does an analogous remark apply to relational data? If not, why not? Justify your answer.

27.29 If you are familiar with the hierarchic data model, identify as many differences as you can between it and "the semistructured model" as sketched in this chapter.

27.30 Here is a quote from reference [27.4]: "XML avoids the fundamental question of what we should do, by focusing entirely on how we should do it." Discuss.

REFERENCES AND BIBLIOGRAPHY

27.1 Serge Abiteboul, Peter Buneman, Dan Suciu: *Data on the Web: From Relations to Semistructured Data and XML.* San Francisco, Calif.: Morgan Kaufmann (1999).

An "up-to-date examination of the rapidly evolving retrieval and processing strategies for relational and semistructured data" (from the publisher's brochure).

27.2 Tim Berners-Lee with Mark Fischetti: *Weaving the Web: The Original Design and Ultimate Destiny of the World Wide Web by Its Inventor.* San Francisco, Calif.: Harper San Francisco (1999). See also Tim Berners-Lee: "Information Management: A Proposal," the original document describing the Web project, at *http://www.w3.org/History/1989/Proposal.html.* Versions of this document were circulated for comments at CERN but never formally published.

27.3 Phil Bernstein *et al.*: *The Asilomar Report on Database Research, ACM SIGMOD Record 27,* No. 4 (December 1998).

> This paper includes some rather depressing observations on the implications of XML for databases: "Unfortunately, XML is likely to generate chaos for database systems. XML's evolving query language is reminiscent of the procedural query processing languages prevalent 25 years ago. XML is also driving the development of client-side data caches that will support updates, which is leading the XML designers into a morass of distributed transaction issues. Unfortunately, most of the work on XML is happening without much influence from the database system community."

27.4 Bob Boiko: "Understanding XML," *http://metatorial.com/papers/xml.asp* (2000).

27.5 Angela Bonifati and Stefano Ceri: "Comparative Analysis of Five XML Query Languages," *ACM SIGMOD Record 29,* No. 1 (March 2000).

> The five languages are XSL, XQL, Lorel, XML-QL, and XML-GL (XSL is really a stylesheet or formatting language—see Section 27.3—but it can be used to formulate simple queries, as can XSLT also). XSL and XQL support queries involving just one XML document, while the others support queries that span documents. XML-GL provides a QBE-like graphical interface. Lorel and XML-GL include updating facilities. See also reference [27.16].

27.6 Jon Bosak and Tim Bray: "XML and the Second-Generation Web," *http://www.sciam.com* (May 1999).

> This paper includes an excellent, albeit presumably unintentional, argument for *not* using XML as the basis for a new database technology. To quote: "XML [documents have] the structure known in computer science as a tree . . . Trees cannot represent every kind of information, but they can represent most kinds that we need computers to understand. Trees, moreover, are extraordinarily convenient for programmers [*sic*]. If your bank statement is in the form of a tree, it is a simple matter to write a bit of software that will reorder the transactions or display just the cleared checks." Well, yes; these remarks might be accurate as far as they go; but do they go far enough? A study of the history of trees (in other words, hierarchies) in the database context strongly suggests that the answer to this question is *no.* The fundamental point is that even when the data has a naturally hierarchic structure—as (it might be argued) is the case with, for example, departments and employees—it does not follow that it should be *represented* hierarchically, because the hierarchic representation is not suitable for all of the processing we might want to do on the data. And what about data that does not have a "naturally hierarchic" structure? For example, what is the best tree representation for propositions of the form "Supplier *s* supplies part *p* to project *j*"? *Note:* We raised these same objections in Section 25.1 in connection with objects, which are also hierarchic, like XML documents.

27.7 Ron Bourret: "XML and Databases," *http://rpbourret.com/xml/XMLAndDatabases.htm* (November 2002).

> A good introduction and survey. To quote: "This paper gives a high-level overview of how to use XML with databases. It describes . . . the differences between data-centric and document-centric [applications], how XML is commonly used with relational databases, and what native XML databases are and when to use them."

27.8 Peter Buneman, Wenfei Fan, Jérôme Siméon, and Scott Weinstein: "Constraints for Semistructured Data and XML," *ACM SIGMOD Record 30,* No. 1 (March 2001).

27.9 Donald D. Chamberlin, Jonathan Robie, and Daniela Florescu: "QUILT: An XML Query Language for Heterogeneous Data Sources," in Dan Suciu and Gottfried Vossen (eds.), *Lecture Notes in Computer Science 1997*. New York, N.Y.: Springer-Verlag (2000).

27.10 Donald D. Chamberlin: "XQuery: An XML Query Language," *IBM Sys. J. 41,* No. 4 (2002).

> Chamberlin was one of the original designers of SQL [4.9–4.11] and is now a member of the W3C working group responsible for the definition of XQuery. This paper is a useful tutorial—though it does contain some contentious remarks, including this one in particular: "Iteration is an important part of a query language." This claim is in direct conflict with Codd's assertion that "to extract any information [from] the database, neither an application programmer nor a nonprogramming user [should need] to develop any iterative or recursive loops" (the ninth of Codd's "Fundamental Laws of Database Management" [6.2]).

27.11 Andrew Eisenberg and Jim Melton: "SQL/XML and the SQLX Informal Group of Companies," *ACM SIGMOD Record 30,* No. 3 (September 2001); "SQL/XML Is Making Good Progress," *ACM SIGMOD Record 31,* No. 2 (June 2002).

27.12 Daniela Florescu, Alon Levy, and Alberto Mendelzon: "Database Techniques for the World-Wide Web: A Survey," *ACM SIGMOD Record 27,* No. 3 (September 1998).

> This paper is concerned with web data in general rather than XML data specifically. It provides a survey of projects, prototypes, and languages having to do with "the relevance of database concepts to the problems of managing and querying" web data. An extensive set of references is included.

27.13 Hector Garcia-Molina, Jeffrey D. Ullman, and Jennifer Widom: *Database Systems: The Complete Book*. Upper Saddle River, N.J.: Prentice Hall (2002).

27.14 Elliotte Rusty Harold: *XML Bible* (2d ed.). New York, N.Y.: Hungry Minds, Inc. (2001).

27.15 International Organization for Standardization (ISO): *XML-Related Specifications (SQL/XML) Working Draft,* Document ISO/IEC JTC1/SC32/WG3:DRS-020 (August 2002).

> A tutorial based on an earlier version of this document can be found in reference [26.32]. See also reference [27.11].

27.16 Dongwon Lee and Wesley W. Chu: "Comparative Analysis of Six XML Schema Languages," *ACM SIGMOD Record 29,* No. 3 (September 2000).

> The six languages are XML Schema, XDR, SOX, Schematron, DSD, and what in this chapter we called the DTD definition language. Of these six, the last is clearly the weakest, while XML Schema is among the strongest. See also reference [27.5].

27.17 Philip M. Lewis, Arthur Bernstein, and Michael Kifer: *Databases and Transaction Processing: An Application-Oriented Approach*. Boston, Mass.: Addison-Wesley (2002).

27.18 Jason McHugh and Jennifer Widom: "Query Optimization for XML," Proc. 25th Int. Conf. on Very Large Data Bases, Edinburgh, Scotland (September 1999).

> A report on experience with the optimizer component of Lore, "a DBMS for XML-based data supporting an expressive query language [called Lorel]."

27.19 Theodor Holm Nelson: "A File Structure of the Complex, the Changing, and the Indeterminate," Proc. 20th Nat. ACM Conf., Cleveland, Ohio (August 24–26, 1965). See also Theodor Holm Nelson: *Literary Machines*. Sausalito, Calif.: Mindful Press (1993; 1st edition published in 1982).

> Nelson's 1965 paper (in which the term *hypertext* was coined) builds on pioneering work by Vannevar Bush (Memex, 1945) and Douglas Engelbart (NLS: oNLine System, 1963).

27.20 Fabian Pascal: "Managing Data with XML: Forward to the Past?" *http://searchdatabase .techtarget.com* (January 2001).

> In reference [27.6], Bosak and Bray effectively propose taking functionality that ought to be part of the DBMS and moving it into application programs instead. Pascal argues that such a proposal is a retrograde step.

27.21 Igor Tatarinov, Zachary G. Ives, Alon Y. Halevy, and Daniel S. Weld: "Updating XML," Proc. 2001 ACM SIGMOD Int. Conf. on Management of Data, Santa Barbara, Calif. (May 2001).

> Proposes a set of updating extensions to XQuery and an implementation that maps the updates through "XML views" to underlying SQL data.

27.22 The Unicode Consortium: *The Unicode Standard, Version 4.0.* Reading, Mass: Addison-Wesley (2003).

27.23 Jennifer Widom: "Data Management for XML," *http://www-db.stanford.edu/~widom/xml-whitepaper.html* (June 17, 1999).

27.24 W3C: "Document Object Model (DOM) Level 3 Core Specification Version 1.0 Working Draft," *http://www.w3.org/TR/DOM-Level-3-Core* (February 26, 2003).

27.25 W3C: "Extensible Markup Language (XML) 1.0" (2d ed.), *http://www.w3.org/TR/REC-xml* (October 6, 2000). See also Tim Bray: "The Annotated XML 1.0 Specification," *http://www.xml.com* (follow the link "Annotated XML").

27.26 W3C: "XML Information Set," *http://www.w3.org/TR/xml-infoset* (October 24, 2001).

27.27 W3C: "XML Path Language (XPath) Version 2.0 Working Draft," *http://www.w3.org/TR /xpath20* (May 2, 2003).

27.28 W3C: "XML Schema Part 0: Primer; Part 1: Structures; Part 2: Datatypes," *http://www.w3 .org/TR/xmlschema-0/, -1/, -2/* (May 2, 2001).

27.29 W3C: "XQuery 1.0: An XML Query Language Working Draft," *http://www.w3.org/TR /xquery* (May 2, 2003).

> *Note:* The following W3C documents are also relevant to XQuery:
>
> - "XML Query Requirements Working Draft," *http://www.w3.org/TR/xquery-requirements* (May 2, 2003)
> - "XQuery 1.0 and XPath 2.0 Data Model Working Draft," *http://www.w3.org/TR/xpath-datamodel* (May 2, 2003)
> - "XQuery 1.0 and XPath 2.0 Formal Semantics Working Draft," *http://www.w3.org /TR/xquery-semantics* (May 2, 2003)
> - "XQuery 1.0 and XPath 2.0 Functions and Operators Working Draft," *http://www.w3 .org/TR /xpath-functions* (May 2, 2003)
> - "XML Query Use Cases Working Draft," *http://www.w3.org/TR/xquery-use-cases* (May 2, 2003)

27.30 XML:DB: "XML Update Language Working Draft," *http://www.xmldb.org/xupdate/xupdate-wd.html* (September 14, 2000).

> XML:DB is an open industry consortium (not a standards body) that is "chartered with the development of XML database specific specifications" [*sic*]. It was formed in 2000 because "XML databases . . . have much greater applicability than just the World Wide Web." XUpdate is intended as an update language for XML data.

APPENDIXES

There are four appendixes. Appendix A is an introduction to a new implementation technology called *The TransRelational*™ *Model*. Appendix B gives further details, for reference purposes, of the syntax and semantics of SQL expressions. Appendix C contains a list of the more important abbreviations, acronyms, and symbols introduced in the body of the text. Finally, Appendix D (online) provides a tutorial survey of common storage structures and access methods.

The TransRelational™ Model

A.1 INTRODUCTION

In the field of scientific endeavor, an idea emerges from time to time that is so startlingly novel, and so dramatically better than anything that went before, that it can truly be described as a breakthrough. The relational model provides the obvious example in the database world; almost everything in this book stands as testament to the radical nature and impact of that one brilliant idea. And now we are witnessing the birth of what looks set to be another major breakthrough: **The TransRelational™ Model**. In this writer's opinion, the TransRelational Model—invented by Steve Tarin, and abbreviated hereinafter to just *TR*—is likely to prove the most significant development in this field since Codd gave us the relational model, nearly 35 years ago.

We should say immediately that TR is not intended as a replacement for the relational model; the "trans" in "transrelational" does not stand for *beyond* as it does in (e.g.) "translunar," it stands for *transform*. It is true that TR and the relational model are both abstract models of data, but TR is at a *lower* level of abstraction (i.e., it is closer to physical storage); in fact, TR is designed to serve among other things as an implementation vehicle for the relational model. As you might recall, we said near the end of Chapter 18 that "a radically new approach to DBMS implementation has [recently] emerged, an approach that has the effect of invalidating many of the assumptions underlying" conventional approaches to implementation. TR is that new approach.

We should explain a little more of the background before we start getting into technical details. TR as such is really a specific application of a more general technology known, after its inventor, as the **Tarin Transform Method**. The Tarin Transform Method —which is the subject of a United States patent [A.2]—is intended as an implementation technology for data storage and retrieval systems of many kinds (not just DBMSs), including, for example, data warehouse systems, data mining tools, SQL systems, web search engines, native XML systems, and so on. By contrast, the subject of this appendix—that is, the TransRelational Model as such—merely represents the application of that more general technology to the implementation of relational systems in particular. As will soon become clear, however, that general technology is especially well suited to the implementation of relational systems in particular; indeed, it was conceived with that specific objective very much in mind.

Now we can begin our technical discussions. A good way to think about TR is in terms of the familiar goal of *data independence* (physical data independence, to be precise). Data independence means there is a sharp distinction between the logical and physical levels of the system, and that sharp distinction in turn means there has to be a **transform** between the two levels, mapping the logical level to the physical and *vice versa*. However, most of today's DBMSs employ what might almost be regarded as the *identity* transform, mapping base relvars to stored files and tuples in such relvars to stored records in such files. In such a system, what is stored at the physical level can be regarded, at least to a first approximation, as a **direct image** of what the user sees at the logical level (see Fig. A.1). One consequence is that such systems do not really provide very much data independence. Another is that the data is necessarily sorted into just one physical sequence in storage, with the result that indexes and other redundant structures are needed to support access to the data in other sequences. Yet another is that complex optimization is needed in order to achieve acceptable performance. And yet another is that the task of database administration becomes much more difficult than it ought to be.

The transforms used in TR, by contrast, are much more sophisticated. Here are some immediate consequences of that fact:

- TR provides much more data independence than direct-image systems do or can.

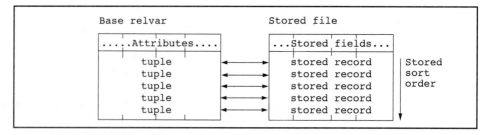

Fig. A.1 Direct-image implementation

- TR effectively stores the data in many different physical sequences at the same time, thereby doing away with the need for indexes and the like.

- Optimization in TR is much simpler than it is with direct-image systems; often, there is just one obviously best way to implement any given relational operation.

- Performance in TR is orders of magnitude better than it is with a direct-image system. In particular, join performance is linear!—meaning, in effect, that the time it takes to join 20 relations is only twice the time it takes to join 10 (loosely speaking). It also means that joining 20 relations, if necessary, is feasible in the first place; in other words, the system is *scalable.*

- The system is much easier to administer, because far fewer human decisions are needed.

- There is no such thing as a "stored relvar" or "stored tuple" at the physical level of the system at all!

In this appendix, we take a brief look at the way TR works. Naturally we do not have room to cover everything; to keep our discussion within bounds, therefore, we have decided to ignore (a) updates and (b) secondary storage; in other words, we adopt the fiction that the database is (a) read-only and (b) in main memory. Please do not conclude that TR is good for read-only, main-memory databases only, however—it is not. For a detailed description of all aspects of TR, including update operations and databases stored on disk, see the tutorial book by the present author [A.1].

A.2   THREE LEVELS OF ABSTRACTION

A relational system implemented using TR can be thought of as involving three levels of abstraction: the relational (or user) level, the file level, and the TR level (see Fig. A.2).

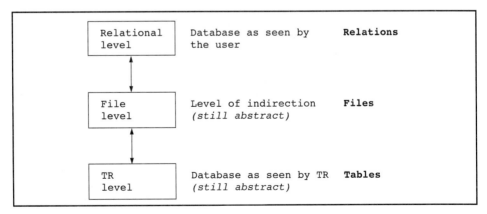

Fig. A.2   The three levels of abstraction

- At the top level, data is represented in terms of *relations,* made up of tuples and attributes in the usual way.

- At the bottom level, data is represented in terms of a variety of internal TR structures called *tables,* and those tables are made up of rows and columns. *Please note immediately that those tables, rows, and columns are not the SQL constructs of the same name, nor do they correspond directly to relations, tuples, or attributes at the user level.*

- The middle level is a level of indirection between the other two: Relations at the upper level are mapped to *files* at this level, and those files are then mapped to tables at the lower level. Moreover, those files are made up of records and fields; records correspond to tuples, and fields to attributes, at the top level. *Note:* Do not be misled by the terminology into thinking the files are physically stored; they are still an abstraction of what is physically stored, just as the relvars are (and just as the TR tables are too, come to that). However, it would not be wrong to think of them as "slightly more physical" than the relvars (and rather less physical than the TR tables).

From this point forward, we will be careful always to use relational terminology at the top level, file terminology at the middle level, and table terminology at the bottom level. We will also assume for simplicity that all relvars and relations are *base* relvars and relations specifically, barring explicit statements to the contrary.

The first step in mapping a given relvar to an appropriate TR representation, then, is to map that relation to a file, with records corresponding to the tuples and fields corresponding to the attributes. For example, Fig. A.3 shows one possible file corresponding to our usual suppliers relation. Within such a file, records have a top-to-bottom ordering and fields have a left-to-right ordering, as the record numbers and field numbers in the figure are meant to suggest. However, the orderings in question are essentially arbitrary; thus, for example, the suppliers relation could map equally well to any of 2,880 different files— 120 different orderings for the five records,[1] and 24 different orderings for the four fields. On the other hand, those 2,880 different files are at least all *equivalent* to one another, in the sense that they all represent exactly the same information; thus, it is sometimes convenient to regard them, not so much as 2,880 different files as such, but rather as 2,880 different *versions* of "the same" file.

Field sequence:		1	2	3	4
		S#	SNAME	STATUS	CITY
Record sequence:	1	S4	Clark	20	London
	2	S5	Adams	30	Athens
	3	S2	Jones	10	Paris
	4	S1	Smith	20	London
	5	S3	Blake	30	Paris

Fig. A.3   A file for the usual suppliers relation

[1] Not all of those 120 orderings can be obtained by means of a simple ORDER BY, of course (the one shown in Fig. A.3 cannot, for example).

A file such as that shown in Fig. A.3 can now be represented by tables at the TR level and can be reconstructed from those TR tables. In fact (important!), many different versions of the same file can all be reconstructed from the same TR tables equally easily (using the term *versions* in the sense just explained—that is, record and field orderings might be different, but content remains the same); we will see how this works out in the next section. Within those TR tables, rows have a top-to-bottom ordering and columns have a left-to-right ordering. And (important again!) a row-and-column intersection within such a table, which we will call a **cell**, can be addressed via [*i,j*]-style subscripting, where *i* is the row number and *j* is the column number.

Details of the mapping of files to TR tables are deferred to the next section. Here we just stress the point that it is nothing like the direct-image kind of mapping discussed in Section A.1. In particular, rows in TR tables do *not* correspond in any one-to-one kind of way to records at the file level, nor *a fortiori* do they correspond in any one-to-one kind of way to tuples at the relational level. By way of illustration, Fig. A.4 shows a TR table, the **Field Values Table**, corresponding to the file of Fig. A.3; observe in particular that, as claimed, the rows do not correspond in any obvious way to the records shown in Fig. A.3.

In order to be able to reconstruct the file of Fig. A.3 from the Field Values Table of Fig. A.4, we need another table, the **Record Reconstruction Table** (see Fig. A.5). Note that the values in the cells of that table are not supplier numbers or status values (and so on) any longer—despite the column labels—but are *row numbers* instead. For further explanation, see the next section.

Column sequence:	1	2	3	4
	S#	SNAME	STATUS	CITY
Row sequence: 1	S1	Adams	10	Athens
2	S2	Blake	20	London
3	S3	Clark	20	London
4	S4	Jones	30	Paris
5	S5	Smith	30	Paris

Fig. A.4   Field Values Table for the file of Fig. A.3

Column sequence:	1	2	3	4
	S#	SNAME	STATUS	CITY
Row sequence: 1	5	4	4	5
2	4	5	2	4
3	2	2	3	1
4	3	1	1	2
5	1	3	5	3

Fig. A.5   Record Reconstruction Table for the file of Fig. A.3

A.3   THE BASIC IDEA

The crucial insight underlying the TR model can be characterized as follows. Let r be a record within some file at the file level. Then:

> **The stored form of r involves two logically distinct pieces, a set of field values and a set of "linkage" information that ties those field values together, and there is a wide range of possibilities for physically storing each piece.**

In direct-image systems, the two pieces are stored together; in other words, the linkage information in such systems is represented by *physical contiguity.* In TR, by contrast, *the two pieces are kept separate*—the field values are kept in the Field Values Table, and the linkage information is kept in the Record Reconstruction Table. And it is that separation that is the fundamental source of the numerous benefits that TR is able to provide.

The Field Values Table

Now, you probably worked out for yourself how the Field Values Table of Fig. A.4 was derived from the file of Fig. A.3: Basically, each column of the table contains the values from the corresponding field of the file, *rearranged into ascending sort order.* Note immediately, therefore, that no matter what order the records of the file appear in initially, we wind up with the same Field Values Table (in our example, all 2,880 versions of the file map to the same Field Values Table). Moreover, even though we are not yet in a position to describe how that table is used (we need to discuss the Record Reconstruction Table first), we can mention a few points that should make at least intuitive sense right away:

- The fact that each column of the Field Values Table is in sorted order is clearly going to help with user-level ORDER BY requests. For example, a request to see suppliers in city name sequence should not require a run-time sort, nor an index.

- The same is true of a request to see suppliers in *reverse* city name sequence (i.e., descending sort order)—the implementation can simply process the Field Values Table bottom to top instead of top to bottom.

- Analogous remarks apply to *every single attribute;* that is, the Field Values Table effectively represents *many different sort orders* simultaneously (in effect, a sort order in both directions on every individual attribute).

- Requests involving specific value lookups—for example, a request to see suppliers in London—can be implemented by means of an efficient binary search. And, again, analogous remarks apply to every attribute.

We close this subsection by observing that the Field Values Table can be thought of as a kind of *bridge* between the user perception of the data (meaning the original user-level relation and/or the corresponding file) and other internal TR structures. In particular, the Field Values Table is the only TR table that contains user data as such—all of the rest contain internal information (typically pointers), information that makes sense to TR but is not directly relevant to, or exposed to, the user at all.

The Record Reconstruction Table

Fig. A.6 shows the Field Values Table from Fig. A.4 side by side with the Record Reconstruction Table from Fig. A.5. Observe that the two tables are *isomorphic;* indeed, there is a direct one-to-one correspondence between the cells of the two tables, as we will see in a moment (i.e., both tables have the same number of rows and columns as the file of Fig. A.3 has records and fields, respectively). Observe too that, as noted in Section A.2, the entries in the Record Reconstruction Table cells are not supplier numbers or supplier names (etc.) any longer; instead, they are **row numbers**, and those row numbers can be thought of as **pointers** to the rows of the Field Values Table or the Record Reconstruction Table or both, depending on the context in which they are used. (For this reason, the columns in the Record Reconstruction Table really ought not to be labeled S#, SNAME, and so on, as shown in the figure; however, keeping those labels helps to make certain later explanations easier to follow.)

Before we explain how the Record Reconstruction Table is built, let us take a look at how it is *used*. Consider the following sequence of operations.

	1	2	3	4		1	2	3	4
	S#	SNAME	STATUS	CITY		S#	SNAME	STATUS	CITY
1	S1	Adams	10	Athens	1	5	4	4	5
2	S2	Blake	20	London	2	4	5	2	4
3	S3	Clark	20	London	3	2	2	3	1
4	S4	Jones	30	Paris	4	3	1	1	2
5	S5	Smith	30	Paris	5	1	3	5	3

Fig. A.6   Field Values Table of Fig. A.4 and a corresponding Record Reconstruction Table

Step 1: Go to cell [*1,1*] of the Field Values Table and fetch the value stored there: namely, the supplier number S1. That value is the **first** field value (that is, the S# field value) within a certain supplier record in the suppliers file.

Step 2: Go to the *same* cell (that is, cell [*1,1*]) of the Record Reconstruction Table and fetch the value stored there: namely, the row number 5. That row number is interpreted to mean that the *next* field value (which is to say, the **second** or SNAME value) within the supplier record whose S# field value is S1 is to be found in the SNAME position of the **fifth** row of the Field Values Table—in other words, in cell [*5,2*] of the Field Values Table. Go to that cell and fetch the value stored there (supplier name Smith).

Step 3: Go to the corresponding Record Reconstruction Table cell [*5,2*] and fetch the row number stored there (*3*). The next (**third** or STATUS) field value within the supplier record we are reconstructing is in the STATUS position in the **third** row of the Field Values Table—in other words, in cell [*3,3*]. Go to that cell and fetch the value stored there (status 20).

Step 4: Go to the corresponding Record Reconstruction Table cell [*3,3*] and fetch the value stored there (which is *3* again). The next (**fourth** or CITY) field value within the supplier record we are reconstructing is in the CITY position in the **third** row of the Field Values Table—in other words, in cell [*3,4*]. Go to that cell and fetch the value stored there (city name London).

Step 5: Go to the corresponding Record Reconstruction Table cell [*3,4*] and fetch the value stored there (*1*). Now, the "next" field value within the supplier record we are reconstructing looks like it ought to be the *fifth* such value; however, supplier records have only four fields, so that "fifth" wraps around to become the *first*. Thus, the "next" (first or S#) field value within the supplier record we are reconstructing is in the S# position in the first row of the Field Values Table—in other words, in cell [*1,1*]. But that is where we came in, and the process stops.

Clearly, the foregoing sequence of operations reconstructs one particular record from the suppliers file—to be specific, the one shown as record number *4* in Fig. A.3:

	S#	SNAME	STATUS	CITY
4	S1	Smith	20	London

By the way, note how the row-number pointers we followed in the foregoing example form a *ring*—in fact, two isomorphic rings, one in the Field Values Table and one in the Record Reconstruction Table (see Fig. A.7). *Note:* For obvious reasons, the rings are also called *zigzags,* and the reconstruction algorithm is known informally as *the zigzag algorithm.*

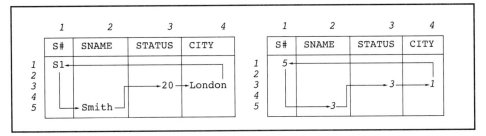

Fig. A.7 Pointer rings (examples)

As an exercise, try reconstructing another supplier record for yourself. If you start with cell [2,1] in the Field Values Table, you should obtain record 3 from Fig. A.3. Likewise, starting with cell [3,1] gives record 5; starting with cell [4,1] gives record 1; and starting with cell [5,1] gives record 2. *Observe the net effect:* If we process the entire Field Values Table in supplier number order by going top to bottom down the S# column—that is, if we carry out the record reconstruction process five times, starting successively with cells [1,1], [2,1], [3,1], [4,1], and [5,1]—then we reconstruct a version of the entire suppliers file in which the records appear in ascending supplier number order. In other words, we have implemented the following SQL query:

```
SELECT  S.S#, S.SNAME, S.STATUS, S.CITY
FROM    S
ORDER   BY S# ;
```

Likewise, to implement this query—

```
SELECT  S.S#, S.SNAME, S.STATUS, S.CITY
FROM    S
ORDER   BY S# DESC ;
```

—all we have to do is process the supplier number column of the Field Values Table in reverse order and do the reconstructions starting from cell [5,1], then [4,1], and so on. And we do not have to do a run-time sort in either case, nor do we have to use an index.

What is more, precisely because the pointers in the Record Reconstruction Table form rings, we can enter those rings at any point. When we apply the reconstruction algorithm, therefore, we can start at any cell we like. For example, if we start with cell [1,3]—that is, the first cell in the STATUS column—we obtain the record:

	S#	SNAME	STATUS	CITY
3	S2	Jones	10	Paris

(More precisely, we obtain a version of this record in which the left-to-right field ordering is STATUS, then CITY, then S#, then SNAME.) Following on down the STATUS column—that is, starting the reconstruction process successively with cells [2,3], [3,3], [4,3], and [5,3]—we eventually obtain the entire suppliers file in ascending status order:

```
SELECT  S.STATUS, S.CITY, S.S#, S.SNAME
FROM    S
ORDER   BY STATUS ;
```

In analogous fashion, if we process the Record Reconstruction Table in sequence by entries in the SNAME column, we obtain the suppliers file in ascending supplier name order; likewise, if we process it in sequence by entries in the CITY column, we obtain the file in ascending city name order. In other words, the Record Reconstruction Table and the Field Values Table together represent all of these orderings simultaneously—without (to repeat) any need for either indexes or run-time sorting.

Now consider the following query, which involves a simple equality restriction:

```
SELECT  S.S#, S.SNAME, S.STATUS, S.CITY
FROM    S
WHERE   S.CITY = 'London' ;
```

Since the CITY column (like every column) of the Field Values Table is kept in sorted order, a binary search can be used to find the cells containing London. Given the Field Values Table of Fig. A.6, those cells turn out to be [2,4] and [3,4]. Zigzags can now be constructed by following the pointer rings running through cells [2,4] and [3,4] of the Record Reconstruction Table. In the example, those zigzags look like this:

```
[2,4], [4,1], [3,2], [2,3]
```

and

```
[3,4], [1,1], [5,2], [3,3]
```

Superimposing these zigzags on the Field Values Table, we obtain the field values for the desired records:

	S#	SNAME	STATUS	CITY
1	S4	Clark	20	London
4	S1	Smith	20	London

The Field Values Table and the Record Reconstruction Table together offer direct support for many other user-level operations too, in addition to simple ORDER BYs and equality restrictions. In fact, most if not all of the fundamental relational operations—restrict, project, join, summarize, and others (not to mention the operation of *duplicate elimination,* which is needed internally, even in true relational systems)—have implementation algorithms that rely on the ability to access the data in some specific sequence. By way of example, consider join. We saw in Chapter 18 that *sort/merge* is a good way to implement join. Well, TR lets us do a sort/merge join without having to do the sort!—or, at least, without having to do the *run-time* sort (the sort is done when the Field Values and Record Reconstruction Tables are built, which is to say at load time, loosely speaking). For example, to join suppliers and parts over city names, we simply have to access each of the two Field Values Tables in city name sequence and do a merge-style join.

One important implication of all of the foregoing is that life becomes much easier for the system optimizer; to be more specific, the access path selection process (see Chapter 18) becomes much simpler—even completely unnecessary, in some cases. Another implication is that many of the auxiliary structures (indexes, hashes, etc.) found in traditional DBMSs become unnecessary too. Yet another implication is that physical database design becomes much easier, involving as it does far fewer options and choices, and the same is true for performance tuning.

Building the Record Reconstruction Table

Consider the effect of applying various sort orderings to the file of Fig. A.3. For example, suppose we sort by ascending supplier number; then we get the records in the sequence *4, 3, 5, 1, 2.* Let us call that sequence "the permutation corresponding to ascending S# ordering" (*the S# permutation* for short). Other permutations are as follows:

- `Ascending SNAME  : 2, 5, 1, 3, 4`
- `Ascending STATUS : 3, 1, 4, 2, 5`
- `Ascending CITY   : 2, 1, 4, 3, 5`

These permutations are summarized in the following *Permutation Table,* in which cell [*i,j*] contains the record number within the suppliers file of the record that appears in the *i*th position when that file is sorted by ascending values of the *j*th field.

	1 S#	2 SNAME	3 STATUS	4 CITY
1	*4*	*2*	*3*	*2*
2	*3*	*5*	*1*	*1*
3	*5*	*1*	*4*	*4*
4	*1*	*3*	*2*	*3*
5	*2*	*4*	*5*	*5*

As the table shows, the S# permutation (to repeat) is the sequence:

`4, 3, 5, 1, 2`

The *inverse* of this permutation is the sequence:

`4, 5, 2, 1, 3`

This inverse permutation is that unique permutation that, if applied to the original sequence *4, 3, 5, 1, 2,* will produce the sequence *1, 2, 3, 4, 5.* (If *SEQ* is the original sequence *4, 3, 5, 1, 2,* then the fourth entry in *SEQ* is *1,* the fifth is *2,* the second is *3,* and so on.) More generally, if we think of any given permutation as a vector *V,* then the inverse permutation *V'* can be obtained in accordance with the simple rule that if $V[i] = i'$, then $V'[i'] = i$. Applying this rule to each of the permutations in our given Permutation Table, we obtain the following *Inverse Permutation Table:*

	1	2	3	4
	S#	SNAME	STATUS	CITY
1	4	3	2	2
2	5	1	4	1
3	2	4	1	4
4	1	5	3	3
5	3	2	5	5

Now we can build the Record Reconstruction Table. For example, the first (S#) column can be built as follows:

> Go to cell [*i,1*] of the Inverse Permutation Table. Let that cell contain the value *r;* also, let the next cell to the right, cell [*i,2*], contain the value *r'*. Go to the *r*th row of the Record Reconstruction Table and place the value *r'* in cell [*r,1*].

Executing this algorithm for $i = 1, 2, ..., 5$ yields the entire S# column of the Record Reconstruction Table. The other columns are built analogously. *Note:* As an exercise, we strongly suggest that you work through this algorithm and build the complete Record Reconstruction Table. Doing this exercise should give you the insight to understand why the algorithm works. Incidentally, note that the Record Reconstruction Table is built entirely from the *file*—the Field Values Table plays no part in the process at all.

The Record Reconstruction Table Is Not Unique

In our discussions in the previous subsection, we said (among other things) that the CITY permutation for the suppliers file of Fig. A.3 was the sequence *2, 1, 4, 3, 5*. Noting, however, that suppliers S1 and S4 are both in the same city, as are suppliers S2 and S3, we might equally well have said the city permutation was *2, 4, 1, 3, 5*—or *3, 1, 4, 2, 5*, or *3, 4, 1, 2, 5*. In other words, the CITY permutation is not unique.[2] It follows that the Permutation Table is not unique, and hence the Record Reconstruction Table is not unique either. Given a particular user-level relation, however, it turns out that there are always certain Record Reconstruction Tables that are "preferred," in the sense that they display certain desirable properties that Record Reconstruction Tables in general do not. The details are beyond the scope of this appendix, however; see reference [A.1] for further discussion.

A.4   CONDENSED COLUMNS

Consider Fig. A.8, which shows a possible file corresponding to our usual parts relation; Fig. A.9, which shows the corresponding Field Values Table; and Fig. A.10, which shows a corresponding "preferred" Record Reconstruction Table.

---

[2] The same is true for the STATUS permutation, but not as it happens for the SNAME permutation (and obviously not for the S# permutation).

	1	2	3	4	5
	P#	PNAME	COLOR	WEIGHT	CITY
1	P1	Nut	Red	12.0	London
2	P2	Bolt	Green	17.0	Paris
3	P3	Screw	Blue	17.0	Oslo
4	P4	Screw	Red	14.0	London
5	P5	Cam	Blue	12.0	Paris
6	P6	Cog	Red	19.0	London

Fig. A.8 A file for the usual parts relation

	1	2	3	4	5
	P#	PNAME	COLOR	WEIGHT	CITY
1	P1	Bolt	Blue	12.0	London
2	P2	Cam	Blue	12.0	London
3	P3	Cog	Green	14.0	London
4	P4	Nut	Red	17.0	Oslo
5	P5	Screw	Red	17.0	Paris
6	P6	Screw	Red	19.0	Paris

Fig. A.9 Field Values Table for the file of Fig. A.8

	1	2	3	4	5
	P#	PNAME	COLOR	WEIGHT	CITY
1	4	3	2	1	1
2	1	1	4	6	4
3	5	6	5	2	6
4	6	4	1	4	3
5	2	2	3	5	2
6	3	5	6	3	5

Fig. A.10 Record Reconstruction Table for the file of Fig. A.8

Observe now that the Field Values Table of Fig. A.9 involves a considerable amount of *redundancy*—for example, the city name London appears three times, the weight 17.0 appears twice, and so on. **Condensing** the columns of that table simply eliminates that redundancy. The result is thus a table in which each column contains just the pertinent *distinct* values, as shown in Fig. A.11. Points arising:

1. It is legitimate, and indeed desirable, to apply the condensing process *selectively*. In particular, there is no point in condensing column P#, because part numbers are unique.

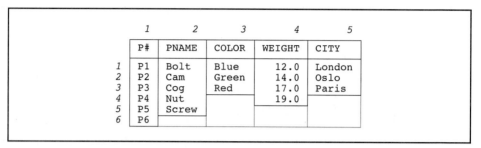

Fig. A.11   Condensed version of the Field Values Table of Fig. A.9

2. Field values in condensed columns are effectively *shared* across records of the parts file. For example, the city name London in cell [*1,5*] is shared by three part records: namely, those for parts P1, P4, and P6. One consequence is that update operations, especially INSERT, have the potential to run faster than before, because they might be able to use field values that already exist, effectively sharing those values with other records; for example, consider what happens if the user inserts a part tuple for part P7, with part name Nut, color Red, weight 18.0, city London. As noted in Section A.1, however, update operations in general are beyond the scope of this appendix.

3. Condensed columns constitute a kind of data compression, of course (albeit a kind not typically found in conventional direct-image implementations)—but notice how *much* compression they can provide. For example, imagine a Department of Motor Vehicles relation representing drivers' licenses, with a tuple for every license issued in (say) the state of California, for a total of perhaps 20 million tuples. But there are certainly not 20 million different heights, or weights, or hair colors, or expiry dates! In other words, the compression ratio might quite literally be of the order of a million or so to one.

Row Ranges

Back to Fig. A.11. Needless to say, we cannot *just* replace (e.g.) the original three appearances of the city name London by one such appearance, because we would be losing information if we did. (The condensed CITY column contains three values, but there are six parts. How would we know which part is in which city?) So we need to keep some additional information that, in effect, allows us to reconstruct the original *un*condensed Field Values Table from its condensed counterpart. One way to do this is to keep, alongside each field value in each condensed column in the Field Values Table, a specification of *the range of row numbers* for rows in the uncondensed version of that table in which that value

	P#	PNAME		COLOR		WEIGHT		CITY	
		1		*2*		*3*		*4*	*5*
1	P1	Bolt	[1:1]	Blue	[1:2]	12.0	[1:2]	London	[1:3]
2	P2	Cam	[2:2]	Green	[3:3]	14.0	[3:3]	Oslo	[4:4]
3	P3	Cog	[3:3]	Red	[4:6]	17.0	[4:5]	Paris	[5:6]
4	P4	Nut	[4:4]			19.0	[6:6]		
5	P5	Screw	[5:6]						
6	P6								

Fig. A.12   Condensed Field Values Table with row ranges

originally appeared, as shown in Fig. A.12.[3] For example, consider cell [*3,4*] in that figure, which contains the weight value 17.0. Alongside that weight value appears the row range "[*4:5*]." That row range means that if the Field Values Table were to be "uncondensed," as it were, then the weight value 17.0 would appear—in the WEIGHT column, naturally, which is to say in column *4*—in rows *4* to *5,* inclusive, within that uncondensed table.

Incidentally, do not confuse a specification of the form [*4:5*] with one of the form [*4,5*]. The former (with a colon separator) denotes a certain range of row numbers, as just explained; the latter (with a comma separator) is a subscript that identifies a certain cell, at a certain row-and-column intersection.

There is another point to be made regarding row ranges. Take another look at (for example) column *3,* the COLOR column, in the Field Values Table of Fig. A.12. Clearly, that column specifies exactly (a) the set of COLOR values that currently appear in the parts file, together with (b) for each such value, the *number of times* that value appears in that file. In other words, the column can be regarded as a **histogram**, as shown in Fig. A.13. In general, in fact, the overall condensed Field Values Table with its row ranges can very usefully be thought of as a set of histograms, one for each condensed column. One consequence of this fact is that queries that conceptually involve such histograms are likely to perform well (consider, e.g., the query "How many parts are there of each color?"). See Section A.6.

To continue with the same point for a moment: If the Field Values Table can be thought of as a set of histograms, then the Record Reconstruction Table—as we already know from the previous section—can effectively be thought of as a set of **permutations**. For example, if we reconstruct the parts file using column 3 of the Record Reconstruction Table of Fig. A.10, we obtain a version of the file that is ordered by part color; in other

---

[3] We have deliberately made the row ranges in the figure look like the intervals of Chapter 23, but in fact that row range information could be physically represented in numerous different ways. One way would be to store just the beginning or the end of the range. Another would be to replace the ranges by counts. And so on.

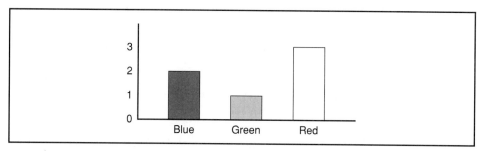

Fig. A.13   Color histogram (based on Fig. A.12)

words, we get what we might call a "COLOR permutation" of that file. Thus, we can characterize the TR representation of any given set of data, informally, as a set of histograms plus a set of permutations (of the data in question). Such histograms and permutations are, in essence, what the TR representation is really all about.

Implications for Record Reconstruction

Condensing the Field Values Table clearly destroys the one-to-one relationship between cells of that table and cells of the Record Reconstruction Table. It follows that the record reconstruction algorithm we have been using so far will no longer work. However, it is easy enough to fix this problem, thus:

> Consider cell $[i,j]$ of the Record Reconstruction Table. Instead of going to cell $[i,j]$ of the Field Values Table, go to cell $[i',j]$ of that table, where cell $[i',j]$ is that unique cell within column j of that table that contains a row range that includes row i.

By way of example, consider cell *[3,4]* of the Record Reconstruction Table of Fig. A.10, which appears (of course) in column *4*—the WEIGHT column—of that table. To find the corresponding weight value in the Field Values Table of Fig. A.12, we search the WEIGHT column of that table, looking for the unique entry in that column that contains a row range that includes row *3*. From the figure, we see that the entry in question is cell *[2,4]* (the corresponding range of rows is *[3:3]*), and the required weight value is 14.0. As an exercise, use the Record Reconstruction Table of Fig. A.10 together with the condensed Field Values Table of Fig. A.12 to reconstruct the parts file in its entirety (start with column 5 in order to obtain the result in ascending city name sequence).

A.5   MERGED COLUMNS

In the previous section, we discussed condensed columns, which can be characterized as a way of sharing field values across records—but the records in question all came from the same file. **Merged** columns, by contrast, can be characterized as a way of sharing field values across records where the records in question *might or might not* all come from the same file. The basic idea is that distinct fields at the file level can map to the same Field Values Table column at the TR level, just as long as the fields in question are of the same data type.

We begin with an example involving just one file. Consider the bill-of-materials relation MMQ depicted in Fig. A.14 (a variation on Fig. 4.6 from Chapter 4). First we show what happens in this example *without* merged columns; then we take a look at how the situation changes if we apply the merged-column technique. Thus, Fig. A.15 shows a possible file corresponding to the relation of Fig. A.14; Fig. A.16 shows the corresponding condensed Field Values Table; and Fig. A.17 shows a corresponding "preferred" Record Reconstruction Table.

MMQ	MAJOR_P#	MINOR_P#	QTY
	P1	P2	2
	P1	P3	4
	P1	P4	1
	P2	P3	3
	P2	P4	8
	P2	P5	6
	P3	P4	3
	P3	P6	4
	P5	P6	3

Fig. A.14   The bill-of-materials relation MMQ

	1	2	3
	MAJOR_P#	MINOR_P#	QTY
1	P3	P4	3
2	P1	P3	4
3	P2	P4	8
4	P1	P4	1
5	P2	P5	6
6	P3	P6	4
7	P1	P2	2
8	P5	P6	3
9	P2	P3	3

Fig. A.15   A file for the bill-of-materials relation of Fig. A.14

	1	2	3
	MAJOR_P#	MINOR_P#	QTY
1	P1 [1:3]	P2 [1:1]	1 [1:1]
2	P2 [4:6]	P3 [2:3]	2 [2:2]
3	P3 [7:8]	P4 [4:6]	3 [3:5]
4	P5 [9:9]	P5 [7:7]	4 [6:7]
5		P6 [8:9]	6 [8:8]
6			8 [9:9]

Fig. A.16   Condensed Field Values Table for the file of Fig. A.15

	1	2	3
	MAJOR_P#	MINOR_P#	QTY
1	1	2	3
2	2	6	1
3	4	3	4
4	3	1	7
5	5	9	9
6	7	4	2
7	6	8	8
8	8	7	6
9	9	5	5

Fig. A.17   Record Reconstruction Table for the file of Fig. A.15

Now we can start our examination of merged columns. Going right back to relation MMQ (Fig. A.14), it is clear that attributes MAJOR_P# and MINOR_P# are of the same type, and hence that fields MAJOR_P# and MINOR_P# of the corresponding file are of the same type, too. They can therefore be mapped to the same column of the Field Values Table. Fig. A.18 shows what happens. Points arising:

1. Columns MAJOR_P# and MINOR_P# have been merged into a single column. That column contains all of the field values (i.e., part numbers) that previously appeared in either column MAJOR_P# or column MINOR_P# in the table before merging. Duplicates have been eliminated.

	1		2
	MAJOR_P# + MINOR_P#		QTY
1	P1 [1:3]	[:]	1 [1:1]
2	P2 [4:6]	[1:1]	2 [2:2]
3	P3 [7:8]	[2:3]	3 [3:5]
4	P4 [:]	[4:6]	4 [6:7]
5	P5 [9:9]	[7:7]	6 [8:8]
6	P6 [:]	[8:9]	8 [9:9]

Fig. A.18   Field Values Table of Fig. A.16 after merging the first two columns

2. Each cell in the merged column thus contains a single part number, together with *two* row ranges. The first row range indicates which rows of the uncondensed Field Values Table the corresponding part number appears in as a "major" part number; the second indicates which rows of that uncondensed Field Values Table the corresponding part number appears in as a "minor" part number. Those row ranges are basically the same as they were in the previous version of the Field Values Table, except for occasional appearances of the special *empty* row range "[:]," which is used when the indicated part number does not appear at all in the corresponding column of the uncondensed Field Values Table (for example, P1 never appears as a "minor" part number).

3. In the merged table, the merged column is column *1* and the QTY column is column *2* (after all, the table now does have just two columns, not three). Column *2*, the QTY column, is the same as it was in Fig. A.16.

4. The Record Reconstruction Table remains unchanged.[4] However, columns *1* and *2* of that table now both correspond to column *1* (the merged column) of the Field Values Table; column *1* refers to the first row range in that merged column and column *2* to the second. Column *3* of the Record Reconstruction Table now refers to column *2* of the Field Values Table.

There are many advantages to the merged-columns idea; here we describe just one. It has to do with join operations. Suppose we want to join relation MMQ to itself, matching minor part numbers in "the first copy" (as it were) of the relation with major part numbers in "the second copy." Then we can tell *in a single pass* over the merged Field Values Table just which tuples join to which! For example, row *3* of that table (which contains the part number P3) shows a "minor part number" row range of [*2:3*] and a "major" one of [*7:8*]. It follows immediately that the second and third tuples in "the first copy" of relation MMQ both join to the seventh and eighth tuples in "the second copy." And similar remarks apply to all of the other rows of that merged Field Values Table. In effect, therefore, we can do a sort/merge join without doing the sort (as noted earlier in this appendix) *and without doing the merge, either!*[5]

Note: Of course, there is no such thing as the "second" tuple, or the "third" tuple, or the "*i*th" tuple for any value of *i*, in any relation; the tuples of a relation are unordered. What we really meant by such sloppy phrasing was as follows:

- Let *F1* be the file reconstructed from the Field Values Table of Fig. A.18 by processing column MAJOR_P# of the Record Reconstruction Table of Fig. A.17 in top-to-bottom sequence. Then "the first copy" of relation MMQ is the file *F1,* and "the *i*th tuple" of that copy is that unique tuple of relation MMQ that corresponds to the *i*th record in *F1.*

- Likewise, let *F2* be the file reconstructed from the Field Values Table of Fig. A.18 by processing column MINOR_P# of the Record Reconstruction Table of Fig. A.17 in top-to-bottom sequence. Then "the second copy" of relation MMQ is the file *F2,* and

---

[4] Actually it can be improved in a variety of ways, but the details are beyond the scope of this appendix.

[5] More accurately, the sort and the merge are not done *at run time;* instead, they are done ahead of time, when the Field Values and Record Reconstruction Tables are built (basically at load time).

"the *i*th tuple" of that copy is that unique tuple of relation MMQ that corresponds to the *i*th record in *F2*.

We close this section by repeating the point that the merged-columns idea can be used across files as well as within a single file. In the case of suppliers and parts, for example, we might have just one Field Values Table (both merged and condensed) for the entire database, with one column for supplier numbers (from relvars S and SP), one for part numbers (from SP and P), one for city names (from S and P), and so on. As a matter of fact, since TR allows us to include values in the Field Values Table that do not actually appear at this time in any relation in the database, we might regard TR as a true "domain-oriented" representation of the entire database. See reference [A.1] for further discussion.

A.6   IMPLEMENTING THE RELATIONAL OPERATORS

In this section, we briefly consider what is involved in using TR to implement certain of the relational operators. We base our examples on the relvars S and SPJ from the suppliers-parts-projects database (sample values are shown in Fig. A.19). A merged and condensed Field Values Table is shown in Fig. A.20, and "preferred" Record Reconstruction Tables are shown in Fig. A.21.

Restrict

Consider the restriction query:[6]

```
SPJ WHERE QTY = 200
```

To implement this query, we do a binary search on column QTY of the Field Values Table (Fig. A.20), looking for a cell containing the value 200; note that such a cell must be unique if it exists at all, because the column is condensed. If the search fails, we know immediately that the result of the query is empty. In the case at hand, however, the search finds cell [2,7], which contains, in addition to the specified QTY value, the row range [3:6]. It follows

S	S#	SNAME	STATUS	CITY	SPJ	S#	P#	J#	QTY
	S1	Smith	20	London		S1	P1	J1	200
	S2	Jones	10	Paris		S1	P3	J2	100
	S3	Blake	30	Paris		S2	P1	J1	200
	S4	Clark	20	London		S2	P1	J2	500
	S5	Adams	30	Athens		S2	P2	J2	500
						S3	P1	J1	100
						S3	P2	J2	500
						S3	P3	J1	200
						S3	P3	J2	200

Fig. A.19   Relvars S and SPJ (sample values)

---

[6] We use **Tutorial D**, not SQL, as a basis for all remaining examples in this appendix.

	1	2	3	4	
	S#	SNAME	STATUS	CITY	
1	S1 [1:2]	Adams [1:1]	10 [1:1]	Athens [1:1]	
2	S2 [3:5]	Blake [2:2]	20 [2:3]	London [2:3]	
3	S3 [6:9]	Clark [3:3]	30 [4:5]	Paris [4:5]	
4	S4 [:]	Jones [4:4]			
5	S5 [:]	Smith [5:5]			

	5	6	7
	P#	J#	QTY
	P1 [1:4]	J1 [1:4]	100 [1:2]
	P2 [5:6]	J2 [5:9]	200 [3:6]
	P3 [7:9]		500 [7:9]

Fig. A.20 Merged Field Values Table for suppliers and shipments

	1	2	3	4		1	5	6	7
	S#	SNAME	STATUS	CITY		S#	P#	J#	QTY
1	5	5	4	5	1	2	1	2	2
2	4	4	2	1	2	8	2	3	6
3	2	2	3	4	3	3	3	4	1
4	3	3	5	2	4	4	7	5	3
5	1	1	1	3	5	5	8	1	8
					6	1	9	6	9
					7	6	4	7	4
					8	7	5	8	5
					9	9	6	9	7

Fig. A.21 Record Reconstruction Tables for suppliers and shipments

immediately that cells [3,7], [4,7], [5,7], and [6,7] of the shipments Record Reconstruction Table:

a. Contain row numbers for the cell in the Field Values Table that contains the QTY value 200 (and indeed they do all include the row number 2)

b. Contain row numbers for the "next" cell in the shipments Record Reconstruction Table

Zigzags can therefore be constructed by following the appropriate pointer rings in the shipments Record Reconstruction Table. In the example, those zigzags look like this:

```
[3,7], [1,1], [2,5], [2,6]
[4,7], [3,1], [3,5], [3,6]
[5,7], [8,1], [7,5], [4,6]
[6,7], [9,1], [9,5], [6,6]
```

Following these zigzags through the shipments Record Reconstruction Table and accessing the Field Values Table accordingly, we obtain the desired result:

S#	P#	J#	QTY
S1	P1	J1	200
S2	P1	J1	200
S3	P3	J1	200
S3	P3	J2	200

For a second example, consider a query that involves a "<" restriction instead of an "=" one:

```
SPJ WHERE QTY < 150
```

It should be clear that this query too is easily handled, this time by:

a. Doing a *sequential* search on column QTY of the Field Values Table

b. Reconstructing all corresponding records, and hence user-level tuples, for each cell encountered during that search

c. Stopping as soon as we find a cell in column QTY of the Field Values Table that contains a QTY value of 150 or greater

Result:

S#	P#	J#	QTY
S1	P3	J2	100
S3	P1	J1	100

Now consider this example:

```
SPJ WHERE S# = S# ('S3') AND QTY = 100
```

By means of searches on the S# and QTY columns of the Field Values Table, we discover from the applicable row ranges that there are four shipments with supplier number S3 but only two with quantity 100. The best strategy is therefore to use the zigzags associated with quantity 100 and check during record reconstruction to see whether the supplier number is S3, stopping reconstruction of the record in question if not. Result:

S#	P#	J#	QTY
S3	P1	J1	100

Finally, we consider the effect of replacing the AND by an OR:

```
SPJ WHERE S# = S# ('S3') OR QTY = 100
```

We can implement this query by, first, finding all tuples for supplier S3, and then finding all tuples not already found in the first step that have QTY value 100 (or the other way around). Assuming, reasonably enough, that the two steps are executed in such a manner that the two results produced are ordered in the same way (in ascending S# order, say), then they can be merged to produce the desired overall result:

S#	P#	J#	QTY
S1	P3	J2	100
S3	P1	J1	100
S3	P2	J2	500
S3	P3	J1	200
S3	P3	J2	200

Project

To compute (say) the projection SPJ{S#,P#,J#}, we simply go through the usual reconstruction process for shipments, but skip the reconstruction step for attribute QTY in each record. By contrast, to compute (say) the projection SPJ{S#,P#}—which unlike the previous example involves some duplicate elimination—it is desirable to process the Record Reconstruction Table for shipments in a sequence that will deliver tuples according to the major-to-minor ordering S#-then-P# (or P#-then-S#); duplicates will be adjacent in this ordering and thus can easily be eliminated. We omit further details here, except to say that "preferred" Record Reconstruction Tables are preferred precisely because they support such orderings.

Summarize

Consider this query:

```
SUMMARIZE SPJ PER S { S# } ADD COUNT AS SHIP_COUNT
```

Here is the result:

S#	SHIP_COUNT
S1	2
S2	3
S3	4
S4	0
S5	0

Now, the S# column of the Field Values Table looks like this (see Fig. A.20):

	S#
1	S1 [1:2]
2	S2 [3:5]
3	S3 [6:9]
4	S4 [:]
5	S5 [:]

Thus, it should be clear that the desired result is directly and immediately obtainable from the row ranges in this column.

Here is another example (note our use of the BY variant of SUMMARIZE here):

```
SUMMARIZE SPJ BY { S# } ADD MIN ( QTY ) AS MNQ
```

To see how this query is implemented, consider supplier S2. From the row range *[3:5]* for this supplier in the Field Values Table (Fig A.20), we know that the rows of the shipments Record Reconstruction Table that apply to this supplier are rows *3, 4,* and *5*—that is, the applicable *cells* of that table are *[3,1]*, *[4,1]*, and *[5,1]*, respectively. Following the zigzags to the corresponding QTY cells in that table, we find that those cells contain pointers to the Field Values Table rows *2, 3,* and *3,* respectively. Since the QTY column (like *all* columns) in that table is kept in ascending order, it is immediately clear that the *minimum* QTY value for supplier S2 is the one in row *2* of the Field Values Table: namely, the QTY value 200.

Join

We have already indicated in earlier sections what is involved in implementing joins. Here we just mention a few additional points:

- Since TR effectively always does a sort/merge join but the sort and the merge are done ahead of time, run-time join costs are additive (linear), not multiplicative. Reference [A.1] gives an example involving a join of five relations, where the TR implementation takes five seconds and a brute force implementation (see Chapter 18) would take over three trillion years, or some 200 times the age of the universe (!).

- The more relations that need to be joined, the more the gain. In other words, the more complex the query, the more significant the TR advantage is over direct-image systems.

- Because all joins are implemented the same way, there is no need to do the complex access path selection process that direct-image systems have to do.

- Moreover, that access path selection process that direct-image systems have to do is of dubious accuracy anyway, because of the difficulty of estimating intermediate result sizes (among other reasons).

Union, Intersect, and Difference

As a basis for examples in this subsection, let us extend the database to include the parts relvar P, with its usual sample values. Let us also extend the CITY column of the merged Field Values Table to include part city names and corresponding row ranges. That column will look like this:

```
       ┌─────────────────────────┐
       │ CITY                    │
       ├─────────────────────────┤
     1 │ Athens [1:1] [  :  ]    │
     2 │ London [2:3] [1:3]      │
     3 │ Oslo   [  : ] [4:4]     │
     4 │ Paris  [4:5] [5:6]      │
       └─────────────────────────┘
```

Now consider operations of the form

```
X { CITY } op Y { CITY }
```

where *X* is S or P, *Y* is the other one, and *op* is UNION, INTERSECT, or MINUS. The use of the merged CITY column in the Field Values Table in implementing such operations should be obvious. In essence:

- *UNION:* A given city name appears in the result if and only if it has a nonempty row range for suppliers or parts or both. In other words, the union is just the set of all city names in the merged column.

- *INTERSECT:* A given city name appears in the result if and only if it has a nonempty row range for both suppliers and parts.

- *MINUS:* If *X* is S, a given city name appears in the result if and only if it has a non-empty row range for suppliers and an empty one for parts. Similarly, if *X* is P, a given city name appears in the result if and only if it has a nonempty row range for parts and an empty one for suppliers.

All of these operations can clearly be implemented in a single pass over the CITY column in the merged Field Values Table.

Closing Remarks

There is much, much more that could be said on the question of using TR to implement the relational operators, but the examples discussed in this section should be sufficient to give the general idea. We close with a few miscellaneous observations:

- Direct-image implementations sometimes have to materialize intermediate result relations. So does TR, but such materialization (a) tends to be needed less often, and (b) is more efficient when it does need to be done (largely because of all the presorting), in TR than it is in direct-image systems

- Candidate key (uniqueness) and foreign key (referential) constraints can be implemented very efficiently in TR, thanks to the fact that the Field Values Table is typically both condensed and merged.

- Here is a quote from Codd's very first paper on the relational model [6.1]:

    Once aware that a certain relation exists, the user will expect to be able to exploit that relation using any combination of its attributes as "knowns" and the remaining attributes as "unknowns," because the information (like Everest) is there. This is a system feature (missing from many current information systems) which we shall call (logically) *symmetric exploitation* of relations. Naturally, symmetry in performance is not to be expected.

    But TR gives us symmetry in performance, too!—or, at least, it comes much closer to doing so than direct-image implementations do—thanks to the separation of field values from linkage information, which effectively allows the data to be physically stored in many different sort orders at the same time.

A.7 SUMMARY

We have very briefly described **the TR model**, a radically new approach to implementing relational DBMSs. The TR model represents a specific application of a more general technology known as the **Tarin Transform Method**, which is intended as an implementation technology for data storage and retrieval systems of many kinds (not just DBMSs). The Tarin Transform Method is the subject of a United States patent [A.2] and is the intellectual property of a company called Required Technologies, Inc. (*http://www.requiredtech .com*).

We have discussed what the TR model looks like for read-only, main-memory databases. Although our discussion has unfortunately had to be quite superficial, we hope it was sufficient to give a sense of how TR differs significantly from conventional, direct-image technology. At the same time, many questions will doubtless have occurred to you. For example:

- Can the Field Values and Record Reconstruction Tables be maintained efficiently in the face of arbitrary updates to the database?

- Since the Record Reconstruction Table is isomorphic to the original file—in effect, to the original relation—but has a pointer in every cell instead of a data value, might not TR require much more storage than a conventional direct-image implementation?

- In a disk-based system, will not the zigzagging mean a lot of random access and terrible performance? And can binary search be made to work efficiently on the disk?

And so on. Such questions are indeed serious ones, but (sadly) this is not the place to address them; suffice it to say that they can be and have been addressed satisfactorily, and the solutions have been implemented. For more information, see references [A.1] and [A.2].

REFERENCES AND BIBLIOGRAPHY

A.1 C. J. Date: *Go Faster! The TransRelational™ Approach to DBMS Implementation.* To appear.

The present appendix is heavily based on this book, but the book goes into much more detail and covers many additional topics. In particular, it covers update operations and databases stored on disk, and it addresses the questions raised in Section A.7.

A.2 U.S. Patent and Trademark Office: *Value-Instance-Connectivity Computer-Implemented Database.* U.S. Patent No. 6,009,432 (December 28, 1999).

This is the original patent on the Tarin Transform Method; it is the intellectual property of a company called Required Technologies, Inc. (*http://www.requiredtech.com*). Note, however, that the Tarin Transform Method has been extended considerably beyond what was described in that original patent. In particular, it now encompasses a variety of update techniques and methods for dealing with disk-based databases (see reference [A.1]). Also, note the title of this reference: The original patent was formulated in terms of (among other things) what it called *value stores, instance stores,* and *connectivity stores.* By contrast, the present appendix and reference [A.1] use the terminology of *Field Values Tables* and *Record Reconstruction Tables,* in the belief that these latter terms are more user-friendly in certain respects and better reflect the essence of what is really going on.

SQL Expressions

B.1	Introduction
B.2	Table Expressions
B.3	Boolean Expressions

B.1 INTRODUCTION

Table and boolean expressions are the heart of the SQL language. In this appendix we present a BNF grammar for such expressions; we also elaborate on the semantics of such expressions in certain cases. However, we deliberately omit:

- Details of scalar expressions
- Details of the RECURSIVE form of WITH
- Nonscalar *<select item>*s
- The ONLY variants of *<table ref>* and *<type spec>*
- The GROUPING SETS, ROLLUP, and CUBE options on GROUP BY
- BETWEEN, OVERLAPS, and SIMILAR conditions
- Everything to do with nulls

We should also explain that the names we use for syntactic categories and SQL language constructs are mostly different from those used in the standard itself [4.23], because in our opinion the standard terms are often not very apt. In particular, we abbreviate *<table value constructor>* and *<row value constructor>* to just *<table constructor>* and *<row constructor>*, respectively.

B.2   TABLE EXPRESSIONS

Here first is a BNF grammar for *<table exp>*s:

```
<table exp>
   ::=    <with exp> | <nonwith exp>

<with exp>
   ::=    WITH [ RECURSIVE ]
              <table name> [ ( <column name commalist> ) ] ]
              AS ( <table exp> )
              <nonwith exp>

<nonwith exp>
   ::=    <join table exp> | <nonjoin table exp>

<join table exp>
   ::=    <table ref> [ NATURAL ] JOIN <table ref>
                      [ ON <bool exp>
                      | USING ( <column name commalist> ) ]
        | <table ref> CROSS JOIN <table ref>
        | ( <join table exp> )

<table ref>
   ::=    <table name> [ [ AS ] <range var name>
                        [ ( <column name commalist> ) ] ]
        | ( <nonwith exp> ) [ AS ] <range var name>
                        [ ( <column name commalist> ) ] ]
        | <join table exp>

<nonjoin table exp>
   ::=    <nonjoin table term>
        | <nonwith exp> UNION [ ALL | DISTINCT ]
          [ CORRESPONDING [ BY ( <column name commalist> ) ] ]
              <table term>
        | <nonwith exp> EXCEPT [ ALL | DISTINCT ]
          [ CORRESPONDING [ BY ( <column name commalist> ) ] ]
              <table term>

<nonjoin table term>
   ::=    <nonjoin table primary>
        | <table term> INTERSECT [ ALL | DISTINCT ]
          [ CORRESPONDING [ BY ( <column name commalist> ) ] ]
              <table primary>

<table term>
   ::=    <nonjoin table term> | <join table exp>

<table primary>
   ::=    <nonjoin table primary> | <join table exp>

<nonjoin table primary>
   ::=    TABLE <table name>
        | <table constructor>
        | <select exp>
        | ( <nonjoin table exp> )

<table constructor>
   ::=    VALUES <row constructor commalist>

<row constructor>
   ::=    <scalar exp>
        | ( <scalar exp commalist> )
        | ( <table exp> )
```

```
<select exp>
    ::=    SELECT [ ALL | DISTINCT ] <select item commalist>
              FROM <table ref commalist>
                 [ WHERE <bool exp> ]
                    [ GROUP BY <column name commalist> ]
                       [ HAVING <bool exp> ]

<select item>
    ::=     <scalar exp> [ [ AS ] <column name> ]
          | [ <range var name>. ] *
```

We now proceed to elaborate on the particular case of *<select exp>*s, which are arguably the most important case in practice. A *<select exp>* can be thought of, loosely, as a *<table exp>* that involves no JOINs, UNIONs, EXCEPTs, or INTERSECTs—"loosely," because, of course, such operators might be involved in expressions that are nested inside the *<select exp>* in question. As the grammar indicates, a *<select exp>* involves, in sequence, a SELECT clause, a FROM clause, an optional WHERE clause, an optional GROUP BY clause, and an optional HAVING clause. We consider each in turn.

The SELECT Clause

The SELECT clause takes the form:

```
SELECT [ ALL | DISTINCT ] <select item commalist>
```

Explanation:

1. The *<select item commalist>* must be nonempty[1] (see later for a detailed discussion of *<select item>*s).

2. If neither ALL nor DISTINCT is specified, ALL is assumed.[2]

3. Assume for the moment that the FROM, WHERE, GROUP BY, and HAVING clauses have already been evaluated. No matter which of those clauses are specified and which omitted, the conceptual result of evaluating them is always a table (possibly a "grouped" table—see later), which we will refer to as table *T1* (though that conceptual result is in fact unnamed).

4. Let *T2* be the table that is derived from *T1* by evaluating the specified *<select item>*s against *T1*.

5. Let *T3* be the table that is derived from *T2* by eliminating redundant duplicate rows from *T2* if DISTINCT is specified, or a table that is identical to *T2* otherwise.

6. *T3* is the final result.

We turn now to an explanation of *<select item>*s. There are two cases to consider, of which the second is just shorthand for a commalist of *<select item>*s of the first form; thus, the first case is really the more fundamental.

---

[1] In fact, all lists and commalists mentioned in this appendix must be nonempty.

[2] In other words, the default in the context of SELECT is ALL. By contrast, the default in the context of UNION, INTERSECT, or EXCEPT is DISTINCT.

Case 1: The *<select item>* takes the form:

```
<scalar exp> [ [ AS ] <column name> ]
```

The *<scalar exp>* will typically (but not necessarily) involve one or more columns of table *T1* (see point 3). For each row of *T1*, the *<scalar exp>* is evaluated, to yield a scalar result. The commalist of such results (corresponding to evaluation of all *<select item>*s in the SELECT clause against a single row of *T1*) constitutes a single row of table *T2* (see point 4). If the *<select item>* includes an AS clause, the *unqualified* *<column name>* from that clause is assigned as the name of the corresponding column of *T2* (the optional keyword AS is just noise and can be omitted without affecting the meaning). If the *<select item>* does not include an AS clause, then (a) if it consists simply of a (possibly qualified) *<column name>*, then that *<column name>* is assigned as the name of the corresponding column of *T2;* (b) otherwise the corresponding column of *T2* effectively has no name (actually it is given an implementation-dependent name). Points arising:

- Because it is, specifically, the name of a column of *T2*, not *T1,* a name introduced by an AS clause cannot be used in the WHERE, GROUP BY, and HAVING clauses (if any) directly involved in the construction of *T1*. It can, however, be referenced in an associated ORDER BY clause if any, and also in an "outer" *<table exp>* that contains the *<select exp>* under discussion nested within it.

- If a *<select item>* includes an aggregate operator invocation *and* the *<select exp>* does not include a GROUP BY clause (see later), then no *<select item>* in the SELECT clause can include any reference to a column of *T1* unless that column reference is the argument (or part of the argument) to an aggregate operator invocation.

Case 2: The *<select item>* takes the form:

```
[ <range var name> . ] *
```

If the qualifier is omitted (i.e., the *<select item>* is just an unqualified asterisk), then this *<select item>* must be the only *<select item>* in the SELECT clause. This form is shorthand for a commalist of all of the *<column name>*s for *T1,* in left-to-right column order. If the qualifier is included (i.e., the *<select item>* consists of an asterisk qualified by a range variable name *R,* thus: "*R.**"), then the *<select item>* represents a commalist of *<column name>*s for all of the columns of the table associated with range variable *R,* in left-to-right order. (Recall from Section 8.6 that a table name can and often will be used as an implicit range variable. Thus, the *<select item>* will frequently be of the form "*T.**" rather than "*R.**".)

The FROM Clause

The FROM clause takes the form:

```
FROM <table ref commalist>
```

Let the specified *<table ref>*s evaluate to tables *A, B, ..., Z,* respectively. Then the result of evaluating the FROM clause is a table that is equal to the (SQL-style) Cartesian product of *A, B, ..., Z.*

The WHERE Clause

The WHERE clause takes the form:

```
WHERE <bool exp>
```

Let *T* be the result of evaluating the immediately preceding FROM clause. Then the result of the WHERE clause is a table that is derived from *T* by eliminating all rows for which the *<bool exp>* does not evaluate to TRUE. If the WHERE clause is omitted, the result is simply *T*.

The GROUP BY Clause

The GROUP BY clause takes the form:

```
GROUP BY <column name commalist>
```

Let *T* be the result of evaluating the immediately preceding FROM clause and WHERE clause (if any). Each *<column name>* mentioned in the GROUP BY clause must be the optionally qualified name of a column of *T*. The result of the GROUP BY clause is a *grouped table*—that is, a set of groups of rows, derived from *T* by conceptually rearranging it into the minimum number of groups such that within any one group all rows have the same value for the combination of columns identified by the GROUP BY clause. Note carefully, therefore, that the result is thus not a "proper table" (it is, to repeat, a table of groups, not a table of rows). However, a GROUP BY clause never appears without a corresponding SELECT clause whose effect is to derive a proper table from that table of groups, so little harm is done by this temporary departure from the "proper table" framework.

If a *<select exp>* includes a GROUP BY clause, then every *<select item>* in the SELECT clause (including any that are implied by an asterisk shorthand) must be *single-valued per group*.

The HAVING Clause

The HAVING clause takes the form:

```
HAVING <bool exp>
```

Let *G* be the grouped table resulting from the evaluation of the immediately preceding FROM clause, WHERE clause (if any), and GROUP BY clause (if any). If there is no GROUP BY clause, then *G* is taken to be the result of evaluating the FROM and WHERE clauses alone, considered as a grouped table that contains exactly one group;[3] in other words, there is an implicit, conceptual GROUP BY clause in this case that specifies *no grouping columns at all*. The result of the HAVING clause is a grouped table that is derived from *G* by eliminating all groups for which the *<bool exp>* does not evaluate to TRUE. Points arising:

---

[3] This is what the standard says, though logically it should say *at most* one group (there should be no group at all if the FROM and WHERE clauses yield an empty table).

- If the HAVING clause is omitted but the GROUP BY clause is included, the result of the HAVING clause is simply *G*. If the HAVING and GROUP BY clauses are both omitted, the result is simply the "proper"—that is, nongrouped—table *T* resulting from the FROM and WHERE clauses.

- Any *<scalar exp>*s in a HAVING clause must be single-valued per group (as with *<scalar exp>*s in the SELECT clause if there is a GROUP BY clause, as discussed in the previous subsection).

A Comprehensive Example

We conclude our discussion of *<select exp>*s with a reasonably complex example that illustrates some (by no means all) of the points explained in the foregoing subsections. The query is as follows:

For all red and blue parts such that the total quantity supplied is greater than 350 (excluding from the total all shipments for which the quantity is less than or equal to 200), get the part number, the weight in grams, the color, and the maximum quantity supplied of that part.

Here is a possible SQL formulation of this query:

```
SELECT P.P#,
       'Weight in grams =' AS TEXT1,
       P.WEIGHT * 454 AS GMWT,
       P.COLOR,
       'Max quantity =' AS TEXT2,
       MAX ( SP.QTY ) AS MXQTY
FROM   P, SP
WHERE  P.P# = SP.P#
AND    ( P.COLOR = COLOR ('Red') OR P.COLOR = COLOR ('Blue') )
AND    SP.QTY > QTY ( 200 )
GROUP  BY P.P#, P.WEIGHT, P.COLOR
HAVING SUM ( SP.QTY ) > QTY ( 350 ) ;
```

Explanation: First, note that (as indicated in the foregoing subsections) the clauses of a *<select exp>* are conceptually evaluated in the order in which they are written—with the sole exception of the SELECT clause itself, which is evaluated last. In the example, therefore, we can imagine the result being constructed as follows:

1. *FROM:* The FROM clause is evaluated to yield a new table that is the Cartesian product of tables P and SP.

2. *WHERE:* The result of Step 1 is reduced by the elimination of all rows that do not satisfy the WHERE clause. In the example, therefore, rows not satisfying the *<bool exp>*

```
       P.P# = SP.P#
AND    ( P.COLOR = COLOR ('Red') OR P.COLOR = COLOR ('Blue') )
AND    SP.QTY > QTY ( 200 )
```

are eliminated.

3. *GROUP BY:* The result of Step 2 is grouped by values of the column(s) named in the GROUP BY clause. In the example, those columns are P.P#, P.WEIGHT, and P.COLOR.

4. *HAVING:* Groups not satisfying the *<bool exp>*

```
SUM ( SP.QTY ) > QTY ( 350 )
```

are eliminated from the result of Step 3.

5. *SELECT:* Each group in the result of Step 4 generates a single result row, as follows. First, the part number, weight, color, and maximum quantity are extracted from the group. Second, the weight is converted to grams. Third, the two character strings "Weight in grams =" and "Max quantity =" are inserted at the appropriate points in the row. Note, incidentally, that—as the phrase "appropriate points in the row" suggests—we are relying here on the fact that columns of tables have a left-to-right ordering in SQL; the strings would not make much sense if they did not appear at those "appropriate points."

The final result looks like this:

P#	TEXT1	GMWT	COLOR	TEXT2	MXQTY
P1	Weight in grams =	5448	Red	Max quantity =	300
P5	Weight in grams =	5448	Blue	Max quantity =	400
P3	Weight in grams =	7718	Blue	Max quantity =	400

Please understand that the algorithm just described is intended purely as a *conceptual* explanation of how a *<select exp>* is evaluated. The algorithm is certainly correct, in the sense that it is guaranteed to produce the correct result. However, it would probably be rather inefficient if actually executed. For example, it would probably not be a very good idea if the system were actually to construct the Cartesian product in Step 1. Considerations such as these are exactly the reason why relational systems require an optimizer, as discussed in Chapter 18. Indeed, the task of the optimizer in an SQL system can be characterized as that of finding an implementation procedure that will produce the same result as the conceptual algorithm just described (in outline) but is more efficient than that algorithm.

B.3   BOOLEAN EXPRESSIONS

As in the previous section, we begin with a BNF grammar. We then go on to discuss *<like cond>*s, *<match cond>*s, and *<all or any cond>*s in a little more detail.

```
<bool exp>
    ::=   <bool term> | <bool exp> OR <bool term>

<bool term>
    ::=   <bool factor> | <bool term> AND <bool factor>

<bool factor>
    ::=   [ NOT ] <bool primary>

<bool primary>
    ::=   <simple cond> | ( <bool exp> )
```

```
<simple cond>
  ::=    <comp cond> | <in cond> | <like cond> | <match cond>
       | <all or any cond> | <exists cond> | <unique cond>
       | <distinct cond> | <type cond>

<comp cond>
  ::=    <row constructor> <comp op> <row constructor>

<comp op>
  ::=    = | < | <= | > | >= | <>

<in cond>
  ::=    <row constructor> [ NOT ] IN ( <table exp> )
       | <scalar exp> [ NOT ] IN ( <scalar exp commalist> )

<like cond>
  ::=    <char string exp> [ NOT ] LIKE <pattern>
                                    [ ESCAPE <escape> ]

<match cond>
  ::=    <row constructor> MATCH UNIQUE ( <table exp> )

<all or any cond>
  ::=    <row constructor> <comp op> ALL ( <table exp> )
       | <row constructor> <comp op> ANY ( <table exp> )

<exists cond>
  ::=    EXISTS ( <table exp> )

<unique cond>
  ::=    UNIQUE ( <table exp> )

<distinct cond>
  ::=    <row constructor> IS DISTINCT FROM <row constructor>

<type cond>
  ::=    TYPE ( <scalar exp> )
              IS [ NOT ] OF ( <type spec commalist> )

<type spec>
  ::=    <type name>
```

LIKE Conditions

Like conditions are intended for simple pattern matching on character strings—that is, testing a given character string to see whether it conforms to some prescribed pattern. The syntax (to repeat) is:

```
<char string exp> [ NOT ] LIKE <pattern> [ ESCAPE <escape> ]
```

Here *<pattern>* is an arbitrary character-string expression, and *<escape>*, if specified, is a character-string expression that evaluates to a single character. For example:

```
SELECT P.P#, P.PNAME
FROM   P
WHERE  P.PNAME LIKE 'C%';
```

("Get part numbers and names for parts whose names begin with the letter C"). Given our usual sample data, the result looks like this:

P#	PNAME
P5	Cam
P6	Cog

As long as no ESCAPE clause is specified, characters within *<pattern>* are interpreted as follows:

- The underscore character "_" stands for *any single character.*
- The percent character "%" stands for *any sequence of n characters* (where *n* can be zero).
- All other characters stand for themselves.

In the example, therefore, the query returns rows from table P for which the PNAME value begins with an uppercase C and has any sequence of zero or more characters following that C. Some more examples:

`ADDRESS LIKE '%Berkeley%'`	— Evaluates to TRUE if ADDRESS contains the string "Berkeley" anywhere inside it
`S# LIKE 'S__'`	— Evaluates to TRUE if S# is exactly three characters long and the first is "S"
`PNAME LIKE '%c___'`	— Evaluates to TRUE if PNAME is four characters long or more and the last but three is "c"
`MYTEXT LIKE '=_%'` `     ESCAPE '='`	— Evaluates to TRUE if MYTEXT begins with an underscore character (see following text)

In this last example, the character "=" has been specified as the escape character, which means that the special interpretation given to the characters "_" and "%" can be disabled, if desired, by preceding such characters with an "=" character.

Finally, the *<like cond>*

```
x NOT LIKE y [ ESCAPE z ]
```

is defined to be semantically equivalent to:

```
NOT ( x LIKE y [ ESCAPE z ] )
```

MATCH Conditions

A *<match cond>* takes the form:

```
<row constructor> MATCH UNIQUE ( <table exp> )
```

Let *r1* be the row that results from evaluating the *<row constructor>* and let *T* be the table that results from evaluating the *<table exp>*. Then the *<match cond>* evaluates to *TRUE* if and only if *T* contains exactly one row, *r2* say, such that the comparison

```
r1 = r2
```

evaluates to *TRUE.* For example:

```
SELECT SP.*
FROM   SP
WHERE  NOT ( SP.S# MATCH UNIQUE ( SELECT S.S# FROM S ) ) ;
```

("Get shipments that do not have exactly one matching supplier in the suppliers table"). Such a query might be useful in checking the integrity of the database, because, of course, there should not *be* any such shipments if the database is correct. Note, however, that an *<in cond>* could be used to perform exactly that same check.

Incidentally, the UNIQUE can be omitted from MATCH UNIQUE, but then MATCH becomes synonymous with IN (in the absence of nulls).

All-or-Any Conditions

An *<all or any cond>* has the general form

```
<row constructor> <comp op> <qualifier> ( <table exp> )
```

where the *<comp op>* is any of the usual set (=, <>, etc.), and the *<qualifier>* is ALL or ANY.[4] In general, an *<all or any cond>* evaluates to TRUE if and only if the corresponding comparison without the ALL (respectively, ANY) evaluates to TRUE for all (respectively, any) of the rows in the table represented by the *<table exp>*. (If that table is empty, the ALL conditions evaluate to TRUE, the ANY conditions evaluate to FALSE.) Here is an example ("Get part names for parts whose weight is greater than that of every blue part"):

```
SELECT DISTINCT PX.PNAME
FROM    P AS PX
WHERE   PX.WEIGHT >ALL ( SELECT PY.WEIGHT
                         FROM    P AS PY
                         WHERE   PY.COLOR = 'Blue' ) ;
```

Given our usual sample data, the result looks like this:

Explanation: The nested *<table exp>* returns the set of weights for blue parts. The outer SELECT then returns the name of those parts whose weight is greater than every value in that set. In general, of course, the final result might contain any number of part names (including zero).

Note: A word of caution is appropriate here, at least for native English speakers. The fact is, *<all or any cond>*s are error prone. A very natural English formulation of the foregoing query would use the word *any* in place of *every,* which could easily lead to the (incorrect) use of >ANY instead of >ALL. An analogous observation applies to all (any?) of the ANY and ALL operators.

---

[4] ANY can also be spelled SOME.

Abbreviations, Acronyms, and Symbols

1NF	first normal form
2NF	second normal form
2PC	two-phase commit
2PL	two-phase locking
2VL	two-valued logic
2øC	same as 2PC
2øL	same as 2PL
3GL	third-generation language
3NF	third normal form
3VL	three-valued logic
4GL	fourth-generation language
4NF	fourth normal form
4VL	four-valued logic
5NF	fifth normal form (same as PJ/NF)
6NF	sixth normal form
A	ALGEBRA
ACID	atomicity-consistency-isolation-durability
ACM	Association for Computing Machinery
ADT	abstract data type
AES	Advanced Encryption System
ALGEBRA	A Logical Genesis Explains Basic Relational Algebra
ANSI	American National Standards Institute
ANSI/SPARC	literally, ANSI/Systems Planning and Requirements Committee; used to refer to the three-level database system architecture described in Chapter 2
API	application programming interface

ARIES	Algorithms for Recovery and Isolation Exploiting Semantics
AST	automatic summary table
BB	same as GB
BCNF	Boyce/Codd normal form
BLOB	binary large object
BNF	Backus-Naur form; Backus normal form
CACM	*Communications of the ACM* (ACM publication)
CAD/CAM	computer-aided design/computer-aided manufacturing
CASE	computer-aided software engineering
CDO	class-defining object
CIM	computer-integrated manufacturing
CLI	Call-Level Interface
CLOB	character large object
CNF	conjunctive normal form
CODASYL	literally, Conference on Data Systems Languages; used to refer to certain prerelational (actually network) systems such as IDMS
CPU	central processing unit
CS	cursor stability (DB2)
CWA	Closed World Assumption
DA	data administrator
DB/DC	database/data communications
DBA	database administrator
DBMS	database management system
DBP&D	*Database Programming & Design* (originally a hardcopy magazine; later online at *http://www.dbpd.com;* superseded by *Intelligent Enterprise*)
DBTG	literally, Data Base Task Group; used interchangeably in database contexts with CODASYL
DC	data communications
DCO	"domain check override"
DDB	distributed database
DDBMS	distributed DBMS
DDL	data definition language
DES	Data Encryption Standard
DK/NF	domain-key normal form
DML	data manipulation language
DNF	disjunctive normal form

DOM	Document Object Model (XML)
DRDA	Distributed Relational Database Architecture (IBM)
DSL	data sublanguage
DSS	decision support system
DTD	Document Type Definition (XML)
DUW	distributed unit of work
E/R	entity/relationship
EB	same as XB
ECA	event-condition-action
EDB	extensional database
EDI	Electronic Data Interchange
EKNF	elementary key normal form
EMVD	embedded MVD
EOT	end of transaction
FD	functional dependence
FLWOR	*for-let-where-order by-return* (XML)
FTP	File Transfer Protocol (usually "ftp," all lowercase)
GB	gigabyte (1024MB)
GIS	geographic information system
GML	Generalized Markup Language
HOLAP	hybrid OLAP
HTML	HyperText Markup Language
HTTP	Hypertext Transfer Protocol (usually "http," all lowercase)
I/O	input/output
IDB	intensional database
IDMS	Integrated Database Management System
IFIP	International Federation for Information Processing
IEEE	Institute for Electrical and Electronics Engineers
IMS	Information Management System
INCITS	ANSI International Committee on Information Technology Standards (formerly called NCITS, and before that X3)
INCITS/H2	INCITS database committee
IND	inclusion dependence
IS	intent shared (lock); information systems
ISBL	Information System Base Language (PRTV)
ISO	International Organization for Standardization

IT	information technology
IX	intent exclusive (lock)
JACM	*Journal of the ACM* (ACM publication)
JD	join dependence
JDBC	"Java Database Connectivity" (officially just a name, not an abbreviation for anything at all)
K	1024 (sometimes 1000)
KB	kilobyte (1024 bytes)
LAN	local area network
LOB	large object
LSP	Liskov Substitution Principle
MB	megabyte (1024KB)
MLS	multi-level secure
MOLAP	multi-dimensional OLAP
MQT	materialized query table
MVD	multi-valued dependence
NCITS	*see* INCITS
NCITS/H2	*see* INCITS/H2
NF^2	"NF squared" = NFNF = non first normal form (?)
ODBC	Open Database Connectivity
ODMG	Object Data Management Group
ODS	operational data store
OID	object ID
OLAP	online analytic processing
OLCP	online complex processing
OLDM	online decision management
OLTP	online transaction processing
OMG	Object Management Group
OO	object-oriented; object orientation
OODB	object-oriented database (= object database)
OODBMS	object-oriented DBMS (= object DBMS)
OOPL	object-oriented programming language (= object programming language)
OQL	Object Query Language (part of ODMG proposal)
OSI	Open Systems Interconnection
OSQL	"Object SQL"
PB	petabyte (1024TB)

PC	personal computer
PJ/NF	projection-join normal form
PODS	Principles of Database Systems (ACM conference)
PRTV	Peterlee Relational Test Vehicle
PSM	Persistent Stored Modules (part of the SQL standard)
PSVI	Post Schema Validation Infoset (XML)
QBE	Query-By-Example
QUEL	Query Language (Ingres)
RAID	redundant array of inexpensive disks
RDA	Remote Data Access
RDB	relational database
RDBMS	relational DBMS
RID	record ID; row ID
ROLAP	relational OLAP
RM/T	relational model/Tasmania
RM/V1	relational model/Version 1
RM/V2	relational model/Version 2
RPC	remote procedure call
RR	read-read; repeatable read (DB2)
RSA	Rivest-Shamir-Adelman (encryption method)
RUW	remote unit of work
RVA	relation-valued attribute
S	shared (lock)
SGML	Standard GML
SIGMOD	Special Interest Group on Management of Data (ACM special interest group)
SIX	shared intent exclusive (lock)
SOAP	Simple Object Access Protocol
SPARC	*see* ANSI/SPARC
SQL	(originally) Structured Query Language; sometimes Standard Query Language; officially just a name, not an abbreviation for anything at all
SQL/MM	SQL/Multimedia
SVG	Scalable Vector Graphics
TB	terabyte (1024GB)
TCB	Trusted Computing Base
TCP/IP	Transmission Control Protocol/Internet Protocol

TID	tuple ID
TODS	*Transactions on Database Systems* (ACM publication)
TP	transaction processing
TPC	Transaction Processing Council
TR	TransRelational™
U	update (lock)
UDF	user-defined function
UDO	user-defined operator
UDT	user-defined type
UML	Unified Modeling Language
unk	*unknown* (truth value)
UNK	unknown (null)
UOW	unit of work
URI	Uniform Resource Identifier
URL	Uniform Resource Locator
VLDB	very large database; Very Large Data Bases (annual conference)
VSAM	Virtual Storage Access Method
W3C	World Wide Web Consortium
WAL	write-ahead log
WAN	wide area network
WFF	well-formed formula
WORM	write once/read many times
WWW	World Wide Web (usually "www," all lowercase)
WYSIWYG	what you see is what you get
X	exclusive (lock)
X3	*see* INCITS
X3H2	*see* INCITS/H2
XB	exabyte (1024PB)
XML	Extensible Markup Language
XQuery	XML Query
XQL	XML Query Language (not the same as XQuery)
XSL	XML Stylesheet Language
XSLT	XML Stylesheet and Transformation Language
YB	yottabyte (1024ZB)
ZB	zettabyte (1024XB)

∈	belongs to; is a member of; is contained in; [is] in
∋	contains
⊆	is a subset of; is included in
⊂	is a proper subset of; is properly included in
⊇	is a superset of; includes
⊃	is a proper superset of; properly includes
θ	comparison operator (=, <, etc.); polar coordinate
∅	the empty set
→	functionally determines
→→	multi-determines
≡	is equivalent to; is identically equal to
⇒	implies (logical connective)
⊢	implies (metalinguistic symbol)
⊨	it is always the case that (metalinguistic symbol)

Index

The Information Principle (or *The Principle of Uniform Representation*): The entire information content of the database is represented in one and only one way, as explicit values in attribute positions within tuples within relations.

The Golden Rule: No update operation must ever assign to any database a value that causes its database predicate to evaluate to FALSE.

The Principle of Interchangeability (of base and derived relvars): There are no arbitrary and unnecessary distinctions between base and derived relvars.

The Principle of Database Relativity: From the user's point of view, (a) all relvars are base relvars, and (b) which database is the "real" one is arbitrary, just as long as the possibilities are all information-equivalent.

The Principles of Normalization:

1. A non5NF relvar should be decomposed into a set of 5NF projections.
2. The original relvar should be reconstructable by joining the projections back together again.
3. The decomposition process should preserve dependencies.
4. Every projection should be needed in the reconstruction process.
5. (*Not as firm as the first four*) Stop normalizing as soon as all relvars are in 5NF.

The Principle of Orthogonal Design: If A and B are distinct base relvars, there must not exist nonloss decompositions of A and B such that some projection of A and some projection of B in the result have overlapping meanings.

The Principle of Value Substitutability: Wherever the system expects a value of type T, a value of type T' (where T' is a subtype of T) can always be substituted instead.

The Fundamental Principle of Distributed Database: To the user, a distributed system looks exactly like a nondistributed system.

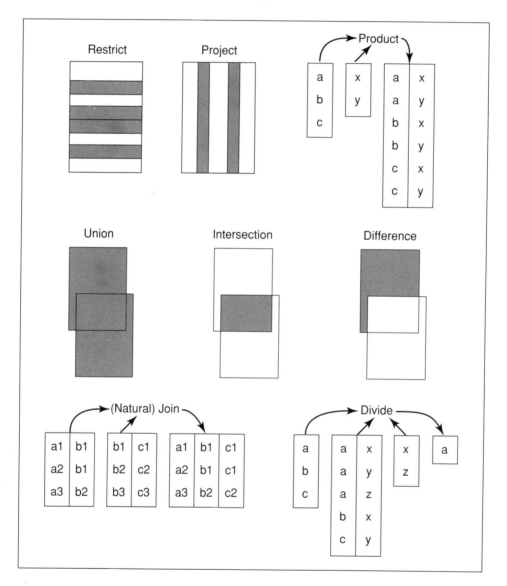

Fig. 7.1 The original eight operators (overview)

S

S#	SNAME	STATUS	CITY
S1	Smith	20	London
S2	Jones	10	Paris
S3	Blake	30	Paris
S4	Clark	20	London
S5	Adams	30	Athens

SP

S#	P#	QTY
S1	P1	300
S1	P2	200
S1	P3	400
S1	P4	200
S1	P5	100
S1	P6	100
S2	P1	300
S2	P2	400
S3	P2	200
S4	P2	200
S4	P4	300
S4	P5	400

P

P#	PNAME	COLOR	WEIGHT	CITY
P1	Nut	Red	12.0	London
P2	Bolt	Green	17.0	Paris
P3	Screw	Blue	17.0	Oslo
P4	Screw	Red	14.0	London
P5	Cam	Blue	12.0	Paris
P6	Cog	Red	19.0	London

Fig. 3.8 The suppliers-and-parts database (sample values)

S

S#	SNAME	STATUS	CITY
S1	Smith	20	London
S2	Jones	10	Paris
S3	Blake	30	Paris
S4	Clark	20	London
S5	Adams	30	Athens

SPJ

S#	P#	J#	QTY
S1	P1	J1	200
S1	P1	J4	700
S2	P3	J1	400
S2	P3	J2	200
S2	P3	J3	200
S2	P3	J4	500
S2	P3	J5	600
S2	P3	J6	400
S2	P3	J7	800
S2	P5	J2	100
S3	P3	J1	200
S3	P4	J2	500
S4	P6	J3	300
S4	P6	J7	300
S5	P2	J2	200
S5	P2	J4	100
S5	P5	J5	500
S5	P5	J7	100
S5	P6	J2	200
S5	P1	J4	100
S5	P3	J4	200
S5	P4	J4	800
S5	P5	J4	400
S5	P6	J4	500

P

P#	PNAME	COLOR	WEIGHT	CITY
P1	Nut	Red	12.0	London
P2	Bolt	Green	17.0	Paris
P3	Screw	Blue	17.0	Oslo
P4	Screw	Red	14.0	London
P5	Cam	Blue	12.0	Paris
P6	Cog	Red	19.0	London

J

J#	JNAME	CITY
J1	Sorter	Paris
J2	Display	Rome
J3	OCR	Athens
J4	Console	Athens
J5	RAID	London
J6	EDS	Oslo
J7	Tape	London

Fig. 4.5 The suppliers-parts-projects database (sample values)